Nineteenth-Century Literature Criticism

Guide to Gale Literary Criticism Series

For criticism on	Consult these Gale series
Authors now living or who died after December 31, 1959	*CONTEMPORARY LITERARY CRITICISM (CLC)*
Authors who died between 1900 and 1959	*TWENTIETH-CENTURY LITERARY CRITICISM (TCLC)*
Authors who died between 1800 and 1899	*NINETEENTH-CENTURY LITERATURE CRITICISM (NCLC)*
Authors who died between 1400 and 1799	*LITERATURE CRITICISM FROM 1400 TO 1800 (LC)* *SHAKESPEAREAN CRITICISM (SC)*
Authors who died before 1400	*CLASSICAL AND MEDIEVAL LITERATURE CRITICISM (CMLC)*
Authors of books for children and young adults	*CHILDREN'S LITERATURE REVIEW (CLR)*
Black writers of the past two hundred years	*BLACK LITERATURE CRITICISM (BLC)*
Short story writers	*SHORT STORY CRITICISM (SSC)*
Poets	*POETRY CRITICISM (PC)*
Dramatists	*DRAMA CRITICISM (DC)*
Major authors from the Renaissance to the present	*WORLD LITERATURE CRITICISM, 1500 TO THE PRESENT (WLC)*

For criticism on visual artists since 1850, see

MODERN ARTS CRITICISM (MAC)

ISSN 0732-1864

R

Volume 42

Nineteenth-Century Literature Criticism

Excerpts from Criticism of the
Works of Novelists, Poets, Playwrights,
Short Story Writers, Philosophers, and Other
Creative Writers Who Died between 1800
and 1899, from the First Published Critical
Appraisals to Current Evaluations

Joann Cerrito
Editor

Jim Edwards
Judith Galens
Alan Hedblad
Michael W. Jones
Jelena O. Krstović
Joseph C. Tardiff
Associate Editors

 **Gale Research Inc.** • *DETROIT* • *WASHINGTON, D.C.* • *LONDON*

MAR   '94

STAFF

Joann Cerrito, *Editor*

Jim Edwards, Judith Galens, Alan Hedblad, Michael W. Jones, Jelena O. Krstović, Joseph C. Tardiff, *Associate Editors*

Patrick L. Bruch, Thomas Carson, Kathryn Horste, Sean McCready, Debra A. Wells, *Assistant Editors*

Jeanne A. Gough, *Permissions & Production Manager*
Linda M. Pugliese, *Production Supervisor*
Donna Craft, Paul Lewon, Maureen A. Puhl, Camille P. Robinson, Sheila Walencewicz, *Editorial Associates*
Jill H. Johnson, Elizabeth Anne Valliere, *Editorial Assistants*

Sandra C. Davis, *Permissions Supervisor (Text)*
Maria L. Franklin, Josephine M. Keene, Michele Lonoconus, Shalice Shah, Kimberly F. Smilay, *Permissions Associates*
Jennifer A. Arnold, Paula M. Labbe, Brandy C. Merritt, *Permissions Assistants*

Margaret A. Chamberlain, *Permissions Supervisor (Pictures)*
Pamela A. Hayes, Keith Reed, *Permissions Associates*
Susan Brohman, Arlene Johnson, Barbara A. Wallace, *Permissions Assistants*

Victoria B. Cariappa, *Research Manager*
Maureen Richards, *Research Supervisor*
Robert S. Lazich, Mary Beth McElmeel, Donna Melnychenko, Tamara C. Nott, Jaema Paradowski, *Editorial Associates*
Karen Farrelly, Julie Leonard, Stefanie Scarlett, *Editorial Assistants*

Mary Beth Trimper, *Production Director*
Catherine Kemp, *Production Assistant*

Cynthia Baldwin, *Art Director*
Barbara J. Yarrow, *Graphic Services Supervisor*
C. J. Jonik, *Desktop Publisher*
Willie F. Mathis, *Camera Operator*

Library of Congress Catalog Card Number 84-643008
ISBN 0-8103-8475-2
ISSN 0732-1864

Printed in the United States of America
Published simultaneously in the United Kingdom
by Gale Research International Limited
(An affiliated company of Gale Research Inc.)
10 9 8 7 6 5 4 3 2 1

The trademark **ITP** is used under license.

Contents

Preface vii

Acknowledgments xi

Preface

Since its inception in 1981, *Nineteenth-Century Literature Criticism* has been a valuable resource for students and librarians seeking critical commentary on writers of this transitional period in world history. Designated an "Outstanding Reference Source" by the American Library Association with the publication of its first volume, *NCLC* has since been purchased by over 6,000 school, public, and university libraries. The series has covered more than 300 authors representing 26 nationalities and over 15,000 titles. No other reference source has surveyed the critical reaction to nineteenth-century authors and literature as thoroughly as *NCLC*.

Scope of the Series

NCLC is designed to introduce students and advanced readers to the authors of the nineteenth century, and to the most significant interpretations of these authors' works. The great poets, novelists, short story writers, dramatists, and philosophers of this period are frequently studied in high school and college literature courses. By organizing and reprinting commentary written on these authors, *NCLC* helps students develop valuable insight into literary history, promotes a better understanding of the texts, and sparks ideas for papers and assignments. Each entry in *NCLC* presents a comprehensive survey of an author's career or an individual work of literature and provides the user with a multiplicity of interpretations and assessments. Such variety allows students to pursue their own interests; furthermore, it fosters an awareness that literature is dynamic and responsive to many different opinions.

Every fourth volume of *NCLC* is devoted to literary topics that cannot be covered under the author approach used in the rest of the series. Such topics include literary movements, prominent themes in nineteenth-century literature, literary reaction to political and historical events, significant eras in literary history, prominent literary anniversaries, and the literatures of cultures that are often overlooked by English-speaking readers.

NCLC continues the survey of criticism of world literature begun by Gale's *Contemporary Literary Criticism (CLC)* and *Twentieth-Century Literary Criticism (TCLC),* both of which excerpt and reprint commentary on authors of the twentieth century. For additional information about *TCLC, CLC,* and Gale's other criticism series, users should consult the Guide to Gale Literary Criticism Series preceding the title page in this volume.

Coverage

Each volume of *NCLC* is carefully compiled to present:

- criticism of authors, or literary topics, representing a variety of genres and nationalities
- both major and lesser-known writers and literary works of the period
- 7-10 authors or 4-6 topics per volume
- individual entries that survey critical response to an author's work or a topic in literary history, including early criticism to reflect initial reactions, later criticism to represent any rise or decline in reputation, and current retrospective analyses.

Organization

An author entry consists of the following elements: author heading, biographical and critical introduction, list of principal works, excerpts of criticism (each preceded by an annotation and followed by a bibliographic citation), and a bibliography of further reading.

- The **Author Heading** consists of the name under which the author most commonly wrote, followed by birth and death dates. If an author wrote consistently under a pseudonym, the pseudonym will be listed in the author heading and the real name given in parentheses on the first line of the biographical and critical introduction. Also located at the beginning of the introduction to the author entry are any name variations under which an author wrote, including transliterated forms for an author whose language uses a nonroman alphabet.

- The **Biographical and Critical Introduction** outlines the author's life and career, as well as the critical issues surrounding his or her work. References are provided to past volumes of *NCLC* in which further information about the author may be found.

- Most *NCLC* entries include a **Portrait** of the author. Many entries also contain reproductions of materials pertinent to an author's career, including manuscript pages, title pages, dust jackets, letters, and drawings, as well as photographs of important people, places, and events in an author's life.

- The list of **Principal Works** is chronological by date of first publication and identifies the genre of each work. In the case of foreign authors with both foreign-language publications and English translations, the title and date of the first English-language edition are given in brackets. Unless otherwise indicated, dramas are dated by first performance, not first publication.

- **Criticism** in each author entry is arranged chronologically to provide a perspective on changes in critical evaluation over the years. All titles of works by the author featured in the entry are printed in boldface type to enable the user to easily locate discussion of particular works. Also for purposes of easier identification, the critic's name and the publication date of the essay are given at the beginning of each piece of criticism. Unsigned criticism is preceded by the title of the journal in which it appeared. Publication information (such as publisher names and book prices) and parenthetical numerical references (such as footnotes or page and line references to specific editions of works) have been deleted at the editors' discretion to provide smoother reading of the text.

- Critical excerpts are prefaced by **Annotations** providing the reader with information about both the critic and the criticism that follows. Included are the critic's reputation, individual approach to literary criticism, and particular expertise in an author's works. Also noted are the relative importance of a work of criticism, the scope of the excerpt, and the growth of critical controversy or changes in critical trends regarding an author. In some cases, these annotations cross-reference excerpts by critics who discuss each other's commentary.

- A complete **Bibliographic Citation** designed to facilitate location of the original essay or book follows each piece of criticism.

- An annotated list of **Further Reading** appearing at the end of each entry suggests secondary sources on the author. In some cases it includes essays for which the editors could not obtain reprint rights.

Cumulative Indexes

■ Each volume of *NCLC* contains a cumulative **Author Index** listing all authors who have appeared in Gale's Literary Criticism Series, along with cross-references to such biographical series as *Contemporary Authors* and *Dictionary of Literary Biography*. Useful for locating authors within the various series, this index is particularly valuable for those authors who are identified with a certain period but who, because of their death dates, are placed in another, or for those authors whose careers span two periods. For example, Fyodor Dostoevsky is found in *NCLC*, yet Leo Tolstoy, another major nineteenth-century Russian novelist, is found in *TCLC* because he died after 1899.

■ Each *NCLC* volume includes a cumulative **Nationality Index** which lists all authors who have appeared in *NCLC*, arranged alphabetically under their respective nationalities, as well as Topics volume entries devoted to particular national literatures.

■ Each new volume in Gale's Literary Criticism Series includes a cumulative **Topic Index**, which lists all literary topics treated in *NCLC, TCLC, LC 1400-1800*, and the *CLC* Yearbook.

■ Each new volume of *NCLC*, with the exception of the Topics volumes, contains a **Title Index** listing the titles of all literary works discussed in the volume. In response to numerous suggestions from librarians, Gale has also produced a **Special Paperbound Edition** of the *NCLC* title index. This annual cumulation lists all titles discussed in the series since its inception and is issued with the first volume of *NCLC* published each year. Additional copies of the index are available on request. Librarians and patrons have welcomed this separate index: it saves shelf space, is easy to use, and is recyclable upon receipt of the following year's cumulation. Titles discussed in the Topics volume entries are not included in the *NCLC* cumulative index.

Citing *Nineteenth-Century Literature Criticism*

When writing papers, students who quote directly from any volume in Gale's Literary Criticism Series may use the following general forms to footnote reprinted criticism. The first example pertains to material drawn from periodicals, the second to material reprinted from books:

[1]T.S. Eliot, "John Donne," *The Nation and Athenaeum*, 33 (9 June 1923), 321-32; excerpted and reprinted in *Literature Criticism from 1400-1800*, Vol. 10, ed. James E. Person, Jr. (Detroit: Gale Research, 1989), pp. 28-9.

[2]Clara G. Stillman, *Samuel Butler: A Mid-Victorian Modern* (Viking Press, 1932); excerpted and reprinted in *Twentieth-Century Literary Criticism*, Vol. 33, ed. Paula Kepos (Detroit: Gale Research, 1989), pp. 43-5.

Suggestions Are Welcome

In response to suggestions, several features have been added to *NCLC* since the series began, including annotations to excerpted criticism, a cumulative index to authors in all Gale literary criticism series, entries devoted to criticism on a single work by a major author, more illustrations, and a title index listing all literary works discussed in the series.

Readers who wish to suggest authors or topics to appear in future volumes, or who have other suggestions, are cordially invited to write the editors.

Acknowledgments

The editors wish to thank the copyright holders of the excerpted criticism included in this volume, the permissions managers of many book and magazine publishing companies for assisting us in securing reprint rights, and Anthony Bogucki for assistance with copyright research. We are also grateful to the staffs of the Detroit Public Library, the Library of Congress, the University of Detroit Library, Wayne State University Purdy/Kresge Library Complex, and the University of Michigan Libraries for making their resources available to us. Following is a list of the copyright holders who have granted us permission to reprint material in this volume of *NCLC.* Every effort has been made to trace copyright, but if omissions have been made, please let us know.

COPYRIGHTED EXCERPTS IN *NCLC*, VOLUME 42, WERE REPRINTED FROM THE FOLLOWING PERIODICALS:

COPYRIGHTED EXCERPTS IN *NCLC*, VOLUME 42, WERE REPRINTED FROM THE FOLLOWING BOOKS:

Carl Jonas Love Almqvist

1793-1866

Swedish novelist, short-story writer, essayist, poet, dramatist, and journalist.

INTRODUCTION

An experimentalist and theorist considered among the finest authors in Swedish literature, Almqvist pursued the Romantic ideal of creating "das Gesamtkunstwerk," a single work unifying all of the arts. To this end, his ambitious *Törnrosens bok,* the multivolume collection for which he is best known, employs a range of literary genres in attempting to relate symbolically "the whole of history from the beginning." Propounding the author's mystical, utopian vision of progressive spiritual perfection, the *Törnrosens bok* also reflects Almqvist's steady movement away from the Romanticism of his early works and toward social Realism. Although critics often contend that Almqvist's focus on social issues in his later years detracted from the artistic quality of his fiction and poetry, he is generally recognized as an exceptional prose stylist whose writings on such subjects as parliamentary reform, foreign policy, education, and theology offer keen insight into the concerns of his day. Moreover, Almqvist's essays on aesthetics, which feature his view of readers as co-creators of literature, have been recognized as important precursors of modern literary theory.

Almqvist was born in Stockholm and raised outside that city on his father's farm. As a youth he studied intensely and absorbed the philosophical and religious thought of his day. He earned his masters degree in 1815, and began writing soon after while employed as a civil servant in the Ministry of Church and Education. Disillusioned with state and ecclesiastical bureaucracy, he resigned his position and moved to rural Värmland in 1824. Almqvist's pursuit of an idyllic life there was short-lived, but his writings during the period were incorporated in the *Törnrosens bok,* the first volume of which appeared in 1831. In the thirties, Almqvist's literary fame grew with the publication of further volumes of the *Törnrosens bok* and of his popular novel *Det går an* (translated as *Sara Videbeck*) in 1839. During this time Almqvist became increasingly interested in politics and began submitting articles to *Aftonbladet,* a liberal newspaper in Stockholm. He continued to write and publish fiction, remaining a prominent figure on the Swedish literary scene until 1851 when, accused of attempting to poison a moneylender, he fled to America. For the next fifteen years he lived in the United States, filling notebooks with writings that have largely remained unpublished. Almqvist returned to Europe in 1865, settling in Bremen, Germany; he died the following year.

Almqvist's early works, which typically fuse various stylistic elements and genres, demonstrate his concern with

aesthetics and his desire to produce an all-encompassing work of art. One such work, the novel *Amorina,* tells the tale of a pious young woman caught in an incestuous love triangle. To its gothic trappings—bloodshed, intrigue, divine intervention, and a family curse—Almqvist added elements of epic and drama to create what he described as a "poetic fugue." Similarly, Almqvist's *Drottningens juvelsmycke* combines both historical and documentary material within the contexts of poetry and fiction. A highly symbolic work based upon the assassination of Swedish King Gustave III, *Drottningens juvelsmycke* centers on the fictional Azouras Lazuli Tintomara, an androgyne involved in the conspiracy, who personifies Almqvist's theme of unity and wholeness. Also written in this early period, Almqvist's *Songes,* for which he composed his own music, are short, dreamlike lyrics focusing on love, death, and the divine.

In his later writings Almqvist increasingly turned his attention toward the social conflicts of mid-nineteenth century Europe. His drama *Marjam,* published in 1839, criticizes what he considered staid Christian dogma. In the same year Almqvist produced his controversial *Det går an,* the story of a man and a woman who meet on a week-long journey from Stockholm to Lidköping. The novel expresses Almqvist's views in favor of love out of wedlock and his belief in a woman's right to work—convictions unacceptable in the Sweden of his day. Also, many of the essays Almqvist wrote in his latter years explicitly assert his social ideas; striking among these is his *Europeiska missnöjets grunder,* which calls for a new and progressive society based on the strength of "the folk."

Critics generally agree that the quality of Almqvist's writing suffered as he began to turn his attention toward journalism and social commentary in the early 1840s. Although Almquist experienced his greatest popularity in this period following the publication of *Det går an,* gaining renown for his critiques of religion and politics, the criminal charge against him and his subsequent exile caused him to fall into general disfavor. In the 1890s interest in his works was partially resurrected during the vogue of Symbolism. Ellen Key called Almqvist "Sweden's most modern writer" in 1894, and by the 1920s he had become the subject of biographical study. While work at midcentury tended to emphasize his aesthetics, recent critics have also taken a renewed interest in his radical and forward-looking political and social ideas.

PRINCIPAL WORKS

Vad är kärlek? (essay) 1816
Parjumouf (novel) 1817
Om brottsliges behandling (essay) 1821
*Amorina (novel) 1822
Törnrosens bok eller fria fantasier, berättade på Jaktslottet
    hos herr Hugo Löwenstjerna (novels, short stories,
    poetry, dramas, essays) 1832-1851
†*Jaktslottet* (novel) 1832
†*Hermitaget* (novel) 1833
†*Hinden* (novel) 1833
†*Drottningens juvelsmycke* (novel) 1834
†*Ramido Marinesco* (drama) 1834
†*Baron Julius K* (novel) 1835
†*Colombine* (drama) 1835
†*Signora Luna* (drama) 1835
†*Araminta May* (novella) 1838
†*Kapellet* (novel) 1838
    [*The Chapel,* 1919]
†*Palatset* (novel) 1838
†*Skällnora kvarn* (novel) 1838
†*"Svenska fattigdomens betydelse"* (essay) 1838
Det går an (novel) 1839
    [*Sara Videbeck,* 1919]
Grimstahamns nybygge (novel) 1839
Människosläkets saga (essay) 1839
†*Marjam* (drama) 1839
†*Ormus och Ariman* (novel) 1839
Ladugårdsarrendet (novel) 1840
†*"Målaren"* (short story) 1840
Gabrièle Mimanso. Sista mordförsöket emot Ludvig Filip
    i Frankrike, hösten 1840 (novel) 1841
    [*Gabrièle Mimanso, The Niece of Abd-el-Kadar, or An*

Attempt to Assassinate Louis Philippe, King of France,
1846]
‡*Songes* (poetry) 1849
†*Europeiska missnöjets grunder* (essay) 1850
§*Dikter i landsflykt* (poetry) 1956
‖ *Murnis; eller, De dödas sagor* (novel) 1960

*The 1822 edition was unfinished and destroyed. A revised edition was published in 1839.

†Published in the multivolume collection *Törnrosens bok.*

‡Although the *Songes* were published in the *Törnrosens bok* in 1849, most were written in the 1820s and '30s.

§These poems were written between 1851 and 1865, while Almqvist was exiled in America.

‖The original manuscript of *Murnis* was completed in 1819. A revised version was published in 1845, but the original was not published until 1960.

CRITICISM

Staffan Björck   (essay date 1972)

[*In the following essay, Björck examines Almqvist's life and career, commenting on principal themes in his writings.*]

Among the naves of older Swedish writers, that of Carl Jonas Love Almqvist is the one most directly associated with North America. Unfortunately, this connection is also the great testimony to his life's tragedy. In his political and social publications there is talk of America as a center for important social experiments: it was that country which Fredrika Bremer—the Swedish pioneer of the women's rights movement—visited on the great journey she began in 1849. But what Almqvist came to require for his own account was the America that could provide asylum and oblivion and at least the illusion of new opportunities to a person who had expended his life in the old world.

When Almqvist set foot on American soil in August, 1851, it was as a criminal, suspected of attempted murder, among other charges. A regimental chaplain, Almqvist had for several years been a client of J. J. von Scheven, an old cavalry captain and notorious moneylender, and in June the rumor was spread throughout Stockholm that he had not only been fraudulent in credit transactions but also had tried to poison Von Scheven by putting arsenic in his gruel. As late as 1970 a professor of law at Uppsala, Stig Jägerskiöld, published a book in which he asserted that the charges which Von Scheven had brought against Almqvist in court had by no means been confirmed. Furthermore—still according to Jägerskiöld—there were some highly influential circles who seem to have been anxious to get rid of the subversive journalist at any price. The question of Almqvist's guilt must be considered as undecided. He himself never made any confession, but he behaved as if he were guilty, and by the very fact that he deserted, both his moral and intellectual integrity was lost. During his years in America he published nothing. A great quantity of verse that has been preserved in handwriting has its definite psychological interest, but the literary quality is extremely uneven.

The original sources of information on Almqvist's years in America are the long and intimate, occasionally somewhat unctious letters he sent to his wife and his two children in Sweden. Here he relates his impressions of the new country and its people at length but he is uncommunicative, on the other hand, about his own private life. Something the letters to his wife discreetly conceal is the fact that in 1854 he entered into a new marriage, namely with a Mrs. Emma Nugent, who was several years older than he and the proprietress of the boarding house in Philadelphia where he took refuge. It was not until the 1920s that a Swedish scholar unveiled the secret of Lewis and Emma Gustawi.

However, Almqvist could never quite settle down in the new country and the new marriage. In the summer of 1865, when he was 72 years old, he gave his life a new direction once more, leaving America for Europe. He came as close to his native country as Bremen, where he lived for a couple of years under the name of Professor Carl Westermann. On September 26, 1866, it was time for the last breakup in his life so rich in departures.

The strange, half-pitiable, half-macabre epilogue to the story of Almqvist's life is in keeping with the quality of ambiguity and evasion that had appeared a great deal earlier. Already in 1834—as if he had anticipated his own fate—he chose as a motto for one of his works: "Two things are white: Innocence—Arsenic." He is among those demonic figures who avoid clear positions and definitive responsibility. Unceasingly, they make their way forward on the narrow edge between life's normal alternatives. As no other Swedish writer, Almqvist put the essence of masquerade and disguise into practice, both in his life and in his poetry. The vast range of the literary register he displays—spanning over all genres and many attitudes—is thoroughly astounding too. An exclusionary haughtiness in theme and form is neighbor to a warm compassion for the people; a fervent sense of patriotism is found beside the most glaring exoticism; utterly sincere piety is entwined with sharp satire in religious matters as well.

Arranged roughly, Almqvist's literary development may be said to look like this: the early production proceeds in a romantic, often extremely romantic style. Then toward the end of the 1830s, he becomes one of Sweden's pioneers in portraying society realistically, gradually to lose himself during his last decade of writing in an assiduous journalistic and *feuilleton* production.

Born in 1793, C. J. L. Almqvist was exactly the same age as the great Romantic poet Erik Johan Stagnelius, Sweden's Keats or Novalis. As a matter of fact, after their studies in Uppsala both of them were simultaneously employed at a government office in Stockholm without seeming to have become closely acquainted. In 1823, when

death discontinued Stagnelius's prolific creativity, Almqvist had also written a good deal—stories, epic fragments, religious manifestos, and other things—but only one work that would acquire lasting importance: that singular kind of compromise between drama and novel which he called *Amorina.* He began printing it in 1822, but an uncle of his, who was a bishop, was horrified by what he read and had the publication suspended. The book first came out in 1839 and didn't have its stage première until 1951, when it made a strong impression: it is possible that our time, more than Almqvist's own, can appreciate the excruciating tragedy in the piece, and likewise its flashing Shakespearean revelations of people and provinces, its fluctuations between elevated scenes and rustic or burlesque ones, and its tone between laughter and despair.

The title figure is a young, sweet, pious woman who has been brought up by a grotesque clergyman, Doctor Libius, and who is tragically driven to madness by the severe complications of life. She is the victim of a love rivalry between the twin sons of Count Falkenburg; their likeness of face but unlikeness of mind is the root of the evil. To crown all, Amorina turns out to be their sister! The soldier Johannes, her and their cousin, is an involuntary instrument for several of the awful misdeeds that are committed in the book. He suffers from a pathological lust for bloodshed and is driven all the more deeply into his degradation by the blind incomprehension of his fellow men. In defense of Johannes, Almqvist anticipates the humane treatment of criminals that first triumphed in our own time. Is it not the duty of society to see to it that a perpetrator of evil deeds is punished? No, answers the poet: "Every criminal is a sick person—he shall be cured."

The piety of the girl Amorina is related—naturally—to that of Almqvist himself. Perhaps its vein of mysticism appears most clearly today in the singularly moving poems called *Songes,* short dreamlike lyric pieces that he wrote during various stages of his life. The music, which he set to them himself, is thoroughly congenial. In the spirit of sectarian piety, Almqvist also loved to gather about himself a circle of fellow believers or disciples. During the second decade of the 1800s he belonged to several societies of this type, in which Swedenborgian thought was united with a worship of the Old Norse. Almqvist was full of enthusiasm for the ethical-pedagogical program of the Manhem Society, in which a religious and patriotic pathos intermingled. Characteristic of this is that magnificent watchword of the ninth grade: *Himmeln och Sverige!* (Heaven and Sweden!)

But shortly after the experiment with *Amorina,* the time was ripe for Almqvist—together with some fellow believers—to make a heroic attempt to put the democratic, Old Norse or Rousseauan program into practice. With the intention of pursuing an "idealized peasant's life," he moved to Värmland's woodlands in western Sweden. Besides his urbane manners, he even laid aside his bourgeois name and called himself Love Carlsson, a name with more of a peasant ring to it. At the same time he got married to a country girl who grew up on his parents' farm. Wordsworth and his friends in the Lake District or Thoreau outside Concord may come to mind. But there is something more radical and more pathetic about Almqvist's experiment, with its ineluctable failure. These experiences from Värmland, however, were not completely wasted. Eventually they were utilized in his writing.

After his return to Stockholm in 1825, Almqvist became a teacher at a secondary school and, in 1829, an esteemed rector at the New Elementary School, where in his first enthusiasm he initiated several teaching reforms. Soon the literary abstinence abated too, and a bit into the 1830s he began publishing a colossal amount. It is channeled into *Törnrosens bok* (*The Book of the Wild Rose*), that magnificent collection which was published in volume after volume in two different versions. The idea for this literary structure is completely in the spirit of late European Romanticism; we may be reminded most immediately of E. T. A. Hoffmann's great fictional works. The framework around the entire romance is braced together by the congenial company at Jaktslottet, where Hugo Löwenstjerna, an old marshal of the royal court, gathers about himself a gallery of friends and relatives who amuse themselves by telling stories and commenting upon them. Most imaginative is the widely traveled and experienced farmer Richard Furumo, who may be said to be a kind of alter ego for Almqvist.

From the overwhelmingly rich material in *Törnrosens bok*—which, moreover, does not include all of Almqvist's production during this period—only a few trends can be mentioned here. His romantic exoticism attempts to escape from the present into different directions, to Celtic themes, to the Middle Ages (with Walter Scott for a guide), to the early Christian world, or to a southern sphere centered around the Mediterranean. The latter is true of the drama *Ramido Marinesco,* an ingenious, iridescent, and moreover very playable variation of the Don Juan theme. The aging seducer tries to mend his ways as "Pater Anselmo," while his son Ramido suffers from a curse: namely, all the young women he falls in love with turn out to be his own sisters!

Poised between history and the present day, Romanticism and Realism, and between epic and dramatic art as well, is the remarkable work *Drottningens Juvelsmycke* (*The Queen's Jewel*), which takes place around the time of the death of Gustaf III. Many authentic persons from the turn of the century make their appearance. One central scene is the murder itself, that notorious masquerade evening at the Opera on March 16, 1792. The occasion, the staging, the locality, everything must have exerted an irresistible attraction upon Almqvist, and in his presentation the theater building grows into a mysterious entity of the same type as Victor Hugo's Nôtre Dame. the bizarre Tintomara also bears a certain resemblance to Hugo's Esmeralda, though she is far more enigmatic. The character of Tintomara is two-sided, androgynous. She is passionately admired and desired by both men and women. The playing card Five of Spades forms the book's symbolic pattern with the central figure surrounded by four admirers, two young fellows, two young girls, intended to love not her but each other. Heartless and helpless, audacious and inaccessible, Tintomara—more than any other character—

embodies the atmosphere that surrounds Almqvist's life and work.

Other pieces in *Törnrosens bok* still very much worth reading are, for instance, *Araminta May,* a capricious erotic novel in the form of letters, and the play *Colombine,* dealing with the misfortunes of a young sweet prostitute; the indisputable sentimentality is successfully balanced by humorous passages, e.g., the droll dialogue between a robust, cursing count and his silly son.

Even more important, however, is the fact that Almqvist, as far as Sweden is concerned, joins the very vanguard of the new realistic portrayal of lower-class life, which appears throughout Europe in the 1830s. Almqvist's stories of common folk are surely the most accessible and esteemed part of his literary production. In *Ladugårdsarrendet* (*The Farm Lease*) and *Grimstahamns nybygge* (*Grimstahamn's New Settlement*) he relates simply and factually the tribulations of settlers on the outskirts of civilization—it is characteristic that it is not established farmers, but settlers, in whom he takes interest. He also amuses himself by interweaving specific advice for agriculture and handicraft, in the hope that others would be able to put it into practice with more success than he himself had!

The story called *Kapellet* (*The Chapel*), . . . takes place on the southeastern seashore of Sweden. In the young clergyman's thoughts, words, and actions is mirrored the vocation that filled Almqvist when he himself was ordained a minister in the summer of 1837. It was his dream that the Christian message would convey also a social awakening. This might lead to a change towards equality of property, reducing the cruel difference of conditions for example between the fisherman's wife and the sexton. But the harvests of the sea are incalculable. By a lucky event, perhaps inserted a little too haphazardly by the author, the poor fisherman's family suddenly becomes wealthy!

While facing afflictions and enjoying success, the simple inhabitants of the archipelago retain a tenacious and cheerful vitality. Thus, the program declaration that Almqvist had delivered in his brilliant essay on "The Significance of Swedish Poverty" was also put into practice. Here the poet made known his democratic conviction that the simple, uneducated populace was the nucleus of the nation, with a buoyant nature that spared it from the fatalities of wealth and made normal poverty easy to bear. Almqvist's basic view of the Swede as independent, proud, and lighthearted served as a guide to the national self-image for years afterward—at any rate as late as Heidenstam. Several of the formulations also have a healthy, metallic ring to them that has made them familiar quotations: "All of us in this country have an iron ruler running right through us that holds us upright: it glows, burns up quickly, and turns to steel, and it bends elastically to one side for a clever hand, but it's also quick to deliver a blow." Despite their long history, the Swedes, Almqvist believed, are still a young people with a youthful disposition. "It's ten o'clock in the morning in the head and the heart."

Among the products of the late 1830s, the long short story or short novel *Det går an* (It Can Be Done, tr. as *Sara Videbeck*) stands in a class by itself, notable both for the impact of its realistic portrayal and the shocking innovation of its ethical program. The story begins on the quay below Riddarholm Church in Stockholm, where *Yngve Frey* is about to depart on a trip across Lake Mälaren. It is certainly one of the first occasions on which a steamship is navigating through Swedish literature; the boat moreover is taken from real life, even down to the timetable. Also in continuation of the story the author brings forward plenty of realistic stuff: the contemporary reader received a good deal of topographical, economic and technical information, presented in the form of traveler's reports, while a late posterity has an incomparable opportunity to call to mind a part of Sweden and Swedish life during the 1830s. The detailed descriptions, e.g., the scenes from the inns along the route or the glimpses of Sara's work as a glazier, give the whole story an authenticity that had been extremely rare in Swedish literature before Almqvist's time.

Against this background of fresh colors the human problems are enacted. Sergeant Albert is—or becomes—a rather passive figure upon which Sara Videbeck's program of life is to be tried. She is the one who has the bright and unconventional mind and the courage to act accordingly. Warned by her parents' failure, Sara revolts against the old patriarchal order. She will not submit to her husband's domestic authority, not professionally, not economically, not sexually. She suggests a life together with Albert unbound and in complete equality.

With the ideas and the claims made in *Det går an* Almqvist was quite in keeping with and partly a great step ahead of the radical movement for reforming the women's role in society by giving them full rights upon reaching their majority, equal inheritance, general education and professional training, more generous opportunities in the labor market, etc. Marriage had not yet been attacked, however, and it was also on this point that *Det går an* aroused the greatest uproar. A great many polemical pamphlets appeared and Almqvist was designated a seducer of youth and destroyer of morality. Also in other ways than with his story he had made himself suspect: in accord with his increasingly vigorous radical convictions, he began in the summer of 1839 contributing to the liberal newspaper *Aftonbladet,* which was heartily detested in the conservative camp. The catastrophe in 1851 became in bourgeois opinion only the late confirmation of the moral degeneration that was indicated with *Det går an.*

Profound changes occurred in Almqvist's professional life too. Bored with his school activity, he had sought a professor's chair in Lund but had been passed by; this course of events deeply disappointed him. After he had been ordained, he abandoned himself to the prospect of a favorable parish, but to just as little avail. And when *Det går an* was published, it had not been lying in the bookstores many weeks before worried parents began to get upset over the idea that their children were being educated by a teacher with such objectionable opinions. Almqvist was induced to request a leave of absence from the rectorship and the following year he was discharged. Moreover, he received an official warning from the diocese in Uppsala, under which he was registered as a minister.

Almqvist now had no other livelihood than that from *Aftonbladet* (though in 1846 he became a regimental chaplain, with an extremely modest income). At least intermittently, he performed his newspaper work with both talent and enthusiasm. Boldly, he became involved in discussions on various political and social questions and also wrote in other genres, for example travel letters from Paris and London. His sketches from the latter city give evidence, for that matter, of Dickens's influence upon him. However, his strained financial situation led him to write potboilers feverishly. During the 1840s he wrote one after the other of a whole series of bulky, very obscure novels, often of a sensational character à la Eugène Sue. The locale is usually Stockholm or other parts of Sweden but may also be Paris, for example, which Almqvist used as the setting for a fantastic novel—*Gabrièle Mimanso*—the plot of which centers around a fictional planned murder of King Louis Philippe of France!

But not even the most unrestrained diligence could prevent his promissory notes from becoming more and more numerous and their amounts from growing larger and larger. Finally, the only alternative was escape.

A considerable time after his physical demise, Almqvist remained dead in literary terms too, but toward the end of the century came the first great renaissance, and in 1894 Ellen Key designated him "Sweden's most modern writer." Later, during the 1900s, the interest in Almqvist has risen in wave after wave. The fact remains evident that as no other writer before Strindberg he set thoughts and passions into movement on a long-range basis when casting doubt upon the ancient order in church and society. Today's discussion of the treatment of criminals and of education, of sex roles and of religious freedom may be said to have originated with him. With his clear-eyed observation of reality and his luxuriant, communicative style, he has presented for us in his Swedish stories an entire epoch in an irresistibly lifelike manner. With his body as well as his fancy, he roamed far outside the boundaries of the national state and language. If not always in reality, then in imagination, he became the indefatigable traveler, full of feeling for "the attraction of the map." Thus he also prepared the way for the international awareness—that sense of the world as your own country—that is gaining ground among the youth of our time. Undaunted, he traversed the realm of esthetic activity and came a long way on the road to the single artistic work joining all the arts ("das Gesamtkunstwerk"). His very sense of life, with its alliance of sombre outlook, blasphemous piety, and cheerful playfulness, corresponds to an important strain in contemporary writing—for example, that of the absurdists. And lastly, long before today's estheticians, Almqvist formulated the idea of the receptor as a co-creator: "The writer and his reader are two factors acting in concert for the work to be accomplished. And the work itself—which cannot be considered finished except to the extent that the letters exist on paper—constantly becomes more and more complete *through* the readers. And because during the course of time these become more and more numerous, it may be said that the writer's work thus constantly continues to be produced, on and on, as long as the world remains."

As long as the world remains. That's a great claim. But this much is certain, that in our own time Almqvist's work will continue to develop further, to be read and to be written about further. More than ever, he seems like a contemporary of the present generation. (pp. 1-13)

Staffan Björck, in an introduction to The Chapel, *by C. J. L. Almqvist, translated by Adolph Burnett Benson, Twayne Publishers, Inc. & The American-Scandinavian Foundation, 1972, pp. 1-13.*

Bertil Romberg   (essay date 1977)

[*In the following excerpt, Romberg discusses Almqvist's narrative technique and use of symbolism in* Sara Videbeck.]

[*Sara Videbeck*] deals with the brave sergeant Albert and Sara Videbeck, the beautiful, energetic daughter of a glazier: their experiences and conversations during a week's journey by steamer and mailcoach from Stockholm to Lidköping persuade them to contract a free marriage. The action extends over a week in summer, and the journey offers an ever changing succession of places and milieux. The steamer and the posting-houses attract different categories of people, from barons and parsons to Dalecarlian women and post-boys. Socially, both Albert and Sara come from a group that would rank somewhere between "better" and "lower" class.

As a work of art, the short novel—or as some prefer, the long short story—is perfect. It was written in a happy mood by a realist delighted with reality.

Sara Videbeck is no fugue, like *Amorina* or *The Queen's Jewel;* it has none of the experimental mixture of genres of the Romantic novel. There is plenty of dialogue in the novel, but no passages arranged in the dramatic dialogue form reminiscent of scenes in a play. The novel dialogue in *Sara Videbeck* is usually introduced by narrative passages, the narrator's comment or account approaches the point of view of the character and moves into the latter's direct speech or conversation by means of introductory formulas. Sixty percent of the text consists of direct speech—that is to say, the views of the actual characters—whereas the narrator's contribution amounts to only forty percent.

Both the dialogue and the narrative of *Sara Videbeck* have been rightly praised as examples of lively, observant, realistic writing. The controversial thesis is presented with genial good humor, and this is also evident from the narrator's own commentary on his writing style and his characters. The narrator intervenes very conspicuously in his fiction, as he did in the Romantic fugues. He discourses on the new steamships and their different classes of passengers, and delights in giving detailed topographic descriptions of Strängnäs and other provincial towns. This omniscient narrator can, with some indignation, inform the reader of the sergeant's mistake when at the end of the novel the latter imagines that his beloved Sara Videbeck has died.

On several occasions the narrator also takes his time discussing various problems of narrative technique: "But as a matter of fact, is it not impossible for a storyteller to follow everything that happened and to tell everything, little things and big things, both what was said and what was not said, what happened and what did not happen?"

But such illusion-breaking additions are not, as in *Amorina,* marked by Romantic humor or Romantic irony; they are rather pleasant additions in an easygoing conversational tone that does not seem to take either thesis or illusion very seriously. They are closer to Dickens than to Laurence Sterne.

. . . . .

The characterization is masterly. The narrator first introduces Albert, whose appearance is described, whose point of view is established, and whose monologue is heard. Albert is curious about a "young female passenger," speculates about her, makes observations, and draws conclusions from them. In the list of passengers he finds her name, status, and domicile, he makes advances, talks to her, is rebuffed, tries again, becomes familiar, and through their conversation gets to know more and more about her—her way of life, character traits, and opinions. Thus we come to know Sara via Albert, and of course we learn about Albert at the same time.

The narrator often views and describes the principal characters directly from his own perspective, but the most important characterization is effected indirectly, that is, when the principal figures are to a great extent left to characterize themselves and each other. This is partly a matter of what they say, and partly a question of their way of saying it. (To this may also be added characterization by gestures and acts.)

Sara and Albert both give long accounts of themselves. It is normal that two lovers should tell each other about their past, their fancies, their opinions; they put each other to the test and lay their cards out on the table.

The two characters thus brought face to face are quite unlike. The impatient and enthusiastic Albert is strong in his opening attack, but it is the cool, sensible, and practical Sara who soon takes over, tightens the reins, and determines the way and the goal of their journey together through life.

In the love scenes Almqvist was extremely careful to emphasize Sara's pure disposition and morals—which explains the apparently cool and noncommittal trait in her character—because the subject of the story could easily be judged offensive by readers of his day. What Sara proposes to Albert is simply sexual intercourse between an unmarried man and an unmarried woman, which at that time was against the law in Sweden. But a certain similarity between Sara and other female characters in Almqvist's work can also be detected. There is undeniably something of animal coeleste about Sara Videbeck.

The novel spans a week, and there is a remarkable exactitude in the chronological course of events.

There is also considerable variation in the ratio between the time it takes to narrate events and the time it took for them to occur. The first day (the steamship tour) fills the first four chapters—that is, fifty-five pages, almost half the novel. The period from the third to the sixth day is summed up in less than one page, and within this time Albert and Sara have made up their minds. In the remaining time they discuss thoroughly their future life together.

A good deal has been said about Almqvist's documentary realism: with all the narrator's details about steamboat decks and posting-house rooms, *Sara Videbeck* has become a living picture of the period, ranking almost as a historical document. The topographical surveys and descriptions have the observant, graphic quality as Almqvist's own travel letters. Sometimes the depiction of the scenery is colored by Albert's point of view, becoming romantically personified, as, for instance, in the somewhat erotic description of the sun setting over Kungsör:

> It was evening. In the west the fairy of the sun had already sunk into the arms of the Kungsör meadows, but a dark-red shimmer of purple still lingered in the sky; it was the last garment that the beautiful fairy had cast off before lying down to sleep under the quilt. Thousands of long red-blue streaks radiated from the shimmer, many of them striped the water and some even lay splashed on the objects on board the steamer.

But these Romantic metaphors are exceptions. As a rule, the descriptions of scenery are matter of fact and concrete: travel poetry of facts.

. . . . .

Among the striking symbols and symbolism in *Sara Videbeck* we first encounter the steamboat trip. It has been suggested that the narrator's digression on modern steamers and antiquated sailing ships has symbolic significance. Steamers are driven by internal combustion, symbolizing people who follow their own feelings and convictions. The old sailing ships, on the other hand, may be taken to represent the clumsy, unwieldy social institutions that drive people where they do not want to go, causing many a shipwreck.

The marriage controversy, one of the elements of the composition, is introduced in the first chapter when Sara throws a ring into the water: gallant Albert has offered it to her when trying to make her acquaintance. Sara's action soon proves to be a symbolic gesture, and the ring that she flung away is later referred to several times. It turns out—quite conventionally—to be a symbol of the shackles of wedlock.

Time after time Sara is described as an "in-betweener," at first in a social sense, but—as Albert's love for her grows—the term acquires a broader significance. It becomes associated with the pane of glass which is not seen "and yet definitely separates the Inside of the little human world from the immense Outside. In the pane itself I can see nothing, but through it, nevertheless, I now see the stars in the sky." Albert's musings on the pane of glass and its nature, and his speculations on the heart of glass and the diamond, also perform the functions of leitmotif and symbols. The pane of glass and the heart of glass also symbolize Sara's pure, chaste, and transparent, but at the same time hard and distant nature.

As already mentioned, the basic theme is the marriage debate. But it is not only the form of marriage and the function of the wedding that Almqvist is attacking in his novel. He is also making a topical argument in favor of women's right to work. Almqvist has stressed the absurdity of Sara not being allowed to pursue a trade even though she is quite capable. The novel was published just in time to support reform measures in the Riksdag of 1840 concerning the rights of majority and the trading rights.

As far as love and marriage are concerned, Almqvist argues in favor of a free erotic liaison—with responsibility and true devotion—as a model for the life shared by woman and man.

To keep love alive, the narrator recommends, through Sara, a busy life of travel. The prescription was recommended still more strongly when *Sara Videbeck* was included in the third volume of the imperial octavo edition of 1850. There, in fact, it was immediately preceded by the short sketch, "Why Do You Travel?" in which he eloquently sets forth all the advantages of traveling: on a journey one has time only to show one's better, more pleasant sides: "I must also add that I have the strange advantage when I travel (alone, that is) that almost everybody meets me in divine mood [. . .] Human beings are like pianos in that they readily return the note that is struck; and they do not sound false except when they are out of tune."

People can certainly be out of tune, but seldom when they are traveling. Consequently we must look upon our whole life as no more than a journey, and all "dwelling-places should be regarded as mere *stopping-places*. Can that be done?" That is how the little essay ends, and *Sara Videbeck*—which ends with the words "It can be done"—may be regarded as the application of these ideas to marriage. As far as we can follow Sara's and Albert's life together, it is lived on a journey, and Albert is also going to travel a great deal in future, so that they may benefit fully from the advantages of mobility. In such an alliance the contracting parties will become happier and better than couples who are forced, by marriage or common domicile, to rub elbows all the time.

Here we find a reflection of Almqvist's own matrimonial situation. It has already been mentioned that his marriage was not a happy one. A letter to J. A. Hazelius in December 1841 gives further evidence:

> My dear Maria is *inwardly* quite angelic in her pure and genuine kindness, in her fairness and love of truth. But *outwardly* hardly anybody can be imagined more cumbersome or difficult for a man who must occupy himself with what he ought to do and would like to do. No shoe is mended, no chair is put in its right place, no turnip is bought without my having to give my opinion five or ten times over and usually then attending to the matter myself. People do not know this and nobody will believe it. Many people think that I have been sitting all by myself, a free and happy dreamer, giving myself up to

all sorts of blissful thoughts. Since you once broached the subject, Janne, I tell you that I have *suffered* and am still suffering. (Letters)

But in spite of everything, he still loves Maria sincerely, Almqvist says, especially in moments of loneliness and when he is away from home. There is in Maria's personality a very strange combination—"at the same time heaven and slovenly chaos"—which makes her difficult to live with.

It is obvious that the discrepancy between husband and wife as to temperament and intellectual level was never to be resolved. But outbursts like the above-quoted example are rare, and in spite of his negative comments on wedding and marriage, Almqvist accepted his own ill-matched marriage, perhaps for practical reasons, perhaps because, in his own way, he always retained his tender feelings toward his wife. During the longest separation of all, his years of exile in America, an unaffected and deep tenderness marks his letters to Maria.

In the appendix to *Sara Videbeck* Almqvist denies that it is a tendentious novel and tries to explain what is meant by "tendency." Almqvist definitely repudiates any mixing of "doctrinaire, agitatorial, or scientific literature with fiction. Both parties—on the one hand, the message, the explanation, the discussion, and on the other, the fiction—will lose through an ill-matched union." Almqvist maintains that only such theoretical arguments as belong organically to the fiction and are justified by it, should be accepted. If not,

> the lessons, however good they may be in themselves, have nevertheless been unartistically inserted into the piece and constitute what in a pejorative sense may be termed *creatures of tendency.* They stand there so to speak on account of the author or rather of the doctrines as such; which is out of place because such things belong to science, not to art.

Thus Almqvist deprecates the "bad," inartistic tendentious literature of his time, with its loosely attached ideas imperfectly integrated into the fiction. That "good" thesis novels may exist is a fact that Almqvist seems to ignore; obviously we cannot speak of a tendency when, for instance, Sara is speaking. Her arguments are "in full accordance with her character and are fully justified by the situation or the incident, for she has every reason and motive to utter them when she does so [. . .] the lessons are not there for their own sake or for the sake of the narrator."

These explanations show Almqvist as an extremely clever theorist of narrative technique.

However, we might then well ask whether the novel fulfills Almqvist's own requirements. His characterization of Sara provides the answer. One thing is obvious: If Almqvist had meant Sara to be a typical glazier's daughter in the 1830's, the opinions that she expresses would certainly have seemed inappropriate in her mouth. On the contrary, Almqvist has emphasized that Sara is *not* typical. On the contrary, he constantly stresses what is unique, uncommon about her. From the very beginning Sara appears to Albert as an in-betweener:

A mademoiselle? Yes, in a way. A burgher's daughter, though of the lowest burgher class. An attractive and strange in-betweener! Not a country girl, certainly not a peasant girl—but not quite better class either. How should such a person be regarded? What should she be called? There is something impenetrable about this intermediate sort.

Albert's speculations about Sara's social status are continued on another level, as if she is quite unfathomable to him. Thus, it seems perfectly consistent for her to have unusual opinions, all the more so as Almqvist motivates them by her personal experiences, particularly her parents' unhappy marriage. It must also be said that the conversations about marriage are introduced quite naturally: the topic is an obvious one for two persons falling in love with each other.

The original version of *Sara Videbeck* was provided with a preface which in 1850 was included in the appendix. In the preface the author is—rightly—convinced that he has a future before him:

> It is said that a fine veil hangs before the future of Europe preventing us seeing distinctly the figures that beckon to us behind it. I think so, too. The veil is not quite transparent, in some places its beautiful drapery hangs in somewhat thicker folds than in others making it less easy to see through it. [. . .] Nobody can or should know the individual fate that awaits us in the future; but the general fate, . . . the general direction . . . is clearly indicated to us.

(pp. 121-28)

Bertil Romberg, in his Carl Jonas Love Almqvist, *translated by Sten Lidén, Twayne Publishers, 1977, 203 p.*

Marilyn E. Johns   (essay date 1980)

[*Johns is an American educator and critic specializing in Scandinavian languages and literature. In the following essay, she argues that* Drottningens juvelsmycke (The Queen's Jewelpiece) *is a quintessentially Romantic novel that demonstrates Almqvist's indebtedness to German philosophy.*]

Friedrich Schlegel's clarion call for "romantische Poesie" rapidly reverberated over the entire literary landscape of Germany and its northern neighbors—a challenge and prophecy whose echoes are still heard a century and a half later. But whereas Schlegel's countrymen continue, albeit sporadically, to do critical homage to him, he is all but forgotten by Scandinavian scholars who prior to the last two decades have restricted themselves almost exclusively to a biographical *modus operandi*. The major critics of Carl Jonas Love Almqvist (1793-1866), the doyen of Swedish Romanticism, hasten to make mention of Almqvist's grounding in German speculative philosophy and literary theory, but are seemingly loath to explore this relationship in any depth, presumably for fear of undermining the author's reputation for creative originality. Rather, they tend to think of him as an early Strindberg—an innovative, extraordinarily gifted, and prolific freak. It is my contention that this is not the case, and that, quite to the contrary, Almqvist's work is decisively influenced by the tradition of German speculative and aesthetic philosophy. Indeed I would venture to say that Almqvist succeeds where even Schlegel himself fails, namely, in the conception and execution of the penultimate Romantic novel.

Drottningens juvelsmycke (*The Queen's Jewelpiece*, 1834) was written in less than three months and comprises the major novel in Almqvist's monumental project, *Törnrosens bok* (*The Book of the Wild Rose*, a collective frame for a great variety of novels, lyric poetry, essays, dramas, and tracts) which was to become the single greatest literary achievement in Sweden during the 1830's or, some would argue, the entire first half of the 19th century. The basic outline of the intrigue has been traced to Moreto and Calderón; the historical, topographical, and orthographical realism to Scott; the psychological technique to Goethe, the coloring to Hugo; and the elements of the fantastic to E. T. A. Hoffmann. But very little work has been done on Almqvist's relationship to Schlegel. To be sure, the extent of his familiarity with the philosopher can only be surmised. We do know that he was a learned academician who read voraciously and who exhibited a very keen interest in German literature in general, but his comments on Schlegel are random at best and occur merely in passing in his theoretical works and his correspondence. Almqvist spent his university years in Uppsala from 1808 to 1815; there he came into contact for the first time with German philosophy and Swedenborgian mysticism, both of which he interpreted sentimentally, assimilating them with his inherited Herrnhutian pietism. He read Kant and Fichte and later came to be a central figure in the German-influenced Swedish literary Romantic circle which published the journal *Phosphorus,* modelled on *Athenäum* in both form and critical posture. Although Almqvist did not join this group until 1820, we do know that he read the Phosphorists' printed manifestoes, including V. F. Palmblad's Schlegelian dialogue on the history of the novel, published in 1812. As early as 1810 P. D. A. Atterbom, who was to become a close friend and admirer of Almqvist's, published in *Phosphorus* a translation of the last chapter of Friedrich Ast's *System der Kunstlehre oder Lehr- und Handbuch der Ästhetik* (1804) which is itself very Schlegelian. Indeed, Schlegel (along with Kant, Schiller, and Schelling) was very much a prominent force in Swedish Romantic critical debate, and Almqvist, as his letters show, was keenly aware of what was transpiring on the German and Swedish cultural scenes at this time. For him to have been ignorant of Schlegel's critical impact would not only have been highly unlikely, it would have been nigh unto impossible.

But even if it were not for Schlegel's omnipresence in Swedish literary debate during the first two decades of the 19th century, Almqvist would probably have been drawn to him anyway by virtue of their sympathetic temperaments. Almqvist underwent a shattering religious crisis in 1813 after which he came to embrace a rather personalized version of Swedenborgianism. He emerged with the ecstatic's overwhelming certainty of a new totalizing vision, with a new dedication to the reconciliation of the earthly and the divine. This ecstatic vision is reflected in

a letter which he wrote to J. A. Hazelius on 1 October 1819: "You know, the more I observe myself, the more I find that I truly have become rapturous [Sw. *svärmisk,* G. *schwärmerisch*], insofar as one takes rapture in its customary definition, namely, *Something extra sensum communem.*" Schlegel too experienced a profound religious conversion, but to a rigidly orthodox Catholicism. It would be, however, fruitless to insist upon a complete equation between Almqvist's and Schlegel's mystical leanings. Almqvist's mysticism is not so exclusively aesthetic as Schlegel's, nor does it so unreservedly agitate for the dissolution of the individual. It is also substantially more religious and less philosophical, but their mutual enthusiasm for a mystical mode of perception undoubtedly made Schlegel's teachings and theories all the more palatable to the young Almqvist.

Before exploring the specific ways in which *The Queen's Jewelpiece* exemplifies Schlegel's theory of the novel, it is perhaps necessary to clear some of the terminological waters which Schlegel himself did much to muddy. The word "Poesie" means three things for Schlegel: it is at one and the same time poetic literature in verse or prose, a human faculty on the same order as imagination or reason, and a universal essence, rather like Soul, which permeates the entire cosmos. Similarly, he uses the word "romantisch" in its vague colloquial sense, in its concrete historical sense, in which it refers to post-classical poetry, and to mean "romanartig." We notice comparable terminological obfuscations surrounding the word "Roman." From Herder's *Humanitätsbriefe,* Schlegel comes to understand the word "Roman" as signifying not only the novel, but also the medieval and early modern romance. "Roman," "Romanpoesie," and "Romantische Poesie" become all but interchangeable. It is not merely a novel, but a kind of "Mischgedicht" which is the best and indeed the only suitable form for expressing the spirit of the Romantic age.

Almqvist shares Schlegel's scepticism towards contemporary judgments on novel form. In his **"Dialogue on the Method of Concluding Pieces,"** Almqvist insists that *The Queen's Jewelpiece* is not a "roman," but is satisfied that it be called "konstverk" or "romaunt." He even goes so far as to say:

> In view of the fact that it [*The Queen's Jewelpiece*] in tone, form, and content is completely unlike what one usually calls *roman,* it struck me as inappropriate to call it such. The pieces in question are, after a fashion, paintings of customs, restrict themselves to specific times and places, occasionally concern familiar historical personages, but like others, I cannot help but observe that a fantasy inherent in the subjects frequently draws the pictures into regions which are foreign to ordinary novels. Nevertheless there suffuses these syntheses a deep and at the same time protean feeling of the entire predilection and tendency which one so often and rightly designates as "romantic." Since, consequently, the problem centers around something which is decidedly romantic without, however, being a *roman,* there hovered between the two the name "romaunt," like an intermediation between an

earthly narrative, on the one hand, and a free flight to foreign mysterious climes, on the other.

Almqvist's desire to expand the generic boundaries of the traditional "roman," his seeking a form in the medieval "romaunt," and finally his interpretation of that form as mediating an immutable conflict between the real and the ideal all are clearly rooted in Schlegelian thought. Almqvist, like Schlegel, is here agitating for "eine Poesie, deren eins und alles das Verhältnis des Idealen und des Realen ist."

Indeed, the whole question of genre for both authors is grounded in a problem of philosophy. . . . [Schlegel's] poetic ideal, which is synonymous with God, asserts the complete fusion and intermingling of "das Fantastische," "das Sentimentalische," and "das Mimische." These terms correspond to several concerns which Schlegel puts forth in his *Athenäum* aphorism 116. The sentimental is "das Sinnliche," "das Geistige," "der heilige Hauch" ("Brief über den Roman". The fantastic is the form which is a semblance of chaos, tempered by an underlying order. It is furthermore suggested that the fantastic form is given a central focus and order by the sentimental theme. And finally, the mimetic corresponds partially to Schlegel's insistence on historical subject matter. There is, then, in romantic poetry an "unendliche Fülle" encompassed within an "unendliche Einheit," all empirical phenomena in their infinite profusion springing from a single source and forming an organic whole.

Even the style in which the *Athenäum* aphorism is written reflects the goal of uniting all that is "getrennt": The radical parataxis of the fragment provides an endless series of concentric unifications, systems which in turn embrace and are embraced by other systems. He would make "Poesie lebendig und gesellig" and "das Leben und die Gesellschaft poetisch." Poetic reflection is itself the "Mittelding" between the real and the ideal. The author establishes a wealth of tensions which keep extending themselves but are never really resolved. He seems to be maintaining that actually a synthesis or unification of these opposites is possible only through their intensification—chaos opposed to order, manifold plentitude to unity, nature to art—a schematization which gives birth in the "Brief über den Roman" to the concept of the arabesque.

Almqvist addresses this same problem in his theoretical essay **"On the Unity of Epism and Dramatism: A Conception of the Poetic Fugue"** in which he maintains that the epic is a specifically heathen art form, extending from the universal to the individual, from necessity to freedom, whereas the drama, which is specifically Christian, traverses the same path in the opposite direction. The lyric forms an intermediary stage which unites them both. But a higher unity, a life for each form within the other, is achieved only in the poetic fugue. The fugue is an expression of totality in musical art, a term which he then applies to both **The Queen's Jewelpiece** and **Amorina,** the cataclysmically Gothic novel from 1839 which was to represent the bankruptcy of Romantic aesthetics for Almqvist. Further explaining the term, he calls the poetic fugue "*a Totality* of alternately dramatic and epic form," and he seems to imply that it also has associations with the musi-

cal fugue's strict scheme of composition with repetitions and variations on a given theme, which provides a mirroring effect not unlike Schlegel's insistence on the self-reflective quality of poetry. It is in keeping with his theoretical works that Almqvist allows the second half of **The Queen's Jewelpiece** to serve as a reflection of and variation on the first half of the novel (a movement strongly reminiscent of *Lucinde*), the entire plot resting on a series of *quid pro quos*. At the center of **The Queen's Jewelpiece** stands Azouras Lazuli Tintomara, an androgynous being who exists in quiet spirituality and is completely sufficient unto herself. Around her mill throngs of desperately divided and fragmented individuals who would use her for their own political or sensual gain. She is a creature of gliding graceful light, struggling in a world of dark, menacing automatons. She embodies a vision of "schöne Seele," an individual in perfect communion with her natural environment; but she is compelled to live in a society which is described in metaphors of mask, masquerade, pantomime, and machinery. Two main plot lines coincide and self-destruct in this enigmatic figure, who herself is finally made a victim of the Schlegelian Romantic paradox and offered up to a higher, more spiritual point of reference. Tintomara is but one in a series of female protagonists to whom Almqvist refers collectively as a "mellanting" (G. *Mittelding*), the literary embodiment of Schlegel's "poetische Reflexion," who hovers at the midpoint between the portrayer and the portrayed, male and female, the real and the ideal.

Since Romantic poetry aspires toward universal harmony, it must of necessity encompass a variety of forms, which leads to Schlegel's concept of "Mischgedicht." His enthusiasm for works with an encyclopedic content and a fusion of the greatest possible variety of forms is the result of his emphasis on artistic "Allheit," "Ganzheit," "Totalität," and "Universalität." This preference leads him to single out Jean Paul for praise because of the complexity of his narrative forms, and to maintain: "Ja, ich kann mir einen Roman kaum anders denken, als gemischt aus Erzählung, Gesang, und andern Formen" ("Brief über den Roman"). Almqvist is Sweden's and possibly Europe's foremost practitioner of this mixed style. He rarely refers to the creative act as writing, but instead speaks of "drawing, forming, composing events, painting characters." Already in **Murnis,** completed in 1819, he combines several genres: the religious epic, visionary poetry, the short story, the *Entwicklungsroman,* and, not least, the myth, the folktale, and the *Kunstmärchen*. This artistic impulse, however, reaches its culmination in **The Book of the Wild Rose,** which, while combining all literary genres, was intended to present a great survey of the history of humanity beginning with the creation, an enterprise characteristic of the Romantic view of the universality of poetry. **The Queen's Jewelpiece** occupies a pivotal position in this herculean undertaking, presenting not only generic synthesis, but also synaesthesia. It combines song, poetry, monologues, epic narrative, drama, epistles, and topographical descriptions, all within a fictitious narrative frame which is still further subsumed under the genre of the historical novel. The constant expansion and contraction of generic limitations derives, as it does in Schlegel, from a profound dissatisfaction with the restrictions of traditional genres, as well as from a deep-seated belief in the cosmic nature of poetry. *The Queen's Jewelpiece* is less a conventionally structured novel than a series of vignettes which comment on preceding tableaux and foreshadow scenes to come. Individually each of them appears as a miniature which is sufficient unto itself, but which nevertheless becomes truly meaningful only in its relationship to its companion pieces, either by negating through romantic irony that which has gone before or by elaborating and extending to a higher plane a preceding motif. The structural impulse behind these vignettes is not unlike that which prompted the form of *Lucinde,* but for Almqvist it results in the most sophisticated pre-Strindbergian novel in Scandinavia, for Schlegel in what we today can only regard as a not very successful experiment.

Schlegel's entire Romantic aesthetics devolves, of course, upon the transcendental aspect of poetry, a fact which predicts not only his theory of "Mischgedicht" but also his insistence on poetry as eternally becoming. His prescription that poetry must be progressive, in a constant state of becoming, and never really "vollendet," prefigures the predominant Romantic aesthetics or the fragmentary or the unfinished, for which his own fragments represent a high-point. This is a concern with which Almqvist is very much in sympathy, as we see most clearly in his "**Dialogue on the Method of Concluding Pieces,**" where he reacts to the contemporary disapproval of the ending of *The Queen's Jewelpiece.* He maintains here that, because events and actions are in reality very seldom fully completed, art too should reflect this universal moiety and be "half obscure, purely intuited, in some ways perhaps eternally inexplicable, inexhaustible." He distinguishes between at least two different modes of authorship—the direct and self-exhausting and the intuitive and suggestive—and considers himself to belong to the latter. Such a perception of art derives from his vision of the fragmented individual. In the same essay, he informs the reader that

> individuals are created in hemispheres . . . ; no one is to be completed except through others, and the whole through everyone. . . . Because every living being, beside his individual wholeness, at the same time, of necessity, is a fragment, a bizarre chill and a dead quality steam forth from everything which appears in naked perfection, unity, and self-sufficiency.

A rejection of an art divorced from other human concerns attends the pivotal role of the reader in the artistic process. For both critics, a work of art unread is not, properly speaking, a work of art, and furthermore that work is superior which inspires active engagement on the part of the reader. Almqvist agitates for an authorship which puts the reader in a perspective, an atmosphere, a wish and desire to go forth in the direction of the subject. The author and his reader become then two cooperating factors, and the work becomes continually more complete through readers. An authorship and its readers ought to be two halves which mutually engage and complete each other, a line of thought which might also have its source in Schelling's characterization of the work of art as "eine bewußtlose Unendlichkeit."

A further elaboration of the same fundamental problem is to be found in Almqvist's essay "**Also on Humor and Style Therein.**" The theories demonstrated there present art not merely as an accurate reflector of life, but also as a willful creator thereof. Art touches feelings and thought processes in such a way that, during the act of contemplation or reading, it mysteriously conjures forth a world which the reader considers his own work. And the final work of art is, then, a point between the work of art itself and the act of reading, that is to say that it extends outwards from us as gentle irony, without, however, being the same as we. We see ourselves as in a mirror, we cannot deny our image, "we sense ourselves in the depths," and gradually we "journey vastly far away from ourselves: are transformed." In order that the reader himself can finally "become poetry," he must be an active participant, and to this end Almqvist solicits reader involvement in *The Queen's Jewelpiece.* In the introductory frame, the demonic narrator Richard Furumo asks that his listeners' "own reflection and lively imagination might kindly fill in and connect [these accounts] into a lovely and pleasing whole." Similarly, the author concludes Book III with an incomplete statement: "Quick, no more weakness, I shall, I shall—," piquing the reader's interest and inviting him to speculate on what course of action is open to Amanda, who is being increasingly entrapped by the machinations of erotic intrigue. In the same tantalizing fashion, we are introduced to J. J. Anckarström, the assassin of Gustaf III, at the masked ball in the Opera House on 16 March 1792, but we are not given his name and can only guess his identity as he lurks within the labyrinthine corridors of the Royal Opera: "The stranger stood quietly and was silent, still his arms seemed to tremble, after the burden he had carried, or because of. . . ." Such ploys to involve the reader in the creation of the narrative culminate in the final scene, for which Almqvist was rather severely taken to task by contemporary critics. The playfully transcendent masquerade of Gustaf III has become a malevolent and byzantine masquerade orchestrated by the machiavellian Reuterholm, whose purpose it is to stage a mock execution of Tintomara in order to terrify her into compliance with his erotic scheming. King Gustaf Adolf, the royal court, and all the upper bourgeoisie are in attendance to watch this spectacle. But romantic irony would have it that Ferdinand, a conspirator against Gustaf III and victim of Tintomara's unwitting charms, has signed on with the execution squad and does not remove his bullets as instructed. His shot rings out as Tintomara's gaze is transfixed by the bullet-like cupola atop Solna church. The shot fades, the landscape recedes into silence, and "with this great pervasive silence . . . the story also is silent." Clearly, this movement is an authorial invitation to reader engagement in the narrative, an engagement that asks that we, like the heroine, transcend the activities and events of the novel itself and fix our vision on a higher frame of reference.

But Almqvist is indebted to Schlegel not only for his development of an aesthetics of reader participation, but also for the concept of arabesque, which Schlegel designates as an idealized synthesis of chaos and order in art, "eine ganz bestimmte und wesentliche Form order Äußerungsart der Poesie." By giving expression to his own caprice or arbitrariness (G. *Willkür*) in seemingly arbitrary and episodic poetry, the author is actually responding to a universal imperative to unite the chaotic into an ordered form. Thus, Schlegel demands a "reizende Symmetrie von Widersprüchen," a "künstlich geordnete Verwirrung" ("Rede über die Mythologie"), an idea inspired by Kant's valorization of the concept in his *Kritik der Urteilskraft*. Almqvist makes this same distinction in his "**Questions of Varying Import**," in which he differentiates the "formal" from the "essential." Like Schlegel's chaos, Almqvist's "essential" is described as a fundamental life force, a throwback to the Greek concept of a primordial fusion of the original elements of the world. As Ernst Behler describes it:

> Systematic order has been imposed on the original state of existence, diminishing the primeval richness of Being. In other words, chaotic order mirrors life and genuine Being, while systematic order is a mere shadow of life.

But for both authors, order can be imposed on the chaotic essence of life and that chaos is itself ordered in the poetic process so that both become one. As Almqvist expresses this idea:

> But in its highest definition, are both these concepts not one? For, though on higher horizons ideas and things appear as differentiated and splintered as possible, there is still a revelation, in the face of which All is One.

Given Almqvist's conviction that art must reflect the chaos and confusion of the world, it is hardly surprising that his critics upbraided him for the novel's loose and disjointed plot, incomplete character conception, and amorphous structure. But the author was very adamant that the structure of the work, although unconventional, was artistically cohesive. He even uses Schlegel's own term when Adolphine desperately seeks a way out of the intrigue which is rapidly enveloping her:

> There must be some way to comb out this tangled silkskein, and since I cannot deny my complicity as the cause behind these many fantastic suspicions, I must hasten to finish painting the arabesque so that it is perfect and we can all understand each other.

But the arabesque has undergone a transmogrification from Schlegel to Almqvist. Schlegel's metaphor of the oriental tapestry has been transformed into one of the labyrinth, a spatial distinction which may to some extent account for the respective successes of their novels. The arabesque and the labyrinth are forms which pervade the entire structure and conception of *The Queen's Jewelpiece*. From the narrative frame centering around Herr Hugo and his salon (a technique which corresponds to the border on Schlegel's tapestry), we move inward toward a bewildering series of tableaux. The reader finds himself first in the middle of a rather melodramatic Scribean erotic intrigue involving two couples each half of which unjustifiably suspects the other of infidelity. He then is caught up in a novelistic reenactment of the murder of King Gustaf III and the political struggles going on behind the scenes. It is here that we are first introduced to Tintomara, who then takes over our interest for the remainder of the novel,

all the while unwittingly causing death, insanity, and destruction all about her. We are presented with lyrical interludes during Tintomara's Rousseauistic communion with nature, with topographical descriptions of the streets of 1790's Stockholm and the bucolic idyll around Kolmården, with pseudoscientific disputations on the nature of androgyny, with social criticism and commentary, and with a depiction of one of the most politically volatile periods in Sweden's history. Characters appear, disappear, and reemerge, colliding with or subsumed by other characters in mad desperate pursuit of the spectre of universal harmony which Tintomara represents, all of them ironically unable to reach or find her because of their ignorant and fragmented natures, which compel them to seek her in the first place. We travel like the characters from vignette to vignette, genre to genre, through the labyrinth of the novel in search of the work's unity, only to discover at the end of the journey that such a unity is to be achieved solely through a transcendence on our part, a transcendence into Schlegel's state of poetic reflection.

For Schlegel, the underlying order of the arabesque lies both in the border of the tapestry and in the less palpable unity of motif and spirit with which the design is suffused. Almqvist follows this organizing principle by adopting a narrative frame for his novel which functions as a distancing mechanism to undercut the immediacy of his material. In order to impart a specifically visual frame of reference, like the pictorial qualities which Schlegel prized so much in Romantic poetry, Almqvist establishes the vivid images of the labyrinth and the five in a deck of cards. Both the playing card metaphor and that of the domino masquerade costumes worn by Gustaf III and the conspirators clearly reinforce the importance of aesthetic "play" within the novel and underline the ongoing contrast between appearance and reality, nature and art, the ideal and the real. *La Sauvage Sauvée*, the ballet in which Tintomara is starring at the Royal Opera, shows her strapped to the ground with a guard on each hand and foot, forming a square in which she is the center, an image likened by Adolfine to the five of spades. This same image recurs several times throughout the novel. When Tintomara is learning to shoot at Kolmården, she takes a five of hearts and blots out the four corners leaving only the one in the center (Ferdinand's heart) which she then shoots away, an action ironically prefiguring her own execution. The mysterious card emerges again, this time as a five of clubs, when the Baroness and the Uncle are playing cards, and the Uncle persistently draws this card, an event which points up the role he too has in making Tintomara an object for his own private gain. In the final scene of the novel she has indeed become the center of the labyrinth, the ace in the center of the number five playing card. She is surrounded by hostile forces who would usurp her strength and harmony, and a small red diamond-shaped piece of paper is placed on her heart for the execution squad. She has become a playing card, a pawn in the designs of all those who meet her and are drawn toward her. One might also, however, consider the visual form of the novel as a descending helix through which the reader passes as he is inexorably drawn down toward the center, a movement which is also across increasingly aristocratic social classes. The irony, of course, lies in the fact that as we are drawn into this center point, we and the characters in the novel become increasingly desperate in our attempt to understand, grasp, and order the enigma which Tintomara represents, all the time descending deeper and deeper into the quagmire of irreconcilable oppositions, while Tintomara is ascending higher and higher away from us.

The novel's strong visual motifs are supported by Almqvist's frequent use of the pictorial. It is not a matter of mere happenstance that this novel has been rendered on the stage by Alf Sjöberg in 1957 and that Hjalmar Bergman worked on a filmatization of it during 1923. Book V in particular presents an inordinately filmic reality. Almqvist describes in a painterly manner the scene in the Royal Opera House where the conspirators meet to carry out their plans for assassination. A narrative camera moves through the ballroom, dollies down dark corridors and abruptly stops when it encounters several shadowy figures in consultation. The atmosphere is so heavy and thick that we do not see faces, but merely hear voices. We then observe close-ups of a young lady and her minutely detailed gestures. Masks and costumes speak forth from this shadowy two-dimensional realm, reinforcing, once again, the underlying philosophical conflict between mask and face, appearance and reality.

The genre's rather flexible form is but one reason why Schlegel chooses the novel to be the ideal mode of Romantic poetry. Another cause may be found in its special capacity for presenting the individuality of its author. According to Schlegel,

> . . . das Beste in den besten Romanen ist nichts anders . . . als ein mehr oder minder verhülltes Selbstbekenntnis des Verfassers, der Ertrag seiner Erfahrung, die Quintessenz seiner Eigentümlichkeit. ("Brief über den Roman")

Since he views modern intellectual history as a process of development toward an ever-increasing subjectivism, he perceives that the only method for the author to overcome his lonely and isolated position is through romantic irony. In view of the fact that the relationship between Almqvist's life and his work has been dealt with at great length elsewhere, I shall not belabor the subject here. Suffice it is to say that **The Queen's Jewelpiece** contains numerous oblique references to Almqvist's personal and professional life and that, far more importantly, these are recounted and woven into the manuscript in a very removed and objective manner. There is in this novel no subjective wallowing in the mire of personal purgatories. Rather, the material has been treated with an attitude which Swedish literary scholars have come to dub post-Inferno Strindbergian resignation. The author has gone beyond the not inconsiderable suffering of his own life and placed it within a framework of objectivity in a characteristically Goethean procedure. A wit and humor, ever keen, have been brought to bear on the agonies of a deeply passionate man, transcending the personal into the universal.

In his considerations of Romantic poetry, Schlegel does not restrict himself to prescription of style, form, philosophical bent, and authorial stance, but also addresses himself to the problem of appropriate subject matter. For Schlegel the emotions of love and Romantic poetry must be treated appropriately. Almqvist follows his theoretician in this dictum. The entire novel whirls about Tintomara and her intrinsic sexual harmony. Each book in the novel is provided with a motto, most of which refer to the erotic subject matter: "Tintomara! two things are white, innocence and arsenic," "Tout à Vous, beau Tristan," "O masquerade of the heart," and "Le mannequin and la mannequine." Although agreeing on the importance of love for romantic poetry, Almqvist and Schlegel differ substantially in their evaluations of that emotion. In contrast to Schlegel's deification of the erotic, Almqvist finds earthly love divisive and destructive. Ferdinand's military comrade expresses Almqvist's ideas on love:

> . . . if only people in this world were crystalline beings, my friend; I mean transparent for one another, so that each one knew the basis of his own character and that of others. Then one could discover and know each other, when genuine similarity and personal sympathy existed. . . . In a better world, I believe firmly that good people could see themselves and others so purely, so clearly, that they would comprehend one another. . . . But here in this world so often tragedies arise as a result of the mist wherein we hover unknown to ourselves and unfamiliar to others.

There is, then, a veil which makes genuine love all but impossible and which is rooted in Almqvist's and Schlegel's perception of the fragmentary and "absurd" nature of this earthly life and those individuals who inhabit it. Both authors seek an expression of perfect love, but for Schlegel there is at least the possibility of attaining to it in this life. In *Lucinde,* Julius desires "die Vollendung des Männlichen und Weiblichen zur vollen ganzen Menschheit"—a unification characterized in strongly androgynous terms. He also realizes that this can be achieved only through the highest degree of love. Almqvist too presents us with a vision of the androgyne, who by her very perfection points up a paucity of genuine love in "normal" human beings. She recalls of course Plato's myth of Aristophanes, and is the very embodiment of the totality free of longing. She represents the union of the Schillerian concepts of "das Tierische" and "das Geistige"—she is an *animal coeleste,* which Almqvist defines as

> not natural or animalistic in the usual lower meaning of the term . . . but rather born of nature and in unity with itself in a divine sense.

Tintomara's perfection lies in a kind of holy inner harmony with herself. It is an idyllic state of happiness which she represents. Her clarity and perfection have not been won through suffering and strife, but are rather the result of a worship of the aesthetic which is unmoved by the tragic conflicts of life. Tintomara becomes a whole cosmology, the center of existence after which Almqvist and the reader are searching. She is simultaneously an angel and an elemental being, both a crystalline divine perfection and a dark mysterious "Naturgrund." She is possessed of certain ingenuous qualities—naïveté, innocence, and natural purity—and according to her mother's pronouncement, chastity, piety, and truth are inbred in her character. She is at the same time beyond conventional morality. She steals because she has no selfish sense of property and is completely free of dogma, functioning socially on an intuitive sense of ethics. Reflection is also a trait with which she is not burdened. Completely unself-conscious, she is a spokesperson for the Romantic ideal of divine instinct which must be incorporated with modern reflection in order to lead to a new synthesis of the conscious and the subconscious. Ordinary humanity is imprisoned within itself by a host of Peer Gyntian wishes, dreams, and desires to which its imperfection gives rise and out of which it longs for escape.

Just as the sentimental is an integral part of Schlegel's aesthetic system, so too is the historical. He agitates on several occasions for the importance of historical subject matter in Romantic poetry. This would seem to be the result of his attempt to expand temporal boundaries, and to universalize the genre. As mentioned before, *The Queen's Jewelpiece* takes the murder of Gustaf III as one of its most integral scenes. In preparation for the novel, Almqvist steeped himself in the protocol for the assassin Anckarström's trial. He had both personal knowledge of and sympathy for this historical era, because his maternal grandmother had participated in the masquerade, Anckarström's wife was his mother's half cousin, and his father had associated with Munck, Liljensparre, and several others of the conspirators. Indeed, there are critics who maintain that *The Queen's Jewelpiece* is primarily a historical novel about Gustavian Sweden. This is, however, a very difficult position to defend, for although some of the events of the novel do historically take place in 1792, the philosophical superstructure is quintessentially Romantic, far removed from the classical values of the Enlightenment which Gustaf III's Sweden embodied.

The Queen's Jewelpiece is, in many respects, not a satisfying novel, because it defies traditional categories of understanding. One does not finish reading it with the sense of having experienced a catharsis or with a feeling of having had particular social, moral, or philosophical values reaffirmed. On the contrary, the author has asked that we work with him in the creation of a work of art and the task has not always been especially easy. He has at one moment ingenuously solicited our engagement in the endeavor, only to trick and manipulate us into following Tintomara ever deeper into the labyrinth. He has switched casts of characters, killed off plot lines, and completely shattered our traditional sense of narrative cohesion. As a narrator, he has promised us omniscience in one scene only to plead ignorance in the next. He has constantly forced us to change generic horses in mid-stream and compelled us to contemplate a never-ending series of dualities while allowing us only a brief glimpse of a significant substructure. He has, quite simply, shown us Tintomara. And we are left, like her lovers, to contemplate this work of art and to seek its unity and harmony in transcendent values, partly intellectual, partly intuitive, aware all the time that we shall succeed no better than they . . . Schlegel would not have been disappointed. (pp. 135-47)

> *Marilyn E. Johns, "Almqvist's Novel 'The Queen's Jewelpiece' and Friedrich Schlegel's Concept of the Novel," in* Monatshefte, *Vol. 72, No. 1, Spring, 1980, pp. 135-48.*

Marilyn Blackwell on Almqvist's realism:

The political goals of Almqvist's generation had not been fulfilled, whether these goals were liberalism, cultural nationalism, Utopian socialism, or, in Almqvist's case, the advent of the new Jerusalem. The retrenching after this defeat was Realism. The very term seems to imply that that which the Romantics sought so singlemindedly and energetically was not possible and that their methods were ineffective. The accompanying delimitation of focus meant that Realism became "force *without* principle, matter *without* mind, mechanism *without* life." The motivation behind this simplification, for Almqvist as well as for his fellow Realists, is still, however, Romantic in spirit—the ideals of nationhood, social order, intellectual unity, the improvement of the human lot. Thus, the eighteenth-century ideal of Progress re-surfaces as a kind of political and social optimism, the kind of optimism which characterizes Victor Hugo's belief in the glorious future of mankind and the eventual triumph of truth and justice and harmony on earth. The unbridled emotionalism and prophetic postures, the exceedingly emphatic message, and the secularized virtues of compassion and charity inform much of Realism as surely as they had Romanticism. Almqvist's *Det går an* is predicated upon precisely such virtues and on an inherent faith in the possibility of the betterment of social and cultural conditions.

> *Marilyn Blackwell, in her* C. J. L. Almqvist and Romantic Irony, *1983.*

Kurt Aspelin   (essay date 1986)

[*In the following essay, Aspelin examines the aesthetic theory, political ideology, and social vision that Almqvist espouses in his works.*]

> What does history say about real *enthusiasm*? If a more indifferent author delineated history, then perhaps he smiles a little at the people who struggled and fell; but he still acknowledges that this is how mankind has moved forward. Who was it then in the entire drama who was frustrated? It was the hangman who ostensibly stood victorious over his victim; it was he who was frustrated. . . . Wisdom which is purely and simply earth-bound is, in most cases, man's greatest, most perfect illusion. "Svenska fattig-domens betydelse" ("The Meaning of Swedish Poverty").

In Malla Silfverstolpe's salon, Carl Jonas Love Almqvist was a strange revelation. He was introduced there at the end of the 1820s by his friend Adolf Frederik Lindblad. He immediately became an object of the attention and admiration of certain patrons of the arts who were in the habit of listening and judging. Here he gained self-confidence and overcame the shyness he usually felt on meeting the great anonymous public. *Amorina* (1822) had been destroyed in the middle of its printing but nonetheless had brought upon him the scorn and distrust of the public, and the failed Värmland experiment had not improved his reputation. He read aloud his romantic dramas and exotic poetic narratives within an immediate circle of connoisseurs and at the piano recited his short, delicately nuanced, and extraordinarily dense *Songes*—creations that, in posterity's judgment, have come to be associated with their amateur singers, charades, and tableaus. One can follow this development in Malla Silfverstolpe's own diaries, which describe this circle in which art was a social necessity. These long pieces are characterized by an idealistic image of the *schöne Seelen* of late romanticism, an image both evocative and typical of its day, and also by an almost indefinable but important element of Swedish *Biedermeier* which imparts to the lifestyle of the participants a perhaps surprising element of narrow-minded and conservative compromise.

But even this circle was not impervious to the violent storm that raged in the outside world. The 1830s became a political decade in which romanticism and aestheticism encountered each other with mutual distrust and indignation. Geijer recorded these changes slowly and thoughtfully. His authority was virtually indisputable; thus, the repercussions were extensive when he increasingly experienced the pressure from the new world developing outside the ivory tower of academia, a world of factories, mass poverty, and a proletariat—that is, everything that could not be accommodated within the conservative, organic philosophy he had previously embraced. Finally he declared publicly that this view was too confining and, in his *Litteraturblad* of 1838, took leave of his former friends. His "defection" created within the circle a rift that could not be mended in spite of many energetic efforts to do so.

But Almqvist? As a matter of fact, he had begun even before Geijer to record how the storm was brewing in the world. For this task he was well equipped with actively receptive antennae, a fact that soon rendered his position within the circle precarious. When he first began attending the salon gatherings, a veritable Almqvist cult feverishly embraced the *törnrosskrifter* [or, the author of the *Törnrosens bok*]. But soon more critical opinions manifested themselves, and even the hostess herself regarded him rather more coolly. Grudges developed quite early between Almqvist and Geijer, which were quickly followed by a sense of both competition and envy. Geijer took on Almqvist's works and ideas with both violence and bitterness—and it is interesting here to note that the *Songes* have been treated much more generously by posterity than have, for instance, Geijer's musical poetry! And even a man such as Ch. E. Fahlcrantz was so suspiciously disposed toward Almqvist that he occasionally acted as the leader of an unofficial anti-Almqvist faction.

Malla Silfverstolpe's diary is still an invaluable source of information as to how heated the debate centering around Almqvist became, both in his presence and in his absence, both in the seances in Uppsala and in the meetings in Stockholm, e.g., in the Lindblad home. Violent arguments broke out when they discussed Saint-Simon's utopian socialist system and his advanced views on the new purified religion of the future. On another occasion, controversy was precipitated by Schiller's revolutionary early drama *Kabale und Liebe,* currently playing in the capital's theatrical repertory. When Silfverstolpe became embroiled in a violent dispute with Almqvist about passion and the fail-

ings of the institution of the family, convention collided with revolt. On both occasions, it was Almqvist who supported the dangerous new ideas concerning a reorganization of society, morality, and family life.

It was then in this salon that Almqvist definitively distinguished himself from his colleagues and showed himself to be a kind of conductor of social currents. It was during this period that the "wild rose" poet acquired his reputation as an ambiguous, dissonant, demonic revelation. He was associated with all that, at the time, was negative and subversive, such as the liberalism of *Aftonbladet* [In a footnote, the translator explains that "*Aftonbladet* was a Stockholm evening daily renowned for its radical politics"], the criticism of the Bible, and authors such as Hugo and Heine. Almqvist was not infrequently likened by his contemporaries to his character Ariman, the dark revolutionary spirit who struggles against Ormus's patriarchal but beneficent law-and-order society of **Ormus och Ariman.** Like him, the poet was seen as a dangerous, "suspicious" person—to employ the label Ormus uses when he enters the name of his enemy in his large book of minutes. According to testimony from several people who knew him, Almqvist's gait was silent and sneaking; suddenly without anyone having noticed him, he appeared in the middle of the room, right next to the others—suddenly and inexplicably. How different he was from the pious, conservative, often scrupulously orthodox Atterbom! And from Geijer! Even after his defection Geijer was securely anchored in society, history, and the family whereas Almqvist was constantly in revolt, escaping anything that would bind him, curious about everything that was new, more because it represented unexplored possibilities for excitement than because it was organically connected with the past.

The explosion came toward the end of the 1830s. In writings published in rapid succession, Almqvist not only created works that were realistic, penetrating depictions of a burgeoning social consciousness but also questioned the most sacrosanct social, moral, and religious assumptions of his day, precisely those assumptions on which his own society founded its authority and with which it legitimized its own existence. In 1839 he took the unprecedented step of engaging himself to write for the liberal, revolutionary journalistic stronghold of the capital, *Aftonbladet.* Atterbom remarked in a letter: "Can this be possible? *He* be delighted to descend into this stinking sewer, and help to stir things up there???" To his earlier friends, who were of a reliable, conservative political opinion, this development was simply a confirmation of their conviction that they had been right all along. Soon it developed that he met with suspicion even his liberal friends, who had begun to discover that his political sympathies were even farther to the left than their own. So during the 1840s his position became all the more difficult, financially and ideologically, right up to his exile in 1851.

In the background there was a complicated net of political and cultural events (difficult to evaluate and insufficiently researched)—offensive and defensive actions from his side and that of his opponents in a situation in which he was increasingly violently attacked by all these "extensions of the very bastions of Power, whose major characteristics are lies, violence, and cunning," as he once put it in a letter from 1838. In his darker hours, he called himself an "enfant perdu." He provided another, more optimistic characterization of himself just as he was about to appear publicly as the apostle of a new epoch and to reveal the extent of his will to revolution—just when he exchanged his feelings of martyrdom for a passion for activity and a commitment to the improvement of his age. He composed his self-diagnosis in a letter from 1837 in which he would see himself as challenger and provocateur: an ill-timed individual who in spite of himself continually provokes and "incites" people around him. Earlier he had resented this role and tried to avoid it, but suddenly he began to intuit that the role was his own and that he ought to play it for all it was worth, that it was his destiny "to be a source of annoyance, an awakener, a figure who provokes great dissatisfaction or great joy, whichever happens to be the case." And he added, in a phrase that is often quoted but deserves to be repeated yet again, "Just imagine . . . if it is my destiny to be a stumbling block? a drywood flame in the stoves of mankind?"

Henry Olsson has stressed the fact that in the depths of Almqvist's nature there lay an essential "revolutionism" that forced him to overthrow all comfortable, middle-of-the-road positions. Almqvist was a spontaneous dialectician. He charged thought with the utmost acerbity and depth of feeling and would then test how far one could take this thought before it became its antithesis. Thus he writes: "As soon as a bare theory or premise enters the picture, I immediately experience a strange desire to let it fly—fly out until it falls." On another occasion he speaks of his "desire to disjoin." According to one of his young admirers, Fredrik Borg, who recalled his acquaintance with Almqvist during his last years in Sweden, he labeled himself sometimes "liberal, sometimes socialist, sometimes communist, sometimes anarchist." He is, he writes in an autobiographical fragment, "a person full of oppositions." He writes further on the fragmentary nature of the human personality in **"Dialog om sättet att sluta stycken"** (**"Dialogue on How to Conclude Pieces"**). An adequate if somewhat imprecise term for this opposition might be romanticism versus realism. Another might be the contrast between, on the one hand, the "wild roseishness and absurdity" that Fröding perceived in him and, on the other, his work on social reforms and his commitment to reality.

The "wild rose-ishness" is in itself fundamental to an understanding of Almqvist. His "desire to disjoin" is always a mere starting point that allows him to immerse himself more deeply in the divine peace that is the single most telling characteristic of the "wild rose" experience. Of course his desire to reform and his rebellious credo of democracy often bring to mind the mode of thought prevalent in Scandinavia during the 1880s, with that period's desire to "question ideas" and its great appetite for a multiplicity of realities. And of course one is constantly forced to associate him with the most advanced programs for reform and revolution current in the Europe of his day—for instance, those of Saint-Simon and Fourier—in order to determine his ideological position and foundation. But his political and social programs also have as their ultimate goal the conveying of mankind to a new kingdom of innocence, a devotion to God and the love of one's fellow man. In the larger European connection—where Almqvist certainly belongs as one of the few truly great Swedish authors—he is a part of that romantic movement which, in the decades before the February revolution of 1848, was to a great extent characterized by a burning utopian mysticism and its concomitant bright dream of sociopolitical and religious renewal.

One can discern Almqvist's posture as an "awakener," as a provacateur, quite early in his life. *Amorina,* for instance, strives to provoke and challenge, to *transform.* One of his brilliant short essays is entitled **"Aven om humor och stil däri"** (**"Also on Humor and Style Therein"**), a draft from the 1820s of a doctrine of art that casts light not only upon *Amorina* and *Ormus och Ariman,* but also upon much later works such as *Columbine* (1835), *Kapellet* (*The Chapel,* 1838), and **"Malaren"** (**"The Painter,"** 1840). Here Almqvist defines humor as a lever that forces people out of their apparent harmony. It is with the help of humor that the artist destroys man's self-complacency and his acquiescence to his miserable condition, thus compelling him through a disharmonious crisis toward true harmony founded on insight and consciousness.

This Almqvistian "aesthetics of disharmony" is, then, dialectically conceived, simultaneously an expression and an image of the opposing realities that he encountered at every turn in the society of his day. This principle of disjunction is simultaneously a prerequisite for and a passage toward true harmony. It breaks up man's conventional mode of apprehension. This disjunction leads man from an insight into all that is ambiguous and bewildering in reality to that point where he, transformed and transfigured, can see the open clarity that characterizes the divine and the paradisiacal. The "drywood flame" of which he writes in his letter of 1837 is to be used to light those who are usually lukewarm and slow to ignite. But they must burn with a cool and steady flame, in quiet peace before the face of God. Thus the innermost secret of the gospel of the priest of the wild rose is man's absorption into the divine, blessed trinity of beauty, goodness, and truth. "God's paradise" is the gently shaded, divinely watered grove to which he would lead his readers—the delightful landscape in the beyond to which he so often returns in his prose writings, meditations, and *Songes* texts, where everything is purer and lovelier than in real life.

Satire, humor, and irony are keys that open the door to this paradise. Almqvist's works represent a constant movement between rebellion and mysticism, a constant play of oppositions; and it is the ardor in them which comprises their fascination. We must not, in our attempt to understand him, eliminate the tension between these poles. It is of the utmost importance to retain the oppositions: to structure them and seek explanations for them. Our conceptions of the great poets shift with different times and different situations. The concept of a "right" classical interpretation exists only in the dead literary history of academia. It is a matter of different interpretations, all conditioned by the interpreter's own perspective and time. An official conception of Almqvist during the 1950s emphasized his "romantic" qualities: the diabolical and playfully imaginative side of his character. One might well see this conception as a mixture of, on the one hand, the fairy-tale drama of flickering fantasy set against a backdrop of poisonous demonism, like that which Alf Sjöberg created in his Royal Dramatic Theater production of *Drottningens juvelsmycke* (*The Queen's Jewelpiece,* 1834) in the middle of the decade and, on the other hand, Gunnar Ekelöf's interest in the brilliant "strountes"—or nonsense poetry—which Almqvist could distill out of a kind of neutral poetic position from which everything is unique, new, and exciting. It is precisely this novel about Tintomara that advances in toward the center—this playful arabesque painting of fantasy realism around the edge of the incomprehensible ambiguity like a baffling phantom in the woods of Kolmården, or on the narrow streets of Stockholm, or in the Royal Opera's artificial world of chiaroscuro, this masquerade novel which in Swedish prose has no equal for artistic invention or multifaceted mystifications. Fifteen years later another conception of him has arisen and is deemed more "relevant": the reformer, the unmasker who formulated arguments and truths that still retain their controversiality today. It is a question of choosing the most suitable features of the author without being tempted to replace one prejudice with another. Great art always poses great questions: *different* great questions. Art is precisely ambiguous—both as an element in a multifaceted historical reality and as an attempt to depict this contradictory reality in its ambiguous language.

In his youth Almqvist suffered from an intellectual contempt for the politics of daily debate. "Politics," he said then, "is the varnish on the painting of Europe." He himself wanted to grasp the truly great problems and view them from the perspective of eternity: he was a prophet who brooded over the innermost secrets of his time. As late as the mid-1830s he speaks with a singular disdain of journalism and the bickerings of the press, and poses instead questions about the fate of Europe, both social and historical, which again had come to his attention and to which he hereafter—because he had committed himself as a leading writer in the daily press—would devote so much energy in seeking a solution.

Even his first writings express a conviction that he was living in the dawn of a completely new world historical epoch, that it was his mission to remold society from the ground up. This is his dream of a new Atlantis, a new Jerusalem, the utopianism he shared with so many European romantic poets and philosophers and the thinkers who inspired them. In his youth he could express his belief in relatively orthodox Swedenborgian terms; he furthermore retained the basic features of Swedenborg's schematics for many years, although in a somewhat modified form that he referred to as "free variations." The new world epoch corresponds from its inception to Swedenborg's New Church. Its coming is accompanied by, in his interpretation of history, a series of earthshaking events, among which are the revolution of 1789 and the triumph of German idealistic philosophy and the art of romanticism. The transformation he dimly perceives in his own day is then universal and all-encompassing in its implications. Thus he maintains in an essay from 1819: "The transformation

of old forms is transpiring on both sides of the earth in those countries which are a part of Christendom. . . . It is obvious that the spirit of universal revolution has not yet completed its undertakings; but less obvious if it has yet begun with full force." Such a transformation implies, he contends in an essay several years later, that "time inexorably marches forward, society *survives,* and mankind increases."

In the writings from his earliest period these grandiose ideas are applied to several different areas. *Vad är kärlek?* (*What is Love?*, 1816) takes issue with the false ideal of womanhood; the writings about the Manhem organization formulate an educational program for the entire nation in the spirit of intense prophetic fantasy; *Om brottsliges behandling* (*On the Treatment of the Criminal,* 1821) contends that a criminal should not be *punished* according to the principle of retribution but rather *reformed*, i.e., returned to the social community. Almqvist even made an attempt to carry out his theories in practical life when, at the beginning of the twenties, he realized his dream of "the idealized farmer." The pioneer experiment in Värmland came, it is true, to an abrupt end and was really a great failure, but it clearly shows how the young Almqvist saw himself as a rebel in his cultural situation. One thinks of the exclamation he placed in Amorina's mouth: "You dead men, the stench of the grave emanates from all of you! Europe smells of corpses!" In the bizarre romantic fugue that constitutes *Amorina* there is much social criticism. For Almqvist, one must revolt against the very foundation of civilization, "the academic world order" (the expression is his), which neglects that which is essential and instead has become mired in dead forms, in a misanthropic, legalistic, hopelessly tangled ball of yarn. The manifestation of this world is the official bureaucratic society to which he had in vain tried to adapt himself and with which he had clashed while working as a copier at His Royal Highness' Chancery—immortalized in his brilliant caricature depicting Ormus, the perfect civil servant liberated from everything spontaneous or human, and the authority which he maintains over the earth from his chancery on the moon. And in *Gudhataren* (*He Who Hated God,* 1839), the sixth book of the *Hunting Seat* series, one can distinguish dazzling observations on the relationship between violence and power. The same deeds that are hailed as courageous and valiant when they are performed by kings and those in power are denigrated as theft and murder when committed by "simple, ordinary people" and are punished accordingly. "The former, on the contrary, over whom one had no control or who, in other words, have been heroes, one could not hang; one therefore idolized them instead. There was no other distinction from the beginning between the gallows and the throne; that is to say, two vertical pieces of wood across which a horizontal piece lies." These words sound like passages from Bakunin's anarchistic tracts.

Much of that cited from Almqvist's early works could just as well have been written by the Almqvist who toward the end of the thirties emerged as a realistic "unmasker" and a radical political journalist. As a democratic reformer he admittedly imparts definitive political and contemporary social implications to his formulations. But the violent and bold personal commitment that was the basis of his open political engagement—as a challenge to the entire Swedish class and civil-servant society, which also was in a position to punish his audacity—was still grounded in the deep conviction, arising out of "utopian mysticism," that he was working toward the divine age. This age promised at one and the same time democratic freedom and the victory of true Christianity. Both are *sub specieaeternitatis* two aspects of the same powerful goal in world development. In several bizarre fantastic works of a mythological-historical bent from around 1840—*Människosläkets saga* (*The Saga of Mankind*) and **"Brev om den skandinaviska Nordens betydelse för Europas fornhistoria"** (**"Letters on the Significance of the Scandinavian North for Prehistorical Europe"**)—Almqvist depicts the development of mankind from the age of paradise at the dawn of history up to the impending new kingdom of peace that will have progressed beyond the horrifying chain of bloody deeds and the acts of cruelty now comprising history. He also perceives two powerful and conflicting forces in this development, the principles of both freedom and repression, which he names—after the two brothers in Genesis—"Abelism" and "Cainism." He seeks their influence in both the past and the present, and he records all the indications that Abelism will be victorious and will introduce a new world epoch in which democratic thought conquers patriarchal repression and hierarchial compulsion in state, church, and family life.

When Almqvist was born, the aftereffects of the French Revolution had quieted down after years of terror and bloodshed. Three years before his exile from Sweden, he was compelled to experience in his homeland—and radically affirm—the impact of the February revolution in Paris in 1848. This was for him "the great lesson" for the oppressive powers of Europe, as expressed in his inspired article in *Jönköpingsbladet* in March of 1848, which comments on these great events and their consequences. The breakthrough of industrial capitalism in Europe's leading countries serves as a background to his works. It created new class relations and social tensions. It brought into focus the problems of political democracy and republicanism and gave birth to the early "utopian" socialists. It also allowed strikes, revolutionary intrigues, and mass poverty to be used as journalistic fodder in the presses of the day. But part of the background is also the breakthrough and culmination of the great romantic artistic wave and its confrontation with burgeoning realism. Soon enough literature became completely preoccupied with social unrest. An author such as Victor Hugo proclaims romanticism to be "liberalism in literature": it is social romanticism which takes over, a movement politically and morally radical and possessed of the ambition to fend off an explosive social reality with a dream of beauty.

In 1838 Almqvist wrote his inspired homage to **"The Significance of Swedish Poverty,"** a poetic nationalistic fantasy that attempts to transform poverty into a positive moral concept. In exactly the same year, because of an unusually severe winter and a drastic crisis in agriculture, mass poverty ("pauperism") in the grim world of reality presented to the country a social problem of the greatest magnitude. One possibility in reading the essay is to bear in mind its pronounced quality of social analysis: its rustic democratic utopia—the dream of a solid connection between the aristocracy and the servants, the aristocracy and the farmer—and its thesis that the Swedish temperament renders impossible the accumulation of capital in Swedish society. In both cases his argument serves to show the inviability of capitalism for Swedish society. But only a short time later Almqvist himself was present to observe the course of European society and study it—the factories, the urban proletariat, worker unrest, and street riots. From Paris and London during the autumn of 1840 he sent a series of brisk and inquisitive travel articles as the foreign correspondent for one of the liberal Stockholm dailies. In them he shows himself to possess a strikingly sharp eye for political and social problems that in reality were very foreign to what was happening in Sweden. This group of articles also admirably illustrates how Almqvist the journalist worked—how he wrote brilliantly and amusingly with quick observations yet with great seriousness and responsibility.

The metaphoric possibilities of modern civilization prove to be useful for formulating the new manifesto. In a little passage in *Det går an* (*It Works*, 1839 [translated as *Sara Videbeck*]), which one might easily miss but which contains a half-serious, half-ironic moral, Almqvist employs the new means of production, steam power technology, to create a symbol of what was happening in his day. It occurs in connection with the steamboat Yngve Frey—the canal boat that leads Sara Videbeck away from the conventional patterns of life and directs her to the possibility of establishing the creative erotic connection which she has thought out on her own and which, in its deepest sense, concerns creation. The narrator comments on her trip:

> Now when one's passage is impelled forward by fire, one goes directly to the goal, without pause, and uses sails no more often than the wind requires. The helmsman must, of course, be familiar with buoys and hidden rocks, that is obvious; but if he knows of them, he can easily avoid them, if he is not an ass. The only great danger with steamboat sailing is the possibility of conflagration; but even here, one can take such precautions with the construction of the firepan that this seldom or never occurs.

To go straight to the goal is to achieve freedom for one who assumes responsibility and possesses common sense. Then he is his own master, dependent upon his own productive possibilities. And if society is established according to such a perspective, it is also possible to eliminate the dangers of the individual's setting fire to himself or exploding from sheer folly. Then one traverses the path from the bare words, the phrase, to the matter itself—reality. In the narrative it is Sara who demonstrates this possibility, and her decision remains as an act of freedom, which we still today are not ready to realize.

The "essence" is, for Almqvist, reality in its untainted manifestation. It revolts against the false power that names have usurped. "The temper of our time is already and becomes increasingly a demand on reality," Almqvist writes in **"Om poesi i sak"** (**"On the Poetry of Essence"**).

This remarkable article from 1839 proposes an aesthetic program that concentrates on a description of reality, in which "the artistic horizon" is the wisdom both of beauty in reality and of reality as (innocent, "paradisiacal") beauty. In this essay, and even more in the programmatic work *Europeiska missnöjets grunder* (*The Foundations of European Discontent,* 1838), which was written at approximately the same time, Almqvist formulates an appeal that sounds like a reveille for all that is new and progressive. The struggle between the new and the old turns into an elemental battle in which the new stands for life, growth, and strength: "Everywhere there is life standing at the door, announcing that it wants to come in, and asking that death be so kind as to give way" (**"Om poesi i sak"**). "The future of Europe is standing in our entryways and wants in. He who does not open his door to the knock will have his door beaten in, will be lucky in the end if splinters do not fly in his face" (*Europeiska missnöjets grunder*). And in a somewhat earlier work, **"De fundersamme"** (**"The Thoughtful Ones"**), he states: "Everywhere it is a question of reality, truth, heart, pure sensibility to nature and to what truly moves us. A thunderstorm rages through the age—and all the letters in the alphabet shudder. They recall with fear that there is a spirit which can kill them."

Almqvist has heard this thunderstorm as a foreboding of the "new life." He consistently returns to the idea that what he is engaged in in his critical work is not theoretical, ivory-tower structures. He does not become bogged down in fanciful speculations as do his literary colleagues—Atterbom and the others, wallowing in their reactionary harmony of complacency—which is the subject of the ironic, malicious dialogue from the middle of the thirties, **"De fundersamme."** In an essay such as **"Poesi och politik"** (**"Poetry and Politics"**) from 1839, he even sketches an aesthetic program that delegates to the author the role of social researcher at the side of and as a complement to the scientific expert. Almqvist himself becomes "the real human being," beyond phrases and literary cliches, with the help of concrete studies and the documentation of reality in varying milieus. One can follow him during his field studies when—notebook in hand, like Zola!—he notes facts and observations about the localities and people he has met during his journeys. Various points recur, integrated into his folklife narratives. From one vantage point they function as a medium of contemporary social criticism and propaganda, filled with factual and moving depictions of contemporary reality. Poverty and oppression, barbaric criminal codes, the fossilization of the church, and the abuse of power are important objects of attack in *Skällnora kvarn* (*Skällnora Mill,* 1838), *Kapellet,* and dramas like *Columbine* and *Marjam,* 1838. Even his novels from the forties are relevant here. They are in line with the more general Swedish novelistic endeavors of the decade whose first goal is to satisfy a new wider bourgeois reading public, hungry for easily accessible, preferably problem-oriented, and suitably radical prose. Often they are dismissed by connoisseurs with a certain superiority; but they represent a very goal-conscious social contribution from the author's point of view, with their amusing realistic images interwoven in "romantic," serial-type intrigues and peppered with sociocritical touches.

It is to his studies in the world of reality that he refers when in *Europeiska missnöjets grunder* he formulates his brilliant analysis of "the folk" as opposed to "the rabble"—by which latter term he means the representatives of the aristocracy that has been debilitated by its power and prestige—or when in **"Syenska fattigdomens betydelse"** he analyzes the conflict, fundamental to society, between farmers and the aristocracy. And it is lessons of this kind that allow him to draw the conclusion that it is the institutions and not the individual members thereof that bear the major responsibility for the derailment of society, for the "European discontent" that he observes everywhere around him. From his studies he knows that it is useless to moralize over the evil and perdition of man. It is a question instead of changing his surroundings.

In a letter from 1840 Almqvist wrote that he had "attacked the prevailing conditions in three separate columns, religious, political, and family life." He returns to this tripartite division when he summarizes his contribution. This division is also the original plan for *Europeiska missnöjets grunder,* which would critically illuminate the three "columns," state, church, and family life—although only the last column is thoroughly treated in the completed work of 1850.

Instead it was mainly in the daily press that Almqvist treated purely political questions: first and foremost in *Aftonbladet* and also later in the more radical *Jönköpingsbladet.* At his best, he is a strikingly agile and effective writer, dangerous as a polemicist but also possessed of a great ability to set right large and difficult fundamental problems of his age and to develop with a tactical eye extensive press campaigns with long-term political goals. His position in his day was a strong one, at least before the "constant writing for his daily bread and butter," about which he complains in the forties, took its toll. His old acquaintance from the circle of Uppsala romantics, the strictly conservative Palmblad, even sees him as a politically important person in his vision of the future, which deals with how the liberal opposition will organize its assumption of power. In the brochure *Politisk camera optica* from 1840, Almqvist takes his place as the "truly popular" minister, who will quickly replace the more moderately liberal government; by his side are several of the most extreme "radicals" of the Stockholm press. With collective power they force through a series of subversive reforms—Palmblad mentions annual parliaments, the abolition of the nobility, and women's suffrage. These examples clearly illustrate the ironic fate to which conservatism so easily falls victim in the eyes of posterity. As a cultural minister, furthermore, Almqvist must make the motion for "a revision of Christianity." The suggestion is referred to as a "committee for pure original Christianity," on which the maker of the motion himself sits together with the *Aftonbladet* journalist Orvar Odd—as well as Sara Videbeck, who seizes the opportunity to plead for the emancipation of women and free marriage.

Almqvist had already given his vision of the "column" of the church in the drama *Marjam.* In this unusually effective but overlooked, tendentious work, he shows how Christianity has degenerated into a collection of "heathen" dogmas and a church that is the instrument of power for the privileged "prelature." As a journalist he also succeeded in connecting his polemics against the church with his more general political criticism of the aristocracy. Often the tone is radical and the stylistic medium coarse irony. Religion becomes a means for the ruling class to fortify its position of social power; this class becomes more than willing to yield heaven to the masses. In an article from *Aftonbladet* from 1839 Almqvist contends:

> But a more fundamental improvement in their earthly condition, some relief from their unnecessary burdens, a greater and less costly participation in the good things which *this* life has to offer—such trivialities the aristocracy has found little reason to bestow on the lower classes, for they apparently still think that the upper classes might suffer in this exchange, since they have received as their lot only the earth, while the working classes on the other hand have received heaven and eternity, which mean much more.

The tone is almost enlightening. But the attack is formulated from the perspective of "genuine" Christianity. For Almqvist, God's pure word and the doctrinal system of dogmatic theology stand in the sharpest possible contrast to each other; the former is a doctrine of love with a minimum of dogma, the latter a sophisticated system of dogmas like the Trinity and the doctrine of satisfaction. Almqvist's Swedenborgian teachings follow him far into his journalistic polemics: the "Christianity *for the second time* or . . . a new Christianity," which he prophesies in reference to the new world epoch, is modelled on very heretical ideas.

Yet it is probably his ideas about the family and the position of women that Almqvist worked on longest and most vehemently. Gradually (and after great struggles) much of that which Almqvist strove for has become a reality and can appear to us today as self-evident. Such proves to be the case for the more fortunate of utopians who in their own time present ideas that strike their contemporaries as shocking. But the independence and freedom in one's erotic life of which Sara dreamed, the open and active trust between the sexes, beyond statutory patterns and conventions, on which Almqvist's program was founded—these are yet to be attained. Almqvist's new concept of the family, his ideas about collective child-rearing, his suggestion about radical intervention in inheritance and property matters are still inflammatory issues. It is in this light that a narrative like **Det går an** still retains its relevance; its literary expressiveness still glitters with a kind of romanticization of reality which in its very vitality has merged with both revolt and liberation.

But if one speaks of the committed reformer and social journalist Almqvist, one must remember that this is only one of his visions. Even the analysis of his authorship constitutes a constant dialogue between oppositions. He did, after all, write during the same period both realistic folklife narratives and the **Songes** poems blazing with fantastic exoticism. At the time when he was preparing his press campaigns against his political opponents, he wrote the little strophe in the novella **Palatset** (**The Palace,** 1838) called "Sinto, mi Sinto," which purports to be Japanese

but which in reality should be seen as the first "lettristic" piece in our literature, comprised only of suggestive word sounds. Even during the forties, a period dominated by journalism and the writing of novels, he could transform himself into a mystic who humbly stutters at the edge of the inexpressible. Alongside his foreign correspondence of 1840-1841 about the "serious side" of France and England, he composed letters to his family at home explicitly adapted to the world of his two Marys and filled with the small matters of "the little life"—chatty, good-humored impressions of the hot spices of the French kitchen and the wonders he had encountered abroad, patriarchal instructions about the management of the home, expressions of yearning for beer-posset and Antuna's gooseberries. "Only Sweden has Swedish gooseberries," says his driveler Seseman in the later America pieces, in a tone in which the bitter longing for home is transposed to farcical parody and thus a brief moment is liberated from this painful sting.

One of Almqvist's recurring thoughts is that the personality of a human being is not fixed and given but rather changes and alters like the most sensitive mimosa. According to this aesthetic, individuals whom the author would describe may not be molded into solid forms; rather their mutability must be allowed a chance. It is true that there is much virtuosity in Almqvist's many changes of role and identity in his works. But they are not virtuosically *empty*. They have a function in his literary world even when they bewilder and confuse. It is therefore wrong to shut him up in Malla Silfverstolpe's salon, however much of the great wide world might be found there, however much "Arimanian" demonism was permissible within its walls. He played the role of inciter and provocateur—"a figure of great suspicion, or of great joy"—in his youth, both in Malla Silfverstolpe's circle and later as a journalist for *Aftonbladet*. His "contradictions" have here their mysterious unity and point of intersection. (pp. 343-58)

Kurt Aspelin, "A Drywood Flame in the Stoves of Mankind: C. J. L. Almqvist, the Period and the Times," translated by Marilyn Johns Blackwell and John Weinstock, in The Nordic Mind: Current Trends in Scandinavian Literary Criticism, *edited by Frank Egholm Andersen and John Weinstock, University Press of America, 1986, pp. 343-59.*

FURTHER READING

Bach, Giovanni. "Swedish Literature." In *The History of the Scandinavian Literatures,* by Bach, et al., edited and partially translated by Frederika Blanker, pp. 87-143. New York: Dial Press Inc., 1938.

   Includes a brief discussion of Almqvist's views on women and marriage.

Blackwell, Marilyn Johns. *C. J. L. Almqvist and Romantic*

Irony. Stockholm: Almqvist & Wiksell International, 1983, 156 p.

Examines several representative works from Almqvist's early years "in light of their philosophical anchoring in German speculative thought and, especially, in Romantic irony, that period's synthesis of philosophy and art."

Richard Burton

1821-1890

(Full name Richard Francis Burton) English essayist, poet, translator, and critic.

INTRODUCTION

Burton was a distinguished Victorian adventurer and a prolific writer who left extraordinarily detailed accounts of his travels in India, Arabia, Africa, and North America, including a famous early description of Mecca entitled *Personal Narrative of a Pilgrimage to El-Medinah and Meccah*. His travelogues are characterized by an objective detachment that has led many critics to consider them closely associated in methodology with the modern disciplines of anthropology, ethnology, archeology, and geography. Burton's analytical approach to non-Western cultures was facilitated by his accomplishments as a linguist—he mastered more than twenty languages and completed numerous translations ranging from Portuguese poetry to Sanskrit philosophy. The most famous of these was *A Plain and Literal Translation of the Arabian Nights' Entertainments,* the first unexpurgated English translation of the ribald tenth-century collection of tales known as the *Arabian Nights.*

Burton was born at Torquay in the county of Hertfordshire, into a prosperous family from the provincial gentry. He spent the first nine years of his life in Tours, in France's Loire region, where he received the rudiments of a classical education. However, after 1830—apart from a brief tenure at public school in England the following year—a decade of instability ensued, with Burton's family moving from one town to another in France and Italy, during which time he acquired only a haphazard education. Finally, Burton was sent to Oxford in 1840 to prepare for a career in the Anglican church. After failing to win a coveted fellowship in classical languages, he deliberately provoked the University authorities and was subsequently expelled in 1842. Shortly afterwards, his father bought Burton a commission in the Indian army. Between 1842 and 1849 Burton learned nearly a dozen oriental languages and gathered material for a series of descriptive writings on Indian civilization, including *Goa, and the Blue Mountains; or, Six Months of Sick Leave.*

In 1853 Burton was granted a furlough of one year, and he soon devised a scheme to visit Mecca and Medina, the sequestered shrines of Islam forbidden to non-Muslims. In April of that year, Burton, disguised as an Afghani doctor, obtained full access to the holy cities, recording his observations in the *Personal Narrative of a Pilgrimage to El-Medinah and Meccah.* Shortly afterwards, he turned his attention to Africa, where he began the exploration of Somalia and eastern Ethiopia. Briefly deterred by his commitment to the Franco-British cause in the Crimean War

(1853-56), Burton subsequently attempted to locate the source of the Nile. After a series of initial explorations in East Africa, early in 1858 he became one of the first Europeans to view Lake Tanganyika, publishing his findings in 1860 in the well-regarded *Lake Regions of Central Africa.* Following a short visit to Salt Lake City, Utah, to study the Mormons, Burton married Isabel Arundel in 1861 and decided to enter the British consular service. He was offered the minor post of consul to Benin and Biafra in what is now Nigeria, and for several years continued his ethnographic survey of Africa's native tribes in the area, as well as in the region of the Congo. In 1864 Burton even arranged for an official audience with Gelele, King of Dahomey, whom he attempted to persuade to cease participating in the slave trade. The published account of Burton's West African years appeared in 1864 as *A Mission to Gelele, King of Dahome.*

Burton was transferred to the consulship of São Paulo, Brazil, in 1865, and then to Damascus, Syria, in 1869. Despite his skill as an administrator, the British government objected to his intervention in the struggle between the town's religious factions, and he was dismissed in 1871. From 1872 until his death in 1890, Burton was kept in a state of de facto exile in the consulship of Trieste, Italy, where he completed his acknowledged masterpiece, his translation of the *Arabian Nights,* begun some years earlier. The work was a great commercial success—the first in Burton's career—but caused a critical uproar due to the inclusion of extensive footnotes that precisely documented the exotic sexual practices of Islamic cults. In Trieste, Isabel Burton grew increasingly alarmed by her husband's projects for translations of erotic Oriental texts; after his death, she destroyed all of his unpublished notes, diaries, and manuscripts.

Translations account for only a fraction of Burton's extensive literary production. Although he made some forays into poetry, Burton's most significant original writings are his volumes on travel and exploration, as well as the notes and appendices to *Arbian Nights.* Burton's reflections on his travels in India, critics have agreed, reveal an intuitive ability in the emerging domain of anthropology—as well as an incipient obsession with the erotic and the grotesque. His first effort in the genre, *Goa, and the Blue Mountains; or, Six Months of Sick Leave,* examines the peoples of the Portuguese colony of Goa, the Malabar Hindus, and the mountain-dwelling Todas, whose practice of polyandry—in which a woman maintains multiple husbands—fascinated Burton. Of the three related volumes that followed, *Sindh, and the Races that Inhabit the Valley of the Indus* has been the most widely praised by critics for its examination of the Indian province and its people from the perspective of both the natural and social sciences. The *Personal Narrative of a Pilgrimage to El-Medinah and Meccah,* however, is considered Burton's most important travel book, both for its wealth of information on the Islamic world and for its sensitive discussion of the Muslim religion. Encyclopedic in its overall vision, the *Pilgrimage* was written in Burton's characteristically digressive, colorful manner, considered excessive by some critics.

Burton employed a similar methodology in the travel books covering his African expeditions. However, many critics have pointed out that his assessment of native African cultures was severe as compared to his general admiration for Indian and Arabic civilization. For example, *The Lake Regions of Central Africa* is marked by an ethnocentric contempt for the native peoples, and his *A Mission to Gelele, King of Dahome* obsessively focuses on the custom of human sacrifice and the practice of slave-trading, painting a picture of the Dahoman people as pathetically degraded. Critics have attributed Burton's shift in attitude here to his rigid adherence to the theory of social Darwinism and to his unconditional acceptance of the tenets of European colonialism, particularly the notion that nineteenth-century industrial civilization is inherently superior to pre-industrial indigenous cultures.

Burton's translation of the *Arabian Nights* has been upheld by many critics as his single greatest literary achievement. The result of twenty-five years of effort, the work confirmed Burton's role as cultural intermediary between East and West, and remains the most complete English edition available. Burton's intention was to render the sto-

ries as if their author had written them in English. While some critics have described the translation as unnecessarily literal and spoiled by archaisms and trite coinages, others have argued that Burton successfully communicated the ribald tone and exotic sensuousness of the original. Nonetheless, the real controversy over *Arabian Nights* did not concern the apparent merits or faults of the translation, but rather focused on Burton's extensive notes and appendices, which included discussions of sex education for women, castration, and homosexuality in Arab culture. Most nineteenth-century reviewers censured Burton for transgressing the limits of Victorian decorum, but modern critics have considered Burton's documentation legitimate scholarship. Indeed, commentators have argued that despite his essentially imperialist outlook, Burton provides in *Arabian Nights* a richer and more sensitive portrait of Islamic civilization than earlier writers, and, in his desire to bring the East and West closer together, Burton's translation came to represent the splendor of the Orient to Victorians.

PRINCIPAL WORKS

Goa, and the Blue Mountains; or, Six Months of Sick Leave (journal) 1851

Scinde; or, The Unhappy Valley. 2 vols. (journal) 1851

Sindh, and the Races that Inhabit the Valley of the Indus (journal) 1851

Personal Narrative of a Pilgrimage to El-Medinah and Meccah. 3 vols. (journal) 1855-56

First Footsteps in East Africa; or, An Exploration of Harar. 2 vols. (journal) 1856

The Lake Regions of Central Africa. 2 vols. (journal) 1860

A Mission to Gelele, King of Dahome. 2 vols. (journal) 1864

Zanzibar; City, Island, and Coast. 2 vols. (journal) 1872

The Kasîdah of Hâjî Abdû El-Yezdî; A Lay of Higher Law, Translated and Annotated by His Friend and Pupil, F. B. (poetry) 1880

The Lusiads. 2 vols. [translator] (poetry) 1880

Camoens: His Life and His Luciads—A Commentary. 2 vols. (criticism) 1881

A Plain and Literal Translation of the Arabian Nights' Entertainments, Now Entitled The Book of the Thousand Nights and a Night. 10 vols. [translator] (stories) 1885

The Memorial Edition of the Works of Captain Sir Richard F. Burton. 7 vols. (criticism, diaries, essays, journals, poetry) 1893-94

Selected Papers on Anthropology, Travel and Exploration (essays) 1924

CRITICISM

John Addington Symonds   (essay date 1885)

[*Symonds was a noted nineteenth-century English critic, poet, historian, and translator. Here, he reviews Burton's translation of the* Arabian Nights, *arguing that it is hypocritical to censor that text when other classical literature circulates in unexpurgated form.*]

There is an outcry in some quarters against Captain Burton's translation of the *Arabian Nights.* Only one volume of that work has reached me, and I have not as yet read the whole of it. Of the translator's notes I will not speak, the present sample being clearly insufficient to judge by; but I wish to record a protest against the hypocrisy which condemns his text. When we invite our youth to read an unexpurgated Bible (in Hebrew and Greek, or in the authorised version), an unexpurgated Aristophanes, an unexpurgated Juvenal, an unexpurgated Boccaccio, an unexpurgated Rabelais, an unexpurgated collection of Elizabethan dramatists, including Shakspere, and an unexpurgated Plato (in Greek or in Prof. Jowett's English version), it is surely inconsistent to exclude the unexpurgated *Arabian Nights,* whether in the original or in any English version, from the studies of a nation who rule India and administer Egypt.

The qualities of Capt. Burton's translation are similar to those of his previous literary works, and the defects of those qualities are also similar. Commanding a vast and miscellaneous vocabulary, he takes such pleasure in the use of it that sometimes he transgresses the unwritten laws of artistic harmony. From the point of view of language, I hold that he is too eager to seize the *mot propre* of his author, and to render that by any equivalent which comes to hand from field or fallow, waste or warren, hill or hedgerow, in our vernacular. Therefore, as I think, we find some coarse passages of the *Arabian Nights* rendered with unnecessary crudity, and some poetic passages marred by archaisms or provincialisms. But I am at a loss to perceive how Burton's method of translation should be less applicable to the *Arabian Nights* than to the *Lusiad.* So far as I can judge, it is better suited to the *naïveté* combined with stylistic subtlety of the former than to the smooth humanistic elegances of the latter.

This, however, is a minor point. The real question is whether a word-for-word version of the *Arabian Nights,* executed with peculiar literary vigour, exact scholarship, and rare insight into Oriental modes of thought and feeling, can under any shadow of pretence be classed with "the garbage of the brothels." In the lack of lucidity, which is supposed to distinguish English folk, our middle-class *censores morum* strain at the gnat of a privately circulated translation of an Arabic classic, while they daily swallow the camel of higher education based upon minute study of Greek and Latin literature. When English versions of Theocritus and Ovid, of Plato's *Phaedrus* and the *Ecclesiazusae,* now within the reach of every schoolboy, have been suppressed, then and not till then can a "plain and literal" rendering of the *Arabian Nights* be denied with any colour of consistency to adult readers. I am far

from saying that there are not valid reasons for thus dealing with Hellenic and Graeco-Roman and Oriental literature in its totality. But let folk reckon what Anglo-Saxon Puritanism logically involves. If they desire an Anglo-Saxon Index Librorum Prohibitorum, let them equitably and consistently apply their principles of inquisitorial scrutiny to every branch of human culture.

> *John Addington Symonds, "The Arabian Nights' Entertainments," in* The Academy, *No. 700, October 3, 1885, p. 223.*

Algernon Charles Swinburne   (poem date 1891)

[*Swinburne was an English poet, dramatist, and critic renowned during his lifetime for his lyric poetry and recognized today for his bold rejection of Victorian mores. The following is Swinburne's tribute to Burton, written the year after Burton's death.*]

Night or light is it now, wherein
Sleeps, shut out from the wild world's din,
    Wakes, alive with a life more clear,
One who found not on earth his kin?

Sleep were sweet for awhile, were dear
Surely to souls that were heartless here,
    Souls that faltered and flagged and fell,
Soft of spirit and faint of cheer.

A living soul that had strength to quell
Hope the spectre and fear the spell,
    Clear-eyed, content with a scorn sublime
And a faith superb, can it fare not well?

Life, the shadow of wide-winged time,
Cast from the wings that change as they climb,
    Life may vanish in death, and seem
Less than the promise of last year's prime.

But not for us is the past a dream
Wherefrom, as light from a clouded stream,
    Faith fades and shivers and ebbs away,
Faint as the moon if the sundawn gleam.

Faith, whose eyes in the low last ray
Watch the fire that renews the day,
    Faith which lives in the living past,
Rock-rooted, swerves not as weeds that sway.

As trees that stand in the storm-wind fast
She stands, unsmitten of death's keen blast,
    With strong remembrance of sunbright spring
Alive at heart to the lifeless last.

Night, she knows, may in no wise cling
To a soul that sinks not and droops not wing,
    A sun that sets not in death's false night
Whose kingdom finds him not thrall but king.

Souls there are that for soul's affright
Bow down and cower in the sun's glad sight,
    Clothed round with faith that is one with fear,
And dark with doubt of the live world's light.

But him we hailed from afar or near
As boldest born of his kinsfolk here
    And loved as brightest of souls that eyed
Life, time, and death with unchangeful cheer,

A wider soul than the world was wide,

Whose praise made love of him one with pride,
    What part has death or has time in him,
Who rode life's lists as a god might ride?

While England sees not her old praise dim,
While still her stars through the world's night
        swim,
    A fame outshining her Raleigh's fame,
A light that lightens her loud sea's rim,

Shall shine and sound as her sons proclaim
The pride that kindles at Burton's name.
    And joy shall exalt their pride to be
The same in birth if in soul the same.

But we that yearn for a friend's face,—we
Who lack the light that on earth was he,—
    Mourn, though the light be a quenchless
        flame
That shines as dawn on a tideless sea.

> *Algernon Charles Swinburne, "Verses on the
> Death of Richard Burton," in* The New Re-
> view, *Vol. IV, No. 21, February, 1891, pp.
> 97-9.*

The Nation   (essay date 1900)

[*In the following excerpt, the critic comments on Burton's translation of* The Arabian Nights, *noting that its
"perversities of style make it unreadable for its own
sake."*]

[Sir Richard Burton] knew *The Nights,* after his erratic
fashion, as no other European ever did. Oriental life,
above and below the surface—a distinction which does not
exist for the East—he knew throughout. He recognized,
too, the precise nature of the charm which went with Galland's version and the Englishings which followed him,
and how that differed from the tone of the original.

> The immortal fragment [he says] will never be
> superseded in the infallible judgment of child-
> hood. Those who look only at Galland's picture,
> his effort to 'transplant into European gardens
> the magic flowers of Eastern fancy,' still com-
> pare his tales with the sudden prospect of mag-
> nificent mountains seen after a long desert
> march; they arouse strange longings and inde-
> scribable desires; their marvellous imaginative-
> ness produces an insensible brightening of mind
> and an increase of fancy-power, making one
> dream that behind them lies the new and unseen,
> the strange and unexpected—in fact, all the
> glamour of the unknown.

The thing could hardly be better put. That he recognized,
too, the weakness of Mr. Payne is evident to every one who
can read between the lines of his references to his immediate predecessor. The style of *The Nights,* the prose and the
verse in all their phases, he understood. The whole problem of the translator lay bare to him. Perhaps he regarded
it as insoluble; perhaps he thought that Mr. Payne had
made the nearest approach possible to a solution. At any
rate, he turned with all deliberation and gave himself to
anthropology as Lane had done to manners and customs.
His great work (1886-1888)—for it is truly great—is a clue
to *The Nights* and to the life therein for the Arabist who

can weigh Burton's judgments and reject his eccentricities.
To the English reader it gives no true idea of the original,
and nothing could be further from being an English classic. No one will ever delight in it; many will study it. Perversities of style make it unreadable for its own sake. Such
phrases as "a red cent," "belle and beldame," "a veritable
beauty of a man," "O, my cuss," "thy hubby," "a Char-
ley," may possibly have Arabic equivalents, but certainly
cannot render those for us. No illusion can survive such
barbarisms. The long, lumbering lope of its verses, too, is
only a degree better than Lane's prose. Its futilities of annotation are a perpetual menace. The fate of the Household Edition brings all to a point: when deprived of un-
publishable matter and relying solely on its English value,
the book was a flat failure. (p. 168)

> *"On Translating 'The Arabian Nights.'—I" in*
> The Nation, *New York, Vol. LXXI, No. 1835,
> August 30, 1900, pp. 167-68.*

Frank Harris   (essay date 1920)

[*Harris was an Irish journalist and writer who served as
the editor of the London* Evening News (1884-86) *and*
Fortnightly Review (1886-94) *and became a noted literary personality during the English decadent movement. Here, Harris presents a portrait of Burton as an
explorer and scholar, combining anecdotal description
and psychological analysis.*]

Raleigh, Sir Walter of that ilk, has always seemed to me
the best representative of Elizabethan England; for he
could speak and act with equal inspiration. He was a gentleman and adventurer, a courtier and explorer, a captain
by sea and land, equally at home in Indian wigwam or English throne-room. A man of letters, too, master of a dignified, courtly English, who could write on universal history
to while away the tedium of prison. Raleigh touched life
at many points, and always with a certain mastery; yet his
advice to his son is that of a timorous prudence. "Save
money," he says; "never part with a man's best friend,"
and yet he himself as a courtier could squander thousands
of pounds on new footgear. One of the best "all-round"
men in English history was Raleigh, though troubled with
much serving which, however, one feels came naturally to
him; for he was always absolutely sceptical as to any afterlife, and so won a concentrated and uncanny understanding of this life and his fellow-men. And yet Raleigh per-
ished untimely on a scaffold, as if to show that no worldly
wisdom can be exhaustive, falling to ruin because he could
not divine the perverse impulses of a sensual pedant.

But in spite of the vile ingratitude of James and his base
betrayal, aristocratic England managed to use Walter Raleigh and rewarded him, on the whole, handsomely. He
played a great part even in those spacious days; was a leader of men in Ireland in his youth, a Captain of the Queen's
Guard in manhood; and, ennobled and enriched, held his
place always among the greatest, and at last died as an
enemy of kings, leaving behind him a distinguished name
and a brilliant page in the history of his country.

But what would the England of today, the England of the
smug, uneducated Philistine tradesmen, make of a Ra-

leigh if they had one? The question and its answer may throw some light on our boasted "progress" and the astonishingly selfish and self-satisfied present-day civilization of till-and-pill.

Richard Burton I met for the first time in a London drawing-room after his return from the Gold Coast sometime in the eighties. His reputation was already world-wide—the greatest of African explorers, the only European who had mastered Arabic and Eastern customs so completely that he had passed muster as a Mohammedan pilgrim and had preached in Mecca as a Mollah. He knew a dozen Indian languages, too, it was said, and as many more European, besides the chief African dialects; was, in fine, an extraordinary scholar and a master of English to boot, a great writer.

I was exceedingly curious, and very glad indeed to meet this legendary hero. Burton was in conventional evening dress, and yet, as he swung round to the introduction, there was an untamed air about him. He was tall, about six feet in height, with broad, square shoulders; he carried himself like a young man, in spite of his sixty years, and was abrupt in movement. His face was bronzed and scarred, and when he wore a heavy moustache and no beard he looked like a prize-fighter; the naked, dark eyes—imperious, aggressive eyes, by no means friendly; the heavy jaws and prominent hard chin gave him a desperate air; but the long beard which he wore in later life, concealing the chin and pursed-out lips, lent his face a fine, patriarchal expression, subduing the fierce provocation of it to a sort of regal pride and courage. "Untamed"—that is the word which always recurs when I think of Burton.

I was so curious about so many things in regard to him that I hesitated and fumbled, and made a bad impression on him; we soon drifted apart—I vexed with myself, he loftily indifferent.

It was Captain Lovett-Cameron who brought us closer together; a typical sailor and good fellow, he had been Burton's companion in Africa and had sucked an idolatrous admiration out of the intimacy. Burton was his hero; wiser than anyone else, stronger, braver, more masterful, more adroit; he could learn a new language in a week, and so forth and so on—hero-worship lyrical.

"A Bayard and an Admirable Crichton in one," I remarked scoffingly. "Human, too," he replied seriously, "human and brave as Henry of Navarre."

"Proofs, proofs," I cried.

"Proofs of courage!" Cameron exclaimed, "every African explorer lives by courage: every day war-parties of hostile tribes have to be charmed or awed to friendliness; rebellious servants brought to obedience; wild animals killed, food provided—all vicissitudes Burton handled as a master, and the more difficult and dangerous the situation the more certain he was to carry it off triumphantly. A great man, I tell you, with all sorts of qualities and powers, and, if you followed his lead, the best of 'pals.'

"No one would believe how kind he is; he nursed me for six weeks through African fever—took care of me like a

brother. You must know Dick really well: you'll love him."

Thanks to Cameron, Burton and I met again and dined together, and afterwards had a long palaver. Burton unbuttoned, and talked as only Burton could talk of Damascus and that immemorial East; of India and its supersubtle peoples; of Africa and human life in the raw today as it was twenty thousand years ago; of Brazil, too, and the dirty smear of Portuguese civilization polluting her silvered waterways and defiling even the immaculate wild.

I can still see his piercing eyes, and thrill to his vivid, pictured speech; he was irresistible; as Cameron had said, "utterly unconventional." Being very young, I thought him too "bitter," almost as contemptuous of his fellows as Carlyle; I did not then realize how tragic-cruel life is to extraordinary men.

Burton was of encyclopædic reading; knew English poetry and prose astonishingly; had a curious liking for "sabre-cuts of Saxon speech"—all such words as come hot from life's mint. Describing something, I used the phrase, "Frighted out of fear." "Fine that," he cried; "is it yours? Where did you get it?"

His ethnological appetite for curious customs and crimes, for everything singular and savage in humanity was insatiable. A Western American lynching yarn held him spellbound; a *crime passionel* in Paris intoxicated him, started him talking, transfigured him into a magnificent storyteller, with intermingled appeals of pathos and rollicking fun, camp-fire effects, jets of flame against the night.

His intellectual curiosity was astonishingly broad and deep rather than high. He would tell stories of Indian philosophy or of perverse negro habits of lust and cannibalism, or would listen to descriptions of Chinese cruelty and Russian self-mutilation till the stars paled out. Catholic in his admiration and liking for all greatness, it was the abnormalities and not the divinities of men that fascinated him.

Deep down in him lay the despairing gloom of utter disbelief. "Unaffected pessimism and constitutional melancholy," he notices, "strike deepest root under the brightest skies," and this pessimistic melancholy was as native to Burton as to any Arab of them all. He was thinking of himself when he wrote of the Moslem, "he cannot but sigh when contemplating the sin and sorrow, and pathos and bathos of the world; and feel the pity of it, with its shifts and changes ending in nothingness, its scanty happiness, its copious misery." Burton's laughter, even, deep-chested as it was, had in it something of sadness.

At heart he was regally generous; there was a large humanity in him, an unbounded charity for the poor and helpless; a natural magnanimity, too; "an unconditional forgiveness of the direst injuries" he calls "the note of the noble."

His love of freedom was insular and curiously extravagant, showing itself in every smallest detail. "My wife makes we wear these wretched dressclothes," he cried one evening. "I hate 'em—a livery of shame, shame of being yourself. Broad arrows would improve 'em," and the revolt of disgust flamed in his eyes.

Like most able, yet fanatical, lovers of liberty, he preferred the tyranny of one to the anarchical misrule of the many. "Eastern despotisms," he asserts, "have arrived nearer the ideal of equality and fraternity than any republic yet invented."

"A master of life and books," I said of him afterwards to Cameron, "but at bottom as tameless and despotic as an Arab sheikh."

Two extracts from his wonderful *Arabian Nights* are needed to give color to my sketch. I make no excuse for quoting them, for they are superexcellent English, and in themselves worthy of memory. Here is a picture of the desert which will rank with Fromentin's best:

> Again I stood under the diaphanous skies, in air glorious as ether, whose every breath raises men's spirits like sparkling wine. Once more I saw the evening star hanging like a solitaire from the pure front of the western firmament; and the after-glow transfiguring and transforming, as by magic, the homely and rugged features of the scene into a fairyland lit with a light which never shines on other soils or seas. Then would appear the woollen tents, low and black, of the true Badawin, mere dots in the boundless waste of lion-tawny clays and gazelle-brown gravels, and the camp-fire dotting like a glow-worm the village centre. Presently, sweetened by distance, would be heard the wild, weird song of lads and lasses, driving, or rather pelting, through the gloaming their sheep and goats; and the measured chant of the spearsmen gravely stalking behind their charge, the camels; mingled with the bleating of the flocks and the bellowing of the humpy herds; while the reremouse flittered overhead with his tiny shriek, and the rave of the jackal resounded through deepening glooms, and—most musical of music—the palm trees answered the whispers of the night breeze with the softest tones of falling water.

And here a Rembrandt etching of Burton storytelling to Arabs in the desert:

> The sheikhs and "white-beards" of the tribe gravely take their places, sitting with outspread skirts like hillocks on the plain, as the Arabs say, around the camp-fire, whilst I reward their hospitality and secure its continuance by reading or reciting a few pages of their favourite tales. The women and children stand motionless as silhouettes outside the ring; and all are breathless with attention; they seem to drink in the words with eyes and mouth as well as with ears. The most fantastic flights of fancy, the wildest improbabilities, the most impossible of impossibilities appear to them utterly natural, mere matters of everyday occurrence. They enter thoroughly into each phase of feeling touched upon by the author; they take a personal pride in the chivalrous nature and knightly prowess of Tajal-Muluk; they are touched with tenderness by the self-sacrificing love of Azizah; their mouths water as they hear of heaps of untold gold given away in

largesse like clay; they chuckle with delight every time a Kazi or a Fakir—a judge or a reverend—is scurvily entreated by some Pantagruelist of the wilderness; and, despite their normal solemnity and impassibility, all roar with laughter, sometimes rolling upon the ground till the reader's gravity is sorely tried, at the tales of the garrulous Barber and of Ali and the Kurdish sharper. To this magnetizing mood the sole exception is when a Badawi of superior accomplishments, who sometimes says his prayers, ejaculates a startling "Astaghfaru'llah"—I pray Allah's pardon—for listening to light mention of the sex whose name is never heard amongst the nobility of the desert.

Even when I only knew Burton as a great personality I touched the tragedy of his life unwittingly more than once. I had heard that he had come to grief as Consul in Damascus—Jews there claiming to be British subjects in order to escape Mohammedan justice, and when thwarted stirring up their powerful compatriots in London to petition for his recall; his superior at Beyrout always dead against him—eventually he was recalled, some said dismissed. I felt sure he had been in the right. "Won't you tell me about it?" I asked him one evening.

"The story's too long, too intricate," he cried. "Besides, the Foreign Office admitted I was right."

When I pressed for details he replied:

"Do you remember the cage at Loches, in which an ordinary man could not stand upright or lie at ease, and so was done to death slowly by constraint. Places under our Government today are cages like that to all men above the average size."

The English could not use Burton; they could maim him.

Englishmen are so strangely inclined to overpraise the men of past times and underrate their contemporaries that many have been astonished at my comparing Burton with Raleigh. But, in truth, both in speech and action Burton was the greater man. He was a more daring and a more successful explorer; an infinitely better scholar, with intimate knowledge of a dozen worlds which Raleigh knew nothing about, a greater writer, too, and a more dominant, irresistible personality. Young Lord Pembroke once slapped Raleigh's face; no sane man would have thought of striking Burton. Aristocratic Elizabethan England, however, could honor Raleigh and put him to noble use, whereas Victorian England could find no place for Richard Burton and could win no service from him. Think of it! Burton knew the Near East better than any Westerner has ever known it; he was a master of literary Arabic and of the dialects spoken in Egypt and the Soudan. Moreover, as he himself puts it modestly, "the accidents of my life, my long dealings with Arabs and other Mohammedans and my familiarity not only with their idiom, but with their turn of thought and with that racial individuality which baffles description" made Burton an ideal ruler for a Mohammedan people. He was already employed under the Foreign Office.

Notwithstanding all this when we took Egypt we sent Lord Dufferin to govern it, and tossed a small consular post to Richard Burton as a bone to a dog. Dufferin knew no Arabic, and nothing about Egypt. Burton knew more than anyone else on earth about both, and was besides a thousand times abler than the chattering, charming Irish peer. Yet Dufferin was preferred before him. Deliberately I say that all England's mistakes in Egypt—and they are as numerous and as abominable as years of needless war have ever produced—came from this one blunder. This sin England is committing every day, the sin of neglecting the able and true man and preferring to him the unfit and second-rate, and therefore negligible, man; it is the worst of crimes in a ruling caste, the sin against the Holy Spirit, the sin once labelled unforgivable. "No immorality," said Napoleon to his weak brother, "like the immorality of taking a post you're not fitted for." No wonder Burton wrote that the "crass ignorance" (of England) "concerning the Oriental peoples which should most interest her, exposes her to the contempt of Europe as well as of the Eastern World." No wonder he condemned "the regrettable raids of '83-'84," and "the miserable attacks of Tokar, Teb, and Tamasi" upon the "gallant negroids who were battling for the holy cause of liberty and religion and for escape from Turkish task-masters and Egyptian tax-gatherers." With heartfelt contempt he records the fact that there was "not an English official in camp . . . capable of speaking Arabic."

Gladstone appointed Dufferin; Gladstone sent Gordon to

Burton in 1883.

the Soudan at the dictation of a journalist as ignorant as himself! Gladstone, too, appointed Cromer, and after Tokar and Teb we had the atrocious, shameful revenge on the Mahdi's remains and the barbarous murders of Denshawi; and a thousand thousand unknown tragedies besides, all because England's rulers are incapable of using her wisest sons and are determined to pin their faith to mediocrities—like choosing like, with penguin gravity.

"England," says Burton, "has forgotten, apparently, that she is at present the greatest Mohammedan empire in the world, and in her Civil Service examinations she insists on a smattering of Greek and Latin rather than a knowledge of Arabic." Here is what Burton thought about the English Civil Service; every word of it true still, and every word memorable:

> In our day, when we live under a despotism of the lower "middle-class" who can pardon anything but superiority, the prizes of competitive service are monopolized by certain "pets" of the *Médiocratie,* and prime favourites of that jealous and potent majority—the Mediocrities who know "no nonsense about merit." It is hard for an outsider to realize how perfect is the monopoly of commonplace, and to comprehend how fatal a stumbling-stone that man sets in the way of his own advancement who dares to think for himself, or who thinks more or who does more than the mob of gentlemen-employees who know very little and do even less. "He knows too much" is the direst obstacle to official advancement in England—it would be no objection in France; and in Germany, Russia, and Italy, the three rising Powers of Europe, it would be a valid claim for promotion. But, unfortunately for England, the rule and government of the country have long been, and still are, in the hands of a corporation, a clique, which may be described as salaried, permanent and irresponsible clerks, the power which administers behind the Minister. They rule and misrule; nor is there one man in a million who, like the late Mr. Fawcett, when taking Ministerial charge, dares to think and act for himself and to emancipate himself from the ignoble tyranny of "the office."

With all its faults the English Civil Service is better than our Parliamentary masters. Like fish, a State first goes bad at the head. Burton used to tell how he came home and offered all East Africa to Lord Salisbury. He had concluded treaties with all the chiefs; no other Power was interested or would have objected. But Lord Salisbury refused the gift. "Is Zanzibar an island?" he exclaimed in wonder, and "Is East Africa worth anything?" So the Germans were allowed twenty years later to come in and cut "the wasp's waist" and bar England's way from the Cape to Cairo.

England wasted Burton, left his singular talents unused, and has already paid millions of money, to say nothing of far more precious things (some of them beyond price), for her stupidity, and England's account with Egypt is still all on the wrong side—stands, indeed, worse than ever, I imagine; for Egypt is now bitterly contemptuous of English rule. Egypt is a source of weakness to England therefore, and not a source and fount of strength, as she would have been from the beginning if the old Parliamentary rhetor had had eyes as well as tongue, and had set Burton to do the work of teaching, organizing, and guiding which your Dufferins, Cromers, Kitcheners and the rest are incapable even of imagining.

The worst of it is that Burton has left no successor. Had he been appointed he would have seen to this, one may be sure; would have established a great school of Arabic learning in Cairo, and trained a staff of Civil Servants who would have gladly acquired at least the elements of their work—men who would not only have known Arabic, but the ablest natives, too, and so have availed themselves of a little better knowledge than their own. But, alas! the chance has been lost, and unless something is done soon, Egypt will be England's worst failure, worse even than India or Ireland.

But I must return to Burton. I should like to tell of an evening I spent once with him when Lord Lytton was present. Lytton had been Viceroy of India, the first and only Viceroy who ever understood his own infinite unfitness for the post.

"I only stayed in India," he used to say, "to prevent them sending out an even worse man."

I asked him afterwards why he didn't recommend Burton for the post; for he knew something of Burton's transcendant quality.

"They'd never send him," he cried, with unconscious snobbery. "He's not got the title or the position; besides, he'd be too independent. My God, how he'd kick over the traces and upset the cart!"

The eternal dread and dislike of genius! And yet that very evening Burton had shown qualities of prudence and wisdom far beyond Lytton's comprehension.

But I must hasten. I found myself in Venice once with time on my hands, when I suddenly remembered that across the sea at Trieste was a man who would always make a meeting memorable. I took the next steamer and called on Burton. I found the desert lion dying of the cage; dying of disappointment and neglect; dying because there was no field for the exercise of his superlative abilities; dying because the soul in him could find nothing to live on in Trieste; for in spite of his talent for literature, in spite of his extraordinary gift of speech, Burton was at bottom a man of action, a great leader, a still greater governor of men.

While out walking one afternoon we stopped at a little café, and I had an object-lesson in Burton's mastery of life. His German was quite good, but nothing like his Italian. He seemed to know the people of the inn and every one about by intuition, and in a few minutes had won their confidence and admiration. For half an hour he talked to a delighted audience in Dante's speech, jewelled with phrases from the great Florentine himself. As we walked back to his house he suddenly cried to me:

"Make some excuse and take me out tonight; if I don't get out I shall go mad. . . . "

We had a great night—Burton giving pictures of his own life; telling of his youth in the Indian Army when he wan-

dered about among the natives disguised as a native (I have always thought of him as the original of Kipling's "Strickland"). His fellow-officers, of course, hated his superiority: called him in derision "the white nigger"; Burton laughed at it all, fully compensated, he said, for their hatred by the love and admiration of Sir Charles Napier (*Peccavi,* "I have Scinde," Napier), hero recognizing hero. It was to Napier, and at Napier's request, that he sent the famous "report" which, falling into secretarial hands, put an end to any chance of Burton's advancement in India— the tragedy again and again repeated of a great life maimed and marred by envious, eyeless mediocrities. What might have been, what would have been had he been given power—a new earth if not a new heaven—the theme of his inspired Report.

I got him to talk, too, about **The Scented Garden,** which he had been working at for some time. Lady Burton afterwards burnt this book, it will be remembered, together with his priceless diaries, out of sheer prudery. He told me (what I had already guessed) that the freedom of speech he used, he used deliberately, not to shock England, but to teach England that only by absolute freedom of speech and thought could she ever come to be worthy of her heritage.

"But I'm afraid it's too late," he added; "England's going to some great defeat; she's wedded to lies and mediocrities." . . . He got bitter again, and I wished to turn his thoughts.

"Which would you really have preferred to be," I probed, "Viceroy of India or Consul-General of Egypt?"

"Egypt, Egypt!" he cried, starting up, "Egypt! In India I should have had the English Civil Servants to deal with— the Jangalí, or savages, as their Hindu fellow-subjects call them—and English prejudices, English formalities, English stupidity, English ignorance. They would have killed me in India, thwarted me, fought me, intrigued against me, murdered me. But in Egypt I could have made my own Civil servants, picked them out, and trained them. I could have had natives, too, to help. Ah, what a chance!

"I know Arabic better than I know Hindu. Arabic is my native tongue; I know it as well as I know English. I know the Arab nature. The Mahdi business could have been settled without striking a blow. If Gordon had known Arabic well, spoken it as a master, he would have won the Mahdi to friendship. To govern well you must know a people— know their feelings, love their dreams and aspirations. What did Dufferin know of Egypt? Poor Dufferin, what did he even know of Dufferin? And Cromer's devoid even of Dufferin's amiability!"

The cold words do him wrong, give no hint of the flame and force of his disappointment; but I can never forget the bitter sadness of it: "England finds nothing for me to do, makes me an office-boy, exiles me here on a pittance." The caged lion!

I have always thought that these two men, Carlyle and Burton, were the two greatest governors ever given to England. The one for England herself, and as an example to the world of the way to turn a feudal, chivalrous State into a great modern industrial State; the other the best possible governor of Mohammedan peoples—two more prophets whom England did not stone, did not even take the trouble to listen to. She is still paying, as I have said, somewhat dearly for her adders' ears and must yet pay still more heavily.

I have found fault with Carlyle because he was a Puritan, deaf to music, blind to beauty. Burton went to the other extreme: he was a sensualist of extravagant appetite learned in every Eastern and savage vice. His coarse, heavy, protruding lips were to me sufficient explanation of the pornographic learning of his *Arabian Nights*. And when age came upon him; though a quarter of what he was accustomed to eat in his prime would have kept him in perfect health, he yielded to the habitual desire and suffered agonies with indigestion, dying, indeed, in a fit of dyspepsia brought on by over-eating. And with these untamed appetites and desires he was peculiarly sceptical and practical; his curiosity all limited to this world, which accounts to me for his infernal pedantry. He never seemed to realize that wisdom has nothing to do with knowledge, literature nothing to do with learning. Knowledge and learning, facts, are but the raw food of experience, and literature is concerned only with experience itself. A child of the mystical East, a master of that Semitic thought which has produced the greatest religions, Burton was astoundingly matter-of-fact. There was no touch of the visionary in him—the curious analogies everywhere discoverable in things disparate, the chemical reactions of passion, the astounding agreement between mathematical formulæ and the laws of love and hatred, the myriad provoking hints, like eyes glinting through a veil, that tempt the poet to dreaming, the artist to belief, were all lost on Burton. He was a master of this life and cared nothing for

any other; his disbelief was characteristically bold and emphatic. He wrote:

> The shivered clock again shall strike, the broken
>   reed shall pipe again,
> But we, we die, and Death is one, the doom of
>   Brutes, the doom of Men.

But, with all his limitations and all his shortcomings, Burton's place was an Eastern throne and not the ignoble routine of a petty Consular office.

> At length the good hour came; he died,
>   As he had lived alone:
> He was not missed from the desert wide,
>   Perhaps he was found at the Throne.

                                                    (pp. 178-97)

> *Frank Harris, "Sir Richard Burton," in* Contemporary Portraits, *Brentano's Publishers, 1920, pp. 178-97.*

Arthur Symons   (essay date 1921)

[An English critic, poet, dramatist, short story writer and editor, Symons initially made his reputation as an adherent of the English decadent movement in the 1890s and established himself as one of the most important critics of the modern era. In the following essay, written in 1921 and later published in his Dramatis Personae, *Symons offers a biographical and critical account of Burton's career, emphasizing his "almost unsurpassable gift for translation."]*

I

One hundred years ago, on March 19th, 1821, Sir Richard Burton was born; he died at Trieste on October 19th, 1890, in his seventieth year. He was superstitious; the fact that he was born and that he died on the nineteenth has its significance. On the night when he expired, as his wife was saying prayers to him, a dog began that dreadful howl which the superstitious say denotes a death. It was an evil omen; I have heard long after midnight dogs howl in the streets of Constantinople; their howling is only broken by the tapping of the bekjé's iron staff; it sounds like loud wind or water far off, waning and waxing, and at times, as it comes across the water from Stamboul, it is like a sound of strings, plucked and scraped savagely by an orchestra of stringed instruments.

In every age there have been I know not how many neglected men of genius, undiscovered, misunderstood, mocked at in the fashion Jesus Christ was mocked by the Jews, scorned as Dante was scorned when he was exiled from Florence, called a madman as Blake used to be called, censured as Swinburne was in 1866, for being "an unclean fiery imp of the pit" and "the libidinous Laureate of a pack of satyrs;" so the greatest as the least—the greatest whose names are always remembered and the least whose names are invariably forgotten—have endured the same prejudices; have been lapidated by the same stones; such stones as Burton refers to when he writes in Mecca:

> On the great festival day we stoned the Devil, each man with seven stones washed in seven waters, and we said, while throwing the stones, "In

---

Swinburne on Burton's translation of the *Arabian Nights*:

> Westward the sun sinks, grave and glad; but far
>   Eastward, with laughter and tempestuous tears,
>   Cloud, rain, and splendour as of Orient spears,
>
> Keen as the sea's thrill toward a kindling star,
> The sundawn breaks the barren twilight's bar
>   And fires the mist and slays it. Years on years
>   Vanish, but he that hearkens eastward hears
> Bright music from the world where shadows are.
>
> Where shadows are not shadows. Hand in hand
> A man's word bids them rise and smile and stand
>   And triumph. All that glorious Orient glows
> Defiant of the dusk. Our twilight land
>   Trembles; but all the heaven is all one rose,
>   Whence laughing love dissolves her frosts and snows.

Algernon Charles Swinburne, in his "To Richard F. Burton: on His Translation of the 'Arabian Nights'," The Athenaeum-Journal of English and Foreign Literature, Science, the Fine Arts, and the Drama, *1886.*

the name of Allah—and Allah is Almighty—I
do this in hatred of the Devil, and to his shame."

Burton was a great man, a great traveler and adventurer,
who practically led to the discovery of the sources of the
Nile; a wonderful linguist, he was acquainted with twenty-
nine languages: he was a man of genius; only, the fact is,
he is not a great writer. Continually thwarted by the English Government, he was debarred from some of the most
famous expeditions by the folly of his inferiors, who igno-
rantly supposed they were his superiors; and, as Sir
H. H. Johnston says in some of his notes, not only was
Burton treated unjustly, but his famous pilgrimage to
Mecca won him no explicit recognition from the Indian
Government; his great discoveries in Africa, Brazil, Syria
and Trieste were never appreciated; and, worst of all, he
was refused the post of British Minister in Morocco; it was
persistently denied him. He adds: "Had he gone there we
might long since have known—what we do not know—the
realities of Morocco."

Still, when Burton went to India, I do not imagine he was
likely to suffer from any hostility on the part of the natives
nor of the rulers. Lord Clive, who, in Browning's words,
"gave England India," which was the result of his incredible victory in 1751 over the Nabob's army of 60,000 men,
was never literally "loved" by the races of India; no more
than Sir Warren Hastings. Still, Clive had genius, which
he showed in the face of a bully he caught cheating at
cards and in his mere shout at him: "You did cheat, go to
Hell!" Impeached for the splendid service he had done in
India he was acquitted in 1773; next year, having taken to
opium, his own hand dealt himself his own doom. So he
revenged himself on his country's ingratitude. So did Burton revenge himself—not in deeds, but in words, words,
if I may say so, that are stupendous. "I struggled for forty-
seven years, I distinguished myself honourably in every
way I possibly could. I never had a compliment nor a
'Thank you,' nor a single farthing. I translated a doubtful
book in my old age, and I immediately made sixteen thousand guineas. Now that I know the tastes of England, we
need never be without money."

Burton first met Swinburne in 1861 at Lord Houghton's
house, who, having given him *The Queen Mother,* said: "I
bring you this book because the author is coming here this
evening, so that you may not quote him as an absurdity
to himself." In the summer of 1865 Swinburne saw a great
deal of Burton. These two men, externally so dissimilar,
had taken (as Swinburne said to me) a curious fancy, an
absolute fascination, for each other. Virile and a mysterious adventurer, Burton was Swinburne's senior by sixteen
years; one of those things that linked them together was
certainly their passionate love of literature. Burton had
also—which Swinburne might perhaps have envied—an
almost unsurpassable gift for translation, which he shows
in his wonderful version of *The Arabian Nights.* He used
to say:

> I have not only preserved the spirit of the origi-
> nal, but the *mécanique.* I don't care a button
> about being prosecuted, and if the matter comes
> to a fight, I will walk into court with my Bible
> and my Shakespeare and my Rabelais under my
> arm, and prove to them that before they con-

demn me, they must cut half of *them* out, and
not allow them to be circulated to the public.

In his Foreword to the first volume of his Translation,
dated Wanderers' Club, August 15th, 1885, he says:

> This work, laborious as it may appear, has been
> to me a labor of love, an unfailing source of so-
> lace and satisfaction. During my long years of
> official banishment to the luxurious and deadly
> deserts of Western Africa, it proved truly a
> charm, a talisman against *ennui* and despondency.
> cy. The Jinn bore me at once to the land of my
> predilection, Arabia. In what is obscure in the
> original there are traces of Petronius Arbiter and
> of Rabelais; only, subtle corruption and covert
> licentiousness are wholly absent.

Therefore, in order to show the wonderful quality of his
translation, I have chosen certain of his sentences, which
literally bring back to me all that I have felt of the heat,
the odor and the fascination of the East.

> So I donned my mantilla, and, taking with me
> the old woman and the slave-girl, I went to the
> Khan of the merchants. There I knocked at the
> door and out came two white slave-girls, both
> young, high-bosomed virgins, as they were
> Moons. They were melting a perfume whose like
> I had never before smelt; and so sharp and subtle
> was the odor that it made my senses drunken as
> with strong wine. I saw there also two great cen-
> sers each big as a mazzar bowl, flaming with
> aloes, nard, perfumes, ambergris and honied
> scents; and the place was full of their fragrance.

The next quotation is from the Tale of the Fisherman and
the Jinn:

> He loosened the lid from the jar, he shook the
> vase to pour out whatever might be inside. He
> found nothing in it; whereat he marvelled with
> an exceeding marvel. But presently there came
> forth from the jar a smoke which spread heaven-
> wards into ether (whereat again he marvelled
> with mighty marvel) and which trailed along
> earth's surface till presently, having reached its
> full height, the thick vapors condensed, and be-
> came an Ifrit, huge of bulk, whose crest touched
> the clouds when his feet were on the ground.

I have before me Smithers' privately printed edition
(1894) of *The Carmina of Caius Valerius Catullus now first
completely Englished into Verse and Prose, the Metrical
Part by Capt. Sir Richard Burton, and the Prose Portion
by Leonard C. Smithers.* Burton is right in saying that "the
translator of original mind who notes the innumerable
shades of tone, manner and complexion will not neglect
the frequent opportunities of enriching his mothertongue
with novel and alien ornaments which shall justify the accounted barbarisms until formally naturalized and adopted. He must produce an honest and faithful copy, adding
nought to the sense or abating aught of its *cachet.*" He
ends his Foreword: "As discovery is mostly my mania, I
have hit upon a bastard-urging to indulge it, by a presenting to the public of certain classics in the nude Roman poetry, like the Arab, and of the same date."

Certainly Burton leaves out nothing of the nakedness that

startles one in the verse of Catullus: a nakedness that is as honest as daylight and as shameless as night. When the text is obscene his translation retains its obscenity; which, on the whole, is rare: for the genius of Catullus is elemental, primitive, nervous, passionate, decadent in the modern sense and in the modern sense perverse. In his rhymed version of the *Attis* Burton has made a prodigious attempt to achieve the impossible. Not being a poet, he was naturally unable to follow the rhythm—the Galliambic metre, in which Catullus obtains variety of rhythm; for, as Robinson Ellis says:

> It remains unique as a wonderful expression of abnormal feeling in a quasi-abnormal meter. Quasi-abnormal, however, only: for no poem of Catullus follows stricter laws, or succeeds in conveying the idea of a wild freedom under a more carefully masked regularity.

As one must inevitably compare two translations of the same original, I have to point out that Burton's rendering is, both metrically and technically, inaccurate; whereas, in another rendering, the translator has at least preserved the exact metre, the exact scansion, and the double endings at the end of every line; not, of course, in this case, employing the double rhymes Swinburne used in his translation from Aristophanes. These are Burton's first lines:—

> O'er high deep seas in speedy ship his voyage
> Atys sped
> Until he trod the Phrygian grove with hurried,
> eager tread,
> And as the gloomy tree-shorn stead, the she-
> God's home he sought,
> There sorely stung with fiery ire and madman's
> raging thought,
> Share he with sharpened flint the freight where-
> with his frame was fraught.

These are the first lines of the other version:—

> Over ocean Attis sailing in a swift ship charioted
> When he reached the Phrygian forests, and with
> rash foot violently
> Trod the dark and shadowy regions of the god-
> dess, wood-garlanded,
> And with ravening madness ravished, and his
> reason abandoning him,
> Seized a pointed flint and sundered from his
> flesh his virility.

II

Burton himself admitted that he was a devil; for, said he: "the Devil entered into me at Oxford." Evidently, also, besides his mixture of races, he was a mixture of the normal and the abnormal; he was perverse and passionate; he was imaginative and cruel; he was easily stirred to rage. Nearly six feet in height, he had, together with his broad shoulders, the small hands and feet of the Orientals; he was Arab in his prominent cheek-bones; he was gypsy in his terrible, magnetic eyes—the sullen eyes of a stinging serpent. He had a deeply bronzed complexion, a determined mouth, half-hidden by a black mustache, which hung down in a peculiar fashion on both sides of his chin. This peculiarity I have often seen in men of the wandering tribe in Spain and in Hungary. Wherever he went he was wel-

comed by the gypsies; he shared with them their horror of a corpse, of death-scenes, and of graveyards. "He had the same restlessness," wrote his wife, "which could stay nowhere long nor own any spot on earth. Hagar Burton, a Gypsy woman, cast my horoscope, in which she said: 'You will bear the name of our Tribe, and be right proud of it. You will be as we are, but far greater than we.' I met Richard two months later, in 1856, and was engaged to him." It is a curious fact that John Varley, who cast Blake's horoscope in 1820, also cast Burton's; who, as he says, had finished his *Zodiacal Physiognomy* so as to prove that every man resembled after a fashion the sign under which he was born. His figures are either human or bestial; some remind me of those where men are represented in the form of animals in Giovanni della Porta's *Fisonomia dell' Huomo* (Venice, 1668), which is before me as I write; Swinburne himself once showed to me his copy of the same book. Nor have I ever forgotten his saying to me—in regard to Burton's nervous fears: "The look of unspeakable horror in those eyes of his gave him, at times, an almost unearthly appearance." He added: "This reminds me of what Kiomi says in Meredith's novel: 'I'll dance if you talk of dead people,' and so begins to dance and to whoop at the pitch of her voice. I suppose both had the same reason for this force of fear: to make the dead people hear." Then he flashed at me this unforgettable phrase: "Burton had the jaw of a Devil and the brow of a God."

In one of his letters he says, I suppose by way of *persiflage* in regard to himself and Burton: "*En moi vous voyez Les Malheurs de la Virtu, en lui Les Prosperités du Vice.*" In any case, it is to entertain Burton when he writes: "I have in hand a scheme of mixed verse and prose—a sort of étude à la Balzac *plus* the poetry—which I flatter myself will be more offensive and objectionable to Britannia than anything I have done: *Lesbia Brandon.* You see I have now a character to keep up, and by the grace of Cotytto I will."

Swinburne began *Lesbia Brandon* in 1859; he never finished it; what remains of it consists of seventy-three galleys, numbered 25 to 97, besides four unprinted chapters. The first, "A Character," was written in 1864; "An Episode" in 1866; "Turris Eburnea" in 1886; "La Bohême Dédorée" must have been written a year or two later. Mr. Gosse gives a vivid description of Swinburne, who was living in 13, Great James Street, and who was never weary of his unfinished novel, reading to him parts of two chapters in June, 1877. "He read two long passages, the one a ride over a moorland by night, the other the death of his heroine, Lesbia Brandon. After reading aloud all these things with amazing violence, he seemed quite exhausted." It is possible to decipher a few sentences from two pages of his manuscript; first in "Turris Eburnea." " 'Above the sheet, below the boudoir,' said the sage. Her ideal was marriage, to which she clung, which revealed to astonished and admiring friends the vitality of a dubious intellect within her. She had not even the harlot's talent of discernment." This is Leonora Harley. In *La Bohême Dédorée* we read:

> Two nights later Herbert received a note from Mr. Linley inviting him to a private supper. Feverish from the contact of Mariani and hungry

for a chance of service, he felt not unwilling to win a little respite from the vexation of patience. The sage had never found him more amenable to the counsel he called reason. Miss Brandon had not lately crossed his ways. Over their evening Leonora Harley guided with the due graces of her professional art. It was not her fault if she could not help asking her younger friend when he had last met a darker beauty: she had seen him once with Lesbia.

III

In 1848 Burton determined to pass in India for an Oriental; the disguise he assumed was that of a half-Arab, half-Iranian, thousands of whom can be met along the northern shore of the Persian Gulf. He set out on his first pilgrimage as Mirza Abdulla the Bushiri, as a *buzzaz,* vendor of fine linen, muslins and *bijouterie;* he was admitted to the harems, he collected the information he required from the villagers; he won many women's hearts, he spent his evenings in the mosques; and, after innumerable adventures, he wended his way to Mecca. His account of this adventure is thrilling. The first cry was: "Open the way for the Haji who would enter the House!" Then:

> Two stout Meccans, who stood below the door, raised me in their arms, whilst a third drew me from above into the building. At the entrance I was accosted by a youth of the Benu Shazban family, the true blood of the El Hejaz. He held in his hand the huge silver-gilt padlock of the Ka'abeh, and presently, taking his seat upon a kind of wooden press in the left corner of the hall, he officially inquired my mother-nation and other particulars. The replies were satisfactory, and the boy Mohammed was authoritatively ordered to conduct me round the building and to recite the prayers. I will not deny that, looking at the windowless walls, the officials at the door, and a crowd of excited fanatics below—

> "And the place death, considering who I was,"

> my feelings were those of the trapped-rat description, acknowledged by the immortal nephew of his uncle Perez. A blunder, a hasty action, a misjudged word, a prayer or bow, not strictly the right shibboleth, and my bones would have whitened the desert sand. This did not, however, prevent my carefully observing the scene during our long prayer, and making a rough plan with a pencil upon my white *ihram.*

After having seen the howling Dervishes in Scutari in Asia, I can imagine Burton's excitement when in Cairo he suddenly left his stolid English friends, joined in the shouting, gesticulating circle, and behaved as if to the manner born: he held his diploma as a master Dervish. In Scutari I felt the contagion of these dancers, where the brain reels, and the body is almost swept into the orgy. I had all the difficulty in the world from keeping back the woman who sat beside me from leaping over the barrier and joining the Dervishes. In these I felt the ultimate, because the most animal, the most irrational, the most insane, form of Eastern ecstasy. It gave me an impression of witchcraft; one might have been in Central Africa, or in some Saturnalia of barbarians.

There can be no doubt that Burton always gives a vivid and virile impression of his adventures; yet, as I have said before, something is lacking in his prose; not the vital heat, but the vision of what is equivalent to vital heat. I have before me a letter sent from Hyderabad by Sarojini Naidu, who says:

> All is hot and fierce and passionate, ardent and unashamed in its exulting and importunate desire for life and love. And, do you know, the scarlet lilies are woven petal by petal from my heart's blood, those quivering little birds are my soul made incarnate music, these heavy perfumes are my emotions dissolved into aerial essence, this flaming blue and gold sky is the 'Very You' that part of me that incessantly and insolently, yes, and a little deliberately, triumphs over that other part—a thing of nerves and tissues that suffers and cries out, and that must die tomorrow perhaps, or twenty years hence.

In these sentences the whole passionate, exotic and perfumed East flashes before me—a vision of delight and of distresses—and, as it were, all that slumbers in their fiery blood.

"Not the fruit of experience," wrote Walter Pater, "but experience itself, is the end. A counted number of pulses only is given us of a variegated dramatic life. To burn always with this hard, gemlike flame, to maintain this ecstasy, is success in life." Alas, how few lives out of the cloud-covered multitude of existences have burned always with this flame! I have said somewhere that we can always, in this world, get what we want if we will it intensely enough. So few people succeed greatly because so few people can conceive a great end, and work toward that without tiring and without deviating. The adventurer of whom I am writing failed, over and over again, in spite of the fact that he conceived and could have executed great ends: never by his own fault, always by the fault of others.

IV

Richard Burton dedicated his literal version of the epic of Camoens "To the Prince of the Lyric Poets of his Day, Algernon Charles Swinburne." He begins:

> My dear Swinburne, accept the unequal exchange—my brass for your gold. Your *Poems and Ballads* began to teach the Philistine what might there is in the music of language, and what marvel of lyric inspiration, far subtler and more ethereal than poetry, means to the mind of man.

In return for this Swinburne dedicated to him *Poems and Ballads,* Second Series.

> Inscribed to Richard F. Burton in redemption of an old pledge and in recognition of a friendship which I must always count among the highest honors of my life.

It was nine years before then, when they were together in the south of France, that Swinburne was seized by a severe illness; and, as he assured me, it was Burton who, with more than a woman's care and devotion, restored him to health. The pledge—it was not the covenant sealed between the two greatest, the two most passionate, lovers in the world, Iseult and Tristan, on the deck of that ship which was the ship of Life, the ship of Death, in the mere drinking of wine out of a flagon, which, being of the nature of a most sweet poison, consumed their limbs and gave intoxication to their souls and to their bodies—but a pledge in the wine Swinburne and Burton drank in the hot sunshine:—

> For life's helm rocks to windward and lee,
> And time is as wind, and waves are we,
> And song is as foam that the sea-waves fret,
>   Though the thought at its heart should be deep
>   as the sea.

It was in July, 1869, that Swinburne joined the Burtons and Mrs. Sartoris at Vichy. As I have never forgotten Swinburne's wonderful stories about Burton—besides those on Rossetti and Mazzini—I find in a letter of his to his mother words he might really have altered.

> If you had seen *him,* when the heat and the climb and the bothers of travelling were too much for me in the very hot weather—helping, waiting on me—going out to get me books to read in bed—and always kind, thoughtful, ready, and so bright and fresh that nothing but a lizard (I suppose that is the most insensible thing going) could have resisted his influence—I feel sure you would like him (you remember you said you didn't) and then—love him, as I do. I never expect to see his like again—but *him* I do hope to see again, and when the time comes to see him at Damascus as H. B. M. Consul. (pp. 241-58)

V

I have been assured, by many who knew him, that Richard Burton had a vocabulary which was one of his inventions; a shameless one—as shameless as the vocabularies invented by Paul Verlaine and by Henri de Toulouse-Lautrec, which are as vivid to me as when I heard their utterance. These shared with Villiers de Isle-Adam that sardonic humor which is not so much satire as the revenge of beauty on ugliness, the persecution of the ugly: the only laughter of our generation which is as fundamental as that of Rabelais and of Swift. Burton, who had much the same contempt for women that Baudelaire imagined he had, only with that fixed stare of his that disconcerted them, did all that with deliberate malice. There was almost nothing in this world that he had not done, exulted in, gloried in. Like Villiers, he could not pardon stupidity; to both it was incomprehensible; both saw that stupidity is more criminal than even vice, if only because stupidity is incurable, if only because vice is curable. Burton, who found the Arabs, in their delicate depravity, ironical—irony being their breath of life—might have said with Villiers: *"L'Esprit du Siècle, ne l'oublions pas, est aux machines."*

Every individual face has as many different expressions as the soul behind it has moods; therefore, the artist's business is to create on paper, or on his canvas, the image which was none of these, but which those helped to make in his own soul. I see, as it were, surge before me an image of Swinburne in his youth, when, with his passionate and pale face, with its masses of fiery hair, he has almost the

aspect of Ucello's Galeazzo Malatesta. Burton's face has no actual beauty in it; it reveals a tremendous animalism, an air of repressed ferocity, a devilish fascination. There is almost a tortured magnificence in this huge head, tragic and painful, with its mouth that aches with desire, with those dilated nostrils that drink in I know not what strange perfumes. (pp. 261-62)

Arthur Symons, "A Neglected Genius: Sir Richard Burton," in his Dramatis Personae, *The Bobbs-Merrill Company, 1923, pp. 241-62.*

Desmond MacCarthy   (essay date 1931)

[*MacCarthy was one of the most influential literary critics in England during the first half of the twentieth century. A member of the Bloomsbury group, which also included Leonard and Virginia Woolf, John Maynard Keynes, E. M. Forster, and Lytton Strachey among its number, MacCarthy was guided by their primary tenet that "one's prime objects in life were love, the creation and enjoyment of aesthetic experience, and the pursuit of knowledge." According to his critics, MacCarthy brought to his work a wide range of reading, serious and sensitive judgment, an interest in the works of new writers, and high critical standards. In the following excerpt he provides a brief overview of Burton's life and career, emphasizing the uniqueness of his personality.*]

The chief authority on the life and works of Sir Richard Burton is Mr. Norman M. Penzer, F.R.G.S., who published in 1923 an annotated bibliography, and a year later selected papers from Burton's contributions to learned societies and other magazines. Burton was one of the remarkable personalities of his time, and Elizabeth, not Victoria, should have been his Queen. But he has been unfortunate in his biographers. His wife wrote a long two-volume account of him in which there was no sense of proportion; it was written from a personal point of view. In a book of 1,200 pages she devoted eleven to his Pilgrimage to Mecca and twenty-six to his journey to Harar, and these were two of the most important of Burton's journeys. His niece, Miss Stisted, wrote to correct what she thought misleading statements in that book, and Mr. Thomas Wright in 1906 published two unsatisfactory volumes in which he devoted much space to showing Burton's great indebtedness to Payne in his translation of the *Arabian Nights.* There was also an earlier biography written in 1887, by Francis Hitcham, of which I know nothing; but it is, according to Mr. Penzer, more adequate, in spite of some inaccuracies. In short, the life of Sir Richard Burton, who combined with such furious energy the pursuits of a scholar, anthropologist and explorer, is an extraordinarily difficult biography to write without making mistakes. It is on Mr. Penzer himself should devolve the honour of writing *the* life of Sir Richard Burton. It would be a fine lasting book.

In a fragment of autobiography which is one of the few lively pieces of writing from Burton's pen, he says that as a little boy he used to ask himself in front of forbidden fruit, "Do I dare to eat it?" Then, when he had settled the question in the affirmative, he immediately ate it. The attraction that Burton exercised throughout life was the spell that audacity exercises upon others. He was violent, explosive and romantic, but his emotional explosions were not empty detonations; they drove him onwards with the directness of a projectile. He lived for adventure, and he pursued his ends with determination. Nothing could stop him. Fevers, wounds, starvation, disappointments were part of the glory of achievement; slights, slanders, poverty, and neglect made him roar and curse, but never daunted him. He took "Honour not Honours," as his motto. He grabbed at the gear of the world whenever he could, but he never sacrificed a genuine interest for the sake of getting his hands on it. The money he got for his anthropologically annotated *Arabian Nights,* however, did more than old age to mellow his defiant attitude towards the world. He and his wife had been once reduced to a last £15. He had been always full of schemes for rehabilitating his battered fortunes; at one time it was the colonization of the Gold Coast, where, to use his own words, "he discovered several gold mines"; at another time it was the exploitation of sulphur in Iceland; at another it was the discovery of ancient gold and turquoise mines in Midian, and once it was a patent pick-me-up for the liverish. All these ventures, except the last—and from that, too, doubtless he drew some of the stuff of romance, which his own energy breathed into everything he undertook—brought him the excitement and experience his nature craved. The ship of his hopes always started under full canvas; she never brought her treasure home, but the navigator had had his brush with the elements and his gamble with fate. He would return still restless, still unremunerated, but consoled.

At last he found his Eldorado. He found it in the exercise of a peculiar intellectual curiosity. He was an anthropologist by instinct, and ever since his early years in India he had been fascinated by the customs of sexual religion and the various and devious ways in which the sex instinct may manifest itself. This had blackened his reputation with the military authorities. He went on accumulating an enormous mass of curious observations and facts in the course of his subsequent Eastern travels, and during the time he was consul at Trieste these stores of information became a source of considerable profit to him. He poured them out in the notes to his translation of the *Arabian Nights* and to various erotic Eastern books produced by the Kama Shastra Society. These like his *Arabian Nights* sold at high prices to subscribers. Burton himself was convinced that his information was of the highest importance to the study of anthropology.

His conversation at times was garnished with such facts, and he had in younger years, at any rate, quite an abnormal relish for shocking the squeamish and defying the respectable. He would boast, "I'm proud to say I have broken every Commandment in the Decalogue." You or I, reader, might say such a thing (probably with approximate truth) without producing much effect. But when such statements came from a man (look at his portrait by Leighton in the National Portrait Gallery!) in whose dark, savagely-scarred face, truculent jaw, thick chest and smoky-bright eye could be felt the force of a tempestuous vitality, they were believed; especially when followed by a laugh of a peculiar shrill ringing quality, not unlike the

chirrup of a pebble skimming and hopping over a frozen pond; a laugh disquietingly incongruous from a huge fort of a man. To women he was courteous, with the kind of elaborate consideration which we describe as old-fashioned, but he could also be ominous. "What are your intentions, Captain Burton?" a match-making mother once asked him; "Entirely dishonourable, Madam, entirely dishonourable."

Next to the spell which his audacity threw over those who met him, his most fascinating characteristic was the restless activity of his brain. It did not wink and go out like a crazy lighthouse, as is the case with most of us. His translations of Camoens (his favourite poet) and Catullus were the work of odd moments during many years. There is a story of some late guest at a London evening party stumbling across Burton on the stairs, at work upon the Portuguese poet. It is not difficult to realize the fascination which so much mental energy exercised in the person of a man who also appealed to the imagination as the most daring adventurer of his time. What power of attracting others lay behind his ferocious exterior, and a voice and carriage that made the timid feel insignificant, there are many stories to show. Affection often seems more precious when it shows behind violence and brutal outspokenness. Even if there was nothing god-like about Burton it is not difficult to understand how Swinburne could have written after the death of his friend,

> He rode life's lists as a god might ride.

Burton wrote more than fifty volumes; he excelled the sedentary in concentration, but never did so energetic and romantic a personality produce so much heavy reading. The truth is, Burton had a good deal of the pedant in him. The bent of mind, which helped to make him a wonderful linguist and a collector of Eastern dialects, made him also delight in the headlong accumulation of facts. Pedantry, though its results are so prosaic, is often itself the result of a romantic temperament. The energy and interest with which Burton sat down to give an account of a journey was equal to that of an imaginative writer on the scent of a story; only that energy went in the direction of accumulation and rapidity, not of construction and vivid writing. He is at his best in the **Pilgrimage to Mecca,** in a series of lectures published under the title of **Wanderings in Three Continents,** and in the papers edited by Mr. Norman Penzer. As a rule the shorter the space he allowed himself the better he wrote.

One of his books I mean to get, **Wit and Wisdom from West Africa: A Collection of 2,859 Proverbs, Being an Attempt to Make Africans Delineate Themselves.** His translation of Catullus is not good; the interest of it lies in the notes on the passages which are usually not translated at all. His thoughts were not original and he was no poet:

> Do what thy manhood bids thee do, from none
> but self expect applause,
> He noblest lives and noblest dies who makes and
> keeps his self-made laws—

are specimens of the few lines among the many he wrote, which have the ring and vigour of his own personality in them. Those lines were written out of himself. He tried a good many religions; Sufism, Roman Catholicism, Mohammedanism, Agnosticism seemed in turn to him to be the best attitude towards the world. To the last two he was on the whole most constant. He combined scepticism with superstition. He threw out of his pockets the little relics and Catholic charms his wife used to drop perpetually into them, but he liked to keep horse chestnuts in little bags against the evil eye, and he believed in the curative properties of silver, laying florins on his eyes when they were tired or tying silver coins round his gouty foot. His fame as an explorer will endure. He may be also remembered as a linguist and an anthropologist, but the intensity of his fame among those who meet him in the precincts of their own subjects will depend upon the appeal he makes to their imaginations as a man:

> Give me a spirit that on life's rough sea
> Loves to have his sails filled with a lusty wind,
> Even till his sail-yards tremble and his masts
>   crack,
> And his rapt ship, run on her side so low
> That she drinks water and her keel ploughs air.

(pp. 46-51)

*Desmond MacCarthy, "Sir Richard Burton,"
in his* Portraits, *1931. Reprinted by Macgibbon & Kee Ltd., 1949, pp. 46-51.*

Jonathan Bishop   (essay date 1957)

[In the following excerpt, Bishop probes the psychological foundation of Burton's literary personae, arguing that "his exploits imply that . . . the rules of civilization, Moslem or English, become mere paint and costume, rigmaroles to be memorized but not believed."]

We all have in the back of our minds an image of the typical Victorian explorer, forcing his way through wild nature and wilder men, reaching his goal by will-power, guns, and money, a worthy representative of the audience his *Travels* would subsequently entertain. Morally, as well as politically, he is an imperialist; his achievement is the extension of home values to alien contexts. He may have his eccentricities, but his didactic effectiveness depends on his essential anonymity. His prose style is as simple as his function.

No individual Victorian perfectly exemplifies this post-Victorian image, though some are very close. No one, however, seems to diverge from it as far as Sir Richard Burton. Brought up irregularly by expatriate parents, Burton contrived to be sent down from Oxford in 1842 in order to join the East India Company's service. Once in India his energy, curiosity, and command of native languages made him an invaluable agent for Sir Charles Napier, then engaged in reducing to order the newly acquired province of Sind. Five years of intelligence work, often in disguise, was climaxed by an investigation of the homosexual brothels of Karachi. His private report, accidentally circulated among superiors already irritated by Burton's insubordinate spirit, blasted his career. In 1853 he persuaded the Royal Geographical Society to finance an expedition to Mecca and Medina in the guise of a Mohammedan pilgrim. A year later he repeated his feat and reached

Harar in Abyssinia. A third expedition to Berberah with three other Indian Army officers failed when a mob of natives attacked the camp. The Crimean War suggested to Burton the possibility of raising a troop of irregulars. Troubles with the authorities frustrated this scheme. In 1856 he joined with Speke, one of his companions at Berberah, on a large scale expedition to Central Africa. He emerged the discoverer of Tanganyika, but quarrels with Speke soured the achievement. A trip to Salt Lake City was followed by marriage and the commencement of a new career as consul. His duties in Africa, Brazil, and the Near East were varied by exploration and scholarship. The climax of his official life, the Consulate at Damascus, came to an end in a welter of native and administrative intrigue. In 1872 he was shelved in Trieste, where for years he worked on his translation of the *Arabian Nights,* finally published in 1885. He died in 1890, leaving behind a memory of romantic individualism which still echoes in print if not in life. Burton's modern reputation is the stronger for his divergence from the Victorian explorer-type.

Pungency, curiosity, and agility are refreshing alternatives to the flat simplicities of so many traveller's reports. And his enjoyment of his own skill as an actor, a man who could slip through alien worlds perfectly disguised as a native citizen, suggests a style of freedom more acceptable than the plain assertiveness of his rivals. His exploits imply that, viewed from the side, the rules of civilization, Moslem or English, become mere paint and costume, rigmaroles to be memorized but not believed.

His biographers tend to praise him for this theatrical adroitness uncritically. They make much of his scrupulous skill in obeying the rules of Moslem pilgrimage and his casual contempt for English respectabilities, as if the two together made a single admirable whole of "unconventionality," in which we should take vicarious satisfaction. But the problem is more complicated than that. Where should we look to find Burton's identity? And what functions do his several masks, as man of action and as writer, perform for him?

We see him, as a young man in India at the beginning of his life, picking up details of native customs with the combined zeal of a pedant and an actor. As he writes up his experiences, description of detail involves description of personal acts: "Stooping low and ejaculating the '*Ao Bacheh!*' as though I loved her, I approached, knelt down to her, put forth my left hand and turning the dying bird upon its back, drew my knife across its throat with the usual religious formula."

To the reader the self that comes before us is triumphantly Western; we should remember that in the eyes of those who saw the actions they were done by a man as nearly an Easterner as he could be. Of this Burton contrives matter for boasting before us: " 'But you, Sahib,' concluded the Ameer, 'hold your hawk just like a Beloch; and you look a very Sayyid. You must be a Moslem!' " (*Falconry in the Valley of the Indus*).

At the time this was written Burton may well have felt an uncomplicated pride in hearing such half-jocular praise. Acting as a native was a role satisfying enough to permit him to reject contemptuously the ordinary behavior of Englishmen in the East. His national self, when he was in this mood, was something to subvert or make fun of, in the simple spirit of the young man breaking the rules of childhood, which, during his early years in India, he certainly was. Yet there was, even at this time, evidence of a double mind. The more expert he became in his part, the more special lore he accumulated and put to practice, the more chances he willingly took of ignominious or dangerous exposure. We get an impression of a man momentarily fearful lest his English self be *too* well concealed, and therefore flirting with self-exposure. Such a proceeding could perform a double duty. If he was not discovered, he could feel renewed satisfaction in the efficacy of his lore, and consequently a renewed sense of the self the lore expressed; if exposure did befall him, his actual self, the concealed essence behind the theatricalities, would stand as it were naked, not merely in the eyes of a hostile world but in his own. The second contingency never occurred; at least, if it ever did, the occasion went unrecorded. Rumors circulated during Burton's lifetime that he *had* been discovered during the Meccan pilgrimage, and had had to kill a man to preserve his secret. Burton always denied this, and there is certainly no reason to believe it; what the anecdote seems to embody is a suspicion that the deception was too skillful to be real; some more ordinary feat must underlie so fictional an exploit. And Burton seems to have shared some of his compatriots' suspicion of the mock-self, or rather of the true self which could value a mock-self as extravagantly as the tone of his books implied he did. Consider an early remark:

> You see how it is that many of our eminent politicals—men great at Sanskrit and Arabic, who spoke Persian like Shirazis, and had the circle of Oriental science at their fingers' ends; clever at ceremony as Hindoos, dignified in discourse as Turks, whose 'Reports' were admirable in point of diction, and whose 'Travels' threatened to become standard works, turned out to be diplomatic little children in the end, which tries all things. They had read too much; they had written too much; they were a trifle too clever, and much too confident. Their vanity tempted them to shift their nationality; from Briton to become Greek, in order to meet Greek on the roguery field; and lamentably they always failed (***Unhappy Valley***).

This self-criticism is, to be sure, doubly modified. For one thing, when he wrote it Burton could not have been aware how true it would prove. And besides, it appears as a concealed joke; the passage makes fun of the figure to whom the book is supposedly addressed. "You" here is "John Bull" and John Bull, Burton tells us behind his hand, will not guess who he is talking about, nor understand the real bitterness beneath the jocularity, a bitterness which we who read the passage can now, if we feel generous, consider pathetic. "John Bull" will feel confirmed in his "enormous national self-esteem"; this is itself a joke. But it is also serious. The nearer Burton got to the end of his life, and the more he could appreciate the literal truth of his youthful prediction, the clearer his decision became. His wife quotes him as saying to her, as he dictated his autobi-

ography in the seventies, that "no man ever gets on in the world, or rises to the head of affairs, unless he is a representative of his nation" (Isabel Burton, *Life*), and if we have any doubts who this representative should be, we have only to turn to such expressions of admiration as those he used to praise his friend Drake for standing by him in Syria, when he spoke of the "real worth" of a "true-hearted Englishman, staunch to the backbone, inflexible in the course of right, and equally disdainful of threats and promises" (***Unexplored Syria***).

With such a remark we seem to come full circle, and face to face with the kind of character of which Burton seemed at first the polar opposite. His sincerity is difficult to judge. Was he despairing of the actor's self when he said such things, anxious only to return to sanity and simplicity? Or was he trying on still one more role, the most difficult of all to impose on the world of shifting enemies and treacherous friends which for him was official England? We cannot ever be sure; it seems safest simply to recognize a variability of mood, and not attempt to call one real and the other the mask.

It is equally difficult to assay the degrees of literality and theatricality that are present when Burton complains of injustice. Burton the victim of ill-treatment is one of the roles for which he is best remembered, and about which, even now, there is least doubt. His long years as a consul in insignificant ports do seem a strange waste of talents for which an intelligent government might have found better uses. And his modern biographers find themselves falling easily into the tactics of a defense attorney, and spend pages rousing the indignation of their readers that a man of such heroic gifts should be so ill-treated by the petty world. There seem to me to be two reasons to doubt the applicability of this pattern to Burton's case. In the first place, the pattern is itself a shaky construction. We need not assume that wherever there is tension or suffering, there are two sides, of which one must be innocent and the other guilty. Secondly, this pattern is, strictly speaking, inconsistent with the other roles Burton played. For it presupposes an absolute moral universe, in which a good man may expect to prevail, or if he does not, to feel that his suffering is the result merely of an oversight, which will be put right as soon as the attention of the proper quarters is called to it. This moral universe need not be supernatural. The ultimate dispenser of justice may be a government, or the press, or public opinion, as well as divine Providence. The seat from which redress is sought is not important as long as the victim believes it to exist, and to be open to his appeal. But Burton, as a connoisseur of human behavior, was accustomed to treat absolutes as social inventions which are created by men for human purposes. As such they are worthy of the curiosity of the scholar. They should never be literally believed. So far as he held this view Burton was not in a position to profit morally by a system for which, on other occasions, he expressed contempt. He could, consistently with his sceptical role, consider himself badly treated, but he could not consider himself unfairly treated. He had rejected England, ostentatiously; he could not, in good conscience, expect England to reward him.

And yet, of course he did; such inconsistency is a psychological commonplace. Burton wished to be "Ruffian Dick" and at the same time be loved by the world he shocked; and his obstinate inability to see how such immaturity might disgust the world is a part of his flaw. We should remember that Burton did in fact have opportunities to make his genuinely extraordinary gifts yield him a respectable career. Both in India at the beginning of his career and in Damascus in middle age he found himself in positions nobody else could have filled with every circumstance in his favor. In each case he was forced to withdraw. The immediate responsibility for his failures can be assigned to others: to Napier who failed to destroy a report meant for his eyes only, and to the Consul-General at Beirut whose jealous intrigue brought about Burton's recall from Damascus. The ultimate cause of both events is certainly the protagonist's personality: scandal, conflict, injustice, and defeat are a part of Burton's life-style. It is possible to see him as goading the world into behaving badly when it would not have done so of its own accord. His wife's very different motives helped contribute to the stability of the image of a victim of injustice in the eyes of posterity. She wished him to be perfect, and so failures had necessarily to be placed on other shoulders; her hero worship reinforced his sense of grievance while he was alive, and made a belief in his victimization an essential part of his reputation on his death.

Instability of attitude appears in Burton's prose style as well as in his grievances. Consider an early effort to describe something fairly simple, a native boat:

> . . . his Pattimar.
>
> His what?
>
> Ah! we forget. The gondola and barque are household words in your English ears, the budgerow is beginning to own a familiar sound, but you are right—the "Pattimar" requires a definition. Will you be satisfied with a pure landsman's description of the article in question **(Goa)**

which will not (he goes on to say) embody a pretended acquaintance with larboards and starboards; these are things "we" don't understand. The actual description of the boat doesn't start until the bottom of the second page, and even then Burton affects to let the reader do the work; if "you" will "sketch . . . fill up . . . throw in" the proper details you will have a pattimar "in your mind's eye." The details themselves appear as picturesque adjectives, each a little extravagant for the context: "Very long, very high,—dark, musty,—high,—eternal," and "bilious-looking." This self-conscious foolery tells us little about the pattimar but a good deal about Burton's hopes and fears. He seems to anticipate exaggerated reactions: "What a charming facetious fellow!" or "Why the devil doesn't he come to the point?" Both are reactions to the personality of the author. We gather that Burton's boat will disintegrate unless each of its dimensions is comically embellished. The result is partially self-defeating; life becomes vivid but no more foreign than the voice of the man who describes it. Self-assertion is here a symptom of an anxiety which only a continued effort to hold on to the reader can allay. The os-

tensible purpose, to interest this reader in an alien world, is secondary to Burton's obsessive need to remind someone of his own existence. His style throughout his work is a means to ensure that a self would always be present in rhetoric if not in life.

Burton is often unsure which self this will be. He speaks in the sentence above as a brash young Englishman only just less ignorant than the home reader, and much of **Goa** and **Falconry in the Valley of the Indus** is written in this tone. Before **Goa** is over, though, Burton's self-destructive restiveness breaks through, and he commences toying with this safe, if callow, role. He was bored in a convalescent hill station, so he describes the life there by telling his reader what "you" do there, playing billiards, smoking cigars, calling on dull people in the rain. Before he gets far "you" have become the pert officer he has himself pretended to be up to now, and that young man is shown up for the idle booby he is. The reader has been tricked into an indulgence which recoils upon himself. And so Burton, who needs the reader's approval more than most authors, does his best to subvert it.

The best of the five books describing Burton's Indian period is **Scinde; or the Unhappy Valley,** a book which deserves rediscovery. One reason for its easy-going charm is Burton's momentary solution of his rhetorical problem. In the **Unhappy Valley** his "you" or mock reader has become a full-fledged character, John Bull, a "dear, fat, old, testy, but very unbloodthirsty *papa de famille,*" whom Burton affects to lead about the countryside, introducing him to its curiosities. Such a device saves his real reader from the jocular contempt Burton plays on his creation, for no one would identify with so ridiculous a symbol of home interest in foreign parts. We can sit back and enjoy the book without feeling affronted. But before he is finished the note of bitterness returns.

Burton reminds his guest not to forget his souvenirs. "Have you all your curios, your treasures, safe and sound?" As he imagines what these would be, Burton's satiric powers run away with him: "Your cigar cases, worsted boxes, work-boxes, etius and inkstands, cut out of the bhan-trees and covered over with successive coatings of contrasting colours, into which are punched grotesque and complicated patterns? The reed *fauteuil?*—it will make a capital chair for the garden of your suburban villa, and another famous tale-trap. The grass sandals worn by the people of the hills? Your dagger and signet-ring, with the 'Jan Bool'? Your handsome posteen, and your embroidered leather coat?" (**Unhappy Valley**). This list, embodying his exacerbated sensitivity to English conventionalities, is also a parody of his own relation to those at home, who must read his books with the same motives with which they listen to the tales of the returned John Bull. Burton's knowledge of Oriental life is, as far as the world is concerned, of the same value as the physical "curios" he holds up to such scorn, mere picturesque scraps of information. The ultimate end of his adventures into native life is a return to the parlor from which he was so anxious to escape.

The most interesting act of his Sind career goes unmentioned, and the record he made of it is lost. We know from the Terminal Essay in the last volume of the *Arabian Nights* that Sir Charles Napier, hearing of homosexual brothels in Karachi, and fearful lest his troops be corrupted, employed Burton, who he knew could pass among the natives in disguise, as his agent to investigate and report, promising that his account would not pass beyond himself. Burton disappeared into the Sindian underworld and on his return wrote a full description. Napier presumably enjoyed the report; the conqueror of Sind was, from all accounts, just the reader Burton had been looking for; and his matter, for once, was automatically interesting. Sexual customs are bound to seem more significant than any other kind of social behavior, and the man who could find them out would prove to a heroic degree his curiosity, his power to shift into an alien world, his devilish ingenuity. To our respect for these qualities is added a shiver of fascinated disgust—did Burton feel obliged to take advantage of the services these brothels offered? His modern biographers enjoy titillating their readers with such thoughts, aware that Burton's authority as a hero is strongly charged with a glamor we most convincingly explain as sexual in origin. Yet the insinuation is easily put aside; we know that Burton was not circumcised until just before his expedition to Arabia, and he could therefore scarcely have risked any behavior which would have at once proved him an infidel at any time before that operation. His information must have come from hearsay eked out by observation, like most of the non-sexual material that fills his respectable books.

Napier read his report, but neglected to destroy it or return it to Burton. On Napier's recall it was sent to the Bombay Government "with sundry other reports" by accident or malice and there read by hostile officials who, Burton felt, saw to it that his career was blasted. His most interesting adventure had found the worst possible reader. The incident is a grotesque episode in his struggles for an appropriate tone.

The climax of his life is of course the journey through Arabia. The main outlines of his exploit are sufficiently familiar not to need repeating here. For once he succeeded in performing an extraordinary action and in fully accounting for it in a single book. His choice of action was inspired. A pilgrimage to Mecca in disguise allowed him to employ the knowledge he had accumulated in Sind on an affair of as great secrecy and daring as the trip through the Karachi brothels, with the advantage that blasphemy could be publicized as perversion could not. And his style matched the action. Hence, perhaps, the exuberance with which the book was written, and the popularity it still retains. He threw himself into the adventure with fanatic care; entering Egypt as a Persian gentleman, he shifted to the role of Darwaysh or Dervish, and finally to that of a Pathan, which he maintained to the end. His justification for the second of these transformations explains the delight they all gave him. "No character in the Moslem world is so proper for disguise as that of the Darwaysh. It is assumed by all ranks, ages, and creeds; by the nobleman who has been disgraced at court, and by the peasant who is too idle to till the ground; by Dives, who is weary of life, and by Lazarus, who begs his bread from door to door."

The role of Darwaysh stands for his theatrical power generally, which enables him to dominate in imagination the whole of that society his disguises allow him to penetrate, by seizing on the weakness of each division within it. His is the universal knowledge of the underworld, aware of each man's criminal side and so equipped to govern by manipulation and secrecy. Above all, Darwayshhood means ideal freedom; since the role does not identify its player as a member of any one group or an inhabitant of any one place, it embodies the drive to detach oneself from local commitments which makes up so great a part of the glamor of Burton's career.

When Burton finally settles on his disguise, he becomes a Pathan merchant who has lived all his life in Rangoon, and sets about acquiring a medical reputation. The role of doctor shares some advantages with that of Darwaysh; Burton shows himself a man of knowledge, whose trade makes men of all classes his suppliants. As a doctor he is sure of respect from the Moslems wherever he goes. As a *pretended* doctor he is something else. "This is what I did," his tone says, "Was I not a clever fellow; so clever I can afford to look a fool in your eyes." For his sarcastic attitude towards the absurdity of his patients is allowed to touch himself. He depreciates the world by depreciating the self which so punctiliously humors it. His jokes at his Egyptian patients' efforts to assert their dignity embody a judgment on the English. "If you" the argument runs, "are willing to pride yourselves on the skill with which you satisfy the absurd requirements of life, and demand a reward in the form of respect for your dignity as a victim of convention, I will explain you to yourselves by parody, exaggerating your behavior in an alien context."

Burton's medical career in Cairo embodies in miniature a good part of the meaning of his whole Arabian exploit. Certainly the strain of buffoonery continues through the book, sometimes in curious ways; he risks discovery at one point by his willingness (for no good motive) to get drunk with a psychotic Albanian; at another he boasts of gaining power over his fellow pilgrims by lending them money with the intention of gaining credit among them by cancelling the debt later on. This stratagem exposes his own petty cunning to as much criticism as the greedy dishonesty of the Moslems; but he is unabashed; to succeed on the terms he has set himself is to become a minor rogue, and Burton is confident that his heroic claims are reinforced by the frank charlatanism on which they are based.

There is no point in rehearsing here the tale of his adventures on the way to the holy cities. Something new does fitfully appear when he enters Medina and commences the holy visitations and ceremonies a pilgrim is expected to go through. We expect to hear of these as we have heard of other customs, religious as well as secular; it seems for a moment odd that Burton should fail to employ so striking an opportunity for the use of his light cunning tone; indeed, it may seem inconsistent of him not to do so at the center of the book. Yet his manner of describing these traditional religious acts is less invaded with his own personality than any other such description in the book. He speaks seriously and fully, in the manner of a man with an interesting subject, but no private case to prove. The total impression the book makes is blasphemous, but this section of it is not. As he tells us what he did, it is for once hard to distinguish the man from his role, and we are tempted to try to account for this by pointing to some quality in the experience itself. Burton in later life flirted with the notion that he was a Mohammedan more than anything else; he became a Sufi in India; now he had made the obligatory pilgrimage; here he was acting in every respect as a pious Moslem; who could question the reality of an allegiance he had earned with such pains? The Moslem religion is not, we might notice, a theatrical one to Moslems themselves. They are not aware, as Christians have tended to be, of a difference between their daily selves and the selves defined by their religious language. Moslem ritual is closely connected with the minute details of ordinary existence, each of which is connected with prayers and practices, which, for a pious man, sanction it in God's eyes. This means that to become or to pretend to become an inhabitant of a Moslem country is to become a member of Islam. Hence, perhaps, the meaninglessness of the charge of apostasy or insincerity to Burton's ears, which we have already glanced at. For if one became a Moslem by becoming a Pathan pilgrim, and if religion meant a series of actions, then he who performed the acts became as good a member of the faith as any man born in it. The doubleness of Burton's self-definition, as an Englishman and as a Moslem, here falls away. And as a consequence the tongue-in-cheek tone with which that doubleness is brought before the reader momentarily vanishes. He is simply what he was obliged to do, and a simple thoroughness is his only duty to his reader.

But this does not last; he falls back and becomes aware of the ambiguity of his position. Characteristically, this awareness takes the form of tactless self-assertion. The climactic moment of the Pilgrimage is a glaring exception to the observation I have just made. "There it lay at last," he says, as he arrives to make his circumambulation of the Ka'abah, and flourishes a few adjectives: "gloomy, strange, unique"; "I may truly say that, of all the worshippers who clung weeping to the curtain, or who pressed their beating hearts to the stone, none felt for the moment a deeper emotion than did the Haji from the far-north" (*Pilgrimage*). He flirts for a moment with feelings that may at the time have included the range from which he here disassociates himself: "But, to confess humbling truth, theirs was the high feeling of religious enthusiasm, mine was the ecstasy of gratified pride." The truth, if it is the truth, is not humbling. Why should he affect at such a moment to think himself the moral inferior of the dirty fanatics around him? We know he does not really place himself beneath them, nor is he ordinarily ashamed of pride. But he must remind himself and his reader who he is. It is typical that he should do so jauntily and inaccurately.

The trip to Harar which followed is the same thing over again. Once more there is a mysterious city, the adoption of a disguise, a solitary journey, diplomacy, and escape. Our interest in the exploit is diminished, as often with Burton, by the mere fact that it is a repetition of an action he has already done well. It is as if he could think of no way to improve upon a pattern of behavior which, for

once, had proved entirely successful. *First Footsteps in East Africa* is chiefly memorable for the details of native life, which spill from sentence to sentence, from text to footnote. Burton's addiction to footnotes, which starts as the result of a conflict between the narrative order and the order of a treatise, ends in destroying all order, for it encourages continual self-interruption and permits him to put off permanently the toil of deciding what is relevant and what not. Such a style echoes and defines a reality broken into minor pieces, each charged with the vigor of the observer, no one piece taking precedence over the others or suggesting a formula for organizing the mass. This is not altogether a bad thing; Burton's appeal is to idle curiosity, a state of mind prepared to entertain for a second or two odd scraps of knowledge, and see the mysterious city of Harar as a network of "narrow lanes, up hill and down dale, strewed with gigantic rubbish heaps, upon which repose packs of mangy or one-eyed dogs." We remember that Arabia, Sind, and Goa have been dingy and old; sometimes these qualities have been unpleasant to the traveler but more often the minor insignificancies of half-civilized scenes have pleased him.

After his short and quarrelsome service in the Crimea, Burton found a new role. He decided to explore the sources of the Nile. Burton's attitude toward exploration is cynical. He is very conscious of the audience at home, who have read too many books on African travel. Yet: "The theme has remoteness and obscurity of place, difference of custom, marvellousness of hearsay; events passing strange yet credible; sometimes barbaric splendour, generally luxuriance of nature, savage life, personal danger and suffering always borne (in books) with patience, dignity, and even enthusiasm" (*Zanzibar*). And he is aware that the public that wants these things will reward the man who brings to light "the Coy Fountains" concealed for so long. The question is, has he the necessary talent? Can he adapt himself as easily to the duties of a British explorer as to those of a Moslem pilgrim? Would it not be too close an approximation to the behavior he has been at such pains to escape?

There was even something ludicrous in such activity to the cosmopolitan eye. In a later book he fancied "a band of negro explorers marching uninvited through the Squire's manor, strewing his lawn and tennis-ground with all manner of rubbish, housing their belongings in his dining-and-drawing-and best bedrooms, which are at once vacated by his wife and family; turning his cook out of his or her kitchen; calling for the keys of his dairy and poultry-yard, hot-houses and cellar; and rummaging the whole mansion for curios and heirlooms interesting to the negro anthropologist" (*Gold Coast for Gold*). A *tu quoque* revenge on the public that provided moral sponsorship of such an expedition as he contemplated might very well have its appealing side. Then too, the sources of the Nile were a mystery, and he had made a career of penetrating mysteries, of aggrandizing himself at their expense. The Nile sources were as worthwhile a goal as Mecca; better than Harar because better known to the public. He had made a mess of his Crimean service; he had cut his Indian traces; only by piling one exploit on another could he maintain the reputation which had to serve as his substitute for professional credit.

One senses that the quarrel with his companion, Speke, which grew up in the course of the journey and led to such disastrous results to both men in the years following, was in part due to the fact that Speke, the scientist and Himalayan athlete, seemed to fit the conventional role of explorer so closely. *He* knew nothing of the natives, had no curiosity, despised black skins, and would have his way at all costs. In Burton's eyes Speke came to represent everything that was most despicable in the Anglo-Indian character. But as we have seen, Burton's contempt for that character was mixed with jealousy and self-doubt. The quarrel with Speke was a revival of his quarrel with his own unresolved identity.

The experience of exploration proved agonizing and incoherent. The journey seems to have no form of its own. Day by day his men attempt to desert, the negro chiefs prevaricate and steal, Speke is incompetent, and both men fall sick with fever, which turns all their impressions to a painful blur and makes an overpowering sense of weakness and fear of failure their master emotion. The only relief comes during short rests at the Arab trading stations, where Burton can feel himself for a while "at home." Tanganyika is eventually achieved, but the all-important question regarding the direction of the flow of the river at its northern head is left unsolved; Speke's diplomacy was insufficient to persuade their guides to lead them through enemy country. On the return Speke is sent to see if there is anything in the story of a still larger lake to the northeast; he returns to claim he has discovered the source of the White Nile. Burton irritably dismisses an intuition his companion cannot support with geographical arguments, and they regain the coast, near enemies.

As in the case of his Indian life, Burton failed to concentrate his experience in a single book. His report (1859) to the Royal Geographical Society is straightforward but dull; *The Lake Regions of Central Africa* (1860) and *Zanzibar* (1872) are evidence of hard work flavored with self-pity. Personality does reappear in *The Nile Basin* (1864) written to defend his theories about the sources of the Nile against the arguments advanced by his old rival Speke, but only as paranoid rancor. In effect, the only part of the experience of Central Africa with which Burton could find himself vitally involved, and therefore the only part he could express in words that (however unpleasantly) bear the indispensable signature of an individual voice, was that which could be abstracted as a problem in geography, and made a vehicle for a personal fight.

I have already quoted from some of the books Burton wrote during his consulships, to illustrate some general point about the selves his career exhibits, and this is the only interest they are likely to have even for Burton specialists. All we see as we look over these books and the experiences they record are *succedanea* (to use a favorite Burtonism) for exploration, meaningless repetition in a minor key of earlier themes. He goes to Salt Lake City, as an almost conscious self-parody of his pilgrimage to Mecca; he climbs mountains and travels down rivers. The most interesting of these later expeditions, to Burton him-

Burton in West Africa.

self, is his attempt to find gold in Midian, which he wished his reader to consider a sequel to the Pilgrimage. It was in fact the very reverse in every respect but the setting. He went as the leader of an expedition, with the support of the Egyptian government; he tried twice to find gold; a third expedition was cancelled on Ismail's fall from power. Burton's two books on his efforts show him as a pompous, irritable snob, gracious to those in power: "I need hardly say that his Highness at once saw the gist of the matter . . . " and venomous to underlings whose efforts to find gold proved disappointing: "We must not be too hard upon M. Marie. He is an engineer, utterly ignorant of mineralogy and of assaying; he was told off to do the duty, and he did it as well as he could—in other words, very badly" (*Land of Midian Revisited*). Burton returned to Cairo with twenty-five tons of dirt and had it exhibited elaborately to the world. As with his Tanganyika argument, he would not be persuaded he was anything but a success. He sailed to Trieste convinced again he was the victim of injustice.

At the end of his life he began a new career as a translator. The *Arabian Nights* was a great triumph, and Burton knew very well why. The notes and Terminal Essay to that work revive the long-buried Karachi report in a form that made his Sindian knowledge presentable, though just barely, to the British public. Here was a topic on which he could challenge the *"mauvaise honte,* the false delicacy, and the ingrained prejudices of the age" on terms most congenial to himself. In these notes and essay his tone regains the vigor and intimacy of his best years, leaving behind the diseased egotism of the later books of exploration. He is talking on a subject he knows better than any man living, a subject that *must* be interesting to all; above all a subject which permits a direct challenge to the conventional world. The role of ethnologist is at hand to defend him should he need defense. He and his reader can get together and talk over, as fellow men of the world, the curious possibilities of another civilization. Burton's specialty is pederasty. The section of the Terminal Essay devoted to this branch of the subject is exhaustive. There are two stories in the *Nights* which involve pederasty, and Burton makes the most of them, but it is clear that the amount of space devoted to this lore is not determined by its relevance to the *Nights* themselves.

Sexuality does enter his travel books in various places. It is glanced at in the **Pilgrimage** and in **First Footsteps,** and much of the interest of his trip to Utah or to the king of Dahomey lies in the sexual secrets of these communities. But Burton learned nothing about polygamy or the Amazons that any bookish traveler who took the trouble might not learn. The *Nights* are in a different class to the degree that Burton convinces us that his unique familiarity with sex in the Moslem world derives from practical experience.

It is difficult to assess the relevance of this old man's hobby to the geographical adventures it replaces. We may dismiss it as simply the fantasy life of impotence in both author and reader, the faint echo of the old Sindian adventure, which meant so much once, and serves at last to warm the heart of a sick failure. Yet when Burton is remembered, he is thought of as the pilgrim of Mecca, and the translator of the *Nights;* to the public these are the only successful things he ever did. It would be comforting if we could make some meaningful connection between the two roles of sexual investigator and heroic adventurer. The most obvious explains something, but not all; we may read his geographical exploits as simple metaphors for sexual curiosity, and interpret the penetration of the sacred secrets of Arabia or Africa as the symbol of an interest heroes share with cowards, which simply came to the surface when its possessor was too old for either the real or the symbolic act. But this solution makes the merely verbal daring of an old man more real than the practical audacity of youth, and an extraordinary action a substitute representation of a common fantasy. Such an answer is harder to explain than the problem it seeks to solve. Yet the problem is real; the interest of his mysterious journeys is importantly if obscurely qualified by his sexual curiosity.

I should guess myself that the connection is to be made by bringing to mind Burton's didactic appeal, his authority as a counter-image to the heroics of more conventional men. That Burton should make sex his prime secret, the secret only he is able to find out and communicate, power-

fully enhances his authority, his suggestion that freedom for the self lies in superior knowledge, and that by *knowing* the world, by breaking it down into a group of customs and rituals, we render these customs and rituals innocuous. For no convention is so threatening as that which embodies societies' views of sexual behavior.

Yet the role of scholar, even of important secrets, is not in itself a solution to the problem of identity; as Burton practised it, it amounts to one more negative gesture in a life made up of rejections. We can see him announcing that he is not an ordinary Anglo-Indian, an ordinary explorer, an ordinary consul; now he asserts in effect that he is not inhibited by false shame. What he is is still undecided. His life remains essentially putative and rhetorical, a theatrical gesture exploiting the attitudes it rejects.

To press any distance into the personality Burton displays to the world is to discover uncertainty, failure, perhaps shoddiness. But these qualities do not so much expose his unfitness to stand as an example of a type of heroic development as illustrate in pathological form key aspects of that type. His egotism, for example, can be seen as one more symptom of that inability to make up his mind who he was which provided the motive force to so much in his career. When he had no other role to act he acted Richard Burton; if he could not decide who Richard Burton was, his wife would decide for him. And the vulgarity is a product of his excessive anxiety to discover a sympathetic reader, who could help to identify him by forgiving and admiring the self his words created. That protean restlessness on which his exploits were based accounts for the misapplications as well as the triumphs of his personal power. (pp. 119-35)

Jonathan Bishop, "The Identities of Sir Richard Burton: The Explorer as Actor," in Victorian Studies, *Vol. 1, No. 2, December, 1957, pp. 119-35.*

S. N. Ray   (essay date 1960)

[*Below, Ray evaluates the eclectic approach to Eastern thought in Burton's poem* Kasidah.]

Its thirteen editions, published at varying intervals between 1880 and 1923, have failed to secure for Sir Richard Francis Burton's **Kasidah** even a casual mention in any authoritative history of Victorian poetry. Its eclectic thought and general heedlessness of the finer graces of verse and poetic imagery have evidently stood in the way. Yet one cannot help feeling that it deserved better of the critics for its manifest sincerity, refreshing intellectuality, and certain ancillary interests which are not altogether negligible. It is certainly the most earnest attempt ever made by a European to build up a philosophy of life equally on Western and Eastern thought; it is the only Victorian poem to oppose stoicism to 'doubt'; it had possibly something to do with Swinburne's change-over from neo-paganism to humanism.

The **Kasidah** was composed in 1853 during intervals of privacy on Burton's journey back from Medina. Redolent of the loneliness of desert travel, it opens with 'a sore lament that the meetings of this world for ever take place on the highway of separation':

> Why meet we on the bridge of Time
> To change one greeting and then to part?
> We meet to part, yet asks my sprite,
> 'Part we to meet?'. . . .
> Why must we bear this yoke of 'Must'?
> Alas, the birthday's injury!

Then it passes in review the answers to this sphinx-riddle given by the wise and the foolish teachers of humanity, and finds them alike inadequate. 'The contradictions, the infinite sorrowfulness and the dark end of all existence' still stare humanity in the face. Yet looking into his own life as he lives it, a man finds that he is not all forlorn. There is joy for him in the exercise of his affections and in self-cultivation. It must be on these verities then that man must build his life: 'It is most hard to be a man having his sole consolation in self-cultivation and the pleasures of the affections, but this is unquestionably the best and only ideal.'

> Do what thy manhood bids thee do;
> From none but self expect applause;
> He noblest lives and noblest dies
> Who makes and keeps his self-made laws.
> All other living is living death.

None of the known faiths can be a substitute:

> I've tried them all, I find them all
> So tame, so drear, so dry;
> My gorge ariseth at the thought,
> I commune with myself, I cry.

In this extremity,

> Better the myriad toils and pains
> That make the man to manhood true. . . .
>
> This be the rule that guideth life:
> With ignorance wage eternal war,
> To know thyself for ever strain;
> The ignorance of thy ignorance
> Is thy fiercest foe, thy deadly bane.
> To seek the true, to glad the heart,
> Such is the life of the Higher Law. . . .
>
> Then if Nirvana round our life
> With nothingness, 'tis haply best,
> Thy toils and troubles, want and woe
> Find at last their guerdon, Rest. . . .
>
> Wend now thy way with brow serene
> Fear not thy humble tale to tell.

The whispers of the desert wind and the tinkling of the camelbell waft you a message of hope and call you to a happy beyond.

Burton had to begin his quest with stupendous negations. There is no God 'uncreated by man in his own image'; the soul is 'fancy as opposed to the body which is a fact, at best a convenient term denoting the sense of individual identity'; conscience is not the still small voice of God, but 'a geographical and chronological accident'; 'the will is in truth never free'; truth is not absolute, 'not an unchanging name'; law does not postulate a law-giver; Nature was never created, but its material and spiritual principles

have existed from all eternity, suffering endless revolution 'without the intervention of a deity'; 'revelation and a future state of rewards and punishments' are puerile fabrications'; 'there are no doors to human knowledge other than the five senses', no incarnation or prophet having ever originated an idea not conceived through the senses; there is no virtue in 'mere belief' and repentance, and no sin in 'mere unbelief'.

The positive ideas, as against these negations, are: the present life is 'all sufficient for an intelligent being'; 'the law under which man is born lays it down that man should travail to better himself'; there is happiness to balance unhappiness in human life, and it is an undeniable fact of experience that 'evil is constantly rising into good'; 'the mind is more than mere brain action, it includes the sentiments which yield joy and cry out against annihilation'; by being true to himself, by rejecting 'creed' which is an accident like birth, by following 'the stern commonsense of mankind' and Reason, which is 'life's sole arbiter, the magic labyrinth's single clue', eschewing ignorance and error by the light of 'dry reason', man may follow the Higher Law, as Burton calls his philosophy, and attain to *Arhatship*.

The philosophy of the **Kasidah** is in substance a vindication of individual divinity, achieved through a synthesis of Socratic, Stoic and scientific rationalism with Sufism, Jainism and Buddhism. It has been described as 'an eastern version of humanism blended with the sceptical or scientific habit of mind.' So much indeed of Eastern thought has been compressed within its small compass, that the **Kasidah,** on its first appearance, was taken to be 'the work of an Eastern polyglot with cosmopolitan tendencies'.

Burton's use of Eastern thought is openly eclectic. Where Sir William Jones or Edwin Arnold interprets with sympathy, Burton selects according to his need elements of Eastern thought which would fit into his individual philosophy. He accepts the Sufi's view of the soul that it is superfluous to seek an 'I' within the I, but will have nothing to do with his mysticism or gnosticism. He borrows the Jain idea of 'Chain of the Universe', and Manu's conception of the human body as a house made of bone, blood, muscles and tendons, without making any use of the Jain philosophy or Manu's elaborate code of ethics. He makes extensive use of Buddhism, citing Buddha in support of atheism, adopting the Buddhist hatred of ignorance and repudiation of the ultra-rational element in faith, and building his philosophy of progress on the Buddhist conception of *Arhatship*. But he will have nothing to do with the doctrine of rebirth which Buddhism retains.

Notwithstanding this eclecticism, Burton may be said to have made a more intimate use of Eastern thought than any European orientalist, and on this score alone the **Kasidah** deserves to be redeemed from critical neglect.

Burton's knowledge of the East was primarily acquired in India. During the seven years he spent in the country, coming out as a young officer in the East Indian Army in 1842, Burton gave himself entirely to the study of Eastern philosophy and religion, and perfected himself in Arabic and Islamic doctrine and practice, earning for himself, by the way, the nickname of 'The White Nigger' in the Officers' Mess, and qualifying for his subsequent visit to Mecca and Medina in the disguise of an Afghan pilgrim.

Lady Burton, who edited her husband's works, wrote about the *Kasidah:* 'It will appeal to all large hearts and brains for its depth, its height, its breadth, its pathos, its melancholy and despair. It is the very perfection of romance; it seems as the cry of the soul wandering through space, looking for what it does not find. I do not believe that this poem has its equal; it is unique.' It may be that Lady Burton's estimate is too personal. In integrity of thought and emotion and sheer poetry it is far surpassed by Fitzgerald's *Omar.* But it is impressive in its intrepid intellectuality which gives to the whole something of an emotional overtone. And historically it has the distinction of being the only Stoic poem in the Victorian era, an era which, unsure of itself, might ignore, or compromise with, 'doubt', luxuriate in its unease or break down under its stress, seek refuge from it in art, neo-paganism, or epicureanism, but could never look it squarely in the face. It is surprising that this unique testament of faith has passed into virtual oblivion, notwithstanding its high seriousness, its author's fame as an explorer and as an orientalist, and his known place in Swinburne's affection.

That Burton was a power in Swinburne's life has not been duly recognized in any study of Swinburne's poetic development. The two came together early in 1861, when on the rebound from thwarted love-making, Swinburne had landed on De Sade's

> On n'est point criminel faire la peinture
> Des bizzarres penchants qu' inspire la nature.

His instincts so confirmed, he was 'ashamed no more at the tendencies of his own nature.' Their meeting at Fryston Hall, under the auspices of Monckton Milnes, was designed to be one of those encounters of opposites in which Milnes delighted. But instead of the expected mutual disapproval, 'a fast and enduring friendship' sprang up between 'the Herculean explorer' and 'the frail Pre-Raphaelite model', both being rebels and iconoclasts at heart, and each admiring in the other what he himself lacked. Sustained by exchange of letters, and deepened by close association during Burton's two furloughs home in 1865 and 1869 and later stays in England, even to the violation of the Putneyan captivity, this friendship has been recorded by Swinburne with a rare warmth of feeling in many of his letters, in the Dedication of *Poems and Ballads* (Second Series), in a deeply appreciative sonnet and two feeling elegies. What impressed Swinburne most in Burton's personality were his superb courage and profound wisdom. Burton was to him 'a demigod of daring' superior even to Raleigh, in physical courage, and spiritually.

> A living soul that had the strength to quell
> Hope the spectre and fear the spell,

who 'eyed lifetime and death with unchangeful cheer'. 'The boldest born of the bravest', Burton was the redeemer of 'such as are clothed round with faith that is one with fear.' Burton's 'full soul'

> . . . held east and west in poise,

> Weighed man with man, and creed of man's
>   with creed,
> And age with age . . .
> And found what faith may read not and what
>   may read.

And the East was the fountainhead of his wisdom:

> Still sunward here on earth his flight was bent,
>   towards 'the glorious orient glowing, defiant
>   of the dark.'

It was Burton's influence which gave the right direction to Swinburne's aberrant genius in the sixties. Without crossing the fundamental urges of Swinburne's nature, Burton found for them healthier, but still exciting, channels. He endorsed Swinburne's plan of outraging Victorian prudery while Rossetti and Meredith and others demurred to many items in the forthcoming *Poems and Ballads* which Swinburne had set his heart on publishing whole, assured by the success of *Atalanta* that he could carry through his project by the sheer power of his verse. By leading Swinburne a hectic round of sociabilities, and introducing him to the bizarre 'tribal feasts' of the Cannibal Club, Burton drew Swinburne away from the degrading society of Howell, the shady Anglo-Portuguese, and Solomon, the pervert Jewish painter. And though Italy and Mazzini had a great deal to do with it, Swinburne's emergence from neo-paganism to humanism in the late sixties was decisively influenced by Burton.

Certain ideas in Swinburne's *Hymn of Man* and *Hertha* are strongly suggestive of the *Kasidah.* Subscribing to Mazzini's credo that 'Humanity is a Collective Being—a Man who lives and works for men,' *Hymn of Man* has yet no room for Mazzini's God, between whom and the individual man Humanity is mediator. In *Hymn of Man,* in fact, he never existed except in man's fancy: 'the god that ye make you', 'the God of your making'. *Hertha,* which has further outgrown Mazzini, reiterates the idea: 'the God of your fashion', 'the God that ye made', finally, 'the Gods of your fashion'. In blazoning forth this un-Victorian idea of a man-made God, Swinburne may have been heartened to have found that as early as 1853 the *Kasidah* had made it the cornerstone of its philosophy: 'there is no God uncreated by man in his own image.' Creed, next, is abhorrent equally to Swinburne and Burton. The ethics of *Hertha,* too, are identical with the ethics of the *Kasidah:* 'to be man with thy might' of *Hertha* corresponding exactly to *Kasidah's* 'Do what thy manhood bids thee do,' and 'man to manhood true'. Finally, the philosophy of *Hertha* which, materializing with Darwinism the pantheism of the East, makes life, change and growth events in a natural, compulsive process of 'becoming', is not unlike the concept of the Jain Chain of the Universe which Burton borrows to symbolize the cosmic law of 'flux'. Personal contact may, indeed, account for these fundamental agreements, but not quite to the exclusion of the possibility of Swinburne's having read the *Kasidah* in manuscript. (pp. 107-13)

S. N. Ray, "Burton's 'Kasidah' of Haji Abdu-el-Vezdi," in The Indian Journal of English Studies, *Vol. I, No. 1, 1960, pp. 107-13.*

Byron Farwell   (essay date 1964)

[*In the following excerpt from his biography of Burton, Farwell discusses Burton's annotated translation of the* Arabian Nights.]

[Burton's] translation of *The Arabian Nights* was a labour of love. It had to be. [His wife] Isabel said, 'He loved his work, and he was sorry when it was finished.' He undoubtedly was. In the *Nights* Burton found escape—escape from his routine consular duties (such as they were), escape from unpleasant or uncongenial surroundings, escape from his over-solicitous wife and comfortable home, escape from the thoughts of what he might have been and the position in which he now found himself.

In his Foreword to the *Nights* he told how his work had been a charm against ennui and despondency during his 'long years of official banishment' in West Africa and Brazil. It became 'impossible even to open the pages without a vision starting into view' and 'the Jinn bore me at once to the land of my predilection, Arabia'. Sinking into this escape world populated by medieval Arabs, he brought forth into the light of Victorian Britain a unique masterpiece. The value of the work lies not in the excellence of the translation—others have produced more technically accurate versions—but in the spiritual and intellectual qualities which he brought to the stories. The *Nights* enabled him to make use of the vast storehouse of knowledge tucked away in his retentive memory and his over-laden notebooks, providing him with a vehicle to carry his ideas, opinions, prejudices, facts, fancies and a curio chest of anthropological oddities to a public that received them with astonishment and delight.

Burton was not the first person to attempt a translation of that collection of tales known in Arabic as *Alf Laylah Wa Laylah,* but his ten-volume work with its six-volume supplement is the most complete and the most famous; no one has attempted to duplicate his efforts since its publication. The first man to bring these stories to the attention of the Western world was Antoine Galland who, between 1704 and 1717, published *Mille et Une Nuits, Contes Arabes Traduits en Francais.* It was designed for popular consumption and it proved very popular indeed; Galland's translation was in turn translated into other languages, including English. The first original effort in English was by Henry Torrens in 1838, but he died before he could complete his work. The man who might have made a translation as complete as Burton's was Edward William Lane, for he had a vast and intimate knowledge of Arabic life. But he was too timid: his translation, published between 1839 and 1841, was designed for 'the drawing-room table' and he 'thought it right to omit such tales, anecdotes, &c., as are comparatively uninteresting or on any account objectionable'.

Burton's only serious competitor was John Payne, who published his translation in 1882–4 through the Villon Society. Although Burton dedicated Volume II to Payne ('to express my admiration of your magnum opus . . . '), it was only natural that given Burton's temperament and capacity for criticism some of his caustic and unkind comments should result in a scholarly rivalry between the two men and their separate translations. This rivalry continues to exist today among those who still read the *Nights,* and outraged defenders of Payne point accusing fingers at Burton, claiming that he plagiarized whole passages from Payne's book—which he did.

Burton's object was 'to show what "The Thousand Nights and a Night" really is'. He aimed to 'preserve intact, not only the spirit, but even the *mécanique,* the manner and matter'. The structure of the *Nights* is not unique in either occidental or oriental literature, but in a work of such vast proportions it is often confusing to a modern reader. The story that provides the frame encompassing all the other tales is the familiar account of how the beautiful Shahrazad, the daughter of the Wazir, encouraged by her sister Dunyazad, so amused and delighted King Shahryar for 1001 nights by her story-telling that each morning he refrained from cutting off her head in order that he might hear the end of the story or the telling of a new tale she had promised him. King Shahryar had embarked upon his programme of executing maidens after a single night in his bed because he and his brother were convinced of the worthlessness of women. Presumably, the nimble-witted Shahrazad succeeded in proving that women are of some value, for in the end the king married her and, we hope, since each night's tale was interrupted only by the dawn, allowed them both to get some sleep.

The work as a whole is divided both artificially by the nights and somewhat more naturally by the unrelated stories. The interruption of the dawn causes the reader almost as much annoyance as it did King Shahryar since, as in a soap opera, the end of the last tale is repeated at the beginning of the next night's episode. Some stories continue for many nights.

The confusing aspect of the work is caused by the stories within stories within stories, like those schoolboys' tablets that show a picture of a boy holding the tablet, which in turn shows a boy holding the tablet, which in turn. . . . We have, for example, Shahrazad telling the story of 'The Fisherman and the Jinni' in which is told the 'Tale of the Wazir and the Sage Duban' in which is told three other stories. The reader must keep all of these frames in mind if he is to work his way out (successfully) to the original story knowing who is telling what story to whom.

Most English- and French-speaking persons, if asked to name the best-known tales from *The Arabian Nights,* would probably name 'Aladdin' and 'Ali Baba and the Forty Thieves'. Yet, curiously enough, 'Alladdin' is not at all like the familiar children's story and the story of Ali Baba does not appear at all—at least, no known Eastern manuscript of the tale exists. The story of Ali Baba first became known through the French version of Galland. While Galland's repute as an honest scholar would make it appear unlikely that he invented the tale, his source for the story has never been found. From the French both stories made their way in their familiar innocent form into English and were well known to English-speaking children long before Burton's day. A cynical guess would be that Galland himself altered Aladdin and invented Ali.

The great charm of Burton's translation, viewed as literature, lies in the veil of romance and exoticism he cast over the entire work. He tried hard to retain the flavour of oriental quaintness and naïveté of the medieval Arab by writing 'as the Arab would have written in English'. The result is a work containing thousands of words and phrases of great beauty, and, to the Western ear, originality. Arabic, if we can trust Burton, contains the most beautifully phrased clichés of any tongue in the world.

The ideas and emotions displayed in the Nights are elemental ones, earthily expressed. The tales concern life's fundamentals: death, old age, marriage, anger, revenge, fear, pain, love, regret, loyalty, beauty, religious faith, temptation, sickness, delight, luck—the gamut of life's experiences and feelings. All are told in a simple, direct manner with little subtlety or sophistication: all black and white without shadings. Some are mere sex fantasies or gross day dreams of glittering wealth. There are no great ideas in the *Nights;* no thought-provoking theories or philosophies. There is only folk wisdom, sometimes crudely and often beautifully expressed.

'Man may not be trusted with woman, so long as eye glanceth and cyclid quivereth,' expresses the basic distrust of the medieval Arab. Here, too, is one of Burton's favourite quotations: 'Death in a crowd is as good as a feast.' Some of the adages might with little change be heard from a French peasant woman, an Aunt Jemima, or almost anybody's mother: 'Speak not of whatso concerneth thee not, lest thou hear what will please thee not.' Still others carry an atmosphere that seems so foreign and out of our time that it repels: 'Three things are better than other three; the day of death is better than the day of birth, a live dog is better than a dead lion, and the grave is better than want.'

For the most part, the thoughts of the characters in the tales are concerned with the practical matters of their everyday life—revenge, for example. Far from being an evil passion, revenge is one of life's sweet enjoyments: 'It is not for any save King Afridun to kill them, that he may gratify his wrath.' And this speech: 'Whoso would solace himself with seeing the beheading of Nur al Din bin al Fazl bin Khakan, let him repair to the palace! So followers and followed, great and small, will flock to the spectacle, and I shall heal my heart and harm my foe.' The deed of revenge is always described in some detail and when it is done there is no repentance nor mercy for the victim's soul: 'Then I took up a great stone from among the trees and coming up to him smote him therewith on the head with all my might and crushed in his skull as he lay dead drunk. Thereupon his flesh and fat and blood being in a pulp, he died and went to his deserts, The Fire, no mercy of Allah be upon him.' Nor is the enjoyment of revenge, no matter how ghastly the form, considered an unladylike entertainment. After a horrible description of the destruction of an enemy army by friendly demons we find: 'And this was high enjoyment for Janshah and his father and the Lady Shamsah.'

Anger, of course, is the concomitant of revenge, and they knew how to be angry in the land of *The Arabian Nights.* There was, for example, the woman who 'raged with exceeding rage and her body-hair stood on end like the bristles of a fretful hedgehog'. There were even some among the Arabs of the Nights who were permanently angry and one is described as 'a man of wrath and a shedder of blood'.

But anger was seldom so strong that it prevented elaborate vilification, particularly among women. Here is but a part of a speech by one young girl to another:

> If one joke with thee, thou art angry; if one sport with thee, thou art sulky; if thou sleep, thou snorest; if thou walk, thou lollest out thy tongue! If thou eat, thou art never filled. Thou art heavier than mountains and fouler than corruption and crime. Thou hast in thee nor agility nor benedicite nor thinkest thou of aught save meat and sleep. When thou pissest thou swishest; if thou turd thou gruntest like a bursten wine-skin or an elephant transmogrified. If thou go to the water-closet, thou needest one to wash thy gap and pluck out the hairs which overgrow it; and this is the extreme of sluggishness and the sign, outward and visible, of stupidity. In short, there is no good thing about thee, and indeed the poet saith of thee. . . .

And here follows a bit of poetry as vulgar as the preceding speech.

Death is a common enough occurrence in the *Nights* but it is nevertheless dreadful. Beautiful and terrible words such as these often provide the happy ending to a tale: 'And they led the most pleasurable of lives and the most delectable, till there came to them the Destroyer of delights and the Sunderer of societies and they became as they had never been.' When the Arabs of the *Nights* drained 'the cup of death' they were 'numbered among the folk of futurity and heirs of immortality'. Death came in many guises. Often it was a camel with a bell around its neck. Sometimes it was disguised in human form and spoke to its intended victim:

> 'Verily the Lord of the House sent me to thee, nor can any doorkeeper exclude me, nor need I have leave to come in to kings; for I reck not of Sultan's majesty neither of the multitude of his guards. I am he from whom no tyrant is at rest, nor can any man escape from my grasp: I am the Destroyer of delights and the Sunderer of societies.' Now when the king heard this a palsy crept over him and he fell on his face in a swoon; but presently coming to himself, he asked, 'Art thou then the Angel of Death?' and the stranger answered, 'Yes'.

It is this grim figure who caused the craven terror of even the noblest characters: 'We lost the power of thought and reason and were stupefied for the excess of our fear and horror,' says one hero. Sometimes the emotion is even more graphically described, as when it was said that 'fear fluttered the scrotum below his belly'.

When misfortune struck, whatever its form, none could grieve and despair as these folk. Usually the world grew black in their sight and sometimes they cried out, 'I am a lost man! Verily we are Allah's and to Allah we are returning' or 'What is the worth of mine eyes if they do not weep?' One man walked from a room with 'grief scattering from his body'. The causes of these laments vary, but once it was simply from 'eating too much of the world'.

But life had its sunny side as well, and it was as bright as the dark side was black. Then one could 'joy with exceeding joy', particularly if one was 'suckled at the breast of fond indulgence and was reared in the lap of happy fortune'. For even kings were happy in those days and of one it was said that 'his subjects joyed in him and all of his days were gladness'. Sometimes when friends or lovers met 'they embraced and fell to the ground senseless for excess of joy'. And a man was welcomed by being told that 'this thy day with us is white as milk'. There was wonder in the world then, too, and a man looked at a carved wooden horse and 'marvelled with exceeding marvel and was confounded at the beauty of its form', or he could see 'a mansion whose beauties would beggar the tongue'. And he would sometimes ask incredulously, 'And is all this in the world?'

Most of the beauty of the Arabs' world was to be found in women, of course, and they reserved their choicest expressions for them. They were frequently compared to 'the moon at its full' or to 'the rising full moon'. Some of the women had 'dewy lips sweeter than syrup' or 'a mole like a dot of ambergris on a downy site'. Princess Dunya was a typical beauty and she is perhaps best described by the effect she created: 'Taj al-Muluk looked upon her and fed his eyes on her beauty and loveliness (but she knew it not); and every time he gazed at her he fainted by reason of her passing charms.' Dunya, it will be noted, created this effect without even trying; others created a similar sensation by working at it. Shams al-Nahar, for example, walked into a room 'as she were the moon among the stars swaying from side to side, with luring gait and in beauty's pride'. And a slave-girl walked towards Ala-al-Din (Aladdin, of course, but presented by Burton in the unexpurgated tale as much more worldly and less wholesome) 'swinging her haunches and gracefully swaying a shape the handiwork of Him whose Boons are hidden; and each of them stole one glance of the eyes that cost them a thousand sighs'.

Much attention was given to the way in which a woman walked. There was a handmaiden who moved 'with the gait of a gazelle in flight and fit to damn a devotee, til she came to a chair, whereon she seated herself'; and another who went 'walking with a voluptuous gait and ravishing all beholders with her lithe and undulating pace'.

But perhaps the best single description of the ideal *Arabian Nights* girl is found in the four hundred and twenty-first and the four hundred and twenty-second nights where we find this passage:

> The girl is soft of speech, fair of form like a branchlet of basil, with teeth like chamomile-petals and hair like halters wherefrom to hang hearts. Her cheeks are like blood-red anemones and her face like a pippin: she has lips like wine and breasts like pomegranates twain and a shape supple as a rattan-cane. Her body is well-formed with sloping shoulders dight; she hath a nose like the edge of a sword shining bright and a forehead brilliant white and eyebrows which unite and eyes stained by Nature's hand black as night. If she speak, fresh young pearls are scattered from her mouth forthright and all hearts

are ravished by the daintiness of her sprite; when she smileth thou wouldst ween the moon shone out her lips between and when she eyes thee, sword-blades flash from the babes of her eyes. In her all beauties to conclusion come, and she is the centre of attraction to traveller and stay-at-home. She hath two lips of cramoisy, than cream smoother and of taste than honey sweeter. . . . And she hath a bosom, as it were a way between two hills which are a pair of breasts like globes of ivory sheen; likewise, a stomach right smooth, flanks soft as the palm-spathe and creased with folds and dimples which overlap one another, and liberal thighs, which like columns of pearl arise, and back parts which billow and beat together like seas of glass or mountains of glance, and two feet and hands of gracious mould like unto ingots of virgin gold.

Sometimes the sight of all these bulks of sex produced rather untidy results: it was said of one woman that 'all who looked on her bepissed their bag trousers, for the excess of her beauty and loveliness'.

Often one feature of a woman proved exceptionally pleasing. There was one young man who 'took her feet and kissed them and, finding them like fresh cream, pressed his face on them'. There was a woman who 'tucked up her sleeves from a forearm like fresh curd, which illuminated the whole place with its whiteness and Sharrkan was dazzled by it'. This particular hero was always impressed with hands and arms and Sharrkan once told a girl that 'my ecstacy cometh from the beauty of thy fingertips'. A large rump was much admired and picturesquely described: a woman 'tucked up her trousers and displayed two calves of alabaster carrying a mound of crystal'. The creator of all these fine parts of women's anatomy is not forgotten: Describing a breast that is 'a seduction to all that see it', an admirer adds, 'glory be to Him who fashioned it and finished it!'

One has the feeling in many passages that the teller of the tales or the character describing the charms of some 'high bosomed virgin' was often carried away with his own powers of description and that the girl herself comes off appearing rather ungainly. Try to imagine a creature with 'breasts like two globes of ivory, from whose brightness the moons borrow light, and a stomach with little waves as it were a figured cloth of the finest Egyptian linen made by the copts, with creases like folded scrolls, ending in a waist slender past all power of imagination; based upon back parts like a hillock of blown sand, that force her to sit when she would lief stand, and awaken her, when she would fain sleep'.

These women 'cool of eyes and broad of breast' were not unaware of their physical qualities and social accomplishments, nor were they above boasting of them. One heroine says modestly, 'If I sing and dance, I seduce, and if I dress and scent myself, I slay. In fine, I have reached a pitch of perfection such as can be estimated only by those of them who are firmly rooted in knowledge.' If they felt their charms were not sufficiently appreciated, they were capable of calling out, 'O man, dost thou not behold my beauty and loveliness and the fragrance of my breath; and knowest thou not the need women have of men and men of women?' They were often bold and brazen, these women from *The Arabian Nights.* Princess Budur, a well-brought-up young lady, awoke in the night to find a strange young man asleep beside her. She was quite taken with him and called out, 'My life on thee, harken to me; awake and up from thy sleep and look on the narcissus and the tender down thereon, and enjoy the sight of naked waist and navel; and touzle me and tumble me from this moment till break of day!' Perhaps many of these young girls received the unpuritan advice of one lovely who asked, 'And what is the medicine of passion, O nurse mine?' and is told, 'The medicine of passion is enjoyment.'

Not all women are beautiful, however, even in *The Arabian Nights.* There were a few—usually old ones, it is true—who were as ugly as others were beautiful: 'Now this accursed old woman was a witch of the witches, past mistress in sorcery and deception; wanton and wily, deboshed and deceptious; with foul breath, red eyelids, yellow cheeks, dull-brown face, eyes bleared, mangy body, hair grizzled, back humped, skin withered and wan and nostrils which ever ran.' This particular dame had morals to match her appearance and 'could not exist without sapphism or she went mad'.

But fortunately for the male characters in the *Nights,* most of the women were designed to love and be loved. Certainly no one ever experienced such violent reactions to love as did the men of these tales when 'delight got hold of them'. One confessed, 'I was drowned in the sea of her love, dazed in the desert of my passion for her.' And later he tells his love, 'If I offered my life for thy love, it were indeed but little.' Another proclaims, 'I will never part with thee, but will die under thy feet.' And still another announces, 'O mistress mine, I am thy slave and in the hollow of thy hand.' A youth describes how 'she took leave of me and went away and all my senses went with her'. The women respond in kind, however, with such sentences as, 'O my lord, my life hath been lived in vain for that I have not known the like of thee till the present.'

But the men seek 'that which men seek in women' and it is doubtful if world literature contains more graphic or more crude descriptions of coition. Sometimes it is stark and brutal as in this speech: 'O strumpet, I am the sharper Jawan the Kurd, of the band of Ahmad al-Danaf; we are forty sharpers, who will all piss our tallow into thy womb this night, from dusk to dawn.' More often, though, the act of love, if not always legal, is at least committed by two lovers. On a wedding night a bride 'did off her clothes' and the groom was happy to find her 'a pearl unpierced and a filly unridden'. But always the description of copulation itself is in the grossest terms—even irreverent—as in the story of Ali Shar and Zumurrud where Ali 'threw himself upon her as the lion upon the lamb. Then he sheathed his steel rod in her scabbard and ceased not to play the porter at her door and the preacher in her pulpit and the priest at her prayer-niche, whilst she with him ceased not from inclination and prostration and rising up and sitting down, accompanying her ejaculations of praise and of "Glory to Allah!" with passionate movements and wrigglings and claspings of his member and other amorous

gestures . . . ' And this is not the crudest passage to be found in the *Nights.*

If a man is denied the object of his passion, he sickens and often dies. This side of the story is usually quickly passed over when the man in question is not the hero of the tale, as when an unfortunate young man 'went out sore afflicted and sadly vexed and, returning home, felt sick, for his heart had received its death blow; so he presently died'. Tellers of the tales often find this a convenient way to rid themselves of characters no longer needed in their stories. Women, too, are often sick with longing, but they rarely die; they only lose sleep: 'she has not tasted sleep by reason of her heart being taken up with thee'.

When lovers finally meet, the meeting does not always seem satisfactory—at least by Western standards. Take the case of Ali bin Bakkar and Shams al-Nahar. Shams was 'burned with love-longing and desire; and passion and transport consumed her'. Ali was in a similar state. Then, 'she rose from the sofa and came to the door of the alcove, where Ali met her and they embraced with arms round the neck, and fell down fainting in the doorway; whereupon the damsels came to them and carrying them into the alcove, sprinkled rose-water upon them both'.

But love is not quite everything in life. There is also friendship—between men, never women. For a friend, the *Nights* tell us, 'is not like a wife, whom one can divorce and re-marry: nay, his heart is like glass: once broken, it may not be mended'. Tired of love stories, King Shahryar sometimes asked Shahrazad for tales of loyalty and friendship: 'Say me, hast thou any story bearing upon the beauty of true friendship and the observance of its duty in time of distress and rescuing from destruction?' She had indeed. In one tale a man says to his sick friend, 'Were thy healing at the price of my head, I would cut it off ere thou could ask me; and, could I ransom thee with my life, I had already laid it down for thee.' Caliph Harun al-Rashid has trouble getting to sleep one night and his faithful eunuch Mansur says to him, 'O my lord, strike off my head; haply that will dispel thine unease and do away the restlessness that is upon thee.'

Sinning or doing good, the Arab is always pious. Then, as now, religion played an important part in the daily life of bad Moslems as well as good ones and the name of Allah is frequently on their lips; they 'say the say that ne'er yet shamed the sayer, "There is no Majesty and there is no might save in Allah, the Glorious, the Great!"' Few Europeans ('Franks') or Christians ('Nazarenes') appear in the tales. When they do, they are inevitably villains. It is a Nazarene who, knowing the Arabs' greatest weakness, suggests the following plot to gain control over a Moslem enemy: 'I will tempt him to abjure his faith, and on this wise: we know that the Arabs are much addicted to women, and I have a daughter, a perfect beauty, whom when he sees, he will be seduced by her.' It is little wonder that no deed is proclaimed more virtuous than the killing of such abhorrent unbelievers.

After women and wine, it was poetry and song that most delighted the soul of the Arab in the *Nights.* ' "Prose is a wordy thing, but verses," rejoined the Caliph, "are pearls on a string." ' They quoted poetry when they were sad ('Needs must I recite somewhat of verse; haply it may quench the fire of my heart'), and when they were happy ('Oppression and depression left her and gladness took mastery of her, and she repeated these verses . . . '); and when 'tormented with the displeasures of memory'. Over-excitement inevitably stimulated poetry ('For excess of emotion he broke into verse'). But poetry and song also created violent emotion, as in this passage: 'Then she went on to sing . . . til our senses were bewitched and the very room danced with excess of delight and surprise at her sweet singing; and neither thought nor reason was left in us.' Sultan and peasant, they all recited or improvised verses and they often conversed in poetry: a fisherman, hearing a girl's sad love story 'wept and made moan and lamented; then, recalling what had betided him in the days of his youth, when love had mastery over him and longing and desire and distraction were sore upon him, and the fires of passion consumed him, replied with these couplets. . . . '

The verses themselves—at least as they appear in translation, and Burton's translations are no worse than others—seem poor things indeed to evoke so much emotion. Even Burton, fond as he was of Arabic poetry, confessed that much of it was bad. To one set of verses in the *Nights* he attached a footnote saying, 'It is sad doggerel.' They contribute nothing to the stories and, like songs in a bad operetta, are frequently introduced at inappropriate times. In his Terminal Essay, which covers a goodly portion of Volume X, Burton discusses the technical and historical details of the verses at great length. According to his count, there were 'no less than ten thousand lines' of poetry in the first ten volumes, plus uncounted thousands more in the six supplementary volumes. Sometimes, when poetic lines translated by Burton in one story are repeated in another, he used the translations of other scholars for variation. But, in general, one version is as bad as another. Rhymed and alliterative prose in the texts created another problem for the translator, but, as can be seen from some of the quotations used here, Burton was more successful in his handling of this type of material.

While Burton used a large number of coined and archaic words in his translation of the *Nights,* he did not overdo their use as he did in his translation of Camoens. There are still many words such as 'grievouser', and even 'grievousest', but some of his coined words are not unapt, as when he speaks of brigands who live by 'violenting' mankind. Most Arabic scholars declare that Burton was not as exact and literal in his translation as Payne, but he succeeded admirably in catching the spirit and conveying the expression rather than capturing the precise meaning of each word. Phrases such as 'she snorted and snarked' are certainly expressive, although Burton himself might have been hard put to define 'snarked', since in his usage it obviously does not mean snored and is redundant if it means snorted. One of the words he invented—or, more correctly, resurrected from Middle English—has become a part of the English language and can be found in most dictionaries: the word is 'ensorcel', meaning to bewitch or enchant. While he was still Victorian enough to avoid most of those four-letter words attributed to the Angles and

Saxons, he sometimes used old variants of them, such as the old Norse word 'skite', and 'coynte'. 'I have carefully Englished the picturesque terms and novel expressions in all their outlandishness,' he said.

As much of Burton's fame as a translator is due to his remarkable footnotes as to his translation of the text. It is probably safe to assume that, in his published works as a whole, no man, not even the most scribbling college professor, ever wrote more footnotes than did Richard Burton. In the *Nights* his passion for footnotes reached full flower. Here, for once, it enhances and makes unique his literary efforts. Because he had lived among so many diverse kinds of people and had studied their customs so intimately, he was able to add a curious gloss to the text he was translating. These notes, written at the end of a long and active life, form, as he said, 'a repertory of Eastern knowledge in its esoteric phase'. He felt that he had a unique contribution to make. 'The accidents of my life, it may be said without presumption . . . have given me certain advantages over the average student, however deeply he may have studied.' The footnotes in the *Nights* are also illuminating footnotes on his own life, for they range far from the text and many are written in a very personal vein.

There is every type of footnote represented in the *Nights,* from scholarly comments on points of Arabic grammar to regular essays on subjects suggested by words or phrases in the text, but the most delightful perhaps are those ingenuous notes that act as a personal gloss on the stories, almost as though Burton himself was an Egyptian fellah listening to the story being told in the coffee house and believing every word he heard. He makes such asides as, 'My sympathies are all with the old woman who rightly punished the royal lecher', and 'The young man must have been a demon of chastity.' When a girl in the story strikes her husband Burton notes, 'Which probably would not be the last administered to him by the Amazonian young person, who after her mate feared to approach the dead blackamoor must have known him to be cowardly as Cairenes generally are.' He could also sigh, 'Poor human nature! How sad to compare its pretensions with its actualities.'

Sometimes Burton stands outside the story but gives his comments on the tales themselves. Of the 'Story of the Three Witches' in Volume VI he says, 'It is the grossest and most brutal satire on the sex, suggesting that a woman would prefer an additional inch of penis to anything this world or the next can offer her.' Of another story he says, probably with tongue in cheek, 'I remark with pleasure that the whole of this tale is told with commendable delicacy. O si sic omnia!' When a character called Abu Nowés makes his appearance in the tales, Burton issues a warning: 'All but anthropological students are advised to "skip" over anecdotes in which his name and abominations occur.' Abu Nowés, the story tells us, 'loved to sport and make merry with fair boys and cull the rose from every brightly blooming cheek'.

Some of the stories contain anecdotes so revolting that even Burton was repelled by them, although this did not prevent him from translating them and commenting upon them. In one tale, for example, a woman bakes bread from dough that had been used as a dressing for a 'corroding ulcer' on a man's spine. Burton had heard the story before and says, 'This nauseous Joe Miller has often been told in the hospitals of London and Paris. It is as old as the Hitopadesa [i.e. *'Pilpay's Fables',* about the thirteenth century].'

Sometimes Burton comments on his own translation. 'The original is intensely prosaic—and so am I,' he says at one point. When he uses the versions of previous translators of the *Nights* he notes, 'I have borrowed from Mr. Payne', 'I give Torrens by way of specimen', or 'I quote Lane'. The other translators are sometimes praised for certain aspects of their work, but more often they are damned or scorned. Noting that Lane omitted a certain story, he says, 'probably he held a hearty laugh not respectable'.

Burton also used his footnotes to attack fellow authors and to get back at critics of his own earlier books. A book called *The Natural History of the Bible* is frequently scored and its author ridiculed for 'his painfully superficial book'. Andrew Lang, a critic who spoke unfavourably of his *Book of the Sword* in *Academy* is ticked off for an introduction he wrote to *Grimm's Household Tales*: 'It is curious that so biting and carping a critic, who will condescend to notice a misprint in another's book, should lay himself open to general animadversion by such a rambling farrago of half-digested knowledge as that which composes Mr. Andrew Lang's Introduction.'

There are many odd scraps of biographical material embedded in the footnotes, such as the fact that he believed in always wearing a nightcap 'however ridiculous', and that a eunuch's wife once told him how different kinds of eunuchs are made. There are many references to his own books and he takes advantage of the opportunity to correct mistakes he had made in some of them. He also lays to rest a story that had circulated about him for years: it was said that during his pilgrimage to Mecca he had once been caught urinating while standing up instead of squatting as is the practice of Arab males. To prevent disclosure, he was said to have killed the Arab who saw him. Not true, said Burton.

All his life Burton had been a keen observer of men and their manners, customs and perversions. That he did not always learn from what he saw does not detract from his merit as an observer and reporter. Some curious bits and pieces of things he had seen or experienced turn up in the footnotes. He noticed, for example, that women of the 'trading classes of Trieste' walk with 'a "wriggle" of their own'; that only occidentals say 'damn *it*' while 'damn *you*' is understood the world over; that Eastern women lie naked between sheets in hot weather; that 'the beauties of nature seem always to provoke hunger in Orientals, especially Turks, as good news in Englishmen'. Whether from experience or hearsay, he also records that 'the most terrible part of a *belle passion* in the East is that the beloved will not allow her lover leave of absence for an hour'. In addition, Burton also set down a number of statements as fact which there is little likelihood of his having observed directly but which are recorded as though he did; he says, for example, that in Egypt 'a favourite feminine mode of murdering men is by beating and bruising the testicles'

and that 'apes are lustfully excited by the presence of women'.

Above all, the footnotes in the *Nights* serve as a vehicle for Burton's hatreds, prejudices and opinions. All of the races, nations, professions and classes of people he had vilified in books and articles over the previous forty years are again abused, often in the identical words he had used earlier. He sometimes adds unusual theories to account for the deficiencies he noted in other people as when he states that the 'mildness and effeminacy' of the Hindus is probably due to their habit of defecating twice a day. He believed that his own race was vastly superior to all others and that Englishmen were the cream of that race and the best qualified to rule over other peoples. But neither this conviction nor his own position as a government official prevented him from attacking what he regarded as the absurdities and the stupidities of his own government and the many defects he found in the English character. He believed hypocrisy to be one of the great faults of his countrymen: 'hypocrisy being the homage vice pays to virtue; a homage, I may observe, nowhere rendered more fulsomely than among the so-called Anglo-Saxon race'. One of his main complaints against the British Government was that it did not rule in as iron-fisted a manner as he thought necessary and he contrasted the attitude of his own government unfavourably with that of oriental nations: 'In the East men respect manly measures, not the hysterical, philanthropic pseudo-humanitarianism of modern government which is really cruellest of all.' Government in Eastern countries, he said, 'is a despotism tempered by assassination. And under no rule is a man socially freer and his condition contrasts strangely with the grinding social tyranny which characterizes every mode of democracy or constitutionalism, i.e., political equality.' Always in favour of hard measures, he said, 'There are indeed only two efficacious forms of punishment all the world over, corporal for the poor and fines for the rich, the latter being the severer form.'

East and West are often contrasted, always to the disadvantage of the latter, in religious matters. As he grew older, Burton became more and more anti-Christian. Isabel's missionary efforts were a complete failure. Burton thought that 'theologians . . . everywhere and at all times delight in burdening human nature'; that 'every race creates its own Deity after the fashion of itself'; and that 'the heaven of all faiths, including "Spiritualism", the latest development, is only an earth more or less glorified even as the Deity is humanity more or less perfected'. In Christianity he found the doctrine of original sin most distasteful to him and he called it 'a most sinful superstition'. He believed that the Bible had been 'hopelessly corrupted'. Of all faiths, he found that of Islam more to his taste. Islam was to him a 'religion of common sense' which, for example, would permit cannibalism when it was necessary to save human life and allowed polygamy where it was necessary to increase the population. He thought the Moslem call to prayer, 'beautiful and human', was far more pleasant than 'the brazen clang of the bell'. He would have strongly disapproved of the modern custom in Arabia of replacing the human muezzin with a loudspeaker that plays a record of the prayer call.

He also gave his views on morality in the footnotes. 'Morality is, like conscience, both geographical and chronological,' he said, adding, 'but strange and unpleasant truths progress slowly, especially in England.' He again put forward his theory that women are more passionate in low-lying lands and in hot damp climates and vice versa. His opinion of women in general was low. He believed 'women corrupt women more than men do' and he contended that only an ignorant girl could be seduced: 'A man of the world,' he said, 'may "seduce" an utterly innocent . . . girl. But to "seduce" a married woman! What a farce!'

Burton regarded himself as an expert on the subject of sex, with which a goodly portion of the *Nights* is concerned, and often makes authoritative statements that would lead one to believe that his experience was both vast and intimate: 'An uncircumcised woman,' he said, 'has the venereal orgasm much sooner and oftener than an uncircumcised man, and frequent coitus will injure her health.' How much of Burton's store of sexual lore was gleaned from first hand experience and how much from what he had heard and read is difficult to say, but he always presented his facts and theories in such a way as to lead his readers to assume that he was absolutely sure of his ground, although in many instances this was certainly not the case. But regardless of his sources or his methods of research, and in spite of the fact that many of his conclusions are certainly suspect, no man before him had ever taken his scientific interest in the subject. There are footnotes on drugs used to prolong coition, a lizard that acts as an aphrodisiac, modes of circumcision, and lust among lepers.

There was no subject too sacred or too profane for Burton to take up in his footnotes. Whether or not he ever actually wrote 'A History of Farting', he certainly had made a study of the subject and frequently makes reference to it in his footnotes. His excuse for this is the frequent use of the phenomenon in his text and that, in Arabic, 'even serious writers like Al-Hariri do not, as I have noted, despise the indecency'. He has only scorn for 'polite men' who translate by 'fled in haste' the Arabic expression 'farted for fear'. He himself does not hesitate to translate the Arabic nickname Abu Zirt as 'Father of Farts' and even tells a personal anecdote on the subject to illustrate the effectiveness of Egyptian beans:

> I was once sitting in the Greek quarter of Cairo dressed as a Moslem when arose a prodigious hubbub of lads and boys, surrounding a couple of Fellahs. These men had been working in the fields about a mile east of Cairo; and, when returning home, one had said to the other, 'If thou wilt carry the hoes I will break wind once for every step we take.' He was as good as his word and when they were to part he cried, 'And now for thy bakhshish!' which consisted of a volley of fifty, greatly to the delight of the boys.

The footnotes in the *Nights* range far and wide, if seldom deep, covering the entire range of Burton's interests—swords and swordsmanship, the use of narcotics by American negroes, the necessity for removing body hairs in hot climates, a theory on laughter, points for judging the physical condition of a good slave and a 500-word essay on breeds of horses. It was a characteristic of Burton that once he acquired a theory or a prejudice, he never changed or relinquished it. So, at the end of his life, as when he had been a youth at Oxford, he is still protesting that English schools should teach their scholars to pronounce and write *y* instead of *j* in words of semitic origin.

Burton concluded his first series on *The Arabian Nights* with what is essentially one long footnote that covers 199 pages of Volume X. This is the famous 'Terminal Essay'. It consists of notes and comments on the origins of the stories, the translations that have been made in Europe, the manner and matter of the *Nights,* and the rhymed prose and poetry. But primarily this 'Essay' owes its fame to the section called 'Social Conditions as Shown in the Nights' which covers more than a third of the article. There are four subsections: A—Al-Islam, B—Women, C—Pornography, and D—Pederasty.

In the first of these subsections he states that from his own viewpoint, 'All the forms of "faith", that is, belief in things unseen, not subject to the senses, and therefore unknown and (in our present stage of development) unknowable, are temporary and transitory: no religion hitherto promulgated amongst men shows any prospect of being final or otherwise than finite.' He himself was an adherent of no religion. He appears to have believed in some sort of providence—which he usually referred as 'Provy'—but not the deity of any existing religion. 'The more I study religions,' he wrote, 'the more I am convinced that man never worshipped anything but himself.' But he makes it quite clear that he preferred Islam to Christianity. 'There is no more immoral work than the "Old Testament" ', he said, 'Its deity is an ancient Hebrew of the worst type, who condones, permits or commands every sin in the Decalogue to a Jewish patriarch, *qua* patriarch.' He cites passages in the Bible of 'obscenity and impurity'; he lists other passages containing 'horrors forbidden to the Jews, who, therefore, must have practised them'; and still another series of Biblical passages are cited of which he says, 'For mere filth what can be fouler.' This part of the essay is an outright attack upon Christianity. While he does not accept wholeheartedly the teachings of Mohammed, he uses Islam to make comparisons with Christianity that are never to the credit of the latter. Beliefs aside, much of his argument is both illogical and unfair, as when he compares a Moslem saying ('cleanliness is next to godliness') with a purely local Christian practice ('even now English Catholic girls are at times forbidden by Italian priests a frequent use of the bath as a signpost to the sin of "luxury" ').

'Women, all the world over, are what men make them,' Burton maintained in his section on women. Isabel would undoubtedly have agreed with him, although she would not have agreed with his views on sex education. Burton believed that young men should be taught 'the art and mystery of satisfying the physical woman' and cited the existence of a few of the many books to be found in all oriental countries designed to end all sexual mysteries.

He roundly condemned the practice of avoiding the subject of sex, saying, 'The mock virtue, the most immodest modesty of England and of the United States in the xix century, pronounces the subject foul and fulsome: "Society" sickens at all details; and hence it is said abroad that the English have the finest women in Europe and least know how to use them.'

After a short defence of the pornography to be found in the *Nights,* Burton moves, naturally enough, into the subject of pederasty:

> There is another element in The Nights and that is one of absolute obscenity utterly repugnant to English readers, even the least prudish. It is chiefly connected with what our neighbours call *Le vice contre nature*—as if anything can be contrary to nature, which includes all things. Upon this subject I must offer details, as it does not enter into my plan to ignore any theme which is interesting to the Orientalist and the Anthropologist. And they, methinks, do abundant harm who, for shame or disgust, would suppress the very mention of such matters: in order to combat a great and growing evil deadly to the birthrate—the mainstay of national prosperity—the first requisite is careful study.

Burton had made a careful study of *Le Vice.* In the course of his many travels he had not neglected to continue the study he had begun as a subaltern in Karachi. His conclusion was that the causes of pederasty were geographical and climatic rather than racial and that there was a 'Sotadic Zone' within which the offence was considered a mere peccadillo.

While there is no evidence that Burton took more than a scientific interest in this subject, he does relate several unscholarly anecdotes which obviously amused him. After telling how men caught in the harem are given to the grooms and slaves who force the opening with a sharpened tent peg, he relates with relish how a certain 'well-known missionary' with a 'conversion-mania' was once subjected to this indignity. With even less excuse he tells how a 'man cannon' was made by one Shaykh Nasr, Governor of Bushire:

> A grey-beard slave was dragged in blaspheming and struggling with all his strength. He was presently placed on all fours and firmly held by the extremities; his bag-trousers were let down and a dozen peppercorns were inserted ano suo: the target was a sheet of paper held at a reasonable distance; the match was applied by a pinch of cayenne in the nostrils; the sneeze started the grapeshot and the number of hits on the butt decided the bet.

At the end of the 'Terminal Essay' Burton sounded a defiant note to all critics, maintaining that his free treatment of subjects normally considered taboo would be a national benefit and that men had been crowned for lesser services than he had here rendered. While admitting that the work as a whole contains errors, shortcomings and lapses, he quickly adds, 'Yet in justice to myself I must also notice that the maculae are few and far between.'

Burton sat back and awaited the criticisms and doubtless wondered how much his venture would cost him. To his surprise and pleasure, the ten-volume work was both a critical and a financial success. Sold by private subscription, the completed *Nights* realized £11,000 profit—more than all of his other books combined. The gold he had sought in Midian and West Africa was found buried in that literary work which he had used to escape the realities of his world. Burton believed it was the pornography in the *Nights* that made it a success, and he told his wife, 'Now that I know the tastes of England, we need never be without money.' (pp. 364-82)

> *Byron Farwell, in his* Burton: A Biography of Sir Richard Francis Burton, *Holt, Rinehart and Winston, 1964, 431 p.*

Michael Foss   (essay date 1969)

[*Below, Foss examines the themes and intentions of Burton's* Pilgrimage to El-Medinah and Meccah *in the context of nineteenth-century English travel literature on Arabia.*]

In 1855, Victorian England, which even then had assembled much of the world into orderly arrangements shining with imperial virtues, discovered that a large chunk, quite close to home, still lay hidden. Europeans had subdued India, meddled in China, possessed the Indies (both East and West), penetrated the Amazon and the Congo, and were even now opening up the territories of the American West. Yet here was Arabia, some million square miles of difficult topography, still uncaptured by the good forces of Christianity, liberalism, science and capitalism.

Here was a forgotten frontier, all the more compelling because of its close proximity to Europe, and its connections with the European past through the mystery of Islam, whose wars with Christianity had scarred all the eastern and southern border lands of Europe. Since Arabia was almost waterless, full of desert, rocks and snakes, and liable to outbreaks of fanatical religion among armed tribes, quick to take offence, the bearers of European benefits preferred to work upon the African jungle, or the American plains. But Arabia could not stay immune forever from European influence; the dangers of a rugged and forbidden land have their own appeal to the boldest adventurers. And the publication, in 1855, of Captain Richard Burton's *Pilgrimage to Al-Madinah and Meccah* showed the Victorian public that the challenge of Arabia had been taken up by a very intrepid traveller indeed.

The first thing to be said about Burton's *Pilgrimage* is that it added practically nothing to the European knowledge of Arabia, Hijaz, the *haj*, or Mecca. Over the centuries, a thin but steady trickle of western Christians had advanced into various parts of Arabia, and had left reliable descriptions. The Renaissance Italian adventurer, Lodovico Bartema (or Varthema), had accompanied the Syrian pilgrims in the character of a Mameluke. He visited Medina and Mecca, and continued south to Yemen.

In 1763, Carsten Niebuhr visited Yemen with a party of scientific Danes, and wrote an account of great accuracy and value. In 1807, a certain Domingo Badia approached Mecca as a portentous Moor, one Ali Bey, and was permitted to make the pilgrimage in the greatest style. In 1814 he published a detailed description of the Holy City,

Burton's mausoleum in the Catholic cemetery at Mortlake.

European riff-raff and vagabonds whose fortunes directed them to Arabia. Thomas Keith, late of the 72nd Highlanders, and now the Agha of Mamelukes, was for a short while, in 1815, governor of Medina, the Holy City of the Prophet's Mosque. There was, then, no shortage of European information on Arabia.

But Burton's narrative caused more of a stir than the scientific accounts of his predecessors. Part of the interest may be put down to the extraordinary person and personality of the author—that large and somehow shambling figure, gaunt-faced and bearded, his cheeks scarred where a spear had passed through them. A pioneer explorer in central Africa, a linguist who seemed to master every language he touched and the composer of some *Critical Remarks on Dr Dorn's Chrestomathy of Pushtu,* could not but have a certain appeal. And as his life continued to be violent and preposterous (once, in Buenos Aires, he took Wilfrid Blunt, his successor as an Arabian traveller, by the thumbs and attempted to put that cool and diplomatic young man under a spell) he remained a romantic in the public eye. Though Burton's *Pilgrimage* has much correct information about tribes and customs, religion and literature, town-planning and topography, it is not a detached, scientific work. It is a work of imagination, and as a travel book, it is closer to Marco Polo and even to *Gulliver's Travels* than it is to the journals of Niebuhr and Burckhardt. He saw with the eyes of a poet (he later wrote a long quasi-eastern poem called *Kasidah*), and like all poets Burton recreated the country he saw according to his own specifications.

Despite Burton's easy familiarity with Arabic, his pithy comments and his acute observations, it is doubtful whether his words lead to the heart of Arabia any more than Polo's fabulous pronouncements tell much about China. Those who followed Burton's guide were likely to enter into a land of subtle unreality designed to satisfy a poet's need.

It should not have mattered. Later European travellers to China soon shook off Marco Polo's spell. But Arabia continued to be illuminated by the poet's shifting light. For the rest of the nineteenth century, the men who informed England most successfully of that frontier land were poets all—Palgrave, Blunt and Doughty. In the late nineteenth century, an age of scientific rationalism, the rediscovery of Arabia was not a reflection of scientific investigation, but of the distorting mirror of the imagination. Perhaps the English public could accept no other presentation; for whereas explorers of unknown countries started with few preconceptions, the Arabian traveller from Europe took with him the historical memories of over a thousand years of conflict with Islam. He necessarily entered into the "fabled" land of the Arabian Nights.

He entered, too, the land of Mohammed, whose religion had successfully asserted a spiritual, intellectual and moral dignity equal to that of Christianity. The public in England perhaps felt that the Arabian traveller had a duty to this past, part mythical and part real. The mystery of a thousand odd years is not to be lightly set aside; and although Burton, Palgrave, Blunt and Doughty, in the name of reality, had many harsh things to say about Arabia and

and recounted all the ceremonies of the *haj.* In the same year, Johann Burckhardt made the journey to Medina and Mecca and left an account that was so complete and trustworthy that Dr Hogarth, the historian of Arabian discovery, commented: "After Burckhardt, there was little but minor detail left to glean about either the society or the topography of the chief centres of population in Hijaz, Mecca, Taif, and Jidda".

Nor was the relatively accessible Hijaz the only part described; Yemen, Muscat, and even dangerous Nejd, cut off by Beduin tribes and Wahhabi fanaticism, had their visitors. In 1819, Captain George Sadlier, an English soldier with no knowledge of Arabic and ignorant of all desert ways, set out from Muscat on an embassy of congratulation to Ibrahim, the Egyptian general then subduing Arabia. This most improbable and most English figure accomplished what no European had done since the beginning of Islam: he crossed the peninsula from Muscat to Yambo, passed, as the Arabs said, "like a bale of goods" from hand to hand. Though he had little understanding of what was happening around him, he wrote a detached and quite accurate eye-witness report of what he saw. And besides these respectable travellers, there was the usual crowd of its peoples, in their robes of disguise, on camelback, or hawk on wrist, they preserved the essential distance between East and West, and satisfied the public.

The four writers were very different types of men, and would have been uneasy together. Burton had a touch of the superman, compounded of action, bombast and ability; he was endearing—if difficult—and faintly comic. Palgrave ran a very changeable course; coming from a respectable English Jewish family, he was never very happy about his background. He became in turn a lieutenant in the Bombay Native Infantry, a Jesuit in Madras and Syria, an Arabian traveller and confidential agent of the French, an ex-Jesuit, British Consul at Trebizond, and finished as Consul-General in Uruguay. He became reconciled to the Catholic Church and wrote *Vision of Life,* a long and tedious poem in imitation of Dante.

Blunt was very much the gentleman, bred for the diplomatic service, and always cultured and affluent. On his own admission, a voluptuary in his twenties, then a fighter for social justice and nationalism both in Egypt and in Ireland. A breeder of Arab horses in Sussex, the anticipator of Haeckel's Monism, he was a vain, intelligent, honest and independent man. But again his life was slightly ludicrous, his conduct something between playacting and despair. Desmond MacCarthy pictured him in his old age, "nid-nodding in Arab robes", in his English panelled hall so full of incongruities:

> All the objects which surrounded him roused a romantic curiosity: the obsolete long gun above the mantelpiece; the portrait of the poet painted by himself at the age of 14 . . . ; the beaded camel-charms, ostrich eggs, blazing blue butterflies, bunches of immortelles; . . . and last, but not least, the magnificent romantic sheikh himself, asleep, beard on breast, in his chair opposite me.

Doughty was less flamboyant than the other three, a quiet, scholarly man from a family dedicated to patriotic duty. He inherited from six admirals, three generals, a bishop and a judge or two, gravity, uprightness and devotion to hard work. He took upon his shoulders the Muse's burden and laboured at the task. His poetry is more copious, but not much better, than that of the other three.

These four writers, though joined together by Arabian adventure, were not great admirers of each other. The fastidious Blunt did not entirely approve of Burton; nor did Palgrave. Few had anything good to say of Gifford Palgrave: he was considered an unreliable opportunist, and perhaps a traitor to his country (that Jesuit connection and the confidential mission for France). Doughty won a certain amount of reverence; Blunt called his knowledge "the most complete among Englishmen, of Arabian things", and T. E. Lawrence called *Arabia Deserta* "the first and indispensable work upon the Arabs of the desert". But Burton, a greater Arabist than either Doughty or Lawrence, wrote huffily of the same work:

> Mr. Doughty informed me that he had not read what I have written on Arabia; and this I regret more for his sake than for my own. My *Pilgrimage* would have saved him many an inaccuracy.

It is to be expected that four literary men would have rather different reasons for going to Arabia. Both Burton and Doughty had some pretence of scientific discovery. Burton's journey to Mecca was financed by the Royal Geographical Society, and was undertaken chiefly to acquire the title of *haji,* a useful preparation for further Arabian journeys. But Burton did not return for many years, and then only to look for gold in Midian. Though Burton rather prided himself on his "anthropology" and his "geography", with him the dilettante of science was inextricably mixed with the adventurer and wanderer.

In 1875, Doughty, the philological scholar, while travelling in Palestine heard of strange inscriptions at Medain Salih, on the route to Mecca. His expedition, which began with scientific curiosity, led to two years of painful wandering in the character of a healer among the tribes of north western Arabia. The real reasons for Palgrave's journey of 1862-3 are hidden in the tangles of politics and his personality, but when he published his *Journey in Central and Eastern Arabia,* in 1871, he was able to find a respectable rationalisation. He wished to find out about the central Nejd, the least known part of Arabia:

> But of the interior of the vast region, of its plains and mountains, its tribes and cities, of its governments and institutions, of its inhabitants, their ways and customs, of their social condition, how far advanced in civilisation or sunk in barbarism, what do we as yet really know, save from accounts necessarily wanting in fulness and precision?

Blunt's introduction into the desert land was more casual and romantic. With his wife, Lady Anne, he had been drawn to the Moslem lands of North Africa and the Near East. At the end of 1877, they first visited Arabia, followed in the next year by a more extended trip "to penetrate into Central Arabia and visit Nejd, the original home and birthplace of the Arabian horse". Whether captivated by the people or the horses, Blunt soon professed "enthusiastic feelings of love and admiration" for the "Arabian race".

Whatever their initial purpose might have been, all four men pursued some visionary gleam beyond scientific interest. Drawn by the dangerous attraction of the forbidden land, they might be expected to have a particular sympathy for Arabia. Burton liked the free and easy independence of the desert tribes. The town Arabs of Hijaz, he thought, were ruined by commerce and greed. "Price", he wrote, "pugnacity, a peculiar point of honour and a vindictiveness of wonderful force and patience, are the only characteristic traits of Arab character which the citizens of Al-Madinah habitually display". And this he contrasted with the "chivalry among the 'Children of Antar' which makes the society of Badawin so delightful to the traveller". "The best character of the Badawi," he wrote too, "is a truly noble compound of determination, gentleness and generosity".

The other Englishmen also seem to be full of superlatives. Palgrave is pleased by the hospitality and conversation of the Beduin. To Blunt, Arabia was a "first love" and a "sacred land", "a romance which more and more absorbed me, and determined me to do what I could to help them to preserve their precious gift of independence". Doughty, in the curious dialect of his book, delighted in the "cheerful musing Beduin talk, a lesson in the traveller's school of mere humanity". In another place he recalled the peace to be found among privation:

> In a land of enemies, I have found more refreshment than upon the beds and pillows in our close chambers—Hither lies no way from the city of the world, a thousand days pass as one daylight; we are in the world and not in the world, where Nature brought forth man, an enigma to himself, and an evil spirit sowed in him the seeds of dissolution.

But soon the euphoric strain ceased. The tone becomes sharp and critical.

For Burton, even the admired Beduin have "ravenous and sanguinary propensities". He called them "savages and semi-barbarians" and said that their valour was "fitful and uncertain". Palgrave was especially contemptuous, and his book is full of unflattering portraits such as this one of two Sherarat Beduins: "utter barbarians in appearance no less than in character, wild, fickle, reckless, and the capacity of whose intellect was as scanty as its cultivation". Poor Doughty, who suffered much from being known as a *Nasrany* (Christian), wrote that "he had but one good day in Arabia; that all the others were made bitter to him by the fanaticism of his hosts".

Even Blunt finally despaired of Islam, though he met his greatest disappointments in North Africa and Egypt. In 1897 he was attacked and roughly treated by the Senussi at Siwah. He entered in his Diaries:

> My experience of the Senussi at Siwah has convinced me that there is *no* hope anywhere to be found in Islam. I had made myself a romance about these reformers, but I see that it has no substantial basis. . . .

"Islam's chance is gone," he wrote towards the end of his life; thirty years of his life had been devoted to Arab affairs, and now that effort was "absolutely thrown away". At the end of their journeys into Arabia, all four men carried most conspicuously the burdens of despair and disillusion.

What were they after? Certainly not Islam. Only Blunt showed some temporary stirrings towards the Moslem religion. The others were unimpressed. Palgrave, as befitted a Jewish-Jesuit, was highly scornful of the Wahhabi fanatics he found in Nejd. Burton, a great admirer of Mohammed himself, defended Islam against Palgrave's attack, pointing out that the Wahhabi sect was like "Calvinism" and not representative of the true Islamic religion. But Burton's own account of the practices at Medina and Mecca shows that he was not the greatest advocate of Meccan religion.

Doughty was so far from Islam that he dared to call himself a *Nasrany* and suffer the consequences. Indeed, all four men were far more concerned with Christianity, than they were with Mohammedanism. Burton flirted with Catholicism (he particularly admired Cardinal Newman),

and even, according to his wife, died a Catholic. Palgrave at the time of his Arabian journey was under the discipline of the Jesuits. Blunt was educated by Catholics at Stonyhurst and Oscott, and his life was a series of hesitations towards Catholicism, though he could never quite bring himself to join. Doughty retained throughout his life the austerity and moral fervour of his Protestant upbringing. Here, in fact, were four Europeans moulded by Christianity, and they very firmly refrained from becoming anything else.

But they were not typical of their race and religion, and each one had felt some disquiet concerning his western background. They failed, for different reasons, to respond to the roseate glow of what their fellow Victorians assured themselves was progress. They withdrew slightly from western ways, not to abandon them, but to test them. And the best touchstone to test the quality of western life was surely Arabia, the heart of Islam.

For Arabia was not only the physical frontier of Europe, it was also the frontier of the western mind. Beyond the frontier lay Islam, self-sufficient, complete. A journey to Arabia permitted Victorian Englishmen to make a pilgrimage such as Bunyan might have recommended; beset by the physical and mental perils of the way, a man might review his relationship to western material progress. We are "pilgrims, all of us, in what Bunyan calls 'the wilderness of this world'," says Sheikh Hafiz Wahba in his introduction to Lady Evelyn Cobbold's book on the *haj.* Arabia is preeminently the land of the pilgrim; it also has its share of the "world's wilderness".

As creative men on journeys of mental discovery, Burton, Palgrave, Blunt and Doughty tried to make Arabia feed their European hopes and fantasies. But, their desires naturally differed widely. Restless Burton, fretted by the confines of Europe, looked for hardships to set against his hustling spirit, and then yearned for peace for that same spirit. "Voyaging is victory," he said with the Beduin:

> In the desert, even more than upon the ocean, there is present death: hardship is there, and piracies, and shipwreck, solitary, not in the crowds when, as the Persians say, 'Death is a Festival'.

And the reward for this toughness was the Arab *kayf:*

> The savouring of animal existence; the passive enjoyment of mere sense; the pleasant languor, the dreamy tranquility, the airy castle-building, which in Asia stand in lieu of the vigorous, intentive, passionate life of Europe.

Burton, whose own boldness was assumed, saw that the Arabs only practised their daring from necessity. He felt his was a more admirable case. He believed in his superiority and advocated English imperialism, which he saw as a triumph of the "vigorous, passionate life" of Europe. He questioned England, not for its imperial expansion, but because it was not expanding aggressively enough.

Arabia was a playground for his spirit, and as an Englishman he was not to be pushed around. He was annoyed by Doughty's meek acceptance of misfortune:

> I cannot for the life of me see how the honoured

name of England can gain aught by the travel of an Englishman who at all times and in all places is compelled to stand the buffet from knaves that smell of sweat.

Palgrave's is perhaps the most straightforward case; there is less philosophising in his account, and less "science"; he was interested in people, and he makes no attempt to hide his clear prejudices. As a Catholic he could not approve of Islam, but as a Jew and an Arabist comparable to Burton, he was most at home in Arabia. In Nejd, he travelled a more dangerous route than the other Englishmen, and though he is not complimentary, one feels he captured the flavour of the place. But for Palgrave, Arabia was only a transitory stage in his spiritual progress. Born a Jew, he transmuted himself into a Catholic (and a Jesuit at that), looked at and rejected the reformed Mohammedanism of the Wahhabi sect, lapsed from Catholicism, flirted with Shintoism, then returned to the Catholic Church. Out of this spiritual progress he composed his long poem the *Vision of Life.*

The book on Arabia which captivated most Englishmen was Charles Montagu Doughty's *Arabia Deserta,* published in 1888. Blunt and Lawrence, among others, considered this the wisest, the most perceptive and most useful account of Arabia. This is curious, for Doughty was the least qualified by training and temperament for Arabian travels. As an Arabist he was certainly inferior to Burton and Palgrave, and he could not abide Islam. Explaining why he was so unwise as to travel as a *Nasrany,* he said, "I could not find it in my life to confess the barbaric prophet of Mecca and enter, under the yoke, into their solemn fools' paradise". "The Mohammedan theology," he added, "is ineptitude so evident that it were only true in the moon".

Sincere, humane and brave he sought his impossible grail, and was gloomy because it existed no more in Arabia than it did anywhere else. For if Blunt was a chevalier, Doughty was an antiquarian. It seems as if his hold on contemporary reality was rather shaky. Some years studying Old English literature in the thin atmosphere of the Bodleian had led to the delusion that Victorian England should display the heroic virtues of the saga. Similarly, when he first heard of the inscriptions at Medain Salih, he set out eagerly, not in search of Arabian reality, but of the Old Testament world.

He thought the nomad Beduin led the life "followed by their ancestors, in the biblical tents of Kedar". He thought he would return to the days of "the Hebrew Patriarchs", and hoped to be "better able to read the bulk of the Old Testament books, with that further insight and understanding, which comes of a living experience."

The future historian may be able to say what effect four literary men, who misunderstood or disregarded Islam, had on English thinking about Arabia and the Arab world. Writers with their hearts in England, who took the experience of their Arabian days to set their western lives in order are perhaps not the best guides to a foreign civilisation. The poet is the riskiest type of political forecaster; his eye is inevitably on other things. Yet T. E. Lawrence is our witness that these writings, and especially Doughty,

were the English handbooks for Arabian excursions. Lawrence, in an introduction to *Arabia Deserta,* said the work "became a military text-book, and helped to guide us to victory in the East". And he emphatically approved Doughty's method, the method of people who:

> In the same circumstance of exile they reinforce their character by memories of the life they have left. In reaction against their foreign surroundings they take refuge in the England that was theirs. They assert their aloofness, their immunity, the more vividly for their loneliness and weakness.

This was Lawrence's way, for he was a literary man too, working his vanity and self-pity into *The Seven Pillars of Wisdom,* just as Doughty had worked his loneliness and his old Testament morality into the twisted sentences of *Arabia Deserta.*

But this was the slanted vision which led the British (guided by Lawrence) to put their faith in the Sherifate of Mecca, and to discount the Wahhabi dynasty of Riyadh. Lawrence had good authority; Burton, Palgrave, Blunt and Doughty had discounted the Wahhabi sect. Wahhabism was obnoxious to European dreams. But a detached eye that could read Islam, might have seen differently. (pp. 38-42)

Michael Foss, "Dangerous Guides: English Writers and the Desert," in The New Middle East, *No. 9, June, 1969, pp. 38-42.*

Edward W. Said   (essay date 1978)

[*Said is a Palestinian-born American critic and scholar of comparative literature. Here, he reviews Burton's contribution to nineteenth-century Orientalism, affirming that such works as* Pilgrimage to Meccah *reveal an inherent conflict "between individualism and a strong feeling of rational identification with Europe (specifically England) as an imperial power in the East."*]

[Burton's] Oriental narratives are structured as pilgrimages and, in the case of *The Land of Midian Revisited,* pilgrimages for a second time to sites of sometimes religious, sometimes political and economic significance. He is present as the principal character of these works, as much the center of fantastic adventure and even fantasy (like the French writers) as the authoritative commentator and detached Westerner on Oriental society and customs (like Lane). He has been rightly considered the first in a series of fiercely individualistic Victorian travelers in the East (the others being Blunt and Doughty) by Thomas Assad, who bases his work [*Three Victorian Travellers: Burton, Blunt and Doughty,* 1964] on the distance in tone and intelligence between his writers' work and such works as Austen Layard's *Discoveries in the Ruins of Nineveh and Babylon* (1851), Eliot Warburton's celebrated *The Crescent and the Cross* (1844), Robert Curzon's *Visit to the Monasteries of the Levant* (1849), and (a work he does not mention) Thackeray's moderately amusing *Notes of a Journey from Cornhill to Grand Cairo* (1845). Yet Burton's legacy is more complex than individualism precisely because in his writing we can find exemplified the struggle between individualism and a strong feeling of national identification with Europe (specifically England) as an imperial power in the East. Assad sensitively points out that Burton was an imperialist, for all his sympathetic self-association with the Arabs; but what is more relevant is that Burton thought of himself both as a rebel against authority (hence his identification with the East as a place of freedom from Victorian moral authority) and as a potential agent of authority in the East. It is the *manner* of that coexistence, between two antagonistic roles for himself, that is of interest.

The problem finally reduces itself to the problem of knowledge of the Orient. . . . As a traveling adventurer Burton conceived of himself as sharing the life of the people in whose lands he lived. Far more successfully than T. E. Lawrence, he was able to become an Oriental; he not only spoke the language flawlessly, he was able to penetrate to the heart of Islam and, disguised as an Indian Muslim doctor, accomplish the pilgrimage to Mecca. Yet Burton's most extraordinary characteristic is, I believe, that he was preternaturally knowledgeable about the degree to which human life in society was governed by rules and codes. All of his vast information about the Orient, which dots every page he wrote, reveals that he knew that the Orient in general and Islam in particular were systems of information, behavior, and belief, that to be an Oriental or a Muslim was to know certain things in a certain way, and that these were of course subject to history, geography, and the development of society in circumstances specific to it. Thus his accounts of travel in the East reveal to us a consciousness aware of these things and able to steer a narrative course through them: no man who did not know Arabic and Islam as well as Burton could have gone as far as he did in actually becoming a pilgrim to Mecca and Medina. So what we read in his prose is the history of a consciousness negotiating its way through an alien culture by virtue of having successfully absorbed its systems of information and behavior. Burton's freedom was in having shaken himself loose of his European origins enough to be able to live as an Oriental. Every scene in the *Pilgrimage* reveals him as winning out over the obstacles confronting him, a foreigner, in a strange place. He was able to do this because he had sufficient knowledge of an alien society for this purpose.

In no writer on the Orient so much as in Burton do we feel that generalizations about the Oriental—for example, the pages on the notion of *Kayf* for the Arab or on how education is suited to the Oriental mind (pages that are clearly meant as a rebuttal to Macaulay's simple-minded assertions)—are the result of knowledge acquired about the Orient by living there, actually seeing it firsthand, truly trying to see Oriental life from the viewpoint of a person immersed in it. Yet what is never far from the surface of Burton's prose is another sense it radiates, a sense of assertion and domination over all the complexities of Oriental life. Every one of Burton's footnotes, whether in the *Pilgrimage* or in his translation of the *Arabian Nights* (the same is true of his "Terminal Essay" for it) was meant to be testimony to his victory over the sometimes scandalous system of Oriental knowledge, a system he had mastered by himself. For even in Burton's prose we are never directly *given* the Orient; everything about it is presented to us by way of Burton's knowledgeable (and often prurient) interventions, which remind us repeatedly how he had taken over the management of Oriental life for the purposes of his narrative. And it is this fact—for in the *Pilgrimage* it is a fact—that elevates Burton's consciousness to a position of supremacy over the Orient. In that position his individuality perforce encounters, and indeed merges with, the voice of Empire, which is itself a system of rules, codes, and concrete epistemological habits. Thus when Burton tells us in the *Pilgrimage* that "Egypt is a treasure to be won," that it "is the most tempting prize which the East holds out to the ambition of Europe, not excepted even the Golden Horn," we must recognize how the voice of the highly idiosyncratic master of Oriental knowledge informs, feeds into the voice of European ambition for rule over the Orient.

Burton's two voices blending into one presage the work of Orientalists–*cum*–imperial agents like T. E. Lawrence, Edward Henry Palmer, D. G. Hogarth, Gertrude Bell, Ronald Storrs, St. John Philby, and William Gifford Palgrave, to name only some English writers. The double-pronged intention of Burton's work is at the same time to use his Oriental residence for scientific observation *and* not easily to sacrifice his individuality to that end. The second of these two intentions leads him inevitably to submit to the first because, as will appear increasingly obvious, he is a European for whom such knowledge of Oriental society as he has is possible only for a European, with a European's self-awareness of society as a collection of rules and practices. In other words, to be a European in the Orient, and to be one knowledgeably, one must see and know the Orient as a domain ruled over by Europe. Orientalism, which is the system of European or Western knowledge about the Orient, thus becomes synonymous with European domination of the Orient, and this domination effectively overrules even the eccentricities of Burton's personal style.

Burton took the assertion of personal, authentic, sympathetic, and humanistic knowledge of the Orient as far as it would go in its struggle with the archive of official European knowledge about the Orient. In the history of nineteenth-century attempts to restore, restructure, and redeem all the various provinces of knowledge and life, Orientalism—like all the other Romantically inspired learned disciplines—contributed an important share. For not only did the field evolve from a system of inspired observation into what Flaubert called a regulated college of learning, it also reduced the personalities of even its most redoubtable individualists like Burton to the role of imperial scribe. From being a place, the Orient became a domain of actual scholarly rule and potential imperial sway. The role of the early Orientalists like Renan, Sacy, and Lane was to provide their work and the Orient together with a *mise en scène;* later Orientalists, scholarly or imaginative, took firm hold of the scene. Still later, as the scene required management, it became clear that institutions and governments were better at the game of management than individuals. This is the legacy of nineteenth-century Orientalism to which the twentieth century has become inheritor. (pp. 194-97)

*Edward W. Said, "Pilgrims and Pilgrimages,
British and French," in his* Orientalism, *Pantheon Books, 1978, pp. 166-200.*

Glenn S. Burne   (essay date 1985)

[*In the following excerpt, Burne evaluates Burton's overall literary achievement and unique perspective on Eastern civilization.*]

When Burton died in 1890, the many obituaries that appeared were for the most part positive, the writers of these notices coming to his defense for a variety of reasons: outrage at Isabel Burton's destruction of her husband's manuscripts; the strong sense that Burton's achievements had not been properly recognized and rewarded by British officialdom; and a genuine admiration for the man himself. He was praised for his contributions to the new sciences of anthropology and ethnology, for his awesome energy which resulted in his collecting and classifying "an incredible mass of fascinating and often obscure facts and information, his insatiable curiosity which led him to explore almost every path of learning, especially the by-paths." He wrote forty-three volumes about his explorations and travels, of which the *Pilgrimage to Al-Madinah and Meccah* and *The Lake Regions of Central Africa* are recognized classics. Also receiving special praise are *First Footsteps in East Africa* and *City of the Saints,* which has been described as the best book on the Mormons published in the nineteenth century. In the field of archeology Burton was admittedly a dilettante, but as a linguist and translator his reputation seems secure. He not only mastered twenty-five languages along with another fifteen dialects, but he compiled vocabularies of little known languages wherever he found them, for the benefit of travelers who would follow him.

In the end it was undoubtedly translation that was his most satisfying work—translation which for all its flaws possessed the integrity, brilliance, and vigor of the man himself. He moved with astonishing ease from the Hindustani of *Vikram and the Vampire,* to Portuguese for Camoen's *Lusiads,* to Arabic for *The Arabian Nights* and *The Perfumed Garden,* to Neapolitan Italian for *Il Pentamerone,* to Sanskrit for the *Kama Sutra* and *Ananga Ranga,* and to Latin for his *Priapeia* and Catullus. For these achievements, as well as his travel books, Burton has been justly admired; but the same writers who praised him could also misjudge him, claiming, for example, that "his cast of mind was so original that not only did he not borrow from anyone else, but he was disposed to resent another's trespassing upon such subjects as he considered his own." To the contrary, Burton was not especially "original" in his attitudes and beliefs, and he was openly generous in his crediting his predecessors and fellow explorers. He read and quoted all works he could find that antedated his own, and, with the notable exception of his personal quarrel with John Speke regarding the headwaters of the Nile, he was always ready to give credit where due, and to assist, from the stores of his own knowledge and experience, young explorers and scholars who sought his advice. And to those who were admitted to his intimacy, "the man was greater than what he did or what he wrote."

This last notion, that the man was greater than his works, has been expressed by a number of critics: it is implicit in recent biographies and flatly stated by Alan Moorehead and Fawn Brodie, and it invites further consideration of just who and what was the "man himself." Since the present study is concerned with Burton as a writer, it is through his published works that we must see and judge him—works that have provoked persistent questions about Burton's character. There are some recurrent themes that run through Burton's writings which, while not diminishing the magnitude of his achievement, serve to call into question in some critics' minds the authenticity and value of many of these writings: Burton's blatant racism, and his obsession with the more sensational aspects of sexuality. Another trait that characterizes Burton's life and writing was his penchant for disguise, for assuming roles, which had a marked effect on his literary work.

From the time he was a teenager, when he assumed the role of *croquemort* in order to participate in the collecting and burial of cholera victims in Naples, Burton delighted in theatrical disguises. Sometimes in costume—as a Persian merchant in India, an Indian doctor in Egypt and Arabia, and Moslem merchant in Somaliland—and sometimes without costume, he assumed and shed new roles up to his death, including such diverse roles as soldier, swordsman, explorer, anthropologist, archeologist, mining speculator, responsible consul, man about town, Arab sheikh, and, in between, devoted husband. He brought to all these roles his characteristic courage, enthusiasm, energy, and dramatic posturings, along with earnestness and exhaustive scholarship. But it is no doubt true that "the wild diversity of these roles served also to obscure the real man and the nature of the 'demon' that drove him from one to another." Each of his books, whatever else it was about, reveals him testing a new identity.

Burton's early books of travel show him frankly searching for fame as a pioneering explorer; he then sought renown as a scientist and scholar; and ultimately he claimed the world's admiration through his translations and personal writings. But throughout his life, despite his many successes, he seems to have suffered from depression, anguish, and guilt. His books, especially those he wrote and translated in his later years, suggest that he sought in the amassing of facts about human relationships, love, and sexuality a compensation for the apparent failures of his personal life. In matters of sexual relations, as in most everything else in his life, he fled from the conventional and the sanctioned; he was drawn to the exotic and forbidden. His writings indicate that he once had an Indian mistress, that he had a brief passionate affair with a Persian woman, and even made an abortive attempt at seducing a nun. His travel books contain strong hints about sexual experiences with the women of Africa. All of this seems "normal" enough, but what has bothered many of Burton's critics has been his repeated emphasis on what they considered unsavory aspects of sexuality—how eunuchs become eunuchs, bizarre and often sadistic circumcisions, clitorectomies, and other mutilation rites, and the fact that he probably wrote more extensively than any other man of his time about pederasty.

There is no question that Burton's work in providing translations of Eastern erotica has had an important effect on subsequent writing on the subject. Twentieth-century scholars on the subject have acknowledged Burton's pioneering and generally salutary contributions to candid and more accurate information about human relations. Another central aspect of his writing is equally important but more subject to controversy: the "image" of the African and the "Oriental" (meaning in Burton's case the people of India and the Near East) that emerges strongly from Burton's travel books.

Burton's writings on India and Arabia did much to create the image of the Middle Eastern "Oriental" in nineteenth-century British minds. It is a blurred image, however, due in part to Burton's inability, as we have seen, to sustain a consistent point of view. For Burton, as some of his biographers and commentators have observed, was a curiously "divided" man. But then most British travelers who wrote of India and the Middle East were divided in some important sense, and it is the special form of their individual inner conflicts that creates the quality which distinguishes their writings as literature. Indeed, recent studies of travel writing tend to view such works not so much as sources of information about the countries visited as revelations of the unique sensibility and values of the writer and his culture. Just as Charles Doughty's view of *Arabia Deserta* (1888) was conditioned by his love of the English past, and as Wilfrid Blunt's anti-imperialism reflects a tension between practical politics and a thoroughly romantic conception of the East, so Burton's writings reveal a man struggling with, and usually failing to resolve, many personal tensions which determined his reactions to the Orient. An examination of these inner conflicts shows Burton to be a man without a firm personal and cultural position from which to view and judge other cultures. He never discovered who or what he was himself, and so his views of others remain inconsistent and contradictory. Only in his two works on Arabia—*Pilgrimage* and *The Arabian Nights*—did he so involve himself in Al-Islam, with imagination and sympathetic insight, as to create works of relative coherence and literary quality. Only when in successful Moslem disguise and enjoying total acceptance in the Islamic world did Burton approach a degree of respite from his painfully divided nature. But even there, as we have seen, the divisions remained.

This "divided Burton" is probably to a great extent the cause of the divided criticism his books have received. From the time his works began to appear in the 1850s to the present, opinion has been sharply divided as to the quality of Burton's writing and the accuracy of his portrayal of African and Eastern peoples and cultures. One of his better biographers thinks that Burton's four books on India were just thrown together without regard for organization or "appropriateness" and are filled with "literary and philosophical rubbish." One of his other biographers, however, considers Burton's two books on the Indian province of Sind to be "solid brilliant ethnological studies," as does the English scholar who edited one of his books on Sind. And regarding Burton's main book on Arabia, *Pilgrimage,* opinions are equally divided. While *Pilgrimage* shows considerable improvement over the India books, the writing is unequal in quality and has led some critics to deplore his lack of literary talent. An anonymous contemporary reviewer criticized *Pilgrimage* for its "levelness of recital which brings the more momentous passages upon the reader suddenly as if he had collided with someone in turning a corner." One of his admirers admitted that Burton "was a man of genius; only, the fact is, he is not a great writer. . . . There can be no doubt that Burton always gives a vivid and virile impression of his adventures; yet, as I have said before, something is lacking in his prose; not the vital heat, but the vision of what is equivalent to vital heat."

Two authors who have special qualifications for judging Burton's works also expressed contrary views. T. E. Lawrence does not say much directly about Burton's style, but makes his judgment evident by indirect means. In his letters and prefaces he indicates his preferences among earlier travel writers, and he makes it clear that he judged travel books primarily on what he considered to be their literary quality. Here Burton did not score very well. Lawrence refers infrequently to Burton, indicating a "disapproving literary rather than scientific judgment." On the other hand, Lawrence greatly admired Doughty's *Travels in Arabia Deserta* and Kinglake's *Eothen.* Doughty's book was "a work of art": "Its value doesn't lie in its exactness to life in Arabia (on which I can pose as an authority), but on its goodness as writing." Alan Moorehead, however, sees Burton's literary abilities differently. Commenting on his books on Africa, Moorehead says that Burton "is a natural writer. He feels at ease with his pen just as other men are at ease in their conversation. Similes, witticisms, flights of imagination, scientific speculations and historical theories pour out of him in a babbling irrepressible stream. The language is Johnsonian, the tone is by turns ironic, boistrous, pedantic, argumentative, and just occasionally downright sardonic."

Critics have also been unable to agree on the accuracy of Burton's portrayal of the East and of his understanding of the Middle Eastern mind. One biographer says flatly that Burton failed utterly to comprehend the Arab's character and psychology, whereas another says that of the various writers on Arabia—Blunt, Doughty, Lawrence, Palgrave, Burton—only Burton solved "the riddle of the Arab," only he "saw eye to eye with the Arab." In one perceptive study of Burton, Blunt, and Doughty, a scholar points out that these three travelers, with differing feelings about British imperialism and differing temperaments, "came to three different views, each of which was thought to be the proper understanding of the Arab world." It is all too easy, he says, to point out the limitations of these views (he thought Burton's picture of the Arab was "too grotesque") and that "it is much more difficult to understand the temperaments and sensibilities which made these views so colorful; but the attempt is extremely rewarding in that it involves three fascinating men in an extremely lively period in human history."

Another writer describes all three of these travelers, Burton, Blunt, and Doughty, as "dangerous guides" to the cultures of the Arabian deserts, because they all—even Burton who is acknowledged to be an accomplished Orientalist—wrote a species of "fiction": their works are primarily works of the imagination, carrying on, consciously or not, the romantic literary traditions of *The Arabian Nights*. Edward Said, picking up on these arguments and working straight out of Thomas Assad (whom he cites), claims that Burton, as narrator and "principal character" of his books, was as much "the center of fantastic adventure and even fantasy as the authoritative commentator and detached Westerner on Oriental society and customs." He sees Burton as the first in a series of "fiercely individualistic Victorian travelers in the East" but adds that "Burton's legacy is more complex than individualistic precisely because in his writings we can find exemplified the struggle between individualism and a strong feeling of national identification with Europe (specifically England) as an imperial power in the East." For all Burton's sympathetic self-association with the Arabs, he was nevertheless, and always, the imperialist. But what is most relevant, according to Said, is that "Burton thought of himself both as a rebel against authority (hence his identification with the East as a place of freedom from Victorian moral authority) and as a potential agent of authority in the East. It is the manner of that coexistence, between two antagonistic roles for himself, that is of interest" [*Orientalism*, 1978].

Whatever these critics may have thought of Burton's qualities as writer and observer, they all agree on the central point emerging here: that Burton was a curious and complex man whose writings reflect an interestingly divided nature. It is apparent, when one considers his biography, that Burton's conflicting attitudes toward other societies and races have their roots in his own early life. Since he never really had a home, he never identified closely with any society. He spent his childhood years wandering with his family in southern France and Italy, speaking the local languages and absorbing the local cultures. He returned to England only when he had to, and, on the occasions he was obliged to spend some time among his countrymen, he almost always alienated them. When in "respectable" company he usually said the very things most likely to shock and offend his listeners, and he preferred the company of the bohemian literary fringes of society. After being thrown out of Oxford University and shipping out to India as an officer in the Bombay Army, he offended most of his fellow officers and superiors and sought the company of the native Indians. As he gained in knowledge and expertise, he became increasingly critical of the English military and civil service, constantly pointing out their ignorance of Indian culture and ineptitude in dealing with the peoples they were supposed to govern. But he could also irritate the Indians, when he wrote his books, with his condescension, his undisguised sense of white English superiority, and tendency to refer to the darker races as barbarians or "semicivilized."

It was at this point that his inner conflicts began to become apparent, paralleling his obvious inability to conform to the expectations of his fellow Englishmen. He was never happier than when in Indian, Afghan, or Arabian disguise, assuming a fictitious identity and mingling with the Indian and Arabian peoples, yet he longed to be admired and accepted by the English reading public. Early in life

he asserted, with some bravado, that for the strong man every region is his home, but later in life he confessed that he wished he belonged to some "English parish" that might admire his accomplishments and welcome him home. Ultimately, it seems, his loyalty was not to England but to the British Empire, or to the *idea* of the Empire in its noblest aspirations. He could not abide life among his fellow Britishers, in general, but he did make some lifelong friends, attesting to his capacity for loyalty to a select few. He greatly admired many Eastern values and life-styles, especially in matters of relations between the sexes, and he likened Victorian morality to a cage of unhealthy ignorance and oppression. He sincerely felt that England sorely needed the sexual wisdom and knowledge of the East, which did little to recommend him to the proper Victorians; yet he described many of the legal and criminal practices of the Indians, especially as regards the power of the husband over the wife, as barbaric. He praised the Arabian spirit of independence, as shown in Arab resistance to Turkish domination, yet condemned that same spirit, in later years, when the Arabs and Egyptians refused to submit to British rule. And while stressing his belief in the white Europeans' right to rule the world, he preferred the Moslem religion to all others and was extremely sarcastic regarding Christian missionary efforts at conversion.

These inconsistencies in dealing with Eastern cultures stem from other, more personal, factions at war within him. Burton presented himself to the world both as a man of action and as a scholar, as a learned linguist and as a rough-neck brawler and libertine whose persona, as narrator in his travel books, was that of the confident conqueror of cultures, peoples, and hostile regions of the world. Yet in his secret soul he was a sensitive artist, a poet, and lifelong friend of Swinburne. Publicly Burton was a master of the arts of boxing, horsemanship, and swordsmanship; he published a book on the proper use of the bayonet (later adopted by the German and British military), advocated the use of the "dum-dum" bullet, and advised harsh punishments for maintaining both military and civil discipline; yet three of his chief idols were Cardinal Newman, Disraeli, and Lord Byron. And in Disraeli and Byron he saw embodiments of his own aspirations: they were both men of action and successful men of letters. Burton's description of Disraeli, in which he likened him to Byron, could apply equally well to himself: both his two idols had "that exceeding sensitiveness, that womanly (not effeminate) softness of heart which finds safety in self-concealment from the coarse, hard, and cruel world that girds it." Burton took infinite pains to hide what he felt to be the poetic or "womanly" side of his nature, but it emerged when he published, anonymously, his efforts at poetry.

So, in sum, what do we find in Burton and his books on the East? We find a man whose writings on India are rich in colorful detail, personal anecdotes, history, geography, and learned discourses on languages and customs, along with prejudice, humor, sarcasm, and sometimes disenchantment. He was essentially a romantic who sought a world of exotic beauty, freedom, excitement, and sensuous fulfillment in the Orient, whereas he often found, as he describes in his first encounter with Bombay, a real world of poverty and disease, rats and congestion, and the stench of Hindu funeral burning-grounds. He had trouble forgiving India her imperfections, and he also berates the Empire for its failing, through ignorance and social clumsiness, to live up to its promise. He lavishes loving detail in describing the joys of his adventures among the Orientals, while hoping that his books will earn him respect from scholars and an admiring British audience. He developed a love for Al-Islam—her culture and religion, which he defended from Western critics in his posthumous *The Jew, The Gypsy, and El-Islam*—while in *Pilgrimage* he reveals, on nearly every page, his assumption of British superiority in general and his own in particular. While relishing his associations with most Arabs, he is critical of the city-dwellers, and he writes most affectionately of the desert people, the Bedouins, whose character and way of life he greatly admired—especially the Arabian "kayf," which, while encouraging surrendering oneself completely to the sensuous enjoyment of the moment, to a kind of "animal existence," is yet in Burton's view a product of a highly intelligent society.

Perhaps, of all the commentators on Burton's divided vision of the East, Edward Said is most provocative in his interpretation of the way in which Burton's preference for Eastern life coexists with his commitment to the Empire. Said suggests (to reduce greatly a complex argument) that it was Burton's mastery, his deep knowledge of the Oriental culture as an intricate system of codes, beliefs, and practices, that provides his British dominance and control over his Oriental experiences. Burton's books are a "testimony to his victory" over the intricate "system of Oriental knowledge." This is in itself a form of imperialism: "To be a European in the Orient, and to be one knowledgeably, one must see and know the Orient as a domain to be ruled over by Europe." In this way, the voice of Burton the individualist and the voice of the British Empire are coalesced.

We do not know if Burton would agree with this view—that his double vision became one through his masterful display of knowledge—but it is clear that he was fully aware of his divided nature and need for "coalescence." Later in life, during periods of serious illness and delirium in West Africa and Brazil, he felt acutely that he had been split into two persons. For many years he lived with the conviction that he had a dual nature, seeing with two different sets of eyes, perpetually at war within himself. So he was not surprised, when being fitted with eye-glasses, to discover that his eyes measured differently and required very different lenses. "I always told you that I was a dual man," he said to his wife, "and I believe that that particular mania when I was delirious is perfectly correct."

It may be true that Burton's knowledge of the East gave him a sense of imperial dominance, but his knowledge and dominance of himself remained always incomplete. On the surface he was opinionated and dogmatic, but fundamentally he was never sure of who or what he really was, where he belonged, or what he believed. It is the dramatic tension arising from his contradictions, and his quest for wholeness, that give vitality and human interest to his writings on the Orient. The impact of the East was strong enough to bring into temporary prominence Burton's na-

tive imaginative sympathies and emotional sensibility. This strength is first evidenced in many passages in *Pilgrimage* and reemerges in his later writings on Moslem East Africa, his own later poetry dealing with Oriental subjects, his books of Eastern erotica, and his translations of *The Arabian Nights*. But in addition to stimulating his emotional and imaginative faculties, the East provided Burton with material to indulge his urge to live robustly, his love for adventure, his penchant for the curious and "anthropological," and his staunch support for British imperialism. It has been said that "Burton found everything he needed in the East, or rather, that he was able to turn everything he found in the East to his own use. He was temperamentally susceptible to the romantic charms which the West is prone to ascribe to the East and he fell in love with them; but he was practical and matter-of-fact enough to appreciate the dowry as well."

Burton returned to his first love, but only after his long and at times unpleasant detour through darkest Africa and the wilds of the New World. He engaged in many dramatic adventures and wrote some good books; and he also became involved in bitter feuds and discrediting controversies, embarked on a fruitless search for gold in the Midian, and wrote some dull books. Yet never did he diminish his earliest and, in a sense, spurious fame as "the first European to have penetrated the holy cities of Islam." This exploit, the emphasis upon its hazards reinforcing European convictions about the ferocity of the Moslems, and "the strangeness, the incomprehensible otherness, of their shrines," seemed to have "ushered in a new period of western fascination with Arabs and things Arabic." The fascination was already there, as we have seen, and Burton served to reinforce it. Also, his journey served to lift forever a certain darkness that had, for the Europeans at least, lain over Mecca for a thousand years. Mystery had been replaced by knowledge. Indeed, it has been remarked that Burton's success made it unnecessary, as it were, for any other European to risk the journey to Mohammed's birthplace. It had been done and described, once and for all.

Yet the romance remained, at least as regards the desert. For it was the vast deserts of Arabia, and its enduring nomads who had learned to be as tough and fierce as their homeland, that increasingly drew the fascinated attention of Europe and especially England. Burton had helped create the myth of the noble Bedouin, a myth not without a basis in fact, a myth that would grip the Western imagination and fuel the popular arts for decades to come: painting, literature, light opera, and later the movies were all to exploit the image of the romantic desert sheik. This mirage was to draw into Arabia "a succession of lusty adventurers anxious to fling aside western dress and even, when they could, western characteristics, in order to woo and win the admiration and what was even better, the acceptance of the peripatic Arab of the desert."

Thus, whatever scholars may think of Burton as an anthropologist, or as a literary artist, his books on the East, and especially *Pilgrimage,* have had a permanent impact on the Western world's conception of the Orient, just as Richard Burton himself, as dramatized in his books, helped model our image of the nineteenth-century hero. (pp. 135-45)

Glenn S. Burne, in his Richard F. Burton, *Twayne Publishers, 1985, 168 p.*

FURTHER READING

Biography

Brodie, Fawn M. *The Devil Drives: A Life of Sir Richard Burton.* New York: W. W. Norton & Co., 1967, 390 p.
Study of Burton's life emphasizing his wife's role in shaping his career.

Burton, Isabel. *The Life of Captain Sir Richard F. Burton.* 2 vols. New York: D. Appleton & Co., 1893.
Exhaustively detailed portrait of Burton by his wife, Isabel.

Dearden, Seton. *Burton of Arabia: The Life Story of Sir Richard Francis Burton.* New York: Robert M. McBride & Co., 1937, 334 p.
Study of Burton's life and career purporting "to describe the most important of [Burton's] achievements in fuller detail than previous biographers, and to offer a brief pointer to the rest."

Hastings, Michael. *Sir Richard Burton: A Biography.* New York: Coward, McCann & Geoghegan, 1978, 288 p.
Biographical study focusing on Burton's foreign adventures.

McLynn, Frank. *Burton: Snow upon the Desert.* London: John Murray, 1990, 428 p.
Psychobiographical portrait of Burton incorporating previously overlooked archival material.

Wright, Thomas. *The Life of Sir Richard Burton.* 2 vols. London: Everett & Co., 1906.
General account of Burton's life and career.

Criticism

Mukerji, Dhan Gopal. "The Testament of Burton." *The Modern Review* LI, No. 1 (January 1932): 47-50.
Analysis of Burton's *Kasidah,* "the only poetical work of its kind in the English language."

Pastner, Carroll McC. "Englishmen in Arabia: Encounters with Middle Eastern Women." *Signs—Journal of Women in Culture and Society* 4, No. 2 (Winter 1978): 309-23.
Outlines "the major components of [the] stereotype of a sector of womanhood" as represented in the works of Burton and other English explorers.

Additional coverage of Burton's life and career is contained in the following source published by Gale Research: *Dictionary of Literary Biography,* Vol. 55.

Thomas Babington Macaulay

1800-1859

English historian, essayist, and poet.

INTRODUCTION

Macaulay is considered one of England's greatest historians and among the most popular and influential writers of the nineteenth century. His non-fiction writings, most notably *The History of England from the Accession of James II* and *Critical and Historical Essays Contributed to the Edinburgh Review,* have been praised for their scholarship and vivid prose style, while his volume of poetry, *Lays of Ancient Rome,* was an influential best seller. An ardent reformer, Macaulay sought to instruct as well as to inform through his writings, helping to shape and defend such Victorian ideals as the belief in individual liberty, progress, and the rights of private property.

The oldest of nine children, Macaulay was born in Leicestershire to a prosperous merchant and shipowner who was one of the leaders of the Clapham Sect, a group of evangelical Christians who were instrumental in abolishing slavery in the British Empire. Macaulay was a precocious child who had an advanced vocabulary at four and wrote a universal history of the world at eight. He possessed a remarkable memory which made him, when he matured, a "living encyclopedia" and a brilliant conversationalist. A prodigious reader and a student of languages, he immersed himself in Greek, Latin, and a half-dozen modern languages. He entered Cambridge in 1818, where, although he failed the honors examination in mathematics, he won many prizes. He was elected a fellow of Trinity College in 1824. The next year Macaulay began writing for the *Edinburgh Review,* a journal which was largely a forum of the Whigs, who advocated limiting the power of the monarchy. His immediate success helped bring him a seat in Parliament in 1830. Once in Commons, he worked to pass the Reform Bill of 1832 and became known for his riveting speeches. In 1834 he took a seat on the Supreme Council of India, where he was instrumental in implementing an English-language curriculum for Indians and drafting a code of criminal justice that still forms part of the Indian legal system. Macaulay left India in 1838. Elected to Parliament again the following year, he joined the cabinet as Secretary of War (1839-41) and later served as Paymaster General (1846-47). In 1847 he lost his seat because his Edinburgh constituents were angry at his support (of subsidizing) a Catholic college in Ireland; they later reconsidered and reelected him in 1852. But that year he had a stroke and, absorbed in the writing of his history, he never again took an active role in politics. He was raised to the peerage as Baron Macaulay of Rothley in 1857. Two years later he died and was buried in Westminster Abbey.

Macaulay's association with the *Edinburgh Review* lasted nearly twenty years, and his contributions to that journal comprise the most significant part of his early writing. In 1843 he gathered many of these essays, slightly reworking some, and published them in three volumes entitled *Critical and Historical Essays Contributed to the Edinburgh Review.* The topics vary from studies of John Milton and John Dryden to a review of Leopold von Ranke's *History of the Popes.* The collection was an immediate best seller, but Macaulay was dissatisfied with what he considered the overly popular and topical style of his essays. He published them only reluctantly, because a pirated American edition contained many errors, and its publishers paid him no royalties in spite of brisk sales. Modern critics find the *Essays* to be written in a style that, though clearly partisan, is certainly the ancestor of the one in which he wrote the *History.* According to the distinguished historian David Knowles, "nothing has really replaced the *Essays,* taken in bulk, as a sketch of the seventeenth and eighteenth centuries, and as the first brilliant overture to the *History."* Macaulay's *Lays of Ancient Rome,* which appeared in 1842, were meant to be re-creations in English of four lost ballads upon which Livy and other historians based their studies of the early Roman republic. Macaulay never claimed to be a great poet, and critics, noting his thumping rhythms and simplistic characterizations, have agreed with him. Yet his poems were reprinted many times (often in school editions) in the nineteenth and twentieth centuries because they reflect the values that the Victorians wanted to transmit to their children—for example, the stern patriotism of Horatius, who with two comrades defends a bridge on the Tiber against an entire army, "For the ashes of his fathers, And the temples of his gods."

Begun on his return voyage from India, Macaulay's magnum opus, *The History of England from the Accession of James II,* was originally projected to extend from 1685 to probably the Reform Bill of 1832. But the five volumes that he was able to produce cover only seventeen years. The first two volumes appeared in 1848, and they were awaited with such anticipation that a traffic jam developed outside his publisher's shop on their day of issue. The last volume, edited by his sister Hannah, appeared posthumously in 1861. In addition, Macaulay published in 1854 a volume of his speeches, most of which he had reconstructed from memory, and he contributed five articles to the *Encyclopedia Britannica* that are considered among his finest works and were republished in 1857 as *Biographical and Historical Sketches.*

Macaulay's reputation as a historian rests largely on the *History,* although critics are divided as to its quality. Its strong emphasis on political narrative seems out of date to many twentieth-century historians, but Macaulay's famous third chapter describing the social, economic, and intellectual state of England in 1685 has been called a forerunner of modern social history. Most scholars agree that Macaulay had the capacity to organize a vast quantity of material and present it in a clear and vivid manner. Some have suggested that he used the techniques of the realistic novel—for instance, the colorful portrayal of villains and heroes—to develop his story smoothly. Other critics maintain, however, that the rhetorical effects he incorporated interfered with the accuracy of his presentation. Macaulay has also been criticized for his Whig partisanship, advocacy of material prosperity, and fervent belief in industrial as well as moral progress; yet some historians have pointed out that Macaulay was not so much a Whig as a "trimmer," a flexible politician who always opposed bigotry and rigidity, even when he found it in his own party.

The last writer to consciously model himself on the great historians of ancient Greece and Rome, Macaulay saw history as a form of didactic literature, and his works are gracefully written treatises filled with ethical lessons. Although producing this kind of history won him fame, his reputation has waned because many of the values he so confidently defended, while they do not seem wrong, appear a little naive from a distance of more than a century. The role of the historian, too, is conceived differently today: in the words of Peter Gay, it is to understand, not to teach. Modern historians prefer to see themselves as scientists who examine social and economic problems and are not content with simply constructing political narratives. Nevertheless, critics agree that few writers have had such a command of the popular literature (for example, pamphlets, treatises, and broadsides) for the period that

Macaulay studied, and that he presented that material honestly and memorably.

PRINCIPAL WORKS

*Critical and Miscellaneous Essays. 5 vols. (essays) 1842-44
Lays of Ancient Rome (poetry) 1842
Critical and Historical Essays Contributed to the Edinburgh Review. 3 vols. (essays) 1843
The History of England from the Accession of James II. 5 vols. (history) 1848-61
*Speeches. 2 vols. (speeches) 1853
The Speeches of the Right Honorable Thomas Babington Macaulay Edited by Himself (speeches) 1854
Biographical and Historical Sketches (essays) 1857
The Marginal Notes of Lord Macaulay (marginalia) 1907
The Complete Works of Lord Macaulay. 20 vols. (essays, poetry, and history) 1910
The Letters of Macaulay. 6 vols. (letters) 1974-81

*These citations refer to American editions published without the author's permission.

CRITICISM

Edgar Allan Poe   (essay date 1849?)

[*Considered one of America's most outstanding men of letters, Poe was a distinguished poet, novelist, essayist, journalist, short story writer, editor, and critic. In the following essay, he reviews the* Critical and Historical Essays *and concludes that Macaulay is a fine writer and original thinker who nonetheless confuses the inductive with the analogical method of reasoning. Since the date of this piece is not known, Poe's death date is used to date the essay.*]

Macaulay has obtained a reputation which, although deservedly great, is yet in a remarkable measure undeserved. The few who regard him merely as a terse, forcible, and logical writer, full of thought, and abounding in original views—often sagacious and never otherwise than admirably expressed—appear to us precisely in the right. The many who look upon him as not only all this, but as a comprehensive and profound thinker, little prone to error, err essentially themselves. The source of the general mistake lies in a very singular consideration, yet in one upon which we do not remember ever to have heard a word of comment. We allude to a tendency in the public mind towards logic for logic's sake; a liability to confound the vehicle with the conveyed; an aptitude to be so dazzled by the luminousness with which an idea is set forth as to mistake it for the luminousness of the idea itself. The error is one exactly analogous with that which leads the immature poet to think himself sublime wherever he is obscure, because obscurity is a source of the sublime, thus confounding obscurity of expression with the expression of obscurity. In the case of Macaulay—and we may say, *en passant,* of our own Channing—we assent to what he says, too often because we so very clearly understand what it is that he intends to say. Comprehending vividly the points and the sequence of his argument, we fancy that we are concurring in the argument itself. It is not every mind which is at once able to analyze the satisfaction it receives from such Essays as we see here. If it were merely *beauty* of style for which they were distinguished,—if they were remarkable only for rhetorical flourishes,—we would not be apt to estimate these flourishes at more than their due value. We would not agree with the doctrines of the essayist on account of the elegance with which they were urged. On the contrary, we would be inclined to disbelief. But when all ornament save that of simplicity is disclaimed,—when we are attacked by precision of language, by perfect accuracy of expression, by directness and singleness of thought, and above all by a logic the most rigorously close and consequential,—it is hardly a matter for wonder that nine of us out of ten are content to rest in the gratification thus received as in the gratification of absolute truth.

Of the terseness and simple vigour of Macaulay's style it is unnecessary to point out instances. Every one will acknowledge his merits on this score. His exceeding *closeness* of logic, however, is more especially remarkable. With this he suffers nothing to interfere. Here, for example, is a sentence in which, to preserve entire the chain of his argument,—*to leave no minute gap which the reader might have to fill up with thought,*—he runs into most unusual tautology.

> The books and traditions of a sect may contain, mingled with propositions strictly theological, other propositions, purporting to rest on the same authority which relate to physics. If new discoveries should throw discredit on the physical propositions, the theological propositions, unless they can be separated from the physical propositions, will share in their discredit.

These things are very well in their way; but it is indeed questionable whether they do not appertain rather to the trickery of thought's vehicle than to thought itself—rather to reason's shadow than to reason. Truth, for truth's sake, is seldom so enforced. It is scarcely too much to say that the style of the profound thinker is never closely logical. Here we might instance George Combe—than whom a more candid reasoner never, perhaps, wrote or spoke—than whom a more complete antipode to Babington Macaulay there certainly never existed. The former *reasons* to discover the true. The latter *argues* to convince the world, and, in arguing, not unfrequently surprises himself into conviction. What Combe appears to Macaulay, it would be a difficult thing to say. What Macaulay is thought of by Combe, we can understand very well. The man who looks at an argument in its details alone, will not fail to be misled by the one; while he who keeps steadily

in view the *generality* of a thesis will always at least approximate the truth under guidance of the other.

Macaulay's tendency—and the tendency of mere logic in general—to concentrate force upon minutiæ, at the expense of a subject as a whole, is well instanced in an article [in *Critical and Miscellaneous Essays*] on Ranke's *History of the Popes.* This article is called a review—possibly because it is anything else—as *lucus* is *lucus a non lucendo.* In fact it is nothing more than a beautifully written treatise on the main theme of Ranke himself, the whole matter of the treatise being deduced from the *History.* In the way of criticism, there is nothing worth the name. The strength of the essayist is put forth to account for the progress of Romanism by maintaining that divinity is not a progressive science. The enigmas, says he in substance, which perplex the natural theologian, are the same in all ages, while the Bible, where alone we are to seek revealed truth, has always been what it is.

The manner in which these two propositions are set forth is a model for the logician and for the student of *belles lettres;* yet the error into which the essayist has rushed headlong, is egregious. He attempts to deceive his readers, or has deceived himself, by confounding the nature of that proof from which we reason of the concerns of earth, considered as man's habitation, and the nature of that evidence from which we reason of the same earth regarded as a unit of that vast whole, the universe. In the former case the *data* being palpable, the proof is direct; in the latter it is purely *analogical.* Were the indications we derive from science of the nature and designs of Deity, and thence, by inference, of man's destiny—were these indications proof direct, no advance in science would strengthen them; for, as our author truly observes, "nothing could be added to the force of the argument which the mind finds in every beast, bird, or flower"; but as these indications are rigidly analogical, every step in human knowledge—every astronomical discovery, for instance—throws additional light upon the august subject *by extending the range of analogy.* That we know no more to-day of the nature of Deity, of its purposes—and thus of man himself—than we did even a dozen years ago, is a proposition disgracefully absurd; and of this any astronomer could assure Mr. Macaulay. Indeed, to our own mind, the *only* irrefutable argument in support of the soul's immortality—or, rather, the only conclusive proof of man's alternate dissolution and rejuvenescence *ad infinitum*—is to be found in analogies deduced from the modern established theory of the nebular cosmogony. Mr. Macaulay, in short, has forgotten that he frequently forgets, or neglects, the very gist of his subject. He has forgotten that analogical evidence cannot, at all times, be discoursed of as if identical with proof direct. Throughout the whole of his treatise he has made no distinction whatever. (pp. 318-21)

Edgar Allan Poe, "Criticism: Macaulay's Essays," in his Edgar Allan Poe: Representative Selections, *revised edition, Hill and Wang, 1962, pp. 318-21.*

Walter Bagehot   (essay date 1856)

[*Regarded as one of the most versatile and influential authors of mid-Victorian England, Bagehot wrote several pioneering works in the fields of politics, sociology, economics, and literary criticism. In the following excerpt from a review written after the publication of the third and fourth volumes of the* History, *Bagehot admires Macaulay's ability to delineate character and to entertain through a wealth of informative detail, but he regrets that Macaulay's insensitive nature does not seem to allow him to understand men of passion or strong religious feeling.*]

Why, it is often asked, "is history dull? It is a narrative of life, and life is of all things the most interesting." The answer is, that it is written by men too dull to take the common interest in life, in whom languor predominates over zeal, and sluggishness over passion.

Macaulay is not dull, and it may seem hard to attempt to bring him within the scope of a theory which is so successful in explaining dullness. Yet, in a modified and peculiar form, we can perhaps find in his remarkable character unusually distinct traces of the insensibility which has been ascribed to the historian. The means are ample: Mr. Macaulay has not spent his life in a corner; if posterity should refuse—of course they will not refuse—to read a line of his writings, they would yet be sought out by studious inquirers, as those of a man of high political position, great notoriety, and greater oratorical power. We are not therefore obliged, as in so many cases even among contemporaries, to search for the author's character in his books alone; we are able from other sources to find out his character, and then apply it to the explanation of the peculiarities of his works. Mr. Macaulay has exhibited many high attainments, many dazzling talents, much singular and well-trained power; but the quality which would most strike the observers of the interior man is what may be called his *in*experiencing nature. Men of genius have in general been distinguished by their extreme susceptibility to external experience. Finer and softer than other men, every exertion of their will, every incident of their lives, influences them more deeply than it would others. Their essence is at the same time finer and more impressible; it receives a distincter mark, and receives it more easily than the souls of the herd. From his peculiar sensibility, the man of genius bears the stamp of life commonly more clearly than his fellows; even casual associations make a deep impression on him: examine his mind, and you may discern his fortunes. Mr. Macaulay has nothing of this. You could not tell what he has been. His mind shows no trace of change. What he is, he was; and what he was, he is. He early attained a high development, but he has not increased it since; years have come, but they have whispered little; as was said of the second Pitt, "He never grew, he was cast." The volume of "speeches" which he has published place the proof of this in every man's hand. His first speeches are as good as his last; his last scarcely richer than his first. He came into public life at an exciting season; he shared at the time in that excitement, and that excitement still seems to quiver in his mind. He delivered marvellous rhetorical exercises on the Reform Bill at the time; he speaks of it with marvellous rhetorical power

even now. He is still the man of '32. From that era he looks on the past. He sees "Old Sarum" in the seventeenth century, and Gatton in the civil wars. You may fancy an undertone in his mind running somewhat thus: The Norman barons commenced the series of reforms which "*we* consummated;" Hampden was "preparing for the occasion in which I had a part;" William "for the debate in which I took occasion to observe." With a view to that era every thing begins; up to that moment every thing ascends. That was the "fifth act" of the human race; the remainder of history is only an afterpiece. All this was very natural at the moment; nothing could be more probable than that a young man of the greatest talents, entering at once into important life at a conspicuous opportunity, should exaggerate its importance; he would fancy it was the "crowning achievement," the greatest "in the tide of time." But what is remarkable is, that he should retain the idea now; that years have brought no influence, experience no change. The events of twenty years have been full of rich instruction on the events of twenty years ago; but they have not instructed him. His creed is a fixture. It is the same on his peculiar topic—on India. Before he went there he made a speech on the subject; Lord Canterbury, who must have heard a million speeches, said it was the best he had ever heard. It is difficult to fancy that so much vivid knowledge could be gained from books—from horrible Indian treatises; that such imaginative mastery should be possible without actual experience. Not forgetting, or excepting, the orations of Burke, it was perhaps as remarkable a speech as was ever made on India by an Englishman who had not been in India. Now he has been there he speaks no better—rather worse; he spoke excellently without experience, he speaks no better with it,—if any thing, it rather puts him out. His speech on the Indian charter a year or two ago was not finer than that on the charter of 1833. Before he went to India he recommended that writers should be examined in the classics; after being in India he recommended that they should be examined in the same way. He did not say he had seen the place in the mean time, he did not think that had any thing to do with it. You could never tell from any difference in his style what he had seen, or what he had not seen. He is so insensible to passing objects, that they leave no distinctive mark, no intimate peculiar trace.

It is characteristic of such a man that he should think literature more instructive than life. Hazlitt said severely of Mackintosh, "He might like to read an *account* of India; but India itself, with its burning, shining face, was a mere blank, an endless waste to him. Persons of this class have no more to say to a plain matter of fact staring them in the face than they have to a hippopotamus." This was a keen criticism on Sir James, savouring of the splenetic mind from which it came. As a complete estimate, it would be a most unjust one of Macaulay; but it cannot be denied, that there are a whole class of minds which prefer the literary delineation of objects to the actual eyesight of them. An insensible nature, like a rough hide, resists the breath of passing things; an unobserving retina will depict in vain whatever a quicker eye shall not explain. But any one can understand a book; the work is done, the facts observed, the formulæ suggested, the subjects classified. Of course it needs labour, and a following fancy, to peruse the long lucubrations and descriptions of others; but a fine detective sensibility is unnecessary; type is plain, an earnest attention will follow it and know it. To this class Mr. Macaulay belongs; and he has on that very account characteristically maintained that dead authors are more fascinating than living people. "Those friendships," he tells us,

> are exposed to no danger from the occurrences by which other attachments are weakened or dissolved. Time glides by; fortune is inconstant; tempers are soured; bonds which seemed indissoluble are daily sundered by interest, by emulation, or by caprice. But no such cause can affect the silent converse which we hold with the highest of human intellects. That placid intercourse is disturbed by no jealousies or resentments. These are the old friends who are never seen with new faces, who are the same in wealth and in poverty, in glory and in obscurity. With the dead there is no rivalry. In the dead there is no change. Plato is never sullen. Cervantes is never petulant. Demosthenes never comes unseasonably. Dante never stays too long. No difference of political opinion can alienate Cicero. No heresy can excite the horror of Bossuet.

But Bossuet is dead; and Cicero was a Roman; and Plato wrote in Greek. Years and manners separate us from the great. After dinner Demosthenes *may* come unseasonably; Dante might stay too long. *We* are alienated from the politician, and have a horror of the theologian. Dreadful idea, having Demosthenes for an intimate friend! He had pebbles in his mouth; he was always urging action; he spoke such good Greek; we cannot dwell on it,—it is too much. Only a mind impassive to our daily life, unalive to bores and evils, to joys and sorrows, with head in literature and heart in boards, incapable of the deepest sympathies, a prey to books, could imagine it. The mass of men have stronger ties and warmer hopes. The exclusive devotion to books tires. We require to love and hate, to act and live.

It is not unnatural that a person of this temperament should preserve a certain aloofness even in the busiest life. Mr. Macaulay has ever done so. He has been in the thick of political warfare, in the van of party conflict. Whatever a keen excitability would select for food and opportunity, has been his; but he has not been excited. He has never thrown himself upon action, he has never followed trivial details with an anxious passion. He has ever been a man for a great occasion. He has been by nature a *deus ex machinâ*. Somebody has had to fetch him. His heart was in Queen Anne's time. When he came, he spoke as Lord Halifax might have spoken. Of course, it may be contended that this is the *eximia ars;* that this solitary removed excellence is particularly and essentially sublime. But, simply and really, greater men have been more deeply "immersed in matter." The highest eloquence quivers with excitement; there is life-blood in the deepest action; a man like Strafford seems flung upon the world. An orator should never talk like an observatory; no coldness should strike upon the hearer.

It is characteristic also that he should be continually thinking of posterity. In general, that expected authority is most ungrateful; those who think of it most, it thinks

of least. The way to secure its favour is, to give vivid essential pictures of the life before you; to leave a fresh glowing delineation of the scene to which you were born, of the society to which you have peculiar access. This is gained, not by thinking of your posterity, but by living in society; not by poring on what is to be, but by enjoying what is. That spirit of thorough enjoyment which pervades the great delineators of human life and human manners, was not caused by "being made after supper out of a cheeseparing;" it drew its sustenance from a relishing, enjoying, sensitive life, and the flavour of the description is the reality of that enjoyment. Of course, this is not so in science. You may leave a name by an abstract discovery without having led a thorough or vigorous existence; yet what a name is this! Taylor's theorem will go down to posterity,—possibly its discoverer was for ever dreaming and expecting that it would; but what does posterity know of the deceased Taylor? *Nominis umbra* is rather a compliment; for it is not substantial enough to have a shadow. But in other walks,—say in political oratory, which is the part of Mr. Macaulay's composition in which his value for posterity's opinion is most apparent,—the way to interest posterity is to think but little of it. What gives to the speeches of Demosthenes the interest they have? The intense, vivid, glowing interest of the speaker in all that he is speaking about. Philip is not a person whom "posterity will censure," but the man "whom I hate;" the matter in hand not one whose interest depends on the memory of men, but in which an eager intense nature would have been absorbed if there had been no posterity at all, on which he wished to deliver his own soul. A casual character, so to speak, is natural to the most intense words; externally even they will interest the "after world" more for having interested the present world; they must have a life of *some* place and *some* time before they can have one of all space and all time. Mr. Macaulay's oratory is the very opposite of this. Schoolboyish it is not, for it is the oratory of a very sensible man; but the theme of a schoolboy is not less devoid of the salt of circumstance. The speeches on the Reform Bill have been headed, "Now, a man came up from college and spoke thus;" and, like a college man, he spoke rather to the abstract world than to the present. He knew no more of the people who actually did live in London than of people who would live in London, and there was therefore no reason for speaking to one more than to the other. After years of politics, he speaks so still. He looks on a question (he says) as posterity will look on it; he appeals from this to future generations; he regards existing men as painful prerequisites of great-grandchildren. This seems to proceed, as has been said, from a distant and unimpressible nature. But it is impossible to deny that it has one great advantage; it has made him take pains. A man who speaks to people a thousand years off will naturally speak carefully: he tries to be heard over the clang of ages, over the rumours of myriads. Writing for posterity is like writing on foreign postpaper: you cannot say to a man at Calcutta what you would say to a man at Hackney; you think "the yellow man is a very long way off: this is fine paper, it will go by a ship;" so you try to say something worthy of the ship, something noble, which will keep and travel. So writers like Macaulay, who think of future people, have a respect for future people. Each syllable is solemn, each word distinct. No other author trained to periodical writing has so little of its sloven-liness and its imperfection.

This singularly constant contemplation of posterity has often coloured his estimate of his social characters. He has no toleration for those great men in whom a lively sensibil-ity to momentary honours has prevailed over a consistent reference to the posthumous tribunal. He is justly severe on Lord Bacon:

> In his library all his rare powers were under the guidance of an honest ambition, of an enlarged philanthropy, of a sincere love of truth. There no temptation drew him away from the right course. Thomas Aquinas could pay no fees, Duns Scotus could confer no peerages. The 'Master of the Sentences' had no rich reversions in his gift. Far different was the situation of the great philosopher when he came forth from his study and his laboratory to mingle with the crowd which filled the galleries of Whitehall. In all that crowd there was no man equally quali-fied to render great and lasting services to man-kind. But in all that crowd there was not a heart more set on things which no man ought to suffer to be necessary to his happiness,—on things which can often be obtained only by the sacrifice of integrity and honour. To be the leader of the human race in the career of improvement, to found on the ruins of ancient intellectual dynas-ties a more prosperous and a more enduring em-pire, to be revered to the latest generations as the most illustrious among the benefactors of man-kind,—all this was within his reach. But all this availed him nothing, while some quibbling spe-cial pleader was promoted before him to the bench,—while some heavy country gentleman took precedence of him by virtue of a purchased coronet,—while some pander, happy in a fair wife, could obtain a more cordial salute from Buckingham,—while some buffoon, versed in all the latest scandal of the court, could draw a louder laugh from James.

Yet a less experience, or a less opportunity of experience, would have warned a mind more observant that the bare desire for long posthumous renown is but a feeble princi-ple in common human nature. Bacon had as much of it as most men. The keen excitability to this world's tempta-tions must be opposed by more exciting impulses, by more retarding discouragements, by conscience, by religion, by fear. If you would vanquish earth, you must "invent heav-en." It is the fiction of a cold abstractedness that the possi-ble respect of unseen people can commonly be more de-sired than the certain homage of existing people.

In a more conspicuous manner the chill nature of the most brilliant among English historians is shown in his defec-tive dealing with the passionate eras of our history. He has never been attracted, or not proportionably attracted, by the singular mixture of heroism and slavishness, of high passion and base passion, which mark the Tudor period. The same defect is apparent in his treatment of a period on which he has written powerfully—the time of the civil wars. He has never in the highest manner appreciated ei-ther of the two great characters—the Puritan and the Cav-alier—which are the form and life of those years. What

historian, indeed, has ever estimated the Cavalier charac-ter? There is Clarendon—the grave, rhetorical, decorous lawyer—piling words, congealing arguments, very stately, a little grim. There is Hume—the Scotch metaphysician—who has made out the best case for such people as never were, for a Charles who never died, for a Strafford who would never have been attainted,—a saving, calculating north-countryman,—fat, impassive,—who lived on eight-pence a day. What have these people to do with an enjoy-ing English gentleman? It is easy for a *doctrinaire* to bear a *post-mortem* examination,—it is much the same whether he be alive or dead; but not so with those who live during their life, whose essence is existence, whose being is in ani-mation. There seem to be some characters who are not made for history, as there are some who are not made for old age. A Cavalier seems always young. The buoyant life arises before us rich in hope, strong in vigour, irregular in action; men young and ardent, framed in the "prodigality of nature," open to every enjoyment, alive to every pas-sion, eager, impulsive; brave without discipline, noble without principle, prizing luxury, despising danger, capa-ble of high sentiment, but in each of whom the

> Addiction was to courses vain;
> His companies unlettered, rude, and shallow,
> His hours filled up with riots, banquets, sports,
> And never noted in him any study,
> Any retirement, any sequestration
> From open haunts and popularity.

We see these men setting forth or assembling to defend their king and church; and we see it without surprise: a rich daring loves danger; a deep excitability likes excite-ment. If we look around us, we may see what is analogous. It has been said that the battle of the Alma was won by the "uneducated gentry;" the "uneducated gentry" would be Cavaliers now. The political sentiment is part of the character. The essence of Toryism is enjoyment. Talk of the ways of spreading a wholesome Conservatism throughout this country: give painful lectures, distribute weary tracts (and perhaps this is as well—you may be able to give an argumentative answer to a few objections, you may diffuse a distinct notion of the dignified dullness of politics); but as far as communicating and establishing your creed are concerned—try a little pleasure. The way to keep up old customs is, to enjoy old customs; the way to be satisfied with the present state of things is, to enjoy that state of things. Over the "Cavalier" mind this world passes with a thrill of delight; there is an exultation in a daily event, zest in the "regular thing," joy at an old feast. Sir Walter Scott is a curious instance of this. Every inci-dent, habit, practice of old Scotland was connected and in-separably associated in his mind with strong genial enjoy-ment. To propose to touch one of those institutions, to abolish one of those practices, was to touch a personal pleasure—a point on which his mind reposed, a thing of memory and hope. So long as this world is this world, will a buoyant life be the proper source of an animated Conser-vatism. The "church-and-king" enthusiasm has even a deeper connection with this peculiar character. Carlyle has said, in his vivid way, "Two or three young gentlemen have said, 'Go to, I will *make* a religion.'" This is the exact opposite of what the irregular enjoying man can think or conceive. What is he, with his untrained mind and his changeful heart and his ruleless practice, to create a creed? Is the gushing life to be asked to construct a cistern? is the varying heart to be its own master, the evil practice its own guide? Sooner will a ship invent its own rudder, devise its own pilot, than the buoyant eager soul will find out the doctrine which is to restrain it. The very intellect is a type of the confusion of the soul. It has little arguments on a thousand subjects, hearsay sayings, original flashes small and bright, struck from the heedless mind by the strong impact of the world. And it has nothing else. It has no systematic knowledge; it has a hatred of regular attention. What can an understanding of this sort do with refined questioning or subtle investigation? It is obliged in a sense by its very nature to take what comes; it is overshadowed in a manner by the religion to which it is born; its conscience tells it that it owes obedience to something; it craves to worship something; that something, in both cases, it takes from the past. "Thou hast not chosen me, but I have chosen thee," might his faith say to a believer of this kind. A certain bigotry is altogether natural to him. His creed seems to him a primitive fact, as certain and evident as the stars.—The political faith (for it is a faith) of these persons is of a kind analogous. The virtue of loyalty assumes in them a passionate aspect, and overflows, as it were, all the intellect which should be devoted to the topic. This virtue, this need of our nature, arises, as political philosophers tell us, from the conscious necessity which man is under of obeying an external moral rule. We feel that we are by nature and by the constitution of all things under an obligation to conform to a certain standard, and we seek to find or to establish in this outer sphere an authority which shall enforce it, shall aid us in compelling others and likewise in mastering ourselves. When a man thoroughly possessed with this principle comes in contact with the institution of civil government as it now exists and as it has always existed, he finds what he wants—he discovers an authority; and he feels bound to submit to it. We do not, of course, mean that all this takes place distinctly and consciously in the mind of the person; on the contrary, the class of minds most subject to its influence are precisely those which have in general the least defined and accurate consciousness of their own operations, or of what befals them. In matter of fact, they find themselves under the control of laws and of a polity from the earliest moment that they can remember, and they obey it from habit and custom years before they know any thing else. Only in later life, when distinct thought is from some outward occurrence forced upon them, do they feel the necessity of some such power; and in proportion to their passionate and impulsive disposition they feel it the more. It has in a less degree on them the same effect which military discipline has in a greater. It braces them to defined duties, and subjects them to a known authority. Quieter minds find this authority in an internal conscience; but in riotous natures its still small voice is lost if it be not echoed in loud harsh tones from the firm and outer world:

> Their breath is agitation, and their life
> A storm whereon they ride.

From without they crave a bridle and a curb. The doctrine of non-resistance is no *accident* of the Cavalier character,

though it seems at first sight singular in so eager, tumultuous a disposition. So inconsistent is human nature, that it proceeds from the very extremity of that tumult. They know and feel that they cannot allow themselves to question the authority which is upon them; they feel its necessity too acutely, their intellect is untrained in subtle disquisitions, their conscience fluctuating, their passions rising. They know that if once they depart from that authority, their whole soul will be in tumult. As a riotous state tends to fall under a martial tyranny, a passionate mind tends to subject itself to an extrinsic law—to enslave itself to an outward discipline. "That is what the king says, boy; and that was ever enough for Sir Henry Lee." An hereditary monarchy is, indeed, the very embodiment of this principle. The authority is so defined, so clearly vested, so evidently intelligible; it descends so distinctly from the past, it is imposed so conspicuously from without. Any thing free refers to the people; any thing elected seems self-chosen. "The divinity that doth hedge a king" consists in his evidently representing an unmade, unchosen, hereditary duty.

The greatness of this character is not in Mr. Macaulay's way, and its faults are. Its license affronts him; its riot alienates him. He is for ever contrasting the dissoluteness of Prince Rupert's horse with the restraint of Cromwell's pikemen. Its deep enjoying nature finds no sympathy. The brilliant style passes forward: we dwell on its brilliancy, but it is cold. He has no tears for that warm life, no tenderness for that extinct joy. The ignorance of the character, too, moves his wrath: "They were ignorant of what every schoolgirl knows." Their loyalty to their sovereign is the devotion of the Egyptians to the god Apis, who selected "a calf to adore." Their non-resistance offends the philosopher; their license is commented on with the tone of a precisian. Their indecorum does not suit the dignity of the historian. Their rich free nature is unappreciated; the tingling intensity of their joy is unnoticed. In a word, there is something of the schoolboy about the Cavalier—there is somewhat of a schoolmaster about the historian.

It might be thought, at first sight, that the insensibility and coldness which are unfavourable to the appreciation of the Cavalier would be particularly favourable to that of the Puritan. It might be thought that a natural aloofness from things earthly would dispose a man to the doctrines of a sect which enjoins above all other commandments abstinence and aloofness from those things. In Mr. Macaulay's case it certainly has had no such consequence. He was bred up in the circle which more than any other has resembled that of the greatest and best Puritans—in the circle which has presented the evangelical doctrine in its most celebrated, influential, and not its least genial form. Yet he has revolted against it. The bray of "Exeter Hall" is a phrase which has become celebrated: it is an odd one for his father's son. The whole course of his personal fortunes, the entire scope of his historical narrative, show an utter want of sympathy with the Puritan disposition. It would be idle to quote passages; it will be enough to recollect the contrast between the estimate—say of Cromwell—by Carlyle and that by Macaulay, to be aware of the enormous discrepancy. The one's manner evinces an instinctive sympathy, the other's an instinctive aversion.

We believe that this is but a consequence of the same impassibility of nature which we have said so much of. M. Montalembert, in a striking *éloge* on a French historian—a man of the Southey type—after speaking of his life in Paris during youth (a youth cast in the early and exciting years of the first revolution, and of the prelude to it), and graphically portraying a man subject to scepticism, but not given to vice; staid in habits, but unbelieving in opinion; without faith and without irregularity,—winds up the whole by the sentence, that *"he was hardened at once against good and evil."* In his view, the insensibility, which was a guard against exterior temptation, was also a hindrance to inward belief: and there is a philosophy in this. The nature of man is not two things, but one thing. We have not one set of affections, hopes, sensibilities, to be affected by the present world, and another and a different to be affected by the invisible world: we are moved by grandeur, or we are not; we are stirred by sublimity, or we are not; we hunger after righteousness, or we do not; we hate vice, or we do not; we are passionate, or not passionate; loving, or not loving; cold, or not cold; our heart is dull, or it is wakeful; our soul alive, or it is dead. Deep under the surface of the intellect lies the *stratum* of the passions, of the intense, peculiar, simple impulses which constitute the heart of man; there is the eager essence, the primitive desiring being. What stirs this latent being is another question. In general it is stirred by every thing. Sluggish natures are stirred little, wild natures are stirred much; but all are stirred somewhat. It is not important whether the object be in the visible or invisible world: whoso loves what he has seen, will love what he has not seen; whoso hates what he has seen, will hate what he has not seen. Creation is, as it were, but the garment of the Creator: whoever is blind to the beauty on its surface, will be insensible to the beauty beneath; whoso is dead to the sublimity before his senses, will be dull to that which he imagines; whoso is untouched by the visible man, will be unmoved by the invisible God. These are no new ideas; and the conspicuous evidence of history confirms them. Every where the deeply religious organisation has been deeply sensitive to this world. If we compare what are called sacred and profane literatures, the depth of human affection is deepest in the sacred. A warmth as of life is on the Hebrew, a chill as of marble is on the Greek. In that literature itself the most tenderly-religious character is the most sensitive to earth. Along every lyric of the great Psalmist thrills a deep spirit of human enjoyment; he was alive as a child to the simple aspects of the world; the very errors of his mingled career are but those to which the open, impulsive, warm-breathed character is most prone; its principle, so to speak, was a tremulous passion for that which he had seen, as well as that which he had not seen. It is no paradox, therefore, to say, that the same character which least appreciates the impulsive and ardent Cavalier is also the most likely not to appreciate the warm zeal of an overpowering devotion.

Some years ago it would have been necessary to show at length that the Puritans came at all near to this idea. The notion had been that they were fanatics, who simulated zeal, and hypocrites, who misquoted the Old Testament. A new era has arrived; one of the great discoveries which the competition of authors has introduced into historical researches has attained a singular popularity; the beam has gone into the opposite extreme. We are rather now, in general, in danger of holding too high an estimate of the puritanical character than a too low or contemptuous one. Among the disciples of Carlyle it is considered that having been a Puritan is the next best thing to having been in Germany. But though we cannot sympathise with every thing that the modern expounders of the new theory are prone to allege, and though we should not select for praise the exact peculiarities most agreeable to the slightly grim "gospel of earnestness," we are thoroughly aware of the great service which they have rendered to English history. No one will now ever overlook, that in the greater, in the original Puritans—in Cromwell, for example—the whole basis of the character was a passionate, deep, rich, religious organisation.

This is not in Mr. Macaulay's way. It is not that he is irreligious; far from it. "Divines of all persuasions," he tells us, "are agreed that there is a religion;" and he acquiesces in their teaching. But he has no passionate self-questionings, no indomitable fears, no asking perplexities. He is probably pleased at the exemption. He has praised Lord Bacon for a similar want of interest.

> Nor did he ever meddle with those enigmas which have puzzled hundreds of generations, and will puzzle hundreds more. He said nothing about the grounds of moral obligation, or the freedom of the human will. He had no inclination to employ himself in labours resembling those of the damned in the Grecian Tartarus— to spin for ever on the same wheel round the same pivot. He lived in an age in which disputes on the most subtle points of divinity excited an intense interest throughout Europe; and no where more than in England. He was placed in the very thick of the conflict. He was in power at the time of the Synod of Dort, and must for months have been daily deafened with talk about election, reprobation, and final perseverance. Yet we do not remember a line in his works from which it can be inferred that he was either a Calvinist or an Arminian. While the world was resounding with the noise of a disputatious philosophy and a disputatious theology, the Baconian school, like Alworthy seated between Square and Thwackum, preserved a calm neutrality,— half-scornful, half-benevolent,—and, content with adding to the sum of practical good, left the war of words to those who liked it.

This may be the writing of good sense, but it is not the expression of an anxious or passionate religious nature.

Such is the explanation of his not prizing so highly as he should prize the essential excellences of the Puritan character. He is defective in the one point in which they were very great; he is eminent in the very point in which they were most defective. A spirit of easy cheerfulness pervades his writings, a pleasant geniality overflows in history: the rigid asceticism, the pain for pain's sake of the Puritan is altogether alien to him. Retribution he would deny; sin is hardly a part of his creed. His religion is one of thanksgiving. His notion of philosophy—it would be a better notion of his own writing—is *illustrans commoda vitæ.*

The history of the English Revolution is the very history for a person of this character. It is eminently an unimpassioned movement. It requires no appreciation of the Cavalier or of the zealot; no sympathy with the romance of this world; no inclination to pass beyond, and absorb the mind's energies in another. It had neither the rough enthusiasm of barbarism nor the delicate grace of high civilisation; the men who conducted it had neither the deep spirit of Cromwell's Puritans nor the chivalric loyalty of the enjoying English gentleman. They were hardheaded sensible men, who knew that politics were a kind of business, that the essence of business is compromise, of practicality concession. They drove no theory to excess; for they had no theory. Their passions did not hurry them away; for their temperament was calm, and their reason calculating and still. Locke is the type of the best character of his era. There is nothing in him which a historian such as we have described could fail to comprehend, or could not sympathise with when he did comprehend. He was the very reverse of a Cavalier; he came of a Puritan stock; he retained through life a kind of chilled Puritanism: he had nothing of its excessive, overpowering, interior zeal, but he retained the formal decorum which it had given to the manners, the solid earnestness of its intellect, the heavy respectability of its character. In all the nations across which Puritanism has passed you may notice something of its indifference to this world's lighter enjoyments; no one of them has been quite able to retain its singular interest in what is beyond the veil of time and sense. The generation to which we owe our revolution was in the first stage of the descent. Locke thought a zealot a dangerous person, and a poet little better than a rascal. It has been said, with perhaps an allusion to Macaulay, that our historians have held that "all the people who lived before 1688 were either knaves or fools." This is, of course, an exaggeration; but those who have considered what sort of person a historian is likely to be, will not be surprised at his preference for the people of that era. They had the equable sense which he appreciates; they had not the deep animated passions to which his nature is insensible.

But though Mr. Macaulay shares in the common temperament of historians, and in the sympathy with, and appreciation of, the characters most congenial to that temperament, he is singularly contrasted with them in one respect—he has a vivid fancy, they have a dull one. History is generally written on the principle that human life is a transaction; that people come to it with defined intentions and a calm self-possessed air, as stockjobbers would buy "omnium," as timber-merchants buy "best middling;" people are alike, and things are alike; every thing is a little dull, every one a little slow; manners are not depicted, traits are not noticed; the narrative is confined to those great transactions which can be made intelligible without any imaginative delineation of their accompaniments. There are two kinds of things—those which you need only to *understand*, and those which you need also to *imagine*. That a man bought nine hundredweight of hops is an intelligible idea—you do not want the hops delineated or the man described; that he went into society suggests an inquiry—you want to know what the society was like, and how far he was fitted to be there. The great business-

transactions of the political world are of the intelligible description. Mr. Macaulay has himself said:

> A history, in which every particular incident may be true, may on the whole be false. The circumstances which have most influence on the happiness of mankind, the changes of manners and morals, the transition of communities from poverty to wealth, from knowledge to ignorance, from ferocity to humanity,—these are, for the most part, noiseless revolutions. Their progress is rarely indicated by what historians are pleased to call important events. They are not achieved by armies, or enacted by senates. They are sanctioned by no treaties, and recorded in no archives. They are carried on in every school, in every church, behind ten thousand counters, at ten thousand firesides. The upper current of society presents no certain criterion by which we can judge of the direction in which the under current flows. We read of defeats and victories; but we know that nations may be miserable amidst victories, and prosperous amidst defeats. We read of the fall of wise ministers, and of the rise of profligate favourites; but we must remember how small a proportion the good or evil effected by a single statesman can bear to the good or evil of a great social system.

But of this sluggishness of imagination he has certainly no trace himself. He is willing to be "behind ten thousand counters," to be a guest at "ten thousand firesides." He is willing to see "ordinary men as they appear in their ordinary business and in their ordinary pleasures." He has no objection to "mingle in the crowds of the Exchange and the coffee-house." He would "obtain admittance to the convivial table and the domestic hearth." So far as his dignity will permit, "he will bear with vulgar expressions." And a singular efficacy of fancy gives him the power to do so. Some portion of the essence of human nature is concealed from him; but all its accessories are at his command. He delineates any trait; he can paint, and justly paint, any manners he chooses.

"A perfect historian," he tells us,

> is he in whose work the character and spirit of an age is exhibited in miniature. He relates no fact, he attributes no expression to his characters, which is not authenticated by sufficient testimony; but by judicious selection, rejection, and arrangement, he gives to truth those attractions which have been usurped by fiction. In his narrative a due subordination is observed—some transactions are prominent, others retire; but the scale on which he represents them is increased or diminished, not according to the dignity of the persons concerned in them, but according to the degree in which they elucidate the condition of society and the nature of man. He shows us the court, the camp, and the senate; but he shows us also the nation. He considers no anecdote, no peculiarity of manner, no familiar saying, as too insignificant for his notice, which is not too insignificant to illustrate the operation of laws, of religion, and of education, and to mark the progress of the human mind. Men will not merely be described, but will be made intimately

known to us. The changes of manners will be indicated, not merely by a few general phrases, or a few extracts from statistical documents, but by appropriate images presented in every line. If a man, such as we are supposing, should write the history of England, he would assuredly not omit the battles, the sieges, the negotiations, the seditions, the ministerial changes; but with these he would intersperse the details which are the charm of historical romances. At Lincoln Cathedral there is a beautiful painted window, which was made by an apprentice out of the pieces of glass which had been rejected by his master. It is so far superior to every other in the church, that, according to the tradition, the vanquished artist killed himself from mortification. Sir Walter Scott, in the same manner, has used those fragments of truth which historians have scornfully thrown behind them in a manner which may well excite their envy. He has constructed out of their gleanings works which, even considered as histories, are scarcely less valuable than theirs. But a truly great historian would reclaim those materials which the novelist has appropriated. The history of the government, and the history of the people, would be exhibited in that mode in which alone they can be exhibited justly, in inseparable conjunction and intermixture. We should not then have to look for the wars and votes of the puritans in Clarendon, and for their phraseology in *Old Mortality;* for one half of King James in Hume, and for the other half in the *Fortunes of Nigel.*

So far as the graphic description of the exterior mode of life goes, he has undeniably realised his idea.

This union of a flowing fancy with an insensible organisation is very rare. In general a delicate fancy is joined with a poetic organisation. Exactly why, it would be difficult to explain. It is for metaphysicians in large volumes to explain the genesis of the human faculties; but, as a fact, it seems to be clear that, for the most part, imaginative men are most sensitive to the poetic side of human life and natural scenery. They are drawn by a strong instinct to what is sublime, grand, and beautiful. They do not care for the coarse business of life. They dislike to be cursed with its ordinary cares. Their nature is vivid; it is interested by all which naturally interests; it dwells on the great, the graceful, and the grand. On this account it naturally runs away from history. The very name of it is too oppressive. Are not all such works written in the *Index Expurgatorius* of the genial satirist as works which it was impossible to read? The coarse and cumbrous matter revolts the soul of the fine and fanciful voluptuary. Take it as you will, human life is like the earth on which man dwells. There are exquisite beauties, grand imposing objects, scattered here and there; but the spaces between these are wide; the mass of common clay is huge; the dead level of vacant life, of commonplace geography, is immense. The poetic nature cannot bear the preponderance; it seeks relief in selected scenes, in special topics, in favourite beauties. History, which is the record of human existence, is a faithful representative of it, at least in this: the poetic mind cannot bear the weight of its narrations and the dullness of its events.

This peculiarity of character gives to Mr. Macaulay's writing one of its most curious characteristics. He throws over matters which are in their nature dry and dull transactions,—budgets, bills,—the charm of fancy which a poetical mind employs to enhance and set forth the charm of what is beautiful. An attractive style is generally devoted to what is in itself specially attractive; here it is devoted to subjects which are often unattractive, are sometimes even repelling, at the best are commonly neutral, not inviting attention if they do not excite dislike. In these new volumes there is a currency-reform, pages on Scotch Presbyterianism, a heap of parliamentary debates. Who could be expected to make any thing interesting of such topics? It is not cheerful to read in the morning papers the debates of yesterday, though they happened last night; one cannot like a Calvinistic divine when we see him in the pulpit; it is awful to read on the currency even when it concerns the bank-notes which we use. How, then, can we care for a narrative when the divine is dead, the shillings extinct, the whole topic of the debate forgotten and past away? Yet such is the charm of style, so great is the charm of very skilful words, of narration which is always passing forward, of illustration which always hits the mark, that such subjects as these not only become interesting, but very interesting. The proof is evident. No book is so sought after. The Chancellor of the Exchequer said "all members of parliament had read it." What other books could ever be fancied to have been read by them? A county member—a real county member—hardly reads two volumes *per* existence. Years ago Macaulay said a History of England might become more in demand at the circulating-libraries than the last novel. He has actually made his words true. It is no longer a phrase of rhetoric, it is a simple fact.

The explanation of this remarkable notoriety is, the contrast of the topic, and the treatment. Those who read for the sake of entertainment are attracted by the one; those who read for the sake of instruction are attracted by the other. He has something that suits the readers of Mr. Hallam; he has something which will please the readers of Mr. Thackeray. The first wonder to find themselves reading such a style; the last are astonished at reading on such topics—at finding themselves studying by casualty: only a buoyant fancy and an impassive temperament could produce a book so combining weight with levity. (pp. 359-75)

[Macaulay's] peculiarities of character and mind may be very conspicuously traced through the **History of England,** and in the **Essays.** Their first and most striking quality is the *intellectual entertainment* which they afford. This, as practical readers know, is a kind of sensation which is not very common, and which is productive of great and healthy enjoyment. It is quite distinct from the amusement which is derived from common light works. This is very great; but it is passive. The mind of the reader is not awakened to any independent action: you see the farce, but you see it without effort; not simply without painful effort, but without any perceptible mental activity whatever. Again, it is contrasted with the high enjoyment of consciously following pure and difficult reasoning: this sensation is a sort of sublimated pain. The highest and most intense action of the intellectual powers is, like the most intense action of the bodily, on a high mountain. We climb and climb: we have a thrill of pleasure, but we have also a sense of effort and anguish. Nor is the sensation to be confounded with that which we experience from the best and purest works of art. The pleasure of high tragedy is also painful: the whole soul is stretched; the spirit pants; the passions scarcely breathe: it is a rapt and eager moment, too intense for continuance—so overpowering, that we scarcely know whether it be joy or pain. The sensation of intellectual entertainment is altogether distinguished from these by not being accompanied by any pain, and yet being consequent on, or being contemporaneous with, a high and constant exercise of mind. While we read works which so delight us, we are conscious that we are delighted, and are also conscious that we are not idle. The two opposite pleasures of indolence and exertion seem for a moment combined. A sort of elasticity pervades us; thoughts come easily and quickly; we seem capable of many ideas; we follow cleverness till we fancy that we are clever. This feeling is only given by writers who stimulate the mind just to the degree which is pleasant, and who do not stimulate it more; who exact a moderate exercise of mind, and who seduce us to it insensibly. This can only be, of course, by a charm of style; by the inexplicable *je ne sais quoi* which attracts our attention; by constantly raising and constantly satisfying our curiosity. And there seems to be a further condition. A writer who wishes to produce this constant effect must not appeal to any single separate faculty of mind, but to the whole mind at once. The fancy tires, if you appeal only to the fancy; the understanding is aware of its dullness, if you appeal only to the understanding; the curiosity is soon satiated unless you pique it with variety. This is the very opportunity for Macaulay. He has fancy, sense, variety, abundance; he appeals to both fancy and understanding. There is no sense of effort. His books read like an elastic dream. There is a continual sense of instruction; for who had an idea of the transactions before? The emotions, too, which he appeals to are the easy admiration, the cool disapprobation, the gentle worldly curiosity, which quietly excite us, never fatigue us,—which we could bear for ever. To read Macaulay for a day, would be to pass a day of easy thought, of pleasant placid emotion.

Nor is this a small matter. In a state of high civilisation it is no simple matter to give multitudes a large and healthy enjoyment. The old bodily enjoyments are dying out; there is no room for them any more; the complex apparatus of civilisation cumbers the ground. We are thrown back upon the mind, and the mind is a barren thing. It can spin little from itself: few that describe what they see are in the way to discern much. Exaggerated emotions, violent incidents, monstrous characters crowd our canvas; they are the resource of a weakness which would obtain the fame of strength. Reading is about to become a series of collisions against aggravated breakers, of beatings with imaginary surf. In such times a book of sensible attraction is a public benefit; it diffuses a sensation of vigour through the multitude. Perhaps there is a danger that the extreme popularity of the manner may make many persons fancy they understand the matter more perfectly than they do: some readers may become conceited; several boys believe that they too are Macaulays. Yet, duly allowing for this defect, it is a great good that so many people should learn

so much on such topics so agreeably; that they should feel that they can understand them; that their minds should be stimulated by a consciousness of health and power. (pp. 380-81)

[The style of Macaulay] is a diorama of political pictures. You seem to begin with a brilliant picture,—its colours are distinct, its lines are firm; on a sudden it changes, at first gradually, you can scarcely tell how or in what, but truly and unmistakably,—a slightly different picture is before you; then the second vision seems to change,—it too is another and yet the same; then the third shines forth and fades; and so without end. The unity of this delineation is the identity—the apparent identity—of the picture; on no two moments does it seem quite different, on no two is it identically the same. It grows and alters as our bodies would appear to alter and grow, if you could fancy any one watching them, and being conscious of their daily little changes; the events are picturesque variations; the unity is a unity of political painting, of represented external form. It is evident how suitable this is to a writer whose understanding is solid, whose sense is political, whose fancy is fine and delineative.

To this merit of Macaulay is to be added another. No one describes so well what we may call the *spectacle* of a character. The art of delineating character by protracted description is one which grows in spite of the critics. In vain is it alleged that the character should be shown dramatically; that it should be illustrated by events; that it should be exhibited in its actions. The truth is, that these homilies are excellent, but incomplete; true, but out of season. There is a utility in unseen portrait, as Lord Stanhope says there is in painted. Goethe used to observe, that in society, in a *tête-à-tête* rather, you often thought of your companion as if he was his portrait: you were silent; you did not care what he said; but you considered him as a picture, as a whole, especially as regards yourself and your relations towards him. You require something of the same kind in literature: *some* description of a man is clearly necessary as an introduction to the story of his life and actions. But more than this is wanted; you require to have the object placed before you as a whole, to have the characteristic traits mentioned, the delicate qualities drawn out, the firm features gently depicted. As the practice which Goethe hints at is, of all others, the most favourable to a just and calm judgment of character, so the literary substitute seems required as a steadying element, as a summary, to bring together and give a unity to our views. We must see the man's face. Without it, we seem to have heard a great deal about the person, but not to have known him; to be aware that he had done a good deal, but to have no settled, inbred, ineradicable notion what manner of man he was who did them. This is the reason why critics like Macaulay, who sneer at the practice when estimating the works of others, yet practise it at great length and with great skill when they come to be historians themselves. The kind of characters whom Macaulay can describe is limited—at least we think so—by the bounds which we indicated just now. There are some men whom he is too impassive to comprehend; but he can always tells us of such as he does comprehend, what they looked like, and what they were.

A great deal of this vividness Macaulay of course owes to his style. Of its effectiveness there can be no doubt; its agreeability no one who has just been reading it is likely to deny. Yet it has a defect. It is not, as Bishop Butler would have expressed it, such a style as "is suitable to such a being as man, in such a world as the present one." It is too omniscient. Every thing is too plain. All is clear; nothing is doubtful. Instead of probability being, as the great thinker expressed it, "the very guide of life," it has become a rare exception—an uncommon phenomenon. You rarely come across any thing which is not decided; and when you do come across it, you seem to wonder that the positiveness, which has accomplished so much, should have been unwilling to decide any thing. This is hardly the style for history. The data of historical narratives, especially of modern histories, are a heap of confusion. No one can tell where they lie, or where they do not lie; what is in them, or what is not in them. Literature is called the "fragment of fragments;" so little has been written, and so little of that little has been preserved. So is history a vestige of vestiges; few facts leave any trace of themselves, any witness of their occurrence; of fewer still is that witness preserved; a slight track is all any thing leaves, and the confusion of life, the tumult of change sweeps even that away in a moment. It is not possible that these data can be very fertile in certainties. Few people would make any thing of them: a memoir here, a Ms. there—two letters in a magazine—an assertion by a person whose veracity is denied,—these are the sort of evidence out of which a flowing narrative is to be educed—of course, it ought not to be too flowing. "If you please, sir, to tell me what you do *not* know," was the inquiry of a humble pupil addressed to a great man of science. It would have been a relief to the readers of Macaulay if he had shown a little the outside of uncertainties, which there must be—the gradations of doubt, which there ought to be—the singular accumulation of difficulties, which must beset the extraction of a very easy narrative from very confused materials.

This defect in style is, indeed, indicative of a defect in understanding. Mr. Macaulay's mind is eminently gifted, but there is a want of graduation in it. He has a fine eye for probabilities, a clear perception of evidence, a shrewd guess at missing links of fact; but each probability seems to him a certainty, each piece of evidence conclusive, each analogy exact. The heavy Scotch intellect is a little prone to this: one figures it as a heap of formulæ, and if fact *b* is reducible to formula B, that is all which it regards; the mathematical mill grinds with equal energy at flour perfect and imperfect—at matter which is quite certain, and at matter which is only a little probable. But the great cause of this error is, an abstinence from practical action. Life is a school of probability. In the writings of every man of patient practicality, in the midst of whatever other defects, you will find a careful appreciation of the degrees of likelihood; a steady balancing of them one against another; a disinclination to make things too clear, to overlook the debit side of the account in mere contemplation of the enormousness of the credit. The reason is obvious: action is a business of risk; the real question is the magnitude of that risk. Failure is ever impending; success is ever uncertain; there is always, in the very best affairs, a slight probability of the first, a contingent possibility of the non-

occurrence of the second. For practical men, the problem ever is to test the amount of these inevitable probabilities; to make sure that no one increases too far; that by a well-varied choice the number of risks may in itself be a protection—be an insurance to you, as it were, against the capricious result of any one. A man like Macaulay, who stands aloof from life, is not so instructed; he sits secure: nothing happens in his study; he does not care to test probabilities; he loses the detective sensation.

Mr. Macaulay's so-called inaccuracy is likewise a phase of this defect. Considering the enormous advantages which a picturesque style gives to ill-disposed critics; the number of points of investigation which it suggests; the number of assertions it makes, sentence by sentence; the number of ill-disposed critics that there are in the world; considering Mr. Macaulay's position,—set on a hill to be spied at by them,—he can scarcely be thought an inaccurate historian. Considering all things, they have found few certain blunders, hardly any direct mistakes. Every sentence of his style requires minute knowledge; the vivid picture has a hundred details; each of those details must have an evidence, an authority, a proof. A historian like Hume passes easily over a period; his chart is large; if he gets the conspicuous headlands, the large harbours, duly marked, he does not care. Macaulay puts in the depth of each wave, every remarkable rock, every tree on the shore. Nothing gives a critic so great an advantage. It is difficult to do this for a volume; simple for a page. It is easy to select a particular event, and learn all which any one can know about it; examine Macaulay's descriptions, say he is wrong, that X is not buried where he asserts, that a little boy was one year older than he states. But how would the critic manage, if he had to work out all this for a million facts, for a whole period? Few men, we suspect, would be able to make so few errors of simple and provable fact. On the other hand, few men would arouse a sleepy critic by such startling assertion. If he finds a new theory, he states it as a fact. Very likely it really is the most probable theory; at any rate, we know of no case in which his theory is not one among the most plausible. If it had only been so stated, it would have been well received. His view of Marlborough's character, for instance, is a specious one; it has a good deal of evidence, a large amount of real probability, but it has scarcely more. Marlborough *may* have been as bad as is said, but we can hardly be *sure* of it at this time.

Macaulay's "party-spirit" is another consequence of his positiveness. When he inclines to a side, he inclines to it too much. His opinions are a shade too strong; his predilections some degrees at least too warm. William is too perfect, James too imperfect. The Whigs are a trifle like angels; the Tories like, let us say, "our inferiors." Yet this is evidently an honest party-spirit. It does not lurk in the corners of sentences, it is not insinuated without being alleged; it does not, like the unfairness of Hume, secrete itself so subtly in the turns of the words, that when you turn to prove it, it is gone. On the contrary, it rushes into broad day. William is loaded with panegyric; James is always spoken evil of. Hume's is the artful pleading of a hired advocate; Macaulay's the bold eulogy of a sincere friend. As far as effect goes, this is wrong. The very earnestness of the affection leads to a reaction; we are tired of having William called the "just;" we cannot believe so many pages; "all that" can scarcely be correct. As we said before, if the historian's preference for persons and party had been duly tempered and mitigated, if the probably good were only said to be probably good, if the rather bad were only alleged to be rather bad, the reader would have been convinced, and the historian escaped the savage censure of envious critics.

The one thing which detracts from the pleasure of reading these volumes, is the doubt whether they should have been written. Should not these great powers be reserved for great periods? Is this abounding, picturesque style, suited for continuous history? Are small men to be so largely described? Should not admirable delineation be kept for admirable people? We think so. You do not want Raphael to paint sign-posts, or Palladio to build dirt-pies. Much of history is necessarily of little value,—the superficies of circumstance, the scum of events. It is very well to have it described, indeed you must have it described; the chain must be kept complete; the narrative of a country's fortunes will not allow of breaks or gaps. Yet all things need not be done equally well. The life of a great painter is short. Even the industry of Macaulay will not complete this history. It is a pity to spend such powers on such events. It would have been better to have some new volumes of essays solely on great men and great things. The diffuseness of the style would have been then in place; we could have borne to hear the smallest minutiæ of magnificent epochs. If an inferior hand had executed the connecting-links, our notions would have acquired an insensible perspective; the best works of the great artist, the best themes, would have stood out from the canvas. They are now confused by the equal brilliancy of the adjacent inferiorities.

Much more might be said on this narrative. As it will be read for very many years, it will employ the critics for many years. It would be unkind to make all the best observations. Something, as Mr. Disraeli said in a budget-speech, something should be left for "future statements of this nature." There will be an opportunity. Whatsoever those who come after may find to say against this book, it will be, and remain, the "Pictorial History of England." (pp. 382-87)

Walter Bagehot, "Mr. Macaulay," in The National Review, *London, Vol. II, No. IV, April, 1856, pp. 357-87.*

William Makepeace Thackeray   (essay date 1860)

[*One of the most important English novelists of the nineteenth century, Thackeray is best known for* Vanity Fair: A Novel without a Hero *(1847-48), a satiric look at upper-class life. In the following excerpt, he praises not only Macaulay's memory and erudition, but also his great heart and passion for literature.*]

[With] regard to Macaulay's style there may be faults of course—what critic can't point them out? But for the nonce we are not talking about faults: we want to say *nil nisi bonum*. Well—take at hazard any three pages of the **Essays** or **History;**—and, glimmering below the stream of the narrative, as it were, you, an average reader, see one, two, three, a half-score of allusions to other historic facts, characters, literature, poetry, with which you are acquainted. Why is this epithet used? Whence is that simile drawn? How does he manage, in two or three words, to paint an individual, or to indicate a landscape? Your neighbour, who has *his* reading, and his little stock of literature stowed away in his mind, shall detect more points, allusions, happy touches, indicating not only the prodigious memory and vast learning of this master, but the wonderful industry, the honest, humble previous toil of this great scholar. He reads twenty books to write a sentence; he travels a hundred miles to make a line of description.

Many Londoners—not all—have seen the British Museum Library. I speak *à cœur ouvert,* and pray the kindly reader to bear with me. I have seen all sorts of domes of Peters and Pauls, Sophia, Pantheon,—what not?—and have been struck by none of them so much as by that catholic dome in Bloomsbury, under which our million volumes are housed. What peace, what love, what truth, what beauty, what happiness for all, what generous kindness for you and me, are here spread out! It seems to me one cannot sit down in that place without a heart full of grateful reverence. I own to have said my grace at the table, and to have thanked heaven for this my English birthright, freely to partake of these bountiful books, and to speak the truth I find there. Under the dome which held Macaulay's brain, and from which his solemn eyes looked out on the world but a fortnight since, what a vast, brilliant, and wonderful store of learning was ranged! what strange lore would he not fetch for you at your bidding! A volume of law, or history, a book of poetry familiar or forgotten (except by himself who forgot nothing), a novel ever so old, and he had it at hand. I spoke to him once about *Clarissa.* "Not read *Clarissa!*" he cried out. "If you have once thoroughly entered on *Clarissa,* and are infected by it, you can't leave it. When I was in India, I passed one hot season at the hills, and there were the governor-general, and the secretary of government, and the commander-in chief, and their wives. I had *Clarissa* with me: and, as soon as they began to read, the whole station was in a passion of excitement about Miss Harlowe and her misfortunes, and her scoundrelly Lovelace! The governor's wife seized the book, and the secretary waited for it, and the chief justice could not read it for tears!" He acted the whole scene: he paced up and down the Athenæum library: I daresay he could have spoken pages of the book—of that book, and of what countless piles of others!

In this little [essay] let us keep to the text of *nil nisi bonum.* One paper I have read regarding Lord Macaulay says "he had no heart." Why, a man's books may not always speak the truth, but they speak his mind in spite of himself: and it seems to me this man's heart is beating through every page he penned. He is always in a storm of revolt and indignation against wrong, craft, tyranny. How he cheers heroic resistance; how he backs and applauds freedom struggling for its own; how he hates scoundrels, ever so victorious and successful; how he recognizes genius, though selfish villains possess it! The critic who says Macaulay had no heart, might say that Johnson had none:

and two men more generous, and more loving, and more hating, and more partial, and more noble, do not live in our history.

The writer who said that Lord Macaulay had no heart could not know him. Press writers should read a man well, and all over, and again; and hesitate, at least, before they speak of those αιδοια. Those who knew Lord Macaulay knew how admirably tender, and generous, and affectionate he was. It was not his business to bring his family before the theatre footlights, and call for bouquets from the gallery as he wept over them. (pp. 133-34)

> *William Makepeace Thackeray, "Nil Nisi Bonum," in* The Cornhill Magazine, *Vol. I, No. 2, February, 1860, pp. 129-34.*

An excerpt from *The History of England*

In every experimental science there is a tendency toward perfection. In every human being there is a wish to ameliorate his own condition. These two principles have often sufficed, even when counteracted by great public calamities and by bad institutions, to carry civilization rapidly forward. No ordinary misfortune, no ordinary misgovernment, will do so much to make a nation wretched, as the constant progress of physical knowledge and the constant effort of every man to better himself will do to make a nation prosperous. It has often been found that profuse expenditure, heavy taxation, absurd commercial restrictions, corrupt tribunals, disastrous wars, seditions, persecutions, conflagrations, inundations, have not been able to destroy capital so fast as the exertions of private citizens have been able to create it. It can easily be proved that, in our own land, the national wealth has, during at least six centuries, been almost uninterruptedly increasing; that it was greater under the Tudors than under the Plantagenets; that it was greater under the Stuarts than under the Tudors; that, in spite of battles, sieges, and confiscations, it was greater on the day of the Restoration than on the day when the Long Parliament met; that, in spite of maladministration, of extravagance, of public bankruptcy, of two costly and unsuccessful wars, of the pestilence and of the fire, it was greater on the day of the death of Charles the Second than on the day of his Restoration. This progress, having continued during many ages, became at length, about the middle of the eighteenth century, portentously rapid, and has proceeded, during the nineteenth, with accelerated velocity.

> *Thomas Babington Macaulay, in his* History of England from the Accession of James II, *Longmans, 1848.*

Walter Waddington Shirley (essay date 1860)

[*Shirley was regius professor of ecclesiastical history at Oxford and editor of several volumes of the historical Rolls Series. In the following excerpt, he notes Macaulay's organizational skill and the honesty with which he defended his Whig views, but finds him lacking in creativity and flexibility.*]

It is too late and too soon to speak further of Lord Macaulay. The verdict of his contemporaries has been recorded; the verdict of posterity cannot be anticipated. Before the grave in the Abbey had been closed, a hundred rapid and brilliant pens had said almost all that could be said of the great man who had ceased from his labours. The brilliancy of our periodical literature is as marvellous as its rapidity. Leading articles which would have brought fortune and permanent fame to Addison or Steele appear every morning in the columns of the *Times,* and are forgotten before the second edition is published. That the sentence pronounced upon our great men by those organs of public opinion should be more brilliant than accurate, more antithetical than sound, is of course to be looked for. A man penning an article at midnight which is to be read in Paris on the following afternoon, has no time for nice discrimination or minute analysis. He selects the striking peculiarities of a character, the salient points of a career, and on these he bases an estimate which, though impressive and picturesque, is necessarily exaggerated.

Notwithstanding the conviction we have expressed, a few 'last words' may, without impropriety, be now added. Two bulky volumes of **Miscellaneous Writings** have been recently published, and some of the contents—one piece in particular—place Lord Macaulay's character in what the public may justly consider a new light.

I should not speak honestly, or to the best of my belief, if I said that Macaulay belonged to the very highest order of minds. I do not think that he did. In no department except the historical did he show pre-eminent capacity, and even his **History** is open to the charge of being only a splendid and ornate panorama. His was not a creative intellect—it could not have fashioned a *Midsummer's Night's Dream,* a *Faust,* or *The Cenci.* He wrote spirited lyrics in which the traditions and associations of a historic people are handled with consummate judgment; but we miss the spontaneous and unsystematic music, the inartificial and childlike grace of the true ballad. The lyrist is the creature of impulse, and Macaulay was never impulsive. Lofty, unimpassioned, self-restrained, he never confesses to any of the frailties of genius. He had great natural powers, no doubt; his memory was prodigious and exact; his understanding just and masculine; still, it seems to me that he was in everything indebted more to art than to nature. He is the highest product of a profound and exquisite culture. This of course detracts from the quality of his handiwork. Only the work of authentic genius is imperishable. The work of the artificer, however elaborate, however curiously finished, does not survive. But Macaulay unquestionably *had* genius of a kind: the genius which moulds the results of immense industry into a coherent and consistent whole. This is a fine and a most rare gift; and we are not wrong when we assert that its owner must always be (even when not of the highest order) a man of genius. Associated with the somewhat artificial constitution of his powers, is the want of flexibility which he shows. There is no great virtue in the agility of the jester or the suppleness of the mimic; but Macaulay wanted that natural lightness and *airiness* of touch which characterizes the working of a thoroughly creative mind. He assailed pigmies with eighty pounders. His heavy metal did its work well; but it smashed right and left, the small as well as the great, without comparison or a nice discrimination. He is one of the greatest masters of the English tongue. The ordered march of his lordly prose, to use once more a worn-out simile, is stately as a Roman legion's. Still it is ponderous, compared at least with the unaffected freedom and the flexible life of Shakespeare's, or Fielding's, or Charles Lamb's. But the art with which this defect is concealed is, like every other detail in Lord Macaulay's art, perfect in its way. The style is ponderous, but there is no monotony. Short sentences, which, like the fire of sharpshooters through cannon, break the volume of sound, are introduced at stated intervals into each paragraph. A Martial or Junius-like epigram follows the imposing burst of eloquence with which Burke or Brougham might have clenched a great harangue. There is no slovenliness in these finished pages. But to make the severe and jealous supervision too obvious might break the spell. So any avowal of the labour that has been expended is studiously avoided. An air of negligence is at times affected. Colloquial expressions are introduced. The immense industry is covertly disowned.

Lord Macaulay's elaborate polish has proved, we think, exceedingly valuable to our rapid, perplexed, and somewhat incoherent age. Too many of our ablest men are apt to speak and think in heroics. Their likings and dislikings are equally violent and equally valueless. That there is something fascinating in the passionate theology and philosophy of the age, we all admit. The fanatic in politics and religion makes many converts; toleration is a plant of a slow, laborious, and difficult growth. Lord Macaulay was no fanatic. He was neither a moral nor an intellectual bigot. A rhetorician by temperament, he was saved from the sins of the rhetoricians by his vigorous manliness, his justice of judgment, and his admirable sense. It cannot be said that his speculations on any topic were very profound; but, as far as they went, they were clear, accurate, above all luminous. His logic, if not exhaustive, was exact and incisive. He seldom undertook any argument which he had not mastered. He never indeed quite rose to the height of the great argument of Puritanism; but, accepting the limited data with which he started, his conclusions were irresistible. There were spiritual capacities and mental needs in the heroes of the Commonwealth which provoked them into action, and which made them what they were to England. These Macaulay never comprehended; his plummet could not fathom them; they lay beyond the reach of his even temper and unimpassioned intellect. His critical creed was marked by the same narrowness. He considered Samuel Rogers a greater singer than Samuel Coleridge. He relished the exquisite refinement of the *Italy,* and he respected a writer who was at once a finished gentleman and a fastidious poet. The uncouthness, the slovenliness, the eccentricities, the want of taste and judgment of the Windermere brethren, were sins that he could not tolerate. Nay, perhaps he was altogether incapable of understanding the vague and fitful feelings which they tried to render, and which give a peculiar charm to the muse of Shelley and Tennyson. He insisted that whatever was said should be said clearly—should be written in words which men could read as they ran:

> This song was made to be sung at night,
> And he who reads it in broad daylight
> Will never read its mystery right,

And yet—it is childlike easy.

'Nonsense,' he in effect replied; 'if there is anything whatever to be read, it will read much better in the daylight than in the dark.' Such a creed, of course, can only be held by one who is destitute of the supremest elements of the poetic faculty—by a critic who has never been pursued by the haunting forms that people the twilight of the imagination. Thus he seldom reached entire historical truth or entire critical truth. It is a thousand pities that he did not write a history of the reign of Queen Anne. Both the poets and the politicians of that age (with one superb and sombre exception) were men whom he could thoroughly gauge. His picture of that brilliant group of versatile, accomplished, witty, corrupt, and splendid gentlemen, would have sparkled like the life which it represented. He would have described with inimitable effect statesmen who were wits and poets, and poets who were wits and statesmen. But his hand faltered when he had to register grander passions and darker conflicts. The spiritual pains, the stormy struggles which tore England asunder in the seventeenth century, were put aside by him with disrelish. The men who embodied and represented this mental strife in the nation—these disorganized aspirations after a Divine kingdom and governor—were treated with coldness and disrespect. The strongest, richest, most unconventional, most complicated characters become comparatively commonplace when he touches them. The virtue is taken out of them. Even the men he most admires are reduced to the most ordinary types. The historical Whig—steady, sagacious, moderate, never unselfishly imprudent, never honestly intemperate—is his ideal of human nature. A very good one in its way; though one sometimes fancies that the reckless and blundering devotion of these simple country gentlemen and yeomen to the falsest of kings is more generous, and perhaps even more heroic. (pp. 438-41)

It was an immense advantage to have at the head of our literature a man who thought calmly, who spoke moderately, who wrote fastidiously, whose enthusiasm was never intemperate, whose judgment was never excited. This great potentate in letters opposed to the license of speculation and the riot of the imagination, a simple theory of morals, a simple system of politics, and a simple code of criticism. Many new men and things he did not recognise that were both good and true; that he did not recognise them arose possibly from some mental defect; but this very narrowness of intellectual sympathy enabled him effectively to stem the current. Men who are perplexed by the controversy of subtle motives and complicated passions seldom think with clearness or act with decision. And this simplicity of mental insight in Macaulay must not be confounded with intellectual rigidness or the barrenness of theory. It was a simplicity more historical than logical. A Frenchman similarly gifted would have arrived at universal suffrage and electoral districts; but Macaulay, with his historic culture and his English associations, could not become a political dogmatist. So instead of driving him into democracy or absolutism, it made him, on the contrary, regard with hearty admiration the rough adjustments, the intricate compromises, the balanced inconsistencies, which are so unmeaning to the strictly scientific intellect, but on which old and historic societies *must* rest.

Lord Macaulay was thus, alike by inheritance and temperament, a Whig. As such, in the cant of the day, he may be considered a 'representative man.' Whiggery has had no more characteristic, no more illustrious interpreter. Had he been endowed with wider aspirations or broader sympathies, he would not have represented his party so faithfully as he did. Tory and Radical politicians are frequently men of fervid imagination. They require to be so. The Conservative, who invests the constitution with a halo of mysterious sanctity, borrows the colours from his imagination; the Radical who sighs for an ideal republic,—the Milton who dreams of a perfectly ordered commonweal, whose king is God,—exerts the constructive powers of the imagination, no less than religious or philosophical enthusiasm. But the Whig is thoroughly practical. He is satisfied with things as they are: having no blind attachments, however, he does not object to reforms, especially if they effect no change. But he does not expect much from them—as he does not venerate the venerableness of the Constitution, so neither does he hail the approach of the *civitas Dei.* A temperate respect is about the warmest political emotion of which he is capable. Even his prejudices are not immoderate. Lord Macaulay was a great man, but he was a Whig great man. The subtleties of the imagination did not perplex him, nor did the contradictions of the moral life. Wordsworth's description of a creature 'moving about in worlds not realized,' would have been singularly inapplicable to that compact, serene, and luminous mind. It was not agitated by 'the obstinate questionings of sense and outward things' which have troubled the sagest men; nor by those high instincts

> before which our mortal nature
> Doth tremble like a guilty thing surprised.

None of these dim and perilous tracks of the spirit were trodden by Lord Macaulay.

That Lord Macaulay's just and well-balanced intelligence did good service to us, we have admitted; but that it is sufficient for the Whig to continue to be what Lord Macaulay was, or that he can contrive to do good service of any kind by a servile imitation of his model, we do not admit. The present condition of the Whigs shows on the contrary that a party which appropriates none of the elements of the current life and thought must perish. The Whig in 1860 is intellectually, if not politically, dead. A party whose notions of National Reformation are exhausted by a six-pound franchise, betrays a poverty of thought that cannot be tolerated even in our governors. On Lord Macaulay himself the traditions of his party exercised a questionable influence. In his *History,* English political life becomes an affair of the Senate rather than of the people. We lose sight of the nation in the constitution. Those slowly-matured national convictions which alone work out great constitutional changes are disregarded, or at least are made to play a less important part in the development of society than a wordy debate in the Commons, or a conflict between the two Houses on a question of privilege.

It has been said that Lord Macaulay wanted 'heart.' A certain coldness of manner and temperament undoubtedly

characterized him. He had the reserve of the English gentleman—which, be it remembered, represents the self-respect and restraint as well as the shyness of the islander. Of his private life (though those best qualified to judge speak very warmly of unaffected kindness and wide charities) I cannot speak; and of his writings it is enough to say, that whenever right or truth is menaced his vindication glows with manly fervour. . . . (pp. 441-42)

> *Walter Waddington Shirley, "A 'Last Word'*
> *on Lord Macaulay," in* Fraser's Magazine for
> Town & Country, *Vol. LXII, October, 1860,*
> *pp. 438-46.*

Leslie Stephen   (essay date 1876)

[*Stephen is considered by many scholars the most important literary critic of the Victorian era after Matthew Arnold. In the following excerpt, he states that in spite of Macaulay's lack of a speculative intellect, his vigor and his ability to compress his great learning into clear language and vivid images make him one of England's greatest historians.*]

[Macaulay's] intellectual force was extraordinary within certain limits; beyond those limits the giant became a child. He assimilated a certain set of ideas as a lad, and never acquired a new idea in later life. He accumulated vast stores of knowledge, but they all fitted into the old framework of theory. Whiggism seemed to him to provide a satisfactory solution for all political problems when he was sending his first article to *Knight's Magazine* and when he was writing the last page of his *History.* "I entered public life a Whig," as he said in 1849, "and a Whig I am determined to remain." And what is meant by Whiggism in Macaulay's mouth? It means substantially that creed which registers the experience of the English upper classes during the four or five generations previous to Macaulay. It represents, not the reasoning, but the instinctive convictions generated by the dogged insistance upon their privileges of a stubborn, high-spirited, and individually short-sighted race. To deduce it as a symmetrical doctrine from abstract propositions would be futile. It is only reasonable so far as a creed, felt out by the collective instinct of a number of more or less stupid people, becomes impressed with a quasi-rational unity, not from their respect for logic, but from the uniformity of the mode of development. Hatred to pure reason is indeed one of its first principles. A doctrine avowedly founded on logic instead of instinct becomes for that very reason suspect to it. Common sense takes the place of philosophy. At times this mass of sentiment opposes itself under stress of circumstances to the absolute theories of monarchy and then calls itself Whiggism. At other times, it offers an equally dogged resistance to absolute theories of democracy, and then becomes nominally Tory. In Macaulay's youth, the weight of opinion had been slowly swinging round from the Toryism generated by dread of revolution, to Whiggism generated by the accumulation of palpable abuses. The growing intelligence and more rapidly growing power of the middle classes gave it at the same time a more popular character than before. Macaulay's "conversion" was simply a process of swinging with the tide. The Clapham Sect, amongst whom he had been brought up, was already more than half Whig, in virtue of its attack upon the sacred institution of slavery by means of popular agitation. Macaulay—the most brilliant of its young men—naturally cast in his lot with the brilliant men, a little older than himself, who fought under the blue and yellow banner of the *Edinburgh Review.* No great change of sentiment was necessary, though some of the old Clapham doctrines died out in his mind as he was swept into the political current.

Macaulay thus early became a thorough-going Whig. Whiggism seemed to him the *ne plus ultra* of progress: the pure essence of political wisdom. He was never fully conscious of the vast revolution in thought which was going on all around him. He was saturated with the doctrines of 1832. He stated them with unequalled vigour and clearness. Anybody who disputed them from either side of the question seemed to him to be little better than a fool. Southey and Mr. Gladstone talked arrant nonsense when they disputed the logical or practical value of the doctrines laid down by Locke. James Mill deserved the most contemptuous language for daring to push those doctrines beyond the sacred line. When Macaulay attacks an old Non-juror or a modern Tory, we can only wonder how opinions which, on his showing, are so inconceivably absurd, could ever have been held by any human being. Men are Whigs or not-Whigs, and the not-Whig is less a heretic to be anathematized than a blockhead beneath the reach of argument. All political wisdom centres in Holland House, and the *Edinburgh Review* is its prophet. There is something in the absolute confidence of Macaulay's political dogmatism which varies between the sublime and the ridiculous. We can hardly avoid laughing at this superlative self-satisfaction, and yet we must admit that it is indicative of a real political force not to be treated with simple contempt. Belief is power, even when belief is most unreasonable.

To define a Whig and to define Macaulay is pretty much the same thing. Let us trace some of the qualities which enabled one man to become so completely the type of a vast body of his compatriots.

The first and most obvious power in which Macaulay excelled his neighbours was his portentous memory. He could assimilate printed pages, says his nephew, more quickly than others could glance over them. Whatever he read was stamped upon his mind instantaneously and permanently, and he read everything. In the midst of severe labours in India, he read enough classical authors to stock the mind of an ordinary professor. At the same time he framed a criminal code and devoured masses of trashy novels. From the works of the ancient Fathers of the Church to English political pamphlets and to modern street ballads, no printed matter came amiss to his omnivorous appetite. All that he had read could be reproduced at a moment's notice. Every fool, he said, can repeat his Archbishops of Canterbury backwards; and he was as familiar with the Cambridge Calendar as the most devoted Protestant with the Bible. He could have re-written *Sir Charles Grandison* from memory if every copy had been lost. Now it might perhaps be plausibly maintained that the possession of such a memory is unfavourable to a high

development of the reasoning powers. The case of Pascal, indeed, who is said never to have forgotten anything, shows that the two powers may co-exist: and other cases might of course be mentioned. But it is true that a powerful memory may enable a man to save himself the trouble of reasoning. It encourages the indolent propensity of deciding difficulties by precedent instead of principles. Macaulay, for example, was once required to argue the point of political casuistry as to the degree of independent action permissible to members of a Cabinet. An ordinary mind would have to answer by striking a rough balance between the conveniences and inconveniences likely to arise. It would be forced, that is to say, to reason from the nature of the case. But Macaulay had at his fingers' end every instance from the days of Walpole to his own in which Ministers had been allowed to vote against the general policy of the Government. By quoting them, he seemed to decide the point by authority, instead of taking the troublesome and dangerous road of abstract reasoning. Thus to appeal to experience is with him to appeal to the stores of a gigantic memory; and is generally the same thing as to deny the value of all general rules. This is the true Whig doctrine of referring to precedent rather than to theory. Our popular leaders were always glad to quote Hampden and Sidney instead of venturing upon the dangerous ground of abstract rights.

Macaulay's love of deciding all points by an accumulation of appropriate instances is indeed characteristic of his mind. It is connected with a curious defect of analytical power. It appears in his literary criticism as much as in his political speculations. In an interesting letter to Mr. Napier, he states the case himself as an excuse for not writing upon Scott. "Hazlitt used to say, 'I am nothing if not critical.' The case with me," says Macaulay, "is precisely the reverse. I have a strong and acute enjoyment of works of the imagination, but I have never habituated myself to dissect them. Perhaps I enjoy them the more keenly for that very reason. Such books as Lessing's *Laocoon,* such passages as the criticism on *Hamlet* in *Wilhelm Meister,* fill me with wonder and despair." If we take any of Macaulay's criticisms, we shall see how truly he had gauged his own capacity. They are either random discharges of superlatives or vigorous assertions of sound moral principles. He compares Miss Austen to Shakespeare—one of the most random applications of the universal superlative ever made—or shows conclusively that Wycherley was a corrupt ribald. But he never makes a fine suggestion as to the secrets of the art whose products he admires or dislikes. His mode, for example, of criticising Bunyan is to give a list of the passages which he remembers, and, of course, he remembers everything. He observes, what was tolerably clear, that Bunyan's allegory is as vivid as a concrete history, though strangely comparing him in this respect to Shelley—the least concrete of poets; and he makes the discovery, which did not require his vast stores of historical knowledge, that "it is impossible to doubt that" Bunyan's trial of Christian and Faithful is meant to satirize the judges of Charles II. That is as plain as that the last cartoon in *Punch* is meant to satirize Mr. Disraeli. Macaulay can draw a most vivid portrait, so far as that can be done by a picturesque accumulation of characteristic facts, but he never gets below the surface or details the principles whose embodiment he describes from without.

The defect is connected with further peculiarities, in which Macaulay is the genuine representative of the true Whig type. The practical value of adherence to precedent is obvious. It may be justified by the assertion that all sound political philosophy must be based upon experience: and I at least hold that assertion to contain a most important truth. But in Macaulay's mind this sound doctrine seems to be confused with the very questionable doctrine that in political questions there is no philosophy at all. To appeal to experience may mean either to appeal to facts so classified and organically arranged as to illustrate general truths, or to appeal to a mere mass of observations, without taking the trouble to elicit their true significance, or even to believe that they can be resolved into particular cases of a general truth. This is the difference between an experimental philosophy and a crude empiricism. Macaulay takes the lower alternative. The vigorous attack upon James Mill, which he very properly suppressed during his life on account of its juvenile arrogance, curiously illustrates his mode of thought. No one can deny, I think, that he makes some very good points against a very questionable system of political dogmatism. But when we ask what are Macaulay's own principles, we are left at a stand. He ought, by all his intellectual sympathies, to be a utilitarian. Yet he abuses utilitarianism with the utmost contempt, and has no alternative theory to suggest. He ends his first Essay against Mill by one of his customary purple patches about Baconian induction. He tells us, in the second, how to apply it. Bacon proposed to discover the principle of heat by observing in what qualities all hot bodies agreed, and in what qualities all cold bodies. Similarly we are to make a list of all constitutions which have produced good or bad government, and to investigate their points of agreement and difference. This sounds plausible to the uninstructed, but is a mere rhetorical flourish. Bacon's method is really inadequate, for reasons which I leave to men of science to explain, and Macaulay's method is equally hopeless in politics. It is hopeless for the simple reason that the complexity of the phenomena makes it impracticable. We cannot find out what constitution is best after this fashion, simply because the goodness or badness of a constitution depends upon a thousand conditions of social, moral, and intellectual development. When stripped of its pretentious phraseology, Macaulay's teaching comes simply to this: the only rule in politics is the rule of thumb. All general principles are wrong or futile. We have found out in England that our constitution, constructed in absolute defiance of all *à priori* reasoning, is the best in the world: it is the best for providing us with the maximum of bread, beef, beer, and means of buying bread, beer, and beef: and we have got it because we have never—like those publicans the French—trusted to fine sayings about truth and justice and human rights, but blundered on, adding a patch here and knocking a hole there, as our humour prompted us.

This sovereign contempt of all speculation—simply as speculation—reaches its acme in the **"Essay on Bacon."** The curious naïveté with which Macaulay denounces all philosophy in that vigorous production excites a kind of

perverse admiration. How can one refuse to admire the audacity which enables a man explicitly to identify philosophy with humbug? It is what ninety-nine men out of a hundred think, but not one in a thousand dares to say. Goethe says somewhere that he likes Englishmen because English fools are the most thoroughgoing of fools. English "Philistines," as represented by Macaulay, the prince of Philistines, carry their contempt of the higher intellectual interests to a pitch of real sublimity. Bacon's theory of induction, says Macaulay, in so many words, was valueless. Everybody could reason before it as well as after. But Bacon really performed a service of inestimable value to mankind; and it consisted precisely in this, that he called their attention from philosophy to the pursuit of material advantages. The old philosophers had gone on bothering about theology, ethics, and the true and beautiful, and such other nonsense. Bacon taught us to work at chemistry and mechanics, to invent diving-bells and steam-engines and spinning-jennies. We could never, it seems, have found out the advantages of this direction of our energies without a philosopher, and so far philosophy is negatively good. It has written up upon all the supposed avenues to inquiry, "No admission except on business;" that is, upon the business of direct practical discovery. We English have taken the hint, and we have therefore lived to see when a man can breakfast in London and dine in Edinburgh, and may look forward to a day when the tops of Ben-Nevis and Helvellyn will be cultivated like flower-gardens, and machines constructed on principles yet to be discovered will be in every house.

The theory which underlies this conclusion is often explicitly stated. All philosophy has produced mere futile logomachy. Greek sages and Roman moralists, and mediæval schoolmen, have amassed words and amassed nothing else. One distinct discovery of a solid truth, however humble, is worth all their labours. This condemnation applies not only to philosophy, but to the religious embodiment of philosophy. No satisfactory conclusion ever has been reached or ever will be reached in theological disputes. On all such topics, he tells Mr. Gladstone, there has always been the widest divergence of opinion. Nor are there better hopes for the future. The ablest minds, he says, in the **"Essay upon Ranke,"** have believed in transubstantiation, that is, according to him, in the most ineffable nonsense. There is no certainty that men will not believe to the end of time the doctrines which imposed upon so able a man as Sir Thomas More. Not only, that is, have men been hitherto wandering in a labyrinth without a clue, but there is no chance that any clue will ever be found. The doctrine, so familiar to our generation, of laws of intellectual development, never even occurs to him. The collective thought of generations marks time without advancing. A guess of Sir Thomas More is as good or as bad as the guess of the last philosopher. This theory, if true, implies utter scepticism. And yet Macaulay was clearly not a sceptic. His creed was hidden under a systematic reticence, and he resisted every attempt to raise the veil with rather superfluous indignation. When a constituent dared to ask about his religious views, he denounced the rash inquirer in terms applicable to an agent of the inquisition. He vouchsafed, indeed, the information that he was a Christian. We may accept the phrase, not only on the strength of his invariable sincerity, but because it falls in with the general turn of his arguments. He denounces the futility of the ancient moralists, but he asserts the enormous social value of Christianity.

His attitude, in fact, is equally characteristic of the man and his surroundings. The old Clapham teaching had faded in his mind; it had not produced a revolt. He retained the old hatred for slavery; and he retained, with the whole force of his affectionate nature, a reverence for the school of Wilberforce, Thornton, and his own father. He estimated most highly, not perhaps more highly than they deserved, the value of the services rendered by them in awakening the conscience of the nation. In their persistent and disinterested labours he recognized a manifestation of the great social force of Christianity. But a belief that Christianity is useful, and even that it is true, may consist with a profound conviction of the futility of the philosophy with which it has been associated. Here again Macaulay is a true Whig. The Whig love of precedent, the Whig hatred for abstract theories, may consist with a Tory application. But the true Whig differed from the Tory in adding to these views an invincible suspicion of parsons. The first Whig battles were fought against the Church as much as against the King. From the struggle with Sacheverel down to the struggle for Catholic emancipation, Toryism and High-Church principles were associated against Whigs and Dissenters. By that kind of dumb instinct which outruns reason, the Whig had learnt that there was some occult bond of union between the claims of a priesthood and the claims of a monarchy. The old maxim, "No bishop, no king," suggested the opposite principle, that you must keep down the clergy if you would limit the monarchy. The natural interpretation of this prejudice into political theory, is that the Church is extremely useful as an ally of the constable, but possesses a most dangerous explosive power if allowed to claim independent authority. In practice we must resist all claims of the Church to dictate to the State. In theory, we must deny the foundation upon which such claims can alone be founded. Dogmatism must be pronounced to be fundamentally irrational. Nobody knows anything about theology, or, what is the same thing, no two people agree. As they don't agree, they cannot claim to impose their beliefs upon others.

This sentiment comes out curiously in the characteristic Essay just mentioned. Macaulay says, in reply to Mr. Gladstone, that there is no more reason for the introduction of religious questions into State affairs than for introducing them into the affairs of a Canal Company. He puts his argument with an admirable vigour and clearness which blinds many readers to the fact that he is begging the question by evading the real difficulty. If, in fact, Government had as little to do as a Canal Company with religious opinion, we should have long ago learnt the great lesson of toleration. But that is just the very *crux.* Can we draw the line between the spiritual and the secular? Nothing, replies Macaulay, is easier; and his method has been already indicated. We all agree that we don't want to be robbed or murdered: we are by no means all agreed about the doctrine of Trinity. But, says a churchman, a certain creed is necessary to men's moral and spiritual welfare, and therefore of the utmost importance even for the pre-

vention of robbery and murder. This is what Macaulay implicitly denies. The whole of dogmatic theology belongs to that region of philosophy, metaphysics, or whatever you please to call it, in which men are doomed to dispute for ever without coming any nearer to a decision. All that the statesman has to do with such matters is to see that if men are fools enough to speculate, they shall not be allowed to cut each other's throats when they reach, as they always must reach, contradictory results. If you raise a difficult point, such, for example, as the education question, Macaulay replies, as so many people have said before and since, Teach the people "those principles of morality which are common to all the forms of Christianity." That is easier said than done! The plausibility of the solution in Macaulay's mouth is due to the fundamental assumption that everything except morality is hopeless ground of inquiry. Once get beyond the Ten Commandments and you will sink in a bottomless morass of argument, counter-argument, quibble, logomachy, superstition, and confusion worse confounded.

In Macaulay's teaching, as in that of his party, there is doubtless much that is noble. He has a righteous hatred of oppression in all shapes and disguises. He can tear to pieces with great logical power many of the fallacies alleged by his opponents. Our sympathies are certainly with him as against men who advocate persecution on any grounds, and he is fully qualified to crush his ordinary opponents. But it is plain that his whole political and (if we may use the word) philosophical teaching rests on something like a downright aversion to the higher order of speculation. He despises it. He wants something tangible and concrete—something in favour of which he may appeal to the immediate testimony of the senses. He must feel his feet planted on the solid earth. The pain of attempting to soar into higher regions is not compensated to him by the increased width of horizon. And in this respect he is but the type of most of his countrymen, and reflects what has been (as I should say) erroneously called their "unimaginative" view of things in general.

Macaulay, at any rate, distinctly belongs to the imaginative class of minds, if only in virtue of his instinctive preference of the concrete to the abstract, and his dislike, already noticed, to analysis. He has a thirst for distinct and vivid images. He reasons by examples instead of appealing to formulæ. There is a characteristic account in Mr. Trevelyan's volumes of his habit of rambling amongst the older parts of London, his fancy teeming with stories attached to the picturesque fragments of antiquity, and carrying on dialogues between imaginary persons as vivid, if not as forcible, as those of Scott's novels. To this habit—rather inverting the order of cause and effect—he attributes his accuracy of detail. We would rather say that the intensity of the impressions generates both the accuracy and the day-dreams. A philosopher would be arguing in his daily rambles where an imaginative mind is creating a series of pictures. But Macaulay's imagination is as definitely limited as his speculation. The genuine poet is also a philosopher. He sees intuitively what the reasoner evolves by argument. The greatest minds in both classes are equally marked by their naturalisation in the lofty regions of thought, inaccessible or uncongenial to men of inferior stamp. It is tempting in some ways to compare Macaulay to Burke. Burke's superiority is marked by this, that he is primarily a philosopher, and therefore instinctively sees the illustration of a general law in every particular fact. Macaulay, on the contrary, gets away from theory as fast as possible, and tries to conceal his poverty of thought under masses of ingenious illustration.

His imaginative narrowness would come out still more clearly by a comparison with Mr. Carlyle. One significant fact must be enough. Every one must have observed how powerfully Mr. Carlyle expresses the emotion suggested by the brief appearance of some little waif from past history. We may remember, for example, how the usher, De Brézé, appears for a moment to utter the last shriek of the old monarchical etiquette, and then vanishes into the dim abysses of the past. The imagination is excited by the little glimpse of light flashing for a moment upon some special point in the cloudy phantasmagoria of human history. The image of a past existence is projected for a moment upon our eyes, to make us feel how transitory is life, and how rapidly one visionary existence expels another. We are such stuff as dreams are made of:—

> None other than a moving row
> Of visionary shapes that come and go
>   Around the sun-illumined lantern held
> In midnight by the master of the show.

Every object is seen against the background of eternal mystery. In Macaulay's pages this element is altogether absent. We see a figure from the past as vividly as if he were present. We observe the details of his dress, the odd oaths with which his discourse is interlarded, the minute peculiarities of his features or manner. We laugh or admire as we should do at a living man; and we rightly admire the force of the illusion. But the thought never suggests itself that we too are passing into oblivion, that our little island of daylight will soon be shrouded in the gathering mist, and that we tread at every instant on the dust of forgotten continents. We treat the men of past ages quite at our ease. We applaud and criticise Hampden or Chatham as we should applaud Peel or Cobden. There is no atmospheric effect—no sense of the dim march of ages, or of the vast procession of human life. It is doubtless a great feat to make the past present. It is a greater to emancipate us from the tyranny of the present, and to raise us to a point at which we feel that we too are almost as dreamlike as the men of old time. To gain clearness and definition Macaulay has dropped the element of mystery. He sees perfectly whatever can be seen by the ordinary lawyer, or politician, or merchant; he is insensible to the visions which reveal themselves only to minds haunted by thoughts of eternity, and delighting, with Sir Thomas Browne, to lose themselves in an *O altitudo*. Mysticism is to him hateful, and historical figures form groups of individuals, not symbols of forces working behind the veil.

Macaulay, therefore, can be no more a poet in the sense in which the word is applied to Spencer, or to Wordsworth, both of whom he holds to be simply intolerable bores, than he can be a metaphysician or a scientific thinker. In common phraseology, he is a Philistine—a word which I understand properly to denote indifference to the higher intellectual interests. The word may also be defined, however, as the name applied by prigs to the rest of their species. And I venture to hold that the modern fashion of using it as a common term of abuse is doing real mischief. It enables intellectual coxcombs to brand men with an offensive epithet for being a degree more manly than themselves. There is much that is good in your Philistine, and when we ask what Macaulay was, instead of showing what he was not, we shall perhaps find that the popular estimate is not altogether wrong.

Macaulay was not only a typical Whig, but the prophet of Whiggism to his generation. Though not a poet or a philosopher, he was a born rhetorician. His parliamentary career proves his capacity sufficiently, though want of the physical qualifications, and of exclusive devotion to political success, prevented him, as perhaps a want of subtlety or flexibility of mind would have always prevented him, from attaining excellence as a debater. In everything that he wrote, however, we see the true rhetorician. He tells us that Fox wrote debates, whilst Mackintosh spoke essays. Macaulay did both. His compositions are a series of orations on behalf of sound Whig views, whatever their external form. Given a certain audience—and an orator supposes a particular audience—their effectiveness is undeniable. Macaulay's may be composed of ordinary Englishmen, with a moderate standard of education. His arguments are adapted to the ordinary Cabinet Minister, or, we may say, to the person who is willing to pay a shilling to hear an evening lecture. He can hit an audience composed of such materials—to quote Burke's phrase about George Grenville—"between wind and water." He uses the language, the logic, and the images which they can fully understand; and though his hearer, like his schoolboy, is ostensibly credited at times with a portentous memory, Macaulay always takes excellent care to put him in mind of the facts which he is assumed to remember. The faults and the merits of his style follow from his resolute determination to be understood of the people. He was specially delighted, as his nephew tells us, by a reader at Messrs. Spottiswoode's, who said that in all the *History* there was only one sentence the meaning of which was not obvious to him at first sight. We are more surprised that there was one such sentence. Clearness is the first of the cardinal virtues of style; and nobody ever wrote more clearly than Macaulay. He sacrifices much, it is true, in order to obtain it. He proves that two and two make four, with a pertinacity which would make him dull, if it were not for his abundance of brilliant illustration. He always remembers the principle which should guide a barrister in addressing a jury. He has not merely to exhibit his proofs, but to hammer them into the heads of his audience by incessant repetition. It is no small proof of artistic skill that a writer who systematically adopts this method should yet be invariably lively. He goes on blacking the chimney with a persistency which somehow amuses us because he puts so much heart into his work. He proves the most obvious truths again and again; but his vivacity never flags. This tendency undoubtedly leads to great defects of style. His sentences are monotonous and mechanical. He has a perfect hatred of pronouns, and for fear of a possible entanglement between "hims" and "hers" and "its," he will repeat not merely a substantive, but a whole group of substantives. Sometimes, to make his sense unmistakable, he will repeat a whole formula, with only a change in the copula. For the same reason, he hates all qualifications and parentheses. Each thought must be resolved into its constituent parts; each argument must be expressed as a simple proposition: and his paragraphs are rather aggregates of independent atoms than possessed of an organic unity. His writing—to use a favourite formula of his own—bears the same relation to a style of graceful modulation that a bit of mosaic work bears to a picture. Each phrase has its distinct hue, instead of melting into its neighbours. Here we have a black patch and there a white. There are no half tones, no subtle interblending of different currents of thought. It is partly for this reason that his descriptions of character are often so unsatisfactory. He likes to represent a man as a bundle of contradictions, because it enables him to obtain startling contrasts. He heightens a vice in one place, a virtue in another, and piles them together in a heap, without troubling himself to ask whether nature can make such monsters, or preserve them if made. To any one given to analysis, these contrasts are actually painful. There is a story of the Duke of Wellington having once stated that the rats got into his bottles in Spain. "They must have been very large bottles or very small rats," said somebody. "On the contrary," replied the Duke, "the rats were very large and the bottles very small." Macaulay delights in leaving us face to face with such contrasts in more important matters. Boswell must, we would say, have been a clever man or his biography cannot have been so good as you say. On the contrary, says Macaulay, he was the greatest of fools and the best of biographers. He strikes a discord and purposely fails to resolve it. To men of more delicate sensibility the result is an intolerable jar.

For the same reason, Macaulay's genuine eloquence is marred by the symptoms of malice prepense. When he sows on a purple patch, he is resolved that there shall be no mistake about it; it must stand out from a radical contrast of colours. The emotion is not to swell by degrees, till you find yourself carried away in the torrent which set out as a tranquil stream. The transition is deliberately emphasized. On one side of a full stop you are listening to a matter-of-fact statement; on the other, there is all at once a blare of trumpets and a beating of drums, till the crash almost deafens you. He regrets in one of his letters that he has used up the celebrated, and, it must be confessed, really forcible passage about the impeachment scene in Westminister Hall. It might have come in usefully in the *History,* which, as he then hoped, might come down to Warren Hastings. The regret is unpleasantly suggestive of that deliberation in the manufacture of eloquence which stamps it as artificial.

Such faults may annoy critics, even of no very sensitive fibre. What is it that redeems them? The first answer is, that the work is impressive because it is thoroughly genuine. The stream, it is true, comes forth by spasmodic gushes, when it ought to flow in a continuous current; but it flows from a full reservoir instead of being pumped from a shallow cistern. The knowledge and, what is more, the thoroughly assimilated knowledge, is enormous. Mr. Trevelyan has shown in detail what we had all divined for ourselves, how much patient labour is often employed in a

paragraph or the turn of a phrase. To accuse Macaulay of superficiality is, in this sense, altogether absurd. His speculation may be meagre, but his store of information is simply inexhaustible. Mr. Mill's writing was impressive, because one often felt that a single argument condensed the result of a long process of reflection. Macaulay has the lower but similar merit that a single picturesque touch implies incalculable masses of knowledge. It is but an insignificant part of the building which appears above ground. Compare a passage with the assigned authority, and you are inclined to accuse him—sometimes it may be rightfully—of amplifying and modifying. But more often the particular authority is merely the nucleus round which a whole volume of other knowledge has crystallised. A single hint is significant to a properly prepared mind of a thousand facts not explicitly contained in it. Nobody, he said, could judge of the accuracy of one part of his *History* who had not "soaked his mind with the transitory literature of the day." His real authority was not this or that particular passage, but a literature. And for this reason alone, Macaulay's historical writings have a permanent value which will prevent them from being superseded even by more philosophical thinkers, whose minds have not undergone the "soaking" process.

It is significant again that imitations of Macaulay are almost as offensive as imitations of Carlyle. Every great writer has his parasites. Macaulay's false glitter and jingle, his frequent flippancy and superficiality of thought are more easily caught than his virtues; but so are all faults. Would-be followers of Mr. Carlyle catch the strained gestures, without the rapture of his inspiration. Would-be followers of Mr. Mill fancied themselves to be logical when they were only hopelessly unsympathetic and unimaginative; and would-be followers of some other writers can be effeminate and foppish without being subtle or graceful. Macaulay's thoroughness of work has, perhaps, been less contagious than we could wish. Something of the modern raising of the standard of accuracy in historical inquiry may be set down to his influence. The misfortune is that, if some writers have learnt from him to be flippant without learning to be laborious, others have caught the accuracy without the liveliness. In the later volumes of his *History* his vigour began to be a little clogged by the fulness of his knowledge; and we can observe symptoms of the tendency of modern historians to grudge the sacrifice of sifting their knowledge. They read enough, but instead of giving us the results, they tumble out the accumulated mass of raw materials upon our devoted heads, till they suggest the wish for a fire in the State Paper Office.

Fortunately, Macaulay did not yield to this temptation in his earlier writings, and the result is that he is, for the ordinary reader, one of the two authorities for English history, the other being Shakespeare. Without comparing their merits, we must admit that the compression of so much into a few short narratives shows intensity as well as compass of mind. He could digest as well as devour, and he tried his digestion pretty severely. It is fashionable to say that part of his practical force is due to the training of parliamentary life. Familiarity with the course of affairs doubtless strengthened his insight into history, and taught him the value of downright common sense in teaching an average audience. Speaking purely from the literary point of view, I cannot agree further in the opinion suggested. I suspect the *History* would have been better if Macaulay had not been so deeply immersed in all the business of legislation and electioneering. I do not profoundly reverence the House of Commons tone—even in the House of Commons; and in literature it easily becomes a nuisance. Familiarity with the actual machinery of politics tends to strengthen the contempt for general principles, of which Macaulay had an ample share. It encourages the illusion of the fly upon the wheel, the doctrine that the dust and din of debate and the worry of lobbies and committee-rooms is not the effect but the cause of the great social movement. The historian of the Roman Empire, as we know, owed something to the captain of Hampshire Militia; but years of life absorbed in parliamentary wrangling and in sitting at the feet of the philosophers of Holland House were not likely to widen a mind already disposed to narrow views of the world.

For Macaulay's immediate success, indeed, the training was undoubtedly valuable. As he carried into Parliament the authority of a great writer, so he wrote books with the authority of the practical politician. He has the true instinct of affairs. He knows what are the immediate motives which move masses of men; and is never misled by fanciful analogies or blindfolded by the pedantry of official language. He has seen flesh-and-blood statesmen—at any rate, English statesmen—and understands the nature of the animal. Nobody can be freer from the dominion of crotchets. All his reasoning is made of the soundest common sense and represents, if not the ultimate forces, yet forces with which we have to reckon. And he knows, too, how to stir the blood of the average Englishman. He understands most thoroughly the value of concentration, unity, and simplicity. Every speech or essay forms an organic whole, in which some distinct moral is vigorously driven home by a succession of downright blows. This strong rhetorical instinct is shown conspicuously in the *Lays of Ancient Rome,* which, whatever we might say of them as poetry, are an admirable specimen of rhymed rhetoric. We know how good they are when we see how incapable are modern ballad-writers in general of putting the same swing and fire into their verses. Compare, for example, Aytoun's *Lays of the Cavaliers,* as the most obvious parallel:—

> Not swifter pours the avalanche
>   Adown the steep incline,
> That rises o'er the parent springs
>   Of rough and rapid Rhine,

than certain Scotch heroes over an entrenchment. Place this mouthing by any parallel passage in Macaulay:—

> Now, by our sire Quirinus,
>   It was a goodly sight
> To see the thirty standards
>   Swept down the tide of flight.
> So flies the spray in Adria
>   When the black squall doth blow,
> So cornsheaves in the flood time
>   Spin down the whirling Po.

And so on in verses, which innumerable schoolboys of in-

ferior pretensions to Macaulay's know by heart. And in such cases the verdict of the schoolboy is perhaps more valuable than that of the literary connoisseur. There are, of course, many living poets who can do tolerably something of far higher quality which Macaulay could not do at all. But I don't know who, since Scott, could have done this particular thing. Possibly Mr. Kingsley might have approached it, or the poet, if he would have condescended so far, who sang the bearing of the good news from Ghent to Aix. In any case, the feat is significant of Macaulay's true power. It looks easy; it involves no demands upon the higher reasoning or imaginative powers: but nobody will believe it to be easy who observes the extreme rarity of a success in a feat so often attempted.

A similar remark is suggested by Macaulay's *Essays.* Read such an Essay as those upon Clive, or Warren Hastings, or Chatham. The story seems to tell itself. The characters are so strongly marked, the events fall so easily into their places, that we fancy that the narrator's business has been done to his hand. It wants little critical experience to discover that this massive simplicity is really indicative of an art not, it may be, of the highest order, but truly admirable for its purpose. It indicates not only a gigantic memory, but a glowing mind, which has fused a crude mass of materials into unity. If we do not find the sudden touches which reveal the philosophical sagacity or the imaginative insight of the highest order of intellects, we recognize the true rhetorical instinct. The outlines may be harsh, and the colours too glaring; but the general effect has been carefully studied. The details are wrought in with consummate skill. We indulge in an intercalary pish! here and there; but we are fascinated and we remember. The actual amount of intellectual force which goes to the composition of such written archives is immense, though the quality may have something to be desired. Shrewd common sense may be an inferior substitute for philosophy, and the faculty which brings remote objects close to the eye of an ordinary observer for the loftier faculty which tinges everyday life with the hues of mystic contemplation. But when the common faculties are present in so abnormal a degree, they begin to have a dignity of their own.

It is impossible in such matters to establish any measure of comparison. No analysis will enable us to say how much pedestrian capacity may be fairly regarded as equivalent to a small capacity for soaring above the solid earth, and therefore the question as to the relative value of Macaulay's work and that of some men of loftier aims and less perfect execution must be left to individual taste. We can only say that it is something so to have written the history of many national heroes as to make their faded glories revive to active life in the memory of their countrymen. So long as Englishmen are what they are—and they don't seem to change as rapidly as might be wished—they will turn to Macaulay's pages to gain a vivid impression of our greatest achievements during an important period.

Nor is this all. The fire which glows in Macaulay's history, the intense patriotic feeling, the love of certain moral qualities, is not altogether of the highest kind. His ideal of national and individual greatness might easily be criticised. But the sentiment, as far as it goes, is altogether sound and manly. He is too fond, it has been said, of incessant moralising. From a scientific point of view the moralising is irrelevant. We want to study the causes and the nature of great social movements; and when we are stopped in order to inquire how far the prominent actors in them were hurried beyond ordinary rules, we are transported into a different order of thought. It would be as much to the purpose if we reproved an earthquake for upsetting a fort, and blamed it for moving the foundations of a church. Macaulay can never understand this point of view. With him, history is nothing more than a sum of biographies. And even from a biographical point of view his moralising is often troublesome. He not only insists upon transporting party prejudice into his estimates, and mauls poor James II. as he mauled the Tories in 1832; but he applies obviously inadequate tests. It is absurd to call upon men engaged in a life-and-death wrestle to pay scrupulous attention to the ordinary rules of politeness. There are times when judgments guided by constitutional precedent become ludicrously out of place, and when the best man is he who aims straightest at the heart of his antagonist. But, in spite of such drawbacks, Macaulay's genuine sympathy for manliness and force of character generally enables him to strike pretty nearly the true note. To learn the true secret of Cromwell's character, we must go to Mr. Carlyle, who can sympathise with deep currents of religious enthusiasm. Macaulay retains too much of the old Whig distrust for all that it calls fanaticism fully to recognize the grandeur beneath the grotesque outside of the Puritan. But Macaulay tells us most distinctly why Englishmen warm at the name of the great Protector. We, like the banished cavaliers, "glow with an emotion of national pride" at his animated picture of the unconquerable Ironsides. One phrase may be sufficiently illustrative. After quoting Clarendon's story of the Scotch nobleman who forced Charles to leave the field of Naseby, by seizing his horse's bridle, "no man," says Macaulay, "who had much value for his life, would have tried to perform the same friendly office on that day for Oliver Cromwell."

Macaulay, in short, always feels, and, therefore, communicates, a hearty admiration for sheer manliness. And some of his portraits of great men have therefore a genuine power, and show the deeper insight which comes from true sympathy. He estimates the respectable observer of constitutional proprieties too highly; he is unduly repelled by the external oddities of the truly masculine and noble Johnson; but his enthusiasm for his pet hero, William, or for Chatham or Clive, carries us along with him. And at moments when he is narrating their exploits, and can forget his elaborate argumentations and refrain from bits of deliberate bombast, the style becomes graphic in the higher sense of a much-abused word, and we confess that we are listening to genuine eloquence. Putting aside for the moment recollection of foibles, almost too obvious to deserve the careful demonstration which they have sometimes received, we are glad to surrender ourselves to the charm of his straightforward, clear-headed, hard-hitting declamation. There is no writer with whom it is easier to find fault, or the limits of whose power may be more distinctly defined; but within his own sphere he goes forward, as he went through life, with a kind of grand confidence

in himself and his cause, which is attractive and at times even provocative of sympathetic enthusiasm.

Macaulay said, in his Diary, that he wrote his *History* with an eye to a remote past and a remote future. He meant to erect a monument more enduring than brass, and the ambition at least stimulated him to admirable thoroughness of workmanship. How far his aim was secured must be left to the decision of a posterity, which will not trouble itself about the susceptibilities of candidates for its favour. In one sense, however, Macaulay must be interesting so long as the type which he so fully represents continues to exist. Whig has become an old-fashioned phrase, and is repudiated by modern Liberals and Radicals, who think themselves wiser than their fathers. The decay of the old name implies a remarkable political change; but I doubt whether it implies more than a very superficial change in the national character. New classes and new ideas have come upon the stage; but they have a curious family likeness to the old. The Whiggism, whose peculiarities Macaulay reflected so faithfully, represents some of the most deeply-seated tendencies of the national character. It has, therefore, both its ugly and its honourable side. Its disregard, or rather its hatred, for pure reason, its exaltation of expediency above truth and precedent above principle, its instinctive dread of strong religious or political faiths, are of course questionable qualities. Yet even they have their nobler side. There is something almost sublime about the grand unreasonableness of the average Englishman. His dogged contempt for all foreigners and philosophers, his intense resolution to have his own way and use his own eyes, to see nothing that does not come within his narrow sphere of vision, and to see it quite clearly before he acts upon it, are of course abhorrent to thinkers of a different order. But they are great qualities in the struggle for existence, which must determine the future of the world. The Englishman, armed in his panoply of self-content, and grasping facts with unequalled tenacity, goes on trampling upon acuter sensibilities, but somehow shouldering his way successfully through the troubles of the universe. Strength may be combined with stupidity, but even then it is not to be trifled with. Macaulay's sympathy with these qualities led to some annoying peculiarities, to a certain brutal insularity, and to a commonness, sometimes a vulgarity of style which is easily criticised. But, at least, we must confess that, to use an epithet which always comes up in speaking of him, he is a thoroughly manly writer. There is nothing silly or finical about him. He sticks to his colours resolutely and honourably. If he flatters his countrymen, it is the unconscious and spontaneous effect of his participation in their weaknesses. He never knowingly calls black white, or panders to an ungenerous sentiment. He is combative to a fault, but his combativeness is allied to a genuine love of fair play. When he hates a man, he calls him knave or fool with unflinching frankness, but he never uses a base weapon. The wounds which he inflicts may hurt, but they do not fester. His patriotism may be narrow, but it implies faith in the really good qualities, the manliness, the spirit of justice, and the strong moral sense of his countrymen. He is proud of the healthy vigorous stock from which he springs, and the fervour of his enthusiasm, though it may shock a delicate taste, has embodied itself in writings which will long continue to be the typical illustration of qualities of which we are all proud at bottom—indeed, be it said in passing, a good deal too proud. (pp. 566-81)

> Leslie Stephen, "Hours in a Library: Macaulay," in The Cornhill Magazine, Vol. XXXIII, May, 1876, pp. 563-81.

George Saintsbury (essay date 1895)

[*A prolific writer, Saintsbury composed influential histories of English and European literature as well as numerous critical works. In the following excerpt, he surveys Macaulay's literary effort, and although he believes him to be at times untrustworthy and shallow in his treatment of historical figures, he admires his partisanship and his ability to create interest in history and literature.*]

Macaulay, though not low-born, was born quite in the middle class; he inherited nothing worth speaking of; and he did not devote himself to any of the ordinary paying professions. Whether—a circumstance over which his biographers skim rather lightly—he did definitely rat at an early period of life from Toryism to Liberalism does not very much matter. He was born a Liberal of the type which he was to do so much to multiply and foster; and if his hoisting of that flag was a little prompted by considerations of probable profit, we may very well set the thing off against a very similar incident in the career of Canning in the generation before, and agree to say nothing about it.

From almost his earliest manhood Macaulay's life was a sort of cascade of fallings on his feet. He came just at the period when clear, brilliant, confident, and rather shallow review-writing was at its best paid and most honoured apogee. He came at the time when there were still rotten boroughs to bring forward a young man of talent, and when a young man of talent could make his position sure by denouncing the rotten boroughs on which he had risen. In the Reform Bill debates there was no young man of anything like his talent on the other side, and the one young or youngish man who would have been too much for him in position and natural eloquence, as well as a fair match for him in scholarship and knowledge, Stanley, was by historical accident on the same side. In society he coincided with the period of breakfasts, and belonged to a party in which there was nobody to match him as talker except Sydney Smith, who was getting old. When it was necessary to provide for himself solidly, the least troublesome and most paying of all appointments left for any one to obtain came in his way. He stayed in India long enough to pick up a competence and not long enough to damage his health. He had no tastes, either domestic or luxurious, which could interfere with this independence, or impose on him a longer servitude. He came home and settled down to his own ideal life: a little politics, a great deal of historical literature, and as much society as he chose, without any obligations of family estate or office to force more on him. His great history fell on the very nick of time to suit its merits, and the famous twenty thousand pound cheque symbolised at once those merits and their reward. And then too he had the crowning felicity of an opportune

death. Had Macaulay lived to the age of Lord Sherbrooke, something like Lord Sherbrooke's fate might—indeed I think must—have been his, though the few years' difference between them must have given him a slight advantage. It is almost terrible to think of the feelings of the man who prophetically described Mr. Gladstone half a century ago, when he found himself face to face with the choice of ceasing to be a Liberal or becoming a Gladstonian.

Yet Nemesis has been even with him (as she always is) for all these good things, and for the enormous popularity which was partly their result and partly their complement. Almost immediately after his death began a steady dead set of critical depreciation, which, unhasting, unresting, has attacked him ever since and which for some years past has spread from the critics to the vulgar. The decriers of Macaulay have been a strangely miscellaneous band. It was not to be expected that the Tories whom he affected to despise should like him; or that the Evangelicals, who regarded him as a renegade, and the Dissenters, who looked on him as the inheritor of the wicked wit of Sydney Smith, should love him. But he managed to attract hosts of enemies of the most heterogeneous kinds. It used to be a tradition in Oxford (I never saw the passage and I apologise to Mr. Smith if it is not true) that Mr. Goldwin Smith even in the fullest days of his Liberalism called Macaulay "a shallow scoundrel." Mr. Matthew Arnold, as is well known, exhausted his elegant quiver on the *Lays of Ancient Rome,* and was evidently often thinking of Macaulay when he denounced the British Philistine. The tribe of Dryasdust hated him because he was not merely an omnivorous reader but a brilliant writer; and the devotees of historical philosophy could not forgive him his obstinate superficiality and the calm assumption which accompanied it that there was nothing beneath the surface. Although one considerable Mediævalist, Mr. Freeman, used to take his part, for reasons not very difficult of discovery, it was impossible for any other student of the older ages not to resent the bland ignoring of something like a thousand years of English history which made Macaulay constantly infer, and sometimes almost say, that nobody need look beyond the Great Rebellion.

Also I am afraid it must be said, though it will make one devoted Macaulayan who is a great friend of mine wroth, that the number of Macaulay's enemies in a certain sense is sure to increase by just so many people as undertake a serious study of any person or period with whom or which he has dealt. It is the general if not the universal result in such cases that the inquirers declare that Macaulay, if not thoroughly dishonest, is at least thoroughly untrustworthy. It is not that he is a partisan,—history without partisanship is to my fancy, in the old phrase of King Henry the Fifth, like "beef without mustard." Nor is it that he is, in history, deliberately unfair. In his anonymous work, where a man ought to be most careful, I fear he sometimes was. Some of the imputations on Croker in the **"Boswell"** Essay are utterly inexcusable, even if we did not know, as we do, that the reviewer took up the book he intended to review with a determination to "slate" it. But having had occasion to examine more than one part of the *History* carefully and documents in hand, I do not think that this sort of unfairness is often to be found there. Unfortunately, another sort which is common in the *Essays* is common also in the *History.* I do not hold that Macaulay, unless (as in the Warren Hastings case) he was himself misled by his authorities, ever advances against his "black beasts" anything which is positively untrue. I do not urge that he often suppresses, in a way with which much fault can be found, anything which makes in their favour. But he has a less gross, perhaps, but a worse and more dangerous fault than any of these. He is constantly misleading by innuendo suggestive of the false, by epithets, by generalisations, by rhetorical extensions of the actual fact or text. He finds in his document, let us say, that A. on not certain authority was accused on a particular occasion of doing or saying such and such a thing. This translates itself in the pages of the *History* into a general charge against A. of being notoriously in the habit of saying or doing it. A particular phrase is reported of a particular person: Macaulay always turns it to "men began to say," or something of that kind. In short, the most careful student, the most experienced critic, never quite knows where to have this great historian on a subject which he, the student or critic, has not yet examined for himself; and when he does examine for himself he too often has to ask himself, Is it possible that these colourings and baits to the unwary, these suppressions by dint of shading, and suggestions by careless scattering of adjectives and adverbs, can have been made without a deliberate *parti pris,* without the aim of the advocate whose admitted and professional privilege it is to throw dust in the eyes of the jury if he possibly can?

Something else has to be added. They have made Macaulay into school-books, and it is well known that, if it be possible to instil disgust and horror of an author into all but the few whom the not perhaps quite equal Jove of literature has specially loved, it can be done most easily and completely by setting them to learn him at school.

And so my Lord Macaulay of late—though I do not know that the great heart of the people has yet been affected about him, or that that Australian book-shelf of which we have all heard has yet been denuded of the *Essays*—has begun to fall rather on evil days. The set against him has spread from the highest to the lowest rank of critics; the lady novelist has lifted up what it may be almost improper to call her heel against him; you see superior gibes to his address in those curious periodicals of scraps and patches which appear more than anything else to satisfy the literary hunger and thirst of the end of the nineteenth century. It is whispered, apropos of the miserable Montgomery, and in connection with the present influentially supported movement for roasting all reviewers gratis, that Macaulay was one of the wicked critics who delight to "slate" good authors. Fond as we are nowadays of rehabilitations, the rehabilitator has not come to him. In short, Nemesis is upon him: the deferred discount of that twenty thousand pound cheque has to be paid, and it is heavy. (pp. 79-87)

. . . . .

I do not know that there have been any very striking vicissitudes in my own opinions of Macaulay. I used to delight in the *Essays* when I was a young boy, and I do not delight in them much less now that I am neither a boy nor young. But I think I always had a kind of inkling of the defects,

which has gained in precision and definiteness, but has not, I think, deepened much. I still think that, on any subject which Macaulay has touched, his survey is unsurpassable for giving a first bird's-eye view, and for creating interest in the matter. Of course for those readers who have what is called "the faith of the charcoal-burner," who must be permitted to repose absolute implicit reliance on every detail of the narrative, every clause of the creed set before them, or who else will be miserable, Macaulay is the most dangerous of all possible guides. But it must be an exceedingly moderate intelligence which does not pretty quickly perceive the classes and kinds of subject on which he is to be taken with grains of salt, an exceedingly sluggish and clumsy intellect which cannot apply these grains with sufficient discretion.

And he certainly has not his equal anywhere for covering his subject in the pointing-stick fashion. You need not—you had much better not—pin your faith on his details, but his Pisgah sights are admirable. Hole after hole—a very sieveful of holes indeed—has been picked in the **"Clive"** and the **"Hastings,"** the **"Johnson"** and the **"Addison,"** the **"Frederick"** and the **"Horace Walpole."** Yet every one of these papers contains sketches, summaries, *précis,* which have not been made obsolete or valueless by all the work of correction in detail. As a literary critic, again, Macaulay is far from impeccable. His sympathies were not very wide, and they were apt to be conditioned by attractions and repulsions quite other than literary. Although he had had a strictly classical education, although he early showed remarkable mastery of literary form himself, it cannot be said that this form was ever the object of any but a very subordinate share of his attention. It is amazing, when one has long been familiar with his essay— an extremely interesting one—on Temple, and then comes to be familiar with Temple's own work, to find how little Macaulay seems to have relished or realised Temple's purely literary excellence. He was a good Italian scholar and something of a Dantist; yet his remarks on the second of the three great poets of the world are wofully narrow and inadequate. I feel morally certain that he could not have been the Miltonian that he was if Milton had been a Cavalier and a Churchman; and I doubt whether it was not necessary for him to make up his mind (as he did on next to no evidence) that Bunyan served in the Parliamentary army before he could give a voice to his admiration of *The Pilgrim's Progress.* Even when politics did not interfere, it is obvious that his interest in literature as a round of sketches of ethics, of manners, of political life in the wide sense, altogether overtops his interest in it as literature. On Spenser, he has, as everybody knows, fallen into one of his rare blunders of fact. He had read, as he had read everything, the minor Elizabethans; but they excite no rapture in him. It is admitted that he has made Bacon, no very deep metaphysician at best, shallower and more exoteric still in his exposition of him. It is "man in relation to the Town" that he, like his beloved Addison, really cares for.

Enough was said in the former paper on this subject of the defects of Macaulay as a historian; and indeed they are not deniable by any competent judge who is not for the nonce a mere advocate. But the merit which has been allowed to his *Essays,* that of extraordinarily vivid presentation of the subject, must be allowed here to a still greater degree, inasmuch as it is shown on a far greater scale and in much more difficult matter. With part of the period which Macaulay's *History* covers I happen, as has been said, to have acquainted myself in considerable detail and by going to the original authorities. Nobody can possibly be more opposed to Macaulay's general views on the politics of that period than I am. And yet I am disposed to think and say, without the least conscious intention of paradox and with much deliberate guarding against it, that of no other period of English history does an idea so clear, vivid, and on the whole accurate exist in so large a number of people, and that this is due to Macaulay. The fact is that the power of making historical periods and transactions real and living is an exceedingly rare power, and that Macaulay had it. Since his day we have had a numerously attended school of historians who have gone beyond even Macaulay in book-devouring, who have as a rule confined themselves more than he did to single periods, and who have sometimes exhausted their powers of picturesque writing and their readers' patience in severely accurate detail. Not one of them, to my thinking, has achieved the success of making his period living and actual as Macaulay has. The picturesque people hide the truth with their flashes and their flourishes. The Dryasdusts dole it out in such cut and dried morsels, with such a lack of art, such a tedious tyranny of document and detail, that the wood almost literally becomes invisible because of the trees.

As for the *Lays of Ancient Rome,* and the not very numerous but very remarkable minor verse which completes them, the history of that division of Macaulay's works is the most startling and the best known of all. When the *Lays* first appeared, they took the world by storm, and they held it for many years pretty well unquestioned. Nobody in his senses, of course, ever took them for the highest poetry: they cannot in that respect pretend to vie even with their own author's curious fragment on **"The Last Buccaneer,"** or his exquisite **"Jacobite's Epitaph."** But in one of the kinds of poetry just below the very highest they exhibited accomplishment and mastery quite wonderful, and gave the poetical satisfaction to thousands, and probably millions, who were not fitted to receive it from higher things. Then arose Mr. Matthew Arnold and denounced them as "pinchbeck," and the large number of persons who about five and twenty years ago were convinced that to get "culture" you must go to Mr. Arnold, at once echoed "pinchbeck," and vowed that they had never thought them anything else. Those, however, who had not exactly waited for Mr. Arnold to form their opinions of classical and romantic perfection, were not, I think, much disturbed by this contempt. And in fact "pinchbeck" is about the unluckiest epithet that Mr. Arnold could have selected. Pinchbeck in the literal sense pretends to be gold, and pinchbeck in the transferred sense means anything which pretends to be something it is not. Now the *Lays* pretend to be nothing that they are not; they aim at nothing more than a rattling spirited presentation in easy ballad rhyme of picturesquely told incidents. There is no doubt plenty of pinchbeck in English verse. There is the pinchbeck that imitates Greek tragedy and the pinchbeck that imitates mediæval imagery; there is pinchbeck which would fain

be French and pinchbeck which would fain be philosophical. I am not quite certain that some of Mr. Arnold's own verse, exquisite as is the best of it, is not pinchbeck in its affectation of a sort of pseudo-philosophic attitude dashed with sceptical modernism, and corrected by classic form. But there is no pinchbeck in the *Lays* because there is no pretence. Gold perhaps they are not; silver I think they are; copper an unkind or partial judgment may call them. But not twenty Mr. Arnolds shall ever persuade me that they are base metal,—metal which shams a higher stuff.

I think the publication of Sir George Trevelyan's excellent life of his uncle [*The Life and Letters of Lord Macaulay,* 1876] began a reaction in favour of Macaulay, and I think that reaction, though not very sudden or violent, is solidly founded and will go on. The pedants indeed are, I hear, raging at him more than ever; but they can do little harm; and the average half-educated journalist has begun to leave off thinking it fine to sneer at him. He will never of course regain the position that he held during the last decade of his own life and for a few years afterwards: and I should be sorry if he did. For his thought was no doubt distinctly *borné* and sometimes almost vulgar; his style was sometimes flashy and almost always deficient in the finest distinction; he was a terribly partial historian; and in every department of literature he was insensible to, and incapable of recognising, *nuances,* half-tones, delicate contrasts, subtle gradations. But on the other hand he had that rarest and most precious power of attracting his readers to, and interesting them in, subjects that were not merely frivolous or ephemeral; his mental attitude was sturdy, honest, shrewd; he had a stout and noble patriotism; his very partisanship, his very advocacy, had something manly and downright in its unfeigned and unmistakable character; and fatiguing as his "snip-snap" sometimes is, utterly disgusting as are imitations of it, yet any one who speaks of Macaulay's style with contempt seems to me to proclaim himself fatally and finally as a mere "one-eyed man" in literary appreciation. Of the merits and defects of that curious generation of middleclass Liberalism

---

Macaulay on the proudest moment of his life, in a letter dated 1850:

I have seen the hippopotamus, both asleep and awake; and I can assure you that, awake or asleep, he is the ugliest of the works of God. But you must hear of my triumphs. Thackeray swears that he was eye-witness and ear-witness of the proudest event of my life. Two damsels were just about to pass that doorway which we, on Monday, in vain attempted to enter, when I was pointed out to them. 'Mr. Macaulay!' cried the lovely pair. 'Is that Mr. Macaulay? Never mind the hippopotamus.' And, having paid a shilling to see Behemoth, they left him in the very moment at which he was about to display himself to them, in order to see— but spare my modesty. I can wish for nothing more on earth, now that Madame Tussaud, in whose Pantheon I once hoped for a place, is dead.

Macaulay, quoted by G. O. Trevelyan, in his The Life and Letters of Lord Macaulay, *Longmans, 1876.*

which flourished in England from 1830 to 1860, he is probably the most striking example; and even if he were not this, he is a very great man of letters, and an almost unsurpassed leader to reading. (pp. 88-97)

> *George Saintsbury, "Macaulay" and "Macaulay (concluded)," in his* Corrected Impressions: Essays on Victorian Writers, *Dodd, Mead and Company, 1895, pp. 79-87, 88-97.*

G. K. Chesterton   (essay date 1909)

[*Chesterton was an eminent man of letters and a Roman Catholic apologist best known for his* Father Brown *mysteries and the fantasy* The Man Who Was Thursday *(1908). In the following essay, first published in the* Daily News *in 1909, Chesterton notes that Macaulay is able to translate his passion for his subject into an exciting narrative and to discover grandeur even in unsympathetic characters.*]

We have all heard of prophets and poets being unpopular; and also of unpopularity as a thing that may purify the soul. But there is this further and rather odd fact—that every great man must go through a period of unpopularity, not while he is alive, but shortly after he is dead. That after eclipse is essential because in that is settled the difference between temporary and eternal oblivion. The prophet and the quack are alike admired for a generation, and admired for the wrong reasons. Then they are both forgotten, for no reason at all. But if the man is a mere quack he never returns. If he is a great man he returns, and he returns for the right reasons.

We need not dwell on the obvious instances of this. Dr. Johnson was enthroned as a cold arbiter, and dethroned as a cold arbiter. Now he has been restored as a most hot and human Christian soul, and Christians can never forget him. Dickens was adored for Little Nell, and then despised for Little Nell. It is only when Little Nell is quite dead and out of the way that he can be sufficiently adored for Dick Swiveller. Of these once popular figures there is one who has not yet recaptured his popularity. Just as a little while ago it was thought cultured to sneer at Dickens, so it is still thought cultured to sneer at Macaulay. Perhaps I had come myself to be too much under that cloud of disillusion; for when I opened Macaulay's *History* by accident the other day I was startled by the unmistakable roll of rich style and real greatness in the thing.

Macaulay's popularity was shallow; he was popular for the wrong reasons. The wit of those ringing and arresting sentences is constantly coarse and unfair, though I wish it were more often remembered that this old lucid cleverness really had to be clever; whereas our vague culture is quite free to be stupid. Wit is lower than humour; but sham humour is much easier than sham wit. You can pretend that you have made an atmosphere; you cannot pretend that you have made a pun. Similarly many a modern professes that his style has the nameless charm of Newman, because he could not possibly invent one clever antithesis of Macaulay. Still, Macaulay's mere wit and logic are shallow, and would not make him great. What is it, after all, that makes him great?

This, I think, makes him great and even eternal; that he had the high passion of history. He understood the word glory; the glory of man as a thing like the glory of God.

The only difference between the warrior and the poet is that the warrior seeks this thing in the future and the poet or the historian in the past. Macaulay had the music of history in him, just as Walter Scott had it. He was passionately traditional. There is one unquestionable test of this: he was fond of proper names. Some of the best lines of Scott's poetry consist entirely of the names of places. Some of the strongest sentences of Macaulay hang wholly on words like Milton or Rome.

There is something that is higher than impartiality, and Macaulay possessed it; poetical justice; the living impartiality of the imagination rather than the dead impartiality of the reason. He sometimes made good men bad and bad men good in the heat of political prejudice; but he always made them men, and even great men. He slandered his opponents, but he did not belittle them. He had a high pleasure in mixing with heroic affairs; he liked to crowd his stage with men of stature and presence; he had a warlike sort of wish to see villains worthy of his heroes. Though he was not enough of a Christian to love his enemies, he was enough of a heathen to admire them; and a heathen is the next best thing. Take the case of the celebrated Graham of Claverhouse, afterwards Lord Dundee. Macaulay starts, by prejudice or purpose, indecently or even insanely against the man. He is really unreasonable in the whole affair of the Covenanters. Claverhouse, I imagine, was an ordinary officer of Dragoons, a type that does not always specialize in the Christian virtues, in the later seventeenth century, a time when the Scotch nobility and gentry were cynical and gross. It was his merely military duty to put down a rebellion of men whom you may call prophets or maniacs according to taste, but who were utterly exceptional, ruthless, and beyond common reason; who gave no quarter in battle, and wished to persecute every other religion upon earth. I daresay Claverhouse did wrong; just as any bullnecked English officer would probably do wrong in dealing with some swarm of alien fanatics. But that is all. Macaulay gives a picture of harmless and laborious peasants trampled down in blood by a monstrous fiend in top-boots, who dances on them apparently for fun. In the first few pages about John Graham, Macaulay describes a beast rather than a man. Whether he was like that in real life we need not elaborately discuss. One thing is certain: that he does not remain like that in Macaulay's *History.*

As soon as Dundee begins to play his great part at the very crisis of the English kingship, an extraordinary impression begins to grow. Macaulay begins to like him. Macaulay is mad for the Revolution; and he becomes quite fond of Dundee because he came so near to frustrating the Revolution. Macaulay is glad with every cell of his brain that James II should go. Yet he is thrilled through every drop of his blood when the arresting voice of Graham calls James like a trumpet to remain. When Dundee is mounted, and rides down the street, Macaulay's prose moves to the tune of Walter Scott. Stroke after stroke changes the beast to a prince of chivalry. Macaulay talks of the calm magnanimity of this monster. He goes out of his way to mention that he reproved the rapine of the clans; that he held heroic language in the council of the chiefs; and that on the eve of his last battle he asked for peril as a favour, that he might show that he was a soldier as well as a general. When the claymores come cleaving their way down Killiecrankie, Macaulay is almost a Jacobite. The last words of the great persecutor of the Covenant are lofty and unselfish; and in death he is as pure as Hector. I know no more singular change of tone in the description of one man.

This is a striking instance of what I may call the abstract enthusiasm of Macaulay. He had a passion for the cause; but he also had a passion for the subject, for the period and everybody in it. A stranger and stronger case still is that of Marlborough. If ever there was a moral dwarf, a spiritual monkey, it was he. He was a lump of littleness just large enough to be seen. He combined all despicable qualities in combinations hitherto untried. He was a thrifty profligate. He was an unpatriotic militarist. He sold his sister and his country, not madly, like a gambler, but quite quietly and explanatorily. It is almost incredible that any man, or even any animal, should be such an object of contempt. And yet Macaulay is so carried away with the great Whig Crusade, the great story that he is telling, that when dealing with one who played a large part in it, he cannot help making the man magnificent, although the part was base. He tells all the truths about Marlborough that I have cited, without the least doubt or favour; and yet he gives the impression that he has been describing a great man.

I have heard that somebody has started something else which is called scientific history, and I once tried to read it. It appears to avoid the dangers of describing great men by the bright and simple solution of not describing men at all. By this method the historian looks down on all the movements of men as if they were ants. If I want truth I must confess that I prefer Macaulay. I prefer to look up at men as if they were angels, even if they are angels of darkness. (pp. 107-11)

> *G. K. Chesterton, "The Case for Macaulay,"*
> *in his* A Handful of Authors: Essays on Books
> & Writers, *edited by Dorothy Collins, Sheed*
> *and Ward, 1953, pp. 107-11.*

Lytton Strachey   (essay date 1928)

[*Strachey was a literary critic and biographer whose iconoclastic reexaminations of historical figures revolutionized the course of modern biography. In the following essay, originally published in* The Nation and the Athenaeum *in 1928, he argues that Macaulay's Whig bias severely compromised the quality of his* History of England.]

In Apollo's house there are many mansions; there is even one (unexpectedly enough) for the Philistine. So complex and various are the elements of literature that no writer can be damned on a mere enumeration of faults. He may always possess merits which make up for everything; if he loses on the swings, he may win on the roundabouts. Macaulay—whatever the refined and the sublime may say to the contrary—is an example of this. A coarse texture of mind—a metallic style—an itch for the obvious and the emphatic—a middle-class, Victorian complacency—it is all too true; Philistine is, in fact, the only word to fit the case; and yet, by dint of sheer power of writing, the Philistine has reached Parnassus. It is a curious occurrence, and deserves a closer examination.

What are the qualities that make a historian? Obviously these three—a capacity for absorbing facts, a capacity for stating them, and a point of view. The two latter are connected, but not necessarily inseparable. The late Professor Samuel Gardiner, for instance, could absorb facts, and he could state them; but he had no point of view; and the result is that his book on the most exciting period of English history resembles nothing so much as a very large heap of sawdust. But a point of view, it must be remembered, by no means implies sympathy. One might almost say that it implies the reverse. At any rate it is curious to observe how many instances there are of great historians who have been at daggers drawn with their subjects. Gibbon, a highly civilised scoffer, spent twenty years of his life writing about barbarism and superstition. Michelet was a romantic and a republican; but his work on mediæval France and the Revolution is far inferior to his magnificent delineation of the classic and despotic centuries. Macaulay's greatnephew, Professor Trevelyan, has, it is true, written a delightful account of the Italian Risorgimento, of which he is an enthusiastic devotee. But, even here, the rule seems to apply; one cannot but feel that Professor Trevelyan's epic would have been still more delightful if it had contained a little of the salt of criticism—if, in fact, he had not swallowed Garibaldi whole.

As for Macaulay's point of view, everyone knows it was the Whig one. In reality this is simplifying too much; but, however we may describe it, there can be no doubt that Macaulay's vision was singularly alien to the England of the latter years of the seventeenth century. Like Gibbon, like Michelet, like the later Carlyle, he did not—to put it succinctly—understand what he was talking about. Charles II, James II—that whole strange age in which religion, debauchery, intellect, faction, wit and brutality seethed and bubbled together in such an extraordinary *olla podrida*—escaped him. He could see parts of it; but he could not see into the depths; and so much the better: he had his point of view. The definiteness, the fixity, of his position is what is remarkable. He seems to have been created *en bloc*. His manner never changed; as soon as he could write at all—at the age of eight—he wrote in the style of his **History**. The three main factors in his mental growth—the Clapham sect, Cambridge, Holland House—were not so much influences as suitable environments for the development of a predetermined personality. Whatever had happened to him, he would always have been a middle-class intellectual with Whig views. It is possible, however, that he may actually have gained something from Holland House. The modern habit of gently laughing at Whigs and Whiggery is based on a misconception. A certain *a priori* stuffiness which seems to hang about that atmosphere is in reality a Victorian innovation. The true pre-Reform Bill Whig was a tremendous aristocrat—the heir to a great tradition of intellectual independence and spiritual pride. When the Hollands' son travelled as a youth in Italy he calmly noted in his diary that someone he had met had a face "almost as stupid as the Duke of Wellington's"; the young Fox was a chip of the old block. Such surroundings must have been good for Macaulay. It was not only that they supported his self-confidence—he had enough of that already—but that they brought him into touch with the severity, the grandeur, and the amenity of an old civilisation. Without them he might have been provincial or academic; but he was not so; on every page of his work one sees the manifest signs of the culture and the traffic of the great world.

Thus Macaulay's Whiggism was a composite affair—it was partly eighteenth century and partly Victorian. But the completeness with which it dominated him gave him his certainty of attitude and his clarity of vision. It enabled him to stand up against the confusion and frenzy of the seventeenth century and say, very loudly and very distinctly, what he thought of it. So far so good. The misfortune is that what he thought was not of a finer quality. The point of view is distinct enough, but it is without distinction; and Macaulay in consequence remains an excellent but not a supreme historian. His Whiggism was in itself a very serious drawback—not because it was a cause of bias, but because it was a symptom of crudity. The bias was of the wrong kind; it was the outcome of party politics, and the sad truth is that, in the long run, party politics become a bore. They did not, indeed, succeed in making Macaulay a bore; that was impossible; but, though he is never dull, one constantly feels that he might have been much more interesting. Too often he misses the really exciting, the really fascinating, point. And how can one fail to miss a great deal if one persists in considering the world from one side or other of the House of Commons?

A certain crudity, a certain coarseness of fibre—the marks of a party politician—are particularly obvious in those character sketches of great persons which form so important a part of Macaulay's *History.* Within their limits they are admirably done; but their limits are too narrow. They lack colour; they are steel engravings—unsatisfactory compromises between a portrait in oils and a realistic snapshot. One has only to compare them with Clarendon's splendid presentments to realise their inadequacy. With what a gorgeous sinuosity, with what a grandiose delicacy, the older master elaborates, through his enormous sentences, the lineaments of a soul! Beside them the skimpy lines and cheap contrasts of Macaulay's black and white are all too obvious.

But the Whig politician was not only crude; he was also, to a strange degree, ingenuous and complacent. A preposterous optimism fills his pages. The Revolution of 1688 having succeeded, all was well; Utopia was bound to follow; and it actually had followed—in the reign of Victoria. Thus he contrasts with delight, almost with awe, the state of Torbay at the time of William's landing and its condition in 1850. In 1688 "the huts of ploughmen and fishermen were thinly scattered over what is now the site of crowded marts and of luxurious pavilions." A description of the modern Torquay becomes irresistible. "The inhabitants are about ten thousand in number. The newly-built churches and chapels, the baths and libraries, the hotels

and public gardens, the infirmary and the museum, the white streets, rising terrace above terrace, the gay villas peeping from the midst of shrubberies and flower beds, present a spectacle widely different from any that in the seventeenth century England could show." They do indeed.

The style is the mirror of the mind, and Macaulay's style is that of a debater. The hard points are driven home like nails with unfailing dexterity; it is useless to hope for subtlety or refinement; one cannot hammer with delicacy. The repetitions, the antithesis, resemble revolving cogwheels; and indeed the total result produces an effect which suggests the operations of a machine more than anything else—a comparison which, no doubt, would have delighted Macaulay. The descriptive passages are the most deplorable. In a set-piece, such as the account of Westminster Hall at the impeachment of Hastings, all the horrors of a remorseless rhetoric are made manifest. From the time of Cicero downwards, the great disadvantage of oratory has been that it never lets one off. One must hear everything, however well one knows it, and however obvious it is. For such writers a dose of Stendhal is to be recommended. Macaulay, however, would not have benefited by the prescription, for he was a hopeless case. The tonic pages of the *Chartreuse de Parme* would have had no effect on him whatever. When he wished to state that Schomberg was buried in Westminster Abbey, he *had* to say that "the illustrious warrior" was laid in "that venerable abbey, hallowed by the dust of many generations of princes, heroes and poets." There is no escaping it; and the incidental drawback that Schomberg was not buried at Westminster at all, but in Dublin, is, in comparison with the platitude of the style, of very small importance.

The curiously metallic quality in Macaulay's writing—its hardness of outline, its slightly hollow ring—is so characteristic that it is difficult not to see in it the indication of some profound psychological state. The stout, square man with the prodigious memory and the inexhaustible capacity for conversation, was apparently a normal human being, except in one direction: he never married, and there seems no reason to suppose that he was ever in love. An entertaining essay might perhaps be written on the sexlessness of historians; but it would be entertaining and nothing more: we do not know enough either about the historians or sex. Yet, in Macaulay's case, one cannot resist the conclusion that the absence from his make-up of intense physical emotion brought a barrenness upon his style. His sentences have no warmth and no curves; the embracing fluidity of love is lacking. And it is noticeable how far more effective he is in his treatment of those whom he dislikes than of those whom he admires. His Marlborough is a fine villain. His James II is a caricature, with a queer vitality of its own—the vitality of a marionette. But his William of Orange is a failure—a lifeless image of waxwork perfection. Macaulay's inability to make his hero live—his refusal to make any attempt to illuminate the mysteries of that most obscure and singular character—epitomises all that is weakest in his work.

Probably the futility of his æsthetic judgments was another effect of the same cause. Whenever he writes of pure poetry—in the essay on Byron, for instance—he is plainly at sea; his lack of sensibility becomes painfully obvious. A true child of his age, he had a profound distrust, amounting at times to an actual hatred, of art. That Queen Mary should have ruined her father, turned him out of his kingdom, and seized his throne for herself—all that was no blemish at all on her character: was she not acting upon strictly Whig principles? But one fault she did have. She was responsible for "a frivolous and inelegant fashion." She was the first person in England to form "a vast collection of hideous images, and of vases on which houses, trees, bridges and mandarins were depicted in outrageous defiance of all the laws of perspective." Queen Mary, in fact, liked china; and that could not be forgiven her.

The weaknesses are obvious, and the strength, suitably enough, is obvious too. History is primarily a narrative, and in power of narration no one has ever surpassed Macaulay. In that he is a genius. When it comes to telling a story, his faults disappear or change into virtues. Narrowness becomes clarity, and crudity turns into force. The rhetoric of the style, from being the ornament of platitude, becomes the servant of excitement. Every word is valuable: there is no hesitation, no confusion, and no waste. It is clear from his journal that Macaulay realised the dominating importance of this side of his work. He laboured at his purely narrative passages for weeks at a time, with the result that they are masterpieces. Nobody who has once read them can ever forget his account of the trial of the Bishops, the siege of Derry, and the battle of Killiecrankie. To write so is to write magnificently, and if one has to be a Philistine to bring off those particular effects one can only say, so much the better for the Philistine. But it is not only in certain passages that Macaulay triumphs. His whole *History* is conditioned by a supreme sense of the narrative form. It presses on, with masterly precipitation, from start to finish. Everything falls into place. Unsatisfying characters, superficial descriptions, jejune reflections, are seen to be no longer of importance in themselves—they are merely stages in the development of the narrative. They are part of the pattern—the enthralling, ever-shifting pattern of the perfect kaleidoscope. A work of art? Yes, there is no denying it: the Philistine was also an artist. And there he is—squat, square and perpetually talking—on Parnassus. (pp. 169-80)

> *Lytton Strachey, "Six English Historians: Macaulay," in his* Portraits in Miniature and Other Essays, *Chatto & Windus, 1931, pp. 169-80.*

A. L. Rowse   (essay date 1944)

[An English historian, poet, and critic, Rowse is the author of numerous studies of Elizabethan history and literature that have been praised for their lively prose style and exhaustive knowledge. In the following essay, originally published in The English Spirit: Essays in History and Literature *(1944), he examines the reasons for the popularity of Macaulay's* Critical and Historical Essays, *a work that Rowse characterises as easily accessible and high spirited, but written by an author with a con-*

ventional outlook, "a Philistine of genius" who helped shape Victorian attitudes.]

Not the least among the number of remarkable books whose publication distinguished the year 1843 was Macaulay's *Essays.* We owe their appearance at that time to the Americans. Macaulay had previously considered publishing his reviews in book form and turned the idea down. For all his cocksure certainty he was a modest man. He did not think so highly of his essays as the public did. "The public judges, and ought to judge, indulgently of periodical works," he wrote to the editor of the *Edinburgh Review.* "They are not expected to be highly finished. Their natural life is only six weeks." But his hand was forced in the matter. When, not content with collecting and publishing his reviews (without permission or remuneration) in the United States, American publishers sent over copies in their hundreds to this country, Macaulay was forced to act. We have reason to be grateful. So far from being confined to a natural life of only six weeks, the *Essays* have survived a hundred years. Few works have been so severely criticised, or shown to have more serious errors; and yet there is no doubt that they will go gaily on to their second century. To what do they owe their survival?

First and last, they owe it to their immense readability. The inscription upon Macaulay's statue in the ante-chapel of Trinity at Cambridge, which says that he was the first to write annals in such a way that the truth was more readable than fiction, has an element of exaggeration in it, when you think of Gibbon and Hume before him, not to mention Tacitus. But all the same it lays hold of the essential fact about Macaulay: he is the most readable of historians. The difficulty with him is not, as with some others (the uncongenial Freeman, for example), to take him up, but to put him down: the eye races through those exciting, easy pages, fearful lest the chapter or the essay come to an end too soon. And the *Essays,* though not up to the standard Macaulay reached in the *History,* reveal this particular quality at its highest.

Whatever we may think of his point of view, and however much we must take exception to what he says, there is no doubt about the pleasure he has given now to generations and will continue to give. Sir G. O. Trevelyan says that the demand for Macaulay varies with the demand for coal. It is a pleasant nineteenth-century thought. But I can imagine no more cheerful and stimulating companion for winter evenings in war-time, in conditions of the black-out. As Macaulay himself says of the pleasures of reading: "Plato is never sullen. Dante does not stay too long."

And the *Essays* are incomparable for young people who are just beginning to take an interest in things of the mind. How many people owe their first intellectual stimulus to the *Essays*! (The appreciation of the *History,* a maturer work, comes later.) Arthur Balfour, in his *Autobiography,* has expressed the obligation of those hundreds of people, with minds worth speaking of, for whom the *Essays* opened a door to higher things. One can see why this should be: for all that Macaulay was a man of affairs, and even a man of the world, there was something curiously unadult, ungrown-up about him. After Dickens the most famous writer of his day, he remained something of a boy to the end of his life. (Some people—it is obvious that Strachey was one of them—have the impression that we do not know all there is to be known about Macaulay.)

What, then, are the qualities which make the *Essays* such a prodigious success?

They have a power of holding the attention in a most extraordinary way. And this arises from the fact that their style is essentially conversational—but the conversation is dramatic, declamatory, exciting. In fact the *Essays* are debates. Macaulay in his usual generous way gave Southey the credit for first hitting upon this form of historical essay; he merely said that he had improved upon it. But what life and vivacity Macaulay gave to it! You can hear the voice, the torrent of that astonishing conversation, which made some people protest (cf. Greville's *Memoirs*), though, like Greville, they usually ended by submitting, fascinated, conquered by him. Again and again one has the sensation of listening to a wonderful discussion among that brilliant circle of young men at Cambridge, or to the famous talk at Holland House. There is all the dramatic excitement of opposing ideas being argued out. There are the intellectual high spirits on every page—always an irresistible quality. There is plenty of good knock-about fun. One cannot but enjoy his attack on Montgomery's *Poems*—would there were someone with a pen like his to deal with the Montgomerys of our day!—or his onslaught upon the intolerable prolixity of Professor Nares:

> The work of Dr. Nares has filled us with astonishment similar to that which Captain Lemuel Gulliver felt when first he landed in Brobdingnag, and saw corn as high as the oaks in the New Forest, thimbles as large as buckets, and wrens of the bulk of turkeys. The whole book, and every component part of it, is on a gigantic scale. The title is as long as an ordinary preface: the prefatory matter would furnish out an ordinary book; and the book contains as much reading as an ordinary library. We cannot sum up the merits of the stupendous mass of paper which lies before us better than by saying it consists of about two thousand closely printed quarto pages, that it occupies fifteen hundred inches cubic measure, and that it weighs sixty pounds avoirdupois. Such a book might, before the Deluge, have been considered as light reading by Hilpa and Shallum. But unhappily the life of man is now three-score years and ten; and we cannot but think it somewhat unfair of Dr. Nares to demand from us so large a portion of so short an existence.

And so on.

I used to think that this might be somewhat unfair on poor Dr. Nares; but having tried to read his book, I now sympathise with Macaulay.

Besides high spirits, ceaseless vivacity, great sense of phrase, a vivid historical imagination, clear-cut and accurate, something more is needed to explain his success as a writer. On the technical side the clue is to be found in his admirable, his infallible power of construction. Whatever it may be, whether argument, or scene, or narrative, he carries the reader irresistibly along with him. Other factors help to explain his almost unexampled success with the public in his own time. He was a deeply conventional man, a Philistine of genius; his work appealed to, was the very expression of, the conventionalism, the Philistinism of the Victorian age. He was a moralist of a rather crude kind, he spoke straight to the heart of a society which, almost inexplicably to us, saw everything in crudely moral terms. To him, as to them, everything was either black or it was white. And so we get the fatiguing antithesis in which he saw, altogether too simply, the characters of Warren Hastings, Clive, Marlborough, Bacon, Dr. Johnson, Horace Walpole. Whatever we may think of it as history, there is no doubt that it makes for good reading.

Macaulay's defects were the defects of his qualities. He was very square-cut, definite, downright. Altogether too much so. He had much of the positiveness of the eighteenth century about him. His taste was formed on Addison, that proto-Victorian, and the writers of the age of Queen Anne. This meant a great limitation of sympathies—though, even then, those were broader than many of his latter-day critics realise. It was Macaulay, somewhat surprisingly, who said: "We know no spectacle so ridiculous as the British public in one of its periodical fits of morality." (If it had not been for that magisterial "we," it might have been Matthew Arnold speaking.) His essay on the Restoration dramatists shows him a good deal less sympathetic to Puritanism than might have been feared from the son of Zachary Macaulay, brought up in the strictest circle of the Clapham sect, the darling child of Hannah More.

The pity is that Macaulay had such power, such unique vividness, that when he was wrong, as he often was, he has impressed his own version upon the English mind more firmly than the truth. His treatment of Warren Hastings and Marlborough are outstanding cases in point. One might almost say that his misrepresentation of Hastings was responsible for the Indian attitude towards the history of our rule in India. What people other than the English would have been so careless of their own case, so unjust to themselves, as to prescribe the reading of Macaulay's essay on Warren Hastings in their schools and universities? The English have a singular faculty for depreciating their great men. (Is it perhaps a form of superiority-complex?) Most people must still be under the impression that Marlborough, though a great soldier, was a bad hat. That is the view that Macaulay has fixed upon us. It is quite untrue that he was a bad man: he was a cold, wonderfully controlled man; but in addition to his genius, he was not without a heart. The Prime Minister's life of his ancestor has disproved Macaulay once and for all.

Nevertheless, the exaggeratedly high standards which Macaulay stood for were an important element in forming the Victorian outlook. Though the Victorians kidded themselves a lot, they were genuinely high-minded; which we are not—and we lose something by it.

It is interesting to note Macaulay's own modest estimate of his *Essays*:

> In spite of the applause and the profit, neither of which I despise, I am sorry that it had become necessary to republish these papers. There are

few of them which I read with satisfaction. Those few, however, are generally the latest, and this is a consolatory circumstance. The most hostile critic must admit, I think, that I have improved greatly as a writer. The third volume seems to me worth two of the second, and the second worth ten of the first.

That gives a very useful little clue to the correct estimation of the *Essays.* What is needed is a dependable guide to them for the use of the unwary. (pp. 208-12)

> *A. L. Rowse, "Macaulay's 'Essays'," in* Victorian Literature: Modern Essays in Criticism, *edited by Austin Wright, Oxford University Press, Inc., 1961, pp. 208-12.*

In a fictional dialogue Matthew Arnold criticizes Macaulay's style:

'Explain yourself,' said I; 'why do you call Mr. Hepworth Dixon's style middle-class Macaulayese?' 'I call it Macaulayese,' says the pedant, 'because it has the same internal and external characteristics as Macaulay's style; the external characteristic being a hard metallic movement with nothing of the soft play of life, and the internal characteristic being a perpetual semblance of hitting the right nail on the head without the reality. And I call it middle-class Macaulayese, because it has these faults without the compensation of great studies and of conversance with great affairs, by which Macaulay partly redeemed them.'

> *Matthew Arnold, in his* Friendship's Garland, *Smith, Elder, & Co., 1903.*

Robert Livingston Schuyler (essay date 1948)

[*For the better part of a career that spanned sixty years, Schuyler was associated with Columbia University, where he wrote and edited numerous books and articles on British and American history. In the following excerpt, he examines the reasons for the widespread popularity of Macaulay's* History, *describing the historian as an excellent storyteller whose confident belief in the theory of progress somewhat restricted his vision.*]

Few popular men of letters, presumably, have been indifferent to their vogue in their own day or to their reputation in the future. In the case of Macaulay there is explicit evidence of sales-consciousness and fame-consciousness. A few days after the publication of the first two volumes of his *History* Macaulay wrote in his journal, one of the most self-revealing of diaries: "Black says that there has been no such sale since the days of *Waverley.* The success is in every way complete beyond all hope. . . . I think, though with some misgiving, that the book will live." And later, predicting that Herodotus would still be read with delight a thousand years thereafter, he said: "We must do our best to be read too." The well-known ambition which he cherished for his *History*—that it would for a few days "supersede the last fashionable novel on the tables of young ladies"—was amply realized, as is shown by the

facts and figures concerning its sales given by Sir George Otto Trevelyan, Macaulay's nephew, in his classic biography of his uncle [*The Life and Letters of Lord Macaulay,* 1876]. The annual sale, according to Trevelyan, writing about 1875, often surpassed that of the best-selling novel of the current year.

The first installment of Macaulay's *History* was published in 1848, and if in this its centennial year the public in the English-speaking world were to be polled on the question, "Who is the greatest historian of England?", I believe that Macaulay would be an easy winner. He is no longer read to the same extent, to be sure, as in his own day and during the following generation. Publishers still find it profitable to reprint his *History* and his *Essays* from time to time, but his reputation today is largely traditional. To say this, however, is to say that Macaulay's writings must have made, as we know that they did make, a tremendous impression upon England and her cultural offspring. Nor should we overlook the influence of Macaulay in non-English-speaking countries. Trevelyan tells us that the *History* was translated into German, Dutch, Danish, French, Italian, Spanish, Polish, Bohemian, Russian, Hungarian and Persian. The surprising thing about it today is not that it is not read more widely, but that it is read at all. It deals with only a brief period, even though an important one, in English history; facts unknown to Macaulay have been brought to light by later investigation; literary taste has undergone changes since his day; and the belief that he held in a progress which has operated in the past, at least for many centuries, and which can be counted upon to operate in the future, has been shaken, to put it mildly. (pp. 161-62)

It was while Macaulay was in India [as a member of the Legislative Council] that the idea of writing a great historical work began to take shape in his mind. "I am more than half determined to abandon politics," he wrote to a friend at the end of the year 1835, "and to give myself wholly to letters; to undertake some great historical work which may be at once the business and the amusement of my life." The idea remained nebulous for some time, but there gradually emerged the conception of a history of England from the Revolution of 1688 to the early nineteenth century. After his return to England in 1838 he wrote to Napier:

> The first part, (which, I think, will take up five octavo volumes), will extend from the Revolution to the commencement of Sir Robert Walpole's long administration; a period of three or four and thirty very eventful years. From the commencement of Walpole's administration to the commencement of the American war, events may be dispatched more concisely. From the commencement of the American war it will again become necessary to be copious. These, at least, are my present notions. . . . How far I shall bring the narrative down I have not determined. The death of George the Fourth [1830] would be the best halting-place. The *History* would then be an entire view of all the transactions which took place between the Revolution which brought the Crown into harmony with the Parliament, and the Revolution which

brought the Parliament into harmony with the nation. But there are great and obvious objections to contemporary history.

It was not, however, until after the Whig defeat in the General Election of 1841, which terminated Macaulay's tenure of office and gave him greater leisure for research and writing, that he set to work seriously on his *History.* He had come to the conclusion that he ought to begin his narrative with the accession of James II, and his first two volumes, published by Longman and Company in 1848, constituted a detailed history of the reign of that monarch. Political and other activities prevented Macaulay from giving his whole time to what was now his chief interest, and the illness from which he never fully recovered diminished his physical vigor though it did not affect his mental powers. He came to realize that the chronological scope of the *History,* as he had at first conceived it, must be greatly reduced. It became clear in time that he would not even be able to cover the reign of Queen Anne, and in the end the *History,* which, as Macaulay announced in its opening paragraph, was to have extended to a time within the memory of men still living, did not come this side of the reign of William III.

We do not have to infer Macaulay's ideas about history and historianship entirely from his historical writings. While he was still in his twenties he wrote a famous essay on history which was published in the *Edinburgh Review* in 1828. It was soon after this that he entered Parliament, years of political activity lay ahead of him, and he could not have foreseen that the world would judge him primarily as a historian. Yet so far as I know he never retracted any of the essential views expressed in the essay. Macaulay's conception of historianship was a lofty one. "To be a really great historian," he said, "is perhaps the rarest of intellectual distinctions," and he found no practitioners of the craft who even approximated to his ideal. He paid his respects to the ancient historians but indicated in what ways they fell short—Herodotus, who "perpetually leaves the most sagacious reader in doubt what to reject and what to receive"; Thucydides, deficient in the power of generalization; Livy, completely indifferent to truth, concerned only with "the picturesque effect of his book, and the honor of his country"; Tacitus, unrivaled among historians in the delineation of character, but carrying "his love of effect far beyond the limits of moderation." Modern historians, in general, had adhered more strictly to truth than their ancient predecessors—they had been less fictional. "Whether the historians of the last two centuries tell more truth than those of antiquity may perhaps be doubted. But it is quite certain that they tell fewer falsehoods."

It was the business of the historian, Macaulay insisted, to interpret as well as to narrate. "The writer who does not explain the phenomena as well as state them, performs only one half of his office." In the philosophy of history the moderns, in his opinion, had surpassed the ancients. The best of them "far excel their predecessors in the art of deducing general principles from facts." They had, however, fallen into a great error—they had distorted facts to suit general principles.

They arrive at a theory from looking at some of the phenomena; and the remaining phenomena they strain or curtail to suit the theory. . . . In every human character and transaction there is a mixture of good and evil: a little exaggeration, a little suppression, a judicious use of epithets, a watchful and searching scepticism with respect to the evidence on one side, a convenient credulity with respect to every report or tradition on the other, may easily make a saint of Laud or a tyrant of Henry the Fourth.

Macaulay took Hume as an example of this kind of misrepresentation; Gibbon, too, he found censurable on this score. And modern historians had sadly neglected the art of narration, "the art of interesting the affections and presenting pictures to the imagination."

No history, Macaulay recognized, could present the whole truth; "but those are . . . the best histories which exhibit such parts of the truth as most nearly produce the effect of the whole." History, in other words, must needs be selective, and "he who is deficient in the art of selection may, by showing nothing but the truth, produce all the effect of the grossest falsehood." In this art of selection, Macaulay found, modern historians had been woefully deficient. They had conceived of history much too narrowly.

> The perfect historian is he in whose work the character and spirit of an age is exhibited in miniature. He relates no fact, he attributes no expression to his characters, which is not authenticated by sufficient testimony. But, by judicious selection, rejection, and arrangement, he gives to truth those attractions which have been usurped by fiction. . . . If a man, such as we are supposing, should write the history of England, he would assuredly not omit the battles, the sieges, the negotiations, the seditions, the ministerial changes. But with these he would intersperse the details which are the charm of historical romances. . . . Sir Walter Scott . . . has used those fragments of truth which historians have scornfully thrown behind them in a manner which may well excite their envy. He has constructed out of their gleanings works which, even considered as histories, are scarcely less valuable than theirs. But a truly great historian would reclaim those materials which the novelist has appropriated. The history of the government, and the history of the people, would be exhibited in that mode in which alone they can be exhibited justly, in inseparable conjunction and intermixture. We should not then have to look for the wars and votes of the Puritans in Clarendon, and for their phraseology in Old Mortality; for one half of King James in Hume, and for the other half in The Fortunes of Nigel.

This protest against the unduly restricted scope of history was written long before the Germans discovered the virtues of *Kulturgeschichte* and still longer before James Harvey Robinson began to make blueprints for what he called "The New History." Macaulay was evidently thinking of modern historians, especially of modern English historians, though as a matter of fact Hume had not entirely omitted social history. Macaulay knew well enough that there was nothing startlingly novel about social history, which was as old as Herodotus. But social history had undoubtedly been neglected by the moderns, though Voltaire had revived it for the eighteenth century. The third chapter of Macaulay's own *History* is one of the most celebrated pieces of social history ever written in the English language. Macaulay said that it was the hardest chapter of all to write, and this was because the social history of England had been so little studied. He made much greater use of newspapers than any of his predecessors had done, and his understanding of seventeenth-century social types, such as the squire and the parson, owed much to his reading of the contemporary drama. He devoured all the ballads, satires and lampoons of the reigns of James II and William III—the period which his *History* covers in detail—that he could lay hands on.

In his essay on history, however, Macaulay was silent regarding the most important developments that had already taken place for the study and writing of history, the beginnings of that revolution in historiography which occurred in the nineteenth century. These developments lay outside the realm of history as literature, which, for Macaulay, was always history par excellence, and while he was not wholly ignorant of them, he failed to grasp their full significance. In Germany Niebuhr was at work rewriting the history of ancient Rome on the basis of critical investigation of the sources, the earlier volumes of the *Monumenta Germaniae Historica* were coming from the press, and the foundations of scientific history were being laid. In England a Record Commission had been in existence for years and had important publications to its credit; government archives and other manuscript collections had been explored and catalogued; scholars such as Francis Palgrave, Macaulay's senior by twelve years, were at work in the public records. It is a significant fact that the most popular of English historians remained throughout his life aloof from this "new" history and its practitioners—scholars like Benjamin Thorpe, whose publications included the first modern edition of the laws of the Anglo-Saxon kings, and John Kemble, ardent collector of Anglo-Saxon charters, of whom Maitland said, "Kemble's work often requires correction; but if Kemble's work had not been, there would be nothing to correct." Macaulay was not associated, so far as I know, with any collective enterprise for advancing historical knowledge. He did nothing that I have heard of to forward the training of historians. Though he was far from lacking in the faculty of critical judgment, and could attack historical writers with vigor and vehemence, not to say with vituperation, he did nothing for historical criticism as a discipline. Sir Charles Firth, who gave us the best edition of Macaulay's *History* and wrote an extensive commentary on it [*A Commentary on Macaulay's History of England,* 1938], after remarking that the development of a more scientific method of treating historical evidence was one of the great achievements of the nineteenth century, observed that Macaulay stood quite outside this movement.

In 1840 the *Edinburgh Review* published an article of Macaulay's which bore the title **"Von Ranke"**. The peg on which it was hung was an English translation of Ranke's *History of the Popes,* but all—literally all—that Macaulay said about the book or the author was that the German original was known and esteemed wherever German literature was studied, that it was "the work of a mind fitted both for minute researches and for large speculations," and that it was written in "an admirable spirit, equally remote from levity and bigotry, serious and earnest, yet tolerant and impartial." This was cool praise for what has been called the masterpiece of the father of scientific history. Macaulay once met Ranke. It ought to have been a dramatic episode, this meeting of the great literary historian and the great scientific historian. But the drama was on the comic side. The story as told by the chatty Charles Greville in his Diary illustrates amusingly the invincible talkativeness—perhaps one should say the extraordinary conversational power—which was a characteristic of Macaulay, at any rate until his later years. Ranke was on a visit to England, and Macaulay was asked to meet him. Greville writes:

> I went prepared to listen to some first-rate literary talk between such luminaries . . . but there never was a greater failure. The professor, a vivacious little man . . . could talk no English, and his French, though spoken fluently, was quite unintelligible. On the other hand, Macaulay could not speak German, and he spoke French without any facility, and with a very vile accent. It was comical to see the abundance of his matter struggling with his embarrassment in giving utterance to it, to hear the torrent of knowledge trying to force its way through the impediment of a limited acquaintance with the French language and the want of habit of conversing in it. But the struggle was of short duration. He began in French, but very soon could bear the restraint no longer, and broke into English, pouring forth his stores to the utterly unconscious and uncomprehending professor.

It is preëminently as a stylist, using that word in its broadest sense, that we usually think of Macaulay—and rightly so. That is how he thought of himself, and how competent critics, generally, have thought of him. "Where he set his stamp," said John Morley, a severe critic of Macaulay, "has been upon style; style in its widest sense . . . style, that is to say, in its relation to ideas and feelings, its commerce with thought, and its reaction on what one may call the temper or the conscience of the intellect." There are, of course, two sides to historianship—intake and outgo, research and presentation. Macaulay, conceiving of history as essentially a branch of literature and anxious above everything else to be read, was more greatly concerned with historical composition and its problems than with historical research and its problems.

It would be a serious mistake, however, to suppose that Macaulay was indifferent to research. He thought of himself as a diligent investigator, and, compared with many of his predecessors, he was. "He reads twenty books to write a sentence," said Thackeray, "he travels a hundred miles to make a line of description." Buckle in his *History of Civilization* spoke of Macaulay's "immense research." Wilbur C. Abbott, no mean authority on seventeenth-century English history, wrote an essay on Macaulay in which he said that "contrary to a widely accepted but wholly erroneous opinion, Macaulay made few statements without evidence to back them, and the tale of his researches is an amazing chronicle." Firth, on the other hand, was of the opinion that the defects of Macaulay's *History* were mainly owing to his underestimate of the importance of the research side of historianship.

Macaulay's topographical investigations are good examples of the pains he took to be accurate as well as colorful. "I must go down into Somersetshire and Devonshire to see the scene of Monmouth's campaign, and to follow the line of William's march from Torbay," he wrote to Napier. Trevelyan informs us that Macaulay spent two days in Londonderry.

> He penetrated into every corner where there still lurked a vestige of the past, and called upon every inhabitant who was acquainted with any tradition worth the hearing. He drove through the suburbs; he sketched a ground-plan of the streets . . . he walked four times round the walls of the city for which he was to do what Thucydides had done for Platæa.

And he kept detailed records of his findings.

Macaulay's descriptions of places may not always have been accurate, though they were seldom lacking in vividness. His description, for example, of Glencoe, scene of the famous massacre in the Scottish Highlands which cast a sinister shadow on the character of Macaulay's hero, William III, distinctly has "atmosphere," but critics have denied that it is truthful. If we accept the testimony of Andrew Lang, who went prowling around Glencoe, the atmosphere is mostly a product of Macaulay's imagination, and we are left wondering whether Macaulay may not have had reasons other than an abstract devotion to truth for giving the clan of the Macdonalds and their glen a bad name.

With his characters, also, Macaulay took great pains. The portraits in the spacious gallery of his *History* may not all be good likenesses. Leslie Stephen said that Macaulay was fond of representing a man as a bundle of contradictions because this enabled him to obtain striking contrasts. Be this as it may, however, his portraits were based upon evidence obtained from research, even if the evidence was not always trustworthy. Macaulay, to be sure, had no gifts of psychological insight to enable him to unravel men's motives or read their hearts, but his characters are something more than the empty names we encounter in the pages of so many historians.

Macaulay, it should be remarked, did not resort to vicarious research. He had a sound appreciation of the value to the historian of delving into old journals and pamphlets for himself. It no more occurred to him to employ assistants to do his investigation for him than to hire ghost writers to write his *History.*

After the publication of the first two volumes of the *History* Macaulay, describing the work that lay ahead of him, wrote as follows in his journal, early in 1849:

> I will first set myself to know the whole subject; to get, by reading and travelling, a full acquaintance with William's reign. I reckon that it will take me eighteen months to do this. I must visit Holland, Belgium, Scotland, Ireland, France.

The Dutch archives and French archives must be ransacked. I will see whether anything is to be got from other diplomatic collections. I must see Londonderry, the Boyne, Aghrim, Limerick, Kinsale, Namur again, Landen, Steinkirk. I must turn over hundreds, thousands, of pamphlets. Lambeth, the Bodleian and the other Oxford Libraries, the Devonshire Papers, the British Museum, must be explored, and notes made. And then I shall go to work.

The pith and marrow of this is in the last sentence. The historian's main work, as Macaulay conceived it, did not begin till his research had been completed. What Macaulay has to teach historians today, and what they can learn from him if they will, lies in the field of historical presentation. Any practiced writer, reading Macaulay, would perceive that he labored to attain clarity and to produce the effects he desired. The following extracts from his journal in 1850 leave us in no doubt about this:

> How little the all-important art of making meaning pellucid is studied now! Hardly any popular writer, except myself, thinks of it. Many seem to aim at being obscure.

> After breakfast I fell to work on the conspiracy of the Jacobites in 1690. This is a tough chapter. To make the narrative flow along as it ought, every part naturally springing from that which precedes,—to carry the reader backward and forward across St. George's Channel without distracting his attention,—is not easy. Yet it may be done. I believe that this art of transition is as important, or nearly so, to history, as the art of narration.

> My account of the Highlands is getting into tolerable shape. To-morrow I shall begin to transcribe again, and to polish. What trouble these few pages will have cost me! The great object is that, after all this trouble, they may read as if they had been spoken off, and may seem to flow as easily as table talk.

Macaulay understood the advantages of reading aloud as a means of improving the form of his writing. "He reads his works to us in the manuscript," his sister Margaret wrote in her journal, "and, when we find fault, as I very often do with his being too severe upon people, he takes it with the greatest kindness, and often alters what we do not like." When he was working on the second installment of his *History* he noted in his journal: "I read a portion of my *History* to Hannah and Trevelyan [her husband] with great effect. Hannah cried, and Trevelyan kept awake."

Freeman in his *Methods of Historical Study* paid a tribute to Macaulay as a writer which deserves to be quoted:

> I can see Macaulay's great and obvious faults as well as any man, I know as well as any man the cautions with which his brilliant pictures must be studied; but I cannot feel that I have any right to speak lightly of one to whom I owe so much in the matter of actual knowledge, and to whom I owe more than to any man as the master of historical narrative. Read a page of Macaulay; scan well his minute accuracy in every name and

phrase and title; contrast his English undefiled with the slipshod jargon which from our newspapers has run over into our books; dwell on the style which finds a fitting phrase in our own tongue to set forth every thought, the style which never uses a single word out of its true and honest meaning; turn the pages of the book in which no man ever read a sentence a second time because he failed to catch its meaning the first time, but in which all of us must have read many sentences a second or a twentieth time for the sheer pleasure of dwelling on the clearness, the combined fulness and terseness, on the just relation of every word to every other, on the happily chosen epithet, or the sharply pointed sarcasm.

Macaulay as a historian exhibited some traits which can hardly be reconciled with the austere ideals of historianship which he himself had voiced as a young man in his essay on history. One was his assurance and positiveness. Lord Melbourne, so it is told, once said that he wished he could be as cocksure about anything as Macaulay was about everything. That, it is true, was before Macaulay had become primarily a historian, and there is evidence that the cocksureness abated somewhat as the years passed by. But the old Adam in him was never entirely extinguished. Walter Bagehot, in a penetrating essay on Macaulay written toward the close of the latter's life, put this very well:

> Everything is too plain; all is clear, nothing is doubtful. . . . You rarely come across anything which is not decided. . . . This is hardly the style for history . . . it would have been a relief to the readers of Macaulay if he had shown a little the outside of uncertainties which there must be, the gradations of doubt which there ought to be, the singular accumulation of difficulties which must beset the extraction of a very easy narrative from very confused materials.

Bagehot was probably attributing his own feeling about history to the run of Macaulay's readers in thinking that they would have been better pleased if their author had dwelt more in the twilight of uncertainty. It is more likely that the brilliant sunlight of Macaulay's certainty swelled the ranks of his readers, that his garb of infallibility was one of the elements of his success. It would have been hard indeed to combine the doubts and cautions, the qualifications and tentativenesses, which Bagehot would have welcomed, with the style that made Macaulay the most popular of historians.

Macaulay used sources that had not been used by previous historians, and he had a much more extensive factual basis for the period he covered, especially for the reign of William III, than any of his predecessors. William's reign, as Firth observes, was comparatively untrodden ground, and it was here that Macaulay did his most original work and made his chief contribution. Many of the sources which he used for this period, including diplomatic correspondence in the French, Dutch and Spanish archives, had not been used for historical purposes before. There were, however, sources which for one reason or another, and sometimes for quite valid reasons, Macaulay did not use. Much material that is easily accessible to students of history today was not so to him. The publication of those great series of calendars of the British state papers, for example, had not yet been begun, and Macaulay did not make very extensive use of the original papers themselves, then preserved in the State Paper Office. The Historical Manuscripts Commission, with its massive array of volumes of reports on correspondence and papers in private libraries and family archives, was still in the future, and fuller acquaintance with contemporary private letters would have modified Macaulay's ideas on a number of matters. And of course Macaulay did not have the advantage of the many monographs and other secondary historical writings relating to the period of his *History* that have been published since his day. Yet he habitually wrote as if all the relevant evidence were before him. Again and again he was positive when he ought to have been tentative, definitive when he ought to have been provisional.

Nor did Macaulay invariably adhere to the highest standards for the ascertainment of historical truth. From the standpoint of the best critical historical scholarship of his day, as represented, let us say, by Ranke, he was often deficient. He did not always weigh his evidence with sufficient care, and, as Firth remarked, he was not always consistent in his estimate of the trustworthiness of sources, as when he deemed Jacobite pamphleteers undeserving of belief when they attacked William III but entitled to serious consideration when they attacked the Duke of Marlborough. Macaulay often pointed out defects, as well as merits, in authorities that he used, but he was not impartially critical. Firth was fully justified in saying that Macaulay's attitude toward his authorities was "a little too much that of the advocate who cross-examines hostile witnesses very severely, and tears their evidence to pieces, but is careful to ask no awkward questions of those who testify on behalf of his clients." Historians really ought not to have clients or heroes.

In a review of Macaulay's third and fourth volumes published in *Fraser's Magazine* (February 1856) Kemble did full justice to the extensiveness of Macaulay's researches and to the new evidence he had produced. He believed, however, that Macaulay had sometimes allowed himself to be deceived through failure to take a sufficiently critical attitude toward his authorities; and he called attention to what he regarded as some serious errors of omission. He concluded by emphasizing the paramount defect which, he declared, pervaded the volumes under review, namely, "the striving to exalt William at the expense of every one with whom he is brought into contact . . . the distortion of view which presents our foreign relations in so untrue a light, and, for the sake of displaying one giant, peoples all Europe with pigmies."

Macaulay was not successful in getting inside the minds of men from whose beliefs and ideals he differed. Active participation in party politics is not the best of apprenticeships for a historian, and, while Macaulay's partisanship diminished as he grew older, there is a sense in which he always remained a Whig of 1832. He never attained that catholicity of outlook that comes only to those who have questioned the accepted maxims of their day and class and party. Macaulay's mind was not easily accessible to new ideas and points of view. A conspicuous illustration of this is to be found in his attitude toward the literature of his own day. Contemporary English poetry, he wrote in 1836, had little attraction for him, and in 1850 he declared, also in a private letter, that the previous twenty-five years had produced hardly a volume that would be remembered in the year 1900. Few predictions could have been more infelicitous and none more indicative of a mind closed to the merits of contemporary developments in the literature of his own country. Who would guess from what Macaulay said that this quarter-century, which he found so destitute of great writing, gave to the world—to mention only a very few of its literary products—works that made Carlyle a celebrity, poems that established securely the fame of Tennyson, Dickens' *Pickwick Papers,* Thackeray's *Vanity Fair,* and Charlotte Brontë's *Jane Eyre?* Macaulay, as his nephew remarked,

> was not fond of new lights, unless they had been kindled at the ancient beacons; and he was apt to prefer a third-rate author, who had formed himself after some recognised model, to a man of high genius whose style and method were strikingly different from anything that had gone before. In books, as in people and places, he loved that, and that only, to which he had been accustomed from boyhood upwards. . . .

This lack of mental flexibility was probably related to Macaulay's habit of forming historical opinions on partial and insufficient evidence and adhering to them tenaciously thereafter, a practice which he had censured in his essay on history. Firth commented on this lack of open-mindedness in Macaulay and pronounced it to be a permanent source of weakness in him as a historian. "He formed an opinion about the character of a man from only part of the evidence, and having formed it he was unaffected by further evidence . . . he made the new evidence square with the preconceived opinion by any device which occurred to him."

Macaulay was not in sober fact the perfectly unchanging person depicted by Bagehot, yet Bagehot showed insight into Macaulay's psychology, the inexperiencing character of his mind, and it is easy to allow for some exaggeration:

> What he is, he was; and what he was, he is. He early attained a high development, but he has not increased it since; years have come, but they have whispered little. . . . He came into public life at an exciting season, he shared of course in that excitement, and the same excitement still quivers in his mind. . . . He is still the man of '32; from that era he looks on the past. . . . That was the "fifth act" of the human race; the remainder of history is only an afterpiece. All this was very natural at the moment. . . . But the singularity is that he should retain the idea now; that years have brought no influence, experience no change. . . . It is the same on his peculiar topic—on India. Before he went there he made a speech on the subject. . . . It is difficult to fancy that so much vivid knowledge could be gained from books—from horrible Indian treatises. . . . Not forgetting or excepting the orations of Burke, it was perhaps as remarkable a speech as was ever made on India by an English-

man who had not been in India. Now he has been there he speaks no better,—rather worse; he spoke excellently without experience, he speaks no better with it.

Macaulay undoubtedly thought of himself as historically-minded. As has been said, he appreciated the importance of the historian's soaking himself in first-hand sources and thus transporting himself in spirit to the times of which he was treating. "After breakfast to the British Museum," he wrote in his journal while he was working on the second installment of his *History,* "I turned over three volumes of newspapers and tracts. . . . I found some curious things . . . but the chief advantage of these researches is that the mind is transported back a century and a half, and gets familiar with the ways of thinking, and with the habits, of a past generation." In a marginal comment in the beginning of his copy of Strype's *Life of Cranmer* he wrote: "I like his old-fashioned style. He writes like a man who lived with the people of an earlier age. He had thoroughly imbued himself with the spirit of the sixteenth century." Some critics of the first installment of the *History* had suggested that Macaulay had appealed to sentiments and prejudices of his own day. Macaulay himself denied this. He wrote in his journal, in October 1849:

> I have seen not less than six German reviews, all in the highest degree laudatory. This is a sufficient answer to those detractors who attribute the success of my book here to the skill with which I have addressed myself to mere local temporary feelings. I am conscious that I did not mean to address myself to such feelings, and that I wrote with a remote past, and a remote future, constantly in my mind.

The implication seems to be that Macaulay recognized that preoccupation with the present on the part of a historian is a defect.

A confident belief in Progress seems to have been the keynote of Macaulay's philosophy of history. It is sounded at the beginning of the first chapter of the *History,* in the third paragraph:

> . . . the history of our country during the last hundred and sixty years is eminently the history of physical, of moral, and of intellectual improvement. Those who compare the age on which their lot has fallen with a golden age which exists only in their imagination may talk of degeneracy and decay: but no man who is correctly informed as to the past will be disposed to take a morose or desponding view of the present.

It is true that the writer of these words was the same person who in private expressed such unfavorable opinions of contemporary men of letters, who referred in his journal to "the general sterility, and miserably enervated state of literature," which sounds like talk of "degeneracy and decay" and a "desponding view of the present" in that phase of culture, the literary, which meant most to Macaulay. The general tone of the *History,* however, leaves no doubt that Macaulay thought of himself, and wished to be thought of, as an exponent of the doctrine of Progress.

At the beginning of his third chapter Macaulay emphasized the differences between the England of 1685 and the England of his own day. History, if it is executed in a spirit of historical-mindedness, will not exaggerate the similarities between past and present. On the contrary, it will, incidentally and implicitly, show differences as well as resemblances. But if, as in Macaulay's case, differences are always represented as redounding to the exaltation of the present and the disparagement of the past, the contrasts that are drawn do more harm than good, for they tend to obscure the principle of historical relativity, the principle, that is, that everything that existed in the past was relative to the conditions of its age and ought to be viewed in that context. Consider, for example, Macaulay's remarks about Bristol:

> Pepys, who visited Bristol eight years after the Restoration, was struck by the splendor of the city. But his standard was not high, for he noted down as a wonder the circumstance that, in Bristol, a man might look round him and see nothing but houses. It seems that, in no other place with which he was acquainted, except London, did the buildings completely shut out the woods and fields. Large as Bristol might then appear, it occupied but a very small portion of the area on which it now stands.

Now the impression which the reader ought to get from the testimony of Pepys is that Bristol in the period of the Restoration was a large and splendid city—in relation, of course, to other English cities of that time. The fact that it would not seem large and splendid if compared with the great English cities of Macaulay's time has nothing to do with the case. Why, Bristol was actually so densely built up that one could not see the woods and fields for the buildings. Think of that! The testimony of Pepys throws a vivid ray of light upon what Maitland called the rusticity of old English towns. Macaulay, however, by his ill-advised comment, goes far to spoil Pepys's testimony for the modern reader. He casts discredit on Pepys's standard of municipal splendor for the (historically speaking) very bad reason that it was not Macaulay's standard, and he belittles the magnitude of Bristol in the seventeenth century because Bristol was still larger in the nineteenth century.

Exaltation of the present and depreciation of the past is not confined to Macaulay's third chapter, though this chapter contains more instances of it than any other. A reviewer of Macaulay's first two volumes, writing in *Blackwood's Magazine* (April 1849), did not greatly exaggerate when he declared that Macaulay's object was "to show that, in *every* respect, the present age is incomparably happier and more virtuous than those which have preceded it." In the opinion of one of Macaulay's biographers, J. Cotter Morison [*Macaulay,* 1882], "Macaulay's constant preoccupation is not to explain his period by previous periods, but to show how vastly the period of which he treats has been outstripped by the period in which he lives. Whatever may be the topic . . . the comparison always made is with subsequent England, not previous England."

Yet Macaulay, I think, did not really disdain the past. His preoccupation with his *History* and aloofness from current events during his later years seem to show this. "Ab-

sorbed in his *History,*" says Trevelyan, "he paid little attention to what was passing at Westminster." And Macaulay himself wrote in his journal in January 1855, when the second installment of the *History* was approaching completion and the Crimean War was raging: "Odd that here, within a few yards of all the bustle of politics, I should be as quiet as a hermit . . . buried in old pamphlets and broadsides; turning away from the miseries of Balaklava to the battle of Steinkirk. . . ."

Why, then, did Macaulay in his *History* so frequently draw, or suggest, contrasts between past and present so favorable to the present? Probably the desire to diminish social discontent had something to do with it. Macaulay knew, of course, about Chartism and other expressions of working-class unrest in his day, he knew about what Carlyle called "the-condition-of-England-question," but his optimism, which remained unshaken, was strengthened by his historical studies. He believed that knowledge of the past made for content, not discontent, with the present. "It is, in some sense, unreasonable and ungrateful in us," he wrote in the *History,* "to be constantly discontented with a condition which is constantly improving."

But perhaps Macaulay's habit of juxtaposing past and present was less the result of a belief in Progress or of a desire to lessen "present discontents" than a device to increase what would today be called "reader appeal," like his use of analogy. Speaking of this latter, Firth says:

> The problem he had to solve, since he wished to secure the largest possible audience, was how to interest the mass of people who live entirely in the present and care nothing about the past for its own sake. What does interest such people is usually the politics of the day. Hence Macaulay never fails to refer to modern analogues to the seventeenth-century problems he is discussing.

He knew that his readers would be flattered to be informed by an eminent historian how superior they were to their seventeenth-century ancestors. It should not be forgotten that Macaulay's ruling passion as a historian was his eagerness to be read.

How are we to account for the tremendous impression made by Macaulay's *History* and his other historical writings? It was from Macaulay that most of his countrymen derived, and perhaps still derive, directly or indirectly, their most abiding historical ideas. His influence upon the English-speaking world has been incalculable. Yet Macaulay had, it seems to me, qualities and points of view that were positive and serious disqualifications for writing history that intrinsically deserved to survive. He had strong biases which affected his handling of historical evidence, his treatment of historical events, and his estimate of historical characters; he was wanting in psychological insight; he was unduly eager to produce desired literary effects; he was given to dogmatic assertiveness; he was unable, too often, to overcome an anxiety to give the impression of being a specialist in omniscience; and he was too much disposed to view conditions of the past from the standpoint of middle-class Victorian complacency and self-satisfaction.

What, then, is the explanation of Macaulay's immense popularity? Perhaps the answer is not far to seek, after all.

Macaulay's *History* appeared at a moment that was most favorable for its success. The first two volumes, it will be remembered, were published in that year of European revolutions, 1848; and English readers could hardly fail to contrast the Glorious Revolution which their ancestors had enjoyed a hundred and sixty years before with the inglorious revolutions which foreigners were suffering at the time—to the great enhancement, of course, of English self-esteem and patriotic pride.

> All around us [Macaulay wrote] the world is convulsed by the agonies of great nations. Governments which lately seemed likely to stand during ages have been on a sudden shaken and overthrown. The proudest capitals of Western Europe have streamed with civil blood. . . . Meanwhile in our island the regular course of government has never been for a day interrupted. . . . And, if it be asked what has made us to differ from others, the answer is that we never lost what others are wildly and blindly seeking to regain. It is because we had a preserving revolution in the seventeenth century that we have not had a destroying revolution in the nineteenth. . . .

In foreign countries, too, the success of the *History* was partly, if not principally, owing to the current interest in revolution, in the conflict between absolute monarchy and constitutional government of which the English Revolution of 1688 was an early instance.

More important, no doubt, than the timeliness of the *History* were Macaulay's literary gifts. If he was not on a level with the world's supreme literary figures, he was at any rate a first-class storyteller, with a sense for the pictorial and the dramatic such as no historian of England before him had possessed. His genius for narration was the most obvious factor in his popularity. He aroused the same kind of human interest in actual historical events that novelists aroused in fictitious events.

Macaulay was master of a style of perfect clarity, exceptional cogency, and metallic incisiveness and brilliancy. It is doubtful whether an obscure sentence could be found in all his writings. He knew how to say exactly what he meant to say, and what he meant to say his readers were glad to hear.

The great majority of them were members of the middle class, and he was thoroughly in harmony with them in his social and political outlook—"one of the middle-class crowd in his heart," Morley called him. He confirmed their confidence in the progress of civilization in general and the beneficence of Victorian liberalism in particular.

And, finally, Macaulay never forgot his readers—which perhaps goes far to explain why readers have never forgotten him. (pp. 174-93)

> *Robert Livingston Schuyler, "Macaulay and His History—A Hundred Years After," in* Political Science Quarterly, *Vol. LXIII, No. 2, June, 1948, pp. 161-93.*

J. H. Plumb   (essay date 1956)

[*Plumb is an English historian and biographer well known for his studies of eighteenth-century England. In the following excerpt, he argues that in spite of Macaulay's limited emotional range, his photographic memory, appetite for learning, and ability to express himself clearly make him one of England's greatest historians.*]

On the day in November 1848 when the first volume of Macaulay's *History of England* appeared, Ludgate Hill was jammed with carriages struggling to get to Messrs. Longman in Paternoster Row. Three thousand copies were sold in ten days and the pace began to increase rather than slacken. The time came when Robert Longman pressed a cheque for £20,000 on Macaulay on the grounds that he had too much money in his own account. At a guinea a volume this was a prodigious achievement for Victorian times. Although Macaulay naturally thought well of his work, its public reception astonished even him. The reviews were almost uniformly as eulogistic as they were lengthy, but the book was far more than a success of metropolitan literary society. "At Duckinfield, near Manchester, a gentleman who thought that there would be a certain selfishness in keeping so great a pleasure to himself, invited his poorer neighbours to attend every evening after their work was finished, and read the History aloud to them from beginning to end. At the close of the last meeting, one of the audience rose, and moved, in north country fashion, a vote of thanks to Mr. Macaulay 'for having written a history which working men can understand.' " His success at Windsor was as great as at Manchester. The Prince Consort was so deeply impressed by his book that he immediately offered Macaulay the vacant chair of Modern History at Cambridge, which Macaulay immediately declined on the grounds that if he were to lecture well he would be forced to give up his *History.* And if he were to write the *History,* his lectures would be bad. Some years later, Queen Victoria recognized Macaulay's unique position in English life and letters by making him a peer—the first writer to achieve such a distinction.

It is obvious from the great financial rewards and public honours which Macaulay's literary works brought him that he wrote very much what his time and generation wished to read. Certainly his own sympathy with his age was greater than that commonly found amongst the great historians. Gibbon who, alone of English historians, can be compared with Macaulay to the latter's disadvantage, offended a considerable section of his reading public by his ironic treatment of the mysteries of the Christian religion. Although perfectly in harmony with the philosophic attitude of the Enlightenment, Gibbon displayed a complete detachment from the aspirations and ideals of the active part of the nation to which he belonged. Macaulay, however, was totally involved in his age—in it he found an echoing response to his own boundless energy and eupeptic confidence. Indeed, it is remarkable how closely Macaulay's character mirrors the strength and weakness of the early Victorian period. And his success must partly lie in the fact that the men and women who read him so eagerly, felt as he felt and believed as he believed: his truth was their truth. That this was so is also borne out by the fact that Macaulay now seems not only far below Gibbon in quality and achievement, but also below Michelet, below Burkhardt, even below Ranke. He lacked the range of Gibbon, the imagination of Michelet, the penetration of Burkhardt, and the wisdom of Ranke. Nor has his scholarship worn so well as theirs. Even so, his qualities still claim for him a place amongst the great historians of the nineteenth century. It is likely that he will always maintain that place, and always be quite widely read. For this reason: in temperament he was very close to a fairly common variety of human personality. To make this clear, Macaulay and his time need to be described in a little more detail. (pp. 17-18)

Macaulay possessed a formidable mental equipment in which the most outstanding and remarkable gift was his photographic memory. After having read *Paradise Lost* twice, he could recite without fault the bulk of the poem. He himself said that if Shakespeare's works were to have been destroyed, he could have reproduced them entirely from memory. A memory of such proportions naturally strengthened Macaulay's self-confidence: on questions of fact he was always right; time and time again he triumphed over less exact men. Such a faculty fed his self-assertiveness, and, as he believed that his judgment was based on knowledge, he had few doubts about the validity of his attitudes. A powerful sense of certainty pervades all that Macaulay wrote and there can be little doubt that this was strengthened by the absolute accuracy of the facts which he could recollect.

Yet essentially Macaulay's was a selective memory controlled and exercised by those preconceptions which were the very fibres of his personality. The facts were fitted into his pattern of judgment. They demonstrated the virtues of liberty and progress or they could be used to show the iniquity of those men who tried to oppose their development. Facts never became the object of imaginative exercise. Macaulay never tried to feel through them, irrespective of judgment, to the reality of times alien to his own world. He remembered what was useful to his own sharp, confident vision. The irrelevant was, however, meaningless to him. His memory was neither the stimulator of curiosity nor its servant; it was a weapon of didacticism.

A fabulous memory was not the only outstanding quality of Macaulay's intellectual make-up. He possessed an immense appetite for learning. As soon as he could read, he was wolfing down universal histories, plays, sermons, poems, classics. He mastered languages with ease and delighted in mathematical exercises—throughout his life he had a passion for doing long arithmetical calculations in his head. To memory and appetite was added order. There was nothing ragged or diffuse about Macaulay's interests. He quickly reduced his knowledge to a system. His earliest essays, even his earliest letters are remarkable for the lucidity of their arrangement and the aptness of the facts and quotations used to illustrate his arguments. And finally to this impressive list of intellectual qualities must be added a sense of style as personal as it was powerful. At the age of five, a servant of Lady Waldegrave's scalded his legs with hot coffee and when asked some minutes later how he did, he replied "Thank you, Madame, the agony has somewhat abated." And for the rest of his life his style re-

mained formal, balanced, and frequently pompous. His public performances, either in essays or in speeches, were also loaded with erudition, yet he was never dull. All that he had to say was too pungent, too vigorous, and too decided to allow a reader's interest to decay.

Macaulay, was, therefore, extravagantly well endowed. He possessed a mind of exceptional range and almost incredible accuracy. His intellectual energy displayed volcanic force, but the rapid, almost torrential, flow of his thought was confined by a strict sense of form and order. Few men have been equipped with Macaulay's ability to reduce a complex mass of fact and argument to a clear and lucid exposition. And yet these qualities were matched by weaknesses which have grown more apparent with time.

Macaulay's emotional make-up was exceedingly simple; as simple as his mind was complex. Although in his journal he left a detailed record of his daily feelings, it is almost devoid of those emotional experiences which provide the structure of most men's lives. Macaulay was never in love. His strongest attachment was to his family. When his sister, Hannah, decided to marry, he was surprised, pained, and then resigned to the separation, realizing his own obtuse folly in never having considered such a possibility. That blow was probably the most grievous personal loss that he ever experienced and he adjusted himself to it very quickly. Time and time again in his diary he refers with pleasure to the sustained happiness of his life. On his fiftieth birthday he wrote "Well, I have had a happy life. I do not know that anybody whom I have seen close, has had a happier. Some things I regret; but, on the whole, who is better off? I have no children of my own, it is true; but I have children whom I love as if they were my own, and who, I believe, love me. I wish that the next ten years may be as happy as the last ten. But I rather wish it than hope it." His last sentence refers to his fear of death, one of his only terrors throughout his early life. He could, however, have "hoped it" for this fear weakened as death itself approached and he met it with the same serenity with which he lived so much of his life.

Yet although there was an inner core of tranquility, Macaulay was not devoid of strong feeling. He was insatiably ambitious and when writing his *History* he was constantly preoccupied with speculations as to how it would be regarded in the year 2000 or 3000. He thoroughly savoured and enjoyed the great fame which came to him and felt that it was a proper reward for his unflagging industry and his concentration of purpose. Furthermore his feelings about public affairs or individuals could be intense: the reform of Parliament, the abolition of slavery, the duties of Englishmen in India, or Byron, Boswell, or Horace Walpole—all aroused in him strong feelings. Heredity, education, and temperament gave him a bias towards decided moral attitudes in which powerful feeling was blended with absolute certainty of right or wrong. This moral passion in Macaulay, so much in tune with the atmosphere of his age, sprang very largely from the simplicity of his own feelings. It was easy for him to condemn Byron for his sexually disordered life; after all, he had never known Byron's temptations. The lack of any sympathy with the strong, surging, animal passions which could destroy and ruin men, was a serious defect in a man who aspired to be an historian of genius. Yet the fault lay deeper than this. It was not the moral weaknesses of men such as Boswell and Byron that disturbed Macaulay so profoundly. There was a deeper jealousy at work.

Both in character and in intellect Macaulay was in the last analysis a simple man—simple and lucid—no matter how intricate the surface machinery might appear to be. On occasion he could be hot and choleric yet always about surface matters. He lacked the roots of life, sexual passion, and the sense of tragedy that it arouses—the biting, painful sense of the transience of living and loving men. Oddly enough the cool-tempered Gibbon, so much more detached from life than Macaulay, felt these things much more strongly. At the heart of Macaulay's being there was immaturity, an inhibition of passion which led him to distrust it in other men. But unfortunately for Macaulay creative energy is usually fertilized by the chaos of passionate life—not always, but frequently. Consequently Macaulay never penetrates to the heart of human existence. His attempts at poetry are dreadfully banal—the metrical exercises of a clever boy in which the emotional situations have been taken from literature and not from life. The same sterility, the same artificiality of feeling, is present in most of the great descriptive passages of his *History.* Although his account of the seige of Londonderry is a *tour de force* of narrative skill, the human figures are two-dimensional, conventional characters, lacking the convincing reality which a more imaginative and creative writer would have given them.

The banality and limitation of Macaulay's emotional range was one of the grave faults of character which weakened his powers as a writer, but it was not the only one. Creative thinking often works very mysteriously, one might almost say in darkness. Suddenly there is a moment of illumination; inconsistencies are resolved, interrelations discovered, and a new vision of reality received. In Macaulay's mind, however, there was no darkness, no obscurity, no inconsistency, nothing unrelated. Everything was lucid and certain. Macaulay lacked doubt; lacked the confused, groping, searching mind which is often so much more creative, except perhaps in mathematics, than a mind of absolute clarity. And, paradoxically enough, though Macaulay loved facts, he did not possess a really enquiring mind. At first sight that may seem a fantastic statement, yet it is true. Macaulay took pleasure in being accurate, yet he did not love facts for their own sake, but merely to arrange them in patterns to his own satisfaction. The patterns were those of a conventional and accepting mind. He viewed the Revolution of 1688 as did the average Whig reader of his day. His vast learning became merely a brilliant illustration of commonplace ideas, for his ideas were rarely formed by his knowledge. His knowledge decorated his convictions. He saw the seventeenth century in terms of his own political beliefs, and in terms of his own morality; and he was quite content to do so. This, of course, was a crippling handicap to an historian for it produced satisfaction and decision too quickly. Lacking curiosity and suspicion, Macaulay had little or no interest in ferreting out facts for their own sake. The hope of a new or startling revelation never sent him searching in strange places for

new sources. Compared with other great nineteenth-century historians he added remarkably little that was new to our knowledge of the past. Accepting too easily facts which suited his didactic argument, Macaulay committed grave errors of scholarship. Forster, Paget, and Spedding had little difficulty in marshalling convincing evidence against judgments that Macaulay had made with too great confidence on too little evidence.

This severe limitation of curiosity in Macaulay to the accumulation of the knowledge which he wanted, was responsible for his greatest weakness as an historian: his lack of grasp of the intricacy of human character and his over-confident judgment of it. True, his own emotional deficiencies had severely restricted his experience of the dark, passionate, tumultuous side of life, yet often creative men have lived lives as quiet as Macaulay's. They, however, have been haunted by imagination, or known the jungles buried in their own hearts, so that they were able to appreciate the difficulties and confusions of more active men. But for Macaulay the precepts of morality were as clear as those of politics and as simple. The complexity of character was lost on him and he depicted the men and women of his *History* and *Essays* in simple terms of good and bad. He never sought beyond the obvious. In consequence, Macaulay was far more successful in describing action or political debate than he was in portraying human beings.

Macaulay was, therefore, a man of formidable learning, fluent, confident, decisive in his judgments. But beneath a powerful intellect there lay a simple, rather childlike, heart. Although he was a thrusting, ambitious man with a muscular, forceful mind, yet in certain fields of human experience he was curiously opaque. His lack of subtlety or of real creative depth proved to be no obstacle to his success. The men and women of his time loved to hear certainties; confidence was a part of the air they breathed.

Although as a child Macaulay had spent hours writing vast verse dramas and world histories, it proved quite impossible for him as a young man to follow a literary career. Indeed, though he wrote a good deal, he probably did not in his early youth desire such a career. Precise scholarship did not appeal to him; and he was drawn irresistibly to politics where his intellectual capacities and immoderate fluency were bound to make him famous as well as redoubtable. His success was immediate, and within a short time he could fill the House of Commons as no other speaker could. He was no debater, no orator in the usual sense. He spoke in a loud, clear, unmodulated voice without gesture. One of the parliamentary reporters of the time described his manner in these terms.

> Vehemence of thought, vehemence of language, vehemence of manner were his chief characteristics. The listener might almost fancy he heard ideas and words gurgling in the speaker's throat for priority of utterance. There was nothing graduated, or undulating, about him. He plunged at once into the heart of the matter, and continued his loud resounding pace from beginning to end, without halt or pause. This vehemence and volume made Macaulay the terror of the reporters; and, when he engaged in a subject outside their ordinary experience, they were fair-

ly nonplussed by the display of names and dates, and titles. He was not a long-winded speaker. In fact, his earnestness was so great that it would have failed under a very long effort.

Although he became one of the great speakers of the Commons, he was not, considering his abilities, a successful politician. He quickly lost his Tory principles, much to his father's regret, and became an ardent disciple of moderate Whig reform. He had no use for Brougham whom he considered to be an immoral, as well as a dangerous, radical. He strongly disapproved of Socialist or Jacobin sentiments—indeed he detested Wordsworth's *Prelude* because he thought its political implications too revolutionary. He believed passionately in orderly progress, gradual reform, and in the ultimate triumph of technology through liberal education. He was convinced that it was England's singular destiny to disseminate these virtues through the world. For Macaulay the 1851 exhibition was the crowning glory of human achievement. He wrote in his diary of his visit to the Crystal Palace, "I made my way into the building; a most gorgeous sight; vast; graceful; beyond the dream of the Arabian romances. I cannot think that the Caesars ever exhibited a more splendid spectacle. I was quite dazzled, and I felt as I did on entering St. Peter's." This was the demonstration of England's industrial majesty, the final justification of the long struggle for civil and religious liberty. "The history of England," declared Macaulay, "is emphatically the history of progress" and by progress he meant what he saw about him in the Great Exhibition—material progress—for he believed that the amelioration of the conditions in which man lived made him more virtuous. Macaulay saw in Francis Bacon the first great exponent of this empirical philosophy and he realized that many would mock him for his materialist outlook. "Some people," he wrote, "may take the object of the Baconian philosophy a low object but they cannot deny that, high or low, it has been attained." And after dismissing ancient philosophy as sterile and useless, he hammers home in a passionate, breathless passage the victories of empirical philosophy:

> It has lengthened life; it has mitigated pain; it has extinguished diseases; it has increased the fertility of the soil; it has given new securities to the mariner; it has furnished new arms to the warrior; it has spanned great rivers and estuaries with bridges of form unknown to our fathers; it has guided the thunderbolt innocuously from heaven to earth; it has lighted up the night with the splendour of the day; it has extended the range of the human vision; it has multiplied the power of the human muscles; it has accelerated motion; it has annihilated distance; it has facilitated intercourse, correspondence, all friendly offices, all despatch of business; it has enabled men to descend to the depths of the sea, to soar into the air, to penetrate securely into the noxious recesses of the earth, to traverse the land in cars which whirl along without horses, and the ocean in ships which run ten knots an hour against the wind. These are but a part of its fruits, and of its first fruits. For it is a philosophy which never rests, which has never attained, which is never perfect. Its law is progress. A

point which yesterday was invisible is its goal today, and will be its starting-post to-morrow.

This outlook has been criticized as philistine, blinkered, nerveless, unimaginative. At the time that Macaulay was beginning his praise, Carlyle, Disraeli, and others were brooding over the suffering and poverty which the Industrial Revolution had brought into being—a fact which many observers were quick to seize on. Aesthetes and philosophers deplored the frank materialism of Macaulay's outlook and modern commentators have not been much more sympathetic. Professor Geyl, Macaulay's most perceptive critic, maintains that this "religion of progress" prevented Macaulay from being a really great historian. "That feeling," he writes, "of absolute certainty about the superiority of the present and about the unqualified beneficence of the gradual increase of the technical and scientific knowledge at the disposal of mankind . . . must lead the historian to view the past in terms which may be entirely irrelevant and result in a picture lacking in the truth of intimacy . . . to my way of thinking, however stimulating and instructive and powerfully intelligent I may find Macaulay's work, this mental attitude toward the past is in the deepest sense unhistoric" [*Debates with Historians* 1955]. Since Macaulay wrote the prevalent mood of European society has been one of doubt if not of despair—at least in literary and philosophic circles—and it is a mood that naturally enough is deeply antipathetic to Macaulay's own.

And yet in what way was Macaulay wrong? The material progress of mankind is the one certain, glorious triumph which no one can deny. Treating history polemically, and it can be treated polemically, Macaulay was quite right, incontrovertibly right, and in no way unhistorical except in so far as he attributed a conscious and deliberate purpose to man's evolution. But history can be more than polemics: it is also a quest for reality in which suffering, ignorance, folly, decay, and failure are as valid as happiness, knowledge, wisdom, growth and success. These are the realms which more imaginative and sensitive historians, such as Ranke or Burkhardt, have made their own, and because their works have recreated a more complex and accurate reality, their scholarship is both more profound and more durable. Yet unsubtle, dogmatic, and philistine as Macaulay was, he still has the best of the argument. Man's prime reason for self-congratulation is his triumph over the material universe.

For Macaulay life and history were all of a piece, the unfolding pattern of virtue, justice, progress. A gigantic, if naïve, faith infused his attitude to present politics as well as to the historic past. The same direct, materialistic commonsense made him very effective on specific political issues, but it rendered him too unyielding, too unsupple for the shifty world of high politics, where more imagination and more sense of reality would have served him better. Although he reached cabinet rank before he was forty (as Secretary of War), his greatest achievement in public life was not in politics but in administration during his residence in India as a member of the Supreme Council, particularly the time that he spent as President of the Commission of Public Instruction and afterwards as President of the Law Commission.

A caricature of Macaulay, 1847.

The tasks which Macaulay tackled while he held these posts in India were completely commensurate with his abilities. His minute on Indian Education is a masterly summary of the complexity of native languages, customs, and educational methods, and the difficulties which would face India unless a common language were found to meet the needs of a more uniform and complex administration and of the growth of technology. He then planned a scheme of education, primary, secondary, and technical, including the production of qualified teachers; as might be expected his attention to detail was absolute and reached down to text-books and grammars. As President of the Law Commission he set about reducing the wild chaos of Indian customary law and argued strongly for the introduction of the principles of British justice, with the consequence that one of the greatest benefits conferred by the British on India has been a reasonably unified, coherent, and wise system of law. The brilliance of Macaulay's administrative ability is thus partly responsible for the excellence of Indian education and justice. On these questions the strength of his mind and character had full play; his weaknesses were of no importance. A comprehensive factual knowledge and a sense of relevance were more apt than creative imagination or a knowledge of fellow men

and women. And his empirical philosophy was fully justified.

Politics and administration provided large opportunities for the exercise of Macaulay's singular talents; the majority of men might have been content with his achievements and the rewards which they brought. Undeniably they gave Macaulay deep satisfaction, but curiously enough they proved in the end inadequate. He had never ceased to be drawn to literature; he had started to scribble as a child and he could not stop. From the age of 24 he wrote regularly for the *Edinburgh Review,* and what he contributed was so novel, so exciting, that his reputation was quickly made. Macaulay in his very first essay used the pretext of a review to write a short biography of the subject of the book under discussion—in this case, Milton.

Biography had not, in Macaulay's day, become an important, regular part of the yearly output of books. Apart from Boswell's *Johnson* it was still largely a matter of short memorial sermons or pamphlets or huge and tedious compilations of ill-edited letters and memoirs. In his essays Macaulay provided something quite new and original. Usually after a few paragraphs displaying the profound ignorance of the author's knowledge of his subject, and of course the superiority of Macaulay's, he settled down to give a short biographical sketch in which his judgments were as rapid, authoritative, and final as the style was flamboyant and pungent. As Macaulay could compress a massive quantity of material into a short space and without the least confusion or congestion, he was able to give a remarkably comprehensive account not only of a man, but of the time in which he lived. Macaulay in these essays set out deliberately to startle the mind and he sought paradox rather than avoided it. He wrote them too with magnificent journalistic verve—once read, never forgotten. To give some idea of their flavour here is a passage on Horace Walpole:

> The conformation of his mind was such that whatever was little seemed to him great, and whatever was great seemed to him little. Serious business was a trifle to him, and trifles were his serious business. To chat with bluestockings, to write little copies of complimentary verses on little occasions, to superintend a private press, to preserve from natural decay the perishable topics of Ranelagh and White's, to record divorces and bets, Miss Chudleigh's absurdities and George Selwyn's good sayings, to decorate a grotesque house with pie-crust battlements, to procure rare engravings and antique chimneyboards, to match odd gauntlets, to lay out a maze of walks within five acres of ground, these were the grave employments of his long life. From these he turned to politics as to an amusement. After the labours of the print-shop and the auction-room, he unbent his mind in the House of Commons. And, having indulged in the recreation of making laws and voting millions, he returned to more important pursuits, to researches after Queen Mary's comb, Wolsey's red hat, the pipe which Van Tromp smoked during his last sea-fight, and the spur which King William struck into the flank of Sorrel.

In everything in which Walpole busied himself, in the fine arts, in literature, in public affairs, he was drawn by some strange attraction from the great to the little, and from the useful to the odd. The politics in which he took the keenest interest, were politics scarcely deserving of the name. The growlings of George the Second, the flirtations of Princess Emily with the Duke of Grafton, the amours of Prince Frederic and Lady Middlesex, the squabbles between Gold Stick in waiting and the Master of the Buckhounds, the disagreements between the tutors of Prince George, these matters engaged almost all the attention which Walpole could spare from matters more important still, from bidding for Zinckes and Petitots, from cheapening fragments of tapestry and handles of old lances, from joining bits of painted glass, and from setting up memorials of departed cats and dogs. While he was fetching and carrying the gossip of Kensington Palace and Carlton House, he fancied that he was engaged in politics, and when he recorded that gossip, he fancied that he was writing history.

Rarely before had the public been regaled with such language or treated to the opinions of a scholar so absolutely confident of the morality and wisdom of his judgments. Naturally his essays brought him great popularity and his literary fame grew as he made his way in the world of politics. Macaulay himself, however, did not set great store by these essays: he did not realize that he was helping to create a new taste for short, vivid biographical studies and he himself thought of his work as being merely ephemeral. Yet he drew a deeper satisfaction from these brief excursions into literature than he did from most of his public activities and the fortunate combination of a valuable legacy with his defeat at the General Election of 1847, brought about his decision to retire from politics and devote himself entirely to history. The last twelve years of his life were spent in writing a *History of England* from 1688 to the nineteenth century. It was planned on a monumental scale to challenge comparison with the world's greatest historians—Thucydides, Herodotus, and the rest—for Macaulay's ambition was as grandiose as his conception.

He failed even to complete the reign of William III and he was honest enough to admit that his work fell short of the highest achievements in the writing of history. Nevertheless, it remains one of the great historical works in the English language, second only to Gibbon's. And probably at no time in his life could Macaulay have written a better one, for by the time he settled down to write his history his mind was formed, his style perfected, and his experience completed. His beliefs were straightforward yet unshakable. He put his trust in those same virtues which his evangelical father and mother had bred in him: honesty, loyalty, charity, industry, and absolute respect for the Christian ideals of marriage and family life. If a man lied, took bribes, dabbled in treason, or fornicated, he was a bad man, so Shaftesbury and Marlborough were bad men; an occasional peccadillo, especially if discreet, could be forgiven, as William III was forgiven for having a mistress, but the combination of immorality and chicanery to be found in a Shaftesbury was too much for Macaulay. These simple black and white judgments are couched in absolute

terms: the *need* in a Shaftesbury or a James II for the life that they led is never explored.

Macaulay's characters, however, had to pass more than moral tests. They were required to have discovered the right side in politics. Macaulay believed that the prosperity, liberty, and political freedom of his own time was the result of those seventeenth-century struggles between King and Parliament, between Church and Puritan, and between Tory and Whig. Prosperity and imperial greatness marched with liberty, toleration, and Whig doctrine. William, Prince of Orange, became the embodiment of the good—the hero of the Victorian world and a maker of the nation. Although this estimate contains more truth, perhaps, than many modern critics of Macaulay would allow, it is altogether too simple, too *determined* to carry conviction. It leaves out the muddled, chaotic, stumbling nature of human activity, and in doing so distracts rather than clarifies the reality which Macaulay hoped to depict. And of course he is baffled, totally baffled, by a character as complex as the 2nd Earl of Sunderland who, after acting as James II's confidant almost to the Revolution, reappears shortly after it as the trusted adviser of William III himself.

To some extent historical events, too, had to be forced into the same mechanical pattern and they are judged by Macaulay as men are judged, according to whether they aided or thwarted the Whig cause. It was quite impossible for him to see that the Tories were largely responsible for the Revolution of 1688 although the facts stared him in the face. Indeed for a modern scholar his history of political management is naïve and jejeune, weak in analysis, and unscholarly in detail. He attempted the impossible task of forcing the politics of William's reign into a rigid dichotomy of Whig versus Tory. Once more his love of clarity bedevilled the truth. He would have men and events clear cut and therefore got them wrong. The rigidity of his intellect and the simplicity of his heart are implicit in almost every page that he wrote.

Glaring as these faults are, the *History* remains a great book. By the time Macaulay was forty-seven he was naturally fully aware of his literary abilities. He knew that he possessed admirable skill in narrative, for his fabulous and accurate memory and his disciplined schematic mind could hold the complete, detailed story that he wished to tell, ready for his pen. His great set pieces, like the Siege of Londonderry or the Massacre of Glencoe, were written straight out of his head, once he had digested and memorized his materials. This, of course, gave them a wonderful fluency and unity. And although he frequently altered his words and rewrote considerably, he never had to verify the detail which he knew with such absolute certainty.

Furthermore, he had developed his style to the point where it was a complete reflection of his thought and feeling so that the full flavour of his truculent, virile personality could be savoured in every paragraph. Few historians have been so easy to read or so easy to remember once read. The authority with which he wrote induced a ready acceptance of his vision of history in the mind of his reader. Also his great intellectual powers and his personal experience of politics enabled him to recreate the political debates of William's reign in a way which can, perhaps, never be bettered. He gives the excitement of a battle to the struggles in the Commons. In some aspects of his history, too, Macaulay showed great originality. He realized from his knowledge of his own times that the political structure of a country is deeply influenced by its economic interests and by the pattern of its society, so he devoted considerable space to depicting the social habits of the late Stuart times and gave many pages, and very admirable ones, to the foundation of the Bank of England and the Recoinage.

In spite of all the criticism which can be levelled against it, the **History** remains a great work of literature and scholarship. And so do Macaulay's essays. In a hundred years England has not produced an historian of his stature. He was an intellectual giant and although he lacked the imagination, the poetry, the sense of tragedy which is present in the very greatest writers, these were almost all that he lacked. Every other quality that a great writer needs he possessed in abundance: he was able to project his mind and personality into words so forcibly that his history has become a part of our common heritage. And what some choose to regard as his prejudices command both admiration and respect. He believed in liberal virtues and had faith in man's capacity to control and order not only history but the world about him. Although this led him to many false and intolerant judgments, they should not blind critics to the basic truth of Macaulay's conviction. In the material world in which he took such optimistic delight, man has made undeniable progress by the use of those qualities that Macaulay possessed in such abundance—memory, order, intelligence. (pp. 19-31)

J. H. Plumb, "Thomas Babington Macaulay," in University of Toronto Quarterly, *Vol. XXVI, No. 1, October, 1956, pp. 17-31.*

G. S. Fraser   (essay date 1960)

[*Fraser was a Scottish journalist, educator, and translator who also published several volumes of poetry as well as books on literary criticism, like* The Modern Writer and his World *(1953). In the following essay, he focuses on Macaulay's prose style, praising his magazine essays, but agreeing with Matthew Arnold that although Macaulay's* History *has a brilliant exterior quality, it lacks an inner life.*]

Macaulay's style—the style of his essays even more than of his great history—was, of all the great Victorian English styles, the most strikingly and lastingly imitable. Nobody, today, attempts to write like Carlyle or Ruskin, or even like that master of an uneccentric pure conversational prose, Newman. To do so would be like dressing up in a dead man's clothes. But when I come upon a middle-page article in *The New Statesman*, say, by Professor Trevor-Roper or Mr. A. J. P. Taylor, I often fancy that I am reading a Macaulay who has had, drastically, to condense himself; the old machinery of allusion, point, and antithesis, of the periodic sentence coming down with a snap or a bang at the end, still works. And I remember, also, the excitement with which a young friend of mine, now a political commentator on one of our respectable daily pa-

pers, announced to me that he had discovered Macaulay's essays. No critic and no imaginative writer today at all resembles Macaulay. But he is still a useful model in the field of high popularisation, in the prose of opinion, information, political persuasion. His heirs are not only among the popular historians and the political journalists. There is more than a touch of Macaulay's manner, for instance, in the less technical writings of Bertrand Russell.

If the influence has been lasting, it was also immediate. Sir George Otto Trevelyan's fine biography of his uncle catches almost uncannily the structure and emphasis of Macaulay's sentences; the style of Trevelyan's *The Early History of Charles James Fox,* an even more vivacious and sparkling book, is just that of Macaulay, with the addition of a touch of genuine aristocratic insouciance which Macaulay, a middle-class convert to Whiggism, never quite caught. Matthew Arnold deplored the prevalence in the late 1860's and early 1870's of what he called 'middle-class Macaulayese', but in fact the student of history and politics can trace Macaulay's influence, more fruitfully, in aristocratic writers; in, for instance, Lord Rosebery's excellent short life of the younger Pitt, in Lord Curzon's speeches, in Sir Winston Churchill's impressive life of his father. It can be traced, in fact, in unexpected places. I do not know if anyone has ever closely examined the prose style of the greatest of Victorian historical scholars, Lord Acton. Opposing almost everything, except the passion for liberty, that Macaulay stood for, he seems to me often to be imitating, perhaps unconsciously and certainly rather ineptly, Macaulay's manner. His prose is full of antitheses, of summary allusions, of pointed sentences, which do not quite come off, because they carry too heavy a burden of thought and learning. The greatest of Victorian critics, Matthew Arnold, brought the whole weight of his own rhetoric, his own 'heightened and telling way of putting things' to the demolishment of Macaulay's rhetoric; but, it would seem, with surprisingly little practical effect. Our most widely read living English historian is Macaulay's great-nephew, George Macaulay Trevelyan; and his style is very much Macaulay's style, with a subtler rhythm and with finer lights and shades.

'Where did you get that style?' asked Lord Jeffrey, when Macaulay first exploded, like a Roman candle, in the *Edinburgh Review.* But his wonder was not the wonder, mixed with perturbation, which he felt about the style of the young Carlyle. Macaulay's taste in literature was a conservative one; if one wants to know what a good critic he might have been, one has to read not his published essays but his marginal notes on Livy or Ovid or Thucydides. Vernacular literature was still, for him, something to be judged by the standards of Greece and Rome in their classical periods. The most recent English writer for whom he had a quite whole-hearted admiration was Jane Austen. He disliked Ruskin, he disliked Carlyle, he was too sharply opposed to everything that Newman stood for to appreciate Newman (though he recognised, grudgingly, his gifts). He was in a real sense old-fashioned not only in his tastes but in his opinions; one of the last important contemporary books he read was John Stuart Mill's essay on liberty, and Mill seemed to him like a man crying out 'Fire!' in the middle of Noah's flood. He thought Wordsworth's *Prelude* a poorer *Excursion*. He read, voraciously, sentimental novels with happy endings, as a public man today reads detective stories, he enjoyed Dickens rather condescendingly, as a public man today enjoys P. G. Wodehouse. He admired Byron and Shelley and Scott, he admired some things in Wordsworth but not what today we think his greatest things, but he felt that the early Victorian age was, on the whole, a day of small men both in literature and politics. He was, in his latter years, a wholehearted Palmerstonian in politics. The strength of his style, its confidence, comes from the two facts that he accepted unquestioningly the surface forward flow of his age, and rejected, just as unquestioningly, its deeper undertow.

His style, in the essays, in its dependence on point, balance, an abundance of not too recondite literary and historical allusion, periodic order, sharp antithesis, is essentially the old *Edinburgh Review* style, the style of Jeffrey or Sidney Smith, handled, however, without Jeffrey's scrupulosity or Smith's bubbling fun, handled with a new breadth, a new, sometimes harsh vividness, perhaps a new coarseness. It is never slovenly or straggly; it has no obscurities, and no fine shades. Though it is a rapid style, with an effect of very forcible impetus, even of rush, it never leaves even the most obtuse reader struggling hopelessly in its wake. In its use of diverse exemplification and concealed repetition—many concrete instances of even the most obvious generalisation, and the generalisation itself clothed in a succession of different phrases—it is very much the style of an orator. It hammers its points home; it illustrates them to a degree, for the more quick-witted reader, almost of tedium. It can rise, it perhaps rises too often, to a peroration; but it can also make a joke. Its tone is rather difficult to define, or even to describe. It is perhaps not unlike the tone, today, of a good university extension lecturer with the knack of handling, or subduing, almost any kind of audience. There is no deep intimacy, but there is a confidence that one will be listened to. Macaulay keeps at a certain dignified distance from the reader, but he is extremely aware, at the same time, of the importance of holding the reader's attention. He is friendly, he is vivacious, at times he almost verges on familiarity. He is not completely at ease, he is stretching himself, but he has a reassuring awareness of how much—how much information, what sound and yet surprising ideas, what a fertile field of illustration—he has to stretch. He is quite at the opposite pole from those writers whom Mr. John Holloway calls the Victorian sages, Carlyle, Ruskin, Arnold, Newman. He does not speak out of any deep inner uneasiness; his purpose is neither self-exploration nor, crudely and obviously, self-expression. Rather he seems often to be exploiting the possibilities of a rhetorical medium almost for the medium's own sake. If we want to know something about his simple, pathetic, generous, and honourable inner life—a life almost entirely dependent for its happiness on books, on daydreams, and on intense family affection divorced from sex—we have to turn to his nephew's biography, and to the extracts from Macaulay's letters and journals included in that. His biographer was well aware of this vulnerable and touching privacy of the central man:

> It may . . . be taken for granted that a desire exists to hear something authentic about the life of a man who has produced works which are universally known, but which bear little or no indication of the private history and personal qualities of the author. [George Otto Trevelyan, *The Life and Letters of Lord Macaulay,* 1887]

The style, Trevelyan seems to be implying there, is in Macaulay's case *not* the man. It is, of course, a style with an unmistakable external individuality about it. Yet the critical reader has an uneasy sense that it is a machine; a machine that, once set in motion, will carry the writer on, almost without his own effort, almost without his own volition.

It carries on the biographer as well as his subject. Sir George Otto Trevelyan has, for instance, this to say about Zachary Macaulay's affection for West Africa:

> But for the absence of an Eve, he regarded the West Coast of Africa as a veritable Paradise, or, to use his own expression, as a more agreeable Montpelier. With a temper which in the intercourse of society was proof against being ruffled by any possible treatment of any conceivable subject, to the end of his life he showed faint signs of irritation if anyone ventured in his presence to hint that Sierra Leone was unhealthy.

There is the note of Macaulay, there, in the doubling of literary and familiar or *mondain* allusions ('a veritable Paradise' doubled with 'a more agreeable Montpelier'). It is like Macaulay not to be able to mention Paradise without mentioning Eve. It is mildly amusing that Zachary Macaulay, in the innocence of his emancipating enthusiasm, should have enjoyed a climate which nearly all Europeans found oppressive and exhausting, if not actively dangerous. In case anybody has not seen the little joke, it is rubbed in in the next sentence. Zachary Macaulay is presented as a fantastically urbane man, who would never lose his temper in any conceivable circumstances but who would show 'faint' irritation if there were even a 'hint' that the climate of Sierra Leone was, not deadly, but merely 'unhealthy'. The reader is left with a sense of good-natured superiority to a saintly simpleton with a crotchet, a modern equivalent of Dr. Primrose or Parson Adams. For a portrait of Zachary Macaulay, a caricature is substituted; and Trevelyan himself must, in his heart, know that it is a caricature. He has himself depicted Zachary Macaulay as a Tory Evangelical utterly obsessed with African emancipation. Would such a man have remained unruffled by a conversation which treated lightly either the Christian faith or the horrors of the slave trade? Trevelyan also describes Zachary Macaulay as a kind but difficult parent, who inflicted long sermons on his children, and who was considerably ruffled by Tom's absorption in profane literature and by Tom's switch-over, at Cambridge, from Evangelical Tory to Erastian Whig politics. This is almost a better example than any in Macaulay's own works of the difficulty, in Macaulayan rhetoric, of telling the plain truth. The plain truth would be something like this; that Zachary Macaulay, though a very polite, patient, and tolerant man in all discussions where his central faith and purpose were not engaged, had an almost irritable defensive affection for West Africa.

There are plenty of examples of this kind of distortion, the exigent simplifications of rhetoric ironing out the awkward complications of fact, in Macaulay's own essays. Take these sentences on Byron:

> The young peer had great intellectual powers; yet there was an unsound part in his mind. He had naturally a generous and feeling heart; but his temper was wayward and irritable. He had a head which statuaries loved to copy, and *a foot the deformity of which the beggars in the street mimicked.*

I have read many contemporary accounts of Byron and I recently visited Newstead Abbey and looked both at the testimony of his shoemaker and at a pair of his shoe-lasts. I cannot think that he was ever mocked in the streets, except just possibly in Aberdeen, in his schooldays. The lame foot seems to have been of the same size as the sound foot; the ankle could not support the lame leg, which was perhaps a little shorter than the sound one. Byron's clothes, his boots, his mode of walking and standing were all calculated to make his deformity, which in any case was of a weakening rather than a dis-figuring kind, as inconspicuous as possible. Macaulay must have known all this; the rhetorical machine carried him away, he could not resist a coarsely effective antithesis. Or take the even more notorious sentences on Boswell:

> If he had not been *a great fool,* he would never have been a great writer. Without all the qualities which made him the *jest and torment* of those among whom he lived, without the officiousness, the inquisitiveness, the effrontery, the toad-eating, the *insensibility to all reproof,* he would never have produced so excellent a book.

The subtle psychological penetration which is everywhere evident in the life of Johnson ought to have made it obvious to Macaulay that Boswell was, at least, not a fool *qua* writer. Nobody lives so long as Boswell did at the centre of the best intellectual company of his day who is merely the 'jest and torment' of his friends, and Macaulay must have known Johnson's own lively and sincere tribute to Boswell's charm as a travelling companion. We know today more about Boswell than Macaulay did, but there is plenty of evidence of his extreme 'sensibility to reproof' in the great biography itself. Again, the steam-roller rhetoric crushes the truth flat.

It was this coarseness in the fibre, not of Macaulay's private and intimate self, but of his public rhetoric that Matthew Arnold never tired of attacking. The most vivacious attack comes in *Friendship's Garland,* in a conversation with Arminius von Thunder-ten-Tronckh reported by Adolescens Leo of the *Daily Telegraph:*

> Now I detest this German lecturer and his oracles, but I am above everything, a man of letters myself, I never refuse to listen to a remark upon style. 'Explain yourself,' said I; 'why do you call Mr. Hepworth Dixon's style middle-class Macaulayese?' 'I call it Macaulayese,' says the pedant, 'because it has the same internal and exter-

nal characteristics as Macaulay's style; the external characteristics being a hard metallic movement with nothing of the soft play of life, and the internal characteristic being a perpetual semblance of hitting the right nail on the head without the reality. And I call it middle-class Macaulayese, because it has these faults without the compensation of great studies and of conversance with great affairs, by which Macaulay partly redeemed them.'

In the essay on Joubert, Arnold calls Macaulay 'the great apostle of the Philistines', and describes him as:

> a born rhetorician; a splendid rhetorician doubtless, and beyond that, an *English* rhetorician also, an *honest* rhetorician; still beyond the apparent rhetorical truth of things he could never penetrate; for their vital truth, for what the French call the *vraie vérité,* he had absolutely no organ . . .

Elsewhere he speaks of:

> the confident shallowness which makes [Macaulay] so admired by public speakers and leading-article writers, and so intolerable to all searchers for truth . . .

Arnold's most sustained attack, an attack a little qualified by a tribute to Macaulay's attractiveness to the reader who is just beginning to 'awake to the intellectual life', comes in the excellent essay, *A French Critic on Milton:* I quote some key phrases and sentences from a passage running over several pages (it will be noticed that Arnold repeats the general characterisation of Macaulay's style, especially the remarks on its mechanical and external quality, its lack of inner life, already uttered by Arminius):

> A style to dazzle, to gain admirers everywhere, to attract imitators in multitude! A style brilliant, metallic, exterior, making strong points, alternating invective with eulogy, wrapping in a robe of rhetoric the thing it represents . . . [The] writer has not for his aim to see and utter the real truth about his object . . . Substantial meaning such lucubrations can have none. And in like manner, a distinct and substantial meaning can never be got out of the fine phrases about 'Milton's conception of life uniting all the voluptuousness of the Oriental haram, with all the pure and quiet affection of the English fireside' . . . the phrases are mere rhetoric . . . The immense popularity of Macaulay is due to his being pre-eminently fitted to give pleasure to all who are *beginning* to feel enjoyment in the things of the mind . . . The Bible and Shakespeare may be said to be imposed upon an Englishman as objects of his admiration; but as soon as the common Englishman, desiring culture, begins to choose for himself, he chooses Macaulay. Macaulay's view of things is, on the whole, the view of them he feels to be his own also . . . But with the increasing number of those who awake to the intellectual life, the number of those also increases, who, having awoke to it, go on with it, follow where it leads them . . . To be satisfied with fine writing about the object of one's study, with having it praised or blamed in accordance with one's like and dis-

likes, with any conventional treatment of it whatever, is at this stage of growth seen to be futile. At this stage, rhetoric, even when it is so good as Macaulay's, dissatisfies [Matthew Arnold, *Mixed Essays,* 1879].

It would, I think, be a futile exercise in paradox to attempt to refute Arnold's general judgement, especially on Macaulay as a literary critic. The rhetoric is much less harmful to the controversial pieces on political thought, like the attacks on Southey, on James Mill, and on Gladstone. Of these, the Southey essay is the worst in tone and temper; I find the Mill essay sane and sympathetic; and I agree with Gladstone himself in finding the Gladstone piece, on Gladstone's early book on the relations of Church and State, a model of controversial courtesy. Perhaps the finest of all the political pieces for tone, however, is the shortish essay on Lord Holland; Macaulay wrote it rather reluctantly, egged or nagged into doing so by Lady Holland, and the style somehow catches something of the easy stateliness of the old Whig society. There are no occasions for violent and coarse antithesis; something of the serene harmony of Lord Holland's own temperament chastens Macaulay's style. The masterpieces, however, among the essays are those which are almost pure narrative; the Clive, the Warren Hastings, the two essays on Chatham, the political part of the essay on Horace Walpole, the Frederick the Great. In these, the great historian is learning his trade. The best defence of Macaulay against Arnold, I think, or the best palliation of Arnold's case for the prosecution, is Macaulay's own view of his achievement as an essayist; a view remarkably modest.

In 1838, Lord Brougham, politically powerless and morally isolated, had, after scamping his contributions to the *Edinburgh Review* for many years, determined to exert himself as if he were a young writer struggling into note. Macaulay, writing to the editor of the *Edinburgh Review,* MacVey Napier, commented:

> [Brougham's contributions] are, indeed, models of magazine writing, as distinguished from other sorts of writing. They are not, I think, made for duration. Everything about them is exaggerated, incorrect, sketchy. All the characters are either too black, or too fair. The passions of the writer do not suffer him to maintain even the decent appearance of impartiality. And the style, though striking and animated, will not bear examination through a single paragraph. But the effect of the first perusal is great; and few people read through an article in a review twice.

Brougham hated Macaulay, who had all his own gifts, combined with two things that Brougham lacked, perfect honour and loyalty in political relations, and a self-knowledge that took in not only scope but limitations. Macaulay did not love Brougham; and in our enemies we have a particularly sharp eye for our own faults in an exaggerated form. All that Macaulay says of Brougham might be said, by a hostile critic, of Macaulay himself. But, unlike Brougham, Macaulay had the gift of self-criticism. Writing again to Napier, in 1842, he says:

> The public judges, and ought to judge, indulgently of periodical works. They are not expect-

ed to be highly finished. Their natural life is only six weeks. Sometimes their writer is at a distance from the books to which he wants to refer. Sometimes he is forced to hurry through his task in order to catch the post. He may blunder; he may contradict himself; he may give an immoderate extension to one part of his subject, and dismiss an equally important part in a few words. All this is readily forgiven if there be a certain spirit and vivacity in his style. But, as soon as he republishes, he challenges a comparison with all the most polished and symmetrical of human compositions . . . My reviews are generally thought to be better written, and they certainly live longer, than the reviews of most other people; and this ought to content me. The moment I come forward to demand a higher rank, I must expect to be judged by a higher standard.

Macaulay, also, was as keenly aware as Matthew Arnold himself that his gifts were not those of a literary critic. He refused, for that reason, in 1838, to review Lockhart's life of Scott. He wrote to Napier:

> I have written several things on historical, political, and moral questions of which, on the fullest reconsideration, I am not ashamed, and by which I would be willing to be estimated; but I have never written a page of criticism on poetry, or the fine arts, which I would not burn if I had the power. Hazlitt used to say of himself, 'I am nothing if not critical'. The case with me is directly the reverse. I have a strong and acute enjoyment of works of the imagination; but I have never habituated myself to dissect them. Perhaps I enjoy them the more keenly, for that very reason. Such books as Lessing's *Laocoon,* such passages as the criticism on *Hamlet* in *Wilhelm Meister,* fill me with wonder and despair. Now, a review of Lockhart's book ought to be a review of Sir Walter's literary performances. I enjoy many of them;—nobody, I believe, more keenly;—but I am sure that there are hundreds who will criticise them far better. Trust to my knowledge of myself. I never in my life was more certain of anything than of what I tell you, and I am sure that Lord Jeffrey will tell you exactly the same.

He had a very sound measure of himself. The essays are, like Brougham's, exaggerated, incorrect, sketchy. But they have proved, unlike Brougham's, to be made for duration. Macaulay lived, from his childhood on, in books; a life of great affairs and intense affections never got him out of books; as an orator urging through the great Reform Bill, as an administrator reshaping the system of law and education in India, as a conversationalist at Holland House, he remained an eager and confident and very intelligent schoolboy, stepping out of his library, his mind full of everything that he had read. His great, and not really unwholesome influence, on political and popular historical writing, suggests odd reflections about how little of the subtlety and maturity of the personal life, of great imaginative literature, ever gets into the discussion of public affairs; about how much we are always ruled by intelligent schoolboys. But in our own age, even more than in Arnold's, there is a great public that is just *'beginning* to feel enjoyment in the things of the mind'. And that public might do much worse than turn to what Arnold rightly called Macaulay's honest and English rhetoric; it might turn to Mr. Colin Wilson. (pp. 9-19)

G. S. Fraser, "Macaulay's Style as An Essay-ist," in A Review of English Literature, *Vol. 1, No. 4, October, 1960, pp. 9-19.*

Emerson rejects Macaulay's materialism:

The brilliant Macaulay, who expresses the tone of the English governing classes of the day, explicitly teaches, that *good* means good to eat, good to wear, material commodity; that the glory of modern philosophy is its direction on "fruit;" to yield economical inventions; and that its merit is to avoid ideas, and avoid morals. He thinks it the distinctive merit of the Baconian philosophy, in its triumph over the old Platonic, its disentangling the intellect from theories of the all-Fair and all-Good, and pinning it down to the making a better sick chair and a better wine-whey for an invalid;—this not ironically, but in good faith;—that, "solid advantage," as he calls it, meaning always sensual benefit, is the only good. The eminent benefit of astronomy is the better navigation it creates to enable the fruit-ships to bring home their lemons and wine to the London grocer. It was a curious result, in which the civility and religion of England for a thousand years, ends, in denying morals, and reducing the intellect to a sauce-pan.

Ralph Waldo Emerson, in his English Traits, *Philips, Sampson and Company, 1856.*

Gilbert Highet   (essay date 1960)

[*A Scottish-born writer and critic, Highet was a classical scholar and distinguished educator as well as a literary personality for a weekly radio program in New York. Among his many publications is* The Classical Tradition; Greek and Roman Influences on Western Literature *(1949). In the following excerpt, Highet recounts his experience reading Macaulay's* The Lays of Ancient Rome *and deems the poems an excellent introduction to the classics as well as effective propaganda for the values of a democratic society.*]

In a certain sense, everything which is written to be read (if it is not pure fact like a railroad timetable) is propaganda, because it attempts to present a point of view, and to convince the reader that it should be accepted. Never was there a greater fallacy (or falsehood) than the dogma that an author is interested only in 'art for art's sake,' that he is producing simply patterns of words without meaning, that he wishes to make no impact on the intellect and emotions of his readers, that he does not wish to *change* them. Still, one of the problems of writing is that it is hard to convey propaganda without becoming obvious, and thereby evoking disbelief or contempt. The whole subject is full of questions which have not yet been thoroughly analyzed. For instance, would you say it was easier to write effective propaganda in prose, or in poetry? Allowing for the fact

that, nowadays at least, it is easier to write prose of any kind than it is to write poetry of any kind, it is actually more difficult to convey a propaganda message in prose than it is in poetry. This is because poetry (like music) makes a more immediate appeal to the emotions, while prose asks to be meditated and criticized. Prose makes us think; poetry sets our hearts beating faster and more strongly. It was a wise man who said that he believed if a man were permitted to make all the ballads, he need not care who should make the laws of a nation.

One strikingly effective dose of propaganda in poetry has been well known to me ever since I was a schoolboy; but it is only in the last few years that I have realized how strong the dose is, how carefully it was devised, and how skillfully it was mixed in with the poetry. It worked on me in two different ways, and, I think, I really believe, it changed my whole life—and changed it unconsciously, as propaganda is designed to do. I think it may have changed the lives of quite a large number of people, and although its efficiency is now diminished to the vanishing point, it worked very well for several generations.

It is a short book containing only four poems, published in Britain in 1842. Its title is *Lays of Ancient Rome.* Its author was a brilliant intellectual who turned into a wise and farsighted statesman: Thomas Macaulay. It is unusual nowadays for politicians to publish volumes of poetry, but that was an age of many talents. One of Macaulay's contemporaries continued to write novels even after he became Prime Minister of Britain.

Some people have called the *Lays of Ancient Rome* tinsel and sham. I cannot agree. On their own level they are good, sound poetry; it is the same level, roughly, as Sibelius's *Finlandia* or Tchaikovsky's *1812 Overture.* The style in which they are written is now out of fashion, but in appreciating poetry one must try to ignore fashion. They are ballads, written in the same vigorous, cantering meter as the original English and Scottish ballads, and obviously inspired also by the romantic poetry of Sir Walter Scott. They are retellings of boldly exciting episodes in the very early history of ancient Rome.

The most famous, **"Horatius,"** tells the splendid story of the invasion of Rome by the Etruscans from the north, which was stopped by a single warrior: Horatius himself, who, with two comrades, held the bridge across the river Tiber until it was cut down behind him, and then (though wounded and wearing full armor) jumped in and swam back to safety. The most pathetic, **"Virginia,"** shows us a Roman father stabbing his daughter to death in the city street, to save her from being enslaved and dishonored by a brutal nobleman. The broadest and deepest, **"The Battle of the Lake Regillus,"** describes another invasion of Rome by the Etruscans, who are determined to break the young republic and put Etruscan kings back on the throne; but, with divine assistance, the Romans smash them in a tremendous conflict. The duels between individual champions in this ballad still stir my blood. I do not know, and scarcely even care, who the heroes are and what place they have in history. It is enough to know that they are brave and to watch them fight.

Mamilius spied Herminius,
    And dashed across the way.
'Herminius! I have sought thee
    Through many a bloody day.
One of us two, Herminius,
    Shall never more go home.
I will lay on for Tusculum,
    And lay thou on for Rome!'

The last and most mystical of these poems, **"The Prophecy of Capys,"** takes us right back before the foundation of the city, shows us the twins, Romulus and Remus, asserting their rights, and gives us a forecast of the future prowess and warlike mastery of the Romans yet to be. Tough people, the Romans, their toughness symbolized in the she-wolf which suckled the twins when they were cast out, and kept them alive for their future vengeance.

The ox toils through the furrow,
    Obedient to the goad;
The patient ass, up flinty paths,
    Plods with his weary load;
With whine and bound the spaniel
    His master's whistle hears;
And the sheep yields her patiently
    To the loud clashing shears.

But thy nurse will bear no master,
    Thy nurse will bear no load;
And woe to them that shear her,
    And woe to them that goad!
When all the pack, loud baying,
    Her bloody lair surrounds,
She dies in silence, biting hard,
    Among the dying hounds.

No, no; I am convinced that, though bright, this is not tinsel nor silver foil; this is true steel. Here is a Roman soldier volunteering to hold the bridge while his comrades hack it to pieces behind him.

Then out spake brave Horatius,
    The Captain of the Gate:
'To every man upon this earth
    Death cometh soon or late.
And how can man die better
    Than facing fearful odds,
For the ashes of his fathers
    And the temples of his Gods?'

Not only is that good poetry of its kind, but I am certain that it is true. I believe that is how men feel in those simple, primitive times when right is right and wrong is wrong, and liberty is far more important than life. I believe that is how the Romans felt in those days; and, for all their terrible barbarities and weaknesses, they gave an example of patriotism to all later history. And it is bound to move any citizen of a free republic to watch the overthrow of a brutal despotism and the assertion of democracy and freedom. The Tarquins, the dynasty of Etruscans who ruled Rome as kings until their expulsion, are the villains of two of these fine ballads. You remember the infamous crime which actually caused the Romans to rebel against them: the rape of the Roman lady Lucretia, who killed herself after being outraged by the Tarquin prince Sextus. Macaulay never tells this story, but it is always in the background, everyone knows it, and it is deeply, pas-

sionately felt. The evil prince appears in the Etruscan army as it moves toward the bridge.

But when the face of Sextus
    Was seen among the foes,
A yell that rent the firmament
    From all the town arose.
On the house-tops was no woman
    But spat towards him and hissed,
No child but screamed out curses,
    And shook its little fist.

In the second battle, at Lake Regillus, Sextus is the first to retreat, but he is not quick enough.

And in the back false Sextus
    Felt the good Roman steel,
And wriggling in the dust he died
    Like a worm beneath the wheel.

I am not ashamed to admit that I got the same kind of pleasure out of these poems at the age of ten or eleven as boys nowadays get out of motion pictures of Western adventure; and frankly, I still find the walkdown, with hero and villain shooting it out in the empty street, less thrilling than a hand-to-hand duel with cold steel.

Then, whirling up his broadsword
    With both hands to the height,
He rushed against Horatius
    And smote with all his might.
With shield and blade Horatius
    Right deftly turned the blow.
The blow, though turned, came yet too nigh:
It missed his helm, but gashed his thigh;
The Tuscans raised a joyful cry
    To see the red blood flow.
He reeled, and on Herminius
    He leaned one breathing-space;
Then, like a wild cat mad with wounds,
    Sprang right at Astur's face.
Through teeth, and skull, and helmet,
    So fierce a thrust he sped
The good sword stood a handbreadth out
    Behind the Tuscan's head.

Macaulay's first aim in writing these poems was historical reconstruction. He was doing the same sort of thing (on a smaller scale) as Shakespeare in writing *Macbeth* or Vergil in writing the *Aeneid:* giving a picture of a vanished age. He obviously liked thinking about the Romans when they were still uncorrupted; he admired their energy and their heroism.

But he had a second motive, a very peculiar one. He was by vocation a historian. Therefore he had to keep thinking about the sources for the history of the past. Now, we have several histories (in Greek and Latin) of the early days of Rome; but they were written many generations after the events they describe. Therefore the question is: on what were they based? Were there written records of those far distant days which the historians could use? And if so, what were the records like? Were they like the Bible, mainly a prose narrative? Or were they more like the *Iliad,* a vivid but incomplete group of poetic scenes? A German historian called Niebuhr, one of the founders of modern historiography, proposed that the early history of Rome as it has come down to us was based not on any continuous record, but rather on ballads describing single adventures, like that of Horatius at the bridge: poems which did not attempt to analyze economic forces or strategic problems, which admitted and enjoyed phenomenal adventures and miraculous interventions, and which blended much imagination and emotion with a smaller proportion of hard fact. None of these poems has survived; we hear of them only remotely and vaguely; but it is far from improbable that they existed. In the *Lays of Ancient Rome* Macaulay is trying to show what they would look like; and, allowing for the change from Italic to Anglo-Saxon styles, he succeeded very handsomely.

But, where does the propaganda come in? I never noticed it when I read these poems as a schoolboy. I simply enjoyed them—as I enjoyed reading the authentic ballads of 'Edward' or 'Sir Patrick Spens.' Still, looking back, I am absolutely certain that these poems were among the most potent initial forces which made me give up my life to the study of the classics. Beginning a strange pair of ancient languages at the age of eleven, studying nouns and verbs and trying to translate simple sentences, I felt merely curiosity about their peculiar structure, but I could not feel much emotional interest in the people who spoke them—until I read the *Lays of Ancient Rome* and saw that the Romans were real, that they had character, that they were in fact more exciting than the drab city dwellers I saw all around me and perhaps more like my Covenanting Scottish ancestors.

These poems were therefore propaganda for the classics. But they contained a more subtle dose of propaganda than this. As you read them (at least when you are young and malleable) you are convinced that kings are cruel despots; that monarchy means tyranny; that hereditary aristocracy is a cloak for privilege and vice and crime; and that the worthiest way to live is as a citizen of a free republic, such as Rome was when it threw off the monarchy of the Tarquins. Now, Macaulay was a 100% Liberal. His father had been one of the most powerful propagandists for the abolition of slavery, and Macaulay himself was a Whig member of the first Reform Parliament. In the year 1842, when the *Lays* were published, the young Queen Victoria had been on the throne for only four years; she was still unpopular, and three attempts had been made to assassinate her. It would therefore have been possible for a man like Macaulay to say openly that the monarchy ought to be abolished and that Great Britain would be happier and more stable as a republic. It would have been possible, but it would have been indiscreet and injudicious. It would have been rabble-rousing rather than constructive political thinking, at that time. What Macaulay could do was to present the Whig point of view both emotionally—through these poems and others—and intellectually—through the superb *History of England* which he was then preparing to write, and which is in fact a history of the overthrow of the royal house of Stuart. In another poem, less well known than the *Lays,* he shows us the triumph of Cromwell over King Charles I, and describes Charles in a phrase of unforgettable bitterness:

> The Man of Blood was there, with his long essenced hair.

These words have the same fiery conviction behind them that makes us, in the *Lays of Ancient Rome,* side with Horatius and the free Romans against the Tarquins and false Sextus. And it was that conviction, subtly instilled into me while I was still a schoolboy and thought I was enjoying poetry, not reading propaganda, that prepared my mind to approve democracy, with all its risks and dangers, rather than the powers and privileges of hereditary aristocracy, and to prefer a republic to a monarchy. This is an important choice. It was not an easy choice to make. When I made it, the step was taken with full intellectual understanding of its meaning. But the emotional preparation for the step, without which it would surely have been far more difficult, was made when I was still a little boy, and read and reread the *Lays of Ancient Rome.* (pp. 197-204)

> *Gilbert Highet, " 'Lays of Ancient Rome': Propaganda and Poetry," in his* The Powers of Poetry, *Oxford University Press, Inc., 1960, pp. 197-205.*

William A. Madden   (essay date 1968)

[*Madden is an American educator and scholar who is the editor and author of numerous books and articles on Victorian studies. In the following excerpt, he closely examines the attributes of Macaulay's prose style and speculates on factors which influenced it. According to Madden, Macaulay's emotional immaturity is responsible both for his attempt to find in historical research a refuge in the past and for his failure to develop a consistent style for writing history.*]

Two early commentators passed judgments on the writings of Thomas Babington Macaulay which are of interest to the student of Victorian prose style. Sir George Otto Trevelyan, in his authoritative *Life and Letters of Lord Macaulay,* contrasted Macaulay's writings and those of contemporaries like Dickens and Thackeray, arguing that the latter had told their own stories in their books, whereas Macaulay's writings gave "little or no indication of the private history and personal qualities of the author." Gladstone, in reviewing Trevelyan's biography, observed that Macaulay's style was "a thing above the heads of common mortals," but amidst the "blaze of glory, there is want of perspective, of balance, of breadth"; in this, according to Gladstone, Macaulay's style was a "mirror which reflected the image of himself."

These early views, the one separating Macaulay the writer from Macaulay the man and the other separating the content from the form of Macaulay's prose, raise for the critic of prose style the "biographical" question: to what extent is an author "in" his writings? Several recent studies have touched suggestively on this question as it bears upon Macaulay. By exploring the interplay between Macaulay's histrionic temperament, the pressures exerted by his immediate environment, and the style of his prose, they have concluded that Macaulay's style does in fact exhibit clear traces of the personal qualities and the private history of the man himself. In the following remarks I propose to carry this more recent view one step further by discriminating between the basic structure of Macaulay's prose—the stylistic form which embodies his fundamental mode of awareness—and the various surface structures by means of which he adapted his basic style not only to the needs of his Victorian audience but, as I will argue, to urgent private needs as well.

Macaulay's basic conceptions, already fixed by the time he had reached the age of twenty-five, were shaped in large measure by an environment which contained diverse elements not easily reconcilable for those who were exposed to them. In Macaulay's case there was, first of all, the Evangelical atmosphere of his boyhood at Clapham Common, dominated by the strong presence of his father and a moral code which stressed earnest conscientiousness and hard work as correctives to the idle imagination and the indolent flesh. Somewhat later there was the liberal world of eighteenth-century literature and philosophy which Macaulay absorbed through his extensive adolescent readings and which in manner, tone, and ambience were almost the very opposite of Evangelical. Finally, there was the highly charged political and literary climate of England between 1815 and 1825 in which Macaulay came of age. The most important as well as the most obvious consequence of the interaction of these disparate pressures was Macaulay's rejection, while in his early twenties at Cambridge, of his father's Evangelical theology and Tory politics on the one side, and of the democratic politics and religious agnosticism of the Philosophical Radicals on the other.

Details regarding this important event are sparse, but it is possible to isolate at least some of the elements which must have entered into Macaulay's decision. It seems clear, for example, that his rejection of his father's religion was a result of his instinctive reaction against the "sullen" Clapham environment of his childhood, which E. M. Forster has described as lacking a "feeling for poetry" [*Marianne Thorton: A Domestic Biography, 1797-1887*]; At the same time, Macaulay retained the strict Clapham moral principles as well as the Evangelical distrust of human reason, its suspicion of "fictions" (with the important exception of moral fables), and its indifference to natural beauty. His subsequent readings in the eighteenth century, in addition to helping to undermine his childhood religion, did much to shape Macaulay's literary tastes, to reinforce his identification of reason with "common sense," and to strengthen his attachment to liberty. Finally, the effects of the contemporary climate seem to have been twofold: imaginatively, Macaulay discovered Romanticism very early and assimilated something of its spirit through his reading of Scott's poetry and novels; politically, he reacted against the brutalities of Peterloo and became convinced of the necessity for moderate reform if England were to be saved.

The attitudes to which this combination of pressures led Macaulay combined negative and positive elements. Negatively, he was convinced that ultimate questions of theology, "the grounds of moral obligation or the freedom of the human will," were insoluble enigmas which had puzzled mankind for a hundred generations and would always remain enigmas that the imagination, *contra* Wordsworth and the other Romantics, was essentially uncreative, having but two functions—either to lie by inventing fictions, or to make more vivid and telling truths already known on other grounds; and that philosophical reason was equally limited, since man was no more granted intuition into ultimate truths through philosophical speculation than he was through imaginative fictions. The positive assumptions that Macaulay adopted, in effect, filled the void left by these negations. For the Evangelical faith in a personal God directly concerned with each man's inmost thoughts and most ordinary acts he proposed faith in the revelatory value of facts; physical, moral, and intellectual events, history in its broadest sense, provided men with their one avenue to truth. In place of imaginative or philosophical intuition he proposed the method of induction working upon observed facts—the "common sense" reasoning used by man from time immemorial—as the single source of knowledge in moral as well as physical science. And for the two great "principles" which had formerly moved masses of men—religious zeal and chivalrous love or honor—he substituted the intellectual and political ideal of liberty, the freedom of every man to think and act without coercion. Rejecting tradition and authority as reservoirs of wisdom, Macaulay proposed the free clash of ideas in an open intellectual market as the necessary condition both for truth and for progress. The fruitful results of this clash were guaranteed by the hidden hand of an unseen Providence which regulated it, irrespective of individual hopes and intentions.

These negative and positive assumptions, conventionally included under the rubric of "Whiggism," underlay Macaulay's formulation of a theory of style. The theory entailed three major criteria, the most important of which was that language had first of all to be clear. "The first rule of all writing—that rule to which every other is subordinate—is that the words used by the writer shall be such as most fully and precisely convey his meaning to the great body of his readers. All considerations about the purity and dignity of style ought to bend to this consideration. To write what is not understood in its whole force [is] absurd." This emphasis upon clarity was closely related to Macaulay's optimistic view of the simplicity and obviousness of truth. His two other criteria, that of force (referred to obliquely in the above passage) and that of charm, were dictated, on the other hand, by his pessimistic view of human nature as represented by the average audience: if language had to be clear in order to be understood, it had to have charm also in order to attract and hold readers, and force in order to persuade them.

Macaulay's evaluation of the English prose tradition was determined by these basic assumptions. He greatly admired the clarity of eighteenth-century prose, its "everyday language" represented by the tradition running from Addison to Jane Austen, while condemning the embellishments of Augustan "elegance" and of Johnson's "learned" language. At the same time, he admired the simplicity and force of the Evangelical style of preaching, a tradition which went as far back as Bunyan, even though he rejected the theology for which that language had been the traditional vehicle. And he praised the vividness and coloring of Burke, Scott, and Southey while deprecating what he regarded as their suborning of reason by their having let their imaginations run loose. The novelty of Macaulay's own style, which so impressed Lord Jeffrey when he first encountered it ("the more I think, the less can I conceive where you picked up that style"), can be traced to his eclectic assimilation of the quite different Evangelical, eighteenth-century, and Romantic canons of good prose. They appear not only in his theory of style and in his assessment of earlier English prose but also in the varying surface styles which play above the basic structure of his own prose.

The basic structure of Macaulay's style was shaped by his unquestioned faith in the obviousness of truth, and more particularly by his belief that out of the clash of opposing opinions truth and progress irresistibly emerged. A passage in the representative essay **"Sir James Mackintosh"** (1835), because of its close adaptation of style to theme and the relative absence of the complicating surface styles which elsewhere often veil the basic structure of his prose, may serve to exemplify Macaulay's style as it embodies the characteristic focus and movement of his mind. It is necessary to quote at some length.

> As we would have our descendants judge us, so ought we to judge our fathers. In order to form a correct estimate of their merits, we ought to place ourselves in their situation. . . . It was not merely difficult, but absolutely impossible, for the best and greatest of men, two hundred years ago, to be what a very commonplace person in our days may easily be, and indeed must necessarily be. But it is too much that the benefactors of mankind, after having been reviled by the dunces of their own generation for going too far, should be reviled by the dunces of the next generation for not going far enough.
>
> The truth lies between two absurd extremes. On one side is the bigot who pleads the wisdom of our ancestors as a reason for not doing what they in our place would be the first to do; who opposes the Reform Bill because Lord Somers did not see the necessity of Parliamentary Reform; who would have opposed the Revolution because Ridley and Cranmer professed boundless submission to the royal prerogative; and who would have opposed the Reformation because the Fitzwalters and Mareschals, whose seals are set to the Great Charter, were devoted adherents to the Church of Rome. On the other side is the sciolist who speaks with scorn of the Great Charter because it did not reform the Church; of the Reformation, because it did not limit the prerogative; and of the Revolution, because it did not purify the House of Commons. . . . The former error bears directly on practical questions, and obstructs useful reforms. It may, therefore, seem to be, and probably is, the more mischievous of the two. But the latter is equally absurd; it is at least equally symptomatic of a shallow understanding and an unamiable temper: and, if it should ever become general, it will, we are satisfied, produce very prejudicial effects. Its tendency is to deprive the benefactors of mankind of their honest fame, and to put the best and the worst of men of past times on the same level. The author of a great reformation is almost always unpopular in his own age. He generally passes his life in disquiet and danger. It is

> therefore for the interest of the human race that the memory of such men should be had in reverence, and that they should be supported against the scorn and hatred of their contemporaries by the hope of leaving a great and imperishable name. To go on the forlorn hope of truth is a service of peril. Who will undertake it, if it be not also a service of honour?

In subject, tenor, and mode the passage reveals Macaulay's mind in a style admirably suited to articulate that mind's basic rhythm of predication. The subject is history and politics, the actions of men *en masse*. In tenor it holds to a middle range; there is a slight heightening in the rhetorical "Who will undertake it, if it be not also a service of honour?", but there is not, as often in Macaulay, either high panegyric or low invective. In mode it is expository and refutative in the manner of reasoned debate, neither urgent and highly colored nor entirely dispassionate. The diction is simple and abstract and thus appropriate to the statement of a general principle, yet the proper names alluded to by way of offering inductive support for the generalizations move the style in the direction of concreteness.

The expressed theme of the passage, and the controlling frame of Macaulay's basic mode of thinking, is contained in the proposition that "the truth lies between two absurd extremes." It is doubtful that Macaulay's attachment to this view had a specific source; it was available to him in various contexts and in writers as different from one another as Aristotle, Bacon, Montesquieu, and the Scottish common sense philosophers. What is of interest to the student of style is its effect upon Macaulay's linguistic organization of his experience. The axiom of a philosopher of the opposed school—Coleridge's insistence that "extremes meet"—suggests a world of discourse from which Macaulay was excluded by his aversion to "extremes." This aversion was undoubtedly related to the confused intellectual and political climate in which Macaulay grew up, charged as that climate was by the antagonisms of Evangelical Toryism and Radical atheism in religion and politics and by the counterclaims of Augustan decorum and Romantic enthusiasm in literature. The proposition that the truth lies between extremes, as expressed by Macaulay, represented less a reasoned philosophical position than a pragmatic cast of mind which had been formed and was made permanent by an unstable and sometimes threatening environment working upon an extraordinarily sensitive and retentive temperament. This habit of mind appears everywhere in Macaulay's prose and affects his handling of almost every topic of which he treats.

A style which organizes itself at its deepest level around the proposition that the truth lies between two absurd extremes may be described as antithetical. The stylistic frame which embodies the conception is capable of accepting a wide range of "extremes," and of operating in various ways: logically, to point to a golden mean; dialectically, in analyses of the historic process; ethically, in the recommendation of prudence; and rhetorically both in the black-and-white mode of conventional antithesis and in the shock of paradox ("Mr. Fox wrote debates. Sir James Mackintosh spoke essays.") But whatever the materials to which it is applied or the manner in which Macaulay applies it, the frame preserves a fixed form . . . in which A and B represent extremes of thought or feeling or behavior, between which lies truth, poise, or prudence. The form may be used for purposes either of simple contrast, in which case C is muted, or of pointing to a desiderated mean (in the above passage C is muted, but the implied mean between bigot and sciolist is, of course, the author himself). The extremes may be those of the "charm of the past" and the "charm of novelty," pointing to their proper blend in the true statesman; to those of theory and fact, pointing to their ideal blend in true history; or to those of superstition and atheism, pointing to the true religious mean of what might be described as vague and reverent deism. The "distance" separating the extremes may vary. Applied to politics the antithetical form encompasses the broad abstractions of tyranny and anarchy, the more limited ones of King and English people, or the specific ones of Tory and Whig, and thus points to the ever more sharply defined middle ground of constitutional government, the English settlement, or the Trimmer. In religion it can narrow from the wide extremes of superstition–atheism, through Papist–Puritan, to High Church–Low Church Anglican.

The antithetical mode of thought and style was so instinctive for Macaulay that on occasion it proved embarrassing; having yielded to its demands, he had sometimes to ignore its consequences. In the early essay **"Dante,"** to cite just one example, the argument that true religion must satisfy both the mind and heart, like Protestantism, and the imagination, like Greek mythology, points Macaulay to Roman Catholicism as the ideal blend of the "awful doctrines" of the one and what Coleridge called the "fair humanities" of the other. But having fallen into the pattern, Macaulay ignores its logic in order to avoid drawing an unacceptable conclusion. The habit was also capable of degenerating into a stylistic tic. The "coarseness" which G. S. Fraser has traced ["Macaulay's Style as an Essayist," *A Review of English Literature* 1, No. 4 (October 1960)] in Macaulay's essays is one result. The rigidity of the form explains also why critics have found Macaulay's prose "metallic," its forever giving, as Matthew Arnold noted, the impression of hitting the nail on the head without the reality. The style is often brilliantly effective in Macaulay's treatment of politics and politicians; in the search for a mean which will be acceptable to parties of the extremes, the compromises reached through practicing the "art of the possible" seem cogent. In his literary essays and the non-political parts of his historical essays, on the other hand, the form can be either falsifying or irrelevant, and sometimes both.

The discussion of poetry in the **"Milton"** essay not only reveals the limitations of the antithetical style but suggests the existence of a complexity in Macaulay himself which that style could neither disguise nor adequately realize. Having set up the antithesis of reason and imagination and the postulate that as the former improves the latter declines, Macaulay can find no adequate mean, since the triumph of reason is seen as a good. Yet the pull of the antithetical form (as well as the claims of Macaulay's own imagination) results in the curious remark that "perhaps

no person can be a poet, or can even enjoy poetry, without a certain unsoundness of mind, *if anything which gives so much pleasure ought to be called unsoundness* (italics added). Here the triumph of the "extreme" of reason over the "extreme" of imagination would not only violate the formula but would also, apparently, do violence to Macaulay's deepest instincts. In a later essay he was to confess that reason and imagination are "powers scarcely compatible with each other," and that their "happy and delicate combination" would require an "intellectual prodigy" whose like we might expect to see even less quickly than we might hope to see "another Shakespeare or another Homer." But, the reader may ask, if human progress requires the decline of imagination, why seek a mean at all? Is the pleasure given by poetry sound or it is not?

The inner tension which lay behind Macaulay's evasions in **"Milton"** appears more broadly in his prose in the interplay between its deep antithetical structure and the various surface-structures by which he amplified, qualified, and, at times, ignored his basic commitments to the proposition that extremes are in their very nature absurd. These surface styles are of three kinds, for which I would suggest the names oratorical, judicious, and histrionic.

The oratorical element in Macaulay's prose reflects the lasting influence of his early Evangelical training within the Clapham circle. In answer to Lord Jeffrey's query about where Macaulay had got his style, G. M. Young suggested [*Victorian Essays,* 1962] that Macaulay picked it up from the pulpit of the preacher Daniel Wilson. Wilson, later a bishop in India, was an Evangelical of the school of Simeon and Venn, the former an adviser to the Clapham circle and the latter the Clapham rector under whose pulpit Macaulay sat as a child. The influence of this school is evident both in the themes of Macaulay's early poetry—**"Epitaph on Henry Martyn"** (1812), **"Sermon in a Churchyard"** (1825), a translation of the **"Dies Irae"** (1826)—and in the style of his prose. The stylistic ideal of Clapham Evangelical preaching, described by Simeon in the handbook which he prepared for young Evangelical ministers, was "scrupulous care in construction—UNITY in the design, PERSPICUITY in the arrangement, and SIMPLICITY in the diction." The objective was not "new and remarkable views," which were merely "self," but "God's truth," and in teaching God's truth the minister had of course to make his personal faith felt by his listeners. Simeon was himself anxious to communicate the intense fervor of his feelings in his sermons: "his whole soul was in his subject and he spoke and acted exactly as he felt."

The Evangelical ideal of personal force combined with intellectual clarity and simplicity was also Macaulay's. His assumption in the remark on style cited above, that there is a "great body" of readers needing to be persuaded, like his preoccupation with "force," suggests the influence of the Evangelical concern with reaching large numbers as well as its belief that fallen human nature was likely to be obdurate to the Word even when it was clearly stated. The truth to be conveyed by a writer, Macaulay observed in his early essay **"History,"** must be "not merely traced on the mind, but branded into it." In the open intellectual market of the early nineteenth century, as in the economic, only the strong could survive.

The Evangelical element is evident in Macaulay's preference for "strong plain words, Anglo-Saxon or Norman-French" to a learned diction in which "nobody ever quarrels, or drives bargains, or makes love"; in his frequent use of anecdote and allusion; in the caricatures by means of which he pillories the morally corrupt and enshrines the good; and especially in the constant "presence" of an authorial voice urgent with moral passion—vehement, rapid, repetitive, scornful, and eulogistic by turns. Although Macaulay admired the "energy" of Dante's style in the *Divine Comedy* and the "passionate appeals" of the Earl of Chatham's Parliamentary speeches, the rhythm of his own oratorical style is closest to that of the Evangelical tradition of Bunyan, Whitfield, and Simeon. It may even be that his stylistic addiction to antithesis originated in the long English tradition of the Evangelical sermon:

> While they are singing the songs of the drunkard, you are singing songs and hymns: while they are at a playhouse, you are hearing a sermon: while they are drinking, revelling, and misspending their precious time, and hastening on their own destruction, you are reading, praying, meditating, and working out your salvation with fear and trembling.

The underlying rhythm of this passage from a Whitfield sermon is close to that in which Macaulay writes, for example, of Barère:

> We have had amongst us intemperate zeal for popular rights; we have had amongst us also the intemperance of loyalty. . . . Compared with him, our fiercest demagogues have been gentle; compared with him, our meanest courtiers have been manly. Mix together Thistlewood and Bubb Doddington; and you are still far from having Barère.

Macaulay's oratorical voice normally expresses itself in an abundance of superlatives in diction, in a repetitive clausal structure, in series of short declarative sentences, and in allusions that both color and simplify the meaning. The passage from the Mackintosh essay cited earlier illustrates in a mild way Macaulay's addiction to superlatives ("*boundless* submission," "*very* prejudiced," "*absolutely* impossible," "*always* unpopular"), to an emphatic diction ("dunces," "bigot," "reviled," "scorn"), and to doubling ("a shallow understanding and unamiable temper," "disquiet and danger," "scorn and hatred," "great and imperishable"). Macaulay's oratorical style is sermonic, especially, in the sense of its persuading by character rather than by argument. When most intense the effect is one of almost Pauline earnestness. "Whatsoever things are false, whatsoever things are dishonest, whatsoever things are unjust, whatsoever things are impure, whatsoever things are hateful, whatsoever things are of evil report, if there by any vice, and if there by any infamy, all these things, "we knew, were blended in Barère."

Trevelyan reports that as a result of Zachary Macaulay's stern biblical principles, his son's "infant fancy was much exercised with the threats and terrors of the Law [of Sinai]." Although Macaulay eventually abandoned the Clapham religion, it seems unlikely that so impressionable a child could ever forget the power or the rhythms of the language in which its theology had first been communicated to him. If the truth had not only to be asserted, but "branded" into the reader's mind, the vividness, force, and diction of Evangelical preachers who converted large, uninformed, inattentive congregations by sheer pressure of style, could hardly be improved upon. It is significant that Macaulay greatly admired Bunyan, of whom he wrote: "In employing fiction to make truth clear and goodness attractive, he was only following the example which every Christian ought to propose to himself." It was an example which Macaulay was to recommend to historians in particular, and one which he followed in his own writings.

A second surface style is reflected in the judicious mode by which Macaulay's prose renders a quite different authorial voice, that of "a cool and philosophical observer." In this mode the stylistic canons of clarity and force translate into an abstract diction and an epigrammatic structure, while the heavy oratorical irony gives way to wit. Using the distinction by which Macaulay himself discriminated between the "hanging judge" prose of Hallam and the "mild, calm, and impartial" prose of Mackintosh, his own oratorical style is that of the hanging judge and his judicious style that of the detached observer who has calmly weighed the evidence. The essay on Barère illustrates the mordant irony of the former: "We sink under the contemplation of such exquisite and manifold perfection; and feel, with deep humility, how presumptuous it was in us to think of composing the legend of this beatified athlete of the faith, St. Bertrand of the Carmagnoles." Macaulay concluded this vitriolic essay by observing that to attack Barère was "no pleasure" but "a duty," because Carnot's attempt "to enshrine this Jacobin carrion . . . has forced us to gibbet it." The irony of the more dispassionate essay on Gladstone's *Church and State,* on the other hand, is milder and wittier, although still characteristically heavy: "There is no harm at all in inquiring what course a stone thrown into the air would take, if the law of gravitation did not operate. But the consequences would be unpleasant, if the inquirer, as soon as he had finished his calculation, were to begin to throw stones in all directions. . . . " The conclusion of the essay is likewise more judicious: "We dissent from his opinions, but we admire his talents; we respect his integrity and benevolence; and we hope that he will not suffer political avocations so entirely to engross him, as to leave him no leisure for literature and philosophy."

Macaulay's frequent use of the epigrammatic structure characteristic of a judicious style gives to much of his prose a pithiness and balance which makes it aphoristic in the Baconian tradition, the seeming fruit of prolonged and searching deliberation. It appears in the Mackintosh passage in the political applications of proverbial lore: "As we would have our descendants judge us, so ought we to judge our fathers"; "The author of a great reformation is almost always unpopular in his own age." Such aphorisms can take a philosophical, moral, or historical turn: "The noblest earthly object of the contemplation of man is man himself;" "Where there is elevation of character there will be fastidiousness;" "A dominant religion is never ascetic." The emergence of the epigrammatic "Senecan" style in English prose during the Renaissance has been connected with the new searching into causes, the nervous questioning and probing of Bacon, and with the decline of positiveness in philosophy. Unlike the Ciceronian periods of a Hooker—the style of "those who have a system in which they can trust"—the terse Senecan phrasing of the Baconians expressed the hesitations and the doubts of rationalists, and, in the looser "baroque" complications of its later forms, was much more congenial and persuasive to the average middle-class reader, untrained in the classics, than the learned oratorical style of High Church divines. Yet Macaulay, we know, instinctively disliked the epigrammatic style of Seneca, whose "affectation," he said, he found "even more rank than Gibbon's. His works are made up of mottoes. There is hardly a sentence which might not be quoted." This dislike had its source in Macaulay's aversion to doubt, his dislike of mystification in language as well as in thought (he noted in his essay on Pitt that mystification could effectively serve the political orator's purposes, but this was another matter). His own judicious style moves on the surface of his prose, a strategy for presenting the voice of the "cool and philosophical observer" while the underlying antithetical style, the style of a man who has a system in which he trusts, does its work.

The third and the most original element in Macaulay's prose, that which gives it its distinctive "charm," was the creation of what was earlier referred to as Macaulay's histrionic temperament. The biographical evidence indicating that Macaulay's temperament was innately histrionic is impressive, and it is the histrionic element which sets off his prose from the *Edinburgh Review* style with which it has obvious affinities. We know from Marianne Thornton's diary that in his boredom with the scientific toys introduced by the Clapham elders into their children's parties, Macaulay showed very early a distaste both for science and for the earnest practicality of the Clapham circle. The histrionic activities at these parties, on the other hand, the masquerades, magic-lantern shows, dramatic speeches, and games, were Tom Macaulay's delight. What is of interest to the student of style is the fact that this "play" instinct survived in extraordinary strength in the adult Macaulay. The story of his attending as a boy one of Lord Teignmouth's Twelfth Night parties at Clapham Common in the disguise of Napoleon is echoed in Trevelyan's report of his directing the family fun in Great Ormond Street twenty years later: "Macaulay, who at any period of his life could literally spend whole days in playing with children, was master of the innocent revels. Games of hide-and-seek, that lasted for hours, . . . were varied by ballads, which, like the scalds of old, he composed during the act of recitation, while others struck in with the chorus." This "play" impulse was related to Macaulay's addiction to novel-reading and his love of imaginatively recreating and putting into language the worlds which he encountered in his reading. His mother wrote to a friend, when Macaulay was only eight, that her son was "so fired with reading Scott's *Lay* and *Marmion,* the former of which he got entirely, and the latter almost entirely, by heart, merely from his delight in reading them, that he determined on writing himself a poem in six cantos which

he called 'The Battle of Cheviot'." Later, when he began his formal schooling, Macaulay compensated for his intense loneliness by reading "widely, increasingly, more than rapidly," so that he was, in Trevelyan's words, "lost in books," and this capacity to "lose" himself in what he read likewise persisted into old age. When over fifty, while reading the *Iliad* during a walk, he reported that he was forced to turn into a bypath "lest the parties of walkers should see me blubbering for imaginary beings, the creations of a ballad-maker who has been dead two thousand seven hundred years." Rereading *Clarissa* in this same period, he said that he very nearly "cried his eyes out."

Macaulay's histrionic temperament is evident in his prose in two ways. The first involves a simple act of imaginative displacement from the present into the past of the kind illustrated by a passage in the early essay **"On the Athenian Orators."**

> Let us, for a moment, transport ourselves, in thought, to that glorious city. Let us imagine that we are entering its gates, in the time of its power and glory. A crowd is assembled round a portico. All are gazing with delight at the entablature; for Phidias is putting up the frieze. We turn into another street; a rhapsodist is reciting there: men, women, children are thronging round him: the tears are running down their cheeks: their eyes are fixed: their very breath is still. . . . We enter the public palace; there is a ring of youths, all leaning forward, with sparkling eyes, and gestures of expectation. Socrates is pitted against the famous atheist, from Ionia. . . .

Like the "scenes" from novels, memoirs, and histories which he endlessly enacted with his sisters, the passage exhibits a preoccupation with the historical past, with the visually vivid and concrete, and with action, especially the verbal action of dialogue. The second histrionic activity which appears in the prose is mimetic. Here the term "histrionic" is used, in the sense given it by Francis Fergusson in his study of the theater, to designate a temperament characterized by an instinctive tendency to perceive, discriminate, and imitate actions. The most sustained example of this, of course, is Macaulay's *History.*

That the basic impulse behind the *History of England from the Accession of James II* was histrionic in both of the above senses is evident in several ways, most obviously in Macaulay's belief that his most ambitious work would be distinguished from his earlier writings, which he had come to regard as "rubbish fit to be burned," and from all previous histories, by its being as entertaining as the latest novel on the Victorian drawing-room table. It would be "fun" to read. It is likewise evident in the way in which Macaulay went about preparing himself. His "research" consisted chiefly of readings, heavily literary in nature, which brought the lives and times of the past vividly before his imagination, a method that has been attributed to Scott: "to treat every document as the record of a conversation, and [to] go on reading till you hear people talking." "I begin to see the men," Macaulay noted in his journal after a day in the British Museum, "and to understand all their difficulties and jealousies." The histrionic intent is evident, finally, in Macaulay's anxiousness to impose a dramatic unity upon his vast materials. "The talent which is required to write history bears a considerable affinity to the talent of a great dramatist," he once wrote, the difference being, in Macaulay's view, that the dramatist "creates" fictions while the historian "disposes" facts. Even when treating the lives of individuals Macaulay habitually looked for dramatic coherence, although he sometimes found his materials recalcitrant. Writing on Pitt, he complained that "his was not a complete and well-proportioned greatness. The public life of Hampden or of Somers resembles a regular drama, which can be criticized as a whole, and every scene of which is to be viewed in connection with the main action. The public life of Pitt, on the other hand, is a rude though striking piece, a piece abounding in incongruities, a piece without any unity of plan." The more material there was for the historian to "dispose," of course, the greater the opportunity he had to arrange it; the very wealth of the materials involved in writing the *History* was, therefore, from the "dramatic" point of view, an asset to Macaulay as a writer. Precisely because no historian could present the "whole truth," but must, like the artist, unify his materials through the manipulation of "perspective"—a manipulation evident in the great care which Macaulay exercised in managing his proportions and transitions—the writing of the *History* was for Macaulay essentially an imaginative effort.

As the creator of a plausible drama, Macaulay's first task in the *History* was to draw his readers' attention away from the immediate context—T. B. Macaulay, the well-known Whig politician, addressing the Victorian reader of the 1840's disturbed by fears or hopes of revolution—and focus it upon the "context of situation" necessary for appreciating the "single act" of the drama he is about to unfold. He accomplishes this task in his opening chapters. The first chapter lifts the reader out of his immediate environment to a Pisgah-like eminence and there endows him with a vision like that which Macaulay attributed to Moses: "There we see the great Law-giver looking round from his lonely elevation on an infinite expanse; behind him a wilderness of dreary sands and bitter waters . . . ; before him a goodly land, a land of promise, a land flowing with milk and honey. While the multitude below saw only the flat sterile desert on which they had so long wandered . . . he was gazing from a far higher stand on a far lovelier country. . . . " Seen from the vantage point of this imaginary Mount Pisgah, the true nature of the action in the *History* comes into perspective. The function of chapter one is to provide a perspective of "centuries" from which to interpret the "single act" which is to form the central matter, and to establish that single act within the larger context of an "eventful drama extending through ages."

This larger drama begins in a universal darkness from which, Macaulay tells us in his first chapter, there mysteriously emerged in England's remote past an obscure tribe whose character and way of life in no way indicated the greatness for which they and their descendants were "destined." It is as though an unpredictable mutation had silently introduced mankind to the possibility of a higher form of existence. In a metaphor which, like that of Moses

on Mount Pisgah, reminds us of Macaulay's debt to his Evangelical background, he portrays Christianity ("the first of a long series of salutary revolutions") as a Noah's ark carrying within itself amid the universal darkness the seed of this higher form of life. The Church, we are told, "rode, amidst darkness and tempest, on the deluge beneath which all great works of ancient power and wisdom lay entombed, bearing within her that feeble germ from which a second and more glorious civilisation was to spring." The Victorian reader thus had his attention engaged through a familiar rhetoric, while his point of view was being established: he was to witness, from an Archimedian perspective outside earthly space and time, a cosmic action written by a "hidden hand."

The effect of this perspective upon our response to the famous third chapter, "The State of England in 1685," is worth noting. From what may be called the Clapham point of view, chapter three simply states that human nature does not change, that in the seventeenth as in the nineteenth century power bred bullies, powerlessness sycophancy, courage freedom, balance truth. From the "Whig" point of view, on the other hand, the reader is told that the history of England between 1685 and 1848 was one of continuous physical, moral, and intellectual improvement; the reader cannot doubt in which direction the tide has moved. From the histrionic point of view, however, chapter three serves a quite different purpose: the reader is made to feel that although England in 1685 was in part the same as and in part worse than England in 1848, it was above all a more *interesting* place than England either before or since. It was the moment, in fact, when the direction of the tide of history became clear. The reader is prepared, that is, not for an Evangelical sermon or a Whig speech, but for an exciting drama, and chapter three brings the reader down from his Pisgah-like eminence to a seat in front of the stage on which this drama is to unfold.

When subordinated to Macaulay's histrionic powers, the oratorical and judicious surface styles of his prose are subtly transformed. The oratorical pattern becomes dramatic through Macaulay's translation of conventional moral-allegorical abstractions—Sneak and Bully, Moloch and Belial—into the historical figures of Penn and Jeffreys. We are told of the youthful, well-intentioned Penn, for example, that "attacked by royal smiles, by female blandishments, by the insinuating eloquence and delicate flattery of veteran diplomatists and courtiers, his resolution gave way," and the reader is thus prepared to find later that Sneak/Penn does not scruple "to use a bishopric as a bait to tempt a divine to perjury." The private morality of individual actors and the political bias of the Whigs and Tories are thus firmly subordinated to the central action. Similarly, the judicious style becomes dramatically relevant in the summaries and explanations with which Macaulay brackets individual events and in the imagined deliberations of persons, parties, or the English people rendered in monologues that contain the *dianoia* of Macaulay's drama. Most notable, however, is the alteration in the basic rhythm of predication by which Macaulay organizes his material. What one critic has called the pattern of tension-crisis-resolution gives to the *History* the purpose-passion-perception rhythm of drama proper.

The principal effect of Macaulay's histrionic style, I believe, is to communicate a sense of the inevitability of the action. The reader had been informed in the prologue chapters that Britain became England because the Normans happened to decide not to return to the Continent, that England became great because she happened to be an island, and that at one point the future of the entire nation was determined by an act of "insane bigotry" on the part of a single individual. Even William III, great though he is, is caught up in an action larger than he. That William should have been at hand at the very moment when the eyes of all England looked about for help "in great perturbation" is merely one example both of Macaulay's skill in handling transitions and of the many "rare concurrences" in the *History* by which, in Taine's phrase, Macaulay converted a trial into a drama. "Those who seem to lead the public taste are, in general," Macaulay once wrote, "merely outrunning it in the direction which it is spontaneously pursuing"; without Copernicus there would still have been a Copernican revolution. In repeatedly calling the reader's attention to "what might have been," Macaulay is not concerned in his *History* to stress the importance of individual choice; on the contrary, its effect is to heighten the reader's sense of the fatality of events which have actually occurred. The effect, that is, to persuade the reader that without William III there would still have been a Glorious Revolution. We do not, as in the essays, merely pass moral or political judgments upon the characters; rather, we watch them enact their appointed destinies:

> And now the time for the great hazard drew near. The night was not ill suited for such an enterprise. The moon was indeed at the full, and the northern streamers were shining brilliantly. But the marsh fog lay so thick on Sedgemoor that no object could be discerned there at the distance of fifty paces.
>
> The clock struck eleven; and the Duke with his body guard rode out of the castle. He was not in the frame of mind which befits one who is about to strike a decisive blow. The very children who pressed to see him pass observed, and long remembered, that his look was sad and full of evil augury.

The end of the action is foreshadowed in the commencement: all is fated, and all is fascinating. In the cohering myth of the action the "errors" of individuals (and the historical inaccuracies of the dramatist) become irrelevant. The play is the thing.

Despite Macaulay's immense learning and remarkable artistry, the consensus of critical opinion is that the *History* remains a flawed literary work. Why this should be so is suggested, first of all, by the need to refer to Macaulay's *styles* rather than to his *style*. Whatever the reasons, he was unable to integrate the various stylistic modes which he had inherited into a coherent and compelling work of literary art; the styles simply coexist in a prose in which the major tensions evident are those between reason and imagination, and between Macaulay's impulse to engagement and his impulse to detachment. These tensions, and the several styles in which they are expressed, might be represented diagrammatically, thus:

	(a) ENGAGED	(b) DETACHED
(A) IMAGINATION	*oratorical* (Clapham)	*histrionic* (Scott)
	moral	narrative
	forceful—biased	vivid—irrelevant
(B) REASON	*antithetical* (Whig)	*judicious* (Gibbon)
	dogmatic	relativist
	clear—pre-emptive	impartial—platitudinous

The styles least compatible appear in opposite boxes: the oratorical (imaginative-engaged) and the judicious (rational-detached); the antithetical (rational-engaged) and the histrionic (imaginative-detached). The styles which were relatively compatible are in the vertical columns (a) and (b), while those less so but still capable of reinforcing one another on occasion are in the horizontal columns (A) and (B). The adjectives in each box are meant to suggest the virtue and vice peculiar to each style, and the names in parentheses the prose traditions upon which Macaulay drew.

Viewed chronologically, and in the light of this diagram, the total body of Macaulay's prose falls roughly into three periods: the early writings, in which the histrionic and judicious styles predominate, with the former being limited to occasional displacements of the kind exemplified in **"On the Athenian Orators"**; the writings of the middle period, roughly from 1825 to 1840, composed during Macaulay's politically active years and dominated by the oratorical "force" and antithetical "clarity" of the fully engaged Macaulay; and the *History* and late essays on Clive and Hastings, in which the histrionic element emerges in strength and spreads over large surfaces of the prose.

In seeking an explanation of why even in his mature period Macaulay did not succeed in integrating the various components of his prose, the critic is brought back to the "biographical" question mentioned at the beginning of our inquiry. It is hardly an exaggeration to say that, despite the excitement which it generates, there are few more redundant, less suspenseful works in English literature than the *History.* Macaulay leaves the reader in no doubt as to either the outcome of the narrative or how he is to feel toward it ("the general effect of this chequered narrative will be to excite thankfulness in all religious minds, and hope in the breasts of all patriots.") But it is not merely foreknowledge that makes the *History* wearisome; audiences frequently know in advance the outcome of dramas which can nevertheless awaken excitement and pleasure each time they are re-enacted. The monotonousness of the *History* can be traced rather to the simplistic moral and intellectual patterns which are embodied in the sustained Clapham "force" and the relentless Whig "clarity" of so much of the writing. The pre-emptive nature of the basic style and the simplifications and irrelevancies which it imposes affect Macaulay's handling of sublime and trivial matters alike. We are told, for example, that "it is only in Britain that an age of fable separates two ages of truth;" the antithetical form, operating on momentum, produces a statement which neither relates logically to the matter in hand nor generates a truth—if it is a truth—which has interesting general implications. Macaulay's unexpressed

purpose in such remarks is to celebrate England's uniqueness, but the particular virtue of a nation's having two ages
of truth separated by an age of fable is hardly self-evident.
On a more trivial level the antithetical form operates in
such categorical assertions as "inns will be *best* when the
means of locomotion are *worst,"* (italics added), a statement which issues, we feel, out of a fixed stylistic habit
rather than out of disinterested inquiry. At the same time,
accompanying and often working against the grain of the
basic antithetical mode are those other styles to which I
have referred. At times forceful, at times judicious, at
times lucid, and often brilliantly dramatic, Macaulay's
style is never all of these at once. Because he cannot bring
his various interests together, we are led to the conclusion,
not that the style is the man himself, but that the styles
are the fragments of the man. Surface clarity and brilliance is belied by an underlying evasiveness.

The biographical clue to Macaulay's inward tensions, and
therefore to the unevenness of his performance as writer,
is provided by Trevelyan, who documents the close link
between Macaulay's life-long interest in games, day-
dreaming, play-acting, and books, and his deep emotional
attachment to his two sisters, Hannah and Margaret. Hannah, the elder sister, later recalled that Macaulay's notion
of perfect happiness "was to see us all working round him
while he read aloud a novel, and then to walk all together
on the Common, or, if it rained, to have a frightfully noisy
game of hide-and-seek." As the children at Clapham
Common grew older the games became more sophisticated, but they retained their histrionic quality. Trevelyan
writes:

> The feeling with which Macaulay and his sister
> regarded books differed from that of other peo-
> ple in kind rather than in degree. When they
> were discoursing together about a work of histo-
> ry or biography, a by-stander would have sup-
> posed that they had lived in the times of which
> the author treated, and had a personal acquain-
> tance with every human being who was men-
> tioned in his pages. Pepys, Addison, Horace
> Walpole, Dr. Johnson, Madame de Genlis, the
> Duc de St. Simon, and the several societies in
> which those worthies moved, excited in their
> minds precisely the same sort of concern, and
> gave matter for discussions of exactly the same
> type as most people bestow upon the proceed-
> ings of their own contemporaries. The past was
> to them as the present, and the fictitious as the
> actual.

Towards the end of his life Macaulay attributed a great
part of his literary success to the habit of "castle-building"
with his sister, a habit, he wrote, "which [Hannah] and I
indulge beyond any people I ever knew."

Against this background Trevelyan's account of two crises
through which Macaulay passed during his thirties is of
great interest. Prior to this time Macaulay had confined
the exercise of his powerful histrionic impulse almost entirely to the domestic circle provided by his sisters; his
public life, like his public prose, was business-like, hard-
headed, engaged. Yet, according to Macaulay, it was his
private life with his sisters which sustained him in his public role, a role which he came increasingly to dislike.

Against the background of this early history, Trevelyan
informs us that in 1832, when Macaulay's sister Margaret
announced her engagement, the shock to Macaulay was
so great that he "never again recovered [his] tone of thorough boyishness"; he was even led to doubt "whether his
scheme of life was indeed a wise one; or, rather, he began
to be aware that he had never laid out any scheme of life
at all." Macaulay's initial response to this first crisis was
to "lay it on" his political opponent; he felt, he said, "a
fierceness and restlessness within me quite new and almost
inexplicable." His second and more enduring reaction was
to revive a plan that had long lain at the back of his mind,
to write a history of England that would be read with pleasure for many generations.

If the mere engagement of one sister was so disturbing in
1832, the death of that sister two years later while Macaulay was in India, and the simultaneous engagement of the
other sister who had accompanied him there, was certain
to create a major psychological crisis. Hannah's engagement first came to Macaulay's knowledge in 1834, and its
effect is revealing. He wrote from India to Margaret (of
whose death in England meanwhile he was as yet unaware):

> I feel a growing tendency to cynicism and suspi-
> cion. My intellect remains; and is likely, I some-
> times think, to absorb the whole man. I still re-
> tain (not only undiminished, but strengthened
> by the very events which have deprived me of ev-
> erything else) my thirst for knowledge; my pas-
> sion for holding converse with the greatest
> minds of all ages and nations; my power of for-
> getting what surrounds me, and of living with
> the past, the future, the distant, and the unreal.
> Books are becoming everything to me.

When he learned shortly afterwards of Margaret's death,
he was staggered. Trevelyan merely notes that he "did
what he might to drown his grief in floods of official
work." According to his letters, however, Macaulay found
his salvation not in work, but in literature. "Even now,
when time has begun to do its healing office, I can not
write about her without being altogether unmanned. That
I have not utterly sunk under this blow I owe chiefly to
literature. What a blessing it is to love books as I love
them—to be able to converse with the dead, and to live
amidst the unreal!— . . . I have gone back to Greek literature with a passion quite astonishing to myself."

Macaulay's response to his second crisis duplicated the
pattern of his response to Margaret's engagement in 1832;
an initial fierce aggression, followed by a renewed interest
in a long historical work which "may be at once the business and the amusement of my life." The aggressive phase
appeared in Macaulay's immediate impulse to "strike
hard at an assailant of Macintosh" in the first essay which
he wrote following the "great blow." "The disgraceful im-
becility, and the still more disgraceful malevolence, of the
editor have, as you will see," he wrote to a friend, "moved
my indignation not a little." The attack on the moral character of the editor of Mackintosh's *History* was repeated
in the next essay, **"Bacon,"** the first half of which deals
with Bacon's moral turpitude and the second half with an
extended defense of the thesis that "great and various as

the powers of Bacon were, he owes his wide and durable fame chiefly to this, that all those powers received their direction from common sense."

Behind the vehement reassertions of his Clapham moral categories and his Whig "common sense" philosophy in the **"Mackintosh"** and **"Bacon"** essays lay, one suspects, a disturbing fear which was closely related to Macaulay's determination in the late 'thirties to turn once and for all from politics to literature, and to give free play to those histrionic powers which he had formerly exercised in private with his sisters. In the course of the Bacon essay he remarked that even in the best living relationships there is something unpredictable and tentative, something therefore unsatisfactory: "fortune is inconstant; tempers are soured; bonds which seemed indissoluble are daily sundered." With the dead, on the other hand, there was no rivalry. "In the dead there is no change. Plato is never sullen. Cervantes is never petulant. Demosthenes never comes unseasonably. Dante never stays too long. No difference of political opinion can alienate Cicero. No heresy can excite the horror of Bossuet." In short, the world of the past, of the dead, of the unreal, held no threat; events, passions, and arguments had been forever decided by men perpetually fixed in their admirable or shameful fates. In his *History,* I would argue, Macaulay was seeking refuge in the past, and in the very act of re-creating that past seeking for himself and vicariously for his sisters the only kind of immortality of which he was sure.

In effect, therefore, the *History* transferred Macaulay's private emotions to the public realm. Intending to record the facts of history as he saw them, he could not see that he saw them through a selective vision rooted in a private need to find meaning and pleasure, now forever lost to him in private life, in the communal life of his country's past, out of the need to integrate the private emotional, moral, and intellectual elements in his experience in a comprehensive public myth. From this point of view Macaulay's life and his greatest work may be read as a reversal of the more usual process described by Péguy: *tout commence en mystique et finit en politique.* In his *History,* as in his public life, Macaulay began in politics and ended in myth. The proper histrionic title of his *History* might be *A Nation's Progress, or Paradise Provisionally Gained: The Epic Story of the Growth of Liberty, Science, and Prosperity.*

Towards the very end of his life, when news of the India Mutiny of 1857 reached him, Macaulay again underwent a symptomatic "unmanning" like that which he had experienced in India in 1834: the thing he most loved in his last years was England itself and that too now seemed to be threatened. In this connection, the fact that the *History* remains a monumental fragment, covering but fifteen of the more than one hundred years of English history which Macaulay had originally intended to treat, is of interest. In losing himself in the past, Macaulay was driven by pressures which he did not understand any better than he had understood why his sister's engagement had made him fierce and restless or why her death had renewed his interest in Greek literature, and these pressures led him to adopt a mode of procedure which assured the defeat of his ostensible plan. To have realized that plan, to have

brought the history of England down to the real and threatening present, would have meant leaving that "past and unreal" world in which he essentially lived in his later years and in which his preconceptions were secure, his emotional life unthreatened, and his histrionic temperament free to exercise itself without restraint.

If the juxtaposition of styles in the *History* may be seen as an expression of incompatible impulses in Macaulay himself, it now seems clear that to have organized and integrated these diverse elements would have required on Macaulay's part, not greater intellectual prowess, but a deeper moral, intellectual, and imaginative penetration of his experience. It was Macaulay's misfortune, it might be argued, to have been cut off by the conditioning and pressures of his early years from the sources of those large connecting metaphors drawn from poetry, religion, or the unconscious which have enabled other writers to use histrionic powers less impressive than his for the highest artistic purposes. Privately, we know, Macaulay took great delight in poetry and in what has been described as the great anthology of poetic myths, Plato's dialogues, but publicly he felt obliged to denounce both Plato and poetry. Having rejected religion in the form in which he had first experienced it at Clapham, he refused for the remainder of his life to re-examine the possibility of ever discovering anything by that route; his mature creed, stated in **"Bacon,"** was "much hope, little faith." Finally, the poverty of his private emotional life, severely exposed by the India crisis, made it unsafe for him to turn to that inward life where other writers have discovered linkages provided by the ancestral memory which is the private storehouse of great metaphors. In writing the *History,* therefore, Macaulay's histrionic temperament was inhibited by a style characterized at its deepest level by the connecting of things under the pressure of fear and avoidance.

Finally, it is worth noting that the *History* makes its dramatic quality felt through direct experience of the style, not through reading the synopses in which handbooks of literature attempt to indicate its "meaning." And it is therefore only in a direct encounter with the prose that we can both gauge its intrinsic interest as a work of art and, in addition, through our experience of the tensions expressed in the style, gain some insight into the Victorian sensibility which Macaulay did so much to shape. Like Macaulay's Victorian reader, what we remember when we finish the book is the "going back," the displacement in time, and the re-living of events the most memorable aspects of which have little to do with the history of England's material, moral, and intellectual progress. The complications of the latter story vanish from our memory while the general excitement of the drama and the vivid details linger: the rush of armies, the sneers of courtiers, Monmouth ascending the tower at Sedgemoor, the bravery of Argyll asleep in his death cell as he awaits the rope, the absurdity of Lodowick Muggleton, the smuggling of Father Huddleston into Charles II's death room, the imposing mask of William III, the beseiged defenders at Londonderry shouting, "No surrender!" For these things we can be grateful to Macaulay's histrionic powers, while at the same time we sense that this brilliant and boyish man was crippled by habits of thought and feeling which diminished or dismissed large areas of experience which he chose not to confront. Macaulay is certainly "in" his prose, and nowhere more completely or more revealingly than in his most famous work. (pp. 127-51)

> *William A. Madden, "Macaulay's Style," in* The Art of Victorian Prose, *edited by George Levine and William Madden, Oxford University Press, Inc., 1968, pp. 127-53.*

Gladstone on Macaulay's consistency and great memory:

It would be difficult to point out any great and signal change of views on any important subject between the beginning of his full manhood, and the close of his career. His life is like a great volume; the sheets are of one size, type, and paper. Here again Macaulay becomes for us a typical man, and suggests the question whether the conditions of our nature will permit so close and sustained a unity to be had without some sacrifice of expansion? The feature is rendered in his case more noteworthy by the fact that all his life long, with an insatiable avidity, he was taking in whole cargoes of knowledge, and that nothing which he imported into his mind remained there barren and inert. On the other hand, he was perhaps assisted, or, as a censor might call it, manacled, by the perpetual and always living presence in his consciousness, through the enormous tenacity of his memory, of whatever he had himself thought, said, or written, at an earlier time. It may even be, as he himself said, that of the whole of this huge mass he had forgotten nothing. It cannot be doubted that he remembered a far larger proportion, than did other men who had ten or twenty times less to remember. . . . His mind, like a dredging-net at the bottom of the sea, took up all that it encountered, both bad and good, nor even seemed to feel the burden. Peerless treasures lay there, mixed, yet never confounded, with worthless trash.

> *W. E. Gladstone, in* The Quarterly Review, *1876.*

Herbert Butterfield   (essay date 1973)

[*Butterfield was a well known historian who for many years was master of Peterhouse at Cambridge and regius professor of history. Among his many books and articles is* The Whig Interpretation of History (*1931*). *In the following essay, he finds Macaulay to have the mentality of an ordinary man "writ very large" but also to be a scholar who can place his characters in their proper historical context.*]

Somewhere near the end of the 19th century, three of the real heavyweights of English historical scholarship, Lord Acton, Bishop Stubbs and Bishop Creighton, set themselves to decide who was the greatest historian the world had ever produced: and the first name considered was that of Macaulay, the name which, at the finish, was unanimously agreed upon. Probably a little later than this, three equally imposing figures—Lord Acton once more, Theodor Mommsen and Adolf von Harnack—addressed themselves to the same question somewhere in Germany.

Again, the first name mentioned was that of Macaulay. And this was the name eventually accepted.

It was Acton, the man present on both occasions, who narrated the story, and it would have been just like him to be the one to propose that question for discussion. I suspect it was he, moreover, who threw the name of Macaulay into the arena: for, in spite of his long hostility to the man, and in spite of the fact that in this period he was assembling formidable criticisms of him in his manuscript notes, he entertained the idea that nobody would ever surpass Macaulay in writing Macaulay's own kind of history. Macaulay himself had a more modest view of his achievement. He always held that Thucydides had the supremacy; and, according to his first biographer, this was the one thing that 'put him out of conceit with himself'.

During the present year, Professor John Clive, of Harvard, has produced a large first volume of a biography of Macaulay [John Clive, *Macaulay: The Shaping of the Historian,* 1973]—a volume packed with fresh detail and profound reflections, taking us up to the moment when the hero, in his late thirties, decides to leave politics for literature. In Macaulay's case childhood and youth are very important: his younger sister suggested that his great clarity of style must have owed something to his constantly talking to younger members of his family, perpetually explaining things to them.

The earliest biography of Macaulay, written by his nephew George Otto Trevelyan, had revealed him as a sentimental soul, a man who 'positively lived on the associations of his own past'. He would be profoundly moved by the sight of a sixpenny print that he remembered to have hung in his schoolroom, or by the discovery of a copy of a novel which he had read in his undergraduate days and which he knew to be 'execrable trash'. Nothing gave him more pleasure than a sight of the inn at Durham where he had dined as a young barrister on circuit—a house where the food itself had been bad. And he dotingly remembered the place on a shelf where he had first discovered the *Lyrical Ballads,* and so come to know 'The Ancient Mariner'.

Professor Clive adds the point that Macaulay, later in life, would recall how, in his undergraduate days, somebody might enunciate a proposition, but then all the possible answers would rush into his head at once. Nor did he seem able to have any politics except the opposite to what was professed by the person who happened to be speaking to him at the moment. When he wrote youthful poetry, he liked to celebrate first one side in a historical conflict and then the other side—first the Cavaliers, for example, and then the Roundheads. Professor Clive tells us that his poems seem to carry the deepest feeling when he is expressing a point of view which is the antithesis to what he really held himself. He wonders whether 'deep down' there was not in Macaulay a sympathy with lost causes, which would come out when he was writing verse: or whether one must look to some fault of character in him, 'some streak of contrariness'. I suspect we should ask our students to write a defence of Metternich or an apology for Stalin. There can scarcely be any better training for a historian than exercises in the interpretation of people not like-minded with oneself.

Macaulay left Cambridge in 1823 and very quickly became a famous essayist. I am not sure that his latest biographer, in dealing with the articles published during the following decade and a half, has quite found the way of tracing from them the development of the man's ideas. The essays show that from a very early stage Macaulay's notion of general history—of a history of England, at any rate—was greatly influenced by the historical novelists, particularly Sir Walter Scott. Professor Clive does draw our attention to the fact that in 1828, Macaulay negotiated with the Society for the Diffusion of Useful Knowledge, and had the idea of producing a history of the Stuarts for that body. Already, at the age of 28, he was considering a large-scale work, and envisaging the needs of a class of readers who might be lacking in formal education. This year, 1828, is clearly an important one in his development, and his essay on 'History' complains that, while a decent work of biography always drew crowds to the circulating libraries, the histories of great empires, written by eminent men, stood on the shelves unread. He confessed that the writer who produced the sort of history he himself was calling for, would have to be an intellectual prodigy. 'We should sooner see another Shakespeare or another Homer,' he said. Later he said there were good historical essayists but nowadays some of the functions of the historian had been taken over by the historical novelists. It was they who gave flesh and blood, gave the impression of reality, to historical figures, who were too often presented as though they were merely personified qualities in an allegory. By 1835 he was seriously thinking of embarking on a big work, and he wrote that a history of the kind he had in mind would be 'more required in the circulating library' than the latest novel.

Instead of covering 150 years, as he had hoped, his *magnum opus* turned out to have the revolution of 1688 as its great theme. It is curious to see how far he was from being romantic about this episode. In the essay on Hallam, also written when he was 28, he had stated that this revolution took its character from the vices of the times: vices, however, which it was to be the means of reforming. The event had been useful in its consequences, but nobody ought to call it a 'Glorious Revolution'—it had carried no glory for anybody except William of Orange. 'The transaction was, in almost every part, discreditable to England,' Macaulay wrote. 'That the enterprise succeeded without bloodshed was principally owing to an act of ungrateful perfidy, such as no other soldier ever committed. Throughout the whole transaction, no commanding talents were displayed by any Englishman. It was fortunate for our civil government that the revolution was in a great measure effected by men who cared little about their political principles.' This depreciatory attitude to the event that was to be his central theme can be found in his very early article on Milton, where he makes the point that poor James II was harassed and expelled, if you please, by his nephew and his two daughters. We know why Macaulay's thoughts began to move into this particular groove. He was trying to convert his contemporaries: so often they exulted in the 'Glorious Revolution' but balanced this by their disapproval of what they regarded as the rebellion against Charles I. Macaulay was the incorrigible undergraduate orator who sometimes allowed his debating points to run away with him. He de-

scribed the reign of William III as the nadir of national prosperity, the nadir of national character. Clearly, he presents us with paradoxes if we try to see him as a Whig historian.

At the beginning of his famous *History* it becomes plain that he is far from regarding himself as one of those historians who are always on the side of the Whigs, seeing them as the perpetual agents of liberty. He sees organised parties emerging in England in the autumn of 1641, at the time of the Grand Remonstrance. An important reason for their rise is the temperamental difference between men, he says: some of them prone to fear, distrustful of change and sentimental about the past, others more ready to take risks, rushing into the future without looking back. Unlike many historians, he takes each party at its best, realising that there are strong arguments on both sides: he expounds 'the reasoning of the most enlightened Royalists' and then that of what he calls the equally virtuous and noble people arrayed against them. He points out that the Cavaliers had 'sturdy English hearts', and says they were not the kind of people who would have tolerated a despotism. Even in the early essay on Milton he had written: 'We cannot refrain from looking with complacency on the character of the old Cavaliers.' When he deals with the dispensing power, the Royal power to override the law, he finds something to be said on both sides: a candid Tory would agree that the case for it can't really be established, a candid Whig wouldn't insist that the case against it could be clinched. As he develops his interpretation of English history in the *Essays,* he sees the Whigs of the age of Walpole very much as the Tories saw them at the time: they were the engineers of the great system of corruption. George III tries to rectify that evil, but fails to realise that the remedy is even worse than the disease. In any case, Macaulay regards it as wrong to portray George III as though he were another Stuart despot. And he criticises the general unreasonableness of the Whigs and their history—lashes them because in the Napoleonic era they refused to allow merit to the Duke of Wellington.

It is as a person outside the conflict that Macaulay inquires why English historiography is so cursed by partisanship. He holds that because the country combines constitutional change with ancient rights, 'every source of information as to our early history has been poisoned by party spirit.' In no other country are statesmen so much under the influence of the past, but for that very reason there is no country where historians are so much under the influence of the present. A Frenchman has no reason for falsifying his history because in his case constitutional rights spring out of a comparatively recent revolution. But in England the motive for falsification becomes irresistible, and historians are always advocates. 'From the commencement of the long contest between the Parliament and the Stuarts,' says Macaulay, 'down to the time when the pretensions of the Stuarts ceased to be formidable, few questions were practically more important than the question whether the administration of that family had or had not been in accordance with the ancient constitution of the kingdom. Every Whig historian was anxious to prove that the old English government was all but republican, every Tory historian to prove that it was all but despotism.'

In his mentality and his emotional structure—in his moral indignations and in his copious tears—Macaulay showed himself of quite common fibre: perhaps the ordinary man, though the ordinary man writ very large. He was constitutionally incapable of understanding people like Cardinal Newman or Archbishop Laud, but he was greatly impressed by Catholicism and was greatly alienated by Gibbon's unfairness to the Christians. Though he tried to be popular, no historian wrote more consciously for posterity, and he was right when he said that he made no concession to contemporary fashion, for the things that limited his work were genuine intellectual constrictions. He was aware of some of his faults and he couldn't credit the success of the *History* in the United States, because, he said, his work was so thoroughly insular. He confessed that he had written too passionately against the Stuarts and that this might have reduced the damage he had meant to do them.

One important feature of Macaulay's work appears in his first article for the *Edinburgh Review,* an article written when he was 24. It was his insistence on the social context in history, on the necessity for social description, on the relevance of all this to the moral life. Both his virtues and his weaknesses in this whole field—as well as his own avowals—suggest that the chief influence in all this was again Sir Walter Scott—a man whom the Marxist writer George Lukacs greatly exalted for the way he related human conduct to historical situations. One result of this was Macaulay's famous Chapter Three on 'The State of England in 1685'; and another was his constantly repeated thesis that violence, corruption and apostasy in the reign of Charles II didn't imply the same personal viciousness that they would today. Even the Whig corruption in the 18th century has to be explained by reference to conditions, he says. Robert Walpole couldn't have governed by any other method.

The idea of progress has a fundamental importance for him, but he urged that it was precisely this that made it essential to envisage the 17th century as a world thoroughly different from our own. It was precisely this, therefore, that made it inexcusable for a modern thinker to regard the past with contempt. As historians, we ought to put ourselves into the situation our ancestors were in, and, as Macaulay said, 'put out of our minds, for a time, all the knowledge which they, however eager in their pursuit of truth, could not have, and which we, however negligent we may have been, could not help having'. He constantly shows how the former age differs from the present and makes this one of his main professional functions. It was 'too much' if the benefactors of mankind, 'after being reviled by the dunces of their own generation for going too far, should be reviled by the dunces of the next generation for not going far enough.'

As Professor Clive, I think, realises, the faults in Macaulay are due less to the Whig interpretation, or even to his notion of progress, than to subtler defects of mind and imagination and sympathy, together with perhaps too much facility in some of the inferior arts—all of which put limits to what otherwise was an amazing achievement. (pp. 826-27)

Herbert Butterfield, "Reflections on Macaulay," in The Listener, *Vol. 90, No. 2333, December 13, 1973, pp. 826-27.*

Jane Millgate   (essay date 1973)

[*Millgate is an English-born educator and critic who has written a number of books on nineteenth-century literature. In the following excerpt, she analyzes Macaulay's treatment of character in his* History, *focusing on his portrayal of William III.*]

Macaulay praised Addison, in his essay of 1843, as 'an observer of life, of manners', and sought to capture in his own pages something of his predecessor's vivid impression of social reality. But he also praised Addison for his observation 'of all the shades of human character,' and for his capacity to embody his perceptions in specific characterizations:

> And what he observed he had the art of communicating in two widely different ways. He could describe virtues, vices, habits, whims, as well as Clarendon. But he could do something better. He could call human beings into existence and make them exhibit themselves.

Macaulay is here making a distinction between the methods of the Clarendonian 'characterists'—whose epitomizations compose the individual traits of their subjects into static portraits—and the ways in which novelists create individualized men and women who reveal themselves progressively in their actions, words, and feelings. The *Spectator* essays thus represent for Macaulay a landmark in literary history, a bridge between two kinds of narrative—between seventeenth-century historical writing and the eighteenth-century novel—and fascinate him as a practising historian by the possibility they suggest of annexing to history proper methods of characterization developed in the borderland between factual reporting and fictional invention.

The difficulty with Macaulay's attempts to invoke the methods of fiction for the purposes of characterization is that he seems almost instinctively to restrict himself to the kind of portraiture which presents men whole rather than as they gradually develop. In the depiction of social groups and types his method does sometimes recall certain kinds of Restoration play or eighteenth-century novel, or even the *Spectator* essays themselves. Yet despite the play of colour and detail around the basic outlines of such portraits, the final impression is of a clarity and fixity not so very different in structural and narrative effect from Macaulay's more orthodox historical Characters: his nameless squires and clerics are still very much counters in the pattern of historical explanation, and they remain lively compilations rather than living beings. Here is Macaulay's description of the life of a young chaplain:

> A young Levite—such was the phrase then in use—might be had for his board, a small garret, and ten pounds a year, and might not only perform his own professional functions, might not only be the most patient of butts and of listeners, might not only be always ready in fine weather

for bowls, and in rainy weather for shovelboard, but might also save the expense of a gardener, or of a groom. Sometimes the reverend man nailed up apricots, and sometimes he curried the coach horses. He cast up the farrier's bills. He walked ten miles with a message or a parcel. If he was permitted to dine with the family, he was expected to content himself with the plainest fare. He might fill himself with the corned beef and the carrots: but, as soon as the tarts and cheesecakes made their appearance, he quitted his seat, and stood aloof till he was summoned to return thanks for the repast, from a great part of which he had been excluded.

As the picture of the squirearchy which precedes this clerical portrait has perhaps suggested, we are not very far here from the neighbourhood of Squire Western, and upon encountering a couple of pages later, among the references to Fletcher, Vanburgh, Shadwell, and Swift, one to *Tom Jones* itself, the reader has a sense of being carried, if not absolutely into the territory of fiction, then well into that debatable border land of which Macaulay had written in his History essay of 1828.

The issue is not so much that reliance on literary sources for which Macaulay was criticized as soon as his first two volumes appeared—though his debt to such material is undoubtedly heavy—but rather the historian's use of fictional modes of presentation. Macaulay himself clearly believed not only that the light literature of the seventeenth and eighteenth centuries was the richest source of information, but that it could also supply appropriate models for the creation of typical portraits of whose truth the final test was essential rather than particular. Macaulay moves with great ease from statistical and factual evidence, through particular examples, to individualized portraits of an irresistible vitality; but the technique is in the end illegitimate, for in calling into being a young Levite with so specific and concrete a daily round Macaulay pushes out of his *History* the many other clergymen with different functions and habits. A single simplified image usurps the place that might have been supplied by a more comprehensive survey, and Macaulayan particularity—with its corned beef and carrots—achieves here not simply vividness and economy, but serious distortion. When general characterization merges into allegory the historian has wandered too far into the land of fiction.

Macaulay had written of Addison that he 'could call human beings into existence and make them exhibit themselves'. And he was certainly aware that this power of dynamic self-revelation had taken various and subtle forms in the works of fiction which succeeded Addison's pioneering achievements. In the Madame D'Arblay essay of 1843 he gives a eulogy of Jane Austen which speaks of her portrayal of clergymen very different from his own young Levite:

> She has given us a multitude of characters, all, in a certain sense, common-place, all such as we meet every day. Yet they are all as perfectly discriminated from each other as if they were the most eccentric of human beings. There are, for example, four clergymen, none of whom we should be surprised to find in any parsonage in the kingdom, Mr Edward Ferrars, Mr Henry Tilney, Mr Edmund Bertram, and Mr Elton. They are all specimens of the upper part of the middle class. They have all been liberally educated. They all lie under the restraints of the same sacred profession. They are all young. They are all in love. Not one of them has any hobbyhorse, to use the phrase of Sterne. Not one has a ruling passion, such as we read of in Pope. Who would not have expected them to be insipid likenesses of each other? No such thing. Harpagon is not more unlike to Jourdain, Joseph Surface is not more unlike to Sir Lucius O'Trigger, than every one of Miss Austen's young divines to all his reverend brethren. And almost all this is done by touches so delicate, that they elude analysis, that they defy the powers of description, and that we know them to exist only by the general effect to which they have contributed.

In the same essay Macaulay denied the highest rank to writers like Ben Jonson and Mme D'Arblay who depicted characters in terms of humours; the greatest praise must be 'reserved for the few who have excelled in the difficult art of portraying characters in which no single feature is extravagantly overcharged.'

Clearly Macaulay did not aspire to the company of Jane Austen, but was prepared to settle, in his own practice, for something closer to the 'humours' tradition, no doubt feeling that for the purposes of an historical narrative an individual like Judge Jeffreys or a composite figure like the Tory squire of the third chapter almost demanded to have single features 'extravagantly overcharged'. In choosing to rely, on the one hand, on the methods of the historical Character and, on the other, on those of the literary caricature Macaulay was settling for the one supreme advantage which both these forms possessed—clarity. The advantages for exposition and argument of sharp and colourful emblems seemed to him to be indispensable, and since his conception of history was essentially unheroic, a matter not so much of particular men as of patterns of events and forces, he no doubt regarded the loss of complexity in human presentation as a small price to pay for the clear delineation of the course of events. Macaulay's purpose was not, after all, to discriminate a Henry Tilney from an Edmund Bertram, but to impress upon his readers the social and economic disadvantages experienced by seventeenth-century minor clerics; not to dramatize the hero of a novel in all his individual complexity and developing life, but to present with clarity the role of a William the Third in the pattern of history.

It is hardly surprising that a man who knew his Clarendon and Burnet as well as Macaulay should have been influenced by the tradition of the seventeenth-century English Character. As David Nichol Smith has pointed out, that tradition was essentially the creation of seventeenth-century historians and memoirists, and although undoubtedly influenced by classical and French models, and probably by the example of the English drama, it remained essentially true to its historical origins. Although characterizing yielded place to the biographical impulse in the course of the eighteenth century ('When the facts of a man's life, his works, and his opinions claimed detailed treatment, the fashion of the short character had passed'), the compact and finite Character form retained considerable attractions for the historian with many protagonists to portray.

For the Character-writer the life of his subject is perceived as a whole rather than as something developing in time; qualities and actions are treated of in essence rather than in sequence; works and opinions are invoked as illustrations in the service of a static judgment and not as the motive power by which a dramatic presentation is moved forward. The Character-writer views his subject either as outside of time or from some point after the subject is assumed to have fully displayed himself—often, indeed, when the subject is dead. The aim is to present what a man adds up to in the end rather than to portray the actual process of addition; change thus tends to be seen as a two-dimensional pattern of variation, and if development be depicted at all it is generally in terms of demonstrated fulfilment or of the completion of some already perceived design.

The great attraction of the Character method for Macaulay was that it lent itself perfectly to his instinct for seeing patterns and wholes in the most diverse materials; it also allowed him to achieve superlative clarity and precision of presentation, as in the brilliant Character of Halifax in chapter II of the *History.* The method's limitations become apparent as the reader encounters in later chapters a Halifax who seems never to change or grow; the experience is one of continual reinforcement rather than of renewed freshness of perception, and the expository advantage of clarity has now to be seen as off-set by the narrative disadvantage—especially if the *History* is to be compared with certain kinds of drama and novel—of lack of development and surprise. The influence of the seventeenth-century Character is, however, discernible in the *History* in almost every kind of portrait, from the briefest to the most extended, and it is discernible above all, compact with all its strengths and weaknesses, in the full-scale treatment of William the Third, Macaulay's central figure.

William the Third had provided the subject of the Cambridge Prize Essay of 1822, with which Macaulay achieved his first public success as an essayist; one of the last episodes of the *History* on which Macaulay worked just before his own death in 1859 described the death of William. It seems symbolically appropriate that Macaulay's career should be thus framed, for no character is more central to his conception of English history or to the validity of the *History of England* as a work of literature. The survival of the Prize Essay allows us to compare an early presentation of William with that in the first two volumes of the *History,* and what immediately emerges from such a comparison is the extent to which the essentials of Macaulay's mature conception of William are already present in the Prize Essay, and in remarkably complete form. As G. O. Trevelyan acutely remarks, the essay seems 'just such as will very likely be produced in the course of next Easter term by some young man of judgment and spirit, who knows his Macaulay by heart, and will paraphrase him without scruple' [G. O. Trevelyan, *The Life and Letters of Lord Macaulay,* 1876]. Trevelyan's

comment might perhaps be emended to read 'parody him without scruple', for the carefully balanced sentences with their frequent antitheses verging all too often on the paradoxical, represent an earlier and cruder version of that style with which Macaulay was to astonish both the editor and the audience of the *Edinburgh Review.* The antitheses are employed not only to exhibit the contradictory elements in William's make-up—the contrast, for example, between his insignificant appearance and his courage and energy on the battlefield—but to oppose him at every point to Louis XIV, whose portrait occupies the first position in the essay's gallery. It is with an attempt to epitomize the distinction between the two kings that the Character of William ends:

> On a general comparison of the qualities of the two great antagonists, we may pronounce that the character of William was suited to the domestic hearth, that of Lewis to the courtly circle;—that William appeared to most advantage on the field of battle, and Lewis in the chariot of triumph.

The desire to 'pronounce' betrays Macaulay into too neat an antithesis, for although William's tenderness for his wife has been mentioned in the portrait, the insistence on the 'domestic hearth' conflicts with an earlier emphasis on hunting and warfare. The encouragement which the Character as a genre gave to such pronouncing was undoubtedly one of its attractions for Macaulay, but in the course of his career he learned both to select with more care the details out of which he contrived his epigrammatic effects, and to balance the advantages of climax and finality against the desirability of smoother and more cohesive transitions.

Surprisingly enough, William remains almost unmentioned in Macaulay's writings between the Prize Essay of 1822 and the *History* of 1848. He makes his reappearance in chapter II of the *History,* where his future role is insisted upon from the first:

> a few days after William's [William II of Holland's] death, his widow Mary, daughter of Charles the First, King of Great Britain, gave birth to a son, destined to raise the glory and authority of the House of Nassau to the highest point, to save the United Provinces from slavery, to curb the power of France, and to establish the English constitution on a lasting foundation.

This is followed, not by a full-scale Character of William, but by a narrative of Dutch sufferings during the conflict with France, thus reversing the order Macaulay had adopted in 1822, when the Character of William preceded the account of these same events. In the *History* the full depiction of William must wait until chapter VII, but we are given in the meantime sufficient details of his actions as a young man to illustrate his potential for fulfilling the destiny marked out for him: 'Young as he was, his ardent and unconquerable spirit, though disguised by a cold and sullen manner, soon roused the courage of his dismayed countrymen.' The resistance of William and the Dutch is thrown into particularly sharp relief, coming as it does just after the description of Charles II's subservience to Louis and its culmination in the secret clauses of the Treaty of

Dover, and as if to drive the point about William's military determination home, the paragraph ends with a description of Louis' withdrawal from the scene of battle 'to enjoy the adulation of poets and the smiles of ladies in the newly planted alleys of Versailles.' Yet it is perhaps inaccurate to speak of passages about Charles and Louis setting off the presentation of William: at this early stage in Macaulay's narrative these men are balanced one against the other in a mutually defining pattern, and if any figure is dominant it is that of Louis. For all the insistence on William's destiny, Macaulay does not allow his figure early prominence, reserving the major emphasis for the moment when his actions become crucial to the history of England.

Macaulay's arrangement sustains an appearance of following William's development: the young Stadtholder is presented in chapter II, and, in chapter VII, William at thirty-six poised for some intervention in the affairs of England. The formal Character in chapter VII is distinct from the overview of the Prize Essay in that it is associated with a particular moment in time, the year 1687. Yet, despite this very specific placing, the picture is painted with all the insight that nineteenth-century knowledge and the historian's assessment of the significant can supply. It begins, appropriately enough, with visual details, as William's various portraits are invoked as a way of linking the nineteenth and seventeenth centuries:

> His external appearance is almost as well known to us as to his own captains and councillors. Sculptors, painters, and medallists exerted their utmost skill in the work of transmitting his features to posterity; and his features were such as no artist could fail to seize, and such as, once seen, could never be forgotten. His name at once calls up before us a slender and feeble frame, a lofty and ample forehead, a nose curved like the beak of an eagle, an eye rivalling that of an eagle in brightness and keenness, a thoughtful and somewhat sullen brow, a firm and somewhat peevish mouth, a cheek pale, thin, and deeply furrowed by sickness and by care. That pensive, severe, and solemn aspect could scarcely have belonged to a happy or a good-humoured man. But it indicates in a manner not to be mistaken capacity equal to the most arduous enterprises, and fortitude not to be shaken by reverses or dangers.

William is, in fact, seen here from a combination of three different perspectives: the contemporary one of his captains and counsellors, that of men of later generations who view his portraits, and that of the historian who interprets the features in terms of demonstrated capacity for action in historical situations. Throughout the presentation which follows Macaulay manipulates these viewpoints, giving the reader something of the detail through which William can be known as a living being; but the dominant impression is still determined by that pattern of significances, as opposed to particulars, which comprises the historian's essential portrait.

After the visual opening, William's early life is surveyed in order to illustrate both his inherent characteristics and the effects of his education and experience. Although the emphases—on his ability to keep his own counsel, his military courage even in defeat, and his aversion to religious persecution—have a special relevance for his subsequent as well as his earlier career, the appearance of restricting the portrait to what could be known of William at thirty-six is firmly maintained, even though the limits are stretched to include material for which only later events could be said to supply the full evidence. Macaulay no doubt has William's behaviour at the death of Mary in mind when he comments: 'When death separated him from what he loved, the few who witnessed his agonies trembled for his reason and his life.' But the specific occasion is not, in fact, mentioned here, and it is only in the richly detailed survey of the material provided by the Bentinck correspondence that the 1687 dateline is absolutely crossed; even then, Macaulay's footnotes alone reveal that the specific instances of what were no doubt recurrent feelings and attitudes are sometimes drawn from letters written later in William's life.

It is through the account of William's friendship with Bentinck that his private as well as public self is brought into the picture—the other side of the medallist's impression given in the opening portrait. It is by the same means that the description of William is gently extended beyond the finite, generalized form of the Character so as to include considerable biographical detail. This movement outwards from the static portrait to link up with the narrative thread of the *History* is continued in the accounts of William's feelings for his mistress, Elizabeth Villiers, his relationship with Mary, and Bishop Burnet's intervention between husband and wife in order that the course both of marriage and of history might run smooth. Transition and arrangement here are handled with great skill, Macaulay effecting an easy shift from portrait to narrative and on again to another portrait, very different in kind from William's, that of Bishop Burnet. Since William's role is to assume steadily greater importance in the events which follow, the more open-ended portrait has its own appropriateness, and by thus extending the Character Macaulay is able to make full use of what was fresh primary material, the details of the Bentinck friendship as revealed by William's personal correspondence.

It is undoubtedly true, as Macaulay's critics were quick to point out, that William is let off very lightly for his infidelities, and that Macaulay seems to accept too readily Burnet's account of the estrangement between William and Mary and of a subsequent reconciliation easily achieved through the dropping of a shrewd hint or two by the Bishop himself. The story is a delightful one and effects a splendidly concrete introduction to the Character of Burnet, but Macaulay's use of it does indeed seem somewhat uncritical, and the spirited defence of Burnet as an historian, in text and footnote, serves to heighten rather than diminish this impression. The simple explanation, as the critics saw it, was that, when it came to William and Mary, Macaulay was disingenuous or gullible, or both. In his 1837 essay on Bacon, Macaulay had criticized Basil Montagu for proceeding 'on the assumption that Bacon was an eminently virtuous man', commenting: 'This mode of defending Bacon seems to us by no means *Baconian*. To take a man's character for granted, and then from his character to infer the moral quality of all his actions, is surely a process the very reverse of that which is recommended in the *Novum Organum.*' There are some grounds for charging Macaulay, in his presentation of William, with failing to live up to the standards and procedures he had himself earlier advocated.

But the matter can also be looked at in a way which at least throws a somewhat happier light on Macaulay's motivation, for he seems not to have sought to give a false impression, but to have wanted very much to give a clear impression. William's faults are admitted from the first—even in the brief sketch in chapter II there is an allusion to the stains attaching to his name following the death of De Witt and the Massacre of Glencoe—but they are deliberately underplayed by Macaulay in order that those qualities which enabled William to become the chief agent of the Glorious Revolution may be seen to predominate. For Macaulay, historical truth undoubtedly meant historical significance as well as historical fact—as in his summary dismissal, in the Milton essay, of those defenders of Charles I who invoked the king's private virtues to excuse his public conduct: 'A good father! A good husband!—Ample apologies indeed for fifteen years of persecution, tyranny, and falsehood!' Because he did not see all facts as equal in importance, Macaulay did not hesitate to emphasize good qualities in William and evil ones in James: in keeping with his basically developmental concept of history, he believed that in relation to the larger course of events these were the qualities which counted. This is, of course, a dangerously relativistic view, but it is not the deliberate dishonesty of which Macaulay has been accused. The affair with Elizabeth Villiers, even the Massacre of Glencoe, seemed to Macaulay to be relatively unimportant in comparison with the courage and decisiveness which enabled William to seize his opportunities in 1687 and 1688 and to steer a steady course through all the difficulties of his ensuing reign.

For Macaulay, historical events were the products of a complex of forces—economic, geographic, social, religious, racial. He never sought to define the working of these forces in any coherent theory, but awareness of their operation affects his conceptions of individuals. Particular men, with their personal strengths and weaknesses, desires and fears, have a part to play in influencing the course of events, and are to be held morally accountable for that part; but they do not dominate. Evidence of this general view can be found in almost any of Macaulay's essays, although it is expressed more crudely and absolutely in the earlier works than in the later. Men are repeatedly presented as products of historical situations rather than as controllers of destiny: a particular conjunction of events may provoke a 'plain Buckinghamshire Esquire' like Hampden into obstructing 'the path of tyranny'; in 1678 or 1679, 'there would have been an outbreak, if [Oates and Bedloe] had never been born.'

This last quotation comes from the Mackintosh essay of 1835, the most extreme Whig document Macaulay ever composed, the article which lays the greatest stress on crucial events rather than crucial figures. It was in this essay

that Macaulay wrote of those who wished to bring William of Orange over to England:

> Their first object was to seat William on the throne; and they were right. We say this without any reference to the eminent personal qualities of William, or to the follies and crimes of James. If the two princes had interchanged characters, our opinion would still have been the same. It was even more necessary to England at that time that her king should be a usurper than that he should be a hero. There could be no security for good government without a change of dynasty.

This is the language of the polemicist, not of the judicious historian; all attempt at authorial detachment is surrendered and Macaulay identifies himself completely with one side of the question. Whatever reasons affected the emotional violence and lack of control of the article on Mackintosh, its very extravagance makes it in some ways the clearest, most unguarded statement of some of Macaulay's fundamental beliefs about men and history. Written shortly before he began seriously to contemplate his major work, the essay ends with paragraph after paragraph of insistence on what England owed to the Revolution, *not* what she owed to William—who is, indeed, barely mentioned.

Even when the more extreme assertions and tones of the Mackintosh essays are discounted and allowance is made for developments in Macaulay's thinking in the late 1830s and 1840s, there remains little doubt that when he embarked upon his ***History*** he believed that without William there would still have been a Revolution, although it would naturally have taken a different course. And he almost certainly saw that Revolution rather than William's part in it as his essential subject. Although the character of William was a vital element in the exposition Macaulay intended to offer his readers, it is clear from the choice of the Character genre as the basic means of portraiture that for the major as much as for the minor figures Macaulay felt individual psychology must give way to the analysis of that larger course of events in which any individual was only a contributory factor.

Yet by the end of the first two volumes of the ***History*** William's part in the Revolution has won for him pride of place: 'For the authority of law, for the security of property, for the peace of our streets, for the happiness of our homes, our gratitude is due, under Him who raises and pulls down nations at his pleasure, to the Long Parliament, to the Convention, and to William of Orange.' The contrast with the end of the Mackintosh essay, where the Revolution rather than William receives the tributes, is clear. In the course of writing his first two volumes not only has Macaulay's historical sense of the part played by William become heightened, but his imaginative commitment to his hero has grown accordingly. And the reader whose sense of William's personality and role has been created by the preceding narrative readily acquiesces in the prominence given to William in the final words of this first complete section of the ***History.***

But William's story is not finished by the end of volume II. His reign in England remains to be narrated, and the question which faces the critic of the later volumes is whether there is any development in Macaulay's basic methods of characterization to correspond to his changed conception of the agency of William in events. While it would be a mistake to emphasize this latter change too strongly—Macaulay was always to see William as a man whose lines of action were severely restricted by historical circumstances—something more than the essentially static portraiture of volumes I and II was clearly required. There is certainly evidence in the *Journal* that Macaulay was anxious about the success of the second pair of volumes, yet he seems to have been concerned chiefly because they could not match the first two in variety or vitality of incident or portrait rather than because they called for any radically different approach to questions of characterization or narration.

In chapter XI, the first of volume III, Macaulay gives considerable space to William's habits, manners, and mode of behaviour once he became king of England, and shows how coldness and abruptness of manner and simple foreignness—particularly when contrasted with the gaiety and sociability of Charles II—served to alienate the king from his subjects. Since William's lack of personal attractiveness formed part of the sketch in chapter II and of the fuller portrait in chapter VII, the details of chapter XI constitute a fleshing out of an already established outline, and only the emphasis on the effects of William's personality is new. Macaulay makes very clear the significance of these effects: the failure to win the hearts of others which to an ordinary man would be a personal misfortune can be to a king a political disaster. And every detail presented in this chapter is recorded on the political as well as the personal scale: an item may be trivial, but it is never insignificant. When William gobbles up the green peas without leaving any for his sister-in-law this registers not merely as domestic ill-manners but also as an insult to an English princess by a foreign king.

As volumes III and IV proceed, the reader feels more and more that whether he views William's social behaviour in chapter XI, his religious attitudes in chapter XIV, or his military conduct in chapter XVI, he is simply being supplied with further details in a pattern already laid down in the first two volumes. As with the presentation of Halifax, all is reinforcement; nothing is surprise. This is undoubtedly as Macaulay felt it should be with the characters of a history. He saw the historian's duty when handling character and event as a matter of extracting significance from the variety and complexity of the life of the past, rather than of seeking to give an impression of that life for its own sake. It seems likely, however, that Macaulay's inclusion of so many vivid episodes and so much social detail may have been prompted, at least in part, by some recognition of the life-denying effect of perpetual dedication to selection of the significant. The vitality of some of the more obvious glowing set pieces may be characterized as a compensatory effect, and the same is true of some of the lesser details as well: in the absence of a continuous attempt at lifelikeness we are given lively anecdotes of green peas.

For Macaulay the omniscience of the historian was very different from that of the novelist. It is not the knowledge which pertains to the creator of characters, but rather that long view of the 'philosophic historian' which he attributed to Halifax. Such a view takes cognizance of all sides of a question and is deliberately detached from a contemporary perspective on events; indeed, when employed from the standpoint of the nineteenth century, it knows the outcome of all the events. But although motives are analysed and the validity of various arguments balanced against each other, the vision is limited to that of the shrewd interpreter of words and deeds; for the historian, unlike the novelist, cannot move freely inside the heads and hearts of his protagonists, nor can he place them in invented situations of a deliberately revelatory kind.

G. M. Trevelyan has argued that Macaulay's great failing was 'a disastrous habit of attributing motives', and he goes on to remark that Macaulay 'was never content to say that a man did this or that, and leave his motives to conjecture; he must always needs analyse all that had passed through the mind of his *dramatis personae* as if he were the God who had created them' [*Clio: A Muse, and Other Essays Literary and Pedestrian*, 1913]. While there is little doubt that Macaulay was too free in ascribing base motives to those he saw as villains—Penn, Marlborough, and James II, for example—Trevelyan's emphasis on creation seems slightly wide of the mark. Macaulay rarely analyses what passes through the minds of his characters; he does, however, attempt—and sometimes with considerable success—to give semidramatized form to the arguments which *might* have occurred to the figures concerned. This partial dramatization is intended to create an impression similar to that available to the novelist, the creator of character, and it is in a way a tribute to Macaulay that Trevelyan mistakes it for the same thing. But it remains in the end interpretation rather than creation, and the liveliness we perceive pertains to the manipulation of the arguments and positions rather than to any attempt at a realistic portrayal of the idiosyncratic movement of an individual mind operating through thought patterns as personal as a particular accent or tone of voice.

One of the most striking examples of Macaulay's use of a technique of semi-dramatization so as to give the impression of entering the mind of a character is the presentation in chapter XV of William's position when the Whigs prevent the amnesty he desires. 'The King watched these events with painful anxiety.' Macaulay tells us, and then, in a series of brief sentences, he lists the causes of this anxiety as they might well have occurred to William himself. But even here there is no attempt to catch the precise quality of William's mental processes, and when Macaulay goes on to sum up what must have been William's feelings—'The King felt that he could not, while thus situated, render any service to that great cause to which his whole soul was devoted'—the supportive details are only of a kind available to a shrewd observer. What Macaulay does do is heighten the already established rhythm of short sentences so that it builds up into a rhetoric of grievances and self-justification:

> As for the turbulent and ungrateful islanders,
> who detested him because he would not let them
> tear each other in pieces, Mary must try what

she could do with them. She was born on their soil. She spoke their language. She did not dislike some parts of their Liturgy, which they fancied to be essential, and which to him seemed at best harmless. If she had little knowledge of politics and war, she had what might be more useful, feminine grace and tact, a sweet temper, a smile and a kind word for every body. She might be able to compose the disputes which distracted the State and the Church. Holland, under his government, and England under hers, might act cordially together against the common enemy.

These are the slightly peevish rhythms of injured merit as a state of mind, rather than the idiolect of Dutch William meditating on the ingratitude of seventeenth-century England. The realism pertains to the emotion rather than to the personality.

This faithfulness to the patterns and tones of mental and emotional situations does much to give the appearance of life to the detailed presentation of William in the later volumes of the *History,* even though it finally contributes more to our understanding of his predicament than to our sense of him as a man. And in certain of the more dramatic episodes Macaulay can draw on William's actual words and gestures to create something of the impression of a living, breathing man at the centre of events. Thus Macaulay's powerful visualizing imagination is applied to particularly good effect in the account of William's campaign in Ireland and the Battle of Boyne in chapter XVI. On the day of the Boyne William was the cynosure of all eyes, and his success in the battle ensured that his sayings and doings were treasured and subsequently recorded in such works as Story's *Impartial History of the Wars of Ireland.* Macaulay combines such contemporary details with information derived from nineteenth-century topographical works, such as Wilde's account of the River Boyne, and from his own visit to the scene of the battle, in order to achieve a concrete particularity of effect capable of surviving the process of selection—as strongly active here as elsewhere in the *History.* We retain a sense of watching events as they happen, and when Macaulay insists, as the campaign starts, that 'William was all himself again,' the reader feels for once that he is watching the actual as well as the essential William.

Anecdote is once more invoked—this time to illustrate William's sprightliness rather than his morose greed—but the gracious acceptance of the cherries carries a lesser burden of implication than the gorging of the peas, for many details of word, gesture, and action contribute to the depiction of William's deportment at this time. Actual words are quoted sparingly, and the historian's discriminating hand has clearly chosen them for their significance; even so, they do serve to capture something of the texture of William's mood. We are given his dry comments as he views the enemy forces—'I am glad to see you, gentlemen, . . . If you escape me now, the fault will be mine'; the deliberately calm understatement when he is wounded—'There is no harm done, . . . but the bullet came quite near enough'; the brief indulgence in sarcasm at the expense of the traitor Richard Hamilton—'Your honour! . . . your honour!'; and the growl of disapproval at the Reverend Mr Walker's pushing so far into the thick

of battle as to get himself killed at the ford—'What took him there?' Each phrase combines typicality and authenticity and in this episode at least the balance is maintained.

A skilfully managed evocation of material which must have presented itself to the mind of William occurs in a passage which precedes the account of the battle itself. In the course of his description of Ireland at the time of William's arrival Macaulay shifts from a nineteenth-century perspective, comparing the Belfast of William's day with the Belfast of the present, through a seventeenth-century perspective—'Not a human being was to be found near the road, except a few naked and meagre wretches who had no food but the husks of oats, and who were seen picking those husks, like chickens, from amidst dust and cinders'—to the viewpoint of William himself:

> Perhaps he [William] thought how different an aspect that unhappy region would have presented if it had been blessed with such a government and such a religion as had made his native Holland the wonder of the world; how endless a succession of pleasure houses, tulip gardens and dairy farms would have lined the road from Lisburn to Belfast; how many hundreds of barges would have been constantly passing up and down the Laggan; what a forest of masts would have bristled in the desolate port of Newry; and what vast warehouses and stately mansions would have covered the space occupied by the noisome alleys of Dundalk. 'The country,' he was heard to say, 'is worth fighting for.'

This is, of course, another example of Macaulay's favourite device of definition by comparison, but the substance of the passage has a concreteness whose effect is amplified by the appropriateness of these thoughts to the particularized perspective of William. The contrast between Holland and Ireland is full of significance for the conduct of William and James, and for the different traditions of government they represent; it is not, however, to this significance alone that the reader responds, but to the way in which the depth of William's feeling about Holland is here powerfully dramatized, and to the representation of his mind in the actual process of making comparisons and discriminations. An added poignancy attaches to the passage in that he who perhaps had these or similar thoughts is also the person who might have effected beneficial changes in Ireland; yet the nineteenth-century reader, aware of the larger perspectives earlier invoked, knew that although material improvements had occurred, sectarian bitterness persisted in Ireland with a fierceness and a potential for violence almost the equal of the seventeenth-century situation.

The actual words quoted at the end of the passage are both the historian's justification for what precedes them and the final concrete touch driving home the point of the meditation. It is for some similar fusion of the historical sense with the presentation of an individual mind in action at particular realized moments in time that the reader yearns at other points in the narrative of William's career in these final volumes. All too often the lack of particularity combines with the very coherence of the presentation to transform the attitudes and actions which so neatly illustrate the original Character into the movements of a puppet on the historian's string. All too often we are told about William; all too rarely does he become the vehicle of perceptions. It is no doubt unreasonable to expect Macaulay to combine the impression of particularized life with the treatment of whole areas of William's thought and behaviour: not only was he unable to draw at all points on the kind of detailed material available for the narrative of the Battle of the Boyne, but he must have felt that an equally particular and personal presentation of every episode would be proper only to a biography of William, not to a history of England. Yet it is because the later volumes of the *History*—in their detail and in their concentration on William as the centre of all the threads of action—approximate so frequently to the patterns of biography that the reader wishes for further glimpses of William from a contemporary perspective, and more frequent opportunities to see with William's eyes. Macaulay would no doubt have considered too sustained a dramatization of the narrative from the point of view of William to be a betrayal of his demonstrative and explicatory function as an historian. The stress on historical significance none the less becomes increasingly artificial and oppressive, squeezing the life out of the actors who go so regularly through the authenticated motions.

There remains in the end a hollowness at the heart of the three later volumes of the *History* which makes them less satisfying than the original pair. It is not simply a matter of those silent qualities in the early volumes which are easily recognizable at a first reading—the series of highly-coloured episodes and dramatic personages, the rich and varied gallery of Characters, the wealth of social detail—for a closer examination reveals not only that some of these effects are relatively crude, but that the later volumes handle more detailed and complex material with considerable subtlety: monetary matters in William's reign are much less exciting than the Bloody Assizes, but Macaulay none the less manages to present clearly a mass of historical detail and to hold the reader's interest as he does so. Yet the hollowness remains, and can only be accounted for by the absence of the Prince of Denmark from the play. Although so much of the detail and the structure of the final volumes is brought to bear on the figure of William, such material can function only as further amplification of the static and finite Character of chapter VII. There is no movement in the central figure to correspond to the slow, detailed forward movement of events. In concentrating on what he saw as the vital elements in William, Macaulay denied him vitality as a personality. The death of William which Macaulay, himself a sick man, was so anxious to get down on paper, represents not the concluding moments in a career but the final touches in a portrait. We know already about the calm religious faith, the love for Mary, the quietness and stoicism, which are here exhibited, and some readers may even feel a sense of relief that they will never be reminded of them again.

The Character, in the expanded form in which Macaulay learned to employ it, provides a most effective way for the historian to capture his personages. It controls them as temporal beings, taking their attributes out of the dimen-

sion of time so that their function in the pattern of events can be clearly seen at every point, not merely when the narration of their careers is complete. Details later revealed become illustrations controlled by the net of the initial Character rather than existential moments in their own right. For the presentation of a figure as continuously crucial to the narrative as William, however, the tension between the static conception of the man and the dynamic process of events becomes in the end too great, so that the portrait designed for maximum coherence and clarity seems finally inadequate.

In the end the history of England defeats Macaulay, and it defeats him, ironically enough, in the person of William the Third. For not only did Macaulay allow the *History* to grow in length far beyond the proportions he originally envisaged, but he also came to see William's role as overreaching the bounds allotted to any individual in the conception of history with which he began. In crediting a single individual with a considerably greater influence on events than his own earlier ideas would seem to allow, and in depicting that influence in action in the detailed terms of the *History,* Macaulay was confronting himself—without fully recognizing the fact—with a new set of problems. The old solutions worked out in his essays for the handling of character, biography, and history were not adequate to the continuous presentation of the life and personality of a man who influenced not only contemporary events but the whole subsequent course of English history. In paying tribute to William at the end of volume II Macaulay was acknowledging that influence without having to come to terms with the difficulties of presenting it; in the later volumes those difficulties became steadily more obtrusive and more intractable.

Although Macaulay had always had a Whig conception of the crucial significance of the seventeenth-century revolution, he had never—even in the 1822 Prize Essay—attempted a narration of that revolution in combination with a presentation of the figure of William. The heroes in his major narrative and biographical essays are not shown in conjunction with events absolutely vital to the whole course of English history—for Macaulay, indeed, there were perhaps only two such moments, the 1640s and 1688 (with the possible addition of 1831-2). Clive, Hastings, even Pitt can all be assimilated to a view of the movement of history which lays emphasis on patterns of events and the general historical moment rather than on the mastery of individual men. But in dealing with William in the detailed, progressive narrative of the *History,* the old conceptions simply would not work.

It is not that room for William should have been found in that shadowy heroes' alcove Macaulay had half-granted to the figures of Julius Caesar, Cromwell, and Napoleon; a complete shift to some kind of heroic view of history was never in question. What the later volumes of the *History* seem clearly to require is a more complex view of the interaction of men and events, the acknowledgment of a temporal dimension to human personality and of the capacity of men to affect events—and be affected by them—continuously and variously in the course of time. The retention of the static Character form in the presentation of

William—for all the expansion of detail with which it is endowed—not only indicated Macaulay's failure to perceive the problem of character and history in a new way, but effectively prevented him from evolving a solution for it.

In this vital matter of characterization the *History* was the end of the line which began with the essays. And Macaulay's failure to complete the *History,* particularly when taken in conjunction with his paradoxical anxiety to get at least to the death of William, indicates an instinctive recognition of the impasse to which he had been brought by the articulation of his conception of seventeenth-century history through a combination of the static portraiture of men with an insistence on the dynamic of events. Walter Bagehot, one of the most perceptive critics ever to discuss Macaulay, had considerable praise for his powers of portraiture, commenting in a review article of 1855: 'No one describes so well what we may call the *spectacle* of a character' [Walter Bagehot, "Mr Macaulay," *The National Review* 2, No. IV (April 1856)]. The spectacle of William of Orange is sharp and clear, but it increasingly impedes, by its fixity, the flow of Macaulay's narrative.

Macaulay was above all else an historian, and he became trapped within his historian's role. He needed always to be absolutely certain as to the point in time from which he was viewing his subject, and this was at once a great strength and a great weakness. It enabled him to lead a contemporary audience back into the past without any danger of forgetting the nineteenth-century perspective and the wisdom of hindsight which later events provided. His position was always one of omniscience: not only did he know, or seem to know everything about the men and events he described, he also knew so much about other times and places which could be brought relevantly to bear for purposes of definition or expansion. But because he could not in the end control his knowingness—any more than he could control that vast outpouring of allusion and opinion with which he astounded his acquaintances as a young man—he could not escape to a shifting vantage point from which to view his characters inside of time. He always saw them whole, and so he always saw them dead. This mattered very little within the limited, largely two-dimensional conventions of the essay. But when, by its detailed tracking of men and events through that small handful of years at the end of the seventeenth century, and by its assimilation of that colourful presentation of the social surface normally associated with the novel, the *History* reached towards some more essentially dynamic narrative form, Macaulay could not relinquish his omniscient stance. From an historian's point of view this may have been no bad thing, but when the *History* is considered as a work of literature, with structural and narrative needs of an organic kind progressively generated within itself, then the static quality associated both with the nineteenth-century perspective and with the presentation of the personages as Characters can only be seen as reducing to a spectacle a work which might have been so much more. (pp. 161-80)

> *Jane Millgate, in her* Macaulay, *Routledge & Kegan Paul, Ltd., 1973, 224 p.*

Peter Gay   (essay date 1974)

[*Gay is a distinguished professor of modern history who has used techniques of psychoanalysis in his studies. He has written many books and articles, including* The Rise of Modern Paganism (*1966*) *and* Education of the Senses (*1984*). *In the following essay, Gay discusses the variety found in Macaulay's rhetorical style, his relationship to his family, and his commitment to the liberal politics of his day.*]

The failings of Macaulay's style have been thoroughly explored; it is unlikely that the most unsympathetic reader will discover any new grounds for complaint. In Macaulay's lifetime, wits found its extravagances ample provocation for lampoons; after his death, serious students of literature raised the most far-reaching objections to his way of writing. A formidable array of essayists and historians— Thomas Carlyle and Walter Bagehot, Matthew Arnold and Lord Morley, Sir Leslie Stephen and Sir Charles Firth—condemned it as verbose, artificial, overemphatic: a virtuoso's instrument played not to interpret the music but to glorify the performer. Macaulay's most discriminating readers found his style wearisome and ultimately profoundly irritating, the style of an orator who smuggles onto the printed page tricks suitable to a debate in the House of Commons, if there. As a committed public speaker, he exaggerates his points, constructs false antitheses, grows heated beyond measure, expands immense ingenuity underlining the obvious and proving the self-evident. He argues all the time: he is always making a case, and sounds as sure of it as only a debater can. His airs and graces, his acrobatic pirouettes, far from concealing, only advertise the essential corruptness of his historical work: he is an advocate rather than a historian, and, to make things worse, a Whig advocate. He professes to detest— and, worse, he really detests—what he is too limited to grasp: the subtler points of philosophy, the mysteries of poetry, the sheer historical interest of personages or causes he does not find sympathetic. Matthew Arnold called Macaulay a philistine, in fact the "Prince of Philistines," a verdict with which Leslie Stephen, with all due caution, concurred; Gladstone called him vulgar—in Greek. All his critics conceded Macaulay the quality of clarity, but he seemed to them clear with illegitimate means and for illegitimate purposes. With Macaulay, clarity somehow becomes a vice.

I do not intend to minimize the gravity of the case against Macaulay. His rhetorical self-indulgence and his Whiggish bias are too blatant to be denied. Some of his mannerisms are impossible to defend; his work is marked by a failure of restraint and of taste. And, as his detractors rightly observed, it is not only the tone that is in question; with Macaulay, as with . . . [some other historians], the style is most, if not all, of the man. His way of writing raises uncomfortable doubts about his way of thinking as a historian. He rarely seeks simply to understand; he judges, dealing out marks like an imperious and far from impartial teacher. Lord Morley, reading in Macaulay's *History of England,* found it "full of cleverness, full of detailed knowledge, extraordinarily graphic and interesting. But," he added, "I cannot make myself like the style. That is not the way in which things happen" [entry for May 9, 1905, in Lord Morley, *Recollections,* 1917]. This is a devastating indictment: it is, of course, the historian's business to record the way in which things happen.

Yet it seems to me that we have done to Macaulay what he did to others. We have judged him from our perspectives rather than his, and we have done this because we live in an age to which the mentality of a Macaulay is unhappily a stranger. Whigs, I think I can safely say, make the modern temper uncomfortable; Tories, their sense of tragedy intact, suit it far better. Macaulay, writes Pieter Geyl ["Macaulay in his Essays," in his *Debates with Historians,* 1955], speaking for this temper, "rouses distrust and annoyance"; lacking all true historical empathy, "vituperative" and "cocksure," his "writing of history strikes us as decidedly old-fashioned." There is much truth in this. But Macaulay's style has other, more attractive aspects. And, in addition, it has many more personal and cultural resonances than are immediately apparent; its surfaces hide a richly complex man, living in a richly complex age.

We must, as the Scholastics would have said, distinguish. I want to submit in evidence three samples of Macaulay's prose. "Such a scene as the division of last Tuesday I never saw, and never expect to see again." The time is March 1831, the stage the House of Commons, the occasion the decisive second reading of the Reform Bill, the recipient of this letter Thomas Flower Ellis, Macaulay's best and, apart from his sisters, only friend.

> If I should live fifty years the impression of it will be as fresh and sharp in my mind as if it had just taken place. It was like seeing Caesar stabbed in the Senate House, or seeing Oliver taking the mace from the table, a sight to be seen only once and never to be forgotten. The crowd overflowed the House in every part. When the strangers were cleared out and the doors locked we had six hundred and eight members present, more by fifty-five than ever were at a division before. The Ayes and Noes were like two vollies of cannon from opposite sides of a field of battle. When the opposition went out into the lobby— an operation by the bye which took up twenty minutes or more—we spread ourselves over the benches on both sides of the House. For there were many of us who had not been able to find a seat during the evening. When the doors were shut we began to speculate on our numbers. Every body was desponding. "We have lost it. We are only two hundred and eighty at most. I do not think we are two hundred and fifty. They are three hundred. Alderman Thompson has counted them. He says they are two hundred and ninety-nine." This was the talk on our benches. I wonder that men who have been long in parliament do not acquire a better coup d'oeil for numbers. The House when only the Ayes were in it looked to me a very fair house—much fuller than it generally is even on debates of considerable interest. I had no hope however of three hundred. As the tellers passed along our lowest row on the left hand side the interest was insupportable—two hundred and ninety-one— two hundred and ninety-two—we were all standing up and stretching forward, telling with the tellers. At three hundred there was a short

> cry of joy, at three hundred and two another— suppressed however in a moment. For we did not yet know what the hostile force might be. We knew however that we could not be severely beaten. The doors were thrown open and in they came. Each of them as he entered brought some different report of their numbers. It must have been impossible, as you may conceive, in the lobby, crowded as they must have been, to form any exact estimate. First we heard that they were three hundred and three—then the number rose to three hundred and ten, then went down to three hundred and seven. Alexander Baring told me that he had counted and that they were three hundred and four. We were all breathless with anxiety, when Charles Wood who stood near the door jumped on a bench and cried out—"They are only three hundred and one." We set up a shout that you might have heard to Charing Cross—waving our hats—stamping against the floor and clapping our hands. The tellers scarcely got through the crowd: for the house was thronged up to the table, and all the floor was fluctuating with heads like the pit of a theatre. But you might have heard a pin drop as Duncannon read the numbers. Then again the shouts broke out—and many of us shed tears—I could scarcely refrain. And the jaw of Peel fell; and the face of Twiss was as the face of a damned soul; and Herries looked like Judas taking his neck-cloth off for the last operation. We shook hands and clapped each other on the back, and went out laughing, crying, and huzzaing into the lobby. And no sooner were the outer doors opened than another shout answered that within the house. All the passages and the stairs into the waiting rooms were thronged by people who had waited till four in the morning to know the issue. We passed through a narrow lane between two thick masses of them; and all the way down they were shouting and waving their hats; till we got into the open air. I called a cabriolet—and the first thing the driver asked was, "Is the Bill carried?" "Yes, by one." "Thank God for it, Sir." And away I rode to Grey's Inn—and so ended a scene which will probably never be equalled till the reformed Parliament wants reforming. . . .

This fine victory was, as we know, only temporary; the Reform Bill did not receive the royal assent until more than a year later, in June 1832, after a prolonged and intense political crisis complete with elections, resignations, and threats to swamp a recalcitrant House of Lords. In these proceedings, Macaulay took a prominent part. He had entered the House of Commons in 1830; he was just turning thirty, already widely appreciated as a lucid and forceful essayist. On March 2, 1831, just three weeks before the historic vote he reported to Ellis, Macaulay rose to speak in behalf of the bill that Lord John Russell had introduced the preceding day. It was one of his best performances, like the others memorized and memorable. The House sat silent, intently trying to catch his rapid delivery, for Macaulay was, though a great speechwriter, a bad speaker. "Turn where we may, within, around, the voice of great events is proclaiming to us, Reform, that you may preserve." This was his peroration:

Now, therefore, while every thing at home and abroad forebodes ruin to those who persist in a hopeless struggle against the spirit of the age, now, while the crash of the proudest throne of the continent is still resounding in our ears, now, while the roof of a British palace affords an ignominious shelter to the exiled heir of forty kings, now, while we see on every side ancient institutions subverted, and great societies dissolved, now, while the heart of England is still sound, now, while old feelings and old associations retain a power and a charm which may too soon pass away, now, in this your accepted time, now, in this your day of salvation, take counsel, not of prejudice, not of Party spirit, not of the ignominious pride of a fatal consistency, but of history, of reason, of the ages which are past, of the signs of this most portentous time. Pronounce in a manner worthy of the expectation with which this great debate has been anticipated, and of the long remembrance which it will leave behind. Renew the youth of the State. Save property, divided against itself. Save the multitude, endangered by its own ungovernable passions. Save the aristocracy, endangered by its own unpopular power. Save the greatest, and fairest, and most highly civilised community that ever existed, from calamities which may in a few days sweep away all the rich heritage of so many ages of wisdom and glory. The danger is terrible. The time is short. If this bill should be rejected, I pray to God that none of those who concur in rejecting it may ever remember their votes with unavailing remorse, amidst the wreck of laws, the confusion of ranks, the spoliation of property, and the dissolution of social order.

Four years after this speech, in 1835, while he was in India as a legal member of the Supreme Council, he began pondering the historical work that would make him immortal; four years after that, in 1839, he began to write it. Late in 1848, the first two volumes of his *History of England* finally appeared. The work has no wholly representative passages; like Gibbon, Macaulay had occasion to narrate battles and invasions, describe ways of living, depict character, and moralize over the course of events. Devoted craftsman that he was, he varied his manner to do his matter justice. But in any passage of sufficient length, he is sure to deploy most of his techniques.

If we would study with profit the history of our ancestors [this is from the beginning of his famous third chapter on social history] we must be constantly on our guard against that delusion which the well known names of families, places, and offices naturally produce, and must never forget that the country of which we read was a very different country from that in which we live. In every experimental science there is a tendency towards perfection. In every human being there is a wish to ameliorate his own condition. These two principles have often sufficed, even when counteracted by great public calamities and by bad institutions, to carry civilisation rapidly forward. No ordinary misfortunes, no ordinary misgovernment, will do so much to make a nation wretched, as the constant progress of physical knowledge and the constant effort of

every man to better himself will do to make a nation prosperous. It has often been found that profuse expenditure, heavy taxation, absurd commercial restrictions, corrupt tribunals, disastrous wars, seditions, persecutions, conflagrations, inundations, have not been able to destroy capital so fast as the exertions of private citizens have been able to create it. It can easily be proved that, in our own land, the national wealth has, during at least six centuries, been almost uninterruptedly increasing; that it was greater under the Tudors than under the Plantagenets; that it was greater under the Stuarts than under the Tudors; that, in spite of battles, sieges and confiscations, it was greater on the day of the Restoration than on the day when the Long Parliament met; that, in spite of maladministration, of extravagance, of public bankruptcy, of two costly and unsuccessful wars, of the pestilence and of the fire, it was greater on the day of the death of Charles the Second than on the day of his Restoration. This progress, having continued during many ages, became at length, about the middle of the eighteenth century, portentously rapid, and has proceeded, during the nineteenth, with accelerated velocity.

The three passages I have just quoted are clearly the work of one mind. Yet they are far from identical in their techniques. The letter is intimate and spirited, the speech is hectoring and biblical, the passage from the *History,* though consistently rhetorical, is notably flexible. Macaulay's stylistic repertoire is larger than its dominant tone would indicate. It is as untrue to say that all his writings are disguised orations as it is to say that his orations are spoken essays. He has every string to his lyre except perhaps true simplicity, and there are moments when he rises even to that. His letter to Ellis, presumably a spontaneous performance, shows how rapidly he could compose a finished piece of reportage. Writing a week after the dramatic moment, Macaulay faces the problem that haunts every historical storyteller—his reader knows the end of the story: 302 to 301 for the bill. But Macaulay piques Ellis' interest by dwelling on the uncertainty of that ending (" 'We have lost it.' . . . I had no hope however of three hundred. . . . First we heard . . . then the number rose"). Without evident compunction, Macaulay, pulling on his reader's lapel, emphatically characterizes the event as exciting ("the interest was insupportable . . . we were all breathless with anxiety"); but also, more subtly, he dramatizes the suspense ("two hundred and ninety-one— two hundred and ninety-two"). He lends his moment, visible as it is on its own, the stilts of the most extraordinary historical parallels ("like seeing Caesar stabbed . . . or seeing Oliver taking the mace from the table"). He makes his narrative brilliantly visual by making it wholly concrete ("we spread ourselves over the benches. . . we were all standing up. . . . all the floor was fluctuating with heads like the pit of a theatre"). He does not disdain pathos ("many of us shed tears") or, writing as he is to a friend, the homely cliché ("you might have heard a pin drop"). And he completes his report by constructing a dialogue suitable for the stage, with laconic question and laconic response, neatly illustrating the popularity of the Whig program and the blessings of a deferential society ("the first thing the driver asked was, 'Is the Bill carried?' 'Yes, by one.' 'Thank God for it, Sir.' "). Yet, throughout all this agile narrative, Macaulay also sounds a deeper, more natural note, a pure boyish exuberance that will not be denied ("And the jaw of Peel fell . . . and Herries looked like Judas taking his neck-cloth off for the last operation"). Macaulay is not too starchy to admit that it had been sweet to fight, sweeter still to win.

When he ventures onto the public stage, Macaulay resolutely suppresses all such levity. In the House of Commons, he is grave, urgent, humorless. The emphatic music of his sentences resounds like the rhythmic beating of a drum in the jungle, designed less to inform than to arouse. That is the point of Macaulay's insistent eightfold reiteration of "now," a technique he borrowed from the rhetoric of the Bible and intensified for his own secular assignment. That is the point also of his equally insistent short sentences, either beginning with the same word ("Save property. . . . Save the multitude. . . . Save the aristocracy. . . . Save the greatest, the fairest, the most highly civilised community") or cast in the same shape ("The danger is terrible. The time is short.") Here is the demagogy of a connoisseur steeped in the oratory of the ages, employed for the delectation of other connoisseurs, Macaulay's fellow MPs. The Commons dearly loved a rousing speech, and hankered after the good old days of parliamentary oratory, the 1790s, when giants like Pitt and Fox and Burke had harangued and swayed the House. While Macaulay does not scruple on occasion to play on the widespread fear of violent upheaval, his is a demagogy less of message than of tone, a half-instinctive, half-calculated appeal to inarticulate, indeed unconscious, inner periodicities. Yet if this is demagogy, it is elevated; the concreteness of Macaulay's letter to Ellis has given way to circumlocutory grandiosity: "while the roof of a British palace affords an ignominious shelter to the exiled heir of forty kings," is a roundabout and rather precious way of alluding to France's former king, Charles X, dislodged by the Revolution of 1830, and living at Castle Lulworth in Dorset. Considering the five hundred bottles of Bordeaux that the royal family had remembered to bring along to sweeten the bread of exile, Macaulay's choice of adjective—"ignominious"—seems a little strained. But Macaulay was interested in decorum and in the resounding effect, not in mundane details that might spoil them. His paraphrase of St. Paul's familiar *Epistle to the Romans* ("Now it is high time to awake out of sleep: for now is our salvation nearer than when we believed,") underscores Macaulay's sense that he is addressing himself to the most solemn of occasions. His sober statesman's warning ("Reform, that you may preserve"), which carried reminders of the conservative authority of Burke and the populist threat of Cobbett, redoubles that solemnity.

The *History* is something rather different. It is ingratiating, like all Macaulay's work, but since with the *History* he is courting popularity with a new public, he adapts his devices to its tastes within the limits of his convictions. He is still making points ("we must be constantly on our guard . . . and must never forget"), but at a less feverish, less ominous temperature than in his speeches. He is still laying down obiter dicta ("In every experimental sci-

ence. . . . In every human being. . . . "), but he now takes the time to prove, or at least elaborate, his assertions, and to press his argument in more leisurely fashion. He is still inescapably orotund, employing the single phrase, "that it was greater," four times in a single sentence to link his evidence into an iron chain. Yet he is sensitive to the perils of repetitiousness; what makes for power in speeches may make for boredom in books. Whether his sentences are monotonous or not depends on the taste of the reader. But it is certain that he tried to avoid monotony. That long sentence beginning, "It has often been found" has the contours of a sleigh ride. Starting on level ground, it picks up momentum as it slides downhill with its list of two- and three-word phrases ("profuse expenditure, heavy taxation"), further accelerates with a rushing sequence of single words ("seditions, persecutions"), and then coasts gently to a stop with a neat antithesis ("not been able to destroy . . . able to create"). In general, though, Macaulay likes his sentences to be short and perspicuous: "But at the court Jeffreys was cordially welcomed." Macaulay is, of course, describing Lord Jeffreys, notorious for the Bloody Assizes.

> He was a judge after his master's own heart. James had watched the circuit with interest and delight. In his drawing room and at his table he had frequently talked of the havoc which was making among his disaffected subjects with a glee at which the foreign ministers stood aghast. With his own hand he had penned accounts of what he facetiously called his Lord Chief Justice's campaign in the West. Some hundreds of rebels, His Majesty wrote to The Hague, had been condemned. Some of them had been changed; more should be hanged; and the rest should be sent to the plantations.

Macaulay's youthful affection for Ciceronian antithesis and Augustan balance did not diminish: "But the liberality of the nation had been made fruitless by the vices of the government" is one of his summaries; "To bend and break the spirits of men gave him pleasure; and to part with his money gave him pain. What he had not the generosity to do at his own expense he determined to do at the expense of others" is one of his characterizations, this one of King James II.

The profusion of parallel clauses in Macaulay's writings suggests that he perceived history as a succession of dilemmas, debates, and combats—between conscience and ambition, bravery and cowardice, Protestants and Catholics, Cavaliers and Roundheads, Whigs and Tories, passive obedience and manly rebelliousness. For Macaulay, history was a vast antithesis. His character sketches, which he scatters across his *History* with a liberal hand, simulate the complexity of human beings by wallowing in antithetical traits. And those paired lists he called the "declamatory disquisition," with which he sets out first the claim of one, then those of the other party, are simply antitheses writ large. The declamatory disquisition, a technique he had learned from ancient historians, illustrates collective aspirations or grievances not by quoting the words of historical individuals, but by constructing an embracing summary. Macaulay begins the great Chapter 9 of his *History*, which he will crowd with such historic action as the English expedition of William and the flight of James, with an extensive examination of the English conscience, divided to its depths between those who feel compelled to obey the king no matter what his crimes, and those who argue that under extreme circumstances rebellion is justified. Macaulay strews this debate with another favorite device, the rhetorical question that drags its answer behind: "What Christian really turned the left cheek to the ruffian who has smitten the right? . . . Was there any government in the world under which there were not to be found some discontented and factious men who would say, and perhaps think, that their grievances constituted an extreme case?"

This narrative manner involves the reader, and is brilliantly calculated to keep his interest at a continuously high pitch. Macaulay's book is long, but he vigorously labors to make it seem short. In his essay on history, an early effort, Macaulay had lamented the decline of the narrative genre and praised "the art of interesting the affections and presenting pictures to the imagination." He practiced that art by moving the story along with apt quotations, changes of pace, and finely contrived opening sentences, which point forward like arrows: "The acquittal of the Bishops," thus begins Chapter 9, *was not the only event* which makes the thirtieth of June 1688 a great epoch in history." Much like Ranke, he likes to hint at what might have happened: recounting the trial of the seven bishops, which ended with their sensational acquittal, he observes, with disarming ingenuousness, "that they would be convicted it was scarcely possible to doubt." Stirred by the improbability of the actual outcome, the reader reads on.

Performing all these acrobatic rhetorical feats, Macaulay never forgets to be concrete. Following his own advice, he presents pictures to the imagination where later historians might have offered footnotes, charts, or tables. In 1685, "There was scarcely a rural grandee," he writes about the Tory opposition to a standing army,

> who could not tell a story of wrongs and insults suffered by himself, or by his father, at the hands of the parliamentary soldiers. One old Cavalier had seen half of his manor house blown up. The hereditary elms of another had been hewn down. A third could never go into his parish church without being reminded by the defaced scutcheons and headless statues of his ancestry, that Oliver's redcoats had once stabled their horses there.

His declamatory disquisitions are models of concreteness, and when Macaulay has a dramatic moment to relate, he nurses its details with an experienced storyteller's affection. "It was ten o'clock. The coach of the Lieutenant of the Tower was ready"—so begins his celebrated account of the execution of Monmouth. "When William caught sight of the valley of the Boyne, he could not suppress an exclamation and gesture of delight"—so begins his equally celebrated account of the battle of the Boyne. In fact, Macaulay imaginatively translates even the social history of Chapter 3 into pictures that can be comprehended without effort:

> Of the old baronial keeps many had been shat-

tered by the cannon of Fairfax and Cromwell, and lay in heaps of ruin, overgrown with ivy. Those which remained had lost their martial character, and were now rural palaces of the aristocracy. The moats were turned into preserves of carp and pike. The mounds were planted with fragrant shrubs, through which spiral walks ran up to the summer houses adorned with mirrors and paintings.

Macaulay is here really analyzing the decline of the military nobility, but the one long word in the passage is the indispensable "aristocracy." Instead of bearing the burden of abstract concepts, the reader can, as it were, see the decline from the martial to the pastoral, with the ivy on the ruins, the carp in the moats, and the pictures on the walls. With the fragrant shrubs, he can even smell it.

. . . . .

To probe beneath these techniques to the feelings that underlie them is to encounter expansiveness and anxiety, the first candid, even aggressive, the second concealed and sublimated. Macaulay's versatility does not bespeak incoherence; his style expresses the unity of his intentions and, though more reluctantly, the strenuousness of his execution. Macaulay fervently wishes to please and to persuade, and to persuade by pleasing. This is continuously hard work; Macaulay wrote a great deal, but his apparent ease of execution does not preclude continuing travail—he just did not wrestle with himself in public. "What labour it is to make a tolerable book," he confided to his private notebook on February 6, 1854, "and how little readers know how much trouble the ordering of the parts has cost the writer!" Whatever contrivance Macaulay chose to adopt, his writing emerges from an intense self-consciousness. He has wrought and polished every phrase; he grants his reader not a moment of the relief that stretches of plain writing would provide. Thomas Carlyle, himself scarcely a relaxed writer, saw this strenuousness plain. "Macaulay is well for a while," he said in the late 1830s, "but one wouldn't *live* under Niagara." While, as I have suggested, Macaulay fits his style to his readers, he does not pay them the ultimate compliment of letting them make their own discoveries. Much like a provincial hotel keeper of the old days, he constantly reappears to ask if everything is satisfactory.

Of the two essential qualities that make up Macaulay's temper and inform Macaulay's style—expansiveness and anxiety—the first, being more public in its origins and its effects than the second, is also easier to comprehend. Macaulay was expansive in a quite literal sense. If he avoided repetitiousness in adjoining sentences or monotony within a single paragraph, he escaped neither vice in the longer stretches: he is never content to report only once an irony that amuses him, or an interpretation he is the first to offer. That James II owed his throne to the Anglican clerics whom he mistreated once he became king, that it was the seventeenth-century practice to blame the misconduct of rulers on evil counsellors, are observations that Macaulay presses upon his readers with the insistence of a nervous hostess. He was aware, regretfully, that the historian must select from the profusion of the past, and so he bravely made his choices. But when he erred, he did not err on the side of economy.

Macaulay, indeed, lengthened his history by shortening its time span. In 1838, when he began to think about it seriously, he wanted it to reach from 1688 to 1832, beginning with the "Revolution which brought the Crown into harmony with the Parliament," and ending with the "Revolution which brought the Parliament into harmony with the nation." When he published the first volumes of the *History* ten years later, this grand harmonious design still dominated his mind: "I propose to write the history of England," runs the opening sentence, "from the accession of King James the Second down to a time which is within the memory of men still living." These two volumes were already gluttonous in their consumption of space: apart from the two introductory chapters, which provide a glance backward, they covered only three years, the reign of James II. And Chapter 3, the most original and most famous chapter in these two volumes, did not advance chronology in any way; it provided an extensive survey of English society—population, cities, classes, popular taste—in the year 1685. The chapter was intimately relevant, and in a sense introductory, to the political drama that King James was about to launch, but it stands very much on its own, as the partial fulfillment of Macaulay's commitment to treat, as he said in an introductory passage, more than "battles and sieges" or the "rise and fall of administrations." He proposed to "relate the history of the people as well as the history of the government, to trace the progress of useful and ornamental arts, to describe the rise of religious sects and the changes of literary taste, to portray the manners of successive generations and not to pass by with neglect even the revolutions which have taken place in dress, furniture, repasts, and public amusements." In view of this ambitious commitment he made to his reader, and from the perspective of modern social history which, among all branches of history, has doubtless advanced the most since Macaulay's day, Chapter 3 did not fulfill his promise. He returns to its chief preoccupations only rarely—it is like an overture whose themes make only sporadic appearances in the opera for which it was written—and in any event, he did not live to balance it with a similar chapter surveying England's society in more recent times. It is not complete, and far from adequately analytical, though, looking backward instead of forward, it is an immense leap beyond the occasional forays that David Hume made into social history, and an advance beyond the brilliant intuitions that Voltaire had offered. With all its failings, Chapter 3 permitted social history to become a serious discipline, and the measure of its success is the question it compelled later historians to raise—even about the chapter itself.

But whatever our final judgment, the point here is that this chapter did nothing to speed up the pace of Macaulay's *History* and served instead to slow it down. The great success of Chapter 3, and the enormous success of the two volumes with the history-reading public, induced Macaulay to revise his scheme, and to study, with even greater diligence than he had planned, the pamphlets and the battle sites of the reign of William III. He never got beyond his hero. The fifth volume of his *History* was published posthumously in 1861; it concluded with a fragmentary account of the last days and the death in 1702 of Dutch William. Incomplete as it was, the history retained Macaulay's celebrated specificity to the end. "When his remains were laid out, it was found that he wore next to his skin a small piece of black silk riband. The lords in waiting ordered it to be taken off. It contained a gold ring and a lock of the hair of Mary." A history once designed to span a century and a half had contracted, by expanding, into a history covering every inch of seventeen years. This was the reward, and the penalty, of expansiveness.

Macaulay's expansiveness also set the tone of his *History.* Lord Melbourne is reported to have said that he wished he could be "as cocksure about anything as Macaulay is about everything," while Walter Bagehot complained that in Macaulay's writings "You rarely come across anything which is not decided. . . ." This, he added, making a charge that was rapidly becoming familiar, "is hardly the style for history." Macaulay does seem to know everything—a posture that tempts skeptical readers to wonder how much he really knows. He describes the thoughts and feelings of his characters as though he had been inside them: Sunderland in 1688 is haunted by "visions of an innumerable crowd covering Tower Hill and shouting with savage joy at the sight of the apostate, of a scaffold hung with black, of Burnet reading the prayer for the departing"; William of Orange, reflecting on the foreign policy of Louis XIV, "smiled inwardly at the misdirected energy of his foe." Macaulay's sweeping, magisterial assertions tolerate no exceptions. When the public learns that James II's queen, Mary of Modena, is pregnant, "From the Prince and Princess of Denmark down to porters and laundresses nobody alluded to the promised birth without a sneer." Nobody? Macaulay the historian seems to be enjoying ubiquity as well as omniscience.

This manner does Macaulay a disservice. It was doubtless, as Sir Charles Firth has observed, the secret of his public success. It permitted him to realize, and greatly surpass, his expressed ambition to "produce something which shall for a few days supersede the last fashionable novel on the tables of young ladies." His cavalier and casual way of citing his authorities, which has the same origin, may irritate the scholar, but it did not trouble the reader to whom Macaulay was principally addressing his work. Yet the accuracy of his lofty simplicities and of his liberal allusions to pamphlets and novels and diaries and road maps was guaranteed by an immense and voracious study of obscure sources, unpublished documents, and earlier historians. Most writers have read less than they get credit for; Macaulay had read more.

The confident manner was the way to the public's heart. The first two volumes sold 13,000 sets in four months; volumes three and four, twice that number in half the time. In about a quarter of a century, Longmans sold more than 140,000 sets of the *History* in Great Britain alone. This meant an average of 6,000 sets a year for a population of over twenty million—though an unprecedented figure for a work of history, Macaulay reached a relatively small reading public. He could therefore write for people he, in a sense, knew and to whom he did not have to explain everything, much though he loved to explain everything. Popular as he intended his *History* to be, he could presuppose relatively cultivated and well-informed readers who caught literary allusions and historical instances without needing the prompting of a condescending footnote.

But, while Macaulay found his general reading public immensely supportive, his expansiveness rested, as it were, on a narrow social base. Somewhat uneasily, but, in the end, triumphantly, he made himself a part of England's intellectual aristocracy; his certainty, on the surface so unruffled, reflects his sense that he was on the right track, in the right place, and not alone. Macaulay could hear reassuring supportive echoes wherever he turned. He was a meritorious officer in a select and influential army, all of whose generals were cousins. This is not a farfetched metaphor. In nineteenth-century England, intellectual leadership was the business of a few extended families. A few ramified clans translated the classics, edited the journals, headed the colleges, reformed the schools, advanced the sciences, and wrote the laws. There was some circulation within this elite, and much adroit renewal: the leading families rarely let a promising recruit get away. They coopted him, or her, by marriage. The intellect was on the march in England, and these were its shock troops.

Thomas Babington Macaulay struggled to be in the vanguard, carrying the flag. His life is a splendid instance of the careers open to the talented from the middling classes. He came from a respectable family of exemplary piety, with few connections, and average income—indeed, had its piety been less absorbing, its income would have been more ample. Macaulay made his way into the favor of the Whig aristocracy, though not without qualms and hesitations, and was created Baron Macaulay in 1857, for his literary attainments. He remained a bachelor, but his beloved sister Hannah married Charles, later Sir Charles, Trevelyan, who was to become a distinguished public servant and civil service reformer. Charles' son, Macaulay's nephew, George Otto, later Sir George, Trevelyan, became a fine modern historian and his uncle's first biographer; Sir George's son, aptly named George Macaulay Trevelyan, became a famous historian in his own right and master of Trinity College, Cambridge, which his even more famous great-uncle had attended. G. M. Trevelyan married the daughter of the novelist Mrs. Humphry Ward, who was Matthew Arnold's niece, thus joining the Macaulays to the Arnolds who, in turn, formed connections with the Huxleys and the Penroses.

It was a clan but not a sect, a brittle troop of high-strung individualists. Many of them achieved eminence in their fields—in economics, in literature, in art criticism, in government, less in the church, but impressively in history—and they did not always agree. Nor were they all Whigs of Macaulay's persuasion, or of any persuasion. But they offered him an intelligent audience and a foretaste of immortality. Macaulay longed for immediate popularity. But, sounding like Stendhal, he liked to caress in his mind the applause of the ages: "Corragio," he wrote in his Journal in 1850, "and think of A.D. 2850." Unlike Stendhal though, Macaulay found his public in his lifetime. At home in his world, sure of the understanding of the elite

and the approval of the larger public, Macaulay was naturally confident about his work and hopeful for the future.

That was the public Macaulay. There was also a private Macaulay, and he is far more elusive. To the extent that his formal style was meant to protect, rather than express, his character, it gives his biographer little help—it is at this point, when style becomes a mask rather than remaining a face, that the study of style reaches its limits, and independent evidence becomes indispensable. Yet his style is not wholly uninstructive for the private Macaulay. It becomes indiscreet when, instead of being confident, it proclaims confidence. It gives involuntary testimony with such favorite words as "voluptuary": he characterized himself, if unwittingly, in characterizing the Earl of Dorset as an "intellectual voluptuary."

Perhaps the best opening to the inner Macaulay is the point I have already made: Macaulay was a performer anxious to please. Now, the person he wanted to please most, whom he addresses, if unconsciously, all the time, is his father. John Clive, in his penetrating biography of the young Macaulay [John Clive, *The Shaping of the Historian,* 1973], both begins and concludes with the historian's father, and justly so. Zachary Macaulay was prominent in what Sydney Smith, the wit, called the Clapham sect, a party of earnest Evangelicals devoted to the religion of the heart and the improvement of the world. William Wilberforce, the antislavery agitator, was its most famous member. The group was small, its influence enormous. The Claphamites relied on arguments that plain Christians, weary and suspicious of theological refinements, could understand: the experience of conversion, the primacy of Scripture, the sincerity of belief, the need for action. They occupied strategic posts in English society: some were Members of Parliament; some were prosperous merchants; some, like Zachary Macaulay, were respected public servants. Tom Macaulay grew up in the midst of this sect, early familiar with the good, sober talk of men of affairs and early imbued with the heavy obligations of sainthood. He was a precocious child, a notable prodigy, anxiously loved by his mother, adored by his sisters, and spoiled by his astonished acquaintances. His father loved him in his own Claphamite way; not without affection, he undertook to keep his son's ego within bounds—it would not do for sinful Christians to be proud.

The Claphamites' devout, unwearied quest for self-improvement entailed close and candid attention to the imperfections of others. This was not cant or self-indulgence: criticisms were unsparing but mutual, and to proffer them responsibly was among the Evangelicals' highest duties. Young Macaulay felt the lash of paternal admonition all too often. As an apprentice Evangelical, he might have smitten the other's cheek; as a dutiful son, he did not dare—and in fact did not wish—to retaliate. In 1824, already a young man of great promise, Tom Macaulay delivered a powerful oration against the slave trade before the Society for the Mitigation and Abolition of Slavery, which his father had founded the year before. It was a great occasion; the Claphamites were there in force, and even a member of the royal family consented to grace the platform. The speech was a triumph, a foretaste of the parliamentary speeches Macaulay would deliver only a few years later. Applause was prolonged and enthusiastic, and the father had tears of pride in his eyes. But as the two walked home together, Zachary Macaulay told his son, "By the way, Tom, you should be aware that when you speak in the presence of royalty, you should not fold your arms." That this sort of severity was hard for the father to sustain seems likely; that a rebuff at such a moment was a devastating affront to the son is certain. This was sadistic propriety masquerading as parental wisdom.

It is the way of the world that men try hardest to please those significant figures whom they please the least. Easy victories bring little satisfaction; repeated failures encourage reiterated effort, to the moment of ultimate gratification or ultimate resignation. As Macaulay grew up, went to Cambridge, and entered the world, he continued to pacify his father, to seek his elusive applause. After he lost his religious faith, Macaulay moderated his language in controversy for his father's sake, stopped for a time sending contributions to a high-spirited quarterly because its tone offended his father, was desolated when he failed in mathematics at Cambridge because he feared his father's reproaches—his mother, in any event, begged her husband to spare the son at least for a while. Even after he had been in politics for some years, when he was in his thirties, Macaulay would take positions in which he did not quite believe because he hoped they would make Zachary Macaulay happy. He felt himself fortunate, he told his sister Hannah in 1831, that he had managed to soften ambition "into a kind of domestic feeling." This, he wrote, "I owe to my dear mother, and to the interest which she always took in my childish successes. From my earliest years, the gratification of those whom I love has been associated with the gratification of my own thirst for fame, until the two have become inseparably joined in my mind." This letter demonstrates that with Macaulay, as with others, infantile patterns survived, suitably transmogrified, in the man. It makes plain that among his intimate audience, his mother was easy to please. What it leaves unsaid is that the most important target of his desperate anxiety was his father.

One powerful ingredient in Macaulay's inner life, then, was his yearning for his father's approval. Another ingredient, quite as powerful, was his passionate love for two of his younger sisters, Hannah and Margaret. Even remembering the unbridled effusiveness of much nineteenth-century correspondence, the profuse employment of extravagant epithets, and the easy equating of affection with love, we cannot escape the conclusion that Macaulay's feelings for his sisters were extraordinary in their intensity and erotic in their essence. He called his love for them his "greatest enjoyment" and his "strongest feeling"; he addressed Hannah as "my dear girl, my sister, my darling—my own sweet friend," and told her how he pined "for your society, for your voice, for your caress." While he bravely steeled himself for the inevitable day that his sisters would marry, when they did, he suffered bouts of depression resembling breakdowns; in the midst of his gratifying political activities and arduous legal labor, he wept, professed that his heart was broken, and declared that, when Hannah married Trevelyan, "the work of more than twenty years" had "vanished in a single month."

This is not the voice of a man deficient in sexual passion, but of one who has steered his sexuality into a sheltered harbor. To love one's sister was safe; it was a love inhibited in its aim—unless, of course, one was Byron. But why should Macaulay pour all his passion into this kind of ungratified—if gratifying—incest? At this point, conjecture must supply the want of adequate evidence. Macaulay's love for his father was a prolonged strain, the intermittent but protracted siege of an impregnable fortress punctuated by desertions from so impossible a task, by "idle reading," and by sloppy attire. Significantly, his sister Hannah recalled later in life that Macaulay's faults "were peculiarly those that my father had no patience with." On the other hand, Macaulay's love for his mother included large portions of voluptuous regression; he would fondly recall the motherly touch, her lavish intimate care during illnesses he welcomed for the sake of her closeness. Ambivalence is the lot of humanity, and Macaulay had his share, but it was in his relation to his father that it emerged most visibly, though rarely into open consciousness. Behind the screen of the son's poignant affection there was rage and, I think, rivalry.

Another bit of evidence adds a significant piece to the mosaic of Macaulay's character: his volubility. Macaulay was a great talker, and, like other great talkers, a bad listener. He was given to one-sided conversations and rapid-fire delivery. Sydney Smith was once asked how he had spent the night. "Oh, horrid, horrid, my dear fellow!" he replied. "I dreamt I was chained to a rock and being talked to death by Harriet Martineau and Macaulay." Others had this nightmare in their waking hours. When a delegation of Quakers waited on Macaulay to protest against his malicious caricature of William Penn in the *History,* Macaulay complacently noted in his journal that he had completely routed them: "They had absolutely nothing to say," a remark we are entitled to take literally. But the compulsive talker, though the target of easy jokes, is a wounded being, driven by his neurosis either to blurt out dreadful secrets, or to get in a word edgewise before he is interrupted. I would suggest that the great orator was unconsciously terrified that no one was listening to him. His offerings had been spurned and so, half in hope and half in despair, he made them over and over again. The only arena in which Macaulay could permit himself to be a voluptuary was in the realm of the intellect.

. . . . .

For Macaulay, psychological needs and social realities happily coincided. No one wholly escapes his early past, least of all Macaulay. What loomed large for Macaulay the young boy, and what was symbolized by the heroic stature of his pious and exigent father, was the Evangelicalism of the Clapham sect. As his religious beliefs faded, as he extricated himself from the mire of biblicism, he retained the energy of the Claphamites, their detestation of evil and their solemn desire to aid good causes. In fact, his dramatic perception of history as a combat between two clearly delineated forces translated the Evangelicals' view of things into secular terms. Similarly, to celebrate progress in history, and to insure its future advance, was to translate early injunctions into mature conduct.

Such translations are commonly called a secular religion, but this term, which has been used to explain the most incongruous phenomena, merits the historian's suspicion. A fervent conviction that emerges after a religious belief has gone may be its functional replacement; it may give the sense of exaltation, the certainty of salvation, or the pleasure of ritual that the now discarded faith once gave. But the two may be independent of one another; and, even if they are psychological equivalents, it remains a difficult question just which half of the term—*secular* or *religion*—deserves emphasis. Normally, it is *religion* that has borne the weight. But *secular* has its own claims. What may matter is not that a set of convictions resembles, or even replaces, a religion with its irrational tenacity and its resistance to empirical evidence, but that it permits a scientific appraisal of the world. Secularization is never a small step.

With Macaulay, certainly, the emphasis must be on the adjective. The precise contours of his religious views have not been fully traced, but he obviously detested religious enthusiasm, rejected miracles and the literal inspiration or even the symbolic supremacy of the Bible, and softened the stern doctrine of original sin into the anthropological commonplace of human fallibility. Macaulay was reticent about his beliefs—understandably so. The coarse candor and widespread freethinking of the eighteenth century had been replaced, decades before the accession of Victoria, by a new emphasis on respectability and a measure of public piety among the ruling orders. It was not until 1858, the year before Macaulay's death, that the House of Commons admitted a member—Lionel de Rothschild—unable to take the oath, previously required, that he was a Christian. And it was only in the following year that Darwin's shattering *Origin of Species* appeared. Before then it had been neither prudent nor common to profess oneself an agnostic, let alone an atheist, and even later it remained rare. Lacking public professions, the student of Macaulay must depend on the tenor of his work, and on a rare philosophical remark—and that one marginal—that has been drafted to do heavy duty for the understanding of Macaulay: "But," the eighteenth-century skeptic Conyers Middleton had written, "if *to live strictly and think freely; to practise what is moral and to believe what is rational,* be consistent with the sincere profession of Christianity, then I shall acquit myself like one of its truest professors." Underlining the critical passage, Macaulay added a note, *"Haec est absoluta et perfecta philosophi vita."* For Macaulay, then, the absolute and perfect life of the philosopher amounted to strict living and free thinking, moral practice and rational belief. If that is Christianity, Macaulay was a Christian. But it is not, and, it is reasonable to conclude, neither was Macaulay.

While Macaulay did not make a god of God, he did not make a god of progress either. His confidence in progress was grounded in realities that offered daily tributes to optimism. Whether one accepted Macaulay's definition of what constitutes progress or not, few—even among devout and sophisticated Christians—had any question that progress itself is desirable. And once one accepted his definition, there could be no doubt that the evidence for progress was overwhelming. Macaulay's style fits into this progress with ease. The amplitude of his periods, his accu-

mulative prose, aptly mirrors the improvements all around him. Its very leisureliness demands time for reading. It breathes and presupposes opulence. It suggests comfortable chairs, warming fires, expensive slippers, China tea, efficient servants, long weekends, and high dividends. In this expansive culture, money was time, and Macaulay's *History* a fitting companion to the long novel, the long poem, and the long dinner. For Macaulay, the message of progress was more than a psychological weapon, it was also a report on contemporary history.

Macaulay was not wholly naïve about the signs of the times. G. M. Young [*Victorian England,* 1953] has called him an Augustan, and the implication that he was, in his style of thinking as much as in his style of speaking and writing, a son of the eighteenth century, is highly suggestive. In decisive ways, Macaulay was not a beginning but an end. But he was heir to more than the English Augustans. He was heir also to the Western Enlightenment, both in his belief in progress and in his reserve. The philosophes, . . . surrounded their confidence with caution, and believed that all progress must somehow be paid for. Macaulay reiterated, in his speeches, his essays, his *History,* that it is better to be cultivated than barbaric, better to live in cities than in hovels, better to have the truths of science than the fancies of religion. But "rude" ages, he acknowledged, had advantages—candor and spontaneity—that advanced cultures tend to dissipate. Gains to reason meant losses for poetry. And the forward march of civilization is not likely to go on unchecked forever. A new barbarism may come, and some future traveler may visit what are now the monuments of Western greatness to see only their ruins.

But these were shadows in a panoramic picture essentially bright. As Macaulay insists in his *History* and often elsewhere, life, despite grievous setbacks, had improved and is improving. In the famous peroration to Chapter 3 of his *History,* Macaulay proffers this conviction in the most concentrated form. He deplores the inclination to imagine "the England of the Stuarts as a more pleasant country than the England in which we live." Nostalgia is human; it springs from mankind's "natural impatience of the state in which we actually are," which disposes us to exaggerate the happiness of bygone times. This very discontent is a source of improvement, because, "if we were perfectly satisfied with the present, we should cease to contrive, to labour, and to save with a view to the future." Yet, natural as it is, nostalgia is an illusion, a mirage. Minds have softened and matured; diseases have been extirpated and life has been lengthened; fathers, husbands, teachers, and jailers have grown far more humane; games and politics alike are infinitely less coarse under Victoria than they had been under William. Most impressive, the poor are fewer in number and better off than ever before. "Every class doubtless has gained largely by this great moral change: but the class which has gained most is the poorest, the most dependent, and the most defenceless."

Much as Macaulay loved the classics, and intimately as he knew them, he found himself in the camp of the moderns in whatever battles the ancients and moderns were still fighting. He derided the fashion of praising ancient poets simply because they were ancient, and he invidiously compared the poetry of Plato with the philosophy of Bacon. Indeed, Bacon was, in Macaulay's eyes, a decisive turning point in human history. He had created a system of thought that permitted mankind to glimpse the power of practical thought—the unlimited potential of reason, reasonably employed, to make life not just a little prettier but a great deal better. In a vast essay on Bacon—almost a book—that added up to over 50,000 words, Macaulay in 1837 rehearsed once more the benefits of true philosophy: longer life, better health, faster communications, in short, greater power over nature.

Macaulay cheerfully acknowledged the materialistic edge to this kind of appraisal. Bacon's philosophy principally benefited what cultivated men were pleased to disdain as the low side of life. It improved existence without producing—or promising—Utopia. It sustained the body, even if it did not perfect the spirit. Yet, as the essay itself testifies, Macaulay by no means underestimated the force of the spirit: after all, it was Bacon's philosophy that had fathered the scientific and industrial revolutions. But, fond as Macaulay was of the father, he was even fonder of the offspring. "The wise man of the Stoics would, no doubt, be a grander object than a steam-engine. But there are steam-engines. And the wise man of the Stoics is yet to be born." His choice of metaphor is anything but accidental; Macaulay, far from being afraid of the machine, unhesitatingly celebrates it. He recognized and welcomed the transforming power of the railway; its fatal impact on the stagecoach and its invasion of the English landscape did not give him pause. If it had harmful effects, they were consequent not upon the invention of the machine but rather upon the unregulated activities of the financiers; Macaulay spoke in behalf of governmental regulation of the railways in order to protect a national asset. Surveying the archaic English legal system, Macaulay compared it unfavorably with the industrial system—a system more modern, more aesthetically satisfying than the antique jumble of rules under which Englishmen were tried in court. "Can there be a stronger contrast," he asked rhetorically, "than that which exists between the beauty, the completeness, the speed, the precision with which every process is performed in our factories, and the awkwardness, the rudeness, the slowness, the uncertainty of the apparatus by which offenses are punished and right vindicated?" No wonder Macaulay should find the Great Exhibition of 1851 dazzling and exceedingly romantic; no wonder that Ruskin should find Macaulay naïve.

But glorious and palpable as progress was, Macaulay did not find it to be automatic. He joined the demand of the Evangelical that men should do good to the confidence of the liberal that they can do good: effort is necessary but it can be effective. It was this principled posture, rather than social origins or social ambition, that made Macaulay proudly confess himself a Whig: "I entered public life a Whig;" he told the electors at Edinburgh in 1839, "and a Whig I am determined to remain." But he immediately added that he used the name "in no narrow sense." It defined, not loyalty to a book or a favorite statesman, not even to a party for its own sake, but to a set of values that this party embodied. Arbitrary rule, corrupt politics, reli-

gious intolerance, inhumane laws were all unmitigated evils, and it was the Whigs who had, despite some regrettable lapses, opposed them all. In his characteristic vein, Macaulay enumerates the progressive posture of the Whigs for the past two centuries and more; the phrase "It was that party," uttered seven times, is the knot that securely holds the pearls of Whig policy together on a string of humane endeavor. And now, as under Elizabeth, the Stuarts, and the Hanoverians, the Whigs remain faithful to their purpose: "To the Whigs of the nineteenth century we owe it that the House of Commons has been purified. The abolition of the slave trade, the abolition of colonial slavery, the extension of popular education, the mitigation of the rigour of the penal code, all, all were effected by that party; and of that party, I repeat, I am a member." It was electioneering talk of this sort, which he blithely imported into his essays and into passages of his *History,* that moved Leslie Stephen to observe that Macaulay "was not only a thorough Whig, but pretty much convinced that all *but* Whigs were fools."

For the debater and reformer, this stance had its advantages; for the historian it presented pitfalls hard to avoid. It compelled Macaulay, much against his conscious intention, to mitigate as only human the failings of those he admired while he pilloried as detestable the failings of those he detested. His historical sympathy was by no means always dormant; on many occasions his liberal sense of justice, susceptibility to paradox, and sheer immensity of information made him notice what he might have liked to overlook. His long essay on Bacon, for one, dwells with almost painful relish on Bacon's cruelty and corruption, and excuses them not one bit. Yet often enough (to borrow an anachronistic device from Mommsen) Macaulay falls into the error of perception that the *New York Times* detected in its correspondents covering the Republican Convention of 1952, when they regularly called the managers of Eisenhower's campaign the "Eisenhower organization," and the managers of Taft's campaign the "Taft machine." The Whigs were Macaulay's Eisenhower, the Tories his Taft.

Whiggism left its tracks across the entire range of Macaulay's historical exploration. At the very time that Ranke was proclaiming the historicist principle that would oblige historians to see every epoch as equally close to God, Macaulay saw the past partly as a prologue to the present, a time to get away from and improve upon. What imperiled his historical work was not so much that he made partisan moral judgments, but that he made moral judgments at all. Yet, once again, it is important to recognize Macaulay's capacity for distance and objectivity. The past was a moral drama, and, as a drama, it was interesting for its own sake. No reader of his history can miss his noble, and often strikingly successful, efforts to transport himself to the seventeenth century, and to take his readers with him on his voyage. Again and again, Macaulay visualizes events through the eyes of the past and assesses them with its standards. "Like Macaulay's Victorian reader," one recent student of Macaulay's style has observed, "what we remember when we finish the book is the 'going back,' the displacement in time, and the re-living of events the most memorable aspects of which have little to do with the his-

tory of England's material, moral, and intellectual progress."

This testimonial to Macaulay's history-mindedness—for
displacement in time and reliving of events is precisely
that—is valuable precisely because it forms part of an indictment, from a critic convinced that Macaulay's way of
"losing himself in the past" is the product of a psychological malaise, the studied avoidance of troubling emotional
problems which Macaulay "chose not to confront." That
Macaulay was driven by demons of denial, that his style
functioned among other things as a suit of armor against
intolerable realities, is a proposition to which I have devoted much of this essay. But we cannot have it both ways:
critics used to take what they considered Macaulay's present-mindedness as a symptom of his political passions;
critics are now taking what they consider his past-
mindedness as a symptom of his fear of life. Whether
Whig or neurotic, Macaulay, it seems, cannot win. This
has been so for a long time; as far back as Gladstone, readers have taken Macaulay's style as a mirror of his defects
rather than of his virtues.

I submit that a more generous estimate is possible and
would be more just. Macaulay, I think, was right to think
of himself as something better than a professional Whig.
He was, in the largest sense of that difficult modern word,
a liberal. His parliamentary speeches, his essays, insofar
as they touch on such matters, and his ***History,*** are a volu-
ble testament to his decency. The causes he stood for and
supported with all his considerable dialectical skills—
Catholic emancipation, removal of Jewish disabilities, educational reform, intellectual liberty, and, after a time of
hesitation and self-instruction, state intervention in setting
limits to the working day—were causes characteristic for
a humane and generous-minded man. Like many liberals
in his time, Macaulay was prone to bouts of hysteria over
the threat of red socialism, but his fears did not compel
him to repudiate the causes in which he believed; they simply confirmed his earliest political impulse, to work for the
timely and far-reaching reforms that would make revolution unneccasary.

Macaulay's proverbial clarity deserves the same complex
response. It was in part a sign of superficiality, in part evidence for his inability to grasp the tragic dimension in
things, in part the didactic streak that urged him to teach
when, at least as a historian, his principal task should have
been to understand. But it was a sign also of his impatience
with cant and obfuscation, his desire to get to the bottom
at least of those things that he recognized to be deep. It
expressed the expansive energy that characterized the age
in which he lived. I am not arguing, with so many, that
the vices of Macaulay's style were his own, its virtues the
virtues of his age. In both the historian and the age, virtues
and vices were thoroughly intermingled. But that he
should have been clear, hopeful, energetic, and opulent is
scarcely vicious. His gravest sin, venial rather than mortal,
is complacency, and he had some reason even for that. We
see more deeply now than Macaulay, but then our world
is a far sadder place than his. That his style is a style as
inappropriate to our time as it was appropriate to his is a
reflection far less on his time than on ours. (pp. 97-138)

Peter Gay, "Macaulay: 'Intellectual Voluptuary'," in his Style in History, *Basic Books,
Inc., 1974, pp. 95-138.*

Froude on Macaulay as representative of his age:

'The fear of the Lord' the Hebrews declared 'to be the beginning of wisdom.' The Greeks thought that the highest
knowledge could be obtained only through pain and mortification. Macaulay never seems to have known either pain
or mortification. He succeeded in everything which he undertook; and if there be any lesson which is taught only in
the school of severity, that lesson he never learnt. A defect
of some kind there undoubtedly was in him. We admire, but
he fails deeply to interest. He rarely stirs our enthusiasm;
he never touches our deepest emotions. In the midst of his
brilliancy his writing is commonplace, though it is commonplace of the very highest kind. . . . Opinions may
change. The present century has repudiated the philosophy
of the past. The next may repudiate the present; and the
same causes which have occasioned Macaulay's unbounded
popularity in his own time may condemn him to oblivion
hereafter. Whatever changes may be before us, however, the
nineteenth century can never cease to be interesting to the
future student. Macaulay has been its most characteristic
and typical representative.

J. A. Froude, in Fraser's Magazine, *1876.*

Joseph Hamburger   (essay date 1976)

[*Hamburger is a professor of political science and coau-
thor, with Lotte Hamburger, of* Contemplating Adultery: The Secret Letters of a Victorian Woman *(1991).
In this excerpt, Hamburger states that Macaulay saw in
the political divisions of the seventeenth century a close
relationship to parties of his own day and believed in the
necessity of finding a middle way between radicals and
reactionaries.*]

A great deal is learned about a political outlook by knowing whether it hopefully cultivates aspirations for high
achievements or more modestly aims to avoid disaster—
whether it is animated by optimism and vision or by foreboding and nightmares. In Macaulay's case it was a matter
of nightmare. Despite his reputation for optimism, there
was about his thinking an atmosphere of gloom. Not that
society was without its achievements and good prospects.
But all this was vulnerable, for political skill and good
sense might not be sufficient, and passion and shortsight-
edness could well prevail.

When Macaulay looked beneath the surface to discern the
forces that shaped events, he saw two classes in postures
of mutual antipathy; these classes existed in all societies,
though the issues that divided and the purposes that motivated the contestants naturally varied. In the seventeenth
century the conflict was between religiously inspired political dissenters and the Stuarts; in his own day, between the
Radicals and the largely aristocratic ruling class. In all societies there would be established classes and those discontented with them. They threatened each other, but above

all they undermined the social order. The discontented were, or could become, rebellious: they threatened anarchy. But even more serious, in Macaulay's view, was the unyielding response of the established, privileged classes, who typically sought to suppress rebelliousness without relieving understandable grievances. Because this class instinctively wished to suppress and even persecute, it threatened tyranny. It was not a matter of choosing between them, anarchy from one, tyranny from the other, for the success of either could be only temporary. The predominance of either would always provoke a strong and effective reaction by the other, and, once this happened, a third alternative was not likely to be available; for it was the diminution of the center that made possible the prominence and the success of the extremes. (pp. 3-4)

With the benefit of hindsight that looks back on the nineteenth century as one of comparative stability, Macaulay's concern [about the growth of the Radical movement] may appear to have been somewhat fanciful. In retrospect, the governing class was, on the whole, conciliatory; even the Tories soon demonstrated a willingness to yield to popular pressure and genuine grievance, as the events of 1829 and 1846 indicate. And most of the discontented were relieved before they became totally disaffected; over the decades most potentially rebellious groups were given a sense of attachment to society. Yet in Macaulay's time a rational and sophisticated person need not have expected this outcome. Symptoms of disaffection were to be found in various places: agricultural workers burned hayricks and broke threshing machines; the beginnings of trade-union organization led to strikes, some of them violent; there had been cases of machine-breaking in factories; and even some of the middle classes, many of them not enfranchised, were organizing extraparliamentary opposition to established institutions. Furthermore, as mentioned, during Macaulay's youth, and until he was almost thirty, the government's response to these discontents was determined by the ultra-Tories: it was uncompromising and unyielding, anxious to extend and strictly enforce the law.

Macaulay interpreted contemporary developments in the light of his understanding of historical change, particularly the change that occurred during the seventeenth century. He put forth what can be called a theory of history as early as 1822 in his remarkable **"Essay on the Life and Character of King William III,"** which was awarded the Greaves Prize at Trinity College. In it he described society as simultaneously threatened by resistance bordering on rebellion and by coercion leaning to despotism. British government and society "were in a state not of amalgamation, but of conflict,—not of equilibrium but of alternate elevation and depression." As a consequence there were alternating conditions of anarchy and despotism. This situation had prevailed throughout history, and the pattern of alternating regimes during the seventeenth century was to be understood in these terms. Thus the pendulum had swung between the early Stuarts and the Puritans and parliamentary forces; then back to Charles II, who was threatened by Whig rebellion during the early 1680s; and then, with James II, back once more in the direction of despotism, which produced renewed resistance.

The nation might not reach the extreme of anarchy or despotism, but movement in the direction of either created a fear that it would continue, and it was this fear that brought about the reverse movement. Thus, in the 1680s, "civil war, anarchy, regicide were apprehended from the violence of the [Whig] opposition." Consequently "the people rallied round the throne, and seemed eager to expiate turbulence by servility." Generalizing, Macaulay noted that the friends of liberty tended to outrage moral feelings and offend worldly interests by seeking excessive vengeance for past abuses and urging too great change; the result was to "alarm the timid, disgust the good, and drive a nation to seek in slavery a refuge from commotion."

Each extreme provoked its opposite. "Anarchy in turn generated tyranny. Tyranny had now again produced resistance and revolution." In an unfortunate society there was an alternation from one condition to the other:

> Each is the cause and the effect of its antagonist. Since the first recorded origin of government they have followed each other in perpetual succession, reciprocally producing and produced. Society, when once drawn out of that happy central point in which alone it can repose, continues to oscillate between these extremes, instead of resting again in the medium.

The remedy for this condition was to establish that "central point" that provided for order without despotism and liberty without anarchy. This would be achieved by bringing the two antagonistic forces into a state of amalgamation and harmony. Those who feared despotism would have to recognize the value of order, and those who feared anarchy would have to recognize the value of liberty. William III was significant because he interrupted the cycle and took a major step toward achieving harmony.

Macaulay applied this type of analysis in his historical writing, not only about England but about France as well, and also in his diagnosis of contemporary politics. In the prize essay of 1822 it was stated as a matter of generalization that still had relevance to politics. It is not surprising, then, that Macaulay's first sustained analyses of the contemporary political situation, published in the later 1820s, were couched in the same terms.

In these later essays he again saw the most important political struggle as taking place between the government—and particularly the Tory party, representing the privileged, landed class—and what he called the lower orders, for whom the Radical politicians were the spokesmen. Ignoring the conventional contests between Government and Opposition, Tories and Whigs, Macaulay thought that "the history of our country, since the peace of 1815, is almost entirely made up of the struggles of the lower orders against the government, and of the efforts of the government to keep them down." Both were extreme parties. Those among the lower orders "who have any opinions at all are democrats already," i.e., Radicals. In addition, there was a "Republican sect"—what might be called a Radical intelligentsia—that was antitraditional, zealous, and arrogant. Analogous to the Puritans and Jacobins, these men, who were educated and from the middle class, could provide the leadership to a growing Radical Movement. On the other side, the government also adopted an extreme position, as the suspension of habeas corpus and the antisedition laws made clear. From the one side there was suppression; from the other, hostility and the threat of rebellion.

If a conflict between these extreme parties occurred, it would be the consequence of unyielding Tory policy provoking those with grievances into a revolutionary posture. The working classes normally lived at a marginal level of existence; thus the vast body of laborers and artisans usually had legitimate grievances arising out of distress and privation. They were also prone to be radical because "it is on persons in this station that the abuses of our system press most heavily; while its advantages, on the other hand, are comparatively little felt by them." Already inclined to radicalism, in this situation they could easily become openly hostile. A Tory government could not exist for one year "without incensing the lower classes of the English to frenzy, by giving them up to the selfish tyranny of its aristocratical supporters." It would not be too much to say of the working classes "that in a season of distress, they are ripe for any revolution."

The revolutionary opposition to the Tory government would include the middle class as well, for it too would be provoked into a revolutionary posture. Normally the middle class had an interest in moderation and an inclination to it as well. Without endorsing Radicalism, it looked for improvements; and without being blindly loyal, it had a stake in the prevailing institutions. But its moderation could not be counted on. If its growing desire to see the removal of faults in the system were disappointed, the middle class would be made more radical. They would enter into an alliance with the working classes, placing "at the head of the multitude persons possessing all the education, all the judgement, and all the habits of co-operation, in which the multitude itself is deficient." Then the Radical intelligentsia would take on greater importance, and a potentially large and numerous revolutionary party would appear. Something like this had begun to emerge at the time of the queen's trial in 1820, and it would take place again if the Tories (that is, the non-Canningite Tories) returned to office. Committed, as Macaulay saw them, to a policy of suppression and opposed to change, they "would goad every Reformer in the country into a Revolutionist" and make an alliance between middling and lower orders inevitable.

Macaulay's fear was not the conventional fear of a revolution in which the masses overwhelm the governing and propertied classes. Of course he had the conventional picture of radicalism as a kind of anarchy, and he feared its spread among the angry working classes. But he had an equally frightening view of the extreme opposition to it as a kind of despotism, and he saw evidence of this in the willingness of the government to suppress radicalism. One side was angry; the other was afraid and had great strength. What Macaulay feared was that antagonism between two powerful and determined groups—a powerful extraparliamentary opposition, dominated by doctrinaire Radicals, and the government, dominated by the ultra-Tories—would cause the political process to be monopo-

lized by impassioned spokesmen for extreme views; there would be "an insolent oligarchy on the one side and infuriated people on the other." At the end of this road there was the nightmare of civil war.

Macaulay's observation of political conflict in the post-Waterloo period led him to believe that the situation threatened to take on some of the characteristics that prevailed in the seventeenth century, and this perception was reinforced by his belief that there was a tendency in all societies to develop in this way. This is the context of Macaulay's rationale for reform and for his defense of the Canning coalition government in 1827. By putting the ultra-Tories into opposition, the Canning coalition would prevent the radicalization of middle-class reformers and the incensing of the working classes, and it would keep at bay the threat of an alliance between middle and working classes. It in fact caused a split in the Tory party. Thus Canning's success would isolate both extremes—Tories and Radicals—and prevent their growth. At the same time, the coalition government was expected to take measured steps toward commercial reform and Catholic emancipation. This gave hope that the middle classes would remain moderate and that the center would be maintained.

This hope was short-lived, since the Canningite government lasted for so brief a period. With the return of the ultra-Tories under Wellington, Macaulay again felt that the greatest problem was the push to the extremes. He feared a retreat from the center by those who admired either rebellion or oppression but nothing between. There were those who "cannot be a friend to liberty without calling for a community of goods, or a friend to order without taking under [their] protection the foulest excesses of tyranny." And again, "There are those who will be contented with nothing but demolition; and there are those who shrink from all repair. There are innovators who long for a President and a National Convention; and there are bigots." The alternative was to find a government that would reconcile antagonists and judiciously reform the system of representation. Such a policy, "by so widening the base of the government as to interest in its defence the whole of the middling class . . . [would] succeed in averting a struggle to which no rational friend of liberty or of law can look forward without great apprehensions."

Meanwhile Macaulay felt apprehensive, for during the late 1820s, with the ultra-Tories dominant and the Whigs still in opposition (not having been in office for a generation, except for their meager participation in the short-lived Canningite governments), conflict between an insensitive and even oppressive government and a discontented and rebellious people appeared to be increasingly likely:

> Already we seem to ourselves to perceive the signs of unquiet times, the vague presentiment of something great and strange which pervades the community; the restless and turbid hopes of those who have every thing to gain, the dimly-hinted forebodings of those who have every thing to lose. Many indications might be mentioned, in themselves indeed as insignificant as straws; but even the direction of a straw, to bor-

row the illustration of Bacon, will show from what quarter the hurricane is setting in.

This was the mood with which he faced the Reform Bill agitation, and it was the expectation of this kind of conflict that shaped his interpretation of the constitutional crisis of 1831-32.

In his nightmare of civil conflict Macaulay pictured the antagonists in the postures that characterized the religious conflicts of the seventeenth century. There would be two extreme antagonists—the visionaries and the defenders. On the one side were enthusiasm and zeal, which created in the discontented both unrealistic expectations and destructive wishes. On the other side, among the defenders of order, there were dogmatism and fear, which made them unwilling to allow changes. Religion provided the model of the sectarian zealot who manipulated mass passions, thereby giving reality to the threat of anarchy and revolution. And it also provided an example of the misguided, unyielding defender of order who persecutes and suppresses, thereby helping to undermine what he would defend. Religion also provided the model for the way these two types of antagonists would engage each other. Doctrinaire, dogmatically assured, and hostile, they would be uncompromising in battle, bitter in defeat, and without mercy when victorious. These ingredients would create the pattern of historical change outlined in 1822.

When Macaulay encountered immoderate Radicalism, with its sweeping criticisms of established arrangements and its utopian standards of judgment, he understood it in the context of religious radicalism. The religious enthusiasts had bred political Radicalism; and he thought that the secular political Radicals of his own time called on passions that had a religious dimension. Both encouraged discontent, criticism, and, in the end, separatism and rebellion, and Macaulay used such terms as "zealot," "demagogue," "sectarian," and "enthusiast" interchangeably for both.

Because their religious outlook had political implications, the Puritans, especially during the reign of Charles I and the Civil War, typified the religionists on whom Macaulay based his image of all other radicals. The Independents, the root-and-branch men, were, "to use the kindred phrase of our own time, radicals." Encouraging men to seek guidance directly from the deity, the Puritans undermined other institutions besides the church; they were opposed to established churches, but they tended to be antiauthoritarian in politics as well. Religious fanaticism became political and thereby threatened the established order. Solely concerned with their relation to the deity, the Puritans felt "contempt for terrestrial distinctions. The difference between the greatest and meanest of mankind seemed to vanish, when compared with the boundless interval which separated the whole race from him on whom their own eyes were constantly fixed." In the political realm, although the Puritan "prostrated himself in the dust before his Maker . . . he set his foot on the neck of his king." The religious zeal of these fanatics was the source of their single-mindedness and immutable purpose in debate and in battle.

Against this background, it is noteworthy that Macaulay

thought of the disciples of Jeremy Bentham and James Mill—the so-called Philosophic Radicals—as playing a role comparable to the Puritans' in the mid-seventeenth century:

> Even now [1827], it is impossible to disguise, that there is arising in the bosom of [the middle class] a Republican sect, as audacious, as paradoxical, as little inclined to respect antiquity, as enthusiastically attached to its ends, as unscrupulous in the choice of its means, as the French Jacobins. . . . Metaphysical and political science engage their whole attention. Philosophical pride has done for them what spiritual pride did for the Puritans in a former age; it has generated in them an aversion for the fine arts, for elegant literature, and for the sentiments of chivalry. It has made them arrogant, intolerant, and impatient of all superiority. These qualities will, in spite of their real claims to respect, render them unpopular, as long as people are satisfied with their rulers. But under an ignorant and tyrannical ministry . . . their principles would spread as rapidly as those of the Puritans formerly spread, in spite of their offensive peculiarities.

Of course Macaulay was aware of the differences. But when he thought of the way in which the Radical intelligentsia of his day might lead the combined middle and working classes in revolution, he pictured its leaders as being like the Puritans.

Turning to the other side, he saw the defenders of the established order as tradition-bound and rigid, insisting on maintaining particular institutional forms instead of looking beyond the forms to the purposes that might be compatible with a variety of institutional arrangements. Uncompromising and determined to maintain society as it was, they were willing to persecute and suppress in order to stamp out any demand for change. In Macaulay's view, they were bound to be ineffective, for such methods provoked without eliminating demands; indeed, instead of eliminating the enemy, they strengthened him. The typical spokesman for this outlook was Laud, and he was assimilated, in Macaulay's mind, to the Tories. Like him, they wished to preserve and to do so by suppressing anyone who challenged existing arrangements; like him, they were dogmatic, intolerant, and unyielding. Macaulay saw the Tory prosecutions of the press and their restrictions on expression of grievances during the post-Waterloo years as comparable, at least in intention and rationale, to Laud's persecution of the Puritans. To Macaulay, Laud was the archetypical Tory, and contemporary Tories were modern-day Lauds.

With Laud and the Puritans as prototypes of Tories and Radicals, the earlier struggle became the model for Macaulay's nightmare of civil war in the nineteenth century. The parallel did not depend on the survival of intense religious feeling. Macaulay was aware of the progress of secularization and of course welcomed it. Yet he assumed that destructive conflict would continue to be a problem, for it arose from circumstances that were ubiquitous. When institutions violated the prevailing sense of justice and ceased to satisfy needs, governing establishments would become the object of distrust and anger, and the established classes would become fearful and vindictive. This could take place in connection with issues of economic policy and party politics, just as it had in the seventeenth century, in connection with religious and constitututional questions. There would be zeal, distrust, and hostility over questions of economics and class, just as there had been over religion. There would be enthusiasm and exclusiveness; and there would be dogmatism and intolerance. There would be rejection of established institutions; and there would be rigid defenses of them. With both visionary critics and orthodox defenders of the social order in mind, Macaulay was sensitive to the way that class differences in his own time could develop into conflict similar to that of the seventeenth century. Thus his descriptions of Lord Eldon and Laud were interchangeable; and his image of the fanatic was the same, whether he had a militant Puritan or a Jacobin or certain contemporary Radicals in mind.

Macaulay's preoccupation with civil conflict, and his belief that it originated in the mutual hostility of fanatical spokesmen at the extremes, affected his attitude to religion. When combined with fear, anger, and discontents, religion encouraged men to be immoderate and pushed them to extremes. It then became, in Macaulay's eyes, fanaticism, indeed, a sort of madness. It was not Augustan tastes that led him to disapprove of religious enthusiasm; much more emphatically, it was his observation that intense religion caused men to conduct themselves in ways that were politically undesirable. He regarded those possessed by it as having a disease. If the disease became epidemic, it was awesome, for it had the strength to convulse nations, cause revolutions, and sustain fierce wars—including civil wars. On the other hand, if intense religiosity did not exist, there would be a better chance that fear and anger would be reduced and discontents relieved by adjustments made through the political process. Then the political realm would be uncontaminated by aspirations and enmities associated with religion, and politics could be practiced without the distorting effects of utopian desires for change and romantic dreams of restoration. Politicians could then debate, adjust, compromise. With religion kept moderate, conciliatory politics would become possible. But if it became extreme, religion was a source of conflict and an obstacle to conciliation.

It was not religion as such, but religious fervor that Macaulay opposed. Tepid, conventional religion was acceptable, for it was useful to society. It restrained appetites, consoled those in want and calamity, allowed one to go to the grave without despair, and was "the restraint of those who are placed above all earthly fears." Thus he defended the Church of England for serving these purposes and for being a bulwark against fanaticism. He was also critical of those who were immoderately antireligious in public. Voltaire's "hatred of Xtnty is positively a disease." He disapproved of the poet Thomas Campbell as "the only man whom I ever heard talk against Christianity boisterously and indecently in a large mixed company," adding, however, with evident gratification, that no one answered him.

Observing a connection between religious extremism and civil conflict, Macaulay in his historical writings was se-

vere on those who displayed intense religiosity. Bunyan and Fox and many others he described as being bizarre and sometimes dangerous. Contemporary manifestations of religiosity, whether appearing among the prominent or the obscure, he treated with disdain and ridicule. Although lacking the potential for great consequence that he associated with religion in the seventeenth century, intense religion in his own time seemed to remind him of past threats to the political order. The examples are innumerable. There are unsympathetic references to Joanna Southcote, Quakers, and Muggletonians. His *Journals* record the visit of "a mad Swedenborgian" who pestered him with "his grievances and his revelations." Even when he recalled the Evangelical preacher Buchanan, whom he admired, he could not help mentioning that his many fine qualities were combined "with a little or rather not a little fanfaronade and humbug." The Methodists elicited the same reaction. "The controversialists [among them] . . . are so absurd and malignant that one is always against the last speaker." Although these judgments may have reflected Macaulay's personal religious outlook, they were also consistent with the political criteria with which he evaluated religion. Thus, while religiosity rarely failed to elicit his disdain, neither did it fail to excite his sense of danger.

His depreciatory comments were especially directed at anything Puritanical. He visualized a Puritan household at the time of the Restoration as one in which there were "Geneva bands, heads of lank hair, upturned eyes, nasal psalmody, and sermons three hours long." Apart from being distasteful, such an austere environment was self-defeating, because it might send forth one who would become the greatest rake of his time, one whose dissoluteness would make the most dissolute Cavalier stand aghast. A favorite Macaulay bugbear was Exeter Hall, which was associated with enthusiastic religious movements. It was his reference to the "bray" of Exeter Hall during the debate on the Maynooth grant that caused outrage, especially among some of his Edinburgh constituents. He was equally affronted by assertive Catholicism. He found the Puseyites annoying; Tract Ninety was "the quintessence of Jesuitism." He confessed feeling "the same disgust at the Anglo Catholic and Roman Catholic cants which people after the Restoration felt for the Puritan cant"; and he wrote, "I hate Puseyites and Puritans impartially." Macaulay knew that the power of religion was diminishing in the face of science and reason, but religious extremists in his own time symbolized the fanaticism that would always be a problem, and they reminded him of the way that visionaries, by working on the discontented, can bring nations nearer to civil war.

It was his refusal to participate in the strong sectarian feelings of his constituents that led to his only experience of electoral defeat. In 1845 he supported the Conservative proposal to make a modest government grant to Maynooth, a Catholic college in Ireland. A large body of his constituents turned against him. Feelings ran high, and at his election meetings in 1847 he was frequently interrupted with hisses and groans. He had served as Member for Edinburgh since 1839 and had been reelected twice, but now he was defeated, an experience that must have given personal meaning to his observation about Catholic emancipation: that "it proved far less easy to eradicate evil passions than to repeal evil laws." Long after this defeat, during another encounter with militant Protestant feeling in Edinburgh, he commented on "the excessive malignity and unreasonableness of the voluntaries. I have no particular love for establishments and priests," he said, "but the rancour of these men disgusts me." In a different context, but probably with these events in mind, Macaulay wrote about "the bigotry of the schismatics who domineered in the north," and he criticized a seventeenth-century Scottish politician (Melville) for having shrunk "from uttering a word so hateful to the theological demagogues of his country as Toleration."

These views about the political uses and the potentially dangerous consequences of religion are not inconsistent with what is known about Macaulay's personal religious beliefs. It is difficult to be certain about them, for he was reticent and guarded. When asked on the hustings, he professed belief in Christianity in tepid and conventional language. He sometimes attended church, believing that one should pay a decent respect to forms. In the same spirit, and from prudence and in deference to his father as well, he restrained in public his powerful impulse to ridicule religiosity; but behind this conventional posture Macaulay's real views were almost certainly more skeptical and irreverent, although they must have varied over the years. One finds him engaged in a debunking skepticism and enjoying mildly blasphemous verse, which suggests that he shared the doubts of his "advanced" contemporaries. One may even speculate that he had himself in mind when he noted that "in every age there are many concealed atheists who keep their opinions to themselves." If he did, such moments must have been few; but there were many others when his observation about the typical Roman Catholic country gentleman of the seventeenth century was applicable to him: "he held his hereditary faith, as men generally hold a hereditary faith, sincerely, but with little enthusiasm." The frequency of such possibly autobiographically inspired observations suggests that Macaulay was without strong religious commitment. Gladstone sensed this, for in commenting on Macaulay's religious views he concluded that "there are passages which suggest a doubt whether he had completely wrought the Christian dogma, with all its lessons and all its consolations, into the texture of his mind" [*Gleanings*]. Living at a time when many educated contemporaries bravely faced challenges to their religious beliefs and suffered agonies of doubt, Macaulay does not appear to have shared such experiences. He recognized the reality of strong religious feeling in others, but he could not quite believe in its necessity. Applied to the context of his own time, his observation on Shakespeare's religious creed appears relevant. Shakespeare, Macaulay thought, "was probably rather floating between, as the mass of a nation will do during some great national change of faith." Situated somewhere between conventional views and the agnosticism that was to become frequent later in the century—and perhaps nearer to the latter—Macaulay too seems to have faced change by "floating between."

His readiness to be irritated by religiosity may have been related to his exposure to it among his own family. His father, Zachary Macaulay, was an active and prominent member of the Evangelical group associated with Clapham, and his mother came from a Quaker family. The piety and intense religious commitment of the Clapham side seems to have predominated during Macaulay's youth. It was carried so far as to discourage the reading of novels, but this did not prevent Macaulay from becoming an avid reader of fiction, including what he admitted to be "trash." His father apparently had hoped that he would devote himself to the church and take orders. As an adult he certainly recalled the words, the atmosphere, and the sayings of some of the prominent members of the group. The Clapham sect, as it came to be known, proselytized vigorously. It was responsible for such organizations as the Sunday School Society, the Religious Tract Society, the Church Missionary Society, and the British and Foreign Bible Society. It also tried to spread the influence of Christian principles, both within the Anglican community and in the wider social realm as well. This was evident in the Society for the Reformation of Manners and in the influential Anti-Slavery Society. Macaulay's father, in addition to playing a leading role in the antislavery movement, was editor of the *Christian Observer,* an evangelical periodical heavily laden with theological discussion, sermons (many of them composed by Zachary), reviews of religious books, biographical sketches of religious figures, reports on organizations in which the Evangelicals were interested, and comments on manners and customs in the light of a religious understanding. The contents of the *Christian Observer* provide a clue to the spirit in which Macaulay's family life was conducted.

Macaulay reacted against most of this. In addition, although less important, his mother's Quaker connection should be kept in mind, not only when one is considering his personal antipathy to the Quakers and his harsh historical judgments of them, but also as one tries to understand his reaction to religiosity. Given his mixed religious background, his observation on Sir William Temple appears to have autobiographical significance. Temple, he said, was one "who had been disgusted by the morose austerity of the Puritans, and who, surrounded from childhood by the hubbub of conflicting sects, might easily learn to feel an impartial contempt for them all."

The Evangelical background, in addition to its religious emphasis, included a political theme that had great significance for Macaulay. Zachary and most of the other prominent Evangelicals were not orthodox Tories; yet, despite their renowned humanitarianism, they exemplified that part of Macaulay's image of the Tory as one who repressed and persecuted. In 1802 the Evangelicals founded the Society for the Suppression of Vice, and Zachary was "an active member," serving on its executive committee and soliciting funds for it. The Society was part of the reaction to the French Revolution. Noting "that a general disrespect prevails for authority," and holding that "without the security of laws, the corrupt propensities of man could not be restrained, nor moral order and human society exist," it defined its object as being "to assist the state in the preservation of moral and religious order." Among its methods was the initiation of prosecutions (which the law allowed, even though it was a private body), including prosecutions for blasphemous libel. Many Radical editors, publishers, and vendors faced this charge, though it was their politics, as well as their irreligion, that was often the target. Although the Society thought of itself as avoiding the political realm and did not initiate prosecutions for sedition, its prosecutions for blasphemous libel had a political dimension, since those prosecuted—men like Carlile and Davidson—were Radicals and had political purposes in publishing the religious doctrines that made them vulnerable to prosecution. In 1819, for example, Richard Carlile faced a prosecution initiated by the Society; Carlile was guilty of the "foulest sedition, and the most horrible blasphemy," according to Zachary.

Despite his genuine concern about economic distress, Zachary was nervous about the breakdown of social order, and he wanted the government to be even more vigorous in its prosecution policy. He thought the ignited state of Manchester was due largely to "the criminal supineness of the Government in not having more vigilantly laboured to repress the host of seditious writers, the *Black Dwarfs, Medusas, Deists, Observers* [all Radical journals], (not meaning, of course, one [*Christian*] *Observer*), which have been so industriously exciting the evils which now threaten to overwhelm the country." He wanted the government to do nothing less than to accomplish "the radical extirpation of these grand germinal movers of sedition and rebellion." He defended the Peterloo magistrates and approved of the Six Acts. After the Peterloo trials, Zachary said, "We are congratulating ourselves on the conviction of Burdett and Hunt." Young Macaulay, when he portrayed the imprudent Tory policy that could provoke revolution, had attitudes like these in mind.

Macaulay's rejection of Evangelicalism, far from being simply a matter of theological differences or personal uncongeniality, was directly connected with his evaluation of religion in political terms. He could see two politically relevant dangers in Evangelicalism. First, his fear that religion could too easily become enthusiastic and fanatical made him unsympathetic to any movement devoted to stimulating religiosity. Second, and much more important, Macaulay could not approve his father's eagerness to suppress political radicalism nor the Evangelicals' initiative in such matters. Indeed, in the light of Macaulay's understanding of the twin dangers to constitutional stability, Zachary and the Evangelicals were particularly objectionable, for they seemed to combine a touch of both the fanatical enthusiasm of the Puritans and Laud's inclination to persecute.

Alert to the "religious" dimension of politics, and having adopted categories of analysis derived both from the history of religious and political conflict, particularly of the seventeenth century, and from the literature of antiquity, as evidenced in the prize essay of 1822, Macaulay began his political career (and his preparations for his career as a historian) with the assumption that the most important political task was to control the inevitable centrifugal tendencies that made destructive civil conflict a real possibility. Because his political orientation had these origins, his historical writings were intimately connected with his responses to contemporary politics. Indeed, when he first wrote (in 1822) about the problem of civil conflict in the

seventeenth century, Macaulay observed that "at the present period [it] suggests reflections peculiarly solemn and important." (pp. 5-20)

> *Joseph Hamburger, in his* Macaulay and the Whig Tradition, *The University of Chicago Press, 1976, 274 p.*

Gertrude Himmelfarb   (essay date 1982)

[*A specialist in the study of Victorian thought, Himmelfarb has written numerous articles and books, including* Victorian Minds: Essays on Nineteenth Century Intellectuals (*1968*) *and* Poverty and Compassion: The Moral Imagination of the Late Victorians (*1991*). *In the following essay, she discusses Macaulay in the context of trends in historiography, maintaining that Macaulay's sense of intimacy with the past is a source of strength, not weakness, and his emphasis on political events is refreshing in light of modern social history.*]

"Who now reads Bolingbroke?" Burke asked, thus casually, irrevocably, consigning him to the ash-heap of history. So the modern historian may be tempted to ask, "Who now reads Macaulay?" Who, that is, except those who have a professional stake in him—professional in a very special sense, not historians who might be expected to have an interest in one of their most illustrious predecessors, but only those who happen to be writing treatises or monographs on him. In fact, most professional historians have long since given up reading Macaulay, as they have given up writing the kind of history Macaulay wrote.

Yet there was a time when anyone with any pretension to cultivation read Macaulay. It is often said that he was so widely read because he was so brilliant a stylist, so readable. This should not be taken to mean that he was easy to read, a "good read," as the English say. Even his essays were formidable—fifty-page disquisitions on Nugent's Memorials of Hampden or Mahon's War of the Succession, or the controversial hundred-and-twenty-page essay on Bacon. More popular and more formidable still were the five volumes of the *History of England from the Accession of James II,* some 2,500 pages covering fifteen years. Nor was it only the leisured classes who read the *History* (or, as one might suspect, bought and bound it for display on their shelves). The lending libraries did a thriving trade in it. Mudie's, the largest of the lending libraries, bought over two thousand copies of the volumes as they appeared, and business was so brisk that they had to set aside a special room to handle them. A gentleman living on the outskirts of Manchester invited his poorer neighbors to his house every evening after work and read the entire *History* aloud to them. At the end of the last reading one of them rose and moved a vote of thanks to the author "for having written a history which working men can understand," a motion the gentleman dutifully reported to Macaulay.

Today it is all one can do to get a graduate student in history to read, let alone understand, Macaulay. If the *History* is, as is commonly thought, a paean to progress, the history of the *History* is a sad testimonial to the cultural regression of our own times. Macaulay was pleased to think of his work as in a direct line of descent from Thucydides's *History of the Peloponnesian Wars;* he admitted that his was far inferior to that greatest of all histories, but it aspired to the same standard of greatness. He also privately confessed that he had been sustained, through all his years of research and writing, by the hope that his work would be remembered in the year 2000 or even 3000—not as arrogant a thought as it might seem considering the fact that Thucydides survived considerably longer than that. That remark was quoted in 1959, the centenary of his death, by a commentator who thought it safe to predict that Macaulay would indeed be read half a century hence, "if there are any readers left." It is not clear whether that ominous proviso referred to a nuclear holocaust or simply to the death of the written word as the result of television or a debased mass culture. What was not anticipated was that professional historians would turn against Macaulay, making him seem as unreadable and unmemorable as Bolingbroke.

In *A Liberal Descent: Victorian Historians and the English Past,* John Burrow makes a valiant attempt to revive our interest in Macaulay and three other historians of a later generation, William Stubbs, Edward Freeman, and James Anthony Froude. His account is sensitive, sympathetic, thoughtful; if one has any criticism it is that he makes too modest a claim on our attention. For he invites us to consider these historians not so much as historians of England recording momentous events in the past—Macaulay on the English Revolution, Stubbs on the "ancient constitution," Freeman on the Norman Conquest, Froude on the Reformation—but as Victorians reflecting in their histories ideas and attitudes peculiar to their own times. *A Liberal Descent,* we are told, "is intended as a study in Victorian culture and intellectual history based on the premise that one of the ways in which a society reveals itself, and its assumptions and beliefs about its own character and destiny, is by its attitudes to and uses of its past." This is surely not what Macaulay had in mind when he hoped to be read in centuries to come—as a specimen of Victorian culture rather than as an historian of the Glorious Revolution. Yet he and the others could hardly complain, since they themselves insisted, as Burrow amply demonstrates, on the "continuity of the past," the relevance of their subjects and their works to their own times.

Burrow himself is sympathetic to that idea of continuity, and it is almost ruefully that he announces a break in continuity between the Victorians and ourselves. His book has a pervasively elegiac tone, testifying to a kind of history, and the culture that produced that history, which is over and done with, which we can only understand and enjoy in its "remoteness." Macaulay, possibly even Stubbs, Burrow suspects, may continue to be read, but for the most part the great Victorian histories are the "triumphal arches of a past empire, their vaunting inscriptions increasingly unintelligible to the modern inhabitants"—monuments occasionally visited, he adds (in an uncharacteristically brutal expression, revealing a bitterness he does not normally allow himself), "as a *pissoir,* a species of visit naturally brief."

Burrow does not elaborate upon the reasons for this break

in continuity, tantalizingly stopping short of those recent tendencies in historiography, like social history or the "new history," which would help explain it. But we must be grateful to him for rescuing "Whig history" from the odium that has enveloped it for half a century. In his famous *Whig Interpretation of History,* first published in 1931, Herbert Butterfield discredited the kind of history he associated with the Whigs, a history that distorts the past by reading it in terms of the present, that looks to the past for the origins and development of those institutions, traditions, and principles which the present deems notable and admirable, that judges the past by the standards of the present, and that makes of the past a battleground between the forces of light and darkness. For the classic Whig historian—Macaulay—history is the gradual, inevitable progress of political and religious liberty and constitutional, representative government. For the radical or Marxist historian it is the progress of democracy, equality, and socialism. In either case the integrity of the past is violated by the imposition of a specious pattern of progress and an anachronistic set of ideas.

Butterfield's book was a valuable corrective to the reductivist, determinist mode of history which belittles or obscures the complexities, contingencies, and discontinuities of the past, all those aspects of the past which were unique to it, which made it radically different from, rather than vaguely reminiscent of, the present. But the attempt to dissociate the past completely from the present, to counter a too intrusive "present-mindeness" with a too austere "past-mindeness," also has its perils, for it precludes, as Butterfield himself recognized, anything but the most antiquarian or narrowly monographic history. Burrow alludes to but does not dwell on Butterfield's thesis (except to remind us that Butterfield himself, in *The Englishman and his History,* written during the war, confessed his satisfaction with the Whig view of history, which had had such benign political consequences for England). But Burrow implicitly restores the balance in favor of Whig history by considering, seriously and respectfully, what it was that Macaulay and the others celebrated in the past, what of the past they wanted to revivify, and what of the present they wanted to legitimize by establishing its continuity with the past.

Burrow subtly shifts the grounds of the argument by changing the terms of discourse from the "Whig tradition" to the "liberal descent" of the title. The expression is Burke's.

> Always acting as if in the presence of canonized forefathers, the spirit of freedom, leading in itself to misrule and excess, is tempered with an awful gravity. This idea of a liberal descent inspires us with a sense of habitual native dignity, which prevents that upstart insolence almost inevitably adhering to and disgracing those who are the first acquirers of any distinction.

One wishes Burrow had also quoted the preceding sentence, in which Burke urges us to look upon "our liberties in the light of an inheritance," or the earlier paragraph which makes the point more sharply:

> The idea of inheritance furnishes a sure principle

of conservation, and a sure principle of transmission; without at all excluding a principle of improvement. It leaves acquisition free; but it secures what it acquires. . . . By a constitutional policy, working after the pattern of nature, we receive, we hold, we transmit our government and privileges, in the same manner in which we enjoy and transmit our property and our lives.

The Burkean idea of the "inheritance" of liberty is more compelling than the familiar idea of the "progress" of liberty. "Progress" says nothing about the mechanism by which liberty advances, nothing about the means by which the past evolves into the present; it only asserts that there is such an evolution, as if it were foreordained, inherent in the nature of man and history. It might even be the kind of "metaphysical" principle Burke so abhorred. The "inheritance" of liberty, on the analogy of the inheritance of property, is more concrete and substantive. It suggests the several stages through which liberty, like property, passes: the original act of acquisition, the protection of that acquisition, the acquisition of additional liberty (or liberties—the plural is more appropriate to this metaphor), and the transmission of what has been so laboriously acquired and preserved. It also suggests, as the idea of progress does not, that what has been acquired can be lost or taken away, in whole or in part (again the plural form is more fitting). Far from being assured by some providential order, liberty in this image is seen as vulnerable and precarious, in need of all the laws, institutions, conventions, and principles which encourage its acquisition and transmission.

Burrow assimilates Macaulay into the "Burkean tradition," and there is much to justify this. It might have been Burke writing that magnificent passage in the *History*: "As our Revolution was a vindication of ancient rights, so it was conducted with strict attention to ancient formalities. . . . When at length the dispute had been accommodated, the new sovereigns were proclaimed with the old pageantry." Yet Macaulay was an imperfect Burkean, more of a "trimmer," a compromiser and conciliator, as Joseph Hamburger has argued, than a Whig. (It is revealing that Macaulay twice contemplated writing about Burke and twice abandoned the project, once after being well into it; that missing essay is a conspicuous gap in his corpus.) Burke's reverence for tradition, history, established institutions, and conventions was rooted in a theory of natural law: "the great primeval contract of eternal society, linking the lower with the higher natures, connecting the visible and invisible world, according to a fixed compact sanctioned by the inviolable oath which holds all physical and moral natures, each in their appointed place." For Burke expediency, compromise, prudence, and the pragmatic accommodation to "circumstances" were the means, not the ends, of policy. For Macaulay, lacking any such commitment to natural law, they were the ends, the only principles of government.

Macaulay was not even comfortable, as Burrow points out, with the idea of the "ancient constitution," although he sometimes invoked it for rhetorical and polemical purposes. The ancient constitution had for him the double liability of being reactionary and revolutionary: reactionary

in not acknowledging the debt liberty owed to modernity, revolutionary in threatening to subvert the distinctive institutions of modernity—the monarchy, most notably—by appealing to the ancient ideal of a republic. In the battle of the ancients and moderns, Macaulay was unequivocally on the side of the moderns. (His *Lays of Ancient Rome* Burrow dismisses as a *jeu d'esprit*.) Liberty, he maintained, was not ancient; it was peculiarly modern. "In almost all the little commonwealths of antiquity, liberty was used as a pretext for measures directed against everything that makes liberty valuable." It was England, not Greece or Rome, that gave birth to the traditions he cherished.

> Senate has not to our ears a sound so venerable as Parliament. We respect the Great Charter more than the laws of Solon. The Capitol and the Forum impress us with less awe than our own Westminster Hall and Westminster Abbey. . . . Our liberty is neither Greek nor Roman; but essentially English. It has a character of its own—a character which has taken a tinge from the sentiments of the chivalrous ages, and which accords with the peculiarities of our manners and of our insular situation. It has a language, too, of its own, and a language so singularly idiosyncratic, full of meaning to ourselves, scarcely intelligible to strangers.

For all their difference, however, Macaulay and Burke belonged to a common tradition, that "liberal descent" which both took to be the glory of England. (pp. 41-4)

And in treating respectfully their common commitment to the "continuity of the past" [Burrow] is also implicitly suggesting that the "Whig interpretation" is not necessarily the fallacy Butterfield made of it. For the Victorians, he points out, it was more often the past that informed the present than the reverse ("We are Cavaliers or Roundheads," William Lecky said, "before we are Conservatives or Liberals"). And in Burrow's account their sense of an intimate relationship between past and present becomes a source of strength rather than weakness—of imagination, passion, and sheer force of mind.

This is an important message to derive from the Victorians. But another message emerges when we contrast them to our own culture and the current mode of historical writing. The Victorian historian could take for granted what we no longer can: not only the continuity of past and present but the political nature of that continuity. Whatever period he traced his descent from, the principles he identified with that period were essentially political; and those principles were transmitted by way of political institutions and traditions. To Burrow, taking his stance with the Victorian historian and Victorian culture, this is so obvious it needs no saying. Today, however, with social history displacing political history as the primary mode of historical scholarship, one can appreciate how crucial that political dimension was both to Victorian history and to Victorian culture—indeed, to the very idea of a continuity between history and culture.

Historians have always written social history, in some form and to some degree. The famous third chapter of Macaulay's *History,* on the state of England in 1685, covers many of the subjects that are now the preoccupation of the social historian: population, agriculture, mining, the growth of towns and of London, modes of travel, inns, coffee houses, newspapers, books, science, the arts, the various social classes, the "common people," child labor, pauperism, wages, the standard of living. But this is only one of six chapters of the first volume of the *History.* Moreover, as Jacques Barzun has pointed out, it appears in the middle of the volume, not at the beginning or end as one might expect; the political narrative is already well under way by the time it begins, so that this chapter is a static interlude in an otherwise dramatic tale. The current mode of social history, the "new history," is far more ambitious, laying claim if not to all of history, as some social historians would like ("total history," as it is called), at least to the dominant, determinant part of history. Even subjects that look political, the staples of the old history—a parliamentary reform act, for example—are "socialized" by the new historians, analyzed in terms not of parliamentary debates or constitutional changes but of social classes and economic interests. More often the subjects themselves are unpolitical: the family, popular culture, social mobility, work, leisure, sex, death, crime, insanity.

This is not to say that social history does not have political implications. It most certainly does, and more blatantly than conventional political history. The most popular kind of social history is the most populist kind: the much vaunted "history from below," the history of the "anonymous masses," of those people who led lives so ordinary that they never made the pages of history, never emerged from the obscurity of their anonymity. Historians now vie with each other in plumbing the depths of that "history from below," in rescuing from oblivion one submerged group after another: working men, women, and children, racial and ethnic minorities, and the "outcasts" of society—deviants, criminals, the insane. One of the latest examples of this genre is *A Mad People's History of Madness,* consisting of extracts from writings by the mad ranging from the medieval mystic Margery Kempe to the modern novelist Mark Vonnegut. Hailed by one reviewer as a "welcome contribution to history from below," it will no doubt soon be faulted for being insufficiently "from below," including as it does such eminences as Kempe and Vonnegut rather than the lowly, anonymous inhabitants of Bedlam and Bellevue.

In contrast to this new form of social history (and such other modes of the "new history" as psychoanalytic or quantified history), Victorian history was insistently political. The Victorians shared, not only with each other but with their predecessors going back to Herodotus and Thucydides, an essentially political conception of both the past and the present. They assumed that the polity—some kind of polity, ancient or modern, folk or state, Whig or Tory, national or imperial—was the bearer of that tradition (or inheritance, as Burke would say) which made for the continuity of past and present, present and future. They also assumed that politics was a higher form of activity, realizing the higher purposes of human beings, engaging their higher natures, involving them in a higher, more rational form of life than the activities of daily life. When Macaulay prepared his readers for the chapter that was to deal with the "history of the people as well as the history of the

government," with art and science, religion and literature, manners, dress, furniture, and amusements, he added that he would "cheerfully bear the reproach of having descended below the dignity of history." But it never occurred to him to descend so far below the dignity of history as to make these subjects the whole or even the major part of his work.

It took a new breed of historian to find in daily life the dignity and essence of history, to make of it the "infrastructure" while relegating politics to the "superstructure," the realm of "epiphenomena." By now, after only two decades of the "new history," this reversal of values, a truly Nietzschean "transvaluation of values," has so captured the imagination that an eminent social historian can defend his enterprise by citing a common mistranslation of Aristotle: "Man is a social animal." What Aristotle said, in fact, is that "man is a political animal," that only in the *polis*—not in the "household" or in the "village"—is man truly human, decisively different from "bees or any other gregarious animals." And the *polis* differs from society precisely in its political organization, the government, laws, constitution, institutions, and traditions by means of which—and *only* by means of which, Aristotle believed—man consciously and rationally fulfills his distinctively human purpose, the "good life." The Victorian historian understood this instinctively, as he also instinctively looked for his roots in the past, a political past. The new social historian, rejecting any such "elitist" idea as the good life, seeking only to understand *any* life, indeed regarding it as a triumph of the historical imagination to explore the lowest depths of life (as in that *Mad People's History of Madness*), may be forgiven for misquoting Aristotle; one is only surprised to find Aristotle's name invoked at all. (pp. 45-7)

Gertrude Himmelfarb, "Who Now Reads Macaulay?" in The New Criterion, *Vol. I, No. 4, December, 1982, pp. 41-7.*

In an 1883 letter to Mary Gladstone, Lord Acton discusses Macaulay:

When you sit down to Macaulay, remember that the *Essays* are really flashy and superficial. He was not above par in literary criticism; his Indian articles will not hold water; and his two most famous reviews, on Bacon and Ranke, show his incompetence. The essays are only pleasant reading, and a key to half the prejudices of our age. It is the *History* (with one or two speeches) that is wonderful. He knew nothing respectably before the seventeenth century, he knew nothing of foreign history, of religion, philosophy, science, or art. His account of debates has been thrown into the shade by Ranke, his account of diplomatic affairs, by Klopp. He is, I am persuaded, grossly, basely unfair. Read him therefore to find out how it comes that the most unsympathetic of critics can think him very nearly the greatest of English writers.

Lord Acton, in Letters of Lord Acton to Mary Gladstone, *Macmillan, 1904.*

Bernard Semmel   (essay date 1982)

[*Semmel is a professor of history with a strong interest in the British Empire. Among his publications are* Imperialism and Social Reform (*1960*) *and* Jamaican Blood and Victorian Conscience (*1962*). *In the following excerpt, he argues that Macaulay's genius is derived from his ability to combine the insights of practical politics with a deep knowledge of history.*]

Thomas Babington Macaulay, the Victorian historian and statesman, wished to unite the fruits of the contemplative and active lives, and to join theory and pragmatic experience, in his writings as well as in his political life: this was, as I hope to show, at once his most characteristic quality and his most useful legacy. For the most part, the masters of philosophy and of rhetoric in the ancient and medieval worlds had insisted on the separation of the members of antinomies. There were defenders of matter and those of the spirit, partisans of liberty and those of order, proponents of free will and advocates of determinism. Such philosophical conflicts were seen in purely speculative terms, the formulation of an intellectual ideal unsullied by its opposite. Where such ideals had to be applied in practice, however, the philosophers understood that a proper balance of the contradictions was to be preferred, for life could not be forced into extremes without unhappy results. They consequently recognized that antinomies in some way expressing this distinction, as for example the classic one of the *vita activa* and the *vita contemplativa,* constituted special cases, requiring a careful mix of both members. Macaulay represented this balanced view of the ancients, at a time when systems drawn from theory, from contemplation alone, were becoming the intellectual and political fashion.

Since the Renaissance, a number of thinkers of a logical bent, and persuaded of the absolute truth of their designs, have condescendingly dismissed this moderation of the ancients, and have tried to impose the principles of one or another ideal conception upon the every-day life of society. These enthusiasts and zealots, who have unfortunately dominated recent political discourse, have tried to construct societies upon visions derived from a philosophical or a divine purpose which they saw as immanent in the moral or physical universe. In this way, Savonarola attempted to realize the imaginings of his monastic contemplation by transforming the life of fifteenth-century Florence, and Calvin to incorporate his understanding of God's intent in the Genevan theocracy he established some decades later. Similarly, though his devotion was not to a divine plan but to a moral ideal, Robespierre inflicted his conception of Virtue on revolutionary France. In our own time, adherents of quasi-religious, secular faiths, following both Hegel and Marx, have moved to create a synthesis of theory and practice, or, in their term, *praxis* (which they see as practice thoroughly permeated by theory), and this from the standpoint of believers in a transcendent purpose embodied in an inevitable course of History.

Macaulay was convinced that those whose vision had been formed by either action or contemplation alone were the makers of catastrophe—inept politicians whose apparent practicality fomented revolution or rigid ideologues who

became enemies of liberty. The religious and metaphysical impulses of a Calvin or a Marx would have been foreign, indeed abhorrent, to him. Although his field of contemplation was History, as was that of the adherents of Hegelian *praxis,* he saw not divine or providential patterns but merely human and circumstantial ones, which he tried to interpret according to the facts of a particular case. His was a more commonsensical effort to bring abstractions into line with real circumstances, an ambition that helped to define his views in both politics and history.

When I began my graduate work, a number of writers, disparagingly and I think mistakenly, described the Whig historians, whose patron was Macaulay, as envisioning a history in which the protagonists were motivated exclusively by such lofty sentiments as a concern for the Anglican Church and the divine right of kings, on the one hand, or for the liberty of the individual and the rights of parliament, on the other. The rival history, they wished us to understand, was a more sophisticated, more realistic product. Its master, Sir Lewis Namier, saw politics not as motivated by principles or ideas, which he thought mere trimmings, but rather in terms of economic interests, or as struggles for power or status. Namier's perspective—his interest in economic and psychological motives—was akin to the crude Marxism and Freudianism which by the 1930s and 1940s were well on their way to becoming the academy's Establishment. Namierite history was widely praised, particularly in contrast to what was decried as the merely belletristic interests of Macaulay and his successors.

But even a cursory reading of the Whigs, I discovered, cleared them of the charge of neglecting the material or psychological motives in active politics. They viewed them, indeed, as of the highest importance. This did not, however, prevent their seeing ideas as frequently decisive. The Namierites, in their deliberate effort to describe merely the impulses of instinct and interest, which they thought the only valid ones, failed to comprehend the full meaning of events. Macaulay, on the other hand, had attempted, with some success, to capture the vital balance between the role of ideas and of interests in history. And, of course, the Whig historians, like Macaulay and his grand-nephew and twentieth-century successor, G. M. Trevelyan, could write in exciting and illuminating fashion, while Namier and his disciples were unconcerned with prose style, as they were with ideas and ideals, and seemed deliberately to cultivate literary awkwardness.

That Macaulay's opinions as a historian and as a liberal statesman were intimately linked has been cited as among his chief faults. Rather than regard this as reprehensible, as do those who think history a thoroughly scientific inquiry, I thought it inescapable. It pleased me that Macaulay had built his political positions on a historical base. How else could a contemplative statesman determine his course? I was gratified, too, that he used his historical subjects to set down the fruits of his own political experience, and this without falling into the error of an ahistorical present-mindedness. For a serious historian, as opposed to a mere antiquarian, could not be indifferent to the problems of his own time and society. The life and the writings of Macaulay, then, supplied me with impressive arguments for a useful interaction of the *vita activa* and the *vita contemplativa,* and of pragmatism and principle.

Macaulay was conscious of the efforts made by an elite of contemplative statesmen throughout Western history to unite thought and action, and he identified his own political posture and principles with certain of those figures. What he saw as success in this sphere was not simply the fact of an intellectual in politics: this could prove a disaster, as he well understood. Rather, he admired those who had so merged theory and practice as to have risen above mere doctrinaire and sectarian concerns in the interest of a civilized and improving society. This position left him an admirer of a select pantheon which included Cicero, Machiavelli, Milton, and Burke, and these were joined by a subspecies of scholarly men of action, among whom were Caesar in the ancient world, Lords Somers and Halifax in the seventeenth, and the younger Pitt in the eighteenth century. When still at Cambridge, Macaulay had been warned by his father against radicalism, and at that time he had set his father's worries to rest by assuring him that "my opinions, good or bad," did not come from the Radicals, "but from Cicero, from Tacitus, and from Milton." It is interesting that the young Macaulay could already identify with the republican historian Tacitus who denounced the infamies of the later Caesars, even as he himself would choose, as an English Tacitus, to denounce those of the Stuarts. But his chief models among the ancients were Cicero and Caesar, despite their shortcomings, for he saw the politics of his own time in the light of their examples.

Macaulay's nephew and biographer, Sir George Otto Trevelyan, regretted that his uncle had never written an essay on Cicero with whose political predicament he sympathized, and whose principles he admired. He had especially approved of Cicero's "zeal for popular rights," as it appeared in his oration against Verres, a corrupt proconsul in Sicily. The Roman statesman's great fault was that he had at times acted as the agent of an aristocratic class that he himself really despised. (In **"Fragments of a Roman Tale,"** a story concerning the Catalinarian conspiracy published while the historian was still at Cambridge, Macaulay praised a "moderate" Caesar, who had opposed both the "oligarchical tyranny," and the demagogic Catalinarians.) The ideal which was to be among the foremost in Macaulay's politics, and even his poetry, was that of the *concordia ordinum,* the harmony between the classes which had been Cicero's chief object in Rome. At the age of twenty, Macaulay struck at revolutionary demagoguery in **"A Radical War Song,"** which depicted the libertine anarchy that would follow an English revolution. In his once well-known **"Horatius,"** he described the class harmony that the Rome of the early republic had enjoyed and to which England might aspire, if only the English aristocrats, like the Roman patricians of the early republic, would be prepared to give up everything for their country so that the rich and poor might live "like brothers" in a just society. This had been Cicero's life-long ideal, and was one of the reasons, Trevelyan observed, though the Roman's practice at times fell short of his prin-

ciples, that Macaulay regarded Cicero as one of "the foremost men of all the ages."

Machiavelli also occupied a prominent position among Macaulay's heroes. The sixteenth-century Florentine was in many respects his *beau idéal:* "the qualities of the active and contemplative statesman," the essayist declared, were blended "into a rare and exquisite harmony" in the Renaissance writer and politician. Machiavelli was an artist as well as a statesman: his comedy, *Mandragola,* in Macaulay's view, was superior to the plays of Goldini, and inferior only to the best of Molière, while his political writings were far superior to those of an over-praised Montesquieu. Defending Machiavelli against those who had made him seem an incarnation of the Devil, Macaulay brilliantly portrayed the political and personal morality of the northern city-states of Renaissance Italy which made the best of men prefer the qualities of an Iago to those of a blundering and gullible Othello, with whom the less sophisticated audiences of Renaissance England sympathized. Given the climate of opinion in sixteenth-century Italy, there was therefore no personal taint in Machiavelli's espousal of morals which would have utterly defiled a northerner; indeed, the Florentine's "public conduct was upright and honorable." Machiavelli, moreover, understood, as few of his contemporaries did, that Italy's troubles stemmed from the use of mercenary armies composed of men and officers with no interest in the welfare of the state. The solution the Florentine had proposed was the establishment of a citizen army, a militia. How could this diagnosis and remedy fail to delight a Whig whose view of the history of his own country and of all of Europe was, as we shall see, drawn along similar lines? But Macaulay did not depict Machiavelli as a doctrinaire even on this point, but always as a contemplative statesman, acutely conscious of the particular circumstances of each case—a practical Whig, ready to employ the devices of Iago for the sake of liberty.

While still at Cambridge, Macaulay defended Milton against critics who saw him as a reckless revolutionary and the tool of a Cromwellian despotism—this in a dialogue set in 1665 that he had constructed between Milton and the royalist Abraham Cowley. The future historian of the 1688 revolution saw the Puritan poet as the Apostle of Liberty. The earlier revolution was necessary, the Milton of the dialogue argued, because Charles I was not merely a tyrant and a bigot, but because he had proved himself so treacherous and deceitful that no one could feel any security in his promises, though the poet granted the inadvisability of the royal execution. Milton asked Cowley to compare the virtuous and relatively free England during Oliver Cromwell's reign with the base and shameful state of affairs since 1660, and suggested the usefulness of another rebellion. The royalist, arguing the advantages of just one member of the antinomy, could see *anarchism* as the only fruit of a new rebellion, and declared that he himself preferred *despotism,* to which Macaulay's Milton, an advocate of a liberal balance, replied:

> When will rulers learn that, where liberty is not, security and order can never be? We talk of absolute power; but all power hath limits, which if not fixed by the moderation of the governors,

will be fixed by the force of the governed. . . . Small, therefore, is the wisdom of those who fly to servitude as if it were a refuge from commotion; for anarchy is the sure consequence of tyranny. That governments may be safe, nations must be free. Their passions must have an outlet provided, lest they make one . . . therefore would I say to all kings, let your demagogues lead crowds, lest they lead armies; let them bluster, lest they massacre. . . . I hold that, as freedom is the only safeguard of government, so are order and moderation generally necessary to preserve freedom.

For Macaulay, as for Milton, revolution was to be avoided, but not at the price of the loss of liberty, which would of itself foment upheaval and lawless bloodshed.

In a celebrated *Edinburgh Review* article on the poet in 1825, which was to make the young essayist famous virtually overnight, Macaulay proclaimed John Milton the embodiment of the union of the contemplative and active lives, as "the glory of English literature" as well as "the champion and martyr of English liberty." The author of *Paradise Lost* had lived at a time of "the great conflict between Oromasdes and Arimanes, liberty and despotism, reason and prejudice" in which "the destinies of the human race were staked on the same cast with the freedom of the English people." While the Revolution had undoubtedly taken many awkward turns, had produced many outrages, such violent events were a necessary consequence of great repression; while the immediate effects of revolution were often "atrocious crimes," in the end "the final and permanent fruits of liberty are wisdom, moderation, and mercy." And Milton's greatest glory was his battle for the most valuable freedom, his struggle against "moral and intellectual slavery," and for "the liberty of the press and the unfettered exercise of private judgement." The Puritan poet had joined the Cromwellians because he saw "free conscience" as their objective. Milton was neither a hot-headed rebel nor an advocate of despotism, but a contemplative statesman who had truly understood the political circumstances of his time. For the choice did not lie "between Cromwell and liberty, but between Cromwell and the Stuarts," and the future historian of that dynasty saw Milton as having chosen well, as was proved by the succeeding reigns of Charles II and James II, thirty years which were "the darkest and most disgraceful in the English annals."

When the *Edinburgh Review* solicited an essay on Edmund Burke from him in 1844, Macaulay turned down the request, observing that there was simply too much to be said on the subject for a single article; certainly, Burke seems everywhere present in the many essays Macaulay devoted to the eighteenth century. A constant, if sometimes submerged, theme of these pieces was the splendor of the principles and the practical wisdom of Burke, and of his admirer, the younger William Pitt. In his article on Warren Hastings, for example, even when taking issue with his hero on the justice of Hastings' impeachment, Macaulay described Burke as "the greatest man then living." Burke was first of all a Whig, and like Macaulay a venerator of the 1688 Revolution. Also, like Macaulay himself, Burke was a man of letters in politics, a contem-

plative statesman who could write brilliantly about a wide range of subjects, from the principles of aesthetic criticism to those of commercial policy. Though the Tories saw the younger Pitt as the founder of their modern party, Macaulay agreed with Burke who had described him, at least for the first part of his government from 1783 to 1792, as "an enlightened Whig." To be a Whig was above all to be "an honest friend of civil and religious liberty," and this was a test that both Burke and Pitt amply met. In the latter part of his life, in reaction to the excesses of the French Revolution, Pitt was to turn to a course of repression, and to lead a party the principles of which were to become illiberal, harsh, and arbitrary. Yet his earlier interest in freedom of the press, parliamentary reform, and a free trade, and his opposition to the slave trade and life-long championship of Catholic emancipation had earned him Macaulay's devotion. By nature, Pitt had been no friend of "war nor arbitrary government," the Whig essayist proclaimed. Although events had forced such a course upon him, as they had upon Burke who also supported the repressive policies of the 1790s, Pitt, like Burke, was at bottom "a lover of peace and freedom."

Macaulay, in the best Whig tradition, was, as were Burke and Pitt in the 1780s and Milton a century earlier, a friend to religious liberty and an enemy of bigotry. His first speech in parliament, urging the removal of all the barriers to Jewish participation in English political life, is probably his best remembered in this connection. In this address, he anticipated Disraeli's better-known remark when he suggested that when Britain was as "savage as New Guinea," and Athens and Rome were but rude settlements, the Jews had had palaces, fleets, philosophers, historians, and poets. Macaulay sought out bigotry in all its guises: for example, he chided the nonconformists, particularly the Wesleyans, who seemed so ready to use against the Unitarians the arguments and methods the Churchmen employed against dissenters like themselves. "The truth is, that bigotry will never want a pretence," Macaulay observed. In speech after speech, he defended the Irish against the injuries inflicted by centuries of British rule: England governed Ireland as she would a newly-conquered territory in India, he complained, not by teaching respect for the laws, but by military force. In a fierce debate in 1845, he favored the granting of financial support for the Catholic training-college at Maynooth, arguing that though Catholicism might contain religious error, the nation could not permit the millions of Roman Catholics of Ireland to live without the solace offered by religion, or the restraints of religious discipline. The Protestant voters of Edinburgh defeated Macaulay at the next general election for such clearly heretical views. (pp. 22-30)

The starting point of Macaulay's *History* was a natural one for a Whig: the Glorious Revolution and the establishment of political and religious liberty in the reign of William and Mary. Two previous Whig politicians, both much admired by Macaulay, had already written partial histories of the period—the leader of the party at the end of the eighteenth century, Charles James Fox, and its intellectual mentor in the first third of the nineteenth, Sir James Mackintosh. Both Fox and Mackintosh were men who had joined the intellectual life with one of active politics. As Macaulay had observed in an essay in 1835:

> Both had thought much on the principles of government; yet they were not mere speculators. Both had ransacked the archives of rival kingdoms, and pored on folios which had moldered for ages in deserted libraries; yet they were not mere antiquaries. They had one eminent qualification for writing history: they had spoken history, acted history, lived history. The turns of political fortune, the ebb and flow of popular feeling, the hidden mechanism by which parties are moved, all of these things were the subjects of their constant thought and their most familiar conversation.

Yet as historians and politicians, the two earlier Whigs had had contrasting virtues: Fox was by far the greater orator, but his work on the reign of James II resembled a parliamentary report more than sober and judicious history; on the other hand, if "Mr. Fox wrote debates," then "Sir James Mackintosh spoke essays." Macaulay, it is clear, saw himself as possessing potentially greater talents in both these realms.

In the *History,* Macaulay wished to display how "from the auspicious union of order and freedom, sprang a prosperity of which the annals of human affairs had furnished no example"; how England had risen from "a state of ignominious vassalage" to "the place of umpire" among the powers; how her public credit, commerce, and maritime strength had made other empires, ancient and modern, seem insignificant. The historian took as his province the period from the accession of James II in 1685, until "a time which is within the memory of men still living." In fact, however, he brought the narrative only to the death of William III in 1701, in part because he was enthralled by the details of the Glorious Revolution and the post-revolutionary Settlement, in part because he suffered from cardiac difficulties which were to end his life, too soon, in 1859. In the early pages of the work, Macaulay declared his intention of telling the history not only of the statesmen but of the common people (their religions, arts, manners, amusements), and thus "cheerfully bear the reproach of having descended below the dignity of history." Although he would describe "great national crimes and follies," Macaulay was convinced that "the general effect of this checkered narrative will be to excite thankfulness in all religious minds, and hope in the breasts of all patriots."

Perhaps the best known part of the first two volumes was Chapter III, Macaulay's description of the state of England in 1685. It was a remarkable accomplishment, and, in some respects, still serves as a model for social historians. Macaulay saw English history as one of a steady, continuous progress that became "portentously rapid" in the eighteenth century, and achieved an even more "accelerated velocity" in the nineteenth. The picture he drew of England at the accession of James II possessed, as a well-drawn historical tableau must, a dynamic quality, a consciousness of the past as well as of the future growth of population, of the economy, and of knowledge and the sciences. In enlivening prose, Macaulay described the state of the army and the navy, of the upper classes and the yeo-

manry, of the towns and the spas; he depicted the coffee-houses, the London police, the stage coaches and highwaymen, schools, post office, newspapers, inns; he wrote of the education of women, and the immorality of literature; he set down the wages of the laboring classes and discussed the surprising prevalence of child labor in the seventeenth-century clothing factories.

This last observation prompted Macaulay to suggest that "the more carefully we examine the history of the past, the more reason shall we find to dissent from those who imagine that our age has been fruitful of new social evils"; "that which is new is the intelligence which discerns and the humanity which remedies them." On the so-called "condition of England" question which has intermittently absorbed modern historians, Macaulay thus took the optimistic position, which has come to be regarded as the insensitive position. Aside from his loss of access to the common lands, brought about by the improvement of agricultural methods in the eighteenth century, in Macaulay's view the common man of the nineteenth century had benefited enormously from the progress of civilization. Life was now more secure, health was better provided for, and, in consequence, the life span had increased greatly. The historian spoke of the "mollifying influence of civilization": there were fewer beatings in the workshops, in schools, and within the family; there was an enormous increase in compassion for the criminal and in public entertainment; no one in 1685 had sought to protect the child laborer or the black slave or the Indian widow, as people would a century and a half later. Macaulay rejoiced that his own was "a merciful age" in which "cruelty is abhorred," and observed that while every class had gained from this change, "the poorest, the most dependent, and the most defenceless" had gained the most.

Macaulay took note of the peculiar nostalgia of his countrymen and their belief that the England of the seventeenth century was somehow a more desirable place in which to live than the England of Victoria. We overrate the happiness of past generations, he argued, because we are impatient with the faults of our own; but this very impatience served as a goad to continued improvement. There had been, however, no golden age in the past, "when farmers and shopkeepers breakfasted on loaves, the very sight of which would raise a riot in a modern workhouse," and "when men died faster in the purest country air than they now die in the most pestilential lanes of our towns." Macaulay predicted that in the twentieth century workers would be "little used to dine without meat"; that the average life span would increase by several years; that "numerous comforts and luxuries . . . unknown, or confined to a few," would be enjoyed by "every diligent and thrifty workingman." "And yet," Macaulay concluded, "it may then be the mode to assert that the increase of wealth and the progress of science have benefited the few at the expense of the many"—an accurate prediction!

Insofar as the *History* had a central theme, it was that of the uniqueness of English development, which for Macaulay accounted for the many blessings enjoyed by the subjects of Victoria. What had kept England a limited monarchy, on the pattern that prevailed throughout Europe during the fourteenth and fifteenth centuries, Macaulay inquired, while the monarchies of the continental countries had turned absolute in the sixteenth century? In France and in Spain, where the power of the sword and that of the purse had engaged in mortal combat, the parliaments had yielded their fiscal powers to princes whose armies not only protected their kingdoms from foreigners but imposed an absolute royal authority on all classes within the nation. In England, on the other hand, protected by the Channel from invasion, the parliament had maintained and even extended its power because of the King's increasing dependence on the revenues it raised, and because it had acted to prevent the establishment of a great standing army, by means of which continental monarchs had made themselves supreme. The Cromwellian military despotism had confirmed for Englishmen the supreme importance of resisting the establishment of a standing army, as opposed to a popular militia. That a standing army was a threat to liberty became a leading Whig principle from the seventeenth century onward. In all this, Macaulay argued along the lines followed by Machiavelli over three centuries earlier.

In this great year of European revolutions, 1848, in which the first volumes of his *History* were published, Macaulay saw the "peculiar character" of the Glorious Revolution as a consequence of this special English development. Because the limited monarchy of the Middle Ages had survived, the revolutionary changes of 1688 were limited and relatively peaceful; on the continent, on the other hand, after the revolution of 1789, the rebels against a hated absolute rule were "impatient to demolish and unable to construct," and "the violent action of the revolutionary spirit" was followed by an "equally violent" reaction. If Charles I and Strafford had succeeded in establishing the centralized, bureaucratic state at which they had aimed, and had formed a disciplined royal standing army to repress popular discontent, England, too, would have suffered from such bloody and unproductive uprisings. But English parliamentary institutions had remained vigorous, and England in 1688 consequently experienced a revolution which was "strictly defensive."

The Glorious Revolution had been "a vindication of ancient rights," rather than an uprising based upon doctrines of natural rights, of equality or popular sovereignty, Macaulay argued, following the reasoning of his much-admired Burke. "To us, who have lived in the year 1848, it may seem almost an abuse of terms to call a proceeding, conducted with so much deliberation, with so much sobriety, and with such minute attention to prescriptive etiquette, by the terrible name of Revolution." Yet this least violent of revolutions had confirmed the victory of the popular element in the constitution over the monarchical, and had saved liberty. It had provided toleration for religious Dissenters, laid the foundation for the freedom of the press, and established the bases for an independent judiciary and a greater popular control of the legislature. It had been the fount of "every good law" necessary "to promote the public weal, and to satisfy the demands of public opinion" in the future.

"The highest eulogy which can be pronounced on the rev-

olution of 1688," Macaulay concluded, "is this, that it was our last revolution." Englishmen saw that they could secure necessary improvements constitutionally, without violence. It is difficult to resist quoting the peroration, written in November 1848, after the savage uprisings throughout the continent:

> All around us the world is convulsed by the agonies of great nations. Governments which lately seemed likely to stand during ages have been on a sudden shaken and overthrown. The proudest capitals of Western Europe have streamed with civil blood. All evil passions, the thirst of gain and the thirst of vengeance, the antipathy of class to class, the antipathy of race to race, have broken loose from the control of divine and human laws. Fear and anxiety have clouded the faces and depressed the hearts of millions. Trade has been suspended, and industry paralyzed. The rich have become poor; and the poor have become poorer. . . . Europe has been threatened with subjugation by barbarians, compared with whom the barbarians who marched under Attila and Alboin were enlightened and humane. The truest friends of the people have with deep sorrow owned that interests more precious than any political privileges were in jeopardy, and that it might be necessary to sacrifice even liberty in order to save civilization.

Meanwhile, in England, all was different:

> . . . in our island the regular course of government has never been for a day interrupted. The few bad men who longed for license and plunder have not had the courage to confront for one moment the strength of a loyal nation, rallied in firm array round a parental throne. And, if it be asked what has made us to differ from others, the answer is that we never lost what others are wildly and blindly seeking to regain. It is because we had a preserving revolution in the seventeenth century that we have not had a destroying revolution in the nineteenth. It is because we had freedom in the midst of servitude that we have order in the midst of anarchy. For the authority of law, for the security of property, for the peace of our streets, for the happiness of our homes, our gratitude is due, under Him who raises and pulls down nations at his pleasure, to the Long Parliament, to the Convention, and to William of Orange.

Macaulay's principal purpose had been served in the first two volumes of the *History,* but the final three cannot be thought, as has been suggested, entirely anticlimactic. In the second two volumes, published in 1857, Macaulay again revealed himself as one able to paint memorable portraits of the men and events of the age, as in his description of the last days of Judge Jeffreys, the character of the Quaker George Fox, and the terrible slaughter at Glencoe in 1692. Macaulay also displayed an ability to present complex economic questions for the general reader, notably in his brilliant discussion of the origin of the national debt, in the course of which he set down another tribute to Edmund Burke, and in his description of the establishment of the Bank of England. In the fifth volume, published posthumously in 1862, Macaulay was to turn his attention to the controversies concerning the restoration of a sound currency, subjects which he remarked were "not such as have generally been thought worthy to occupy a prominent place in history," but which no historian could now dare to ignore. Nor can we pass over Macaulay's illuminating discussion of the early efforts at parliamentary reform, and his learned as well as entertaining account of the moves to achieve greater liberty of the press.

In the posthumous final volume, Macaulay reopened the question of a standing army, so critical to the main theme of his earlier volumes. The issue, as it was to present itself in 1697, was perceived rather differently from the way it had been previously, for this was a time when, the historian argued, the national interest and a concern for liberty were in delicate balance. Having served as the war secretary in the cabinet of Lord Melbourne after his return from India in 1839, Macaulay could the better appreciate the position of one of the heroes of his *History,* the contemplative statesman, Lord Somers. In past times, Macaulay observed, the hostility to a permanent military force had been both "reasonable and salutary"; in the late 1690s, however, the ancient principle had begun to run counter to the national need. The Whig ideologues—like John Trenchard and his supporters who wished to disband William's army—routinely cited the usual sectarian "claptraps and historical commonplaces" and declared it "a fundamental principle of political science that a standing army and a free constitution could not exist together." They cited the city-states of Greece, the Roman Republic, the Italian republics of the Middle Ages, and the French and Spanish monarchies—even as Macaulay had earlier—as well as the more recent example of Cromwell's model army. Both sides in the controversy agreed that Britain required a military force for its defense, but the wielders of the Whiggish argument saw a popular militia as in all ways preferable to a standing army. The more practical-minded protagonists of a standing army, on the other hand, pointed to the large regular forces kept by France, a past and potential enemy, and warned that if England supported an army, it ought not to be an inefficient milita. But our ancestors, Macaulay observed, "were secure where they ought to have been wary and timorous where they might well have been secure."

Understanding the reasons for the deep antagonism to a standing army, and even to a considerable degree influenced by them, Lord Somers, himself a student of ancient literature, countered the precedents cited by the Whig doctrinaires by historical arguments of his own. He chose to steer a middle course. Somers warned that England had to make "a choice between dangers." What might be a risk when considering her internal policy, might be "absolutely essential to her rank among European Powers, and even to her independence," Macaulay observed, in describing Somers' position. "All that a statesman could do in such a case was to weigh inconveniences against each other, and carefully to observe which way the scale leaned." This had been the message of Somers' treatise known as the Balancing Letter in which he had recommended a temporary army, fixed annually by parliament, which would effectively serve the purposes of a regular standing army but would constitute no threat to liberty. This was, of course,

the compromise that England finally adopted, one which, in Macaulay's view, had helped to preserve both her freedom and her security. This political expedient had been the amalgam of both principle and the experience of practical political life.

Macaulay regarded the position of Somers and that of another contemplative statesman of the seventeenth century, Lord Halifax, as he did his own. Like Somers, he wished to be "one who looked on the history of past ages with the eye of a practical statesman, and on the events which were passing before him with the eye of a philosophical historian." Certainly Macaulay's temper was the pragmatic one of the Balancing Letter: principles, such as the opposition to a standing army, had sometimes to yield to the facts as they were to be found in the particular case of England's new circumstances. This was one of the fruits of Macaulay's union of the active and contemplative lives, as it had been for Somers, and also for Halifax. The latter, we know, has achieved an unsavory reputation as an unprincipled Trimmer. For the Whig historian, however, Halifax, in what some regarded as constant shifts, had behaved with a steady intelligence:

> to have been the foremost champion of order in the turbulent Parliament of 1680, and the foremost champion of liberty in the servile parliament of 1685; to have been just and merciful to Roman Catholics in the days of the Popish Plot, and to [extreme Protestant] Exclusionists in the days of the Rye House Plot; . . . this was a course which contemporaries, heated by passion, and deluded by names and badges, might not unnaturally call fickle, but which deserves a very different name from the late justice of posterity.

Macaulay might well have desired as an appropriate obituary for himself, in his dual role as historian and statesman, what he concluded of Halifax:

> For what distinguishes him from all other English statesmen is this, that, through a long public life, and through frequent and violent revolutions of public feeling, he almost invariably took that view of the great questions of his time which history has finally adopted.

"Nothing is easier," Macaulay declared in a speech to the House of Commons in 1833, "than to write a theme for severity, for clemency, for order, for liberty, for a contemplative life, for an active life, and so on": "when we come to the real business of life, the value of these commonplaces depends entirely on the particular circumstances of the case." To argue only one side of hoary antinomies was for the rhetorician or the idealogue, not for the contemplative statesman who was Macaulay's ideal. The latter understood the need that both parts of an antinomy be put into balance. He acted on the basis of a right historical reason, even as the good historian never forgot the practical side of politics. Macaulay was a man whose understanding of both history and political realities had taught him to be wary of unbending abstractions that became all too swiftly irrelevant to the facts. Yet an exclusively practical interest in the day-to-day necessities of the State, a concern not informed by historical understanding, was equally dangerous. If the first frequently led to the imposition of a tyranny based on an inflexible ideology, the second, ignorant of history, was likely to repeat its grossest errors, and to incite rebellion.

History had proved that to impose the conceptions of the contemplative upon the active life led to dogmatism and fanaticism. The seventeenth-century Puritan enthusiasts, despite all their virtues, were condemned by Macaulay for their bigoted vision of what God had commanded. Similarly, the philosophical Radicals of the nineteenth-century, in Macaulay's view, might as readily move to a system of repression, erected on a rigid logic, in their effort to secure their moral goal of "the greatest happiness of the greatest number." When the contemplative man turned to political action, he usually found himself unfitted for the thousand acts of petty ruthlessness that the necessities of power imposed. A determined ideologue, however, might adjust all too well, so confident would he be of the truth of his vision. He became a Savonarola, a Calvin, a Robespierre, or a Lenin.

Macaulay, possibly uniquely, seems to have turned to politics primarily so that he might write his *History,* a circumstance which helped to remove him from many of the severities of the contest for power, and to have spared him the intellectual and moral deformities to which that struggle, unalloyed, often gives rise. His parliamentary skills had helped to secure him the independent income necessary to scholarship. His political services, not only on the backbenches but in cabinets, had given him the experience in matters of state to which he had attributed both Fox's and Mackintosh's virtues as historians. Persuaded, as he was, that he had contributed to having eased the path of his country through the difficult days of the 1830s and 1840s, when England was threatened by social upheaval, he wished to erect for posterity a literary monument which would memorably embody the lessons he had learned from historical models, lessons which his career in active politics had confirmed. This was a worthy ambition, and its realization sufficiently compensates for his defects as a writer of history.

Mill was probably right in seeing Macaulay's faults as much like those of his countrymen in the hey-day of the *Pax Britannica.* If, at times, we despair that Macaulay did not have a sufficient sense of the tragic in history, was too complacent in his view of the speical position of England or of the benevolent role of the middle-classes, and too naive concerning the inevitability of progress, we can attribute these deficiencies not only to his own temperament, but to the somewhat repellent self-satisfaction of his class and his nation during this period. Not that Macaulay was unaware of the faults of early Victorian society, but his social conscience, clearly different from that of a Carlyle or a Dickens or a Mill, and in good part shaped by his sense of the long sweep of historical development, made it possible for him to achieve what some of his contemporaries, and certainly posterity, thought an unfeeling detachment. That he was correct in seeing the condition of the industrial workers as better than that of their predecessors, for example, or in his view that there would be further improvement, somehow did not and does not excuse an apparent

lack of sensitivity to an era, like our own, which prides itself on this quality. Nor, if we are to judge by the success of Dickens, would a display of such sensitivity have deprived Macaulay of the coveted place of his *History* on every lady's boudoir table in his own time.

But Macaulay was the contemplative statesman, not the sentimental reformer. He avoided the great sin of the political intellectual who has become the captive of a sectarian doctrine, whether that creed stemmed from the French Revolution in his day or the Russian in ours. Like Burke who denounced inflexible Jacobin "abstraction" in favor of principle derived from experience, Macaulay saw ideology as subversive of the liberal precepts tested by history and validated by the consensus of the best minds of the past. Because the principles he thought important were not part of a metaphysical system, which an ideological age demands as a sign of seriousness, our somewhat narrow-sighted and present-minded generation has dismissed them as conventional or even hypocritical pieties. But we have not advanced so far that we can easily set aside Macaulay's opposition to tyranny and bigotry, his rejection of an imposed vision of a single Truth, and his devotion to both liberty and order, passions he shared with Milton and Mill. Macaulay was the pragmatic liberal who was guided by the lessons of the past, as well as the historian who understood the realities of politics, an appropriate model for a society which wishes, in its course of improvement, to preserve freedom. (pp. 34-44)

> *Bernard Semmel, "T. B. Macaulay: The Active and Contemplative Lives," in* The Victorian Experience: The Prose Writers, *edited by Richard A. Levine, Ohio University Press, 1982, pp. 22-46.*

FURTHER READING

Beaty, Richmond Croom. *Lord Macaulay: Victorian Liberal.* Norman: University of Oklahoma Press, 1938, 387 p.
    Emphasizes Macaulay's political career and provides the historical background to make it intelligible.

Carleton, William G. "Macaulay and the Trimmers." *The American Scholar* 19, No. 1 (Winter 1949-50): 73-82.
    Argues that Macaulay wrote his *History* not as a Whig, but as a historical relativist and moderate.

Clark, Harry Hayden. "The Vogue of Macaulay in America." *Transactions of the Wisconsin Academy of Sciences, Arts, and Letters* XXXIV (1942): 237-92.
    Surveys the American reaction to Macaulay's works and to the scholarship on Macaulay.

Clive, John. *Macaulay: The Shaping of the Historian.* New York: Alfred A. Knopf, 1973, 499 p.
    Traces Macaulay's personal and intellectual development through the late 1830s.

Das Gupta, R. K. "Macaulay's Writings on India." In *Historians of India, Pakistan, and Ceylon,* edited by C. H. Phillips, pp. 230-40. London: Oxford University Press, 1961.

Perceives more wisdom in Macaulay's comments on India than is usually attributed to them.

Davies, Godfrey. "The Treatment of Constitutional History in Macaulay's *History of England*." *The Huntington Library Quarterly* II, No. 2 (January 1939): 179-204.
Assesses Macaulay's accuracy as a historian and claims that he did not understand William III or Parliament after 1688.

Davis, William A., Jr. " 'This is My Theory': Macaulay on Periodical Style." *Victorian Periodicals Review* XX, No. 1 (Spring 1987): 12-22.
Questions whether the lively, high-spirited style of the *Essays* was sincere.

Firth, Charles Harding. *A Commentary on Macaulay's History of England.* London: Macmillan, 1938, 375 p.
Points out omissions and errors in the *History*, but notes that professional historians are usually kinder to Macaulay than other critics.

Fong, David. "Macaulay: The Essayist as Historian." *Dalhousie Review* 51, No. 1 (Spring 1971): 38-48.
Contends that Macaulay views history in literary terms and that there is an organic relationship between the *Essays* and the *History*.

Geyl, Pieter. "Macaulay in His Essays." In his *Debates with Historians*, pp. 30-47. Cleveland: Meridian Books, 1958.
Finds Macaulay to be too much a prisoner of his own biases to treat the past objectively.

Gray, Donald. "Macaulay's *Lays of Ancient Rome* and the Publication of Nineteenth-Century British Poetry." In *Victorian Literature and Society: Essays Presented to Richard D. Altick*, edited by James R. Kincaid and Albert J. Kuhn, pp. 74-93. Columbus: Ohio State University Press, 1984.
Explains the great popularity of the *Lays* by their affirmation of the virtues and tactics that Macaulay hoped would triumph in the world.

Jann, Rosemary. "Thomas Babington Macaulay: History as Whig Via Media." In her *The Art and Science of Victorian History*, pp. 66-104. Columbus: Ohio State University Press, 1985.
Maintains that Macaulay was representative of a transitional state of the Victorian mind that enjoyed the strangeness of the past, but wanted to be reassured that the world was rational and progressive.

Jones, Frederick L. "Macaulay's Theory of Poetry in 'Milton'." *Modern Language Quarterly* 13, No. 4 (December 1952): 356-62.
Discusses how Macaulay misunderstood the intent of Thomas Love Peacock's *Four Ages of Poetry* and developed his theory that as society grows more rational, it also becomes less capable of producing great poetry.

Knickerbocker, William S. "Suet with No Plums: Restoring Thomas Babington Macaulay." *Sewanee Review* XLVII, No. 2 (April-June 1939): 242-52.
Perceives Macaulay as a spokesman for the middle class and the idea of progress through nonviolent ("noiseless") revolution.

Knowles, David. *Lord Macaulay, 1800-59.* Cambridge: Cambridge University Press, 1960, 31 p.
Depicts Macaulay as a master of historical narrative who gives us a sense of the greatness of human beings.

Levine, George. "Macaulay: Progress and Retreat." In his *Boundaries of Fiction: Carlyle, Macaulay, Newman*, pp. 79-163. Princeton: Princeton University Press, 1968.
Suggests that the *History* has many characteristics of a skillfully constructed realist novel, but that Macaulay's use of literature to escape from reality prevented him from understanding historical characters to whom he was unsympathetic.

Morley, John. "Macaulay." In *Nineteenth-Century Essays*, edited by Peter Stansky, pp. 73-97. Chicago: Chicago University Press, 1970.
A well-known biographer, editor, and politician of the nineteenth century characterizes Macaulay as a second-rate rhetorician. This essay was written in 1876.

Munroe, David. "Macaulay, the Study of an Historian." *Queen's Quarterly* XLVI (Spring 1939): 38-47.
Portrays Macaulay as a great historian who spent a disproportionate amount of his time on William III's reign.

Paul, Herbert. "Macaulay and His Critics." In his *Men & Letters*, pp. 284-313. London: John Lane, The Bodley Head, 1901.
Represents Macaulay as a major historian who combined deep knowledge with high literary skill, and who was open and honest about his Whig partisanship.

Praz, Mario. "Macaulay." In his *The Hero in Eclipse in Victorian Fiction*, translated by Angus Davidson, pp. 102-17. London: Oxford University Press, 1969.
Depicts Macaulay as a middle-class historian who was a great storyteller.

Trevelyan, George Otto. *The Life and Letters of Lord Macaulay.* 2 vols. London: Longmans, Green, and Co., 1876.
The definitive biography, written by Macaulay's nephew.

Trevor-Roper, Hugh. Introduction to *Critical and Historical Essays*, by Thomas Babington, Lord Macaulay, pp. 7-23. New York: McGraw-Hill Book Company, 1965.
Asserts that Macaulay was a bad judge of men, but an excellent judge of political situations and a brilliant writer.

Weber, Ronald. "Singer and Seer: Macaulay on the Historian as Poet." *Papers on Language and Literature* III, No. 3 (Summer 1967): 210-19.
Defines Macaulay's ideal historian as a prophet with the logical mind of a philosopher and the imagination of a poet.

Wedgwood, C. V. "Macaulay's *Lays*." *A Review of English Literature* 1, No. 4 (October 1964): 29-37.
Claims that the *Lays of Ancient Rome* are superior to most mid-nineteenth-century verse on a similar subject.

Yoder, Edwin M., Jr. "Macaulay Revisited." *South Atlantic Quarterly* LXIII, No. 4 (1964): 542-51.

    Praises Macaulay as a vivid portraitist.

Additional coverage of Macaulay's life and career is contained in the following sources published by Gale Research: *Concise Dictionary of British Literary Biography, 1832-1890,* **and** *Dictionary of Literary Biography,* **Vols. 32, 55.**

Pierre and Jean

Guy de Maupassant

The following entry presents criticism of Maupassant's novel, *Pierre et Jean* (1888; *The Two Brothers;* also translated as *Pierre and Jean*). For discussion of Maupassant's complete career, see *NCLC,* Vol. 1.

INTRODUCTION

Pierre and Jean is a story of adultery, fraternal rivalry, jealousy, and betrayal that has, since the time of its first publication, been recognized as Maupassant's finest novel. Praising the work for its sensitive and perceptive portrayal of human psychology, critics note that in *Pierre and Jean* Maupassant was able to realize his goal of exploring the thoughts and feelings of his characters without abandoning the objective narrative style he favored. In addition, the novel has been lauded for its economical yet powerful prose style and symbolic sophistication.

According to the diary of Maupassant's companion Hélène Lecomte du Nouy, *Pierre and Jean* was written in 1887 and was inspired by the experience of an acquaintance of Maupassant's, who had received a substantial inheritance from a family friend. Lecomte du Nouy also notes that, after deciding to set the story in the port city of Le Havre, Maupassant traveled there to gather accurate details of setting. The novel first appeared in serial form in the journal *Nouvelle Revue* in December of 1887 and January of 1888 and was published in book form later in 1888, accompanied by a preface entitled "The Novel" in which Maupassant attempted to define his approach to the novel as a literary genre.

Pierre and Jean is the story of two brothers of the Roland family. The drama begins when the Rolands learn that an old family friend, Léon Maréchal, has died and left his entire fortune to one of the sons, Jean. Jean's brother Pierre, a young doctor, is troubled by the bequest and begins to suspect that Jean is in fact the illegitimate son of Maréchal. From this point forward the story revolves around Pierre and the torment he endures in suspecting his mother of marital infidelity. Eventually he insists that his mother show him an old portrait of Maréchal in her possession, and his misgivings are confirmed when he immediately detects a resemblance between Maréchal and Jean. In a tense scene in Jean's sitting room, Pierre's composure breaks, and he divulges to his brother his suspicions about Jean's dishonorable birth. He then flees. Mme. Roland has overheard everything and confesses to Jean her youthful affair with Maréchal. After the quarrel Jean forms the conviction that Pierre must go away, and suggests to him the position of ship's doctor on the steam ship *Lorraine*. The novel concludes with Pierre boarding the *Lorraine*. In his exile he is shown to be in confusion and disillusionment, unable to come to terms with his mother's past.

Though considered a difficult and ambiguous work, *Pierre and Jean* has been acknowledged as Maupassant's most artistically successful novel. It had its greatest popularity in England and France during the late nineteenth century. Like Maupassant's other works, however, it virtually disappeared from the critical literature for the first half of the twentieth century. A number of studies written in the early 1950s signalled the beginning of a continuous period of scholarly interest in *Pierre and Jean*. The most salient feature of modern commentary on the novel is the lack of agreement about the fundamental meaning of the work. The novel's earliest postwar critics tended to see the novel as an exploration of the destructive effects of jealousy and adultery, as represented by Pierre and Mme. Roland. G. Hainsworth has judged the significance of *Pierre and Jean* to be the problematic relationships between the sexes, as represented in Pierre's rivalry with Jean over the widow Mme. Rosémilly. Subsequent critics have identified various other elements as central to *Pierre and Jean*: illegitimacy and doubtful paternity—which Maupassant, in his stories, showed an almost obsessive interest in; the relations of parents and children; self-discovery; alienation and existential loneliness; and societal victimization of the innocent. Some critics have concentrated on wordplay and symbolism, such as the motif of the fog, in their efforts to decode the meaning of the story and to expose Maupassant's ways of using language. A multiplicity of interpretations has also been applied to the main characters of the novel. Early modern critics invariably treated Pierre as the protagonist of *Pierre and Jean*. More recent studies have given greater emphasis to Pierre's complex relationships to the other characters of the novel. Members of the tightly-knit Roland family and the subsidiary characters are now commonly viewed as players within dynamic relationships, bound together by powerful emotional and psychological ties.

Adding to the critical debate surrounding *Pierre and Jean* are the apparent contradictions many critics have seen between this work and Maupassant's critical essay "The Novel." Maupassant's purpose in the essay is to distinguish between the so-called "objective novel" and the "novel of [psychological] analysis". His higher regard for the objective novel is clear in the essay. He defines it this way: "[writers of the objective novel] aim at giving us an exact representation of what takes place in life, carefully avoiding any complicated explanation, any dissertation upon motives, and they limit themselves to showing us people and the things that happen." However, *Pierre and Jean* is thoroughly psychological in its interests and its presentation of character. Some maintain that this seeming contradiction can be resolved by accepting at face value Maupassant's disclaimer at the beginning of "The Novel" that his essay was not intended as an apology for *Pierre and Jean* but concerns the writing of novels in general. Sullivan, however, has maintained that Maupassant concluded that the unadorned objective technique he had employed in his earlier novels was insufficient to describe the behavior of a character as complex as Pierre Roland.

Pierre and Jean has been praised for its tight narrative structure and, especially, for the economy of the text, in which Maupassant achieved a spareness and control of language that has been called mathematical. *Pierre and Jean* was a departure for Maupassant; critics have admired the way he stretched the boundaries of his art by giving it a new psychological dimension while at the same time achieving a precision and technical control of his objective method that had eluded him in his earlier novels.

CRITICISM

Anatole France   (essay date 1887)

[*A French novelist, journalist, short story writer, and editor, France was a leading figure in French letters from 1890 to 1922. In the following review, first published in 1887 in the newspaper* Le Temps, *France praises* Pierre and Jean *and discusses the literary theories Maupassant put forth in the novel's prefatory essay.*]

M. Guy De Maupassant gives us to-day, in the same volume, thirty pages of æsthetics and a new novel [*Pierre et Jean* with its preface entitled **"LeRoman"**]. I shall surprise no one when I say that the novel is of great value. As for the æsthetic, it is of the kind one might expect from a practical and resolute intellect, naturally inclined to find the things of the mind simpler than they are in reality. One discovers in it, together with good ideas and better instincts, an innocent tendency to take the relative for the absolute. M. de Maupassant lays down the theory of the novel as the lions would lay down the theory of courage if they knew how to speak. His theory, if I understand it rightly, comes to this: there are all sorts of ways of writing good novels, but there is only one way of estimating them. He who creates is a free man, he who judges is a helot. M. de Maupassant shows himself equally imbued with the truth of both these ideas. According to him there exists no rule for producing an original work, but there exist rules for judging one. And those rules are stable and necessary. "The critic," he says, "ought only to appreciate the result according to the nature of the effort." The critic ought "to search for everything which least resembles the novels already written." He ought to have no "school prejudices"; he ought not "to preoccupy himself with tendencies," and yet he ought "to comprehend, distinguish, and explain all the most opposing tendencies, the most contrary temperaments." He ought. . . . But what ought he not? . . . I tell you he is a slave. He can be a patient and stoical slave like Epictetus, but he will never be a free citizen of the republic of letters. And yet I am very wrong in saying that, since, if he is good and docile, he will elevate himself to the destiny of that Epictetus who "lived poor and infirm and dear to the immortal gods." For that sage retained in slavery the dearest of treasures, inward liberty. And that is precisely what M. de Maupassant takes away from the critics. He takes from them even "feeling." They must understand everything; but he absolutely forbids them to feel anything. They will no longer know the troubles of the flesh nor the emotions of the heart. Bereft of desire, they will lead a life sadder than death. The notion of duty is sometimes terrifying. It unceasingly troubles us by the difficulties, the obscurities, and the contradictions that it brings with it. I have experienced this in the most diverse conjunctions. But it is whilst receiving M. de Maupassant's commandments that I recognise the full rigour of the moral law.

Never did duty appear to me at once so difficult, so obscure, and so contradictory. In truth, what is more difficult than to appreciate a writer's effort without taking into consideration whither that effort tends? How can one favour new ideas and at the same time hold the balance evenly between the representatives of originality and those of tradition? How can one at the same time single out and ignore the tendencies of artists? And what sort of a task is it to judge by pure reason of works that spring only from feeling? This, however, is what is demanded of me by a master whom I admire and whom I love. I feel, in truth, that it is too much, and that so much ought not to be exacted from human and critical nature. I feel myself overwhelmed, and at the same time—shall I say it?—I feel myself exalted. Yes, like the Christian on whom his God enjoined labours of charity, works of penitence, and the immolation of his whole being, I am tempted to exclaim: "I must be something since so much is asked of me."

The hand that humiliated me uplifts me at the same time. If I am to believe the master and teacher, the germs of truth are laid up in my soul. When my heart is full of zeal and simplicity, I shall discern literary good and evil, and I shall be a good critic. But this pride totters as soon as it is uplifted. M. de Maupassant flatters me. I know my own irredeemable infirmity and that of my colleagues. For the study of works of art we shall never possess—neither they nor I—anything more than feeling and reason, that is to say the least precise instruments that are in the world. Therefore we shall never obtain certain results, and our criticism will never elevate itself to the rigorous majesty of science. It will always float in uncertainty. Its laws will never be fixed, its decision will never be irrevocable. Far different from justice, it will do little ill and little good, if indeed to amuse refined and eager spirits for a moment is to do little good.

Leave it then unfettered, since it is innocuous. It has some right, it seems, to the freedom you so haughtily refuse it while you grant that freedom with a just liberality to works called original. Is it not the daughter of imagination like them? Is it not in its own way a work of art? I speak of it with absolute disinterestedness, being by nature very detached from things, and inclined to say each evening with the author of "Ecclesiastes": "What profit hath a man of all his labour?" Moreover, I do hardly any criticism, properly speaking. That is a reason for remaining impartial. And perhaps also I have still better ones.

Well, without, as you see, allowing myself to fall into the least illusion in regard to the absolute truth which it expresses, I hold criticism to be the most certain mark that distinguishes truly intellectual ages; I hold it to be the honorable sign of an instructed, tolerant, and polite society. I hold it to be one of the noblest branches with which the aged tree of letters decorates itself in the autumn of its days.

Now, will M. Guy de Maupassant permit me to say, without following the rules he has laid down, that his new novel, *Pierre et Jean,* is very remarkable, and discloses a very vigorous talent? It is not a purely naturalist novel. The author knows this well. He is conscious of what he has done. This time—and it is not for the first time—he has set out from an hypothesis. He said to himself: "If such an event took place in such circumstances, what would be the result?" Now, the starting-point of the novel of *Pierre et Jean* is so singular, or at least so exceptional, that observation is almost powerless to show its consequences. To discover them it is necessary to have recourse to reasoning and to proceed by deduction. That is what has been done by M. Guy de Maupassant, who is, like the devil, a great logician. Here is what he has *imagined:* A sentimental jeweller's wife of the Rue Montmartre, whose husband, to whom she had borne a little boy, was a very common-place tradesman, pretty Madame Roland felt painfully the emptiness of her existence. A stranger, a customer, who had come to the shop by chance, fell in love with her and told her so with delicacy. He was a M. Maréchal, a civil servant. Divining in him a tender and prudent soul like her own, Madame Roland loved and gave herself. She soon had a second child, another boy, of

whom the jeweller believed that he was the father, but whom she knew to have been born under a happier influence. Between this woman and her lover there were profound affinities. Their intimacy was prolonged, harmonious, and concealed. She only broke with him when the tradesman, retiring from business, took his wife, now past middle-age, and the children, already grown up, to Havre. Madame Roland, tranquil and pacified, lived on her secret memories, which had in them nothing bitter, for bitterness, they say, only belongs to faults committed against love. At forty-eight she could congratulate herself on an episode that had rendered her life charming, without costing her anything of her honour as a respectable middle-class woman and mother of a family. But suddenly we learn that Maréchal has died and appointed the second of the Roland boys as his sole legatee.

Such is the situation, I was going to say the hypothesis, from which the novelist has started. Am I not right to affirm that it is a strange one? Maréchal had, during his lifetime, shown the same affection for the two little Rolands. Doubtless he could not, in the depths of his heart, love them both the same. Nothing was more natural than that he should prefer his own son. But he felt that his preference could not be disclosed without indiscretion. Why did he not understand that this same preference would be even more indiscreet if it burst forth suddenly in a posthumous and solemn act? Why was it not evident to him that he could not favour the second of these children without exposing their mother's reputation to suspicion? Moreover, would not the most natural delicacy inspire him to treat both brothers with equality, out of consideration for the fact that they were alike the children of her whom he had loved?

No matter! M. Maréchal's will is a fact. That fact is not improbable; we can, we should, accept it. What will be the consequences of that fact? The novel has been written, from the first line to the last, to answer this question. The lover's too expressive legacy suggests no reflection to the husband, who is a simple-minded man. The worthy Roland has never understood or thought of what there might be in the world save jewellery and gudgeon-fishing. He attained at a stroke and perfectly naturally to supreme wisdom. At the time of her love-affair, Madame Roland, who was not an artificial creature, could deceive him without even lying. She has nothing to fear on that side. Jean, her younger son, also finds natural a legacy by which he benefits. He is a quiet, ordinary boy. Besides, when one is preferred to another, one does not bother oneself much by asking why. But Pierre, the elder, accepts less easily a disposition which is to his disadvantage. It appears, to say the least, peculiar to him. At the first mention of it to him outside his home, he thinks it odd. He is painted for us as an honest enough soul, but hard, discontented, and jealous. He has, above all, an unhappy temperament. When suspicions have entered, there is no more rest for him. He piles them up whilst wishing to dissipate them; he makes a regular inquiry. He gathers indications, he collects proofs; he troubles, frightens, overwhelms his unhappy mother whom he adores. In the despair of his betrayed piety and his lost religion, he spares that mother no contumely, and he proclaims to his adulterine brother the secret he has surprised and ought to keep. His conduct is cruel and monstrous, but, given his nature, it is logical. I have heard it said: "Since he commits the unpardonable wrong of judging his mother, he ought at least to excuse her. He knows what old Roland was, and that he was a fool." Yes, but if he had not had the habit of despising his father, he would not spontaneously have made himself his mother's judge. Besides, he is young and he suffers. These are two reasons why he should be pitiless. And do you ask what is the issue? There is none. From such a situation there can be no issue.

The truth is that M. de Maupassant has treated this unthankful subject with the sureness of talent which he possesses so fully. Strength, flexibility, proportion, nothing is lacking in this robust and masterly story-teller. He is vigorous without effort. He is consummate in his art. I do not insist. My business is not to analyse books: I have done enough when I have implanted some worthy curiosity in the well-disposed reader; but I ought to say that M. de Maupassant deserves every eulogy for the manner in which he has drawn the figure of the poor woman who pays cruelly for a happiness that went unpunished for so long. He has shown, with sure and rapid touch, the somewhat vulgar but not unattractive grace of that "tender book-keeper's soul." He has expressed with a subtlety that has no irony in it the contrast of great feeling in a petty existence. As for M. de Maupassant's language, I shall content myself with saying that it is true French, for I know not how to give higher praise. (pp. 26-33)

> *Anatole France, "M. Guy de Maupassant, Critic and Novelist," in his* On Life & Letters, *second series, translated by A. W. Evans, Dodd, Mead and Company, 1924, pp. 26-33.*

Henry James   (essay date 1888)

[*As a novelist James is valued for his psychological acuity and complex sense of artistic form. Throughout his career, James also wrote literary criticism in which he developed his artistic ideals and applied them to the works of others. Among the numerous dictums he formed to clarify the nature of fiction was his definition of the novel as "a direct impression of life." The quality of this impression—the degree of moral and intellectual development—and the author's ability to communicate this impression in an effective and artistic manner were the two principal criteria by which James estimated the worth of a literary work. James admired the self-consciously formalistic manner of contemporary French writers, particularly Gustave Flaubert, which stood in contrast to the loose, less formulated standards of English novelists. On the other hand, he favored the moral concerns of English writing over the often amoral and cynical vision which characterized much of French literature in the second half of the nineteenth century. His literary aim was to combine the qualities of each country's literature that most appealed to his temperament. James's criteria were accepted as standards by a generation of novelists that included Ford Madox Ford, Joseph Conrad, and Virginia Woolf. In the following excerpt, James describes* Pierre and Jean *as Maupassant's best novel, while also pointing out its limitations.*]

The first artists, in any line, are doubtless not those whose general ideas about their art are most often on their lips—those who most abound in precept, apology, and formula and can best tell us the reasons and the philosophy of things. We know the first usually by their energetic practice, the constancy with which they apply their principles, and the serenity with which they leave us to hunt for their secret in the illustration, the concrete example. None the less it often happens that a valid artist utters his mystery, flashes upon us for a moment the light by which he works, shows us the rule by which he holds it just that he should be measured. This accident is happiest, I think, when it is soonest over; the shortest explanations of the products of genius are the best, and there is many a creator of living figures whose friends, however full of faith in his inspiration, will do well to pray for him when he sallies forth into the dim wilderness of theory. The doctrine is apt to be so much less inspired than the work, the work is often so much more intelligent than the doctrine. M. Guy de Maupassant has lately traversed with a firm and rapid step a literary crisis of this kind; he has clambered safely up the bank at the further end of the morass. If he has relieved himself in the preface to *Pierre et Jean,* the last-published of his tales, he has also rendered a service to his friends; he has not only come home in a recognisable plight, escaping gross disaster with a success which even his extreme good sense was far from making in advance a matter of course, but he has expressed in intelligible terms (that by itself is a ground of felicitation) his most general idea, his own sense of his direction. He has arranged, as it were, the light in which he wishes to sit. If it is a question of attempting, under however many disadvantages, a sketch of him, the critic's business therefore is simplified: there will be no difficulty in placing him, for he himself has chosen the spot, he has made the chalk-mark on the floor. (pp. 243-44)

. . . . .

It is very much a mark of M. de Maupassant that on the most striking occasion, with a single exception, on which his picture is not a picture of libertinage it is a picture of unmitigated suffering. Would he suggest that these are the only alternatives?

The exception that I here allude to is for *Pierre et Jean,* . . . . Is it because in this masterly little novel there is a show of those immaterial forces [of patience and renunciation], and because Pierre Roland is one of the few instances of operative character that can be recalled from so many volumes, that many readers will place M. de Maupassant's latest production altogether at the head of his longer ones? I am not sure, inasmuch as after all the character in question is not extraordinarily distinguished, and the moral problem not presented in much complexity. The case is only relative. Perhaps it is not of importance to fix the reasons of preference in respect to a piece of writing so essentially a work of art and of talent. *Pierre et Jean* is the best of M. de Maupassant's novels mainly because M. de Maupassant has never before been so clever. It is a pleasure to see a mature talent able to renew itself, strike another note, and appear still young. This story suggests the growth of a perception that everything has not been said about the actors on the world's stage when they are represented either as helpless victims or as mere bundles of appetites. There is an air of responsibility about Pierre Roland, the person on whose behalf the tale is mainly told, which almost constitutes a pledge. An inquisitive critic may ask why in this particular case M. de Maupassant should have stuck to the *petit bourgeois,* the circumstances not being such as to typify that class more than another. There are reasons indeed which on reflection are perceptible; it was necessary that his people should be poor, and necessary even that to attentuate Madame Roland's misbehaviour she should have had the excuse of the contracted life of a shopwoman in the Rue Montmartre. Were the inquisitive critic slightly malicious as well, he might suspect the author of a fear that he should seem to give way to the *illusion du beau* if in addition to representing the little group in **Pierre et Jean** as persons of about the normal conscience he had also represented them as of the cultivated class. If they belong to the humble life this belittles and—I am still quoting the supposedly malicious critic—M. de Maupassant *must,* in one way or the other, belittle. To the English reader it will appear, I think, that Pierre and Jean are rather more of the cultivated class than two young Englishmen in the same social position. It belongs to the drama that the struggle of the elder brother—educated, proud, and acute—should be partly with the pettiness of his opportunities. The author's choice of a *milieu,* moreover, will serve to English readers as an example of how much more democratic contemporary French fiction is than that of his own country. The greater part of it—almost all the work of Zola and of Daudet, the best of Flaubert's novels, and the best of those of the brothers De Goncourt—treat of that vast, dim section of society which, lying between those luxurious walks on whose behalf there are easy presuppositions and that darkness of misery which, in addition to being picturesque, brings philanthropy also to the writer's aid, constitutes really, in extent and expressiveness, the substance of any nation. In England, where the fashion of fiction still sets mainly to the country house and the hunting-field, and yet more novels are published than anywhere else in the world, that thick twilight of mediocrity of condition has been little explored. May it yield triumphs in the years to come!

It may seem that I have claimed little for M. de Maupassant, so far as English readers are concerned with him, in saying that after publishing twenty improper volumes he has at last published a twenty-first, which is neither indecent nor cynical. It is not this circumstance that has led me to dedicate so many pages to him, but the circumstance that in producing all the others he yet remained, for those who are interested in these matters, a writer with whom it was impossible not to reckon. This is why I called him, to begin with, so many ineffectual names: a rarity, a "case," an embarrassment, a lion in the path. He is still in the path as I conclude these observations, but I think that in making them we have discovered a legitimate way round. If he is a master of his art and it is discouraging to find what low views are compatible with mastery, there is satisfaction, on the other hand in learning on what particular condition he holds his strange success. This condition, it seems to me, is that of having totally omitted one

of the items of the problem, an omission which has made the problem so much easier that it may almost be described as a short cut to a solution. The question is whether it be a fair cut M. de Maupassant has simply skipped the whole reflective part of his men and women—that reflective part which governs conduct and produces character. He may say that he does not see it, does not know it; to which the answer is, "So much the better for you, if you wish to describe life without it. The strings you pull are by so much the less numerous, and you can therefore pull those that remain with greater promptitude, consequently with greater firmness, with a greater air of knowledge." Pierre Roland, I repeat, shows a capacity for reflection, but I cannot think who else does, among the thousand figures who compete with him—I mean for reflection addressed to anything higher than the gratification of an instinct. We have an impression that M. d'Apreval and Madame de Cadour reflect, as they trudge back from their mournful excursion, but that indication is not pushed very far. An aptitude for this exercise is a part of disciplined manhood, and disciplined manhood M. de Maupassant has simply not attempted to represent. I can remember no instance in which he sketches any considerable capacity for conduct, and his women betray that capacity as little as his men. I am much mistaken if he has once painted a gentleman, in the English sense of the term. His gentlemen, like Paul Brétigny and Gontran de Ravenel, are guilty of the most extraordinary deflections. For those who are conscious of this element in life, look for it and like it, the gap will appear to be immense. It will lead them to say, "No wonder you have a contempt if that is the way you limit the field. No wonder you judge people roughly if that is the way you see them. Your work, on your premisses, remains the admirable thing it is, but is your 'case' not adequately explained?"

The erotic element in M. de Maupassant, about which much more might have been said, seems to me to be explained by the same limitation, and explicable in a similar way wherever else its literature occurs in excess. The carnal side of man appears the most characteristic if you look at it a great deal; and you look at it a great deal if you do not look at the other, at the side by which he reacts against his weaknesses, his defeats. The more you look at the other, the less the whole business to which French novelists have ever appeared to English readers to give a disproportionate place—the business, as I may say, of the senses—will strike you as the only typical one. Is not this the most useful reflection to make in regard to the famous question of the morality, the decency, of the novel? It is the only one, it seems to me, that will meet the case as we find the case to-day. Hard and fast rules, *a priori* restrictions, mere interdictions (you shall not speak of this, you shall not look at that), have surely served their time, and will in the nature of the case never strike an energetic talent as anything but arbitrary. A healthy, living and growing art, full of curiosity and fond of exercise, has an indefeasible mistrust of rigid prohibitions. Let us then leave this magnificent art of the novelist to itself and to its perfect freedom, in the faith that one example is as good as another, and that our fiction will always be decent enough if it be sufficiently general. Let us not be alarmed at this prodigy (though prodigies are alarming) of M. de Maupassant, who is at once so licentious and so impeccable, but gird ourselves up with the conviction that another point of view will yield another perfection. (pp. 281-87)

> *Henry James, "Guy de Maupassant," in his* Partial Portraits. *1888. Reprint. The University of Michigan Press, 1970, pp. 243-87.*

An excerpt from "The Novel," Maupassant's preface to *Pierre et Jean*

The realist, if he is an artist, will try not to show us a commonplace photograph of life, but to give us a more complete view of it, more striking, more convincing than reality itself.

To tell all would be impossible, for it would necessitate at least a volume per day to enumerate the multitudes of insignificant incidents that fill our lives.

So a choice has to be made, and this is the first blow to the theory of the whole truth.

> *Guy de Maupassant, in his* "The Novel" *in* Pierre et Jean, *Penguin Books, 1979.*

Artine Artinian   (essay date 1941)

[*In the following excerpt, Artinian summarizes critical reaction to* Pierre and Jean *immediately after its publication in 1887-88.*]

According to the testimony of Mme Lecomte du Nouy, Maupassant was working on . . . *Pierre et Jean,* in the summer of 1887; she had noted in her journal, under date of June 22, that the author had read to her the first pages of his novel, inspired, as were many of his works, by a *fait-divers:* a friend having just come into an inheritance of eight million francs from an acquaintance of the family, Maupassant decides to develop his interpretation of this unusual news item. And he immediately makes plans to go to Le Havre for a first exploration of the setting of his story. Moreover, as René Dumesnil points out, the theme of the adulterine child is a favorite with our author, who had previously treated it in several of his tales before doing so in *Mont-Oriol* and finally as the central theme of *Pierre et Jean.*

It first appeared in *La Nouvelle Revue,* in December, 1887, and January, 1888, before being published in book form under the Ollendorff imprint on the eighth of January. Its appearance in book form had been, indeed, retarded by a week because *Le Figaro* was first to publish the study on the novel which was in turn to serve as preface to the work.

This preface, justly famous to-day as the most detailed account of Maupassant's literary principles, was very close to the heart of the author; so it is not surprising that *Le Figaro,* having without permission omitted portions of it in its January 7th number, was threatened with a lawsuit by its indignant author. In a letter to Mme Juliette Adam, founder and editor of *La Nouvelle Revue,* Maupassant

wrote of the preface in the following terms: "C'est une étude très travaillée sur le roman actuel dans toutes ses formes, et j'espère qu'elle fera un peu discuter. . . ."

He must have been more than gratified by the results. This manifesto inspired so much discussion, in fact, that it nearly detracted attention from what is considered to be one of Maupassant's outstanding achievements.

The always sympathetic Maxime Gaucher of *La Revue Bleue,* who five years earlier had been one of the first to salute a master in the author of *Une Vie,* was now the first to applaud *Pierre et Jean:*

> C'est une oeuvre exquise. Caractères observés sur le vif, intérêt dramatique, relief des figures, netteté et sobriété des détails, touche puissante et en même temps délicate, style coloré et original, sans qu'on sente un moment l'affectation ou le désir d'étonner, art savant de composition sous une apparente négligence d'allures, on ne sait à quoi il faut le plus applaudir.

The critic cannot reconcile, however, the completely useless preface which he finds attached to such a novel "très bien fait". And he finds it especially useless if the novelist intended thereby to defend himself. For there is no need of defense, as proved by the fact that the questionable themes treated by Maupassant have been overlooked in favor of his superior talent. In fact, the critic affirms that the only principle he wants to retain from that preface is the principle developed by Maupassant to the effect that no such thing as the *roman bien fait* exists. The critic mentions that particular principle because he believes it to be untrue; and the author's own *Pierre et Jean* is the best proof of its invalidity. . . . (pp. 93-4)

The anonymous notice which appeared the following day in *La Revue des Deux Mondes*—was it the purist Brunetière, who had already reproached Maupassant on the same score?—finds the intrigue interesting and capably handled, but criticizes the liberties which the author still insists on taking:

> On peut regretter que M. de Maupassant mette dans la bouche de ses personnages quelques expressions que l'on penserait ne pas y rencontrer, et il nous semble que le récit aurait gagné quelque chose à cette épuration; mais il paraît que l'école à laquelle appartient M. Guy de Maupassant tient absolument à cette maniére de dire.

Anatole France, who had first spoken—and in the highest terms—of Maupassant the year before, again praises our author lavishly, less as critic than as novelist, however. He finds in the author's exposition of literary tenets exactly what might have been expected from a practical and resolute mind such as Maupassant's: a tendency to consider intellectual matters as more simple than they actually are, a tendency to confuse the relative with the absolute. But the novel itself is "d'une grande valeur"; it is "fort remarquable et décèle un bien vigoureux talent." . . . (p. 95)

The day following Anatole France's notice in *Le Temps,* Edmond Lepelletier of *L'Echo de Paris* stated that zealots of both the short story and the novel would surely agree that *Pierre et Jean* "est un livre excellent, d'un style pur, aux mailles solides, forgé sur la bonne enclume et fait de main d'ouvrier." Viguier of *L'Evénement* would place Maupassant several steps ahead of the young writers who were making a place for themselves in letters. It must be admitted that the first hundred pages of his *Une Vie* and a few *nouvelles* come close to being masterpieces. As for *Pierre et Jean,* its author demonstrates once more that he possesses the major quality of a novelist, that of creating outside of himself characters that live. But this praise on the part of Viguier is immediately followed by a not over subtle criticism:

> Il excelle, sinon à restituer dans son intégrité la vie de ses personnages, du moins à offrir l'apparence de la vie. Je veux dire que l'auteur de l'histoire émouvante et simple de *Pierre et Jean* se préoccupe surtout de définir ses personnages par une série d'actes congrus et qu'il néglige—volontairement, je crois—d'expliquer les mobiles de ces actes.

The reviewer for *L'Illustration* agrees with Viguier's judgment that Maupassant's characters are of flesh and blood:

> Avec M. Guy de Maupassant, on ne risque guère de tomber dans l'abstraction. Il a le don de la vie, et ce don il le possède aussi bien dans son style que dans ses personnages. . . .
>
> (p. 96)

About ten days after Anatole France's article in *Le Temps,* that periodical carried another long study on Maupassant, this time by Edmond Scherer, entitled "L'Artiste et le critique". As the title indicates, the brunt of the review is directed at the essay on the novel. But before plunging into the discussion at hand, Scherer states that he would like to establish at least a semblance of an equilibrium by not ignoring altogether the second part of Maupassant's work. . . . Scherer confesses, in regard to the dissertation which introduces the novel, that going to it after reading the epic of *Pierre et Jean* is like coming out of a room where the light is nearly blinding to enter into another where it is practically dark: whereas the narrative is clarity itself, the theoretical study, on the other hand, is nothing but confusion. According to the critic, the moment Maupassant begins to discuss theories, he gives the impression of playing with ideas whose very significance he does not realize. He fails utterly in the defense of his own thesis; for, after extolling the realistic novel, he suddenly declares that the artist "est obligé de choisir les faits, de corriger les événements, de moins donner le vrai que l'illusion du vrai. . . ." According to Scherer the primary principle of all literature, as of all art, is to interest; this principle Maupassant acknowledges when he extols the injunctions given him by Flaubert, that he should learn "à regarder au lieu de simplement voir." This is excellent counsel, but both master and pupil "ont eu le tort d'appliquer exclusivement à la notation des choses matérielles. L'école réaliste en est venue là qu'elle pourrait tout aussi bien s'appeler l'école descriptive." That is not the least of their sins, moreover; not only do they indulge in a superabundance of descriptions, but they take pride in not retreating before any reality, in giving us "le laid . . . l'ignoble, qui attire tant d'êtres." Regardless, too, of their claim to be

judged only by their peers, the *public* should be taken into consideration, that large reading public which they try to attract. . . . (pp. 97-8)

As we might have expected, Firmin Boissin of the *Polybiblion* did not fail to express his indignation at this latest fruit of Maupassant's pen, although acknowledging the comparative purity of *Pierre et Jean.* He deplores Maupassant's esthetics, according to which an author may say anything he desires so long as he expresses it in irreproachable style; he deplores also the author's indifference to the moral significance of his work, as to whether its influence might be salutory or corruptive. But he has only praise for the author's handling of the powerful and dramatic struggle between mother and son. . . . (p. 98)

> *Artine Artinian, in his* Maupassant Criticism in France: 1880-1940, *King's Crown Press, 1941, 228 p.*

G. Hainsworth   (essay date 1951)

[*In the excerpt below Hainsworth explains the difficulty of establishing the true subject or meaning of* Pierre and Jean.]

[*Pierre et Jean*] has never been evaluated, to our knowledge, as an application of the theory expressed in [Maupassant's] preface, that a novel ought at one and the same time to offer a recognizable picture of 'reality' and formulate *indirectly* the author's ideas. Critics have rarely seen further than the prima facie subject: Pierre's jealousy of Jean's legacy and his tragic discovery of his mother's sin. But this explicit theme is interwoven with, and qualified by, Pierre's subconscious jealousy of Mme Rosémilly. Pierre's rivalry with his brother in this respect, though stated by the author in chapter I and again by Jean in chapter VII, escapes entirely Pierre himself in his attempts at auto-analysis. Its reality and above all its importance for the whole of Pierre's behaviour is brought out not only in various details, explicit or otherwise, which stress Pierre's solitude and bachelorhood, but also in a number of passages where a significant association of ideas is made to reveal his subconscious thoughts. So in chapter II, when Pierre concludes that he must be 'gratuitously' envious *of the legacy,* since *the first thing it had made him think of* was Mme Rosémilly, 'whom he does not love', and the fact that Jean would now be able to marry her. The conversation at Marowsko's on the naming of a new liqueur (*groseille, grosélia, groséline* or *groseillette?*) which leads without transition in the text to Pierre's blurting out the news of the legacy, illustrates the same association of ideas: 'ɢʀoseille'—ʀosémilly)—the legacy. Thus conditioned by subconscious jealousy in respect of Mme Rosémilly, Pierre's attitude towards his mother is largely presented, in its manifestations, and without Pierre being aware of the fact, as that of male towards female, and the two strands are brought together remarkably in chapter VI where Pierre, watching Mme Rosémilly and Jean, suddenly attacks his mother: 'J'apprends comment on se prépare à être cocu'.

The novel therefore appears, in its widest terms, and this is its originality of idea, a juxtaposition and an equation (which anticipates Freud) of (*a*) the relations of parents and children, (*b*) the relations of the sexes. The picture of woman here is once again *à la Schopenhauer:* her practical sense, her preoccupation with what is immediate, her short memory; but all this does not make for the greater glory of the male, whose intellectual and moral pretensions remain a mere phantasmagoria. It is almost, in the end, as if Maupassant reduced everything to mere movement in space—the female rooted in the present (thus forgetful), the male gifted with mobility (thus capable of being trapped)—and the insistence throughout on the motive of fishing and more especially on the question of ships entering and leaving harbour corresponds broadly to this conception.

The first chapter, while stating the whole idea in terms of the rowing match and of the opposite attitudes of the two sexes in the fishing-boat, contains, in the description of the *Prince Albert*'s approach, symmetrical with the departure of the *Lorraine* in the last chapter, a symbol which, applicable indifferently to son, lover or husband, links the two themes that run through the book. Chapters II-V develop Pierre's physical and moral alarms and excursions, what he takes for his concern with the family honour and what is indeed the possessive instinct of the male. Chapter VI, set against a wide natural background and where, while Jean courts, or rather is trapped by Mme Rosémilly, Pierre *snarls* both at them and his mother, constitutes a summary and a turning-point. In chapters VII-VIII, Jean's relations with his mother and his self-deception as to the motives of his own conduct are conceived on similar lines to Pierre's above, and chapter IX, after certain *rappels,* returns the male to his roving. Although the general pattern may appear less free than that of *Bel-Ami,* the detailed execution, with its interweaving of concrete detail, symbol, overt and covert psychological notation, and with its pervading irony, which is far from excluding the pathetic, involves a subtlety of impersonal technique such as to make *Pierre et Jean,* so simple in subject and so frank in its idea, outstanding amongst Maupassant's novels. (pp. 15-17)

> *G. Hainsworth, "Pattern and Symbol in the Work of Maupassant," in* French Studies, *Vol. V, No. 1, January, 1951, pp. 1-17.*

Edward D. Sullivan   (essay date 1954)

[*An American educator, Sullivan is the author of* Maupassant the Novelist, *as well as a book on Maupassant's short stories. In the excerpt below, he discusses Maupassant's preference for the objective novel and asserts that the psychological approach he uses in* Pierre and Jean *represents an extension of, rather than a departure from, this objectivity.*]

Mont-Oriol brought Maupassant to the end—a dead end—of his first conception of novelistic technique. He saw the inadequacy of this novel in spite of his publisher's lavish praise, and began to reflect deeply on the nature of his art. He could continue to turn out short stories with facility, and he did, but he had to write novels as well, and here there was no "natural" method of producing them,

for his instinctive technique had taken him as far as he could go. His reflections on the novel as a form resulted in the celebrated preface to *Pierre et Jean,* called simply **"Le Roman."** This little essay is not, however, a chart of the road he is about to follow, and he specifically denies that the theories set forth in the preface apply to the novel with which it was printed. **"Le Roman"** is rather a summary of the artistic and novelistic credo, derived from Flaubert, on which all his past work had been based. There is nothing new here; all the ideas had been expressed and developed much earlier in his newspaper articles. . . . He had reached a critical point, he recognized that he could not go on as before, compiling novels out of various fragments, but before pushing on, he felt the necessity of putting on paper the basic tenets of his creed as a novelist, hoping to obtain from this exposition a hint as to the direction he should follow. As a result, **"Le Roman,"** which is drawn up at a crucial period mid-way in his career as a novelist, points backward to *Une Vie, Bel-Ami,* and *Mont-Oriol,* and applies specifically to them. The last three novels, *Pierre et Jean, Fort comme la mort,* and *Notre Cœur,* do not represent a denial of the principles of the preface, but are rather an extension of them. The purely objective method he advocates was adequate to treat the rather primitive characters and situations of the three early novels, but, given other situations and more complex and reflective people, some other way had to be found to present them fully. The problem was to penetrate deeply into the psychology of his characters, since the basic action of the novel was henceforth to be internal, and yet do this without compromising the objectivity he so highly prized. *Pierre et Jean* is the result of this effort to extend the objective technique to make it supple enough to deal with a purely psychological drama.

The starting point of *Pierre et Jean,* the shortest and undoubtedly the best of his novels, was very different from his earlier works. Instead of composing by addition or accumulation, he operated this time by expansion and development. The earlier linear structure of a number of separate incidents strung out in time and attached to a character or a place gives way to the centripetal structure of a single situation among a restricted group of characters, wherein every action and word drives inward to the center which is the mind of Pierre. Coming after *Mont-Oriol* which was larded with extraneous incidents and superfluous documentation, *Pierre et Jean* provides a sharp contrast with its severe economy, its concise but evocative description, its exclusion of all padding. As he frees himself from the stringent limitations of objectivity and moves into the dimension of psychology, he finds the substance of his novel not in extent but in depth, not by padding but by probing.

It is obvious from his earliest essays that Maupassant considered the psychological novel a rather absurd form, and although in his more generous moments he granted authors the right to work in that form, he frequently expressed his own antipathy to it. He repeats the same strictures in the very preface to what is generally considered a psychological novel, and insists that no man can penetrate the mind of another and explain all his secret thoughts and motives. Yet the contradiction between the theories of the preface and the practice of the novel itself is more apparent than real, if one examines *Pierre et Jean* closely. He has not turned away from the objective technique but has extended it, at the same time keeping it within very definite limitations. It is these limitations, in fact, which lend sobriety and power to the novel. Given the nature of his subject, a purely objective presentation, revealing the inner motive by an artistic description of the externals, would be too cumbersome: what goes on in the mind of a man seated on a dock may revolutionize his whole life without revealing anything of the nature of his conflict to the most discerning bystander. Maupassant is impelled therefore to expose for us what goes on in the mind of his character, but this presentation operates within precisely defined limits which are a logical result of Maupassant's preoccupation with objectivity. The author never makes his presence felt in the story, his role is that of the skilled observer, ubiquitous but not omniscient. Much of the action is revealed by this careful, unobtrusive, objective reporter, which is Maupassant's favorite technique. But frequently the author is obliged to relate what Pierre is thinking, and these excursions into "psychology" represent simply a shifting of the point of view: he tells what goes on in Pierre's mind, without comment, as if he were merely reporting what Pierre had revealed to him. At no point does the author assume a superior position and analyze his character's thoughts; he knows no more about Pierre than Pierre knows of himself; it is exactly as if a confession or journal written in the first person singular had been transformed into a narrative in the third person by a self-effacing scribe. Pierre's motives are not explained except insofar as he himself explains them; we fumble in hypotheses based on the subconscious only when Pierre becomes aware of them. There is no external analysis; in this framework, the author can never be more subtle or penetrating than his character, and for Maupassant's purposes in this book that is sufficient.

The central idea of the novel is the theme of paternity, a theme that seems to have obsessed Maupassant. René Dumesnil, who made an interesting classification by subject of all of Maupassant's stories, writes:

> Maupassant est hanté par certains sujets et principalement par celui qui trouvera dans *Le Champ d'Oliviers* son expression définitive et parfaite; l'enfant, l'enfant ignoré de son père, l'enfant abandonné sciemment ou non, et qui a poussé comme une mauvaise graine livrée aux caprices des saisons. Sous ses formes les plus diverses, ce problème de la responsabilité morale du père revient plus de trente fois dans les quelque deux cent cinquante nouvelles que Maupassant a laissées.

In *Pierre et Jean* the situation is studied not from the point of view of one of the principals, father or son, but from the point of view of the brother, or rather the half-brother, of the son whose parentage is questioned. The focus of the book is on Pierre Roland and his anguish as the truth is gradually revealed to him that his brother Jean is not Roland's son, but the fruit of an adulterous liaison of Mme Roland and an old friend of the family, Léon Maréchal. The crisis develops when the calm bourgeois life of the Roland family in Le Havre is shattered by news of Maréchal's death and by the fact that he has left his fortune to Jean. Pierre accepts the news of his brother's good fortune calmly and with only a twinge of jealousy at first. He is indignant at the suspicions of some of his acquaintances who are surprised that the money was not left to both sons equally, especially since Pierre was the older. From his initial concern over his mother's reputation, not doubting her innocence, and the propriety of accepting the legacy under such conditions, he arrives after painful analysis and investigation at the moral certainty that the implication is all too true and that Jean is Maréchal's son. In a crucial scene all his pent-up anger and distress burst forth and he tells Jean the truth. Jean is shocked, but stands by his mother—and the legacy—and the situation is resolved by Pierre's leaving home and accepting a post as ship's doctor.

The entire book is tightly constructed around this single situation, the effect of a legacy, and further, everything is seen from a single angle, that of Pierre. His reactions are the real subject of the book, and all the other characters are seen through him. There is simply no place for the leisurely superfluities of the earlier novels. *Pierre et Jean* is therefore much closer to his usual short story technique, and, by its brevity and simplicity more a *nouvelle* than a novel. The framework of the short story is filled out, not by multiplication of events but by the enlargement of the psychological dimension. Since this excursion into psychology is controlled by his preoccupations with objectivity, it is worth making a close analysis of this masterpiece in order to try to reveal the nature and limits of Maupassant's art.

The first chapter is a remarkable example of concise and economical exposition, presenting the characters, laying the groundwork of the entire novel and at the same time moving through a dramatically presented scene. It opens abruptly with an exclamation "Zut!" uttered by M. Roland, annoyed that the fish are no longer biting. By a skillful mixture of dialogue and exposition we see the chief characters, grouped here in Roland's sail boat, and are given a glimpse of their past. The party includes M. Roland, a retired jeweler with a passion for sailing; his wife, "une femme d'ordre, une économe bourgeoise un peu sentimentale, douée d'une âme tendre de caissière"; their older son, Pierre, who had tried various professional studies and now, having won his degree as a doctor, was ready to begin his practice; the younger son, Jean, who had just completed his law studies; and finally, their neighbor Mme Rosémilly, a young and attractive widow. The two brothers are quite different, and there has always been a certain rivalry between them, which has become more marked in the presence of Mme Rosémilly. Their contrasting natures and their latent jealousy are discreetly established to foreshadow the real subject of the book: "Mais une vague jalousie, une de ces jalousies dormantes qui grandissent presque invisibles entre frères ou entre sœurs jusqu'à la maturité et qui éclatent à l'occasion d'un mariage ou d'un bonheur tombant sur l'un, les tenait en éveil dans une fraternelle et inoffensive inimitié."

Having set forth his background and outlined his charac-

Pierre walking the fog-shrouded streets of Le Havre before dawn. From a wood engraving by G. Lemoine after an illustration by Géo Dupuis.

ters, Maupassant refers back to the conversation during which the fishing trip was planned, then brings us again to the "Zut!" and we are once more in the present as the party starts home. On the way we get a further sketch of Mme Roland, her sentimental, poetic nature, "sa taille autrefois très souple et très mince," and we see the rivalry of the two brothers expressed in their juvenile efforts to outrow one another. Details of the setting, the boats, the coast-line, the port of Le Havre, are filled in as we proceed.

That evening the local notary brings the news of Léon Maréchal's death and announces that Jean is named his sole heir. From this point on every element of the writing is charged with intensity and significance; each person reacts in his own way, normally, precisely as one would expect from what we know of them, yet each phrase that is uttered, simple though it is, has a resonance that carries through the rest of the novel. One detail, the significance of which is not immediately apparent, is the stipulation in Maréchal's will that if Jean refuses the inheritance, the estate will pass to the "enfants abandonnés." M. Roland is overjoyed by the unexpected good fortune and cavorts about the room, but his wife is reserved, as if in a dream, and says simply, "Cela prouve qu'il nous aimait." In this simple scene, simply reported without comment, innocent remarks, pregnant with meaning no one is aware of as yet, mark the beginning of the drama and prefigure what is to ensue. Pierre breaks in with a perfectly natural question,

but it is the first step on the long and tortuous path he is to follow: "Vous le connaissiez donc beaucoup, ce Maréchal?" Roland replies with his usual empty effusion, relating how Maréchal went for the doctor when Jean was about to be born, and naïvely quotes what he supposes Maréchal must have said: "Tiens, j'ai contribué à la naissance de ce petit-là, je vais lui laisser ma fortune." Mme Roland, again with an apparently guileless remark, goes right to the heart of the matter when she says of this fortune: "Elle tombe du ciel pour Jean . . . mais Pierre?" Her husband retires and the chapter ends: "Mme Roland se remit à songer devant la lampe qui charbonnait."

This first chapter gives an admirable exposition, starting in the present and weaving in the past with extreme economy. Nothing is superfluous: every word plays its part in presenting the scene or in evoking what we should know of the past and the nature of the people involved. Every development in the rest of the novel is a natural outgrowth of elements contained in the first chapter: the rivalry over Mme Rosémilly, and Pierre's jealousy over her seeming preference for Jean; the fact that both Pierre the doctor and Jean the lawyer are looking for offices, which will bring them into conflict at a crucial moment later; the central problem, Pierre's suspicions, are suggested unobtrusively, for he has begun his investigation without being aware of it. The point of view throughout the chapter is that of the omniscient author, or, more exactly, the ubiquitous author. He knows something of the past of these characters and he acts as observer, giving no more information than could an alert witness, adding a few shrewd deductions of his own. He is in a privileged position but he does not analyze; he gives either his observations directly, or deductions based on his observations.

From this point on our attention is centered almost entirely on Pierre, and we find him restlessly strolling about the port of Le Havre, finally sitting down on a bench on the quai to examine himself, wondering why he feels a certain "malaise." We are told directly that "Il avait l'esprit excitable et réfléchi en même temps, il s'emballait, puis raisonnait, approuvait ou blâmait ses élans; mais chez lui la nature première demeurait en dernier lieu la plus forte, et l'homme sensitif dominait toujours l'homme intelligent." This brief analysis is repeated by Pierre himself as he meditates on the dual nature of man, on the conflict between "l'être instinctif" and "l'être pensant," and he concludes that the reason for his restlessness can only be his subconscious jealousy of Jean, especially since the fortune would allow his brother to marry Mme Rosémilly. He probes further, deciding that since he has a low opinion of the widow and does not want her anyway, his envy is all the more base, "C'est donc de la jalousie gratuite."

Woven into Pierre's examination of conscience is a description of the background: the harbor, the lights of ships and lighthouses, the sights and sounds of the port. These brief descriptive notes do more than merely set the stage, however; certain elements possess a symbolic value which accompanies and reinforces the evolution of Pierre. The fog, especially, whirls and eddies through the novel as a discreetly handled "objective correlative." The fog in Pierre's mind as he tries to see his way clear through the chain of circumstances is matched by the haze and fog of the harbor setting. As he meditates here on the quai, only slightly troubled about himself and without suspecting anything untoward in the legacy, the night is clear and lights are visible, but there is nevertheless a "brume nocturne" which filters the light of the stars. Once engulfed in the fog, Pierre will never be able to emerge completely or dispel it entirely.

He meets his brother on the quai, congratulates him on his good fortune, and muses on the ships entering and leaving. He expresses his nostalgia for foreign lands: ". . . j'ai des désirs fous de partir, de m'en aller avec tous ces bateaux, vers le Nord ou vers le Sud . . . mais voilà il faudrait de l'argent, beaucoup . . . ," a banal idea but it prepares the final resolution of the situation that is being built up.

From this slight feeling of "malaise" Pierre is driven to suspicion and speculation by two major incidents, aided by a series of lesser but nonetheless significant annoyances. The first is occasioned by his visit to his friend Marowsko, a Polish refugee pharmacist. When he tells Marowsko of his brother's fortune, the old pharmacist repeats several times: "Ça ne fera pas un bon effet," and refuses to explain other than by saying: "Dans ce cas-là, on laisse aux deux frères également, je vous dis que ça ne fera pas un bon effet."

Pierre does not reflect much on this statement, but sets off next morning in search of an apartment and office, and is annoyed that the family began lunch without him in their eagerness to arrive at the notary's office to accept the legacy. Finding just the apartment he needs, he hopes his brother can advance him the rent. Then the second incident: his conversation with the waitress in a café whom he knew casually. He tells her of his brother's inheritance and her remark reinforces Marowsko's: "Vrai, ça n'est pas étonnant qu'il te ressemble si peu!" Now it is suddenly clear to him what others are suspecting and he concludes that Jean should refuse the inheritance for the sake of his mother's reputation, although Pierre himself does not believe for a moment that the suspicion could be founded in fact. He is however upset enough to spoil the dinner in celebration of the legacy by his warnings to his father about over-indulgence.

After a night's sleep he feels better, more kindly disposed, and thinks that perhaps the waitress, like all prostitutes, was eager to tear down the reputation of any honest woman. He reflects that he would not even have understood the implications of her remark had it not been for the "levain de jalousie qui fermentait en lui." Or perhaps she had had no such evil thought at all. There is a certain ambiguity in this examination of Pierre's mind at the beginning of Chapter IV; it seems at first that Maupassant himself is analyzing Pierre's reactions, but actually what we have is clearly Maupassant's summary of Pierre's self-examination, and the author remains strictly within the limits of Pierre's knowledge of himself. Consequently it is Pierre, not the author, who takes us briefly into the subconscious when it occurs to him that all his suspicions have been dredged up from the depths of his mind:

> Il se pouvait que son imagination seule, cette imagination qu'il ne gouvernait point, qui échap-

pait sans cesse à sa volonté, s'en allait libre, hardie, aventureuse et sournoise dans l'univers infini des idées, et en rapportait parfois d'inavouables, de honteuses, qu'elle cachait en lui, au fond de son âme, dans les replis insondables, comme des choses volées; il se pouvait que cette imagination seule eût créé, inventé cet affreux doute. Son cœur, assurément, son propre cœur avait des secrets pour lui; et ce cœur blessé n'avait-il pas trouvé dans ce doute abominable un moyen de priver son frère de cet héritage qu'il jalousait. Il se suspectait lui-même, à présent, interrogeant comme les dévots leur conscience, tous les mystères de sa pensée.

The only function of the author here is to turn the results of Pierre's self-examination into indirect discourse.

Immensely cheered and relieved by his reflections, Pierre goes for a sail, and through him Maupassant, who was probably happiest when afloat, describes the joyous sensation of sailing a small boat. Pierre is happy and dreams of a brilliant future in his newly-found apartment. But this joyous interlude is cut short by the intrusion of the fog, the physical fog from the sea which is the concomitant of the misty uncertainty of his mother's position. The old sailor with him says suddenly, "V'là d'la brume, m'sieu Pierre, faut rentrer." He returns to find his mother and Jean enthusiastic over the office-apartment they have just rented for Jean's law practice. It is the same one Pierre had wanted, but he lacked money for a deposit. He is furious but manages to conceal it. Then in the middle of the meal he asks abruptly, "Comment l'aviez-vous connu, ce Maréchal?" Troubled by jealousy and anger, his suspicions are rekindled, although this is conveyed simply by an objective report of the conversation. What he learns is not reassuring: he was three years old when the family first knew Maréchal, who, a little later, had been extremely helpful when Pierre had scarlet fever. Why then did he leave all his money to Jean? Pierre goes out into the fog which is still thick. He calls on Marowsko but senses the old man's suspicions and his hesitancy to push the subject very far. He leaves, pondering the motive behind Maréchal's legacy; it is not jealousy that stirs him now, but the fear lest he himself believe that Jean is Maréchal's son. He must know for certain, must remove all suspicion. The fog still surrounds him: he leaves Marowsko "et se replongea dans le brouillard de la rue."

He goes toward the jetty to settle down to examine the facts. He is startled by the lament of a fog-horn, "le cri des navires perdus dans la brume . . . ce cri de détresse qu'il croyait avoir jeté lui-même." The horns of other ships add a chorus of blasts, and closer at hand the port siren wails in reply. Seated on the jetty, "dans ces ténèbres lugubres et mugissantes," he tries to recall all he ever knew of Maréchal: he recalls his elegance and refinement, realizing Maréchal could never have been the friend of M. Roland, "pour qui le mot 'poésie' signifiait sottise." Suddenly he remembers that Maréchal was blond, like Jean, and that there used to be a portrait of him in the house. Had his mother hidden it because of too striking a resemblance? He groans: "Et soudain, comme si elle l'eût entendu, comme si elle l'eût compris et lui eût répondu, la sirène de la jetée hurla tout près de lui. Sa clameur de monstre surnaturel, plus retentissante que le tonnerre, rugissement sauvage et formidable fait pour dominer les voix du vent et des vagues, se répandit dans les ténèbres sur la mer invisible ensevelie sous les brouillards." He half convinces himself that his mother could never have been Maréchal's mistress, but bitterly reviewing the situation, he asks, why not? In a rage he turns to go and the siren goes off almost in his face. Shapes appear in the fog, ships entering the port, their names announced by the pilot—the *Santa Lucia* from Naples, an English ship from India. Again he dreams of foreign countries, unconsciously seeking the only way out of the fog.

By now Pierre's concern is not so much that his mother's reputation will be damaged by acceptance of the legacy but rather that his suspicions may be proven valid. It is no longer a question of public opinion: "Il aurait voulu que tout le monde accusât sa mère pourvu qu'il la sût innocente, lui, lui seul!" Looking at his brother closely, he fails to find any resemblance between Jean and M. Roland. He asks his mother to find the portrait of Maréchal and, unable to endure the presence of his family, goes off to Trouville for the day, which he spends on the beach. Disgusted by all the women there who adorn themselves not for their husbands but for their present or future lovers, he sees the beach only as "une halle d'amour."

At dinner in the evening he again refers to the portrait of Maréchal; his mother a little reluctantly goes to look for it and finds it immediately. Pierre takes it, notes the resemblance between Jean and Maréchal, almost blurts it out, and rather ostentatiously looks from Jean to the picture and back again. After dinner there follows a dreadfully intense silent scene, Pierre striding up and down looking first at the picture on the mantel, then at his mother. When Mme Rosémilly is announced, Mme Roland seems even more troubled, and Pierre guesses that his mother fears a woman will be quick to see the resemblance. He hides the picture, which alarms his mother still more, and disappears without a word.

In the weeks that follow, Pierre's suspicions, so obvious to his mother, bring about a daily crisis of dumb suffering between them. He cannot refrain from torturing her by his actions or by thinly veiled references. During this protracted tension the whole family goes for a day's outing to Saint-Jouin, where Jean comes to a decision and proposes to Mme Rosémilly. Here there is a shift of point of view: Pierre leaves the center of the stage and is replaced by Jean. Jean's thoughts are disclosed without commentary by the author, followed by the admirably objective scene of the proposal, culminating in the practical-minded Mme Rosémilly's "exposé net de la situation." Pierre and his mother witness the scene from a distance and his bitter remark, "J'apprends comment on se prépare à être cocu," sends her flying in anguish to her other son.

On their return to Le Havre they inspect Jean's new apartment. During the absence of the others, the two sons find themselves together in the salon, where Pierre's slighting remarks about "the widow" involve them in a dispute which leads to Jean's announcement that he is going to marry her. Pierre has reached the breaking point; exasperated, he flings at his brother that it is dishonorable to accept "la fortune d'un homme quand on passe pour le fils d'un autre," and reveals what is common gossip. He pours it all out, "la tumeur venait de crever," and he rushes out blindly. Here the author intervenes with a comment on Jean: "Il était de la race des temporiseurs qui remettent toujours au lendemain . . . , one who had never faced any problems in his life and who was now overwhelmed by this catastrophic revelation. His mother, who has overheard everything, confesses to Jean her guilt and in a long speech she divulges the history of the Maréchal affair. She agrees not to run away, but meanwhile what can be done about Pierre?

Maupassant, after presenting almost entirely in dialogue this long crucial scene in Jean's apartment with a profoundly dramatic effect, turns to an analysis of Jean's reaction, so different from that of Pierre, who had been hurt "dans la pureté de son amour filial." Jean is more concerned with the effect on "ses intérêts les plus chers." Maupassant goes on to explain that the suddenness of the shock had swept away any moral prejudices he might have had and that he was not, in any case, "un homme de résistance" but one who preferred above all to escape embarrassing complications. But some solution is necessary. All of this analyzing by the author, explaining Jean by deductions and comparisons which Jean himself does not make, is rarely applied to Pierre. This serves to keep Pierre the central figure since we have the illusion of being told the story as if directly by him, from his point of view. The shift of point of view in the scene between Jean and his mother is necessary to impart to the reader that knowledge which Pierre seeks, but which he can never find. He can never completely dispel the fog.

Jean debates whether he should not refuse the legacy and has about convinced himself that he should renounce all claim, when a steamer whistle in the port gives him an idea. At breakfast the surface of things has been glossed over and the brothers behave as if nothing had happened. Jean leads the conversation to a discussion of a new ship, the *Lorraine,* which is about to make its maiden voyage, and reports what salary is earned by the captain, the purser, and the ship's doctor. Pierre, already intent on the idea of getting away, understands the drift of the conversation, and it is generally agreed than an effort should be made to get him the post of doctor on the *Lorraine.*

Jean and his mother pay a visit to Mme Rosémilly. Maupassant takes over with a survey of her apartment from his own point of view, a merciless portrait of a sentimental bourgeois décor, with a particularly heavy-handed irony in the description of the pictures on the wall. This and the distressingly coy conversation on the coming marriage strike what sounds like a false note, though there is some justification for the scene at this point. From the moment that Pierre understands that the post of ship's doctor provides a solution to his problem, there is a marked decrescendo, the affair is settled, only a few threads remain to be gathered, and perhaps the acid description of Mme Rosémilly's apartment has at least the function of marking this *détente.*

Everything is in fact settled: Pierre gets the position as doctor on the *Lorraine,* yet he alone is still uncertain about

Jean's birth. He does not know whether his mother confessed or denied to Jean, nor does he know with absolute certainty himself that she is guilty, although he is almost sure that she is. He makes his preparations for departure, and as he waits for the sailing date we are shown two scenes which parallel those at the beginning which had set off the whole train of action. The whole dénouement in fact matches exactly the opening scenes and marks the return to an equilibrium that is however not quite the same. Again Pierre visits Marowsko, this time to say good-bye, which fills the old man with consternation for he was counting on Pierre's practice to build up his pharmacy. As he leaves him Pierre thinks, "Personne n'aura pour moi un regret sincère." Again he remembers the waitress ("Elle avait raison, après tout.") but the *brasserie* is full, the waitress busy and totally indifferent to his departure.

On the day of the sailing the family gathers in his cabin for an intolerably awkward scene. There being nothing left to say, Pierre lectures on the pharmaceutical properties of the contents of his medicine chest to fill up the silence. The family leaves him at last to wave good-bye to him from their small boat. Here we are effectively back at the beginning again, with the Rolands and Mme Rosémilly in the boat, only this time Pierre has been eliminated. It is only after they wave and the steamer passes that M. Roland ("le bonhomme comptait si peu") learns by accident that Jean is to marry Mme Rosémilly.

It is no accident that the fog symbol reappears at the very end. The last words of the novel as Mme Roland turns again to the sea as the steamer fades into the distance, are: "Mais elle ne vit plus rien qu'une petite fumée grise, si lointaine, si légère qu'elle avait l'air d'un peu de brume." Maupassant in his manuscript wrote: "si légère qu'elle semblait un nuage," but changed it in proof. Pierre is pursued by "un peu de brume," never able to rid himself of it completely for he never *knows* the truth absolutely as does Jean or the reader. This bit of haze that remains carries back through the book to the first sign of it which was "la lampe qui charbonnait" at the end of the first chapter as Mme Roland mused over the news of the inheritance.

The theme of *Pierre et Jean* was deeply rooted in Maupassant's consciousness and one that he treated in short stories and novels from every possible angle. He appears to have been obsessed by speculation on what happens to children who are the product of illicit or adulterous love affairs, especially children who grow up unaware of their true parentage. In a short story "Le Testament," written in 1882, he used the device of a will to reveal that the third son of a family was really the son of the lover, all the mother's fortune being left to this younger son, who then assumed the family name of his true parent. Yet this story, while it is obviously linked to *Pierre et Jean,* is actually a by-product of his work on *Une Vie,* the mother in the shorter work being a curious combination of Jeanne's mother and Jeanne herself. "L'Attente," also written in 1882, is perhaps closer to the treatment of *Pierre et Jean,* since it deals with the effect on a son when he discovers his mother has a lover. But it is idle to look for a single "source" in a short story for the novel. Dumesnil's classification of the stories by subject shows this single theme

treated an extraordinary number of times both before and after *Pierre et Jean.* Mme Lecomte du Nouy's statement that the idea for the novel was suggested by the fact that a friend of his was left a large fortune by "un commensal de la famille," may be true or simply a pleasant fiction, but does not in any case add anything to our knowledge of the novel.

What is probably more instructive is a glance at what has been left out of the novel, sources that Maupassant wisely refrained from utilizing, which is essentially what distinguishes *Pierre et Jean* from the earlier novels. We have been particularly struck by the tight structure of this novel, its concentration, its unique concern with the subject at hand, eliminating any extraneous material. The first three novels are crammed with anecdotes and sketches which sometimes fill out the background and enrich it but which most often, in *Une Vie* and *Mont-Oriol,* are simply gratuitous padding. In *Pierre et Jean* he happily overcame this desire to pad, not that materials were lacking, but by definite artistic choice. One very revealing example of this is contained in the episode of the Roland family's trip to Saint-Jouin. They lunch at the inn there, are provided by the proprietress with clothing and equipment for crayfishing. The proprietress of the inn, who is known as "la belle Alphonsine" is but briefly described and plays her role at the edge of the scene. Now Maupassant had written in the *Gil Blas* of August 1, 1882 a sketch of the curious and picturesque innkeeper of Saint-Jouin, "la belle Ernestine," and in the course of the article remarked three times what a wonderful character she would be in a novel. In view of his past record, it is remarkable that Maupassant was able to bring in this personage without lingering over her at all; for he saw that though she was splendid material for a novel she had no function whatsoever in *Pierre et Jean.*

As far as one can see, there are no real textual borrowings from earlier works. Certain favorite ideas or leit-motivs recur but are generally brief and quite different in form from previous versions. For example, the theme of man's solitude and his desire for the companionship of marriage is expressed by Pierre as he wanders on the quai early in the story. The nearest thing to a textual borrowing is a description of the ship leaving for Trouville, which resembles the account of the same scene as given earlier in a story "Découverte." In the story he began thus: "Quand on fut sorti du port, le petit bâtiment fit une courbe rapide, dirigeant son nez pointu sur la côte lointaine entrevue à travers la brume matinale. . . . " In *Pierre et Jean* we read: "Le petit paquebot sortit des jetées, tourna à gauche et soufflant, haletant, frémissant, s'en alla vers la côte lointaine qu'on apercevait dans la brume matinale. . . . " This may be nothing more than a new evocation of a familiar scene rather than a rewriting of an earlier text, but, in any event, Maupassant refrained from dumping into the novel his ready-made description.

One more item of source material should be mentioned since the connection has apparently not been made before. Pierre Borel and Léon Fontaine have written: "Pour essayer de se faire expliquer le secret de ses effroyables migraines, il questionnait invariablement le pharmacien de la localité où il se trouvait. À Etretat, que de soirées il a passées dans l'arrièreboutique du pharmacien Leroy! À Bezons, il avait d'interminables conversations avec un pharmacien polonais" ["Maupassant avant la gloire," *Revue de France,* October 1, 1927]. Undoubtedly this Polish pharmacist is the base on which he built Marowsko.

The real source of *Pierre et Jean,* however, remains hidden in Maupassant's mind, in the circumstances, whatever they were, which drove him to treat again and again in his fiction the theme of doubtful paternity. That obsession produced many fine stories and this tight little masterpiece of a novel. He had freed himself from the limitations of the novel by addition, had extended and made more supple his technique, resisting the temptation to develop extraneous incidents which so vitiated the earlier novels. He had produced a novel virtually without a blemish, but he could not stop there. He continued the process of liberation in his next two novels, but he moved falteringly, without the absolute control he showed in *Pierre et Jean,* and he moved into an alien field, as if against his will. (pp. 102-19)

Edward D. Sullivan, in his Maupassant the Novelist, *Princeton University Press, 1954, 199 p.*

Unsigned review of *Pierre et Jean:*

Among the novels of M. Guy de Maupassant *Pierre et Jean* probably ranks as the author's masterpiece, and though it is hardly to be compared to some of his short stories, it is of so episodical a nature that it may be said to possess the qualities of his short stories without the defects of his sustained romances. It is a very serious psychological study and in this respect rather remarkable among M. de Maupassant's works, which usually pursue a different method. His exposition of this method, however, is singularly enough prefixed to *Pierre et Jean* as a Preface, and is well worth reading for the light it throws on the way of working of the most celebrated writer of *Contes et nouvelles* of our time, if not for the value of the principles it advocates. . . .

Review of Maupassant's Pierre et Jean *in* The Book Buyer, *April 1880.*

Robert J. Niess   (essay date 1959)

[*In the excerpt below, Niess questions the emphasis the critic Edward D. Sullivan places on fog symbolism in* Pierre and Jean. *Niess finds more importance in darkness (as a symbol of concealment and flight) and in light (symbolizing dawning certainty and understanding). Sullivan's essay is excerpted above.*]

In the continuing appraisal and reappraisal of French realism being carried on by scholars and critics, one fact is becoming clearer and clearer: that the old charge of obviousness so often brought against the realists and their novels is in reality baseless and that realism as a whole offers just as fertile a field for the perspicacious reader as romanticism or as symbolism itself. We find with each new article

on Flaubert, for instance, that his lexicon always carries a double burden of direct statement and of implied meaning, philosophical, social, ironic, emotional. Not a page of his is without its little significant fact, its signpost, its 'epiphany' not a line he wrote can now be taken to mean certainly one thing and only one thing. Always there is the suspicion, and it is normally well founded, that if we look closely enough we will see that the detail, the metaphor, the simile, the description, the dialogue is to be taken in two senses and if we are content to read Flaubert for direct meanings only, then we are content to read only something less than half of what he consciously put into his pages.

Guy de Maupassant was, of course, his aptest pupil and it is certainly becoming more and more evident, as the critics sift his style and the scholars turn his manuscripts inside out, that a very great part of what seems obvious at first glance is really not so obvious at all, or at least, if obvious in its primary meaning, it also carries meanings and hints that are not so clear and not so apparent. While Maupassant clearly never was the subtle technician his godfather was, it is still possible to read a good many of his works with an eye to symbolic motif and to draw some rather interesting conclusions about this author who is dismissed by altogether too many moderns with the contemptuous sniff that he is anything but 'intelligent.' Intelligent he was not, if we take men like Gide to represent the party of intelligence, but he was not so obtuse as some of the younger critics make him out to be either and a host of short stories, plus a handful of novels, are there to prove it. They prove, it would seem, that it is very nearly as risky to take him at face value as Flaubert and that he was as capable as the greater man of letting his true meaning be carried by the 'sous-en-tendus,' by the hints, the signposts, by the symbols, in a word.

Pierre et Jean, it seems to me, is one of the best proofs of Maupassant's skill at this artistic kind of dissimulation. Some of its symbols seem to have such importance in its economy that it may not be an exaggeration to claim that they hold the key to its true meaning and to Maupassant's intentions and aims.

One of Maupassant's best critics, Professor Edward D. Sullivan, appears to be in agreement with me here, although he does not go so far as I in this kind of interpretation. In his excellent *Maupassant the Novelist,* Professor Sullivan goes to some lengths in discussing the frequently recurring fog symbol in *Pierre et Jean* and from his analysis of its appearances and general role in the story comes to a conclusion as to the fundamental meaning of the work that is highly original, though not, perhaps, entirely comprehensive. His belief is that the fog symbol, recurring as frequently as it does, was certainly no accident and that through it Maupassant intended us to conclude that Pierre, who is of course the central figure, never arrives at complete certainty about his mother's guilt or innocence and remains to the end in doubt and apprehension. In his discussion of Chapter IV of the novel, the chapter in which Pierre first begins to think seriously of the possibility of a sin on his mother's part, Sullivan says this:

Woven into Pierre's examination of conscience

is a description of the background: the harbor, the lights of ships and lighthouses, the sights and sounds of the port. These brief descriptive notes do more than merely set the stage, however; certain elements possess a symbolic value which accompanies and reinforces the evolution of Pierre. The fog, especially, whirls and eddies through the novel as a discreetly handled 'objective correlative.' The fog in Pierre's mind as he tries to see his way clear through the chain of circumstances is matched by the haze and fog of the harbor setting. As he meditates here on the quai, only slightly troubled about himself and without suspecting anything untoward in the legacy, the night is clear and the lights are visible, but there is nevertheless a 'brume nocturne' which filters the light of the stars. Once engulfed in the fog, Pierre will never be able to emerge completely or dispel it entirely.

A little later, Sullivan adds this: "The shift of point of view in the scene between Jean and his mother is necessary to impart to the reader that knowledge which Pierre seeks, but which he can never find. He can never completely dispel the fog." And lastly, as he terminates his analysis of the work, he remarks: "It is no accident that the fog symbol reappears at the very end [. . .] Pierre is pursued by 'un peu de brume,' never able to rid himself of it completely, for he never *knows* the truth absolutely as does Jean or the reader."

This explanation is original, ingenious and attractive, but perhaps not completely acceptable nonetheless, for there can be little real doubt that Pierre understands the situation as clearly as anyone—indeed, one might argue that it is the gradual growth of understanding on his part that is the very core and meaning of *Pierre et Jean,* not the growth of jealousy, as the most frequent interpretation has it. It would seem that Pierre's knowledge of what his mother has done is in fact clearer and more comprehensive than her own knowledge of her sin or Jean's realization of it after she has told him of her youthful love for Maréchal, for Pierre arrives at his certainty by a long process of analysis, reasoning and weighing of the evidence; he comes to a moral certainty that is more certain than her own personal knowledge of what she has done, more certain because based on intellectual and emotional processes, while hers is corrupted by sentiment and by the need to justify herself. And surely Pierre's certainty is more certain than Jean's, for Jean seems hardly concerned in the matter at all and his knowledge is corrupted, like his mother's, by self-interest and sentiment. If there is anyone in the novel who really *knows,* who is not in the fog, it is surely Pierre, and it is the process of discovery, of the elimination of the fog of doubt and ignorance, that forms the true subject of the novel.

It is possible to argue this way because other symbols in *Pierre et Jean* clearly counterbalance and contradict the fog symbols; they form a subtle and skillful opposition which is in effect a rendering of the process of the growth of knowledge in a human mind. This duel of opposite symbols quite changes the meaning of the story from a tale of jealousy or an account of doubt to the history of the acquisition of a horrible certainty, and it is this conflict of oppo-

site tendencies, symbolized by opposite motifs, which gives the book its tragic sense. These motifs, largely but not completely found in the first half of the book, consist in the main of two kinds, fog, smoke and sleep symbols on the one hand, symbolizing doubt and confusion, and light symbols on the other, representing, seemingly, the penetration of knowledge into an unwilling mind.

To understand the opposition of these symbols it is necessary to keep the structure of the novel fairly carefully in mind. This is the march of events:

Chapter I, of course, presents all the main characters with their dominant traits, and further includes the all-important fact of the legacy left to Jean by an old friend of the Roland family, one Maréchal. In the second chapter, Pierre, now clearly the central figure, begins to speculate on the reasons for the curious provisions of the legacy which so advantaged his brother and which left him completely aside and as he does, the first beginnings of jealousy appear in his mind. As yet, there is no suspicion of his mother, but when he visits an old friend of his, the Polish pharmacist Marowsko, the seeds of doubt are planted by a remark made by the old man and the novel is on its way to the dénouement. In Chapter III Pierre, still the central figure, begins to examine his own life in the light of his brother's advantages and his jealousy of him grows with the realization that he has wasted his own years and has nothing to show for his education. But the significant fact of this chapter is again provided by a remark of a second person, this time a waitress in a café he frequents. She points out, when he has told her of his brother's inheritance, that "ce n'est pas étonnant qu'il te ressemble si peu," thus putting in words an obscure sentiment that has been torturing Pierre for hours already and which is almost at the point of becoming a recognizable emotion. Pierre is so upset by her observation that he succeeds in ruining a dinner given by his family for Jean. Chapter IV, almost without external events of any consequence, is devoted to Pierre's analysis of the situation and to the gradual replacement of jealousy as his dominant emotion by a growing sense of certainty that his mother has sinned and that Jean is not Roland's son at all, but Maréchal's. But he is not yet completely satisfied that his intimate conviction is justified in fact and the chapter ends on an ambivalent note. In Chapter V, Pierre persuades his mother to produce an old portrait of Maréchal and makes a brief visit to Trouville, where on the beach all the evidence falls into place and he becomes convinced that his suspicions of his mother are justified. On his return, he begins the slow torture of his mother which will rend the family and eventually drive him from home for good. Chapter VI provides a diversion in the action and is concerned largely with a fishing expedition undertaken by the whole family, during which Jean finally screws up his courage to the point of asking Mme Rosémilly, an attractive young widow, to become his wife. In Chapter VII, the dramatic highlight of the novel, Pierre discloses his suspicions to Jean and later their mother tells Jean the truth about her liaison with Maréchal. Chapter VIII is largely concerned with plans for obtaining a position for Pierre as ship's doctor on the Lorraine, for it is evident to everyone but M. Roland—"le bonhomme comptait, si peu"—that

Pierre can no longer live with either Jean or his mother. In the concluding chapter, Pierre finally departs from Le Havre, a victim of his own certainty of his mother's sin.

Now let us look at the symbols which seem to carry the sense of the work. First, the symbols of uncertainty, ignorance, oblivion and hesitation: smoke, fog, night and sleep. It is notable that the greater part of the important action of the novel, that is, the psychological action in Pierre's mind, the process of discovery and complete realization of his mother's fault, takes place at night. I do not think this is just accidental or the result of an old convention; it seems rather, that Maupassant may have wanted to stress by this circumstance the ignorance in which Pierre finds himself as to the events of the past, the ignorance which his bitter psychological investigation finally dispels. But these night scenes in themselves would not be sufficient to impart the sense of what Maupassant is driving at and they are reinforced by fairly frequent references to smoke and fog, which, like night, appear to represent the opposite of enlightenment. The references to smoke, while less frequent than those to fog, are more widely scattered in the novel, occurring from the first to the last chapter and appearing nearly every time the sea is mentioned. One of them in particular, the last one, seems significant and I shall return to it later.

The fog symbols are almost entirely concentrated in Chapter IV, the chapter in which Pierre faces the problem posed by the inheritance directly for the first time and comes to something like certainty of his mother's guilt. The first of them occurs when Pierre is out sailing with Papagris, the sailor. After some hours of beautiful weather on the water, the old man points out to him:

> V'là de la brume, M'sieu Pierre, faut rentrer.

> Il leva les yeux et aperçut vers le nord une ombre grise, profonde et légère, noyant le ciel et couvrant la mer, accourant vers eux, comme un nuage tombé d'en haut.

> Il vira de bord, et vent arrière, fit route vers la jetée, suivi par la brume rapide qui le gagnait. Lorsqu'elle atteignit la *Perle,* l'enveloppant dans son imperceptible épaisseur, un frisson de froid courut sur les membres de Pierre, et une odeur de fumée et de moisissure, l'odeur bizarre des brouillards marins, lui fit fermer la bouche pour ne point goûter cette nuée humide et glacée. Quand la barque reprit dans le port sa place accoutumée, la ville entière était ensevelie déjà sous cette vapeur menue, qui, sans tomber, mouillait comme une pluie et glissait sur les maisons et les rues à la façon d'un fleuve qui coule.

Some hours later, after Pierre has obtained from his parents certain apparently innocuous but really significant details about the relationship of Maréchal to the family, he leaves the house and walks through the streets of Le Havre:

> Elles étaient ensevelies sous le brouillard, qui rendait opaque, pesante et nauséabonde la nuit. On eût dit une fumée pestilentielle abattue sur la terre. On la voyait passer sur les becs de gas qu'elle paraissait éteindre par moments. . . .

Still later, when Pierre has arrived at something like the terrible certainty which will ruin his life, he has this climactic experience:

> . . . soudain, comme si elle l'eût entendu, comme si elle l'eût compris et lui eût répondu, la sirène de la jetée hurla tout près de lui. Sa clameur de monstre surnaturel, plus retentissante que le tonnerre, rugissement sauvage et formidable fait pour dominer les voix du vent et des vagues, se répandit dans les ténébres sur la mer invisible enseveli sous les brouillards.

> Alors, à travers la brume, proches ou lointains, des cris pareils s'éleverent de nouveau dans la nuit. Ils étaient effrayants, ces appels poussés par les grands paquebots aveugles.

There does not seem to be much doubt that Maupassant was here deliberately trying to convey the idea of uncertainty, groping, hesitation, ignorance, the mental state against which the truth must struggle for possession of Pierre's mind.

But these 'passive' symbols are reinforced by a more 'active' symbol, sleep, if the paradox may pass. Of the book's nine chapters, no less than five end with references to Pierre's sleep or to his efforts to sleep. Chapter II, for example, in which the first glimmerings of suspicion enter his mind, ends thus: "Pendant quelque temps, puis il entendit Jean qui marchait doucement dans la chambre voisine, puis il s'endormit après avoir bu deux verres d'eau." Chapter III, where the waitress really arouses his doubts about his mother, has these as its final lines: "De la fin de cette soirée il n'eut guère souvenir. On avait prie le café, absorbé des liqueurs, et beaucoup ri en plaisantant. Puis il se couche, vers minuit, l'esprit confus et la tête lourde. Et il dormit comme une brute jusqu'à neuf heures le lendemain." Chapter IV, where he comes almost to certainty, closes in this way: "Il avait accumulé les prouves ainsi qu'on dresse un réquisitoire . . . Alors il rentra pour se coucher, et, à force de volonté, il finit par s'assoupir." No reference to sleep terminates Chapter V, where Pierre finally and clearly arrives at certainty, but this is understandable; it seems that here Maupassant is indicating by this break in the established rhythm that the truth, which is revealed to Pierre so disastrously by the 'moment privilégié' of Trouville, is simply too strong to be fought against, that it cannot be shut out by any means.

But again, Chapter VI, the fishing expedition, ends by a reference to sleep that may be significant: "La mer montant les chassa vers les pêcheurs qu'il rejoignirent, puis tout le monde regaga le côte. On réveilla Pierre qui feignit de dormir; et le dîner fut trés long, arrosé de beaucoup de vins." It is notable that Pierre is not asleep but only pretending to be and here, it would appear, Maupassant is attempting to indicate that Pierre's efforts to blot out the truth have been resumed, after the Trouville incident has lost some of its impact, but that those efforts are fruitless, so great is the evidence now. Lastly, Chapter VII, which contains the dramatic climax of the novel, the revelation by Madame Roland to Jean that he is Maréchal's son, and the chapter which ends the psychological action of the book, closes with these brief words: "Seul dans la maison,

Pierre ne dormit pas et l'avait entendu revenir." Again, Pierre cannot sleep—here he does not even try, and by this last reference Maupassant surely means us to understand that from now on oblivion, concealment, flight are finally impossible for Pierre, that he is now condemned to know the truth for the rest of his ruined life.

These darkness symbols of concealment and flight are balanced by a series of opposite symbols, all of them dealing with light, a motif that seems to represent the progressive invasion of Pierre's mind by the truth which he seeks at all costs to blot out from his consciousness. All of them occur in the chapters which have most importance for the psychological progress of the novel and they cease, significantly, when the truth has finally penetrated Pierre's mind. In Chapter II, containing the beginning of Pierre's suspicions, he goes out to wander in the city in order to try to discover the cause of the vague malaise which has seized him at the news of the legacy. Almost immediately "il ne sentit attiré par les lumière du café Tortoni, et il s'en vint lentement vers la façade illuminée." A little later in the same chapter the most impressive of these light symbols appears [the light of innumerable beacons along the coastline.] (pp. 511-17)

Still later in this same chapter, when Pierre visits the old

Pierre, unable to sleep, sinks down on the stairwell. Wood engraving by Dupuis/Lemoine.

pharmacist, the light symbol reappears, this time in the form of "un seul bec de gaz."

There are no similar passages in Chapter III, but in IV, where Pierre approaches but does not quite attain certainty, he again wanders to the port of Le Havre in quest of an answer to his unspoken problem. There the symbol recurs:

> Lorsque'il se fut assis à l'extrémité du môle et ferma les yeux pour ne point voir les foyers électriques, voilée du brouillard, qui rendent le port accessible la nuit, ni le feu rouge du phare sur le jetie sud, qu'on distinguait à peine cependant. Puis se tournant à moitié, il pose ses coudes sur le granit et cache sa figure dans les mains.

Later, in the same setting, it comes again: "Pierre se retourna et aperçut son oeil rouge [i.e., the signal light], terni de brume. Puis, sous la clarté diffuse des feau électrique du port, une grande ombre noire se dessina entre les deux jetées." But perhaps the best example of this symbol occurs in Chapter V, where Pierre attains complete moral certitude; here the symbol is quite evidently employed expressly for the purpose of enlightenment and there can be no real doubt that Maupassant intended us to conceive the dazzling light of the beach at Trouville as a parallel to the moment of intuition which Pierre experiences as he witnesses the scene and which finally and completely convinces him of his mother's guilt. . . . True enough, light is not specifically mentioned [in that scene], but there was no necessity for mentioning it, for Maupassant knew that every reader would immediately identify a beach scene with sunlight, and moreover the colorful presentation of the ensemble could only evoke the presence of dazzling light.

Once more, it seems significant that the light symbols cease when Pierre has reached certainty; they have served their purpose, there would be no point in continuing it.

There remains only one detail, the fact that the very last lines of the novel contain one last reference to smoke. The family had just seen Pierre off on the Lorraine: "Comme ils allaient quitter le quai et prendre le boulevard François-Premier, la femme se retourna encore une fois pour jeter un dernier regard sur la haute mer; mais elle ne vit plus rien qu'une petite fumée grise, si lointaine, si légere qu'elle avait l'air d'un peu de brume." Do these lines prove Sullivan's point, that Pierre goes away still uncertain as to the true facts of the case? Perhaps, but not necessarily. They may mean something quite different: that Pierre has indeed come to certainty that he knows the truth, but that his mind and soul, as human minds and souls will do, are attempting to blot out what he ineluctably knows, that they are trying to return to the blessed oblivion which for Maupassant, that tortured soul, meant the only happiness man can know here below. (pp. 518-19)

Robert J. Niess, " 'Pierre et Jean': Some Symbols," in The French Review, *Vol. XXXII, No. 6, May, 1959, pp. 511-19.*

Ernest Simon   (essay date 1960)

[*In the following excerpt, Simon addresses Edward Sullivan's argument, excerpted above, concerning Maupassant's use of the objective technique in* Pierre and Jean. *He discusses the "hybrid character" of the novel, noting the analytical is clearly dominant over the objective technique.*]

> Je n'ai point l'intention de plaider ici pour le petit roman qui suit. Tout au contraire les idées que je vais essayer de faire comprendre entraîneraient plutôt la critique du genre d'étude psychologique que j'ai entrepris dans **Pierre et Jean.**
>
> [Guy de Maupassant, **"Le Roman"**]

To someone who has just finished reading the preface to **Pierre et Jean,** this opening passage of Maupassant's essay on the novel might be the source of some puzzlement; for the most fundamental assertion contained in this preface is indeed that the novelist's art admits no general rules of composition and that it must include all *genres* and all methods. Why then did Maupassant think that the principles of his novel did not agree with those of its preface?

Maupassant must have realized that, in spite of his efforts toward impartiality, his preference for the naturalistic novel, the novel of objective observation in the manner of Zola, stood out very clearly in that section of his preface where he compares the objective novel to the novel of psychological analysis. Whereas he limits himself to a brief and precise description of the psychological novel, he discusses at much greater length his theory of the objective novel, and he is pleased to indicate all its advantages: the objective novel is closer to the facts of human existence where psychology is hidden under actions and words; it is " 'plus vraisemblable,' for those living around us do not tell us the motives that determine their actions." Furthermore, since we can know approximately only the functioning of our own mind and not that of others, it follows that an author who writes a pure psychological novel "can only substitute his own psyche for that of all his characters, for he cannot change his sense organs, which are the only links between ourselves and outside reality." In the whole preface the only declaration in support of the psychological novel is the following:

> Mais si, au seul point de vue de la complète exactitude, la pure analyse psychologique est contestable, elle peut cependant nous donner des œuvres d'art aussi belles que toutes les autres méthodes de travail.

After all the arguments marshalled in support of the objective novel, this is admittedly a rather feeble affirmation.

Inevitably, Maupassant's obvious preference for the objective technique in the preface to **Pierre et Jean** has influenced various interpretations of the novel. A. Artinian, in *Maupassant Criticism in France, 1880-1940,* reports that in a somewhat hostile review written in 1888, the critic Firmin Boissin admitted:

> Ce qu'il y a de mieux dans ce roman, je viens de le dire, c'est la partie psychologique. M. de Maupassant s'y est infligé un démenti à lui-même:

dans sa préface, il méprise la psychologie et dans son roman il prouve que l'on peut très bien allier les qualités du psychologue à celles du peintre.

André Vial, in *Guy de Maupassant et l'art du roman,* places the novel somewhere between the "Roman de mœurs" and the pure "roman d'analyse"; but Edward D. Sullivan's study, *Maupassant the Novelist,* proposes the thesis that **Pierre et Jean** represents not the application of an analytical method, but, on the contrary, an *extension* and refinement of his favorite objective technique. According to Mr. Sullivan, "**Pierre et Jean** is a psychological novel, but in this case the objective method has been used and adapted to the particular problem presented by the subject."

The different views of Maupassant's novel are, of course, dependent upon different conceptions of the criteria that distinguish a psychological from an objective novel. Maupassant too had his own criteria; and as the quotation at the head of this study shows clearly enough, he thought that **Pierre et Jean** was a novel of psychological analysis. Since it remains true, on the other hand, that in this same preface Maupassant voices just as clearly his preference for the objective method, it is possible that he wanted to meet a challenge and prove to himself as much as to his audience that psychological analysis "can produce results as beautiful as those of any other method."

It remains to be seen, however, whether the author did not unconsciously follow his natural inclination toward the objective method; whether he himself was not mistaken about his novel; and whether the principles of analysis that he puts into practice in the novel really do coincide with those he discusses in the preface.

These principles are very clearly outlined. The psychological novel seeks to indicate "les moindres évolutions d'un esprit" and the motives that determine the characters' actions. Facts in themselves are of only very secondary importance; they are the novel's pretext rather than its subject. The real subject is found in the motives and in the reactions of the mind "acting under the impulse of interests, passions and instincts."

The objective novel, on the other hand, limits its scope to an exact representation of what happens in life. To do this, it must carefully avoid complicated explanations and dissertations about motives and describe only characters, actions and events. Psychology must be hidden in the narrative as it is hidden under the facts of existence. With such an objective method, the characters' states of mind must be suggested in actions and gestures that enable the reader to guess their motives and their subjective reactions. In short, according to Maupassant, the objective novel must "hide psychology instead of displaying it."

Considered in its large, over-all characteristics, **Pierre et Jean** conforms rather closely to the main criteria of the psychological novel as outlined by the author. Outside events are relatively unimportant for the development of the narrative. Jean's inheritance is only the starting point of a moral and psychological drama. It is the pretext of the novel, the necessary first cause of Pierre's internal struggle, but it remains in itself a minor factor in the novel's subsequent development. The truly important event, Madame Roland's adulterous love affair, happened long before the chronological start of the action and remains unknown to everyone, including the reader, until the story is well under way. This event, almost forgotten even by Madame Roland, grows in importance for the novel's development in direct proportion to the importance it assumes in Pierre's mind. In other words, we are not dealing here with a true "roman de mœurs." The inheritance and the money it brings to Jean do not play the determining role that money plays in Balzac's novels, for example, or that poverty and alcohol play in *L'Assommoir*. Jean's inheritance is merely the mechanism that sets off Pierre's "crise de conscience," which is the true subject of the book.

The incident of Jean's inheritance has then a purely psychological value, and the drama is wholly subjective. Maupassant has refused to exploit the usual dramatic potentialities of events, and without the struggle going on in the young man's soul there would be no novel. There is, so to speak, a visual concentration on the character's mind, and it is the exploration of that mind by means of a sustained analysis that is the subject of the book. What we see in it above all is the psychological study of a man torn between his jealousy, his rancor, his filial love and his moral consciousness. As soon as Pierre objectifies his conflict by revealing it to this brother, as soon as he ceases to question his own conscience, the novel stops, for it is the psychological study that is the motive force behind the action.

Thus considered in large outline, *Pierre et Jean* may be said to conform to Maupassant's main criterion for the psychological novel: a concentration of interest on the mental activity of the characters rather than on events and actions. It now remains to examine in greater detail the technique of the novel and, in particular, the practice of the analytical technique.

Mr. Sullivan has dealt in some detail with the question of Maupassant's analytical technique. According to him, Maupassant's method in *Pierre et Jean* is not an analytical one, but simply a modification of his usual objective technique:

> The problem was to penetrate deeply into the psychology of his characters, since the basic action of the novel was henceforth to be internal, and yet to do this without compromising the objectivity he so highly prized. *Pierre et Jean* is the result of his effort to extend the objective technique to make it supple enough to deal with a purely psychological drama.

What this thesis fails to take into account is Maupassant's own criteria of objectivity and subjectivity as outlined above. For Maupassant, the great difference between the two types of novel resides precisely in a difference of method, in a shift of point of view. His conception of the analytical novel is that it displays the psychology of its characters and describes their mental activities directly from the inside. The objective novel, on the contrary, proceeds by indirection; it reveals the hidden motives of its characters only to the extent that the author succeeds in suggesting them through events, actions and spoken words. The very

idea of an objective direct description of psychological states would thus be, for Maupassant, a contradiction in terms.

Mr. Sullivan bases his thesis on the fact that the description of Pierre's mind is effected chiefly by means of the young doctor's introspection, without any intervention on the part of the author. According to him, Maupassant then is not analyzing his character but merely reporting his thoughts:

> Maupassant is impelled . . . to expose for us what goes on in the mind of his character, but his presentation operates within precisely defined limits which are a logical result of Maupassant's preoccupation with objectivity. The author never makes his presence felt in the story, his role is that of the skilled observer, ubiquitous but not omniscient. . . . At no point does the author assume a superior position and analyze his character's thoughts; he knows no more about Pierre than Pierre knows of himself.

Four pages later, however, Mr. Sullivan mitigates the too absolute implications of this last statement when he acknowledges that Maupassant does indeed at times take the position of the omniscient author. He remarks about the first chapter of the novel that "the point of view throughout the chapter is that of the omniscient author, or more exactly, the ubiquitous author." Thus, even if we admit for the moment Mr. Sullivan's contention that Pierre's extended self-analysis represents an effort toward an objective technique, it is more than probable that Maupassant did not apply this technique exclusively or consistently. Furthermore, at no point in his preface does Maupassant suggest a distinction between psychological analysis conducted by the author and that conducted by the subject himself. Indeed, the only distinction he admits is that between objective description and direct analysis.

In an observation pertaining to the beginning of Chapter Four, Mr. Sullivan suggests how Maupassant may have put his "objective technique" into practice in the novel as a whole: "The only function of the author here is to turn the results of Pierre's self-examination into indirect discourse." Mr. Sullivan, of course, does not imply that Maupassant consciously employed represented discourse as an objective technique, but rather that it was an inevitable corollary of his general efforts toward greater objectivity in the kind of psychological analysis he was attempting in *Pierre et Jean*. Perhaps too, represented discourse was, for Maupassant, a technique he had learned from his master Flaubert. Furthermore, he may also have used represented discourse to mitigate the fundamental "invraisemblance" he saw in the pure psychological novel. We remember that in the preface Maupassant preferred the objective technique chiefly because of its greater verisimilitude, its closer coincidence with actual situations. It is indeed much more likely that Pierre himself should follow the flow of his reflections and transmit them to the reader by means of represented discourse than to presuppose an omniscient author who knows all that goes on in his character's mind.

In fact, Maupassant abandons represented discourse as

soon as it is no longer "vraisemblable." Very often, some-times even in the same paragraph, represented discourse suddenly changes into direct analysis by the author. This stylistic process occurs most frequently when it is a ques-tion of giving the reader an insight that the subject himself does not possess, as in the following passage:

> Il se releva tout à coup avec la résolution d'aller faire une petite visite à Mme Rosémilly.
>
> Puis il se rassit brusquement.

So far we have straight, objective reporting by the author; but then, the style shifts quite suddenly to represented dis-course, which transmits Pierre's thoughts to the reader:

> Elle lui déplaisait, celle-là? Pourquoi? Elle avait trop de bon sens vulgaire et bas; et puis, ne sem-blait-elle pas lui préférer Jean?

At this point in the passage there is another sudden shift of point of view, and Maupassant steps in as the omni-scient author:

> Sans se l'avouer à lui-même d'une façon nette, cette préférence entrait pour beaucoup dans sa mésestime pour l'intelligence de la veuve, car, s'il aimait son frère, il ne pouvait s'abstenir de le juger un peu médiocre et de se croire supé-rieur.

The author intervenes here because Pierre cannot, in all likelihood, think clearly about a thing he does not admit to himself. What we have in this last passage is obviously more than just "Maupassant's summary of Pierre's self-examination," as Mr. Sullivan quite rightly concludes after having analyzed another passage; and the scope of the psychological analysis here goes well beyond "the lim-its of Pierre's knowledge of himself." There are numerous instances like the above, where the omniscient author steps in to supplement Pierre's self-knowledge.

It is also apparent from the above example that Maupas-sant's method becomes increasingly analytical as his char-acter's reactions become less conscious or more complex. It is noteworthy too, that the other characters are de-scribed in the objective manner of Maupassant's short sto-ries. A few passages of description or dialogue suffice to establish the personalities of Père Roland, Capitaine Beau-sire, Madame Roland and Madame Rosémilly. These are simple people, without any psychological complexity. Even Madame Roland's growing anguish is readily com-prehensible in its origin and immediate causes. Maupas-sant, accordingly, never needs—and indeed never uses—the analytical technique to describe these more or less pe-ripheral characters.

Nor does he use it at the beginning to describe Jean. He too is a rather simple man, less intelligent than his brother, whose reactions at first are eminently predictable. Mau-passant therefore limits delineation of his personality to a few objective descriptions like the following:

> Maintenant, il se taisait de nouveau, mais la clarté de son œil, la rougeur de ses joues, jusqu'au luisant de sa barbe, semblaient pro-clamer son bonheur.

And again:

> Dans la façon dont il riait, dont il parlait avec une voix plus sonore, dont il regardait les gens, à ses manières plus nettes, à son assurance plus grande, on sentait l'aplomb que donne l'argent.

But when it comes to describing Jean's much more com-plex reactions at the moment when he has just heard his brother's revelation, the author again abandons the objec-tive technique to give us a direct view of his character's mind. . . . (pp. 45-51)

This method, which seeks to adapt narrative technique—whether objective or analytical—to the degree of psycho-logical complexity, is even more apparent in the case of Pierre himself. His simpler characteristics, as well as those already well known to the reader—his jealousy, his ran-cor, his feeling of superiority—are always indicated objec-tively by means of simple dialogue (direct discourse) most often preceded by a very brief adverbial expression. . . .

A somewhat higher degree of complexity, where Pierre is just beginning to analyze himself, is presented in mono-logue form by means of direct discourse preceded by a ver-bal expression like: *il pensait, il se disait, il se demandait,* etc.— (p. 51)

As has already been indicated above, the third and fourth degrees of still greater psychological complexity are ren-dered by means of represented discourse and direct analy-sis by the author. The relatively simple exposition of the young man's state of mind at a given moment of his inter-nal crisis is executed through represented discourse. But the deeper analysis of the motives that determine his thoughts is carried out by the omniscient author who steps directly into the narrative in order to illuminate his char-acter's mind. [An] example will show how these various techniques are put into practice:

> Il se disait: "Pourquoi ce Maréchal a-t-il laissé toute sa fortune à Jean?"

This is the second degree of complexity. Pierre is starting to analyze his situation; his thoughts are clear and straightforward. Hence, the author first uses direct dis-course, then suddenly intervenes:

> Ce n'était plus la jalousie maintenant qui lui fai-sait chercher cela, ce n'était plus cette envie un peu basse et naturelle qu'il savait cachée en lui et qu'il combattait depuis trois jours, mais la ter-reur d'une chose épouvantable, la terreur de croire lui-même que Jean, que son frère était le fils de cet homme!

We have here an investigation of the deeper motives that are pushing Pierre to seek out the truth. Finally, the last paragraph brings a second shift in point of view and in technique:

> Non, il ne le croyait pas, il ne pouvait même pas se poser cette question criminelle! Cependant il fallait que ce soupçon si léger, si invraisem-blable, fût rejeté de lui, complètement, pour tou-jours. Il lui fallait la lumière, la certitude, il fal-lait dans son cœur la sécurité complète, car il n'aimait que sa mère au monde.

There is here a shift from the analysis of motives to a simpler exposition of Pierre's state of mind; we have, therefore, a lesser degree of psychological complexity; and Pierre's thoughts are transmitted to the reader through Pierre's introspection, i.e., by means of represented discourse.

Mr. Sullivan has rightly emphasized, as an example of objective technique in *Pierre et Jean,* the many descriptions of the foggy atmosphere of Le Havre, which corresponds symbolically to Pierre's confused and indecisive frame of mind. The leitmotif of the fog is more than a setting for the action; it also reinforces in the reader's mind the psychological portrait whose general outline might be lost in the progressive accumulation of small details. In this connection, Mr. Sullivan's thesis carries its full weight, for Maupassant uses the objective technique of the large overall symbol to the advantage of psychological analysis.

Pierre et Jean then can be said to present the hybrid character that Vial has discovered in it—with the reservation, however, that the analytical clearly dominates the objective technique. It seems that, although Maupassant did not want to abandon entirely his favorite objective technique, he was aware of the limitations that this method imposed upon him in the study of character. Objective description, which was adequate to present simple characters without any psychological complexity, is no longer adequate to probe an intelligent, introspective mind in conflict with itself like Pierre's. To this end he needed the greater flexibility offered by more direct analytical techniques; and he used these techniques whenever the psychological complexity of his characters required it. (pp. 51-2)

> Ernest Simon, "Descriptive and Analytical Techniques in Maupassant's 'Pierre et Jean'," in The Romanic Review, *Vol. LI, No. 1, February, 1960, pp. 45-52.*

Murray Sachs   (essay date 1961)

[*A Canadian critic, Sachs has published studies of Anatole France, Gustave Flaubert, and women writers of Quebec. In the following excerpt, he reviews several critical studies of* Pierre and Jean *to illustrate fundamental disagreements about the meaning of the novel. Sachs describes* Pierre et Jean *as a novel of self-discovery in which Pierre is left, in the end, devoid of illusions.*]

[In *The French Review* XXXII, No. 6, May 1959], Professor Robert J. Niess offered a very sensitive analysis of some of the symbols which support and underline the action in Maupassant's novel, *Pierre et Jean.* This discussion of symbols was a notable enrichment of the pioneer work on this novel done by Professor Edward D. Sullivan who, in his *Maupassant the Novelist* (Princeton, 1954), called attention to the symbolic importance of the fog which insistently accompanies Pierre's anguish throughout the book. Paradoxically, however, these two studies, which complement each other so enlighteningly, have at the same time served to expose the differences of opinion which exist as to what the book as a whole *means.* For on this point Sullivan and Niess are not in agreement. In Sul-

livan's view, the fog symbol carries the whole meaning of the book: it is a study, he feels, of Pierre's struggle with a crisis of doubt and uncertainty, which he can never dispel. Niess, on the other hand, points to the interplay of light symbols with the fog symbols, and argues that "it is the process of discovery, of the elimination of the fog of doubt and ignorance, that forms the true subject of the novel." And both these critics reject the traditional interpretation, lately argued with some additional refinements by M. André Vial [in *Guy de Maupassant et l'art du roman,* 1954], that *Pierre et Jean* is primarily a study of jealousy.

Now, we have Maupassant's own word that it is a serious matter when the meaning of one of his novels can come into question. In the essay **"Le Roman,"** which stands as the preface to *Pierre et Jean,* Maupassant declares that realistic novelists, such as himself, seek, not to entertain us, "mais de nous forcer à penser, à comprendre le sens profond et caché des événements." Accordingly, his skill as a novelist must lie in "le groupement adroit des petits faits constants d'où se dégagera le sens définitif de l'œuvre." Must we then conclude that, in *Pierre et Jean,* his skill has faltered, inasmuch as the work has given rise to conflicting definitions of its "sens définitif"? Or is it rather, perhaps, that his critics have misread the book? It is the contention of this essay that neither is the case. Maupassant's skill was never greater than in *Pierre et Jean,* and the three critics mentioned have, each from a different standpoint, been validly perceptive. But each has, it seems to me, defined only part of the book's total meaning. I should like, therefore, to offer a suggested reading of this novel which embraces, gratefully, the insights of Vial, Sullivan, and Niess, but which, as a statement of its theme, satisfies more completely the content of the work as a whole.

It is well known that the starting point of *Pierre et Jean* was a newspaper *fait divers* which Maupassant had seen, reporting the strange legacy left by a bachelor to the son of his best friends. It seems indisputable that Maupassant's initial idea was to explore the possible effects of such a legacy, supposing it to be motivated by illegitimate fatherhood. René Dumesnil has, moreover, demonstrated statistically, in his classification of Maupassant's stories by themes, that Maupassant was attracted obsessively by the themes of illegitimacy and adultery as they affect children. It is understandable, therefore, that all interpretations of *Pierre et Jean,* including those of Vial, Sullivan, and Niess, have tended to regard the illegitimacy of Jean and the adultery of Mme. Roland as being at the very center of Pierre's crisis, and hence at the center of the book's meaning.

Yet this stress on illegitimacy and adultery is surely misleading. Between the conception of the original idea and its final formulation, Maupassant obviously went through a radical shift of focus in his approach to the material. Though we have no record of the stages through which his thinking went, we can compare the starting point and the end result. If he began with an event: an inheritance which suddenly reveals illegitimacy and adultery within a family, he certainly ended with total absorption in a personality: that of one member of the family, and a member who was not, as a matter of fact, part of the story at the outset. For the original anecdote involved but a single son. It was doubtless to heighten the drama and add density to the narrative that Maupassant decided to posit two sons, the one legitimate, the other not. And perhaps it was the novelty of the point of view which suggested to Maupassant the idea of centering the novel on the reactions of the legitimate son. But at this point we meet the mysterious chemistry of artistic creation, which resists precise analysis. For we can only suppose that the effort to call into full flesh-and-blood being the character of Pierre Roland slowly enticed Maupassant into a shift of focus. His attention was transfixed by the complexities of the personality he was seeking to understand. It is clear, at any rate, that the legacy, the illegitimacy, and the adultery, became relegated in this process to secondary status. They became simply mechanisms of the plot, rather than its thematic center. They reveal Pierre's character, and are but the accidental catalysts of a crisis which, given the personality with which Pierre was endowed, would have had to occur sooner or later anyway. For *Pierre et Jean,* as Maupassant finally wrote it, emerged as the story of Pierre Roland's self-discovery, forced upon him by a crisis which exposed the hollowness and immaturity of the illusions by which he lived. It is not what Pierre discovers about the illegitimacy of his brother, or the adultery of his mother, but what he discovers about himself, that forms the center, the theme, the "sens définitif" of this novel.

It may help to understand further how such a radical shift of focus could have come about, if it is noted how much of himself Maupassant (consciously or unconsciously) put into the character of Pierre. This assimilation of the author's self into that of his protagonist became inevitable, probably, once Maupassant elected to make Pierre Roland his main character. For then the Roland family came to resemble, in important respects, Maupassant's own: a sensitive, intelligent, but volatile older brother, a less rewarding and less interesting younger brother, a mother who is a "mal mariée," a father held in low esteem, and finally, the intense attachment of the older brother to his mother. We must also note that the psychological analysis demanded by such a subject forced Maupassant, by his own principles, to draw heavily on his own personality. Had he not said, in **"Le Roman,"** that "celui qui fait de la psychologie pure ne peut que se substituer à tous ses personnages dans les différentes situations où il les place. . . . C'est donc toujours nous que nous montrons . . . "? It is no accident that Pierre, like his creator, is a brooding, insecure person, probingly and penetratingly curious about himself and others, yet also regularly impelled to flee the reality he thus uncovers, and seek solace in the gentle rocking of a boat on the ocean. The slow process by which the exploration of this character, so like himself, displaced Maupassant's interest from the elements which first attracted him to the material, seems thus entirely natural, and even inherent in the circumstances of creation. And in this same absorptive process by which the focus shifted, we may perhaps discern the secret of the striking fact about this novel, that its hero, whose behavior is often pusillanimous and even hateful, nevertheless engages our sympathy and understanding, and emerges in our mind as somehow morally superior to all the other characters.

Maupassant has obviously given too much of himself in this book for his protagonist's travail to be allowed to seem anything less than deeply moving. For all his remarkable objectivity of tone and style in this novel, Maupassant is passionately and personally present in this tragic study of Pierre Roland's enforced confrontation with the truth of his own self.

If we now test this definition of the theme against the action of the book, we can indeed perceive that, at each stage of the unfolding drama, Pierre does seem to find more of self-knowledge than of understanding of his family. The action proper begins, after a chapter of exposition, with Chapter II. We see Pierre brooding over the vague malaise that has harassed him since Jean's inheritance was announced. Quickly he faces the apparent truth: that he is jealous of Jean. But far from seeing in this discovery a moral problem for himself, or a threat to his family, Pierre is pleased! He has found out something about himself. "Il se sentait mieux, content d'avoir compris, de s'être surpris lui-même, d'avoir dévoilé l'autre qui est en nous." If he is pleased, rather than pained, it is because he does not yet see that his jealousy, no momentary aberration, has characterized his behavior since Jean was born. Pierre has made, without fully knowing it, the initial discovery in the chain which will destroy his image of himself, and his illusory self-esteem. Significantly, however, after the initial pleasure of discovery, Pierre is disquieted enough by his jealousy to seek a characteristic solace in contemplation of the sea, and in thoughts of exotic travels. The pattern of Pierre's reactions is more or less repeated at the end of Chapter II, when Marowsko says: "Ça ne fera pas un bon effet." There is no pleasure of discovery here, for Pierre does not at all recognize consciously the remark's implications. Yet it is the still unsuspected beginning of the destruction of his ideals. Pierre is obscurely upset by the remark, enough to be *impatienté.* And the two glasses of water he needs before falling asleep surely mean that he has been drained dry by emotional stress, though he is not aware of its origin.

Chapters III and IV develop both these strands further. Pierre's growing awareness of his jealousy, and his anxious doubts about what Marowsko implied, always retain a self-centered character. Each new discovery is a painful revelation to Pierre—but of himself, more than of the family. Thus, when he realizes that his bad behavior at Jean's party, in Chapter III, is pure jealousy, he proceeds to drown his shame in alcohol. The hint of the *fille de brasserie* that Jean must be Maréchal's son stuns him—but chiefly because it threatens his own image of his mother. His violent reaction excludes Jean, whose mother she also is, and his father. Nor can he think of Mme. Roland in any capacity but that of *his* mother: "L'émotion qu'il ressentit à l'idée de ce soupçon jeté *sur sa mère* [italics added] fut si violente qu'il s'arrêta." Naturally enough, when, brooding in the fog at the end of Chapter IV, he comes to consider the likely truth about the meaning of the legacy, the hardest hurdle for his mind to jump is the question of whether or not his mother had actually committed adultery. "S'était-elle donnée? . . . Mais oui, puisque cet homme n'avait pas eu d'autre amie." And the hurdle taken, he is so violently distressed that the urge to kill wells up in him. He is dimly but painfully aware of the destruction threatening his notion of purity, which is enshrined in his idealized picture of his mother, and which is a key anchor in his life.

The self-centered quality of this extraordinarily violent but still unconsciously motivated reaction emerges clearly through the events of Chapter V, which follow directly from it, and which push its meaning through to the conscious level of Pierre's mind. The next morning, having fled to Trouville to escape his thoughts, Pierre suddenly has a distorted and hallucinatory vision of the beach scene as a squalid and shameless "halle d'amour." Then later that day, his mother's lie about Maréchal's portrait finally shatters the last of Pierre's desperate hopes. The certainty that she committed adultery is now absolute for Pierre. And at this, the searing pain of seeing an ideal sullied, and an illusion destroyed, which had remained unarticulated in nameless fury at the end of Chapter IV, and which was veiled in symbol by the vision of the beach at Trouville, surges into overt expression in Pierre's conscious thoughts. No device can any longer conceal from Pierre the crushing disillusionment which this discovery represents: "Il regardait sa mère, qui avait menti. Il la regardait avec une colère exaspérée de fils trompé, volé dans son affection sacrée. . . . Mais oui, elle l'avait trompé dans sa tendresse, trompé dans son pieux respect. Elle se devait à lui irréprochable, comme se doivent toutes les mères à leurs enfants."

Thus, at the end of Chapter V, Pierre has come face to face with two glaring and major cracks in the structure of illusions by which he sustains himself. His self-esteem is seriously compromised by the discovery of his jealousy. And the only genuine affection in his life, his love for his mother, has turned out to be falsely based. Feeling betrayed in his idealism, and ashamed of his inner self, he now lashes out in fury at the world which has wounded him: he begins to torture his mother. The inevitable result of this is to expose still more his own inadequacies, and to torment himself even more deeply. While Chapter VI seems mainly given over to Jean's comic pursuit of Mme. Rosémilly, we are aware throughout that Pierre's inner tension is mounting unbearably. Finally, in the climactic moment of Chapter VII, when the building pressure within Pierre can be contained no longer, he explodes. He pours out the whole tale of his suspicions and sufferings in the presence of Jean, and in the hearing of his mother, in the next room. But once again, the meaning of the action is fundamentally personal to Pierre. He does not speak to inform, or even to hurt, his hearers. His need is to relieve his own insupportable tension: "Il semblait maintenant avoir oublié Jean et sa mère dans la pièce voisine. Il parlait comme si personne ne l'écoutait, parce qu'il devait parler, parce qu'il avait trop souffert, trop comprimé et refermé sa plaie."

All action in the novel ends at this point, for there remains only to assess the consequences of the events for all concerned. By his explosion, Pierre has irrevocably altered the family's relationship among its members. He has made his own continued contact with his mother, and with his brother, impossible on the old basis. Moreover he is left outside the new relationship which his mother and his brother were forced to establish after his outburst. He can never know what passed between them. In short, Pierre has made himself a complete outsider to his family, and his departure from Le Havre is necessary. The practical details by which this is achieved are set forth in Chapter VIII. But Chapter IX deals with the more important consequences. For, Pierre's explosion has also torn away the last shred of pretense, the remaining refuge still possible from the terrible reality about himself which has been unfolding through these events. His illusions have become untenable. As the book ends, Pierre is deeply shaken, disillusioned, and terribly, totally alone. He finds himself isolated, and unavoidably face to face with himself. Ironically, the confrontation with truth takes place on a transatlantic liner, once the symbol of adventure, romance, and escape to him, but now a confining, unstable prison in his anguished view. Events have thus brought him to the point where he can no longer flee, in mind or body, from the truth about himself. At the painfully late age of thirty, Pierre Roland will now, we realize, be compelled at last to grow up.

Thus the meaning of *Pierre et Jean,* the "sens profond et caché des événements," lies in the process of exposure by which the protagonist comes to see the illusory nature of his ideals and his self-image. The process of exposure begins, accidentally, with the announcement of a legacy. But it is clear that the seeds of the process have long been present. The legacy sets in motion a *crise de conscience* for Pierre, in which he traverses accesses of jealousy, the torment of doubt, the pain of certainty, and the horror of his own sadistic impulses. But these are only stages along Pierre's inescapable path toward self-knowledge; until, at the end, he stands, stripped bare of illusions, face to face with the crushing, implacable truth.

It is entirely just, of course, to point out that the action of the novel, set in motion by the legacy, also has important and shattering consequences for Jean and for Mme. Roland. Things can never be the same again for either of them, any more than they can for Pierre. Yet the consequences are surely, by any standards, most profound and far-reaching for Pierre. Hence it was on these consequences that Maupassant rightly concentrated his creative powers and insight—and it is these consequences which give the novel its core of meaning. (pp. 244-50)

William Sharp on Maupassant's economical literary style:

Not a page is wasted by this master of his craft, not a paragraph expended where a brief sentence would suffice, not a touch laid that could be dispensed with. One may read *Pierre et Jean* with pleasure, apart from the interest of the story; it has all the satisfying completeness inevitable to a work wherein the author has known exactly the effect he wished to produce, with tact and skill to apply that knowledge supremely well.

William Sharp, in The Academy, *October 25, 1890.*

Murray Sachs, "The Meaning of Maupassant's 'Pierre et Jean'," in The French Review, *Vol. XXXIV, No. 3 January, 1961, pp. 244-50.*

Elliott M. Grant   (essay date 1963)

[*Grant is a prolific writer on French literature whose works include studies of Victor Hugo and Emile Zola. In the following excerpt, Grant addresses the various critical interpretations of Pierre Roland and adds his own theory about the duality of Pierre's nature.*]

Recent discussions of Maupassant's **Pierre et Jean** have centered on the symbolism and meaning of the novel. [In his *Maupassant the Novelist,* 1954] Professor Sullivan sees in the recurring fog that accompanies Pierre's anguish a symbol of the doubt and uncertainty with which he struggles but which he never completely conquers. Professor Niess, on the other hand, finds in the frequent use of light an indication that the fog of doubt and ignorance is finally dispelled [*The French Review,* May 1959]. Professor Sachs maintains [in *The French Review,* January 1961] that the true significance of the novel is the revelation of a man's character to himself. In developing with great skill this thesis, Professor Sachs has illuminated an idea, glimpsed but not fully revealed by Professor André Vial [in his *Guy de Maupassant et l'art du roman,* 1954]. And the latest comer, Professor Cogny, combines harshness and sympathy in his concluding remarks on Pierre Roland [in the introduction to his edition of *Pierre et Jean,* 1959] when he pictures the pitiless young man departing disillusioned, distressed, and resigned into the unknown future he has been forced to accept. For this critic, Maupassant's comment on a society which victimizes the innocent appears to be a central meaning of the book.

While I find myself in basic agreement with Professors Sachs and Vial and in accord with Niess that before the end of the book Pierre has certainly discovered the truth (though I doubt that Professor Sullivan meant to imply that he hadn't), and while I have no quarrel with M. Cogny's views (except perhaps to question whether Maupassant intended to give social significance to his story), there is another aspect of the novel that needs to be emphasized. Pierre Roland represents, I believe, the complexity of human nature. He is, to paraphrase Racine's famous characterization of Phèdre, neither wholly good, nor wholly bad. I should like, therefore, in a brief analysis, to show how Maupassant discloses to the reader, possibly even more than to Pierre himself, the double nature of his protagonist. Here we shall perhaps find the "true meaning" of the book.

This duality in Pierre's character is suggested in the very first chapter. We are told that he is "exalté, intelligent, changeant et tenace, plein d'utopies et d'idées philosophiques." The next paragraph calls him "rancunier," and his jealousy of his brother is indicated soon after, but labelled at this point harmless (*inoffensive*). His idealism, hinted at in the first characterization, is defined more clearly when the author speaks of "ses enthousiasmes, ses tentatives avortées, tous ses élans impuissants vers des idées généreuses et vers des professions décoratives." Only a minor test of this man is offered in this first chapter. It

occurs in the rowing scene when Jean outdoes his brother and Pierre is shown as "humilié et rageur." The less attractive side of his personality is here momentarily revealed, and confirmed several pages later when he mutters something ungracious about the widow. The chapter ends in the Rolands' apartment with the news of Jean's inheritance. Pierre, alone, has put a leading question: "Vous le connaissiez donc beaucoup, autre-fois, ce Maréchal?" the import of which is understood by nobody, not even himself.

Both Pierre and Jean, too stimulated by the news for immediate sleep, leave the apartment separately for a nocturnal stroll; the second chapter is devoted to Pierre's promenade and to his reflexions which furnish a new test of his character. "Il se sentait' mal à l'aise, alourdi, mécontent comme lorsqu'on a reçu quelque fâcheuse nouvelle." He finally realizes, after searching his conscience, that he is jealous of his brother's good fortune. The better side of his nature at once condemns this jealousy, this "jalousie gratuite, l'essence même de la jalousie." He tells himself that he must treat that ("Faut soigner cela"). So that when a little later he meets his brother, the reader is prepared but nevertheless impressed to hear him congratulate Jean in the most unselfish and affectionate terms. At this point the balance is surely tipped in favor of the good that is within him.

Soon, however, events strain this goodness to the utmost. The conversation with the barmaid suggests the frightful possibility of Jean's illegitimate birth and gives significance to Marowsko's obscure reaction. The dinner celebrating Jean's inheritance and the leasing of the apartment which Pierre himself had hoped to acquire are obvious irritants. His growing memories of the past, culminating in his recollection of the miniature of Maréchal contribute inevitably to his suspicions and, therefore, to his anguish. During these two chapters the two sides of his nature are alternately revealed. His jealousy leads him to plague his father during the dinner, and his irritation over the apartment causes him to probe more deeply and pointedly into his parents' friendship with Maréchal. On the other hand, his better nature shows itself in the remorse, however brief, that he feels at spoiling his father's pleasure and above all in his self-condemnation for suspecting his mother. "Je suis fou, pensa-t-il, je soupçonne ma mère."

Chapter V brings to Pierre the destruction of his lingering hopes. It opens with an account of his sleepless night dominated by his suspicions, his fears, his passionate desire for reassurance. To escape from all this he flees to Trouville where the beach scene appears to him in a "distorted and hallucinatory vision" (if I may quote Professor Sachs) as "a squalid and shameless *halle d'amour.*" Then, on returning home, his mother's lie about Maréchal's portrait convinces him that all his suspicions and fears were only too justified. Before this chapter has ended he begins to torture his mother, deliberately and effectively. While it gives him a measure of satisfaction, it also causes him pain and anguish. For, again, Maupassant suggests Pierre's double nature by stating that he is "torturé et satisfait pourtant." The revelation of the good in Pierre, as well as the bad, is what previous critics have tended to minimize.

The first part of Chapter VI defines still more clearly the conflict in Pierre. He has now brought his mother to the point of nervous breakdown, and while, again, he feels some satisfaction at this, he is at the same time torn by remorse. . . .

But he is unable to stop, and in the second part of the chapter during the excursion to Saint-Jouin and Jean's pursuit of Mme Rosémilly which Maupassant relates in semi-comic terms, we have a concrete example of his sadistic impulse. For he says to his mother, as from a distance they watch Jean and the young widow: "J'apprends comment on se prépare à être cocu." And when Mme Roland in revolt defends the young woman as being "la droiture même," he jeers: "Ah! ah! La droiture même! Toutes les femmes sont la droiture même . . . et tous leurs maris sont cocus. Ah! ah! ah!" Yet even in this scene, in which the cruel side of Pierre's nature is uppermost, Maupassant does not forget to show the other. We glimpse it in that vision of Pierre stretched out flat on the beach, "comme un cadavre, la figure dans le galet: c'était . . . Pierre, qui songeait, désespéré." Is not this despair synonymous, at least in part, with remorse?

The climax comes in Chapter VII. If there was ever, in literature, a case of the irresistible outburst of repressed emotions, it is surely here. A quarrel with Jean leads to an explosion in which Pierre pours out all his recent suspicions and all his suffering, unchecked even by the knowledge that their mother is within hearing. His need, as Professor Sachs puts it admirably, is to "relieve his own insupportable tension": "Il semblait maintenant avoir oublié Jean et sa mère dans la pièce voisine. Il parlait comme si personne ne l'écoutait, parce qu'il devait parler, parce qu'il avait trop souffert, trop comprimé et refermé sa plaie." Certainly in this scene the cruel side of his nature seems to be uppermost. Yet we see that the cruelty results from suffering, and before the scene ends, Pierre's better nature struggles to the surface. "Tiens, je suis un cochon d'avoir dit ça!" he cries, and flees from the apartment. Let us note that he is the first to condemn himself.

This self-condemnation continues into the last chapter of the book. "Il vivait maintenant dans la maison paternelle en étranger muet et réservé. . . . Un remords le harcelait d'avoir dit cette chose à Jean. Il se jugeait odieux, malpropre, méchant, et cependant il était soulagé d'avoir parlé." But he has, as Professor Sachs says, made "continued contact with his mother, and with his brother, impossible on the old basis." He is forced into a virtual exile represented by his acceptance of an appointment as medical officer on a transatlantic liner.

What has he learned from this whole experience? He has, indeed, discovered something about himself. He has found within his nature a streak of cruelty, a touch of sadism. He has unveiled, as the novelist puts it, "l'autre qui est en nous." We should notice that Maupassant wrote *nous,* not simply *lui,* thus giving a more universal significance to his characterization of Pierre than would otherwise be the case. At the same time, this "other" man does not triumph easily. As Professor Vial says, we see in Pierre a "tumultueux combat" between the good and bad demons that inhabit him. Is it not, therefore, clear that even as Racine

makes us feel compassion for some of his characters caught in a kind of *engrenage* from which they seem unable to escape, Maupassant, too, inspires compassion for Pierre Roland wrestling with a problem which is certainly not of his own making, finally condemned to a life of a "forçat vagabond, uniquement parce que sa mère s'était livrée aux caresses d'un homme." He has not, admittedly, reacted to the problem with perfect nobility and iron self-control. He has, in short, displayed some of the weaknesses that exist in many men, perhaps, indeed, in most men. Does not this analysis of the double nature of Pierre Roland constitute for the reader the interest, the lesson, and, therefore, the meaning of the book? And is not this also a principal reason (though not the only one) why more than one critic has seen in *Pierre et Jean* a "chef-d'œuvre classique"? (pp. 469-73)

Elliott M. Grant, "On the Meaning of Maupassant's 'Pierre et Jean'," in The French Review, *Vol. XXXVI, No. 4, February, 1963, pp. 469-73.*

Paul Ignotus   (essay date 1966)

[*Ignotus is a Hungarian-born British writer, whose* The Paradox of Maupassant *is considered an important modern study of Maupassant. In the excerpt below, Ignotus discusses the recurring theme of illegitimacy in the works of Maupassant and looks at the concept of the psychological novel as exemplified in* Pierre and Jean.]

Why was Maupassant so tormented by [the subject of illegitimacy]? Some suspected a secret about his three alleged children. Others thought that he must have had doubts about the identity of his own father; the gossip about his mother and Flaubert may have reached him. This was an obvious assumption, but there was nothing to substantiate it; nothing except, perhaps, the fact that when Jean Lorrain referred to him as to one of the 'Flaubert-Zola stud', he reacted in a pathological way—preparing to challenge Lorrain to a pistol duel one day, and running away from the whole problem on another in a state of lethargic depression. It was a rude remark, no doubt, but why should he have taken it to heart more than he did any other abuse by unsuccessful colleagues? Was it because the word 'stud', when applied to Flaubert, may have alluded to biological links? All these are guesses. The fact is that his writings in which the problem of hidden or mistaken paternity is touched upon are innumerable; the industrious *Maupassantien,* Dr Pierre Cogny, advised by his elders, MM. Vial and Dumesnil, enumerated some forty short stories relevant to the subject, but added that his list was far from complete [preface to the 1959 edition of *Pierre et Jean*]. Disguised or not, a feeling of *alarm* about such a possibility seems to be ubiquitous in his works. And the book in which he exposed it most fully was his fourth novel, published early in 1888, *Pierre et Jean.*

Pierre and Jean are brothers; the former a penniless doctor, the latter a penniless lawyer, in Le Havre. With meagre parental support, they manage somehow; the modest and monotonous pleasures of provincial middle-class youth keep them going. Unexpectedly, the younger, Jean, inherits a large fortune from an old friend of the family. This should make them all happy; Jean is a good boy, he will certainly be generous with his close relatives, including Pierre who has dreamt much of touring faraway countries, entertaining glamorous women . . . Pierre cannot really feel that he has been deprived of anything since he has never claimed or counted on even a fraction of that money. Yet, as he went out for a stroll:

> He felt uneasy, oppressed, discontented, as when one has received disturbing news. Yet it was not any precise thought that afflicted him. . . . [And after a while] he began to ask himself the question: 'Ought this to be Jean's inheritance?' Yes, it was possible after all.

This fraternal jealousy was followed by an alarming suspicion of his mother: and this suspicion turned out to be true. The mother confessed. It was shattering, but had to be endured; they suddenly sensed the frustrated woman that their mother had been; could they condemn her for what little colour had mixed in her drab life? And, anyway, what could they do? Money was money; besides Jean was engaged to a pretty mercenary-minded little bourgeoise, who found it natural to take stock of incomes and expenses at the peak moments of amorous scenes. Understanding, horror of complications and a desire for comfort decided the course to be taken.

Pierre et Jean is a beautiful novel. Maupassant was at grips with the trend of 'psychology' when writing it. He had always had an aversion to analysing souls directly; the art of the novelist should, he urged, rather consist in making the 'intimacy of souls' *visible*. In his essay attached to *Pierre et Jean,* in defiance of the fashion symbolized by his friend, Bourget, he reiterated this point; but in the novel itself, he allowed himself to be more 'psychological' than he had been before—as he himself emphasized in an article he wrote later. The novel was not like Bourget in any way; it was his own, lyrical and self-tormenting 'intimacy' breaking through the 'visible' crust under which he liked to hide it; but the encouragement to loosen up came from the climate of the fashion which he contradicted. His giving in did not amount to more than a deep breath; the story is undistorted Maupassant, made even more touching by some slight weakness.

This novel was based, as his fictions had always been, on a true story, partly read, it seems, in the *faits-divers* and partly heard from Mme Hermine Lecomte du Nouÿ. As to its *milieu,* this was once again the middle classes of Normandy with which he had always been familiar; but a spark of what he had picked up in the *salons* helped him to broaden his sight of their 'great miseries'. It was not his most perfect work; the admirable terseness of his style had to some extent to be sacrificed in this excursion towards the 'souls'; but it was an excursion well worth taking. His love of factuality did not abandon him; nor his fondness for topographical accuracy, strangely dissolved in his meditative visions, for instance, when describing Pierre's evening stroll:

> After taking a few steps he stopped to gaze at the harbour. On his right above Sainte-Adresse the two electric beacons on the headland of la Hève,

like two monstrous twin cyclops, cast their long and powerful beams on the sea. Projected from the two neighbouring sources, the two parallel rays descended like the tails of two giant comets, following a straight and immeasurable path from the summit of the cliff to the depth of the horizon. Then on the two jetties two other fires, offspring of these colossi, indicated the entrance to le Havre; and beyond, on the other side of the Seine, one could see still more, many more, fixed or winking, with flashing or dimmed lights, opening and closing like eyes, the eyes of the ports, yellow, red and green, keeping a look-out on the darkened sea covered with ships, living eyes of the hospitable earth saying merely by the regular and invariable mechanical movement of their eye-lids: 'It is I. I am Trouville, I am Honfleur, I am the river of Pont-Audemer.'

How many names of localities which cannot possibly mean anything to most readers! Who knows Sainte-Adresse, who knows the river of Pont-Audemer? One would expect a mass of such names to strike one as senseless and tiresome. Far from it—they grow into poetry, acquire the radiation of mythological figures. There seems to be some truth in the belief of Naturalist writers that no fact, however trivial, is ultimately unimportant; its authenticity exerts a magic even on those unable to check it. (pp. 206-09)

> *Paul Ignotus, in his* The Paradox of Maupassant, *University of London Press Ltd., 1966, 288 p.*

Robert Willard Artinian   (essay date 1972)

[*In the following essay, Artinian credits Maupassant with having created, in* Pierre and Jean, *a new type of psychological novel, in which the main character analyzes himself, rather than being analyzed by the narrator.*]

One of the innovations of Maupassant the novelist that becomes immediately apparent on reading *Pierre et Jean* is that instead of analyzing his characters for the reader in the traditional manner of the psychological novel, the author presents the reader with a character who analyzes himself: the author's presence, unusually subtle, does not call attention to itself. Where it is betrayed, however, is through the selection and rendition of images and metaphors. These clearly reveal the manner in which Maupassant colors the narrative of *Pierre et Jean,* conscientiously annotating the position of his protagonist, and by extension casting a moral judgment upon the world he has presented. As this is essentially a novel of obsession, the imagery which surrounds the obsessions of Pierre has been chosen to demonstrate the manner in which it develops in parallel with his torment.

The images used to depict first the envy and jealousy directed at Jean, then the notion of his illegitimacy, evolve from the vague and nebulous toward more precise, more clearly defined representations, becoming more insistent as Pierre's mind ineluctably circles around these *idées fixes*. The first such image occurs after the news of Jean's inheritance is formally made known. Pierre leaves the house to walk in the port.

> Il se sentait mal à l'aise, alourdi, mécontent comme lorsqu'on a reçu quelque fâcheuse nouvelle. Aucune pensée précise ne l'affligeait et il n'aurait su dire tout d'abord d'où lui venait cette pesanteur de l'âme et cet engourdissement du corps. Il avait mal quelque part sans savoir où; il portait en lui un petit point douloureux, une de ces presque insensibles meurtrissures dont on ne trouve pas la place, mais qui gênent, fatiguent, attristent, irritent, une souffrance inconnue et légère, quelque chose comme une graine de chagrin.

The central notion of a *petit point douleureux* tends to suggest both something very precise, the fact of Pierre's pain, as well as something vague and ambiguous, the location of the pain, its source (" . . . *meurtrissures dont on ne trouve pas la place, . . .* "). It is of course the indefinable quality of the *malaise* which is underlined in this passage. Pierre does not know what to think and does not know that it is the news of the inheritance which disturbs him. This is suggested by the use of the simile *"mécontent comme lorsqu'on a reçu quelque fâcheuse nouvelle."* The haziness is further enhanced by the fact that the entire passage tends to alternate between two domains, the physical and the psychological. Thus on the one hand the author presents the *point douloureux,* the *meurtrissure,* and on the other, verbs of psychological application: *gênent, fatiguent, attristent, irritent.* Finally there are figures which unite the physical and metaphysical worlds, the *engourdissement du corps* and the *pesanteur de l'âme.* The climax of the passage occurs at its concluding simile, *comme une graine de chagrin.* Drawing together the physical *graine* with the psychological *chagrin,* Maupassant suggests an image of growth, of expansion and development, which is the essence of ***Pierre et Jean.***

The next figure builds upon the foundation laid by the first passage:

> Comme il n'était pas encore quatre heures, et qu'il n'avait rien à faire, absolument rien, il alla s'asseoir dans le Jardin public; et il demeura longtemps sur son banc, sans idées, les yeux à terre, accablé par une lassitude qui devenait de la détresse.

The representation is again vague, again occurring during a solitary promenade by Pierre, and again plays on the blending of the physical (*lassitude*) and the psychological (*détresse*), linked by a verb of expansion (*devenait*). A bit farther on the *malaise* is somewhat more clearly defined: *"Et la pensée de l'heritage de son frère entra en lui de nouveau, à la facen d'une piqûre de guêpe; mais il la chassa avec impatience, ne voulant point s'abandonner sur cette pente de jalousie."* Here Maupassant is able to suggest two crucial ideas; he reinforces the notion of growth and development present in both preceding texts by employing the figure of a *pente;* and he changes the emphasis from the ambiguous balance between physical and psychological to a definitely physical point of view: *piqûre de guêpe.* In this respect Maupassant is fulfilling the requirements set forth in his study **"Le Roman"** which precedes ***Pierre et Jean***

(and which is too often referred to as the "preface"—it is not): that the inner man reflects his condition externally:

> . . . au lieu d'expliquer longuement l'état d'esprit d'un personnage, les écrivains objectifs cherchent l'action ou le geste que cet état d'âme doit faire accomplir fatalement à cet homme dans une situation déterminée.

The progression of the *idée fixe* is enhanced by its next figurative representation:

> En toute autre occasion il n'aurait certes pas compris, pas même supposé possibles des insinuations de cette nature sur sa pauvre mère, si bonne, si simple, si digne. Mais il avait l'âme troublée par ce levain de jalousie qui fermentait en lui.

This is a particularly effective image as it is again one of growth and development, blends the spiritual and physical worlds, and, further, because Maupassant introduces an element of moral stress: the contrast between the pure mother and impure suspicions of Pierre, between the neutral if not healthful *levain* and the unquestionably pejorative fermentations. Finally the jealousy is crystallized: *"Et cette pensée brusque, violente, entra dans l'âme de Pierre comme une balle qui troue et déchine: '. . . pourquoi a-t-il laissé toute sa fortune à mon frère et rien à moi?' "* Immediately one becomes aware that Maupassant is expanding an earlier image: *The piqûre de guêpe* has become a devastating bullet, tearing at the inner man:

> Et une souffrance aiguë, une inexprimable angoisse entrée dans sa poitrine, faisait aller son concour comme une loque agitée. Les ressorts en paraissaient brisés, et le sang y passait à flots, librement, en le secouant d'un ballottement tumultueux.

Pierre experiences a catastrophic disintegration, here expressed in almost surrealistic images: the shred of cloth waving, suggesting fragmentation, defeat; the mechanical view of the complete breakdown of the physical (and therefore spiritual) man. Pierre has entered into a nightmarish world: *"Alors, à mi-voix, comme on parle dans les cauchemars, il murmura: 'Il faut savoir. Mon Dieu, il faut savoir'."* Nightmarish, because he is aware that truth would destroy: *"Plus il songeait, moins il doutait. Il se sentait traîné par sa logique, comme par une main qui attire et étrangle vers l'intolérable certitude."* Any revelation of truth is viewed as both inevitable, inexorable and destructive as suggested by Maupassant's choice of vocabulary: *étrangle, intolérable.* The representation of Pierre's obsessions thus far has followed increasingly physical lines, moving away from the vagueness and abstraction of the first figures of speech with symbols of growth and expansion.

The climactic image occurs as one would expect at the crisis point of the novel, when Pierre, unable to control himself, blurts out his findings to Jean while his mother listens from the next room:

> Mais il fallait qu'il vidât soi coeur! et il dit tout, ses soupçons, ses raisonnements, ses luttes, sa certitude, . . . Il parlait comme si personne ne

l'écoutait, parce qu'il devait parler, parce qu'il avait trop souffert, trop comprimé et reformé sa plaie. Elle avait grossi comme une tumeur, et cette tumeur venait de crever, éclaboussant tout le monde.

In this one passage Maupassant artfully unifies all the metaphorical structures which preceded it. Pierre, out of control, is shown acting mechanically, almost in spite of himself, responding to the stimuli of *la fatalité*. What has been growing inside him can no longer be contained, the figures of growth, *graine, pente, levain, fermentation,* have reached their fruition. The growth, from *point douloureux, meurtrissure, piqûre, plaie,* has finally produced a *tumeur*. And this tumor, being malignant, must break or be broken. The swelling-up, *trop comprimé,* can no longer be tolerated, Pierre can contain his knowledge no longer. To underscore his extreme necessity Maupassant employs the verb *falloir* with the imperfect subjunctive, *vidât,* thus calling attention to the act of *vidange* and to its effect, *éclaboussant tout le monde,* Pierre, Jean, Madame Roland next door, and their entire universe.

The efficacy of this metaphoric structure resides in the fact that it not only implies a part-whole relationship but also allows emphasis on visual and sensorial perception and, finally, because large-scale double meanings emerge when it is combined with other images. That the emphasis should begin with a delicately constructed balance between the physical and mental worlds and then gradually be slanted toward their insistence on pain, both physical and mental, and finally come to climactic fruition with the symbol of the tumor seems abundantly justified. When one considers that in this "new psychological novel," where the main narrative point of view is Pierre, and in particular the mind of Pierre, where the author does not analyze but where the character analyzes himself, the self-analysis is all the more enhanced by the fact that the metaphors do not simply appear gratuitously, but clearly originate from Pierre, and from a discipline which is his own: For Pierre's mind is that of a medical doctor, and in this context the figures of *point douloureux, meurtrissure, piqûre, plaie, tumeur,* acquire supreme relevance. It is a significant testimony to the art of Maupassant the novelist that he was able to maintain his esthetic distance and not intervene in the narration, but instead was able to present only that which was clearly pertinent, to the extent that even his use of imagery was determined entirely by his narrative point of view. This scrupulous adherence to this adopted vantage point, the insistence on subtly remaining in the background of the narrative and not intruding upon it, reveal Maupassant as anticipating the techniques of modern fiction as exploited later by Proust, Camus, and Robbe-Grillet. (pp. 225-29)

> *Robert Willard Artinian, "'Then, Venom, to Thy Work': Pathological Representation in 'Pierre et Jean'," in* Modern Fiction Studies, *Vol. 18, No. 2, Summer, 1972, pp. 225-29.*

John Raymond Dugan   (essay date 1973)

[*In the following excerpt, Dugan discusses the importance of the setting of* Pierre and Jean.]

There can be no doubt that the natural setting is meaningful in *Pierre et Jean.* The city of Le Havre, whose presence [can be] noted in the stories, was at the end of the last century as closely identified with the sea as it is to this day. It is against this backdrop that Maupassant works out his tense drama of parental identification. Right from the opening lines the sea, presented in great detail during the course of the novel, is paralleled with the introduction of the main characters, all out for a boating excursion and some fishing. Chapter Two returns us to the waterfront as Pierre wrestles with the suspicion that has been stirred in his mind by the news at the end of chapter one. And again in chapter four, in a contemplative mood, he is attracted to the sea. In Chapter Six all the major figures of the novel are brought to the coast for their second fishing excursion, set among the rocks and pools left by the ebbing tide at the base of the Norman cliff. The terrain is again familiar to the reader of Maupassant's short stories. Chapter Nine comes back to the sea, and in concluding the novel, Maupassant presents us with the vastness of its horizon as Pierre's ship disappears. The initial scene, in its point of view, has a great deal in common with the opening pages of *Mont-Oriol.* And in a way comparable to that considered in *Une vie* and in *Bel-Ami* the novel begins and ends outdoors. Again the protagonist is seemingly emprisoned for eternity by his environment. A picture painted in words is the last view we have of Pierre, and this time the central figure's presence is only suggested by the ship. It is as if he were swallowed up, finally and pitilessly. The cycle is completed from the scene of activity and conversation against a maritime background in which we look inward towards the shore, to the scene of vast emptiness, the limitless horizon of the concluding lines.

There emerges from this novel a very curious pattern of fluctuation from exterior to interior. With surprising regularity the action moves from one to the other, from confined space to infinity within a chapter or from chapter to chapter. The exterior world again in this work, certainly one of the author's most powerful, represents an essential tool of his art.

The other outstanding manifestation of the outside world in this the briefest of his novels is undoubtedly the fog. It too is an understandable and logically acceptable part of the physical setting. As Sullivan points out, there can be no misunderstanding about its close symbolic relationship to Pierre himself, but I feel that to explain it fully, its counterpart, the sea, must be carefully examined along with it. Both are limitless in dimensions, but the one is an ever-changing infinity of clarity and expansiveness while the other is confused, static and retractive.

The fact then that external nature functions in a most profound way here is easily demonstrable. What we would seem to be witnessing in the novel of Maupassant would appear to be not a marked shift in the attention devoted to the exterior but an evolution with regard to its narrative significance, a change in the author's interpretation of his world.

Turning then to the indoor scenes we find that in the course of the narrative there are really only three interiors of any real importance, the Roland household, Madame Rosémilly's and Jean's apartments.

The latter half of the first chapter takes place in the dining room and salon of the Roland home. All we are told of the first room is that it is small, and on the main floor. Of the second, nothing but its location. Here upstairs, they receive Monsieur Lecanu the notary. We return to the same dining room at the beginning of the third chapter and again the scene is totally devoid of descriptive material. At the end of this chapter, the description of the dinner celebrating Jean's unexpected good fortune is concentrated on the table itself. Chapter Seven provides the first real evidence of description of an interior, but not the interior of the family residence. It is rather the much discussed apartment which Jean has been able to rent and which Pierre silently covets. Jean and his mother have spent much time and money furnishing it in a fashion suitable to the younger son's taste, of which Pierre quite obviously disapproves. The description is thus not simply a reflection of the taste and character of Jean and Madame Roland, but a concrete manifestation of Jean's material success, of Pierre's greater refinement of taste, and of his jealousy. And it is precisely in this environment that Pierre can no longer restrain himself. The crisis has been brought about by a number of factors, culminating with the visit to these new surroundings. As in "Hautot père et fils", the *décor* here is no longer a simple reflection, comment on, or projection of character, albeit this element is very much a part of the technique. Reality is now playing a subtler, deeper and indeed much more vital rôle. It would appear to be acquiring more life than in the author's earlier novels.

It is, significantly enough, in the subsequent chapter that we first visit the apartment of Madame Rosémilly. On entering her salon we are treated to a lengthy description of four engravings hanging on the walls. Their poetic banality, their "sensation de propreté et de rectitude", coupled with the bourgeois bad taste of the rest of the décor, is sufficient evidence both to Pierre and to the reader that any permanent relationship between Madame Rosémilly and himself is quite out of the question. Again the *décor* is imbued with a direct function in the advancement of plot, for it is not simply a reflection of the proprietress' taste, but a clear statement of her relationship with the two brothers.

This novel then represents a noticeable progression from its predecessors. As we saw only suggested by the circumstances surrounding the basic choice of milieu in *Mont-Oriol*, we see clearly proven here by the Roland home that the habitat-inhabitant interrelationship is no longer required by Maupassant to establish character. On the other hand, this kind of description, like its external counterpart, is becoming more exclusively selective and more deeply meaningful within the overall concept of the work.

Travel in the large sense is not a major device of *Pierre et Jean,* but the little family boat, the "Perle" serves to unite the participants in the drama as the novel opens, in much the same way as the coach in "Boule de Suif". All the major characters of the novel are closely confined in a limited space, and their relationships are quite clearly defined from the outset. However the "Perle" will assume

deeper meaning in the fourth chapter when Pierre ventures out in her alone. She strikes out as if:

> . . . animé d'une vie propre, de la vie des barques, poussée par une force mystérieuse cachée en elle.

The whole of the setting can by this means take on an independence culminating in the enveloping fog. In its capacity for action it too speaks to Pierre with its silence. The same shift in emphasis we have already observed is operative here as well.

The depiction of character in *Pierre et Jean* is, as one might expect, much less dependent on the descriptive element than heretofore observed. We have seen that the major characters of the novel are gathered together in the opening chapter in a fashion common in Maupassant.

But just what do we see of them? Pierre is dark and clean shaven, Jean blond and bearded. And their rowing prowess is a direct reference to the rivalry up to now only latent in their relationship. Something of their past, their education and profession is rapidly sketched in. Madame Rosémilly is blond. Madame Roland is putting on weight since the family came to Le Havre, and we are told something of her romantic, Emma Bovary-type temperament.

If these are the only ascertainable facts then the physical appearance of his characters cannot be a major concern of Maupassant here. Only those details which contribute to the explanation of the human, interior relationships in the novel are deemed noteworthy.

But, curiously enough, physical appearance is in reality the keystone of the book. It is Pierre's friend the waitress who first suggests the possibility of his brother's illegitimacy, and from that point on the portrait of the deceased Léon Maréchal dominates Pierre's quest. He even goes so far as to study his brother's face in repose in order to try to decipher the truth, but again we the readers see only his blond hair and beard. It is very late in the book that the vital piece of evidence makes its appearance, and we are given only the briefest account of the miniature portrait from a visual point of view. Pierre remarks on its resemblance to his brother, but there is no clearly established evidence for this within the text itself. Maréchal has, we are told, the same forehead and the same beard, and nothing further is filled in. Just how they are alike we are not told. The colour of the hair, remembered earlier by Pierre, becomes the only really concrete link between his brother and the deceased as far as the reader is concerned.

The descriptive occupies a new and deeper rôle in this novel. Appearance speaks to Pierre, but does not reveal itself to the reader for more than a fleeting moment. The visual has no meaning for Maupassant in itself, but integrated into the psychological structure of the work, its muted presence speaks with eloquence. And it has become so completely a part of the fictional universe that we lose sight of it. We are concerned not with the portrait, but with the reactions of Pierre, of his mother, and to a lesser degree of his father, to the object in question. This is not a Flaubertian symbol, a little significant detail, but an object which, exterior to all the people directly involved in the situation, is meaningful to everyone. Like the apartment of Hautot père's mistress, it requires interpretation within the work and by those involved in order to be developed. It contains within its frame a whole tale of illegitimacy and marital infidelity, of feminine longings and love. Maréchal's physiognomy *per se* is meaningless.

What we would appear to be witnessing is not really a marked change of direction in the novel, but rather a gradual evolution with regard to Maupassant's position in relation to the physical world and his interpretation of it. (pp. 45-9)

> *John Raymond Dugan, in his* Illusion and Reality: A Study of Descriptive Techniques in the Works of Guy de Maupassant, *Mouton, 1973, 209 p.*

An excerpt from *Pierre et Jean*

Suddenly the sailor said:

'Fog coming up, M'sieu Pierre, we must get back.

He looked up and saw to the north a grey shadow, dense but insubstantial, filling the sky and covering the sea, hurrying towards them like a cloud that had dropped from the heavens.

He turned about and with a following wind made for the jetty, pursued by the scurrying fog that was catching up fast. When it reached the *Perle*, blanketing it with its intangible thickness, a cold shiver ran over Pierre's limbs, and a smell of smoke and damp, that strange smell of sea fogs, made him shut his mouth so as not to taste the damp, freezing vapour. By the time the boat reached its usual mooring in the harbour the whole town was already shrouded in this light vapour that, though it did not actually fall, wetted everything like rain and flowed over houses and streets like a river.

Guy de Maupassant in his Pierre et Jean, *Penguin Books, 1979.*

Mary Donaldson-Evans   (essay date 1981)

[*In the following excerpt, Donaldson-Evans opposes the trend in current criticism of* Pierre and Jean *to see its meaning in terms of binary opposites or dualities. She argues, instead, that tensions within the novel are ruled by the dynamics among triads, or configurations of three characters.*]

A gradual shift in focus has marked the series of critical studies which, since the 1950's, have been devoted to **Pierre et Jean,** the fourth of Maupassant's six completed novels. Most of the early analyses concentrated upon Pierre's role and tended to exclude the other characters from consideration. More recent examinations, taking their cue from the novel's title, have generally regarded **Pierre et Jean** as a study in binary oppositions. Singling out Pierre as the true hero who struggles against bourgeois values in his quest for self-knowledge, A. H. Wallace contrasts him to Jean, whom he views as hopelessly ordinary,

having neither the ambition nor the intelligence to raise himself above the mediocrity of his middle class milieu [*Guy de Maupassant,* 1973]. Charles Castella, through his Marxist analysis of the novel, sees the two men as engaged in a *quête démonique,* their desires being mediated by each other rather than by any genuine worth of the desired object [*Structures romanesques et vision sociale chez Guy de Maupassant,* 1972]. And Marie-Claire Ropars-Wuilleumier, in her perceptive and provocative study of the novel, asserts that the struggle between the brothers, which can be discerned at several levels of the text, is in fact the structuring principle of the entire work ["Lire l'écriture," *Esprit,* 12 (Déc. 1974)].

While it is indisputable that an understanding both of Pierre's psychological struggle and of the fraternal jealousy which characterizes his relationship with Jean is essential to an appreciation of the text, these two viewpoints do not by any means exhaust the possible interpretations of the novel or even explain the many apparent paradoxes, which have all too rarely been recognized, let alone resolved. It is true that the work itself appears to justify both theories: Pierre *is* the central character for six of the novel's nine chapters, and the "dualité obsessionnelle" discerned by Jean Paris in Maupassant's works is certainly operative here, as suggested not only by the title but by the frequency of the figure two which occurs more than one hundred times in the novel ["Maupassant et le contre-récit," in *Le Point aveugle,* 1975]. However, I believe that such interpretations unjustly ignore the novel's complexity (**Pierre et Jean** has often, and falsely in my view, been seen as too obvious) and that the opposition between the brothers, underlined and affirmed from the first chapter to the last, is in fact symbolic rather than real, meaningful only in the context of their relationship with the novel's female protagonists. Moreover, I would like to postulate and, I hope, defend the thesis that, as a direct consequence of this relationship, the novel's basic structuring device is not the duality of a binary opposition but rather the triad, and that it is the number three, that mystical number par excellence, which provides the key to the *architecture secrète* of **Pierre et Jean.**

Perhaps the first clue to the novel's hidden complexity is to be found in the interpretations of the critics. It has frequently been noted (by Vial, Lanoux, and Hainsworth as well as by Ropars-Wuilleumier, Wolfzettel, Wallace, and others) that certain of the protagonists possess a *Doppelgänger* in the novel, a claim which should be simple enough to verify. However, curiously enough, there is widespread disagreement as to the identification of these doubles. According to the most commonly held view, Madame Rosémilly and Madame Roland would be symbolic doubles, Pierre Roland could be identified with his father, while a third couple would be formed by Jean and his natural father Maréchal. There is ample justification for these assertions. In addition to the common first syllable of their married names, the two women are "ménagères accomplies, éprises d'ordre, de propreté et d'économie." Pierre Roland is closely associated with *le père* Roland and not only phonetically (*père* and *Pierre* being but a phoneme apart) but through their shared love of the sea, their unwitting complicity in uncovering Madame Roland's past

(Roland senior functioning as an adjuvant on Greimas' actantiel model), and Pierre's identification of himself with the cuckold. Finally, Jean Roland, the son of his mother's lover to whom he bears a family resemblance, is clearly regarded, at least by his mother, as Léon Maréchal's reincarnation.

Although most of the critics are quick to see the resemblance between Madame Rosémilly and Madame Roland, not all subscribe to the notion that the sons reduplicate the roles of their respective fathers. Lanoux and Wallace have pointed out—and with reason—that the somnolent, *terre-à-terre* Jean appears in some ways to be Roland's son whereas Pierre, in his refinement and sensitivity, is more akin to Maréchal. However, this apparent contradiction ceases to be one as soon as we view each of the main characters existing, not merely in duplicate, but in *triplicate*. Wolfzettel has perceived a link between the vulgar café waitress and the other two women and indeed, this nameless waitress becomes for Pierre the incarnation of womanhood, encompassing both his mother and Madame Rosémilly, when he discovers the former's past transgressions. As for the two brothers, both composites of the same two men (Roland and Maréchal), are they not in fact two faces of the same being, complementary rather than antithetical, Pierre being identified with Roland by his *role* and Maréchal by his *character,* forming a perfect chiasmus with Jean who is the novel's lover (hence duplicating Maréchal's *role*) but who, like Roland, is characterized by a thick-headed *bonhomie* throughout the novel?

Maupassant, it is true, insists frequently upon the striking differences which characterize the two men. We are told in the first chapter that Jean is "aussi blond que son frère était noir, aussi calme que son frère était emporté, aussi doux que son frère était rancunier." It is tempting indeed to look upon this opposition as the novel's most salient feature, the basis for any study of its symbolism, particularly in light of Barthes' explanation of the symbolic code as being founded in part upon the formal device of antithesis. Yet there is something troubling, even paradoxical, about such a dichotomy, for Maupassant subverts it at every turn of the text and the result is a *mundus inversus,* the meaning of which is not easily penetrable. Pierre is older than Jean by five years, yet it is Jean who appears more mature, who serves as an example for his older brother, and Pierre is told repeatedly in his youth to model his behavior upon that of his younger sibling ("Regarde Jean et imite-le.") Even in the term of endearment used to address Jean, there is a contradiction: "Dans la famille, on appelait toujours Jean 'le petit' bien qu'il fût beaucoup plus grand que Pierre." The paradox extends to the sons' respective professions as well: Pierre, a physician, is incapable of curing his own psychological malady, described metaphorically as an ailment which has grown from a "grain de chagrin" to a "tumeur." Likewise incapable of curing his mother despite his father's pleas, he is in fact the cause of her suffering. Indeed, Pierre lacks all of the qualities generally associated with a physician; rather, he is characterized by his investigative mind, his strong sense of logic, his judgmental attitudes. His lawyer brother, on the other hand, appears as the antithesis of the legal mind: unquestioning and refusing to pass judgment ("Il n'était

pas un juge, lui, même un juge miséricordieux, il était un homme plein de faiblesse et un fils plein de tendresse"), it is he who finds a "cure" for Madame Roland's suffering, who, after listening sympathetically to her pathetic revelation, soothes her, bathes her forehead in vinegar, gives her sweetened water to fortify her; it is Jean, in short, who embodies the concern, the gentleness, the compassion which Pierre as a physician would be expected to demonstrate. And the paradoxes do not end here, for the illegitimate son Jean reaps all of the benefits, both material and social, usually associated with legitimacy, while Pierre, the legitimate son, is *déshérité,* banished, deprived not only of the financial security which is usually the prerogative of the legitimate son, but of all sense of belonging as well. In the end, it is he who becomes the outcast by fleeing "cette maison qui n'était plus sienne, ces gens qui ne tenaient plus à lui que par d'imperceptibles liens."

As was the case with their mutual resemblance to certain aspects of the novel's fathers, I believe that such apparent contradictions can best be understood if one looks upon the brothers as chiasmic, complementary, interlocking with each other like two pieces of a jigsaw puzzle, rather than as irreconcilably antithetical rivals. The anecdote which provided the source of **Pierre et Jean** appears to substantiate this view of the Brothers Roland. According to Madame Lecomte du Nouy, the novel's genesis was an inheritance of 8 million francs which one of Maupassant's acquaintances had been willed by a friend of the family:

> Il paraît que le père du jeune homme était vieux, la mère jeune et jolie. Guy a cherché comment le don d'une pareille fortune pouvait s'expliquer; il a fait une supposition qui s'est imposée à lui.
> (Quoted in the Conard edition of **Pierre et Jean**)

The transformation which Maupassant effected on this simple *fait divers,* that of the addition of a brother defined not merely by his *difference* from the beneficiary of the will but by his *opposition to him,* is highly suggestive. Half-brothers, Pierre and Jean appear indeed to be half-men, the symbolic transposition of pre-psychoanalytical theories which were already in the wind in the 1880's and with which Maupassant was certainly familiar through his friend Dr. J. M. Charcot. Not only had Freud studied with Charcot in 1885-1886, but Pierre Janet, an eminent neurologist and one of the leading promoters of experimental psychology in France, had also been influenced by Charcot's concepts. Although Janet's first book, which dealt with the disintegration of the ego as a cause of hysteria, did not appear until 1889, hence too late to have served as an inspiration for **Pierre et Jean,** Janet had already published several articles in the *Revue Philosophique* by the mid-1880's, including one, entitled "Les actes inconscients et le dédoublement de la personnalité," which appeared in 1886. There can be little doubt that Maupassant was aware of Janet's theories, given the former's keen interest in medicine, and it seems quite plausible that he intended the brothers to be symbols of psychological *dédoublement* and of consciousness and unconsciousness respectively. Seen in this light, Pierre, whose growing awareness of his mother's past transgressions forms the very nucleus of the novel, would represent the conscious self which

Pierre detects no resemblance to their father in his sleeping brother Jean. Wood engraving by Dupuis/Lemoine.

Maupassant calls "l'être pensant," the moralizing, self-aware *moi* whose driving forces are those of anguish and guilt, forces opposed to sexuality. Jean, on the contrary, who is unconscious both figuratively and literally through much of the novel, appears as the incarnation of "l'être instinctif" and hence of the *pulsions sexuelles* which Pierre tries unsuccessfully to repress. That Madame Roland is the primary object of such sexual desires is manifest throughout, and is symbolized both by Pierre's relationship to the maternal sea and by his hallucinations which are rife with Freudian implications. On one occasion, the sight of an Italian ship arriving in port provokes a phallic vision of the volcanic eruption of Vesuvius with, at the foot of the volcano, fireflies darting about "dans les bosquets d'orangers de Sorrente ou de Castellamare." The referential accuracy of the description does not in any way obliterate its *sens caché,* and it is not by chance that the thought of Castellamare (*chateau de la mer/chateau de la mère*) awakens in Pierre feelings of nostalgia and tenderness:

> Que de fois il avait rêvé de ces noms familiers,
> comme s'il en connaissait les paysages.

He longs to escape to this paradise of his imagination but realizes that he cannot: "Mais non, il fallait rentrer, rentrer dans *la maison paternelle* et se coucher dans son lit" [Italics here and throughout the essay are the critic's.]. The *chateau de la mer/mère* which he ardently desires (a desire clearly belonging to his *pulsions sexuelles*) thus contrasts sharply with the *maison paternelle,* a prison of solitary confinement ("*son* lit"). This opposition finds an echo later in the novel in the striking disparity between Jean's elegant apartment on the Boulevard François Ier (evocative, by its address, of a Renaissance castle and lovingly decorated by his mother) and Pierre's minuscule shipboard cabin which, as Ropars-Wuillemier has pointed out, is a mere extension of the house, being characterized above all by its narrowness. Moreover the bed, "tabernacle de la vie," which plays such an important role in Maupassant's creative universe, becomes symbolic of the brothers' destinies, and Jean's bed, "très large, une vraie couche de ménage, choisie par Madame Roland," stands in direct opposition to Pierre's shipboard berth, "étroit et long comme un cercueil." Nor is the allusion to death gratuitous, for if Jean's apartment signals for him the commencement of a new, conjugal life, Pierre's *chambrette* and his departures are associated with separation and death, as we shall see later.

It is obvious that Jean's "victories" represent the fulfillment of Pierre's unconscious desires and that, furthermore, these desires are in close relationship with the *pulsions oedipiennes.* Even the meal scenes underline the opposition which characterizes the two *demi-frères* and, through a culinary metaphor, make it clear that they are to be seen as symbols of complementarity. In one important episode, Pierre, arriving a few moments late for lunch, finds nothing to eat but a cold, dry cutlet, left for him "dans le plat *creux,* au milieu de la table." The adjectives *froide* and *sèche* which qualify the cutlet appear to be symbolic of the role of *mère castratrice* which Madame Roland plays increasingly with respect to Pierre, and the stark epithet *creux,* evoking hollowness and depth, contrasts with the adjectives of ascension and plenitude which characterize the delicacies offered Jean at the banquet held in celebration of his newly acquired wealth. Seated "à la place de son père," hence characterized by his relationship to his mother who looks lovingly at him, "rose de bonheur, le regard brillant," Jean is presented with "un énorme bouquet . . . [qui] s'élevait comme un *dôme* pavoisé, une *pyramide* de pêches magnifiques . . . un gâteau *monumental* gorgé de crème fouettée et couvert de clochettes de sucre fondu, une *cathédrale* en biscuit." In addition to the obvious allusion to Jean's deification (to which corresponds Pierre's humiliation), the architectural metaphors describing Jean's flowers and his exotic *friandises* suggest the complement of the concave *plat creux* from which Pierre had taken his unappetizing leftovers. Furthermore, the epicurean delights proffered to Jean evoke both the tropical lands Pierre dreams of visiting, as Ropars-Wuilleumier has noted, and the maternal breast. The allusions to warmth, sweetness and softness which figure in the description are strongly evocative of the *mère nourricière,* and Madame Roland's nurturing role is clearly symbolized not only by the feast itself but by her tenderness towards her son Jean. This touching scene is profoundly disturbing to the guilt-ridden *moi conscient,* and Pierre finds himself playing quite literally the role of *trouble-fête,* a role which will be his for the duration of the novel and which will in the end be the source of his physical alienation.

The nature of Pierre's relationship to his mother can be understood, not only through a symbolic reading of the text, but at the literal level as well. The reader is told that his love for her is exclusive and that he believes her to be "plus criminelle envers lui qu'envers son père lui-même." Furthermore, his most profound desires—those of prostrating himself before her, caressing her, holding her in his arms—are carried out by Jean, the symbol of his unconscious self, "l'autre qui est en nous," in the forgiveness scene during which it becomes clear that the most important woman in Jean's life, as in Pierre's, is his mother. It is not mere coincidence that Jean and Madame Roland conclude a pact of solidarity on the very day on which Jean and Madame Rosémilly decide to wed. The tender forgiveness scene between mother and son is in marked contrast to the cold, "reasoned" engagement episode, and Jean's marriage to Madame Rosémilly appears as little more than the legitimization and resolution of his Oedipal love. Jean is blond because he is innocent, unfettered by the feelings of guilt and remorse suffered by his conscious

other half. Moreover, Pierre's fate—an endless ocean voyage, lacking destination, a continual *va-et-vient* between two ports—seems perfectly suited to the anguish and indecision which are by definition those of the conscious self. Condemned to a perpetual *flânerie,* Pierre, despite his frenetic mental activity and high ideals, is *impuissant,* unfinished, an *avorton,* for he is a prisoner of his own emotional process whose movement is comparable to the ebb and flow of the sea. It is little wonder, then, that Jean the Unconscious should triumph, and Pierre's statement regarding his own duality must be given its full metaphoric value:

> Chez lui la nature première demeurait en dernier lieu la plus forte, et l'homme sensitif dominait toujours dominait toujours l'homme intelligent.

Maupassant's suggestion of complementarity where the brothers are concerned is by no means the only example of his subtlety, as a close study of his lexicon quickly reveals. It is surely not coincidental that the name chosen for the adulteress has an historical antecedent in the person of Madame "Manon" Roland, the Revolutionary figure who had loyally warned her husband of her love for another man and who was viewed by the 19th century as the personification of virtue. Moreover, in a tale of doubtful paternity and handsome strangers, an author who could so mischievously name the cuckold's two friends *Papagris* and *Beausire* was certainly not unaware of the myriad possibilities of onomastic word play. Such playful choices carry over into toponymy as well. That, in the first chapter, Roland stops at the Place de la *Bourse* and gazes in silence at the sailing ships moored in the Bassin du *Commerce* while seagulls hover in the sky above like vultures, waiting for debris to be thrown into the water; that the pretty Madame Roland lives on the rue de la *Belle Normande,* while Madame Rosémilly, known for her craftiness, has an apartment on the route de *Sainte-Adress;* that Jean and Madame Rosémilly become engaged to be married on the beach at Saint-*Jouin* (phonetically suggestive of certain forms of the verb *joindre*), that Pierre's view of women as potential whores, hawking or at least promising their sexual wares outside the accepted channels of betrothal and marriage becomes crystalized as he observes their antics on the beach at *Trouville*—these choices, and others, establish a secret communication between author and reader, become metaphoric *clins d'oeil,* amusing, revealing, impossible to ignore. Nor is it by chance that Pierre's professors, "[qu]'il . . . jugeait des ânes," have names suggesting beasts of burden; or that a ship evoked in the first chapter, *La Normandie,* is named for the province of Maupassant's mother's birth, whereas the last ship to be mentioned in the novel, *La Lorraine,* suggests the paternal influence (Gustave de Maupassant having had his origins in the province). Like the paradoxes which are inherent in the characters and roles of Pierre and Jean, these choices are not gratuitous, and they suggest an interpretation which gives full recognition to the "procédés rigoureux de composition" which Jean Paris has so rightly discerned in Maupassant's works. Such an interpretation, rejecting the long-held theory that **Pierre et Jean** surrenders all its meaning in the first chapter, must look beyond the obvious when dealing with the novel's structure as well.

We have already seen that the traditional view of **Pierre et Jean** in terms of binary opposition is an overly simplistic one and that it may be more useful and more productive to see the major characters, not in terms of doubles, but rather in groups of three. Indeed, a close reading of **Pierre et Jean** would seem to suggest that the number three, rather than two, is the principal structuring device in the novel, as evidenced both by its frequency throughout the work and by the predominance of the triad or three-person relationship. To understand this role, we must briefly re-examine the events of the novel in order to lay bare the tripartite pattern which reverberates throughout the text and which, like the technique of *mise en abîme,* can be isolated at all levels of the narrative.

Let us begin with the obvious and indulge in some basic statistics. The novel contains nine chapters and six principal characters. The numeral three, *trois,* appears thirty-four times, multiples of three appear an additional nineteen times, and the word triangle occurs twice. These figures are not in themselves convincing, but their relationship to the novel's major events and in particular to Pierre, the protagonist, give them special significance. Pierre is thirty years old when his younger brother Jean inherits the fortune of an old family friend, Léon Maréchal. Pierre's reaction to this event can be expressed as a trichotomous sequence: tormented, first by jealousy of his brother's good fortune, secondly by the fear that an inheritance which benefited only one son would cast doubt upon his mother's reputation, finally by his own certitude that his mother had indeed engaged in an adulterous affair with Maréchal, Pierre flees three times to the harbor. During the course of the novel, Pierre pays three visits to his friend the pharmacist Marowsko, departs three times by boat, spends three hours sailing the family yacht, learns that he was three years of age when his parents met Maréchal, and is prevented from renting an apartment ideally suited to his needs because he is unable to make the down-payment on the annual rental of 3000 francs. The novel is set in three cities, contains three family outings, three old sailors and three women (I am excluding the Roland family maid whose role is episodic and related to setting rather than plot). Moreover, the events which are characterized by a three-fold repetition are also marked by an evolutionary movement. For example, Pierre's estrangement from his family is symbolized by the three boat trips which are to progressively distant places; his three visits to the port are characterized by an increasing inability to find solace in this aquatic setting, once so comforting to him; the women are presented in reverse order of anonymity: from Louise Roland, who is granted both first name and last, we move to Madame Rosémilly, *la veuve,* who, lacking a first name in the novel, is defined by her role as a widow and by her cupidity; finally we are introduced to the nameless café waitress who represents the vulgarity and the immorality which Pierre has discovered in his mother and which, from his jaundiced perspective, he has extended to include all women.

In addition to the main plot of which Pierre is the protago-nist, there are two others, as indicated by the shifting narrative point of view. The first of these is Jean's; the second, as we shall see later, is Madame Roland's. The narrative of which Jean is the center is also tripartite, the division being 1) Jean's inheritance and the accompanying celebration; 2) (which is casualy linked to one): the acquisition and furnishing of an elegant apartment; and 3) the promise of marriage given by Jean to Madame Rosémilly. Pierre's drama, which is synchronic with Jean's, is psychological, dominated by elements of what for Barthes is the hermeneutic code, whereas Jean's plot is composed of external events. The relationship between Jean's narrative and Pierre's is one of cause and effect, action and reaction. Each new "victory" of Jean triggers a new stage of Pierre's moral dilemma.

If the events which either befall Jean or are initiated by him have a causal relationship with the *péripéties* of Pierre's drama, the reverse is not the case, and Pierre's narrative in no way contaminates Jean's. It is true that there is one point in the novel when Jean's ascensional movement appears to be threatened: this occurs when Pierre reveals to Jean the secret of their mother's past. However Jean refuses to let this information interfere with his happiness, concluding logically, in justification of his egotistical decision to keep the inheritance, that he will refuse his share of Roland's legacy, since he is the son of another. While outwardly noble, this sacrifice is an empty one in view of Roland's modest means, yet it is functionally important in the narrative structure, for it widens the gap between Pierre's descending trajectory and Jean's ascension and prevents Pierre from blocking his brother's upward movement.

It is clear that Jean's plot, set in a comic mode and ending in a promise of marriage, is antithetical to Pierre's narrative, tragic in that it leads not to a union, but to an irreconcilable separation which can be equated with death.

In addition to the two interrelated plots of which Jean and Pierre are the subjects, there is a third which, because it lies outside the chronology of the novel, has consistently been neglected by critics. This is Madame Roland's extra-marital affair with Léon Maréchal. It could be objected that this affair takes place long before the novel begins and hence cannot be regarded as an integral part of the novel's narrative structure. I would like to propose that the contrary is in fact true for the following reasons: the details of Madame Roland's relationship with Maréchal are provided, like clues to a mystery, not in a single expository passage as a kind of *Vorgeschichte* or *pré-texte.* Rather, they are scattered throughout the novel, in chapters 1, 3, 4, 5, and 7. This jumbled narrative sequence, with all of its elements (setting, characterization, motivation) is reconstructed for the reader, not by an omniscient narrator, but rather in turn by three characters, Roland Senior, Pierre Roland, and Madame Roland. The story of this affair unfolds in conjuction with the novel's two other narrative sequences and if its development is not linear, it is very much a part of the novel, having as great an influence as Jean's successes upon Pierre's destiny. Indeed, it functions as an ever-widening narrative space, propelling Jean along the upward slope he had begun to climb even before the inheritance is revealed and, by the same token, sending Pierre downward to the fate which will be his. The increasing invasion of the present by the past corresponds directly to the growth of what one could call the extra-temporal *récit,* for the complete story of the affair, based not upon Roland's anecdotes nor upon Pierre's conjecture, but rather upon Madame Roland's own authority, is provided only in Chapter 7. It is interesting to note that there are three principal "intrusions" of the long past liaison, three distinct moments in Pierre's trial of his mother, corresponding roughly to his preliminary suspicions, subsequent investigation and final accusation. Moreover, each stage is associated with one of the novel's three female protagonists.

The first interference of the adulterous affair occurs in the first chapter when Jean's inheritance is revealed. Although certain details provided at this moment suggest the possibility of an extra-marital affair, it is only in retrospect that their meaning becomes clear. Chronologically, the news of the inheritance coincides with the disclosure that Madame Rosémilly prefers Jean to Pierre, a preference already prefigured by Jean's victory in the rowing competition with Pierre earlier the same day in the presence of Madame Rosémilly and for her benefit. This first intrusion thus stands in direct relationship to the first of the novel's important triads: Jean—Pierre—Madame Rosémilly. Pierre is disgruntled, troubled, suspicious, but he knows not of what and, examining his conscience, concludes that his malaise must be caused by jealousy of his brother's good fortune.

The second stage of Pierre's *prise de conscience* takes place in Chapter 3 and is associated with the café waitress. In Chapter 2, Pierre had shared with Marowsko the news of the inheritance. Marowsko's dismay, and his cryptic words ("Ça ne fera pas un bon effet") had troubled Pierre, but it is not until the *bonne de brasserie* remarks, upon learning of Jean's inheritance, "Vrai, ça n'est pas étonnant qu'il te ressemble si peu!" that the implications of the legacy become clear to him. This moment, too, has its triadic counterpart, for shortly before Pierre tells her of the inheritance, the café waitress indicates her fascination with Jean and it is in fact her implied preference for his brother which impels Pierre to relate the story of the legacy. The second triad, Pierre—Jean—*serveuse,* is thus a mere variant of the first one, with a lone woman who is pursued, however briefly, by Pierre, and who expresses, overtly or in veiled terms, a predilection for his younger brother Jean. Although a distributional analysis would prove the café waitress to be a minor character, functionally her role is very great since it is she who initiates Pierre's investigation of his mother. It is on the basis of her words that, in the chapter which follows, Pierre imagines first an outline, then a detailed if incomplete picture of his mother's relationship with Maréchal.

The final touches are added by Madame Roland herself shortly after Pierre, who is now certain of his mother's guilt, has openly accused her of adultery. In the confession scene which follows Pierre's departure, Madame Roland reveals to Jean that Pierre's convictions regarding her relationship with Maréchal are indeed accurate. On a sym-

bolic level, she "writes" the closing chapter of her own saga, for she relates to Jean how her affair with Maréchal came to an end. This final intrusion of the past corresponds to the novel's most important triad, that of Madame Roland, Pierre and Jean. Prefigured throughout the novel, Madame Roland's choice of Jean is made explicit in the confession scene during which she begs her younger son to stay with her in order to protect her from Pierre who has been transformed into her inquisitor by his discovery of her infidelity. This scene between Madame Roland and Jean represents the fusion of their destinies and their dyadic alliance against Pierre who is seen as a threat to their happiness. Later that night, as she slips into bed beside her sleeping husband, Madame Roland is overcome by "l'émotion retrouvée des adultères anciens." This evocation of her adulterous affair brings immediately to mind the extra-temporal triad, Madame Roland—Maréchal—*le père* Roland, for which the novel's principal triad is in fact a metaphor.

Clearly, the apparent antithesis between the brothers, rather than an end in itself, is, at the level of plot, nothing more than a vehicle for the basic chosen/rejected opposition, and the triad is restored as soon as one poses the question "Chosen by whom?" "Rejected by whom?".

What conclusions can be drawn from this preponderance of the figure three in Maupassant's novel? From the perspective of the triadic relationships, the obvious interpretation is, as we have seen, the Oedipal one. Freud and Lacan notwithstanding, modern family behaviorists have tended to prefer to the Oedipal theory the "triangle" concept which they consider more flexible and according to which the two-person relationship or dyad, basically ephemeral, always forms a triad under stress. Several examples of such "triangling-in," as the phenomenon is called, could be isolated in *Pierre et Jean,* from the triangling-in of Maréchal by Madame Roland when her dyadic union with Roland became unbearable, to Pierre's triangling-in of Jean by revealing to him the secret of their mother's adulterous past.

From the viewpoint of what I see as the novel's third narrative sequence, another interpretation imposes itself. Of the three characters who provide, in turn, details of Madame Roland's relationship with Maréchal, only Pierre is truly creative. Roland's contributions are anecdotal, and he himself is completely unaware of their significance. Madame Roland's confession is nothing more than a confirmation of Pierre's hypothesis and an attempt to justify her adultery to her illegitimate son, Jean. Pierre, on the other hand, must labor to reconstruct an event which took place when he was but a young child. Neither his own memory nor the bits of information provided unwittingly by his father are sufficient to indict his mother. Rather, Pierre himself must, through his logic, but also through his imagination, weave the isolated strands of narrative into a whole, recognizable fabric. The narrative construct which emerges in Chapter 4 is the product of this effort, and Pierre appears as author with respect to this *récit.* This role has been prepared for him throughout the first three chapters: his vivid imagination, his predilection for symbolic discourse, his literary judgments, his verbal creativi-

Pierre berates his mother for her infidelity. Wood engraving by Dupuis/Lemoine.

ty, his extreme sensitivity—all identify him with the writer. Pierre's *récit* is provided for the reader in the form of an interior monologue. The intense moral suffering which is the result of his *re*-creation of his mother's affair is relieved only after he has objectivized the story by sharing it with Jean in *l'acte narratif.* He is purged through this experience, and only the anguish of his isolation remains. Here, too, the triadic configuration dominates, not only in the narrative context, but in the circumstances of the *énonciation.* It is not by chance that Madame Roland is in the next room when Pierre tells Jean of his illegitimacy and that she hears every word, for it is she who is the real *destinataire* of his narrative message, Jean's role being rather like that of the psychologist whose sole function is to serve as intermediary between two people for whom unmediated conversation has become impossible. Clearly, the importance of the triad in **Pierre et Jean** cannot be overestimated. Indeed, the three-person relationship which informs the structure is the basis for all of the tensions among the characters. It is significant that the novel's only truly contented character, the one to whom Maupassant ironically gives the first word and the last in the novel, is the one who consistently remains uninvolved, who is never successfully triangled-in by the other charac-

ters, who is completely unaware of the novel's many triads, even the one of which he was once himself a part. Indeed, so ignorant is Monsieur Roland of the tragedy which is rending his family that when, alluding to his mother's infidelity, Pierre tells his father that he is mourning a woman who lost her virtue, a woman whom he had loved too much, Roland does not pursue the conversation, ironically judging "que ces choses-là ne regardent pas les tiers." Roland is quite literally the *tiers exclu* and his exclusion, based upon his own stupidity and ignorance, serves as a foil for Pierre's voluntary exclusion, founded upon his awareness of his mother's past. Pierre's departure on the liner "Lorraine" represents at once a death, as the novel's symbolism makes abundantly clear, and a descent into the hell of his own destiny, rendered spatially by Pierre's descent into the bowels of the ship where there awaits him a Dantesque sight of ragged, foul-smelling emigrants, lying in heaps upon the floor. Condemned to minister to these wretched creatures, he who had once dreamed of capturing the rich, elegant clientèle of Le Havre and of choosing his mistresses from among them, Pierre is, like the emigrants, both a failure and an exile. Judge of his mother' conduct, he has himself been judged and found guilty, and his expulsion is a punishment for his arrogance and for the moralistic attitude which he had adopted as a cover for his anguish. Pierre's fate can be seen, not only as a continuation of the ultimately senseless agitation and aimless movement of his life, but also a final loss of identity. *Pierre d'achoppement* for his brother, *pierre de touche* with regard to his mother, *pierre philosophale* from Marowsko's point of view, the protagonist had been aptly named. With his departure, Pierre is rendered incapable of playing the triple role promised by his name. Equilibrium is restored to the family structure and the novel ends, not only with his elimination, but with the formation of a new and potentially stable triad, Madame Rosémilly—Madame Roland—Jean. The petit-bourgeois logic with which the cashier-mother justifies this substitution and balances the books ("Elle avait perdu un fils, un grand fils, et on lui rendait à la place une fille, une grande fille", is a further example of Maupassant's bitter irony: the son to whom Madame Roland is referring is Pierre, not Jean, and her statement subverts the usual referent of the cliché according to which the parents of the betrothed do not lose a son but gain a daughter (or vice versa). This transaction places Pierre squarely in the debit column.

Jean's triumph is absolute: he has robbed his older brother of the very thing he held most dear, his mother, and has condemned him to a life of exile, forever wandering the seas. Yet the ultimate tragedy of Pierre's destiny should not blind us to the fact that this tragedy derives its power from the subtlety, the irony and the playfulness of an author who—it is often overlooked—once expressed the desire to be "un satirique destructeur, an ironique féroce et comique, un Aristophane ou un Rabelais." It is a measure of his ludic cynicism that the attributes which in the normal course of events should guarantee Pierre's success (legitimacy, seniority and sensitivity) are usurped by the illegitimacy, juniority and insensitivity of his half-brother Jean, an irony underscored by the fact that Pierre, not Jean, is made to feel the villain. This subversion of accepted symbolic and narrative conventions which Maupassant practices in the role reversal of Pierre and Jean, his superimposition of a triadic structure upon the apparently clear grid of binary oppositions, as well as the complex and subtly amusing onomastic word play everywhere evident in the novel reveal that Maupassant's writing has a depth and density which has been recognized all too rarely. Upon closer examination, the "simple" and "obvious" Maupassant has proven himself capable of weaving an unexpectedly intricate web, whose fine mesh has ensnared many a reader, blissfully unaware of all but the most obvious strands. *Caveat lector!* (pp. 204-19)

> *Mary Donaldson-Evans, "Maupassant 'Ludens': A Re-Examination of 'Pierre et Jean',"* in Nineteenth-Century French Studies, *Vol. IX, Nos. 3-4, Spring-Summer, 1981, pp. 204-19.*

James Grieve (essay date 1982)

[*In the following excerpt, Grieve points to Pierre's self-exile at the end of* Pierre and Jean *as the indication that the meaning of the novel is alienation and existential loneliness.*]

In his **"Etude sur le Roman,"** Maupassant, speaking of novels in general, refers to *le sens définitif de l'œuvre,* an expression which seems to suggest that he believed one could reduce any given novel to a statement of its "true meaning". Certainly, in recent years, many of the scholars conducting the discussion and reassessment of Maupassant as a novelist of greater cunning and complexity than he was once credited with have tended to assume that **Pierre et Jean** can be reduced to a single "true meaning" or a "true subject", to "what the book as a whole *means*", to "the meaning of the book", or "the real subject of the book".

This apparent will to discover a single strand of theme in **Pierre et Jean** is all the more surprising since one of the earliest seekers of meanings concealed in this novel and presumed to be revealed by symbolism, G. Hainsworth, himself warned a generation ago that "critics have rarely seen further than the prima facie subject: Pierre's jealousy of Jean's legacy and his tragic discovery of his mother's sin" ["Pattern and Symbol in the work of Maupassant," *French Studies* V, 1951].

What these few recent readings of **Pierre et Jean** have surely demonstrated, albeit collectively and implicitly, is that there is more to this apparently simple novel than was once believed—that there is, indeed, no such thing as *the* meaning of it. Whether one accepts, with Vial, that the novel deals with *les effets funestes de l'existence d'un enfant adultérin;* or, with Cogny, that this novel represents Maupassant's *pensée sur le problème de la famille,* or, with Lanoux, that the book's most central concern is *le thème de la bâtardise;* or, with Sullivan, that "the central idea of the novel is the theme of paternity"; or, with Simon, that it is "the exploration of [a] mind by means of a sustained analysis that is the subject of the book"; or whether one takes seriously Hainsworth's various theories that the book not only is concerned, in important measure, with "the relations of the sexes" but is a reworking of *Hamlet* as well as being "a general study of human relations and a kind of contrast between man and woman", what must surely be apparent to the reader of **Pierre et Jean** is that most of these statements go some way towards defining a more or less evident intent of the novelist. However, what must equally be conceded is that, by virtue of their very multiplicity, none of these definitions has a greater claim to definitiveness than any of the others; and even that, taken together, they do not entirely account for important and seemingly incongruous ingredients in the recipe of the novel's plot, aspects of its theme and elements of its symbolism.

In a book that strikes by its economy of resources, the character of Marowsko seems anomalous. If the book is merely an analysis of jealousy or a variation on the theme of adultery-illegitimacy, or even a study of relations between man and woman, why did Maupassant feel the need to include this Polish chemist, surely as incongruous in Le Havre in the 1880s as Zola's Russian anarchist Souvarine in Montsou in the (supposed) 1860s? The technical answer to the question: why Marowsko? is probably: Because Pierre needs a confidant and his unfocused feelings need a catalyst. The only trouble with that explanation is that, though it accounts for the presence of a confidant-character, it explains none of the incongruities of Marowsko (his foreignness, Pierre's admiration of him, his aloneness, his suggested resemblance to Marat) that made one wonder about his inclusion in the first place. Nor does the fact that Maupassant in younger days is said to have consulted a Polish chemist in the Paris region about his headaches help explain why such an apparent anomaly should turn up in a novel supposedly about bastardy and/or jealousy, set in a provincial town and written many years later. Pierre may well need a confidant and a catalyst; but does this novel need a Marowsko? This is the question that needs an answer. Yet, nobody offers an adequate solution to the mystery, not even Cogny who recognizes the character is *curieux*.

In similar vein, one might ask: If this really is a novel about "the complexity of human nature", rivalry between two incompatible half-brothers or "Pierre's subconscious jealousy of Mme Rosémilly", then what do any of those "true meanings" have to do with the final chapter, with its striking but apparently incongruous passage of description of the emigrants?

A third question that is raised by these "true meanings" is this: If the design of *Pierre et Jean* does indeed show the symmetry between the first and last chapters that every commentator seems to agree to see in it while not demonstrating it, then should one not expect that concealed pattern in the shape of the novel to have some functional bearing on one of its themes? And, if one defines those themes as "the double nature of Pierre", or obsession with adultery and children born out of wedlock, then how does that final chapter relate in symmetry to the opening chapter as a symbolic counterpoint to some such theme? In what pertinent way does the final exile of Pierre illustrate or serve as the consummation of his "double nature" or of Maupassant's alleged obsession with illegitimacy, or of any of the other competing hypotheses offered as solutions to that riddle: the supposed "meaning" of *Pierre et Jean*? If those *are* among the themes of this novel, should one not expect to find them vividly portrayed in the first and last chapters?

When one considers Maupassant's own practice in the final chapters of his own novels, one realises that it is not only in the work of the type of novelist he deprecates in his **"Etude sur le Roman"**—

> qui transforme la vérité constante, brutale et déplaisante, pour en tirer une aventure exceptionnelle et séduisante

that one finds endings which come as the aesthetic climax and definitive statement of whatever themes the novelist has been treating. Can one not say of the ending of *Pierre et Jean* what Maupassant so ingenuously says of the *idéaliste* novel?

> Les incidents sont disposés et gradués vers le point culminant et l'effet de la fin, qui est un événement capital et décisif satisfaisant toutes les curiosités éveillées au début.

The ending of any novel, even an anti-novel, must have an important bearing on any meaning that a reader can give to that novel. What if Mme de Clèves lived happily ever after with Nemours? What if Emma Bovary did not commit suicide or Werther ran off with Lotte's younger sister? In *Pierre et Jean,* as in any novel, "Something begins", as Professor Kermode says, "that must have a consonant end" [*The Sense of an Ending,* 1968]. The way the novel ends must, in other words, tell us something about what the novelist has been about from the outset. If this novel does deal primarily with jealousy, where is the consonance in its end? To use Barbara Herrnstein Smith's formulation [in *Poetic Closure,* 1968]: a book does not merely stop or cease; it concludes. Where is the necessary relationship between adultery discovered and the conclusion of Pierre's departure? Or, if the book really is about a Hamlet-like situation between son and mother, where is the climactic closure one would expect between son and mother to state that theme at its most pointed? Can one not say of the conclusion of *Pierre et Jean* what has been said of the coda in Beethoven: it is "part of the aesthetical plan and intention of the whole [work] with a definite purpose and a relevancy to all that has gone before"?

If one accepts that the conclusion of this novel is not an arbitrary appendage, a purely random set of events stuck on now that the plot is over, but is more precisely a closure that says something thematic about the *portée,* the *valeur d'ensemble* of the work, then it surely follows that the theme that it rounds off must have something to do with Pierre's departure and the feelings he has about it, since that departure and those feelings are what the final chapter is about.

Pierre et Jean, seen as a totality, from the end, is not a story of bastardy or jealousy. It is, first and foremost, the story of how a young man is severed from his family and learns through this experience something about existential aloneness; it is a story of how, from belonging in an atmosphere of togetherness, with his family, looking forward to a future of indefinite fulfilments, he grows into a state of belonging nowhere, a state that is little more than the sterile expectation of death. It is the story of how a man full of *élans* and *enthousiasmes,* is converted to pessimism, solitude and alienation. At its most evident, on the level of events, the novel tells a story of that form of emotional exile known as alienation—Pierre's alienation from his fellowman and from a previously held and comforting worldview.

Without wishing to lay claim to having discovered "the" meaning of *Pierre et Jean,* I feel that none of the other hypotheses fits the complete evidence nearly so well as does this one—the jealousy theme, for instance, is played out by the end of chapter VII, a third or more of the novel is unconcerned with it; the "problem of hidden or mistaken paternity" cannot be demonstrated to be more than the merest narrative skeleton; and the notion of the book as "a general study of human relations and a kind of contrast between man and woman" is so facile and vague that it could probably be argued to fit any evidence.

Pierre's departure is usually seen as no more than the adventitious resolution of a dilemma that constitutes the main thematic concern of the book—as Sullivan says 1972]: "The situation is resolved by Pierre's leaving home", which suggests that for Maupassant the conclusion is merely a way of disposing of a situation that could equally well have been resolved, say, by Pierre's committing suicide, or becoming an alcoholic (like the drop-out in **"Garçon, un bock!"**) or a recluse like M. Parent. My suggestion is that it makes more sense to see the conclusion not as mere resolution of the development, but as the structural point of the development, the technical reason for there being a dilemma in the first place. If Maupassant set out to write a novel of the discovery of alienation through exile, he needed there to be some precipitating crisis which could lead to that discovery. And for that crisis, he chose one of those stock situations of illegitimacy-revealed that he had so often drawn on before. The view of Sullivan not only downgrades the conclusion's pertinence to the theme; it is because he takes that view that he does not *read* the conclusion. Nor, for the same reason, does he read the beginning.

A large point in favour of my reading of the novel as a study of exile and the discovery of alienation is that this reading includes the first chapter and the last. Previous interpretations have seen little more in the opening than a mere "chapter of exposition", a schematic presentation of "all the main characters with their dominant traits" or a demonstration of the "duality in Pierre's character". Now, it is true that the first chapter does those things. But it also does something much more important—it shows in close detail the atmosphere of family stability, the torpid normality of shared life, against which the bleakness of Pierre's fate, once he has discovered his alienation, will stand out and horrify. In dealing with alienation, as Walter Kaufmann says [in "The Inevitability of Alienation," in R. Schacht's *Alienation,* 1970],

> We are concerned with a relationship between A and B. . . . A is usually specified. . . . But B also needs to be specified.

In chapter I, Maupassant is specifying B. Let Pierre be A. In order for the story of his exile to be effective and affecting, what he is to be exiled from—closeness, family contacts, habitual actions, optimism—must be well established; and that can be shown to be one of the most thematic intents of Maupassant in composing this opening chapter. The Roland family is shown here to be a well integrated unit, joined by habits, positive feelings, communal activities, by clearly defined and interdependent roles and relationships and even by slight tensions of long standing. It is this comforting background that corresponds to what, much later in the novel, Maupassant will sum up for Pierre as

> les racines de toutes ses tendresses . . . , un lit immobile et tranquille . . . , le mur solide enfoncé dans la terre qui le tient, . . . la certitude du repos à la même place, . . . le toit qui résiste au vent . . . la chaleur du logis fermé.

In this atmosphere of comfort and belonging, Jean and Pierre laugh together; they make similar reactions to their father, telling the same fibs, as often before, about how many fish they have caught; they come down to Le Havre from Paris on the same occasions so as to *partager les plaisirs de leur père;* both plan to settle in Le Havre, close to their parents; their feelings for each other are laced with a harmless envy, which is managed without fuss by their mother. This opening scene is made up in large measure of what Maupassant calls *les menus faits de la vie commune,* so that the transformation that will overtake Pierre shall seem all the more disastrous. Both sons take simultaneously to courting the young widow; both of them make a point of arranging the fishing trip in the *Perle;* as one, they comply with their father's suggestion to row homewards, each going through exactly the same motions as the other to pull up their lines, put away their fishing tackle and make ready to row; and, as they row, it is *ensemble, d'un même effort.*

The three men walk through the town together, their shared silence suggesting their unity; all four members of the family react in the same way to the announcement that *un m'sieu d'chez l'notaire* has called three times during their absence; all four agree on the likely explanation of this visit; all four go simultaneously to wash before dinner; all four feel some embarrassment at the presence of Mme Rosémilly. The last two glimpses the reader has in this chapter of the brothers show them doing, once more, the same things: they sit in matching chairs, in matching postures, one on each side of the table; then, one after the other, they go out for a walk.

Such a concentration on the spontaneous sameness of the actions and responses, not only of the two brothers but of the groupings of three or all four members of the family, supports the view that one very basic structural purpose of Maupassant in writing this first chapter was to emphasize the positive, supportive ambience of the family life and shared view of the world which have hitherto nourished Pierre and favoured all his *indécisions, ses enthousiasmes, ses tentatives avortées,* the ambience from which he is soon to be cruelly severed by his discovery of what Maupassant elsewhere calls *l'autre face des choses, la mauvaise.* In a novel which is to be so much concerned with the horrors of aloneness, the opening chapter impresses by its presentation of the simple joys of togetherness. It is also remarkable how this aspect of the opening chapter is ignored by other readers—I say above that Sullivan does not *read* this chapter: he gives two whole pages of circumstantial discussion of the first chapter, full of quotations, without once mentioning this aspect, which quite clearly bulks large in Maupassant's intentions. Another example of the same thing is to be seen in Vial, who stresses the antithesis, the jealousy and the contrasts between the natures of Pierre and Jean [*Guy de Maupassant et l'art du roman,* 1954].

This positive ambience of togetherness, of belonging, of shared habits and comforting view of the world makes not only for the hideousness of Pierre's destiny as a solitary exile, but also for that previously noted symmetry in the form and meaning of the first and last chapters. Reversed symmetry might be a better name for it: at the beginning, the family is united; at the end, it is broken. In chapter I, an ocean-liner arrives to a chorus of excitement; in chapter IX, another ocean-liner leaves, to a muted lament. The first day is gentle and reassuring (*la mer plate, tendue comme une étoffe bleue, immense, luisante, aux reflets d'or et de feu . . . ciel rose . . . surface paisible et luisante de la mer)*; the last day hints at harshness (*la mer polie semble froide et dure comme de l'acier*). The mood of the opening is one of contentment and of promises about to be fulfilled; the mood of the ending is one of unfulfilment and bitterness never to be relieved.

One of the book's most memorable images is an image of exile—the description of the emigrants crammed into the 'tween-decks of the *Lorraine*. It seems also to be an element in this pattern of reverse symmetry apparently designed by Maupassant to reinforce his theme of alienation. The emigrants, bound for exile, look like a reminder in the last chapter of a similar image in the first chapter, with a surprisingly similar, yet different, import. I refer to the two paragraphs of description of the fish caught by the Roland men and stored in a basket in the boat. Between this passage, right at the beginning, and the passage on the emigrants, right at the other end of the book, there are two similarities and one difference. The first similarity lies in the use of certain words by Maupassant to describe the similar predicaments of the fish and the emigrants. Five words (other than articles, prepositions and the like) appear in both passages: *bêtes, odeur, efforts, puanteur* and *vaguement*. Other words, while not exactly similar, express the idea of the imminent and inevitable death that awaits both conglomerations of victims: on the one hand, *palpitation d'agonie, l'air mortel, impuissants;* and on the other, *grouillants, écrasés, ils espéraient ne point mourir, stériles* and *lutte acharnée, reprise chaque jour en vain*. Apart from these repetitions or resemblances of actual words, the two passages manage to suggest a second similarity: that the fish and humans are interchangeable; that their lot is the same. They are out of their elements, piled higgledy-piggledy on top of one another, hapless victims of a world that is cruel and bent on their destruction, symbolic reminders of the plight that will become, and has become, Pierre's. One of the aesthetic superiorities of *Pierre et Jean* over some of Maupassant's other novels is that the pessimism about human existence which he made characters like Norbert de Varenne in *Bel-Ami* or Gaston de Lamarthe in *Notre Cœur* expound editorially, as it were, is here understated, conveyed largely by the symbolism of such passages.

The difference between the two passages is that the first is, on the face of it, a positive image of life, and the second a negative image. This difference is part of that reverse symmetry already alluded to. At first reading, the catch of fish is just another part of the family atmosphere of plenitude, promise and satisfaction that the novelist builds up in his opening scene. The mood of the piece, conveyed by adjectives like *bienveillant, doux, saine* and *plein*, is optimistic. It is only when the similarity with the other much later, bleakly negative passage on the condemned exiles is noticed that the possibility of an ironic ulterior motive in Maupassant's use of such symbols arises. Seen from that point of view, the resemblance between the crush of doomed fish and the crush of doomed people seems an ironic pointer to the ultimate fate of Pierre, as he sees it—a brief life of loneliness, pointless struggle, unfulfilment and death. The resemblance is underlined by the expression used of Pierre: *élans impuissants*, reminiscent of the *efforts*

impuissants of the fish and the *efforts stériles* which Pierre sees in the emigrants.

There are other such ironic hints at the importance of this theme of exile and alienation. In chapter II, for instance, when Pierre goes out for his walk, Maupassant tells us: *il avait choisi la solitude,* which looks, in its immediate context, like a banal statement. But, from the wider context of the book as a whole, it takes on the appearance of an irony prefiguring a meaning not to be made apparent until much later in the novel's development and in its eventual closure—for much of the reader's experience of Pierre is to be of a solitary brooding figure, sitting on the breakwater in chapter II, wandering the streets alone in chapter III, sitting on the pier in chapter IV, prowling about the house or the beach at Trouville in chapter V, lying by himself on the shingle at Saint-Jouin in chapter VI, or finally disappearing on the stern of the ship at the very end of chapter IX. Also, he has few contacts with anyone: two brief encounters with the lonely Pole, Marowsko, two even briefer with the girl in the café and one with a sailor.

All the mentions of ships, and Pierre's latent exoticism and yearnings for distant places that accompany those mentions, must surely be seen, too, as ironic hints at the theme of exile:

> Moi, quand je viens ici, j'ai des désirs fous de partir, de m'en aller avec tous ces bateaux, vers le Nord ou vers le Sud. . . . Ce serait rudement chic de pouvoir s'offrir une promenade par là-bas.

Before he knows it, this is exactly what he will be doing—and it won't be *rudement chic*. Or again, as he imagines the joys of travelling to far-away places like the bay of Naples, Vesuvius, Sorrento or Castellamare:

> Que de fois il avait rêvé de ces noms familiers, comme s'il en connaissait les paysages. Oh! s'il avait pu partir, tout de suite, n'importe où, et ne jamais revenir, ne jamais écrire, ne jamais laisser savoir ce qu'il était devenu,

he gets up and walks away *comme un officier qui fait le quart sur le pont,* another ironic hint from his destiny, at it were, that that is exactly what he will be doing before very long, except that he will not be enjoying it. There is for Pierre a heady glamour in the thought of exile; it presumably goes back to those *utopies* of which he is full. These imagined glimpses of departure and travel in exciting distant lands are like coded warnings from his fate that he cannot decipher. In real exile, however, he will not be the person he imagined savouring the experience, *libre, sans entraves, heureux, joyeux*, able to enjoy *les blondes Suédoises ou les brunes Havanaises*, but the morose and sterile pessimist of the final pages, to whom departure and travel mean only a solitude resembling death, a solitude foreshadowing death.

The character Marowsko takes his place in this view of the world created by Pierre's romantic imagination as another ambivalently ironic image of the ultimate meaning of exile. A refugee from Poland (despite the unPolish name that Maupassant gives him), he reminds Pierre of Marat. P. Cogny wonders about this similarity [in his edition of

Pierre et Jean, 1959]—is it, he asks, because there is something of the charlatan about both Marowsko and about Marat? (How Cogny feels this about Marowsko, I do not see; there is no suggestion to this effect by Maupassant, nor does Cogny substantiate his notion). Or is it because of the similarity of their names? Or perhaps because Marat was at one time, like Marowsko, a political refugee? This last hypothesis of Cogny's comes closest to an explanation of the main role, apart from that of confidant-catalyst, played by this character in the novel. For the important thing about Marowsko is that, like Marat at a certain period of his life, he lives in exile; and this is surely the thing about him that most impresses the susceptible and inexperienced Pierre. In Pierre's imagination, full as it is of untried fancies about foreign parts, Marowsko is no charlatan. On the contrary, he has *séduit l'imagination aventureuse et vive de Pierre Roland,* to whose mind he partakes of that glamour of exile we have already perceived in Pierre's response to the ships visiting Le Havre and to their destinations as he imagines them to be. He seems to Pierre a romantic figure, full of resourcefulness, dash and derring-do, and with dastardly secrets in his past. His exile thus seems to Pierre an exotic impressive state, pregnant with the promise of imprecise fulfilments. It is only when Pierre himself stands on the brink of exile, when his feeling of estrangement from his hitherto homely background has irreparably damaged his way of seeing the world, that he is able to glimpse through Marowsko another meaning in exile: abandonment by all other human beings, hopelessness, a futile waiting for death, summed up by Marowsko's words: *"Je n'ai plus qu'à mourir de faim, moi".*

It is in chapter V, exactly half way through the novel, that these hints at exile give way to Pierre's actual suffering from the feelings of alienation from home, self and family. Before going on his day-trip to Trouville, he goes in to kiss his mother—

> Il lui sembla tout à coup qu'il ne l'avait jamais vue. . . . ce sourire, cette voix si connue, si familière, lui paraissaient brusquement nouveaux et autres de ce qu'ils avaient été jusque-là pour lui.

As soon as he walks onto the beach at the seaside resort, he is assailed by other symptoms of estrangement:

> Pierre marchait au milieu de ces gens, plus perdu, plus séparé d'eux, plus isolé, plus noyé dans sa pensée torturante, que si on l'avait jeté à la mer du pont d'un navire.

His feeling of alienation from people is, at first, most virulently provoked by the women, whose prettiness and frivolity remind him of his mother's betrayal. It spreads later to include all others at Trouville and makes him seek to avoid contact with anyone:

> Pierre, nerveux, exaspéré par ce frôlement, s'enfuit, s'enfonça dans la ville.

Next, it infects his relations with his father and brother, from whom he feels potently estranged:

> il les regardait en étranger qui observe, et il se croyait en effet entré tout à coup dans une famil-

le inconnue. . . . Sa famille! . . . . C'était fini, c'était brisé.

From this point on, the images of exile and solitude, and hints of the death they prefigure, become darker and more premonitory. Pierre lies on the shingle, *un corps étendu sur le ventre, comme un cadavre, la figure dans le galet.* Jean, making his arrangements for Pierre's exile, is visited by *une émotion bizarre et imprévue. . . , l'émotion des séparations et des adieux sans espoir de retour.*

Pierre's estrangement from the others is consummated by his scene with Jean in chapter VII, after which *il s'enfuit,* one of the many precipitate exits made by this character which prefigure his definitive exit from the family unit. By chapter VIII he has accepted the irreparable emotional rift between himself and his family and is obsessed with a longing to consummate it physically, filled with

> un besoin de fuir intolérable, de quitter cette maison qui n'était plus sienne, ces gens qui ne tenaient plus à lui que par d'imperceptibles liens.

In that same chapter, as Mme Roland visits the younger Mme Rosémilly, Maupassant dwells on more transparent symbols of exile and the death that by this stage exile seems to mean: these are the four engravings which decorate the walls of the widow's sitting-room. Showing two women, one younger than the other, each of whom is parted from a loved man by a sea voyage and by hinted death, they stand as a counterpoint to Mme Roland's feelings and forebodings about Pierre's departure and unlikely return.

The last chapter, the chapter of Pierre's physical exile, the chapter of the emigrants and of the severance of Pierre's last contacts with Marowsko and with the serving-girl, is the richest in allusions to his feelings of alienation: *il vivait maintenant dans la maison paternelle en étranger muet et réservé.* Maupassant now expresses this obsessive estrangement in imagery suggestive of imprisonment, burial or death. Pierre reads of his appointment to the position of ship's doctor like a *condamné à mort à qui on annonce sa peine commuée.* He founders in his alienation as in a *cloaque de misère;* he feels like a *chien perdu,* a *bête sans abri,* an *être errant qui n'a plus de toit.* Does one not sense in these pages, with their heartfelt lyricism of despair, that this is Maupassant rising for his last great aria of the book? Is he not here reaching the climactic fulfilment of his narrative? In the horrific metaphysical experience that is here happening to Pierre (the discovery of his existential isolation, that *solitude de la vie* that Maupassant himself discovered shortly after the death of Flaubert), does there not lie much of the pessimistic point of the whole novel, much of that cruelty that Maupassant warned his mother would be found in it? One surely has the feeling that the whole work was conceived and executed with the express purpose of leading Pierre Roland and the reader to this very spot, this crock of dross at the rainbow's end. Here, more forcefully than in the black short story **"Solitude,"** Maupassant is describing what for him was the basic human condition, an elemental animality of experience which is usually concealed by the fallacious consolations of human contact, a condition that is vulnerable to *les forces brutales du monde,* and to *l'insécurité de tous les lendemains futurs,* a condition that amounts to *un danger et une constante souffrance,* and to *une fuite continue, régulière, exaspérante.*

Solitude and exile seem to mean much the same as each other for Maupassant. Both are antitheses of *élan,* which was a component of the personality of Pierre Roland before he discovered his aloneness. Solitude and exile seem also to be the outcome of any emotional effort towards another person:

> Quoi que nous tentions, quoi que nous fassions, quels que soient l'élan de nos cœurs, l'appel de nos lèvres et l'étreinte de nos bras, nous sommes toujours seuls. [Guy de Maupassant, **Contes et nouvelles**]

Maupassant even reads the obelisk in the Place de la Concorde as a symbol of exile, solitude and alienation:

> . . . tendant le bras vers le haut obélisque de granit, debout sur le pavé de Paris et qui perdait, au milieu des étoiles, son long profil égyptien, monument exilé, portant au flanc l'histoire de son pays écrite en signes étranges, mon ami s'écria: "Tiens, nous sommes tous comme cette pierre".

The story **"Solitude"** is barely a story at all, of course. It is, like many another unsatisfying story, a monologue; it has no characters, no interaction, no plot. It is a diatribe in which a barely disguised Maupassant editorializes at will on one of his favourite pessimistic themes. But it may well be that, in writing **"Solitude"** in 1884, Maupassant had rid himself of the need to express directly all the virulence of his feeling on the subject of emotional exile. And this may be why, three years later, he put no "editorializing" character such as Gaston de Lamarthe or Norbert de Varenne into **Pierre et Jean,** to spout the truth and make sure the reader took the point. Whatever the case may be on that, each of these two works, short story and short novel, complements and enlightens the other; no proper study of alienation in Maupassant can ignore either.

Pierre, then, like a *condamné au milieu d'autres prisonniers,* is not only the victim of a specific malfunction of life, unfortunate but random; he is *condamné à cette vie de forçat vagabond* because he is not, like his father, one of those *simples d'esprit* who will be for ever protected from a demoralizing insight into the real horrific nature of existence. From now on his life will be *emprisonnée;* he lies in a bunk that is *étroit et long comme un cercueil.*

These hints of alienation as a prefiguration of death are now aptly followed by Pierre's vision of the emigrants, crammed together like trapped fish or damned souls in an underworld while other lost wraiths seek their way in a higher circle of hell. It is this vision of the emigrants, and the parallel they imply to Pierre between their fate and his own very similar one, that bring to a head all his revulsion at *cette existence d'abominable misère,* consummating his total severance from his past and suggesting that death is not far away—his mother now wears black, *comme si elle eût porté un deuil,* her cheeks are *de cire blanche,* she believes she will never see him again and the kisses blown by Pierre are *des baisers d'adieu* (the *d'adieu* being, as the

manuscript variant shows, an afterthought by Maupassant which serves as another reminder of the emotional finality of this parting).

The text's last ironic comment on Pierre's experience of exile is to be heard in the roar of applause that goes up from the crowd as his ship weighs anchor, to acclaim *ce départ magnifique*—a Flaubertian touch, showing the mocking disparity not only between this sad reality and Pierre's previous unrealistic fancies about the glamour of sea-voyages to exotic lands, but also between the private dispiriting meaning of the departure for him (and his mother) and the exalting quality of the same moment for his father and the rest of the world. A *départ magnifique* is certainly what Pierre had always imagined exile to be; he now discovers that this was a pipe-dream, an illusion of promise that fails him as surely as he fails to live up to the promises of his former view of the world and himself. It may be this failure which is to be heard in another ambivalent and ironic commentary on Pierre, from one of the novel's other exiles: *"Vous autres Français, vous ne tenez pas vos promesses."* Exile, for Marowsko, is a broken promise, as it now is for Pierre, too. Exile is no longer one of those exotic places, those distant, appealing lands that Pierre had once fantasised about visiting, those

> pays aux grandes fleurs et aux belles filles pâles ou cuivrées, . . . pays aux oiseaux-mouches, aux éléphants, aux lions libres, aux rois nègres, . . . pays qui sont nos contes de fées à nous qui ne croyons plus à la Chatte blanche ni à la Belle au bois dormant. . . .

Exile is now nothing more than a sterile *terre inconnue, à l'autre bout du monde.*

This new reading of **Pierre et Jean** has no pretensions to exclusivity or definitiveness. It adds a thread to those already identified in Maupassant's skilful weaving of his skein of subject matters. (pp. 133-44)

> *James Grieve, "Intimations of Mortality: Another of the Meanings of Maupassant's 'Pierre et Jean',"* in Australian Journal of French Studies, *Vol. XIX, No. 2, May-August, 1982, pp. 133-47.*

Robert M. Viti   (essay date 1989)

[*In the following excerpt, the critic proposes that the natural forces that form the physical surroundings in* Pierre and Jean —*the sea, wind, sky, and light—can also be seen as principal agents in the action of the narrative.*]

In the rehabilitation of Maupassant the novelist, which began in earnest in this country during the 1950s, Maupassant the critic has acted as inspiration and guide, especially in the case of **Pierre et Jean.** This is not surprising since Maupassant's theoretical study, **"Le Roman,"** precedes the fictional text. The novelist refers to his own work as "[une] étude psychologique" and, although he is quick to point out that his more general statements do not necessarily pertain to **Pierre et Jean,** it is difficult not to apply his thoughts about "le Romancier d'aujourd'hui [qui] écrit l'histoire du cœur, de l'âme et de l'intelligence à l'état normal" to the novel which follows. To psychology is added complexity, since the "objective" novelists force us "à comprendre le sens profond et caché des événements" and "cachent . . . la psychologie au lieu de l'étaler." Professors Sullivan, Niess, Sachs, Grant and Freimanis follow Maupassant's lead and take the novel as a complex psychological study of Pierre's confrontation with a difficult truth, a work which demonstrates the novelist's powers of "dissimulation," a book whose "true meaning [is] carried by the 'sous-entendus,' by the hints, the signposts, by the symbols, in a word" [Robert J. Niess, "*Pierre et Jean:* Some Symbols," in the *French Review* 32, No. 6 (1959)]. More recently, two critics, although not much interested in the novel's psychological aspects, proclaim its complexity: Marie-Claire Ropars-Wuilleumier uses it as the basis of a whole theory of reading [in "Lire l'écriture," *Esprit* 12 (Dec. 1974)]; and Mary Donaldson-Evans argues that even this array of criticism fails to recognize and do justice to the novel's "hidden complexity" and to the "depth and density" of Maupassant's writing "Maupassant *Ludens:* A Re-Examination of *Pierre et Jean,*" *Nineteenth-Century French Studies* 9, Nos. 3-4 (1981)].

Most recently of all, however, Robert Lethbridge, while not denying the work's psychological interest, terms it "a novel working *between* two existing modes," that is, the psychological and naturalist novels. Side by side with the study of Pierre's state of mind, the text presents "human beings subject to fatalities beyond their control . . . Human dramas are played out against the backdrop of the cycle of the seasons . . . , the sea and the stars, reducing their protagonists to the insignificance of insects . . . What they achieve is purely by chance" [Robert Lethbridge, ed., *Maupassant: Pierre et Jean,* 1984].

It is not my intention, either, to dispute the importance of psychology and complexity in *Pierre et Jean;* the perceptive and sensitive studies of the critics mentioned above are, I believe, convincing in this regard. The novel is in fact a powerful study of the movement in an individual psyche from illusion and ignorance to disillusion and knowledge, and that knowledge is the discovery of a hostile universe. However, following Lethbridge's lead, I would like to suggest that the central focus of the novel lies not merely in the mind of Pierre, nor in the light, fog, and smoke as symbolic representations of his state of mind, but also in these elements themselves and in the sea, sky, and earth as separate, distinct entities that have a reality of their own. Psychology and the effects of these natural elements on the characters are never totally absent. Individual characters, including Pierre, invest them with meaning, side with one element or another and live out destinies which result from such a choice, but in my view the natural forces which impose themselves on the novel's human characters can also be considered principal agents in the action. Aided by the news of Maréchal's legacy to Jean, Pierre indeed learns that his ideal, embodied by his mother, is a false, illusory one; however, the elements of Maupassant's universe do not simply represent this knowledge, do not just mirror it, they seem to bring it about. The human drama is dominated by and can itself be said to mirror a large-scale cosmic struggle. If Pierre's

fate is a tragic one, it is only because he has been swept up in a larger universal battle.

Let me begin with Pierre in whose fate most critics find the novel's meaning. How can his role be characterized? One view would be that he is an active, almost obsessive seeker of the truth, of the light, however painful and disillusioning, be it about himself, his mother or the world; that Pierre, once put on the scent, possesses "une ténacité de chien qui suit une piste évaporée." There seems to be some inner necessity which, despite all his attempts to the contrary, compels him to continue his search, "malgré lui." As he says to himself in considerable anguish: "Il faut savoir. Mon Dieu, il faut savoir." He is, after all, at least initially attracted by the café Tortoni's bright lights and is at ease in the sunshine aboard *la Perle.* The irony of such a reading is obvious: Pierre himself causes his own misfortune, he actively destroys his own ideal because of his unflagging inquisitiveness. The web which ensnares Pierre, the "engrenage" which Grant posits [in "On the Meaning of Maupassant's *Pierre et Jean,*" the *French Review* 36, No. 5 (1963)], is, then, an internal one, an integral part of Pierre's personality.

But is this view the only justifiable one? Besides being the hunting dog following the scent, Pierre is also "une bête chassée." Stalked by whom? by what? Perhaps by his own need to know, but he often has the impression that his feelings have a life of their own, that they are imposed or impose themselves upon him. In Chapter V, after a few fitful hours of sleep, his "oppression douloureuse" seems to invade him: "Il semble que le maleur . . . se soit glissé, durant [son] repos dans [sa] chair elle-même, qu'il meurtrit et fatigue comme une fièvre." The portrait of Maréchal, the culminating step in the revelation of the truth about his mother, appears to Pierre to be "une personne vivante, méchante, redoutable, entrée soudain dans cette maison et dans cette famille." Are these but the hollow excuses that some misguided, displaced Romantic hero, forced, he contends, by some cruel destiny to bring about his own unhappiness, uses as a pretext to excuse his own conduct and to distance himself from the consequences of his own acts? Again, perhaps. But there is a good deal of evidence in the novel to justify Pierre's perception of outside, sinister forces which seem to control his fate, of an *engrenage extérieur.*

Chapter I not only introduces the main characters, it places them in a historical and geographical context. The Parisian Roland family is now in Le Havre where the elder Roland has retired to indulge in his passion, "un amour immodéré de la navigation et de la pêche." We are told that his two sons, Pierre and Jean, had stayed on in Paris to complete their schooling, but had spent vacations in Le Havre "[pour] partager les plaisirs de leur père." Both have now decided to reside in the town and before settling down to work "prenaient un peu de repos dans leur famille." Inland Paris clearly stands in contrast with seaside Le Havre: for Roland, the capital is the humdrum, quotidian "comptoir," which he leaves in favor of his exotic "barque"; for Pierre and Jean Paris is also a place of work, of study, whereas Le Havre represents playful marine pleasure. Mme Roland shares her husband's love for the sea, a pleasure he seldom allows her to experience, so that on this particular day, "Cette sortie en mer l'avait ravie . . . et elle savourait ce plaisir rare et nouveau." She is rocked by the water into a dreamy numbness, able only to murmur: "Dieu! que c'est beau cette mer!" Although we are not immediately aware of it, the sea also has a dream-like reality for Pierre, representing as it does the opening to far-off fairytale lands. Le Havre, by its proximity to the sea, seems to be what its name announces: a haven to which the Roland family has retreated (*prendre la retraite* would seem to apply to the entire family, not just to le père Roland) to find a dreamy tranquillity.

A haven, besides denoting a shelter *to* which one retreats, implies some kind of threat *from* which one flees. The Roland family has come from Paris, and even though in the description of the fishing expedition, the capital, although set in opposition to Le Havre, certainly does not seem the origin of any threat, once the party reaches land, the harmony of the day's activities is shattered. I am referring, of course, to the revelation of Maréchal's legacy. Even before we know that a legacy is involved, we are prepared for an important event by the mysterious message the maid communicates and the disconnected manner in which she conveys it. The air of suspense is heightened by the family's conjecturing and especially by Pierre's fear that the notary's visit might bring bad news. However, the mystery is solved quickly, at least on one level, with the arrival of M. Lecanu and his announcement that Jean has inherited Maréchal's fortune. My particular interest in the legacy is not what it says or to whom it is given, although these are obviously of great importance; rather, I am interested in

the origin of the legacy, *where* it comes *from*. Léon Maréchal is the source, but the way in which he is described seems to equate him with a geographical entity, Paris. He is, to le père Roland, "Un Parisien enragé; il ne quitte pas le boulevard." His rabid enthusiasm for the streets of Paris is reminiscent of Roland's fanatical love of the sea, to which it stands in stark contrast. This man who, we learn much later in the novel, had promised many times to visit Le Havre has finally done so. It is significant that the Rolands had come from the sea to meet the capital's representative along the "rue de Paris."

The other source of the legacy is the sky. As Roland says at the end of Chapter I: "la fortune nous tombe du ciel." Of course, *tomber du ciel* is a common expression indicating unexpectedness or surprise. I attach importance to it for two reasons: first, because it is repeated on two other occasions in the first chapter and once again in Chapter IV ("un bonheur tombant sur l'un";/"un peu d'aisance leur tombant du ciel"; and when Pierre contemplates "la fortune tombée sur son frère"); and second, precisely because it is a common expression. A.-J. Greimas has formulated what is for him "une règle pratique de la lecture de Maupassant: chaque fois qu'il rencontre dans le texte un *lieu commun*, le lecteur est invité à le considérer comme le temps fort du récit et à y chercher 'un sens profond' " [*Maupassant, la sémiotique du texte: exercises pratiques,* 1976]. Just as the fundamental themes Greimas posits in his study of "Deux Amis" are expressed in such common places as "C'est la vie," "C'est la mort" and "C'est la guerre," so too the important role of the sky is revealed in the triteness of being "heaven-sent." The intrusion of

The Roland family sailing in the harbor of Le Havre. Wood engraving by Dupuis/Lemoine.

the legacy, and of its two sources, Paris and the sky, has broken the unity and peace of the family represented by the idyllic *partie de pêche,* for it has forced Mme Rosémilly to be on her way as a matter of politeness, caused first Jean and then Pierre to leave the house almost immediately after the notary and has engendered an uneasiness in Mme Roland about the disadvantageous position in which Pierre has been placed. Only the elder Roland is unaffected, as he continues to be throughout the novel, considering the occurrence "une veine, une rude veine." Despite the old man's contentment, the sanctuary of Le Havre seems under attack.

A look back at the fishing party reveals that the seemingly minor disruptions of the general harmony take on an additional importance and represent a more serious menace. The sky, more specifically the bright sun-filled sky, prevents Roland from catching fish. As he says: "si le soleil chauffe, le poisson ne mord plus"; and again: "Je n'essayerai plus jamais de pêcher l'après-midi. Une fois dix heures passées, c'est fini. Il ne mord plus, le gredin, il fait la sieste au soleil." The "air mortel" in which the captured fish is struggling in vain is inimical also to the designs of the fanatical fisherman. Moreover, the rowing competition is initiated because of the presence of another "alien" element represented in the person of Mme Rosémilly (she alone among the characters on *la Perle* has a negative reaction to the sea and thus, like Paris and the sky, stands in opposition to it) who considers the ocean as a danger to security, having lost her husband to it. Hence her response to Mme Roland's ecstatic "Dieu! que c'est beau cette mer!": "Oui, mais elle fait bien du mal quelquefois." The Rolands' desire for peace and tranquility, represented by their retreat to Le Havre from Paris, is indeed threatened by Maréchal's legacy and the sea seems menaced by the sky's brilliance and by the land. The general movement of the attack is from land to sea, from Paris to Le Havre, from east to west, the movement of the sun.

Pierre is not the only character affected by the struggle of the elements, but he is the human center of attention throughout most of the novel, having cast his lot with the sea. However, despite what other critics of the novel maintain, it is my contention that the great majority of his actions after the first chapter only continue his initial retreat to Le Havre. Although at first seemingly attracted by the light, he will not actively seek it as the source of some knowledge or truth, but in fact will do everything he can to run from it, even though he is unsure for quite a while why. In fleeing the light he will seek, repeatedly and obsessively, his beloved ocean. The light, instead of simply reflecting in a rather passive way a growing state of mind that Pierre's actions bring about, is presented as and will continue to be an outside, autonomous, cosmic force which imposes itself on him, in spite of himself. Just as the sea will be defeated and overwhelmed by land and light, Pierre's flight to the sea will be overtaken by the attack of the land, and his attempts to hide in the fog, in the night and in sleep will be thwarted by the relentless pursuit of the sun and its surrogates, electric and gas lights, which act as unsettling reminders of the brilliant sky. Once able to flee the land and on the point of living his ideal life at sea at the end of the novel, however, he suddenly sees his

world in a "new light," or rather so dominant and malefic a force is the light that it seems to transform his universe and stand it on its head. Pierre's complaints of mysterious outside forces inexorably carrying him along seem justified. Indeed, they are among the elemental forces of the universe in which he finds himself.

With the opening paragraph of Chapter II, it is immediately apparent that Pierre will not easily escape the enemy forces. The menace of the land is once again present in the name of the street he follows, the rue de Paris. The manner in which it is described—"éclairée, animée, bruyante"—seems to conjure up the real *Ville-Lumière* and thus blend the dual threats of land and light. At first attracted by the brightly lit café Tortoni, Pierre decides to make for the sea. However, here again he is met by an array of light, dominated by two menacing lighthouses, "semblables à deux cyclopes monstrueux et jumeaux." Even the reflected light of the sun is present when the moon rises in the night sky. Pierre is possessed by an almost uncontrollable desire to flee toward exotic lands, as he says to Jean, whom he finds seated at the end of the breakwater. Upset by his brother's presence, and no doubt by the unexpectedly bright lights, Pierre can think of no other refuge but Marowsko's pharmacy, a natural choice when we learn that the old man is a kindred spirit, having fled Poland first for Paris and then for Le Havre (again the "retreat" from east to west), where he expects life to be better since he believes that Pierre will provide him with "une belle clientèle." However, even here, Pierre has not succeeded in escaping the light, although the threat seems diminished, represented only by "un seul bec de gaz [qui] brûlait au-dessus du comptoir." Marowsko's reaction to Pierre's story of the legacy, "Ça ne fera pas un bon effet," upsets the young doctor again and his final recourse is to return home and shut out the light in sleep.

When Pierre decides to set sail on *la Perle* in Chapter IV, all the important opposing forces are present: the sea, of course, the light of the bright, clear sky and even, it seems, the land, which appears to have replaced the sea, with the boat's progress over the water compared to that of a plough through a field: "L'avant ouvrait la mer, comme le soc d'une charrue folle, et l'onde soulevée, souple et blanche d'écume, s'arrondissait et retombait, comme retombe brune et lourde, la terre labourée des champs." The fog which a short time later rolls in seems sent by the sea, having as it docs "l'odeur bizarre des brouillards marins." It blocks the sun and envelops first the boat and then the entire city. The fog is an active ally of the sea since the tiny droplets of water floating in the air and causing an intense diffusion of light act as a protective cover employed by Le Havre and the sea against the attack of the light. This particular fog even resembles the flow of a body of water, "une vapeur menue qui . . . mouillait comme une pluie et glissait sur les maisons et les rues à la façon d'un fleuve qui coule," and, for the time being at least, helps the sea to repulse the attacks of the sky and land.

Unable a short time later to stand the suffocating atmosphere of his parents' house, Pierre almost exactly retraces the route he had taken through the city in Chapter II, going first this time to Marowsko's and then to the sea, seeking relief from "le germe secret d'un nouveau mal." The old chemist again affords only a brief respite, for the "bec de gaz" is still burning and the conversation again turns to the subject of the inheritance. Pierre hurries to the water's edge, "satisfait d'entrer dans ces ténèbres lugubres et mugissantes." He must close his eyes, for despite the fog, as the text makes clear, lights are still visible and he wants to avoid them: "il ferma les yeux pour ne point voir les foyers électriques . . . ni le feu rouge du phare sur la jetée sud." In fact, Pierre's attempts to "see" Maréchal and arrive at the truth seem unimportant to him. The "certitude" he seeks is the equivalent in his mind of "sécurité complète"; after finding it, "il n'y penserait plus, plus jamais. Il irait dormir." However, even shutting his eyes is to no avail since the truth of Maréchal's relationship reveals itself, culminating in the vision of Maréchal's blond hair. The light thwarts every attempt to block it, penetrating even "les ténèbres sur la mer invisible ensevelie sous les brouillards." Pierre is again tempted to flee into the sea and escape to an idealized Italy, but returns home, able to sleep only by the force of his will.

Chapters V and VI signal the total victory of the light. When Pierre decides to go once again to the seaside, this time by boat to Trouville, the fog is no longer there to protect him: "Le brouillard s'etait dissipé, il faisait beau, très beau." It is on the beach, dominated by the dazzling light of the sun and the bright colors of the bathers' clothing and paraphernalia, that he realizes that his ideal of purity, embodied by his mother, is but an illusion. After returning home, he seems to understand that an exterior evil force, represented by Maréchal, has destroyed his ideal, that "une main inconnue et malfaisante, la main d'un mort, avait arraché et cassé, un à un, tous les liens qui tenaient l'un à l'autre ces quatre êtres." The family outing to Saint-Jouin in Chapter VI serves only to underscore the totality of the light's dominance. Pierre is completely passive; he has nothing to do with the decision to go to the seashore, almost as if he knows the scene which awaits him at the water's edge. It is significant that the family rejects the idea of going by sea and decides instead to go by land. The surrounding countryside is bathed in brilliant sunlight: "les blés jaunes éclairaient la campagne d'une lueur dorée et blonde. Ils semblaient avoir bu la lumière du soleil tombée sur eux." The seaside panorama is once again dominated by the sun; in fact, the light is so overwhelming that it seems to have engulfed the water and made it its own: "Le ciel plein de lumière se mêlait tellement à l'eau qu'on ne distinguait point du tout où finissait l'un et où commençait l'autre." Seated side by side in an uneasy silence contemplating the cloudless horizon, Pierre and his mother "pensaient en même temps: 'Comme il aurait fait bon, autrefois'." The "autrefois" which they both wistfully call up is at once their past relationship before the legacy and the sanctuary of Le Havre before it succumbed to the attack of the light.

With the advent of the sun's supremacy and after his angry confrontation with Jean, Pierre's insuperable need to take flight returns. It will do him no good, however, to retreat *to* the sea; now that the light reigns supreme, his only recourse is to flee *into* the sea; and it is the light's ally, Paris, which pushes him off the edge into the water. The

text makes it clear that the letters sent from the capital by Pierre's former professors are the deciding factor in his obtaining the post of ship's physician on the *Lorraine.* Jean leaves no doubt about the efficacy of the recommendations when he, only a bit dishonestly, congratulates his brother: "Tu dois cela certainement aux lettres de tes professeurs." Pierre's desire to be rid of the land and to join the sea seems fulfilled, and he is at first happy at the prospect of life on a poeticized ocean: "il sentait sa souffrance adoucie un peu par la pensée de ce départ et de cette vie calme, toujours bercée par l'eau qui roule, toujours errante, toujours fuyante." But the light allows him only a brief and fleeting sense of well-being, cruelly transforming Pierre's world and leaving him confused and disillusioned. So powerful is the light that in this alien new world everything he holds dear, all his values and attachments are turned upside down, beyond recognition.

In the *mundus inversus* of the novel's final chapter, there occur three scenes which repeat events that had taken place earlier: Pierre's visit to Marowsko, which parallels his actions in Chapters II and IV; the conversation with the waitress in the *brasserie,* where he had gone in Chapter III; and the family outing on *la Perle,* with which the novel had opened. However the similarity of the two sets of scenes is only superficial; for Pierre, the three scenes in Chapter IX are the opposite of what they represented earlier. Instead of a pleasant conversation with a friend, Pierre is confronted by Marowsko's bitter charge of desertion. At the *brasserie,* the girl's businesslike coolness replaces her instant recognition and ingratiating *tutoiement* of the previous meeting. Pierre's announcement of his trip to far-off, exotic America is met by Marowsko's hostility and the barmaid's indifference. The sailing of the family boat, once the depiction of tranquillity and family unity, now represents only pain and separation.

To demonstrate how different this new world which Pierre inhabits really is, even the natural elements have changed polarity. The fog is now clearly an agent of the sky, no longer the protective aid and ally of the sea, and is used to describe his new sadness, "[qui] l'enveloppa comme ces brumes qui courent sur la mer." The lands he will visit are not only "lointaines," but also "malfaisantes." The mist which follows the ship on the last page of the novel is ironic and futile, for Pierre must know that the sun will inevitably follow and burn off its last vestiges. The water has also changed. The rain, the winds, storms at sea will attack Pierre and represent now "toutes les forces brutales du monde." The land now signifies to him the security of solidity and immobility, a protection against the sea "qui roule, qui gronde et engloutit." Trees, gardens, streets and houses now stand for openness and freedom; what confronts Pierre in the future is but the bondage of a galley slave: "rien que de l'eau et des nuages." "[Son] lit immobile et tranquille" in his parents' house is replaced by "son petit lit marin, étroit et long comme un cercueil." Once "[un] chien qui suit une piste évaporée," then "une bête chassée," Pierre has become "[un] chien perdu" in a universe he does not recognize or comprehend.

The only element seemingly absent from the novel's last chapter is the light. Of course, it need not be mentioned explicitly, so decisive was its victory in Chapters V and VI. It is present, however, and ominously so. Exasperated by his encounters with Marowsko and the waitress, Pierre goes to the water's edge one last time before his departure. There he is met by his father, Papagris and Beausire, who are returning to land aboard *la Perle*. Sensing their undisturbed air of contentment, Pierre says to himself: "Bienheureux les simples d'esprit." What he leaves unsaid, and what the reader fills in almost immediately is the second part of the beatitude from the fifth chapter of Matthew: "car le royaume des cieux est à eux!" This, of course, is a subversion of Christ's message, for these are not the humble of whom he spoke, but the dim-witted inhabitants of the now-dominant order who, because they have no allegiance, since they have not taken sides in the cosmic struggle, indeed because they are unaware of any battle at all, are unaffected and unchanged. Roland's beloved sea is literal: a place to sail and catch fish. It stands for nothing else; it is what it appears to be. Roland is the quotidian, the absence of dreams, the complete unawareness of even the possibility of their existence. After all, "il était de ceux que rien ne trouble," a man "si terre à terre, si lourd, pour qui le mot 'poésie' signifiait sottise." This is precisely what saves him.

There is another, more ruthless "pauvre d'esprit" (Pierre refers to him in these terms), one who more actively than the elder Roland participates in and benefits from the light's ascendancy, one who stands in opposition to Pierre from the very title of the novel on, namely, Jean. He is, after all, the son of Maréchal and is therefore closely identified with both Paris and the light. Furthermore, he, like Roland, represents an ironic subversion of Christ's humble masses, since his major objectives are self-contentment and self-enrichment. He is the only main character who seems to have no relationship, happy or sad, with the sea. However, he actively "deprives" Pierre of the sea on two occasions: when Pierre finds him seated on the breakwater in Chapter II (Pierre is annoyed "d'avoir été privé de la mer par la présence de son frère"); and by renting the apartment which Pierre had chosen, thereby depriving him of "une délicieuse salle à manger . . . ayant vue sur la mer." It is precisely in Chapter VI that Jean begins to replace Pierre as the focus of attention among the characters; his dominance corresponds exactly with the light's victory. When Pierre's revelations about Mme Roland threaten to thwart his rise, Jean is quick to find a remedy. On the point of being forced to renounce his father's fortune, of having to act like "un honnête homme" and idealistically accepting poverty (as a true Christian "pauvre d'esprit" would) and donating his money to the poor, he is called to his true destiny by the light: "Ses yeux regardaient le bec de gaz qui brûlait en face de lui de l'autre côté de la rue." He immediately thinks of Mme Rosémilly and quickly finds a reason to accept the inheritance. By pledging allegiance to his real father—"Puisque je suis le fils de cet homme que je le sais et que je l'accepte, n'est-il pas naturel que j'accepte son héritage?"—he openly swears at the same time to carry out the legacy's mission. It is Jean who comes up with the idea of Pierre's serving as ship's physician on the *Lorraine,* and therefore helps Paris (in the form of the professors' recommendations) to exile Pierre and separate his now outcast brother from a world whose agent he, Jean, becomes and in which he is now dominant.

Pierre is not the only one to suffer as a result of the triumph of the skies; his mother's life is also irrevocably altered. Mme Roland had followed her husband to Le Havre in part to forget the unhappy end of her love affair with Maréchal. Her peaceful world is destroyed by Maréchal's return in the form of the legacy. At one and the same time she is reminded that her ideal of perfect love is false—as she says to Jean: "Comme c'est misérable et trompeur, la vie! . . . Il n'y a rien qui dure"—and her own ideal of herself is blemished, for her son Pierre learns that she was unfaithful and she is forced to recount the whole story to her other son Jean. But Mme Roland is a character who partakes of both the ideal and real worlds, who is at home with the sea and the world of work which Paris represents. Her soul is compared to "un livre de comptes" and Pierre himself notes that "elle savait le prix de l'argent, ce qui ne l'empêchait point de goûter le charme du rêve." Therefore, although she suffers, she also prospers. Donaldson-Evans has astutely noted that Mme Roland substitutes Mme Rosémilly for her loss of Pierre. This "cashier-mother" shows herself at home in the *mundus inversus* when she "balances the books" by subverting "the usual referent of the cliché according to which the parents of the betrothed do not lose a son but gain a daughter (or vice versa)" ("Maupassant *Ludens*"): "Elle avait perdu un fils, un grand fils, et on lui rendait à la place une fille, une grande fille."

Robert Lethbridge is certainly correct when he contends that "*Pierre et Jean* is a deceptive text. . . . it is clearly about deception." More precisely put, perhaps, it is a subversive text, which establishes relationships, patterns, and ideals only to turn them under, be they concerning purity, love, humility, politics or the family order. Pierre and his shadow figure, Marowsko, find their world completely turned on its head and end up disillusioned and defeated, casualties of the cosmic battle of sky and land against sea. Moreover, this disillusionment is the Truth of the new order proclaimed by the Savior on the mountain; this defeat is inevitable, as predictable as the sun's inexorable passage from east to west. (pp. 445-55)

Robert M. Viti, "The Elemental Maupassant: The Universe of 'Pierre et Jean'," in The French Review, *Vol. LXII, No. 3, February, 1989, pp. 445-55.*

Trevor A. Le V. Harris   (essay date 1990)

[*In the excerpt below, Harris perceives the meaning of* Pierre and Jean *as a complex of parallelisms, equations, and analogies that Maupassant develops as the framework of his narrative.*]

[*Pierre et Jean,* Maupassant's fourth novel,] has always excited a positive critical response and for many readers is a perfect illustration of the precision and economy of his prose style. At the same time, these qualities of the prose have been placed at the disposal of a psychological analysis of considerable subtlety. Indeed, Sullivan, among others, see *Pierre et Jean* as a clear statement of Maupassant's secession from Naturalism and a corresponding move towards the 'psychological' novel [*Maupassant the Novelist,* 1972]. It would not be an exaggeration to say that, in spite of its diminutive proportions, *Pierre et Jean* is deemed to be a great work, the brevity of the text belying the intricacy of the composition. This is a novel which is subtle without being cumbersome, complex but compact.

In a sense, however, attempting to justify any analysis on the grounds of universal critical fervour is apt to miscarry, since universal critical censure would constitute an equally potent reason for interest in the text. It is, more simply, the conflicting interpretations of the novel, in themselves an indication of the rich curiosity it arouses, which justify further attempts to release an adequate reading. To judge by the flurry of articles which ran for some time through the pages of a number of prominent periodicals, the 'meaning' of the novel is indeed elusive, although the commentaries invariably turn on a consideration of *Pierre et Jean* as a drama of marital infidelity, illegitimacy and filial jealousy. The standard position, even in the most recent assessments of the novel, seems to be that the serious focus of the text is the character of Pierre. Typical, in this respect, is Louis Forestier's position. He qualifies Pierre as 'la figure centrale autour de laquelle tourne tout le livre' [Maupassant's *Romans,* edited by Forestier, 1987]. Although the main themes of the novel are among those Maupassant often treats elsewhere, Forestier underlines the fact that the emphasis is on Pierre's personal reaction to his mother's adultery and, more especially, on his jealousy towards his illegitimate brother Jean. In this way, Forestier argues, Maupassant's themes are subordinated to 'la formule psychologique à laquelle il est en train de se rallier'.

And yet, without underestimating the importance of these themes for an understanding of *Pierre et Jean,* it is possible to argue, in addition, for the importance of a number of structural aspects of the text and to see *Pierre et Jean* as an extended instance of the intricate regulation [seen in many of Maupassant's works]. Indeed, Maupassant's approach to his narrative material in this novel is so carefully controlled that it evokes the methodology of the mathematician who has set about solving a difficult problem or algebraic formula, so that the development of the novel approximates to a series of arithmetical operations. The constituent elements of the text and the relationships between these are reworked and rearranged until the narrative arrives at a solution in which the correct values and positions are ascribed to each element in the novel's narrative 'equation'. Putting the same point in more general terms, one could say that the extraordinary economy, poise and balance of this text are a function of the careful manipulation of structures of symmetry and asymmetry.

At the end of the first chapter an inheritance is announced. Jean Roland, younger son of a retired Parisian jeweller now established in Le Havre with his family, is the sole heir to the fortune of Léon Maréchal, an old friend from the Roland family's Paris days. The sums concerned are considerable, 'une vingtaine de mille francs de rente'. Not surprisingly, this piece of news has an important effect on the family; not least on the main beneficiary of the legacy,

Jean, who leaves the house to go for a walk and to ponder his unexpected good fortune. A few moments later Jean's elder brother, Pierre, also decides to go for a stroll. His route takes him down to the harbour, where he pauses for a moment to consider his own reaction to the announcement of his brother's windfall:

> Puis ayant fait encore quelques pas, il aperçut un homme assis a l'extrémité du môle.
>
> Un rêveur, un amoureux, un sage, un heureux ou un triste? Qui était-ce? Il s'approcha, curieux, pour voir la figure de ce solitaire; et il reconnut son frère.
>
> 'Tiens, c'est toi Jean?'
>
> 'Tiens . . . Pierre . . . Qu'est-ce que tu viens faire ici?'
>
> 'Mais je prends l'air. Et toi?'
>
> Jean se mit à rire:
>
> 'Je prends l'air également.'

On a first reading all this is innocent enough. But such a cluster of improbable concurrences appears more than a little strange. Pierre and Jean both react in the same way to the news announced at the end of chapter 1. They both go out for a walk. They both go down to the harbour. They both make for the harbour wall. Is all this merely coincidence? The language of these lines stresses the identity of the two sets of actions: both Jean and Pierre have the same reflex exclamation, 'Tiens', and both say 'je prends l'air'. Nor is this an isolated case of repetition. Later in the novel, to take another example of the same kind, Pierre finds an attractive apartment in town and decides to rent it, only to discover soon afterwards that Jean has seen the same flat and has already paid his deposit. Pierre and Jean are contestants, runners, as it were, in the same race. But it is Jean who invariably gets there first, a point illustrated by the impromptu rowing-competition Pierre and Jean have in chapter 1. Pierre may be cited first in the title of the novel; elsewhere, in all their other contests, Jean beats him to it.

It is a race which we, as readers, watch from two quite different angles: from head on, as it were, and from the side. The foreshortening of the first narrative perspective induces us to perceive the two men as running abreast, while narrative details from the second viewpoint clearly contradict this assessment and underline Jean's lead over his brother. The result is a constant uncertainty in the reader's mind as to the precise positions of Pierre and Jean in relation to each other. They seem now to be identical, now to be fundamentally different. The title of the novel itself incorporates both of these possibilities, since the two proper names lead us to expect two separate characters and, by the same token, the existence of two discrete personalities, while the simple conjunctional link between the two names evokes the possibility of an equivalence. The following, from the first page of the text, is an early illustration of the presentation of Pierre and Jean as simultaneously equivalent and different:

> Ses deux fils, Pierre et Jean, qui tenaient l'un à

bâbord, l'autre à tribord, chacun une ligne en-
roulée à l'index, se mirent à rire en même temps
et Jean répondit. . . .

By virtue of their symmetrical arrangement in space and
the uniformity of their physical attitude, Pierre and Jean
are closely linked: this is the shot, as it were, from camera
one. But this equivalence is modified by the fact that it is
Jean who speaks while Pierre remains silent. It is as
though the narration were expressing a quantitative preference for Jean, a point underlined a few lines further on
in the text. As the family prepares to return to harbour at
Le Havre after a day's fishing, Roland asks his two sons
how many fish they have caught. On this occasion, although Pierre speaks first, Jean's 'quatre ou cinq' beats
Pierre's 'trois ou quatre'. The balance is again tipped in
Jean's favour. The syntactic balance is also upset by a series of oppositions in the descriptions of Pierre and Jean
which precede each of the answers. Pierre has 'favoris
noirs', while Jean is 'blond'. Pierre is 'rasé', whereas Jean
is 'très barbu'. In addition, Jean is 'calme', Pierre is 'emporté', Jean is 'doux', but Pierre is 'rancunier'.

These oppositions, however, are in their turn quickly in-
validated by a further switch back to narrative sentences
which again emphasise the equivalence of the two characters: 'Tous les deux prenaient donc un peu de repos dans
leur famille, et tous deux formaient le projet de s'établir
au Havre . . . '. Or, again: 'Tous deux tirèrent leurs fils,
les roulèrent, accrochèrent dans les bouchons de liège les
hameçons nettoyés et attendirent'. The equivalence of the
intentions in the first example and the uniform and mechanical character of the rapid set of reactions in the second underline the extent to which the two characters are
ironically reduced from any status they might have as individuals to mere reproductions of each other.

The oscillation between seeing Pierre and Jean as equivalents and seeing them as fundamentally different finds one
of its clearest expositions in the last lines of chapter 1:

> Les deux frères, en deux fauteuils pareils, les
> jambes croisées de la même façon, à droite et à
> gauche du guéridon central, regardaient fixe-
> ment devant eux, en des attitudes semblables,
> pleines d'expressions différentes.

Our uncertainty regarding the exact relationship of Pierre
and Jean persists, but that uncertainty could not receive
a more precise formulation. Indeed, the narratorial presentation in this case is so schematic as to border on self-
parody. 'Here', says the narrator, 'are two people who are
exactly the same but different. Do not be misled by the
symmetry.' The resulting sentence is something of a paradox consisting of two discrete levels or movements. In the
first movement, Pierre and Jean are identical. Their context, their physical placement in relation to the room and
their posture are all identical. But all of this is overturned
by the difference in their facial expressions, the neat, almost fastidious symmetry of the first movement merely
serving to emphasise the asymmetry of the second.

As we saw a moment ago, the asymmetry or difference
which lurks under the apparent similarity between Pierre
and Jean always operates in Jean's favour. Even in the
most innocuous narrative sentences which place the two

brothers in a hierarchical relationship to each other, it is
always Jean who has the edge over Pierre. It is possible to
interpret these moments in the text as contributing to the
thematic development of the text, Jean's 'quatre ou cinq'
as against Pierre's 'trois ou quatre' being construed, for example, as a way of articulating Jean's ribbing of his elder
brother. And yet, those places in the text at which the narration accords Jean a greater prominence than Pierre can
be deemed to constitute purely formal devices designed to
act as a narratorial anticipation of the fact that it is Jean
who inherits and not Pierre. It is, in a sense, narrative
'fate' from the outset that Jean should come off better than
his brother.

This may require a little clarification, since some readers
will undoubtedly wish to point out that Jean's quantitative
superiority over his elder brother is, quite simply, a method of characterisation used by Maupassant to indicate to
the reader that Jean is intrinsically more resolute or 'better' than Pierre. Jean wins out, we might argue, because
of greater abilities, greater gifts or a stronger personality.
Such a claim, however, does not stand up to closer examination. It is true that there are aspects of Jean's personality which appear to argue in his favour and to the detri-
ment of our interpretation of Pierre. Notwithstanding the
significant age-difference between the two men, for example, Jean completes his studies at the same time as Pierre.
But the narration makes it clear that this is a consequence
of Jean's lack of imagination and plodding nature, rather
than evidence of any native talent or genius. Pierre may
have taken longer to knuckle down, but he manages to become a doctor 'après d'assez courtes études', suggesting a
vacillating but more talented individual. In this sense, the
two cancel each other out, dogged persistence playing fitful intelligence and Jean maintaining the upper hand
where his parents are concerned, purely because his own
brand of effort and application is more acceptable to their
petit-bourgeois vision of things.

All of which is equivalent to saying that Jean's prestige
comes from other characters and not least from the narrator, but not from himself. His superiority to Pierre is the
consequence of a gift, the result of an arbitrary donation
rather than any deliberate decision or ambitious behaviour
on his own part. The prestige which the narrator gives to
Jean in the opening pages of the text constructs an expectation in the mind of the reader: Jean is somehow better
than Pierre. The expectation is duly fulfilled at the end of
the first chapter with the announcement by the notary, Lecanu, that Jean is to inherit Maréchal's fortune. Although
the event is perfectly contingent, it somehow seems quite
logical. And yet, we the readers have surely been hood-
winked. We have been very neatly softened up by the narrator for the news of Jean's inheritance, but spuriously so.
We are the victims, in fact, of something approaching a
narratorial confidence trick, since the manner in which the
text paves the way for Jean's financial good luck, on the
one hand, and the nature of that good luck, on the other,
are fundamentally inconsistent with each other, Jean's
new wealth being passed off as a logical consequence of
earlier remarks of a quite different order. But even those
earlier remarks, as we have already hinted, are spurious,
in the sense that Jean's superiority over Pierre is never

really convincing. Jean and Pierre are, in many respects, each other's equal.

Maréchal's preference, therefore, is an illogical one and certainly confuses Pierre, since it does not respect this parity or symmetry between the two brothers. Marowsko, Pierre's pharmacist friend and occasional drinking-companion, is suspicious of Maréchal's decision, pointing out that 'ça ne fera pas un bon effet', while another casual acquaintance, the barmaid in a local café, is more direct in her response to the news of Jean's inheritance, pointing out mischievously that 'án'est pas étonnant qu'il te ressemble si peu'. It is the glaring asymmetry in the decision by Maréchal which prompts Pierre to investigate the reasons for the inheritance, the inconsistency of the decision being all the more inexplicable given the perfect symmetry which had characterised the relationship between Maréchal, Pierre and Jean in the past. Of Maréchal's home and habits Pierre dimly recalls that

> Deux bonnes le servaient, vieilles toutes deux, qui avaient pris, depuis bien longtemps sans doute, l'habitude de dire 'monsieur Pierre' et 'monsieur Jean'.
>
> Maréchal tendait ses deux mains aux jeunes gens, la droite à l'un, la gauche à l'autre, au hasard de leur entrée.

The studied balance of the gestures made by Maréchal and the symmetry in the constitution and behaviour of those in his service underline what, to Pierre's mind, had been a meticulous equality in Maréchal's attitudes to the two brothers, a strategy whereby Maréchal carefully avoided any favour or fancy. Pierre's investigation, however, with its implacable and ultimately pernicious logic, brings him at length to the supposition that Maréchal's scrupulous evenness in his treatment of the two men had been a social expedient and that the reason for Maréchal's decision to leave his entire fortune to Jean is that they are father and son respectively. The symmetry, in short, was a lie.

Pierre's ruminations about his mother's conduct and Maréchal's subsequent legacy bring with them weighty implications. The blatant asymmetry created by Maréchal's decision must either be corrected or, at the very least, concealed in order to avoid a public scandal. The social consequences of a revelation of the complete truth would, Pierre realises, be disastrous for the Roland family. But Pierre never manages to negotiate with Jean in finding this socially acceptable solution to the problem. This fact, followed by Pierre's embittered disclosure to Jean of the truth about Maréchal's legacy, means that the solution will inevitably entail Pierre's exclusion from the family unit. The main difficulty here is to arrange that exclusion to appear as natural and logical as possible. Pierre's departure is the most powerful aspect of the unjust logic which prevails in the novel and which forces the true Roland son to cede his place to the illegitimate pretender. At the same time, of course, Pierre's exile also implies a heavy satire on the community which evicts him, intent as that community is on keeping up appearances and retaining the material comforts which the generous legacy provides.

Following Pierre's wild outburst in chapter 7, during which he reveals everything he has discovered or thinks he has discovered about his mother, Maréchal and Jean, it is Jean who takes the upper hand. The concealment of the truth, however clumsily achieved, is now the only solution to the problem. Pierre's exile to the role of ship's doctor aboard the *Lorraine*, is the solution Jean applies to the question he has set himself: 'Comment l'écarter?' This is a way of restoring symmetry to the Roland family unit, not only in the sense that it neatly masks the asymmetry caused by Maréchal's decision and revealed by Pierre's bitterness, but also in the sense that it creates a pleasing sexual symmetry within that group. The projected marriage between Jean and Mme Rosémilly will allow the Roland family to continue to expand, a form of Darwinist natural selection which ensures the future viability of the Roland 'species'. In addition, it is another instance of the fundamental sexual motivation for all our acts which Maupassant, following Schopenhauer, sees as the overriding principle in Jean's conduct. The narration makes it very clear that it is Mme Rosémilly's attractive physical appearance, 'la cheville mince, la jambe fine, la hanche souple', which determines Jean's decision to propose to her.

With Pierre's exclusion, the composition of the family group has therefore been modified from the original distribution at the beginning of the novel, where Pierre and Jean had been linked in a congenial rivalry and their parents in complacent estrangement, with Mme Rosémilly as a free-floating element waiting to be incorporated into the family structure. The arrangement at the end of the novel leaves the relationship between Roland and his wife unaltered, if not undisturbed as far as Mme Roland is concerned, but inverts the positions of Mme Rosémilly and Pierre, the latter becoming 'l'autre', the foreign, ostracised element now ejected from the structure. The interchange of Mme Rosémilly and Pierre which permits the final harmony is neatly passed off as a parody of the conventional, tearful behaviour a mother displays at the news of her offspring's betrothal, as Mme Roland consoles herself with the fact that, if she has lost a son, then she has gained a daughter—the irony being that the lost son is not the one who is about to get married.

The intermediate stage which had preceded this final configuration was one of fundamental disequilibrium which, if allowed to persist, would have caused the whole family unit to explode. With Pierre's revelation of the truth about Jean, the latent tension of the initial structure gives way to a powerful, if tacit, resentment and torture, throwing the whole system of relationships off-balance and threatening to leave Mme Roland out on a limb. Jean's selfishness and the self-interested behaviour of the whole family demand that he become reconciled with his mother and bring to a successful conclusion his marriage contract with Mme Rosémilly, the corollary of which is the exclusion of Pierre as an unwelcome agitator. This last point both upholds and yet lends a different emphasis to André Vial's assessment of the novel as a narrative concerning 'l'adultère et l'enfant adultérin, agents de désorganisation de la famille' [*Guy de Maupassant et l'art du roman*, 1954]. While it is clearly the case that Mme Roland's adultery and Jean's existence are the factors which, in one sense, are responsible for the disorganisation of the Roland family, it must also be said that they are largely passive factors. It is not until Maréchal, posthumously, and Pierre decide to activate them that they constitute a tangible threat. In this respect, much of the responsibility for the disorganisation of the family needs to be placed on Pierre, whose obsessive search for the truth, it might be argued, sets that disorganisation in train much more effectively than had Maréchal's irresponsible legacy.

In one sense this argues in favour of the importance of Pierre within the overall scheme of the novel. Louis Forestier underlines, in what are no doubt some of the most balanced pages on the character of Pierre, that *'Pierre et Jean* est surtout l'étude du cas psycho-pathologique de Pierre' and that the main part of the story 'se déroule dans le psychisme d'un homme'. But what is equally important is that Pierre's obsessions about the precise details of Jean's ancestry are thrown in to such clear relief by virtue of the type of reaction they provoke in others. It is the conflict between Pierre's values and his family's which generates the drama, not Pierre's values alone. *Pierre et Jean* is not just a story about Pierre, but also a story about Pierre's relationship with his society, and the two facts cannot be divorced from each other.

If the solution to the difficulties caused by Maréchal and Pierre is successful at all, it is because it plays on the community's desire for order. At the end of the novel, as Forestier points out, 'Pierre, le fauteur de trouble, est éliminé et l'ordre se rétablit pour les autres personnages'. We must be careful, however, to give the term 'order its full weight here. The restoration of order to the community of *Pierre et Jean* is made possible by that community's refusal of all imbalance or irregularity. It is a society erected on principles of tidiness, neatness, system and symmetry. Mme Rosémilly's home, for example, is subjected to an 'ordre invariable', her lounge curtains, having 'des plis si droits et si réguliers qu'on avait envie de les friper un peu'. Mme Roland, too, is consumed by a desire for order. Even if one accepts, as she arranges the contents of Jean's wardrobe, that her behaviour might be seen as maternal devotion to a son, there is still something too precise, almost mathematical, about the order she introduces, changing 'l'ordre établi pour chercher des arrangements plus harmonieux' and dividing 'tout le linge en trois classes principales, linge de corps, linge de maison et linge de table'.

The social body of which Pierre was once a member stifles and ultimately ejects him not for reasons of morality, but because he refuses to conform or to imitate the established norm, to enter into the contract of convention which regulates the behaviour of those around him. He threatens to become an isolated figure who cannot be incorporated into any available structure of symmetry. This is a society which cannot handle Pierre because of his difference. It cannot cope with his individualism. We learn early in the novel that even as a child Pierre's difference was perceived as a negative element, invariably provoking the parental reprimand, 'regarde Jean et imite-le!' But Pierre does not fall into line. He consequently becomes an outsider, a difference which cannot be incorporated into the family. In short, he becomes 'l'autre'. When Jean, during the fishing-trip to Saint-Jouin, tells his mother of his intention to marry Mme Rosémilly, Mme Roland instinctively looks around for Pierre: 'elle aperçut là-bas sur la plage un corps étendu sur le ventre, comme un cadavre, la figure dans le galet: c'était l'autre, Pierre, qui songeait, désespéré'.

Pierre's exclusion, consequently, must be seen as an instance of the victory of social myth over personal truth, of collective legend over individual history. Pierre, the legitimate Roland son, is exiled, and Jean, Maréchal's son, is allowed to usurp his brother's rightful place within the Roland family.

It is the power of social conventions which allows the majority of the characters to live this comforting and indulgent lie. Indeed, the ability of habit and convention to convert myth to truth is so strong in *Pierre et Jean* that *le vrai* and *le faux* are brought together, confused and ultimately fused into a relationship of identity through inversion. Jean and Roland, for example, although in no way physically related, appear strikingly similar. Both have languid, placid personalities. Their sleep, especially, is presented as identical. Jean is prey to 'un sommeil animal et profond', while Roland delights in an 'invincible repos'. Conversely, Roland's true son is quite unlike his father. In one of his many moments of bitterness, Pierre acknowledges this absence of any bond between father and son, exclaiming 'nos tendances ne sont pas les mêmes'. By the same token, Pierre realises that the apparent links between Roland and Jean are a sham. . . .

The distance and difference between nature and artifice have been abolished, new values reassigned to them by a system of conventions. The conventions which sustain the relationship between Roland and Jean draw their power to convince all those who need to be convinced by them from the fact that the characters are favourably disposed towards the neat, comforting lie. It is clear very early in the narration how Roland, for example, delights in distortion of the truth. Whenever the Roland family goes out on a fishing-trip in *La Perle,* Pierre and Jean invariably humour their father by lying about the number of fish they have caught: 'ils faisaient chaque fois le même mensonge qui ravissait le père Roland'. Mme Roland, too, with her incurable sentimentality, shows a marked preference for the fictitious and a concomitant escapism from the irksome demands made on her by reality. The sentimental and melodramatic pictures which adorn Mme Rosémilly's living-room walls alert us to a similar tendency in her. The first shows 'la femme d'un pêcheur agitant un mouchoir sur une côte, tandis que disparaît à l'horizon la voile qui emporte son homme'. In the second, the same woman, on her knees in a conventional pose of grief, watches 'la barque de l'époux qui va sombrer'. . . .

The spruce, virtually disinfected order of Mme Rosémilly's home extends even to her pictures, which form two neatly related pairs. This fact is eloquent enough in respect of the character of Mme Rosémilly herself, but, in terms of the concept of symmetry in relation to the novel as a whole, the description of her four *gravures* deserves more detailed consideration. Mme Rosémilly's behaviour elsewhere suggests very strongly that her own penchant for melodrama and her affected behaviour in general are both under attack here. No doubt Maupassant's implied criticism of Mme Rosémilly's manufactured attitudes embodies an important comment on the hypocrisies and ridiculous self-delusions to which many of his characters are prone. It is difficult to see how one could deny the presence of a satirical element here, and dwelling on this further would perhaps be taking a sledge-hammer to crack a nut.

But picking up the overt mockeries of the description does not exhaust its importance and should not be allowed to obscure the broader implications of Maupassant's manipulation of the symmetry principle. If one looks again at the first sentence in the passage just quoted, there is a very important sense in which the notion of symmetry can be deemed to be operating at a more subtle level: 'Les deux autres gravures représentaient des scènes analogues dans une classe supérieure de la société.'

There is something decidedly odd about this little sentence. It seems, at first, to be an innocent, almost off-hand statement, a straightforward denotative remark. And yet, there is something in its brevity which should make us suspicious. It is an ostentatiously simple sentence, drab, almost banal in its brevity. The full interest of the sentence and of the passage in which it is situated, proves to be located in the notion of analogues, not only in relation to the 'analogues' openly acknowledged by the narration in the description of Mme Rosémilly's pictures, but also in the way these lines represent a pivotal element in a tight analogical structure connecting that description to the opening and closing sequences of the novel. In the opening lines of the text, it is the *Prince-Albert* which passes close to *La Perle*. In the last chapter, the *Lorraine*, with Pierre aboard, steams past, the Roland family watching, again, from *La Perle*. Mme Rosémilly's engravings depict two parallel maritime departures. Precise verbal echoes illustrate the link between the different sequences. For example, the 'oeil mouillé de larmes et de regrets' of the young woman in the second pair of pictures is echoed by Mme Roland's 'yeux aveuglés par les larmes' at the end of the novel in the description of Pierre's departure. Or, again, the 'femme d'un pêcheur agitant un mouchoir' in the first pair of engravings recalls the moment when, at the beginning of the narrative, watching the *Prince-Albert*, Mme Roland and Mme Rosémilly 'agitèrent leurs mouchoirs'. Once more, therefore, artifice and nature become blurred, the characters merely rehearsing scenes already performed within the pictorial fictions within the fiction.

The symmetries generated by the description of Mme Rosémilly's engravings do not end there. Not only does it look back to the beginning of the text and forward to the end, alluding to a symmetry outside it, but it is also structured, itself, as a precise symmetry. The balance of the opening and closing pages of the narrative is reproduced here, since there are two pairs of *gravures* rather than one. Mme Rosémilly's taste for the symmetrical dictates that a single narrative pair of pictures would appear odd: odd because, mathematically, not an even number. The structures of balance and evenness are further emphasised by the fact that the two pairs of pictures are inversions of each other. In the first pair we have a man leaving a woman, in the second a woman leaving a man. In both pairs the man dies or is assumed to die. In the first case, however, the man dies at sea as his loved one watches helplessly from the shore, while in the second the woman has left the man on land and is at sea when he dies.

The description of Mme Rosémilly's private art collection, therefore, is not merely a mockery of her sentimentality and affectation, but also a powerful image of the insincerities which govern the behaviour of the characters in general. The neatness and arrangement which the characters favour and of which Mme Rosémilly's living-room is an especially schematic example cannot be reduced to a benign dig at bourgeois bad taste or a middle-class preoccupation with hygiene. The symmetries which we have been exploring function rather as an image of conventional modes of behaviour carefully designed to camouflage a more confusing and disturbing reality. The compulsion towards balance and symmetry which is the normal currency in the characters' interpersonal relationships and which is the prime value in their existence is clearly a permanent pose. This is demonstrated by using Pierre as a centre of consciousness and having him reveal the differences which lurk beneath the apparent similarities, searching for the truth behind 'la grimace de la vie'. Pierre is detached from the other characters of the novel. He is our point of reference and through him we come to know the truth about Jean. At least, this is what the narration of the novel would have us believe, and many readings of this text take as axiomatic Pierre's role as a source of sincerity.

But to what extent can Pierre really be deemed to remain outside or above those whom he investigates and judges? One of the most admirable qualities of this novel is the way in which the relative merits and demerits of the social 'grimace' are played off against each other. The text appears to argue in favour of Pierre and against the absence of moral rectitude in the solution to the problems posed by Maréchal's legacy. And yet, Pierre's apparent detachment from the prevailing dogma is itself compromised. He, too, becomes incorporated into the novel's structures of symmetry in the final tableau, as the *Lorraine* steams out of Le Havre—a figure, as it were, in yet another picture.

At the ethical or psychological level, Pierre certainly appears to be the innocent party in all of this. At the same time, however, the text is sufficiently scathing at his expense to force the reader to reappraise his assessment of the character. Pierre may seem to be the *fons et origo* of all truth, but his many negative and unattractive qualities cause him to be perceived as quite unreasonable. It is Hainsworth who points out [in the 1966 edition of *Pierre et Jean*] that 'he represents a mass of imperfections, about which we must not complain . . . but which hardly recommend him as a reasonable human being'. Jean's plodding docility, for example, hardly seems more reprehensible than his brother's inconstancy. Moreover, Pierre's choice of the medical profession is implicitly criticised in the sense that his vocation as healer is clearly inconsistent with the cruelty he shows towards his mother. His behaviour, which, by his own admission, resembles that of a judge, and his emotional violence towards his whole family further undermine the case in favour of Pierre's 'truth'. Despite his evident cynicism, it is difficult to dismiss entirely the suspicion that Pierre's detachment is itself a posture, a form of affectation. His penchant for solitude and interior monologue extends to the attribution of positive values to non-expression: he is drawn to 'la rare conversation de Marowsko, dont il jugeait profonds les longs silences'. His views on femininity, and especially on motherhood, are shown to be shot through with an impossibly naïve idealism: he believes that his mother 'se devait à lui irréprochable, comme se doivent toutes les mères à leurs enfants'. The narration does not hesitate to mock Pierre's inflated, melodramatic appreciation of himself. When Roland asks him one evening why he always looks so despondent, Pierre answers, 'c'est que je sens terriblement le poids de la vie'. Although Pierre may feel himself to be morally superior to those around him, he none the less also strikes a pose, creating his own mythical persona for himself, a fact which means that he is ultimately trapped into a resemblance with the other characters which reduces, if it does not totally eradicate, his apparent individualism.

Conversely, although Jean is responsible for securing Pierre's exile aboard the *Lorraine* and might in this respect be seen as the villain of the piece, it is he who gradually usurps the mantle of reasoned argument from his elder brother. It is true that there is much in the narration which militates against any sort of favourable interpretation of Jean. He is presented as someone who is always vaguely ridiculous and, at times, resoundingly so. The narrator's overt mockery of the way in which Jean convinces himself that he ought to keep Maréchal's fortune is a particularly mordant attack on his self-interest. His first reaction when he discovers the truth about Maréchal and his mother is to admit that the decent thing to do is refuse the inheritance. The inevitable consequences of that decision, however, are brought home to him as, gazing absentmindedly from his bedroom window, he sees a young woman making her way home. His thoughts, 'dans son âme où l'égoïsme prenait des masques honnêtes', turn immediately to Mme Rosémilly and he grows despondent as he understands that his return to poverty would almost certainly prevent his marriage to her. He then searches for a way round the problem which might leave his conscience in peace. His solution is a comic masterpiece of spurious reasoning: 'Puisque je ne suis pas le fils de celui que j'avais cru être mon père, je ne puis plus rien accepter de lui, ni de son vivant, ni après sa mort. Ce ne serait ni digne ni équitable. Ce serait voler mon frère'. What Jean conveniently omits from his reasoning, of course, is that Roland's legacy will be paltry by comparison with Maréchal's, so that the attempt to re-establish a symmetry between the two brothers is really quite vacuous. Moreover, Jean is already in possession of Maréchal's bequest, while Pierre will have to wait until Roland's death.

The comic effect of passages such as this one could not exactly be described as endearing. And yet, the manner in which Jean attempts to sidestep his conscience—indeed, the fact of his having a bad conscience at all—argues in favour of a more positive reaction to him as a character. The silent confrontation between Jean's mean pragmatism

and idealistic altruism is one with which the vast majority of readers could be held to have some degree of familiarity. Hainsworth has argued that Pierre's faults make him a 'profoundly human' character. Surely the same could also be said of Jean. Despite the fact that some readers would argue that it is rather quotidian when placed alongside the loftier moral concerns of Pierre, Jean's dilemma is a painfully realistic one. Even if one asserts the ethical vacuity of Jean's reasoning in justifying his acceptance of Maréchal's money, it is equally clear that Pierre's ruthless pursuit of the truth and his subsequent revelation of this are both dictated by envy and jealousy. His action is wholly destructive and in the process he is guilty of genuine cruelty to his mother. It is Jean, ironically, who nurses Mme Roland following Pierre's violent confession of the truth about her past with Maréchal. If myth triumphs over truth in *Pierre et Jean,* we must conclude that it is because that society perceives Jean's reasonable lie as more acceptable than Pierre's unreasonable truth.

The cruel fate which befalls Pierre at the end of the novel, however, would seem to represent something of a stumbling-block when attempting to square Pierre's 'reward' with Jean's. And yet, even here the cruelty of Pierre's exile is perhaps more apparent than real. His appointment as a ship's doctor aboard the *Lorraine* is in many ways appropriate for the restless, inconstant man that he is. There is, furthermore, something rather too insistent about Pierre's dramatic sentiments at his departure which seems to reinforce the affectedness noted earlier. It is, in fact, rather difficult to argue that Pierre's attitude on leaving France is a genuine chagrin. He had, after all, made it quite clear to Jean much earlier in the narrative that the idea of leaving France held a great attraction for him. Sitting on the harbour jetty with Jean, Pierre remarks, 'quand je viens ici, j'ai des désirs fous de partir, de m'en aller avec tous ces bateaux, vers le nord ou vers le sud'. Some readers may not wish to admit the force of the pun, but there is clearly a sense in which Pierre's new life at sea in fact reunites him with the *mer* he loves so much.

Pierre et Jean confuses our perception of the two principal characters to a point where the apparently sound moral reaction to their respective actions founders on the personal motives each character has for acting in the way that he does. The 'innocent' Pierre behaves in a reprehensible manner towards his mother and family, while the 'guilty' Jean conducts himself in a manner which, if not always justifiable, is none the less human and humane. It is this blurring or relativisation of the conventional moral categories which establishes a new symmetry between Pierre and Jean. This does not mean that we are merely restored to the symmetry between the two characters which had prevailed at the beginning of the text, for our perception of the new equivalence we detect is inevitably enhanced by the asymmetrical interlude we now see as misleading. What Pierre and Jean really *are* has been made clearer by presenting them for a time as what they were not. The initial symmetry was shown to be unstable in the sense that differences could be seen to exist between the two characters. And yet, having explored those differences, it becomes clear that Pierre and Jean are indeed identical. But, rather than standing in a relationship of perfect equivalence, they are systematic *inversions* of each other. We can see this if we oppose the two basic categories truth and acceptability: Pierre can be defined as possessing the first and lacking the second, while the opposite is true of Jean. At this point, if we turn again to the early descriptions of the two brothers, one can see quite readily that Jean is a meticulous inversion of Pierre, each detail of their appearance and their physical and moral character taking its place in a neat system of oppositions:

Pierre	Jean
favoris noirs	blond
rasé	très barbu
trente ans	beaucoup plus jeune
emporté	calme
rancunier	doux

The identity between the two characters is reasserted in their respective situations at the end of the novel. Jean's lavish apartment, with its 'grand entre-sol', 'galerie vitrée' and 'salle à manger en rotonde', would appear to be different in many ways from Pierre's 'chambrette', with its 'petit lit marin' and 'hublot'. There is, however, a clear link between them. Jean's apartment has 'deux portes sur des rues différentes' and 'deux salons', while Pierre's new appointment means that he will spend 'plus de la moitié des mois à terre dans deux villes superbes, New York et Le Havre'. One half of Pierre's new existence will be spent on land, the other at sea. In Jean's case, the 'grand entre-sol' opens onto roads, while the dining-room looks out across the sea. In both cases, the land and the sea assume equal importance. (pp. 61-78)

[Elsewhere] we examined the fundamental importance of binarism as a structuring principle of this text, noticing the proliferation of pairs of terms, of which the novel's title is the most obvious example. The extent to which we must take Pierre and Jean as in some way equivalent to each other is also demonstrable at the level of the overall patterning of the text, in the sense that their respective importance as centres of narrative attention is also subjected to a rigorous parallelism. This is clearly visible in the shifting focus of the narrative, which, despite the traditional emphasis on Pierre as the centre of consciousness of the text, develops to Jean's advantage as the narrative progresses.

There is, perhaps, a tendency to feel a shade uncomfortable with this kind of argument, suspecting that the neatness and reductiveness come from the reader rather than the text. And yet, doubleness, whether in the form of binarism, duplication or inversion, undoubtedly constitutes the main focus of the novel. Throughout **Pierre et Jean,** the narrative is inhabited by a constant and pervasive binarism. The possible list of examples is long indeed. Illustrating the point briefly here, the reader notes that M. Rosémilly dies at sea 'deux ans auparavant': the meeting between the Roland family and Lecanu to discuss Jean's inheritance takes place at 'deux heures'; on the evening when his suspicions about Jean are first aroused, Pierre, before going to bed, drinks 'deux verres d'eau'; Mme Roland obtains a reduction of 'deux cents francs'; on the rent of Jean's new apartment; during his outing to Trouville, Pierre falls asleep on 'deux chaises'; the journey to Saint-Jouin necessitates 'deux heures de marche'; and so on.

Balance and symmetry are again hinted at on the onomastic level of the text, another inversion concealing the identity in the relationships between Pierre and Marowsko, on the one hand, and Jean and Maréchal, on the other. The names of the two older men are phonologically related, although the fact that they have the same first syllable appears to be rendered insignificant by the obvious difference between the endings. Here too, however, contrast can be seen as operating a significant inversion. Whatever the exact pronunciation of the two names, one of them is quite definitely marked as not French, and the contrast foreign/French in the names Marowsko/Maréchal at once articulates one of the major differences and the underlying identity between Pierre and Jean. It is Pierre, clearly linked to Marowsko (himself an exile) in the novel, who will have to spend half of his life out of France, while Jean will spend all of his time in France. At the same time, the initial syllable of each name points to the importance of the sea in the lives of both brothers: *mar/mer.*

The extent to which Maupassant is sensitive to such wordplay and word association is illustrated by Marowsko's role in an intricate chain of linguistic echoes which all point to the life of exile that Pierre will be forced to lead. After the announcement of Jean's inheritance, Roland's maid brings tea and biscuits. The biscuits are packed 'en de profondes boîtes de ferblanc', which, the narration adds, are often 'soudées en des caisses de métal pour les voyages autour du monde'. It is precisely journeys around the world to which Pierre is condemned at the end of the novel, and the 'profondes boîtes' and 'caisses de métal' prefigure the ship and Pierre's 'chambrette' and 'petit lit marin'—the latter being likened to a coffin, the last *caisse,* prepared for the final *grand voyage.* Moreover, the 'fades et cassantes pâtisseries' which the maid serves up are described by the narration as fit only for 'des becs de perroquet', while Marowsko is described as having 'un grand nez d'oiseau' and 'un air triste de perroquet'. The final linguistic clue to the existence of an intricate analogical and lexical link between the tea-drinking scene, Marowsko and Pierre's eventual exile is to be found in the description of Pierre's cabin with its 'bibliothèque de fioles', recalling the *fiole* of liqueur Marowsko gives Pierre when he visits the old chemist soon after the scene in which the tea is served. The role of word association is pointed up still further during Pierre's visit to Marowsko as the two men attempt to find a suitable name for the chemist's latest concoction. They hit on the name 'groseillette' and after a few moments Pierre finds himself talking to Marowsko about Jean's inheritance. The reader strongly suspects that the word 'groseillette' has evoked 'Rosémilly'—the major consequence of Jean's new wealth, of course, being that it enables him to marry the young widow.

Marowsko is also linked to Pierre in the sense that he lives an incomplete existence. Pierre's inconstancy and his career vacillations find a concrete echo in the curiously similar characteristics, both physical and moral, which the narration attributes to Marowsko:

Il remuait et agissait par gestes courts, jamais

complets, jamais il n'allongeait le bras tout à fait, n'ouvrait toutes grandes les jambes, ne faisait un mouvement entier et définitif. Ses idées semblaient pareilles à ses actes; il les indiquait, les promettait, les esquissait, les suggérait, mais ne les éconçait pas.

The parallelism between Pierre—Marowsko and Jean—Maréchal also takes its place in another set of parallelisms, equations, analogies and inversions structuring the whole narrative. If Maréchal is Jean's real father, and Marowsko, in a sense, Pierre's foster-father—Pierre actually refers to him as 'le père Marowsko'—then they are not the only father-figures in the text. There is, of course, Roland. But two other characters also carry in their names or nicknames the mark of paternity: Beausire and Papagris. This profusion of sires clearly constitutes, at one level, an ironical commentary on Roland and on the fact that his status as the father of the Roland family is undermined by the events of the novel. But, by extension, the multiplication of fathers in the novel must also be seen to reduce not only the notion of paternity, but also that of origins, to a point where its status, like that of the moral categories represented by Pierre and Jean, becomes relativised. The text introduces a number of analogous elements, eliminating the apparent uniqueness or authority of a given fact, the variety of identical or inverted elements creating a system of similitude which effectively calls into question the very idea of a reliable point of reference or origin.

Indeed, the narration of *Pierre et Jean* floods the novel with analogies. It is not simply that the text shows a predilection for metaphor or simile, but rather that each element of the narrative is aligned with another, apparent differences being engulfed by a structure of correspondences. The animate and the inanimate are juxtaposed so that each category assumes the characteristics of the other. The result is not a mere personification or dehumanisation of the thing or person described, but an equation in which the same basic drives and properties govern the entire system of relationships between the elements of the text. A given person, object or action has a corollary, parallel or correspondence somewhere in the framework in which it finds itself. For example, as his suspicions about Jean become clearer, Pierre is increasingly disturbed:

> Sa détresse, à cette pensée, devint si déchirante qu'il poussa un gémissement, une de ces courtes plaintes arrachées à la gorge par les douleurs trop vives. Et soudain, comme si elle l'eût entendu, comme si elle l'eût compris et lui eût répondu, la sirène de la jetée hurla tout près de lui.

Instead of being a straight metaphor for Pierre's anguish at this point, in which case Maupassant would surely have omitted his groan altogether, and instead of being a melodramatic echo of Pierre's moral agony, this brief description, largely because of the repetition of the expression *comme si,* keeps both metaphor and melodrama at a distance. Instead, these lines hint at the existence of a parallel context which does not merely symbolise Pierre's pain, but mirrors or repeats it, revealing a network of reciprocities and interconnections between levels normally held to be discrete. The following lines on *La Perle* are a more schematic instance of the same technique: 'L'avant ouvrait

la mer, comme le soc d'une charrue folle, et l'onde soulevée, souple et blanche d'écume, s'arrondissait et retombait, comme retombe, brune et lourde, la terre labourée des champs'. In syntactic terms this is clearly a simile. And yet, the sentence demonstrates an identity existing between two activities normally held to be opposed. In one sense, this juxtaposition of apparent opposites is typical of what we might like to call the creative mind, although, arguably, it is more typical of poetry than of prose. But the approach is also typical of Maupassant's vision of things, seeing the similar in even the most disparate situations, eliminating their respective specificities. Such parallelisms can lead, as in the following example, to an unsettling confusion in which each element of the equation resembles the other so closely that it is impossible to separate them or to say which of the two should, as it were, take precedence or be considered as the origin. Indeed, the notion of originality, in this world of constant reflection, no longer has any validity. . . .

And this is precisely the relationship which pertains between Pierre and Jean, the two men being confused to the point where the true value of the title is not *Pierre et Jean,* but rather, Pierre = Jean. In terms of character analysis, we have an extended instance of the relationship between Hautot, father and son, examined in the previous chapter, since Pierre and Jean, too, are identical, interchangeable characters, neither being able to assert himself as different from or more original than the other. On a social level, the implications of this view of character are profoundly disturbing, in the sense that Maupassant seems to be arguing against the possibility of difference or originality in the people he presents to his reader. The narrative argument of *Pierre et Jean* appears to place all of its eggs in the moral basket, but then to sabotage any confidence the reader might have in this level of the text, Pierre's supposed moral superiority being snuffed out by reason of his resemblances to the ethically bankrupt Jean. The novel, in fact, seems to deny the very possibility of the existence of the truly individual man, able to place himself above the questionable conduct of others, since Pierre, for all his pretentions, is embittered, not detached, the victim of the same social contagion as the other characters, contaminated by the same dubious drives and patterns of behaviour. (pp. 78-82)

Trevor A. Le V. Harris, in his Maupassant in the Hall of Mirrors: Ironies of Repetition in the Work of Guy de Maupassant, *The Macmillan Press Ltd., 1990, 230 p.*

FURTHER READING

Biography

Lerner, Michael G. *Maupassant.* New York: George Braziller, 1975, 301 p.
    Biography of Maupassant in which Lerner briefly treats the autobiographical elements of *Pierre et Jean.*

Criticism

Lethbridge, Robert. "Maupassant, Scylla and Charybdis." *French Studies Bulletin,* No. 9 (Winter 1983-84): 6-8.

    Takes issue with an essay by Geoff Woollen (cited below) on Maupassant's preface to *Pierre et Jean.*

Schaffer, Aaron. Introduction to *Pierre et Jean,* by Guy de Maupassant, pp. ix-xxix. New York: Charles Scribner's Sons, 1936.

    Biographical sketch which addresses the relationship of Maupassant's work to that of Flaubert, Zola, and the Goncourts. Schaffer also discusses Maupassant's artistic objectives.

Woollen, Geoff. " 'Roland furieux' and 'Le roman d'analyse pure'." *French Studies Bulletin,* No. 7 (Summer 1983): 10-11.

    Describes *Pierre et Jean* as a work of artistic moderation, embodying the results of Maupassant's experiment to create a work of fiction midway between the "analytical" and the "objective" novel.

Additional coverage of Maupassant's life and career is contained in the following sources published by Gale Research: *Dictionary of Literary Biography,* **Vol. 123;** *Nineteenth-Century Literature Criticism,* **Vol. 1;** *Short Story Criticism,* **Vol. 1; and** *World Literature Criticism.*

Johann Nestroy

1801-1862

Austrian playwright.

INTRODUCTION

As both a playwright and an actor, Nestroy was associated with the Viennese folk theaters, where melodramas, comedies, and fairy-tale plays were performed for the entertainment of the working classes. Written to showcase his own comedic performances, his works combine adept use of Viennese dialect with a penetrating wit and insight into human behavior to form satirical portraits of characters from all levels of Austrian society. Nestroy viewed his works as pure entertainment and denied that they could be considered serious literature, yet critics note that in their astute social and political commentary and their complicated manipulation of language, his plays represent a major contribution to the development of Austrian drama. Because his humor is largely linguistic and relies heavily on the use of Viennese dialect, Nestroy's comedies have not been widely translated; however, one of his better-known works, *Einen Jux will er sich machen,* was adapted for the American stage by Thorton Wilder as the highly successful *Matchmaker.*

Nestroy was born in Vienna, the son of a lawyer of Czechoslovakian descent. Initially he planned to follow his father in the practice of law and, toward that end, he briefly studied at the University of Vienna. However, pursuing his greater interest in music, he left school to become an opera singer. Soon afterward, Nestroy began performing in non-musical roles and discovered his talent for comedy; by the time he joined the Theater an der Wien in 1831, then under the direction of the noted producer Carl Carl, he had become an exclusively comic actor and had written *Der Zettelträger Papp,* his earliest extant comedy. His first major theatrical success came with the production of *Der böse Geist Lumpazivagabundus oder Das liederliche Kleeblett* in 1833. Throughout the remainder of Nestroy's career he retained his affiliation with Carl, moving with him to the Theater in der Leopoldstadt, later renamed the Carltheater, in the 1840s. After Carl's death Nestroy also served as director of the Carltheater, retiring in 1860. He died two years later at his home in Graz.

Nestroy's works demonstrate the shift from the Romantic, fairy-tale dramas that dominated the Viennese folk theater in the early nineteenth century to the more realistic plays of the later nineteenth century. The early work *Der böse Geist Lumpazivagabundus,* for example, tells the story of two fairy goddesses who conduct an experiment to ascertain whether sudden wealth will improve the lives of three vagabonds. In his later plays Nestroy commonly used urban Viennese settings and concentrated to a greater extent on social and political satire. In *Zu ebener Erde und*

im ersten Stock he examines the social and economic disparity between two Viennese families, one living in the basement of an apartment building, the other inhabiting luxurious quarters above, while in *Freiheit in Krähwinkel* he depicts the comic outcome of a political revolution in a small village.

Critics note that the distinguishing feature of Nestroy's comedies is a pervasive skepticism concerning all human endeavors and all levels of society. In *Freiheit in Krähwinkel,* for example, he satirizes not only the pomposity of the conservative government, but also the excesses of the revolutionaries and the folly of the citizens caught between the two factions. Nestroy also wrote a number of parodies in his later years, transferring the dramatic events of biblical and mythological stories to lower-class neighborhoods in Vienna and depicting their heroes as average, often very flawed, citizens.

Because Nestroy's comedic performances were thought during his career to be the most important element of his works, they were seldom performed in the decades immediately following his death. Early in the twentieth century his works were discovered and championed by the noted German critic Karl Krause, sparking a renewal of interest in Nestroy which led to productions of his works onstage as well as a large body of critical commentary. Since that time, Nestroy's comedies have become a standard part of the repertoires of Austrian theater companies, and a number of actors have made a specialty of recreating the Nestroy roles.

PRINCIPAL WORKS

Friedrich Prinz von Corsica (play) 1822*

Der Zettelträger Papp (play) 1827

Die Verbannung aus dem Zauberreiche oder Dreisig Jahre aus dem Leben eines Lumpen (play) 1828

Der Tod am Hochzeitstag oder Mann, Frau, Kind (play) 1829

Der gefühlvolle Kerkermeister oder Adelheid, die verfolgte Witwe (play) 1832

Genius, Schuster und Markör oder Die Pyramiden der Verzauberung (play) 1832

Humoristische Eilwagenreise durch die Theaterwelt (play) 1832

Der konfuse Zauberer oder Treue und Flatter haftigkeit (play) 1832

Zampa der Tagedieb oder Die Braut von Gips (play) 1832

Die Zauberreise in die Rittenzeit oder die Übermütigen (play) 1832

Der böse Geist Lumpazivagabundus oder Das liederliche Kleeblett (play) 1833

Robert der Teufel (play) 1833

Die Gleichheit der Jahre (play) 1834

Müller, Kohlenbrenner und Sesselträger oder Die Träume von Schale und Kern (play) 1834

Der Zauberer Sulphurelektromagnetikophosphoratus und die Fee Walburgiblocksbergiseptemtrionalis oder des ungeratenen Herrn Sohnes Leben, Taten, und Meinungen wie auch dessen Bestrafung in der Sklaverei und was sich alldort Ferneres mit ihm begab (play) 1834

Eulenspiegel oder Schabernack über Schabernack (play) 1835

Zu ebener Erde und im ersten Stock oder Die Launen des Glücks (play) 1835

Das Haus der Temperamente (play) 1837

[*The House of Humors*, published in *Three Viennese Comedies*, 1986]

Glück, Misbrauch und Rückkehr oder Das Geheimnis des grauen Hauses (play) 1838

Der verhängnisvolle Faschingnacht (play) 1839

Der Erbschleicher (play) 1840

Der Talisman oder Die Schickalsperüken (play) 1840

[*The Talisman*, published in *Three Viennese Comedies*, 1986]

Das Mädl aus der Vorstadt oder Erlich währt am längsten (play) 1841

Einen Jux will er sich machen (play) 1842

Die Papiere des Teufels oder der Zufall (play) 1842

Liebesgeschichten und Heiratsachen (play) 1843

[*Love Affairs and Wedding Bells*, published in *Three Plays*, 1967]

Nur Ruhe! (play) 1843

Eisenbahnheiraten oder Wein, Neustadt, Brünn (play) 1844

Der Zerrissene (play) 1844

[*A Man Full of Nothing*, published in *Three Plays*, 1967]

Die beiden Herren Söhne (play) 1845

Unverhofft (play) 1845

Der Unbedeutende (play) 1846

Der Schützling (play) 1847

Die Anverwandten (play) 1848

Freiheit in Krähwinkel (play) 1848

[*Liberty Comes to Krähwinkel*, 1957]

Martha oder die Mischmonder Markt-Mägde-Mietung (play) 1848

Der alte Mann mit der jungen Frau (play) 1849*

Judith und Holofernes (play) 1849

[*Judith and Holofernes*, published in *Three Viennese Comedies*, 1986]

Alles will den Propheten sehen (play) 1850

Sie sollen ihn nicht haben oder Der holländische Bauer (play) 1850

Mein Freund (play) 1851

Kampl oder Das Mädchen mit Millionen und die Näherin (play) 1852

Heimliches Geld, heimliches Liebe (play) 1853

Tannhäuser (play) 1857

Umsonst! (play) 1857

Lohengrin (play) 1859

*Date of composition

CRITICISM

Thornton Wilder (essay date 1967)

[*A Pulitzer Prize-winning American dramatist, Wilder was renowned for his blending of traditional American values and innovative theatrical techniques. One of his best-known plays,* The Matchmaker, *was based on Nestroy's* Einen Jux will er sich machen, *and in the following excerpt, Wilder praises Nestroy's satiric wit.*]

During the forties and fifties of the last century a famous actor-dramatist of Vienna was observed on a number of occasions, sitting alone in a café in the late afternoon. His manner became increasingly agitated. The hour of seven was approaching when the curtain must rise on his performance. He was trying in vain to call a waiter's attention, but shrank from rendering himself conspicuous. Finally a fellow guest would raise his voice and call out: "Herr Ober, can't you see that Herr von Nestroy wishes to pay his bill?" Yet an hour later this same shy actor, released from his torment at the café-table, would advance toward the audience with an introductory monologue and song, expressing in his carriage and in the glances of his large

brilliant eyes an unbounded insolence. The words he uttered and the pantomime that accompanied them attacked
his public's most cherished illusions. Later, when he rose
to be manager of his company he never directed the productions himself. He lacked the courage to "correct" his
fellow actors' performances. He arrived promptly at rehearsals, letter-perfect in his rôle. When scene-shifters
bumped into him, it was Nestroy who tendered a deferential apology. There have been other examples of writers famous for aggressive and arrogant wit who have been mild
and self-effacing in private conduct. Dr. Sigmund Freud,
who delighted in Nestroy's work, has described wit as "the
retaliation of the underdog."

Satire is aggressive. Cynicism is a devaluation of prevailing standards. What and whom was Nestroy attacking?
Why did his audiences submit to—and even welcome—
the large element in his writing and performance that was
so obviously intended to render them uncomfortable?

Nestroy played in "second class" theaters—in the so-
called *Vorstadt,* the suburbs that had recently been included in the new metropolis. The Viennese aristocracy and
the "nicely" cultivated public attended the Burgtheater
which offered long verse tragedies generally dealing with
antiquity or the Middle Ages (occasionally these were by
great hands; in *Der Talisman* Nestroy alludes to Grillparzer's *Ottokars Glück und Ende*). Nestroy's plays were felt
to be "low." Though the majority of them picture the
emerging newly wealthy middle classes, the parts he wrote
for himself embody figures from a lower level of society—
servants, apprentices, adventurers, and proletariat ne'er-
do-wells.

Satire flourishes when society is passing through a state of
transition, and transition contains elements of social and
cultural revolt. The upward movement of a hitherto de-
pressed stratum is accompanied by pretension, insecurity,
and gaucherie. Two centuries earlier Molière was ridiculing these manifestations in *Le bourgeois gentilhomme, Les
femmes savantes,* and other plays. Goldoni was constantly
occupied with them and often at his best, as in *La casa
nuova.* Beaumarchais laughed and shook his fist. It is not
necessary to be a cardcarrying Communist to observe that
a large part of European literature during the last two centuries—tragic and comic—has been concerned with "class
warfare." Numberless are the works, headed by the Don
Juan and Faust legends, that derive a large part of their
force from the seduction of a peasant girl by a man of privileged background. (Nestroy affords a powerful treatment
of this situation in *Der Unbedeutende.*) Vienna was in social and political ferment. When finally the short-lived
"March Revolution" of 1848 broke out in Austria,
Nestroy himself manned the ramparts and wrote two
comedies to celebrate the victory—disconcerting plays,
however, for his satire was directed at both the oppressors
and the liberators. For cynics there are no Utopias and little hope of meliorism. Satirists, like Swift, Voltaire, and
Gogol, may declare their intention of bettering mankind,
but one is left with an impression of their resigned acceptance of the doctrine of man's imperfectibility. We are
often told that the object of comedy is to expose stupidity,
restrain excess, unmask hypocrisy, and to chastise vice.

Each of the masters returned repeatedly to certain targets:
Aristophanes flayed his contemporaries' passion for political bungling (of little interest to Nestroy); Molière attacked medical quackery and religious hypocrisy (Nestroy
has little to say about doctors and *never* alludes to religion). Most satirists, in so far as they are permitted—
particularly those working in the late Middle Ages and
early Renaissance—have exploited the scatological and
the pornographic. Accounts of Nestroy's performances as
an actor give the impression of having been accompanied
by a constant play of obscene implications, yet scarcely a
word of such matter can be read in the printed texts that
have come down to us. This daring material appeared in
Nestroy's rôle only and was conveyed by him in extem-
pore improvisation and in glance, pause, and gesture. The
censor threatened, critics voiced their outrage, a portion
of the audience protested; but Nestroy could not restrain
himself; his daemon drove him on. Two plays in this volume show very clearly where such material could have
been inserted: Titus in *Der Talisman,* climbing up the social ladder, is the object of infatuation of a succession of
women he despised and insulted; and the scurrilous Nebel
in *Liebesgeschichten* (Moon in *Love Affairs and Wedding
Bells*), pretending to make love to a rich and foolish spinster. In other words, Nestroy is not merely undermining
the sentimental attitude to love, but the very instinctive
drive itself. He depicts a sort of faun for whom one female
is as acceptable as another.

The inner target of Nestroy's satire was the very ethos of
Vienna's newly stabilized bourgeoisie: the pleasure-loving
geniality, the famous *Gemütlichkeit.* In a play *Unverhofft,*
written in the year following *Der Zerrissene* (*A Man Full
of Nothing*), the character played by Nestroy himself says:
"Only an unintelligent man can fail to see the omnipresent
havoc underlying the apparently innocuous *Gemütlichkeit.*" What revolted Nestroy in his native city was not
only the narrowness and coldness of heart that characterize all such milieux, but its predominant and stultifying
characteristic of sentimental complacency—the smugness
of small-town citizens living in a newly conscious metropolis. In the center of every play we find this Nestroy-figure,
this disillusioned but clear-sighted outsider—often amoral, but never self-deluding—exposing the pretension of his
audience, ridiculing their defenses, denouncing their sloth
and the damage inflicted by their mindless subservience to
outworn conventions.

Why did his public find enjoyment in this drastic devaluation of its self-image? Members of a parvenu social stratum are like adolescents, absorbedly self-conscious. They
love to hear themselves discussed. They peer into mirrors.
Even to hear themselves ridiculed becomes a "school of
manners." But they soon tire of mere abuse; the darts
must be accurate. The *vis comica* is always painful, but it
is compelling in proportion to its truth. And Nestroy,
aided by employing *their own dialect,* was unerringly actual. His wit cut to the quick. He walked a perilous tightrope
and often suffered for his insolence. Enormously successful plays alternated with abject failures. (A number of
those failures are now among the most admired of his
works.) Finally, with the years his temper became milder.
The rôles he wrote for himself in *Der Unbedeutende,*

Kampl, and *Mein Freund* are still sharp-eyed and harsh spoken, but at heart they reveal themselves as merely kindly curmudgeons.

Of Nestroy's fifty major plays scholars have found only two which were not adaptations of novels or plays by others—the majority of them from the French. It is astonishing to observe with what fidelity he followed the plot structure of his foreign source. The invention of narrative patterns—"plotting"—did not interest him. Far more astonishing is the alteration he effected through the imposition of his own dialogue and characterization. Consider *Der Talisman,* for example: the young hero of *Bonaventure,* a vaudeville-comedy by Duperty and F. de Courcy, is the conventional young opportunist of French farce who reacts with banal surprise to the succession of wigs that circumstance offers him. In *Der Talisman,* Titus is the social pariah—victim of the prevailing prejudice against red hair—who avidly seizes each opportunity to advance himself. In Nestroy's hands the prejudice against red hair becomes a symbol of all the senseless ideas on which a *gemütlich* public nourishes itself. Titus is *aware* of it and, remaining in close rapport with the audience by means of asides, monologues, and songs, invokes their complicity in his heartless and even cruel advancement. (That is: in the dryness of heart that underlies the *Gemütlichkeit* and that snatches at any occasion for pleasure or wealth, no matter whom one tramples upon.)

Principally, however, Nestroy was forgiven his cynicism because of his extraordinary mastery of language. It is this that has lead to the proverbial assumption in Vienna that "Nestroy is untranslatable," by which is also meant untranslatable even into German (an exaggeration that can be laid to local pride; the distortion imposed by the dialect is less exotic than that found in Hauptmann's Prussian and Silesian plays). Similarly it is said of the great actor-dramatist of Naples today, Eduardo de Filippo, that he is untranslatable even into Italian. Nestroy avails himself of the German language's tendency to compound nouns, forcing adjectival forms from polysyllabic (and polyglot) substantives, wrenching startling associations of ideas from puns, and illuminating philosophical concepts by the use of droll mixed metaphors. Most jokes lose their savor in translation and perish under dissection. The greater part of this verbal acrobacy is entrusted to the Nestroy-figure and hence derives a special fascination in the mouth of a character at the bottom of society. Under a light screen of dialect *he* speaks a highly sophisticated German; his is the only superior intelligence in the play. The same pungency and force are found in the utterances of Shakespeare's clowns—half beggars, the lowest of the servants, parasites at rich men's tables. Through *independence* of *mind* the despised outsider elevates himself to the rank of a penetrating judge of society and its mores. Diogenes, the Cynic, is reported to have lived in a tub. (pp. v-x)

> *Thornton Wilder, in a foreword to* Three Comedies *by Johann Nestroy, translated by Max Knight and Joseph Fabry, Frederick Ungar Publishing Co., 1967, pp. v-x.*

Max Knight and Joseph Fabry   (essay date 1967)

[*In the following excerpt, the critics summarize Nestroy's accomplishments.*]

Nestroy's X-ray eyes saw through sham, pretense, and fraud, and exposed man's miserable motives. In all Nestroy plays the main character was written for himself, and speaks for himself. Buried in slapstick comedy lay his philosophy, his sober view of man: "Two wolves can meet without being afraid of each other, but two men meeting in a dark forest always will think, 'He is a robber.'"

Nestroy saw man as tossed about by a fate that remained completely unconcerned. In one of his early plays, when he was still using the traditional framework of the fairy piece (though he used it as a parody), Father Fate, resting on a cloud, is asked for help by his nephew Stellaris. Fate cuts short all explanations:

> FATE: I know everything. (*To himself*) I don't know a thing, but I'm much too lazy to listen. It's great to be Fate: one does nothing and gets credit for everything.
>
> STELLARIS: Then we may hope?
>
> FATE: Of course. Go ahead and hope! (*Sits down on his cloud and falls asleep again.*)

Nestroy soon discarded the framework of the world of magic and concentrated on man on earth, but fate still remains "a miserable ruler, Nero and Louis XIV wrapped in one." Man is tyrannized by fate as much as by a dictatorial king, but he rebels: "They say that a man's chances are dealt like a card from the deck of destiny—if I could find the cardsharp who dealt mine I'd club him one on the head."

Man's life is sweetened by love which, unfortunately, tends to degenerate into marriage. "Love is a string that ties hearts together, and marriage a rope that ties hands; the string can be broken, but the rope—never." His dim view of marriage may be the result of his own experience: he married very young, divorced his wife when he found her with a lover, and for the rest of his life he had one affair after another while living with a common-law wife whom he, as a Catholic, could not marry.

Nestroy lived in an era when one did not talk about sex, but he did not hide his opinion that sex, next to money and plain human cussedness, is man's greatest motivation. "In the drama of love, the first act is called longing, the second possession. And impatient youth will not stand for an intermission." But some of his most pointed barbs were saved for marriage: "Is there a better opportunity to make someone you hate unhappy than to marry him?" "Love is called happy if it results in what is often the greatest mishap: marriage." "Marriage is always a tragedy, because one of the partners must die—or it doesn't end." Marriage, to Nestroy, was "a mutual life annoyance company," which, however, did not keep him from including one and, more often, several marriages in the conventional happy endings of his plays. "I've never found anything distasteful," he wrote, "in seeing someone else getting married."

The remnants of feudalism are still in evidence in Nestroy's plays. The aristocrat, in his mansion, is the protector of the people in the village and controls the local police. But the newly rich man can now buy the mansion and the power, and this, of course, is comedy. And Nestroy can pour forth his irony against the rich, which censorship does not allow him to do against the establishment, the aristocrats. All problems are solved by money, often come by in the crudest form: a sudden inheritance, an unforeseen treasure, an unexpected gift. Nestroy himself ridicules his own use of unexpected money to bring about happy endings: "Has it happened again?" one of his main characters calls out just before the last curtain. "It's incredible how many rich uncles and aunts die every year so everything will end well!"

Although Nestroy ridicules the rich, he is no social reformer. He is a writer of the people and for the people, but not a participant in the class war. Class distinctions exist—between aristocrats and commoners and, more recently, between the rich and the poor. But Nestroy is as critical of the common people as he is of the rich, the aristocrats, the authorities, fate. Common people, too, sell their souls for money, with down-to-earth rationalizations: "I really shouldn't take your money but one needs money to live, and I live all the time, so I need money all the time." He sees the common man's weaknesses, his laziness, his superstition, his adulation of success, his fickleness. "To get a job would create prosperity, prosperity might grow into wealth, with wealth come new wishes, wishes result in dissatisfaction—no, you don't tempt me, I'd rather remain unemployed." And: "A poor man must eat too. When he smells food, all other passions disappear. He has no anger, no emotions, no sadness, no love, no hate, not even a soul. He has nothing but an appetite."

Nestroy lived at the time when the struggle between absolutism and constitutional freedom was being waged throughout Europe—a Europe that had been stirred up by the successful American and French revolutions. But after Napoleon's defeat, the Holy Alliance among Russia, Prussia, and Austria had resulted in repressive governments for Europe, masterminded by Prince Metternich, Austria's Minister of Foreign Affairs. Only for a brief moment in Nestroy's time, in 1848, Europe stirred again. But when Nestroy joined in manning the barricades even his contemporaries did not know whether this was Nestroy the revolutionary or Nestroy the comedian putting on a parody of a revolutionary. (Just as his contemporaries never knew whether Nestroy, when taking a curtain call—a tall, thin man doubling over from the waist and spreading his long arms—was seriously thanking his fans or caricaturing an actor taking a bow.) Metternich had to flee to England, and Nestroy, for a short time, had his chance to spell out, and not just to hint at, what he thought of censorship. "Censorship is an admission of the rulers that all they can do is to kick ignorant slaves around, they can't govern free people," and "Censorship is a pencil turned into a man or a man turned into a pencil, a line personified, drawn through the products of the mind, a crocodile lurking at the banks of the stream of ideas, ready to bite off the heads of the writers."

He used the brief spell of freedom to write some plays dealing with the political ferment of his time, but when they reached the stage the counter-revolution had been successful and the plays were either emasculated or suppressed. Nestroy's enthusiasm for the people's cause was short-lived; he had had hopes both before and during the revolution, but was disappointed by the way the people used their short victory. "The people are a giant in the cradle who wakes up, staggers about, tramples everything down, and in the end collapses, finding himself in a position even more uncomfortable than in the cradle."

Nestroy has been called a skeptic and nihilist, a poet, a prophet, and a philosopher, and he was all of these. In one mood he could call out bitterly, "What has posterity done for me? Nothing! Well, I'll do the same for posterity!" In another mood he speculated about the significance of daydreams: "If they're full of hope, you're young; if they're full of memories you're old." Soberly he lectured, "Principles are tight clothes—they hinder every movement." But philosophical poetry shows through his criticism of man: "Beautiful days are the privilege of the rich but beautiful nights are the monopoly of the happy"; and, similarly: "In a castle in the air even the janitor in the basement has a view into paradise."

Nestroy was maligned, misunderstood, and ignored by his contemporary critics, but his message comes clearly through in the twentieth century: Imperfect man lives in an imperfect world, and improvement is not possible unless he looks at himself critically and unsparingly. This bitter pill of self-examination is best swallowed in a humorous coating. "Seriousness," said Nestroy, "has a solemn side, a sad side, and many grave sides, but it always has a little spot of electricity from which, with the proper friction, the sparks of humor fly."

When Nestroy came back to Vienna from the provinces in 1831, he continued his established policy of adapting plots and plays from existing sources. He screened German, French, and English plays and novels and took his plots where he found them. This had long been accepted procedure among European playwrights, including Shakespeare and Molière. Europe was still a playwright's paradise; he did not have to invent his plots, he had only to "find" them.

Nestroy raided German (mostly Berlin) farces, French vaudeville plays, English comedies, operettas, operas, and novels, including Charles Dickens' *Martin Chuzzlewit*. In addition, he wrote parodies of works he felt were fake romantic or bombastic, including Richard Wagner's *Tannhäuser* and *Lohengrin*, Giacomo Meyerbeer's *Robert der Teufel*, and plays by Karl von Holtei. In his popular parody of Friedrich Hebbel's *Judith und Holofernes* he poked fun at the sham idolizing of historical and mythological figures, an art which Bernard Shaw later lifted to sophisticated levels.

Nestroy found an ensemble of outstanding comedians in the Vienna Carl Theater and Theater an der Wien. According to an old Viennese saying, a comedian must either be tall and thin, or short and fat, or talented. In Nestroy's repertory theater group he himself was tall and thin, Wenzel Scholz was short and fat, and both were eminently talented. All the plays contain a Nestroy part, a Scholz part, and usually parts written for other members of the cast—for an actor who used to play the part of Hanswurst, the comic character in the old farces, for the great diva, the villain, the dashing young man, the foolish young thing, the old comedienne, the coquettish maidservant. It speaks for Nestroy's creative gift that, in adapting his sources and shaping them into new plays, he never produced stereotypes but rather new challenges for the same actors. In . . . three plays . . . the Nestroy parts include a blasé rich man looking for excitement (*A Man Full of Nothing*), a bitter, basically honest man, crushed by hostility and prejudice (*Talisman*), and a cynical scoundrel ready to make his fortune by fair or foul means (*Love Affairs and Wedding Bells*). When Nestroy adapted borrowed plots he was usually satisfied with writing juicy parts for himself and his colleagues and creating amusing situations, but rarely bothered to change the construction: if the source play was poorly constructed, so was his own. What he was looking for was an opportunity to clown. His plays abound in funny disguises and primitive misunderstandings that lead to colossal and, by modern standards, often unnecessary mixups—people hiding behind curtains, unlikely chance meetings, and just plain fun, even if it interferes with the plot and stops the show. In fact, this is sometimes the purpose.

Nestroy was skillful in transplanting foreign settings to Vienna soil and in pumping blood into the often pale characters of the originals. Under his hands even minor parts became people as his Vienna audience knew them. Most characters of Nestroy's plays who look like prototypes of nineteenth-century Austrians, and some of whom have become part of Austrian folklore, are "foreigners," naturalized by Nestroy's pen. So thorough was the transformation that even people who knew the original play did not recognize the characters when they saw Nestroy's version on the stage.

The plots may have been borrowed, the characters adapted, but the dialogue was unadulterated Nestroy, entirely his own property. His plays are sprinkled with witticisms, puns, and homespun philosophy rolled into quips which were drawn, like iron filings to a magnet, into the parts he wrote for himself. His rapid-fire, hair-raising tongue twisters supported the belief, after his death, that only he could have played these parts.

Nestroy combined literary tradition and innovation. He kept enough of the familiar format of the old Hanswurst comedies to make his audience forget (or pay little attention to) his indictment of the *status quo*. He still used the device of letting his characters talk in asides, to indicate their thoughts. He did not shrink from *deus ex machina* solutions: in his early plays demigods or magicians appeared; later the unexpected denouement came through sudden inheritances, the popping up of a long-lost father, or the discovery of a letter that explained all. Nestroy used verbal "leitmotifs" to identify his characters, a device of many European writers including Dickens ("Barkis is willin'," "I'm confidently expecting something to turn up"), but for comic effect. He also used crudely expressive

names to label his characters—a stupid farmer is named Kraut and a sausagemaker, Lard—a technique still retained in comic strips, where a detective is named Dick Tracy. Nestroy also employed the familiar device (surviving in musicals) of characters forgetting about the plot and singing songs.

Here Nestroy really combined the old and the new. He himself was delighted when he had a chance to sing. His voice may no longer have been good enough for grand opera, but it was capable of presenting three or four little ditties an evening. All his plays are "farces with songs" or "parodies with songs" or, in his early days, "fairy plays with songs." Here again he stands with both feet in the tradition of the Viennese folk comedies, and here again he pioneers. Some of his songs are no more than pleasant excuses for buffoonery. But in most of them—he wrote more than two hundred—the actor steps not only to the footlights but out of the play altogether, and addresses the audience on subjects of general and usually topical interest. The songs are Nestroy's comments on his contemporary world. They are not necessarily concerned with the plot, but always with man, his follies, customs, weaknesses, and anything else that can be got past the censor. Each stanza ends in a punch line that can be passed on with a wink: "Ja, die Männer ham's gut" ("Yes, a man has it made"); "Na, lass' ma an jeden sein' Freud' " ("Let each man be happy, as each man sees fit"); "Das ist wohl nur Chimäre, aber mich unterhalt's" ("This may be all nonsense, but I think it's fun"). The custom of adding stanzas as encores gave Nestroy the opportunity to comment on last-minute events, and netted him fines and jail terms. His songs are the ancestors of the ballads Bertolt Brecht used in his plays and of those ditties that became so popular in the German and Austrian political cabarets during the last years of the Kaiser and between the two world wars, especially during the rise of totalitarianism. These songs abound in innuendo and veiled references, and seem to thrive when freedom of speech is threatened, when people are not allowed to criticize their government openly. In the United States the political *chanson,* by European standards, leads a relatively feeble existence.

Nestroy's greatness, it has been said, rested on his gift of knowing what needed to be satirized, his wit, and his linguistic artistry. Although the latter kept this Austrian Aristophanes from becoming known outside the reach of his local idiom, he was not a dialect writer like Finley Peter Dunne or the authors of such comic strips as the Katzenjammer Kids. He used language as the carrier for the imagery of his wit; he used language on all levels, mother tongue in cheek. He parodied the stilted, lazy elegance of the speech in the Vienna salons; he satirized the would-be smartness of the *nouveaux riches,* mocked the officialese of civil servants, and made full use of the colorful and inventive idiom of the Viennese spoken by the people in the suburbs. Since most of the Nestroy and Scholz parts are "common people," the punchiest lines are spoken in dialect, but even the "lowest" people do not speak dialect all the time. Nestroy effectively played one kind of speech against the other. A cobbler who tries to converse with a nobleman in the highfalutin terms of an aristocrat and, in the midst of it, drops a real lowdown slang word, or a *par-*

venu who is out to impress a nobleman with a diction he thinks is aristocratic, provides for more chuckles than would someone speaking straight dialect.

Nestroy was an educated man, a graduate of Austria's best high school, and a theater-obsessed dropout from the University of Vienna after two years of law study. In his plays he draws some of his quips from classical literature or mythology ("Jupiter set an example for all lovers when he disguised himself as a bull to win Europa, and ever since then, bull has proved effective in winning a girl's heart.") He uses Latin phrases to poke fun at stuffy bureaucrats or to coin verbal monstrosities (one of his characters who is confident of quick success says: "I feel venividivicious today"). A smattering of English, French, Italian, and Spanish helps him to make bilingual puns. In one scene, an uneducated tailor tries to impress a lady by helping her recover a sharp-toothed little dog she has lost in Italy. He dictates a notice: "Cane perduto. Piccolo pooch with quattro footsies. Denti plenti."

But Nestroy's real tool was, of course, German, the language he truly mastered as a virtuoso. He combined Viennese idiom and High German into similes, metaphors, mixed-up proverbs, and gyrating figures of speech. His word creations may have been primitive or ingenious, but they were never an end in themselves; they always conveyed the message he wanted to get across. "The great of the earth are all stars; that's why they can shine only when everything else is dark." "The words of a thousand imps become important, they impress, because the imps are a thousand, and honest people, who won't believe them, are at most ten." One of the most widely quoted passages comes from a scene in which Nestroy, dressed up as a schoolboy, has to take a test in social studies. To the teacher's question, "What is man?" Nestroy's answer is a display of verbal somersaults which, however, never lose sight of the direction in which they are going. Any attempt to translate such gymnastics must be content with imitation:

> Man is a being who occupies the highest stage of creation, who even claims to have been made in the image of God—but God is probably not very flattered. Man is an insect, because he stings, bites, bugs you, gives you the creeps, and is often for the birds. But man is also a fish, because he gets into deep water and does horrible things in cold blood. No less is man a reptile, for he's a snake in the grass. He's a bird, too, because he lives in the clouds, often makes a living out of thin air, and gets upset when he cannot fill the bill. And, finally, man is also a mammal, because he's a sucker.

Nestroy exploited the peculiarities of German, for example its tendency to form excessively long words. He fired word rockets that have up to two dozen syllables, and he enjoyed rattling them off on the stage with the dexterity of a juggler.

Nestroy played with the language like a child who has discovered a new toy. If some of his expressions are clichés today, it must be remembered that he coined them first. Had he been writing in English, he probably would have had no compunction about constructing "progress" as the

opposite to "Congress," in forming from "toy" a diminutive "toilet," or from "infant" a collective "infantry." A second-hand suitor, a dirty laundry maid, a man with a "rhinocerous" nose may have popped up—his audience appreciated such burlesques, but it took two or three generations for the realization that beyond the punning, catchy songs, and cheap mixups, Nestroy had elevated the lowest form of comedy to the level of literature. (pp. 11-23)

> *Max Knight and Joseph Fabry, in an introduction to* Three Comedies *by Johann Nestroy, translated by Max Knight and Joseph Fabry, Frederick Ungar Publishing Co., 1967, pp. 1-27.*

W. E. Yates   (essay date 1972)

[*In the following excerpt, Yates discusses Nestroy's treatment of his original source materials in the parodies* Die verhängnisvolle Faschingsnacht *and* Judith und Holofernes.]

The critical relation to language that is reflected in the roles of the *raisonneurs* is part of a characteristic mistrust of all conventionality which, when directed at literature and the theatre, made Nestroy a natural parodist. And once his youthful folly, **Rudolph, Prinz von Korsika,** was behind him, his critical outlook quickly extended to the conventions of the theatre. This is evident in the comments made by Papp in his first short comedy: in a variant version of the second scene, for example, Papp suggests how plays by Schiller could be rewritten, with happy endings, to make them more entertaining. Then in **Die Verbannung aus dem Zauberreiche** Nestroy's view of the *Ritterstück* is made very clear when Longinus, ostensibly extolling the genre, reduces its content to its stereotyped elements when he sums it up in the formula 'Wut, Götter, Rache, Tod, Mondschein, Verderben, Schwärmerei, Grabesnacht, Himmelslust und Schwerenot' (II, 3). And in his next full-length play, **Der Tod am Hochzeitstage,** he presents a robber in burlesque guise, the sleepy and cowardly Stixlmann, in whose mouth lines from Grillparzer—Jaromir's claim to his birthright of innocence (*Die Ahnfrau* 2839-43)—sound utterly out of key, unreal (I, 2). The point is reinforced in the following scene by a juxtaposition, typical of Viennese parody, of dialect and literary German. Stixlmann has been instructed to execute a robbery: perplexed and frightened, he weeps like the *Naturmensch* he is. 'Wenn das mein' Ahndl sehet, die hat woll'n, ich soll ein Schulmeister werden, wenn das mein' Regerl wüßt', die hat g'meint, ich soll s' heiraten auf Ägidi . . . ' He imagines the prospect of the gallows, and now it is with a much more immediate misery than in the original that he echoes Jaromir's words about the robber's moments of tears, 'Ach der Räuber hat auch Stunden . . . ' (*Ahnfrau* 1860).

The instinct of the parodist is also to be seen in the burlesque use Nestroy makes of the *Zauberstück* convention. His true parodies, however, are only eleven in number. The first two were directed at ephemeral theatrical material: **Der gefühlvolle Kerkermeister** is a parody of a ballet, and *Nagerl und Handschuh* of a *Zauberstück* on the Cinderella theme. Five more parody operas: Hérold's *Zampa,* Meyerbeer's *Robert-le-Diable,* Flotow's *Martha,* and *Tannhäuser* and *Lohengrin* by Wagner. The remaining four, though all contain musical numbers, parody stage plays: one by Ernst Raupach (*Robert der Teufel*), two by Karl von Holtei (*Lorbeerbaum und Bettelstab* and *Ein Trauerspiel in Berlin*) and one by Hebbel (*Judith*). In two cases (*Der gefühlvolle Kerkermeister* and the first Holtei-parody) it seems clear that much of the parody was directed against the acting in performances of the originals. Among the opera parodies it is unfortunately the case that while the two best-known originals are the Wagner operas, Nestroy's *Tannhäuser* (1857) is an adaptation of an earlier parody by a doctor in Breslau, H. Wollheim, while *Lohengrin* (1859) is one of the weakest of Nestroy's later works. Conversely, the best and most incisive of the opera parodies, *Robert der Teufel,* treats an original that is now largely forgotten. Nevertheless it forms, together with *Die verhängnisvolle Faschingsnacht* and *Judith und Holofernes,* the climax of the tradition of parody on the Viennese popular stage.

Nestroy's command of the traditional parodistic techniques is evident in the early parodies. Just as the characters in *Othello* are restyled by Kringsteiner, or the nobles in Schiller's *Fiesco* are transformed into sausage-sellers in Gleich's parody *Fiesko der Salamikrämer* (1813), so in *Zampa der Tagdieb* the nobles of Hérold's opera are reduced to a macaroni-maker and the son of a salami-manufacturer. And just as Meisl works in reinterpretations of motive in his parody of *Die Ahnfrau,* so Nestroy uses the same technique in *Der gefühlvolle Kerkermeister.* 'Ha,' cries the widow Adelheid, who is being importuned by the wicked tyrant Berengario, 'und ich wollte dem Verblichenen treu bleiben, ewig, oder wenigstens doch so lang, bis ich einen nach mein' Gusto g'funden hätt'!' (I, 1). This critical mistrust of false sentiment, in literature as in life, runs throughout Nestroy's early work. (pp. 96-8)

Of all his parodies, the two that lend themselves best to close examination of their textual relation to their respective originals are *Die verhängnisvolle Faschingsnacht* and *Judith und Holofernes,* both parodies of spoken drama as opposed to opera and based primarily on the texts (as opposed to the performance) of the originals. In both Nestroy uses the traditional techniques of parody, but sustains a directness of critical reference to the originals that far surpasses Kringsteiner, Gleich and Meisl.

Die verhängnisvolle Faschingsnacht is directed against Holtei's drama *Ein Trauerspiel in Berlin,* which had not been performed in Vienna but which had been published in 1838. The tragedy it treats is that of a labourer, Franz, and his beloved Dörthe, an honest country girl who is in employment as a servant in a Berlin household. Dörthe's mistress, Amélie, is wealthy and affected: she heaps unjust criticism on Dörthe, and dominates her own second husband, Gustav. Gustav's father, Ehrenthal, is going to offer Franz a job in the country as a forester's assistant; Gustav himself resolves to leave Amélie and the city, but cannot bring himself to, because of his affection for their infant son. Herr Lämmlein, the brother of Amélie's first husband, coveting for his own daughter the fortune Amélie has inherited, bribes her manservant August (who is an ex-convict) to steal the child. August seizes the occasion of a masked ball to bring in his helper, Nante, to carry off the child while August himself steals Amélie's jewelcase; Dörthe, waiting to meet Franz, observes the thieves and follows them to rescue the child. Amélie returns from the ball with an admirer, Herr Richard, but tells him to go and locks herself in Dörthe's room; and when Franz comes in, impatient and jealous, Richard takes him for August and tries to conceal the true position by telling him he has been with Dörthe. Furious, Franz kicks in the door and stabs Amélie dead with a knife which Dörthe lent him earlier to cut his bread. Dörthe finds the child in its basket where Nante has hidden it; and though she is herself arrested as the thief and suspected of the murder, the facts of the case are finally straightened out. The true thieves are arrested, and Franz gives himself up as the murderer. Though he knows now that Dörthe is in fact true to him, he hopes for death rather than life imprisonment; and Dörthe, who will return to the country under Ehrenthal's protection, promises that she will remain true to his memory.

In Nestroy's parody, Helene (= Amélie) is not murdered, but only faints; as a result the murder inquiry in the last act of the original is dispensed with. Otherwise, Nestroy follows Holtei's plot closely. He adds a role (Nani) for Marie Weiler (the première of *Die verhängnisvolle Faschingsnacht* was a benefit performance for her), and the role of Lorenz (= Franz) is expanded into a characteristic Nestroy-role with monologues and *Couplets.* Equivalent cuts are made in the role of Taubenherz (= Herr Lämmlein), who in Holtei is a stereotyped hypocrite. Amélie compares Lämmlein to Tartuffe (II, 2); but Nestroy doubtless saw that any comedy to be drawn from the role would be of a very well-worn kind. Otherwise the characters of the parody correspond closely to those of the original: Nestroy takes the whole action of Holtei's 'tragedy' and rewrites it, turning it into a gay Viennese *Posse.* (pp. 99-100)

The foundation on which his parody is built is the customary transference of the action to a Viennese setting; then he uses in the main five further devices to achieve his parodistic effect. First he may insert comment to gloss the improbabilities of the original. Tatelhuber's description of his son as a 'Tagdieb' is a gloss of this kind; then two scenes later Gustav's (Philipp's) reaction to his child, the exaggerated affection that makes him forget in a moment all his resolves of independence, is summed up in another inserted gloss, again spoken by Tatelhuber: 'Aus dem wär' a prächtige Ammel word'n.' (In Kringsteiner's *Werthers Leiden* a similar effect is achieved through the role of Lenzl, Werther's naively frank mate who accompanies him as he arrives in the Leopoldstadt district.)

Secondly, a technique of simplification and concentration is applied to the feature of the original that Nestroy was most concerned to pick out for ridicule, the strong sense of pride and honour that leads Franz into the tragedy. The account of his proud character that Dörthe gives Ehrenthal in the opening scene is compressed by Nestroy into the short speech in which Sepherl tells of Lorenz's 'ungeheures Ehrgefühl' (I, 4). This kind of concentration of the characterization is a feature of each of Nestroy's best parodies. It will be seen again in his presentation of Holofernes; and it is also displayed in **Robert der Teufel:** 'Wenn ich auch ein Teufel bin, so bin ich doch zugleich zärtlicher Vater,' Bertram declares, and then adds a gloss to underline the point: 'das ist zwar gegen allen gesunden Menschenverstand, aber man tragt's jetzt so' (II, 7).

Thirdly, elements of characterization and of language are caricatured by comic exaggeration. Holtei's second act opens with the sycophantic words of the maid, Philippine: 'Gnädige Frau werden schön sein, wie keine andre'; in Nestroy the insincerity of such a compliment is magnified in Rosine's eulogy: 'Göttlich sehen Euer Gnaden aus; wenn Euer Gnaden eintreten, das wird sein, als ob die Sonn' am Himmel aufging'!' (II, 3). Similarly whereas in the original the philanderer Richard simply mentions his supposed fear that he has a rival, over and above Amélie's husband, in the parody the artificiality of this ploy is brought out in a characteristic purple passage:

HOLTEI	NESTROY
RICHARD . . .Denn ich muß glauben, daß ein beglückter Nebenbuhler—	GECK . . . Ich ahne das Schrecklichste. Nicht Ihr Gatte, nein, ein glücklicher Nebenbuhler ist
AMELIE (*lachend*) Mein Mann!—?	es, der das Flammenschwert vor
RICHARD Ehemänner zählen	dem Paradiese dieses Herzens
nicht. (I, 5)	schwingt. (I, 16)

A fourth technique, one of the most basic in Viennese parody since the mid-eighteenth century, is that of trivialization. This element functions in counterpoint with that of exaggeration, cutting the figures of the original down to size, and so serving to highlight all the more clearly the artificiality of language and feeling that Nestroy caricatures by exaggeration. This is a technique that later provides one of the best moments in the second Wagner parody: the arrival of Lohengrin on a white lamb allows Nestroy to mock at the long farewell that Wagner's hero takes of his swan, for all the artificiality in the repetition 'Leb wohl, leb wohl, mein lieber Schwan!' stands exposed when Nestroy's Lohengrin bids farewell to a mere sheep: 'Leb wohl, leb wohl, mein gutes Schaf!' (I, 3). In **Die verhängnisvolle Faschingsnacht** a similar procedure, also intended to deflate the emotional atmosphere of the original, underlies the alteration of Franz's murder of Amélie to Helene's merely fainting. Or again, whereas in the original Ehrenthal, dressed for the masked ball, appears in costume as a German knight, in the parody Tatelhuber's costume is reduced to that of Harlequin—a reduction which is comically appropriate to the unheroic temper of the original, and which allows Tatelhuber to carry, in the form of the wooden sword of the comic figure, the comic miniature equivalent to the genuine sword of knighthood.

A fifth technique used by Nestroy is to develop elements that exist only in embryo in the original: instead of being merely spoken, ideas are enacted. In Holtei, for instance, Richard and Ehrenthal feel a mutual irritation (II, 4), which is made clearer in the parody by the practical consequences Nestroy develops, with Tatelhuber striking Geck with his *Pritsche* (II, 7). Similar expansions serve to bring out the true character of Geck and the exaggerated strength of feeling of the main figure. In the opening scene of Holtei's play, Dörthe tells Ehrenthal of Franz's jealousy; Nestroy shows us Lorenz's jealousy in action as he piles reproaches on Sepherl for her friendship with Tatelhuber (I, 28). In Holtei, Richard argues with Amélie in defence of Dörthe, saying that she is pretty and 'not without a rustic grace' and that she maintains 'eine unverwüstliche Gutmütigkeit' (I, 6). When Amélie protests, he laughingly accuses her of being jealous. Nestroy draws the consequences of this attitude, and, omitting the serious moralizing in the original, shows instead where Geck's feelings could potentially lead in practice: he embraces Sepherl and has to pass it off with Helene as a mere joke (I, 18-19). One consequence of this expansion which adds to the dramatic effectiveness of Nestroy's play is that the motivation is made much more secure, in that Helene's jealousy is given real grounds; similarly Lorenz's jealousy of Tatelhuber is prepared in advance by the gossip of the women in the market (I, 5; I, 10).

If Nestroy's designation of **Die verhängnisvolle Faschingsnacht** as a 'Posse mit Gesang' is appropriate, this is not because the play lacks parodistic sharpness: his various parodistic techniques genuinely throw light on the deficiencies of the original. But on the parodistic base he builds up a comedy that is also much more than a parody—an expansion which, ironically, we owe at least in part to the Austrian censors, whose refusal to sanction a production of Holtei's play meant that a mere parody would have been lost on the Viennese public. Nestroy adds, in all, seven (short) musical scenes. He adds original scenes of broad comedy, including Tatelhuber's two attacks on Geck (I, 14; II, 7), the scene in which the thieves are shown falling out among themselves (III, 4-5), and the portrait of the comically slow and reluctant policemen (III, 6-7). He adds the secondary action in which Lorenz's advances to Nani (II, 2) lead to his adding to the confusion in the final act by introducing a second basket, full of washing (III, 3); this addition to Lorenz's role is balanced by the advances made by Tatelhuber to Sepherl, which she does not understand (II, 9). Nestroy also heightens the whole mood of carnival confusion by concluding his first act with a light-hearted sequence in which Tatelhuber, wanting to keep watch on Geck, and Geck, wanting to keep watch on Helene, both decide to disguise themselves and as the curtain falls are both (in Tatelhuber's phrase) 'als schönes Geschlecht verkleidet'. Among other motifs Nestroy works into his comedy is the famous scene in which Frau von Schimmerglanz declines Lorenz's wood by turning to her servant with an imperious 'Sage Er ihm: Nein!' (I, 9)—a vignette of unforgettable satirical vividness, which Karl Kraus cites as one of the tiny scenes characteristic of Nestroy's creative power, 'winzige Zwischenszenen, wo ein Satz über die Bühne geht und eine Figur, ein Milieu, eine Epoche dasteht'. It is touches of this kind that, together with the clarity and freshness of its characterization and language, lend **Die verhängnisvolle Faschingsnacht** the undying comic vigour which it has retained, both in print and on the stage, independently of the now forgotten drama it parodies.

No problems about the unfamiliarity of the original faced Nestroy when he came to compose his parody of *Judith,* though since the censors in the *Vormärz* period would not permit biblical material to be performed on the stage it was nearly nine years after its première in Berlin that Hebbel's play received its first Viennese performance. This took place on 1 February 1849 in the Burgtheater, with the dramatist's wife (formerly Christine Enghaus) in the title role and Ludwig Löwe as Holofernes; less than six weeks later, on 13 March, the première of the parody followed in the Carl-Theater. Its exceptional interest is that, by a fortunate coincidence, it is of all Nestroy's parodies the one in which he launches the most concentrated attack on the text of the parodied original, while that original is also the only one of the prose plays he parodied which has remained well known in its own right.

Judith und Holofernes is a one-act piece. The reduction of the material to this size is made possible by three fundamental features of Nestroy's procedure. First, the plot is compressed: whereas in the original Judith visits Holofernes twice (in Acts IV and V), Nestroy telescopes the events of the two occasions into a single visit (sc. 24). Secondly, he eschews altogether the sexual element which is at the heart of Hebbel's original characterization of Judith, but which was considerably diluted in the stage version performed in Vienna (that prepared by Hebbel for the Hamburg production in December 1840) and which it would, moreover, have been wellnigh impossible to treat in parodistic form without insuperable objections from the censors. By substituting for Judith her brother Joab, who dresses up to take her place, Nestroy cuts the material of the first scene of Hebbel's third act, as well as Judith's self-analyses in the last act. Thirdly, he once again concentrates on a single principal feature in the characterization: in this case the arrogant boastfulness of Holofernes. He very effectively parodies Hebbel's hero by concentrating on this one feature, presenting Holofernes as a caricature of bombastic egoism. Indeed, the very starting-point of the parody is the perception that Hebbel's Holofernes is no more than a type, superficially conceived and portrayed. His whole persona and position are summed up in the opening chorus of the parody, one of those comic simplifications that reduce character and motive to their most basic explanations:

> Blitzstrahl ist sein Grimm, Grimm, Grimm,
> Donner seine Stimm', Stimm', Stimm'!
> Weil er uns sonst niederhaut,
> Preisen wir ihn alle laut!

Over a decade earlier Nestroy had drawn a comic sketch of wrathful boasting, in artificial literary language full of exaggerations just like those Holofernes uses, in *Das Haus der Temperamente* (I, II):

> WALBURGA . . . (*nimmt Bücher, welche auf dem Tische liegen und wirft sie wütend nach Hutzibutz*) Fort, Schurke, ehe dich mein Grimm zermalmt!
>
> HUTZIBUTZ (*eilt schnell zur Mitte ab.*)
>
> WALBURGA Tausend Vulkane toben in meiner Brust! Weh dem, der dem Lavastrom begegnet! (*In die Seitentüre ab.*)

(pp. 104-09)

Nestroy's sense of the hollowness of this supposedly dominating, heroic personality also underlies the comic ending of the parody, in which Holofernes is not killed, but a replica of his head has the same effect as his real head in the original: held aloft, it causes the flight of his Assyrian troops. The use of a false head also has a precedent in *Bernadon Die getreue Prinzessin Pumphia* (II, 9), where Kulican makes to 'behead' the Persian king, Cyrus. But the parodistic effect Nestroy derives from the motif is much sharper: just as the opening chorus suggests that the obedience of the Assyrians is only guaranteed by the barbarism which Holofernes' position allows him to exercise, so the implication of the ending is to confirm that his dominating leadership of them depends not on any intrinsic quality in his character, but on his position, which could equally well be filled by a cardboard dummy.

The peculiar weakness in the characterization of Hebbel's Holofernes, which prompts this equation with a mere dummy, lies partly in the extravagance of his language, which needed very little exaggeration for the parodistic effect, and partly in a wide discrepancy between his boasts and his actions: not merely (as is often the case with supposed military heroes in drama) are we shown no action that might justify his pride, but precisely those actions of supposed greatness that we do see are irreconcilable with any kind of greatness, being on the contrary arrogant, arbitrary and vindictive. Nestroy brings this out by expanding a single episode to show its implications. First he reduces the episode to its essential gist:

HEBBEL	NESTROY
HOLOFERNES Was macht die Ebräerin?	HOLOFERNES Chalkol! Wie hat dir die Hebräermaid gefallen, die durch unser Lager zog?
DER HAUPTMANN O, sie ist schön. Aber sie ist auch spröde!	CHALKOL O unendlich! Bei ihrem Anblick fuhr mir's durchs Herz wie—
HOLOFERNES Hast du sie versucht? (*Der Hauptmann schweigt verlegen. Holofernes mit wildem Blick:*) Du wagtest das, und wußtest, daß sie mir wohlgefällt? Nimm das, Hund! (*Er haut ihn nieder.*) (Act V)	HOLOFERNES So vielleicht? (*Durchbohrt ihn mit dem Schwerte.*)
	CHALKOL Ah! (*Stürzt zusammen und stirbt.*)
	HOLOFERNES Ich werd' dir's austreiben, auf Mädeln schaun, die deinem Feldherrn in die Augen stechen! (sc. 22)

By transferring Holofernes' explication of the motive of his anger to after his murder of Chalkol, Nestroy underlines the practical futility of his action. Then he adds two further similar question-and-answer exchanges in quick succession: Holofernes kills another captain for questioning an order, then another for trying to avoid Chalkol's fate:

> HOLOFERNES Nun, Idun, was sagst du? Ist die Hebräerin nicht reizend, packschierlich, schön?
>
> IDUN (*beiseite*) Jetzt leg' ich mir ein Bildl ein bei ihm. (*Laut*) Schön? Hm—ich hab' sie eigentlich gar nicht angeschaut.
>
> HOLOFERNES So wenig Ehrfurcht hast du vor

dem Geschmack deines Herrn? Stirb, Elender!
(*Ersticht ihn.*)

That the opposite approach could produce the same punishment demonstrates the arbitrariness, as well as the futility, of Holofernes' barbarous reaction. And now, the expanded episode completed, Nestroy returns to the original text at exactly the point he left it:

HEBBEL	NESTROY
HOLOFERNES Schafft ihn weg und führt mir das Weib her.	ACHIOR (*meldend*) Die reich-und reizgeschmückte Hebräerin wünscht aufzuwarten.
	HOLOFERNES . . . Laß aber erst 's Zelt ordentlich zusamm'räumen, überall lieg'n Erstochene herum—nur keine Schlamperei! (sc. 23)

Hebbel himself recognized the weakness of the characterization of Holofernes: indeed, as Rommel suggests, something of this recognition may lie behind the way his Holofernes himself admits and tries to explain and justify his loquacity in the fourth act. Shortly after the première in Vienna, despite the success of the occasion, Hebbel was already planning to revise the text; and he singled out the role of Holofernes as needing revision, and as being rather a fleshless skeleton of a figure. In later years he came to see clearly the ridiculous quality of Holofernes' part.

Nestroy's designation for *Judith und Holofernes* is 'Travestie'. Bührmann tries to maintain the distinction, current in German theory of comedy, between 'parody', which trivializes the action and characters but retains the tone and form of the original, and 'travesty', which preserves the action and characters and trivializes the tone and form of the treatment; but this distinction is not always helpful in relation to the Viennese popular stage, since in the parodistic comedies from the *'mythologische Karikaturen'* onwards elements of 'parody' and 'travesty' constantly overlap. This is certainly the case in *Judith und Holofernes.* Essentially, the process to which Nestroy subjects Hebbel's text is the usual one of breaking down the theatrical illusion of the original by forcing juxtapositions with the standards of present (Viennese) reality. One of the effects is a counterpoint between the exaggerated and the trivial, as in *Die verhängnisvolle Faschingsnacht.* When Holofernes is accused of villainy and hatred of the Jews, he slips into the casual tone of a pure Scholz-role: 'Es ist nicht so arg; ich hab' nur die Gewohnheit, alles zu vernichten' (sc. 24). In the same scene, the declaration of the original Holofernes to Judith, 'Du gefällst mir, wie mir noch keine gefiel' (Act IV), becomes 'Aber, auf Ehr', du bist gar kein übler Schneck!' Another feature of this *'Verwienerung'* is that the text abounds in anachronisms, and in inappropriate allusions to 'understanding German' (sc. 24) or to Vienna: 'Da is in ganz Wien, will ich sagen, in ganz Assyrien keiner, der mir's Wasser reicht' (sc. 9). The subject of *Judith* lent itself particularly well to this treatment, since a parallel to Holofernes' siege of Bethulia lay to hand in the immediate recent history of Vienna. Thus the population of the city—which Holofernes renames from 'Bethulien' to 'Bettltuttien' (sc. 9)—are transformed into the Jewish traders and small businessmen of Vienna,

and their language is a pastiche of the German of the Viennese Jews. Their attitudes—a parodistic extension and exaggeration of the fearfulness and bickering in Hebbel's third act, and a parodistic contrast to the fanaticism reported in the fifth act—reflect attitudes to be met in Vienna during the siege and encountered by Nestroy at first hand in the National Guard in the Leopoldstadt district: antipathy towards fighting, a predominant selfish but sober materialism, a quick defeatism, and an utterly reasonable inability to come to terms with the rigmaroles of military discipline:

ASSAD (*kommandierend*) Marsch!

HOSEA Wohin? . . .

ASSAD Links g'schaut!

HOSEA Warum? Links is gar nix! Warum sollen wir schauen links? Was ist da zu sehen? (sc. 17)

The whole sequence (sc. 10-20) colourfully suggests what are the real and natural concerns of these unwilling combatants: Hosea, for instance, plans to make money by buying up all the food in the city (sc. 10) and retains his interest in speculation: 'Exerzieren und versäumen die Börs'—?' (sc. 11). This incursion of satirical elements into parody, designed to present a (comic) sample of reality as a norm against which the artifice of the literary original is tested, is wholly in keeping with the traditional approach of the popular parodists in Vienna. Plard, noting that Nestroy adhered to the traditions of the popular theatre and that he wrote in the first place for the Viennese stage of his own time, not for posterity, advances once again the argument that in treating Hebbel's text in parodistic form he was more interested in creating a viable comedy with two comic roles suitable for himself (Joab) and Scholz (Holofernes) than in literary parody for its own sake; and this conclusion seems to have taken root in the canon of Hebbel criticism. It is, however, a *non sequitur:* the fact that Nestroy wrote for a contemporary public does not stand in logical contradiction to the fact that he intended a literary parody. Indeed, the closeness of the parody in most scenes to the original text (which had been available to Nestroy in published form since 1841) shows that it developed in an essentially literary way, to an extent, indeed, which the casual member even of a well-informed Viennese theatre audience could not be expected to appreciate.

As the classic German parody, *Judith und Holofernes* has attracted much attention from the critics, from those who (like Kraus) can see no merit in the original to those who (like Plard) are more sympathetic to Hebbel, and there is no need now to demonstrate the closeness of original and parody in detail; nearly all the significant parallels are noted by Rommel. It is, however, possible to pick out again in brief summary the principal techniques used by Nestroy in the construction of his text.

First, there is again an element of comic exaggeration. Hebbel's Holofernes, for example, orders that the camels be bridled (Act I); when Nestroy's super-hero calls for his mount, it is not just for any camel, but for 'das buckligste meiner Kamele' (sc. 9). And whereas the Holofernes of the original reproves a captain for anticipating his command, in the parody the offender is demoted and forbidden all thought. . . . (pp. 109-14)

The exaggeration of style and manner here is relatively slight, since Holofernes' part needed little. There is more in Nestroy's treatment of the subservience around him, which becomes a caricature of sycophantic grovelling. . . . (p. 115)

Secondly, as in **Die verhängnisvolle Faschingsnacht,** this kind of exaggeration goes together with a process of concentration. Whole passages of the original are compressed into a single speech that serves to recapture—comically heightened—the basic argument or attitude of the original. The best-known example is the boast of Nestroy's Holofernes, 'Ich möcht' mich einmal mit mir selbst zusammenhetzen, nur um zu sehen, wer der Stärkere is, ich oder ich' (sc. 3). Twenty years earlier Nestroy had caricatured the wrath of Dappschädl in a similar image: 'Nur her, weil ich in der Rage bin, wenn nicht bald wer Schläg' kriegt, so hau' ich mich selber im Zorn' (**Der Tod am Hochzeitstage** I, 13). It is as a mere Dappschädl, a comic figure, that Nestroy's 'Ich oder ich' presents Holofernes; but the line is a distillation and summary of at least three utterances of Hebbel's hero. . . .

Other examples of the same technique include Nestroy's treatment of Holofernes' second monologue, which is compressed into a few lines in scenes 5 and 7; the concentration of Achior's whole description of the Israelites, their unmilitary nature and the might of their God, at the end of Hebbel's first act, into the single sentence, which collapses in the emphatic cliché of colloquial idiom, 'Im Kämpfen sind sie schwach, wenn aber der Himmel für sie Wunder wirkt, da triumphieren sie über ihre Feinde, daß es eine Passion is' (sc. 9); the succinct demonstration, by revealing antithesis, of the ineffectuality of the priesthood: '. . . So träufle mein Wort Erquickung in die schmachtende Seele. Weh! Weh! Dreimal wehe!' (sc. 13); the summary of the ambivalent situation of the original Judith: 'Ich bin . . . / . . . Witwe aus ein' sehr guten Haus, / Und kenn' mich vor Unschuld gar nicht aus' (sc. 24); and the transformation of her introduction of her inspiration at the beginning of the second and third acts into Joab's exclamatory cries: 'Ha, Beleuchtung von oben—! Prophetische Einwirkung von unten—! Begeisterung von allen Seiten—! Schmeichelei—Einschläferei—Betäuberei—Meuterei—Sablerei—!!' (sc. 15). (The artifice of this last outburst is further highlighted when in his next speech Joab slips back into a prosaic casualness: 'Is schon wieder vorbei . . . . ')

Thirdly, direct quotations from Hebbel are again followed either by a reinterpretative adaptation or by a glossing comment of the parodist's own invention. In scene 4, for example, a speech that is very nearly a verbatim transcription is followed by a reply which as it were translates the original into Viennese, thus spelling out—unmasking—the self-conceit of Holofernes' attitude:

HEBBEL	NESTROY
BOTE Nebukadnezar will nicht, daß fernerhin andre Götter verehrt werden neben ihm.	HEROLD Nebukadnezar will nicht, daß ferner andere Götter verehrt werden neben ihm.
HOLOFERNES (*stolz*) Wahrscheinlich hat er diesen Entschluß gefaßt, als er die Nachricht von meinen neuesten Siegen empfing. (Act I)	HOLOFERNES (*für sich*) Da kann man sehen, wie köbig die Könige werden, wenn sie Holofernesse haben, die ihnen die Welt erobern. (sc. 4)

The use of the aside allows Nestroy to practise the same kind of explication of a character's real thoughts that Meisl practises with Berta in *Die Frau Ahndel,* but in a way that is much more closely linked to, and more directly commenting on, the original text. Another example of clarifying paraphrase, which translates the exclamatory rhetoric of the original into colloquial idiom and therewith would-be altruism into mere cringing, can be seen in Nestroy's treatment of the episode in Act III of *Judith* in which Daniel regains his speech; and it is followed at once by an example of quotation and glossing comment:

HEBBEL	NESTROY
ASSAD . . . Gib Befehl, daß die Tore der Stadt geöffnet werden. Unterwürfigkeit findet Barmherzigkeit! Ich sag's nicht meinetwegen, ich sag's dieses armen Stummen wegen, ich sag's wegen der Weiber und Kinder! . . .	ASSAD Unser ganzer Widerstand is eine Dummheit, wir wollen lieber sein schön unterwürfig, dem Holofernes öffnen das Tor, ihm machen ein tiefes Kompliment und sagen: 'Euer Exzellenz sind der Beglücker von ganz Israel!'
DANIEL (*reißt sich von ihm los*) Steiniget ihn! Steiniget ihn!	DANIEL (*plötzlich die Sprache gewinnend*) Steiniget ihn! Steiniget ihn!
VOLK War dieser Mann nicht stumm?	ALLE (*mit Staunen*) Was war das? Der Stummerl red't?
ASSAD (*seinen Bruder mit Entsetzen betrachtend*) Stumm und blind . . . (Act III).	RACHEL Das is nur bei besondere Gelegenheiten der Fall.
	ASSAD Für gewöhnlich is er stumm. (sc. 17)

The insertion of Rachel's comment into a passage that otherwise corresponds closely to the original serves to emphasize the unlikelihood of the apparent miracle; once again the interpolation of the everyday voice serves to distance the audience from the action, to break down the spurious illusion.

Fourthly, Nestroy uses one of the basic forms of travesty in his adaptation of Judith's narration of the story of her marriage with Manasses. Nestroy tells the story, but in verse: in doggerel couplets, with deliberately clumsy rhymes, which by jarring on the ear of the audience or reader serve to make a number of parodistic points. For example, the emotional description of the wedding night is parodied with the help of a mock-sentimental series of alliterations (which have their basis in the original) and a broad dialect rhyme. . . . And the climax of the whole story is deflated when a near-quotation is followed not—as in the original—by a quiet statement of mysterious death, emotional in tone and couched in highly literary language, but by a deliberately anti-climactic 'translation', which again serves to bring out the unlikelihood, the artificiality, of the story. . . . (pp. 115-18)

Nestroy's parody of *Judith* is an important literary landmark. In the preface *Wert und Ehre deutscher Sprache,* which was written in 1927, Hofmannsthal makes the point that the everyday German prose that the writers of his generation inherited from the nineteenth-century age of realism was an artificial and therefore inexpressive language, which he contrasts with the various dialects. Standard German always sounds stilted to Viennese ears, and the popular dramatists of successive generations drew comic effects from it. Nestroy shared this native sense of the artificiality of high-flown literary German and regularly contrasted it with the earthy directness of dialect. What is peculiarly significant in his case is not only the acuteness with which he approached works of literature, but the fact that his exposure of linguistic artificiality coincided historically with the decline that Hofmannsthal later recorded in the vitality of the written German of prose literature; and so it is that his parody of *Judith* takes on the stature of a representative rejection of the literary language of his whole age. (pp. 118-19)

> *W. E. Yates, in his* Nestroy: Satire and Parody in Viennese Popular Comedy, *Cambridge at the University Press, 1972, 207 p.*

M. A. Rogers   (essay date 1977)

[*In the following essay originally delivered at a conference in 1977, Rogers deciphers political references in several of Nestroy's comedies and argues that the humor of his plays is dependent on his political skepticism.*]

Our first consideration in discussing Nestroy's relationship to politics must be the obvious one that he was, by profession, a comic actor and dramatist and hence doubly dependent on the good will of his audience, though it must be made clear that he did not always go out of his way to secure this good will and in the middle of one stormily received performance is credited with having wished that the audience might be mown down by gunfire; it is perhaps worth observing that reactions to new plays by Nestroy tended to be extreme, whether favourable, often without regard to the real merit of the piece, although the sensation on the part of the audience that they, for once, were being attacked by Nestroy's satire seems to have been responsible on one or two occasions. Hence, any political opinions Nestroy may have chosen to express would be subject to modification in the light of the audience's probably reaction: umbrage taken at one joke could lead to the wrecking of the whole play.

Our second consideration must of course be the censorship, whose arbitrary and recherché pencil converted (in a play not by Nestroy) the devil's traditional red trousers into green ones because red trousers were part of the uniform of Austrian generals. In most cases, Nestroy performed his own censorship before the manuscript was ever submitted to central authorities for scrutiny, smuggling into performance, one suspects, the more biting turns of phrase which he had toned down for official approval, whilst deceptively preserving the content. His brushes with the censor were usually on account of extempores of a personally insulting kind—jibes, for instance, at the chief of police in Brno (a pun on his name), a Viennese critic (likewise) and the newly crowned King of Prussia (a sneer at the form of his coronation, which will be discussed later).

Our third, and most important, consideration must be the fact that Nestroy was writing comic plays for performance; that is to say, that anything which appears to be an unambiguous statement of opinion is subject to modification by the nature of the character uttering it, the intonation of the actor playing that part, the context within the play and the fact that the line is intended to be funny. It is this last modification which gives rise to the greatest number of imponderables in our discussion, for we are not talking here about simple irony, or about one character's view designed to balance another's and produce a synthesis: we are talking about the presentation of a statement in such a way as to make us laugh and yet we must allow that this may in no way invalidate the statement. However, it would be naive in the extreme to consider the humorous aspect as mere windowdressing to make the naked statement (if one can talk of such a thing) more attractive or more memorable. We must consider the joke, aphorism or witticism (and for the moment I am unwilling to separate or define such categories) as a whole and see how it is constructed and what the elements are on which it depends and out of which it is made. Let us take, so as not to preempt our discussion of plays written during the Revolutionary period, a relatively harmless observation made by Kern in *Der alte Mann mit der jungen Frau,* IV 9, while looking at the baby of a political fugitive whose wife he has taken into his house:

> Das dicke Gesicht und wie er schläft! Werden sehn, der wird einmal Ratsherr werd'n.
>
> (Look at his fat face and how soundly he's sleeping! You'll see, he'll be a counsellor one day.)

Were we to wish to reduce this to a plain statement, we could say that Nestroy considers corpulence and somnolence as the prime qualifications for becoming a counsellor. However, he is in fact allowing his audience to come to this conclusion, assuming, indeed, that this is already the conventional idea of counsellors that they have in their minds which only needs this encouragement to emerge. If we look more closely at the form of the remark, we can see that it is, in its own way, a pun on the attributes of somnolence and corpulence, which are shared by babies and Ratsherren, just as the constituents of a pun have letters and sounds in common. Of course, puns gain in significance if they can be so presented or are so chosen that the apparently chance relationship between the words is made to seem to parallel some kind of relationship between the things, and the quality of the pun will in general depend upon the degree to which this double correspondence is successfully achieved.

What, however, can we derive from such a joke? Evidently, nothing so simple as the assertion that all counsellors are sleepy and fat; but certainly the expectation that an audience will recognise the likeness and share this view which is openly admitted to be conventional and in the formulation presented here as a joke really does go without saying; were one to set it up as a full-scale false syllogism, one would have to state one's general premiss, but here one merely implies it. So it is possible to derive from a joke the prerequisites for its being written: the writer must assume familiarity on the part of his audience with given conventional views of objects, institutions and people, and, in the case of the pun, with the significance and associations of given words. Here I should like to anticipate the results of my later stylistic analysis by drawing attention to the political vocabulary which arose in 1848 and pointing out that it is primarily with this vocabulary that Nestroy is concerned, and only secondarily with the events of the time. For the vocabulary, after all, has the conventional associations and implications that are necessary for the construction of such a joke as the one we have just examined, and knowledge of it will certainly have been widespread enough for the right effect.

A fourth consideration that must be borne in mind is the difficulty of being sure which passages are intended to have political reference and which are not. Like our own Marie Lloyd, Nestroy was able to convey his own interpretation of words which could never have been guilty of such significance without him. Here, we are reckoning not simply with the context in the play (indeed, the effect we are describing involved in many cases the actor stepping completely out of his role in order to address the audience directly, not even in an aside) but the context in reality, as well as the actor's emphasis. After serving a brief prison sentence for extemporised insult of a Viennese critic, Wiest, Nestroy found himself, in the course of his next stage appearance, as an incurable drunkard locked in by his respectable friend to keep him from going out to the pub, saying (*Lumpazivagabundus* III 12)

> Er hat mich eing' sperrt?—Das hat er nicht nötig—Ich war schon eingesperrt—
>
> (He's locked me up . . . He needn't have done that—I've been locked up before—)

which duly earned its round of applause. Similarly, Wendelin's lament in *Höllenangst* I 7:

> Ich hätt' sollen gar nie in d' Wirklichkeit kommen; solang ich noch ein Traum meines Vaters, eine Idee meiner Mutter war, da kann ich recht eine charmante Idee gewesen sein; aber so viele herrliche Ideen haben das, wenn s' ins Leben treten, wachsen sie sich miserabel aus
>
> (I should never have emerged into reality; as long as I was just a dream of my father's, an idea of my mother's, I may well have been a positively charming idea; but that's the trouble with so many splendid ideas, when they're put into practice, they turn out badly)

can be interpreted as a rueful reflection on the 1848 revolution, in view of its context (there are references in the immediately preceding song) and the date of performance, although there is nothing actually in the text to stipulate this, and it would make very good sense in any case, as part of Wendelin's convention of extreme pessimism—(ibid. I 8):

> WENDELIN. Meiner Seel', ich halt' schon auf die andre Welt auch nix mehr.
>
> EVA. Frevel nit, Sohnerl, die andre Welt ist ja die bess're Welt.

> WENDELIN. Mein Gott, sie kann zehnmal besser sein, und 's is erst noch nicht viel dran.
>
> (WENDELIN. Bleeding hell, I don't think much of the other world either any more.
>
> EVA. Don't blaspheme, son, the other world is the better world.
>
> WENDELIN. My God, it can be ten times better than this one and it still won't be up to much.)

An even more difficult case in point is that of *Judith und Holofernes,* the parody of Hebbel's *Judith,* with a blustering, cruel and cynical general and a besieged town whose inhabitants behave more like the Jews of the Leopoldstadt than those of the Old Testament. The allusions to the siege of Vienna are evident—especially when Holofernes (scene 7) describes his sword as the "Götterfabrik" and continues:

> Was in der neuen Zeit durch Bajonette geht, das richten wir, die grauen Vorzeitler, mit dem Schwert.
>
> (What they do in modern times with the bayonet, we dim figures of antiquity perform with the sword.)

Yet such remarks can all be deduced from the original of the play, which appeared in 1840.

Inasmuch as Nestroy reflects the preoccupations of the times, in that he must employ conventional assumptions held by or at least well known to his audience, the period before the Revolution is virtually devoid of political references. The word Kapitalist turns up in his first full-length play, as a sneer delivered by a couple of young boys to the one-time rich young heir, now aged, an ex-convict and a crossing-sweeper—in point of fact, a young ne'erdowell from Fairyland, sent to earth for moral regeneration by living out thirty years as an earthly scapegrace. The figure of Fate, who steps forward and tells the audience that he does nothing but sleep and yet gets the credit for everything that happens, was apparently removed by the censor from *Die Familien Zwirn, Knieriem und Leim,* but whether because it was taken as blasphemy or an attack on the Government is hard to tell. Even such a potentially fruitful subject as the opposition between rich and poor, diagrammatically displayed on a horizontally split stage in *Zu ebener Erde und erster Stock,* is treated as the occasion for virtuoso juxtaposition, rather than social comment. Both families, the rich and the poor, behave according to convention, or at least according to comically extreme versions of these conventions, and the eventual reversal of their positions is brought about by the generosity of a rich English lord, a fortunate lottery win (remember the lottery) and the inevitable inheritance, combined with the equally inevitable rash speculations and unexpected bankruptcy on the first floor. Even the wicked servant, Johann (the Nestroy role) is in such a long line of thieving servants that in *Die beiden Nachtwandler* (II 23) the suddenly rich and now suddenly poor Faden can say to his one-time apprentice and temporary valet, Strick:

> FADEN. Ich hab' jetzt gar nix mehr, du wirst auch nit viel haben.

STRICK. Ich bin nur einen halben Tag Bedienter g'west, was kann ein Anfänger viel machen? Ich hab' Ihnen halt um dreissig Gulden betrogen, die will ich jetzt ehrlich mit Ihnen teilen.

(FADEN. I haven't anything at all left now, you won't have much either.

STRICK. I was only your servant for half a day, what can a beginner do in that time? I *did* manage to diddle you out of thirty florins, which I'll share with you honestly now.)

Zu ebener Erde und erster Stock simply prefigures the quadripartite stage and structure of *Das Haus der Temperamente,* rather than being a social play. Likewise, *Der Talisman* certainly presents a clear picture of social structures, as Titus Feuerfuchs, his red hair covered by a talismanic wig, makes his way up via the gardener's widow and the lady's maid to the lady herself, altering his manner and his vocabulary at each step, but the structure is utilised and treated as a comic one, and not immediately as the object of criticism. Social consciousness appears to emerge in *Der Unbedeutende,* in which Peter Span, the carpenter, asserts that his best friends are not 'Reiche, sondern Arme—die zwei' (I 14), but this assertion of the importance of the workers and of their simple honesty against the weakness and viciousness of the rich, the aristocrats and their toadying servants smacks of the melodrama in general and its Austrian form in particular, the "Lebensbild" which Nestroy had dismissed in one line in *Der Talisman;* the stock-in trade of such plays was a wishy-washy sentimental radicalism, and the prime practitioner of the art, one Friedrich Kaiser, who wrote for the same management which employed Nestroy, in a watered down version of the master's style, was, appropriately enough, the man chosen to proclaim the constitution on March 15th 1848, of which more later. *Der Schützling* does something similar with the industrial revolution and the idea of progress helping the poor, honest, lower-class individual with engineering ability to his just deserts in society, in this case a rich and beautiful upperclass wife.

After the flood of political activity which began in 1848 had ebbed, the censorship seems to have become milder. Certainly references to contemporary political events are much more common than they were before in the songs which appear in Nestroy's plays, and which were always rewritten for the sake of topicality. One of them, for instance, the famous *Kometenlied* from *Lumpazivagabundus,* in which a drunken cobbler with astronomical pretensions justifies his prediction that a comet is about to destroy the world by pointing out how everything on earth proclaims that the end is nigh, is subject to some kind of political interpretation at all stages, as Ernst Fischer demonstrates in his article in *Sinn und Form,* 1962, and as was evident to contemporaries who heard Nestroy's stressing of the refrain: *Die* Welt steht auf kein' Fall mehr lang'. Additional stanzas and half stanzas, none of them particularly witty, jeer at Cavour, Garibaldi, Louis Napoleon and Nationalism. Nestroy's private correspondence contains a vulgar pun on the Hungarian politician Teleki, a feigned distaste for pork because it all comes from Hungary (cf. *Der Zigeunerbaron*) and the description of Czech nationalists as "Böhmische Dalken"—Bohemian Fools by anal-

ogy with our own gooseberry fool. Only in his last play, *Häuptling Abendwind,* set in the cannibal isles, where they talk thick Viennese dialect and make goulash out of their captives, does Nestroy treat politics in a witty fashion again: the two cannibal chiefs have firmly set their faces against civilisation (scene 7):

> ABENDWIND. Ihre Sprach' soll nicht übel sein, und gelehrt und g'scheit.
>
> BIBERHAHN. Aber für uns nicht national.
>
> ABENDWIND. Nur fatal, dass sie auswärts kein Wort verstehn von uns.
>
> BIBERHAHN. Wenn einen kein Mensch versteht, das ist national. (. . .) O, nur erst den Fortschritt ausgebatzt, dann—!
>
> ABENDWIND. Mein Gott, man will ja eh nix, als dass man seine paar Bananen und sein Stückel G'fangenen in Ruh' verzehren kann.
>
> BIBERHAHN. Freilich, wir sind ja gemütliche Leut'.
>
> ABENDWIND. Recht rare primitive Kerle!
>
> BEIDE (*zugleich aber jeder beiseite*). Nur dann und wann fressen wir einer dem anderen die Gattin weg!
>
> (ABENDWIND: Their language is supposed to be not too bad, learned, you know, clever.
>
> BIBERHAHN. But not ethnic for us.
>
> ABENDWIND. Just a bit of a blow that nobody abroad understands a word we say.
>
> BIBERHAHN. When nobody understands you, that's ethnic. [. . .] Oh, all we need to do is kick our progress, and then . . .
>
> ABENDWIND. My God, all we want is to be left alone to eat our few bananas and our bit of prisoner in peace.
>
> BIBERHAHN. Of course we're just peaceable folk!
>
> ABENDWIND. Really smashing primitive blokes!
>
> BOTH [together]. Just that we have a tendency to eat one another's wives from time to time.)

One final instance must be given of Nestroy's extra-revolutionary political references: his attack on the King of Prussia, for which he was fined. In the Prussian coronation ceremonial, the King put the crown on his own head. As Jupiter in *Orpheus in der Unterwelt,* Nestroy motioned away Mercury who was dressing him to receive a visit with the words: "Die setz' ich mir selber auf". He alludes to the coronation at the same time in a private letter to Ernst, Ritter von Stainhauser, his great friend and the theatre's accountant, likening the King, in his insistence on this ceremonial, to a newly promoted officer who deliberately walks past as many sentries as possible in order to be saluted.

That Nestroy's concern with politics should be superficial, inasmuch as it seems to be directed at the outward signs, as here, is in no way surprising. The very word "politisch" has one association above all and that neither serious nor flattering: craftiness. Where it is used in the refrain of a song, it covers a dog that steals a goose, a man who never pays his debts, a boy who plays on his mother's suspicions of his father to send her out after him, so that he can steal the cream and cake, and a husband who accepts cuckoldry in return for indulgence over loan repayment. Kern, in *Der alte Mann mit der jungen Frau,* I 6, opines that political prisoners cannot have been political enough, otherwise they would never have been caught. We saw, in the brief analysis of one remark, that Nestroy needs ready-made conventional phrases and expectations for his comic structures, and political vocabulary and political symbols—the externals—provide these in large numbers.

On May 25th, 1848, he appeared in *Die Anverwandten,* an adaptation of Dickens's *Martin Chuzzlewit* performed for the first time, written before the revolution, one assumes, tricked out with extraneous references, the first of which (after the Pecksniff hypocrite song, "Ah, die Wahrheit is in gute Händ'.") is to the *Zopf,* the pigtail, symbol of the old system, defined in one of the songs in *Freiheit in Krähwinkel* as "das Zopfensystem" (I 7). By the second song in the play, Nestroy is in the middle of the political vocabulary, the two chamber problem (IV 4):

> Der Hauptpunkt bei d' Kammern is d' Aussicht von Haus,
> Ob's nach rückwärts geht oder vorn' ins Freie hinaus—
>
> (The view's the main thing with a room or a chamber—
> A dead-end backyard or a broad panorama—)

"vertreten", meaning to represent or to wear down the heels of one's boots, and, which caused an uproar in the theatre, Frankfurt. The trouble, of course, was that the natural association with the town was sausage rather than democracy, and Nestroy uses it to characterise the mixture of popular ignorance and popular enthusiasm:

> Gar mancher is als Wähler für Frankfurt 'nein g'rennt,
> Der ausser Frankfurt Würsteln von Frankfurt nix kennt.
>
> (For Frankfurt they cast their votes, eager every one—
> But what does Frankfurt mean to them?—a sausage in a bun!)

A theatre critic there was able to quell the disturbance this reference caused because he happened to be wearing his Academic Legion uniform; this statement in the review sorts well with the third stanza of the song which describes the dilemma over the choice of uniform for the newly armed people. It would seem that the externals deserved as much importance as Nestroy gave them.

The political vocabulary survived after the town itself had been brought back to order by the army of Windischgrätz. The 6th of February, 1849 saw the première of *Lady und Schneider,* a comedy about a tailor obsessed with politics, whose every phrase is a political one, even in conversation with his fiancée; he insists on marriage (I 9):

> Ich verlange die vollständigste Personalunion, unsere Ehe muss der innigste Anschluss werd'n . . .
>
> (I demand a personal act of union, our marriage must be the closest confederation . . .)

A noble lady employs him to create a new ballgown; he misinterprets this as some kind of political intrigue (II 8):

> HEUGEIG'N. Nur mein Aug' hat die Garderob'kästen durchwühlt, mein Geist aber—
>
> BRIDEWELL. Natürlich, Ihr Geist sann auf Neues, Geniales, in dem Alten nur Mängel entdeckend.
>
> HEUGEIG'N (*für sich*). Wenn die Red' nicht politish is, nacher weiss ich's nicht.
>
> (HEUGEIG'N. Only my eyes were sifting through the wardrobes, my thoughts—
>
> BRIDEWELL. Of course, your thoughts were occupied with new things, works of genius, discovering only defects in the old.
>
> HEUGEIG'N [*to himself*]. If that isn't a political speech, then I've never heard one.)

The verb "wühlen", to stir up, also gets special attention; the tailor is impressed with a masked lady's hair (II 13):

> Ich glaub', der ruhigste Staatsbürger möchte in diesen Locken ein Wühler werden.
>
> (I reckon the quietest citizen wouldn't mind getting tangled up in this mass movement.)

Kern (*Der alte Mann mit der jungen Frau,* III 2) uses another sense of the word when he suggests that the political fugitive should become a farmer and "stir up" his paternal soil.

This use of political vocabulary has various implications. The most evident is one that was adumbrated at the beginning of this paper: namely, that it was a familiar convention as far as the audience was concerned, but let us draw from this especially the fact of its having become *conventional*—so conventional that it can be used as a mode of expression for contents that are quite alien to it. It is difficult to decide whether the application of such a procedure implies merely recognition of what has happened or even a certain contempt for such phrases, as in the mock etymology of Ur-Wähler as a watch-stealer (*Lady und Schneider,* I 8). What are we to make of a remark which links the conventional headquarters of hen-pecked husbands in Austria with the little town in Moravia to which the remainder of the parliament had been despatched? When Gabriel criticises his sixty-year old master's reluctance to listen to accusations against his twenty-year old wife, he says:

> Das wird noch a schöne Verfassung werd'n in dem Haus—die kommt nicht von Kremsier, sondern vom Simandl-reichstag in Krems. (*Der alte Mann mit der jungen Frau,* II 7)
>
> (A fine constitution we're going to have in this house—not from Kremsier, but from the hen-pecked husbands' parliament in Krems. [cf. The

French government has gone to Vichy for its health].)

Is this no more than an extension of the political vocabulary already employed by Kern to describe his own domestic situation? When worried about his wife's fidelity, he says (op. cit. II 18):

> —und somit erwachst mir das schöne vormärzliche Recht, geheime Polizei zu etablieren in meinem häuslichen Staat—

> (—and thus I acquire the fine old pre-revolutionary right to establish secret police in my domestic realm.)

Kern's wife is angry that he should pay attention to their servant's allegations, but, as he points out (II 16):

> Dienstboten sind einmal die Pressfreiheit der häuslichen Konstitution.

> (Servants are after all the Free Press in our domestic constitution.)

Are we to see Kern's use of this vocabulary (which would seem in both the cases cited to be emotionally charged in a pro-Revolutionary way) as part of his character—or simply as imaginative phraseology—a manifestation of Nestroy's stylistic habits, with politics supplying images now as well? And is the implied comparison between the rump parliament and the henpecked husbands really intended? The independence of the dialogue from plot or characters, on which we remarked earlier in connection with the first political reference in *Die Anverwandten* would seem to speak in favour of this—the miraculous correspondence of the town's names has been exploited properly.

On the other hand, such evident jokes as Heugeig'n's in *Lady und Schneider,* II 13, when he is asked to measure Linerl's left arm:

> Hm, der Linken Mass *nehmen* ist sehr eine gefährliche Massregel, indem der Linken meistens mehr Mass zu wünschen ware

> (Hmm, taking the measure of the Left is one thing, for the Left to take anything in measure—)

or the exercising of the Jewish army in *Judith und Holofernes,* 17:

> ASSAD. Links g'schaut!

> HOSEA. Warum? Links is gar nix!

> (ASSAD. Eyes left!

> HOSEA. Why should I?—Left there's nothing!)

are surely too trite to be seen as embodying a political opinion of any meaningful kind. Gertainly Heugeig'n's automatic reaction can be seen as precisely that; a compulsion to use political vocabulary is such an evident part of his comic character—no such claim can be made for Kern. On the same level, it would seem, is the exchange in *Verwickelte Geschicht,* I 9, between Fass the radical drayman, and Wachtel, the servant:

> FASS. Ich hab' mich in Ihnen getäuscht, Sie sind ein Konservativer.

> WACHTEL. Man konserviert sich selbst am besten dabei.

> (FASS. I've been deceived in you, you're a conservative.

> WACHTEL. It's the best way to conserve yourself.)

Taking this out of context (it is prepared for by Wachtel's comments on his acquaintance with Fass's radical drinking club, and his pun on "einführen"—he has been "introduced", the club may be "run in") one could make great play with an older, wiser Nestroy forsaking his liberal opinions; especially in view of Fass's presentation of Communism (ibid. I 3):

> FASS. . . . der Reichtum ist das erste, was abgeschafft wird; ohne Teilung gibt's keine Brüderlichkeit.

> KESSEL. Gut, und wenn ich nachher mit meinem Teil fleissig arbeit' und wieder reich werd', während du das Deinige verlumpst, was is es nacher?

> FASS. Wer sagt dir denn, dass wir uns auf *eine* Teilung beschränken? Wir kommen alle Jahr'.

> (FASS. . . . wealth is the first thing that's going to be abolished; without sharing there's no fraternity.

> KESSEL. Right, and if I work hard with my share and become rich again, while you squander yours, what happens then?

> FASS. Who told you we were sticking at one share-out. We're making it an annual event.)

But this is much better explained in terms of a tradition of unprincipled layabouts as comic characters, beginning with Longinus in Nestroy's first full-length play, and including the cobbler Knieriem. Elsewhere, Nestroy's attitude to Communism is not a friendly one; in the last lines of *Lady und Schneider,* "kommunistische Umtriebe" are equated with attempts at cuckoldry, whilst the fourth stanza of the song in III 17 ends with the refrain:

> Ah, wenn d'Freiheit Kommunismus wird, nein,
> Da hört es auf, ein Vergnügen zu sein.

> (When freedom becomes communism, no,
> The pleasure goes out the window.)

However, closer inspection of the rest of the stanza reveals that, as with the cuckoldry at the end of the play, or the ne'erdowell in *Verwickelte Geschichte,* it is in fact merely being brought into relationship with a convention of the Volkstheater:

> "Wir sind arm", sagen s', "der is reich, der muss uns sein Geld geb'n,
> Zu was braucht er's? A Reich'r hat a so 's beste Leb'n!"
> Und für reich halten s' jeden, der ein' schönen Rock tragt,
> O Verblendete! Geht doch zu d' Schneider und fragt!—

("We're poor", they say, "he's rich, he must give
us his money.

What's he need it for? A rich man has a life that
is sunny."
And they think everyone's rich who wears a fine
    coat,
Fools! The tailor, if you ask him, sounds a differ-
    ent note.)

Are we perhaps dealing here with a deliberate attempt at trivialisation—or is Nestroy simply bringing crude and conventionalised versions of politics and political slogans within the set of crude assumptions and conventions with which he constructs jokes and which, by so doing, he shows up for what they are, precisely by overstating them and making them consistent in their conventionality?

Consider how the Volkstheater convention of drinking is related to political vocabulary and aspirations. In *Lady und Schneider* it is done quite subtly in terms of ferment (II 2):

> RESTL (*bedenklich*). Hm, es war alles so gewiss in Bewegung, vormittag schon hab' ich überall Gärung gefunden.
>
> LINERL. Weil der Vater in der Weinhandlung und in der Bierhalle war
>
> (RESTL [*with concern*]. Hm, everything was sort of going round, I found things in ferment everywhere this morning.
>
> LINERL. Because you were in the wineshop and the beerhall)

whilst Fass declares roundly (*Verwickelte Geschichte,* I 3):

> . . . wir trinken fürs Vaterland.

As Heugeig'n sings (*Lady und Schneider,* I 8, stanza 2):

> Und sie tun's Bier nicht schonen
> Diese Assoziationen.
>
> (They don't stint libations
> These associations.)

The third stanza of this song can be used to make the same sort of point from a different direction; for almost a hundred years, it had been the convention for a craftsman figure to see the world in terms of his own trade by means of puns, in an introductory monologue or song, Nestroy himself taking the resemblances on to a metaphysical level. Here the process is ironically reversed, as Heugeig'n, reviewing the economic effects of the Revolutionary period, speaks of all the work the saddlers have done, without ever being paid for it by the people who have changed horses overnight. Politics has become one of the rigidly defined categories of behaviour rich in associations employed within the Volkstheater for the construction of jokes.

It must not be automatically assumed, however, that this sort of treatment necessarily implies scorn for the elements so used. Sketches for *Höllenangst* contain notes for a monologue that would doubtless never have passed the censor. In it, the catchphrases and symbols of the Revolution make a kind of final appearance, a sort of apotheosis:

> Revolutionairs stürmen in der Regel gegen die irdischen Regierungen an. Das is mir zu geringfügig, ich suche das übel tiefer oder eigentlich höher, ich revoltiere gegen die Weltregierung, das heisst gegen das, was man eigentlich Schicksal nennt, ich trage einen unsichtbaren Calabreser mit einer imaginären rothen Feder, die mich zum Giganten macht; Giganten waren antediluvianische Studenten, sie haben den Chimborasso und Lepoldiberg aufeinandergestellt . . . und haben Barrikaden gebaut, um den Himmel zu stürmen.
>
> (As a rule, revolutionaries, attack earthly governments. That's too petty for me, I'm seeking the cause of the evil deeper down, or rather, higher up, I'm rebelling against the way the world's run, against what you call Fate, I'm wearing my invisible revolutionary cap, with an imaginary red feather that makes me into a giant. Giants were antediluvian students, who piled Annapurna on Ludgate and built barricades to storm Heaven.)

We have already remarked on the ingrowing pessimism of Wendelin that functions as a basic assumption behind his aphorisms. We learn later in this grandiose accusation that "Der grösste Fehler des Schicksals ist sein Zopf". The tone in the play itself is much more resignedly despairing (II 17):

> Auch auf Träum; dass s' ausgehn, claub i' fest,
> Unser Freiheitstraum is so a Traum g'west,
> Und ich frag', ob's nicht wahr is und g'wiss,
> Ob d' Freiheit uns nicht aus'gangan is?
>   I lass mir mein' Aberglaub'n
>   Durch ka Aufklärung raub'n,
>   's is jetzt schön überhaupt,
>   Wenn m'r an etwas noch glaubt.
>
> (I believe in dreams too, that may go
> By contraries, isn't that so?
> Our freedom was a dream of that kind,
> So that nowadays—well never mind!
>   Though my superstitions fright'ning,
>   I don't want enlight'ning,
>   It's very relieving
>   To have something to believe in!)

We have reached the point where the symbols of the Revolution have lost their daily relevance and become an impractical mythology. It must be recalled that they were at one time a practical mythology, though a mythology for all that, at least as Nestroy presented them in his play written during and depicting some of the events of the Revolution itself, *Freiheit in Krähwinkel.* Krähwinkel, a *Government Inspector* type of half-horse town, was invented by August von Kotzebue for *Die deutschen Kleinstädterr* and used by later dramatists as a place where any craze could be taken to its ultimate extreme. Vienna could see as much or as little likeness as it wished.

The play has features that we have noted before: automatic reactions to words capable of political interpretation—the furrier is mistrusted because he receives his raw material from absolutist Russia, Klaus, the mayor's subordinate, twitches whenever he hears the word "frei" regardless of context (I 1 and I 2). However, the intentions are grander than in other plays; Ultra, the revolutionary journalist, expresses them:

> Alle Revolutionselemente, alles Menschheitempörende, was sie wo anders in grossem haben, das haben wir Krähwinkler in kleinem. Wir haben ein absolutes Tyrannerl, wir haben ein unverantwortliches Ministeriumerl, ein Bureaukratieerl, ein Zensurerl, Staatsschulderln, weit über unsere Kräfterln, also müssen wir auch ein Revolutionerl und durchs Revolutionerl ein Konstitutionerl und endlich a Freiheiterl krieg'n. (I 8)

> (All the elements of revolution, all the things that outrage humanity that they have elsewhere on a big scale, we Neasdenites have on a small one. We have an absolute mini-tyrant, we have an irresponsible mini-ministry, a mini-bureaucracy, a mini-censor, national mini-debts, far beyond our mini-resources, so we must have a mini-revolution as well, and through the mini-revolution get a mini-constitution and in the end a bit of mini-freedom.)

The play becomes a recipe for revolution, including all the elements in miniature. To begin with, Ultra assumes various disguises in the course of the action, appearing as a Liguorian (the religious order driven out of Vienna), a Russian prince, the European Freedom and Equality Commissioner, Metternich, and finally, as a worker with pickaxe; of this last avatar he says (III 19):

> Ah, mir g'schieht ordentlich leicht, seit ich wieder einem rechtschaffenen Menschen gleichseh'.

> (Ah, I feel a lot better now I look like a proper human being again.)

Indeed, the final tableau of the barricades attempts to show a unity within the revolutionary cause which was already breaking down; the stage directions speak of workers, "Bürger" and students, each in appropriate costumes, manning the barricades together. Elsewhere in the play, other great moments of the revolution are recalled: tableaux representing the 13th of March and the 15th of May appear as the Mayor's nightmares, only to be dispelled by using the government newspaper as a pillow, having been called up by a Katzenmusik, the "traditional" way of showing dislike of prominent people. The expulsion of the Liguorians is presented as a comic spectacle, and innocent Krähwinkler, who have simply gone along to watch the revolution happening are shown as having been maltreated by heartless troops. But there hovers an air of play-acting over the whole enterprise: the European Freedom and Equality Commissioner does not simply have a three-coloured banner, but a seven-coloured rainbow one—the editor of Nestroy's works sees this as a jibe at Friedrich Kaiser's appearance on horseback to proclaim the Austrian constitution, and such an attack would certainly fit with the ironic attitude to ceremony evinced in the later episode of the Prussian coronation.

Moreover, the students (without whom, we are told, no

revolution is possible, and whose appearance puts the reactionaries to flight) are only girls dressed up; it is perhaps worth recalling that one of Nestroy's most successful and frequently repeated roles was in a play called *Zwölf Mädchen in Uniform* (the number of disguised beauties actually varied with the actresses available).

It would seem then that most of the events of the Revolution, with their symbolic significance, had passed into the public domain and were open to the same sort of treatment meted out to other conventional symbols. Even though the use of the tableau-form implies some respect, Klaus's comment in the middle of the same scene certainly does not (I 22):

> Was uns die Freiheit martert! Ich weiss, was ich tu', ich setz' sie in die Lotterie.

> (How freedom's tormenting us! I know what I'll do, I'll put it in the lottery.)

Instead of Grannie's birthday, or his house number, he takes the three significant dates of the Revolution for his lottery ticket; and with the lottery, we are back in the theatre tradition, with the lottery in *Lumpazivagabundas* and *Zu ebener Erde.*

And yet one cannot say that Nestroy is jeering at the Revolution especially. The conviction that there must be students before you can have a revolution is no different in method from another instance of the conversion of observation into an absolute rule: the slowness of absolutist bureaucracy is not accident, but design, and Reakzerl, Edler von Zopfen, lets us into the secret (I 11):

> Was schon über drei Monate hier liegt, können Sie mir gelegentlich zur Unterschrift unterbreiten.

> (Anything that's been here over three months, you can pass to me for signature some time or other.)

If there seems to be too much play-acting in this play, we must recall that the director of Nestroy's company and his employer, Carl Carl, turned out his entire troop, armed with property swords and spears, to take their turn at guarding the barricade in the Jägerzeile, where there was later to be fierce fighting.

Not being a historian, I cannot pass an opinion on the accuracy of Nestroy's presentation, but I can point to the play's popularity and allege that what he presented was by and large acceptable to the theatre-goers who at this stage were still drawn more or less from all strata of society. In dealing in images in this way, he was dealing with assumptions necessarily shared by his audience, whom we can envisage as delighted to have their own historical significance portrayed to them on stage. It is, of course, an idealised revolution, witness the words of the European Freedom and Equality Commissioner (II 16):

> . . . eine unendlich breite Basis, welche sich erst nach und nach auch in die Länge ziehen wird, und zur Vermeidung aller diesfälligen Streitigkeiten gar kein System.

> (. . . an infinitely broad basis, which will even-

tually turn into the long run, and, in order to avoid any possible disagreements, no system at all!)

Insofar as there is criticism of the Revolution in the play, it may be seen in the ironic turn this idealisation takes. Just as, in *Lady und Schneider,* Heugeig'n is obsessed with politics per se and does not care about the exact line involved:

> Sie müssen mich noch wo an die Spitze stellen, sei's Bewegung oder Klub, liberal, legitim, konservativ, radikal, obligarchisch, anarchisch oder garkanarchisch, das is mir alles eins, nur Spitze! (I 10)

> (They must make me top man somewhere, a group or a club, liberal, legitimist, conservative, radical, oligarchic, anarchic, Noah'sarkic—I don't care, so long as I'm the man at the top!)

so, in *Freiheit in Krähwinkel,* the enthusiasm is directed towards and stimulated by, slogans and catchphrases, events that have become images, although their full and true significance is not necessarily appreciated; reactions to these are automatic. The presentation of human behaviour in such terms (for example, the men's curiosity about the Revolution, which they must go and see) is Nestroy's stock-in-trade; there is scarcely a character in his plays who does not have a fixed point or points of view from which to interpret everything that is said to him, certainly the majority of the characters played by Nestroy himself are aware that such reactions exist even if they only make use of them ironically. With such a view of human behaviour implied by his comic methods, for Nestroy to bring anything on to the stage and treat it in that way suggests that the beginnings, at least, of such rigidity and categorisation are there, and, since we are concerned so much with linguistic usage rather than with actual instances that are incapable of statistically valid proof, our judgement of Nestroy's accuracy and justice is bound to be based on the success with which such a presentation is accomplished, the ingenuity, deftness and ease. (Nestroy's concern with linguistic usage is made specially plain in Ultra's discussion of the valuelessness of freedom and right in the plural, a remarkably perceptive observation which is perhaps obscured by the numerous examples of trivial rights and freedoms which follow.) Such a stylistic criterion would, for instance, speak against the "Ur-Wähler" pun, but be in accord with the ambiguity of the ferment that Restl discovers in wine shop and beer hall. It is the comparatively effortless assimilation of revolutionary imagery into the corpus of Volkstheater material that persuades me that Nestroy is essentially right in this instinctive analysis.

It is, of course, in some ways a historical and geographical accident that revolutionary propaganda should fit Nestroy's traditional but rigorously applied methods so well. In modern times, it can be observed that none of Brecht's attempts to write plays about Nazism comes to grips with the nature of the phenomenon because his style forces him to see it as something which it is not. *Rundköpfe und Spitzköpfe,* despite its skill as an ironic and dramatic structure, and in spite of brilliant and savage passages,

is too logical in its inversion of logic and its concentration on the preservation of the capitalist form of society within the ethnic state, whilst *Schweyk im zweiten Weltkrieg* is a cabaret entertainment, and the brilliant cameos of *Furcht und Elend des dritten Reiches* deal more with effects than origins, with individuals rather than the mass. Kraus, with his initial admission of impotence in face of the nothingness of Nazism comes closer to analysing it, because he, like Nestroy, takes readymade material and plays with it until it reveals itself.

At the time of the Revolution, then, inevitably the greatest source of ready-made material was the revolution itself—one need only think of the enormous quantity of posters and broadsheets which appeared, the genuine petition of the Viennese waiters' union rubbing shoulders with the mock demands of the Konstitutioneller Wiener Schuster-Buben-Verein. Nestroy's presentation of the self-dramatising and image-making aspects of the revolution is no different from his presentation of equally self-conscious behaviour in which behavioural models take over from spontaneity both before and after the Revolution. Even Ultra's undeniable eloquence against censorship is, in the long run, no more than the application of stylistic skill to a given subject or cast of mind, as it might be Wendelin's pessimism. For Nestroy, politics in general, and the revolution in particular, did little more than provide fresh material, a new set of vocabulary and externals, whose frightening manipulability and ready separation from their initial significance he could demonstrate and make use of for comic purposes and if, in the long run, everything turned out badly, that was no more than another manifestation of the innately corrupt state of the world which he had presented twenty years before, in a song in his first play, again in the famous *Kometenlied* fifteen years before and repeatedly in the intervening years. This general pessimism, though, and this is the central point one must remember in interpreting Nestroy and evaluating his attitudes, was not simply one of the author's basic tenets, it was a basic assumption employed for comic purposes and without this deep despair, the jokes would not have been funny. To rephrase this a little in terms of our present subject, the political elements which appear in Nestroy's plays supply not only the content, but, and this is what reflects badly upon them, also the comic form. (pp. 147-64)

> *M. A. Rogers, "Nestroy and Politics," in* 1848: The Sociology of Literature, *edited by Francis Barker and others, University of Essex, 1978, pp. 147-65.*

P. M. Potter   (essay date 1978)

[*In the essay that follows, Potter analyzes Nestroy's* Zu ebener Erde und erster Stock, oder die Launen des Glückes *as representative of the point in Nestroy's artistic development at which he grasped the essential characteristics of the* Wiener Volkskomödie *tradition and combined them with his own preferences of material and techniques.*]

While the interest shown in Nestroy's comedies continues undiminished, the principal areas of investigation remain the question of comedy and the works' relation to theatre history. Relatively little attention has been paid, however, to the *Localposse* called *Zu ebener Erde und erster Stock, oder die Launen des Glückes,* which tends to be dealt with too often in general terms or merely referred to in passing, to serve as an example of whatever point is being made, both having the effect of obscuring the relatively complex questions posed by the play in relation to Nestroy's *opus.* Two factors which have tended to militate against a more thorough treatment of the play have been its relative proximity, from a present-day point of view, to the much more widely-known *Lumpazivagabundus,* first performed some two and a half years previously, and the device of the horizontally divided stage, undoubtedly the most immediately obvious feature of the play, but one which has perhaps been given more attention than the content.

Let us start with the technique of the divided stage, if only to assign it its proper role as merely one feature among several, and not the one overriding element in the play. Although Mautner states that Nestroy was not dependent on a previous source for this device, it should be seen as neither more nor less than a development of the baroque stagecraft with its mechanical devices that was still very much in use in the Viennese theatre of Raimund's day and which was used by Nestroy in *Lumpazivagabundus.* Raimund's plays are after all set in two worlds—the world of the spirits and the world of the mortals below or the "niedere Welt" as Hofmannsthal calls it in *Die Frau ohne Schatten,* his own *Zauberstück.* Already, therefore, a horizontal division is implied on the stage, although, being portrayed consecutively not simultaneously, it was not translated into the more specific terms of *Zu ebener Erde. . . .* The fourfold division of the stage in *Das Haus der Temperamente* is another instance of the same technique, for which there is not direct source, although one must suppose that the success of *Zu ebener Erde . . .* influenced Nestroy. What he has done in choosing the device of the divided stage is to appropriate a feature of the baroque and Viennese traditional theatre and to employ it on stage in a de-mythologised manner, translated into social terms, or, in the case of *Das Haus der Temperamente,* into psychological terms.

It is noteworthy that the latter play, from the point of view of characters and plot, is divided essentially into two, both flats on the first floor being linked in all respects (sons, daughters and the fathers' friends) by the love intrigue, and the pattern is identical for the flats on the ground floor. When seen in this way, the essential difference becomes clear, for rather than an interweaving of complementary elements of a single plot, *Das Haus der Temperamente* simply repeats the double action in each flat with only minor variations. O. M. Fontana's comment on both plays that it was Nestroy's principle "ein und dasselbe Geschehen auf verschiedenen Ebenen und von verschiedenen Gesichtspunkten her sichtbar zu machen und sie alle miteinander zu verbinden, so daß die verschiedenen Erlebnisinhalte einander widersprechen, aber auch ergänzen und sich unaufhaltsam in eines zusammenschließen" is therefore totally applicable to neither. The point is surely that in the two plays the identical technique is used for different ends. In *Das Haus der Temperamente,* the divi-

sion of the stage into four is primarily a device to create comedy by allowing repetition, whereas in *Zu ebener Erde . . .* the divided stage serves the intrigue.

[Franz H.] Mautner had in fact little time for this play, calling it "dieses schwächeren der Stücke Nestroys" (*Komödien* [1970]). One is led, however, to wonder why he saw the play in this light. The opinion was obviously not shared by Nestroy's audiences, to whom the play was performed 134 times from its première on 24 September 1835 until 1856, a figure exceeded only by three other of his 83 works. It may perhaps be objected that the development of the play is predictable from the beginning and therefore not of great dramatic merit. Does the fact that a play is obvious imply that it is weak in its construction? One only has to look at Brechtian epic theatre to realise that such is not the case. There is no doubt that much of the impact of *Zu ebener Erde . . .* would be lost without this predictability. "The 'Posse mit Gesang' ", as F. Walla observed in [his essay " 'Fiktion' and 'Fiktionsbruch' in the Comedies of Nestroy," *German Life and Letters,* October, 1972], " . . . has its own laws" and, knowing these laws, one expects from the outset that Adolf and Emilie will be united, that the *Tandlerfamilie* will see better days, that Goldfuchs will come to grief, and one is therefore able to concentrate, not on what happens, but on how it is brought about. Indeed, one is inclined to agree with [Roger] Bauer when he says, "Die besten seiner Stücke laufen ab wie gutfunktionierende Uhrwerke" ["Johann Nestroy," in Bennovon Wiese, ed., *Deutsche Dichter des 19. Jahrhunderts,* 1969]. If the quality of "gutfunktionierende Uhrwerke" is in fact a criterion of merit in Nestroy's works, then we must certainly assign *Zu ebener Erde . . .* a higher place than did Mautner. In the same context it must be added that the clockwork quality of the plot is reflected in Nestroy's masterly control of the divided stage, with its parallel actions and dialogues in contrapuntal patterns.

Another objection possibly implied in Mautner's criticism, and which is perhaps what he had in mind when he wrote of the "etwas blasse, menschenfreundliche Stil des Stückes" (*Komödien*), is the fact that the play relies heavily on artificial means in order to bring about the desired conclusion. The abrupt changes of fortune of the two families are not motivated and are dependent on outside circumstances: the chance purchase of the Lord's coat, the winning of the lottery prize—an obvious example of pure chance as the identical motif, at Fortuna's instigation, in *Lumpazivagabundus* shows—and Adolf's sudden inheritance on the one hand are matched by the behaviour of Goldfuchs' son, the disastrous outcome of Goldfuchs' speculation and the failure of a bank. The fact that all these disasters are reported rather than portrayed gives them an impersonal quality, beyond the control of the characters on stage. At the end of the play it is made clear that one is to interpret these changes as being caused purely by chance:

> 's Glück treibt's auf Erden gar bunt,
> 's Glück bleibt halt stets kugelrund.

In other words, Nestroy has not attempted to justify the changes but has again followed a well-established Viennese tradition, with the difference that the Fortuna-motif has been de-mythologised by the absence of an actual Fortuna figure on stage. It would be wrong therefore to judge the play by the demands of a more sophisticated and realistic theatre and hence one can hardly accuse Nestroy of writing a weak play merely because he adhered to a popular tradition, a tradition to which he continued to adhere in subsequent, more widely acclaimed plays, where the conclusion is brought about by equally improbably means. One has only to think of *Der Talisman* or *Einen Jux will er sich macheu* where Nestroy's awareness that he is following tradition is only too clear: "was 's Jahr Onkel und Tanten sterben müssen, bloß damit alles gut ausgeht—!"

The relationship to Viennese tradition has further given rise to misleading analyses of the play, largely because it was written only two and a half years after *Lumpazivagabundus* and was the next better-known play which Nestroy wrote after the great success of *Lumpazivagabundus.* This proximity, together with a certain similarity in the abrupt changes of fortune, have caused critics to place *Zu ebener Erde* . . . in the same category as *Lumpazivagabundus.* The similarity between the two plays appears at first sight to be strong, particularly when one considers the final scene of each. Bauer describes them, in speaking of Nestroy's early plays in general, as "eine Pirouette des Autors, die wohl vom ganzen damaligen Publikum—oft mit Überraschung—als solche verstanden wurde". Accordingly the play is to be interpreted as an example of Nestroy's cynical treatment of tradition, and of his "Umkehr und parodistische Verneinung des biedermeierlichen Weltbilds seiner Vorgänger" (Bauer), while at the same time apparently conforming outwardly to tradition. There are, however, a number of objections which must be raised against applying such an interpretation to *Zu ebener Erde. . . .*

An analysis of the element of chance will show the diversity of the two plays. To begin with, there is no element of a test in *Zu ebener Erde* . . . , unlike the situation in *Lumpazivagabundus* where Fortuna's intervention is designed to illustrate the power-structure of the *Feenwelt.* In our play the lack of a test motif also removes questions of moral or ethical superiority where an external agency is required to bring about a specified outcome, as is the case in many of Raimund's plays. Fortuna is not therefore to be seen as an instrument of justice (at least not in bringing about the improvement in the fortunes of the Schlucker family) nor as a means of restoring social order. In fact it is the mention of an abstract force of chance in the last scene which takes much of the element of social comment out of the play and enables it to be seen to adhere to the social assumption of the day. On the other hand the last scene is not in contrast to the previous action, but is a direct consequence of it and has been anticipated by previous events.

Again there is no suggestion that Fortuna is directly concerned in the love intrigue, in the sense that Fortuna intervenes specifically to bring about a union of the lovers which would otherwise have been impossible. It is true that Adolf's unexpected good fortune makes the situation considerably easier for the couple, but they had already made plans—albeit incomplete and conventional—for an elopement. Here again one may interpret the Fortuna element as a means by which Nestroy is able to adhere to social conventions in that Adolf's new-found wealth absolves the couple from the necessity of an elopement, which in itself implies a defiance of parental authority. Nestroy is therefore able to avoid the dilemma of having to portray a direct clash between the two conventions, both of which are approved of by society, and having to decide on the victory of one over the other.

Since there is no actual Fortuna figure on stage in this play, the element of chance is not discussed on stage in the manner of *Lumpazivagabundus,* where the reasons for her intervention are clearly specified at the beginning. Hence it is not possible for the audience to be spectators of an intervention which is specifically designed to realise certain previously defined aims. In the case of *Lumpazivagabundus,* the audience's awareness of these aims gave the intervention of Fortuna an ethical purpose, which ultimately turns out to be unethical purpose, which ultimately turns out to be unethical, since the triumph of true love can only be brought about by the triumph of *Liederlichkeit.* For this reason one must draw the conclusion that the role of chance in *Zu ebener Erde* . . . cannot be used to discredit the *genre* as it was in *Lumpazivagabundus,* nor does it oblige the playwright to provide a totally artificial ending in order to appear to uphold convention. Hence this play lies outside Sengle's generalisation that: "Nestroy, der gewiß die Kehrseite der Gemütlichkeit sah, versäumt es nicht, sich mit Hilfe biedermeierlicher Rahmenhandlungen an den herrschenden Geist anzupassen", a comment which clearly applies to *Einen Jux will er sich machen* or particularly to such early plays as *Lumpazivagabundus* or *Weder Lorbeerbaum noch Bettelstab.* As has been shown in examining the treatment of the Fortuna-motif, *Zu ebener Erde* . . . , on the other hand, can be said to adhere to the spirit of the time, without an artificial ending or any other form of "Rahmenhandlung", since the assumptions of the play and the progress of the plot throughout the play lead logically to the conclusion actually given.

The presence of the Fortuna-motif leads us to question another commonly-held view of the play, namely the tendency to link it with the *Besserungsstück.* As the play is not a *Zauberstück* it should not strictly be termed a *Besserungsstück,* but it has several times been included in, or considered together with, this category. The play, it is true, has features similar to that of the *Besserungsstück,* particularly its cyclical structure with the motif of " 's Glück is kugelrund" and in Nestroy's plans for the rehabilitation of Goldfuchs and Johann (see below). Goldfuchs, although scarcely the central figure, is nevertheless the one who, by his downfall, is the most obvious candidate for the process of self-realisation and improvement. His final words in the play, however, are:

> (*Zu Adolf und Emilien, deren Hände er zusammenlegt*):
>
> Nehmt meinen besten Segen!—Mein Beispiel gebe warnend euch die Lehre: Fortunas Gunst ist wandelbar.

These words, as can be seen from the stage directions, are to be taken as part of the final tableau and as such are intended more for the audience than for the characters involved, giving an apparent summing-up of the impact of the play. At first sight the phrase "Mein Beispiel gebe warnend euch die Lehre" could be taken as being within the tradition of the *Besserungsstück,* and perhaps was an attempt to this end on the part of Nestroy himself. The rest of the sentence, however, immediately negates this impression, since, if Fortuna is capricious, how can Goldfuchs' disasters be an example to others? And since this is the only insight which Goldfuchs achieves, it can hardly be said that he has come to realise his own faults with a view to remedying them. Similarly the evidence is lacking that Goldfuchs has been forced to come to terms with his changed situation and to resume life according to new principles, as is the case with the central characters of *Lumpazivagabundus* or of *Müller, Kohlenbrenner und Sesseltrager,* where the three-fold lapse of time is central to both the plot and significance of the play. In addition, Goldfuchs has his virtues which are discernible even before the catastrophe, particularly in his reaction to his son's follies, so that the final scenes can scarcely be said to portray a true change of character. The element of *Besserung* is therefore quite lacking in *Zu ebener Erde. . . .*

In that case could it be said that, after all, the play parodies the *Besserungsstück* and that the ending is merely a cynical attempt by Nestroy to bring the play to a suitable conclusion? This point of view is certainly implicit in Bauer's opinion that the early plays ended with "eine Pirouette des Autors", but it is equally not the case that, in contradiction to the rest of Bauer's comment, his audiences saw the ending of this particular play as such. The *Wiener Theaterzeitung* of 30 September 1835 commented on the play with the words: "Es ist seit langen Jahren auf den Volksbühnen kein Stück erschienen, das sich an Keuschhaftigkeit . . . mit diesem messen könnte." Parody is largely a question of degree and, although *Zu ebener Erde* . . . has much that is illogical and artificial in its plot, it shares these features with the majority of Nestroy's plays. In terms of the Viennese Popular Theatre this play does in fact have a plot which leads naturally to its conclusion, unlike such deliberate parodies as *Lumpazivagabundus* or *Weder Lorbeerbaum noch Bettelstab.*

It could also be objected that the love intrigue, with all the traditional elements of parental opposition, secret meetings and planned elopements, is meant to have the effect of parody. On the other hand all these traditional elements are precisely that and no more, just as is the eventual happy ending. In this play there is no hint that these elements are to be taken at anything other than their face value, unlike, for instance, *Einen Jux will er sich machen* with Marie's automatic "das schickt sich nicht" whenever any of the stock elements are mentioned. The love intrigue in fact plays a considerable part in enabling social convention to survive the upheavals of the third act, since Emilie is no longer faced with marrying beneath herself for love but can look forward to a love match with her social equal, if not superior. Hence far from superficially resolving conflicts by an imposed ending, Nestroy is able in the obligatory happy ending to combine the upholding of social convention with the demands of romantic love.

When one examines the characters, it is certainly the case that Johann, Damian and Christoph all exhibit features which anticipate, in their verbal comedy and attitudes to life, later Nestroy characters, and yet at the same time all three stand apart from the plot of the play, in which they have little real significance, unlike Knieriem, Lorenz (in *Die verhängnisvolle Faschingsnacht*) or Titus Feuerfuchs. Paradoxically it is in the figure of Johann that we have yet another example to show that this play is not as similar to *Lumpazivagabundus* or as typical of Nestroy's works in general as one might suppose. Johann is an intriguer, playing on the weakness and follies of others, as do many of the other characters played by Nestroy himself. At the same time this nature springs from a well-defined view of life and of the aims he expects to achieve, witness his objections to marriage:

> Der Ehstand, wenn er kinderlos is, is um fünfzig Prozent kostspieliger als der ledige; kommt Familie so steigt es auf hundert Prozent;

and to gambling:

> Man verliert Geld und Zeit. Zeitverlust ist auch Geldverlust, also verliert man doppeltes Geld und kann nur einfaches gewinnen.

In the play itself Johann's role is one of dishonest dealings, rather than one of superiority over the other characters which Titus Feuerfuchs displays by his wit. There is a further difference in the fact that, while both are able to manipulate their surroundings to their own advantage, in Titus' case this has the effect of exposing a number of weaknesses and pretensions in the other characters. Johann, however, cannot be said to expose his master's weaknesses since these are made sufficiently evident at other points in the play, nor can his dishonest dealings serve solely as an example of the dangers to which Goldfuchs exposes himself by his weakness since the minor figure of the cook Meridon also takes advantage of his master in the same way. Hence such action has much more the effect of exposing Johann's own fundamentally dishonest character.

It may be objected that the other Nestroy roles in the earlier plays are also not intended to display the weakness of other characters. One reason for this is the fact that the traits of these characters are sufficiently clear without such a figure, as is the case in *Das Haus der Temperamente.* Nevertheless, Johann and Schlankel can be clearly distinguished in that the latter's role is obviously central to the plot as a whole. The basis for their intrigues is also greatly different. Schlankel is motivated by a wish to be in a position of control over events, also taking the form of *schadenfreude.* In Johann's case, motivation is purely material. The figure of Johann cannot therefore be said to contribute to any establishment of a morally superior element in the play by his "Schärfe des Blicks und verblüffende Sicherheit des Auftretens". That his dishonesty subsequently leads to an undignified downfall must prevent us from placing him in the same category as Titus Feuerfuchs or even Knieriem, the latter being at least partially excused by his fatalistic belief in the comet, an unworldly element quite lacking in Johann, and which on the surface enables Nestroy to motivate his rehabilitation: "Ist das ein Glück, Weib, der Komet is aus'blieb'n".

That Nestroy did in fact write additional scenes involving, amongst other things, the rehabilitation of Johann and his marriage to Fanny, implies that at one stage he felt the need to make the play adhere even more closely to prevailing opinions. As it is, even without this additional material, it must be said that the treatment of Johann differs widely from that of similar figures in Nestroy's other works, to the extent that, far from being a means of attacking Biedermeier assumptions, Johann becomes a means of strengthening these very assumptions. In referring to the alternative ending, Rommel wrote: "Es handelt sich bei solchen Planungen um mehr als bloß ein Happy-End", implying that the re-establishment of the situation at the beginning of the play (including Goldfuchs upstairs, the Schluckers below) was an expression of a wish or need on Nestroy's part to make the play comply with the traditions of his age. If this is so, why did this particular ending not become the definitive one? The answer is surely that it did not prove necessary, for, even without it, this is the play in which Nestroy comes closest to the Biedermeier spirit in so many of its aspects.

Although *Zu ebener Erde* . . . aroused, in contemporary critics, hopes that their wish for a move towards the treatment of social themes in the Viennese popular comedy was being fulfilled, there are a number of significant features in this play which differ from Nestroy's later treatment of social themes. Goldfuchs apparently believes that his wealth is inexhaustible and acts accordingly, comedy being created by the incongruity of his attitude towards money as well as by the intrigues of Johann with his master's money. Goldfuchs does not share the vulgarity or self-conscious attitude towards wealth of the *nouveaux riches* Fett (in *Liebesgeschichten und Heiratssachen*) and Zwirn, and similarly his plans for his daughter are motivated by a wish for financial consolidation rather than for social advancement. At the same time the element of "Kleider machen Leute", satirised in the figure of the landlord in *Liebesgeschichten und Heiratssachen,* is largely lacking in *Zu ebener Erde*. . . . One must conclude, therefore, that the social element in this play is, in many respects, a continuation of Raimund's approach in *Der Verschwender* or *Der Bauer als Millionär* rather than a fore-runner of the more radical treatment of the theme in Nestroy's later work.

It is perhaps the supreme paradox of *Zu ebener Erde* . . . that, once Nestroy had freed himself from the magical externals of the *Geisterwelt* in the *Wiener Volkskomödie* tradition, he was able to produce a work that conformed most nearly to the spirit of the same tradition. Seen in this light, the play takes on its true perspective in the overall development of Nestroy's work. He was able to see through the tradition within which he had been working and grasp its essential characteristics, including them in his work in a secularised context, but without discarding those external features which lent themselves to his own preferences in the choice of material and techniques for his

comedies. At the same time Nestroy's further development is anticipated in the figure of Johann, whose successors are truly integrated in the plot of later works, as well as in the plot itself which, farfetched and illogical though it may be, nevertheless has an ending that is a consequence of what has gone before, not a mere "Pirouette" tacked on to satisfy the public's expectations and the playwright's cynicism.

The play therefore represents a transitional phase of Nestroy's work and as such is difficult to place neatly in given categories. It should instead be considered first as a separate entity and the full nature of the various elements in the play dealt with within the context of the play itself. Comparisons with other plays of Nestroy tend to show a contrast rather than a similarity and hence illustrate the misleading nature of the tendency to deal with the play by making passing reference to it as one example among several.

Wit, mastery of the stage, acceptance of tradition and yet a critical outlook, all are there in *Zu ebener Erde* . . . , a play which, in O. M. Fontana's words, gives us "den ganzen Nestroy". (pp. 40-7)

> P. M. Potter, "Nestroy's 'Zu Ebener Erde und Erster Stock': A Reappraisal," in Austrian Life and Literature, 1780-1938: Eight Essays, edited by Peter Branscombe, Scottish Academic Press, 1978, pp. 40-8.

Kurt Corriher (essay date 1979)

[*In the following essay, Corriher maintains that for Nestroy "reason, as the only free element of the individual's existence, is therefore also the factor which defines him."*]

"I think that all men and all women are philosophers," writes Karl Popper, "though some are more so than others." Professional or academic philosophers are more consciously and methodically so than housewives and plumbers, but every human being lives on the basis of some instinctive world view, sometimes more, sometimes less conscious or complete. Johann Nestroy was certainly no philosopher in the academic sense of the word. He functioned at a level between the professional philosopher and the uncontemplative masses of human society. Less methodical than the former, he was nonetheless far more reflective, expressive, and coherent than the latter.

In recent decades literary scholars have shown an increasing tendency to cling to topics which can be neatly demonstrated and which require a minimum of subjectivity. Perhaps because of that trend, Nestroy criticism has held closely to such concretely demonstrable topics as the targets of his satire, linguistic analyses of his language, and technical discussions of his satiric method. How Nestroy perceived the universal dilemmas of human life has been considered a topic too problematic for anything more than broad generalizations. He was, after all, a writer of dialect farce whose chief goal was comic effect. The philosophical expression in his works appears chiefly in reflective monologues, in generalizing songs which are part of a long tradition in Viennese farce, and in countless aphoristic comments which sprinkle the dialogue of Nestroy's plays. The expression is thus fragmentary—often even contradictory. Scholars have chosen not to delve too deeply into this apparent formlessness. "Das Fehlen großer gedanklicher Zusammenhänge," writes Christoph Kuhn [in his *Witz und Weltanschauung in Nestroy's Auftrittsmonologen*], "läßt die Interpretation Nestroyscher Texte zu einem ungewissen Unternehmen werden."

Yet by pursuing inferences and implications it is possible to identify philosophical assumptions which are reasonably coherent and which underlie the whole of Nestroy's work. Through careful investigation and some reasonable speculation, one can gain insights into a philosophy which, though unsystematic and often unconscious, is nonetheless surprisingly consistent. The present study attempts to present one aspect of this Nestroyan thought, his conception of individual identity.

In Nestroy's satirical *Possen* one confronts a world in which human lives are buffeted by utterly irresistible forces. These might be conveniently divided into external forces such as social and economic factors, and internal forces such as hunger, greed, love—all the physical and emotional needs of man which Nestroy constantly satirized and ridiculed. In his *Possenwelt* characters do not determine the action, but are determined by it. They do not create situations, but merely react to given situations, resulting in a runaway action, a chain of events which tumble forward of their own weight and carry the hapless characters with them. In Nestroy we encounter again and again the key concept of *Schicksal*, which was Nestroy's term for that aggregate of forces, both external and internal, which determine men's lives. (In a characteristic refrain from a *Quodlibet* in *Der Talisman*, Titus observes: "Wir sein nix als—Narren des Schicksals" III, 11.) *Schicksal* appeared to Nestroy as random, completely arbitrary in its power, and thus grounded, beyond the limits of human reason, in a great void. [Kuhn argues that] "Schicksal ist ihm höchstes Prinzip. Ihm glaubt und mißtraut er zugleich; denn es widerspricht seinem rationalen Denken zutiefst, eine blinde, willkürliche und ungerechte Macht jenseits aller Vernunft anzunehmen."

In Nestroy's view man is born into a troubled existence. The reality which he confronts and of which he is a part is an ever-changing one. It lacks permanence, both of quality and of being, for death threatens a total and profound annihilation of self.

> DIE ALTE: Etwas Verzweiflung, a bissel Jammer, a wenig Wahnsinn—und am Schluß—mein Gott, sterben müssen wir ja alle—der Tod! (*Der gutmütige Teufel* I, 8)

Suffering, helpless, finite, the individual faces frustration at every level. His actions are determined by the myriad forces of external reality combined with the tyranny of his own emotions and physical needs. Even the quest for understanding is doomed to failure by the irrationality of that void which man encounters at the limits of reason—a void which Preisner describes as "die Leere des offenen Schlundes" [in *Johann Nepomuk Nestroy: Der Schopfer der tragischen Posse*, 1968].

The repetition of one phrase, sentence, or figure of speech is a standard comic device in the tradition of popular comedy. Nestroy employed that device as did many Viennese dramatists before him. Still, it is significant that one phrase held a hypnotic fascination for Nestroy, a phrase which he used in that manner again and again: "Ich kann nichts davor!" This expression of almost frantic helplessness occurs so frequently in Nestroy's *Possen* that one can assume it springs from a deeply rooted impulse. The basis of that impulse was the belief that mankind's striving is doomed to encounter frustration on every level. Thwarted hopes, plans, and desires are fundamental elements of Nestroy's humor. Much of his comic effect stems from the stumbling helplessness of characters in the grip of superior forces:

> TITUS: . . . Die Zurückstoßung meines Herrn Vetters war nicht das einzige Bittere, was ich hab' schlucken müssen. Ich hab' in dem Heiligtum der Lieb' mein Glück suchen wollen, aber die Grazien haben mich für geschmackswidrig erklärt. (*Der Talisman* I, 8)

Ramsamperl's *Couplet* from *Nagerl und Handschuh* expresses this idea of disappointment and thwarted hopes in the form of a reflective generalization:

> Oft rennt einer blindlings in sein Schicksal hinein
> Und glaubt, er wird grad wie im Himmel dann sein.
> Was find't er dann ob'n auf dem Gipfel des Glücks?
> Von allen den schönen Erwartungen nix. (I, 7)

Frustration on the intellectual plane is even more distressing. In its efforts to grasp the nature of existence, the mind is doomed to failure. It cannot cope with the blind irrationalism of fate or the spectre of its own cessation in death—both manifestations of an incomprehensible void. These features of human existence can be described but never explained. They can be identified but not comprehended. Their results are recognizable, but their cause, if one may even speak of such a thing, is lost in the void, beyond the reach of man's faculties. The very foundation of existence appears senseless. Man's reason, which strives to discern order and purpose in existence, is therefore also doomed to frustration.

Faced with this reality, Nestroy concluded that all human striving is vain because it encounters insurmountable obstacles on every level. He was only too aware of the resulting spectre of purposelessness which lurked in the shadows of his scepticism. The pointlessness of life is a problem which torments his characters incessantly and which is in fact the source of the bitterness underlying his cynicism. The ease and incredible frequency with which Nestroy's figures contemplate suicide, for example, is one indication of his concern for life's meaninglessness. When Pitzl, in one of Nestroy's last works, asks, "Was hat man von dieser fünzig bis sechzig Jahre langen Luftschnapperei?" (*Umsonst* I, 9), he is giving voice to a question which looms in the background of every Nestroy *Posse*. Beneath the humor flows a current of bitterness that gives rise to sentiments such as those expressed in this refrain from a song in *Theaterg'schichten:*

> Es is alles ans, es is alles ans.
> Im Narr'nturm, da tanz' ma ans. (II, 25)

Bitterness arises because one's ego recoils from the idea that its existence is without meaning. Nestroy constantly strove to overcome the nihilism inherent in his views, but at best he achieved only a stand-off in his struggle against meaninglessness.

Not surprisingly one also encounters that cousin of meaninglessness, ennui, in Nestroy's works. If life is without meaning and if all human activity is senseless, then profound boredom is the unavoidable result. This existential ennui that surfaced on the stage of Viennese popular comedy a century before it was expounded by such luminaries as Sartre or Heidegger is most clearly represented by "der Zerrissene," Herr von Lips.

One major difficulty in interpreting Nestroy is that one encounters a kind of circular satire. Just as Nestroy tends to doubt all things, so also does he tend to satirize all things, himself included. Thus Lips, who makes satirical comments about the world, is himself an object of satire, for *Der Zerrissene* is in many ways a parody of the sort of *Zerrissenheit* which Nestroy's scepticism produced. This self-parody, consistent in Nestroy's scepticism produced. This self-parody, consistent in Nestroy's work, is actually an additional indication of Nestroy's concept of reality. When satire turns in upon itself, the circle is closed, and we are confronted with yet another manifestation of the *Ausweglosigkeit* and absurdity of a purposeless and senseless existence, an absurdity one also finds in Nestroy's contemporary, Büchner, as well as in modern playwrights such as Beckett and Sartre. The fact that Lips is a parody of, among other things, the Byronic *Weltschmerz* which afflicted the romantic age, in no way invalidates him as a spokesman for Nestroy's own *Zerrissenheit*. Certainly the play is far more than "eine satirische Studie des reichen Bürgers" [quoted from Rio Preisner's *Johann Nepomuk Nestroy: Der Schöpfer der tragischen Posse*, 1968]. When viewed in the context of the *Gesamtwerk,* it is clear that Lips gives direct expression to the existential ennui which is elsewhere only secondarily implied, and thus, despite the element of self-satire which is common throughout Nestroy's work, Lips is a key figure in interpreting Nestroy's world view.

Lips' opening *Couplet* runs in part:

> Bald möcht' ich die Welt durchflieg'n, ohne zu rasten,
> Bald is mir der Weg z'weit vom Bett bis zum Kasten;
> Bald lad' ich mir Gäst' a paar Dutzend ins Haus,
> Und wie s' da sein, so werfet ich s'gern alle h'naus.
> Bald ekelt mich 's Leben an, nur 's Grab find' ich gut,
> Gleich drauf möcht' ich so alt wer'n als der ewige Jud';
> Bald hab' ich die Weiber alle bis daher satt,
> Gleich drauf möcht' ich ein Türk' sein, der s' hundertweis' hat;

> Meiner Seel', 's is a fürchterlichs G'fühl,
> Wenn man selber nicht weiß, was man will! (I,5)

He suffers from what appears to be a groundless dissatisfaction. Although Lips is wealthy and enjoys all the comforts of a privileged place in society, his life seems barren and pointless. In the monologue that follows immediately upon the above *Couplet,* Lips ruminates on the theme of boredom "die enorm horrible Göttin," and speaks dismally of his "ödes, abgeschmacktes Leben." Life appears to him like a prison sentence, a period of time which must be endured but lacks any intrinsic purpose or value. That same idea is elsewhere articulated by Schlicht, who, in another of Nestroy's *Auftrittsmonologe,* refers to a man's life as "nix anders als ein an seinem Geburtstag gefälltes, auf unbestimmte Zeit sistiertes Todesurteil" (*Mein Freund* I, 3), a quote which also illustrates the contribution of the knowledge of death to the feeling of senselessness in one's life. What purpose can there be in a life that must inevitably face annihilation?

The ennui of Herr von Lips is more than the boredom of an idle schoolboy. Its scope is profound. He is bored with the terms of existence. Not only does life contain no meaningful activity, to the man who recognizes its true character it is barren even of diversion:

> WIXER. Du mußt dich zerstreuen.
>
> LIPS. Das is leicht g'sagt, aber mit was?
>
> WIXER. Wir begleiten dich, geh auf Reisen!
>
> LIPS. Um zu sehn, daß es überall so fad is als hier? (I,6)

Lips is not the only Nestroy character who grumbles dejectedly about the tedium of existence (always, of course, within the limited bounds of the harmless *Possenwelt*). Gottlieb complains that a genius is a man who wears a coat "wo der eine Ellbogen über die Torheit der Welt lacht, während der andere über ihre Alltäglichkeit zu gähnen scheint" (*Der Schützling* I,2), and Weinberl laments longingly, "Wenn ich nur einen wiffen Punkt wüßt' in meinem Leben . . . " (*Einen Jux will er sich machen* I, 13).

At the root of all this boredom is that abyss which Nestroy sensed underlying existence. It is a discontent which springs from emptiness, disorientation, the lack of anything to give life stability and purpose. Those thinking characters (like Lips) who compulsively seek the foundation of all they encounter in life invariably trek to the brink of a yawning void and find themselves painfully suspended. Of course these *Possen*-characters rarely express themselves so directly on the popular stage, but a dim and troubling awareness of the vacuum beneath existence is visible behind outbursts such as Irene's in *Das Haus der Temperamente* when she asks ironically, "Ist nicht der Schmerz der Tiefste, welcher grundlos ist?" (I,4).

With Nestroy's pessimistic view of the human condition, his *Possen* take on a deeply ambiguous character. On the one hand lies the wit, humor, and *Spielheiterkeit* of the fictional world of Viennese farce, where there are no earnestly tragic conflicts, and where a happy outcome is always assured. Underlying it however is the expression of Nestroy's bitter disillusionment with the purposelessness and injustice of the world of reality, a disillusionment which enters this jolly *Possenwelt* primarily through his gifted use of irony. Amidst all the wit and laughter, Nestroy's *Possen* betray a current of existential discontent that is sharper, deeper, more bitter by far than Raimund's listless melancholy.

Fearful of life's meaninglessness, tormented by frustration and ennui, Nestroy, at least in his intellectual life, approached dangerously close to despair. The knowledge which his intelligence won for him proved more harmful than beneficial. Thinking, and the reason which he valued so highly, led him to insights which destroyed all peace of mind. "Mir haben die Lehrer in der Schul' schon 's Glück abg'sprochen," claims Peter Span in *Der Unbedeutende,* " 'Das is a g'scheiter Bub!' haben s' gesagt, und da is 's schon vorbei" (I, 14). Yet there are benefits which help hold despair at bay.

The rational mind, the reason which Nestroy relied upon so heavily, is the agent of his scepticism. Reason alone is capable of recognizing illogic and thus, for Nestroy, untruth. Reason is the one element of the individual's being which is not wholly subject to the tyranny of *Schicksal.* Although reason may be ultimately thwarted, it cannot be consistently deceived. It may be unable to penetrate the void, but it is capable of recognizing falsehood, and that recognition is in itself a kind of truth—the only one in

Portrait depicting Nestroy in the role of Sansquartier in Louis Angely's one-act farce Zwölf Mädchen in Uniform.

which Nestroy believed. To establish the illusory nature of something is to establish (albeit negatively) a truth. In short, though reason is limited in its power, it has freedom within those limits, namely the freedom to deny. In rational contemplation reason is at least capable of extricating itself from the morass of illusion which distorts perceptions.

Nestroy's embracing of intellectual freedom can be seen throughout his work. "Nestroy war und blieb zeit seines Lebens ein unerbittlicher Feind gegen Knechtung des Geistes," writes [Alphons Hämmerle in his "Komik, Satire und Humor bei Nestroy," 1947], and Kuhn adds, "Geistige Freiheit ist das Element von Nestroys Weltbetrachtung. Der Dichter ist keiner Ideologie, keinem Glauben verpflichtet." [in his "Johann Nestroy: der Satiriker auf der Altwiener Komödienbühne," in Johann Nestroy, *Gesammelte Werke* I]. [Otto] Rommel has noted that the so-called "Raisonneure" roles which Nestory created for himself represent men who are mercilessly buffeted by the misfortunes of fate, "aber im tollsten Trubel behalten sie den Kopf oben und wahren sich die geistige Freiheit." Nestroy was never willing to relinquish this vital liberty, and it is exercised even by his most harried characters. The famous *Freiheit in Krähwinkel* has long been praised for its defense of political and human rights, but such freedoms were of secondary importance to Nestroy. For him they exist merely within the larger prison of fate. Thus it was not difficult for Nestroy to follow *Freiheit in Krähwinkel* with a second political *Posse* which very nearly repudiates the first. The whole sphere of politics is subsumed within the greater issue of fate versus liberty, on an existential plane. Hämmerle has correctly identified the one freedom for which Nestroy held a true revolutionary's passion:

> Wenn auch diese Posse [*Freiheit in Krähwinkel*], im ganzen gesehen, nicht so sehr ein Preislied auf die Errungenschaft der menschlichen Freiheiten seiner Zeit ist—die Freude hierüber ist in seiner Posse unverkennbar zu spüren—, so schimmert durch alle seine milieubedingten Äusserungen über dies hohe Gut der Menschheit die unbegrenzte Leidenschaft zur einen einzigen Freiheit hindurch, die dem Menschen gegeben ist, nämlich die geistige Freiheit, die den Menschen befähigt, das sich immer wieder neu bildende Lügengespinst zu durchschauen. . . .

Through scepticism reason can rise above even the awesome omnipotence of *Schicksal.* By apprehending it within a mental concept, the individual, at least momentarily, steps outside of it. What lies behind *Schicksal* cannot be conceptualized and thus cannot be manipulated by reason, but reason is at least free to recognize this, its own limitation. The individual's daily life may be determined by the forces of *Schicksal,* but he *can* overcome it on an intellectual plane. Nestroy sees this freedom as an essential positive factor in the life of the individual. *Schicksal* cannot prevent the rational mind from recognizing its tyranny, and, although reason cannot alter the course of *Schicksal,* the ability of reason to comprehend the unjust nature of *Schicksal* grants one a soothing liberty:

Nur eins hat das Schicksal vor den irdischen Tyrannen voraus, nehmlich das, daß man ungeniert darüber schimpfen kann, es nutzt eim zwar gar nix, aber man wird doch wenigstens zu keiner Verantwortung gezogen, und es is das schon eine schöne Sach'.

From the idea of intellectual freedom it is but a short step to Nestroy's concept of identity, his definition of self. Determinism poses special problems for the individual in a search for identity, for if one maintains a doctrine of complete determinism, then the self becomes submerged within greater entities. What is there that delineates the individual from the rest of the world if every action is but the product of indefinable world forces? Where does the world end and the self begin? This, at least, is the question Nestroy faced.

For him the answer lay in that intellectual freedom which he so cherished. Reason, as the only free element of the individual's existence, is therefore also the factor which defines him. It marks the boundary between the self and the chaotic determinants of the world. In critically contemplating the world a man separates himself from it. "I am the being that thinks," Nestroy might have said if he had consciously and systematically elucidated his views.

That Nestroy strenuously maintained a sense of the integrity of self is clear from his conduct both as *Privatmann* and as theater artist. In the former sphere he simply withdrew, protecting his separate identity from the world behind a wall of shyness and timidity. His personality was extremely private. Not only did he not share himself with the world, he went to great lengths to avoid contact with it, as if afraid of being submerged within the homogeneous whirl of life in Vienna. [Hämmerle has stated that] "Abseits von der übrigen Künstlerwelt . . . führte er seine Künstlerexistenz und genoß er sein Wiener Leben . . . In ihm lebte der Bohemien, der, unbeachtet, sich das Treiben der Wienerwelt ansah. . . . " His was not the sort of personality that mixes easily in social settings. He was far too self-aware (the more popular modern term is "self-conscious") to blend into a crowd, and, in any event, he preferred to maintain the distance which allowed him to observe, to think, and to judge.

In the evening when the lights of the theater came up, this *Ichbezogenheit* took on a different form altogether. There, from the security of the stage, the public, Nestroy did not merely withdraw but rather positioned himself *against* the world. His consciousness of self ceased to be passive and became instead an aggressive self-assertion. As early as the first ill-fated engagement in Brünn (where Nestroy was finally obliged to leave the city because of his refusal to stop extemporizing on stage) the actor displayed his rebellious spirit, his fierce resistance to any restrictions or authorities which threatened the integrity of his ego. Throughout his career his struggles against critics, hostile audiences, and even official censorship stemmed, not from any outwardly directed desire to reform society, but from an inner need to defend his own integrity. He never attempted to impress a particular doctrine upon the world as did the contemporary writers of Young Germany, for example, or Austrian *Vormärzdichter* such as Anastasius Grün. He entertained no such ambitions and in fact could not possibly have

done so considering the universal scope of his scepticism. His struggles against a critic such as Wiest, for example, are not argumentative, but blindly personal. They are not in defense of a threatened idea but of a threatened ego. They are manifestations of a never-ceasing fear of the loss of self, a deep and abiding need to reaffirm his own existence as an entity independent of the rest of the world.

This aura of "separateness" pervades his work and was the basis for that sense of alienation which initially gripped his audiences during the thirties. Here was an individual who seemed to be subtly at war with Vienna, with the spectators, with other characters on stage, with society, politics, people—in short Nestroy appeared bent upon keeping the whole world at bay with a barrage of cynical condemnation. Speaking of Nestroy's "durchdringende Geistigkeit," [in *Johann Nestroy und seine Kunst,* 1937, Franz H.] Mautner remarks, ". . . ihre eigentümliche Wirkung war die, daß man nicht etwa den Eindruck hatte, es agiere da oben einer der witzigsten oder weisesten Menschen aus der Mitte des Volkes, sondern einer, der stets in einer gewissen Distanz von ihm verweile und so seine Fehler und Schwächen schärfer und grausamer sehe. . . . "

On a personal level this struggle for a separate self can be seen in the fierce egoism with which Nestroy's characters relate to one another. Again and again they demonstrate that the maintenance of self is their principal concern:

> ARTHUR. Der Mensch ist sich selbst der Nächste, zuerst ich, dann du. (*Umsonst* III, 3)

. . . . .

> TITUS. . . .Meine Stellung hier im Hause gleicht dem Brett des Schiffbrüchigen: Ich muß die andern hinunterstoßen, oder selbst untergehen. (*Der Talisman* II, 20)

. . . . .

> WEINBERL. Was Sie denken, geht mich nix an, *ich* muß es denken, muß es fühlen. (*Jux* I, 13)

The last quotation leads us to the intellectual sphere, where Nestroy's passion for the integrity of the self is dependent upon his concept of intellectual freedom. Only the intellect, more specifically the reasoning faculty, is clearly separate from the world and invulnerable to its contamination. Therein lies the individual's identity, which Nestroy found so essential and defended so vigorously. By reasonably contemplating the world, one establishes one's separateness from it. Small wonder that he was so contemptuous of mystical inclinations with their tendency to surrender the self into a single unitary world existence. Such an attitude was anathema to him. It meant the loss of self and that, for Nestroy, was identical to another phenomenon which terrified him—death. Thus it is more than a descriptive simile to say that Nestroy clung to the freedom of the rational mind as to life itself. For him that freedom was life. It defined life. Without it the self would be lost in the chaos of the world, cease to exist, be dissolved in the void.

Because of the illusory, deceptive nature of the world, the rational mind can affirm only itself. The world offers only illusions which must be negated, but in negating the external world, the sceptic implicitly affirms his own rational mind. Scepticism then becomes the ultimate source of individual identity. If, as for Nestroy, to reason is to doubt, then the maxim formulated earlier assumes its final form as "I am the being that doubts," and a sense of a stable, integral identity is the positive aspect of scepticism. The counterpart of the chaotic world which is ruled by *Schicksal* and the void behind it is orderly reason whose foundation is a real and identifiable self. (pp. 160-64)

> Kurt Corriher, "Nestroy and Individual Identity," in The Germanic Review, *Vol. LIV, No. 4, Fall, 1979, pp. 160-64.*

Kurt Corriher   (essay date 1981)

[*In the following essay, Corriher contends that the concept of rational thought as the basis of human dignity strongly influenced Nestroy's presentation of hope in his plays.*]

At the beginning of the eighteenth century, Josef Anton Stranitzky's traveling acting company settled in Vienna and created a genre which was to survive for over a hundred and fifty years. Until the late nineteenth century dozens of playwrights exploited the natural playfulness and wit of Viennese dialect to produce popular farces in a tradition which became known as the *Wiener Volkstheater.* Through the years, the tradition gave birth to over a thousand plays, but of the many prolific playwrights who contributed, only two produced works of sufficient quality to overcome the restrictions of dialect farce and find an audience in the greater German-speaking world.

Ferdinand Raimund (1790-1836) was the genius of the *Zauberstück* and creator of a world of gentle charm, combined with a warm benevolence toward humanity. Of a very different stamp was his younger contemporary, Johann Nestroy (1801-1862), who became both the last and the worthiest representative of the tradition founded by Stranitzky. With Nestroy, Viennese popular comedy took a radically new turn, achieved its culmination, and then, after his death, quickly faded into the realm of historical phenomena.

Unlike his predecessors, Nestroy did not coddle the sensibilities of his bourgeois audience. He turned what had been more or less harmless entertainment into biting satire, and he gave voice to a world view which was deeply cynical. "Etwas Verzweiflung, a bissel Jammer, a wenig Wahnsinn—und am Schluß—mein Gott, sterben müssen wir ja alle—der Tod!" (*Der gutmütige Teufel* I, 8). This quotation from one of Nestroy's later plays aptly summarizes his reaction to human existence. For Nestroy, the satirist and cynic, life was a battle against hopelessly superior forces. One's own needs and drives, together with the necessities of the external world, formed an aggregate of amoral forces to which Nestroy gave the name *Schicksal.* Man is a puppet, perpetually suffering at the whim of indifferent fate. When Titus, in *Der Talisman,* sings a *Quodlibet* with the refrain: "Wir sein nix als—Narren des Schicksals" (III, 11), he expresses a fundamental aspect of Nestroy's world view.

Differentiating between a playwright's own views and those of his characters is always a problematic undertaking. It is simplified in Nestroy's case, however, by several factors. We have a huge body of literature (83 plays) from which to draw recurring concepts. Moreover Nestroy, like Raimund, was not only a playwright but also the actor who embodied his own central characters onstage. It is widely acknowledged that these Nestroy characters (all of whom exhibit an unmistakable resemblance in basic attitudes) often function as a mouthpiece for their creator. Finally, the traditions of Viennese popular comedy included monologues and songs in which it was customary for the actor to step out of character and speak directly to the audience. Nestroy exploited that opportunity not only for social satire, but frequently for philosophical reflections on human existence. There can be no doubt that at such times Nestroy spoke primarily as author, rather than character.

Scholars have investigated Nestroy chiefly as a satirist. Little has been written about his philosophy, partly because the genre of farce is held in low esteem by most scholars, and partly because it is, with Nestroy, a difficult topic to approach. Nestroy's philosophical expression occurs primarily in the reflective monologues, generalizing *Couplets,* and hundreds of aphoristic comments scattered throughout his dialogue. At best fragmented, and at worst contradictory, Nestroy's philosophical views must be pieced together with the aid of inferences and implications, but in so doing one can establish an outline philosophy with remarkable consistency and coherence.

It soon becomes clear, for example, that Nestroy's world view is fundamentally sceptical. Not only are his characters tossed about like corks on the great ocean of fate, even their desire for some scrap of certainty in human knowledge is doomed to frustration. Peter, in *Der Unbedeutende,* declares that his sister's reputed liaison with a disreputable character is impossible—but then typical second thoughts arise. "Hm—" he muses, "welcher Entdecker hat das schon bemessen, wie weit sich die äußersten Vorgebirge der Möglichkeit ins Meer der Unmöglichkeit hinein erstrecken?" (III, 16).

Nestroy's approach to perception was rigidly rational. He distrusted emotion of any sort, and felt that only the rational mind could free itself from the tyranny of *Schicksal.* Yet even reason cannot penetrate to absolute knowledge. It can only recognize falseness, and hence the relentless negativism of Nestroy's satire. In short he embraced a philosophy of rational scepticism.

Despite the resulting burden of doubt (*from Höllenangst* I, 14: "Zweifeln kann man an allem, und unter zehnmal zweifeit man neunmal gewiß mit vollem Recht"), there were powerful advantages in that philosophy. In negating the world, the sceptic implicitly affirms his own negating faculty, or, in Nestroy's case, the rational mind. The rational mind then becomes the single aspect of man's existence which is independent of the external world, and as such it defines the individual and grants him an identity separate from the chaotic forces of *Schicksal.*

Scepticism, as the realization of intellectual freedom, anchors the Nestroyan individual to a concrete pole of identity—a positive asset in itself. Yet Nestroy's particular brand of scepticism with its severely critical tone, its tendency not only to doubt but to condemn, contains a second benefit, namely the establishment of individual dignity. Dignity is the moral side of identity. The mere recognition of the world's deceptive nature provides the individual with a sense of self by placing him outside of it, but in condemning that world from a moral standpoint, Nestroy also places himself above it. As [Jürgen] Hein writes [in his *Spiel und Satire in der Komödie Johann Nestroys*, 1970] "Der Satiriker erweist die Wirklichkeit als nichtig, die Welt als wertlos und fehlerhaft. Im satirischen Sprechen, welches ein künstlerisches Darstellen ist, befreit er sich von diesem Mangel und erhebt sich über die verkehrte Welt."

Self-esteem is vital to Nestroy's characters. When Titus says of an obsequious servant, "Fahr ab, du bordierte Befehlerfüllungsmaschine!" (*Der Talisman* III, 16) he is betraying not only his contempt for servility but also his own feeling of superiority. Nestroy's characters constantly exhibit this need to feel superior by their compulsion to disparage the people around them, but there are also more direct indications of this concern for dignity. Rarely do his characters endure unanswered insults, for example. Instead they display an exaggerated sense of pride. Peter Spann's struggle for dignity (which is here more appropriate than the term "honor") in *Der Unbedeutende* is one of the clearest examples, and his closing words express the sentiments of a typical Nestroy character: "Wenn Sie wieder einmal mit unbedeutende Leut' in Berührung kommen, dann vergessen Sie ja die Lektion nicht, daß auch am Unbedeutendsten die Ehre etwas sehr Bedeutendes ist" (III, 34).

On the philosophical plane, dignity for Nestory was the moral affirmation of one's identity, that is, the affirmation of an active, sceptical reason. The thinking man who recognizes and condemns the world's injustice is always held in esteem in a Nestroy play. Conversely much of his sharpest wit is reserved for attacking the unthinking who refuse to face reality or insist upon sweetening it with fantasy. The most obvious example is Simplicius in *Gegen Torheit gibt es kein Mittel.* Simplicius is a negative model in every respect. His *Torheit* is equated with idealism and naive optimism, and he earns the contempt not only of the audience but of every other character as well. When at one low point he grimly insists, "Nein, sag' ich, er soll durchaus nix wissen von mir und meiner Misere! Ich bin zu stolz geworden, du glaubst es nicht Anselm, was ich für einen edlen Stolz jetzt hab' " (III, 5), his claim to "edler Stolz" ironically proves Nestroy's contempt for such an unreasoning individual and thus, conversely, his esteem for those who exercise their intellectual freedom. For Nestroy that means those who have learned to be not only sceptical but morally critical. It is not enough merely to mistrust the world. For full dignity, one must also censure it.

Dignity and identity are so closely bound for Nestroy that they may be treated individually only as a heuristic device. Nestroy's scepticism not only separates the individual from the rest of the world, with its deprecating tone it also

exalts him above it. Thus for him identity and dignity are different facets of the same gem. To establish one's identity one must recognize the true nature of existence, but for Nestroy, to recognize it is also to condemn it. Integral parts of that world are its random injustice, its presentation of illusions, its mutability—all *ipso facto* damnable in Nestroy's scheme of values. Just as the freedom to doubt demonstrates one's identity, the freedom to disapprove affirms that identity. It lends a sense of the "rightness" of self as opposed to the rest of existence, a sense of self-worth, a sense of dignity. In Nestroy's world, dignity cannot be achieved by rectitude in the conduct of everyday life because man is not free in that sphere. Fate controls him. Dignity can only be an intellectual matter because the self is defined by intellect.

For those who would protest that Nestroy's cynicism also extends to himself, a note of explanation is necessary: his self-contempt was limited to the unfree aspects of his existence such as emotion, physical weaknesses and passions, or any of the myriad factors which prevent the individual from exercising the dictates of unencumbered reason (thus preventing him from being "morally free" in the usual sense of moral conduct). [Friedrich] Nietzsche, who as a pre-existentialist shares many of Nestroy's philosophical instincts, understands precisely the source of Nestroy's self-esteem: "Wer sich selbst verachtet, achtet sich doch immer noch dabei als Verächter." ["Jenseits von Gut und Böse," in *Nietzsche Werke: Kritische Gesamtausgabe,* 1968] The *Verächter* is the individual's free intellect, the root of personal identity for Nestroy.

His reflective characters rise above *Schicksal* through the power of critical contemplation. Wendelin sums it up clearly in the "Schicksalsmonolog:"

> Revolutionairs stürmen in der Regel gegen die irdischen Regierungen an. Das is mir zu geringfügig, ich suche das Übel tiefer oder eigentlich höher, ich revoltiere gegen die Weltregierung, das heißt gegen das, was man eigentlich Schicksal nennt, ich trage einen unsichtbaren Calabreser mit einer imaginären rothen Feder, die mich zum Giganten macht; . . .

Finally, there is one other facet of identity (other than the moral condemnation of the world) which earns a certain dignity for the thinking man. Confronting existence with uncompromising reason, denying oneself the comforts of illusion, results in a life of suffering. "Mir haben die Lehrer in der Schul' schon 's Glück abg'sprochen," laments Peter in *Der Unbedeutende,* " 'Das is a g'scheiter Bub!' haben s' gesagt, und da is 's schon vorbei" (I, 14). Yet Nestroy clearly saw this acceptance of suffering as an honorable trait in itself, and the price which must be paid for dignity. Accepting pain for the sake of principle is a characteristic of worthy men. One hears that view echoing in the background of statements such as Peter's when he remarks, "Die Gefahr sucht sich in der Regel Opfer, die ringen mit ihr, mit kleine Bub'n gibt sie sich nicht ab" (*Der Unbedeutende* III, 2). Enduring the pain of recognition, denying oneself the comfort of the world's deceptions, facing up to horrifying truths, all these are Sisyphean acts of courage, but unlike Camus, Nestroy does not see any form of happiness as their end result. What he does see is the individual's reward of dignity.

Death presents special problems for this area of Nestroy's thought. Death looms as the termination of reason, thus also of the self together with its claim to dignity. Death is a monster void which swallows all, and so the qualities of dignity and identity are marred by their transitoriness. In the end death will win, and however beneficial man's tiny spark of dignity may be in rendering life bearable, it too will ultimately be extinguished. Still, Nestroy drew some comfort from his intellectual condemnation of the phenomenon of death. By facing it head-on and refusing to accept any illusory compromise, such as the Christian vision of an afterlife, the individual manages to rise above it at least for the duration of his life. Nestroy resisted death with all the moral outrage that his intellect could muster, aware all the while that every man must eventually succumb.

So identity/dignity has a fatal flaw. Confronted with the ineluctability of death it only barely escapes total submersion in order to remain as an imperfect piece of flotsam which helps keep the individual afloat. It gives him something to cling to in life, some protection against the injustices of existence. Identity/dignity at least helps the individual avoid despair.

Another difficult area when dealing with Nestroy's conception of dignity is his so-called "resignation" which surfaced in the early forties and was especially apparent during the middle decade of his creative years. One of his most quoted aphorisms is Schnoferl's weary comment, "Die edelste Nation unter allen Nationen ist die Resignation" (*Das Mädl aus der Vorstadt* I, 12), and indeed Schnoferl is the clearest representative of Nestroy's "resigned" characters. At first glance, especially when viewed without reference to the works as a whole, many of Schnoferl's statements seem to indicate a sort of classic resignation, a meek submission to circumstance. Referring to the woman whom he secretly loves, he cautions, "Jetzt, Schnoferl, sei standhaft, für dich blüht diese Blume nicht, drum handle als Freund und leiste Verzicht auf das, was du nicht erringen kannst!" (I, 11). It sounds very much like a renunciation out of inner humility, but in another famous speech Schnoferl's description of this Nestroyan "resignation" leaves one with the impression that he may not be so meekly acquiescent after all:

> Für mich war die Liebe kein buntes Gemälde in heitrer Farbenpracht, sondern eine in der Druckerei des Schicksals verpatzte Lithographie, grau in grau, schwarz in schwarz, dunkel in schmutzig verwischt. Die pragmatische Geschichte meines Herzens zerfällt in drei miserable Kapitel: zwecklose Träumereien, ab'brennte Versuche und wertlose Triumphe. Wenn der Mensch nie diejenige erringt, wo er eigentlich—wo es der Müh' wert, wo—ich kann mich nicht ausdrücken, mag mich eigentlich nicht ausdrücken—wenn der Mensch nicht Baumkraxler genug war, um die wahren süßen Früchte am Lebensbaum zu erreichen, wenn—ich find' nicht die gehörigen Worte, das heißt, ich findet s', aber grad die g'hörigen täten sich

> nicht g'hören—mit einem Wort, der Mensch verfällt nach einigen Desperationsparoxysmen in eine ruhige Sarkasmus-Languissance, wo man über alles räsoniert und andererseits wieder alles akzeptabel find't.
>
> (I, 5)

Desperation, Sarkasmus, räsonieren, these words cast a heavy shadow of bitterness over the final *akzeptabel,* and leave one with the uneasy feeling that things aren't really acceptable at all.

In fact Nestroy's resignation is never a "sich an die Welt klammernde Demut." It has nothing to do with the Christian ideal of blissful compliance with God's will, acquiescence in the suffering of the world out of deference to the divine wisdom of creation. Such meek submissiveness would be unthinkable for Nestroy. It would completely conradict his concept of individual dignity which stems from the moral condemnation of the world, that is the *refusal* to accept the indignities of *Schicksal.* Humble acceptance of life with all the injustices of *Schicksal* would be a capitulation, a total surrender of dignity, and for that Nestroy, even in his mellowest moment, was never prepared. He could not, and did not write a single *Posse* without an undercurrent of bitter resentment at life's suffering and meaninglessness. The cynicism is indeed muted during the "resigned" forties and early fifties, but those who would interpret Nestroy's resignation as a belated embracing of life and *Schicksal* are being misled by a tone that is only somewhat less acerbic than before.

Nestroy never accepts the world in any moral sense. Purposelessness and *ennui* are never overcome in favor of any sort of resigned, inner well-being. Nestroy's so-called resignation is simply an extension of his rational view of existence. The key to understanding it is to be found in the "Schicksalsmonolog" where Wendelin comments:

> 's Schicksal hat alles, was die von ihm beherrschten Menschen empören muß. Es gibt wohl viele, die 's mit Geduld ertragen, das sind eigentlich recht die G'scheidten, die einsehen, daß es umsonst, und daß ohnmächtige Empörung immer lächerlich ist;

Nestroy's resignation represents the maturation of his idea of life's futility—the purposelessness of existence. It is the acknowledgement, rather than the acceptance of an ugly truth. Referring to Schlicht in *Mein Freund,* [in his dissertation, "Das Lebensegefühl des 'Biedermeier' in der Oesterreichischen Dichtung," 1929] the critic Wilhelm Bietak concludes:

> Es ist dies nicht die Resignation des Biedermeier, die ins Werk tritt . . . ; es ist nicht die Resignation, die ihr Glück in der Beschränkung auf die innere Ruhe und den Seelenfrieden findet, sondern ein Beugen unter das Joch, das jeden Widerstand als nicht der Mühe wert erachtet, ein Hinnehmen des Lebens in seiner Niedrigkeit, das jedes Streben das Leben in höherem Sinne zu gestalten als vergeblich und sinnlos von sich weist. . . .

Resignation appears, not as characters experience inner peace, but when they realize that some imagined joy has in fact no reality. It is accompanied not by contentment, but by disappointment and frustration. It is the resignation of Weinberl when he says, "Jetzt habe ich das Glück genossen, ein verfluchter Kerl zu sein, und die ganze Ausbeute von dem Glück is, daß ich um keinen Preis mehr ein verfluchter Kerl sein möcht' " (***Einen Jux will er sich machen*** IV, 3). Schnoferl's opening *Couplet* in ***Das Mädl aus der Vorstadt*** with the refrain, "Na, der Mensch muß nit alles auf einmal begehr'n," is actually a list of typical human desires paired with the ironic disclosure that in reality their fulfillment does not bring the anticipated pleasure:

> Schad', daß ich nit heiraten tu', das wär' schön,
> Die Seligkeit soll schon ins Aschgraue gehn.
> Wie schön, wenn man ein' Affen mit hambringt
>   auf d' Nacht
> Und 's Weib ein'm acht Tag' drüber Vorwürfe
>   macht!
> Wie schön, wenn man z'erst in Kaffeehaus ver-
>   liert
> Und z' Haus von Weib extra noch ausgemacht
>   wird!
> Wie schön, tut das Schicksal ein' Freund gleich
>   bescher'n!
> Wie lieb, wenn die Kind'r in der Nacht unruhig
>   wer'n!
> Und wie überraschend tut sich oft d' Famili ver-
>   mehr'n!
> Na, der Mensch muß nit alles auf einmal be-
>   gehr'n.
>
>   (I,5)

Bietak has correctly identified the nature of Nestroy's resignation but errs in interpreting it as a surrender of human dignity. In so doing he misunderstands the source of Nestroy's dignity. Nestroy could concede man's helplessness in the face of *Schicksal* precisely because that recognition did not forfeit but rather confirmed man's only true dignity, which lies in the exercise of intellectual freedom and moral judgment. His resignation is not an admission of man's unworthiness but rather an accusation against the unworthiness of an unjust world. It is a recognition that striving is futile, and a refusal to humiliate the self with pointless endeavors. It is a denunciation of fate and an exercise of intellectual freedom, the freedom to reject illusion, and as such it enhances rather than detracts from human dignity. One must note that the above quote from the "Schicksalsmonolog" continues as follows (emphasis added):

> Es gibt wohl viele, die 's mit Geduld ertragen,
> das sind eigentlich recht die G'scheidten, die ein-
> sehen, daß es umsonst, und daß ohnmächtige
> Empörung immer lächerlich ist; *aber deshalb
> sind sie doch immerhin sanfte Aufrührer, servile
> Revolutionäre, zarte Proletarier.*

Nestroy's resignation did indeed have the effect of easing the burden of life's injustice. It did so by enhancing dignity and by mitigating the frustration which results from pointless striving. It appeared during a period of maturity (roughly the decade from 1840 to 1850) when Nestroy's intellectual distance was greatest, allowing him a quieter, more confident approach to the problems of existence. As Rommel writes [in "Johann Nestroy, der Satiriker auf der Altwiener Komödienbühne," in Johann Nestroy, *Gesammelte Werke*, I, 150.], "Die aggressive Schärfe kritischpsychologischer Analyse weicht allmählich einer überlegen ruhigen, humorvollen Betrachtung der Widersprüche des Lebens. . . ." It is crucial to an understanding of Nestroy's thought to recognize that his resignation was not an emotional surrender, but a rational refusal to humiliate the self.

Although the dignity gained through intellectual freedom is a crucial weapon in the battle against despair, it is ultimately insufficient. Nestroy's central characters find it necessary to compromise their strictly rational approach in order to make life bearable. Chief among such compromises is the troubled acceptance of hope.

The word *Hoffnung* occurs abundantly in Nestroy's works, and this frequency of usage alone indicates the prominent position which the concept occupies in Nestroy's world view. The word falls so casually from the lips of his characters that they themselves seem hardly aware of it. It is so deeply and permanently a part of their psychological posture towards life that it becomes a linguistic convention, functioning as a catchword for any thing, person, or event which is positively valued, as when Sidonia, who is urging a romance on her son Ludwig, warns, "Scherze nicht, Ludwig, es gilt die schönste Hoffnung meines Lebens—" (***Kampl*** I, 17). Often the word approaches the status of a euphemism for happiness. Titus, in ***Der Talisman,*** laments, "Das stolze Gebäude meiner Hoffnungen ist assekuranzlos ab'brennt, meine Glücksaktien sind um hundert Prozent g'fall'n, und somit belauft sich mein Aktivstand wieder auf die rundeste aller Summen, nämlich auf Null" (III, 1). However the word may be employed, it never strays radically from its standard nuance of desire coupled with expectation. Nestroy is not unconventional in his use of the term. Yet the concept is a problematic one in his scheme of understanding, and his attitude towards it remained deeply ambiguous.

On the one hand Nestroy clearly saw hope as a comfort for the anguished individual. It is a powerful weapon in the struggle against *Schicksal,* against emptiness and despair. Time and again Nestroy's characters refer to hope as though it were an essential element of individual well-being. Not surprisingly, given Nestroy's scepticism, such references most often take a negative form. Characters complain of the distress resulting from a *lack* of hope. Sometimes that hope has a specific object, as when Sigmund mourns, "Was liegt mir im Grunde an meiner Existenz, da ich leider keine Hoffnung habe, sie je mit Cäcilien teilen zu können!" (***Freiheit in Krähwinkel*** II, 8), or when Fräulein von Blumenblatt observes, "Die Arme! . . . Sie hat ja ganz mein Schicksal: ihr Herz ist schwach, ihre Liebe stark, die Hoffnung klein, die Hindernisse groß—ganz mein Schicksal" (***Jux*** III, 2). Often, however, hope is spoken of abstractly. It appears as a vague (and usually improbable) longing for improvement in the state of one's existence—in fact, for happiness. Thus *Hoffnung* frequently appears in a parallel context with *Glück,* as in the above speech from ***Der Talisman*** or this one from ***Lady und Schneider:*** "Lina Restl!! Das gibt mir den Rest, das raubt mir Glück, Hoffnung, Verstand—alles bis aufs letzte Restl" (II, 16).

The overall impression which one receives from statements such as these is that, in Nestroy's world, hope is essential for survival. Without it life would be untenable. There would be no refuge from the misery and injustice of *Schicksal* other than the limited comfort of dignity. In a typically Nestroyan paroxysm of complaint, Blasius wails:

> Ich bin unglücklich und ich halt's nicht aus, und meine letzte Stunde muß bald schlagen, und ich habe keine Hoffnung mehr, und so verfolgt vom Schicksal wie ich war kein Mensch auf der Welt.

The absence of hope would leave one almost completely at the mercy of *Schicksal* and the void behind it, and thus subject to despair. In fact Blasius continues:

> Wenn ich denk', mein vorig's Leben und mein jetziges Leben, so gehn mir d' Augen über, es stoßt mir 's Herz ab und ich verzweifel'.
> (***Glück, Missbrauch und Rückkehr*** V, 1)

Because hope is an antidote to that despair which constantly threatens the individual, the two terms frequently appear in juxtaposition, sometimes directly and sometimes more subtly:

> GABRIEL. Er war die Hoffnung meiner alten Tage—
>
> BERNHARD. Und jetzt—?
>
> GABRIEL. Ist er der Millionenschnipfer meiner Zukunft.
>
> BERNHARD. Du bist schon wieder ein'kehrt im Rückweg.
>
> GABRIEL. Das wohl, aber bei einem echt Verzweifelten greift nix an.
> (***Kampl*** IV, 9)
>
> . . . . .
>
> ZACKENBURG. . . . "Können Sie mich ohne Mitleid der Verzweiflung hoffnungsloser Liebe preisgeben?"
> (***Kampl*** I, 32)
>
> . . . . .
>
> PITZL. Gieße einSeidlziment Hoffnung in die Zehnmaßpitschen deiner Verzweiflung—
> (***Umsonst*** II, 13)

Hope is essential in avoiding despair because it provides at least a faint taste of what is so sorely lacking in Nestroy's world—the ideal. Ideals are not unknown to Nestroy. Without an internal image of a perfect model, critical judgment would be impossible. Every condemnation implies some ideal against which the condemned entity is being measured. The values expressed in Nestroy's works are of course based on such hypothetical ideal images. His contempt, however, was for those naive souls who believe that the ideal can actually exist and is thus worth pursuing. For him ideals are merely imaginary concepts, required in order for the mind to perceive the shortcomings of reality. And yet Nestroy himself, this sceptic,

this cynic for all cynics, found that facing an ideal-less world was asking too much of the individual. Such unbending honesty would no doubt be noble, but also unbearable. The dignity gained thereby could not alone prevent despair. Fortunately he found in hope a way to mitigate the harshness of reality, a way to restore to life a fragile fragment of the ideal.

Hope is necessarily a positive concept. Its object is in one sense always an ideal, namely happiness. Even though the immediate object of hope may be something quite mundane ("Wir haben Hoffnung auf Barrikaden" [***Lady und Schneider*** II, 1]), the necessary implication is that its acquisition will bring at least some limited form of happiness. Spoken of abstractly (as it frequently is in Nestroy) hope's object is nothing less than the ideal of a felicitous existence.

Hope then is Nestroy's repository for the ideal, the only one he allowed himself. It is a tiny positive flame aglow in the sceptic's negative void, a comfort in the darkness of human existence. Schlicht expresses it with a different metaphor in his plea to Julius: "Laß mir meine frohen Erwartungen! Die Hoffnung is ja der Goldschnitt am Buch des Lebens, die Blätter sind übervoll vom schwarzen Druck der Verhältnisse, und die Traumbilder, die man sich vorgaukelt, sind die einzigen Illustrationen drin" (***Mein Freund*** I, 7).

Obviously there is a conflict in all this. Hope consists of desire *coupled with expectation,* and expectation implies at least the possibility of hope's goal (including its spark of the ideal) being realized. Yet Nestroy admits of no such possibility. *Schicksal* is not only omnipotent, but as a part of the fabric of existence, it is also timeless. The forces which cause suffering, frustration, and finally death are not subject to change. The arbitrariness of *Schicksal* and the void transcend time. How can one who does not believe in improvement still hope?

There is no resolution to this conflict. Nestroy's description of hope as "der Goldschnitt am Buch des Lebens" expresses the decorative (that is illusory) element of the concept, but it also clearly implies an acceptance of hope as an ameliorating element in life. Yet the same man who coined that metaphor also recorded the following aphorism in his notes:

> In der Jugend hat man für grenzenlose Wünsche noch grenzenlose Hoffnungen, später bleiben die grenzenlosen Wünsche, aber die Vernunft löscht die Hoffnung aus, und die ungestümen Wünsche müssen sich nach und nach an der schroffen Wand der Hoffnungslosigkeit den Schädel einstoßen.

This is more nearly the Nestroy we would expect in view of his broad scepticism. The contrasting of *Hoffnung* with the *Vernunft* which extinguishes it is precisely in line with his other basic instincts toward rational exposure of illusion. Because reason does not admit of any ideals it cannot permit hope. Reason perceives that hope's object can never be realized, and that hope is therefore based on illusion. Thus to insist on hope is to compromise reason—and with reason the self and dignity.

Still, Nestroy found that compromise necessary to avoid despair, but he was never comfortable with it, and a deep ambiguity towards the concept of hope is never overcome in his work. On the one hand hope is embraced as an emotional comfort, but on the other despised as a surrender to illusion. That Nestroy granted even a limited, grudging approbation to hope stems from the fact that, in hope, the illusory element is at least banished to a considerable distance. One need not accept the present reality of any ideal, but merely an improbable future possibility—improbable because, as evident in the above examples from Nestroy's work, his characters almost always see hope as extremely dim, tottering on the brink of hopelessness, and never actually being realized except as part of the obligatory happy-end. By far the majority of Nestroy's references to hope are actually complaints against its futility, an indication of his profound discomfort with the concept. Still he recognized its stubborn persistence in the human psyche and paid homage to that persistence in speeches such as these two by Anselm in **Gegen Torheit,** where hope survives in the face of ridiculous odds. About a young woman's vehement rejection of his courtship, Anselm comments, "Dieser Haß—das gibt mir wieder Hoffnung, denn Haß hat sich schon oft in Liebe verwandelt" (II, 17), and about another young woman's marriage to a man (Simplicius) whom she despises: "Wenn man von dem Grundsatz ausgeht, daß gar nichts unmöglich ist, als daß sich eins die Nasen abbeißt, so kann man auch hoffen, daß es a recht gute Eh' werden wird" (III, 17).

Of course the irony in such statements is undisguised, and it is this ironic attitude that helps to salve Nestroy's wounded dignity. It is his way of saying, my emotions are indulging in a shameful illusion, but at least my reason recognizes that fact. In this exchange from **Kampl,** Nestroy's equation of *Hoffnung* with *Luftschloss* is an example of the Nestroyan reason at work, exposing hope as a fool's illusion:

> LUDWIG. Festen Vorsatz in der Brust—ach, alles hab' ich, alles, nur keine Hoffnung im Herzen.
>
> KAMPL. Und das ist grad 's Leichteste. Zum Luftschlösserbauen braucht man nicht einmal ein' Grund, und Sie haben in mir einen Bauplatz gefunden!
>
> (III, 15)

In **Der Zerrissene,** hope is equated with dreams. Lips muses:

> Eben die Träum' verraten mir's, daß es auf die Neig' geht, ich mein', die wachen Träum', die jeder Mensch hat. Bestehen diese Träum' in Hoffnungen, so is man jung, bestehen sie in Erinnerungen, so is man alt. Ich hoff' nix mehr und erinnere mich an vieles, ergo: alt, uralt, Greis, Tatl!
>
> (I, 6)

There are countless other examples of the same attitude. Reason breaks in on hope, exposes its object as chimeric, and thereby reasserts the dignity of the self. Significantly, such statements often occur in songs or *Couplets* where Nestroy was wont to step out of character and generalize:

> In der Stadt hat man d' Wasserfäll nur in der Gestalt,
> Wenn einem a Hoffnung in Brunn' abifallt.
> (*Glück, Missbrauch und Rückkehr* III, 7)

. . . . .

> Wie oft g'schieht nit das,
> Daß man hofft auf was,
> Ein Palast sich herbaut schon im Geist,
> Plötzlich wird daraus
> Nur ein Kartenhaus,
> Was ein einz'ger Blaser niederreißt.
> (*Gegen Torheit* II, 26)

. . . . .

> Wenn man glaubt, man hat das Glück
> Schon sicher in sein' Haus
> Husch, husch, husch, im Augenblick
> Beim Fenster rutscht's hinaus.
> Man schmeichelt sich mit Hoffnung oft,
> Zu Wasser wird das, was man hofft—
> (*Der Talisman* III, 11)

In the strictest intellectual sense Nestroy was forced to reject hope. There is no place for it in a world determined by *Schicksal*. Still the concept is clearly an essential part of Nestroy's world view because of its pervasiveness and special prominence. Facing reality head on, as it were, grants the individual dignity, but dignity alone is not enough to compensate for the despair brought on by recognition. Nestroy saw the need to cheat against reason from time to time and to accept (albeit not without shame) certain irrational comforts. Chief among those comforts was hope. The concept permeates his works, from the earliest through the latest, and he clearly recognized it as a phenomenon occupying a special position in every individual's existence—as Lips puts it, "die wachen Träum', die jeder Mensch hat." (pp. 27-41)

Kurt Corriher, "The Conflict between Dignity and Hope in the Works of Johann Nestroy," in South Atlantic Review, *Vol. 46, No. 2, May, 1981, pp. 27-42.*

Joel Schechter and Jack Zipes   (essay date 1981)

[*In the following essay, the critics contend that Nestroy's characters use language to demonstrate their individual autonomy and achieve self-expression in spite of governmental attempts to restrict free speech.*]

Those among us wondering how theater can survive and protest injustice in reactionary times may find a model in the plays of Johann Nestroy. From the time he began writing plays in 1822 until his death in 1862, Nestroy wrote numerous farces and satires in what Brecht aptly called "slave language." His language, full of puns and comic understatement, was meant to appear harmless to Austrian censors, but the innuendos and disguised criticism of government repression were fully grasped by the Viennese lower and middle classes who attended Nestroy's plays. These spectators were delighted by Nestroy's daring use of slave language; his humorous coded messages set audiences free, at least temporarily, to question and laugh with impunity at the forms of economic and social control Metternich's regime had imposed upon them. Nestroy's theater offered the common people a liberated zone, a political forum where they could see their tradition and needs addressed through subversive satire.

During one brief, utopian moment of his life and times in Vienna, Nestroy did not have to use slave language to conceal his political criticism. Yet he chose to continue this mode of communication with his audience—perhaps because he sensed that the nation's revolutionary impulse would be short-lived. In March of 1848, Prince Klemens Wenzel Metternich, one of the nineteenth century's most repressive political leaders, resigned his position as Chancellor to the Emperor of Austria and fled to England. After his departure a lengthy reign of police surveillance and state censorship ended in Austria. By July of the same year, Nestroy completed his remarkable satire, *Freedom Comes to Krähwinkel*. The play indicated Nestroy's reserve about the future of the Revolution of 1848. To be sure, he was not afraid to attack Metternich. In Act Three, when the reactionary mayor of Krähwinkel wonders how he will defeat the city's radicals at the barricades, a visitor named "Herr Incognitus" enters in disguise. Viennese audiences could easily recognize the visitor as Metternich. The white-haired diplomat advises Krähwinkel's mayor on military strategy and answers questions about money he has deposited in England. Then he departs. The mayor loses the battle by following his visitor's advice, so that Metternich's antirevolutionary strategy continued to fail nightly at each performance. Such is satire's revenge against tyranny.

The fantasy ended, however, when imperial troops recaptured Vienna in October of 1848, and Nestroy's play was abruptly closed. The stage life of his satire lasted a mere three months, not quite as long as the Revolution of 1848. The Revolution's hopes were dashed, but Nestroy could not have been completely surprised; he had already suggested in *Krähwinkel* that the Austrian people feared freedom too much to fight for it. Nestroy was not blind to the foibles of the rebellious Austrians, and he did not refrain from criticizing the lower class oppressed who were apt to be just as petty and banal as their upper class oppressors. Nestroy's satire sought to expose the connections between master and slave while developing a slave language that could subvert this connection.

. . . . .

Johann Nestroy is generally regarded as the most gifted representative of the Austrian folk play tradition. *Freedom Comes to Krähwinkel* shares many of the conventions evident in other folk plays by his contemporaries, Raimund and Meisl; but it departs from their conventions with poignant social and political commentaries developed through highly inventive and satirical slave language. Nestroy's linguistic reflections of class consciousness and conflicts showed the contradictory ways in which the common people sought freedom. Though the satirist's sympathies were always with the lower and lower-middle classes, he ridiculed the customs and daily routines through which they unconsciously blocked themselves from gaining emancipation. This is the reason why some of the most significant modern playwrights in Austria and

southern Germany, such as Ödön von Horváth, Peter Handke, Wolfgang Bauer, and Martin Sperr, have shown a great appreciation of Nestroy.

However, these modern writers are more pessimistic than Nestroy. They tend to depict the despair of common people in totally administered societies where pre-formed language controls thought and emotion. Nestroy never lost sight of the subversive and creative energy of the common person willing to take risks in pursuit of social advancement and social change. With these risks, expressed through their special comic language, Nestroy's characters offer models for change of social relations and political conditions. Two of Nestroy's more formidable satires, *The Talisman* (1840) and *Krähwinkel* (1848) demonstrate how language employed by a representative character embodies this indomitable, exuberant spirit of the common people—and of Nestroy himself.

. . . . .

In *The Talisman,* Titus, the red-haired barber's assistant encounters provincial hatred of people with red hair, until he has the good fortune to acquire a series of wigs which conceal his own hair. At first Titus cannot believe how kindly people treat him. "It all seems one big joke to me when after years of being kicked around I'm suddenly able to charm people. What can I say? When I think about this morning and now, that's quite a change within a period of four to five hours! Yes, time is but the big tailor's helper, who's supposed to alter everything in the workshop of eternity. Sometimes the work goes quickly, sometimes slowly, but it's always done. Nothing can hold it up. Everything gets altered!"

Then Titus breaks into a satirical song; the first stanza both celebrates and mocks man's mutability:

> There once was a man made out of steel who loved to dance furiously.
> Nor was he much afraid of catching colds at the window.
> He ran around and jumped into a career of love-making.
> He gambled and drank the entire night through. He rarely slept at home.
> After ten years his heart beat frantically, his belly acted homopathetically.
> He had to wear flannel pajamas in July
> And a cotton nightcap to boot, or else he'd catch a cold and die.
> Yes, time changes many a thing.

Once Titus starts wearing wigs, his fortune improves not only because his hair color changes, but also because his behavior changes. He mimicks the etiquette and language of the well-heeled to insure that he will be mistaken for one of them. Through his mimickry Nestroy ridicules the assumption that one's language or manners reflect an individual's essence. Titus demonstrates the ability of man to transform himself socially by adopting to new (if false and mutable) conventions as he ascends the social hierarchy. At the same time, Titus is totally conscious of the deception he perpetrates. The village goatherd Salome, an innocent red-haired woman who becomes his conscience, constantly reminds Titus that *authenticity* is preferable to a life of lies. In the end, Titus abandons the wigs—just as Nestroy would prefer straight speaking to the disguises of slave language—and chooses to pursue his career with Salome at his side.

In *Freedom Comes to Krahwinkel* Ultra, the radical journalist, also assumes different false identities to outwit government forces of reaction. Unlike Titus, however, Ultra is a more fully developed individual and consciously pursues a plan so that he can obtain the right to publish his own thoughts; he has no wish to mimic the thoughts of the upper class. This may be why his journal has only 36 readers, and almost everything in it except the restaurant reviews is censored. Many of Ultra's articles come back from the censor as blank sheets of paper. Although Ultra hates the censors, he is honored to be banned: "To have an article struck out by the censor is the highest possible compliment. It shows that your meaning is plain even to the very lowest intelligence." Clearly Ultra wants to reach all levels of society through his writing, and like Nestroy himself, he believes that language can invest his audience with the will and means to risk changing their lives.

When the mayor of Krähwinkel offers Ultra a position as censor in hopes of silencing the journalist's political protests, the radical refuses to be bought. In what is Nestroy's strongest and most overt condemnation of censorship, Ultra tells the mayor that a censor is "a man turned into a pencil, a pencil turned into a man . . . a crocodile that sits on the bank of the river of ideas, snapping off the heads of writers as they swim by." When the mayor exclaims that he has never heard such language as this in Krähwinkel, Ultra agrees, explaining that the city is a century behind the times, and his own speech is only four months old. In other words, his language is no older than the Revolution of 1848. Ultra's vocabulary of freedom and revolution is a form of opposition to government repression. At the same time, it is as vulnerable to usurpation and abuse as the upper class language mimicked by Titus in *The Talisman.*

This usurpation is enacted in Krähwinkel by a hack poet named Sperling, who says he has nothing against freedom since it gives writers a "wide space for riding their Pegasus." Of course, he would not have said this before the revolution arrived in Krahwinkel. Earlier the opportunistic poet recites a paean to police bludgeons (alias knouts), when the reactionaries are still in power. After Krähwinkel's revolution, Sperling praises freedom in doggerel just as servile to fashion as his earlier works:

> On Freedom
>
> Ei, ei!
> We are now free!
> This is completely new
> to live without slavery.
> with a free press's liberty
> and self-government.
> Therefore shout jubilantly
> We are now free.
> Ei, ei! Ei, ei!

After reciting his song, Sperling adds that it is impossible to write anything more sensitive than his splendid paean. And he is probably correct to judge himself incapable of

greater subtlety or sensitivity—which is not to say that he had much of it to begin with. One could cite his verse as reason to reinstate censorship. At the very least, Nestroy's play hints that rhetoric in the name of freedom is as susceptible to cliche and deserving of parody as other forms of language.

. . . . .

In both *The Talisman* and *Krahwinkel,* the protagonists Titus and Ultra humorously demonstrate how slave language can by used by those wary of being exploited. The characters take social and political risks with their language, through puns, witticisms, double entendres, irony and satire that maintain their autonomy and allow them to pursue authentic means of self-expression. They are most free in their songs, which generally offer satirical comments about social conditions.

Nestroy often drew parallels between sexual repression and political oppression in his plays. In *The Talisman,* there are three widows of different social classes who pursue Titus in devious ways while trying to adhere to a social code that will make love respectable. However, it is the natural, unaffected Salome whom Titus chooses in the end, because she expresses herself frankly and directly. Only through a "free" language, suggests Nestroy, is there a possibility for love. All else is sexual play of a diverting kind, or sexual conformity which bars the possibility of love.

In *Krähwinkel,* Klaus, a sanctimonious official informer, tries to prevent his daughter from marrying a junior official named Willibald. Moreover, the mayor wants to blackmail Frau von Frankenfrei, an attractive and outspoken widow, into marriage. Both these men fail in their plots when the social revolution succeeds. Willibald wins Cacilia, and Ultra will evidently marry Frau von Frankenfrei. As with most of Nestroy's characters, Frankenfrei's name symbolically represents her morality—in this case one which is frank and free. Here too a connection is made between love and free language, and between social convention and sexual repression. The Viennese psychoanalysts Freud and Reich could have—and quite possibly had—seen anticipations of their theories of repression in the satire of an earlier Vienna resident, Johann Nestroy.

While Nestroy is still popular in Austria and Germany today, and while he may have had a great influence on various German and Austrian writers, his plays remain almost unknown in the United States. His wordplay and the social and political implications in his writing have hardly been appreciated here. Perhaps, given America's self-image as the land of the free, most of the country's citizens have never sensed a need to develop a slave language. However, times are changing, and it may be time that we carefully examine the most significant Austrian dramatist of the nineteenth century, who knew how to survive and even sing in dark times. (pp. 72-5)

Joel Schechter and Jack Zipes, "Slave Language Comes to Krähwinkel: Notes on Nestroy's Political Satire," in Theater, *Vol. XII, No. 2, Spring, 1981, pp. 72-5.*

Roger A. Crockett   (essay date 1983)

[*In the essay that follows, Crockett argues that several of Nestroy's characters are manifestations of his refusal to accept fatalism.*]

Nestroy's comedies are replete with characters claiming to be fate's victims. *Schicksal,* along with its kin *Zufall* and *Glück,* are personified, cursed, praised, ridiculed, and courted. Nestroy's characters blame fate for a wide range of personal misfortune as well as for the ills of society. Must they, however, be taken at their word? Should it be assumed, as it has been thus far in Nestroy scholarship, that they speak the personal frustrations, the fatalistic philosophy of the author? To deny that they do would require a Nestroyesque skepticism, the sarcastic attitude that "'s is alles nit wahr!" This position is defensible, however. Nestroy's *Volk* is, after all, only a slightly exaggerated reflection of Viennese society. Its dialogues are the banter Nestroy heard every day in the markets and coffee houses, made more literate through his unique wit. What the masses were saying about fate is summarized by Ernst Fischer [in his "Johann Nestroy: Ze seinem hundersten Todestag," *Sinn und Form,* 14 (1962)]:

> In der deutschen und österreichischen Romantik war diese Macht des Schicksals und Ohnmacht des Menschen, diese Verantwortungslosigkeit des Handelnden ("Unsere Taten sind nur Würfe in des Zufalls blinder Nacht!") ein zentrales Thema. Der Wiener Spießbürger schwelgte in der Ausrede auf das Schicksal, auf das "Malör", das ihn, den Harm- und Schuldlosen, immer wieder zu Missetaten trieb.

There is considerable textual evidence that Nestroy was fully aware of the situation Fischer describes and that the excuse of fate is treated satirically. First of all, the personification of fate is eliminated early in Nestroy's career, never to reappear. This is, of course, the character *Fatum* in the comedy *Die Familien Zwirn, Knieriem und Leim,* with the subtitle *Der Welt-Untergangs-Tag*—Nestroy's final magic play, if, indeed, it can be called magic at all. With this comedy, earth is at last free from intervention from above. The inhabitants of Stellaris' extra-terrestial kingdom can do no more than the Viennese audience: watch the play. Like the mortals of the time, the supernatural beings call on *Fatum,* in their great distress. *Fatum,* however, appears as a sleepy old man and admits his total lack of interest in their problems or anyone else's:

> *Fatum:* Ich weiß alles. (Vortretend, für sich.) Ich weiß gar nichts, aber ich bin zu faul, die ganze Geschichte anzuhören. Es ist etwas Prächtiges, das Schicksal zu sein, man tut rein gar nichts, und am Ende heißt es bei allem, was geschieht, das Schicksal hat es getan.

He answers Stellaris' question: "Dürfen wir hoffen?" with the ambiguous: "Ja, ja, hofft nur zu!" Nevertheless, he is still trusted and revered by his supplicants as the chorus sings: "Des Fatums Macht wird alles lenken, . . .".

In the words of Bruno Hannemann: "Der traditionelle Gnadenund Führungscharakter dieser metaphysischen Großmacht, die für jegliche Autorität von Gott bis zum Kaiser anzusehen ist, geht hier in tiefem Schnarchen

unter" [*Johann Nestroy: Nihilistisches Welttheater und verflixter Kerl* 1977]. Then is Nestroy's God dead? Hannemann contends that he is not, but rather that he has become a sleeping bureaucrat: "An der Willkür seiner Entscheidungen leidet der Mensch." Yet to a world looking to the heavens for justice, asleep or dead is a meaningless distinction. *Fatum* makes no further decisions in the affairs of men, arbitrary or otherwise. Nestroy has come as close to asserting that God is dead as he thought the censors and his folk audience would permit. Nestroy's characters do not often realize that the heavens hold no hope for a just solution to earth's problems, but this is the message his audiences were supposed to receive. It is the same message that Brecht would later couch in a proverb cleverly alienated by punctuation:

> Der Mensch denkt: "Gott lenkt".
> Keine Red' davon!

Nestroy expresses this sentiment most forcefully in his introductory monologue as Gottlieb Herb in *Der Schützling:*

> Wie die Welt noch im Finstern war, war der Himmel so hell, und seit die Welt so im klaren is, hat sich der Himmel verfinstert. Die Stern', die sich anno Aberglauben um unser Schicksal so hinabgezappelt haben, sind anno Aufklärung in dieser Qualität erloschen. Wir sind jetzt weit mehr auf die Welt reduziert, an etwas Irdisches muß man sich jetzt anklammern.

While this assertion reaffirms the message of the satirical *Fatum* episode, it is a rare example of Nestroy's candor. The uniqueness of Herb's humanistic doctrine as opposed to the large number of characters professing fatalism has caused the former to be discredited. Again Hannemann writes:

> Allerdings kann Gottlieb Herb mit dieser Hinwendung zum Irdischen weder sich selbst noch die anderen Figuren in Nestroy's Possenkosmos überzeugen. Die überall anzutreffenden Anspielungen auf metaphysische Schicksalsmächte (auch im Schützling) relativieren nicht nur Herbs irdisches Credo, sondern bestätigen geradezu das Gegenteil: . . . .

The "metaphysische Schicksalsmächte" to which Hannemann refers are, of course, irrational and arbitrary. Character after character complains that good fortune, like wealth, is unequally distributed, and that well-laid plans go awry for unforeseeable reasons. These characters are also the ones taken at their word as speaking for the author. Siegfried Diehl suggests that the immoral lifestyle of Knieriem and Zwirn, the vagabonds of *Lumpazivagabundus,* is not only justified but necessary for survival in the face of whimsical fate. Stressing that blind chance rather than Providence is in control of the universe, Rainer Urbach offers a similar interpretation [in his [*Stranitsky und die Folgen: Die Wiener Komöbie und ihr Publikum* 1973].

> Der Zufall macht die Menschen nicht für alle Möglichkeiten frei, sondern nur für die schlechtesten. . . . Die Menschen werden zu Opportunisten der Gelegenheit. "Man muß die

Welt nehmen, wie s' is, und nicht wie s' sein
könnt' ", heißt es für den Realisten in der Komödie, den Zufallsräsoneur.

According to Rio Preisner, Nestroy's earlier works are
characterized by "auswegslose Dialektik von prometheis-
cher Auflehnung und dionysischer Flucht. . . ." [*Johann
Nepomuk Nestroy: Der Schöpfer der tragischen Posse*,
1968].

If, however, we were to refuse to take the fatalistic characters literally, but rather were able to discredit them, we
could establish Gottlieb Herb as the character who most
nearly speaks Nestroy's mind. Fortunately, Nestroy has
already discredited his "victims" of fate by showing how
each one caused his own misfortune.

Central to a study of fate versus human responsibility
must be Knieriem, the comic principal and Nestroy role
in ***Der böse Geist Lumpazivagabundus*** and its previously
discussed sequel, ***Die Familien Zwirn, Knieriem und
Leim***. He is the first, both chronologically and in popularity, of the line of characters who deny responsibility for
their mistakes. Not only the enthusiastic reception of
Lumpazivagabundus, but, of more importance, its provisional conclusion made a sequel inevitable. To tell the
story of Knieriem required more than one play. Furthermore, since the comedy is by no means a true *Besserungsstück*, the forced conversion of Knieriem and Zwirn cannot be permanent. Thus, the first half ends literally up in
the air. In a tableau we see the two vagabonds experiencing an interlude of tranquil family life. To underscore the
fantasy of the closing scene, Nestroy sets it "im Hinter-
grunde in einer sich öffnenden, etwas tieferen Wolkeng-
ruppe." The curtain falls after "Beleuchtung mit griechis-
chem Feuer," an effect otherwise reserved for scenes in
fairyland. So it seems entirely natural that Knieriem and
Zwirn have returned to their old lifestyles as the sequel begins.

While Zwirn exhibits essentially the same vices as Knieriem, it is the latter through whom Nestroy demonstrates
the extremes to which fatalism and irresponsibility can
lead. Two threads run through both comedies: Knieriem's
constant inebriation and his prophecy of the all-
annihilating comet. Knieriem continually looks outside of
himself for the cause of his troubles. For his inability to
hold a job he has a ready explanation:

> *Knieriem*. . . .—und dann hab' ich nichts als
> unverschuldete Unglücksfälle g'habt.—In Bud-
> weis hab' ich mein' Meister g'haut.
>
> *Leim*. Warum denn?
>
> *Knieriem*. Weil ich ein' Rausch g'habt hab', also
> kann ich nix davor. In Altbrünn hätt' ich bald
> ein' Lehrbuben zerrissen.
>
> *Leim*. So was ist aber auch abscheulich. . . .
>
> *Knieriem*. Ich hab' damals einen unsinnigen
> Haarbeutel g'habt, also kann ich nix davor. . . .

Blame for his unbridled intoxication is placed on the
comet, with the result that Knieriem convinces himself of
his unaccountability. Such protestations of innocence for
personally caused misfortune are certainly consistent with

the attitudes of many other characters to be discussed
later. Knieriem, however, goes about avoiding responsibility much more systematically. Instead of simply using fate
as an alibi for stupidity after the fact, Knieriem uses the
inevitability of the comet to justify his immoral conduct
in advance. The question we must ask about the relationship between Knieriem's behavior and the comet is: which
is stimulus and which is response? Is he a drunken vagabond because his belief in earth's imminent doom convinces him that this is the only sensible answer to an absurd situation, or is his belief in the comet strengthened,
even created by a need to justify his debauchery? Simply
stated: Is Knieriem a nihilist or an opportunist? To illuminate this question it is necessary to look more closely at
the comet itself and Knieriem's motives.

In Act II, Scene v, Knieriem declares to the haughty, sta-
tus-conscious Mathilde that the end of class distinction is
at hand: ". . . es wird bald eine Stunde schlagen, wo es
keine Fräuleins und keine Schuster mehr gibt. . . . Der
Unterschied der Stände hat aufgehört; Herrschaft, Bedienter, gnädiger Herr, Bettelmann, Fräul'n und Schuster,
das is irzt alles eine Kategorie." His rhetoric conjures revolutionary images: the comet as omen of the impending
proletarian revolt, moving freely through a disordered
cosmos as described in the *Kometenlied*, destined to strike
an equally chaotic world. The class system is suddenly
eliminated. The world, interpreted here as the absolutist
Austrian state, "steht auf kein' Fall mehr lang."

Of course Nestroy infused his monologues and intercalat-
ed *couplets* with social and political satire. The *Kometenlied* was no exception. Yet Nestroy, while reform-minded,
was no advocate of violent revolution. Indeed, if the comet
were the revolution, it could equalize society only by totally destroying it. It is, rather, on a level other than the political that Knieriem's prophecy will be fulfilled. The comet
will soon equalize the classes, but in another, unexpected
way.

Much like some present-day prophets of doom who capi-
talize on apocalyptic frenzy, Knieriem gathers a circle of
converts to his belief in the impending end of the world.
He assembles his cult to await the appointed hour at the
tavern, the temple of his hedonistic philosophy: pleasure
without responsibility. Here he has attained the status of
high priest. Of all the guests he is the only one who acts
unafraid. Calmly he exhorts his congregation to keep
drinking, reminding them that they will not have to pay
for it. He even preaches what amounts to a sermon in
which the proprietor is condemned for his sins:

> Schaut's, wie den Wirt irzt 's G'wissen druckt,
> Wie ängstlich als er 's Kappel ruckt,
> Er zählt irzt, weil der Tod ihn trifft,
> Wie viele Gäst' er hat vergift't.

Like all priests, however, he promises salvation to his followers:

> Als schuldlos Opfer stirbt der Gast,
> Dem Wirt der Teufel 's Licht ausblast.

The damnation of the proprietor for such a paltry offense
as serving bad wine is yet another example of Knieriem's
well-developed reflex for evasion of responsibility.

While the other patrons genuinely fear the cataclysm, Knieriem revels in the situation and in his starring role. He hardly seems to care that the world is about to end. Rather, he acts like a man who has created for himself an elaborate defense mechanism, convinced others of its validity in order to legitimize it, and yet subconsciously realizes the truth. Knieriem is not only the prophet and high priest of the comet, he is its inventor. Although concern was in fact running high in 1832 because of an Austrian's discovery that the earth's orbit was about to pass through the tail of a comet, this fact is not revealed within the fiction of the play. Nobody else seems to have heard about the comet at all except Leim, who is not alarmed, because a professor assured him nothing would happen. Furthermore, the comet which Knieriem popularizes is his own invention, a product of his imagination, concocted from mathematical calculations and astronomical "observations" made as he staggers home after closing time.

The comet does not predate Knieriem's belief in it, but rather is generated by a need to explain and justify his pre-existing immoral lifestyle. This is not to say that Knieriem is guilty of a conscious deception. A defense mechanism can be effective only if the creator believes in its validity, and Knieriem has long since embraced the fiction. Yet, as convenient as the belief in the comet had been in the intervening years, it cannot maintain a hold over him in the decisive moment. He betrays this in his behavior at the tavern where, free of any apocalyptic fear, he enjoys the fame and power of high-priesthood and the convenient excuse for yet another night of debauchery.

Imbued with the spirit of Lumpazivagabundus, Knieriem sets out with his comet to destroy the world in a figurative sense. The ordered lifestyle which is so abhorrent to him must be counteracted with disorder, represented by the purveyor of cosmic chaos. "Die Welt steht auf kein' Fall mehr lang," he warns, as he attempts to disrupt the world of enlightenment, of responsible human action. For a few hours within his microcosm he succeeds. True to Knieriem's prophecy, at that moment when the comet is supposed to strike, class differences cease to exist. Servants, bourgeoisie, and even the wealthy Madame Leim are all brought to Knieriem's level. His fatalistic following is classless; all are equally and pathetically duped.

It is an absurd premise that so many individuals from all levels of society could allow themselves to be thus deceived on an astronomical subject by a drunken shoemaker. Not only does this cobbler not "stick to his last," but he strays as far afield as possible. This absurd situation serves Nestroy's purpose perfectly, however. Who could possibly be duped by someone so patently unqualified? The answer is obvious: only someone who wants to be. The tavern guests are ready and eager to accept unquestioningly the existence of an absolute, inescapable fate. Knieriem merely lets them discover the comet within themselves, as he once did. Rather than being the cosmic chaos per se or a nihilistic symbol for a meaningless universe, the comet is a catalyst. Its effect is to release the suppressed, irrational elements of the mind, which lurk just below the surface, from their control by the rational.

It should not be seen as a defeat for Knieriem's philosophy

that the world does not end. At that moment when the disciples cower under the table, clutching the wine for which they think they do not have to pay, the comet has already struck. There is temporary anger, embarrassment, but nothing is learned. The people throw Knieriem out of the tavern; they do not leave themselves. The comet is within them, and it will strike again and again.

There is no sequel to *Die Familien Zwirn, Knieriem und Leim.* Yet, like *Lumpazivagabundus,* it has an open conclusion. Knieriem survives the tavern scene unchanged: once a priest of the comet, always a priest of the comet. His temporary displeasure with alcohol and astronomy is a direct result of his being thrown out of the tavern. With his next "thirst" will come a reversion to both. Still he refuses to abandon the comet, which has disappointed him at the end of two comedies:

> Der Komet war nicht pünktlich, ich schau' wie
> a Narr,
> Vielleicht is er schläfrig und schlaft tausend
> Jahr'.
> Auf d'Astronomie hab' ich irzt einen Zorn,
> Und das bloß aus dem Grund, weil ich prügelt
> bin wor'n.

Nestroy does not let his comet sleep nearly that long. The characters of numerous later comedies who ignore responsibility for their actions and seek justification through fatalism are also Knieriem's disciples and worshippers of his comet. When, for example, Rot in *Müller, Kohlenbrenner und Sesselträger* begins his introductory monologue by cursing fate, the audience might initially believe him to be a victim of illness, poverty, or society's prejudice: "Aus der Urne des Schicksals werden die Lose des Menschen gezogen; wenn ich den Buben beuteln könnt', der das meinige gezogen hat,—ich tät's." Rot, after all, is a lackey, a carrier of sedan chairs, required to perform backbreaking work while relying on the generosity of his patrons for tips. The audience does not remain duped for long. Rot admits that he really likes his work. His "Schicksal" is that he must soon give up his profession and marry a woman to whom he once made a promise in a weak moment: " . . . ein unseliges Eheversprechen zwingt mich, morgen dem schuldlosen Stand jugendlicher Freiheit zu entsagen . . .—jetzt erst murr' ich gegen das Geschick. (Er murrt laut.)" Although Rot does not comprehend that he was the "Bube" who drew his own lot, it becomes clear to the audience.

Rot is only one of numerous characters who seek a metaphysical excuse for stupidity. The foolishness of Blasius Rohr is documented step by step in *Glück, Mißbrauch und Rückkehr,* a comedy whose title already foretells the plot's progression. By good fortune alone Blasius, an impoverished scribe, acquires a factory from his uncle. Laziness and stupidity prompt him to sell the factory and buy his way into nobility. At his newly purchased castle in the country Blasius surrounds himself with flatterers who exploit him. He courts a spoiled lady with an ambitious father and rapidly squanders his wealth through mismanagement. When his last misguided project, the installation of gas lighting, backfires and burns the castle to the ground, Blasius suddenly finds himself alone and friendless. Still unaware of his own guilt he laments: "Ich bin unglücklich und ich halt's nicht aus und meine letzte Stunde muß bald schlagen und ich habe keine Hoffnung mehr und so verfolgt vom Schicksal wie ich war kein Mensch auf der Welt."

Certainly something has caught up with Blasius, but only someone as blind to his own folly as he is could call it "Schicksal." Two years earlier in *Der Treulose,* another treatment of self-inflicted misery, Nestroy defined his avenging force which brings fools to justice:

> . . . 's gibt eine Nemesis, die schon in diesem Leben lohnt und strafet, sie geht unfehlbar sichern und bedächtigen Schrittes, sie braucht nicht deinen Jugendsprüngen nachzueilen, des Alters Bleigewicht wird sich auf deines Lebens Schwingen niedersenken, und dann erreicht sie dich mit leichter Müh'. Du hast Böses gesäet, du kannst nichts Gutes ernten.

This warning is directed at Herr von Falsch, whose recently discovered extramarital affairs have prompted his wife to consider leaving for America. It is the last line of the above quotation which distinguishes Nestroy's nemesis from the supernatural avenger of Greek mythology. Falsch is not being warned of absolute divine retribution or of whimsical chance, but of the necessary consequences of his own consciously committed deeds. Nestroy is speaking in terms of historical inevitability, of certain actions leading in time to predictable results. At the time of the warning it was not too late for Falsch to alter the present and with it his future. Of course the admonition goes unheeded, and Falsch must harvest in his old age what he sowed in his youth: deceit and infidelity.

The image of the wheel of fortune appears several times in different comedies. Nestroy uses the wheel as a warning against complacency on the part of those who have achieved a certain degree of social or monetary status. He was aware that the same favorable circumstances one initially exploits to gain the upper hand will not always be present. Those characters who do not take precautions to safeguard their wealth or who foolishly risk it through irresponsible actions fall on fortune's wheel just as they rose. Thus Lips, *Der Zerrissene,* considers himself insulated by his millions. In a moment of boredom he laments:

> Wenn einem kleinen Buben nix fehlt und er is grantig, so gibt man ihm a paar Braker, und 's is gut. Vielleicht helfet das bei mir auch, aber bei einem Bub'n in meinem Alter müßten die Schläg' vom Schicksal ausgehn, und von da hab' ich nix zu riskier'n; meine Gelder liegen sicher. . . .

It is in this mood of invulnerability that Lips makes a hasty, thoughtless decision to marry the first eligible woman he meets that day. This foolish gamble, which leads to jealousy, combat, and flight from the law, is the cause of Lips's fiasco. Ironically the *Schicksalsschläge* of which he speaks are almost immediately forthcoming. They come, however, in the form of the same nemesis which claimed Rot, Blasius, and Falsch.

Three Nestroy characters merit deeper examination. They represent different social classes: Goldfuchs, the millionaire capitalist; Vinzenz, son of a financially independent

widow; and Wendelin, son of a poor shoemaker. Varied, too, are the specific causes of their misery, but it is all ultimately self-inflicted and blamed on fate. This is the common denominator among disciples of Knieriem, who otherwise defy stereotyping as rich or poor.

Like Lips, Herr von Goldfuchs in *Zu ebener Erde und erster Stock* is extremely self-assured. This comedy, with the subtitle *Die Launen des Glückes,* is particularly germane to our study, because it is Nestroy's most visual representation of the wheel of fortune. Nowhere is this motif so integrated into the plot, language, and even the stage construction as in the tale of the poor Schlucker and rich Goldfuchs families. The vertical division of the stage demonstrates the social and financial gulf between the families as graphically as is theatrically possible, yet Nestroy has placed his principals at opposite points on a giant wheel which completes one half turn by the play's end. To the degree that the Schlucker family rises, the Goldfuchs family falls. This parallelism, which leaves the families always one hundred and eighty degrees from each other, gives the impression that fate is indeed turning the gears. This idea is furthered by fatalistic statements from both families. To the poor family parterre, belief in the wheel of fortune is a consolation: " . . . 's Glück is kugelrund; es kann alles noch anders werd'n," whereas to the millionaire it serves as a rationalization after the fall: "Mein Beispiel gebe warnend euch die Lehre: Fortunas Gunst ist wandelbar." Even the closing chorus of the play reaffirms the general acceptance of cyclical fortune by both families:

> 's Glück treibt's auf Erden gar bunt,
> 's Glück bleibt halt stets kugelrund.

All is not as it seems, however. There is no causal connection between the rise of the poor family and the fall of the rich one. The fortune of the former does not create the misfortune of the latter or vice-versa. Therefore there can be no compelling reason for the parallelism within the plot other than Nestroy's desire to remove any realism and render the comedy parabolic. As P. M. Potter notes [in his "Nestroy's *Zu ebener Erde und erster Stock:* A Reappraisal," *Forum for Modern Language Studies,* 13 (1977), borrowing a page from Brecht, the plot's predictability enables the audience "to concentrate, not on what happens, but on how it is brought about." Since the rise of the Schlucker family depends on very different factors from the fall of the Goldfuchs family, we are compelled to analyze the respective fates as independently motivated, parallel plots with different messages for the audience.

To gain wealth rapidly when one has no assets to begin with requires good fortune. The three incidents which rescue the Schlucker family from despair are unexpected, unearned gifts of Providence. As in *Lumpazivagabundus,* Fortuna has shaken her cornucopia over an unlikely recipient. A coat bought by the second-hand dealer Damian belonged formerly to an English lord and contains a thousand pounds in banknotes. Since Damian does not know about the money before the lord's secretary arrives, he can hardly be seen as having earned the reward for its safe return. Salerl's winning the lottery, the second stroke of luck, is also nothing more than blind chance. Finally, that Adolf's real father turns out to be alive and wealthy is a circumstance over which Schlucker has no control but which he is ready and eager to exploit.

The series of events, amounting to the intervention of a *deus ex machina,* accentuates the fairy-tale nature of the plot. To Nestroy's audience, which identified itself much more with the destitute family than with the millionaires, the Schlucker episode offered considerable satisfaction and even a little hope.

In contrast, luck has much less to do with the ill fortune of the Goldfuchs family, despite protestations to the contrary: "Fortunas Gunst ist wandelbar." Although the incidents which drain Goldfuchs of his millions are misfortunes, they result from character weaknesses. Goldfuchs is a man of few personal accomplishments. By his own admission a "geborener Millionär," he finds as his only source of pride the ability to flaunt and squander his money. In his very first appearance he chides his servant Friedrich for thinking that a gulden per stalk is too high a price for asparagus. Seconds later he orders the same servant to discard a fine batiste handkerchief merely because it had fallen on the floor. Secretly pocketing the handkerchief, Friedrich remarks prophetically: "Ich bin kein Wahrsager, sondern nur ein Bedienter, ich glaub' aber all'weil, ich werd' noch was haben, wenn der einmal nix hat" (VI, 11–12). Goldfuchs' vulnerability to flattery, coupled with a refusal to manage his own money, makes him an easy prey for the conniving servant Johann, who embezzles a notable sum from him. Succinctly stated, Goldfuchs is an incurable squanderer. Unlike Raimund, however, Nestroy has no sympathy for his principal. There is no guardian angel to rescue the spendthrift from himself, only the gloating Johann to heap derision upon misery.

The news that his son has wantonly accrued large debts and has been thrown into prison surprises and horrifies Goldfuchs. What else could he have expected, however, from an offspring he raised and in whom he instilled his own attitude toward money. The character of the son mirrors that of the father in his taste for the good life, his irresponsibility, and his disregard for the value of money. The only element of chance in this disaster is its timing. Otherwise it was inevitable that Goldfuchs would eventually pay dearly for implanting his own values in a young man who lacked independent financial means. Once again nemesis, not bad luck, has claimed a victim. This is not yet the devastating blow, however.

Like Lips, Goldfuchs feels insulated by his wealth. He confidently exclaims: "Eine Million ist eine schußfeste Brustwehr, über welche man stolz hinabblickt, wenn die Truppen des Schicksals heranstürmen wollen." Goldfuchs invests most of his fortune in a ship's cargo, a venture expected to pay a fifty percent dividend. Fortune takes the worst possible turn when the ship sinks. Such an unpredictable natural catastrophe would seem to exonerate Goldfuchs from any responsibility for his loss. Nestroy, however, had a different message in mind for the audience. Johann reminds his master gleefully that carelessness rather than fate has brought him near bankruptcy. Goldfuchs had forgotten, or in his delusion of invulnerability had simply not bothered, to have the cargo insured:

> . . . Aber sagen Sie mir nur, wie kann man so ein Geschäft entrieren zur See ohne Assekuranz?—Für was wären denn die Assekuranzanstalten und für was würden all'weil neue errricht't? . . . Kurzum, Sie haben unüberlegt in den Tag hinein'handelt! Da red't man über die jungen Leut'; ja, derweil machen d' alten, wie Sie sein, so dumme Streich'!

This reprimand, ignored thus far in the interpretation of the comedy, is vital to its understanding, for it points out the precise error which led to the millionaire's downfall. It removes the onus from fate and places it squarely where it belongs.

Goldfuchs' last eighty thousand gulden, a small percentage of his erstwhile fortune, is lost in the collapse of a bank. Admittedly, he had no direct or indirect control over this disaster, but it is doubtful, given his wastefulness, that this amount would have lasted very long. As Johann remarks: " . . . wie Sie dumm spekulieren, werden die 80.000 Gulden auch bald hin sein."

How, then, should Goldfuchs' closing line be interpreted: "Mein Beispiel gebe warnend euch die Lehre: Fortunas Gunst ist wandelbar"? Potter reasons correctly that the comedy does not qualify as a *Besserungsstück,* since there is no positive character development in Goldfuchs. His only recognition at the end is the capriciousness of fate. Nonetheless, we cannot agree with Potter that "one is to interpret these changes as being caused purely by chance." That Goldfuchs lays the blame on "Fortunas Gunst" demonstrates only that he still fails to acknowledge his responsibility, but his credibility as a hapless victim of fate has been breached. His example can only serve to deter others, and it is in this regard that his words: "Mein Beispiel gebe warnend euch die Lehre" are ironically fitting. To the young lovers Adolf and Emilie and to the Schlucker family that has just acquired wealth, it appears to be a warning about the pitfalls of fortune. But to the audience, which has the benefit of a higher perspective, Nestroy is directing a strong warning not to follow Goldfuchs' example and invite nemesis through carelessness and stupidity.

Die beiden Herren Söhne is Nestroy's variation on the story of the prodigal son. Concerning this parable Nestroy confides in his posthumously published aphorisms: "Mir war der verlorene Sohn immer verächtlich, aber nicht deswegen, weil er ein Schweinehirt war, sondern weil er wieder nach Hause gekommen ist." At the beginning of the third act the cousins Vinzenz and Moritz are portrayed as figurative swineherds. They reside in an attic hovel with nothing to eat and only one shirt between them. Both suffer the same consequences despite the great difference in degree of their transgressions. They both eloped: Moritz did so out of what he believed to be true love, whereas Vinzenz eloped out of a sense of adventure and to exact revenge on Suse's father. Moritz turned down a job while still under Pauline's influence because it did not pay enough to meet her lavish demands. Vinzenz refused to work out of sheer laziness and a feeling that his wealth was inexhaustible. After squandering all his mother sent him he landed in debtor's prison. To bail him out his mother had to sell everything she owned.

At this point the Biblical Prodigal Son would go home, thereby incurring Nestroy's indignation. For these two sons, however, there is no going back. In Vinzenz's case there is nothing to which to return. He has squandered the entire prospective inheritance. Although Moritz could return, Nestroy chose to rewrite the parable's ending, which he so detested. Moritz is determined not to go home until he has redeemed himself in his father's eyes.

Vinzenz is clearly one of Knieriem's disciples, infused with the spirit of Lumpazivagabundus. Underlying his wastefulness is an exaggerated *carpe diem* philosophy akin to Knieriem's comet obsession. This is evident, for example, in his derisive tirade against Moritz's father:

> Zorn, Groll, Pläne—und wieder Pläne, Zorn, Groll!—Einmal beerbst ihn doch und tust nach-her, was du willst. So ein zorniger alter Herr soll bedenken, daß er heut' oder morgen mäuserlstad da liegen wird, als Pasquill auf seine Pläne und seinen Groll.

The language is bitter and aggressive. Over-all there is little attempt to make Vinzenz the least bit sympathetic. Far more genial and humorous is Knieriem's expression of the same hedonistic philosophy: "Aufs Jahr geht so die Welt zugrund, da zieh' ich halt noch von einem Weinkeller in den andern herum und führ' so ein zufriednes häusliches Leben."

Vinzenz's answer to the uncertainty in planning for the future is simply not to plan:

> Ich rechne nie! Auf die Art kann 's Schicksal mir auch nie einen Strich durch die Rechnung machen, währenddem man als schlauer Berechner und Planmacher alle Augenblick' den Verdruß erlebt, daß ei'm 's Schicksal das Tintenfaß über die Kalkulationen schüttet. (XII, 373)

He carries the fatalist's belief in the futility of planning a step further. It is not only useless, he contends, but actually dangerous, because the future will retaliate: "Die Zukunft ist eine undankbare Person, die grad nur die quält, die sich recht sorgsam um sie bekümmern." Vinzenz's fatalistic statements have prompted Franz Mautner [in his *Nestroy*, 1974] to write: "Hatte Nestroy sich über das dumme 'Schicksal' schon längst mokiert, so wird nun auf dem Weg über Resignation ein tiefer Degout gegen seine Sinnlosigkeit sichtbar, der in einigen folgenden Stücken an Haß grenzen wird." Yet if Nestroy is proposing resignation in the face of fate's "senselessness," why does he permit Vinzenz to disprove so forcefully with his actions what he is advocating with his words? If only those who plan for the future are victimized by it, then it stands to reason that Vinzenz, who does not plan, should be safe inside his shell of inactivity. Then how does it come about that he is impoverished by the third act of the play? It is precisely his unwillingness to look beyond the immediate moment and safeguard his wealth which forces Vinzenz's otherwise unnecessary ruin. Again, as with Rot, Blasius, Falsch, Lips, and Goldfuchs, the agent is not supernatural fate but predictable nemesis.

Like the other fatalistic characters discussed, Vinzenz

cannot distinguish between nemesis and fate. He betrays this inability in a song in the second act. In stanzas two, three, and four we are confronted by victims of circumstance in satirical episodes where it can be said that the mishaps are not self-imposed. Framing these anecdotes, however, are stanzas one and five, which present situations having little to do with fate. In the first, a man becomes intoxicated before an important ball and ruins his chances for marriage and promotion. In the final stanza, parents try to raise a musical genius from the cradle. They give him an expensive piano and the best teachers for ten years with predictable results: "Statt ein' Wunderkind wird er ein ung'schickter Lack!." The refrain for all five stanzas is:

> Da muß man ein' Zorn krieg'n, 's is wahr,
> Man is rein nur dem Schicksal sein Narr!

Jürgen Hein has correctly noted the significance of the discrepancy between the refrain and the fifth stanza in particular:

> Der Refrain scheint durch die Beglaubigungs-formel "'s is wahr" vordergründig die vergeblichen Anstrengungen gutzuheißen und die Schuld des Schicksals zu bestätigen, hintergründig und in Wahrheit aber enthüllt er den "Narren des Schicksals" als Opfer seiner eigenen Dummheit und Unzulänglichkeit. [*Spiel und Satire in der Komödie Johann Nestroys* 1970]

The stupidity of the man who gets drunk before the ball and especially of the parents who try to create musical genius cannot be overlooked. Yet Vinzenz does overlook it in the song just as he ignores his own repeated stupidity. It is predictable, then, that fate gets the blame when the inevitable consequences of his refusal to plan for the future leave him indigent: "'s Schicksal is ein arabischer Partikulier, wir sein seine Kamel', denen er die Lasten auf 'n Buckel legt."

Were more proof required that Vinzenz is a dedicated disciple of Knieriem with respect to his irresponsibility and rationalization, it could be found in his differing attitudes toward education before and after the disaster. The rich Vinzenz boasts of his successful avoidance of education despite his mother's urgings. In poverty, however, he laments how he was raised to live off his wealth. Proof could also be found in Vinzenz's vilification of his mother for the wrong reason: "Mich kränkt eigentlich gar nix, als daß meine Mama an dem ganzen Elend schuld is." Not the fact that she neglected discipline in his upbringing, but rather that she bailed him out of prison angers him. There he was comfortable and without responsibility. Now in the real world again he is subjected to what he considers to be the whim of fate. Vinzenz is hopelessly dependent on fatalism, not only to justify his manner of life, but also to rationalize its consequences.

In Moritz Nestroy has provided an effective antagonist. Whereas Vinzenz debunks his own philosophy by living it to its disastrous conclusions, Moritz further disproves it by pursuing the opposite ideology successfully. With Moritz Nestroy presents a virtuous character, but one with enough weaknesses to be believable. He, too, is a disobedient son whose first step into independence is a misstep, and whose blind love for a pampered social climber leads him into more mistakes. Nonetheless, he is not afraid to pass up easy solutions and take risks in order to redeem himself in his father's eyes.

Despite Vinzenz's protestations of the injustice of fate, there is only one instance in the play when a character is unjustly victimized by circumstances beyond his control. Ironically that character is Moritz, whose prospects for marriage are ostensibly ruined by Vinzenz's surprise appearance at Steinheim's soirée. As devastating as this setback seems, Moritz does not lose sight of his goals or abandon his principles. He is not under the protection of any supernatural force, such as a guardian spirit, any more than cousin Vinzenz is cursed by something outside of himself. There is no *deus ex machina* at the conclusion. Moritz overcomes his own errors, as well as Vinzenz's meddling, by continuing to strive. His striving, though, does not render him worthy of salvation from above. Instead, Moritz's self-redemption is a strong assertion of a tenet, that Nestroy might have expressed thus:

> Wer immer strebend sich bemüht,
> Der kann sich selbst erlösen.

Nestroy gives us relatively few characters like Moritz, far more like Vinzenz. Thus we might conclude that his world view is nihilistic, his solution resignation and capitulation. Yet there is a simple explanation for an abundance of vagabonds and the irresponsible rich. Disciples of Knieriem provide a much greater opportunity for satire than do the virtuous and successful. It should not be concluded that the author sympathizes or identifies with Vinzenz because he lets him rave on about an irrational universe. He is merely providing him the ammunition with which to shoot down his credibility.

The overly superstitious are another excellent source of grist for Nestroy's satiric mill. "So verfolgt mich mein Schicksal, daß ich nur in der Nacht ausgeh'," complains Wendelin, the unhappy victim of his own gullibility in *Höllenangst*. Yet it is clear from the outset that Wendelin's almost pathological superstitiousness, not fate, is the cause of his unhappiness. Nestroy satirized superstition because he saw it, surely, as an enormous obstacle to the liberation of the lower class from manipulation by the rich and power-hungry. Wendelin and the like-minded Dominik Hauskatz of *Die Papiere des Teufels* both believe they have encountered the devil incarnate. They so fear damnation that they let themselves be used as pawns in illicit intrigues.

It is fitting that Nestroy's most fatalistic monologue should have been given to Wendelin. Full of political satire, the so-called "Schicksalsmonolog" was too controversial to be submitted to the censors. Thus it remained unpublished in Nestroy's lifetime. The fragmentary monologue, which also exists as a more compact "Skizze" and as a song, is an expression of impotent rage against the irrationality and injustice of fate. Wendelin declares war on "den gräulichen Absolutismus des Schicksals," which he believes should be forced to accept a constitution, "daß es Rechenschaft ablegen müßt, sowohl über Verschleuderung als Verweigerung seiner Gaben." He adds,

however, that this endeavor is doomed to failure from the outset. One of his major objections to fate is its unadaptability. It has remained autocratic in an age when people are demanding explanations. Fate is likewise bureaucratic, filing away complaints and leaving them eternally unanswered. The only advantage fate has, we read in the second version of the monologue as well as in the song, is that one can complain about it openly without fearing retribution.

Such an expression of fatalism is in character for Wendelin, who believes that fate has disadvantaged him from birth, and who spends the entire comedy running from an imaginary devil. Yet scholars contend that the monologue is nothing less than Nestroy's own nihilistic confession. Christoph Kuhn writes [in his *Witz und Weltanschauung in Nestroys Auftrittsmonologen*, 1966]: "In keinem Auftrittsmonolog hat Nestroy so viel von sich selbst dargestellt wie im Schicksalsmonolog aus *Höllenangst*. . . . Es ist die Welt von Nestroys eigenen Überzeugungen, die im Schicksalsmonolog angeschnitten wird." Concerning Wendelin's demand for an explanation of the injustice in the world, Hannemann concludes: "Darin liegt der Zweifel Nestroys an der Welt und am Himmel: in her Ungerechtigkeit des Schicksals gegenüber dem individuellen Glücksstreben." Hans Weigel considers Wendelin the prototype of the Nestroy revolutionary, referring to him as "der Rebell schlechthin, der Mensch im Widerstand gegen die irdischen Dinge und das, was höherenorts für sie verantwortlich ist" [*Johann Nestroy*, 1912].

Undoubtedly some of the author's own beliefs come through in the monologue. The fact that an accident of birth could determine one's wealth or poverty certainly bothered Nestroy. The bitter dichotomy between rich and poor is a recurring theme throughout his works. Wendelin, though, responds to the seeming irrationality of the situation with despair. As he withdraws into paranoia, his fatalism and superstitiousness deepen. Is this retreat into despair the course which Nestroy endorses, as Diehl asserts ("Nur diesen Zweifel hat der Mensch, dem unberechenbaren Schicksal entgegenzusetzen")? Is it another example of the Sisyphean struggle that Nestroy constantly, though hopelessly, wages against fate, as Preisner contends? Most likely it is neither.

It seems improbable that Nestroy would suddenly justify and glorify a character flaw which he had so often ridiculed. Knieriem imbibes his way through two comedies, denying responsibility for his comportment while laying the blame on the elusive comet. Rot, Blasius, Falsch, Lips, Goldfuchs, and Vinzenz are all fatalistic enough to be blind to their own faults. In each case we are shown the precise error and how it could have been avoided. Yet somehow we are supposed to believe that the defiant fatalist of *Höllenangst* is the mirror of Nestroy's soul. The fact is that Wendelin exhibits the same character flaw as all the others, although, with the exception of Knieriem, he goes about it more systematically. The paradox of Wendelin is that while he is frustrated by his inability to fathom the injustice in the world, he nevertheless draws considerable comfort and security from his feeling of unaccountability. His fatalism shields him from the reality of personal responsibility, which he steadfastly refuses to face:

I laß mir mein' Aberglaub'n
Durch ka Aufklärung raub'n.

Thus he runs from the devil, while unknown to him and in spite of him people in the real world are unraveling the plot and solving his family's problems.

The monologue's more compact variant in Nestroy's sketch ends with the lines, "Nur eins hat das Schicksal vor den irdischen Tyrannen voraus, nehmlich das, daß man ungeniert darüber schimpfen kann, es nutzt eim zwar gar nix, aber man wird doch wenigstens zu keiner Verantwortung gezogen, und es is das schon eine schöne Sach'." It is important to Wendelin not to be called to account, either to temporal authority or to his own conscience. For him fate, or the belief in it, is indeed "eine schöne Sach'." It is a fruitless one, however, for it leads to no positive result: "Da droben is kein Fortschritt zu hoffen."

Kuhn labels Wendelin "ein 'G'scheiter', ein Wissender und ein Zweifelnder." Weigel, borrowing a term from Rommel, calls him: "eine[n] von Nestroys 'geistreichen Dummköpfen.' " The latter designation is more accurate, if we change the emphasis from the adjective to the noun. Despite his literary allusions and complicated logic, Wendelin fails to comprehend the obvious. If no progress is to be hoped for from above, and if all protests are futile, then the logical conclusion should not be difficult to draw. Merely complaining about one's fate is a waste of energy, regardless of the temporary relief it might bring. Responsible corrective and, where possible, preventive action is the solution, but only after the first step, which is enlightenment. This is a step which Wendelin refuses to take.

"'s Schicksal paßt nicht für unsere Zeit," claims the refrain of the song based on the ideas of the monologue and intended for a later comedy. Fate is no longer valid for our time. It has outlived its usefulness and should be replaced by a philosophy of human responsibility for human actions. This, of course, would mean a return to the ideals of the Enlightenment and an end to Biedermeier complacency.

As we have seen, Nestroy's comedies represent a satirical counterpoint to the Biedermeier refrain of man's puppet-like existence. Nestroy has cut the strings from the arms and legs of his characters. No longer marionettes of fate, they are forced to stand on their own despite their resistance. The message from all the disciples of Knieriem, even the most hopelessly afflicted, is ultimately that expressed so candidly by Gottlieb Herb: "Wir sind jetzt weit mehr auf die Welt reduziert, an etwas Irdisches muß man sich jetzt anklammern." (pp. 469-87)

> *Roger A. Crockett, "Disciples of Knieriem: A Reappraisal of Nestroy's Philosophy of Fate," in* The Journal of English and Germanic Philology, *Vol. LXXXII, No. 4, October, 1983, pp. 469-87.*

Craig Decker (essay date 1987)

[*In the following essay, Decker investigates Nestroy's use of language as a means of subverting the oppressive cultural power of social elites in nineteenth-century Austrian society.*]

The *Vorstadt-* or *Volkstheater,* which constituted an integral part of Viennese cultural life during the late eighteenth and early nineteenth centuries, functioned as an independent alternative to the theatrical politics of the Burgtheater. The monarchy both subsidized and determined the Burgtheater's program. It established strict guidelines for controlling the selection of texts as well as their eventual performance. A sense of "refinement" was of primary importance in this selection and staging process. Concerning the "Lustspiel," for example, the Burgtheater statute of 1779 dictated: "Die Sprache sei von der Natur, aber nicht vom Pöbel genommen." The Burgtheater's audience was analogously "nicht vom Pöbel genommen." The economically and socially privileged attended the Kaiser's theater for the glory of art and the monarchy, while representatives of the remaining social classes were conspicuously absent. As Kurt Kahl states in his study of the Burgtheater [*Die Wiener und ihr Burgtheater,* 1974], "Wer deutsch unterhalten werden wollte, ging zum Hanswurst." Hence, the *Volksstück* originated as a response to dissatisfaction with the institutionalized theater of the feudal aristocracy. The genre thus provided the Viennese public sphere with a potential corrective to the state's theatrical hegemony.

In contrast to the classical repertoire of the Burgtheater, the *Vorstadttheater* presented dramas with a more topical and local appeal. Unlike the texts of high theater, the *Volksstücke* existed for all classes. Consequently, the productions were intended to be both thematically accessible and economically affordable to a broad and diverse audience. Reinhard Urbach points to a fundamental difference between the two forms of theater when he writes: "Im Innern der Stadt, in der Hofburg, war das Theater Tempel geworden. Kunst wurde zelebriert. . . . Heilige Ruhe herrschte durch Verbote." The *Volkstheater,* in contrast, "kam . . . dem Publikum entgegen. Hier war das Theater Forum." The socially diverse audience of the *Volkstheater* reflected the egalitarian impulse inherent in the institution's origins. An edition of the *Zeitung für die elegante Welt* from 1804 describes the spectators in the following manner: " . . . hier das Parterre von wohlgenährten fröhlichen Bürgern, die Logen von Personen höheren Ranges [besetzt], die Galerie von arbeitsmüden Menschen der untersten Klassen gefüllt . . ." Artisans, shopkeepers, petty merchants, lower civil servants and members of the working class comprised the majority of the audience. Because the state did not subsidize the *Volkstheater,* the institution depended directly upon its patrons for economic survival. Public opinion, therefore, played a significant role in determining the repertoire. With regard to the impact of the *Vorstadttheater* during the early 1800's, Volker Klotz [in his *Dramaturgie des Publikums,* 1976] writes: "Nirgends sonst in deutschen Sprachgebieten, weder früher noch später, nimmt Theater einen derart großen Raum ein im Freizeitleben seiner Zuschauer; nirgends sonst unterhält es mit ihnen so lebhaften Verkehr."

Despite the popular appeal of the Viennese *Volksstück,* or perhaps even because of it, literary historians have generally concurred with Karl Goedeke's dismissal of the genre in 1881 as "das regional begrenzte, dialektgebundene, anspruchslose, 'bloß' unterhaltende, 'triviale' Lokalstück auf der 'Schaubühne ohne ideale Ansprüche' " [Quoted in Jürgen Hein, "Das Volksstück. Entwicklung und Tendenzen," in *Theater und Gesselschaft: Das Volksstück im 19. und 20. Jahrhundert,* ed. Jürgen Hein, 1973]. Typical references to the *Volksstück* of this period point to its "naive imaginative plots and sly moralizing," presented in the form of "charming and whimsical musical comedies" abounding in "melancholy gentleness" [Werner P. Friedrich, *History of German Literature,* 2nd. ed., 1961]. According to Gerd Müller, the concept of the "traditional 'Volksstück' " largely engenders connotations of "eine Form des leichten Unterhaltungstheaters, das sich auf klischeehafte Problemgestaltung, humorige Verwicklungen und dialektal gefärbte Sprache eingestellt hat."

Critics who perceive the genre in these terms, however, fail to recognize the revolutionary and democratic potential of the *Volksstück,* a potential albeit not fully realized until Nestroy. Indeed, the very fact that a forum for entertainment was being provided to the broad masses as opposed to a select elite indicates a movement toward the democratization of culture. The use of dialect in the theater may have represented a "lack of refinement" in relation to the aesthetically polished language of the classical theater. However, within the socio-historical context of the cultural needs of the people, it provided a representative voice. Nevertheless, in what I would like to characterize as the initial phase of the *Volkstheater,* the revolutionary potential of the theater was not fully actualized in the dramas of such authors as Gleich, Bäuerle and Raimund. These writers tended to ignore the public sphere and concentrate almost exclusively on the private realm of bourgeois life.

Raimund's *Der Alpenkönig und der Menschenfeind* (premiered in 1828) exemplifies the thematic concern of the *Volksstück* of the early 1800's with the necessity for individual as opposed to social transformation. Rappelkopf, the drama's protagonist and an apparently incurable misanthrope, tyrannizes his wife, daughter, and servants. Despite their repeated attempts to alter his behavior, Rappelkopf continues in his oppressive severity. When the Alpenkönig descends from the mountains, however, Rappelkopf's character undergoes a total transformation. The mythical figure subjects the misanthrope to a series of natural and psychological disasters: lightning, flood, and the reappearance of Rappelkopf's three dead wives. The ultimate horror, however, occurs when the Alpenkönig magically transforms himself into Rappelkopf. In taking on the mannerisms, attitudes, and physical characteristics of the protagonist, the Alpenkönig functions as a mirror. The image sufficiently terrifies Rappelkopf and eventually leads to his cure.

In *Der Alpenkönig und der Menschenfeind,* the necessity for change is placed squarely on the individual's shoulders. Raimund depicts the social structure, by contrast, as an absolute and unchangeable entity. Erich Joachim May is largely correct in characterizing the political tendencies of the *Volksstück* at this time in the following manner [in his *Wiener Volkskomödie und Vormärz,* 1975]: "Nicht die Verhältnisse sind veränderbar, sondern nur der Mensch durch die 'erkannte' Einsicht in bestehende Zustände." In this respect, the texts tend to reflect the sentiments of Raimund's "erster Alpengeist": "Doch es kann nichts Schönres geben / als auf Alpenspitzen schweben."

On one level, the bourgeois retreat into the individual domain affirms existing political structures. Klotz and May have suggested that an ideology commensurate with the restorative aims of the Austro-Hungarian monarchy informs the *Volksstücke* of this period. This view, however, is only partially correct, since it discounts the movement towards bourgeois self-criticism embodied in these texts. Rappelkopf does indeed change, illustrating that the individual is not bound up in a predetermined existence. The transformation of his personality, in turn, improves the conditions within his household. Like the domestic milieu in the *bürgerliches Trauerspiel,* the household in Raimund's text represents a microcosm of social organization. It follows then that the *Volksstücke* of this period implicitly indicate the possibility of social transformation, even though these texts maintain a rigid public/private dichotomy.

The appearance of Nestroy's texts marks the second phase of the *Volksstück.* The limitations of his predecessors' contributions are also the preconditions for Nestroy's transformation of them. Gleich, Bäuerle, and Raimund succeeded in establishing a theater intended for and supported by the broad masses. Nestroy subsequently transcended the initial boundaries of the genre by politicizing the private sphere and extending the possibility of transformation into the public sector. His texts thus represent the first full realization of the *Volksstück*'s revolutionary potential.

Nestroy scholars, highly influenced by Karl Kraus, have largely failed to recognize the political dimensions of Nestroy's transformation of the genre. "Nestroy als Meister eines Welttheaters," Hans Mayer has remarked, "das bleibt undenkbar ohne Karl Kraus." In rescuing Nestroy for subsequent generations, Kraus also unfortunately established a problematic and misleading framework for the reception of Nestroy's texts. In his 1912 essay, "Nestroy und die Nachwelt," Kraus examines the continuing validity of Nestroy's dramas. He condemns the impulse towards "Unterhaltung" which he perceives in Nestroy's predecessors, while praising the artistic value of Nestroy's *Volksstücke.* Underlying Kraus's valorization, however, is a disdain for politics and a condemnation of socially engaged literature. He delivers his indictment by contrasting Heine's poetry (synonymous with "das Politische" and "das Unwahre") with Nestroy's satires ("das Menschliche," "das Wahre"). The former represents "die falsche Lyrik"—i.e. that type of literature which responds to and remains within its concrete political context. "Trapped" in the deceit of politics, Heine's poetry perpetuates mendacious political thought and results in "intellektuelle Scheinwerte." Nestroy, on the other hand, rises above the "limitations" of socially engaged literature. His texts, according to Kraus, do not negate concrete political circumstances, but rather politics as a whole: "Ja, er hat den politischen Beruf ergriffen—wie ein Wächter den Taschendieb. Und nicht die Lächerlichkeiten innerhalb der Politik lockten seine Aufmerksamkeit, sondern die Lächerlichkeit der Politik." Kraus commends Nestroy's "volle Inaktualität." Compared to Heine, Nestroy presents a "truer" form of art, grounded in an apolitical depiction of "das Menschliche."

Kraus extends his praise of Nestroy by citing the dramatist's linguistic achievements: "Nestroy ist der erste deutsche Satiriker, in dem sich die Sprache Gedanken macht über die Dinge." Nestroy's thematization of language represents a substantial contribution to the development of the *Volksstück.* Kraus, however, stresses the aesthetic form of Nestroy's language and thus deemphasizes its social content. Indeed, Kraus identifies language as the very means by which Nestroy's texts transcend political reality: "sie ["die wahre Sprache der Lyrik," synonymous with "die Sprache der Satire," which Kraus then equates with "Nestroys Sprache"] ist nie polemisch, immer schöpferisch." Hence, according to Kraus, Nestroy's *Volksstücke* present a linguistic metacritique and achieve their validity through their self-reflexive language games: "Hier lacht sich die Sprache selbst aus." The metacritique of language, Kraus asserts, parallels Nestroy's metaliterary critiques. Severed from their socio-historical context (one referred to disdainfully by Kraus as "der soziale Punkt"), Nestroy's satires are not relevant as critiques of social reality, but rather as satires about satire. The legacy of Kraus's "timelessly aesthetic" evaluation of Nestroy continues to inform Nestroy criticism, as the following passage from Franz H. Mautner's 1974 study of [*Nestroy*] illustrates: "Denn Nestroy war von jeher jener echteste aller Satiriker, dem es nicht um vorwiegend zeitgebundene Übelstände und gewiß nicht um individuelle Fälle zu tun ist, sondern um Durchdringung der ewigen menschlichen Art . . . "

Critics such as Kraus and Mautner have concentrated on Nestroy's linguistic skill and ignored the political critique emerging from it. Ödön von Horváth, who began to employ the *Volksstück* himself in the late 1920's, sensed a more historically bound emphasis in Nestroy's linguistic concerns. In a letter dated three months before his death in 1938, Horváth wrote: "Gott, was sind das für Zeiten! Die Welt ist voller Unruhe, alles drunter und drüber, und noch weiß man nichts Gewisses! Man müßte ein Nestroy sein, um all das definieren zu können, was einem undefiniert im Wege steht!" Horváth's emphasis on Nestroy's ability to define things clearly points to the interrelationship between Nestroy's linguistic and political critiques. Nestroy's thematization of language does not remain solely within the boundaries of the linguistic system itself. It also explores and comments upon that which is "undefined," namely the complex of material reality and social relations which, although mediated through language, is not exclusively constituted by it.

Unlike Kraus, Horváth recognized the integral relationship between form and content, and the way in which language could be used as a means of social criticism. Indeed, an understanding of Nestroy's texts presupposes an understanding of how language functions. Language is not the autonomous aesthetic object Kraus posits, but rather a so-cial medium providing the means for interpersonal exchange and communication. It functions to identify and structure a given community of speakers on the one hand, and to offer a common means for expressing changes within that community on the other. The dialectic which exists between the linguistic system and its cultural context also operates, as speech act theory has demonstrated, upon individual linguistic formulations and their specific contexts:

> The speech act, as a unit of communication, must not only organize the signs but also condition the way in which these signs are to be received. Speech acts are not just sentences. They are linguistic utterances in a given situation or context, and it is through this context that they take on their meaning. [Wolfgang Iser, *The Act of Reading*, 1978].

The context of a specific utterance, however, often negates the possibility of an "ideal speech act"—i.e. one that is free of constraints. The social structures informing dialogue frequently prohibit the participants' equal access to "constative speech acts," that is, those which assert, contest, or deny. Central to Nestroy's exploration of language is his thematization of dialogic constraints. His *Volksstücke* reflect a highly class-conscious society. The rising bourgeoisie challenges a socially and economically decaying aristocracy, while, at the other end of the social hierarchy, the conditions for the formation of a *Kleinbürgertum* and a proletariat are emerging. The social codes governing appearance, behavior and, most importantly, class status have become reified. Rummelpuff, the commander of Krähwinkel's soldiers in *Freiheit in Krähwinkel* (1848), articulates the ways in which individual human worth is socially determined: "Der Mensch fängt erst beim Baron an." The social exclusions which the aristocracy establishes are reinforced through corresponding linguistic exclusions. The "inhuman status" of the lower classes restricts their employment possibilities. Their respective jobs, in turn, restrict their language. The following example from *Der Unbedeutende* (1846), in which Franz, "ein Bedienter," and Rumpf, "ein Schloßwächter," discuss the dubious character of the Baron's secretary, Puffman, illustrates the mechanisms through which social hierarchies translate into linguistic exclusions:

> FRANZ. Wenn man da den Herrn Puffmann dreinbringen könnt', diesen—ich mag gar nicht sagen, wer er ist—
>
> RUMPF. Ruhig, er ist mein Büro-Chef, mir tut's Herz weh, wenn wer über ihn schimpft, weil ich in meiner Stellung nicht nach Gusto mitschimpfen kann.

Throughout their interchange, Rumpf repeatedly reminds Franz what his official station prohibits him from doing and saying. The internal controls which language exercises over speech and silence increase when speech remains externally controlled by social class.

In his texts, Nestroy exposes the various levels of language associated with different social roles and illustrates the relative nature of each. In *Der böse Geist Lumpazivagabundus oder Das liederliche Kleeblatt* (1833), for example, the "vazierende Handwerksburschen" Zwirn and Knieriem are illiterate because they have had no formal education. They cannot read and hence cannot gain access to most sectors of social experience. Despite their inability to act upon the written word, however, they are able to use spoken language to disrupt society's power over them. In fact, their socially marginal position allows them a freedom to agitate through language, a freedom not always available to more elevated social roles.

At one point, Hobelmann reads a letter from his son-in-law to the two journeymen. Zwirn and Knieriem conceal their illiteracy by appealing to Hobelmann's elitism:

> ZWIRN. Sie werden wissen, ein Unterschied der Stände *muß* sein.—Sie sind Meister, wir zwei Gesellen—*ihm den offenen Brief reichend:* lesen *Sie!*
>
> HOBELMANN. Recht gern will ich euch den Gefallen tun. *Liest:* "Liebe Freunde und Brüder! Wie gern wär' ich heute bei Euch—aber—"
>
> ZWIRN. Ehre dem Ehre gebührt.
>
> . . . . .
>
> HOBELMANN. Jetzt sei Er einmal ruhig. *Liest:* "Wie gern wär' ich heute bei Euch, aber meine traurige Lage macht es unmöglich. Ich bin krank—"
>
> ZWIRN. Da sollten S' doch mit ein Doktor reden.
>
> HOBELMANN. Warum denn?
>
> ZWIRN. Sie sagen ja, Sie sein krank.
>
> HOBELMANN. Das schreibt ja der Leim, der ist krank.
>
> ZWIRN. Ja, von wem ist denn der Brief?
>
> HOBELMANN. Von Leim.
>
> KNIERIEM. Von Leim.
>
> ZWIRN. Ah so—von Leim.
>
> HOBELMANN *Liest weiter.* "Ich bin krank und liege in Nürnberg im Spital—"
>
> ZWIRN. Herr Hobelmann, foppen müssen S' mich nicht! ich kann auch grob sein. Wie können S' denn sagen, Sie liegen in Nürnberg im Spital, und stehen da neben meiner.
>
> HOBELMANN. Aber den Brief schreibt ja der Leim.
>
> KNIERIEM. Der Leim.
>
> ZWIRN. Ah so—der Leim.

Although Zwirn and Knieriem initially asked Hobelmann to read them the letter, they continually interrupt him to his chagrin. Through their disruption of the situation, the problem of context emerges. The statement, "Ich bin krank und liege in Nürnberg im Spital—," is perfectly logical if understood within the context of the letter. It appears to contradict itself, however, if Hobelmann's reading of Leim's words is mistaken for Hobelmann's own

words. Zwirn and Knieriem's recontextualization ruptures the textual system within which the letter was written and intended to be received. Equally significant is the fact that by creating such confusion the two journeymen also momentarily destroy an apparently closed social system. Hobelmann becomes so disgusted with their antics that he is no longer able to maintain the superiority which, due to his social status, he should rightfully possess.

Language itself is not the agent which creates or prohibits social equality. Its social application, however, as well as the conditions underlying its use, will determine whether language is to function as an instrument to achieve and maintain political freedom or, as Habermas states [in his "Zu Gadamers *Wahrheit und Methode*," in Apel, et. al., *Hermeneutik und Ideologiekritik,* 1971], "ein Medium von Herrschaft und sozialer Macht," which serves to legitimate institutionalized oppression. In the remainder of this paper I will investigate Nestroy's thematization of language as a means of establishing, maintaining, or subverting social power, using examples from *Der Talisman* (1840) and *Freiheit in Krähwinkel* and concentrating on the socially critical dimensions of Nestroy's *Volksstücke.*

. . . . .

> MELCHIOR. O an den Ort, wo ich war, das war ein klassischer Kaffee.
>
> ZANGLER. Was hat Er denn immer mit dem dummen Wort klassisch?
>
> MELCHIOR. Ah, das Wort is nit dumm, es wird nur oft dumm angewend't.

Nestroy,
Einen Jux will er sich machen

In Nestroy's texts, the aristocracy strives to maintain its economic and political superiority by controlling the stringent behavioral codes regarding dress, demeanor, and speech. These codes, however, provide the very preconditions for the abundant role changing characteristic of Nestroy's texts. The social structure, despite its outward rigidity, does allow for social mobility if one is able to recognize and exploit the relative viability of existing institutions. Nestroy's farce *Der Talisman* demonstrates how his texts subvert social structures by turning their operative codes against themselves. Nestroy's spokesman in *Der Talisman* is Titus Feuerfuchs who, on account of his physical characteristics, is defined by society as an outsider. His red hair, which runs counter to the prevailing norms of outward appearance, segregates him from the closed social system. Through an accident, however, he is able to infiltrate and then advance within it. In Act One, Titus rescues the runaway wagon of the "Friseur" Monsieur Marquis. After the two characters have discussed the circumstances leading to the event, the conversation shifts to the issue of remuneration:

> MARQUIS *Aufstehend:* Ihr Edelmut setzt mich in Verlegenheit; ich weiß nicht, wie ich meinen Dank,—mit Geld läßt sich so eine Tat nicht lohnen—
>
> TITUS. Oh, ich bitt', Geld ist eine Sache, die—

MARQUIS. Die einen Mann von solcher Den-
kungsart nur beleidigen würde.

TITUS. Na, jetzt sehen Sie,—das heißt—

MARQUIS. Das heißt den Wert Ihrer Tat verken-
nen, wenn man sie durch eine Summe aufwiegen
wollte.

TITUS. Es kommt halt drauf an—

MARQUIS. Wer eine solche Tat vollführt.

Here it becomes clear that it is not only a question of who
completes the act, but who completes the sentence as well.
Marquis, continually interrupting Titus, frustrates the latter's constative attempts to assert, deny, or contest. The
monetary debate is thus decided to Marquis' advantage,
since he establishes and dominates the communicative situation.

Although Titus does not receive the financial reward he
desires, Marquis does give him a black wig, as well as some
very helpful advice: "die gefällige äußere Form macht
viel—beinahe alles." These gifts allow Titus to conceal his
true physical identity and enter the society which had previously excluded him. As an outsider, Titus was able to examine the operative social codes. He now adopts them,
subverting the system from within. He recognizes the necessity of manipulating these codes convincingly in order
to get ahead in the world. The most important element for
Titus, however, if his ruse is to succeed, is masterful manipulation of language. Titus is well aware of the power
of speech. An imperious command of language enables
him to draw attention to his speech and thus conceal those
personal attributes which do not comply with accepted social patterns. In his conversation with Salome at the beginning of the drama, Titus displays his ability to exploit the
connotative possibilities of words:

SALOME. Ich versteh' Ihnen net, aber Sie reden
so schön daher—Wer ist denn Ihr Vater?

TITUS. Er ist gegenwärtig ein verstorbener
Schulmeister.

SALOME. Das ist schön. Und ihre Frau Mut-
ter?—

TITUS. War vor ihr'm Tod längere Zeit seine Ge-
mahlin.

SALOME. Ah, das ist schön.

TITUS *Für sich.* Die find't alles schön, ich kann
so dumm daherreden als ich will.

When a society places such emphasis on outer form, one
can easily deceive through language. An impressive formulation, whose contents may be self-contradictory, redundant, or even nonsensical, remains unchallenged. Language, Titus discovers, provides an effective means to gain
and maintain power. The protagonist uses this tool to his
advantage throughout the farce.

As a result of his transformed physical appearance and his
masterful talent for linguistic transformations, Titus finds
a job at the estate of Frau von Cypressenburg. Within the
new social milieu the black-wigged protagonist first encounters the gardener, whose name, appropriately

enough, is Flora. Titus, a "vazierender Barbiergeselle,"
knows absolutely nothing about gardening. By generating
abundant horticultural metaphors, however, he conceals
his ignorance and gives the appearance of extensive experience in the field. Upon first meeting Titus, Flora asks
him about his background:

FLORA. Er ist also—?

TITUS. Ein exotisches Gewächs, nicht auf diesen
Boden gepflanzt, durch die Umstände aus-
gerissen, und durch den Zufall in das freundli-
che Gartengeschirr Ihres Hauses versetzt, und
hier, von der Sonne Ihrer Huld beschienen, hofft
die zarte Pflanze Nahrung zu finden.

Flora disregards his rhetorical embellishments and mat-
ter-of-factly inquires as to Titus's knowledge of gardening.
Avoiding a direct reply, Titus says, "Ich habe Men-
schenkenntnis, folglich auch Pflanzenkenntnis." The re-
tort puzzles Flora, and she requests further explanation.
Titus then embarks on a lengthy excursus in which he
equates the routines of human beings with the existence
of plants, introducing his remarks with the words: "Wer
Menschen kennt, der kennt auch die Vegetabilien, weil
nur sehr wenig Menschen leben, und viele unzählige aber
nur vegetieren." Seeking to conceal his incompetence,
Titus once again exploits the connotative possibilities of
language. Yet his statement does not lack content: it fur-
thers his job prospects and simultaneously indicts the monotony and intellectual deprivation resulting from an exclusively work-oriented existence. The compulsion to produce ultimately leads to the most unproductive results:
"was ich von die Millionär weiß, so führen fast alle aus
millionär'scher Gewinn- und Vermehrungspassion ein so
fades, trockenes Geschäftsleben, was kaum den blühenden
Namen 'Vegetation' verdient." Titus's response is typical
of Nestroy's double-edged use of language. A specific situation (Titus's attempt to demonstrate gardening expertise)
engenders specific forms of speech (garden metaphors).
On one level these figures address the concrete situation.
At the same time, however, they also transcend it, creating
a more encompassing context for the author's social criticism.

As a result of his verbal aplomb, Titus gets the job. Flora's
interest in his gardening abilities equals her interest in him
as a potential replacement for her deceased husband. She
offers to exchange Titus's tattered clothes for the gardener's uniform of her former spouse. The protagonist willingly accepts the clothing. His attire, as well as his speech,
are now more commensurate with his new social role. Yet
Titus has little desire to remain within the estate's lower
ranks. During a subsequent conversation with Flora, Constantina enters the room. Constantina, the "Kammerfrau"
of Frau von Cypressenburg's daughter, is likewise a
widow. Titus quickly realizes that the maid represents a
more direct line of communication to the seat of power.
He promptly takes advantage of the situation, hoping to
advance even further. His dark hair and his flattering
speech endear him instantly to Constantina. As his new
partner, Constantina likewise offers him new clothes.
Titus replaces the gardener's uniform of Flora's former
husband with the hunting uniform of Constantina's de-

ceased spouse. A transformed outer appearance once again leads to transformed speech. Titus complements his new outfit by generating hunting metaphors.

Through Constantina, Titus does come into direct contact with Frau von Cypressenburg. Before his long-awaited meeting with her, however, is a series of farcical encounters which endanger his social ambitions. If he is to be successful, Titus must conceal himself from those characters aware of his true physical characteristics. Salome and Plutzerkern, who knew Titus before he received the wig from Marquis, are both in a position to compromise him. When they enter the house, however, Titus camouflages his identity as convincingly as his language conceals his background. Yet when Marquis pays a visit to the estate and discovers that his beloved Constantina has her heart set on the new arrival, Titus's plans appear to be ruined. The "Friseur" takes revenge upon the rival by removing the black wig while Titus sleeps. The protagonist awakes and begins to dress for his initial meeting with Frau von Cypressenburg. Upon seeing himself in the mirror, and discovering that his wig is missing, Titus exits in a fit of desperation.

Titus remedies the loss by finding a blond wig. Thus when he finally encounters Frau von Cypressenburg, he has undergone yet another physical transformation. The elevated social context of the rendezvous requires yet another level of language. The owner of the estate fancies herself to be a writer. In an aside Titus reminds himself he must speak in a manner consonant with Frau von Cypressenburg's station: "Ich stehe jetzt einer Schriftstellerin gegenüber, da tun's die Alltagsworte nicht, da heißt's jeder Red' ein Feiertagsg'wand'l anziehen." Once again Titus must discuss a subject about which he knows absolutely nothing. As was the case when he conversed about gardening and hunting, however, Titus succeeds in projecting the appearance of knowledge through masterful linguistic formulations. Frau von Cypressenburg asks Titus whether his father is also a hunter. He responds: "Nein, er betreibt ein stilles, abgeschiedenes Geschäft, bei dem die Ruhe das einzige Geschäft ist; er liegt von höherer Macht gefesselt, und doch ist er frei und unabhängig, denn er ist Verweser seiner selbst:—er ist tot." Titus's explanations impress the woman. They also satirically condemn the laziness of her class. Titus criticizes the aristocracy's "stilles, abgeschiedenes Geschäft" from a bourgeois standpoint. Since work represents the highest virtue and legitimation of bourgeois existence, an idle aristocracy appears as decrepit, indeed moribund. Titus denounces the upper class's self-serving use of Christian doctrine. The notion of a "höhere Macht" legitimizes a hierarchical social structure which allows the aristocracy to remain "frei und unabhängig," i.e. "nicht leibeigen." His twofold use of "Verweser" sharpens his critique. The word refers to the political role of the aristocracy (e.g. "Reichsverweser"), while simultaneously condemning its present uselessness and decay. Frau von Cypressenburg, however, like most characters in the text, ignores the content of his speech and concentrates solely on its rhetorical qualities. Her reaction reveals how "pleasing form," the regulator of social reality, also underlies the dominant aesthetic: "Wie verschwenderisch er mit zwanzig erhabenen Worten das sagt, was man mit einer Silbe

sagen kann. Der Mensch hat offenbare Anlagen zum Literaten." In referring to Titus's literary abilities, Frau von Cypressenburg implicitly equates the literati with pretentiousness. Her characterization of the prevailing literary praxis inadvertently criticizes the pomposity of those writers who use a profusion of words to say nothing. Because of her own predilection for verbal excess, she immediately engages Titus as a personal secretary. While she remains ignorant of her self-incriminating words and actions, Nestroy uses her as a vehicle to indict overblown "artistic expression."

With his new job, Titus culminates his rapid ascension of the social hierarchy. A command of "die gefällige äußere Form" has enabled him to advance from an impoverished, outcast apprentice to a fashionable personal secretary. At the beginning of the farce Titus was refused employment at the estate. Now he has considerable influence over the hiring and firing of the domestic personnel. Titus succeeds because the shallowness and self-flattery of the upper class prevent it from recognizing his manipulations. Nestroy censures a society blinded by "pleasing form" and thus incapable of perceiving the gap between appearance and reality. What transpires when such contradictions are exposed informs Nestroy's *Freiheit in Krähwinkel,* a drama which does not investigate the nature of individual mobility but rather the dynamics of social transformation.

In his satirical depiction of political subjugation and revolt, Nestroy explores the dialectical relationship between language and domination. He thematizes how speech can be used to conceal the nature of a specific material conflict. At the same time, however, he also investigates how language can function as a critique of ideology and expose the nature of that very conflict. Nestroy situates the drama in a small town whose name signals its isolation and backwardness. Krähwinkel's inhabitants have been living in peaceful subjugation for years. The city administration has effectively maintained social, political, and economic control. The revolutionary ideals of 1848, having already led to democratic reforms in Vienna, will ultimately infiltrate the remote Krähwinkel as well. When the play begins, it is clear that the absolutist idyll faces a considerable challenge.

The ensuing conflict involves the demand for a democratic system (advocated most prominently by the Nachtwächter and Ultra) to replace Krähwinkel's absolutist regime. The Bürgermeister, who heads the oppressive city government, maintains his tyranny through an elite cadre of officials. Rummelpuff, the commander of the city's troops, and Reakzerl Edler von Zopfen, Krähwinkel's "geheimer Stadtsekretär," guarantee total military and administrative support for the Bürgermeister. Equally vital to the regime's existence, however, is the cooperation of Pfiffspitz, the editor of Krähwinkel's only newspaper. His acquiescence to governmental censorship enables the administration to control not only the socio-political system of the city, but also its sole source of information.

From an administrative standpoint, it is necessary to deny the city's inhabitants access to information that would reveal the truth about Krähwinkel's political functioning. Although the populace does not have access to the press, they can demonstrate publicly. Governmental control, however, aims to suppress this form of political activity as well. The Bürgermeister, addressing a crowd of rebellious Krähwinkler who have gathered in front of his home, reminds them—not without irony—of his tactics of domination: "Meine lieben Krähwinkler, da ich dazu auserkoren bin, an eurer Spitze zu stehen, hab' ich euch stets nach Möglichkeit stumpf zu machen gesucht." The publicly declared policy of "Stumpfmachen" censors both printed and spoken utterances. By depriving the populace of the means of public expression, the administration insures political inequality in the city.

Within the limits of the oppressive social structure, the government employs a political rhetoric dependent upon public misunderstanding achieved through officially encouraged literalism. The play's opening dialogue provides an extreme example of this process:

> NACHTWACHTER. Anders muß's wern, und anders wird's wern, die Zeiten der Finsternis sind einmal vorbei.
>
> PEMPERL. Wenn d' Finsternis abkummt, können d' Nachtwächter alle Tag verhungern.
>
> NACHTWACHTER. Hör auf, Klampferer, mit deine blechenen G'spaß. Wir sitzen hier versammelt, als Kern der Krähwinkler Bürgerschaft, und da kann nur von einer Geistesfinsternis die Red' sein.

In response to Pemperl's literal interpretation of the word "Finsternis," the Nachtwächter points to the fact that "wir sitzen hier versammelt," emphasizing the concrete context of their present democratic gathering as a model for Krähwinkel's future political organization. Pemperl's allusion to the Nachtwächter's immediate needs reflects the material origins of the revolutionary discontent. At the same time, his response also illustrates the crippling effects of the administration's rhetorical strategies upon the populace. Pemperl is unable to recognize the Nachtwächter's use of "Finsternis" as a metaphor. He automatically interprets the word literally—a reaction which raises a central issue in all of Nestroy's texts: the literal versus the metaphorical significance of words. Since metaphors express alternative modes of vision, Pemperl's failure to recognize their use typifies, in this context, the deficient political consciousness in Krähwinkel. The fact that the general populace does not possess the luxury of metaphor is symptomatic of the concrete political freedoms the government denies them.

Those in power recognize the citizenry's linguistic naiveté and exploit it. The administration uses such words as "Recht" and "Freiheit" not to integrate these principles into daily social practice but rather to conceal actual political oppression. The terms do not correspond to Krähwinkel's social reality, yet the majority of the population remains unaware of the discrepancies between the linguistic signifier and its social referent. Ultra, however, undermines the form of the administration's rhetoric by pointing to its content, or, in this case, its lack of content. During his initial monologue he remarks: "Recht und Freiheit sind ein paar bedeutungsvolle Worte, aber nur in der einfachen Zahl unendlich groß, drum hat man sie uns auch immer nur in der wertlosen vielfachen Zahl gegeben." His explanation of this apparent paradox indicts a society enslaved by its inability to comprehend the abuse of linguistic abstraction:

> Was für eine Menge Rechte haben wir g'habt, diese Rechte der Geburt, die Rechte und Vorrechte des Standes, dann das höchste unter allen Rechten, das Bergrecht, dann das niedrigste unter allen Rechten, das Recht, daß man selbst bei erwiesener Zahlungsunfähigkeit und Armut einen einsperren lassen kann. Wir haben ferner das Recht g'habt, nach erlangter Bewilligung Diplome von gelehrten Gesellschaften anzunehmen. Sogar mit hoher Genehmigung das Recht, ausländische Courtoisie-Orden zu tragen. Und trotz all diesen unschatzbaren Rechten, haben wir doch kein Recht g'habt, weil wir Sklaven waren.

The abundance of publicly declared rights is intended to conceal the lack of political freedom in the city. Because those in power create these laws in order to maintain their hegemony, the rights legitimize the privileges of the aristocracy as well as the enslavement of the lower classes. The upper class is granted the right to exploit others, while the dispossessed are given the right to have pseudorights. Ultra goes on to undermine the official manipulation of the term "Freiheit" in an identical fashion. He submits the prevailing linguistic code to the same type of ideology critique informing Büchner's *Der Hessische Landbote*. Büchner condemns Hesse's ruling elite by illustrating the disparity between the emotive use of the word "Gerechtigkeit" and the lack of it in social reality. Justice belongs to the aristocracy; the remainder of the population is subject to the elite's despotic injustice. Analogously, the freedom which exists in Hesse is the freedom of the upper class to tyrannize those beneath it. The enslavement of the lower classes is largely perpetuated by linguistic hierarchies. "[Die Vornehmen] haben feiste Gesichter und reden eine eigne Sprache, das Volk aber liegt vor ihnen wie Dünger auf dem Acker" [Georg Büchner, "Der Hessische Landbote," in *Samtliche Werke und Briefe,* ed. Werner R. Lehmann, 1971]. Justice, the supposed object of the aristocratically controlled language, is denied the majority of the population. This language, in turn, is institutionalized in a series of self-serving laws which similarly remain incomprehensible to the populace. These laws are not designed to promote social equality, but rather to exploit the ignorance of the oppressed, resulting in mass enslavement under the supposed banner of justice: "Diese Gerechtigkeit ist nur ein Mittel, euch in Ordnung zu halten, damit man euch bequemer schinde; sie spricht nach Gesetzen, die ihr nicht versteht, nach Grundsätzen, von denen ihr nichts wißt, Urtheile, von denen ihr nichts begreift." Büchner stresses that words are not synonymous with deeds. His pamphlet exposes the ways in which language is officially manipulated to prevent any political action. Simultaneously, however, *Der Hessische Landbote* also illustrates language's potential as a means of enlightenment and its power as an effective catalyst for implementing social change.

In the course of the drama, Ultra adopts a variety of roles in order to undermine and subsequently restructure Krähwinkel's government. He appears, among other things, as a "Ligurianer," a "Fürst," and a "Diplomat." In assuming these roles, he also adopts the various levels of language, formal gestures, and ideologies of these representative types. His recognition of the discrepancies between form and content and between the word and the deed enables him to use these façades to subvert the political rhetoric associated with them. He undermines the political hegemony of these religious and governmental roles by transforming them into vehicles for the establishment of a new social order. As a central component of his democracy, he advocates a political discourse liberated from the abstractions which have subjugated Krähwinkel's populace and demands a mode of communication which concretely addresses the city's social reality. The contrast between these two uses of language surfaces upon Ultra's initial encounter with the Bürgermeister:

> BURGERMEISTER. Welche Sprache? das ist unerhört in Krähwinkel!

> ULTRA. Ich glaub's weil's um 100 Jahr zurück seid's, und diese neue Sprache ist erst wenig Monate alt. In dieser neuen Sprach' sag ich Ihnen jetzt auch was die Zensur ist. (668)

Ultra proceeds to employ this "new language" to condemn the Bürgermeister and his forms of censorship as well as to inform the city's inhabitants of their political enslavement. As Pfiffspitz's co-worker, he is able to use the newspaper to disclose, rather than conceal, political reality. In contrast to the government's manipulative and evasive verbiage, Ultra's "new language" and political philosophy succeed in overthrowing the oppressive regime and establishing a constitutional democracy in the city.

The principle of subversion is evident on all levels of Nestroy's texts. Ultra's belief in the necessity of transforming existing systems, expressed in his conviction that "Die G'schicht ändern kann i," points to the internal dynamic informing Nestroy's dramas. His *Volksstücke* emphasize the need for reevaluating those social and political institutions which, due to new historical developments, have lost their validity. Nestroy radicalizes the nineteenth-century *Volksstück* into concrete social and political provocations. In discussing Nestroy's transformation of the genre [in his *Die Wiener Komödie und ihr Publikum*, 1973], Reinhard Urbach maintains: "Nach Nestroy hat sich die Wiener Komödie zwischen Kritik der Wirklichkeit und Satire der Sprache zu entscheiden." Urbach's conclusion implies a questionable split between language and social reality. This split, in turn, implies a basic misunderstanding of Nestroy's texts, since it is precisely through his critique of language that his social critique emerges. In thematizing the political dimensions of language, Nestroy's *Volksstücke* transform the genre decisively and initiate the method of social criticism which characterizes its subsequent development. (pp. 44-59)

> *Craig Decker, "Toward a Critical 'Volksstück': Nestroy and the Politics of Language," in* Monatshefte, *Vol. LXXIX, No. 1, Spring, 1987, pp. 44-61.*

FURTHER READING

Bennett, Benjamin. "Nestroy and Schnitzler: The Three Societies of Comedy and the Idea of a Textless Theater." In his *Theater As Problem: Modern Drama and Its Place in Literature,* pp. 93-136. Ithaca: Cornell University Press, 1990.
    Bennett applies his theory of a split between "virtual reader" and "actual spectator" to Nestroy's plays, discussing the tension created between "our critical or satirical perspective and our continued participation in the object of satire."

Evenden, Mike. "Nestroy on Stage." *Theater* 12, No. 2 (1980): 66-71.
    Observes that since Nestroy's death, productions of his plays have failed to capture the playwright's "unique voice."

Harding, Laurence V. *The Dramatic Art of Ferdinand Raimund and Johann Nestroy.* The Hague: Mouton and Co., 1974, 243 p.
    Seeks to revise the notion of Raimund and Nestroy as opposing figures in the Austrian Folk Theater, discussing differences and similarities of plot, characterization, language, and staging in their respective plays.

Huish, Louise Adey. "A Source For Nestroy's *Gegen Thorheit giebt es kein Mittel.*" *The Modern Language Review* 87, No. 3 (July 1992): 616-25.
    Maintains that Nestroy found source material for his plays in the writings of French novelist Paul de Kock.

McKenzie, John R. P. "Political Satire in Nestroy's 'Freiheit in Krähwinkel.'" *The Modern Language Review* 75, No. 2 (April 1980): 322-32.
    Analyzes Nestroy's satire of religion, materialism, and revolutionary ineptitude in *Freiheit in Krähwinkel.*

———. "Nestroy's Political Plays." In *Viennese Popular Theatre: A Symposium,* edited by W. E. Yates and John R. P. McKenzie, pp. 123-38. Exeter: University of Exeter Press, 1985.
    Presents dramatic and historical factors for consideration in evaluating the politics of Nestroy's plays.

Reese, Joe. "*Der Zerrissene* and *L'Homme blasé:* A Closer Look at Nestroy's Source." *Modern Austrian Literature* 23, No. 1 (1990): 54-67.
    Argues that Nestroy's *Der Zerrissene* lacks the thematic subtlety of its French source *L'Homme blasé.*

Schwarz, Egon. "Thalia in Austria." In *Laughter Unlimited: Essays on Humor, Satire, and the Comic,* edited by Reinhold Grimm and Jost Hermand, pp. 41-55. Madison: University of Wisconsin Press, 1991.
    Briefly discusses the "sociosatiric" comedy of Nestroy's *Talisman.*

Seidmann, Gertrud. "Johann Nestroy." In *German Men of Letters, Volume V: Twelve Literary Essays,* edited by Alex Natan, pp. 275-99. London: Oswald Wolff, 1969.
    Provides an overview of Nestroy's comedies, focusing on his use of standard comedic elements.

Walker, Colin. "Nestroy's *Judith and Holofernes* and An-

tisemitism in Vienna." *Oxford German Studies* 12 (1981): 85-
110.

Examines Nestroy's *Judith and Holofernes* within its social and political contexts, accusing the dramatist not of
anti-Semitism but of "insensitivity."

James Robinson Planché

1796-1880

English dramatist.

INTRODUCTION

Planché was a prolific writer, adaptor, and translator who dominated the British popular stage in the mid-nineteenth century. His "extravaganzas," whimsical pieces adapted from diverse sources, combined song, dance, and grand spectacle to entertain and edify his audiences. Seeking to promote what he considered "the best interests of drama," Planché also spearheaded the movement for historical accuracy in stage costuming, an endeavor that demonstrated his talents as an antiquarian and scholar. In addition, he was an integral part of efforts resulting in the Dramatic Authors Act of 1833, reform legislation which protected dramatists from infringement on publication or performance rights.

Planché was born in London to a family of Huguenot ancestry and began acting in amateur theatricals at an early age. In 1818 he wrote *Amoroso,* a burlesque originally intended for his own amateur acting troupe. The play was performed at the Drury Lane theater that same year, and Planché, encouraged by its success, began writing professionally for the stage. In the early twenties Planché wrote undistinguished burlesques and melodramas for various London theaters, including Covent Garden, where in 1823 he suggested that Charles Kemble stage his production of Shakespeare's *King John* in historically correct costume. Planché undertook the research for this staging himself, and, despite reservations on Kemble's part, the production was a great success. In 1831 Planché began working with actress and theater manager Madame Vestris, for whom he produced the majority of his plays. The first of his extravaganzas for her theater, *Olympic Revels; or, Prometheus and Pandora,* was written in collaboration with playwright Charles Dance. This and Planché's subsequent works were great popular successes, and the dramatist continued to produce extravaganzas into the 1860s. In 1866 he was appointed Herald of Somerset in recognition of his scholarly achievements, and in 1872 he produced his last works for the stage, the songs for Dion Boucicault's *Babil and Bijou.* At the time of his death eight years later, Planché was known as the "grand old man of English drama."

Planché's plays were largely constructed from three types of subject matter: classical mythology, fairy tales, and the theatrical events of his day. Featuring word-play and comic allusion to contemporary life, Planché's classical extravaganzas evoked bathos with his absurd use of classical gods and demi-gods to address nineteenth century trivialities. The enthusiastic reception of *Olympic Revels* prompted a series of similar productions: *The Paphian*

Bower, The Deep, Deep Sea, and *Telemachus,* all of which were co-written with Charles Dance and performed as holiday pieces. For Christmas 1836 Planché staged *Riquet with the Tuft,* his adaptation of the French fairy tale *Riquet à la Houppe.* Featuring the talents of such acclaimed performers as Charles Matthews and Madame Vestris, the play was well-received, and was the first in a twenty-year string of Christmas and Easter fairy extravaganzas. Planché's stagings of fairy tales—among them *Puss in Boots, Beauty and the Beast,* and *The Fair One with the Golden Locks*—demonstrated his desire to dignify these well-known stories for presentation in the English theater. In addition, Planché's creation of tragic characters, such as the deformed prince Riquet in *Riquet with the Tuft* or the pitiable Gam-Bogie in *The Yellow Dwarf,* illustrated his intent to expand the strictly comic nature of the extravaganza. A third type of extravaganza devised by Planché, dubbed the dramatic *revue,* parodied the state of the theater in his day. *Success, or a Hit If You Like It,* for example, is a light-hearted allegory in which various personified London theaters (Drury Lane, Covent Garden, Haymarket, and others) vie for the hand of town governor Fashion's daughter Success, establishing a comic forum for Planché's commentary on the principal productions of the season.

Eclipsed by the rise of musical comedy, these and scores of other plays that Planché produced are no longer performed. Planché himself recognized their ephemerality, realizing that his topical humor would not long endure. His plays are presently valued primarily for their commentary on nineteenth-century popular culture. As Donald Roy has written, many of Planché's extravaganzas "constitute a fascinating insight into their times and provide the theatre historian with a positive mine of information and quotation."

PRINCIPAL WORKS

Amoroso, King of Little Britain (play) 1818

The Vampire; or, The Bride of the Isles [adaptor; from *Le Vampire*] (play) 1820

Success; or, A Hit If You Like It (play) 1825

Oberon; or, The Elf King's Oath [adaptor; from the poem by Christoph Martin Wieland] (play) 1826

Charles XII; or, The Siege of Stralsund (play) 1828

The Green-Eyed Monster (play) 1828

The Merchant's Wedding; or, London Frolics in 1638 [adaptor; from *The City Match* by Jasper Mayne and *Match Me at Midnight* by William Rowley] (play) 1828

Olympic Devils; or, Orpheus and Eurydice [with Charles Dance] (play) 1831

Olympic Revels; or, Prometheus and Pandora [with Charles Dance] (play) 1831

The Paphian Bower; or, Venus and Adonis [with Charles Dance] (play) 1832

The Deep Deep Sea; or, Perseus and Andromeda [with Charles Dance] (play) 1833

History of British Costume (non-fiction) 1834

The Loan of a Lover (play) 1834

Secret Service [adaptor; from *Michel Perrin*] (play) 1834

Telemachus; or, The Island of Calypso [with Charles Dance] (play) 1834

The Jewess [adaptor; from *La Juive* by Eugene Scribe] (play) 1835

Riquet with the Tuft [adaptor with Charles Dance; from *Riquet à la houppe*] (play) 1836

Puss in Boots [with Charles Dance] (play) 1837

The Drama's Levée; or, A Peep at the Past (play) 1838

Blue Beard [with Charles Dance] (play) 1839

The Sleeping Beauty in the Wood (play) 1840

The Follies of a Night (play) 1842

The White Cat (play) 1842

The Fair One with the Golden Locks (play) 1843

Fortunio and his Seven Gifted Servants (play) 1843

Grist to the Mill [adaptor; from *La Marquise de Carabas*] (play) 1844

The Golden Fleece; or, Jason in Colchis, and Medea in Corinth (play) 1845

The Birds of Aristophanes [adaptor; from the drama by Aristophanes] (play) 1846

The Invisible Prince; or, The Island of Tranquil Delights (play) 1846

The King of the Peacocks (play) 1848

The Island of Jewels (play) 1849

The Seven Champions of Christendom (play) 1849

King Charming; or, The Blue Bird of Paradise (play) 1850

The Prince of Happy Land; or, The Fawn in the Forest (play) 1851

The Good Woman in the Wood (play) 1852

The Pursuivant of Arms; or, Heraldry Founded upon Facts (non-fiction) 1852

The Camp at the Olympic (play) 1853

Mr. Buckstone's Ascent of Mount Parnassus (play) 1853

The Yellow Dwarf and the King of the Gold Mines (play) 1854

The Discreet Princess; or, The Three Glass Distaffs (play) 1855

Love and Fortune [adaptor; from *La Ceinture de Vénus*] (play) 1859

Orpheus in the Haymarket [adaptor; from *Orphée aux enfers* by Hector Crémieux] (play) 1865

King Christmas (play) 1871

*Babil and Bijou; or, the Lost Regalia [with Dion Boucicault] (play) 1872

The Recollections and Reflections of J. R. Planché (autobiography) 1872

The Extravaganzas of J. R. Planché 5 vols. (plays) 1879

**Planché contributed the songs to Boucicault's play.

CRITICISM

J. Palgrave Simpson (essay date 1880)

[*In the following essay written in the year of Planché's death, Simpson presents an approving retrospective of the dramatist's career.*]

One of the brightest and most genial writers that ever shed sunlight on the British drama has lately gone from among us. Although at a very advanced age—he was eighty-four years old when he departed—his latest little lyrical effusions were replete with all the elegance and grace, and even juvenile freshness and sparkle, which characterised his earlier productions. The buoyant spirit of poetical fancy, and "quirk and quip" and flowing measure, remained unimpaired to the last.

James Robinson Planché was born on the 27th February, 1796, and was descended from a French Huguenot family, which, with many others, fled from France after the revocation of the Edict of Nantes, and settled in England. The foreign name, it is said, had degenerated in English mouths to that of Plank, in spelling as well as in pronunciation; until young Planché, who early evinced a fondness for that archæological research which, in his after years, stood him in such good stead in his life's path towards fame and fortune, insisted, in spite of the jeering of acquaintances on the score of affectation, on restoring the name to its legitimate orthography and accentuation. Subsequently even, when the name was well established and universally recognised, his friends and associates would jestingly fix the date of any theatrical doings, in which he was concerned, as *"Consule Planco."*

This early taste for literature may be supposed to have been derived from his mother, a lady of considerable literary ability. His archæological propensities seem to have been implanted in him from his birth; and the study of antiquity, especially as regarded heraldry and costume, was one of his earliest hobbies.

His connection with the stage would appear to have been decided by a mere freak of fate. When quite a youth he wrote, for private representation by young amateurs among his friends, a burlesque entitled **Amoroso, King of Little Britain.** It was a mere imitation of *Bombastes Furioso, Chrononhotonthologos,* and other (now effete) productions of a school which delighted in turning into ridicule the bombastic fustian of the tragedies of a somewhat earlier period. This not very clever effusion, which, however, was destined to be the parent of a long progeny of bright, witty, and charmingly written extravaganzas, fell, by chance, into the hands of John Pritt Harley, the comedian, who was sufficiently pleased with it to present it to the then managing committee of Drury Lane Theatre, where it was first played in May, 1818, and with very considerable success. The time had not yet gone by when such ultra-burlesque and extravagant productions were still to the taste of the public palate.

This first start, so auspiciously made, determined, there can be no doubt, one of the paths in the youth's future career which led him to distinction. From that time, his literary efforts were chiefly, although far from entirely, devoted to the stage. Dramatic productions of every kind flowed rapidly from his pen, and commanded success wherever they were given.

It must be admitted that most, if not all, of these productions—comedies, comediettas, vaudevilles, farces, burlettas, or whatever they may have been called—were derived from the French stage, and were what is now called "adaptations from the French." But in those days critics had not begun to investigate the sources from which any new dramatic work on the English stage might have sprung. The epithet "original" was never taken with consideration. Planché's pieces were accepted as wholly emanations from his own brain; and among his admirers he was hailed by the denomination of "The English Scribe." "Scribe in English" would have been the juster and truer designation. It must be said for the British dramatist, however, that his adaptations were made with so much ease, and natural freedom, and bright dialogue, that they always acquired the stamp of genuine British ware, and

might have passed for such in the judgment of all but those who had an intimate knowledge of the French stage and its latest productions. Such connoisseurs were rare when Planché commenced his dramatic career. His numerous little pieces, moreover, were so daintily manipulated from the French, and were treated with such a lightness and sprightliness of touch, that they frequently assumed shapes of a higher order than the original could show. In such instances Sheridan's sneer about "stolen children *disfigured* " would have lost its point. Many examples of this adroitness in remodelling might be given. One of the most obvious may be found in **The Loan of a Lover,** adapted from Scribe's *Zoe, ou l'Amant Prêté,* which is in every respect superior to the original piece. It still maintains its place on the English stage. "Custom" has not "made it stale."

Whatever the origin of Planché's dramatic pieces, there can be no doubt that he exercised a considerable influence on the English stage. The two most characteristic qualities of his writings were taste and elegance. Breadth of tone in comedy—power which might in most cases have been more justly looked on as fustian, and sentiment which chiefly displayed itself in maudlin clap-trap—had been the main attributes and aims of most of the dramatists of the first quarter of the century. Planché introduced into his work elements which gave a fresh direction to the comedy writers of the period. True, they were redolent of hair-powder and bedecked with patches; but they had a pleasant smack of elegance and grace; and, although not displaying the breadth of low comedy, the tendency to fine heavily-phrased writing, or the platitudes of artificial sentiment which were the prevailing characteristics of most of his immediate predecessors, they were accepted with delight by the public. In adopting and adapting French models he had imbued himself with the spirit of the French school, and almost founded a new school of his own. "The natural," somewhat heightened in colour by that stage rouge, which is more or less necessary to all dramatic doings, and the due proportions of which were well taught by his foreign prototypes, took the place of stereotyped artificiality.

It was not, however, to the "hundred and one" pieces of this description, varying in importance and in weight, that Planché has owed his principal fame as a dramatic author. His name must be always chiefly remembered in connection with his elegant and graceful "extravaganzas," as he called these freaks of pretty fancy. How he writhed, poor man, with indignation and annoyance, if anyone spoke of them as "burlesques."

It was when Madame Vestris held the reins of management at the Olympic Theatre, and had herself introduced a new era of taste and elegance in costume, decoration, and scenery, besides an entirely new system of natural and, at the same time, effective stage management, that Planché commenced his career of "extravaganza" in collaboration at first with his friend Charles Dance, and stamped favourably on the public mind a fresh species of entertainment, which at once achieved an immense success. In the beginning the lucubrations of the joint authors were founded on classical subjects; and **Olympic Revels,**

Olympic Devils, The Deep Deep Sea, Telemachus, with other similar productions, filled the treasury of Madame Vestris's fortunate little theatre.

When left to himself, Planché's fancy seemed to have turned to fairy tales and legends, as more congenial to his fantastic spirit, and, excepting his *Golden Fleece* (I believe), all his later extravaganzas, produced under the Vestris-Mathews management at Covent Garden and the Lyceum Theatres, were founded on fairy subjects, chiefly selected from the fairy tales of Madame D'Aulnoy. At the Lyceum they followed each other in quick succession at Christmastide and Easter. Fanciful and graceful, and invariably put on the stage with exquisite taste, they always constituted one of the principal attractions of the London dramatic season.

To enumerate all these light and witty effusions of Planché's pen would be only to give a dry catalogue of goneby splendours. But a few among others may be cited from a long list, such as *Puss in Boots, The Sleeping Beauty, The White Cat, Fortunio, The Fair One with the Golden Locks, The Invisible Prince, The King of the Peacocks, The Island of Jewels,* and *The Yellow Dwarf.* Nor should his *pièces de circonstance,* written somewhat after the fashion of the French *revues,* and of a satirical nature, as dealing with events of the day, be forgotten. Among these exceptional sparkling productions—which, however, may be said to have been often "over the heads of the audience"—may be enumerated, *The Drama's Levee, The Drama at Home, The Birds of Aristophanes, Mr. Buckstone's Ascent of Mount Parnassus, Mr. Buckstone's Voyage Round the World;* although these specimens are far from completing the list of these original and witty "skits" on topics of the day.

Eminently successful and highly prized as these vivacious and witty effusions were, illustrated by the prettiest and most graceful melodies in vogue at the period, as well as by exquisite scenery and dresses, they ceased in time, even during their author's life, to maintain a hold on public favour. They grew to be old-fashioned. The graceful extravaganza was gradually elbowed off the stage by the modern burlesque, in which pun was set aside for jingle of words or distortion of syllables; "breakdowns" became a necessary ingredient to catch the public fancy; and music-hall songs were substituted for popular Italian airs. Old playgoers lamented the loss of these bright and delicate fairytales; and an attempt for a return to the old refinements of Planché's pleasant *féeries* was made from time to time. Managers revived, now and then, *The Invisible Prince,* or *The King of the Peacocks,* as refreshers to the popular taste of a more unrefined time. But their efforts were useless. Planché "drew" no longer, in spite of all his bright and sprightly grace. The public palate had learned the smack of the strong brandy of burlesque, and rejected the lighter beverage of extravaganza, even though it may have been champagne, "as washy stuff," lacking all the best elements of intoxication. Those who would now appreciate Planché's style in this species of composition—his graceful sweetly flowing lyrics, his happy parodies, his witty turns of phrase, his fertile power of punning in that old strain in which puns were really "puns," and not mere

ear-catching jingling sounds—must now revert to the collection of his noted extravaganzas, and read what they can no longer see, supplying all the brilliant scenic accessories of other times by the force of imagination.

The collection of Planché's *Extravaganzas,* lately prepared and edited by his friends Dillon Croker and Tucker (Rouge Croix), and published, as a testimonial to the distinguished author, and for his pecuniary advantage, when evil days had fallen on his bright career, will afford the utmost delectation to all, who can appreciate, and revel in, poetic fancy shed over fairy-lore.

It was not only by his clever adaptations and charming extravaganzas, however, that Planché earned distinction on the stage. About the year 1822 he became attached to Covent Garden Theatre, then under the management of Charles Kemble, and altered and adapted to the modern stage many of the old comedies, which had fallen into the "sere and yellow," as unfit for modern representation. Among these were *The Woman Never Vexed, The Merchant's Wedding,* and *The Spanish Curate,* the first of which, more especially, ensured a great success, and was translated (that is to say, Planché's adaptation) into German, under the title of *Die Gebrüder Forster,* a play still holding its place on the German stage. Here, too, he produced his opera of *Maid Marian,* with Bishop's music; and in the year 1826 had "the honour" (as he was wont himself to say) of writing the libretto of *Oberon* for Carl Maria von Weber. His association with the great composer was always looked back on by him with infinite pleasure and pride.

The most solid distinction, however, attained by Planché, was acquired, doubtless, by his archæological knowledge and his antiquarian research. He was early in life affiliated to the leading archæological societies. In historical costume he was considered the great authority of the time. In latter days the study has found other exponents. But when, in 1834, he published his *History of British Costume,* his work was accepted with universal favour, and was long looked on as the text-book for the historian as well as for the stage. It was thus, as the master of knowledge on this subject, that, during his connection with Covent Garden Theatre, he was employed by Charles Kemble to correct and revise the costumes in *King John, Henry IV, As You Like It, Othello,* and *Cymbeline,* which were revived under his direction, and illustrated with dresses from his own designs. Similarly, when connected with the fortunes of the Vestris-Mathews management at Covent Garden Theatre, and afterwards at the Lyceum—a connection which commenced in 1840, and lasted for a long series of years—he was engaged, not only as reader of plays at the theatre and general adviser, but as the supervisor of the costume department.

That the general acknowledgment of Planché's science and research in archæological studies was not confined to the department of costumes, but spread over a far wider field, was evidenced by his appointment to posts at the Heralds' College, first as "Rouge Croix" and then as "Somerset Herald," in which latter capacity he somewhat mystified his correspondents occasionally by signing

"Somerset," and thus puzzling them as to whether or not he was a duke.

As an antiquarian, then, it may be inferred that Planché obtained his highest distinction. But in the literary field he also culled his laurels. A journey through Germany and the Netherlands, in 1826, produced his *Lays and Legends of the Rhine;* and a voyage down the Danube, in the following year, elicited a work on that then almost unknown river: both books were clever, bright, instructive, and pleasant, and commanded considerable attention and vogue. Then, lastly, he has given to the world his *Life and Recollections,* in two volumes of agreeable gossip on men and things, that had passed before him during his long artistic career.

It was when he might have been thought bowed down by the weight of years, at the age of eighty, that he had the courage and spirit and the fresh activity of mind, to commence two works of weight and importance, *The Cyclopædia of Medieval Costume,* followed by *The History of Costume,* both of which works he lived to complete, to his own satisfaction and to the content of the antiquarian student in the world at large.

This active spirit, so varied in accomplishments, so deeply imbued with taste, so full of sweet and genial fancy, has at last passed away. The latter part of his life was unfortunately embittered by family misfortune. But he bravely took to his home a widowed daughter and eight children, for whose sake he still toiled, and struggled with manly fortitude and Christian kindliness. Suffering, also, from excruciating disease, was hard to bear in his old days. But his genial spirit still shone forth throughout all. He delighted to have friends around him, and strove to command his pristine gaiety. But the end came. After a brief battle for life, he murmured to a watching friend, "Take me from my bed." He was helped into his arm-chair; and there in a short time his spirit passed away with a placid smile on his lips. (pp. 95-9)

J. Palgrave Simpson, "James Robinson Planché," in The Theatre, n.s. Vol. II, No. 2, August, 1880, pp. 95-9.

Dougald MacMillan   (essay date 1929)

[*In the following excerpt, MacMillan describes Planché's attempts to instill his extravaganzas with a moral principle.*]

The minor drama of the first half of the nineteenth century, consisting of burlesques, burlettas, melodramas, and so forth, probably deserves the bad name which it has among students of the drama. Some phases of it, nevertheless, present problems of some importance. Planché's burlesques stand out among similar productions of his generation, the work of Burnand and the Brough brothers and Henry James Byron, for example, at least in one particular. Though they were designed to amuse, they were written with serious intent by a man sincerely interested in acted drama; and in them the author desired to express the best thoughts that he was capable of. Though he wrote trifles of the lightest sort, he always endeavored to present,

along with his tomfoolery, a sound moral principle dressed in a sparkling, if sometimes incongruous, costume. Although this may not be an artistic aim of the highest character, Planché's Christmas pieces were among the most popular of their day in spite of their moralizing; and in this fact, it seems to me, lies their importance.

There is evidence in the plays themselves, in Planché's prefaces to them, and in his *Recollections and Reflections* to show to what extent he was really desirous of promoting the welfare of the stage and establishing once more a strong, self-reliant drama in England. In his *revues* he attempted, through satire, to point out the faults of drama as they appeared to him. In addition to pointing out faults, he tried in several ways to improve the drama by exerting what influence he could in practical matters, in attempting to reform the costuming of historical plays, to improve the condition of authors with regard to their copyrights and the condition of his audiences by giving them entertainments that inculcated good moral lessons, and unknown to them to improve their taste in things theatrical by elevating the tone of burlesque and by presenting artistic plays whenever possible. There is a tone of genuine regret, tempered with hope, in his statement, "The rage for mere absurdity which my extravaganzas so unintentionally and unhappily gave rise to has lasted longer than I had anticipated, but there are unmistakable signs, I think, of its subsidence."

In his endeavor to raise burlesque from the state of the "girl and music show," Planché always, he says, attempted to convey some modicum of intellectual stimulus to his audiences. It is true that this desire usually materialized in the shape of a moral. In reply to objections to the seriousness of the conclusions of some of his pieces, *The "Birds" of Aristophanes* (Haymarket, April 18, 1846) particularly, he says, "I do not regret that upon every occasion I endeavoured to 'point a moral,' though my abilities might not enable me to 'adorn a Tale.'" Later (in 1879), in the preface to *The Discreet Princess* (Olympic, Dec. 26, 1855), he adds, "Regardless of the opinion of a few self-constituted judges who contended that a moral was out of place in an extravaganza, and had evidently overlooked the fact that there is no very popular fairy tale without one, I most contumaciously persisted in my error, and on the present occasion, actually selected a subject which had *two.*" These morals are explicit in the first stanza of the final song:

> At Christmas time, whate'er the rhyme,
>   It should contain a moral;
> For giving you a piece with two,
>   With us you will not quarrel.
> So may distress, through idleness,
>   Ne'er make your children smarters;
> But prudence still ensure success
> To your pretty little sons and daughters.

The "Birds" of Aristophanes also furnishes an interesting case. Planché quotes the preface to the 1846 edition of it. He says:

> It has never been advertised or officially entitled
> 'a burlesque.' It is an humble attempt to imitate
> or paraphrase (but not burlesque or travesty)

such portions of the Comedy of *The Birds,* as were capable of being adapted to local and recent circumstances. . . . Notwithstanding the probable disappointment of the lovers of mere absurdity, and the natural mystification of a few good-humoured holiday spectators, the experiment, I am happy to say, was as successful as my poor abilities could make it, and, what is of more consequence, it ensures the future triumphs of superior writers, if such will make the trial.

He does not bow to the decision of his censors, because

> I deny the fact upon which they found their arguments. One critic, for instance, who insists upon comparing **The Golden Fleece,** a burlesque of a tragic subject, with **The Birds,** the paraphrase of portions of a comic one, is shocked at the introduction of Jupiter, and remarks that his language 'was far too earnest; too literal; it was no longer burlesque; it was no less than the voice of offended Heaven.' My only answer is that I never contemplated burlesque. The fable is ended; the allegory over; the moral to be drawn, however trite, is a serious one. I could not too earnestly, too literally point out (the sole aim of the piece)
>
> What dire confusion in the world 'twould breed,
> If fools *could* follow whither knaves *would* lead.
>
> And it is the feebleness, and not the strength or gravity, that I regret, of the language in which the concluding exhortation is couched:—
>
> On wings *forbidden,* seek no idle Fame,
> Let men BE men! and WORTHY OF THE NAME

To this he adds, in the preface to the play in the collected extravaganzas, the following:

> Though partially disappointed, I could not help being amused, and in some degree flattered by the opinions it elicited. For instance, a popular foreign artiste pronounced the piece to be 'Too d—d clever.' Nor did I abandon hope, and the recent success of 'The Palace of Truth,' and still more of 'Pygmalion' upon those very boards have proved that there *is* a public who can enjoy good writing and good acting unassisted by magnificent scenery and undergraded by 'breakdowns.'

It seems that nothing more need be said about the seriousness of Planché's aims in **The Birds** at any rate.

In the preface to **Young and Handsome** (Olympic, Dec. 26, 1856) he says that, because of the subtlety of the satire of the story and the breadth of the humor of the situation, he had no fear that the piece would not take with the audience. "I consequently felt," he continues, "that I might indulge my constant desire to elevate the character of Extravaganza without running the risk of failure from a nonappreciation by the audience of the deeper meaning of the subject."

This consciousness of a serious purpose prevented Planché's sacrificing what he thought was his art to the whims of managers or the degraded taste of the public. . . . He also protests vigorously against the changes

made, in response to popular demand, in his conclusion of **The Red Mask** (Drury Lane, Nov. 15, 1834), based on Cooper's *The Bravo.* Planché followed the novel to a tragic ending; but, he says, the critics denounced it as cruel, unnecessarily brutal, and so on. A happy ending was substituted and the piece ruined, a fact which the manager, Bunn, learned later through the medium of the box-office. The butchering of this play causes the following remarks: "I should be amongst the last to advocate any scenic representation in which good taste and feeling were outraged for a mere *coup-de-théâtre,* or to propose any exhibition tending to brutalize the people." And: "To what is now distinguished as the sensational drama, an objection is justifiably raised, on the ground that the incidents are introduced for the purpose of affecting the nervous system only, and not with the higher motive of pointing a moral, or the development of human passion." He cites *Macbeth* as an example of a play which, if stripped of its "romantic accessories" and its poetry, would be the grossest sort of sensationalism; and he states his sincere conviction that "no drama, however interesting or well acted, can survive, if the curtain falls on 'a lame and impotent conclusion.' "

Somewhat the same idea is found in the preface to **Orpheus in the Haymarket** (Haymarket, Dec. 26, 1865) where Planché objects to the French libretto that he was called upon to rewrite for the English stage and still preserve it in such form that it would fit Offenbach's music. He says,

> It was not the utter subversion of the classical story, which I had faithfully followed in my early extravaganza, 'Olympic Devils,' that I objected to. The idea was whimsical enough, but it was the inartistic mode in which it was carried

The introductory vision to The Vampire.

out, the unmeaning buffoonery forced upon it—
'fooling' which nothing could make 'admirable.'
I wrote the piece as well as I could, freely translating all that was good in it, expunging preposterous absurdities which, however amusing to a
French audience in the hands of some favorite
farçeur, would have been 'perilous stuff' on the
Haymarket stage, and by entirely reconstructing
the two last tableaux, and flinging the whole into
rhyme (the original being in prose), I think I succeeded in elevating the tone and imparting to the
Drama generally a more definite purpose than
the author appeared to have thought it worth his
while to have done although there were several
indications in the dialogue that he was not insensible of the opportunity.

On these principles Planché based his plays. How well his
works were interpreted we cannot now tell. He, himself,
laments the treatment that some of his plays received from
mediocre, or worse, actors in these words, "my old
wounds began to bleed afresh at the recollection of the
mangling I have endured from 'respectable actors.' " And
Fitzgerald says that his plays, which were full of delicate
conceits and classical allusions, "supposed a too high state
of culture in the audience"; and the producers cut and
hacked them, inserting "wheezes" and "bits of fat." We
know that there were exceptions to this rule, especially in
the parts acted by Mathews and Robson, and Planché enters no complaints against his producers on this account.
(pp. 255-59)

One of the most important single acts of Planché's theatrical career was the designing of the costumes for Charles
Kemble's revival of *King John* in 1823. The movement toward reform in theatrical costume had long been under
way; John Philip Kemble had dressed Macbeth as an officer of the 42nd Highlanders rather than in the gold lace
and famous Hessian boots of Garrick's day. In his ***Recollections,*** Planché relates his experiences and recapitulates
the arguments for accuracy in historical costume with
which he won over Charles Kemble to his side and received permission to try his experiment. His idea seems
now to be extremely simple and entirely natural; it was
merely that an historical play should be costumed in accordance with the customs in dress of the period of the action of the play, not of the authorship or of the performance. The older actors objected vigorously to the innovation; and Planché quotes a remark of Mrs. Siddons to her
brother, Charles, to the effect that all that was required of
costumes was that they be "conventional." The success of
this revival, Planché says, was assured when, on the opening night, the first scene was "discovered."

> When the curtain rose, and discovered King
> John dressed as his effigy appears in Worcester
> Cathedral, surrounded by his barons sheathed in
> mail, with cylindrical helmets and correct ar-
> morial shields, and his courtiers in the long tu-
> nics and mantles of the thirteenth century, there
> was a roar of approbation, accompanied by four
> district rounds of applause, so general and so
> hearty, that the actors were astonished, and I felt
> amply rewarded for all the trouble, anxiety, and
> annoyance I had experienced during my labours.

Interest in plays and production naturally led Planché into
a lively concern in the state of the stage in general. Evidence is found in his *revues* of the theatrical seasons. Of
his *revue,* ***Mr. Buckstone's Ascent of Mount Parnassus***
(Haymarket, March 28, 1853), he says, "In this piece, as
in many others, I took the opportunity of promulgating
opinions which might be serviceable to the best interests
of the Drama." Prominent among these opinions was that
that the English should establish and maintain a national
theatre modeled on the plan of the Théâtre Française. In
the same *revue* a character, the Spirit of Drury Lane, says,

> Because of every other hope bereft
> The Drama is to Fortune's mercy left.
> So much is she your slave, that e'en the weather
> Can ruin all the theatres together!
> The State no temple to the Drama gives—
> She keeps a shop and on chance custom lives,
> From hand to mouth. What cares she for dis-
>   grace,
> While Bassinghall Street stares her in the face?
> Will any manager, who's not a ninny,
> To walk the stage give Roscius one poor guinea,
> While he can double his receipts by dealing
> With a man-fly, who walks upon the ceiling?

Similar ideas had been expressed in ***The Drama at Home,***
another *revue,* nearly ten years before the lines just quoted
were written. Drama has just been informed by Portia of
the fact that she is free at last to go wherever she will and
take up her abode at any theatre. She exclaims, "O joyful
day! then I may flourish still!" Punch replies,

> May! Well, that's something; let us hope you
>   will.
> A stage may rise for you now law will let it,
> And Punch sincerely 'wishes you may get it!'

Planché cherished for the rest of his days his notion that
a national theatre would be the solution of many of the
English theatrical problems. The year before his death he
published a pamphlet called ***Suggestions for Establishing
an English Art Theatre,*** in which he proposed the formation of a stock company to finance the establishment of
such a theatre modeled somewhat upon the plan of the
Théâtre Française.

There remains one point about which again it seems wisest
to let Planché speak for himself; that is his conception of
the nature and purpose of burlesque and extravaganza. It
is distinctly stated in several places. The first of these remarks is made in connection with the acting of James
Bland, called "the King of Extravaganza." Planché says,

> In these pieces, . . . James Bland established his
> reputation as monarch of extravaganza, in
> which dominion he so long exercised sovereign
> sway and masterdom, and has never been sur-
> passed by the successors to his throne. His train-
> ing in subordinate characters under the best ac-
> tors of the regular drama, imparted to his tone
> and manner an earnestness, which, while it gave
> point to the epigram, trebled the absurdity of the
> language in which it was conveyed. He made no
> effort to be 'funny,' but so judiciously exaggerat-
> ed the expression of passion indicated by the
> mock-heroic language he had to deliver, that
> while it became irresistibly comic, it never de-

generated to mere buffoonery, but was acknowledged by the most fastidious critic to be 'admirable fooling.' It this true and artistic perception of the nature of burlesque, he has only been equalled by the late Mr. Robson. . . .

The distinction which Planché made between burlesque and extravaganza is expressed in the preface to *The Sleeping Beauty in the Wood* (Covent Garden, April 20, 1840), which, he says, was "announced as an extravaganza, distinguishing the whimsical treatment of a poetical subject from the broad caricature of a tragedy or serious opera, which was correctly termed a 'Burlesque.'" The same idea appears in a speech in *The Camp at the Olympic* (Olympic, Oct. 17, 1853) in which the characteristics of the various forms of the drama are set forth.

> Ballet shall help me to keep up the ball,
> Opera lend me a ballad or romanza.
> *And Fancy make burlesque, extravaganza.*

In the same piece The Spirit of burlesque, Planché says, "most pointedly gave my opinion of his mission" in the following dialogue.

TRAGEDY.	Avaunt, and quit my sight! let the earth hide thee. Unreal mockery, hence! I can't abide thee!
BURLESQUE.	Because I fling your follies in your face, And call back all the false starts of your race, Shew up your shows, affect your affectation, And by such homeopathic aggravation, Would cleanse your bosom of that perilous stuff, Which weighs upon our art— bombast and puff.
MR. WIGAN.	Have you so good a purpose then in hand?
BURLESQUE.	Else wherefore breathe I in dramatic land?
MRS. WIGAN.	I thought your aim was but to make us laugh?
BURLESQUE.	Those who think so but understand me half. Did not my thrice-renowned Thomas Thumb, That mighty mite, make mouthing Fustian mum? Is Tilburina's madness void of matter? Did great Bombastes strike no nonsense flatter? When in his words he's not one to the wise, When his fool's bolt, *spares* folly as it flies, When in his chaff there's not a grain to seize on, When in his rhyme there's not a ray of reason, His slang but slang, no point beyond the pun, Burlesque may walk, for he will cease to run.

Planché very carefully makes his distinction in this manner between the two forms that he indulged in, and he also points out the fact when one of his pieces belongs in neither class. In the speech of April which forms a sort of prologue to *Cymon and Iphigenia* (Lyceum, April 1, 1850) the statement about the play is,

> For it's not a burlesque, nor an extravaganza,
> But a something or other,
> Which pleased your grandmother,
> And we hope will please you in your turn.

These lines are also quoted to describe *Love and Fortune* (Princess's, Sept. 24, 1859) in an attempt to make the audience, and the critics, understand that the piece, which was described as "a dramatic tableau, in Watteau colours," was not a burlesque or extravaganza and was therefore not to be judged by the standards usually applied to those two forms. The piece, however, was unfortunate in the same way that *The Birds,* which also belongs in this category, had been; and it suffered the like fate of being misunderstood. The author defends these two unsuccessful pieces, saying that he thinks they are not inferior to his other plays and "will yet one day justify that opinion." The day has not yet come.

Looking back at the seriousness with which Planché took his work in this decidedly unimportant branch of the drama, one is impressed by the strange combination seen in his plays of eighteenth-century methods and subject matter with the morality and rather stiff elegance of nascent mid-Victorianism. (pp. 259-63)

> *Dougald MacMillan, "Some Burlesques with a Purpose, 1830-1870," in* Philological Quarterly, *Vol. VIII, No. 3, July, 1929, pp. 255-63.*

Dougald MacMillan   (essay date 1931)

[In the following essay, MacMillan describes the origins and attributes of Planché's fairy extravaganzas.]

In a previous brief study of the early burlesque of James Robinson Planché I called attention to the existence of his fairy extravaganzas, which are, in many ways, his most important contribution to the history of English burlesque drama. The use of fairy tales, like that of classical myths, was not new to the English stage in Planché's day; but the well worn stories of the White Cat or Riquet with the Tuft had not in the eighteenth century been used to the same extent as classical stories by the writers of burlettas and pantomime openings. Planché may, safely I think, be said to have given the fairy tale its definite and prominent place on the Victorian stage. The many imitators of Planché's work carried on in classical burlesque and fairy extravaganza the tradition set by Planché, chiefly through the brilliant series of pieces produced by Madame Vestris at Covent Garden and The Lyceum. As the classical burlesques merit attention, so do the fairy extravaganzas call for analysis. An understanding of Planché's pieces will go far toward producing a fairly complete picture of a type of comic drama immensely popular in Victorian London. To accomplish this end, I should like to point out the subjects, sources, and characteristics of these fairy pieces.

Twenty-two of the extravaganzas are little more than dramatizations of French fairy tales, chiefly those of Perrault and Madame D'Aulnoy. The first three were written during the period of collaboration with Charles Dance, the others by Planché alone. Many of the titles are familiar to everyone and the unfamiliar ones are mostly those that Planché made himself to fit his plays, departing deliberately from the titles by which the stories are commonly known. In handling the stories Planché, almost without exception, adhered strictly to the story as it is told in his original. The most noticeable exception to this rule which he made for himself is in the case of *The Yellow Dwarf,* where he has given the tale a happy ending, an obviously necessary change if the piece were to succeed with the holiday audience. In practically every case the dramatist tells us the source of his story, and he usually points with pride to the fact that he has carefully followed his original as far as the actual story goes; he was also much interested in getting the audience to appreciate this faithfulness on his part and in destroying the current misconceptions of his sources, misconceptions that had their origin in the "garbled nursery versions" of the tales that circulated under the title "Tales of Mother Goose" (from Perrault's *Contes de ma Mère l'Oye*), in which the stories were obviously "written down" to small children and deprived of all their subtlety and humor, qualities that are easily discernable in the French originals and in Planché's own translations of them. Though he was probably not as successful in this as the excellence of his object and his own sincerity might have deserved, he certainly succeeded in making his versions of the tales pleasing to the audience and very popular. This is amply proved by the fact that the pieces held the stage for twenty years, many of them in individual cases running from the night of their first production to the openings of their successors at the next holiday season.

It will be observed that Planché, who, when his works are viewed as a whole, displays astonishing versatility, in these extravaganzas has taken his subjects from a very limited field. Except for a few instances all of the important and best extravaganzas have for their plots stories taken from classical mythology or from French fairy tales. He chose his subjects with due care and developed them to the best of his ability, always endeavoring to give the stories their true interpretation, while, at the same time, he made them into amusing nonsense for the delight of his audiences. The humor is derived not from a perversion of the tales or from a distortion of the characters, but from a delicate, whimsical handling of the themes, behind which one can always feel the intelligent sympathy that he has for the original treatment of the subject.

This is particularly true in the case of the fairy pieces. In *Riquet with the Tuft* he has attempted to tell the story in an amusing fashion and at the same time to preserve the subtle pathos of the character of Riquet, the hunchback with the ugly body and beautiful mind, the pathos that is a true part of the tale as it is told by Perrault. And the same quality is seen in *The Yellow Dwarf,* where the character that gives the play its title has much in common with Riquet, though he lacks the pathetic sweetness of disposition that makes the latter character appealing. The same is true, perhaps in less degree, of the other plays. The

Greek gods may participate in all sorts of buffoonery, but they remain gods to the end and act their parts in the usual stories as we have been accustomed to see them. This faithfulness to the story is one of the points in which Planché's burlesques differ from those of his contemporaries, who were usually content to pervert the tales whenever it was necessary by so doing to please the galleries and the managers. In spite of the atrocities of his friends, Planché usually remained true to his ideal of a good story faithfully retold, that he might not do an injustice to his source. And his success proved, frequently in spite of the qualms and fears of managers, that he was right, that the people liked best the old stories told as they were used to hearing them from childhood, with the added spice of clever dialogue and pretty scenes to tickle the adult palate. In the preface to *Telemachus,* Planché says, "In this instance as in every dramatization of a popular subject that I have been concerned in, the well known plot was invariably preserved with the most reverential fidelity, whatever liberties might be taken with the details. . . . Whether this be a merit or not is, of course, a matter of opinion, but it is upon that principle that I have worked throughout my career, and believe that it has been most essential to my success."

It has been necessary in this discussion of the subject matter of Planché's plays to touch on the subject of sources of plots, but this matter must be taken up for more detailed consideration. As is apparent at a glance, few of Planché's plots are original and those few are not among his best works. His ability seems to have enabled him to readjust stories already well known,—sometimes too well known, it seemed,—rather than to invent and construct plots of his own. Even in his original plots, as in *The Irish Post* (1846) or in *Who's Your Friend* (1843), there is little true originality; yet these pieces interest one by the sprightliness of their dialogue and the prettiness and delicate good taste of their construction. The result is that he naturally turned more and more from the presumably original productions of his earlier years (at that time, too, came the acknowledged rearrangements and adaptations) to the carefully constructed plays bearing old names and telling old and loved tales.

Planché's is not the searching parody of a Beerbohm, drawing attention by imitation and concentration to the stylistic mannerisms of the author parodied. His is the humour of the consciously absurd; he plays tricks with the original, he exercises his ingenuity upon it, but he leaves it intact.

—Stanley Wells, in Shakespeare Survey, 1963.

Beginning with *Riquet with the Tuft,* comes the series of burlesques based upon French seventeenth and eighteenth century fairy tales. The sources of these plays offer more interesting material for consideration. The authors whom Planché used as sources are five: Perrault, Mme. D'Aulnoy, Mme. le Prince de Beaumont, Mlle. de la Force, and Mme. de Murat.

Riquet with the Tuft, the first of the fairy pieces, is based on the French *"Comédie Féerie," Riquet à la Houppe,* by Saurin and Brazier, which Planché had seen in Paris in 1821. The story is from Perrault's *"Contes des Fées."* Planché says that *Riquet with the Tuft* "is the only piece of this class [i.e., based on a fairy tale] for any portion of which I am indebted to the French stage." *Puss in Boots* bears on the title page the statement: "Founded on the well known TALE of that extraordinary Animal, as unfolded by the best authorities." Planché's translation of Perrault's tale is called *Master Cat; or, Puss in Boots.* The other plays based on stories from Perrault are *Blue Beard, The Sleeping Beauty in the Wood,* and *The Discreet Princess,* based on *"L'Adroite Princesse"* in Perrault's *Les Contes de ma Mère L'Oye.* The titles are all translations of Perrault's own titles.

Fourteen of the fairy extravaganzas have for their sources tales by Madame D'Aulnoy. All of the tales used as foundations for the plays are also included in Planché's published translations of Madame D'Aulnoy's fairy tales.

The three remaining plays from French sources in this group are *Beauty and the Beast,* from Madame le Prince de Beaumont's *La Belle et la Bête; The Good Woman in the Wood,* from Mlle. de La Force's *La Bonne Femme;* and *Young and Handsome,* from the Countess de Murat's *Jeune et Belle.*

In each case Planché has followed the version of the story as it appears in his own translations of the works of the various authors, always giving a complete story, and sedulously avoiding the "garbled nursery versions" which were well known to his audiences and had been the inspiration of Christmas pantomimes before his day. This avoidance of the nursery tales is more apparent in the spirit of his work than in the actual story itself. One of the characteristics of the original French tales is their humor, which appears in the comments of the author on the actors in the story, and their apparently unconscious criticism of the life around them, that of the court of Louis XIV. Both of these qualities have disappeared from the nursery tales as we, and Planché's audiences, know them. In the original tales, behind his perfect seriousness, we feel the intention of the narrator to poke fun not at the characters in the tales but at the readers of them. This subtle satire contributes largely to their charm. It is something of this air that Planché has tried to preserve in his stage versions of the tales, as in his translations he has tried to keep the original flavor, substituting for the atmosphere of Louis's France that of Victoria's England.

In technical method the fairy pieces resemble quite closely their classical predecessors. . . . That this method is much like that which was used in the eighteenth-century ballad operas and burlettas is at once apparent. In Planché, however, is found a closer coördination between songs and spoken dialogue than in most of the earlier plays. The extravaganzas are in this respect certainly better put together than such pieces as Planché's own earlier works and, in general, the productions of his contemporaries and imitators.

The characters that appear in these little plays are in most cases not developed with any attempt at distinct portrayal. In the fairy pieces, however, there are two exceptions, more remarkable because they are unexpected in drama of this frivolous sort. Riquet with the Tuft and Gam-Bogie, the yellow dwarf, stand out among the other characters of the extravaganzas as exceptional, first in being physically unattractive and in having in their characters and positions a touch of pathos. Riquet is a deformed, repulsive looking prince with a clever mind and a happy disposition. This is not a startlingly original conception, but the character has a sincerity that is unusual in burlesque. He describes his case thus, in a song:

> I'm a strange looking person I own,
>   But contentment forever my guest is;
> I'm by habit an optimist grown,
>   And fancy that all for the best is.
> Each man has of troubles his pack,
>   And some round their aching hearts wear it;
> My burden is placed on my back,
>   Where I'm much better able to bear it.

And so on to much the same effect, reaching the conclusion:

> Thus on all things I put a good face,
>   And however mis-shapen in feature,
> My heart, girl, is in the right place,
>   And warms towards each fellow creature!

The character is, in a manner, appealing; and one is truly glad when the fair princess has him in the end.

The Yellow Dwarf is the one of the fairy extravaganzas which has a tragic ending. The dwarf, Gam-Bogie, in his efforts to keep Allfair, the beautiful lady, in his possession brings about, unintentionally, the death of the two lovers, Allfair and Melidorus. In Madame D'Aulnoy's tale the lovers remain dead but are transformed into two palm trees growing side by side. Planché revivifies them at the end of his play and adds a last, grand scene, for obvious reasons. Gam-Bogie is represented as vicious and vindictive. Most of his speeches are typical of the dialogue of burlesques, but at the end of the play he reveals his character in the speech made after the violent death of Allfair. It is a parody of part of Othello's speech, in the fifth act, in which he curses himself.

> And caused her death to whom I was devoted
> Oh, heavy trial! Verdict: Serves me right!
> Whip me ye devil—winds come, blow me tight!
> Roast me in flames of sulphur—very slow!
> Oh, Allfair—Allfair! Dead—O, O, O, O!

It must be remembered that this appears in a Christmas extravaganza, in which local slang was regarded as humorous; but the conception of the remorse and disappointment of the dwarf is apparent. And the actor, Robson, was able to make a serious impression with it. The language is, despite the slang and the ridiculous rhyme, if anything, perhaps less extravagant than that in *Othello,* whence many of the phrases are taken.

These two characters, however, in which there is some attempt to portray depths of emotion, are exceptions. The characters are not of first importance in the extravaganzas, and most of them are conventional but pleasing. Their most satisfactory quality is, perhaps, the tenacity with which they "stay in character" until the action of the play is over and they address the audience in the finale. Unlike most of his contemporaries, Planché expected his actors not to indulge in "gags" or private jokes with the audience but to play their parts in the drama that they always take seriously regardless of the ridiculousness of their speeches or the effect on the audience. In this laudable object this serious writer of burlesque was not always entirely successful.

The dialogue of most of the extravaganzas is in pentameter couplets. There is some prose in *Puss in Boots* and a good deal in *Riquet with the Tuft.* It is, however, the usual couplet that appears most frequently. Such an abundance of this meter, not especially well written or much varied, is apt to become tiresome, but the audience is saved from tedium by the frequent introduction of songs. (pp. 790-97)

[An] example of a type still found in musical comedy, the plaintive, sentimental song, is found in *Graciosa and Percinet.* Graciosa is tied to a tree in the forest to be devoured by wild beasts. After the following song her fairy lover appears and, of course, saves her.

> True love can ne'er forget;
> Long here I should not fret
> Were I still, Percinet,
> Your darling one;
> This very day you said,
> When first your bow you made
> If I required your aid,
> You'd to me run.
> But "out of mind when out of sight,"
> I'm afraid the proverb's right;
> Of your promise you'll think light,
> And brown I shall be done.
> True love can ne'er forget;
> Long here I should not fret
> Were I still, Percinet,
> Thy darling one!

Another type is found in which the words are parodied after the words of their originals. An example comes from *Fortunio and His Seven Gifted Servants,* though almost any other extravaganza would yield as good results. Here the parody is upon "The Days that we Went Gypsying," once popular. I quote only the first stanza.

> Oh, the days that we got tipsy in, a long time
>   ago,
> Were certainly the jolliest a man could ever
>   know!
> We drank champagne from glasses long, and
>   hock from goblets green,
> And nothing like a cup of tea was ever to be seen.
> All night we passed the wine, nor dreamed of
>   hyson or pekoe
> In the days that we got tipsy in—a long time ago.
> (pp. 797-98)

[It] remains only for me to express my profound conviction that, though these pieces of Planché's and others like them are frequently arrant nonsense in them one finds often a truer key to the spirit of their age than in the works of persons of considerably greater literary respectability; and in the history of the stage of the early nineteenth century they must be considered. (p. 798)

> *Dougald MacMillan, "Planché's Fairy Extravaganzas," in* Studies in Philology, *Vol. XXVIII, No. 4, October, 1931, pp. 790-98.*

Harley Granville-Barker   (essay date 1932)

[*Granville-Barker was an English dramatist, actor, and critic associated with the "New Drama" movement, and as such, emphasized the value of serious drama rather than stereotypical social comedy or melodrama. In the following excerpt, he discusses Planché's importance to Victorian popular theater, and comments on his successful collaboration with actress Madame Vestris.*]

Planché was a much respected veteran. He . . . had written and helped to write some 57 extravaganzas (the name his own adopting), not to mention a hundred or more farces, comedies, melodramas, and librettos for operas besides. He wrote the libretto for Weber's *Oberon,* and one of the disappointments of his life was over Mendelssohn's final recalcitrance (after much making of agreements and evasively polite correspondence) to set to work seriously upon a score for *The Burghers of Calais*—great work that it was to be! By 1872 he can confess to at least a share in 176 plays of one sort or another; 62 of them all his own, the rest collaborations and "liftings", mainly from the French. As to these last, conscience still waited upon international copyright; the early Victorian dramatist held the freebooter's licence handed down from the Elizabethan. Planché, being introduced to Scribe at the Garrick Club with the bland recommendation *"Encore un qui vous a pillé"*, capped it in compliment by *"Impossible de faire même du nouveau sans piller Monsieur Scribe"*. And Scribe smiled politely. Not that there was much profit in the thefts. Thomas Dibdin was reputed to be the "author" of 800 dramatic pieces, no less; but when he died in 1841 at the age of seventy, he had been glad enough of a subscription of £50 a year to keep him from poverty in his decline. Planché himself lived modestly enough and was prodigiously industrious. His 176 plays apart, he was an antiquary of renown, wrote a standard history of British Costume (it was he who persuaded Charles Kemble to stage *King John* with historical accuracy, and so started a movement which has only just run its once salutary course), was attached to the Herald's Office, and, at seventy-six, completing his memoirs, could boast that he was still working as hard as he had ever done during the last fifty years. Yet a Civil List pension of £100 a year was a matter of importance to him. Nor did the receivers—the managers—do much better than the thieves; the theatre was in a wretched state financially. Nobody profited in fact, least of all the public.

Planché, unlike others, readily acknowledged his debt to France, even for the work which was most his own, the extravaganzas. He took the idea, and even the material for the first of them (the first written; its production was long delayed) from a *Folie Féerie, Riquet à la Houppe,* which he saw in Paris in 1821. English burlesque at this time was in an even more deplorable state than play-writing in general. The worst would not find its way into print; one can only hope even now that the best is not exemplified by a concoction entitled *Othello Travestie,* credited to a certain "Maurice G. Dowling, Esq.", which Mr Lacy thought it worth while to publish. With Othello a gibbering nigger, whose speech to the Senate is set to the tune of *Yankee Doodle* and begins

> Potent, grave and rev'rend sir,
>   Very noble massa . . .

—a Desdemona following him to the tune of *Bonnie Laddie* with

> I'll tell you why I loved the Black;
>
>   *Too ral,* etc.
>
> 'Cause ev'ry night I had a knack,
>
>   *Too ral,* etc.
>
> Of list'ning to his tales bewitchin',
> My hair while curling in the kitchen.
>
>   *Too ral,* etc.

—and far worse to follow yet, the scene of her murder (a "comic" murder!) being really too nauseatingly vulgar for quotation; with this for a standard no wonder Planché found his fairy tale unwelcome! Not till he encountered Madame Vestris did he get his chance.

She had her faults, had Madame Vestris; but she was a woman of courage, commonsense, and—timeliest of qualities!—of great good taste. What she did for English drama, at a time when it was more than usually difficult to do anything whatever for that rapscallion art, when you had, managerially, either to be "legitimate" and face almost certain loss in the vast barns of Drury Lane and Covent Garden, or evade the law elsewhere by peppering your plays with songs and dances and pretending they were not plays at all, has been too tardily remembered. She found in Planché's delicate simplicities excellent material for the colour and spice of her acting and singing and dancing: she was accomplished in all three, and had enough vitality besides for the inspiring of the actors around her. We may guess, indeed, that she re-fortified his dilution of the French spirit to something even above its original strength. Between the two of them, at any rate, they seem to have produced a civilised entertainment in this kind. And for fifteen years to come, till, game to the last, she left the theatre to die, Planché, with little interruption, wrote Christmas and Easter plays for her, the Christmas play often lasting till Easter, and the Easter play sometimes seeing the summer through. Here, as such things go, was an achievement to be proud of; and it is worth commemoration.

Simplicity, delicacy and what one can best call innocence; these are the Planché hall-mark. One may add taste and tact, and exact judgment also—he knows when to stop. In no kind of writing do such qualities count for more; there is no substance in it, manner is everything—its good manners, in fact. The trick of his method is old enough, it is, indeed, classic; he makes the sublime not, let us remark, ridiculous, not by any means grotesque, but easy and familiar; and, because he is Planché, pleasantly, good-naturedly familiar. (pp. 106-09)

> *Harley Granville-Barker, "Exit Planché— Enter Gilbert,"* in The Eighteen-Sixties: Essays by Fellows of the Royal Society of Literature, *edited by John Drinkwater, Cambridge at the University Press, 1932, pp. 102-48.*

Kathy Fletcher   (essay date 1980)

[*In the following essay, Fletcher analyzes Planché's adaptation of* The Birds, *comparing it with Aristophanes' original.*]

On 13 April 1846, a new Easter piece, **The Birds of Aristophanes,** *composed by J. R. Planché,* opened at the Haymarket. Unlike previous holiday pieces based upon a classical source, it was not a burlesque of a legend or play, but was an actual adaptation of Aristophanes' masterpiece. As such, it was a unique experiment. Old Comedy was translated, studied, and subjected to critical scrutiny, but, not surprisingly, it was a stranger to the London commercial theatre. With its characteristic open celebration of sexuality, licentious fooling, and pointed political and personal comment, the form stood in total opposition to Victorian standards of decorum and to a system of censorship and licensing.

The Birds is an intriguing little piece of one-act length, which takes its structure and story from Athenian Old Comedy, its performance style from nineteenth-century extravaganza, and its point of view from contemporary conservatism. The play warrants our attention today for reasons other than its attraction as a curiosity. Firstly, it represents a conscious attempt by a practicing dramatist to extend the boundaries of comedy on the English stage. Planché's strategy was to add a literary dimension to one of the "illegitimate" popular forms. Secondly, the piece is an interesting study in adaptation. The premise of the ancient Greek play, that of founding a utopia, was particularly well-suited for a time of social unrest and experimentation. Changes were made by the playwright in order to increase contemporary relevance and response to current social and political movements. Finally, a comparison of Planché's version with the Aristophanic original illustrates two differing conceptions of comedy and suggests certain limitations of the form on the Victorian stage.

An adaptation of Aristophanes is undoubtedly an aberration in the annals of holiday entertainment, but it is perhaps more understandable if one considers the man who created it. James Robinson Planché was naturally inclined to combine the ancient with the modern, the scholarly with the popular. His long and many-faceted career in both the world of scholarship and commercial theatre was checkered with instances of innovation and reform. By 1846, he had already published the first **History of British Costume,** and during the next four decades of his immensely productive life, he wrote numerous scholarly articles, books, and treatises on costume, armor, and heraldry. Today, he is most often remembered in general theatre histories as a leader in the movement toward historically accurate costumes and as a major figure in the vogue for antiquarian productions of Shakespeare. He was instrumental in the implementation of the Dramatic Author's Act (1833), which established the right of the British dramatist to control and charge for performance and publication of scripts. As a playwright, reader, and "superintendent of the decorative departments," Planché made his living in the day-to-day grind of commercial theatre. From 1818 to 1872, he fashioned by his own count, 176 works for the stage, 72 of which he claimed were original. Like most of the working dramatists of the time, Planché was a voracious adapter of foreign plays (most notably French), early English comedies, and contemporary pieces from other genres.

While his body of work encompasses numerous types and sub-types, he was the acknowledged master of "extravaganza." Planché perfected this light and whimsical form and naturalized the French *folie féerie* under its banner. Like so many other dramatic genres from this century, extravaganza was born of the restrictive theatrical laws, enforced until 1843, which permitted the performance of "regular" or spoken drama only at the legitimate or patent houses. Planché skillfully unified the disparate elements of song, dance, and spectacle; extravaganza joined pantomime as one of the exceedingly popular holiday forms. Brought out semi-annually at Christmas and Easter, such pieces were traditionally big moneymakers for the managements and often kept theatres afloat when tremendous losses were sustained from offerings of the "regular" tragic or comic main pieces. Although he possessed the inclinations of a reformer and antiquarian, Planché was always understandably concerned with audience appeal and its consequent affect upon box office receipts. With its combination of ancient Athens and Victorian London, *The Birds of Aristophanes* is perhaps emblematic of the man and his professional position.

Planché related that he conceived the idea for such an adaptation while "casting about for a subject" for yet another Easter piece. He finally "determined to gratify a craving of long standing" and adapt a play by the Greek comic poet "to the modern and local circumstances requisite to interest and amuse London playgoers of the nineteenth century." Planché billed the piece as a "dramatic experiment" and announced in the published text that it had been "undertaken with the view of ascertaining how far the theatrical public would be willing to receive a higher class of entertainment than the modern *Extravaganza* of the English stage, or the '*Revue*' of the French." In retrospect, he declared with characteristic reforming zeal, "So great a step in advance was a hazardous experiment, but it was worth making for the sake of Art and the true interests of the British stage." His professed goal was nothing short of establishing a new comic genre on the English stage—one which utilized the production elements of extravaganza but was imbued with significant content. He hoped to open a field in which "much abler men" than himself "might give the reins to their imagination and

their wit in dramatic form, unfettered by the rules and conventionalities of a regular Comedy" and in which they might be assisted by "Music and Decoration." He recalled in his autobiography, "I was impressed with the idea that I was opening a new stage-door by which the poet and the satirist could enter the theatre without the shackles imposed upon them by the laws of the regular drama. . . . [M]y ambition was to lay the foundation for an Aristophanic drama, which the greatest minds would not consider it derogatory to contribute to."

For this lofty endeavor, Planché chose a play which takes as its premise the creation of a utopia—a topic perhaps more and certainly not less relevant in 1846 than it had been in 414 B.C. For several decades, the men whom we now refer to as the utopian socialists had been theorizing, with varying degrees of practicality and mysticism, about alternatives to the exploitative capitalist economic system and resultant lifestyle. In France, Charles Fourier advocated the reconstruction of society based upon communal associations of producers. Louis Blanc was known for his theory of worker-controlled "social workshops," and in 1840, Pierre-Joseph Proudhon declared, "Property is theft." Furthermore, the actual founding of experimental communities was a fact of nineteenth-century life. In the 1830s, Paris witnessed the rise and fall of a commune established by the followers of the social reformer Saint-Simon. In the United States, Robert Owen set out to build a more perfect society in 1825. His venture in New Harmony, Indiana collapsed several years later, sending Owen back to the British Isles £40,000 poorer. The famous Brook Farm community in Massachusetts which began in 1841, was in trouble by the time Planché composed his play, and was completely dissolved by 1849. In short, the London audience of 1846 did not have to look very far nor think very long to find a contemporary analogy for a character who builds a city in the sky.

If the choice of play was shrewd in terms of subject matter, the selection of Aristophanes as a model for the "hazardous experiment" was also wise in terms of form. Old Comedy shared many formal characteristics with nineteenth-century extravaganza; it was written in verse, was episodic, and utilized singing and dancing. This meant, of course, that the audience was prepared for these extrinsic features. Planché chose to alter one major formal element, a move which probably represents a concession to audience expectation and a tendency by the playwright to rely upon a proven device. Rather than use a multi-actor chorus, he assigned that role to Priscilla Horton, a popular performer of breeches roles. It was her job to comment upon the action and address the audience directly, leaving the chorus of birds from the original a comparatively minor role.

Structurally, however, Planché left the elements of Old Comedy solidly intact. The major characters are introduced in the *prologue;* the birds arrive during a *parados* (marching-on song); the fantastic plan or "happy idea" is laid out in the *agon* (argument); the *parabasis* (address by the chorus) furnishes a mechanism for the playwright to speak directly to his audience; and a series of episodes, separated by choral interludes, shows the "happy idea" being put into practice. In fact, for each structural element in the original there is a corresponding unit in the adaptation, which may be abbreviated but which performs essentially the same function. This holds true for approximately two-thirds of the play. In the final portion, Planché made a radical and very telling departure from his source.

While Planché reproduced the general outline of the story within the Old Comedy structural pattern, he made minor alterations and additions which increased its relevance for the Victorian audience. In the *prologue,* for example, the motivation assigned to the two major characters has a distinctly nineteenth-century ring. Jackanoxides and Tomostyleseron (from Pisthetairus and Euelpides of the original) have left their home in order to, "seek out some blest corner of the earth, / Where folks are not weighed by what gold they're worth. / Where there's no care, no fraud, no toil, no strife, / And we may settle down in peace for life." They search for and find the King of the Birds (played by the popular extravaganza performer, James Bland) and ask him the whereabouts of such a place. After being told that a human utopia does not exist, Jack continues to press the issue with a description of his ideal state.

> But are states all alike? all men enrolled
> Slaves of ambition—worshippers of gold?
> Is there no city now, for instance, where
> To eat, and drink, and sleep, is all men's care?
> Where those who have, to those who have not,
>   give
> Unlaboured for, the means, at least, to live?
> Where there's no pandering to wealth or station,
> No war, no politics, no litigation;
> No bitterness between great and small?

The particular emphasis placed upon escape from a civilization enamored with wealth and the search for a classless society was a contemporary innovation. Aristophanes' wanderers go in search of a carefree life, but their chief complaint about "home" is that Athenians spend an inordinate amount of time suing each other in the law courts.

Given the socialistic rhetoric of Planché's characters, Jack's formulation of the "happy idea" becomes quite ironic. When the two runaways are finally convinced that there is no ready-made human utopia, they come to the realization that the life of a bird is an attractive proposition. After all, it promises free water and seed, little work, no politics, no tailor's bills and no taxes. But Jack, unwilling to completely relinquish the human life, conceives a brilliant plan, "To build on trees then is it not a pity, / When you might found a splendid airy city, / Midway 'twixt earth and heaven, so that admission, / To either would depend on your volition? / Both gods and men you thus would check with ease, / And make with either any terms you please." In an instant, a plan for seizing power and gathering wealth supersedes the search for an ambition-free society. Jack changes from social reformer to entrepreneur.

The King of the Birds looks with favor upon Jack's proposition, and summons the members of the bird kingdom, so that Jack may convince the feathered congregation of his plan's advantages. Planché converted this section, the traditional *agon* or argument, into a parody of British Parlia-

mentary debate. Jack begins his address before "the House" with a version of Othello's speech to the senators, "Most potent, grave, and reverend owls and widgeons, / My very noble and approved good pigeons." He goes on to proclaim the superiority of birds over man, " 'Arms and the man' to sing I deem absurd, / A nobler theme is mine, 'Wings and the bird!' " An ill-timed "Cock-a-doodle-doo!" from the floor touches off a verbal free-for-all in which bird names and terminology are interspersed with political rhetoric. In his more polite moments, Jack refers to his colleague as "the honourable bird," but his anger culminates in the following declaration to the King, "Sir, I am not to be put down by clamour, / Nor knocked down by a factious yellowhammer, / Whom I should blush to call my learned friend." When order is finally restored, Jack whips the gathering into a vengeful frenzy by describing the many ways in which man, the "plumeless biped," has captured, tamed, killed, and eaten birds in the past. He sets his "motion" before the House in the form of a song, which details his plan for construction and operation of the airy city. In essence, the new utopia is to be a miniature London, with "streets, crescents, and squares," run on a model of contemporary bureaucratic procedure. The only difference is that the birds, with Jack as their leader, of course, will be in power. Gods must pay transit duty when they pass through the city on a journey to earth, and humans will be required to have a passport before ascending to heaven. Jack's plan wins unanimous approval, and the birds exit to begin work on their new metropolis.

Just as Planché managed to parody a British institution in the *agon,* he satirized contemporary life in the *parabasis.* In Old Comedy, this direct audience address was traditionally used by the playwright to express political opinion, utter personal grievances, or simply to ask for audience approval. Planché used his female Chorus to remark upon the fantastic nature of life in nineteenth-century England. If any "sensible folks" are inclined to sneer at such "classical fancies" as birds building cities in the air, they should reconsider: "Could not projects as airy, and visions as vain, / Be proved to have sprung from an Englishman's brain?" The Chorus proceeds to remind the audience, living in the midst of the railway boom, of "monstrous" speculations advertised in the *Times* and the *Post,* of bubble companies and of "absurd schemes" championed in the House. After pointing out the seeming impossibility of modern methods of transportaiton ("In the days of Queen Bess, did our forefathers dream / Of the glories of gas, and the marvels of steam?"), the Chorus makes the only direct reference in the play to one of the contemporary social reformers: "And if an Utopia man could secure, / In Harmony birds would beat Owen, I'm sure!"

Another opportunity for pointed topical allusion is furnished by an episode involving three would-be immigrants to the new city. Jack is revealing in his growing power when the Chorus announces that now all humans are "quite crazy to be birds!"; "On 'Change, no sooner was your project known, / Than every other scheme aside was thrown.' " The five Aristophanic visitors of this episode, the dithyrambic poet, soothsayer, astronomer, commissioner, and statute-seller, are changed for contemporary purposes to a poet, architect, and legislator. Planché used the arrival of the Poet, who is also a dramatist, to call attention to dwindling audiences, the precarious financial state of London managements, the takeover of the grand old patent houses by minor entertainers, and his own battle to have lyricists, as well as composers, paid for their work. The hapless Poet is dismissed—who needs lyrics for bird songs anyway? The Architect fares no better in his bid to enter the ideal state. He offers to erect the city in the sky, but then reveals the quality of his workmanship, "My quarrel is with the new Building Act, / I feel my genius cramp'd, sir, upon land. / They stipulate that houses now should *stand!*" When the Legislator appears proffering his services as lawmaker, he refuses to declare himself either a Tory or a Whig, saying he is, "Sometimes one, sometimes 'tother; / In short, 'tis rather difficult to say / What anyone exactly is to-day."

Three undesirable visitors are enough for Jack, and he flees the oncoming hordes from earth. At a vantage point which furnishes a *"Bird's-eye view"* of the new city, he meets the King, who informs him that its construction is now complete. From this moment on, Planché's version departs radically from the original. Aristophanes gave his schemer free rein to the end, and continued to escalate the level of absurdity. Pisthetairus and Euelpides change into birds; a goddess is caught trespassing; Prometheus appears incognito; and a delegation which includes Heracles and Poseidon arrives from Olympus. Pisthetairus drives a hard bargain with the gods and they finally agree not only to yield their sceptre of power to the birds, but also to give Zeus' daughter, Sovereignty, to Pisthetairus in marriage. The triumphant character ascends to heaven and returns with his bride amidst great jubilation and joyous hymns to Hymen.

Planché, however, did not let his play go rollicking to a close. With the King's announcement of the city's completion comes the news that the ideal state is torn by class dissension. The rooks want a rookery; since they cannot afford to live in Peacock Square, they have no place to go. The parrots, goldfinches, and lorys, on the other hand, "are all enraptured with the glories / Of their new palaces and public places, / Where little dirty birds daren't shew their faces." Not everyone is satisfied with the environment of a city in the clouds. The waterfowl complain that the air is too dry; the geese have found there is no grass in the sky, and say "a common's needful for their health." To this demand, Jack replies, "They're always cackling for a commonwealth." It seems that insurrection is brewing everywhere, "there's sad grumbling 'mongst the barndoor fowls, / Their roosting snuggeries are filled with owls; / And every grain and crumb they chance to scratch up, / Some hawk or buzzard's almost sure to catch up." The airy city is rife with class struggle, political discontent, and capitalistic opportunism; it is a mirror image of nineteenth-century Britain with its housing problems, radical movements and intense social and political unrest.

Jack is unconcerned about the trouble and says that this state of affairs is no worse than in the past. The King reminds him, however, that he has raised the hopes of the bird kingdom for the abolition of such problems, "You promised, if they went by your advice, / That it should be of birds the Paradise." Jack is still unwilling to accept blame and begins an exchange which swiftly leads to the message of the piece.

> JACK. Zounds! If amongst themselves they can't agree,
> Why, prithee, should the blame be cast on me?
> I cannot change their nature, can I?
> KING.   Why
> Then change the life they led that nature by?
> JACK. Because I thought them born for better things.
> KING. You thought! Vain fool, know Jove, who gave them wings,
> Put, in his wisdom, limits to their flight;
> Marked out their food by day, their rest by night.
> Think you he gave to man the power of reason
> To stir inferior beings up to treason?
> To snatch from out his hand the regal rod,
> And make each goose believe itself a god?
> Or gave to godlike man that reason's use,
> That he with wings should make himself a goose?

Lest anyone should miss his point, Planché drove it home once more. The scene changes and discovers Olympus with the principal deities enthroned, and the King of the Birds as Jupiter himself. Mere mortals will ever be "discontented with their lot," he declares, and then proceeds to succinctly deliver the moral of the play, "Hence, let wild theorists a lesson take, / And see what monsters of themselves they'd make, / What dire confusion in the world 'twould breed, / If fools could follow whither knaves would lead." Jupiter's stern pronouncement is a far cry from the reveling which closed the Aristophanic version. It is essentially a reprimand for hubris, something more akin to the spirit of tragedy than to Attic comedy. Because he projected a serious purpose for comedy, Planché felt compelled to denounce what he saw as folly. He did not allow the situation, set in motion, to play itself out because he did not trust the absurdity of the action to make its own comment. He did not trust his audience to draw the desired conclusion, but laid it out simply and clearly in rhyming couplets. Such a closing moral was traditional in Victorian extravaganza, and it lent a distinctly paternalistic tone to the holiday entertainment form. It was, however, foreign to the spirit of satire. The altered ending moved *The Birds* away from the province of successful satire and into the realm of fable.

There are other differences in the two versions of the play which reflect two disparate conceptions of the theatre as an institution. On the whole, the sharpness of Aristophanes' wit was considerably dulled in the adaptation. Planché's humor was much less caustic and biting, much more cautious and generalized. In Aristophanes' play, Pisthetairus holds a dedication ceremony just as the city is completed. His abortive attempt at performing a sacrifice is a direct parody of a contemporary religious rite. Had Planché even considered staging an analogous episode (and he certainly would not have), it would never have passed the censors. These were men of an age which dealt with its religion much differently than fifth-century Athens and looked upon its theatre not as a civic and religious celebration where the anarchic spirit was given its due, but as a profit-making business subject to stringent governmental control. Despite any pronouncements to the contrary, the London stage was not fertile soil for the revival of an "Aristophanic drama," in the truest sense of the word, nor was Planché the man to accomplish such a feat.

A leveling tendency is also at work among other elements of the play. Aristophanes' version encompasses extremes of dramatic form. He made frequent use of physical slapstick humor. In their first encounter with the birds, Pisthetairus and Euelpides prepare to defend themselves with pots and pans, and later, Pisthetairus unceremoniously beats his visitors from the stage. Planché steadfastly refrained from using such tomfoolery, a fact not surprising considering the author's pride in having developed a more refined species of holiday entertainment than the preceeding extravaganza and burlesque. At the other end of the spectrum, Aristophanes, the poet, soared to lyrical heights in his choral odes, particularly in the *parabasis.* In fact, *The Birds* has been often regarded by scholars as the pinnacle of Aristophanic verse. Planché's pentameter couplets, which he ordinarily used for extravaganza, tinkle along pleasantly but never approach anything resembling poetic grandeur.

If the adaptation failed to measure up to the incredibly high standards set by the great Athenian poet-playwright, it was nonetheless a pleasing piece of dramatic construction and a noteworthy experiment. The basic theme of the play was cleverly matched to contemporary concern with problems arising from industrialization, capitalism, and the first flailing attempts of socialism. That Planché responded by declaring such problems inherent to human nature and by counseling contentment with god-given lot was indicative of his solidly middle-class stance. This conservative position may have helped to undermine the play as satire. Having clearly identified the birds as an oppressed species and Jack as a reformer, it was a dangerous game to loose the reins as Aristophanes was able to do; a resounding pronouncement by an authority figure (and who more authoritarian than Jupiter?) certainly seemed a much safer and easier proposition.

On a smaller scale, Planché's use of individual topical allusion was exceedingly clever and his parody of Parliamentary debate is still highly amusing. The play, on the whole, is thoroughly charming—a quality which, like it or not, was the most salient characteristic of the Planché extravaganzas. To settle for "charming" may seem a bit anticlimactic for an author who undertook his experiment "for the sake of Art and the true interests of the British stage," but certainly the attempt to restore a major comic writer to the theatre is still worthy of notice.

Planché's plan to test the discernment of his audience had only mildly encouraging results. He recalled in his memoirs, "It was a *succès d'estime,* I am proud to say, with many whose opinion I value highly, but not *d'argent,* as far as the treasury was concerned." Several London critics praised the play highly. The *Times* reviewer was pleased to see Aristophanes staged, although he doubted that many would know enough to appreciate the attempt. The critic for the *Illustrated London News* declared that the piece was too good to elicit "shouts of laughter from the general audience." In some instances, he noted, the allusions were too esoteric, but "the author, however, may rest assured that not a point was missed by the more educated portion of the heavens, although the appreciation was subdued and quiet." Although disappointed that the play was not a popular success, Planché remained convinced of its merit. Over twenty years later, he spoke of *The Birds* and another unpopular experiment, *Love and Fortune* (1859), as his "disregarded darlings," and concluded, "their comparative failure in point of attraction has not in the slightest degree affected my opinion that, both as regards motive and execution, they are not surpassed by any of my more popular productions, or shaken my confidence that they will yet one day justify that opinion."

If *The Birds* did not herald a new era of comic writing on the English stage, it is still of interest historically. It provides evidence of some serious thinking about genre and the function of drama, even within a commercial theatre which has been frequently identified with haphazard construction. It also indicates a tentative willingness on the part of a practicing dramatist to express a conservative political viewpoint on the stage, albeit in a very generalized fashion. While today the adaptation may seem a quite tame and blunted version of the original, Planché obviously considered it to be a significant innovation for the Victorian stage. The play serves as a remainder that each age draws its own comic perimeters, and that it is often difficult to see beyond one's own self-imposed boundaries. (pp. 89-98)

> *Kathy Fletcher, "Aristophanes on the Victorian Stage: J. R. Planché's Adaptation of 'The Birds',"* in Theatre Studies, *Vols. 26 and 27, 1979-80 and 1980-81, pp. 89-98.*

Donald Roy   (essay date 1986)

[In the following excerpt, Roy surveys Planché's extravaganzas.]

[Although some of the earliest of Planché's extravaganzas] were first announced as burlettas, in accordance with the required playbill parlance of the day, they can all more or less conveniently be grouped into three categories: those which make use of figures from Greek or Roman mythology or parody the forms of classical drama, those derived from fairy-tales, and those which Planché dubbed *revues.*

The first of the 'classical' extravaganzas, *Olympic Revels, or Prometheus and Pandora* [1831], originated in a burlesque that he had written some years earlier, shortly after *Amoroso* [1818], but had been unable to place. Borrowed from George Colman's story *The Sun Poker,* which, Planché says, furnished him 'not only with a subject, but suggested a mode of dealing with it', and perhaps inspired by Madame Vestris's recent appearance in a revival of Kane O'Hara's *Midas,* it is a lively, if slight piece, replete with word-play and puns, topical allusions to English life, and a prevailing mood of comic bathos that arises from the incongruity of such utterances in the mouths of classical gods and demi-gods. The dialogue, in rhyming couplets, is liberally punctuated with good-humoured travesties of popular songs or of airs and choruses from operas with which the theatre-going public was familiar, such as *Masaniello, Der Freischütz, The Marriage of Figaro, Guillaume Tell* and *Midas* itself, and it culminates in an appeal to the audience from Vestris in the character of Pandora:

> Smile, ye kind gods, on our Olympic Revels;
> Ye gay gallants, come, banish my blue devils,
> Let not my grapes be sour as the fox's
> But fill with patrons all Pandora's boxes . . .

The extravaganza ran until the end of the season, its reception having much to do with the firm establishment of Vestris as the first woman theatre manager, and, thus successfully launched, the *Olympic Revels* recipe was reemployed with increasing ingenuity, verve and visual display in an annual series of 'classical' extravaganzas, each written with Charles Dance and expressly for performance as a Christmas holiday piece: *Olympic Devils* (1831), *The Paphian Bower* (1832), *The Deep, Deep Sea* (1833) and *Telemachus* (1834).

After an interval of ten years, in 1845, Planché returned to Greek mythology in *The Golden Fleece,* but with a rather different purpose. He had intended to write a straightforward *revue* for Easter, but the interest lately aroused at Covent Garden by the production of Sophocles' *Antigone* in something approaching the original manner, 'on a raised stage and with a chorus' and to music by Mendelssohn, prompted him to make his own comment on that style of presentation—'to burlesque', as he says in his preface, 'not the sublime poetry of the Greek dramatist . . . but the *modus operandi* of that classical period, which really illustrates the old proverbial observation that there is but one step from the sublime to the ridiculous'. By this time Planché was attached as stock-author to Benjamin Webster at the Haymarket, where he remained from 1843 to 1847, another period of intense collaboration which yielded seventeen plays in four seasons, including comedies, farces and above all extravaganzas, which he was specifically contracted to produce at each Christmas and Easter. But Madame Vestris and Charles Mathews were members of the company there, their three-year tenancy of Covent Garden and a brief spell with Macready at Drury Lane having both come to grief, and the subject of *The Golden Fleece* was chosen so as to capitalise on their individual talents, Vestris's early experience as *diva* in Italian opera giving a rhetorical edge to her Medea and Mathews's characteristically relaxed, nonchalant manner as the Chorus enabling him to confide in the audience in an amused and amusing fashion. The effect proved to be well calculated; the play was revived many times, becoming a regular part of Mathews's repertoire, and its treatment even earned Planché something of a reputation among academics as a classical scholar.

The following Easter he went a stage further with *'The Birds' of Aristophanes,* which he sub-titled a 'Dramatic Experiment' and conceived not as a burlesque but as 'an humble attempt to imitate or paraphrase . . . such portions of the Comedy of *The Birds* as were capable of being adapted to local and recent circumstances', his ambition being to open 'a new stage-door by which the poet and the satirist could enter the theatre without the shackles imposed upon them by the laws of the regular drama' and thereby 'lay the foundation for an Aristophanic drama, which the greatest minds would not consider it derogatory to contribute to'. Though only a *succès d'estime,* it is an accomplished piece of work, decidedly free in its paraphrase of the original and more decorous in tone, but nonetheless vigorous and idiomatic throughout and quite trenchant in those passages that offer contemporary comment or satire. Take, for instance, the Chorus's parabasis:

> What in men turned to birds, is too strange to
> be funny,
> When they make every day ducks and drakes of
> their money?
> Why should not the fowls in the air build a palace,
> When there's hope of a submarine railway to
> Calais? . . .

or Jackanoxides' exchanges with the Architect:

> ARCH: . . . My quarrel is with the new Building Act:
> I feel my genius cramp'd, sir, upon land.
> They stipulate that houses now should *stand!*
> A fallacy exploded long ago,
> As ruinous to architects, you know;
> For if your dwellings are to last for ages,
> The half of us will not get workmen's wages.
> JACK: Sir, to be frank with you, I think a swallow,
> Would beat the best half of your builders hollow.
> To talk of architecture is a joke,
> Till you can build a chimney that won't smoke!

and the Poet:

> POET: . . . Of course you'll build a theatre—and there
> I'll satirise them all.
> JACK: Apply elsewhere,
> *I* build a theatre *above*—no, no!
> There are too many to be let below.
>   *Air*—CHORUS—*"Lucy Neal"*
> In dust, at Covent Garden,
>   The mourning Muses sit,
> Misfortune floored the management,
>   And Jullien floored the pit.
> The Northern Wizard conjures,
>   And reckless maskers reel,
> On boards so oft by Kemble trod,
>   By Siddons, and O'Neill.
> Kemble, Young, and Kean,
>   Siddons and O'Neill!

If now ye graced the Drama's side,
How happy she would feel.

Even the final admonition given by Jupiter, warning men not 'to be something they are not' and of the confusion that would ensue if 'wild theorists' were heeded and if 'fools could follow whither knaves would lead' is, for all its safe conservatism, salutary.

After this, the two remaining 'classical' extravaganzas add little of substance. Evidently an attempt to repeat the success of **The Golden Fleece** and written for the Easter following Vestris and Mathews's assumption of control at the Lyceum, **Theseus and Ariadne** (1848) has a rather more fragmentary, adventitious air and lacks some of the earlier play's wittily tongue-in-cheek manner, despite three virtuoso patter-songs for Mathews as a choric Daedalus and a memorable punning of 'baccy' with 'Bacchae'. **Orpheus in the Haymarket** was adapted from Offenbach and Crémieux's *Orphée aux enfers* at Buckstone's request for the first appearance of Louise Keeley at his theatre in 1865.

Planché clearly disliked the *opéra bouffe,* not so much because of its 'utter subversion of the classical story' but rather 'the inartistic mode in which it was carried out, the unmeaning buffoonery forced upon it', so he took it upon himself to make extensive alterations and felt he had 'succeeded in elevating the tone and imparting to the Drama generally a more definite purpose'—a quality which emerges most clearly in tableau 3, when Public Opinion, acting as Chorus, interferes in the action to restore Eurydice to earth and Orpheus, asserting in the process a strong sense of Victorian morality and reproving the deities for their lack of it. There are some good theatrical jokes and, as Planché says in the preface, 'with the addition of pretty scenery, pretty dresses, and some pretty faces . . . the piece went merrily with the audience'; but he was obviously not entirely satisfied with it.

More distinctive still, and buoyantly original throughout his career, were Planché's so-called 'fairy' extravaganzas. Their initial conception owed something to the French *féerie,* which flourished so spectacularly in the early years of the nineteenth century, but in adapting the genre to English taste Planché naturalised it so thoroughly as to make a lasting contribution to the English theatre. His first essay in it was **Riquet with the Tuft,** produced at the Olympic for Christmas 1836, with Charles Mathews as the deformed Prince Riquet and Madame Vestris as the beautiful but foolish Princess Emeralda [*sic*], who in return for the gift of sense bestows on him the gift of love which magically removes his deformities. In view of the known popularity of Planché's classical extravaganzas with the Olympic audience, both performers had grave reservations about this new departure. The form of the piece, too, was unfamiliar. Nursery tales like *Mother Goose, Aladdin* and *Little Red Riding Hood* were of course long established on the English stage as the subject-matter of Easter entertainments and the openings of Christmas pantomimes, but by and large they had been handled in a straightforwardly dramatic (or melodramatic) fashion and, more often than not, as a pretext for spectacle, whereas the *féerie* proper was a more refined confection of whimsy, badinage and

delicate satire, retaining much of the charm of the early eighteenth-century 'contes de fées' by Charles Perrault, the Comtesse d'Aulnoy and others, on which so many of them were based.

In the event, fears about the piece's viability proved totally unfounded: **Riquet with the Tuft** played to crowded houses from Boxing Day until the end of the season and initiated a tradition of fairy extravaganzas which were to come annually from Planché's pen for the next twenty years, all intended for either the Christmas or the Easter holidays— on three occasions, in 1843, 1850 and 1851, there was one for each of the holiday seasons—and produced successively at the Olympic, Covent Garden, Drury Lane, the Haymarket, the Lyceum and, to complete the circle, finally the Olympic again. Increasingly Planché became personally associated with the genre, and in his hands it came to occupy a special place both in the affections of holiday audiences and in the memories of regular theatre-goers. Writing half a century later, Frank Burnand [in his *Records and Reminiscences, Personal and General,* 1904], destined to be a prolific and successful exponent of a related entertainment, recalled that 'the pit of the Lyceum at Christmas time, when Madame Vestris produced one of Planché's extravaganzas preceded by a couple of farces of which Charles Mathews was the life and soul, was something marvellous to see, so jammed and crowded was it'.

Riquet with the Tuft was the only one of these extravaganzas for which Planché was directly indebted to a *féerie, Riquet à la Houppe,* in which he had seen the French comedian Potier years before at the Porte Saint-Martin theatre in Paris. For the remainder he preferred to draw his inspiration from the original fairy-tale itself, following its story-line closely almost without exception but tailoring

Planché as Somerset Herald.

characterisation and business to fit the special gifts of his actors. The first group, **Puss in Boots** (1837) and **Blue Beard** (January 1839) at the Olympic, followed by **The Sleeping Beauty in the Wood** (1840), **Beauty and the Beast** (1841) and **The White Cat** (1842) at Covent Garden, were all written for the Vestris-Mathews company and contained suitable heroines or breeches roles for Madame Vestris, a succession of burlesque kings or other notables for James Bland (a specialist in this 'line') and a couple of 'gagging' clowns for John Harley. At Drury Lane in **Fortunio** (1843), the first of Planché's extravaganzas not connected with the name of Vestris, the transvestite Miss Myrtina was entrusted to a rising newcomer, Priscilla Horton, who then went on to play similar roles alongside Bland in the four fairy extravaganzas produced at the Haymarket, **The Fair One with the Golden Locks** (1843), **Graciosa and Percinet** (1844), **The Bee and the Orange Tree** (1845) and **The Invisible Prince** (1846). After Vestris and Mathews became lessees of the Lyceum, Planché proceeded to write nine fairy extravaganzas for them in seven seasons, beginning with **The Golden Branch** at Christmas 1847 and ending with **Once Upon a Time There Were Two Kings** in 1853, for which Bland rejoined the company to play King Periwigulus the Proud. Opposite him as King Placid the Easy was Frank Matthews, who had been a regular in these roles since 1849, while most of the breeches parts were taken first by Kathleen Fitzwilliam and later by Julia St George; for Madame Vestris, in deference to her advancing years (and declining health), Planché devised a number of matrons and confidantes. Julia St George reappeared in tights in two of the final group of three fairy extravaganzas presented at the Olympic—**The Yellow Dwarf** (1854), **The Discreet Princess** (1855) and **Young and Handsome** (1856); but here the dramatic interest centred upon the series of grotesques he fashioned for Frederick Robson, an actor equally at home on the music-hall stage, who possessed such passionate intensity of feeling to match his comic brilliance that he was capable of controlling the whole mood of a piece.

In the preface to **The Queen of the Frogs** (1851) Planché listed his criteria for a good fairy extravaganza, all of which he had found in its source, *La Grenouille bienfaisante* by the Comtesse d'Aulnoy: 'A plot, the interest of which is sustained to the last moment, and is not in the least complicated; a series of startling and exciting events, the action in which required no verbal explanation, and numerous opportunities for scenic display and sumptuous decoration—what more could be desired?' Evidently he felt that audiences would desire more, for to this basic formula he invariably added the same kind of embellishments as had been used to enliven his classical extravaganzas: elaborate and inventive play on words, spirited or plaintive songs to the music of drawing-room ballads, traditional airs, nursery rhymes and well-known operas (often enough those—such as *Guillaume Tell* and *Norma*—to which Planché had already supplied a 'straight' libretto), and a good deal of witty allusion to topics of a literary, theatrical or social nature, which contrive, as it were, to domesticate the fairy world and assimilate it to the familiar actuality of London life.

The guiding principle behind these references—either in-

congruity or anachronism, or both at once—is fairly simple, but they certainly presuppose the existence of a cultivated and intellectually alert audience. So much is clear even from such 'throwaway' lines as:

> I've looked for you through all the château, Margot;

and

> The lock upon the door at the first landing,
> The only Lock upon my understanding.

Elsewhere the allusiveness can be more extended and potentially more serious in tone. The railway mania of 1845, for instance, the feverish speculation in bubble companies which ruined hundreds of investors for every one it enriched, is dealt with at length in **The Bee and the Orange Tree,** which also unburdens itself of some fairly outspoken comment on the evils of industrial capitalism in general in the song of the ogre, Ravagio:

> . . . And why I'm so plump the reason I'll tell,
> Who lives on his neighbours is sure to live well.
> What sharper, or swindler, or usuring Jew,
> But lives much the same as the Ogres do . . .
> The sempstress wasted by slow decay,
> Has her bones but picked in another way;
> To the weary weaver with sleep o'ercome,
> The factory bell sounds like 'Fee Fo Fum' . . .
> And better swallow infants, fast as pills,
> Than grind their bones to dust in cotton mills.

Again, in **The King of the Peacocks,** performed at Christmas 1848, the burden of the opening scene between the rival fairies Faith and Fickle, who champion the relative merits of tradition and change fuelled by scientific progress, is a commentary on the revolution which had agitated France for most of that year. Twelve years later, on the occasion of the revival of **The Fair One with the Golden Locks** in 1860, a second stanza was appended to the closing song in order to accommodate a reference to the recent annexation of Nice by Napoleon III.

By far the most consistent subject for reference, however, is Shakespeare, whose work Planché plunders for material with a reckless abandon born at once of an obvious love and knowledge of the plays and a certainty of their familiarity with audiences. Frequently he provides the briefest of echoes, single lines or phrases quoted (or misquoted) in passing, as it were, and without the least dramatic emphasis, though some of the puns, such as this in **Once Upon a Time There Were Two Kings** (1853), are irresistible:

> . . . a piano you're not born to play.
> Oh, there be misses, I have here and there heard,
> Play in a style that quite out Erard's Erard.
> Pray you avoid it . . .

Just as frequently, however, it is a question of full-scale, prolonged parody of key speeches, as in **The Fair One with the Golden Locks** (1843) where King Lachrymoso contemplates taking a draught of magic elixir (which turns out to be a bottle of poisonous fly-spray) with the lines:

> Is this a corkscrew that I see before me?
> The handle towards my hand—clutch thee I will!

I have thee not—and yet I see thee still!
Art thou a hardware article? or, oh!
Simply a fancy article, for show.
A corkscrew of the mind—a false creation
Of crooked ways, a strong insinuation! . . .

Even entire scenes are echoed, as in *Graciosa and Percinet,* which has a parody of the closet scene from *Hamlet,* and *The Island of Jewels,* where the storm scene parodies *King Lear* at some length and contains the following exchange between King Giltgingerbread the Great and his son Prince Prettiphello:

> PRINCE: Are you aware, sir, you have no umbrella? (*rain*)
>
> KING: A thought has struck me, rather entertaining,
>   I am a King more rained upon than reigning.
>   My wits are going fast!

Many similar passages could be instanced where the whole effect depends on the audience's ability immediately to recognise and saviour the parallel. Planché's primary object of creating an elegant, urbane kind of humour is amply realised, but it would appear that in performance the parody was susceptible of greater ambivalence of tone. In the hands of a remarkable burlesque actor like Robson, for instance—who many thought, had he lived longer, might have challenged the memory of Edmund Kean in the latter's most celebrated tragic roles—some moments could even partake of the quality of the Shakespearean original. Robson's portrayal of the monstrous Gam-Bogie in *The Yellow Dwarf* was so powerful that, in Planché's words, 'he elevated Extravaganza into Tragedy'. The way in which he handled the dwarf's proposal to the Princess Allfair, which is strongly reminiscent of the wooing scene in *Richard III,* is unfortunately not recorded, but his Othello-like lament over her dead body,

> Whip me ye devils—winds come, blow me tight!
> Roast me in flames of sulphur—very slow!
> Oh Allfair—Allfair!—Dead—O, O, O, O!

moved Thackeray almost to tears: 'This is not a burlesque', he exclaimed, 'it is an idyl'!

To many contemporary spectators, however, perhaps the greatest single attraction of the fairy extravaganzas was their visual excitement. His long apprenticeship as stock-author, with a hand in the mounting of his own and other plays, had made Planché perfectly familiar with the technical aspects of staging, and this knowledge was employed to good purpose in all his work, particularly melodrama, opera and extravaganza, where he exploited the potential of changeable scenery and machines with a sure touch. It was of course an asset above all in fairy extravaganza, capable of making manifest the magic at the heart of the tales themselves and lending an air of enchantment to the entire performance. If this is already evident in the pieces written for the Olympic in the 1830s, it becomes abundantly clear in those destined for the larger stages of Covent Garden between 1839 and 1842 and the Lyceum in the late 1840s and early 1850s, where the full gamut of resources—from dioramas, gauzes and complete *changements à vue* to sophisticated trap-work, flying and mechanical artifices of all kinds—was turned to account, and the extravaganzas themselves grew from one to two acts, as if to accommodate the increased possibilities. At both these theatres Planché was appointed 'superintendent of the decorative department' and was in daily contact with the teams of scene-painters, machinists, property-makers and costumiers. The ingenious deployment of scenic effect in his work during these years betokens not only an acute awareness on his part of what could be made to happen on stage but also a willingness to exercise to the full the technical skill and imaginative powers of his colleagues, who included at one time or another the Grieves, Bradwell and Beverley.

That he had a profound respect for their achievements is borne out by generous comment in his memoirs and prefaces alike. Bradwell, who followed Vestris and Mathews from the Olympic to Covent Garden, he called an 'unequalled machinist', and one can understand why from intriguing stage directions of his which bear witness to trees which change colour, 'close upon' the presumptuous woodcutter and 'beat him with their branches' in *The Sleeping Beauty in the Wood* (1840), and to disembodied hands which appear in all parts of the stage, leading the way, carrying torches, bringing in tables and chairs, shaking the hands and being pressed to the lips of ordinary mortals in *The White Cat* (1842) 'in the most natural and graceful manner without its being possible for the audience to detect the *modus operandi*'. His most lavish praise, however, was reserved for William Beverley, the scene-painter and machinist who first joined the Lyceum company for *The Golden Branch* in December 1847 and remained to collaborate with Planché for almost six years. The extravaganzas produced during this period contain the most dazzling of effects, so dazzling in fact that Planché soon began to have reservations about their value, partly—and understandably—because they made his plays less likely to be revived, but more particularly because in the long run they 'injured the true interests of the Drama'.

Though that experienced theatre-goer, Henry Morley, could write in glowing terms in 1853 about Beverley's ability to create 'a fairy effect . . . of the completest kind' in *Once Upon a Time There Were Two Kings* 'by lengthening the silver skirts of damsels who appear to hover in the air, grouping them into festoons, and giving to their beauty something of a fantastic unearthly character', Planché was later to comment sadly and at some length upon the whole phenomenon of 'unmeaning spectacle' to which that very prowess gave rise. In retrospect, he associated its onset with the sensation occasioned at the end of *The Island of Jewels* (1849) by 'the novel and yet exceedingly simple falling of the leaves of a palm tree which discovered six fairies supporting a coronet of jewels'; thenceforward, 'year after year Mr Beverley's powers were taxed to outdo his former out-doings. The epidemic spread in all directions. The *last* scene became the *first* in the estimation of the management of every theatre, where harlequinades were indispensable at Christmas'. On the Vestris-Mathews management alone the effect was deleterious enough: 'The most complicated machinery, the most costly materials, were annually put into requisition, until their bacon was so buttered that it was impossible to save it. As to me, I was positively painted out'. Fortunately, this objection did not deter him from adapting fairy-tales to the stage until the very end of his full-time career as a playwright.

There remains that group of extravaganzas to which Planché refers as *revues,* or, for want of a snappier English expression, 'dramatic reviews', and defines as 'a running commentary on recent metropolitan events'. Again the model for these was French in origin, and again he claimed to have been the first to introduce the genre to this country with *Success, or A Hit If You Like It,* written for the Yates and Terry company at the Adelphi and presented there in December 1825. This *revue* treated audiences to a good-natured commentary on the main theatrical productions offered to them during the past London season. In it, Fashion, governor of the town for the Emperor Whim, instructs his daughter Success to receive all her suitors, who hail from the English Opera House, Drury Lane, Covent Garden, the Haymarket, the Adelphi and the Italian Opera at His Majesty's, before he, in consultation with the press, will decide who is to gain her hand; in the event they cannot agree, there is a riot, and she is awarded in temporary custody to Long Tom Coffin from *The Pilot,* the play by Fitzball then running at the Adelphi. This of course allowed T. P. Cooke, who was playing Long Tom Coffin at the time, to supply a free sample of his performance in a shop-window context. He also appeared briefly as Zamiel in *Der Freischütz,* a part he had created at the Lyceum in 1824, while Yates gave impressions of Charles Mathews the elder and Charles Young, and John Reeve impersonated Kean in John Howard Payne's tragedy of *Brutus* and Liston in his celebrated role of Paul Pry in Poole's comedy. This all makes for a genial affair, if rather flat-footed for today's reader—as all such pieces must be that rely for their principal effect on topicality and local knowledge.

Planché went on to write another eight *pièces de circonstance* in the same mould, half of them between 1853 and 1855, after he had finally abandoned his life of day-to-day commitment to the London theatre, and as if viewing the theatrical scene from a more dispassionate, not to say valedictory, perspective. All were written for or commissioned by the playhouses he knew best—the Olympic, the Haymarket and the Lyceum—normally as a *bonne bouche* for the holiday audience on Easter Monday, and all but one taking stock of the current state of the theatre. Inevitably ephemeral—a property freely admitted by Planché, though he numbered them 'amongst the most creditable of my original dramatic compositions'—they now present a sadly dated air and are certainly not revivable. On the other hand, they constitute a fascinating insight into their times and provide the theatre historian with a positive mine of information and quotation.

The Drama's Levée, or a Peep at the Past (1838), for instance, shows the Drama 'in a critical state of health' because of rivalry and dissension between her two sons, Legitimate and Illegitimate:

> DRAMA.   . . . Now with their feuds they rend
> my feeble frame,
> And rob me both of fortune and of

fame. (*noise without*)
Hark! There, again!—that worse than O.P. riot;
Why won't they let the Drama die in quiet?
Go, part those children; bid them both appear!
Enter LEGITIMATE DRAMA *in a Roman toga.*

L. DRA.   He whom they own Legitimate is here!

DRA.   You naughty boy! when I'm so very poorly;
You have been fighting with your brother surely.

L. DRA.   I have; because of him I can't get fed,
Whilst he is almost sick with gingerbread.

DRA.   Will you ne'er cease this ruinous debate?
Where's that audacious Illegitimate?
Enter ILLEGITIMATE DRAMA *in a dress half harlequin and half melodramatic.*

I. DRA.   Behold! (*striking an attitude*)

DRA.   Unnatural son!

I. DRA.   Is't thus I'm styled?
I always thought I was your natural child.

L. DRA.   He puns! He'll pick a pocket the next minute!

I. DRA.   I shan't pick yours, because there's nothing in it! . . .

Amid jokes, puns and allusions to contemporary dramatic fare there are other trenchant comments on the burletta and the abiding conflict between the Major and the Minor houses before the 1843 Theatre Regulation Act.

The Drama at Home, or an Evening with Puff (1844), written in imitation of Sheridan's *The Critic,* is an ambitious piece which takes up the story after the promulgation of this act and expounds Planché's 'humble opinions on the unprecedented condition of the English stage' following the abolition of the monopoly hitherto enjoyed by the patent houses and the occupation of Drury Lane and Covent Garden by non-dramatic enterprises. The Drama is now in extremis and wishes to die, but Puff attempts to revive her spirits with harebrained, spectacular projects to pull in an audience, and conjures up brief fragments or tableaux from recent or current productions at a wide range of theatres, concluding with a 'grand anomalous procession' of the various exhibitions on offer in London. The final note is one of cautious optimism: although the removal of legal restrictions has as yet produced 'no rising drama worth the name', merely a collection of sensational or opportunist pieces, there is ample time for things to improve. A much slighter piece, *The New Planet, or Harlequin out of Place* (1847), for which the recent discovery of Neptune provided a convenient, if flimsy, pretext, is little more than a verbal and visual inventory of stage productions, quasi-scientific exhibitions or demonstrations and other entertainments—like the 'mysterious lady' and a troupe of Ethiopian Serenaders—then available to Londoners.

The Seven Champions of Christendom (1849), on the

other hand, the only *revue* not concerned with theatrical matters, took the whole of Europe as its canvas and essayed a commentary on the state of the continent at a time of violent political and social unrest. The risk inherent in tackling such a subject for an Easter Monday audience was even greater than it had been with *The Birds,* but to ignore it, says Planché's preface with characteristic solemnity, 'was impossible, and I had always contended that the mission of the dramatist was of a much higher nature than the catering of mere amusement for the million'. To accommodate it, therefore, to audience expectations he allegorises the action and shows St George and the patron saints of Scotland, Wales, Ireland, France, Italy and Spain overcoming tyranny, ignorance, superstition 'and all the plagues of humanity, in the semblance of the gigantic ogres, witches, sorcerers, demons, dragons, serpents, and venomous vermin in the original legends, with the weapons with which modern science and "the march of intellect" had so powerfully armed them'. Smug and chauvinistic though it is to modern taste, the play was brilliantly successful, again demonstrating Madame Vestris's superiority to purely 'commercial managers' in her willingness to take chances, and subsequently being much anthologised for literary readings.

The last four *revues* all take a close look at the theatrical scene in the 1850s and do so in a mood of palpable anxiety. *Mr Buckstone's Ascent of Mount Parnassus* (1853), a title alluding to Albert Smith's entertainment *The Ascent of Mont Blanc,* which was then enjoying immense popularity at the Egyptian Hall, was commissioned by J. B. Buckstone for the opening of his management of the Haymarket. It shows the new manager pondering what to offer the public 'nightly for forty weeks' and being visited first by the Spirit of Fashion, who gives him some candid advice from the audience's point of view concerning the drama's shortcomings, and then by Fortune, who conjures up specimens of what she has recently favoured, including *The Corsican Brothers* and no fewer than six versions of *Uncle Tom's Cabin,* before he decides that none of this will do and vows to scale his own dramatic Parnassus. Though an equally occasional piece, *The Camp at the Olympic* (1853), written to introduce Alfred Wigan's management of the Olympic, furnishes a more comprehensive survey of the current resources of the English stage in comparison with the recent and distant past; while *Mr Buckstone's Voyage Round the Globe* (1854), which took its cue from Wyld's Great Globe, a scale model of the earth then on display in Leicester Square, presents a curious mixture of comments on the theatre and the state of the world, terminating with the goddess Cybele's advice to the manager:

> And here let all the world take up its quarters.
> Demonstrate to the town the earth's attraction,
> And so give universal satisfaction.

The conceit underlying *The New Haymarket Spring Meeting* (1855) is to equate all the shows vying for public favour in London—exhibitions, scientific and geographical displays, opera and dance as well as drama—with racehorses contesting the Great Metropolitan Handicap at 'Upsand Downs'; and, after seeing a parade of last and this year's runners, Buckstone, as the Lord Mayor's Fool, concludes that:

> The odds are fearfully against the stage . . .

This is very much the message of all these *revues*. In them, as elsewhere, Planché 'took the opportunity of promulgating opinions which might be serviceable to the best interests of the drama', and by the mid 1850s his opinions seem bleak indeed. He sees a beleaguered theatre struggling to withstand massive competition from other entertainments and denied government support:

> The State no temple to the Drama gives—
> She keeps a shop, and on chance custom lives,
> From hand to mouth . . .

To Alfred Wigan's complaint in *The Camp at the Olympic* that 'the Drama's perishing of inanition . . . And sadly empty the dramatic larder' the only remedy that his wife can suggest is an eclectic mixture of the fare that is currently available, in the hope that it will be enough to save their 'experimental Camp'—a stoical conclusion on the manager's part but scarcely redolent of confidence, still less of enthusiasm, on the author's.

In 1853 Planché had given up his London home in order to live in Kent, going so far as to resign his membership of the Garrick Club, and although he was to return in the following year after his appointment as Rouge Croix Pursuivant he never again haunted the theatrical establishment or attached himself to any manager. Instead he accepted occasional commissions, mostly at the Haymarket and the Olympic, for the *revues* and fairy extravaganzas already mentioned, several comedies and one opera. They show no decline in his powers. Indeed, after his sense of being eclipsed by Beverley at the Lyceum he relished the thought of having 'once more to rely upon acting rather than upon scene-painting' and was never prouder of a success than in the case of the scenery-less, action-less *Camp at the Olympic,* where his dialogue had to stand alone. *Love and Fortune,* too, inspired in form by the fairground theatre performances of early eighteenth-century France and subtitled by Planché a 'Dramatic Tableau (in Watteau colours)', is an interesting attempt to marry his own delicate style in verse and sung ditties to the more vigorous idiom of *commedia dell'arte.* While not entirely successful (and a comparative failure when staged by Augustus Harris in 1859), it has considerable charm and is a clear token of his continuing enterprise as a playwright. It is all the more ironic, therefore, that his final exercise should have proved a sad miscalculation. Invited by Boucicault in 1872 to contribute the songs for a 'fairy spectacle' called *Babil and Bijou* to be presented at Covent Garden, the veteran versifier of seventy-six set to work with elation, but in the event found his words heavily cut and finally overwhelmed in a sumptuous four-hour farrago of scenic display, complete with submarine and lunar sets and a huge cast of nearly a hundred exotically attired actors, singers and dancers, the action of which could not be followed without reference to a printed brochure summarising the argument and reproducing Planché's lyrics. Thereafter he was not to be tempted back to the stage, preferring to devote himself to his duties as Somerset Herald which, coupled with his many scholarly pursuits, kept him fully occupied. His health remained good until the last twelve months of his life, and in a letter to an antiquarian friend in 1875 he had written '[I] am in my eightieth year, working harder than I did at thirty.'

So busy a round was it that his output of plays was restricted to a mere dozen in the last twenty-five years of his life, compared with more than 160 in the previous thirty-five. Long before this retrenchment, however, his reputation with contemporary audiences was secure, the product not only of native ability but of sheer professional assiduity. Bunn, for instance, [in *The Stage,* vol. III, 1840] described him as 'my able, industrious, and zealous friend', and a reviewer of *Faint Heart Never Won Fair Lady* at the Olympic called him 'as untiring as untired, and as indefatigable as the fair manageress herself'. To industry, as a direct corollary, he added a complete grasp of the physical realities of stage performance. The opinion of Edward Fitzball, a fellow-toiler in the same theatrical vineyards, must command respect in this connection: 'Planché is a practical author, and one of our cleverest; a little too cautious *perhaps;* he would braid the sunbeams, so carefully, as not to burn his fingers. In the general parlance of theatrical business a practical author means a play writer who looks beyond his steel pen, and quire of foolscap; to the O.P. and to the P.S. . . . he will plumb the depth of his venture, and satisfy himself to the solving of a problem in Euclid, as regards the practicability and possibility of his scenic effect, on the stage, or of any original idea emanating from his own brain' [From Fitzball's *Thirty-Five Years of a Dramatic Author's Life,* 1859]. Pragmatism of this order no doubt helps to explain Planché's great admiration for Scribe and for that other master-craftsman of the *pièce bien faite,* Victorien Sardou. It is perhaps in the same light, too, that one should see his readiness to alter existing 'classic' plays for performance and to collaborate with fellow playwrights or composers in the production of new work, as he did with Charles Dance on all but one of the first ten Olympic extravaganzas, with Weber so successfully on *Oberon,* with Bishop on other operas, and with Mendelssohn to the extent of being prepared to make all and any textual concessions in order to ensure that their aborted opera, *The Siege of Calais,* might see the light of day.

However, the single most obvious mark of Planché's understanding of 'the stage and its necessities' was his ability to write for actors. The weather-eye he kept at all times on the individual strengths and weaknesses of a company enabled him not only to fit parts to star players like Madame Vestris, Mathews, Liston and Bland, but also to make revisions for a new cast on the occasion of a revival, to add, change or suppress songs according to their vocal competence, to write into a given story what he unabashedly called 'introduced characters', or even to choose a whole subject for the benefit of available performers, as he did *Fortunio* for 'some of the best pantomimists of the day' at Drury Lane, or, most conspicuously of all perhaps, *The Yellow Dwarf* and *The Discreet Princess* for the uniquely tragi-comic Robson, in whose interests the former piece was designed to include two 'turns' for which he was already well known in the music-halls, a Lancashire clog hornpipe and a finale to the music of 'Villikins and his Dinah'. Clearly, then, it would be a mistake to bring literary values to bear on Planché's overall style or

even to expect much concern for realism in his dialogue. Whatever importance he attached to realistic costume and décor, his plays were conceived first and foremost as scripts for actors, as vehicles for their peculiar talents or distinctive stage *personae.* He recognised his dependence on them and was generous in his praise for those who were most responsible for his success; his shrewd assessment of Charles Mathews shows that he was also a good judge of the limits of their powers.

Despite this capacity for compromise, Planché seems to have nurtured a genuine seriousness of purpose throughout his working life. At its simplest it is evident even in his attitude to source material. He persistently congratulates himself on fidelity to his originals, both in publishing accurate translations of French fairy-tales to replace the mutilated versions known to nursery children or pantomime audiences, and also in adapting these tales to the stage. It was what prompted him to restore the action of *Blue Beard* to fifteenth-century Brittany and its eponymous villain to the ranks of the French aristocracy, in preference to the 'very magnificent three-tailed Bashaw' found in 'George Colman's well-known and well-worn melodramatic opera'. His rationale is conveniently summarised for us in the preface to *The Prince of the Happy Land,* where he talks of preserving not only the wit and satire that have been lost in these garbled versions of the stories but also the 'moral lessons of the originals'. However commonplace the morals themselves, Planché leaves us in no doubt as to his sincerity in propounding them: 'Regardless of the opinion of the few self-constituted judges who contended that a moral was out of place in an extravaganza, and had evidently overlooked the fact that there is no very popular fairy tale without one, I most contumaciously persisted in my error, and on the present occasion, actually selected a subject which had *two.* This does not prevent him, however, from making his own occasional emendations when he finds those lessons too melancholy, as in the case of *The Yellow Dwarf,* where, having dutifully brought the piece to the required conclusion with the death of the two young lovers and their transmutation into palm trees, he disarmingly provides an alternative happy ending, more suitable to 'a tale of mirth . . . at such a season'.

Similarly, if for more aesthetic reasons, he adopted a conscientious attitude to the translation or adaptation of existing plays from the French. In a note to the published text of *The Jewess,* and subsequently in his memoirs, he indignantly deplored the changes forced on him in his own version of this opera and of *The Red Mask* in deference to the imagined susceptibilities of the public. When he initiated changes of his own it was for one of two, in his eyes, perfectly legitimate reasons: first, to correct historical inaccuracies in the original, as in Scribe's *Gustave III* or in *Fiesco* (where he took issue with Schiller on a point of Italian precedence!); and secondly, to adjust the original to English manners and taste. In so doing Planché not infrequently improved on his source. One of many actors with reason to be thankful for this, Frank Archer, maintained that his comedy *Secret Service* 'gave greater opportunities than the musical play from which it was taken', and the *Examiner* in its review of *The Knights of the Round Table* was merely echoing the consensus of press opinion when it commented: 'What he takes he makes his own by skill and expertness of handling. We have seen adaptations of his clearly better than the originals . . . '

Moreover, in Planché's memoirs and prefaces alike, one repeatedly finds him claiming to have had the higher or long-term interests of the drama ever in mind, one particularly self-righteous passage declaring that 'whatever success I have been fortunate to achieve in the course of my literally life, I have certainly not been indebted for it to any intentional sacrifice of my own principles at the shrine of popularity'. Even allowing for an understandable element of *post hoc* rationalisation here, the sense of purpose seems to be devoutly felt and it is borne out in much of his professional activity. It expresses itself in an almost obsessive desire to reanimate and strengthen English drama in general and to raise the tone of popular dramatic fare in particular. His introduction to English audiences of the *revue* and his acclimatisation of the French *féerie* could, to take a cynical view, be dismissed as acts of theatrical opportunism, but there is no gainsaying the fact that, once having established these forms, he endeavoured to take them further with **The Seven Champions of Christendom** and his adaptation of **The Birds,** for instance, in the service of higher satirical or moral ends. Likewise social satire, albeit of a fairly genial disposition, informed the elegant comedies of manners that he wrote for Vestris and Mathews, like **Hold Your Tongue** and **My Heart's Idol.** His promotion of historical authenticity in costume and realistic staging generally was a sincere crusade, so sincere as to give a sharp edge to his disappointment at their degeneration into a pretext for gratuitous spectacle. He wrote feelingly on this subject in an article published in 1861: 'That I was the original cause of this movement, I do not deny; that . . . I succeeded in the object I had honestly at heart, I am proud to declare; but if propriety be pushed to extravagance, if what should be mere accessories are occasionally elevated by short-sighted managers into the principal features of their productions, am I fairly answerable for their suicidal folly?' The same article bitterly regrets the harmful influence that he has indirectly and unwittingly exercised on traditional pantomime through the 'last scenes' of his Lyceum extravaganzas, which in Beverley's hands became so spectacular as to provoke a mania for transformation scenes and induce rival managers to outdo each other by 'patching' extravaganza on to pantomime 'to the serious injury of both'.

Clearly, Planché was astute enough to be well aware of the dangers of the pictorial approach to production, however closely associated with it he had been. In his work as supervisor of design and stage management at Covent Garden and the Lyceum he certainly cultivated period realism—and there is ample evidence in stage directions and costume lists as well as in contemporary illustrations to show how detailed it could be—but it was always subordinate to the play itself: he was too much a man of the theatre to allow it to develop into heavy-handed antiquarianism for antiquarianism's sake. In fact, his keen historical sense could lead him to eschew spectacle altogether, as in his production of *The Taming of the Shrew* at the Haymarket in 1844, for which he designed sets and costumes as

well as superintending rehearsals. His purpose on this occasion was to restore Shakespeare's text in its entirety, including the induction with Christopher Sly, in preference to Garrick's altered version, *Katherine and Petruchio*, which was still in common use for performance. He therefore took the logical step of abandoning scenery as such in favour of two simple locations, the exterior of the alehouse where Sly was discovered and the nobleman's bedchamber where the comedy itself was performed by the troupe of strolling players in conditions approximating to those of the Elizabethan stage and without a single curtain drop. The experiment was a bold and highly successful one, all the more remarkable in that it anticipated the Elizabethan Stage Society and the work of William Poel by a good half-century.

In his own plays the same sense of period can produce the most delicate and refreshing results, as in his *commedia*-inspired **Love and Fortune** and his spirited adaptation of Garrick's *Cymon* into a 'Lyrical, Comical Pastoral' in rococo style, with much of Arne's original music and *mise en scène* 'in perfect keeping with the time in which it was originally produced'. Both have an intrinsic verve which far transcends mere historical pastiche. Elsewhere in his work, too, whatever his dramatic purpose there is customarily a similar lightness of touch, and, where appropriate, a tremendous sense of fun. Self-sufficient jokes, as distinct from puns, are not common and seem designed to elicit a smile rather than a laugh, though they are certainly worth waiting for, as is Leona's wry comment in **The Queen of the Frogs:**

> Since Orpheus for his wife went to the deuce,
> The custom's fallen quite into dis-use;
> And if to take such journeys men are prone,
> It is for other wives—and not their own.

Even an otherwise indifferent piece can have good moments and erupt into pure comedy, as does **Grist to the Mill** when Francine, masquerading as marchioness to a miserly, atrabilious marquis, bids the latter's nephew 'embrace your uncle, who opens his affectionate arms. (*Aside to Marquis*) Open your affectionate arms.' But most of these moments need to be appreciated in context, depending as they do on the comic momentum that the action of the piece or the continuous flow of banter has built up. Many, indeed, can scarcely be savoured at all without the embodiment of performance, so inextricably geared are they to establish dramatic procedures. Such a moment occurs with King Brown's interrupted enjambement in **The Golden Branch:**

> The bride is on her road! Ah, there's the bother!
> She may arrive ere I can say Jack Rob—(*flourish without*)
> —inson!—She has so! There's a pretty job!

and again with the burlesque stichomythia between Soyez Tranquille, Argus, Florizel and Rosetta in **The King of the Peacocks:**

> SOYEZ. *Avancez,* miss!   (ROSETTA *comes forward.*)
> ARG.   O heavens!
> FLOR.   What do I see?
>   You!

ROSE.   I—myself—
ARG.   Then she herself is—
ROSE.   Me!
ARG. Rosetta!
FLOR.   Sister!
ROSE.   Brother! (*embraces—to*
   ARGUS) Husband!
ARG.   Wife!
   Transported I deserve to be for life!

Much of the best comedy, in fact, is self-referential, making capital out of perceived theatrical conventions and commonplaces. Planché seems not only at his most assured but at his most inventive and original when taking the theatre itself as his raw material. *The Garrick Fever* shows how much farcical business he can generate from a strictly theatrical setting, *A Romantic Idea* how adept he is at the burlesque of genre. Not surprisingly, incidental theatrical satire looms large, not only in the *revues*. The current London scene that Planché knew so well supplied him with targets in plenty, among the most favoured being animal shows and menageries, dioramas, *poses plastiques,* waxworks, the exhibition craze generally, nigger minstrel troupes, ballet and, perhaps the greatest source of competition to the legitimate stage, opera. Opera is also frequently absorbed into the fabric of the extravaganzas as a basis for lunatic spoof. *The Fair One with the Golden Locks* has a 'Grand Scena, on the most approved principle of Modern Operatic Composition', which incorporates recitative, songs and choruses to music from *Norma*, 'The Minstrel Boy' and 'The British Grenadiers'; while in *The King of the Peacocks* a group oath is sung by the king, his cooks and his guards holding rolling-pins to the music of 'Blessing of the Poignards' from *Les Huguenots*. There is also much linguistic guying, whereby the words of familiar Italian arias are replaced by English lyrics which are incongruous but have a similar ring: 'Com' e gentil' from *Don Pasquale* becomes 'Comb it genteelly'; 'La ci darem la mano' from *Don Giovanni* becomes 'Mind you don't let your ma know'; and the recitative and aria from *Tancredi* beginning 'O Patria' opens with 'Oh, pa! try her. Won't you, my great papa, try her', immediately after the singer has announced:

   I will only stay
To sing a song—As opera heroes choose
Always to do, when they've no time to lose.

In Planché's last extravaganza, *Orpheus in the Haymarket* [1865], the vogue for sensational dramas in the 1860s provokes a touch of sarcasm as Pluto darkens the stage, except for a circle of limelight around Eurydice, and prepares to carry her off to the underworld:

   EURY. What ails me? I am losing all sensation!
   PLU. Then for the modern stage you've no vocation!

Moments later, self-conscious theatricality asserts itself quite unashamedly: Public Opinion interrupts an imminent rhyme on the grounds that 'the Licenser' might object to it, and Orpheus strides on to the shadowy stage wondering who has 'turned off the gas in the sky borders'. There are many other such subversions of convention, as in the dual ending to *The Yellow Dwarf* and the references to Planché's own role as author or adapter. Perhaps the

most interesting example of this comes in *The Good Woman in the Wood* where the Fairy Fragrant conveys Dame Goldenheart to the famous 'Cabinet des Fées', whose shelves are lined with volumes of fairy-tales beloved by children, including a section of 'stage editions'; on a desk, centre stage, lies a volume containing the present tale but as yet untitled, which the fairy opens to

         find out how the adapter
   Has worked the story up in the last chapter.

No doubt it was the same propensity that attracted Planché to a late eighteenth-century comedy by Richaud-Martelly, *Les Deux Figaro, ou le sujet de comédie,* which has among its dramatis personae a would-be playwright taking down details of the 'real-life' action, as outlined by Figaro, to form the basis for a comedy he is writing and in turn contributing to the former some inventions of his own. However, this single level of artifice evidently did not satisfy Planché, for he transformed the original into a musical comedy by interpolating songs to the music of *The Barber of Seville* and *The Marriage of Figaro* and complicated the French author's duplication of Figaro still further by introducing a Susanetta figure alongside Susanna.

Undeniably, it is in the extravaganzas that these elements of deliberate theatricality are seen at their best, but they are not sufficient in themselves to account for what Planché called the 'almost unprecedented popularity' enjoyed by the genre, particularly by the fairy extravaganza. Among his contemporaries it seems often enough to have been discussed in the same breath as burlesque, as if there were little or no distinction between the two, but Planché himself had a precise conception of their separateness. *The Sleeping Beauty in the Wood,* the first of his holiday pieces to be performed at Covent Garden, where the use of the term 'burletta' became redundant, was clearly announced in the bills as an extravaganza, 'distinguishing', the preface tells us, 'the whimsical treatment of a poetical subject from the broad caricature of a tragedy or serious opera, which was correctly termed a "Burlesque"'. There are certainly burlesque properties in Planché's work, and he provides an eloquent apologia for the form in the lines spoken by Burlesque in *The Camp at the Olympic,* but he was not primarily or, one suspects, by temperament a writer of burlesque.

Instinctively his preference, and hence the emphasis in his work, lay elsewhere. The epithets most commonly applied to the fairy extravaganzas in their day were 'delightful', 'beautiful', 'brilliant', 'graceful'; they were characterised as 'airy trifles', with lyrics 'as faultless in tone, tact and taste, as they were rhythmically perfect'. For somewhat grudging corroboration from within the playwriting fraternity itself one may again turn to Fitzball, who after quoting Moncrieff's comment on Planché to the effect that 'he wrote in white kid gloves' adds: 'For my own part, I always seemed to entertain an idea that he lived on honey and nectar'. Of those virtues so prized by his audiences some are still faintly detectable from the printed page: an extraordinary verbal facility and skill in versification; an absurd sense of humour held in check by a refinement inimical to excess and vulgarity; a gift for creating eccentrics and grotesques; an imaginative flair for situation and the possibilities of scenic imagery; above all a delicacy of touch which enables comedy to go hand-in-hand with pathos and even with a strain of seriousness. However down-to-earth or jokily familiar his treatment of it, however defused of supernatural menace, there remains an underlying respect for the marvellous. Percy Fitzgerald put his finger on this vital factor when he described Planché's dramatisation of the fairy-tale as 'done with a certain seriousness, very much as it would appear to a child's eye'.

> **The epithets most commonly applied to the fairy extravaganzas in their day were 'delightful', 'beautiful', 'brilliant', 'graceful'; they were characterised as 'airy trifles', with lyrics 'as faultless in tone, tact and taste, as they were rhythmically perfect'.**
>
> *—Donald Roy*

What cannot now be recaptured is the dimension of performance, the qualities of acting and *mise en scène* brought to bear on the written text. That they were considerable, possibly decisive, is suggested by Planché's personal responsibility for design and stage management at most of the theatres with which he was regularly associated, particularly Covent Garden, the Haymarket and the Lyceum. The enthusiasm generated by the scenic splendours of extravaganza, most notably by those from the hand of William Beverley, became legendary, but the visual contribution of precisely realised costume may have been almost as important. The theatre critic Dutton Cook [in his *Nights at the Play,* 1883] had occasion to recall 'that courtly conventional dress of the last century which Mr Planché often favoured in his modernised renderings of fairy stories', in other words the court dress of the later years of Louis XIV and those of Louis XV, the very period in which the stories themselves were originally published. Pictorial evidence confirms both this and the Greek dress worn in the classical extravaganzas, and shows occasional excursions into other periods of European history and other cultures. Whatever liberties Planché may have taken with sartorial detail, his costumes were always firmly anchored in a specific historical period and executed with a conscious sense of design. That this was the case from the earliest days of extravaganza at the Olympic is confirmed by his anecdote in the preface to **Olympic Revels,** recounting his cast's distress at the adoption of historically correct dress: 'Liston thought to the last that Prometheus, instead of the Phrygian cap, tunic, and trousers, should have been dressed like a great lubberly boy, in a red jacket and nankeens, with a pinafore all besmeared with lollipops; others that, as in *Midas,* the costume should be an incongruous mixture of the classical and the farcical'.

As for the style of acting he preferred, Planché's major innovation as stage manager was to insist that the characters of his extravaganzas be played 'straight'. Whatever non-

sense they spoke, however absurdly or grotesquely they were called on to behave, their manner should be intent and matter-of-fact. Again, this was a strategy adopted from the very outset. The preface to **High, Low, Jack and the Game,** presented at the Olympic as early as 1833, attributes the play's success 'above all' to 'the spirit with which the performers entered into the whim of the piece—not attempting to be *funny* but acting it as seriously as possible', while that to **Fortunio,** premiered ten years later, congratulates the company on their 'apparently total unconsciousness of its absurdity'. It was the sheer perfection of this technique in James Bland that earned him the title of the 'monarch of extravaganza'. He had acquired the technique, Planché says, while playing subordinate roles 'under the best actors of the regular drama', and it had imparted to his diction and manner 'an earnestness, which, while it gave point to the epigram, trebled the absurdity of the language in which it was conveyed. He made no effort to be "funny", but so judiciously exaggerated the expression of passion indicated by the mock-heroic language he had to deliver, that while it became irresistibly comic, it never degenerated to mere buffoonery'.

These considerations constrain one to give full weight to Planché's revealing phrase, 'the precise tissue of absurdity on which I had calculated'. It comes in a passage regretting what he saw as an excessive employment of spectacle in the mounting of **Once Upon a Time There Were Two Kings** (with which he had not been personally involved) and it makes clear that his recipe for extravaganza was determined with precision, as much in the staging as in the writing. It was a compound of the fantastic, the poetic, the grotesque and the comic, and it was finely judged to appeal to a wide audience of playgoers, not least the cultivated among them. Henry Morley's evaluation of **Love and Fortune** [in his Journal of a London Playgoer, 1891] as 'exquisite trifling, very fanciful to hear, and very beautiful to see' could have been applied to the extravaganzas as a whole, on which William Archer's apt comment was that they were 'to their successors as Tenniels to Rowlandsons'.

Beyond doubt it was also a recipe that set the seal on his reputation as a dramatist. In his early days he was viewed with contempt by some—'Who are your successful authors? Planché and Arnold, Poole and Kenney; names so ignoble in the world of literature that they have no circulation beyond the green-room' [Philo-Dramaticus (Rev. W. Harness) in *Blackwood's Magazine,* June 1825]—with indifference by many; and Horace Foote's *A Companion to the Theatres* of 1829 records him simply as one amongst many authors of 'comedies and farces'. Yet for the generation of young writers who first encountered Planché's work in its heyday at the Haymarket and the Lyceum he was a master in his chosen field. John Hollingshead summed up their admiration well when he declared that Planché 'raised theatrical extravaganza and burlesque to the dignity of a fine art, and wrote verses to be sung on the stage which could be read with pleasure in the study'.

Naturally, those who aspired to the same success strove to emulate his work. The suppliers of popular dramatic fare in the 1850s, 1860s and 1870s—the Brough brothers, Burnand, H. J. Byron, Robert Reece—borrowed his style of writing for their burlesques and took its word-play much further, until the puns became excruciating or so contorted as to require a bracketed gloss for the benefit of the reader. W. Davenport Adams, who published in 1891 *A Book of Burlesque,* the first attempt at a comprehensive survey of the whole phenomenon, had no hesitation in nominating Planché as 'the founder of modern burlesque', a remark that might well have occasioned a sepulchral revolution in Brompton Cemetery in view of the so-called founder's public repudiation of his mid-century imitators thirty years before, along with their 'jungles of jingles and sloughs of slang'. Another disciple, and the only one whom Planché recognised as a worthy successor, was W. S. Gilbert, and the similarities between the two, mentioned as early as 1870 by Dutton Cook in his review of the first performance of *The Palace of Truth,* have been the subject of much subsequent comment. Gilbert's indebtedness was not confined merely to the inspiration for Pooh-Bah in *The Mikado* (who obviously derives from Baron Factotum, 'Great-Grand-Lord-High-Everything' in *The Sleeping Beauty in the Wood*) and a number of individual patter songs in *Patience, Iolanthe* and *The Grand Duke,* but may have extended to the overall lightness of touch that informs his early fairy comedies as well as the Savoy Operas themselves. Probably the example of Planché, no less than that of Robertson, lies behind Gilbert's tight control over the performance of his work through careful stage management and rehearsal and his rejection of outlandishly comic make-up and costume.

In this connection, too, the debt that Victorian pantomime owed to the staging of Planché's extravaganzas is manifest, above all in the evolution of the spectacular 'transformation scene', the burgeoning of the fairy element and the gradual erosion of the old-style harlequinade. Just as clearly, the 'principal boy' followed in the elegant footsteps of those handsome young princes and other blue-blooded breeches roles that Planché wrote for Eliza Vestris, Priscilla Horton, Kathleen Fitzwilliam and Julia St George. Extravaganza's influence may also be present in the pantomime's adoption of preposterous names for its worthies and villains along the lines of Planché's King Henpeckt the Hundredth, Viscount Verysoso, Killmany O'Gobble Killmore and the Fairy Baneful, and even in its increasing orientation towards audiences of children: as early as 1854, in the concluding verses to *The Yellow Dwarf,* comes the announcement that the piece is intended as a Christmas treat for

> . . . all you young folks who are home for the holidays,
> And children of all growths who hate melancholy days.

But the distaste he felt for the radical changes in pantomime which he had unintentionally abetted is transparent in Planché's testy animadversion upon 'the dull, monstrous, hybrid spectacle which has superseded the bright, lively, and laughable harlequinade of my earlier days'.

Ironically, then, those very features of extravaganza which had assured Planché's reputation became the source of its subsequent undoing. The wit and delicacy of his work was overshadowed by the elephantine punning and coarse, boisterous gagging of mid-century burlesques, with their flippant songs, low dresses and energetic 'breakdowns'; its charm was to be outshone by Gilbert. Planché's scrupulous, realistic approach to staging was lost sight of in doctrinaire antiquarianism on the one hand and extravagant spectacle on the other. To borrow Harley Granville-Barker's neat summation, the 'pattern of [his work] was . . . fated to be clowned as well as painted out of existence'. Unfortunately he lived long enough to see it all happen, but not long enough, fortunately, to see himself consigned within a generation to a footnote in William Toynbee's edition of Macready's diaries with the terse comment: 'He was a prolific writer for the London theatres, but his plays have made no permanent reputation'. Though overtaken by events which contrived retroactively to discredit or diminish it, his achievement during his lifetime was considerable and worthy. His multiple talents, if circumscribed, were unique and original enough to raise him distinctly above the ruck of artisan writers and theatre people; he was content to exercise those talents within the commercial establishment of the theatre as he found it, because for most of his life he had no other source of income, but at the same time he endeavoured with cautious enterprise to advance the cause of theatre as an art.

His obituary in the journal of the British Archaeological Association, understandably emphasising his serious, scholarly accomplishments, offers but a limp tribute: 'In his plays there is an abundance of harmless mirth, but neither coarseness nor vulgarity'. Less respectful to the scholar, but more representative of the popular affection he inspired as a playwright, are some lines addressed to him by Edmund Yates in the 1870s, after he had quitted the theatre for good:

> Then Mr Planché, come once more and doff
>   your herald's tabard!
>   Clear your cobwebs, seize the pen which
>   you have never plied in vain;
> For the bright sword of your wit is growing
>   rusty in its scabbard,
>   And we long to see it flashing in the gas-
>   lamps once again.

(pp. 9-32)

Donald Roy, in an introduction to Plays *by James Robinson Planché, edited by Donald Roy, Cambridge University Press, 1986, pp. 1-35.*

Kathy Fletcher   (essay date 1987)

[*In the following essay, Fletcher examines sexuality and gender roles in Planché's extravaganzas.*]

> One day he lost sight of his retinue in a great forest. These forests are very useful in delivering princes from their courtiers, like a sieve that keeps back the bran. Then the princes get away to follow their fortunes. In this they have the advantage of the princesses, who are forced to marry before they have had a bit of fun. I wish our princesses got lost in a forest sometimes.

George MacDonald, *The Light Princess* (1864)

George MacDonald penned his wish for mythic freedom in an age when restrictions on women's movement and behavior were notoriously severe. As the Victorian cult of domesticity assured the middle-class woman that her place was in the home, it encouraged her to be passive, submissive, and self-effacing. Prescriptive works such as those by Sarah Stickney Ellis urged women to live only through husband and family, to keep the private sphere an uncontaminated refuge of morality and peace while the husband and father engaged the corrupted and corrupting world outside in order to accumulate material wealth. Mrs. Ellis promised her readers that through Christian dispensation woman had been raised from her degraded position as "the first in sin" to a moral and spiritual equality with man, "and from being first his tempter, and then his slave, she has become his helpmate, his counsellor, his friend, the object of his most affectionate solicitude, the sharer of his dignity, and the partaker in his highest enjoyments." Only by becoming the "angel in the house," however, could she insure her own purity, dignity, and self-worth.

In the last fifteen years, scholars have begun to explore the approved, public image of this domestic angel, the realities of the Victorian woman's daily life, and the ways in which restrictive rules of behavior were broken, circumvented, ignored, or changed. Nina Auerbach, in her revisionary study, *Woman and the Demon,* links the severe social, physical, and sexual restrictions wished or imposed upon middle-class women to a pervasive fear of disruptive female power, arguing that "the diluted woman of acceptable convention was one peculiar outgrowth of a broad mythography in which woman, potent, primary, and alone, appropriates all the magic left in her world." Auerbach traces various recurring images of women (such as the Old Maid and the Fallen Woman) to reconstruct a portrait of female power which threatened, at any moment, to obliterate social boundaries. "The repressiveness of Victorian culture is a measure of its faith in the special powers of woman, in her association with mobility and unprecedented change, with a new and strange dispensation, with an unofficial but widely promulgated and frightening mythology."

Auerbach's interpretation has far-reaching implications for the Victorian theatre, particularly the realm of popular entertainment, which drew upon widely held beliefs, both articulated and subliminal, in an effort to attract a large audience to the theatres. As a forum for the exploration of shared fantasy, for cultural reassurance and socialization, the theatre, with its historical sexual associations and its affinity with role playing, reflected complex, often contradictory attitudes toward power relationships and sexual boundaries.

The dynamics of sexuality and gender are particularly evident in the extravaganza, a genre which most effectively theatricalized the growing Victorian fascination with art and literature of fantasy. The form which extravaganza assumed was largely the result of a collaboration between James Robinson Planché and Madame Vestris—a lucrative theatrical partnership which, in itself, challenged accepted notions of social hierarchy and brought a con-sciousness of social reality to the fictional world on the stage.

Now remembered primarily for antiquarianism and costume reform, Planché was a highly successful author and adaptor and widely recognized as creator of the distinctly nineteenth-century form of extravaganza, shaped from the earlier burlesque, ballad opera, French revue, and fairy play. In all, Planché wrote forty-four of these hybrid pieces which combined song, dance, spectacle, and topical allusion. The first, a loosely constructed look at the past theatrical season, was produced in 1825, but the genre began its long reign in public favor with his second extravaganza, *Olympic Revels* (1831, co-authored with Charles Dance), produced by Vestris for her inaugural season as manager of the Olympic Theatre. At first, the subjects came from classical mythology, but in 1836 he turned to eighteenth-century French fairy tales. Planché wrote for other houses and other managers, but the working relationship with Vestris extended over twenty-two years and included productions at Covent Garden and the Lyceum, as well as the little Olympic.

The extravaganza quickly became a familiar feature of the theatrical season. Along with pantomime and burlesque, it appeared each Christmas and Easter, and was treasured by the London audience member as a holiday institution. It shared with the older pantomime a reliance upon transformation and a fantastic, fictional universe, but while the "panto" maintained a strong working-class appeal, the extravaganza was directed especially at a middle-class audience and tended to reflect its standards, concerns, and mores. Planché started to write in this format just as the riotous behavior and manners of Regency London began to evolve into a more decorous Victorian style. Establishing and enforcing rules of conduct became an important concern with many of the middle class intent upon defining and consolidating their position in the increasingly complex social hierarchy.

Vestris's success at drawing a fashionable clientele to the formerly despised Olympic is well documented. Planché wrote that during her management (1831-39) the theatre became "not only one of the most popular and fashionable theatres London ever saw, but served as a life-boat to the respectability of the stage, which was fast sinking in the general wreck." Vestris's subsequent managements of Covent Garden (1839-42) and the Lyceum (1847-56) with Charles Mathews catered to middle-class patrons. The texts of Planché's extravaganzas, relying heavily upon word play and topical allusion, clearly call for an audience more quiet and attentive than the legendary rowdy house for pantomime. In his 1849 review, the *Times* critic felt compelled to observe:

> Boxing-night at the Lyceum is always truly respectable—the galleries quiet, the pit critical, the boxes fashionable. A little extra squeeze at the doors, and a larger display of young ladies and gentlemen than usual, are, in fact, the only signs to distinguish it from any other night in the season. . . . Strange as it may appear, no apples or orange peels were projected from the galleries, and yet the people in the pit seemed as pleased as the gods with Boxing Night.
>
> (Rev. of *The Island of Jewels*)

Planché was regularly praised for delicacy and tact. "It is a rare gift," wrote one critic, "which enables him to distinguish so nicely the exact boundary line between the ludicrous and the vulgar, and which imparts to all his plays a refined expression that never ceases to exert its salutary influence upon the audience" (Rev. of *The Good Woman in the Wood, Times*).

While many Victorians who were greatly concerned with respectability (particularly Evangelicals) did not attend the theatre, the extravaganza provided for many families an acceptable, even traditional, form of entertainment. Much of the extravaganza's appeal, however, was based upon the sexual charms of its actresses, and the importance of sexuality and gender to the extravaganza is unmistakable. Women, girls, and holiday entertainment were inseparable, as the many critics' paeans to physical charms indicate. Planché regularly inserted dialogue to comment on the beauty of the principals. The Duke in *Riquet with the Tuft* (1836), for example, insists that his daughter's (Vestris's) figure is formed "by Medicean rule," and Planché recorded that a prominent feature of the "Bacchanalian procession" of *Olympic Devils* (1831) was "a young Bacchante reclining listlessly on a leopard skin." Reviewers were always appreciative of sights such as "a bevy of nymphs, all of whom had pretty dresses, and not a few those pretty faces and forms which would beseem their characters" (Rev. of *Telemachus*). Reduced to its lowest level, this tendency resulted in the exploitation of supernumerary women and girls essentially as scenery. Dressed in provocative fairy costumes, strapped to complex machinery, and elevated into fantastic compositions, they became decoration for the seemingly magical "transformation scene." The *Morning Chronicle* described a perspective setting in which the branches of "silvery palms" formed cathedral-like arches:

> In this fairy palace, four young ladies with flowing robes thrice their own lengths were arranged, two reclining, two suspended, the means of suspension not being visible. The group was a very beautiful one, and became still more so by the three other young ladies, two of them arrayed in the curved and sweeping robe, and suspended, and the third a fairy, standing, dressed as a warrior, in a chariot. In the front was a plateau of golden leaves, lined with little ballet imps; while, when the whole scene was complete, the personages of the spectacle arranged themselves on either side, and the effect was picturesque, artistic, and beautiful.
> (Rev. of *Once Upon a Time There Were Two Kings*)

The "picturesque" and fanciful world of extravaganza allowed the actress to discard muffling contemporary dress, and an emphasis on physical charms made the persona of the female performer particularly important to this form of entertainment. Public display carried with it a number of prominent associations for the Victorian, since the notion of public versus private life was of special significance in defining sexual roles. In general, the public nature of the actress's profession set her clearly in opposition to the "domestic angel." A special pardon was sometimes allowed for "high art," but the exhibition of her talents for gain condemned the average actress to a social category only slightly above the prostitute's. Indeed, the association of that profession and the theatres early in the century made her sexual conduct particularly suspect, and the morality of the actress was still being debated late in the century.

Those performers who specialized in light entertainment were considered an even greater moral risk. Interested in exploring the boundaries of sex and class, the eccentric diarist Arthur J. Munby made a special point of recording his encounters with female performers from the exalted (he was acquainted socially with Helen Faucit, Lady Martin) to acrobats and ragged street minstrels. At a dinner party in the 1860s Munby met a conventionally beautiful and ladylike young woman, only later to discover that she was the daughter of an extravaganza performer:

> I took down to supper her mother, a pleasant elderly lady, of quiet gentle manners, ladylike, selfpossest: might have been a Bishop's wife. And who was this nice old lady? Why, she was Mrs German Reed—Miss P. Horton; whose legs, as Ormsby said afterwards, used to be familiar objects at the Haymarket, years ago! nay, she is 'entertaining' still. Does this prove the versatility of women? or not rather their wellkept purity in many cases where fools allow it not? And her daughters, so dignified & free from what is theatrical & meretricious—*they* prove something, too, I should think!

The passage is instructive, first, for its identification of Priscilla Horton's legs as "familiar objects." Despite, or perhaps because of, its careful respectability, extravaganza could utilize physical display in a way which tended to reduce the female to a collection of body parts and bordered on the pornographic. More revealing, however, is Munby's astonishment at finding the socially recognized signs of virtue where he least expected it, in the "public" woman, and his pleasure at discovering, contrary to received social wisdom, that Horton's profession had apparently not ruined her capacity for child rearing nor tainted her very feminine daughters.

Many Victorians shared Munby's fascination with the woman performer, if not his compulsion for exploration and record keeping, for if the actress's profession was shameful, it was also alluring. In his article on the changing social position of the actress, Christopher Kent notes the special "symbolic importance" of the actress. While she suffered ostracism from most polite circles, she enjoyed economic independence and a sexual and social freedom denied to the more respectable members of her sex. Auerbach observes that acting "was one of the few professions whereby a woman could transcend her prescribed social function of self-negating service to live out her own myth. . . . The questionable social position of the early Victorian actress enhanced her mythic freedom." While the hard reality of an actress's life might be quite different from the perceived glamor, it was true that those above the profession's lower ranks might enjoy the benefits of a potentially stimulating and lucrative profession which demanded the energetic application of creative talent. Even the very serious Florence Nightingale, chafing against the forced inactivity and puerile amusements of a proper young lady, recorded:

> Women, while they are young, sometimes think that an actress's life is a happy one—not for the sake of the admiration, not for the sake of the fame; but because in the morning she studies, in the evening she embodies those studies; she has the means of testing and correcting them by practice, and of resuming her studies in the morning, to improve the weak parts, remedy the failures, and in the evening try the corrections again.

In general, then, the actress brought with her to the stage a social significance, for in the public imagination, at least, the profession offered a psychic release from the normative prohibitions. Furthermore, the ability to assume and shed a different identity each night, or often within the same night, suggested, perhaps, a deceitfulness, but also a kind of power. The fear, the fascination, and the disapproval which the actress generated fed into the nexus of audience/performer/fictional character, and was of vital importance to the enigmatic extravaganza, as it created at once a world of fantasy yet relied heavily upon the audience's identification with favored performers.

As a glamorous London actress, Madame Vestris's fame was clearly enhanced by her public image as one who flouted bourgeois standards of behavior. Unlike some later Victorian performers such as Marie Wilton or Madge Kendal, there is no indication that Vestris was greatly concerned with social respectability outside her own profession. Early in her career much attention was focused on her private life, as notorious love affairs and her near legendary extravaganza encouraged the concoction of further, completely spurious anecdotes. She remained, for the most part, a Regency personality who was able to function quite well professionally in Victorian London.

As a personality actress, Vestris brought a specific persona to her work. She was known for her physical beauty: dark hair, dark eyes, exquisite figure; and her success as a performer was based in large measure upon her ability to manipulate obvious sexual appeal, seeming innocence, and the appearance of gentility. The *Morning Chronicle's* assessment of Vestris's performance as the heroine of **Blue Beard** (1839) was typical: "Her voice has all its lusciousness, her movements their accustomed grace, and her acting all its fascinating archness." Presumably suggesting a mischievous quality, "archness" was assigned to her time and again in the papers, along with grace, vivacity, spirit, charm, and naiveté. Westland Marston remembered "an occasional air of playful *mutinerie* that increased public favor by her evident consciousness of it." He believed she possessed a "seductive charm of look and manner" and skill in "the art of sending out telegraphic glances," and he fancied it was "her practice of taking the house into her confidence, combined with her coquetry and personal attractions, that rendered Vestris so bewitching to the public." Planché profited by both her talents and her public image, constructing female roles in which she could exploit her abilities, such as the tempting but ingenuous Pan-

dora of **Olympic Revels,** the love-sick Venus of **The Paphian Bower,** and the abandoned Calypso of **Telemachus.**

Already a highly successful performer, Vestris transgressed the sexual expectations of even her own profession when she became a manager. If she had previously embodied the public's conception of a siren, she now invaded the male preserve of hiring, firing, planning, and methodical execution, and part of Vestris's charm was her ability to bridge the traditional masculine and feminine realms. After her death, Planché recalled a "peculiar combination of personal attractions and professional ability, which, for so many years, made her the most popular actress and manager of her day" (**Recollections**). Dubbed the "fair lessee" by the press, she became known for her scrupulous attention to detail in production and her willingness to experiment with managerial techniques. In 1836 Planché hoped to call the attention of other managers to her practices at the Olympic, and praised her careful staging, her refusal to fill boxes with orders or to use puffs, and the institution of early hours "as to enable families to reach their homes before midnight" (Letter to Vestris, **Extravaganzas**). Although he clearly had an enormous respect for Vestris's skill, he felt compelled to mention both the diminutive size of the theatre and the sex of the manager in setting up the Olympic as a model: "Fortunately for yourself, perhaps, your exertions have been confined to a Theatre the direction of which is a recreation, more than a labour; but the model is not less instructive because it is made on so small a scale and preserved in the cabinet of a lady." Many commentators appreciated Vestris's good taste, her fashionable flair, and the lightness of touch which she brought to the decoration of her theatres. The domestic feeling which she managed to suggest in a public space is evident in Matthew Mackintosh's often-quoted description of the Olympic as "so elegant and comfortable that even luxurious west-enders might have fancied themselves at home in their own May-Fair drawing-rooms." Charles Kean's biographer called the theatre "a perfect theatrical boudoir," suggesting both the intimate spatial relationships at the Olympic and the sexual attraction which was carefully and tastefully cultivated in performance.

Vestris and those who wrote for her exploited the novelty of a female manager and, in the best tradition of effective publicity, turned a potential social liability into a professional asset. For her debut at the Olympic John Hamilton Reynolds wrote an opening address which suggested metaphorically Vestris's transformation in and out of various roles considered gender-specific:

> Before you a venturous woman bends!
> A warrior woman—that in strife embarks,
> The first of all dramatic Joan of Arcs.
> Cheer on the enterprise, thus dared by me!
> The first that ever led a company!
> What though, until this very hour and age,
> A lessee-lady never owned a stage!

She moves on from the warrior image to refer to herself in a number of widely different, often contradictory guises in rapid succession, including an omnibus driver and a frustrated housewife:

Madame Vestris as Beauty in Beauty and the Beast.

In this, my purpose, stand I not alone—
All women sigh for houses of their own;
And I was weary of perpetual dodging
From house to house in search of board and
    lodging!

Reynolds thus leads her from the opening male-related images to those more acceptably feminine, and then, in a plea to the audience, she reaches a helpless and dependent state (with a pun on the Olympic as a "minor" theatre):

Oh, my kind friends! befriend me still, as you
Have in bygone times been wont to do;
Make me your ward against each ill designer,
And prove Lord Chancellor to a female *Minor.*

With its final couplet, the speech closes in a welter of sexual cross-reference:

Still aid the petticoat on old, kind principles,
And make me yet a Captain of *Invincibles!*

The appeal is for chivalry, but the final allusion is to Thomas Morton's farce *The Invincibles,* in which Vestris and a "regiment" of women made quite a hit dressed in male military uniforms. The closing address for her first Olympic season, written by Charles Dance, concluded with a promise of more fun and merriment: "At all events, no exertion shall be spared on my part to win from you an admission that 'the women are the best Managers after all.' "

Vestris's adroit, though perhaps largely unconscious, manipulation of sexual appeal sanctioned her emigration to distinctly masculine territory. She could run a theatre quite successfully and still play all varieties of coquette on the stage, and if much of the psychic power of the actress's image originated from her disregard of sexual boundaries and the ability to transform herself, public consciousness of Vestris's various roles must have enhanced her fascination. While she was not a great dramatic actress, and certainly not a "transformer" in the sense of the great tragediennes, as a juggler of sexual roles she was incomparable.

Her own personal style had a great influence on the Planché extravaganzas and, consequently, on the way in which this popular entertainment approached sexual roles. In particular, the transvestite role no doubt became a feature of extravaganza because of its importance in Vestris's career. A descendant of the Restoration and eighteenth-century breeches role, the transvestite performance gave Vestris the license to discard cumbersome petticoats and display her shapely legs. She became identified professionally with male parts in 1820 with her success as the Don in W. T. Moncrieff's *Giovanni in London,* and she made such performances something of a specialty. Leigh Hunt found her Macheath too "genteel," but appreciated her costume:

Her red frock-coat and white trousers become her by the feminine mode of wearing them, and the elegance of her figure, a sort of compromise between the dress of an English buck and that of a Turkish lady. They are masculine enough as a dress, and yet feminine enough for her to wear them with ease. . . . In a word, we never remember an instance of an actress who contrived to be at once so very much of a gentleman and yet so entire and unaltered a woman.

The British Stage and Literary Cabinet insisted that the "incessant performance of gross rakish characters" would ultimately "vulgarize" her style, and labeled the transvestite performance a moral outrage: "Prostitution may be thought a strong expression; but we hold that we are warranted in using it, when a woman's limbs are exposed night after night, and season after season, to the full gaze and libidinous criticism of debauchees, with the sole purpose of raising money by this appeal to the passions of the multitude." The drawing power of the transvestite role, however, was immense, and Vestris had eleven years of celebrity (or notoriety) before performing Orpheus in Planché's *Olympic Devils* (1831) at the age of thirty-four. "Madame Vestris was, as usual," wrote the *Morning Herald,* "quite at home in breeches . . . " (Rev. of *Olympic Devils*). This was Planché's second Olympic extravaganza, but his first to use an attractive actress as mythological hero or fairy-tale prince. Later termed "principal boy" in pantomime, this sort of transvestite role became a standard feature of the two holiday genres simultaneously. Over a period of twenty years Vestris performed seven transvestite roles in the extravaganzas. Her last was in *King Charming,* which opened 26 December 1850. The unusually voluminous costume (which did not expose her legs) was copied from that of the Nepalese ambassador who had been "visible everywhere during the London season." Vestris was by this time fifty-three and intermittently ill. Charles Mathews sometimes assumed her role when she was unable to appear, creating the unusual theatrical situation of a husband and wife performing the same part.

By 1852, Planché recorded, "[t]ime had begun to tell on Madame Vestris," and "with that good taste which never deserted her" she determined that breeches parts "were no longer be *fitting* a lady of her age."

Of the twenty-two major transvestite roles in the Planché extravaganzas (there are numerous minor roles as well), Vestris created the greatest number; Priscilla Horton ranked second with five; Julia St. George performed four, and Kathleen Fitzwilliam, three. Various other actresses played one role only. The number of roles she created for Planché is perhaps not a fitting gauge of Vestris's influence, however, since her control as manager and the legacy of her performance style continued to shape the form even when she did not appear. In 1843, when Planché was writing for a Haymarket company deprived of Madame Vestris, the *Morning Chronicle* concluded that Priscilla Horton had been engaged for the transvestite role of *The Fair One with the Golden Locks* "in default" of the older actress, "for it seemed very evident that the part was written for her." The *Times* noticed in its review of *The Seven Champions of Christendom* (1849) that it was the first extravaganza produced under Vestris's management in which she did not appear:

> So much is that lady associated with the very origin of that particular class of burlesque of which Mr. Planché is the chief inventor, and so admirably has she played in a long series of such productions, that we feel there is something wanting when she does not stand personally before us in one of her graceful fantastic dresses, although we still see the guiding spirit in the general elegance and splendour.

The younger extravaganza actresses, while achieving nothing like Vestris's transcontinental fame, were distinctly categorized as extravaganza performers, and newspaper critics applied with striking regularity the same adjectives they used in describing Vestris's style.

The transvestite role remains something of a puzzle to the modern historian, for the exact nature of the male impersonation is now difficult to determine. A facetious article in *Blackwood's Magazine* in 1845 described "[e]picene princes, whose taper limbs and swelling busts are well worth the scrutiny of the opera-glass." Unlike male impersonators on the popular stage later in the century, nothing in the available evidence suggests a sustained, realistic attempt on the part of the extravaganza actress to recreate or mimic adult male behavior. A certain spirited gallantry was prized, however. Priscilla Horton, for example, was commended for creating "the neatest, smartest young gentleman" in *The Fair One* (*Times*) and for playing a "gallant" hero "with the greatest 'dash' and vivacity" in *The Invisible Prince* (*Times*). While endearing, boyish characteristics were appreciated, particularly in actresses who came after Vestris, it was important to retain certain feminine attributes. The *Illustrated London News* believed that Horton "looked and acted, and sang most charmingly" (Rev. of *Fair One*), and G. H. Lewes remarked that Miss Eglinton made "a seductive prince" (Rev. of *Good Woman*).

There was apparently a fine line of acceptability for such performances in extravaganza. Accolades for Planché's delicacy and tact were related, among other things, to the perceived appropriateness of dialogue for the actress. One reviewer, for example, was impressed that when Planché resorted to slang, "it will invariably be found either that he puts it into mouths that may give utterance to it without offence, or, if he makes it proceed from the lips of ladies, he only goes just so far as not to infringe delicacy." The critic's prime example was a euphemistic reference to a spanking (" 'Twas not on my *top* that he vented his rage") written for a prince (Priscilla Horton) recalling his school days: "this is the way in which Planché just arrives at the verge of vulgarity, the confines of coarseness, without overstepping them, while many others would not have been able to avoid inserting in plain terms the broad antipodes which the word 'top' suggested" (Rev. of *Invisible Prince, Morning Chronicle*).

Extant illustrations for Planché's transvestite roles range from those which depict a mature, shapely woman (the "epicene princes" with "taper limbs and swelling busts" to which *Blackwood's* referred) to those which present a much more androgynous persona, with female curves obscured, but often retaining the small feet and hands of idealized femininity. While boyish qualities may have become more prominent with actresses who followed Vestris, anatomical variations in the iconography seem to have more to do with the artistic stance adopted by the illustrator and whether he chose to emphasize character and story relationships or the sexual appeal of the performer. The same periodical, for example (the *Illustrated London News*), ran wildly different engravings of characters played by Priscilla Horton, from muscular, to androgynous, to lovely and unmistakably feminine.

Costumes reflect the same carefully balanced compromise between masculine and feminine which Hunt noticed in the 1820s. While some costumes used actual breeches, the standard transvestite garment during Planché's career was a picturesque, knee-length skirt worn over tights. This revealed a substantial amount of leg, yet maintained enough feminine characteristics to circumvent most criticism of inappropriateness. In his study of Planché's costume design, Paul Reinhardt comments that certain transvestite garments reproduce in part the contemporary female silhouette. When Horton, for example, is disguised as a statue of Apollo in *The Invisible Prince,* the bodice "is draped, but in a style fashionable in female dress in the 1840's, and the skirt is flared like contemporary fashions though it stops just above the knee." Sumptuousness was thought to further enhance the actresses' charms. The *Times* noted that all seven champions of Christendom "are acted by ladies, and their appearance in glittering armour and waving plumes conduces much to the splendid effect of the piece."

While such costumes seem, to modern sensibilities, largely feminine, it would be a mistake to underplay the masculine nature of the attire. Voluminous Victorian petticoats restricted a woman's movement, and were a physical representation of the prohibitive rules for respectable feminine behavior. Even if the actress did not appear in contemporary male costume, which in any case would not have shown her legs, to discard the requisite baggage of women's dress was in some way symbolic. It meant increased freedom of movement and action and, by implication, the assumption of male autonomy. Some indication of context can be gleaned from the scorn visited upon the model for "rational" female dress adopted by the American Amelia Jenks Bloomer. The short skirt (extending below the knee) and loose, "Turkish" trousers gathered at the ankles (not unlike those in Vestris's King Charming costume) were a distinct failure when Bloomer and her followers attempted to introduce them to London in 1851. The more easily offended of the city's population declared the dress unfeminine, immoral, and theatrical, while the majority of Londoners found a source of laughter for the season. As with most highly visible social topics, Bloomerism found its way into extravaganza, and Planché made fun of women who wore the garment and the feminist stance it suggested in *The Prince of Happy Land* (1851). An ambassador must inform a prince that his beloved has been magically changed into a deer:

> AMB.   What tongue shall tell her tale?
> PRINCE.   Dead!
> AMB.   Worse!
> PRINCE.   False!
> AMB.   Worser! if the dreadful rumour
>   Be true, her Highness has become—
> PRINCE.   A Bloomer!
> AMB.   No, but as much unlike to woman-
>   kind,
>   What'er she was afore, she's now a
> *hind!*

The extravaganza audience was reminded of the discrepancy between the sex of performer and character largely through visual effect. The texts of the plays usually call attention to this fact only indirectly by praise of the character's attractive appearance. Planché occasionally toys more explicitly with sexual ambiguity, as in the double sex change (the Shakespearean device in reverse) which occurs in *The Invisible Prince.* The hero, Leander (played by Priscilla Horton), disguises himself as an Amazon in order to enter an enemy camp:

> PRINCESS. Why, he looks like a woman!
> LEANDER.   I've made bold
>   The habit of an Amazon to
>   borrow;
>   A man your foes shall find me to
>   their sorrow.
>   This woman's garb but hides a
>   lover true,
>   Who'll be your Hero and Leander
>   too.

Even when the dialogue did not refer specifically to sexual identity, audience awareness of the discrepancy was important, as part of the fascination must have been to see traditionally masculine dash and bravery seemingly combined with specifically feminine qualities in one persona.

One of the most interesting roles in this respect was that of Perseus in *The Deep Deep Sea; or, Perseus and Andromeda,* Planché's fifth extravaganza for the Olympic co-written with Charles Dance. Premiering on Boxing Day, 1833, the piece burlesqued, among other things, aquatic

entertainments and featured Madame Vestris as the brave, impulsive hero. Perseus makes his entrance in the second scene, as King Cepheus and Queen Cassiope try to convince their daughter, Andromeda, to marry her Uncle Phineas. "Rich curtains" at a center archway open, and the hero appears mounted on Pegasus (a real pony) *"and bearing the head of* MEDUSA *in a rich velvet bag."* The *Morning Chronicle* noted that Perseus/Vestris arrived "[i]n the nick of time . . . in all the radiance of her own beauty, and with the additional ornament of one of the most splendid costumes we ever saw. . . ."

In the course of the play, Perseus sings Planché's new lyrics to preexisting tunes—this was one of the constant features of extravaganza—and Planché wisely took advantage of Vestris's admired voice. The hero introduces himself to the tune of the nursery ballad "Ride a Cock-horse," describes his first meeting with Andromeda to "We Met! 'Twas in a Crowd," and anticipates a drinking celebration with "Mighty Jove," a duet sung with his "Uncle" Neptune. Just before rushing off to rescue his beloved, Perseus delivers a parody of an aria from *Tancredi,* announcing:

> I will only stay
> To sing a song—As opera heroes choose
> Always to do, when they've no time to lose!

While clearly singing in the persona of the masculine character, Vestris apparently utilized her familiar, winning vocal style. The *Morning Chronicle* commented, "Madame Vestris delighted the audience with several of the finest melodies, with parodial words, certainly; but these, when uttered from her lips, scarcely render the airs less charming."

In response to King Cepheus's objections to a "half-pay captain," Perseus relates his divine lineage and describes his victory over the monstrous Medusa with a tongue-in-cheek daring:

> For as 'tis well by every school-boy known,
> Who looked her in the face was turned to stone.
> So that one glance would make the daring elf
> A lithographic portrait of himself.

In the final scene of the play, Andromeda is bound to a rock as a sacrifice to a sea monster ravaging the country. Perseus arrives just as the monster approaches, kills it (with some help from Neptune), and is awarded the hand of Andromeda. He then foils an attack by the evil Phineus and his soldiers by producing the head of Medusa from his bag and turning them into stone figures: "They'll make a wedding present for my wife—/ A group in marble— modelled from the life."

As a tag to Vestris's performance of Perseus, Planché wrote an appeal to the audience emphasizing differing masculine and feminine responses:

> Your pulses, friends, once more I crave to feel!
> Perseus no more—how flutters now my *own?*
> For, ah! your suppliant away has thrown
> Her manly courage with her manly part,
> And comes with all the woman in her heart.

Not all the transvestite heroes in extravaganza are as volitional as Perseus. In *Puss in Boots,* for example, though he ends up with the kingdom and the beautiful princess, Ralph is mainly the beneficiary of the clever Puss, performed by Charles Mathews. King Charming is more a victim than a hero, being subjected to the machinations of an evil waiting woman. But Perseus is representative of the most heroic of the mythical heroes, such as the later St. George (Kathleen Fitzwilliam) who rescues all of Christendom, or Graceful (Priscilla Horton) in *The Fair One with the Golden Locks,* who begins as a simple messenger, surmounts numerous obstacles, and finally wins the king's own beloved.

Perhaps more than any other single feature, the portrayal of male characters by women illustrates the obsessive concern with sexual definition which pervades the extravaganza. Those "epicene princes" who become heroes within the fictional construct of the play win the love of beautiful women, kill dragons and monsters, brave demons, outwit enemies, and rescue maidens. Without violating the sexual decorum of character, the actress could imaginatively cross, quite safely, sexual boundaries related to both romantic love and behavior considered gender-specific. Transsexual casting was one way to give women the sort of mythic adventures which George MacDonald wished for but did not deliver to his heroine in *The Light Princess;* it allowed the hero-heroines to "get away to follow their fortunes," in contrast to the more traditional princesses "forced to marry before they have had a bit of fun."

The transvestite performance may have provided a vicarious satisfaction for those in the audience who had difficulty integrating the prescriptions for gender behavior with the reality of their own conflicting desires. For others, it was perhaps a way of indulging subliminal belief in feminine power. The transvestite role might acknowledge, in a theatrical context, Auerbach's mythology of transformation, indeed, even the disturbing concept that a woman might turn herself at will into a man and appropriate "male" duties and prerogatives. In the case of Madame Vestris, the fictional adventures reflected the real-life challenges which she faced as a manager in a male-dominated, male-oriented commercial theatre. Yet the tongue-in-cheek tone of extravaganza and the assurance that all order would be restored at the conclusion of the fictional piece assured the rational mind that the social order was not threatened.

Popular entertainment, then as now, was an important means of sexual socialization. Planché and Vestris performed a remarkable balancing act, creating an acceptable entertainment for those greatly concerned with respectability, yet allowing participation on a subliminal level. The plays perhaps functioned as a forum for exploring sexual boundaries, an escape valve for a society greatly concerned with self-improvement, self-discipline, and self-exploration. The extravaganzas are remarkable documents of a social class struggling to clarify and internalize the rules of its own sexuality. (pp. 9-32)

> *Kathy Fletcher, "Planché, Vestris, and the Transvestite Role: Sexuality and Gender in Victorian Popular Theatre," in* Nineteenth Century Theatre, *Vol. 15, No. 1, Summer, 1987, pp. 9-33.*

FURTHER READING

Dircks, P. T. "James Robinson Planché and the English Burletta Tradition." *Theatre Survey: The American Journal of Theatre History* XVII, No. 1 (May 1976): 68-81.
> Traces the origins of Planché's early classical burlesques to the burletta tradition of the eighteenth century.

MacMillan, Dougald. "Planché's Early Classical Burlesques." *Studies in Philology* XXV, No. 2 (1928): 340-45.
> Comments on the method of production and classical subject matter of Planché's early plays.

Wells, Stanley. "Shakespeare in Planché's Extravaganzas." *Shakespeare Survey* 16 (1963): 103-17.
> Addresses Planché's concern with Shakespeare in his stage productions, enumerating various allusions and parodies.

George Sand

1804-1876

(Pseudonym of Amandine-Aurore-Lucile Dupin Dudevant) French novelist, essayist, and dramatist.

INTRODUCTION

One of the most celebrated writers and controversial personalities of nineteenth-century France, Sand wrote prolifically in a variety of genres, producing over eighty novels, three collections of short stories, a four-volume autobiography, numerous essays, twenty-five dramas, and approximately twenty thousand letters. She remains best known for her novels, which have been praised for their vivid depictions of the peasantry and the countryside, insightful studies of human nature, and natural prose style. Although she was one of the most popular novelists of her time, relatively few of her works are studied today. Instead, she is primarily remembered for her bold behavior while living in Paris as a young woman: wearing men's clothing, espousing equal marital rights for women, and engaging in love affairs with prominent artistic figures.

Sand's parents, who married one month before her birth in Paris, were of dissimilar backgrounds: her mother was a bird seller's daughter, while her father was an officer in Napoleon's army and purportedly an illegitimate descendant of Frederic-Auguste de Saxe, King of Poland. Following her father's death when she was four, Sand was entrusted to her paternal grandmother's care and was raised at the family estate of Nohant in Berry. There, she was privately tutored until she reached the age of thirteen, at which time she was sent to the Convent of the English Augustinians in Paris for three years. When she was eighteen, Sand married a local army officer, Casimir Dudevant, and eventually became the mother of two children. Dudevant and Sand soon realized that they were incompatible, and after several restless and unhappy years of marriage, Sand left her husband in 1831 to pursue a literary career in Paris. Following the publication of two novels written in collaboration with her lover Jules Sandeau and signed J. Sand, she began her career in earnest with the novel *Indiana,* writing independently under the name George Sand. For the next several decades, Sand remained a prominent member of the artistic and intellectual community of Paris, due to her considerable literary output as well as her friendships with such figures as Honoré de Balzac and Gustave Flaubert. She also often captured public interest with her romantic involvements, which included relationships with Alfred de Musset and Frédéric Chopin. Sand spent her last years at Nohant, where she died in 1876.

Sand is best known for her bold statements about the rights of women in nineteenth-century society, her exploration of contemporary social and philosophical issues,

and her depiction of the lives and language of French provincials. Several of her important early novels, including *Indiana, Valentine, Lélia,* and *Jacques,* reflect her rebellion against the bonds of marriage and deal largely with the relationships between men and women. Clearly influenced by Byron and Rousseau, Sand crafted Romantic narratives depicting passionate personal revolt against societal conventions and an ardent feminism, attitudes which outraged her early British and American critics. These novels were extremely popular with the reading public, however, and they established Sand as an important literary voice for her generation. Sand's abiding interest in politics and philosophy is evident in such novels as *Consuelo* and *Le meunier d'Angibault (The Miller of Angibault).* These works, dealing specifically with humanitarianism, Christian socialism, and republicanism, have been described by critics as the least plausible of her literary efforts: the tone is often didactic and the plots contrived. Sand is perhaps most renowned for her pastoral novels. Set in her native Berry, *La mare au diable (The Haunted Marsh), François le champi (Francis the Waif),* and *La petite Fadette (Little Fadette)* were inspired by her love of the countryside and her sympathy with the peasants. Realistic in background detail and distinguished by their Romantic idealism, they are considered by many scholars to be Sand's finest novels. The most enduring products of her later years are her autobiography, *Histoire de ma vie (My Life),* and her voluminous correspondence.

From the beginning of her career, Sand's unconventional lifestyle interfered with serious critical assessment of her works. In spite of moral prejudice, which dominated early critical analyses of her works, she eventually won acceptance as an artist during her lifetime. Throughout the first half of the twentieth century, many critical studies of Sand's oeuvre attempted to establish links between her life and works, particularly focusing on Sand's romantic relationships. Since the early 1970s, critics have concentrated on the works themselves, noting especially her bold exploration of such issues as sexual freedom and independence for women. Many feminist critics have lauded Sand for presenting strong, willful heroines, and for exposing the obstacles faced by women—particularly women artists—in the nineteenth century. Writing about *Lélia,* Kathryn Crecelius asserted that the novel "remains a searingly honest cry of a woman artist's soul, an indictment of, and a curse upon, a society in which she had no place." Several commentators have argued, however, that Sand's feminism was limited; she consistently advocated equal rights for women in matters of marriage and divorce, yet she subscribed to conventional views on male and female social roles. As Donna Dickenson has averred, Sand believed "that women are creatures of emotion . . . and that men are blessed with all the brainpower." A number of scholars have explored Sand's pastoral novels, noting in particular her use of fantastic and folktale elements in narratives notable for their evocation of a culture vastly different from that of Parisian society. While some critics have disparaged Sand's tone in these works as patronizing and excessively idealistic, others have praised her insightful characterization and colorful use of language, suggesting that her "rustic" fiction inspired such novelists as Thomas Hardy, George Eliot, and Leo Tolstoy.

PRINCIPAL WORKS

Indiana (novel) 1832
  [*Indiana,* 1881]
Valentine (novel) 1832
  [*Valentine,* published in *The Masterpieces of George Sand,* 1902]
Lélia (novel) 1833
  [*Lélia,* 1978]
Jacques (novel) 1834
  [*Jacques,* 1847]
Lettres d'un voyageur (travel sketches) 1834-36
  [*Letters of a Traveller,* 1847]
André (novel) 1835
  [*André,* 1847]
Mauprat (novel) 1837
  [*Mauprat,* 1847]
Spiridion (novel) 1839
  [*Spiridion,* 1842]

Les sept cordes de la lyre (play) 1840
  [*A Woman's Version of the Faust Legend: The Seven Strings of the Lyre,* 1989]
Le compagnon du tour de France (novel) 1841
  [*The Companion of the Tour of France,* 1847]
Consuelo (novel) 1842-43
  [*Consuelo,* 1846]
Jeanne (novel) 1844
Le meunier d'Angibault (novel) 1845
  [*The Miller of Angibault,* 1847]
La mare au diable (novel) 1846
  [*The Haunted Marsh,* 1848]
François le champi (novel) 1848
  [*Francis the Waif,* 1889]
La petite Fadette (novel) 1849
  [*Little Fadette,* 1849]
Histoire de ma vie. 20 vols. (autobiography) 1854-55
  [*My Life,* 1979]
Elle et Lui 1859
  [*She and He,* 1978]
Le marquis de Villemer (novel) 1861
  [*The Marquis of Villemer,* 1871]
Flamarande (novel) 1875
Correspondance, 1812-1876. 6 vols. (letters) 1883-95

CRITICISM

George Sand   (essay date 1832)

[*In the following preface originally published in the 1832 edition of* Indiana, *Sand defends her first novel against charges of immorality and subversiveness.*]

Should pages of this book incur the grave reproach of inclination toward new beliefs, should severe judges find their tone imprudent and dangerous, one would have to reply to critics that they do too much honor to a work of no importance; that to grapple with lofty questions of the social order, one should feel oneself endowed with immense spiritual force or great talent; and that such presumption has nothing to do with so simple a story, of which the writer created almost nothing. If, in the course of his task, he happened to express laments torn from his characters by the social malaise of which they are victims, if he dared echo their aspirations for a better existence, let the reader blame society for its inequalities and destiny for its whims! The writer is no more than a mirror which reflects them, a machine which traces them; and he owes no one apologies if his prints are exact and his images faithful.

Bear, then, in mind that the narrator did not take as a subject or slogan some scattered cries of pain and anger from the drama of human life. He does not for a moment claim to conceal a profound moral in the form of a tale; he has not come to add a stone to the uncertain edifice of the future, nor to throw one at the crumbling edifice of the past. He knows too well that we live in a time of moral ruin, when human reason needs blinders to soften the all too radiant light that dazzles it. If he had thought himself enough of a scholar to write a truly useful book, he would have tempered the truth rather than have exposed it with its raw colors and cutting lines. Such a book would have had the effect of dark glasses on tired eyes.

Not that he renounces fulfilling this noble and generous task some day; but young as he is, he recounts what he has seen without daring to draw conclusions on this immense process between past and future that perhaps no man of the present generation has the competence to judge. Too honest to conceal his doubts but too timid to set them up as certainties, he relies on your reflection and abstains from weaving preconceived ideas and hardened judgments into the fabric of his story. He performs his craft as storyteller with meticulous care. He will tell you all, even that which is outrageously true; but if you deck him in a philosopher's robe, you will embarrass him, simple entertainer that he is, charged with diverting but not with instructing you.

Had he been more mature or more gifted, he would still not have dared touch the gaping wounds of a civilization in agony. One would have to be so sure of healing them before taking the risk of probing them! He would much rather try to reattach you to ancient ruined beliefs, to old lost devotions, than use his talent—if he had any—to trample on overturned altars. However, he knows that with the prevailing spirit of charity, a sensitive conscience is scorned by public opinion as hypocritical reserve—as, in the arts, a timid bearing is ridiculed as quaint decorum; but he knows that there is honor, if not profit, in the defense of lost causes.

To whoever misjudges the spirit of this book, such a profession of faith will sound like a hopeless anachronism. The narrator hopes that after having heard his story to the end, few listeners will deny the *morality* that emerges from its facts, triumphant as in all human affairs. It seemed to him, on finishing his tale, that his conscience was clear. He flattered himself with having portrayed social misery without too much melancholy, human passion without excessive passion. He muted his strings when they sounded too harshly; he tried to stifle those notes of the soul which should remain silent, those voices of the heart one cannot awake without danger.

You will perhaps do him justice by admitting that he has shown how miserable is the creature who transgresses his rightful bounds, how desolate the heart that rebels against the decrees of his destiny. If he did not give the best possible role to the character who depicts the *law,* if he portrayed as more sullen the other who represents *opinion,* you will find a third who represents *illusion* and who thwarts without pity the vain hopes, the mad endeavors of passion. Finally, you will see that if he did not strew rose petals on the patch of ground where the law fences in our wills like sheep, neither did he plant thorns on the road that leads away from it.

That, I think, should suffice to insure this book against the charge of immorality; but if you insist that all novels end like Marmontel's tales, you will perhaps reproach me for the last pages. You will disapprove the fact that I did not

plunge into misery and abandon that creature who violated human laws throughout the two volumes. Here let the author reply that before being moral, he wanted to be true; that, feeling too young to write a philosophical treatise on the art of bearing with life, he was content with narrating *Indiana,* a tale of the human heart with its failings, its cruelties, its rights and wrongs, its virtues and vices.

Indiana—if you insist on explaining everything—is woman herself, that frail creature charged by the author to represent those passions which are repressed or, if you prefer, suppressed by social laws. She is free will grappling with necessity; she is love butting her head blindly against all the obstacles placed before her by civilization. But the serpent wears and breaks its teeth gnawing obstinately on a file, and the powers of the soul are drained in ruthless combat with the reality of life. Such is what you can gather from this anecdote; it was in this spirit that it was told to him who passes it on to you.

Despite his protestations, the narrator expects reproaches. Honest souls and honorable consciences might take alarm at seeing virtue so harsh, reason so dreary, and opinion so unjust. This terrifies him: for a writer fears nothing more than alienating the faith of men of good will, arousing fatal sympathies in embittered souls, poisoning the raw wounds inflicted by society on impetuous and rebel minds.

Nothing is easier to conquer and more dishonorable to court than success based on illicit appeal to the passions of the times. The author of *Indiana* denies ever having dreamed of this. Should it obtain this result, he would destroy his book, notwithstanding that naïve paternal love that pampers rickety creatures in these days of literary miscarriages.

But he hopes to defend himself by saying that he thought he would better serve his principles with authentic examples than with poetic fantasies. With its aura of sad sincerity, the story will—he thinks—move young, ardent minds. They will find it hard to distrust a storyteller who goes his way recklessly in the world of reality, fraternizing left and right with no greater deference for one side than for the other. To describe a cause as odious or absurd is not to combat but to persecute it. The storyteller's art is perhaps nothing more than awakening to their own true stories the fallen he wants to raise up, the suffering unhappy he wants to heal.

To insist on clearing it of all blame would be giving too much importance to a work which is likely to make little stir. The author thus yields completely to his critics. One sole charge is too serious to be admitted: that of having written a dangerous book. He would rather remain unknown forever than erect his glory on the ruins of his conscience. He thus adds a few more lines to deny this charge he fears most.

Raymon, you will say, is society; egoism is morality and reason. Raymon, the author will answer, is that false reasoning, that false morality by which society is governed. He is a man of honor as the world understands it, because the world never looks close enough to see everything. The good citizen stands by Raymon, and you will not say he is the enemy of order; for he sacrifices his happiness, he sacrifices himself, in the name of social order.

You will then say that virtue was not very brilliantly rewarded. Alas!—others will answer—nowadays virtue triumphs only in the *théâtres du boulevard.* The author will say that he was committed to portraying, not a virtuous society, but one of necessity, and that honor, like heroism, has become rare in these days of moral decadence. Do you think this truth disgusts truly honorable souls? I believe the exact contrary. (pp. 4-10)

> *George Sand, in a preface to her "Indiana," in* George Sand in Her Own Words, *translated and edited by Joseph Barry, Anchor Books, 1979, pp. 3-10.*

George Sand (essay date 1842)

[*In the following excerpt from a preface originally published in the 1842 edition of* Indiana, *Sand explains the development of her views—commenting on those she expressed in her 1832 preface—and reaffirms her position as defender of oppressed people, particularly women, suggesting that her detractors only served to strengthen her beliefs.*]

If I agreed to have the preceding pages [of the 1832 preface to *Indiana*] republished, it is not because they sum up my present belief on the right of society over individuals. It is, rather, because I regard opinions freely expressed in the past as something sacred, which we should neither change nor subdue nor censor in our own way. But now that, having walked through life, I see horizons opening around me, I feel bound to tell the reader what I think of my work.

I was young when I wrote *Indiana,* I was obeying sentiments full of vigor and sincerity which overflowed into a series of other novels based on the same theme: the disequilibrium of the sexes due to society. These novels were all vaguely accused by critics of endangering the institution of marriage. Despite its few insights and its naïve uncertainties, *Indiana* did not escape the indignation of so-called serious minds whose words I was then disposed to accept in all docility. However, though my reason was scarcely mature enough to write on such a serious matter, I was sufficiently adult to judge the thoughts of those who judged mine. However simple the accused might be, however learned his judge, the former has sense enough to know if the sentence of the latter is just or perverse, wise or absurd.

Journalists who pose as defenders or guardians of public morality (I know not by virtue of what mission, since I know not in the name of what faith) severely condemned the temptation of my poor tale. Presenting it as a plea against the social order, they gave it an importance and renown it would never have had on its own. They thus vested with a serious and heavy role a young writer scarcely familiar with basic social ideas, whose only literary and philosophical paraphernalia were a bit of imagination, courage, and love of truth. Sensitive to blame, almost thankful for the lessons others designed to teach him, he examined the indictments brought before public opinion

as to the morality of his thought. Thanks to this study, from which he banished pride, he slowly acquired convictions which, at the start of his career, were mere sentiments, but which have since become principles.

Throughout ten years of research, qualms, and often painful but sincere irresolution, fleeing the role of pedagogue assigned to me by those who wished to invite people to ridicule me, loathing the charges against me of vanity and outrage designed to stir up hate for me, proceeding by analysis of life before seeking its synthesis, I pursued my artistic bent and recounted facts which readers sometimes found credible and portrayed characters which were on occasion recognized to have been painted with care.

I contented myself with this work, seeking to consolidate my convictions rather than unsettle those of others, telling myself that if I were wrong, society would somehow awaken powerful voices to destroy my arguments and make up for my imprudent questions by the wisdom of their replies. Many voices were heard, indeed, warning the public against this dangerous writer; but both public and author still await the wise replies.

Long after having written the preface of *Indiana* with all due respect for established society, I still sought to solve the insoluble problem of *reconciling the happiness and dignity of individuals oppressed by this society, without changing society itself.* Bent over the victims, mingling his tears with theirs, acting as emissary between them and his readers, refusing—prudent defender that he is—to palliate the faults of his clients, invoking the judges' clemency rather than their rigor, the novelist is the true advocate of those abstract creatures who represent our passions and our sufferings before the court of power and the jury of opinion. It is a serious task behind a cover of frivolity, difficult to fulfill, as it should be, troubled as one is by those who would have the form more serious or the matter more trivial.

I do not claim to have accomplished this task with skill. But I am certain of having tried earnestly, in the midst of internal conflicts in which my conscience, now terrified by ignorance of its rights, now stimulated by a heart enamored with truth and justice, marched steadily toward its goal without straying too far or retreating too often.

Initiating the public in this internal struggle by means of a series of prefaces and discussions would have been a puerile measure denoting the vanity of talking about oneself. I refrained from it, as from dealing too rapidly with aspects which remained obscure in my mind. Conservatives found me too bold, innovators too timid. I confess that I had respect and sympathy for both past and future, and in this battle, I found peace only the day when I understood that the one was not necessarily the destruction or desecration, but the continuation and development, of the other.

After ten years of apprenticeship, opened at last to broader ideas which I found not in myself but in the philosophical advances around me (in particular from a few brilliant minds I respectfully interrogated and in general from the spectacle of the sufferings of my fellow creatures), I finally admit that although I was right to doubt myself and withhold my judgment at that time of ignorance and inexperience during which I wrote *Indiana,* my present duty is to take pride in the boldness I have yielded to before and since. I have been reproached for these audacities, but they would have been even bolder had I known that they were legitimate, sincere, and sacred.

Before committing the first novel of my youth to the publicity which a popular edition will give it for the first time, I have now reread it with the severity and detachment I would have had for somebody else's work. Resolved not to retract (one should never retract what has been said or done in good faith) but to condemn myself had I found my youthful inclinations erroneous or dangerous, I found myself in such agreement with the sentiment that inspired *Indiana* (and which would inspire it again if I had to write this story for the first time) that I refused to change anything in it, except for a few awkward phrases and inadequate words. There are certainly many more, and I submit the literary merits of my writings entirely to the lectures of my critics: here I grant them all the competence I lack. I do not deny—I am glad to acknowledge—the undeniable mass of talent at work in the daily press. But that many moralists and philosophers are to be found in this circle of elegant writers I deny resolutely, with all due deference to those who have condemned me and will condemn me again at the first opportunity from the heights of their morality and philosophy.

I repeat, I wrote and had to write *Indiana;* I yielded to a powerful instinct for protest granted me by God, who gives existence to nothing in vain, not even the feeblest creature, and who puts forth His power in the smallest as in the greatest cause. But, then, was it that small, the cause I defended? It is that of half the human race; the suffering of the woman implicates that of the man, as that of the slave his master's; and this I tried to show in *Indiana.* It is said I was pleading an individual cause: as if—assuming I were moved by a personal sentiment—I were the only unfortunate creature of our otherwise peaceful and radiantly happy humanity! From the cries of suffering and sympathy which responded to mine, I now know exactly what to think of that utter felicity of others.

I don't recall having written anything under the influence of egocentric passion. I have never even thought of having to defend myself against it. Those who have read me without prejudice understand that I wrote *Indiana* with an unreasoned but profound and legitimate sense of the injustice and barbarity of those laws which still govern women in marriage, in the family, and in society. I've never had to write a treatise on jurisprudence, but I've had to battle against public opinion, for it is this which retards or accelerates social advancement. The war will be long and hard; but I am not the sole, nor the first, nor the last champion of such a great cause, and I will defend it as long as I live.

As for the sentiment that inspired me at the start, I developed and amplified it even as others fought it and blamed me for it. Unjust, malicious critics taught me more about it than I would have discovered had I been unattacked. In this sense I thank my blundering judges for having enlightened me. The motives behind their judgments have contributed a bright light to my thoughts and conveyed a profound security to my conscience. An open spirit draws profit from everything, and what might discourage vanity intensifies devotion to a cause.

Let no one see in the reproaches uttered to journalists from the depths of a serene and serious heart a sort of protest against the right of criticism entrusted to the French press by public morality. That critics often misuse and misunderstand their social mandate is evident to all; but that the mission itself is providential and sacred no one will deny, unless he be an atheist drunk with progress, an enemy of truth, a blasphemer of the future, or an unworthy child of France. Freedom of thought, freedom to write and speak, sacred conquest of the human mind! What are the petty sufferings and fleeting troubles provoked by your errors or abuses compared to the infinite blessings you promise for the world? (pp. 214-20)

> *George Sand, in a preface to her "Indiana," in* George Sand in Her Own Words, *translated and edited by Joseph Barry, Anchor Books, 1979, pp. 214-20.*

Bertha Thomas (essay date 1883)

[*In the following essay, Thomas discusses Sand's plays and later novels, assessing the extent of their success.*]

There are few eminent novelists that have not tried their hands at writing for the stage; and Madame Sand had additional inducements to do so, beyond those of ambition satiated with literary success, and tempted by the charm of making fresh conquest of the public in a more direct and personal fashion.

From early childhood she had shown a strong liking for the theatre. The rare performances given by travelling acting-companies at La Châtre had been her greatest delight when a girl. At the convent-school she had arranged Molière from memory for representation by herself and her school-fellows, careful so to modify the piece as to avoid all possibility of shocking the nuns. Thus the Sisters applauded *Le Malade Imaginaire* without any suspicion that the author was one whose works, for them, were placed under a ban, and whose very name they held in devout abhorrence. She inherited from her father a taste for acting, which she transmitted to her children. We have seen her during her literary novitiate in Paris, a studious observer at all theatres, from the classic boards of the Français down to the lowest of popular stages, the Funambules, where reigned at that time a real artist in pantomine, Débureau. His Pierrot, a sort of modified Pulchinello, was renowned, and attracted more fastidious critics to his audience than the Paris artisans whose idol he was. Since then Madame Sand had numbered among her personal friends such leading dramatic celebrities as Madame Dorval, Bocage, and Pauline Garcia. "I like actors," she says playfully, "which has scandalized some austere people. I have also been found fault with for liking the peasantry. Among these I have passed my life, and as I found them, so have I described them. As these, in the light of the sun, give us our daily bread for our bodies, so those by gaslight give us our daily bread of fiction, so needful to the wearied spirit, troubled by realities." Peasants and players seem to be the types of humanity farthest removed from each other, and it is worthy of remark that George Sand was equally successful in her presentation of both.

Her preference for originality and spontaneity before all other qualities in a dramatic artist was characteristic of herself, though not of her nation. Thus it was that Madame Dorval, the heroine of *Antony* and *Marion Delorme,* won her unbounded admiration. Even in Racine she clearly preferred her to Mlle. Mars, as being a less studied actress, and one who abandoned herself more to the inspiration of the moment. The effect produced, as described by Madame Sand, will be understood by all keenly alive, like herself, to the enjoyment of dramatic art. "She" (Madame Dorval) "seemed to me to be myself, more expansive, and to express in action and emotion all that I seek to express in writing." And compared with such an art, in which conception and expression are simultaneous, her own art of words and phrases would at such moments appear to her as but a pale reflection.

Bocage, the great character actor of his time, was another who likewise appealed particularly to her sympathies, as the personation, on the boards, of the protest of the romantic school against the slavery of convention and tradition. Her acquaintance with him dated from the first representation of Hugo's *Lucrèce Borgia,* February, 1833, when Bocage and the author of *Indiana,* then strangers to each other, chanced to sit side by side. In their joint enthusiasm over the play they made the beginning of a thirty years' friendship, terminated only by Bocage's death in 1862. "It was difficult not to quarrel with him," she says of this popular favorite; "he was susceptible and violent; it was impossible not to be reconciled with him quickly. He was faithful and magnanimous. He forgave you admirably for wrongs you had never done him, and it was as good and real as though the pardon had been actual and well-founded, so strong was his imagination, so complete his good faith."

The assistance of Madame Dorval, added to the strength of the Comédie Française company, did not, however, save from failure Madame Sand's first drama, *Cosima,* produced, as will be remembered, in 1840. She allowed nearly a decade to elapse before again seriously competing for theatrical honors, by a second effort in a different style, and more satisfactory in its results.

This, a dramatic adaptation by herself of her novel, *François le Champi,* was produced at the Odéon in the winter of 1849. Generally speaking, to make a good play out of a good novel, the playwright must begin by murdering the novel; and here, as in all George Sand's dramatic versions of her romances, we seem to miss the best part of the original. However, the curious simplicity of the piece, the rustic scenes and personages, here faithfully copied from reality, unlike the conventional village and villager of opera comique, and the pleasing sentiment that runs through the tale, were found refreshing by audiences upon whom the sensational incidents and harrowing emotions of their modern drama were already beginning to pall. The result was a little stage triumph for Madame Sand. It helped to draw to her pastoral tales the attention they deserved, but had not instantly won in all quarters. Théophile Gautier writes playfully of this piece: "The success of *François le Champi* has given all our vaudeville writers an appetite for rusticity. Only let this go on a little, and we shall be inundated by what has humorously been called the 'rurodrama.' Morvan hats and Berrichon head-dresses will invade the scenes, and no language be spoken but in dialect."

Madame Sand was naturally encouraged to repeat the experiment. This was done in *Claudie* (1851) and *Le Pressoir* (1853), ruro-dramas both, and most favorably received. The first-named has a simple and pathetic story, and, as usual with Madame Sand's plays, it was strengthened at its first production by the support of some of the best acting talent in Paris—Fechter, then a rising *jeune premier,* and the veteran Bocage ably representing, respectively, youth and age. Old Berrichon airs were introduced with effect, as also such picturesque rustic festival customs as the ancient harvest-home ceremony, in which the last sheaf is brought on a wagon, gaily decked out with poppies, cornflowers and ribbons, and receives a libation of wine poured by the hand of the oldest or youngest person present.

"But what the theatre can never reproduce," laments Madame Sand, "is the majesty of the frame—the mountain of sheaves solemnly approaching, drawn by three pairs of enormous oxen, the whole adorned with flowers, with fruit, and with fine little children perched upon the top of the last sheaves."

Henceforward a good deal of her time and interest continued to be absorbed by these dramatic compositions. But though mostly eliciting during her lifetime a gratifying amount of public favor and applause, the best of them cannot for an instant be placed in the same high rank as her novels. For with all her wide grasp of the value of dramatic art and her exact appreciation of the strength and weakness of the acting world, her plays remain, to great expectations, uniformly disappointing. Her specialty in fiction lies in her favorite art of analyzing and putting before us, with extreme clearness, the subtlest ramifications, the most delicate intricacies of feeling and thought. A stage audience has its eyes and ears too busy to give its full attention to the finer complications of sentiment and motive; or, at least, in order to keep its interest alive and its understanding clear, an accentuation of outline is needed, which she neglects even to seek.

Her assertion, that the niceties of emotion are sufficient to found a good play upon, no one now will dream of disputing. But for this an art of execution is needed of which she had not the instinct. The action is insufficient, or rather, the sense of action is not conveyed. The slightness of plot—a mere thread in most instances—requires that the thread shall at least be never allowed to drop. But she cuts or slackens it perpetually, long arguments and digressions intervening, and the dialogue, whose monotony is unrelieved by wit, nowhere compensates for the limited interest of the action. Awkward treatment is but half felt when subject and situations are dramatically strong; but plays with so airy and impalpable a basis as these need to be sustained by the utmost perfection of construction, concision and polish of dialogue.

Her novel *Mauprat* has many dramatic points, and she received a score of applications for leave to adapt it to the stage. She preferred to prepare the version herself, and it was played in the winter of 1853-4, with moderate success. But it suffers fatally from comparison with its original. An extreme instance is *Flaminio* (1854), a protracted drama, drawn by Madame Sand from her novelette *Teverino.* This is a fantasy-piece whose audacity is redeemed, as are certain other blemishes, by the poetic suggestiveness of the figure of Madeline, the bird-charmer; whilst the picturesque sketch of Teverino, the idealized Italian bohemian, too indolent to turn his high natural gifts to any account, has proved invaluable to the race of novelists, who are not yet tired of reproducing it in large. The work is one addressed mainly to the imagination.

In the play we come down from the clouds; the poetry is gone, taste is shocked, fancy uncharmed, the improbabilities become grotesque, and the whole is distorted and tedious. Madame Sand's personages are never weary of analyzing their sentiments. Her flowing style, so pleasant to read, carries us swiftly and easily through her dissertations in print, before we have time to tire of them. On the stage such colloquies soon appear lengthy and unnatural. The climax of absurdity is reached in *Flaminio,* where we find the adventurer expatiating to the man of the world on "the divinity of his essence."

There is scarcely a department of theatrical literature in which Madame Sand does not appear as an aspirant. She was a worshipper of Shakespeare, acknowledging him as the king of dramatic writers. For her attempt to adapt "As You Like It" to suit the tastes of a Parisian audience, she disarms criticism by a preface in the form of a letter to M. Régnier, of the Comédie Française, prefixed to the printed play. Here she says plainly that to resolve to alter Shakespeare is to resolve to murder, and that she aims at nothing more than giving the French public some idea of the original. In "As You Like It" the license of fancy taken is too wide for the piece to be safely represented to her countrymen, since it must jar terribly on "that French reason which," remarks Madame Sand, "we are so vain of, and which deprives us of so many originalities quite as precious as itself." The fantastic, which had so much attraction for her (possibly a result of her part German origin), is a growth that has hard work to flourish on French soil. The reader will remember the fate of Weber's *Freischütz,* outrageously hissed when first produced at Paris in its original form. Nine days later it was reproduced, having been taken to pieces and put together again by M. Castil-Blaze, and thus as *Robin des Bois* it ran for 357 nights. The reckless imagination that distinguishes the Shakespearian comedy and does not shrink before the introduction of a lion and a serpent into the forest of Arden, and the miraculous and instantaneous conversion of the wretch Oliver into a worthy suitor for Celia, needed to be toned down for acceptance by the Parisians. But Madame Sand was less fortunate than M. Castil-Blaze. Her version, produced at the Théâtre Français, in 1856, failed to please, although supported by such actors as Delaunay, Arnold-Plessy, and Favart. Macready, who had made Madame Sand's acquaintance in 1845, when he was giving Shakespearian performances in Paris, and whom she greatly admired, dedicating to him her little theatrical romance *Le Château des Désertes,* was present at this representation and records it as a failure. But of her works for the stage, which number over a score, few like her *Comme il vous plaira* missed making some mark at the time, the prestige of her name and the exceptionally favorable circumstances under which they were produced securing more than justice for their intrinsic merit. It was natural that she should over-estimate their value and continue to add to their number. These pieces would be carefully rehearsed on the little stage in the house at Nohant, often with the aid of leading professional actors; and there, at least, the success was unqualified.

Her ingenious novel *Les Beaux Messieurs Bois Doré,* dramatized with the aid of Paul Meurice and acted in 1862, was a triumph for Madame Sand and her friend Bocage. The form and spirit of this novel seem inspired by Sir Walter Scott, and though far from perfect, it is a striking instance of the versatility of her imaginative powers. The leading character of the septuagenarian Marquis, with his many amiable virtues, and his one amiable weakness, a longing to preserve intact his youthfulness of appearance as he has really preserved his youthfulness of heart, is both natural and original, comic and half pathetic withal. The part in the play seemed made for Bocage, and his heart was set upon undertaking it. But his health was failing at the time, and the manager hesitated about giving him the rôle. "Take care, my friend," wrote Bocage to Madame Sand; "perhaps I shall die if I play the part; but if I play it not, I shall die of that, to a certainty." She insisted, and play it he did, to perfection, she tells us. "He did not act the Marquis de Bois Doré; he was the personage himself, as the author had dreamt him." It was to be his last achievement, and he knew it. "It is my end," he said one night, "but I shall die like a soldier on the field of honor." And so he did, continuing to play the rôle up till a few days before his death.

More lasting success has attended Madame Sand in two of the lightest of society comedies, *Le Mariage de Victorine* and *Le Marquis de Villemer,* which seem likely to take a permanent place in the *répertoire* of the French stage. The first, a continuation that had suggested itself to her of Sedaine's century-old comedy, *Le Philosophe sans le savoir,* escapes the ill fate that seems to attend sequels in general. It is of the slightest materials, but holds together, and is gracefully conceived and executed. First produced at the Gymnase in 1851, it was revived during the last year of Madame Sand's life in a manner very gratifying to her, being brought out with great applause at the Comédie Française, preceded on each occasion by Sedaine's play, and the same artists appearing in both.

The excellent dramatic version of her popular novel *Le Marquis de Villemer,* first acted in 1864, is free from the defects that weaken most of her stage compositions. It is said that in preparing it she accepted some hints from Alexander Dumas the younger. Whatever the cause, the result is a play where characters, composition and dialogue leave little to be desired.

L'Autre, her latest notable stage success, brings us down to 1870, when it was acted at the Gymnase, Madame

Sarah Bernhardt impersonating the heroine. This not very agreeable play is derived, with material alterations, from Madame Sand's agreeable novel *La Confession d'une jeune Fille,* published in 1864.

If, however, her works for the stage, which fill four volumes, added but little, in proportion to their quantity, to her permanent fame, her dramatic studies added fresh interest and variety to her experience, which brought forth excellent fruit in her novels. Actors, their art and way of life have fared notoriously badly in fiction. Such pictures have almost invariably fallen into the extreme of unreality or that of caricature, whether for want of information or want of sympathy in those who have drawn them.

The subject, always attractive for Madame Sand, is one in which she is always happy. Already in the first year of her literary career her keen appreciation of the art and its higher influences had prompted her clever novelette *La Marquise.* Here she illustrates the power of the stage as a means of expression—of the truly inspired actor, though his greatness be but momentary, and his heroism a semblance, to strike a like chord in the heart of the spectator—and, in a corrupt and artificial age, to keep alive some latent faith in the ideal. Since then the stage and players had figured repeatedly in her works. Sometimes she portrays a perfected type, such as Consuelo, or Impéria in *Pierre qui roule,* but always side by side with more earthly and faulty representatives such as Corilla and Anzoleto, or Julia and Albany, in *Narcisse,* incarnations of the vanity and instability that are the chief dangers of the profession, drawn with unsparing realism. In *Le Château des Désertes* we find further many admirable theories and suggestive ideas on the subject of the regeneration of the theatre. But it fared with her theatrical as with her political philosophy: she failed in its application, not because her theories were false, but for want of practical aptitude for the craft whose principles she understood so well.

It is impossible here to do more than cast a rapid glance over the literary work accomplished by George Sand during the first decade of the empire. It includes more than a dozen novels, of unequal merit, but of merit for the most part very high. The *Histoire de ma Vie* was published in 1855. It is a study of chosen passages out of her life, rather than a connected autobiography. One out of the four volumes is devoted to the story of her father's life before her birth; two more to the story of her childhood and girlhood. The fourth rather indicates than fully narrates the facts of her existence from the time of her marriage till the Revolution of 1848. It offers to her admirers invaluable glimpses into her life and mind, and is a highly interesting and characteristic composition, if a most irregular chronicle. It has given rise to two most incompatible-sounding criticisms. Some have been chiefly struck by its amazing unreserve, and denounced the overfrankness of the author in revealing herself to the public. Others complain that she keeps on a mask throughout, and never allows us to see into the recesses of her mind. Her passion for the analysis of sentiment has doubtless led her here, as in her romances, to give very free expression to truths usually better left unspoken. But her silence on many points about which her readers, whether from mere curiosity or some more honorable motive, would gladly have been informed, was then inevitable. It could not have been broken without wounding the susceptibilities of living persons, which she did right in respecting, at the cost of disappointment to an inqusitive public.

In January, 1855, a terrible domestic sorrow befell her in the loss of her six-years-old grandchild, Jeanne Clésinger, to whom she was devoted. It affected her profoundly. "Is there a more mortal grief," she exclaims, "than to outlive, yourself, those who should have bloomed upon your grave?" The blow told upon her mentally and physically; she could not rally from its effects, till persuaded to seek a restorative in change of air and scene, which happily did their work.

"I was ill," she says, when writing of these events to a lady correspondent, later in the same year; "my son took me away to Italy. . . . I have seen Rome, revisited Florence, Genoa, Frascati, Spezia, Marseilles. I have walked a great deal, been out in the sun, the rain, the wind, for whole days out of doors. This, for me, is a certain remedy, and I have come back cured."

Those who care to follow the mind of George Sand on this Italian journey may safely infer from *La Daniella,* a novel written after this tour, and the scene of which is laid in Rome and the Campagna, that the author's strongest impression of the Eternal City was one of disillusion. Her hero, a Berrichon artist on his travels, confesses to a feeling of uneasiness and regret rather than of surprise and admiration. The ancient ruins, stupendous in themselves, seemed to her spoilt for effect by their situation in the center of a modern town. "Of the Rome of the past not enough exists to overwhelm me with its majesty; of the Rome of the present not enough to make me forget the first, and much too much to allow me to see her."

But the Baths of Caracalla, where the picture is not set in a frame of hideous houses, awakened her native enthusiasm. "A grandiose ruin," she exclaims, "of colossal proportions; it is shut away, isolated, silent and respected. There you feel the terrific power of the Cæsars, and the opulence of a nation intoxicated with its royalty over the world."

So in the Appian Way, the road of tombs, the fascination of desolation—a desolation there unbroken and undisfigured by modern buildings or otherwise—she felt to the full. But whatever came under her notice she looked on with the eye of the poet and artist, not of the archæologist, and approved or disapproved or passed over it accordingly.

The beauties of nature, at Tivoli and Frascati, appealed much more surely to her sympathies. But of certain sites in the Campagna much vaunted by tourists and handbooks she remarks pertinently: "If you were to pass this village" (Marino) "on the railway within a hundred miles of Paris, you would not pay it the slightest attention." Such places had their individuality, but she upheld that there is not a corner in the universe, "however commonplace it may appear, but has a character of its own, unique in this world, for any one who is disposed to feel or comprehend it." In one of her village tales a sagacious peasant professes his profound contempt for the man who cannot like the place he belongs to.

Neither the grottoes and cascades of Tivoli, the cypress and ilex gardens of Frascati and Albano, nor the ruins of Tusculum, were ever so pleasant to her eyes as the popular-fringed banks of the Indre, the corn-land sand hedgerows of Berry, and the rocky borders of the Creuse at Crozant and Argenton. She had not ceased making fresh picturesque discoveries in her own neighborhood. Of these she records an instance in her pleasant *Promenades autour d'un village,* a lively sketch of a few days' walking-tour on the banks of the Creuse, undertaken by herself and some naturalist friends in June, 1857. In studying the interesting and secluded village of Gargilesse, with its tenth-century church and crypt with ancient frescoes, its simple and independent-minded population, in following the course of a river whose natural wild beauties, equal to those of the Wye, are as yet undisfigured here by railroad or the hand of man, lingering on its banks full of summer flowers and butterflies, exploring the castles of Châteaubrun and La Prugne au Pot, George Sand is happier, more herself, more communicative than in Rome, "the museum of the universe."

The years 1858 to 1861 show her to us in the fullest conservation of her powers and in the heyday of activity. The group of novels belonging to this period, the climax of what may be called her second career, is sufficiently remarkable for a novelist who was almost a sexagenarian, including *Elle et Lui, L'Homme de Neige, La Ville Noire, Constance Verrier, Le Marquis de Villemer* and *Valvèdre. Elle et Lui,* in which George Sand at last broke silence in her own defense on the subject of her rupture with Alfred de Musset, first appeared in the *Revue des Deux Mondes,* 1859. Though many of the details are fictitious, the author here told the history of her relations with the deceased poet much too powerfully for her intention to be mistaken or to escape severe blame. That a magnanimous silence would have been the nobler course on her part towards the child of genius whose good genius she had so signally failed to be, need not be disputed. It must be remembered, however, that De Musset on his side had not refrained during his lifetime from denouncing in eloquent verse the friend he had quarreled with, and satirizing her in pungent prose. Making every possible allowance for poetical figures of speech, he had said enough to provoke her to retaliate. It is impossible to suppose that there was not another side to such a question. But Madame Sand could not defend herself without accusing her lost lover. She often proved herself a generous adversary—too generous, indeed, for her own advantage—and in this instance it was clearly not for her own sake that she deferred her apology.

It is even conceivable that the poet, when in a just frame of mind, and not seeking inspiration for his *Nuit de Mai* or *Histoire d'un Merle blanc,* would not have seen in *Elle et Lui* a falsification of the spirit of their history. The theorizing of the outside world in such matters is of little worth; but the novel bears, conspicuously among Madame Sand's productions, the stamp of a study from real life, true in its leading features. And the conduct of the heroine, Thérèse, though accounted for and eloquently defended, is by no means, as related, ideally blameless. After an attachment so strong as to induce a seriously-minded person, such as she is represented, to throw aside for it all other considerations, the hastiness with which, on discovering her mistake, she entertains the idea of bestowing her hand, if not her heart, on another, is an exhibition of feminine inconsequence which no amount of previous misconduct on the part of her lover, Laurent, can justify. Further, Thérèse is self-deceived in supposing her passion to have died out with her esteem. She breaks with the culprit and engages her word to a worthier man. But enough remains over of the past to prevent her from keeping the promise she ought never to have made. When she sacrifices her unselfish friend to return to the lover who has made her miserable, she is sincere, but not heroic. She is too weak to shake off the influence of the fatal infatuation and shut out Laurent from her life, nor yet can she accept her heart's choice for better or worse, even when experience has left her little to learn with regard to Laurent. Clearly both friend and lover, out of a novel, would feel wronged. Thérèse's excuse lies in the extremely trying character of her companion, whose vagaries may be supposed to have driven her beside herself at times, just as her airs of superiority and mute reproach may have driven him not a little mad. Those who wish to know in what spirit Madame Sand met the attacks upon her provoked by this book, will find her reply in a very few words at the conclusion of her preface to *Jean de la Roche,* published the same year.

Most readers of *Elle et Lui* have been so preoccupied with the question of the rights and wrongs of the originals in their behavior to each other, so inclined to judge of the book according to its supposed accuracy or inaccuracy as a matter of history, that its force, as a study of the attraction that so often leads two exceptional but hopeless, irreconcilable spirits to seek in each other a refuge from the isolation in which their superiority places them, has been somewhat overlooked. Laurent, whether a true portrait or not, is only too true to nature; excessive in his admirable powers and in his despicable weakness. Thérèse is an equally faithful picture of a woman not quite up to the level of her own principles, which are so high that any lapse from them on her part brings down more disasters on herself and on others than the misdemeanors of avowedly unscrupulous persons.

Within a few months of *Elle et Lui* had appeared *L'Homme de Neige,* a work of totally different but equally characteristic cast. The author's imagination had still all its old zest and activity, and readers for whom fancy has any charm will find this Scandinavian romance thoroughly enjoyable. The subject of the marionette theater, here introduced with such brilliant and ingenious effect, she had studied both historically and practically. She and her son found it so fascinating that, years before this time, a miniature stage had been constructed by the latter at Nohant, over which he presided, and which they and their friends found an endless source of amusement. Madame Sand wrote little dramas expressly for such representations, and would sit up all night, making dresses for the puppets. In an agreeable little article she has devoted to the subject, she describes how from the crudest beginnings they succeeded in elaborating their art to a high pitch; the *répertoire* of their lilliputian theater including more than twenty plays, their "company" over a hundred marionettes.

To the next year, 1860, belong the pleasant tale of artisan life, **La Ville Noire**, and the well-known and popular **Marquis de Villemer**, notable as a decided success in a *genre* seldom adopted by her, that of the purely society novel.

Already Madame Sand had outlived the period of which she was so brilliant a representative. After the Romantic movement had spent its force, a reaction had set in that was influencing the younger school of writers, and that has continued to give the direction to successful talent until the present day. Of the so-called "realism," Madame Sand said that it was nothing new. She saw there merely another form of the same revolt of nature against affectation and convention which had prompted the Romantic movement, whose disciples had now become guilty of affectation in their turn. *Madame Bovary* she pronounced with truth to be but concentrated Balzac. She was ready to perceive and do justice to the great ability of the author, as to original genius in any school; thus of Tourguénief she speaks with enthusiasm: "Realist to see all, poet to beautify all, great heart to pity and understand all." But she deplored the increasing tendency among artists to give the preference among realities to the ugliest and the most painful. Her personal leanings avowedly were towards the other extreme; but she was too large-minded not to recognize that truth in one form or another must always be the prime object of the artist's search. The manner of its presentation will vary with the age.

> Let the realists, if they like, go on proclaiming that all is prose, and the idealists that all is poesy. The last will have their rainy days, the first their days of sunshine. In all arts the victory remains with a privileged few, who go their own ways; and the discussions of the "schools" will pass away like old fashions.

On the generation of writers that George Sand saw growing up, any opinion pronounced must be premature. But with regard to herself, it should now be possible to regard her work in a true perspective. As with Byron, Dickens, and other popular celebrities, a phase of infinite enthusiasm for her writings was duly succeeded by a phase of determined depreciation. The public opinion that survives when blind friendship and blind enmity have done their worst is likely to be the judgment of posterity. (pp. 213-37)

Bertha Thomas, in her George Sand, *Roberts Brothers, 1883, 302 p.*

Henry James on Sand's motivation to write:

[George Sand] was pressed to write, and she was pressed to write because she had the greatest instinct of expression ever conferred on a woman; a faculty that put a premium on all passion, on all pain, on all experience and all exposure, on the greatest variety of ties and the smallest reserve about them.

Henry James, in his Notes on Novelists, *1914.*

Maximilian Rudwin   (essay date 1927)

[*In the following essay, Rudwin examines elements of the fantastic in many of Sand's works, focusing primarily on her pastoral romances.*]

George Sand . . . retained longer than any other member of the Romantic generation of 1830 a distinct liking for the fantastic. In contrast to the majority of the French Romantics, for whom the employment of the fantastic in fiction was but a part of their aesthetic theories, it was with her a matter of temperament. George Sand had from her tenderest childhood a disposition for the mysterious and marvellous, which her early environment tended to develop still further. The supernatural surrounded on all sides a child who was only too much disposed to enjoy its charms. The superstitions of the peasants of Berry in the midst of whom George Sand passed her childhood took a strong hold on her mind. During the long winter evenings, the hempdresser of Nohant, seated in a corner of the hearth, would tell some lugubrious legend in which figured demons, ghosts or goblins, and the mind of the child who listened to it on her visits to the villagers was kindled.

George Sand's early reading still further increased her natural propensity toward the prodigious. Already as a child, prior to her entry into the convent, she came in contact, as she tells us herself, with the English "roman noir" and read with delight and terror the works of Ann Radcliffe. The effect of this early reading remained with her to the end and can be traced in the works of her maturity. George Sand, just as the other Romantics in France, was, in her treatment of the fantastic, subject to impressions from abroad. In her novel, **le Château des déserts** (written in 1847 and first published in 1851), the supernatural is in the end explained away exactly in the manner of Mrs. Radcliffe. Reminiscences of Lewis' novel, *The Monk*, with which George Sand must have become acquainted at the same time, may be detected in her novel **Lélia** (1833). The monk Magnus, who is in love with Lélia, believes that he has been fascinated by the eyes of the Fiend and is on the point of exorcising him with book and bell. It will be recalled that, in the English novel, Ambrosio also believes that the woman he loves is an incarnation of the Devil.

But greater than English influence on George Sand was that of Germany. The woman novelist, together with the other French Romantics, fell under the spell of the fantastic fiction of the German Romantic School. E. T. A. Hoffmann, the most prominent among the German fantastic fictionists, exerted, as is well known, a very great influence in France. He practically directed the French Romantic movement about the year 1830. At a time when Heinrich Heine could write: "In Germany today Hoffmann has no vogue whatever," all the great French writers of the Romantic generation read and imitated him. George Sand held him in high esteem and employed his stories as models for many of her writings. Her play, **la Nuit de Noël** (1863), is drawn from Hoffmann's

Meister Floh, and her novel **le Diable aux champs** (written in 1851 and first published in 1855-56), also shows the influence of this German storywriter. Her fantastic tales written toward the end of her life, **la Reine Coax** (1872), **le Nuage rose** (1872) and **le Géant Yéocis** (1873) are fully in the manner of Hoffmann.

Goethe was next to Hoffmann in his influence on George Sand. This woman writer was attracted to *Faust* primarily through its fantastic element. The philosophical content of Goethe's great poem first escaped the French Romantics. Their interest was limited to its fantastic parts. George Sand thus counted *Faust* among the great fantastic plays in her **"Essai sur le drame fantastique: Goethe, Byron, Mickiewicz"** (1839).

In her novel, **le Château des déserts** previously mentioned, we find a Witches' Sabbath which recalls the Walpurgis Night in *Faust,* Goethe's influence is especially evident in her fantastic drama, **les Sept cordes de la lyre** (1839), which is no more than a copy of *Faust.* Albertus, the principal character in this play, is an off-spring of the German philosopher. He too is tempted by Mephistopheles in his ambition to wish to know and comprehend all. Supreme wisdom finally fills his soul when he has learned to know love. This play has also a philosophical import. It symbolizes by the harmony of the strings of the lyre the harmony to which humanity should be attuned.

The supernatural figures principally in the pastoral romances of George Sand. This novelist found pleasure in seeking the marvellous among the classes of men who wish to find relief in their imagination from the humdrum rounds of their daily occupations. She wished to show that the countryman, in contrast to the citydweller, still has eyes to behold wonders. The fantastic element seems to George Sand to be one of the forces of the popular mind. It is interesting to note that the writer who had the honor of giving to the peasant his place in literature and who was the first to consecrate a series of great works to the portrayal of rustic life was also the first to discover the part that the marvellous plays in the mind of the peasant. George Sand describes the tiller of the soil with his joys and sorrows, his songs and dances, his beliefs and customs, his traditions and superstitions.

The fantastic not only figures in her fictional writings; it was also deemed worthy of special critical consideration. On the occasion of the exhibition of paintings of rural customs in Berry by her son, Maurice Sand, she wrote an article on the rustic legends of the region. This article, which appeared anonymously under the title **"Légendes rustiques"** in the *Magazin pittoresque* for November, 1857, is also known, on account of its subject-matter, as "Légendes fantastiques."

George Sand was interested in illuminism and occultism and wrote mystic and symbolic books, such as **Consuelo** (1842-43) and its sequel, **la Comtesse de Rudolstadt** (1843-45). In the thirteen "books" of these two novels, the lives of the principal characters are so to say bathed in an atmosphere of mystery and marvel. Count de Rudolstadt, a man of a mystical mind and an adept of occultism, is persuaded that he has seen again the soul of his deceased mother incarnated in an old beggar-woman. When he, in his turn, is laid to rest in the vault of his ancestors, Consuelo believes that she sees him in the magic mirror of Count de Saint-Germain and imagines on several occasions that she hears the sound of the divine bow of his violin.

George Sand, together with the other Romantics, was interested in the Devil. But it must not be inferred that she held a belief in the Devil and all his works. Like all Romantic humanitarians, this woman writer did not believe in a personal Devil and a material hell. Already as a child she was repelled by what she called "the fiction of hell." In her **"Essai sur la drame fantastique"** already mentioned, she brands as an intellectual crime "the frightful belief in eternal damnation, the most guilty notion that one can have of the Deity." Baudelaire, who hated George Sand, remarked a propos of her disbelief in the Devil and hell that she had "good reason to wish to suppress hell."

Satan was to George Sand as to many other Romantics the symbol of revolt and the support of all the weak and downtrodden. In her novel **Consuelo,** she puts into the mouth of the rebel archangel the following words:

> I am not the demon. I am the archangel of rightful revolt and the patron of great combats. Like Christ, I am the God of the poor, the weak and the oppressed.

George Sand, as a good Romantic, admired Milton's Satan and praised the Puritan poet's portrayal of the fallen angel. She says somewhere in her writings: "Milton made the thunderstruck forehead of his rebel angel so noble and so beautiful." In her description of the legends of Berry, she tells of Georgeon, the evil spirit of the Black Valley and mentions the local belief that the Devil holds his Sabbath at the cross of the Bossous.

But George Sand is wary in conjuring the Devil up from his subterranean habitation. In a letter dated September 2, 1838, she praises Hoffmann for making the Devil appear in his "ecstacies" not in person but as a philosophical concept. The appearance of Mephisto in her play previously mentioned must be considered as an exception. The Tempter was brought over bodily from *Faust.* Although the word "diable" appears in a few of the titles of her works, the Devil does not show himself in person in them. The novel, **le Diable aux champs** previously mentioned, does not contain the Devil. Nor is the principal character in her comedy, **le Démon du foyer** (1852), a horned and hoofed individual. The romance, **la Mare au diable** (1846), deals not with the Devil but with Death. This story of a diabolical pond takes its title from the dismal engraving of Holbein's *Laborer,* in which the skeleton Death is represented as skipping along whip in hand by the peasant's side in the field and urging on the team drawing the plough so that he may finish his work and follow him.

In her novels **Consuelo** and **la Comtesse de Rudolstadt** George Sand deals with a medieval sect which is supposed to worship Satan. Our novelist, together with many other members of the Romantic group, wished to bring about a reconciliation of good and evil, aspired to marry Hell to Heaven. Lélia already said that "the spirit of evil and the spirit of good are but one spirit: God." In *Consuelo,* George Sand puts this idea in the mouth of the heretical sect of the Lollards: We read:

> A mysterious and singular sect dreamed . . . of uniting these two arbitrarily divided principles into one single principle. . . . It tried to raise the supposed principle of evil from its low estate and make it, on the contrary, the servant and agent of the good.

George Sand, along with the other Romantics, predicted the day when the Devil should regain Heaven and occupy his former seat at the right hand of the Lord. Further on in this novel the following paragraph will be found:

> In the opinion of the Lollards, Satan was not the enemy of the human race, but, on the contrary, its protector and patron. They held that he was a victim of injustice and jealousy. According to them, the Archangel Michael and the other celestial powers who had precipitated him into the abyss, were the real demons, while Lucifer, Beelzebub, Ashtaroth, Astarte, and all the monsters of hell, were innocence and light themselves. They believed that the reign of Michael and his glorious host would soon come to an end, and that the Devil would be restored and reinstated in Heaven with his accursed myrmidons. They paid him an impious worship and accosted each other by saying, *Celui à qui on a fait tort te salue*—that is to say, He who has been misunderstood and unjustly condemned, salute thee— that is, protect and assist thee.

The French Romantics held views which were already taught by the Gnostics, are found in the books of the Kabbalists and the Magi, and were shared by many medieval sects. The German Luciferians of the thirteenth century, among other heretical sects, believed that Lucifer had been unjustly banished from Heaven and pronounced anathema against St. Michael, his conqueror. In our own country, a Universalist minister, the Reverend Mr. Tillotson, was deposed from his church for wishing to extend its doctrine of universal salvation to Satan. The orthodox teaching is that the Devil cannot do penance and receive pardon like Adam. The Church has always taught that Satan is a devil through all eternity. He is damned beyond redemption. In the Persian eschatology, however, Ahriman will be the last to arrive purified in the paradise. According to the belief of the Yezidis in Asiatic Turkey, the rebel angel will some day be restored.

The belief in the Devil's pardon and restoration to Heaven was also held by several Church fathers. The germ of this belief is in the passage: "Even the devils are subject unto us through thy name" (Luke x. 17). Origen entertained the hope for the Devil's restoration to Heaven. His belief in the salvalibility of the Satanic nature was shared apparently by Justin, Clemens Alexandrinus and afterwards by Gregory of Nyssa and Didymus. Thomas Aquinas, it is said, could hardly be happy from thinking of the irreversible doom of Satan. He passed a night in prayer for the salvation and restoration of the Devil. "O God," he prayed, "have mercy upon thy servant, the Devil." Father Sinistrari, the famous *Consulteur* of the Inquisition, argued that demons were included in the atonement wrought by

Christ and might attain final beatitude. He even intimated, though more timidly, that their father, Satan himself, as a participator in the sin of Adam and sharer of his curse, might be included in the general provision of the Deity for the entire and absolute removal of the curse throughout nature. Saint Theresa did not wish that one should speak ill of the Devil and pitied him for not being able to love.

In a thirteenth century poem, *A Moral Ode,* we find the assertion that the Devil himself might have had mercy had he sought for it.

The idea of the salvation of Satan was a part of the Romantic humanitarian movement which a misanthropic humorist has named "redemptorism," that desire to rescue criminals and courtesans by means of love, that hope of the final triumph of universal good. This ideal found expression in different forms in Goethe, in Burns, in Byron, in Blake, and in Victor Hugo. Goethe intimated that he had written a passage "where the Devil himself receives grace and mercy from God." Byron shared this Romantic belief in the salvation of Satan in predicting a time

> When man no more can fall as once he fell, And even the very demons shall do well!

This ideal has been expressed by Robert Burns in a single verse of his "Address to the De'il", which touches the heart without offending the intellect.

Henry Mills Alden has uttered his belief in the following words:

> Lucifer is the light-bearer, the morning-star, and whatever disguises he may take in falling, there can be no new dawn that shall not witness his rising in his original Brightness.

(pp. 513-19)

> *Maximilian Rudwin, "The Supernatural of George Sand," in* The Open Court, *Vol. XLI, No. 9, September, 1927, pp. 513-19.*

Patricia Thomson   (essay date 1972)

[*In the following excerpt, Thomson surveys the critical response in Great Britain to Sand's early novels.*]

Of all French writers, George Sand made the most impression in England in the 1830s and 1840s. More than Hugo, much more than Balzac, she stood for English readers as a symbol of the post-revolutionary writing of France. It is interesting to see the way in which she gradually impinged on the consciousness of English reviewers.

Her first major novel, *Indiana,* was published in Paris, in May 1832, with great acclaim. Balzac praised its truth and contemporaneity and George Sand herself described its heroine simply as Woman—'l'amour heurtant son front aveugle à tous les obstacles de la civilisation'. *Valentine,* equally passionate and well received, was also an attack on social constraints, on arranged marriages, in particular, and a plea for the supremacy of the heart's affections. It was published in November 1832, but it is not until February 1833 that George Sand is mentioned in English journals. The *Athenaeum,* true to its policy of foreign coverage, gave a largely inaccurate, though picturesque, gossip note on her:

> The writer of *Indiana* and *Valentine,* is now positively known to be Madame Dudevant, a young lady who, some years back, distinguished herself at the age of thirteen by an indomitable wish to escape from her parents and seek out Lord Byron. Frustrated in this, she was subsequently married *à la mode française* to some son of earth most unlike the poet. Doubtful of the success of her productions, she published under the name of her friend Sand, who thus finds himself loaded with a celebrity which, not having enough talent to support, he has confessed the truth; and the lady thus alone stands answerable for works that do more honour to her genius than her delicacy.

It is typical that rumours of her life should have preceded any account of her works. The *Athenaeum,* however, put that right in subsequent issues with a review of *Indiana* and *Valentine* in March, three columns devoted to *Lélia* in September and an account of *Jacques* in December of the following year—so that, by the end of 1834, its readers should have been up to date with George Sand's output.

These reviews set the tone of admiration, mingled with moral outrage, which becomes very familiar in the next decade. From the start, the reviewer is aware that he is dealing with 'a Phenomenon', with the current French favourite, more read than Balzac, as much talked of in the salons as Rossini—and every disapproving comment is nicely balanced by a tribute. In each case, the writer makes very heavy weather of her name—the first, though certainly not the last, masculine pseudonym to trouble English ears. He cannot leave well alone: 'avowedly Mr George Sands but . . . now known to be Mme Dudevant'; 'The lady (who conceals her odd and harsh sounding name—*Dudevant*—under the pseudonym of George Sand) . . . '; 'This George Sand . . . is no other than Mrs Sand, whose real name is Dudevant'. Each time a new combination is tried.

The subversive nature of the earlier works seems largely to have escaped the reviewer. Indeed much escapes him. Sir Ralph Brown (also variously referred to by George Sand as M. Rodolphe Brown, Mr Brown and Sir Brown) was intended to typify a phlegmatic but chivalrous English milord and his dismissal by the reviewer as an absurd Scotchman does argue a certain cursoriness of reading. He is much more disposed to concentrate on the romantic settings and poetic descriptions. What he marvels at, in particular, is the ability of French readers to enjoy tales which are 'love from beginning to end . . . in England, they would not be tolerated, not only on account of their immoral tendency and licentious descriptions but that, really, two volumes of all love and nothing but love, would be palling to English taste'.

By *Lélia,* the formidable nature of George Sand's challenge to accepted ideas is fully realized and the *Athenaeum* reviewer, while still acknowledging her brilliance, pulls out all his stops. 'We cannot look upon it but as an unreal mockery . . . a bold, brazen paradox born, fostered and nourished in the very hot-bed of scepticism, in the whirl and turbulence of Parisian politics, manners and question-

able morality.' Lélia herself is summed up as 'a monster, a Byronic woman—a woman without hope and without soul'. Her melancholy, perverse philosophy has not been uncommon in French novels but 'no woman has heretofore declared herself as a disciple'. Had this book been written in England it 'would have been pursued by the hue and cry of every critic in the kingdom'. As it has not, 'We shall not again dip our pen in this mire of blood and dirt, over which, by a strange perversity of feeling the talent of the writer, and that writer a woman! has contrived to throw a lurid, fearful and unhallowed light'.

Strong words these, and, although it should be remembered that equally violent reactions were aroused in France by *Lélia,* it can be seen that the *Athenaeum* reviewer has the additional impetus of patriotic indignation. What got under the skin of critics on both sides of the Channel was Lélia's total disbelief in progress, her scepticism, her sense of being 'deracinée du présent', her disbelief in conventional ideas of virtue—witness Trenmor, the idealized ex-galley slave. It is ironic that George Sand soon left behind the mood of despair in which she wrote this book but continued to be known as the author of *Lélia,* for it it she crystallized for many Victorians the *mal du siècle* which they were to feel all their lives.

After a lapse of fifteen months, the review of *Jacques* is mild in comparison. George Sand is 'undoubtedly the most gifted and most original female writer of her country and times, a sort of female Jean-Jacques Rousseau'. What must be most deplored about her is her 'perpetual war against the nuptial vow'. But despite this, despite 'the highly heated atmosphere of Parisian life . . . despite some unnatural characters and false philosophy', George Sand has 'deep knowledge of the female heart . . . wonderful truth of feeling and observation . . . rapid and burning eloquence'. She is, in fact, 'a woman of genius'.

The *Athenaeum* series of reviews, then, in 1833 and 1834, was the first official introduction of the English reading public to George Sand's novels, and however adverse some of the comments, readers can have been left in no doubt as to the importance of this new author. Other journals, although less systematic in their treatment of her writings, were similarly aware of their significance. The *Foreign Quarterly Review* in 1834 devoted twenty-six pages to an account of all her novels, including *Rose et Blanche,* her earliest production, written in collaboration with her lover, Jules Sandeau, but treated by the reviewer as a later work. There is still considerable uncertainty about the name of the '*soi-disant* George Sand' and some musings about her reputation—'a lady (as we have been informed, but cannot vouch) of unblemished character . . . a new and radiant, if not perfectly salutiferous star'. Reference is made to the author's own injuries in marriage which account for her excesses—'in the irritation of unhappiness [she] has lost the sensitive pudicity of her sex'—and the falling off from the earlier novels in *Lélia* is deplored—'decidedly the worst . . . a compound of romance, *ultra*-German transcendentalism, and the coldest irony . . . The poet, ex-galley slave, and Lélia herself, are all so mystically metaphysical . . . as actually to bewilder a plain English intellect'—but *Jacques* is noted as a return to the style of *Indiana* and *Valentine.* Like them, it is concerned with matrimonial miseries and George Sand 'would well deserve to be called the *Anti-Matrimonial Novelist*'.

Less barbed, indeed gallant and courtly in tone, showing little critical sense but no ill will, is an article in the *Monthly Magazine* about the same time. It is entitled 'French Authoresses. No. I. Madame Sand', and consists largely of a long extract from *Rose et Blanche* which the writer strangely prefers to *Indiana.* Owning that he is 'partial to the writings of the gentler sex' he pays tribute to France which 'has been always distinguished for the literary talents of her daughters' and to 'the lady who delights in the unpretending cognomen of G. Sand'. Conscious of being somewhat out of his depth, he attempts, a little helplessly, to define her by what she is not:

> We know of no English authoress whom we could select as a parallel to convey an idea of her peculiar manner. She is not so profoundly Malthusian as Miss Martineau, nor so masculine and philosophical as Miss Edgeworth; neither is she a describer of balls and routs and a puffer of tradesmen, like Mrs. Gore. Her style is peculiarly her own.

North of the Border, unmindful of the Auld Alliance, *Blackwood's Magazine* and the *Edinburgh Review* were thundering against the moral anarchy, lack of religious convictions, profligate extravagance, and wild flights of imagination of current French fiction, but seemed strangely ill-informed about the novels of George Sand which they had clearly not read. In fact the *Edinburgh Review* deliberately exempts from censure the tales 'of M. Sand, which are written in a calmer, truer, better spirit than those with which we have been occupied'. As late as 1836, *Blackwood's Magazine* is still so out of touch that a contributor gratefully expresses his indebtedness to an article on Talleyrand by 'Madame Sand, better known by her former name of Madame Dudevant', in these terms:

> We shall . . . borrow largely from this little production. Its authoress is well-known in France as having written several very pleasing and successful romances, and as having, we are told, been formerly enthusiastically, and perhaps platonically, in love with Lord Byron. The paper to which we now allude, is written in a strain of thoughtful and sensitive morality, which pleases us much.

It is instructive to see that only the Byron myth, with an additional innuendo, has so far travelled north. The bland ignorance of *Blackwood's Magazine* of anything other than 'the little production' on which the writer leans so heavily, is not allowed to continue much longer. Two months later, in March, an embarrassed and laborious recantation is published.

> But here we must pause to correct, or, in parliamentary phraseology, to explain, what *Maga* said, in the month of January last, touching that highly gifted but singularly unwomanly, at least unhonest-womanly authoress, Madame Dudevant, *alias* George Sand; whose moral character, however, we beg it may be understood that we

presume not to impeach. We have, we blush to say, shown ourselves precipitate, and, what we are not often, credulous. We spoke of this lady and her novels upon report, upon the strength of French praise, without having seen either; and having now made ourselves better acquainted with the subject, we here solemnly revoke our hearsay verdict, and correct our erroneous statements.

To make amends, he has read no fewer than six of her novels but his primary concern is to put right his gaffe about her matrimonial status, which he explains in all its intricacies. He does not deny that her books are 'clever . . . very clever', but deplores the fact that she writes, 'if not licentiously yet with an utter recklessness', and he proceeds to hold up each novel, in turn, to ridicule. Then, having sponged the slate clean in this satisfactory manner, *Blackwood's Magazine* thankfully abandons the subject for a full decade and leaves the vexed question of 'this lady' for other reviews to handle.

The reading public had not long to wait. The very next month, in April 1836, was launched the most notorious attack of the era on the French novel. It was in the best *Quarterly Review* tradition of vituperation and inaccuracy, and its tone recalled the earlier savaging of Keats and Tennyson. This 'famous-infamous article', as G. H. Lewes was later to call it, was swiftly rebutted by Sainte-Beuve in the *Revue des Deux Mondes* and by the *Westminster Review,* but it did enormous damage in intensifying the prejudices of English novel-readers.

The *Quarterly Review* had already, two years earlier, published a derogatory account of French drama, but the novel article is very much more hostile. The reason for the violence of Croker's attack is soon revealed: the great and steadily growing popularity of the French novel which he feels it incumbent on him to stem. In the curious mélange of authors, listed in increasing order of danger to readers—Paul de Kock, Hugo, Dumas, Balzac, Michel Raymond, Michel Masson, and, finally, George Sand—in the great number of their works to which he refers with particularity, we can see an all-out effort on the part of the *Quarterly* to cover and condemn all possible sources of national infection. It is, as Sainte-Beuve observed with wry mockery, 'une mesure d'hygiène morale, je dirai presque de police locale'.

Quite clearly the contemporary French novel had already made a big impact: Croker would have hesitated to bring this 'mass of profligacy before the eyes of the British public' but 'the novels are seen everywhere . . . they are advertised in a thousand ways over the whole reading world . . . When we see them exhibited even in London in the windows of respectable shops—when they are to be had in circulating libraries . . . nay; *ladies book-clubs*' the obvious duty is 'to *stigmatise* them with a BRAND'. His article, in fact, he hopes will have the same effect as 'labelling vials or packets POISON'.

The source of all the impurity is, of course, Rousseau, the old Apostle of Disorder, but none of the writers is more tainted than George Sand who 'carries to its most pernicious excess this species of demoralizing novel'. He confesses that his surprise and revulsion knew no bounds when he discovered that 'these lascivious tales—disgusting enough if written by a *man,* however young or however vicious, are really the production of a *woman*—a lady—a lady, if not of rank at least of title—of *Madame la Baronne du Devant!*'. He is comically torn between wanting to make the most of the discrepancy between George Sand's gentle birth and her views, and his desire to dispute her right to a title; and he goes on, in a splendid flight of fancy, to suggest that she has chosen the name of Sand in remembrance of the assassinator of Kotzebue: 'A *German* name can hardly have been chosen at random by a *French* writer.' Croker's ignorance as well as his pettiness give cause to marvel, for the very first reference to George Sand, in the *Athenaeum* three years earlier, had made clear the reason for the pseudonym.

But as she has chosen a man's name, he will show her no chivalry. This promise Croker certainly makes good. He presents the plot of each novel in turn in the most ridiculous and distorted light, and lumps them all together in his general condemnation. Sainte-Beuve points out that he speaks, in the same breath, of what is most charming and most open to question in George Sand's novels: 'Indiana et Valentine tombent frappées du même coup que Lélia.' But while it is true that Croker shows no critical sense, he is not unaware that *Lélia* gives him most ammunition.

> We cannot refrain from distinguishing from the impure crowd the revolting romance of *Lelia* of which the heroines—high-born and wealthy heroines, be it observed—are not merely *prostitutes* but *monsters*—the men, convicts, maniacs, and murderers—the incidents such as never before were printed in any book publicly sold—and the work altogether such as in any country in the world but France would be burned by the hangman.

The last clause is blatantly revealing of the Tory distrust and fear of France which underlies the whole review and which is evident in so many articles of the thirties and forties. It is made even clearer when Croker uses the novels as a reflection of the state of moral degeneracy and impurity of the nation, especially since July 1831. When he looks at the Paris press to see if the picture of French life given by the novels is a true one, he shows from the statistics of murders and suicides that it is—conveniently blind to similar evidence of 'profligate and bloody' occurrences in London.

While it is clear that the *Quarterly Review* is using the French novel, and that of George Sand in particular, as a stick to beat the French nation with, the article did her reputation in England much damage. I cannot agree with Moraud that the abuse was so unrestrained that the article did more good than harm by rousing the hostility of other journals. Much of the mud did stick, and both Mazzini and Lewes were to refer feelingly to the ill-effects of the *Quarterly Review*'s attack on the fame of George Sand. Echoes of its distinctive tone of insular righteousness rumble in many subsequent articles and as late as 1850 we find the *Dublin University Magazine* still thankful to Croker for having lit the warning beacons: 'It was well for the morality of our higher and middle classes, and especially for the young, that the memorable article on this subject in a leading contemporary scared the public with the mention of some of the grosser abominations in which many of these writers have dealt.'

The immediate response to the article was mixed. The *Examiner* deplored it, not because it doubted its veracity but because it felt that it would serve for those in need of 'bad books' as a catalogue, 'a complete guide to smutty reading'. The *Westminster Review* briskly described the *Quarterly* as 'a review not famous for the strict honesty of its criticisms' but concentrated rather on clearing France from the aspersions made through her novelists than on the writers themselves—although making it clear that much could, and would, be said in their defence. The *Athenaeum* in the following year ran a long series by Jules Janin on 'Literature of the Nineteenth Century in France', of which the June article is dedicated to 'that writer without a peer whom your prudish and pedantic England has insulted without knowing . . . George Sand'. This is written in such a bombastic and inflated style that readers must have felt it confirmed their worst fears about the meretricious nature of the novelist. There is a great deal of local colour; Janin is concerned in the first instance to set the scene of George Sand's arrival in Paris—'that revolutionised city, heaving and boiling like the lava of a volcano'—and to show her as a Child of the Barricades of the July Revolution. He gets into such a hermaphrodite tangle with his pronouns that the editor of the *Athenaeum* feels it necessary to insert the sober footnote: 'From the manner in which M. Janin has spoken of this writer, it may be necessary to inform the English reader that George Sand is the pseudonym of Mme Dudevant.' The following is a fair sample of Janin, in full flood.

> Shortly after the revolution of July . . . a handsome young man, with quick and penetrating eye, dark hair, and intellectual bearing—lively, laughing, curious and unconstrained—entered Paris. He had, for friends, his ardour, his beauty, his youth, his courage and his hopes . . . George Sand—for he it was—with that miraculous intelligence which is composed of the mingled intelligence of the two sexes, felt himself, at once, as warmly excited as the young conscript in his first battle. Already was her hand groping in the literary ammunition-box, to find there the baton of a marshal of France . . .
>
> George Sand, in his own home, is, by turns, a capricious young man, of eighteen, and a very pretty woman of from five-and-twenty to thirty,—a youth of eighteen, who smokes and takes snuff with peculiar grace, and a *grande dame* whose brilliancy and fancy at once astonish and humble you.

For seven long *Athenaeum* columns this incredible prose flowed from Janin's excitable pen. Apart from a brief apology for *Lélia* 'the blot upon the literary life of George Sand' all is exaggerated praise, from the opening 'Who then is *he*—or who is *she?*—man or woman—angel or demon—paradox or truth?', to the final eulogy. It is a strange article and a strange series for the *Athenaeum* to run, although the friendship of Dilke with Janin no doubt goes far to explain it. With Croker as enemy and Janin as sponsor, George Sand's press was not such as any serious novelist would have welcomed.

But the balance was redressed in 1838, when the *Westminster Review* published its promised article in defence of French fiction. This thoughtful and significant article by 'F.B.' [identified as Francis Burdett in W. F. Poole's *Index to Periodical Literature*] is the first serious attempt in the thirties to understand the appeal of the French novel. The writer makes the somewhat optimistic assumption that the time has now gone by when it can be dismissed as 'immoral' and the time arrived for considering what it has to offer that home produce lacks. What he emphasizes, above all, is the impression given by French writers of vigour and fertility. There had been something 'gigantic and exciting in the recent history of France' and this is reflected in French fiction which is full of questioning, examining, sifting of all external and internal fact in the interests of humanity:

> Behind the apparent life, that other unrealized one; a sort of dreamt life, which has its pains, its gaiety, its love, its separations, without other outward sign than a passing cloud on the brow, a momentary light in the eye. This internal poem, which we never read ourselves, the novel will repeat to us.

The democratic aspect of the fiction, too, has its attraction. The heroes 'not only of Sand but of the mere *litterateurs*' are almost always men of the people and the social condition of women is one of the many questions working in the French mind. George Sand is idealistic and not immoral; she never makes evil agreeable:

> It is against, and not for license, that Sand is contending; for the right of a woman to belong to the man she deems worthy, and while she deems him worthy. How completely is the thing sought always a pure, unselfish, eternal affection! whilst how often are painted (with southern warmth, it is true, and the minuteness of a dissection) the struggles and victory of chastity in woman over force, authority, want, and the tempter within.

In French novels, the manner is as important as the matter:

> And then their style! never, surely, was style carried to a greater perfection; never was literature so rich before in authors who wrote clearly, elegantly, nervously, abundantly . . . Sand's, for instance, so clear, pure, keen, we seem to breathe some mountain air, first delightful, then almost trying to our organs.

In comparison with all this, what have our writers to offer? Only 'good taste, seated principles and prejudices' which are manifest in the silver-fork fiction which the *Westminster* had already attacked three years earlier. 'Our novelists palpably and deliberately reveal to us the puppets they work with.' What we lack is 'the great vitality which is in this literature . . . Though unfinished and immature it will and must one day strongly affect ours.'

What this article makes very clear is that part of the great effect of George Sand, and to a lesser extent of Balzac, derived from their impact at a time when English fiction was

at a low ebb. With the vogue of Scott past, and that of Dickens yet to come, the gap was very inadequately filled by the fashionable and relatively lifeless novels of Bulwer Lytton, Mrs Gore, Lady Blessington, and the young Disraeli. Polite conversation always has trouble in holding its own against a *cri de cœur*. An article in the *Dublin University Magazine*, published three months after the *Westminster* one, makes this point even more convincingly, because the writer in this case has little good to say for French fiction—except that it is preferable to English:

> We must confess that in looking over the contemporary trash poured forth from the press of Paris, our national pride has reason to be anything but exalted at the comparison. The works of our neighbours are, indeed, low enough—mean enough—foul enough, perhaps—but their homage, however depraved or senseless, is still addressed to the human heart . . . they have not yet begun to make for themselves idols of silver and gold.

Like 'F.B.' he complains of the 'puppet personages', the 'innumerable patricians', the stereotyped plots, the stress on 'eating and drinking'—'the quantity of culinary and cellarly lore which Mr. D'Israeli imparts to us is truly valuable'—the yawning boredom of fashionable novels, which 'reflect disgrace, not merely upon our literature but upon our national character in every way'.

George Sand, in particular, was capable of supplying what the English novel had missed—pure romanticism. Scott's brand of the romantic was peculiarly his own; George Sand's was in the great poetic line. Her descriptions recalled Byron, her plea for democracy and sex-equality was Shelleyan (her claim of woman's right to belong to a man only as long as she loves him could be straight from the notes to *Queen Mab*) and it is obvious that English readers were thrilling to the romantic call.

A review article in the *British and Foreign Review* in 1839, on George Sand's recent novels, provides, I think, a more representative judgement than either the *Westminster Review* or the *Athenaeum*. It has been ascribed to H. F. Chorley, who in the 1840s was one of the most prolific general reviewers on the *Athenaeum* staff. The tone of his reviewing has been well summed up by L. A. Marchand. Honest and liberal, but soft centred, Chorley probably mirrored the average opinion of the majority of his readers and his tendency was to be cautiously favourable to French fiction, while falling back frequently on moral strictures, to show his judicial quality. The novels he covers in this review are ***André, Lettres d'un Voyageur, Les Maîtres Mosaïstes, Mauprat,*** and ***Spiridion*** and he is careful to explain why he should be reviewing George Sand at all. He says that the public has become so familiar over the past few years with descriptions of George Sand—of 'the half-sybilline, half-animal countenance poetically rendered by M. Calamatta'—so interested in the countless tales told of her, that he feels their curiosity should be gratified. For she is not a comet, alone in her eccentricity, but a product of her times, of 'that unfathomed chaos of mingled beauty and corruption, in the deepest depths of which [France] was struggling at the time when Madame Dudevant began to write'.

The reviewer is really very much more concerned to show that the dangers of reading George Sand have been exaggerated than to do full justice to her powers. He points out that however startling her opinions may be, they are vague, whether she is pleading for freedom in the relations of the sexes or preaching a universal church. And in this vagueness lies the antidote to the 'otherwise fatal mischievousness' of her views. It is because of the 'particle of diviner nature' in George Sand that she calls up shadows, like Lélia or Trenmor or Jacques, incapable of tempting anyone into the toils of 'a mystic sensuality'. With this skilful, back-handed compliment Chorley indirectly counters Croker's charge that the novels are 'POISON' and then goes on to over-praise one of the gentlest of her short novels, **André,** clearly because it has so little harm in it. The review is rather a job of rehabilitation than criticism, although generous tribute is paid to George Sand's intimate familiarity with all classes of society, which can give such varied portraits as the Marquise in **Valentine** or the rat-catcher in **Mauprat,** her simple and dramatic dialogue, and her power of abstracting from each scene and epoch its own peculiar essence. Chorley contrives to sit on the fence effortlessly. When he deals with George Sand's latest mystical novel **Spiridion,** for instance, he first warns the British reader sternly against insularity, if he is to appreciate it, and then undercuts his advice by pointing out that there is nothing much to appreciate: 'It is but the old tale of the coquette becoming devotee—as sensual in devotion as in coquetry'. Lewes's later description of this article as 'bold in its praise considering the state of opinion at the time' leaves out of account such intemperate tributes as Janin's. But unlike the latter, Chorley would have alienated no one and may well have encouraged some to feel it safe to sample a novel by George Sand.

The final significant article of the decade was published in the *Monthly Chronicle* of 1839. It was by Mazzini, long an admirer of George Sand and her democratic principles. It is time to write in praise of her, he says, for 'her novels are sold and read everywhere, not only in Piccadilly, but we believe even in Albermarle Street'. He considers that 'the anathema hurled against her three years since seems to us singularly to have lost its force'; her latest works are calm, containing 'nothing that can raise a blush in the youngest reader'.

His defence of her is whole-hearted. He stresses her suffering, her struggles, her generosity, her genius. He even defends her smoking: 'Sinners that we are, we are compelled to declare at all risks that we do not consider a cigar decidedly *immoral*'. He defends her right to a private life—an unheard-of claim. He presents **Indiana** and **Jacques** as powerful lessons in morality and is so carried away that he delivers, as in the voice of George Sand, a long impassioned homily to the wife-who-is-about-to-err which sounds more like Dickens than George Sand. Even **Lélia** is not an immoral book, although it is, for the young, a dangerous book, because it shows a world without hope. What George Sand is really attacking in her writing is, like Goethe, the world of individualism and self-interest. It is a heart-warming article because of Mazzini's own sincerity and idealism.

By the 1840s, then, it would have been difficult for any reader not to be aware of what reviewers persisted in calling 'the phenomenon of George Sand'. I have dealt only with the most important articles but there were many passing references to her in journals and Mrs Trollope, G. W. M. Reynolds, and Thackeray had more formally added their praise or censure. And in the next two or three years her books continued to be reviewed steadily, especially in the *Athenaeum,* the *Foreign Quarterly Review,* and the *Westminster Review* which also bring in references to her in discussion of other authors and topics. The writers are frequently torn between their desire to praise the vitality of French literature and their feeling that it is morbid and un-English—though, almost in the same breath, they condemn English insularity and suggest that any attempt to enlarge English horizons is worthy of support. There is no particular party line laid down about George Sand in these journals. The *Westminster Review* is probably most consistently outspoken about her genius and remarkable qualities whereas in the *Foreign Quarterly Review* in 1841 there is a hostile article, 'Rousseau and the Modern Littérature Extravagante' which is designed to bring out what a 'frightful progress in morality has been made since Rousseau'. Most of the blame should be laid upon the doctrine of the equality of the sexes, of which creed George Sand is the apostle:

> An openly avowed hostility to marriage, borne out by a divorce from her husband, the adoption of male attire, a cigar in her mouth, a whip in her hand, and her conversation with young men carried on in the familiar terms of *tu* and *George,* have invested the talent of Madame Dudevant with a kind of apodictical authority.

But the *Foreign Quarterly* was as full of praise as the *Athenaeum* in 1843, when **Consuelo** appeared and it published its review concurrently with the serialization of the novel in the *Revue Indépendante.* The general consensus of opinion was that the second half of the novel was disappointing, 'all false, all writing', in Browning's words, with its Gothic castles and subterranean passages, metempsychosis and trances, dwarfs and wandering musicians, but that the first part made up for it in truth of characterization and eloquence. The *Athenaeum* even found much to admire in the latter part. The Canon's household 'is like the best Flemish painting, with a touch of fancy and elegance not belonging to the artists of the *Pays Bas*', and the reviewer especially praises her description of the kitchen garden—the splendour of artichokes and melons, asparagus and courgettes: 'Never, surely, was a kitchen garden represented in such glowing colours, even by the rapturous imagination of a Brillat-Savarin'. Both reviewers now feel free to assess her primarily as a novelist and this is the line taken by the *Athenaeum* reviewer when he defends the length of his article:

> It is not difficult to explain, why we have devoted so much space to a production so wild as this novel, fuller of extravagancies than even of deep thoughts and marvellous beauties of detail. Be its views right or wrong, distorted or natural, the aim of this novel is to consider the mutual relations of art and society: and the subject is one of great and increasing interest.

What of the less open-minded journals? Either silence or parroting of earlier pronouncements. What does emerge is just how much borrowing, often no doubt unintentional, went on between reviewers. Again and again, those hostile to George Sand fall back on the phraseology of the 1836 *Quarterly;* an account in the *Dublin Review* of 1840 of a number of French novels is a case in point. The writer gets the same emotional effect: 'disgust', 'depravity', 'moral cholera', 'written by a woman!', 'abominations'; he evokes the same political and national implications: 'In how many cases the novelists of that unhappy country have led their readers to the scaffold'. Like Croker, he stresses the popularity and baneful influence of foreign fiction and supplies interesting details of how Belgian publishers reprint Parisian novels at sixpence instead of six shillings and thus propagate the 'moral gangrene' of France in Russia, Spain, Peru, the Brazils and, alas, Britain. 'If a purer sense of national dignity forbids translations, yet those are not wanting who need not such assistance'. Where he differs from the *Quarterly Review* is in his genuine admiration of George Sand's 'most elevated' literary talents. His invective against her is libellous and yet he recognizes and indeed itemizes her virtues as a writer, 'very superior to Mme de Staël—and perhaps equal to Jean-Jacques Rousseau'.

No such weakness is shown by the *Foreign and Colonial*

Drawing of Sand by the poet Alfred de Musset.

Quarterly Review in 1843 in the article which Lewes later described as 'dreadfully unfair—an imitation of the 1836 *Quarterly*'. It was prompted by the publication, the year before, in Paris, of George Sand's collected works and the reviewer has done her the honour of plodding through all thirty-three volumes before making his pronouncements upon her, which are indeed in the same *Quarterly* vein and sound strangely out-dated seven years later. This article, too, stresses the popularity of French literature which 'is naturalised in London as soon as it is born in Paris'. But in case there are still some readers who are ignorant of George Sand, the writer reiterates the usual malicious account of her life, liaisons, garb, name, cigar, appearance—with some additional insults about her 'large hook nose and projecting upper jaw bone'. He admits grudgingly that the novels possess 'some merit' but are untranslatable because of the 'coarseness of subject matter' and then proceeds to slang each novel in turn. The article ends with the ominous pronouncement: 'A few George Sands will soon reduce France to the level of the orang-outang or little better, possibly something worse. Let France look to it, her cup may be fuller than she thinks of the wrath of her God'.

The publication of the collected works of George Sand and Balzac occasioned a very different article the following year from the pen of G. H. Lewes. Published in the *Foreign Quarterly Review,* [July 1844], it is undoubtedly the most important article that had so far been written on George Sand, for Lewes was expressing 'serious convictions formed over five years' very intimate acquaintance with her works' and a growing impatience with biased and ignorant criticism. The five articles which he mentions in his brief survey of George Sand criticism to date are the *Quarterly* of 1836, the arch-villain, the *Westminster*'s spirited reply, the 1839 *British and Foreign Review* which, despite its praise of her, still perpetuated the idea of her as an immoral writer, Mazzini's noble defence, and the last abusive echo of the *Quarterly* in the *Foreign and Colonial Review.* In this outline, Lewes underestimates quite seriously the amount of good criticism and well-balanced analysis that had, in fact, appeared in the columns of the *Westminster Review* and the *Athenaeum,* but he is making the important point that even the best criticism of George Sand has been acutely conscious of the facts of her life: 'Because she was herself unhappy in marriage, people assumed that she wrote against it; the truth being that she advocates marriage, but not its abuses.' His defence of both George Sand and Balzac is in three parts; he considers each as moralist, artist, and entertainer. As moralist, George Sand can be defended because she is earnest. 'She puts forth *convictions* . . . It is incumbent on an author, not that he speak the truth, but what he holds to be the truth'. Unlike Balzac, she does not treat adultery lightly and makes very little use of it in her novels; her heroines are, indeed, singularly chaste. As for her 'social theorising', she is, above all, a democrat and longs for social amelioration but she does not grind specific axes in her novels and what really manifests itself is her sincere longing for truth and her sympathy with greatness of thought and feeling. Like Mazzini, Lewes would keep the young away from **Lélia** not because it is immoral, but because it is, though a 'profound poem . . . the most terrible outcry of scepticism ever heard. The whole anarchy of the epoch is mirrored in its pages'. But it is quite extraordinary that the cry of 'immoral' should so often have been raised against George Sand's novels:

> No-one can have heard of Madame Sand without some grievous charge of immorality; she is the popular symbol of French grossness, with which the imaginations of our immaculate countrymen are horrified . . . Never was there a more notable instance of giving a dog a bad name and hanging him. Madame Sand has been known to travel in androgynous costume; smokes cigars; is separated from her husband, and has been the theme of prolific scandal. The conclusion drawn was, that from such a person nothing but anti-social works could possibly be expected.

Like all George Sand's English enthusiasts, Lewes is enraptured by her style—to which, incidentally, it was allowable to refer with enthusiasm even in otherwise unfavourable notices. It is 'perhaps the most beautiful ever written by a French author'. He goes on to quote at length from *Lélia* which 'we never open . . . at random without feeling as at an open window on a May morn . . . Poetry flows from her pen as water from the rock; she writes as the birds sing: without effort, but with perfect art'.

While George Sand excels Balzac in style, each is equally great in characterization. 'Sand, like a poet, has known and felt life; Balzac has observed it,' but that does not mean that she is not capable of subtle psychological delineation. Her men may be less pleasing than her women but she has some remarkable analyses of egotism.

Lewes feels that he has no need to waste time on George Sand and Balzac as entertainers, 'their popularity speaks for them'. What he does want above all to stress (and it is very clear that Lewes's main preoccupation is with George Sand and not with Balzac) is that a great novelist has acquired undeserved odium in England so that 'although her works are largely read (we have a bookseller's authority for the fact), and her genius is recognised by most of our eminent men, it is rare to see any praise of her not qualified by some concession to the prejudices of the day'. What is needed now is 'a calm dispassionate examination' of her works.

Lewes's article was, I should say, just in time still to be highly relevant. It is not to underestimate his very real devotion to George Sand's writing to remember that he was a good journalist, aware of the strategic moment when an issue was a live one—neither too hot to handle nor too cold to revive. For some of the heat, in fact, was by this time going out of George Sand reviews. This was partly due to increased familiarity with her writings, partly to the nature of the novels themselves. Reviewers felt less threatened by her philosophic, reforming novels than her more passionate, early ones—although the warning note still had to be sounded about them. Earlier, in 1844, the *Edinburgh Review,* in a review of the novels of Mme Hahn-Hahn, the so-called George Sand of Germany, denied any real resemblance between the writers. George Sand had certainly greater genius but she had a deplorable habit of blaming society for all corruption, whereas the German writer took up a much healthier attitude to individual re-

sponsibility. The 'unfortunate' criminal was a particular delusion of George Sand's. But on the whole the novels did seem to be becoming much less morally impeachable and the reviews reflected this change.

Indeed, even as George Sand was becoming more respectable, some reviewers were disposed to regret the apparent loss of her old fire. Both the *Foreign Quarterly Review* and the *Athenaeum,* in 1846, reviewing several of her latest novels, among them **Jeanne, Isidora, Teverino, Le Péché de M. Antoine,** and **Le Meunier d'Angibault** could find only in the last novel any trace of her genius. The *Foreign Quarterly* dismissed **Jeanne** as a failure which could be 'recommended as a novel which even girls may read' (a former accolade now used as an insult) and commented on the paleness of the colours in which she now wrote:

> We had begun to despair of George Sand. The feebleness of the **Comtesse de Rudolstadt** and **Jeanne,**—the carelessness and nothingness of **Isidora** . . . led us to suspect that the cry of 'George Sand has written herself out,' might not be one of envy, but of regret. [But] there came **Le Meunier d'Angibault** to overthrow all our conclusions and once more to awaken our enthusiasm.

Like the *Athenaeum* reviewer, he praises the scenes of the Berry countryside and the characterization of the miller's family, using one of the favourite Victorian encomiums, and one used again and again in reviews of George Sand: 'This is a Dutch painting for life-like effect, with a deeper meaning than any Dutch painter ever cared for'. Chorley's review article in the *Athenaeum* deeply irritated Elizabeth Barrett, who was a worshipper of George Sand. She wrote angrily to Browning of 'this digging and nagging at great reputations' by 'little critics'. Chorley had taken up much the same line as the *Foreign Quarterly Review* but had sounded a patronizing and jeering note quite absent from the other review: 'No matter what may be the progress of her health as a moralist, a palsy is creeping over her powers as a novelist.' In his discussion of what he considers to be her stages as a novelist—gallantry, philosophy, devotion, and now social reform—he is simply enlarging on what he had already said, but these are distinctions for which Elizabeth Barrett has no time and she gives short shrift to his 'infinite trash about the three eras in the Frenchwoman's career . . . as if earnestness of aim was not from the beginning . . . a characteristic of George Sand! Really, it is pitiful.'

George Sand is, then, in the 1840s, despite a greatly increased number of notices of her books, much less of a talking-point for reviewers than she had been in the thirties. There is now not only considerable agreement about her excellence and limitations as a novelist, but, of course, much more competition for the attention of reviewers from English novelists. There is, however, a very interesting resuscitation of alarm about her, when the project of translating her novels was set afoot in 1847. Several of her novels had already been translated but a much larger scheme was now envisaged by a handful of her admirers, under the general editorship of a feminist friend of Mazzini's, Matilda Hays. The *Athenaeum* reviewer, Chorley, is fluttered by it. He sees no reason why she should be made available in translation at all. It is all very well to accept George Sand as an artist of genius but when she sets herself up as a philosopher and moralist, advertised by her admirers as 'the greatest female genius of the day', then she could do a great deal of harm to the uninitiated. She is, after all, a woman whose views have been the outcome of her own particular circumstances and Chorley quotes, in full, in May 1847, his 1839 account of her life in order to show how inadvisable it would be to accept such a woman as prophet. He has clearly taken fright at the fact that George Sand is now being fêted by the Ladies, as he calls them, and fears she may be made easily available for the domestic consumption of the less educated.

Apart from his moral disquiet, he does make two pertinent comments on the translations. These are also voiced by the *Westminster* reviewer, who, unlike Chorley, welcomes the idea as one inaugurated by a kindred spirit, which should make available novels always 'less read than talked about by the British public'. But there are two things wrong with the translations. First, 'the editors have been so anxious to choose harmless novels, that the choice so far is unrepresentative', and secondly, the standard of translation is very bad and does not in any way capture the magic of George Sand's style. In the event, the project had to be abandoned for lack of support, Miss Hays sadly confessing in a preface that they had over-estimated the amount of interest they could depend on, but not before the *Quarterly Review* had been roused from its long and studied silence on the subject of George Sand. Ever since Croker's onslaught of 1836, that journal had ignored her existence, but the revelation that **Le Meunier d'Angibault** was to be translated by a cleric was too much to tolerate. In the index to the *Quarterly Review* of 1847 appears an entry—'Sand, infamous novels of'—which directs the reader's attention to a footnote to an article in which free-love is mentioned: 'See the writings *passim* of that great apostle of pantheism, the 'semivir obscoenus' of France, George Sand.' The note thunders on in fine excommunicatory vein:

> If we are to believe the newspaper advertisements, an attempt is now making by an English *editrix,* assisted among others by a beneficed clergyman of the English Church, to circulate these productions here in an English translation—*omitting the obscenity.* We denounce this scheme, not from any wish to widen the original flood of pollution—God forbid—but in the confidence that the public would not tolerate the undisguised poison, while the *modest* emendation is a smuggler's attempt to conceal the real nature of his infamous cargo—the inevitable moral consequences of Madame Dudevant's avowed creed. If there is really such a person as 'the Rev. E. R. Larkin, Chaplain to Lord Monson, and Rector of Burton by Lincoln' the open connexion of his name with 'The Works of George Sand' appears to us a strange phenomenon.

The *Quarterly Review,* sticking firmly to its imagery of poison and pollution, was alone in its intransigence and ignorance of George Sand's later novels. Even *Blackwood's Magazine,* her old enemy, was capable of admitting a change in her novels and in their attitude to her. In 1848,

reviewing 'A Parcel from Paris', they say, recapping their former strictures: 'We need hardly say that Madame Dudevant is anything but a favourite of ours . . . ', but have to confess that they have found nothing much objectionable in her recent books. But they seem still, in Scotland, after fifteen years, to be as hopelessly at sea as ever with the facts of George Sand's life. The reviewer now confuses her life with that of her heroine, Indiana: 'Ignorant of the world, she allowed herself to be married to a rough old soldier'—but the tone is kindlier. Many of the stories of her 'swaggering and smoking in man's attire, and brandishing pistol and horsewhip with virile energy and effect' may indeed have been exaggerated. They are still cautious about her but at 'the ripe age of forty-four, we may suppose her sobered down a little' and they give a long account of the favourable impression she made on someone who met her and who spoke of a 'sad but serene physiognomy'. The softening process has continued by the next year, when the approval of **La Petite Fadette** is unequivocal: 'We pass on to a lady of a very different stamp, who does not often obtain commendation at our hands; and yet, in this instance, we know not why we should withold approval from George Sand's last novel, **La Petite Fadette,** one of those seductive trifles which only Madame Dudevant can produce'.

It could be said, I think, that the Berry novels at the end of the 1840s completed the acceptance of George Sand by reviewers. The simplicity and rural charm and naturalness of these tales—well-punned as 'the Georgics of France'—were seized upon by them as an indication, not only that George Sand had mellowed, but that a more responsible attitude to the role of the artist was arising on the other side of the Channel. In a two-column review of **François le Champi,** in 1848, the *Athenaeum* asked: 'Is modern French literature approaching to a new phasis? . . . Are we to . . . be permitted once more to breathe the air of Nature? Is the stimulant literature expiring? . . . George Sand . . . has made a strong effort to recall novelists to a right sense of their office . . . she has made this effort critically and consciously.'

So that when, in the *Westminster Review* of 1852, Lewes wrote his well-known article on the lady-novelists, discussing the achievements of such a mixed bag of English women writers as Jane Austen, Mrs Gore, Mrs Marsh, Mrs Trollope, Geraldine Jewsbury, Eliza Lynn, Currer Bell, and Mrs Gaskell, he felt himself at liberty to use the **Œuvres Complètes de George Sand,** not only as a *point de départ* for his observations, but as an example, throughout the article, of what a woman writer was capable of achieving. His two touchstones for feminine greatness were Jane Austen and George Sand and he was obviously writing now, as he had not eight years earlier, without fear of contradiction: 'For eloquence, and depth of feeling, no man approaches George Sand'.

In the twenty years since George Sand had first taken away the breath of reviewers, she had attained in England, not only critical respectability, but tacit recognition as a great writer and important influence. It is noteworthy that throughout Lewes's article, he refers constantly to minor women novelists who are indebted to her, not as a matter of supposition but of fact. . . . What two decades of reviewing have revealed is her gradual acknowledgement by English critics as an important and individual novelist in her own right. (pp. 501-16)

Patricia Thomson, "George Sand and English Reviewers: The First Twenty Years," in The Modern Language Review, *Vol. 67, No. 3, July, 1972, pp. 501-16.*

Annabelle Rea   (essay date 1979)

[*In the essay below, Rea discusses* Mauprat *and François le champi* as examples of Sand's transformation of fairy tales into vehicles for her ideas on social change.]

Until recent years only the life of George Sand was generally deemed worthy of scholarly attention. Neglect of her works drew its source partially from their romantic exaggerations, melodramatic effects and incredible coincidences as well as from the didactic tone of Sand's evangelical socialism. Some, perhaps following the lead of Marcel Proust, even thought of Sand as primarily a children's writer because of the simplicity of certain of her stories. However, the very simplicity of the tales, the familiarity of their motifs, increased the chance of their acceptability to her broad readership; we must not forget that Sand was an enormously successful writer in her time, second only to Victor Hugo in popularity. Her "mission of sentiment and love" led her to want to touch as many readers as possible, not to speak of her need to sell her works to support herself and an extended household.

A closer study of some of Sand's apparently simple stories allows us to note the presence of a number of elements from fairy tales, myths, legends or other archetypal patterns. We can find parallels with the tale of Beauty and the Beast as written in the eighteenth century by Madame de Beaumont or of Erich Neumann's "The Lady of the Beasts" who domesticates the male. We discover Sand's version of Pygmalion and Galatea as well as her interpretation of the mystical union of the androgyne, also treated by her contemporary, Balzac. It is this complex of references which I propose to analyze in two of Sand's works, through a study of her treatment of maternity and marriage, to show that under the surface simplicity lie some highly significant feminist ideas.

A brief look at Sand's life will provide us with necessary background material for this discussion of *Mauprat* and *François le Champi.* We know from *Histoire de ma vie* of the "délices" she experienced in listening to myths and fairy tales or in contemplating their illustrations "with interest and admiration" before learning to read, and of her learning to read through these tales. Nothing can compare, said Sand, with the "first joys of the imagination." We know that this delight continued via the stories she invented as a child and later through Berry folk tales and religious stories.

Her life also provided important raw materials in the matters of marriage and maternity. Her own unfortunate marriage to a man far from her intellectual and cultural equal was to make the issue of marriage one of Sand's most vital

crusades starting with her first novel, **Indiana.** Extremely rich in Sand's background, the question of maternity merits much further exploration. Sand gives a very broad definition to the term: it signifies for her many things, including nurturing, caring, and educating, and ranges from her childhood "true maternal affection" for some of her dolls, her "maternal passion" for small children, her caring in the convent dormitory for smaller, ill children, to her adulthood "strange illusion" while writing **Histoire de ma vie** that she was her young father's mother, and "maternal solicitude" for her dying grandmother. Germaine Bree has spoken and written of the "happy triangle" of Aurore and her two mothers, the one, "the unique object of my love," who shared her daughter's world as a child, and the other, the educator who strove to form her granddaughter's taste and judgment. Sand's biological maternity as well as her maternal concern for several young, weaker lovers contribute to this leitmotif of her life.

Adoption too played an important role in Sand's life. During her convent years, because of her "need to venerate someone," she asked Mother Alicia to serve as her adoptive mother. One might say, for instance, that she "adopted" Frédéric Chopin as her third child or that Augustine Brault was also for some time an adopted child. Adoption, very broadly defined (for example, Fadette and Landry and their children "adopt" all of the poor children of the neighborhood; Indiana and Ralph "adopt" poor, ailing slaves), is a most important theme in the Sand novels. It plays a much greater role than does any biological mother-child relationship except that between an adoring, widowed mother and her grown son. Helene Deutsch's term "rescue fantasy" is most appropriate to the Sand mission.

Deutsch, despite her rigid categorization of traditional passivity as "normal" in women, provides other fruitful concepts for our understanding of Sand in her chapter on adoption [in her *The Psychology of Women: A Psychoanalytic Interpretation,* 1945]. She sees adoption as a means for a woman, "the androgynous woman," to separate sexuality from the nurturing aspects of motherhood. It also avoids, according to her, the narcissistic or Oedipal associations with motherhood. Sand's treatment of adoption enters much more specifically and more frequently into her novels written after age forty. This may serve in some measure to explain the apparent contradiction between the 1834 comment: "but a love without the union of bodies is mystical and incomplete" and the much later, "If I had my life to begin again, I would be chaste."

The two works in which I have chosen to study the elements of fairy tale and myth, **Mauprat** and **François le Champi,** might be replaced by a number of others which will come to the minds of those who know Sand well; these patterns are widely represented in her works. However, **Mauprat** because the savage Bernard comes from a truly bestial milieu, and **François le Champi,** because the themes of maternity and marriage so neatly telescope into one, seem to me the most fruitful choices. Published ten years apart (**Mauprat,** 1837; **François le Champi,** 1847), both are typical of Sand's love stories. In the first, the heroine is alone in a world of men, except for the minor character, Mademoiselle Leblanc, her unattractive maid, while in the second, several other women characters serve as contrasts or comparisons with the heroine who has only one man and two male children around her. The first tells of nobles in a rural setting, and the second, of the lower classes of the country. Despite the many differences, the similar patterns emerge clearly.

The young Bernard de Mauprat is variously treated as a beast, specifically a wolf, guided by instinct or by chance; a barbarian, a brute, and a savage. He lives in a castle "shrouded in perpetual darkness" with his all-male family of outlaws whose debauchery, pillaging, torturing, and general feudal brutality evoke Blue Beard, the thief Cartouche, the Ogre, and Croquemitaine. Bernard, though not as totally corrupt as his grandfather and uncles and who resists the life he leads, is arrogant and often drunk. His only culture comes from a few tales of chivalry, for his mother had died after giving him only "good notions," just enough for him to resist full participation in the activities of La Roche-Mauprat. Women for him existed as two types: "insolent prostitutes" or "stupid victims." For the Mauprats they were objects of scorn and/or animal desire. Edmée appears and incarnates for Bernard the rescuing fairy of one of his legends of chivalry. He desires her because of her beauty. For him only the simple formula held: "She is beautiful, therefore I am in love."

Edmée de Mauprat, Bernard's second cousin, possesses not only great beauty, but extraordinary moral strength, energy, courage, pride and personal ambition. Devoted to her father, she is also tender and consoling to all who need her: the ill, the poor. Her exemplary charity, her reputation and her goodness are not widely known; she has no desire for a brilliant reputation in the outside world. Her closeness to nature is revealed by the flowers and birds that populate her room. Impetuous physical activity, particularly on horseback, is balanced by the passions of intellectual activity. Rousseau instills in the essentially self-educated woman her theory of absolute equality among human beings; Tasso is a favorite among poets; her letter writing style is virile in its precision. However, with her father's old age, she sacrifices her need for physical and intellectual activity to remain at his side, taking up needlework which she terms, with other "feminine occupations," "amusements of captivity." Although she possesses many "virile" qualities, Edmée has moments of weakness, "like the true woman" she is.

While Edmée feels immediate sensual attraction to her cousin, she protects her "honor" as the fiancée of another man, and defends her theories on the difference between desire and love through the knife she carries at all times in the early stages of Bernard's presence. A Freudian interpretation would identify the knife with the penis, giving Edmée equality with the male. Even after Bernard has attained a high level of education, has proven himself in war, the "volcano" of his passion erupts one final time. His bestial side endangers Edmée's honor once again and this time it is her riding whip that serves to tame him. Bernard is punished for this final breakdown by his trial for attempted murder. Edmée's reason has controlled her senses; only when Bernard has attained the same civilized stage will he marry Edmée. Through this parable Sand

clearly reveals what Germaine Brée has termed her "gloriously pre-Freudian" characteristics. However, Sand's fantasies do not all typify those Freudian attributes to women but cross Freud's sexual lines to reveal rather a "person's" fantasies.

Edmée's power over Bernard—she orders him, she defies him—in its early stages backed by the knife, is transferred to the education she arranges for him. Sand stresses her belief that people may be corrected through love, that even one's flaws may be directed toward good ends. The transformation process is termed "giving birth" to a new destiny and sculpting from stone ("tailler ce quartier de roc"); both expressions are highly pertinent to our analysis. The process is painful for Bernard, the brutally uncultured young man, who has entered an incomprehensible world of tenderness and affection between family members, of cordial relations between nobles and peasants, of love of nature, of prayer, of generosity, modesty and liberty. He understands the language of this new world but cannot speak it. During his time at the castle of Sainte Sévère, Bernard begins the essential task of knowing himself, and also learns quickly the matters presented to him. He hears from Edmée that women are not the crafty liars he once thought but rather the weak victims of oppressors whose use of violence and tyranny makes ruse women's only salvation. Edmée becomes for Bernard a Madonna, his "dame," as he moves off to six years of new trials in the American War of Independence and the law court of Bourges before finally attaining his goal of marriage with Edmée. She has molded a husband of whom she will not be ashamed, now worthy of herself; Bernard has raised himself to her level in intelligence and wisdom as well as in the qualities of the heart. As Edmée says: "Est-ce ta faute, malheureux enfant, si depuis sept ans, je te cache le secret de mon affection, si j'ai voulu attendre pour te le dire que tu fusses le premier des hommes par la sagesse et l'intelligence, comme tu en es le premier par le coeur?" ["Is it your fault, poor child, if I've hidden the secret of my affection from you for seven years? I wanted to wait to tell you until you became the first among men in wisdom and intelligence as you are the first by your heart."] Because Bernard serves as the narrator of the story and because modesty is now one of his qualities, we do not learn in detail of the qualities of the reformed beast.

Thus, marriage is a serious commitment which must be carefully considered so it will not become an "enchained future." Perfect equality in marriage, as on the larger scale of society, will ensure the end of slavery. During their long years of harmonious marriage, Bernard "abandons" his life to Edmée's guidance. Her logic and rectitude lead him to defend the Republic against its enemies and, again on her orders, to return home where she has remained, after the defeat of the Republic. Both extraordinary individuals, husband and wife, enjoy high respect in the region.

Bernard's rescuing of Edmée from La Roche-Mauprat, and, reciprocally, Edmée's rescuing Bernard from his bestiality makes the story an example of the Beauty and the Beast motif although the heroine has not accepted bestiality as Beauty does. Edmée has refused the erotic, the violent, in favor of the civilized man. Adoption also appears, although less importantly than marriage. In the most literal sense, the chevalier Hubert, Edmée's father, has requested, twice before the story began, permission to adopt the child Bernard and bring him up as his heir and the intended husband of his only child. He does "adopt" Bernard, but only after the escape of the young man from La Roche-Mauprat. More importantly, Edmée in a sense also adopts Bernard as her child. Her caress recalls to him his mother's final kiss. She carries out her correction of his bad qualities with tenderness; she serves as a mother to him in sending him away from her and receives him with maternal pride on his return. The rescue motif does link the transformation of the beast and the adoption of the "poor child." (Edmée uses this term for Bernard as late as the trial).

Sand uses the same link with the hero of *François le Champi.* The novel's title introduces a dirty, ragged and feverish foundling, stronger and larger than his age, who knows nothing, although he seems to understand what is said to him, who can express nothing and who thus appears to all a perfect simpleton. His eyes express his goodness; he knows to help others, but expresses no reaction to being helped himself, neither astonishment nor pleasure. As a foundling, a "child of sorrow" in the terms of Helene Deutsch, François is a beast in the eyes of the rigidly prejudiced society represented by the heroine's mother-in-law: " . . . je suis sûre qu'il est déjà voleur. Tous les champis le sont de naissance, et c'est une folie que de compter sur ces canailles-là." [I'm sure he's already a thief. All foundling children are from birth and it's madness to count on those scoundrels."]

Madeleine Blanchet's welcoming of the seemingly slow-witted François typifies her generosity, her charitable and democratic acceptance of all persons, and her selflessness. Sand's portraits of others in the novel intensify the heroine's goodness. Her miserly and brutal husband drinks heavily, gambles, and keeps a mistress. Although she has no love of this man to whom she "let herself be married at sixteen," she makes a patient effort to respect him. Other women characters also serve as contrast as do Beauty's Sisters in Mme. de Beaumont's tale: the jealous, greedy and revengeful mother-in-law; the husband's wickedly self-centered, pleasure-seeking mistress whose control over her lover almost ruins his family; the heroine's frivolous, spoiled and self-centered fifteen-year-old sister-in-law; and the foster mother of François, who, while not a bad woman, thinks first of her own survival. Of the women characters only Jeannette, the daughter of the man for whom François works, has certain similarities to Madeleine.

Like Edmée and many others of Sand's heroines, Madeleine Blanchet is physically weak but morally strong. She stands up to her husband, giving him orders and marching off "like a soldier to battle" when her conscience tells her she must. In order to do what she considers right, she is willing to cover up the truth of her actions, to "lie" and "steal" from her miserly husband to feed the needy. She works long, hard hours for others, sleeping and eating little, charitably active as are Edmée and other Sand heroines. She typifies the Sandian nurturer and caretaker as she

cares selflessly for the ill, even her husband and mother-in-law. Madeleine's education puts her into a superior category in her milieu; she reads, she writes, possessing the power with words that characterizes so many Sand heroines. Although outstanding compared with others of her world, Madeleine has done nothing to seek this reputation; she is modest. She is not her husband's rival but complements him, winning his respect despite his undisciplined ways. Because of her difference, however, she feels herself alone; only her duty to her son, Jeannie, counterbalances her dreams of suicide.

Madeleine transforms the foundling child from an outcast and simpleton into a strong, intelligent and articulate, caring man, to whom all the younger women in the book are attracted. As his master, Jean Vertaud, says of him: "Car ce qui me plaît de toi, c'est que tu as le coeur aussi bon que la tête et la main. . . . " ["For what pleases me about you is that you have as good a heart as your head and your hands."] Unlike the biological son who remains essentially a shadow throughout the book, the adopted son takes over as the central figure in the final pages. Madeleine's nourishment of François has been physical through the "stealing" of food from her household; it has been both intellectual and emotional through her instruction in reading and writing and through her maternal love which enabled François to learn about his feelings and to express them, at first only to her. Finally, her nurture has been moral; her self-sacrifice, her uncomplaining caring, her tenderness and consolation have served as models for the foundling child.

With considerable money, transmitted by a priest from his biological mother of whom he knows nothing, François is able to return to rescue the woman who once rescued him. As Madeleine did at the beginning of the book, François now works into the night, cares for her tenderly during her illness, lies, plots and spies according to his pure conscience in order to save her. So much has the strong young man taken on "feminine" characteristics that he is asked by Madeleine's sister-in-law why he does not wear women's clothes and he is teased that soon he will take up spinning and sewing.

Sand has set up a series of parallels to show the equality of François and Madeleine by the end of the book. François was cured of his early fever by Madeleine whom he cures of her illness at the end. Madeleine saves François from his situation as a foundling, even offering to "buy" him from La Zabelle who planned to return him to the orphanage. François buys back the property of Madeleine which had fallen into the hands of the evil mistress of her husband. The reciprocity of many actions underlines their exceptional qualities and their complementary nature. At the time of their decision to marry, the androgynous couple appear almost asexual, except for a slight pressure of François hands:

> mais comme tout en tremblant elle voulait aller du côté où étaient Jeannie et Jeannette, il la retint comme de force et la fit retourner avec lui. Et Madeleine, sentant comme sa volonté le rendait hardi de résister à la sienne, comprit mieux que par des paroles que ce n'était plus son enfant

le champi, mais son amoureux François qui se promenait à son côté.

[But since, trembling all the while, she wanted to go over near Jeannie and Jeannette, he held her back as if by force and made her stay with him. And Madeleine, sensing that his will made him bold enough to resist hers, understood better than through words that no longer was it her child the foundling, but her love François who was walking at her side.]

Before turning to the conclusions that may be drawn from the two novels, it is necessary to answer two questions about Sand's writing that may be raised concerning *Mauprat* and *François le champi.* Sand has published many love stories where love is the purified union of souls. As we know from Simone de Beauvoir's *Le Deuxième Sexe,* love has traditionally been woman's primary occupation. Are these novels, then, "feminine" novels? According to Simone de Beauvoir, the woman in love traditionally waits for her lover to come rescue her; in Sand it is the woman who rescues the man and actively transforms him according to her standards. De Beauvoir also speaks of the woman's activity in daydreaming. Could one not suggest that Sand's novels represent her personal quest for the ideal man and her creation of an imaginary substitute for the often disappointing reality? This transformation of personal fantasies into artistic creations is discussed by Freud in "Creative Writers and Day-Dreaming": "The motive forces of phantasies are unsatisfied wishes, and every single phantasy is the fulfillment of a wish, a correction of an unsatisfactory reality." Albert Thibaudet has resolved the question for us, enabling us to deny that Sand's works represent the "feminine novel," by defining "the true novel" as "an autobiography of the possible."

Other writers have suggested that Sand's life is of far greater importance than her works because of her connections to all the cultural, political and philosophical movements of the day, and because of her living essentially as did men at the time. Samuel Edwards states: [in his *George Sand: A Biography of the First Modern, Liberated Woman,* 1972] "Her life is significant a century after her death, far more because of her accomplishments as a woman than for her books and plays." Even Simone de Beauvoir in *Le Deuxième Sexe* talks about little more than Sand's life. Although Carolyn Heilbrun emphasizes British and American literature in *Toward a Recognition of Androgyny,* she does mention Sand, saying that she "evidences the passionate pull toward androgyny far more in her life than in her works, which rather record the disabilities of womankind." Our study of Edmée de Mauprat and Madeleine Blanchet has not shown us only the "disabilities" of women. Rather, we have seen superior women, as defined in *Mauprat* by Bernard's "brother at arms" in the American War of Independence: "Les hommes s'imaginent que la femme n'a point d'existence par elle-même et qu'elle doit toujours s'absorber en eux, et pourtant ils n'aiment fortement que la femme qui paraît s'élever, par son caractère, au dessus de la faiblesse et de l'inertie de son sexe." ["Men think that woman has no existence of her own and that she must always absorb herself in them, and yet they only love passionately the woman who seems, through the force of her character, to raise herself above the weakness and inertia of her sex."]

Edmée de Mauprat and Madeleine Blanchet, with their androgynous natures, are representative of Sand's heroines. These are physically active women, morally strong, intuitively intelligent, and often more educated than others of their milieu. Hiding their superiority, they concentrate their efforts on educating those around them, especially men, to elevate them to their level. Maternal always, they spend much of their time and energy not only educating but also nurturing the ill and the needy through quietly charitable acts. From time to time Sand speaks of her heroines as having "virile" characteristics, as in the case of Edmée's virile style of writing. Critics have noticed the androgynous nature of certain of Sand's heroines; for example, in his introduction to *La Mare au Diable* Pierre Reboul states: "Jeune Marie, si aimante, si maternelle, mais si virile, si forte—gracieux androgyne!" ["Young Marie, so loving, so maternal, but yet so virile, so strong—graceful representative of androgyny."]

Less often noticed, however, and perhaps of greater significance is the androgynous nature of Sand's men, as they have been created by her women. As James so wisely commented in *Notes on Novelists:* ". . . the moral of George Sand's tale, the beauty of what she does for us . . . is not the extension she gives to feminine nature, but the richness she adds to the masculine." The need for education to change women's situation has been much discussed and Sand did criticize the traditional education given to women, but her originality lies in her proposal that it is even more necessary to revise men's education. Bernard and François are men who practice tenderness and compassion, sensitivity and affection. Bernard retains some of the hardness of his past, is perfectly "virile" enough to battle in war and to father six children, but he abandons himself to his wife's judgment to guide his future. François cares tenderly for the ailing Madeleine while performing clever business manipulations. Both men are in adoration, painted in religious and chivalric terms, before their women, but these women in no measure represent the romantic muse passively posed upon a pedestal.

Neither heroine has rejected the traditional nineteenth-century role of wife and mother but both have themselves finally come to control the conditions of those traditional occupations through their creation of the ideal companion. As Barry states so well: "Over a century of time has brought a certain political equality, but it has yet to bring that equality in life, in marriage, in the family, in the one-to-one relationship of a man and a woman, which, essentially, is what George Sand's life and work are all about." These are women, not passively waiting for a man, not willing to accept man's bestiality, but actively educating, civilizing a future husband. The husband is not a narcissistic choice representing, as Freud believed, "what (women) would have liked to become" but that husband is made by them to become what they will him to be. In our title, maternity—and we continue to refer to maternity through adoption—precedes marriage. Sand's treatment of maternity serves almost as a synonym for education because it is the "rescue" through education that leads to marriage in these works of Sand. Always tailored to the individual, education as we have seen in *Mauprat,* bears the synonyms: "giving birth" and "sculpting." The romantic demiurge, here a woman "sculptor" in rivalry with the gods, creates from an adopted male a future husband. We clearly see the coming together of the complex of Beauty and the Beast, Pygmalion, and the myth of the androgyne. Adrienne Rich indicts the patriarchal system whereby the relationship of a woman and her child has been "manipulated and mutilated." She says, "For me, poetry was where I lived as no one's mother, where I existed as myself." By constructing their own ideal marital situations these heroines of Sand do not have the "disabilities" cited by Heilbrun as much as does Adrienne Rich. Sand's symbol of the patriarchal society attacked by Rich might be La Roche-Mauprat, the all-male society enshrouded in darkness, destroyed during the novel.

The civilizing motif, the taming of the beast in man, and the rescue motif of adoption become one in both novels but more obviously in *François le champi.* Edmée de Mauprat and Madeleine Blanchet have, like Beauty, wed a former Beast. However, they have not accepted and agreed to love man's bestiality, as Beauty did. Both have, like Pygmalion, created the ideal companion but, unlike Pygmalion, they have not created only exterior perfection nor have they received any supernatural aid. These women have, by dint of hard work, suffering, long years of patience, and good example, educated the perfect companion. A close look at Sand's novels shows that she has indeed taken elements from familiar tales but she has transformed these elements so that they serve to illustrate her original ideas.

In these seemingly simple love stories, using the familiar elements of fairy tale and myth, Sand, the eternal optimist, was calling for social change through her ideas on marriage as a union of equals, of a woman and a man who complement each other, both sharing traditionally masculine and feminine qualities; her thoughts on the freedom to love without regard to age or class; her criticism of the male's use of violence and tyranny; her protest for the dignity of women. As she wrote to Flaubert, the close friend of her old age, 1872: "If our advice is sound, if the mirror we hold up to society is accurate enough for man to recognize his reflection, and little by little persuade him to change his image, then we will not have written in vain. . . . " She was of her century in calling for social reform but very much of ours in demanding the kinds of change she called for: "I will lift up woman from her abjection in my person and in my writing." In her *Histoire de ma vie* she writes about her own memories in order to encourage her readers to call forth and know theirs. Perhaps this is her ultimate message: woman must first know herself and then rescue herself by developing her own androgynous qualities and demanding them of her male companions. (pp. 37-47)

Annabelle Rea, "Maternity and Marriage: Sand's Use of Fairy Tale and Myth," in Studies in the Literary Imagination, *Vol XII, No. 2, Fall, 1979, pp. 37-47.*

Nancy E. Rogers   (essay date 1979)

[*In the essay below, Rogers asserts that Sand repeatedly explored the theme of enslavement in her works, though she rarely wrote explicitly on the issue of slavery.*]

The institution of slavery was a central topic of conversation, political discussion, and literature in the first half of the nineteenth century in France. Evidence of its literary importance is provided by Léon-François Hoffmann's lucid and comprehensive study *Le Nègre romantique,* in which the image of the black, especially the slave, is shown to be a collective obsession for the Romantic writers. It was during this period (1815-1848) that the French African colonies were being developed and that the question of slavery in the islands of the Caribbean Sea and the Indian Ocean was being bitterly discussed by French abolitionists and their adversaries. Although the slave trade was officially abolished as early as the Hundred Days, trafficking continued until 1848 when Lamartine, as head of the Provisional Government, signed the decree emancipating the colonial slaves. The remarkable length of Hoffmann's bibliography makes it abundantly clear that the slave question was indeed a popular subject for Romantic writers, some as well known as Balzac, Hugo, and Mérimée, some as obscure as Auguste Bouet and Louis-François Raban.

It is especially interesting to see how many of these literary treatments of slavery were written by women, most of them liberal and humanitarian in stance. Yet, George Sand, possibly the strongest believer in liberation from tyranny among women of her time, receives no mention. The reason is simple: Sand never focused directly on the problem of slavery in her fiction and never made a slave a central personage in her work. It is highly illogical, however, that the woman whom Renan called "the Aeolian harp of our time," the novelist who reflected almost all of the important currents of Romantic thought in her work, would have neglected this vital issue. An examination of her writings between 1832 (the publication of *Indiana*) and 1848 decisively reveals that this was not the case. Instead of writing explicitly about slavery, Sand uses it as a metaphor to describe oppression of any degree or type, a subject which she vehemently discussed in her letters and autobiographical writings and which is reflected to a lesser degree in her fictional works.

Sand's first novel, *Indiana,* largely inspired by Bernardin de Saint-Pierre's *Paul et Virginie,* is perhaps the most overt of her works of fiction in reference to slavery. The heroine is a Creole of Spanish origin, raised on the ile Bourbon and subject to many of the emotional and social disabilities commonly associated with Creoles; for example, she has "toutes les superstitions d'une créole nerveuse et maladive" and is "ignorante comme une vraie créole." In addition, she has a creole "sœur de lait," Noun, who still wears the white apron and madras "à la manière de son pays" and is "pleine de sang créole ardent et passionné," reflecting the literary convention which depicted Creoles as possessing almost unbridled sexuality, a trait which was applied to fictional black slaves as well.

Although slavery as an institution is not a central theme in this novel of love and ill-matched marriages, it is still strongly in evidence, especially in the presentation of Indiana's background and its effect on her attitude towards society and oppression. Her hatred of tyranny and desire for independence were awakened by her reaction to slavery:

> Elevée au désert, négligée de son père, vivant au milieu des esclaves, pour qui elle n'avait d'autre secours, d'autre consolation que sa compassion et ses larmes, elle s'était habituée à dire: "Un jour viendra où tout sera changé dans ma vie . . . "

Her belief in equality for all human beings is described in the following passage in which hatred of slavery and civilization are equally expressed:

> Dieu ne veut pas qu'on opprime et qu'on écrase les créatures de ses mains. S'il daignait descendre jusqu'à intervenir dans nos chétifs intérêts, il briserait le fort et relèverait le faible; il passerait sa grande main sur nos têtes inégales et les nivellerait comme les eaux de la mer; il dirait à l'esclave: "Jette ta chaine, et fuis sur les monts où j'ai mis pour toi des eaux, des fleurs et du soleil."

Perhaps the most explicit statement of the heroine's (and the hero's) anti-slavery sentiments is the couple's humanitarian activity when they return to their beloved ile Bourbon; Ralph states:

> La majeure portion de nos revenus est consacrée à racheter de pauvres noirs infirmes. C'est la principale cause du mal que les colons disent de nous. Que ne sommes-nous assez riches pour délivrer tous ceux qui vivent dans l'esclavage! Nos serviteurs sont nos amis; ils partagent nos joies, nous soignons leurs maux.

This idealistic anti-colonialism indicates the firmness of Sand's egalitarian belief, even though expressed in somewhat unrealistic terms.

Slavery in **Indiana** is hardly limited to the political institution of buying and selling human beings for work in the colonies. Instead, it is used as a metaphor for any kind of subjection of one person to another. The metaphorical use of the noun is hardly original with Sand. Indeed, the 1814 and 1822 editions of the *Dictionnaire de l'Académie* list several figurative uses of *l'esclave*. It is interesting to note, however, that the emphasis here is on slavery as an active process in which one chooses subjection. The first figurative definition is: "Ceux qui par flatterie, par intérêt, *se rendent* [my italics] dépendans de quelqu'un . . . " Another definition is: "On dit aussi d'un homme qui est tellement *attaché* [again, my italics] au service de quelqu'un ou à quelque emploi, qu'il ne peut pas s'éloigner . . . " It is not until the publication of the Littré dictionary in 1863 that *l'esclave* is figuratively described as "dominé par, assujetti à . . . la peur, l'amour, etc." Littré cites many examples from Fénelon, Voltaire, and Racine in which slavery is related to such concepts as the passions, duty, and domestic life. Whether slavery is an active or a passive condition, it is clear from these dictionaries that the term had widespread usage in the sense of subjugation and dependence during the nineteenth century.

In Sand's work the image of slavery is most arresting when applied to the concepts of love and marriage, the two most constant themes in her fiction. Love is conceived of as a romantic master/slave relationship in which the lover is always inferior to his or her beloved, thus illustrating the conception of slavery as a process by which one renders oneself a slave, as described in the *Dictionnaire de l'Académie*. This idea of love as mastery is extended naturally in Sand's *Weltanschauung* to the institution of marriage, in which women, under the Napoleonic Code, had no legal or financial rights and were completely subjected to their husbands. Indiana is often described as "la pauvre captive" and "cette femme esclave," a woman who suffers from the tyranny of both her father and her husband; here, Sand is using the word as Littré defined it in the above citation. Tyranny, however, frequently engenders revolt, and Indiana joins the other rebellious runaway slaves so often depicted in the literature of the time. The young wife escapes for a brief moment but returns to the patriarchal household; later, when her husband discovers her diary and letters, he drags her by her hair and kicks her on the forehead, leaving "cette marque sanglante de sa brutalité à un être faible. . . . " Thus, Indiana is branded as blatantly as any runaway slave recaptured by his master, and her condition is scarcely freer than that of the slaves she lived among and pitied as a child.

Sand continually uses the image of the woman/slave in her correspondence, autobiography, and later novels. Valentine, Lélia, and Consuelo all protest against the humiliating state of women in a patriarchal system, as does Sand in reference to her own situation. It is in her letters, however, where Sand often discusses the condition of women in general, that the most vehement protest against the "tyrannie avilissante" of marriage is registered. The image becomes a means for Sand to apply her most sensitive reasoning to an analysis of the state of womanhood. She sees women as so oppressed that they are incapable of being equal to men on a political or even an intellectual level; time is needed to correct this injustice: "Ayant été plus dégradées, il est impossible qu'elles n'aient pas pris les mœurs des esclaves, et il faudra encore plus de temps pour les en relever. . . . " Until society redresses the wrongs of marriage, women will live in their humiliating state:

> Jusque-là, la femme aura toujours les vices de l'opprimé, c'est-à-dire les ruses de l'esclave . . . Oui, la femme est esclave en principe et c'est parce qu'elle commence à ne plus l'être en fait, c'est parce qu'il n'y a plus guère de milieu pour elle entre un esclavage qui l'exaspère, et une tyrannie qui avilit son époux, que le moment est venu de reconnaître en principe, ses droits à l'égalité civile . . . L'esclave homme peut se révolter contre son maître et reprendre franchement et ouvertement sa liberté et sa dignité. L'esclave femme ne peut que tromper son maître et reprendre sournoisement et traîteusement une liberté et une dignité fausses et détournées de leur véritable but (***Correspondance***, VIII)

Taken as a whole, Sand's opinions on the oppression of women in marriage can be compared to the condition of the black slave as described by Hoffmann, who summarizes the reasons for their continued subjection as follows: (1) lack of education; (2) lack of political power; (3) lack of power before the law; (4) denial of the right to raise their own children; and (5) dependence upon the master as the source of punishment, recompense, food, clothing, etc. Sand sees women as subject to the same deficiencies; like the slaves, women have only three possible methods of confronting their servitude: suicide, collaboration, or revolt. Her novels, letters, and autobiographical writings depict women attempting all three possibilities, always with the same result: failure.

Sand finds slavery a useful metaphor in her works for other conditions besides love and marriage. For example, lack of education is a kind of enslavement from which it is difficult to escape. In a letter to her son Maurice she stresses the importance of education:

> Tu vois quel est l'avantage et la nécessité de l'éducation, puisque sans elle, on vit dans une espèce d'esclavage, puisque tous les jours un paysan sage, vertueux, sobre, digne de respect, est dans la dépendance d'un homme méchant, ivrogne, brutal, injuste, mais qui a sur lui l'avantage de savoir lire et écrire. (*Correspondance,* III)

And in *Lettres à Marcie* she bemoans the inferior education given to women by men; such an education makes a woman a slave and extinguishes her intelligence. Another type of slavery is that of the prisoner, a state especially described in *Lélia,* where Trenmor, the rehabilitated ex-convict, describes his past imprisonment: "Esclave, je goûtai de vives joies dans le sentiment de l'espoir et dans les rêves de l'avenir. Libre, il m'a fallu chercher ces joies promises dans le souvenir de l'esclavage, dans les rêves du passe." Wealth, also, can be a means of enslavement. Valentine, for example, is afraid of being a slave of the opulent life, and Sand warns her son Maurice against becoming enslaved by his grandmother's fortune: "Mieux vaut être un pauvre artiste dans une petite mansarde avec ton vieux George que d'être l'esclave de riches insolents" (*Correspondance,* III).

Sand's republicanism was a conviction inculcated at an early age; she relates in her autobiography how Deschartres's teachings on the advantages of property turned her to communism at the age of twelve. And in a letter of 1835 she writes that "l'amour de l'Egalité a été la seule chose qui n'ait pas varié en moi depuis que j'existe. Je n'ai pas pu accepter de maître même en amour . . . " (*Correspondance,* III). It is not surprising then to find that she extends the metaphor of slavery to include the poverty and oppression of the proletariat, "le peuple," about whom she writes so movingly in her socialist novels. One of the most strident statements of her republican beliefs is contained in a letter to Luc Desage in 1847. This long epistle describes humanity as divided into two groups: "D'un côté *patriciat, aristocratie, tyrannie: synonimes* [sic]—*de l'autre esclavage, servitude, prolétariat: synonimes* [sic]" (Sand's italics). Further developing the slave/proletariat analogy (but finding "le peuple" in worse condition), she continues:

> En Asie, en Russie, etc. il y a des esclaves blancs. En Amérique des esclaves noirs. En France et dans les contrées environnantes, il y a un peuple

libre, mais si pauvre, si pressuré, si trompé, si dépouillé qu'il est, au dire des étrangers, beaucoup plus malheureux que les esclaves. Ceux-là reçoivent des coups, mais on les nourrit. Notre peuple n'est pas battu. Mais il meurt de misère . . . (*Correspondance,* IV)

And in a letter to Maurice in 1848 she compares the worker to the slave:

> Les autres [than Ledru-Rollin, Blanc, etc.] nous ramènent à toutes les institutions de la monarchie, au règne des banquiers, à la misère extrême et à l'abandon du pauvre, au luxe effréné des riches, enfin à ce système qui fait dépendre l'ouvrier, comme un esclave, du travail que le maître lui mesure, lui chicane et lui retire à son gré. (*Correspondance,* VIII)

Freedom for the oppressed, the people, will involve a release from slavery and a choosing of new masters, as Sand affirms in a letter to the Italian radical Mazzini: "Il [le prolétariat] a les instincts de l'esclave révolté, mais il n'a pas les facultés de l'homme libre. Il veut se débarrasser de ses maîtres, mais c'est pour en avoir de nouveaux, fussent-ils pires, il s'en arrangera quelque temps, pourvu que ce soit lui qui les ait choisis" (*Correspondance,* XI). The master/slave confrontation is also used metaphorically to express Sand's hatred of society's hierarchy. For example, she writes to Marie d'Agoult: ". . . je ne permettrai à nul autre de me dire que les derniers ne sont pas les premiers, et que l'opprimé ne vaut pas mieux que l'oppresseur, le dépouillé mieux que le spoliateur, l'esclave que le tyran" (*Correspondance,* III). In 1844 we find her proclaiming that she has "rien de bourgeois dans le sang . . . Je serai avec l'esclave et avec la bohémienne, et non avec les rois et leurs suppôts" (*Correspondance,* VI).

Sand also envisions the slavery of entire groups of people, for example the Slavs, as depicted in *Consuelo,* where she refers to them as "le peuple opprimé et effacé." In that fascinating novel of music and occultism, the people of Bohemia are enslaved by political and religious institutions: ". . . la Bohême est retombée, après bien des luttes, sous le joug de l'esclavage . . . Nos maîtres savaient bien que la liberté religieuse de notre pays, c'était sa liberté politique. Voilà pourquoi ils ont étouffé l'une et l'autre." Even language can be an enslaving instrument; in Bohemia the native language has been lost to the overpowering influence of German spoken by the Austro-Hungarian rulers. As Consuelo says: ". . . je sais à peine l'allemand, cette dure langue que tu hais comme l'esclavage. . . . "

That Sand was interested in and appalled by the institution of "la traite" itself is well evidenced by her correspondence concerning two works on the subject. Fifteen years before the publication of *Uncle Tom's Cabin,* Gustave de Beaumont published *Marie ou l'esclavage aux Etats-Unis* on the subject of racial persecution. In this work Beaumont denounces segregation, as he describes a family the members of which die victims of racism. Sand's letter to Beaumont in 1836 does not directly address itself to the subject of slavery but instead speaks of the problems of a democracy which allows for such prejudices. Sand states:

> Une peinture bien vive, une flétrissure bien

chaude de cette fausse et hypocrite Démocratie, de ces odieux préjugés, sont le plus éloquent plaidoyer en faveur de la raison et de la justice. On ne peut pas lire ce plaidoyer sans concevoir l'espérance que de généreux efforts seront victorieux et hâteront sur la terre le règne de la Vérité. (*Correspondance,* III)

The other novel on the subject of slavery to which Sand warmly responded was the famous *Uncle Tom's Cabin.* In December of 1852 she writes of her enthusiastic reading of this work and expresses the modest desire to write an article praising it: "Il me semble que je serais compétente pour parler de cette brave femme qui m'ennuie et qui me fait pleurer en même temps, avec sa Bible, ses nègres et ses moutards" (*Correspondance,* XI). The resulting article appeared in *La Presse* on 20 December 1852, and later served as a *notice* to the La Bédollière translation, which was published in 1853. Nowhere in this *éloge* of Mrs. Stowe and her art is there any of the inflammatory rhetoric one is accustomed to hear from Sand when writing of the injustices of the world. In fact, the horrors of slavery are totally ignored whereas the tender scenes, inspiring characters, and saintly aspects of the novel (the author is called a saint as well) are commented upon. The only overt reference to the state of slaves in America is the following phrase in which she describes the compassion of Mrs. Stowe: "Grand, généreux et vaste est le cœur qui embrasse de sa pitié, de son amour, de son respect toute une race couchée dans le sang et la fange, sous le fouet des bourreaux, sous la malédiction des impies." This is the closest that Sand's *notice* comes to a political tract. What is especially striking here is that in an article on a novel about slavery, Sand reverts to her old habits of using slavery as a metaphor for other conditions, in this case misery and ignorance:

> Il n'est déjà plus permis aux personnes qui savent lire de ne l'avoir pas lu [le roman], et on regrette qu'il y ait tant de gens condamnés à ne le lire jamais: ilotes par la misère, esclaves par l'ignorance, pour lesquels les lois politiques ont été impuissantes jusqu'à ce jour à résoudre le double problème du pain de l'âme et du pain du corps.

In her preface Stowe herself speaks of the evils of slavery, the unjust and cruel system which destroys the humanity of slaves, and the lack of compassion among the "Christians" who have imposed slavery on the world. And the translator, La Bédollière, sees the novel as containing "tous les éléments d'une révolution" against "le crime de l'esclavage"; his preface contains a chart, based on the census of 1830, which shows the proportion of free men and slaves in the southern United States, in order to demand the emancipation of those slaves. By contrast, Sand's gentle praise and mild rhetoric are almost startling.

It is obvious from her writings that George Sand was vitally concerned with equality among all men. That slavery itself was an important issue to her is also undeniable, as is her belief in the emancipation of slaves. The latter conclusion is reached, however, only by deduction, since explicit references to the institution itself are few. The fact that Sand never overtly attacked the evils of slavery is per-

haps less surprising when we consider the plurality of issues to which she earnestly addressed herself. Sand consistently chose to become involved in struggles against injustices which touched her own life: such causes as legal equality for women, divorce, freedom from oppression for the worker and the peasant, and republicanism were zealously espoused by the novelist. Yet it is clear that the question of slavery was never far from her mind; its dominance and constant use as an image to express Sand's stand on other social problems indicate its importance, conscious or subconscious. Slavery represents the lack of any kind of freedom for Sand, as perhaps most universally seen in this citation from *Histoire de ma vie;* the subject there is marriage, but the vehicle for expressing Sand's vehement belief in liberty is—once again—slavery: "Et puis l'esclavage est quelque chose d'antihumain que l'on n'accepte qu'à la condition de rêver toujours la liberté." (pp. 29-35)

Nancy E. Rogers, "Slavery as a Metaphor in the Writings of George Sand," in The French Review, *Vol. 53, No. 1, October, 1979, pp. 29-35.*

Victor Hugo on Sand's role as a woman writer:

In this age devoted to completing the French Revolution and to beginning the Human Revolution, equality between the sexes being part of equality between men, a great woman was needed. Woman had to prove that she could have all our manly qualities without losing her angelic ones: that she could be strong without ceasing to be gentle: George Sand is that proof. . . . she bequeaths to us the right of woman which draws its proof from woman's genius. . . . Thus the Revolution is fulfilled.

Victor Hugo, as quoted in Renee Winegarten's The Double Life of George Sand, Woman and Writer, *1978.*

Diane Johnson (essay date 1979)

[*Johnson is an American educator, novelist, biographer, and critic. In the excerpt below, she discusses Sand's life and artistic development as depicted in several works, including Sand's autobiography and her correspondence with Gustave Flaubert.*]

A year ago in [*The New York Review of Books* (August 17, 1978)] V. S. Pritchett, reviewing new editions of four of George Sand's novels, observed that the revival of interest in her work is owing at least in part to "opportunism of the women's liberation kind." This "disconcerting sybil," in his wonderful phrase, is, no question about it, a rich topic for hungry feminist scholars and alert publishers. Sand herself remarked of her complete works, "They are endless," and of her rather good novel *Consuelo* . . . and its sequel she could say, only half joking, "Are they mine? I don't recall a single word of them."

If anything the Sand revival has gathered momentum in the past year, still owing to opportunism of the women's liberation kind, but also to the coincidence of these concerns with growing general interest in romantic literature, and, in addition, to the availability in recent years of reliable texts in French of her letters and other autobiographical writings—the monumental edition of *Oeuvres autobiographiques,* prepared by the great French textual scholar Georges Lubin, and the Lubin edition of her correspondence.

It is likely that the autobiography and letters will do more than her novels to enhance her stature in the modern view. Her work is surprisingly readable, full of plots, retaining for all its melodrama a reassuring core of eighteenth-century worldliness: "All this is fine, my dear," says the worldly husband in *Valentine* to his much younger wife when she confides that she is attracted to someone else,

> but it is supremely ridiculous. You are very young. Please accept some friendly advice: a woman should never use her husband as her confessor; it demands more virtue of him than his situation allows. . . . It seems to me that I have done enough for you by closing my eyes. You force me to open them, and thus I have to go away, because the situation between us would no longer be bearable and we could no longer look at each other without laughing.

Her pastoral novels have always been admired; her more sensational novels, like *Consuelo* or *Mauprat,* are better than just entertaining. But her life, with its prodigies of accomplishment and perhaps the most distinguished array of lovers ever assembled, was, like the lives of other great romantic writers of her generation, more interesting yet. And she is at her most interesting when she writes about herself, although her tone is modest, equable, honest, and informed—quite unlike the self-dramatizing reputation she has acquired—and although she leaves out all the scandalous bits.

Two of the following works are of autobiography: *My Life* is a condensed translation of her twenty-volume *Histoire de ma vie,* prepared by Dan Hofstadter, and Joseph Barry's compendium *George Sand in Her Own Words* is a selection from the autobiography, from her travel writings, journals and letters, and from several of the novels. The idea is to present her character, emotions, and opinions, together with a sample of her literary style, and although such hodgepodges are rarely successful, this one largely succeeds; one could even wish both these works were fuller. Next comes an edition of Sand's letters to and from Flaubert, and finally yet another biography of this much-scrutinized woman, of whom at least nine biographies, either new ones or reprints, have been issued in English in the last three years alone.

The lives of artists, like those of religious figures, retain at any period a singular power of example. Why? Perhaps because life itself, for the writer, is a sort of busman's holiday. As with the saint, it is his professional duty to examine matters of behavior and the heart, and we await his expert conclusions. How closely the world watched writers as different as Byron, Charlotte Bronte, Thomas Carlyle, George Sand. Today the writer who would lead an exemplary life is obliged to asceticism. Flesh, for one thing, is

no longer equal to the efforts required to shock us today the way Byron or Sand shocked their contemporaries. Sand was fortunate in her times and, unlike Byron, in her constitution.

Sand herself did not believe that people should watch or be affected by the lives of artists, only by their works: the artist "does neither good nor ill when turning to the right or to the left. His end justifies all." Yet it is the testimony of this excellent woman's life, much more than of her (highly virtuous) works, that we are apt to value.

What Flaubert, like many other artists, thought of Experience is implied by his industry. He stuck to his desk. A "sense of the grotesque has restrained me from an inclination to a disorderly life. I maintain that cynicism borders on chastity," he wrote to Sand, who was always too sincere to be chaste. She in her long life had taken wide risks ("everyone is free to embark either on a great ship in full sail, or on a fisherman's vessel"). But she also put in a lot of time at her desk—she went farther both in life and art than she needed to, and is seen to have collected a reward. Life provides too few of these inspiring examples of people collecting their rewards—mountain climbers, Eagle Scouts, valedictorians—of effort and courage paying off, for us to take them lightly. George Sand's reward was being George Sand, a soul in health. The conclusion of her latest biographer, that she was "in some ways a tragic figure," raises some questions about us, about these days, and about the real meaning of that glib description.

George Sand wrote her autobiography in 1854-1855 when she was fifty, with twenty-two years more of productive life ahead, her most famous novels and most notorious liaisons behind her, and at a time of relative calm after decades of domestic tumult. Adultery and tumult are matters, in general, that she does not discuss, doubtless to the disappointment of her contemporaries, who were accustomed to "confessions" in the style of Rousseau and who were familiar, through gossip and scandal, with the outlines of her affairs.

Instead she writes about the development of her character, her literary interests and her intellectual concerns, with particular emphasis on the origins of these in her early childhood and family relationships. Her purpose in writing, apart from money, was closer to that of Mill or Carlyle, or authors of other nineteenth-century autobiographies, whose formal continuity is provided not by events but by a spiritual or mental theme, in the service of which "facts" can be bent a little. Here, nearly a third of the original work was taken up with family history, including the correspondence of her father with his mother, causing a contemporary to observe that she should have called it "The History of My Life Before I Was Born." It is interesting to note that Sand doctored this correspondence, with the abandon of a novelist, to make it more interesting and affectionate than it really was. All in all, her awareness of the influence of early life (and allowing for the fact that these are selections) produces a work quite modern in effect, and so little emphasis on accomplishments is disarming.

Autobiographies have always been a rich source of error

for biographers, no doubt because although an author has, as Dr. Johnson observed, the "first qualification of an historian, the knowledge of the truth . . . it may plausibly be objected that his temptations to disguise it are equal to his opportunities of knowing it." Modern readers are more familiar than Dr. Johnson with the idea that the autobiographer may also be unwilling or unable to perceive certain truths or patterns in his own life, something biographers are often insufficiently aware of; and sometimes the meaning of autobiographical memories emerges from patterns common to the genre itself. Sand's infant memory of "a blurred train of hours spent sleepless on my little bed and filled with gazing on some curtain fold or flowers in the wallpaper" might suggest to a biographer of Ruskin, for instance, the possibility that the hard view posterity has taken of his ordinarily indulgent parents, which originates in part from his mentioning that they gave him no toys but a bunch of keys and no pastimes but to trace the design in the carpet, has prevailed because the elderly autobiographer was remembering a time in his infancy, before he could walk or talk.

The translator of Sand's autobiography, Dan Hofstadter, remarks in his preface that what she writes is "experience transformed by self-advocacy into melodrama," an opinion belied by the work itself, but nonetheless the view which has prevailed, mostly because, as Curtis Cate deplored in his 1975 biography, she has too long been depicted as "a voracious nymphomaniac, moving insatiably from the exhausted body of one genius to the next in vain search of inexhaustible virility." No doubt but that she was supremely energetic, and remarkable for fitting in so much real life between the hours spent in composition of her tremendous *oeuvre* (tremendous, though in the same scale as her contemporaries Dumas, Balzac, Scott, Sue).

The impression conveyed by her autobiography, however, is one of wisdom, modesty, and calm, perhaps slightly tinged in places with satisfaction:

> I had a sound constitution, and as a child seemed likely to become beautiful, a promise I did not keep. This was perhaps my fault, since at the age when beauty blossoms I was already spending my nights reading and writing.
>
> On the whole, with decent hair, eyes, teeth, and no deformities, I was neither ugly nor beautiful in my youth—a serious advantage, I think, since ugliness prejudices people one way and beauty another. . . . It is best to have a face which neither dazzles nor frightens, and with mine I get on well with friends of both sexes.

Renee Winegarten observes in her biography of Sand [*The Double Life of George Sand, Woman and Writer*] that it was Sand's particular vanity to see herself as "a frank, sober, straightforward person of simple tastes, one who easily forgave injuries and who was really the victim of other people's passions"; and perhaps every autobiographer does indulge some vanity or other. Rousseau was vain of his wickedness and Mill of his reason. But on the whole it is easy to take Sand at her own valuation. She is not a writer with a variety of fictional poses at her command—her heroes and heroines all sound remarkably

alike. And the first person is a difficult voice for dissimulation, let alone for twenty volumes.

Joseph Barry's collection [*George Sand in Her Own Words*] seeks to present Sand's character as it emerges not only from the autobiography but in selections from journals, letters, articles, and in novels, especially the novels which were most widely viewed as autobiographical, particularly *Indiana,* her first novel, a tale of an unhappily married young wife like Sand herself at the time. There are also bits of the controversial *Lélia,* which scandalized and titillated its audience with its hints of lesbian love and complaints about rude sexual behavior in men ("When he had dozed off, satisfied and sated, I would lie motionless and dismayed at his side. Thus I passed many hours watching him sleep"). (pp. 9-10)

The late Ellen Moers, in an excellent introduction to these selections, remarks on the process of "denigration familiar to experts in women's history," by which "the name of George Sand came to mean to most people not an author at all but a target for labels: transvestite, man-eater, lesbian, nymphomaniac." She points out that in Sand's own day she was seen as a great, though controversial, woman, and a great writer. A fresh view of her work may restore her to the reputation of her own time; literary reputations always sink and rise this way. But it seems that the sinking of Sand's was also strongly owing to her sexual behavior, born of the anxiety society apparently feels at women who embellish, in any fashion, traditional female roles. Literary history, for its part, tends to be uncomfortable with books by women which attempt to describe, however mildly and literally, the actual conditions of female life: even the most judicious descriptions are usually taken for dangerous symptoms of rabid feminism. Poor Sand is also in our day attacked as being no feminist, because she disapproved of the vote for women, and of free love, and she enjoyed making jam and doll clothes for her grandchildren.

Certainly she was in advance of her day in advocating divorce and sexual and legal equality for women, and in wanting decent educations for them. The specifics of her views today seem unimportant, but the criteria by which she has been judged in biographies over the years, even by her most sympathetic biographers, remain interesting. Some recent critical comment will serve to illustrate the general tone of disapproval, sometimes strong, sometimes only faint, as here, in *The New York Times* review, by Patricia Meyer Spacks, of Barry's book: "The compilation provides relatively little evidence of Sand's art, but a vivid impression of personality: a woman intense in political and personal passion, opinionated, self-absorbed, ever projecting herself on the external world,"—the kind of personality, in short, that is often congratulated in men and practically required in writers. On the other hand, André Maurois and Curtis Cate, in their biographies, both admire her capacity for "feminine" self-sacrifice.

Sand was aware that her society believed, as society may still really believe, that female character is most becomingly produced in reaction to an array of customary choices (marriage, maternity) rather than by projection. In fact the singular and most admirable thing about Sand was that she seems to have considered herself a free and responsible moral agent, accountable, and capable of theorizing, like a man. If she did slightly despise other women it was because they did not act freely in the world but only in response to it.

Society encourages artificial sexual differences; in fact "there is only one sex." This feeling allows her to be unself-conscious in her enjoyment of "female pursuits," and yet an artist, and the confidante and intellectual adviser of many men, including Gustave Flaubert, seventeen years her junior. They were drawn into close friendship by the patterns of their respective lives—Sand, always generous to genius, was also an old hand at younger men. Flaubert, who had so few human contacts, and had lost his beloved mother during the course of his friendship with Sand, found in her much maternal consolation and support. Their affection seems to have transcended their differences, in age, in political persuasion, in temperament, and in ideas of art, where each embodies the perspectives of his different generation. Sand remained a romantic idealist, and Flaubert was afflicted with the "modern ennui."

Their wonderful letters [collected in *The George Sand—Gustave Flaubert Letters*, translated by A. L. McKenzie] range from art and politics to cold remedies, family gossip, and advice. Sand thinks Flaubert should get married, and that he needs more exercise. There are some famous exchanges on democracy and on literary realism, two topics where they diverged utterly. After the Franco-Prussian war, both were in political despair, but disagreed about the future, and their disagreement is the model of nineteenth-century ambivalence about democracy, which wasn't working out very well. To Flaubert, the Revolution had been "an abortion, a failure," proceeding from the Middle Ages and from Christianity—deplorable epoch, deplorable creed. "The crowd, the common herd will always be hateful." "The idea of equality . . . is opposed to that of justice. . . . People are now not even indignant against murderers." His rather Saint-Simonian remedies are criticism, science, and an end to metaphysics. He also would do away with universal suffrage and compulsory education.

Sand's reply, which grew immensely long and was published in *Le Temps,* implores people not to abandon good will, love of, faith in humanity. Her views are those of the generation of Shelley; Flaubert's like those of many intellectuals of his age, in England as well as in France, and on art as well as on liberty. He deplores romantic sentimentality, and holds it responsible for political ills. She deplores the absence of ideology in his work: "You especially, lack a definite and extended view of life. Art is not merely painting. . . . Art is not merely criticism and satire. . . . I think that your school is not concerned with the substance, and that it dwells too much on the surface. By virtue of seeking the form, it makes the substance too cheap."

Flaubert protests that he is "constantly doing all that I can to enlarge my brain, and I work in the sincerity of my heart. . . . I do not enjoy making 'desolation,' believe me, but I cannot change my eyes! As for my 'lack of conviction,' alas! I choke with convictions. But according to the ideal of art that I have, I think that the artist should not manifest anything of his own feelings, and that the artist should not appear any more in his work than God in nature."

"That desire to depict things as they are, the adventures of life as they present themselves to the eye, is not well thought out, in my opinion," Sand replies. "Depict inert things as a realist, as a poet, it's all the same to me, but, when one touches on the emotions of the human heart, it is another thing." It is the debate in current fiction even now.

They did not resolve their differences, of course, nor did they resent them. When Sand died, six months after this exchange, Flaubert wrote to her son Maurice that it had seemed to him, at the funeral, that he was burying his mother a second time. "Poor, dear, great woman! What genius and what heart! But she lacked nothing, it is not she whom we should pity." (pp. 10-11)

Men liked George Sand better than women did; similarly, she may have been more fortunate in her male than in her female biographers. Renee Winegarten, although able to interpret some of Sand's sexual activities and ambivalence toward female duties with a woman's understanding, has nonetheless something of the tone of a plain woman who doesn't like to think of others being fooled by the ruses of a pretty one: "When she created women who were lonely, a prey to nerves, hysteria and mysterious illnesses; who saw themselves as their husbands saw them (that is, as irresponsible children or virtual idiots) . . . she had not far to look. She had only to examine her own heart, for she herself was one of them." "(If she knew about feminine ruse, it was because she shared it while despising it.)"

Winegarten's is a kind of wound-and-bow view in which Sand tries to compensate for the early loss of her father, and childhood feelings of being unloved, by strenuous efforts to win love and admiration as an adult. Naturally. It seems rather odd for the author of a biography with, ostensibly, a special interest in Sand as someone who seriously contended "on behalf of all women, with the central experiences and issues of womanhood: with daughterhood, with motherhood, and finally, with the desperate need for selfhood," to conclude that for all her success Sand "ultimately remains, through some deep inner flaw, a tragic figure." And she incurs this patronizing judgment, moreover, in part because "she never found an equal partner in life (as distinct from a friend) to accept her on equal terms."

No doubt a view can be defended that all human beings are tragic. By Winegarten's definition, certainly, more are tragic than not (tragic George Washington, tragic Mrs. Gaskell). And are those tragic who enjoy being the superior of their partner in life, as Victorian husbands were admonished to be?

And by what qualities, indeed, do we define a life as successful or tragic? One criterion might be the owner's contentment with it. George Sand did not feel herself to be a tragic figure. Instead is she not better thought of as the very pattern of a successful and lucky human being—generous, kindly, rich in possessions, experience, friendship, independent, accomplished, a woman who lived to be famous and old and whose children survived her, and whose personal qualities of wisdom, humor, toleration, and compassion were acknowledged by all. It's as if we have got so used to looking at lives for their secret disappointments and neuroses, to debunk or to empathize, that we have got out of the habit of remembering that some lives can be really marvelous and inspiring. (pp. 11-12)

Diane Johnson, "She Had It All," in The New York Review of Books, *Vol. XXVI, No. 15, October 11, 1979, pp. 9-12.*

Paul G. Blount   (essay date 1979)

[*In the excerpt below, Blount presents the reactions of several major Victorian writers to Sand's novels, maintaining that their lavish praise stemmed from their preference for romantic rather than realistic fiction.*]

Her prose stirs you like music.

John Stuart Mill

We would say with Theocritus, that her music is more lulling than the sound of water flowing from a rock.

G. H. Lewes

Although Sand's fame among the Victorians rested on many bases, the firmest one of all was their appreciation of her literary talent. Victorians admired her as a stylist; they had a high regard for her characterizations and reveled in her nature descriptions; many preferred her brand of romanticism to the rising realism of the day and felt that she had a message for the age.

Two of her admirers, Mazzini and Lewes, helped set the tone of criticism by their extravagant praise. Mazzini ranked Sand high among contemporary French writers, and George Henry Lewes wrote: "All the beauties of the prose literature of the seventeenth century, put together, would not equal the prose of George Sand. . . . I would say that of all which has been written of the same kind by all the writers of other epochs, I see nothing that can for an instant be compared to certain descriptions—to whole volumes of George Sand." T. C. Sandars was attracted to Sand's appreciation of beauty, reflected in her language as she dealt in self-analysis. A *London Society* writer deprecated critics who saw in Sand "the rhythm of Homer and Virgil, the verve of Juvenal, the sublimity of Dante and the sarcasm of Byron," yet the comment reveals how extravagant their praise often was. Elizabeth Barrett commented to Mary Mitford that she could read a book "upon a walking stick," if it were written eloquently.

Style is music to me. I cannot help my pleasure in the beauty of it. Now, to my mind and ear too, the bare *french* of that wonderful genius Victor Hugo, and of this brilliant monstrous woman Madame Dudevant, is french *transfigured*. . . . It is not french—it is french no more. We recognize nothing like it in Voltaire—and the previous (so-called) classical writers. It is too sweet for french,—and too strong—and above all, too

numerous. It is something like the "voice of the charmer" to me.

Elizabeth called Sand the greatest female genius since Sappho.

John Ruskin labeled Sand "often immoral always beautiful." John Stuart Mill refused to agree with John Morley that Sand's style was the "high-water mark of prose, but yet could not name anybody higher," and admitted that "her prose stirs you like music." The Victorians were joined by readers in other nations who in their praise stopped often just short of idolatry. Henry James wrote that Sand's style had the "odor of hawthorn and the wild honeysuckle." Ernest Renan called Sand the "Aeolian harp of our times," and Alexandre Dumas fils commented that Sand "thinks like Montaigne, dreams like Ossian, writes like Jean Jacques." Turgenev in 1858 made a pilgrimage to Nohant to pay his respects.

Sand's description of nature endeared her to many Victorians, among them Matthew Arnold and her early reviewer Mary Margaret Busk. Even uncomplimentary reviewers, such as one in the *Foreign and Colonial Quarterly Review* of 1843, praised Sand's feeling for nature. The praise endured: a *Blackwood's* reviewer in 1876 writing on "Country Life" was compelled to refer to Sand's idealized view of rural living; although A. Innes Shand, writing also for *Blackwood's* in 1877, found Sand's peasants so idealized that he feared her friends who were inspired by her novels to visit the Berry countryside would never recognize the peasants once they got there. Two critics, Frederic W. H. Myers and Matthew Arnold, selected *Valvèdre* as a superb example of Sand's handling of nature, and John Addington Symonds chose the same novel as his favorite and praised Sand's nature description, finding this "devotion to nature for her own sake and the essential freedom which we regard as the central point of Elizabethanism."

Sand's distinct ability to paint characters also won the praise of many Victorians. Mrs. Busk admired the grandmother in *Valentine* and the rough veterans of the Imperial Army as they appeared in *Jacques.* A critic in the *British and Foreign Review* maintained that poetry was not dead as long as an author could create a heroine like the one in *André;* he admired Marcasse the rat-catcher, also from *André,* and commented: "Nor have the characters in which George Sand is successful that fault so largely destructive of the reader's trustful intimacy with so many of the personages of contemporary French novels. They are not over-wrought; their passions develope themselves in simple and dramatic dialogues; their action is well noted down without a stiff and trammeling minuteness; there is life in their repose."

George Henry Lewes found Sand a poet who created characters while Balzac was a philosopher who merely criticized his. Later when Lewes stated that Sand was prostituting her talent, he still felt she could depict characters well, especially old men and rascals among young men. T. C. Sandars, like Lewes, admired the rascals and saw them as foils for other characters.

Of all the Victorian critics, George Henry Lewes used

criteria that are most respected today. Joseph Mazzini treated her too much like a priestess of a new religious cult, a priestess whose politics he admired. Lewes came closest to meeting Arnold's criterion of "disinterestedness," and two lengthy articles in the *Foreign Quarterly Review* in July 1844 and April 1846 did much to establish Sand's literary reputation in Victorian England.

Lewes's 1844 review came when Balzac and Sand had edited their complete works, six volumes from Balzac, sixteen from Sand. Lewes compared the two writers from three points of view: the author as moralist, the author as artist, the author as entertainer. Sand emerged superior in all three categories. She was moral because she spoke what she believed to be the truth; if there were painful passages, they reflected the evil of her times. On the other hand, Lewes charged, Balzac made adultery seem the "general condition of society." As an artist, Lewes found Sand superior to Balzac in her style, her characterizations, and in what Lewes called her "poetic conceptions." Balzac he found artificial (as when he described nature as a woman dressed for a ball) and he disliked Balzac's attention to detail: "He cannot mention a single room in the house, but he must instantly make an inventory of the furniture, as if with an eye to distraining for rent." Lewes summed up: Balzac gave inventory; Sand gave emotion. *Lélia* he found the "most extraordinary piece of writing extant . . . alternately a hymn on the majesty of nature and an elegy on the nothingness of life." He then quoted a long passage in the original French, commenting that he never encountered such passages without "feeling as at an open window on a fair May morn." He declared her style "perhaps the most beautiful ever written by a French author." In his third category, the artist as entertainer, Lewes admitted Sand and Balzac both had wide reputations but Sand was greater than Balzac because she was "moral," and he explained that by moral he did not mean "sermons in the style of Hannah More." He probably meant something like what Longinus meant in "On the Sublime" when he referred to the "universal theme" that makes up a great literary work. In this Lewes would agree with Matthew Arnold, who was also indebted to Longinus. Arnold found Sand "moral" in this sense, not trivial and topical like Balzac.

In contrasting Balzac and Sand, Lewes revealed a dominant Victorian preference for romanticism over realism. Mazzini shared this Victorian bias. He said that realists like Balzac took as their motto the same cry that was heard in the streets of Naples at the time of a plague: "Have you any dead? Show lights in your windows." The realists, he claimed, took all that was dead, unclean, and unhealthy in society and showed it to view. Such a practice, he said, "unpoeticized" virtue, corrupted the imagination, promoted unbelief, and encouraged suicide.

Lewes and Mazzini had noteworthy Victorians on their side: Elizabeth Browning, who found Balzac deeper in the mire than Sand; John Ruskin, who did not like realistic fiction, which he felt developed in London suburbs "feeding the demands of the rows of similar brick houses which branch in devouring cancer round every manufacturing town," and who consequently found George Eliot the worst kind of Cockney realist. Matthew Arnold felt Sand would establish superiority over Balzac; and Charlotte Brontë preferred Sand to Balzac. As late as 1880, Andrew Lang wrote, "If the battle between the crocodile of Realism and the catawampus of Romance is to be fought out to the bitter end—why in the Ragnarôk [in Norse mythology, the final destruction of the world], I am on the side of the catawampus."

Many Victorians preferred the "catawampus" because they felt the romantic style best expressed a search for the ideal instead of the corrupt and dying side of society. Sand herself saw the conflict and wrote to Flaubert in 1866: "Maybe our sickness was more valuable than the reaction that followed it; than this craving for money, than this search for pleasures untouched by the ideal, than all this unchecked ambition. They do not seem to me to prove that this century has recovered its health."

The Victorian conviction that their age was sick resulted in a characteristic anxiety and melancholia. Arnold speaks of "this strange disease of modern life." Tennyson's poetry is profoundly melancholic. John Stuart Mill relates in his *Autobiography* how he escaped near mental collapse through the reading of literature. Carlyle in *Sartor Resartus* documents a struggle with The Everlasting No. The desire to escape the anxiety and melancholia of the age made many Victorians turn to Sand's romantic search for the ideal, seeking in her works a message to relieve their spiritual malaise.

Most of Sand's biographies record a passage that Sand wrote in English when she was sixteen: "Written *at Nohant, upon my window, at the setting of the sun, 1820:* Go fading Sun. . . . Evening descends to bring melancholy on the landscape. With thy return, beautiful light, Nature will find again mirth and beauty, but joy will never comfort my soul." While this may be a mere adolescent expression and enjoyment of weltschmerz at a low threshold of pain, to her admirers Sand became a child of the century in search of the ideal, seeking a formula for joy; as Matthew Arnold put it, his age needed "joy, but joy whose grounds are true" ("Obermann Once More," ll. 237-238).

Early in the century Mazzini stressed this quality of Sand's:

> I do not speak of glory, which, whatever has been done to prevent it, has crowned her; I know well that she values it but little. I do not even speak of something much more precious,—of the small number of chosen souls, the initiated and precursive of every country, who communicate with her from afar, whom her voice encourages and consoles, who rise up stronger from the perusal of her works, and follow all her steps with love and admiration.

He gave his own personal testimony, citing what Sand's *Lettres d'un Voyageur* had meant to him:

> It was in 1836 that I first met with these *Letters*, . . . My dearest friend had perished in the prisons of Charles Albert; others were condemned to linger there for twenty years; others were dying the slow death of the soul. . . . I had no longer faith in men; no longer faith in myself.

I still believed in God, and had faith in the future of my country; but from time to time doubt swept across my soul with icy wings. . . . I was about to be chased from a land Switzerland which I had learned to love as my second country. This book was to me a friend; a consolation. This sisterly voice, its accents broken by suffering, yet having strength to speak words of encouragement and hope to those "who were yet wandering amid storm and darkness," was sweet to me as is the cradle song to a weeping child. Many others have felt, many will doubtless feel, all I felt then. Travellers themselves through different paths, they will learn from these *Letters* where doubt and discouragement may lead them; and learn also how to regain strength and hope . . . "and the call of a friendly voice, from the height of the next hill, as they ascend the steeps of the lofty mountain," will be to them also, I doubt not, an encouragement and a consolation.

Charlotte Brontë had a similar emotional response to the *Lettres,* and George Eliot wrote her friend Sara Hennell that she hoped Sand's *Lettres* "will do you as much good as they do me."

T. C. Sandars praised Sand's "noble passion" and defined it as "that which elevates us and strengthens us in beauty of sentiment and grandeur of ideas." This "strengthening" was what endeared Sand to Jane Carlyle, Elizabeth Browning, and Matthew Arnold. Balzac recognized the "noble passion" and argued that the foolish things she had done should be to her credit in "the eyes of beautiful and noble souls."

Recognizing Sand's appeal and the need for her kind of romantic search to help cure the sickness of the age, Hippolyte Taine wrote Sand in 1872, just four years before her death:

> If only for our sakes, you must look after yourself for many years to come. Please give us, in addition to what you may be planning in head and heart, some such work as I once asked of you, more popular in tone, more vivid. It should be a sermon and an exhortation for men who have been bruised and wounded, but the tone of it must be that of a rousing call, of the encouragement for which all France is waiting. It is not a social thesis that her people demand, nor yet a moral one. In fact, it is not a thesis at all of which they stand in need, but the sound of frank and generous voices, the voices of maître Favilla, of Champi, or Villemer. They want to be persuaded that there is an heroic world still within their reach, and that the world in which they live could, if only they would stand tiptoe, be made to resemble it.

To stand tiptoe was the experience that Sand afforded many of her readers, and this appeal was a considerable part of her popularity. Although she was admired as one of the first emancipated women and as a political symbol, she was equally admired for her style, her characterization, her nature descriptions, and her search for the ideal. In that search she touched some of the most influential minds of her times, making the heroic seem still possible in an age of the antihero. (pp. 67-75)

> *Paul G. Blount, in his* George Sand and the Victorian World, *The University of Georgia Press, 1979, pp. 67-75.*

Ellen Moers   (essay date 1979)

[*An American educator and critic, Moers garnered praise for her critical studies* The Dandy: Brummel to Beerbohm *(1960),* Two Dreisers *(1969), and* Literary Women *(1976). In the excerpt below, she surveys the critical history of Sand's career.*]

> And now I'm attached to it, this name of mine. . . . I was baptized, obscure and carefree, between the manuscript of *Indiana* which was then my whole future—and a thousand-franc note, which was then my whole fortune. It was a contract, a new marriage between the poor apprentice poet that I then was and the humble muse who had consoled me in my difficulties. God defend me from tampering with the dispositions of destiny. What is a name, anyway, in our revolutionary world? A number for those who do nothing, a sign or emblem for those who work or fight. This name I've been given, I made it myself, and I alone, finally, by my labor. I have never exploited the work of another, never taken, or bought, or borrowed a page, a line from anyone. Of the seven or eight hundred thousand francs that I've earned since I was twenty, I have nothing left, and today as at twenty I live from day to day, by this name which protects my work. . . .

> (*Histoire De Ma Vie,* IV, XIV)

What should that famous name "George Sand" mean to us? A reasoned answer, supplied by Joseph Barry's newly translated anthology, is that George Sand was a writer—a nineteenth-century French writer, who for four and a half decades, from 1831 to 1876, wrote with verve, eloquence, and power well over one hundred volumes of prose: fiction, plays, autobiographies, letters, essays. A prolific and successful but not really a popular writer, as Henry James noted with surprise: none of her works was by the standard of her time or ours a "best-seller," not even *Consuelo,* one of her most important novels, which sold only a few thousand copies. Among writers and intellectuals, however, she reached what might be called a "mass market" everywhere around the world, and their tributes to her as spokesman of the age (surpassing even Dickens, Dostoevski insisted) were touched with reverence and gratitude, as well as hyperbole.

The English critic George Henry Lewes wrote in 1842 that Sand was "the most remarkable writer of the present century. . . . George Sand is infinitely more than novelist. She is a Poet, not of the head alone, but of the heart—a Poet, not writing clever verses, but uttering the collective voice of her epoch. . . . No genius was ever recognized by the many; George Sand may comfort herself with the appreciation of the few." Lewes was only a young man then, and just beginning his career as a critic; but his reverence for Sand as a writer was to prove a bond between him and the two great novelists Lewes most influenced, Charlotte Brontë and George Eliot. They too read George Sand as the genius of their age; they too reverenced the poet and the thinker in the novelist.

Turgenev, Renan, Heine, Dostoevski, the Brownings, the Carlyles, Mill, Ruskin, Taine, Whitman, Marx, Wilde—all testify that, among nineteenth-century intellectuals, reading Sand was something of an addiction. And almost a Victorian parlor game was marking the influence of Sand's novels on other people's fiction, as Marian Evans (the future George Eliot) saw marks of *François le Champi* on Thackeray's *Henry Esmond*. However, a number of the prominent Victorian addicts of Sand's fiction—Emerson, Whitman, Ruskin, Arnold—were people who otherwise had little use for the novel as a form. Matthew Arnold, the most important literary critic of the century, could barely say a good word for Dickens and, devoted as he was to contemporary French literature, never once mentioned the name of Flaubert; but he went on reading Sand's novels all his life.

When she died in 1876, Arnold predicted that "the immense vibration of George Sand's voice upon the ear of Europe will not soon die away"; he was wrong. Within a quarter of a century intellectuals stopped reading Sand. Virtual silence descended on the academy and the critical journals; no more vibrations. Marcel Proust wrote the experience of reading Sand, as a nineteenth-century child, into his *Remembrance of Things Past,* and George Sand's work slipped, with so much else, into *le temps perdu.*

By a reversal of taste as extreme as any in literary history, and by a process of denigration familiar to experts in women's history, the name of George Sand came to mean to most people not an author at all but a target for labels: transvestite, man-eater, lesbian, nymphomaniac. The very texts of some of her volumes had vanished, as French scholars discovered when they began the massive labor of recovering the writer George Sand, for, predictably, the reversal of literary taste was due to be again reversed and Sand was to return to our own time as a writer, not a caricature.

When the revival of interest in Sand's work started quietly in France in the 1930s, it was once again an intellectual phenomenon, beginning with two eminent Frenchmen, Édouard Dolléans and Alain (pen name of Émile Chartier), who happened to be friends. Dolléans was the historian of nineteenth-century working-class movements in France (he also wrote a history of Chartism in England), and he began to write about Sand with the deepest respect because of her own involvement with working-class poets and politics, because of her influential role as champion of *le peuple.* While the critic Alain turned to Sand because of her love of nature and music, her passion and her prose. Alain is best known outside France as the teacher of philosophy whose students brought him fame, notably Simone Weil and André Maurois. And it was Maurois's biography called *Lélia: The Life of George Sand* and published in 1952 that gave the Sand revival wide and international currency.

In the 1960s and 1970s, literary scholars in France and Italy prepared definitive new editions of Sand's novels (including **Consuelo, La Comtesse de Rudolstadt, Indiana, Lélia, Mauprat, La Mare au Diable, François le Champi, La Daniella**) and supplied learned introductory studies of Sand's politics, her knowledge of music and history, her use of dialect and regional lore, her place among the Romantics. Georges Lubin, the dean of Sand scholars, edited her autobiographical writings (which include her masterworks) and since 1964 has been editing Sand's correspondence—thirteen volumes of it for the years through June 1856, with two more decades of Sand's life and presumably ten more volumes still to come. The letters are dazzling. Had she written nothing else, George Sand would be securely known as one of the greatest of all practitioners of the form.

Because of the incredible range of Sand's epistolary relationships and concerns, Georges Lubin's scholarship has perforce reached out to include virtually all the politics and all the arts in mid-nineteenth-century Europe, not to mention the day-by-day chronology of Sand's passionate life as writer, lover, mother, friend, and *châtelaine.* His magisterial edition of the **Correspondance** has formed the basis for the two new scholarly lives of George Sand, both widely read and widely hailed, both by Americans: Curtis Cate (1975) and Joseph Barry (1977). Mr. Barry's particular strength as a Sand biographer—a knowledge of her works which is probably unrivaled in the English-speaking world—is also reflected in [his anthology *George Sand in Her Own Words*].

Both Cate and Barry know far more about Sand's intimate life than did any of her contemporaries, because the documentation at their command is so enormous. Yet the "new" George Sand who emerges from their biographies is remarkably like the "old" George Sand perceived in her own time by those who knew her or who divined her character from her writings. She has a brilliant, well-stocked mind and a warm heart; she has courage, energy, vitality, generosity, responsibility, good humor, and charm; she has aristocratic distinction combined with bohemian informality; she is a wise, passionate, down-to-earth human being, and disappointingly sane. These days we want our writers to be crazies; in the mid-nineteenth century, people wanted their writers to be great men. Their ideal of a writer was Goethe (to whom Sand was often compared) because of the wholeness and fullness of both his active and spiritual life. "Great Men are the inspired (speaking and acting) Texts of that divine Book of Revelation" called "History," said Carlyle, who worshiped Goethe, who made a cult of the writer as Hero, who privately admitted there was "something Goethian" about George Sand but never would have said so in public, because she was a woman.

She was a woman who was a great man: that is what her admirers most wanted to say about George Sand. But words of gender being what they are, suggestions of abnormality and monstrosity cling to their portraits of Sand, all unintentionally and quite the reverse of what her admirers had in mind. Elizabeth Barrett (later Mrs. Robert Browning) began a sonnet to Sand with the line

Thou large-brained woman and large-hearted
    man . . .

and what she intended as a tribute to wholeness came out
sounding grotesque. Similarly, Balzac wrote down his impressions of Sand after a visit to her home in Nohant: "She
is boyish, an artist, she is greathearted, generous, devout,
and *chaste;* she has the main characteristics of a man; *ergo*
she is not a woman."

Flaubert, who wrote the novella *Un Coeur Simple* for
Sand's approval, wept at her funeral and said: "You had
to know her as I did to know how much of the feminine
there was in that great man, the immensity of tenderness
there was in that genius." And Turgenev: "What a brave
man she was, and what a good woman."

Reading George Sand is to encounter a great man who
was all woman, not a phenomenon—though that such a
life, a spirit, a style were possible struck her contemporaries as phenomenal, for they had never known a literary
woman of her kind before. To read Sand is also to return
to a Romantic age, to find the lanes greener, the nightin-
gales thicker, the stars brighter, the breezes softer, the colors brighter, and the tones more heavenly, for Delacroix
is painting, Viardot is singing, Liszt and Chopin are at the
piano; and the hopes of relieving human suffering, of binding all humanity into one golden solidarity, are more dazzling than ever before. Reading Sand, however, is not the
ponderous experience that American and English readers
might expect from our rather Victorian definition of
"greatness of character." George Sand was very French,
and she never took herself very seriously.

In 1831, when she was twenty-six, she set out for Paris to
become a writer—to support herself and her dependents
by writing. High Romanticism was in full sway in France,
and the new writers were named Victor Hugo, Lamartine,
Musset, Vigny, Balzac, Stendhal, Mérimée, Sainte-Beuve.
When she was twenty-seven, George Sand, the author of
Indiana, was one of the names on that Romantic list. With
the speed and energy characteristic of her entire literary
career, she accomplished her apprenticeship in journalism
and fiction, including the writing of dozens of works and
thousands of pages, the making of contacts and finding of
markets, all within fifteen months. She also established a
dual life-style which makes itself felt throughout all her
writings. On the one hand, she was an independent: her
officer father and aristocratic grandmother long dead, her
mother removed, her maiden name (Dupin) and married
name (Dudevant) abandoned, her husband put in his place
by a formal contract of separation. She was a Parisian and
a cosmopolitan, in touch with all that was new in the arts
and in political thought. But on the other hand, she was
a countrywoman in residence principally in her province
of Berry and enmeshed, voluntarily and wholeheartedly,
with human ties: her two children; her country estate of
Nohant, with its servants, peasants, neighbors, its spreading regional associations of memory and legend; and her
lovers and friends. Friends were, as far as George Sand
could manage it, for life; lovers came and went more
quickly, but they too long had a claim on her responsibility and generosity.

Indiana, the novel which first made the name of George

*Engraving of George Sand wearing the men's attire for which she
was famous.*

Sand famous, is in many ways uncharacteristic of her fiction, with its debts to the earlier Romanticism of Madame
de Staël and Bernardin de Saint-Pierre, its small cast of
mainly wealthy characters, its unlikely Bourbon Island
references, its melancholy Englishman. (Yet even Sir
Ralph may be forgiven Sand, if, as has been argued, he inspired the relationship between Ralph Touchett and Isabel
Archer in Henry James's *Portrait of a Lady.*) But already
in *Indiana* the distinctive pleasures of reading Sand make
themselves felt, and the first of these are country pleasures:
country nights, country solitude, country passions, country journeys, the horses and dogs and pastimes, even the
boredom of rainy autumn evenings in the country interior.
It was, however, *Valentine,* her second novel, in which
Sand's originality as landscapist and country chronicler
(and creator of rebellious heroines) overwhelmed readers
such as Matthew Arnold. He responded as a young man
to what he called "the cry of agony and revolt" in Sand's
early fiction; but what Arnold *did* in response was to set
off on a journey into Sand's countryside and Sand's interi-
or at Nohant—a pilgrimage on which he has been followed ever since by untold thousands of enthusiasts of Romantic art and Romantic nature.

At her best, no one has ever surpassed George Sand as the
novelist of Nature, because her style pulsates with a natu-

ral vigor and music and because she was a countrywoman as well as a Romantic. Her range includes not only the mysteries and enchantments of distant horizons and perilous wanderings, of superstition and legend, of ecstatic (and often feminist) solitude; but also the closely observed and dearly loved realities of peasant life: the greeds and frugalities, the labor of the seasons, the farm animals and insects, the stolid silences of illiterate folk radiated with their music and dancing, their enchanting dialect speech. Her *romans champêtres* (*La Mare au Diable, François le Champi, La Petite Fadette, Jeanne, Les Maîtres Sonneurs, Le Meunier d'Angibault*) are those of Sand's novels which have never gone completely out of fashion and to which the English country novelists (George Eliot and Thomas Hardy) were most in debt.

But Sand had something her English imitators did not and that was her grasp of history. "Tout concourt à l'histoire," she wrote, "*tout est l'histoire, même les romans qui semblent ne se rattacher en rien aux situations politiques qui les voient éclore.*" Her country tales and her love stories take place in the churning past and the open future of a world of toppling regimes, shifting classes, and clashing ideologies. Even in *Indiana*, Delmare is the husband he is because he is a displaced Bonapartist, Indiana the wife she is because she is the daughter of slaveholding colonials, and Raymon the lover he is because he is an apologist for constitutional monarchy, his political portrait drawn after that of a minister of the July monarchy, which had come into power two years before the publication of the novel. When Sand gives her heroine views on women's education, as in *Valentine*, they are those of an aristocrat who remembers what happened to her sex and class during the French Revolution. Sand places most of her young heroes in generational conflict with their fathers and offers them as typical *enfants du siècle*. She demonstrates that even the illiterate peasant—as in the interesting study of Patience in *Mauprat*—could be touched by the ideas of the Enlightenment. And in some of the most brilliant sections of *Histoire de Ma Vie*, she presents her own childhood as riven by the class and period ideologies held by her grandmother and her mother and seconded even by their maids.

It can be something of a relief to turn from the slow-moving dreamtime of Thomas Hardy and George Eliot to the faster pace of George Sand's European world, a world, as Marx read it and we still read it today, in revolutionary turmoil. Sand was a shrewd, committed, and radical observer of the half-dozen regimes that rose and fell in France during her lifetime. As Minister (without portfolio) of Propaganda, she played an active political role—greater than any woman before her—in the revolutionary government of 1848. Correspondent of Mazzini, of Gutzkow, of Bakunin, she was in touch with most of radical Europe. In all her work, her fiction and nonfiction, ideology remains a principal excitement, never a bore.

Less interesting to us today, I think, than to her contemporaries is Sand on the passion of love; here there can be the boredom of excess French talk, of impossible chastities, of improbable plots. "I don't care," wrote George Eliot, " . . . whether I think the design of her plot correct or that she had no precise design at all . . . I cannot read six pages of hers without feeling that it is given to her to delineate human passion . . . with such truthfulness such nicety of discrimination such tragic power and withal such loving gentle humour that one might live a century with nothing but one's own dull faculties and not know so much as these six pages will suggest." Sand remains interesting as the chronicler of passion in the occasional scene where, as V. S. Pritchett has put it, "her people and landscapes are silhouettes seen in sheet lightning": for example, the Noun-Raymon love scene in Indiana's bedroom, which made Alfred de Musset first admire before he fell in love with its author.

Today Sand's social thought sustains her love stories rather than the other way around, for her pairings of lovers of different ages and places and classes still convey that aspiration toward a new, humane social order which lifted the hearts of her contemporaries and still has the power to move even our own. A commonplace of Romanticism was the use of human love as the paradigm of social solidarity; but from Friedrich Schiller's (and Beethoven's) *Ode to Joy* to Walt Whitman's *Leaves of Grass*, that theme ordinarily centered on man's love for man, on fraternity. Sand's originality—and it was this that must have attracted Dostoevski to her heroines—was to redefine fraternity from the woman's point of view, as friendship between men and women. Certainly her ideal of marriage, which she despaired of seeing fulfilled under the legal system of her times, was that of the perfect friendship, without rivalry or dominance, of two beings come together in that state of unity and wholeness which, as she wrote Flaubert, is Nature's supreme law.

Friendship seems to me to be George Sand's greatest theme. It pervades her fiction and her politics, shapes her style and her humor, and makes her *Lettres d'un Voyageur*, those exquisitely worded imaginary dialogues of reflection and criticism, her single greatest work. Even the disarray of her novel plots is sometimes excused by her charming finales of communal life, when groups of lovers settle down together for a friendly sharing of work, talk, child raising, and country pleasures that seems to promise more of ecstasy than all their frenetic lovemaking. At the end of *Valentine*, peasants and aristocrats are so united; at the end of *Les Maîtres Sonneurs*, the workers of the fields are united with their rivals, the wandering foresters. In *Valvèdre*, the late novel (1861) which Arnold ranked among her best, Sand's ultimate programmatic fantasy of communality makes friends of scientist, industrialist, and artist, of "new" woman and old, of Protestant, Catholic, and Jew.

Sand worked hard at her friendships, writing marvelous letters, dispensing generous hospitality. A highly skilled domestic manager, she made Nohant (the locale of her own slavery to ceaseless writing) into a haven of comfort and bohemian relaxation for such as Liszt, Balzac, Juliette Adam, the English actor Macready, Turgenev, Flaubert, Pauline Viardot, Delacroix—who were her friends, not her lovers. But her genius for friendship seems to have originated in childhood, the period of her life which, to the despair of scandalmongers, dominates her *Histoire de Ma Vie*.

There Sand opens what to us seems unusual, but for her was her birthright as a French countrywoman: the friendly association between bastard and legitimate half-siblings, between unrelated children raised by the same wet nurse (the Noun-Indiana relationship), between future peasant and future *châtelaine.* Sand wrote, and there is something to it, that her ideas of utopian communism originated in her girlhood participation in the communality of peasant labors and diversions. Certainly she had not a trace of gentility or snobbery, not a shred of vain glory over being a *propriétaire.* Nohant was where her heart was, but Nohant made her neither proud nor wealthy. It was her writing, not her land, that supported her; and of that she was justly proud.

A talk with friends is the manner of her best tales and memoirs and essays and even political propaganda—a manner which Sand raised to the dignity of the grand style. And it is her style, finally, which makes reading George Sand an addiction. "The taste one develops for Sand," wrote the critic Emile Faguet, "is a kind of sympathy. Her style becomes our friend. And we more easily free ourselves of an enchantment than of a friendship." (pp. ix-xxii)

> *Ellen Moers, in an introduction to* George Sand in Her Own Words, *edited and translated by Joseph Barry, Anchor Books, 1979, pp. ix-xxii.*

Jeannee P. Sacken   (essay date 1981)

[*In the essay below, Sacken demonstrates the connection between scenes of nature and plot in* Indiana, *asserting that in the urban settings the characters are repressed, while in the idyllic countryside they find freedom.*]

At the end of *Indiana,* Sir Ralph and Indiana bid adieu to the narrator as he departs: " 'Retournez au monde; si quelque jour il vous bannit, souvenez-vous de notre chaumière indienne.' " This farewell recalls the geographical distance and the social differences between l'île Bourbon and Paris, the gorge of Bernica and the château of Lagny; moreover, it emphasizes the presence of nature imagery as a reinforcement of the thematic development. The incidents which occur on l'île Bourbon, as well as in Paris and at Lagny, convey the theme of physical and spiritual enslavement—a contrast to the Bernica described by Ralph: " 'Tous nos jours se ressemblent; ils sont tous calmes et beaux; ils passent rapides et purs comme ceux de notre enfance. . . . La majeure portion de nos revenus est consacrée à racheter de pauvres noirs infirmes.' " It is at Bernica that Ralph and Indiana discover the happiness, love, and freedom which had eluded them in Paris, at Lagny, and during their previous visits to l'île Bourbon.

Indiana, Ralph, and Delmare are first seen at Lagny where the surrounding environment is unnatural and dream-like. The interior of the house initially suggests the artificiality: the door to the main salon is "une porte surmontée d'Amours nus, peints à fresque, qui enchaînaient de fleurs des biches fort bien élevées et des sangliers de bonne volonté." The ceiling, painted to represent "un ciel parsemé de nuages et d'étoiles," again points to the falseness of the

small, provincial château. When Laure de Nangy subsequently lives at Lagny, she describes the salon walls of which she has painted a pastiche:

> Et cette jolie nature fausse et peignée . . . n'est-ce pas qu'il y avait dans tout cela de la poésie, des idées de mollesse et de bonheur, et le sentiment de toute une vie douce, inutile et inoffensive?

These walls, with their evocation of the pastoral love enjoyed by Louis XV's nobles—itself merely a pretense—are witness to Indiana's and Raymon's love. For Indiana this spiritual love is the perfection of a long-desired ideal, while for Raymon it is only a means to impassion himself, a form of amusement as depicted by the figures on the walls.

Outside the house, the nature is equally artificial. The château's park encloses an orangery replete with rare and exotic plants—foreign to the region—to decorate this "jardin anglais." Despite its semblance of being natural, such a garden with its "arbres taillés" is just as artificial as "le jardin français." Indiana is described as "une belle fleur exotique"—a metaphor which strengthens her suggested affinity with nature; while free at Bernica during her youth, she fails to thrive once transplanted from her natural habitat.

Also in the park is a gazebo, which, when strewn with flowers, serves as the place for Noun and Raymon's frequent *rendez-vous:* " . . . dans le kiosque rempli de fleurs exotiques où elle venait l'enivrer des séductions de la jeunesse et de la passion, il oubliait volontiers tout ce qu'il devait se rappeler plus tard." During two of Raymon's visits to the garden, the description of the rainy or foggy weather suggests a certain unreality. When he meets Noun for the last time in Indiana's room: "La nuit était froide; un brouillard épais enveloppait les arbres du parc, et Raymon avait peine à distinguer leurs tiges noires dans la brume blanche, qui les revêtait de robes blanches." Subsequently traversing the garden for his tryst with Indiana, he encounters similar weather conditions: "Le hasard voulut que cette nuit-là fut blanche et opaque comme l'avaient été les nuits correspondantes du printemps. Raymon marcha avec incertitude parmi les arbres enveloppés de vapeurs." The foggy night acts as an opiate on Raymon, distorting his perception, as did the abundance of flowers and wine during his earlier *rendez-vous* with Noun. Although he is on his way to Indiana, his thoughts are of the dead Noun; and as he is overwhelmed by his conscience for his part in her suicide, the cry of a bird forces him to confuse the natural and supernatural, a cry "qui ressemble exactement au vagissement d'un enfant abandonné; et, quand il s'élance du creux des joncs, on dirait le dernier effort d'une personne qui se noie." Both nature and Raymon are seducers: Raymon, metaphorically described as a "vipère," seduces Noun and Indiana, and then is himself seduced by his hallucinations in the park and in Indiana's room with Noun.

The descriptions of the weather in Paris underscore the fate Indiana suffers at the hands of Raymon and in society. Her trips to Paris occur, symbolically, in winter. It is in Paris after a long winter that the dying Indiana meets and revives during three days of happiness with Raymon "quand la nature commençait à se réveiller." On a subsequent trip, she suffers Raymon's coldness throughout the entire winter until he abandons her on one of "les jours les plus froids de l'année."

While they are living at Lagny, and later in Paris and on l'île Bourbon, the image of the bird suggests Indiana's lack of freedom and her total subjugation to her husband. The initial description of M. Delmare as jealous and suspicious is amplified by his depiction as a *oiseau de proie:* "Il est certain que l'argus conjugal fatigua son œil de vautour sans surprendre un regard." A confrontation between Delmare and Indiana gives evidence of his potential cruelty and demonstrates that Indiana is a prisoner within her marriage:

> Il était tenté de l'étrangler, de la traîner par les cheveux, de la fouler aux pieds pour la forcer de crier merci, d'implorer sa grâce; mais elle était si jolie, si mignonne et si blanche, qu'il se prenait à avoir pitié d'elle comme un enfant s'attendrit à regarder l'oiseau qu'il voulait tuer.

Delmare's cruelty toward his wife is further underscored by the reader's realization that he does, in fact, shoot birds: "[il] s'exerce à tuer les hirondelles au vol." These images and events presage the outburst of Delmare's violence against Indiana: "Sans pouvoir articuler une parole, il la saisit par les cheveux, la renversa, et la frappa au front du talon de sa botte."

On l'île Bourbon, nature is both a negative and positive force for the melancholy Indiana and the brooding Ralph. For both the sight of the sea is painful, reminding Indiana of the life her husband forced her to abandon, and Ralph of his unhappy life in France. Although the house shared by the Delmares and Ralph is isolated in the mountains above the town, both Indiana and Ralph escape to a more profound solitude. Descending the gorges, Indiana finds solace in her thoughts of Paris and Raymon. Her ardent desire to return to France enables her to see the surrounding nature as the concretization of her memories: "Quelquefois les nuages de la côte prirent pour elle des formes singulières: tantôt elle vit une lame blanche s'élever sur les flots et décrire une ligne gigantesque qu'elle prit pour la façade du Louvre. . . . " A retreat to the hidden gorges of Bernica allows Ralph to flee the unhappiness he associates with the sight of the sea just as he was able to seek refuge there when he was cast out of his family as a child. It was there that he helped raise Indiana, herself rejected by her father. A major portion of her limited education consisted in watching the different birds.

For the child Indiana, the observations of the birds' flight across the ocean were a form of amusement. Her adult vision of their flight has a modified significance however: "Le soir, elle suivait de l'œil le vol des oiseaux qui s'en allaient coucher à l'île Rodrigue. Cette île abandonnée lui promettait toutes les douceurs de l'isolement." The sight of the bird in flight has come to mean an escape from the emotional and social shackles imposed on her by her marriage to Delmare. Initially, her daydream allows her to picture herself in a small hut on l'île Rodrigue living freely and in complete isolation from society. Eventually, her

plan is transformed into a flight from her husband to what is merely another form of enslavement—Raymon.

She hopes to accomplish what she believes to be a liberating flight, " 'Au coucher de la lune . . . comme une pauvre pétrelle au fond de quelque récit bien sombre.' " During her escape the canoe also is metamorphosed into a bird: "La pirogue bondit avec élasticité comme un plongeon sur les eaux." The metaphor is repeated: "La goëlette *La Nahandove* les porta, rapide et légère comme un oiseau." It is this last trip back to l'île Bourbon, decided on by both Ralph and Indiana, that actually corresponds fully to the free flight of the bird. For Indiana, the victim of a social enslavement, and for Ralph, oppressed by an inability to express his emotions, the image of the bird in flight symbolizes their ideal of a liberated existence. While on the boat, Indiana regains her physical and mental health and Ralph's true personality begins to emerge from behind his imprisoning, expressionless exterior.

When they are once more in their childhood sanctuary of Bernica, Ralph is able to divulge his repressed love, confessing that he had previously looked to nature as a vicarious lover: " 'Alors, j'étais ivre, j'étais fou; je demandais l'amour aux fleurs, aux oiseaux, à la voix du torrent.' " Although nature seduces, it also reveals the truth, and allows Indiana to live "dans le cœur de Ralph tel qu'il était." With the discovery of their hidden, imprisoned selves, Ralph and Indiana are able to control their lives. This regeneration after social oppression is likened to the continuous renewal of nature after a storm:

> Les arbres, si frais et si beaux quinze jours auparavant, avaient été dépouillés entièrement de leurs feuilles, mais déjà ils se couvraient de gros bourgeons résineux. Les oiseaux et les insectes avaient repris possession de leur empire. . . . Tout revenait à la vie, au bonheur, à la santé.

Nature is ultimately an all-powered and divine force for Ralph and Indiana, and it is here that they are able to find God:

> Pour nous l'univers est le temple où nous adorons Dieu. C'est au sein d'une nature grande et vierge qu'on retrouve le sentiment de sa puissance pure de toute profanation humaine.

Throughout **Indiana** there is a narrative progression from the psychological and marital enslavement and the social hypocrisy at Lagny, in Paris, and on l'île Bourbon to the self-discovery, freedom, and happiness at Bernica. Each thematic shift emerges through the characters' geographical movement, through the significance attached to the descriptions of nature within settings as it changes from the artificial imitations to its real, unadulterated state, and through the use of nature images. So we see that as the image of the bird in flight supersedes that of the birds destroyed by Delmare, the thematic meaning shifts also. Nature initially reflects the destructive cruelty of Delmare, Raymon, and society's treatment of Indiana. By the novel's end, for both Indiana and Ralph, nature is a beneficient, regenerative, and divine force. (pp. 313-17)

Jeannee P. Sacken, "Nature Imagery as Narrative Structure in George Sand's 'Indiana'," in Romance Notes, *Vol. XXI, No. 3, Spring, 1981, pp. 313-17.*

Victor Carrabino   (essay date 1983)

[*In the following excerpt, Carrabino discusses the symbol of the labyrinth in* Consuelo *as a Jungian representation of the title character's quest for identity.*]

If **Consuelo** is George Sand's most ambitious and imaginative novel, it is because the work itself transcends the limits of associations to various individuals, after whom, apparently, the novel was modeled. It is often reported that Consuelo, the *zingarella,* was patterned in part upon Pauline Viardot, an opera celebrity who, during George Sand's times, found her path to stardom quite arduous in spite of her extraordinary musical talents.

Indeed much has been written on George Sand's works. At times she appears to be the mentor of literary pillars such as Dostoievsky, Ibsen, Whitman, and even Proust, just to mention a few. At other times, George Sand is cast aside as a relic of a past century. Yet, one cannot overlook the fact that George Sand has also been revived by Colette, Simone de Beauvoir—among the modern feminists of contemporary French literature. Because of her bizarre social behavior, her maternal love affairs with Chopin and Musset, critics have depicted of George Sand a classical picture of a *femme fatale.* This diabolic woman was influential, it is said, even in the political arena of her times. Some critics have gone to some length to discuss her lesbian tendencies. However, in spite of all these labels, George Sand should be read above all for her keen insight into the human psyche.

Consuelo, the heroine of the novel, is a singer whom the author takes on a long, free-spirited trip through Europe in search of herself. It is this search of the self, of one's identity, that makes the novel of particular interest to us. After all, as George Sand claims: "life is a great riddle, and we should not allow the slightest incident to pass without examining and understanding it".

Consuelo's methodical approach to solving life's riddle is represented by the symbol of the labyrinth, which is a pervasive symbol throughout the novel. Consuelo is not simply a model of Pauline Viardot. She joins the collective unconscious of every human being in search of his own self in his eternal orphic quest of his identity through the limitless boundaries of the psyche.

The effort to reach the center of the labyrinth is what Jung calls the "individuation process": "The state of life dynamism in which consciousness realizes itself as a split and separated personality that yearns and strives toward union with its unknown and unknowable partner, the self " [Edward C. Whitmont, *The Symbolic Quest,* 1973].

Many are the labyrinthine symbols in the novel. One can even suggest, as Jean Sgard claims that both the novel and Consuelo's life have a labyrinthine tapestry. However, no attempt has been made to trace the meticulous trip of Consuelo in the search for her identity and link it to the Jungian Individuation Process. As an archetypal metaphor, the labyrinth in **Consuelo** is not only suggested but it is clearly expressed at different times in the novel. The labyrinth is in fact a most effective pattern to describe man's quest for his identity.

In many solar myths, for example, it is reported that the hero travels perilously through a dark labyrinthine underworld of monsters between sunset and sunrise. The ascension and descension between Life and Death is often represented by a labyrinthine structure. Likewise, the struggle of the individual in his psychological quest of the self is represented by the dark and bright sides of the conscious and unconscious respectively.

Joseph Campbell reports in the *Mythic Hero* that "the labyrinth was the center of activities concerned with those greatest mysteries, Life and Death. There men tried by every means known to them to overcome death to renew life . . . There the living King-god went to renew and strengthen his own vitality by association with the immortal lives of his dead ancestors".

Structurally, the labyrinth is represented by the intersection of several paths, some of which lead to dead-end streets, culs-de-sac, through which one has to discover the road that leads to the center. The labyrinth is built purposely in such a way to delay the individual from easily reaching the center without any suffering and vicissitudes. False promises, envy, deceptions, and illusions are integral obstacles that deprive the individual from reaching the center. Structurally, the labyrinth is a series of concentric circles with a definite center, however, inaccessible. The labyrinth has been equalled, for example, to the mandala which has in fact a labyrinthine structure.

As a symbol of defense, the labyrinth hides something precious, sacred, valuable, unknown. It is through courage, strength, perseverance, and self determination that the individual can reach the center. Only those who have undergone such vicissitudes, the initiated ones, can finally share the fullness and richness of the mysterious revelation.

On the psychological level the labyrinth has also a religious connotation. In the cabalistic tradition, which was later a favorite subject of investigation for the alchemists, the labyrinth played a magical function, which held Solomon's secret. This interpretation of the myth of the labyrinth joins the mystico-ascetic doctrine: in the myriad of sensations, passions, wishes, complex ideas, man, lost in the labyrinth, needs to find the correct way, the road to freedom and knowledge. This going in and out of the psychological labyrinth translates man's spiritual resuscitation. The labyrinth is a viable symbol for man to reach the uncanny realm of his inner self, the most sacred and mysterious interior of man's life.

Consuelo becomes an archetypal hero, this time transvested in female clothes. Actually Consuelo is dressed as a young boy during her journey with Joseph Haydn.

Consuelo was a gypsy, tells us George Sand, "only by profession and metaphorically". There is something picaresque about Consuelo's life. She is destined to wander. Roads fascinate Consuelo: "What is more beautiful than a road? It is the symbol and the image of an active varied life. What capricious windings of this one before me . . .

And this road is the path of mankind, the highway of the universe". Roads are free, appropriate for a free-spirited traveler such as Consuelo. "No wall or fence confines the view. The horizon has no ending, and, as far as the eye can see, the road is a land of liberty".

Consuelo's search becomes thus a constant quest of finding herself, and her role in society, in the name of Art which will ultimately transcend all other quests. Consuelo is in a constant confusion. Once, she exclaims, "I must collect my thoughts and learn to know myself." "Yes", answers Porpora, her mentor "you have said the word, Consuelo; you must have solitude, absolute freedom of action".

The novel opens with Consuelo in Venice as an apprentice of Porpora, a famous musician of the eighteenth century. She is Porpora's star pupil. Consuelo lives in Venice, where canals, bridges, small streets serve as a compliment to Consuelo's psychological labyrinth. When Anzoleto leaves Venice, due to his infidelity with Clorinda, George Sand comments: "Then, abandoning his victims to their fate, Clorinda to her stupefaction and the consequences of the adventure, he swam to the opposite shore, hurried through the dark labyrinth of streets to his lodging".

Consuelo manages to escape from Venice, this time with the help of Porpora, who like Ariadne, serves as a magical thread given to Theseus. Consuelo has just escaped from the first outer circle of the labyrinth, and entered into the next circle, when, a more complex and mysterious circle waits for her. To escape the demonic forces which are a threat to Consuelo's individuation process, namely the road to Art, Consuelo leaves Venice and goes to Bavaria, to the Castle of the Giants dominated by the giant oak tree of Schreckenstein—known as the Rock of Terror. Consuelo's initiation to this new circle becomes a test for her endurance and courage.

In this castle she meets Albert who becomes her mystical mentor, another thread of Ariadne which will liberate Consuelo on the way to Art. However, Consuelo's road is not an easy one. First she must suffer. In fact, tells us Sand "the castle where Albert lives is like a cage, indeed a labyrinth". Amalia, Albert's cousin and promised fiancée, arranged by the family, defines the castle as a cage: "I am a pearl confined in this dismal family of mine as in an oyster, of which this ghastly Castle of the Giants is the hell". This bird held in captivity in this pitiless cage gives us a vivid symbol of the labyrinthine atmosphere in which Consuelo is about to be trapped.

The appearance of Consuelo in Albert's life, when she first arrives at the castle, is forecast by a typical romantic pathetic fallacy. Like the archetypal hero, orphan, often left alone to his destiny, Consuelo leaves the tumultuous atmosphere of Venice to immerse herself in a series of heroic stages. She arrives at the castle during a tempestuous night. The mysterious voice of nature announces Consuelo's arrival: "Do you not hear the wind roaring among the firs of Moërs-Wald, and the voice of the torrent ascending to your ears? There is a soul being driven toward us by the storm at this moment. You will do well, Mr. Chaplain, to pray for those who travel among our perilous

mountains, exposed to the fury of the tempest", exclaims Albert to whom the chaplain replies: "I pray every hour and from the depth of my soul, for those who travel through the rough pathways of life, exposed to the tempest of human passions". It is the emphasis on this demonic night which brings us to the novel's labyrinthine road to Consuelo.

From the time she arrives at this castle, Consuelo's life becomes one of intense search and discovery. She has in fact entered the Dantesque Hall of her psyche: "When the carriage had driven across the drawbridge . . . it seemed to her that she was entering Dante's Hell". Consuelo, the wandered, the fugitive, is aspiring to a new being: "This change of scene, of environment, and of name transported her suddenly into unfamiliar surroundings, where playing a new role, she aspired to become a new being". This rebirth of Consuelo, now Porporina by name, can only be possible by her courage and determination to pursue her destiny to the very end, at whatever cost.

A series of concentric circles awaits Consuelo. Having reached the outer layer of the whirlpool of the psyche, she cannot escape. In the eyes of Consuelo, the structure of the different rooms in the castle resembles that of a labyrinth: "One morning, as she went down very softly, on tiptoe, to avoid awaking anyone, she mistook her direction among the innumerable stairways and endless corridors of the castle, with which she was hardly familiar as yet. Lost in the labyrinth of hall and passages, she crossed a sort of vestibule which she did not recognize, thinking to find an exit to the gardens in that direction". Consuelo must be continuously active to find an exit out of the labyrinth which holds her captive. She must listen to her instincts, discover her true role in life: whether to pursue marriage, or become an opera singer. She knows that the road to art is more difficult: "The roads that lead to art", claims Porpora, "are overgrown with thorns, but some beautiful flowers are plucked in them".

Consuelo's active search plunges her in her psychological labyrinth: "After many detours and much retracing of her steps in the inextricable labyrinth of paths in that forest . . . Consuelo found herself on a sort of plateau". The next concentric circle in the labyrinth of her mind is closing in on her. She is about to face a madman, Zdenko, the guardian of the labyrinth. Her state of continuous disorientation is evident. She loses herself quite easily. "As she retracted her steps toward the castle, Consuelo lost herself in reflections". Driven by "all the perseverance of her strong will", Consuelo must visit the underworld of the castle, penetrate her inner self, the deeper and more intricate concentric circles which will lead to the sacred and mysterious center.

Consuelo enters this circle through a cistern, a well and descends into it. "She ventured to descend several steps. The staircase, which seemed to have been built so that one could reach the water at any of its varying levels, was *spiral* in shape, and made of blocks of granite, either set into or cut from the rock. The slimy, slippery steps offered no support, and descended farther than the eyes could see into a terrifying abyss". Consuelo must discover what mysterious revelations are held back and trapped in the very central entrails of the labyrinth. Notice that Consuelo must fight the water which fills the well. In Jungian analysis, Consuelo's journey can be explained psychoanalytically as the rejoining of the anima—Consuelo—(female principle) with the animus—Albert—(male principle). We know that in archetypal language, water is the male principle, while the moon or the night is the female principle. Consuelo enters into the abyss of her psyche at night. This union, or the search of one for the other can be explained as the union and understanding of the conscious and unconscious.

Consuelo's discovery can also be explained by the myth of Orpheus. She must master the obstacles. As Orpheus had to charm the gods with his music, Consuelo likewise charms Zdenko with bohemian songs and by uttering the magical password: "May he who has been wronged salute thee". As a result Zdenko, like Virgil to Dante, becomes her guide. According to Edward Whitmont in his *The Symbolic Quest,* "One of the oldest images of the mystery of life, death, transformation and return is the labyrinth (the individuation path is also like the labyrinthine spiral), in which we fear to lose ourselves".

Consuelo must reconcile the opposite forces that pull her in opposite directions. She must realize her Self, hence reach unity and wholeness of being. In archetypal language, the most symbolic representations of the Self are "images that point to totality and wholeness . . . as well as to a central entity of order and direction. These encompassing images have circular, square, cubic or global shapes or have some other definite or eternal character" (Whitmont). In fact, according to Whitmont, the "individuation process" can be best expressed in terms of concentric circles and labyrinthine structures, for the course of development in the "individuation process" is a movement toward a center that is more adequately depicted in the ancient and medieval (spiral) labyrinth patterns which are found in many places of worship and burial. The labyrinth is one of the oldest symbols; it depicts the way to the unknown center, the mystery of death and rebirth, the risk of the search, the danger of losing the way, the quest, the finding and the ability to return".

This archetypal and psychological odyssey of man's existence translates Consuelo's immersion in the spiral of the interior labyrinth to the central directive focus of her inner self. Once Consuelo has embarked on her descent, the steps that lead to the abyss, she is faced with a series of dark caves, semicircular balustrades, endless winding staircases. She cannot turn back at this point although "the abyss is so deep that one cannot see the water that is swallowed up in it". Consuelo, in search of Albert, who has not been seen for more than nine days, is determined, as if instinctively, to find him. Albert represents for Consuelo man's *esprit de finesse,* the sacred and mysterious world of Art.

The many hazardous and tortuous paths that she must overcome echo the piercing sound, the constant splashing of water, in fact, a turbulence which translates her inner psychological turmoil: "The echoes of the cavern repeat it again and again, and the awesome splashing of the water lasts even longer. One would say that it was the baying of a demonical pack of hounds. A narrow and difficult path skirts the precipice along one of the walls of the grotto and lead to another obscure gallery, in which the handwork of a man ceases entirely, and which turns from the currents of water and their downward plunge to ascend toward higher levels. That is the road that Consuelo must take, there is no other".

Walking amid innumerable obstacles, Consuelo's confusion must be overcome. At the subterranean gateway of her psyche, Consuelo must fulfill Porpora's prophecy, even though she often finds herself in endless impasses: "Those subterranean galleries which opened before her were a freak of nature, and led to culs-de-sac, or to a labyrinth from which she could not find the way out". Consuelo's heroic pilgrimage raises her to the stature of a mythological heroine. She has, after all, the hallmarks of a hero: "So Consuelo plunged into the mysteries of the underground's labyrinth, among those obstacles without number flight was impossible". However, it is not the flight Consuelo wishes. Penetrating the uncanny labyrinth is Consuelo's primary concern. Finally, helped by Zdenko, a modern Charon, or even Ariadne, who offers Consuelo the keys to the three doors watched by the dog Cynabre (reminiscent of the mythological three-headed dragon-tailed dog), Consuelo finally finds Albert at the feet of an altar where mysterious religious ceremonies are held. Consuelo has conquered the underworld. The rescue of Albert may then be easily interpreted as the rescue of artistic principles in man's life: "Like the hero of a fable, Consuelo, had gone down into Tartarus to rescue her friend". Like Orpheus and Eurydice walking towards life "they were beginning a new life together, leaning on each other, not daring to look behind". Clearly, Consuelo's whole voyage is tinted with archetypal symbols. The violin, for example, that Albert plays only in the inner circle of the labyrinth, near the altar, as if in a solemn pagan, even Dionysian ceremony, allows Sand to speculate on the sacredness of art itself. In Albert, Consuelo has finally met her destiny, the world of Art, for, as Porpora claims, "Art is sacred"—to whom Consuelo replies: "If art is sacred, are we not too, who are its priests and its levites?"

Consuelo's acquisition of the sacred knowledge of art gives her an affirmation that her life is better devoted to music. She is going to be the new priestess of the sacred art, for art and religion, as George Sand convincingly writes, are synonymous: "At the dawn of religion, the stage and temple are one and the same sanctuary . . . The arts are born at the altar's foot—Music and poetry are the loftiest expressions of faith, and the woman who is endowed with genius and beauty is priestess, sybil and teacher". However, the road to art is hazardous, for the "apostleship of art is a combat".

Consuelo's marriage to Albert at the end of the novel, before Albert's deathbed, which makes her a virgin widow, can perhaps be explained as Consuelo's marriage to music. That was her destiny, that was the arduous path that she had to follow. Mircea Eliade, speaking of man's reach of the center [in *The Myth of the Eternal Return,* 1974], the conquest of the Self, claims: "The road is arduous, fraught with perils, because it is, in fact, a rite of passage from the profane to the sacred, from the ephemeral and illusory to reality and eternity, from death to life, from man to the divinity. Attaining the center is equivalent to a consecration, and initiation; yesterday's profane and illusory existence gives place to a new, to a life that is real, enduring and effective".

Consuelo leaves the castle to enter the future labyrinth of her career on the way to fame. However, her mind is set that only music can satisfy her. Now Consuelo is on the stage as the Countess of Rudolstadt—in a world of comedy, as Porpora calls it. He comments: "My noble-hearted child, let us walk gravely through this masquerade which is called the world". Another form of labyrinth. (pp. 79-85)

Victor Carrabino, "George Sand's 'Consuelo': The Search for a Soul," in Festschrift Für Nikola R. Pribić, *Hieronymus Verlag Neuried, 1983, pp. 77-85.*

Albert Smith   (essay date 1985)

[*In the essay below, Smith explores elements of fantasy in three of Sand's dramas, delineating the relationship between Sand's plays and prevailing types of comedic theater in the nineteenth century.*]

Among attempts by French authors in the nineteenth century to expand the expressive capabilities of literature, the exploitation of fantasy, especially on the stage, has received scant attention. Though we may find recognition of fantasy in a particular writer like Hugo or Musset, in so far as awareness of a general tendency is concerned we discover next to nothing in scholarly writing. Yet important critics of the time promoted fantasy, and a considerable number of authors resorted to it. Enough dramatists used elements of fantasy to force the conclusion that it had extraordinary expressive potential.

The Romantics in particular recognized the validity of introducing fantasy into literary works. Charles Nodier and Philarète Chasles, early in the Romantic period, pointed to modern man's need to compensate for the mechanization and regularization of life and suggested that fantasy offered a ready means for meeting the threat of rampant positivism. Later, Victor Hugo, in his work on Shakespeare, called attention to fantasy as one of the great sources of artistic inspiration, citing literary creations which are thoroughly false from the standpoint of objective reality, yet eminently true from the standpoint of what they symbolize.

In the theatre, the Romantics exploited two forms of fantasy, especially: the *commedia dell'arte* and a genre qualified as *romanesque*. Théophile Gautier regularly proclaimed his love for a *comédie romanesque* and for plays using elements of the *commedia*. Nerval in his criticism speaks favorably of the former type of play. Gautier successfully tried his hand at a *pièce romanesque* in *Une Larme du diable* and at a play molded on the Italian comedy in *Pierrot posthume*. Hugo, too, when he no longer felt himself hobbled by the constraints of stage production, wrote several plays which fall within the definition of the *romanesque*, for example, *La Forêt mouillée* et *Mangerontils?* It is no wonder that Musset received the acclaim of discerning contemporaries: a number of his comedies have elements which clearly reflect his partiality for fantasy.

The features of the *commedia dell'arte* are well known: stock masks representing fixed social types; improvised plot with the accent on comic episodes which interrupt a more serious action, usually sentimental; a setting defined not by its historical detail but by its functionality; gesture as well as speech as a means for generating laughter. The character of the *comédie romanesque* is less well known. We find the form described most elaborately by Gautier, first in a chapter of *Mademoiselle de Maupin* and subsequently in his criticism. Here, too, the characters represent types: lovers, servants, peasants, nobles and kings, and clowns. These personages have no relation to any known historical period or locale; their extravagant costumes reflect no specific period or country; the rich and fancifully conceived settings resemble no place in the real world. There is thus no attempt to imitate objective reality in the *comédie romanesque*. Similarly, there is no concern for verisimilitude in the development of plot. Gautier rejects the notions of logic and probability, emphasizing that the events of the moment are more important than a tight plot structure leading to a reasonable dénouement. The cause-and-effect principle is thus suspended. Scenes change capriciously. Gratuitous episodes abound. Digressions are frequent; even the author, says Gautier, may intrude for a few moments to woo the heroine in the hero's place. Animals and objects have speaking roles. Indeed, a key notion in Gautier's conception of the *romanesque* is speech. Though the visual is important, it is the verbal aspect that creates the charm of the *comédie romanesque*. Specifically, the form accentuates speech in itself rather than speech serving to advance the action. And in this form of *discours pour le discours,* it is style that counts: the hallmark of the genre is, for Gautier, brilliant expression. The *comédie romanesque* thus rejects imitation of the observed world to rise above crude reality, as Gautier says, "sur les ailes bigarrées de la folie."

One does not generally associate George Sand with literature of this kind. Yet, together with that *esprit engagé* which is one of her principal traits, we find a not insignificant measure of fantasy in her work. I should like to outline here what I perceive to be elements of fantasy in her theatrical production.

I shall consider three works: **Les Vacances de Pandolphe,** a comedy in three acts first performed at the Gymnase Dramatique in March, 1852; **Comme il vous plaira,** an adaptation of Shakespeare's *As You Like It,* presented at the Théâtre Français in April, 1856; and **Le Diable aux champs,** written in the months just preceding Louis-Napoléon's coup and published finally in 1855.

Les Vacances de Pandolphe resembles a standard *commedia dell'arte.* The characters bear names recalling the Italian heritage of the play: Pascariel, Léandre, Pedrolino, Isabelle, Colombine. Though the setting in which they perform is Italian, it is scarcely notable for its realism. Sand insists that the setting be fanciful, in a style reminiscent of Watteau. She likewise rejects realism in costuming.

Certain costumes must also recall Watteau's paintings of characters from the *commedia*. She has the frayed costume of the down-at-the-heels Léandre exaggerate grotesquely the nobleman's proud indigence. In both setting and costume, stylization and fancy are key concepts.

The action of the play is anything but simple. There are at least three separate plots. One deals with Doctor Pandolphe's frustrated attempts to enjoy a restful vacation. Another focuses on the simple Violette's claim to a rich uncle's inheritance. A third plot turns on the love of Pandolphe's gardener, Pedrolino, for Violette. No one action dominates.

Sand shows at least as much interest in the comic elements in her play as in plot or message. As in the traditional *commedia,* humor derives mainly from antic behavior. The character creating most of the comedy is Pedrolino. He is funny because he is consistently clumsy. His efforts to oblige his employer regularly create chaos. Attempting to move a table, he causes Pandolphe to lose his balance. Fanning the dozing doctor, Pedrolino accidentally whacks him in the face and jolts him awake. In a moment of despair, Pedrolino pulls the corner of the tablecloth to dry his tears. Unfortunately, the table is set, and dishes, silver, and food tumble to the floor. One is reminded of modern farce played so amusingly by Peter Sellers in the various Inspector Clouseau films.

Comme il vous plaira is less frankly farcical. The *comédie romanesque* is not necessarily a matter of buffoonery. Those Romantics drawn to the *romanesque* uniformly cited Shakespeare's original as a model, and *As You Like It* has few truly farcical elements.

Like her contemporaries who favored the *comédie romanesque,* Sand was mainly interested in rejecting realism and in exploiting verbal exchange. Her adaptation of Shakespeare's play naturally has features which would have delighted Gautier. The refusal of historicity and local color is as in the original. It is impossible to determine at what historical epoch the action takes place; and Sand gives no clues which allow pinpointing the scene of the events. Moment and milieu have no bearing on the behavior of the characters, who might be acting in any sylvan locale in a remote past.

Though George Sand made a conscious effort to bring more order into her adaptation than Shakespeare had given to his original, plot structure in *Comme il vous plaira* is far from tight. Digressions and gratuitous scenes are the rule. The author pauses, for example, to allow the jester, Pierre Touchard, to philosophize mockingly on human destiny; or she breaks the main action with an amusing scene between Jacques and the exiled duke's official singer—who unwittingly demonstrates that his voice is awful. As in Shakespeare, there are several plots: in addition to the Roland-Rosalinde action, Sand shows particular interest in the relationship between Célia and Jacques, and she is not without concern for Touchard and Audrey, Roland and Olivier, and Jacques and the exiled duke. Though Sand shows more respect for verisimilitude than did her model, she is not a slave to it. The peripeteia which permits the dénouement, for instance, is wholly un-

expected. Duke Frédéric's decision to relinquish his usurped power and to return the ducal throne to his brother, whom he exiled years before, comes as a total surprise. Nothing in his character or career has prepared us for his change of heart.

As for Gautier, so for Sand, the *romanesque* is characterized by its emphasis on speech. The bulk of the action in *Comme il vous plaira* is taken up with verbal exchanges dealing with different forms of love. Célia attempts regularly to tease the misanthropic Jacques out of his mistrust of amorous relationships; Roland frets over his timid love for Rosalinde, who in turn complains of his apparent refusal to express his passion directly to her; Jacques, appropriately, uses the monologue to elaborate his jaded views on intimate human relations and his attraction to the solitary life. Touchard provides a certain verbal comedy with his physical attraction to Audrey. It is these speeches and exchanges that create the interest in Sand's adaptation. The author is only secondarily concerned with a tightly organized plot.

Le Diable aux champs is not wholly a fantasy piece like *Les Vacances de Pandolphe* or *Comme il vous plaira.* Sand was at pains in this "comédie monstre," as she called it, to make her work timely, specifically to evoke French provincial life in the waning days of the Second Republic. With such a plan in mind, it is natural that she should choose the realistic mode by which to treat her subject. The setting of the work is a detailed imitation of a provincial village. The action occurs at a precise moment— September, 1851. The characters belong to recognizable contemporary social classes—nobles, landed gentry, bourgeois, servants, peasants, priests, and artists. These personages allude constantly to the contemporary political and social situations. Both *moment* and *milieu* are shown to have a bearing on their mentality and thus their actions. The realism extends—as in numerous works by George Sand—even to the speech of the characters. As we move among nobles, bourgeois, and peasants, we encounter varying degrees of grammatical correctness in the language being used, so that we are led to see speech, among other elements, as a marker of social position.

Le Diable aux champs is based, then, upon an awareness of class differences in French society, awareness which further betrays a realistic orientation. Yet into this close imitation of real life, Sand introduces notes which have a distinct ring of fantasy. Already in the midst of a realistic action in Part I, she presents two birds commiserating on the difficulties of avian domestic life and, in addition, reinforcing by their behavior before a puppet which personifies Satan, an idea expressed by the artists a few minutes earlier, that the devil no longer frightens anyone, even the birds. Elsewhere other animals speak—spiders, cranes, beetles, dogs—and in Part VII Sand has the marionettes muse on their unusual metaphysical condition.

Fantasy is also visible in Sand's characterization. Ostensibly realistic, Sand's personages have a striking resemblance to types which Gautier recognized in the *comédie romanesque:* romantic young lovers, vagabond ladies, supportive and resourceful handmaids, caustic clowns, simpleminded valets and peasants, gentle and indulgent kings, and motley-dressed *graciosos.* As in *Comme il vous plaira,* Sand brings on stage in *Le Diable aux champs* several young couples in love: Diane de Noirac and Gérard de Mireville, nobles; Florence and Jenny, from the middle class; and Pierre and Maniche, peasants. We recognize in the courtesan Myrtho the vagabond lady who here, on her own account, has come from Paris in search of the lover who abandoned her. Diane de Noirac's servant Jenny is clearly a loyal and resourceful handmaid. Her lack of education and position in no way prevent her organizing a successful strategy to save her mistress from social disgrace. Were it not for the seriousness with which Sand treats the subject and for the realistic context, we might easily imagine ourselves following the actions of a maid-servant of certain earlier comedies not without kinship to the *romanesque.*

In *Le Diable aux champs* there are peasants aplenty, some evidently simple individuals unaware of what is going on around them. Sand's character Jacques even resembles the misanthropic personage of the same name in *Comme il vous plaira* in his cynicism and his detachment from ordinary human relations. The artists are nothing other than realistically drawn *graciosos,* with their bent for merry-making and wit.

Likewise, the actions of these characters may be seen as partaking of the *comédie romanesque.* The amorous situation of the various lovers is romantic in the extreme. It is principally love that guides them. Diane de Noirac seeks perfect satisfaction in love. At the beginning of the work, Jenny is represented as unconsolable at having been abandoned by her fiancé. Florence has followed her to support her when she falls too deeply into despair. Myrtho lives to take revenge on Diane for having captured her lover, Gérard. The work ends much like *Comme il vous plaira,* indeed, much like the archetypal comedy, with the definitive joining of each set of lovers in a festive union.

Other aspects of *Le Diable aux champs* belong less exclusively to the fantasy theatre: the complex plot, with its plurality of sub-plots; the zig-zagging movement of the action, reflecting George Sand's rejection of linear structure; and the emphasis on verbal exchange. These, as they are used in *Le Diable aux champs,* cannot be conceived as the sole property of fantasy. As Hassan El Nouty has pointed out, the same features occur in Romantic attempts to achieve in the theatre something wholly contrary to the *romanesque,* an ever greater illusion of reality, as evidenced in Vitet, Monnier, and the Musset of *Lorenzaccio.* On balance, we must grant that *Le Diable aux champs* is closer to the realistic than to the *romanesque.* At the same time, because of its evident resemblances to the *comédie romanesque,* we have grounds for viewing the work as a variant of the fantasy theatre.

George Sand was well aware of problems facing the dramatist. She was certainly conscious of the expressive potential of fantasy. Numerous ideas advanced in her works relate directly to what we understand as fantasy theatre. When the artists in *Le Diable aux champs* discuss the odd coloration of objects on their sets and the unusual play of perspective on their miniature stage, they are in effect underscoring Sand's perception that art is really *artifice,* having nothing to do with an exact reproduction of reality. That the *commedia* which they present on their puppet stage is set in no specific time or locale shows that Sand agreed with other theorists of fantasy theatre on the matter of setting: it should be universalized, in order to remove it from what Gautier had already called crude reality, and what Sand herself termed "le réel aride."

Sand sought to avoid the imitation of a gloomy positive reality in most of her dramatic works. She defended strenuously her idealization of character, emphasizing her preference for seeing the world through rose-colored glasses rather than through the mud-stained magnifying glass of the realists. She found particular charm in animals and objects with speaking roles. These, she said, give a peculiar fairy-tale quality to the play which contributes to removing the spectator from the real world. Like Gautier, she preferred types to individuals. She recognized in particular the interest of types from the old *commedia dell'arte:*

> Leurs masques exprimaient des types psychologiques. Pantalon n'était pas seulement un disgrâcieux cacochyme, c'était surtout un avare et un vaniteux. Tartaglia n'eût pas amusé une heure, s'il n'eût été que bègue et myope. C'était un sot et un méchant sot. Le public des atellanes lui-même . . . voulait deviner l'homme moral à travers l'homme physique.

For these types are symbols of eternal human attitudes, of the human psyche itself.

As for plot, Sand repeatedly stressed her attraction to an unhurried, digressive action, which she opposed to the tight linear structure of plays enjoying popular success in her day. A leisurely action, in her opinion, allowed the spectator time to reflect on the characters and events in action on the stage.

Like Gautier before her, Sand saw little validity in the logical development of plot. She has the artists in *Le Diable aux champs* emphasize that the dénouement need in no way determine the action which precedes it. What she particularly liked in the *commedia dell'arte* was its improvisational quality, its lack of predetermined plan. It is thus natural that the *commedia* with puppets performed in *Le Diable aux champs* relies heavily on improvisation. Even the overture music is improvised: "L'ouverture se compose d'un tambour, d'une trompette, d'un mirliton, d'un flageolet et de deux couvercles de casserole, jouant tous ensemble, chacun dans un ton ou dans un rythme différent." To underscore that the *commedia* has no rigid outline to which the actors must adhere, Sand makes the action of the puppet play subject even to external circumstances. That a spectator's comments cause the action to veer from its course is simply a veiled theoretical statement.

We can thus appreciate Sand's discomfort when she considered Shakespeare's *As You Like It* for presentation on the French stage in 1856. It appears to have been her recognition that the public would have rejected Shakespeare's structural liberties that led her to make sometimes major changes in the plot of the English original. As she said, she felt herself obliged to reorganize Shakespeare's material, so as to make the beauties of his delightful yet untidy vision accessible to reason, "cette raison française dont nous sommes si vains et qui nous prive de tant d'originalités non moins précieuses."

Like her contemporaries, George Sand was ultimately interested in the function of fantasy. Philarète Chasles and Gautier before her had expressed their distaste for the material and moral reality around them and for attempts to depict that reality in books and on the stage. Sand, too, was repulsed by contemporary efforts to imitate what she saw as the sordidness of the world, to present to the public, as she said, "une daguerréotype de ses misères et de ses plaies." Also like her contemporaries, she recognized in certain types of literature a means of escape from the drabness of the world. She speaks of a basic human need for fiction, for illusion, in which the individual may forget, for a time, positive realities. Yet, whereas Chasles especially saw fiction only as a means of escape, Sand viewed it in a more affirmative light, emphasizing that fiction, whatever its form, offered the individual another existence, gave him an opportunity to live for a while an impersonal life, detached from material preoccupations. In the kind of fiction which attracted her she found a peculiar brand of pleasure:

> Le plaisir honnête, désintéressé en ce sens qu'il doit être une communion des intelligences; le plaisir vrai avec son sens naïf et sympathique, son modeste enseignement caché sous le rire et la fantaisie. . . . L'amusement proprement dit est pour chacun de nous un joli petit idéal à chercher ou à réaliser au coin de son feu, à la place du jeu où l'on s'étiole et de la causerie où l'on se dispute quand on ne dit pas du mal de tous ses amis. Trouvons autre chose pour nos enfants, n'importe quoi, des comédies, des charades, des lectures plaisantes et douces, des marionnettes, des récits, des contes, tout ce que vous voudrez, mais quelque chose qui nous enlève à nos passions, à nos intérêts matériels, à nos rancunes, à ces tristes haines de famille qu'on appelle questions politiques, religieuses et philosophiques. . . .

The value of pleasure is thus far from empty. Not only does it raise us out of our material concerns; it also teaches us. And here is where we discover the true and enduring character of George Sand. She always viewed literature—fiction as she called it—as a tool for edification. She was unequivocal in assigning this function to dramatic art: "les fictions scéniques n'existent qu'à condition d'enseigner."

An educational aim is clear in the three works under consideration. This is not necessarily a specific lesson which may be drawn from the actions which Sand represents. Her aim is rather the promotion of sympathy for certain moral qualities. Underlying each work—*Les Vacances de Pandolphe* as much as *Comme il vous plaira* and *Le Diable aux champs*—is an unspoken but, nevertheless, discernible respect for uprightness and selflessness, for goodness, honesty, and loyalty—in short for Eros. The theatre of fantasy, as much as any other dramatic form—perhaps more so than many—offered George Sand a means for educating, for leading her reader or spectator out of material preoccupations toward virtue. (pp. 160-68)

Albert Smith, "Theatre," in George Sand: Collected Essays, *edited by Janis Glasgow, The Whitston Publishing Company, 1985, pp. 160-71.*

Kathryn J. Crecelius   (essay date 1987)

[*In the following essay, Crecelius analyzes the controversial nature of* Lélia, *commenting in particular on its concern with the difficulties encountered by a woman artist in the male dominated society of the nineteenth century.*]

Both *Indiana* and *Valentine* firmly established Sand's reputation as a writer. The beauty of Sand's prose was hailed, and her criticisms of men, marriage, and society, tolerantly approved. She was, after all, a member of the iconoclastic romantic generation that had brought new and daring themes to French literature. *Lélia* received a very different reception from that of the first two works. The reaction was sharply mixed, with Capo de Feuillide writing a particularly vituperative attack on the novel that led Sand's friend Gustave Planche to fight a duel with the critic.

Although there was almost universal agreement that the style of *Lélia* was beautiful—"Otherwise, in no other of her novels has the author shown more magic and charm of style"—the form and the ideas were either lauded or castigated. Planche, who had had a strong influence on the evolution of the novel, assured readers of the *Revue des Deux Mondes* that *Lélia* "will begin an explosive revolution in contemporary literature and will give the death blow to purely *visible* poetry." Musset, in a review he never published, denied that *Lélia* would produce a revolution; however, he found the novel original and praised it highly in a letter to Sand as a work that defined her as an author, not a lady novelist. Sainte-Beuve wrote a fairly balanced review for *Le National* and concluded that writing *Lélia* was a courageous act for Sand. "Whatever you might think, *Lélia,* with its faults and excesses, is a book that largely deserved to be written. If the reports of the moment are against it, the very violence of this clamor is enough proof of the audaciousness of the enterprise."

The negative critics did not mince words in excoriating Sand and her novel. *Le Petit Poucet* called *Lélia* a "work of lewdness and cynicism," while the relentless Capo de Feuillide wrote that the novel contained "the prostitution of soul and body." Both he and Léon Gozlan felt that *Lélia* was not a work to be read by women, for it would contaminate them. Since Sand herself was a woman, the implication in these criticisms is that she was somehow corrupt. In fact, Capo de Feuillide compared her to Sade!

The question of the author's gender intervened in the critique of *Lélia* in a different way than in the past. Early critics knew for the most part that G(eorge)(s) Sand was a woman, although some thought they could discern male and female hands at work in *Indiana,* probably because they were aware of her former collaboration with Sandeau. Sand's gender did not play a large role in the evaluation of *Indiana* and *Valentine;* if anything, the fact of her being a woman brought her sympathy or was seen as the cause of her sensitivity to certain issues. With *Lélia,* the situation changed. *Le Petit Poucet* doubted that the author of such a novel could be a woman. The *Journal général de la littérature française* ascribed *Lélia* to a male author and thought that the work would perhaps not be of interest to women. On the other hand, Planche felt that women especially would find in *Lélia* their own history and see the novel as an apologia for their suffering and helplessness, not an accusation against them. Jules Janin published a long article in *L'Artiste* in 1836, reprinted in other periodicals as well, in which he attributes male and female genders to Sand and describes *Lélia* as the work of a woman against women:

> Cette fois, George Sand quittant ce chaste manteau viril dont elle s'était enveloppée avec tant de courage et d'énergie, a voulu se montrer plus qu'une femme, c'est-à-dire dans sa pensée, deux fois plus qu'un homme, et elle est tombée dans les plus graves excès. . . . George Sand, redevenu une femme, dans ce livre qui est écrit contre les femmes, devait ainsi porter la peine de ce déguisement.

> This time, George Sand, taking off the vast virile coat in which she had enveloped herself with so much courage and energy, wanted to show herself more than a woman, that is, in her thought, twice as much as a man, and she has fallen into the gravest excesses. . . . George Sand, having gone back to being a woman, in this book which is written against women, should thus pay the penalty of this disguise.

Sainte-Beuve also devotes fully one-third of his article in the *National* to the question of women authors, whom he applauds for their efforts to win more respect and less idolization for their sex, at least as long as women do not enter *en masse* into writing as a profession. "We especially like to see a noble effort on the part of women to enter into a more equal intellectual partnership with men, to handle all sorts of ideas and to express themselves when necessary in more serious language."

A woman's book, a novel that would corrupt women, a young man's scorn of life—is *Lélia* any of this? How could readers come to such diverse views of the same work? What exactly was *Lélia,* and how can we read the novel today?

Lélia was originally in form and ideas. Both "roman" and "roman-poème," as Sainte-Beuve called it, *Lélia* was and is difficult to classify. It has no conventional plot, particularly as compared with the elaborate plots of Sand's previous work. As Shelley Temchin points out, certain events occupy a disproportionate amount of space, while others are glossed over, so that narrative time (*Erzählzeit*) and time narrated (*erzählte Zeit*) stand in strange relation to each other. *Lélia* is not narrated by one narrator. As in a classical play, each character is allowed several monologues, while the dialogues become *dialogues de sourds.*

The novel is divided into five parts. Part I is mostly an exchange of supposed letters between Lélia and Sténio, with occasional third-person narration. Part II contains a conversation between Magnus and Sténio and more exchanges between Lélia and Sténio. The last two "chap-

ters" or subdivisions of this part are again narrated in the third person and describe Bambucci's ball and Lélia's meeting with Pulchérie. In Part III, Lélia speaks almost exclusively while Pulchérie listens. Part IV is the shortest and consists of third-person narration and letters between Lélia and Sténio. Part V contains the most sustained third-person narration. In *Lélia,* the female character speaks extensively in her own name, for the first time since Aurore Dudevant's early works, and is given responsibility for her own story. Although the first-person narration and minimal novelistic form and content make it easy to identify Lélia with Sand, it should be remembered that however much Lélia derives from her creator, she is a fictional character. As Sand wrote to Sainte-Beuve while the novel was in progress: " . . . [D]on't completely confuse the man [*sic*] with his suffering. . . . [I]n reality, the man is often less than his pain and thus less poetic, . . . and less damned than his demon."

Part prose-poem, related to the epistolary novel, philosophical meditations, gothic novel—*Lélia* is all this and more. Sand's sources were many: Byron is mentioned by several critics; Anne Radcliffe, whom she had read in the convent, is indubitably present; Sénancour and Nodier, as Pierre Reboul exhaustively (and exhaustingly) documents, formed the backbone of her novel. Staël's *Corinne,* which Reboul mentions in passing, was surely a greater influence than has been imagined. Yet *Lélia* resembles none of the works Sand drew upon; she did not improve on any one form, but melded several into a wholly new book whose discontinuous, fragmentary form mirrors its raw emotional content.

Like Corinne, Lélia is an artist. Her family and origins are mysterious, as are Corinne's. There is an explicit comparison between the two women established during the ball scene early in the novel: "The dying Corinne must have been plunged into this same mournful attention when she heard her last poems being declaimed at the Capitol by a young girl." In form, there is also a similarity between the two novels, for *Corinne* is itself an original work, part travelogue, part traditional *récit.* The long epistolary monologues of *Lélia*—if one can so describe the passages, much more than letters, where each character speaks in turn— are reminiscent of Corinne's descriptions of Rome's antiquities.

Corinne's art is clearly defined, if imperfectly portrayed; she is an *improvisatrice* whose oral, spontaneous poetry is by its very nature ill suited to reproduction in a written work. It is always difficult to depict a writer convincingly in a literary work, for unless the author is particularly adept, the character's work can be hard to judge. For three hundred years, critics have been arguing over whether Oronte's sonnet in Molière's *Misanthrope* is a good or bad poem. In *Lélia,* the song Sténio declaims in "Le Vin" has been attributed to Musset, Sainte-Beuve, Ajasson de Grandsagne, or another of Sand's friends. Pierre Reboul also diplomatically states that the verses are not so good that they couldn't be attributed to Sand herself, for she had written occasional poems in the convent, but she seems to have lacked true talent in this literary genre alone. Sand has cleverly avoided the problem of *showing*

Lélia's artistry (to use James's term) by simply calling her an artist without being more precise; the number of times the word "poète" appears in the text, as well as the fact that Lélia writes to Sténio, makes it a likely assumption that Lélia was a writer, if not literally a poet. Lélia is an Artist, a woman artist who represents all forms of artistic endeavor and all exceptional women whose gifts put them sometimes above, often below, the rest of humanity, but surely outside of the usual social circles.

As has been recognized since the novel's publication, *Lélia* owes much to Byron. Planche calls the novel a cross between *Manfred* and Plato's *Phaedo*. Musset found certain pages as beautiful as *Lara,* while Chateaubriand wrote to Sand that she would be the Lord Byron of France. Lélia is a female Byronic hero, a Byronic heroine. She is larger than life, a type, rather than a mimetically *vraisemblable* character, as Reboul insists too often in his edition. She stands alone, unique and exceptional in a changing, disappointing world. She is hypersensitive and, being capable of much, desires more. "Poetry had created other faculties in me, immense, magnificent, and which nothing on earth could satisfy." Like the Byronic hero, too, Lélia is possessed of "heroic Satanism," in Peter Thorslev's phrase. From the very first page of the novel, Sténio asks Lélia if she is an "angel or a demon," a nonhuman creature. In Part IV, he damns her as diabolical for having united him with Pulchérie.

If Lélia derives from Byron's creations, as well as from Faust, with whom she compares herself, she is also firmly fixed in a well-known line of specifically French heroes, the romantic sufferers of the *mal du siècle,* particularly René, Obermann, and Nodier's characters. *Lélia* is a *roman de l'individu,* a personal cry of despair from one who does not fit into society and who sees no way out of her dilemma. Just as Lélia is the first French Byronic heroine, *Lélia* represents the first time the French *mal du siècle* is expressed by a female character. Although Staël was the first woman author to describe the malady of melancholy in *De la littérature* and depicted Oswald as its victim in *Corinne,* neither Corinne nor Delphine really embodies the *mal du siècle* except in the sense that all women were excluded from society and power, and many felt keenly their status as outsiders, unable to act or participate fully in the world. Sand, of course, does insist sharply on this aspect of Lélia's problem, but she does so in a work in which, as in *René* and *Obermann,* the voices of the individual characters and philosophical themes take precedence over fictional plot. Staël's aims were clearly different from Sand's in *Lélia,* even if *Corinne* did serve on several levels as a model. Sand thus arrogated the major theme of both the first and second generation of romantics to herself and to women, and the greatness of *Lélia* lies in its dialectic of general, human despair and that specific only to women. Furthermore, *Lélia* integrates all the separate causes for dissatisfaction, adding literal physical impotence to the spiritual and social powerlessness evinced by previous heroes.

Lélia returns to *Indiana* in its criticism of love, religion, and society as oppressors of all, but of women especially. Sand's portrayal of love in *Lélia* does not differ substan-

tially from that in her previous works. In *Lélia,* though, Sand has made bold to put her critiques in the mouth of a female character, rather than showing her opinions indirectly through the plot or narration.

Lélia speaks specifically of what is known today as "romantic love," that form of passion invented by the post-Rousseau, romantic generation.

> C'est pourquoi nous cherchons le ciel dans une créature semblable à nous, et nous dépensons pour elle toute cette haute énergie qui nous avait été donnée pour un plus noble usage. Nous refusons à Dieu le sentiment de l'adoration. . . . Nous le reportons sur un être incomplet et faible, qui devient le dieu de notre culte idolâtre.

> That is why we seek heaven in a creature like ourselves, and we expend on this creature all that high energy we've been given to use more nobly. We refuse God the emotion of adoration. . . . We transfer it to an incomplete, feeble human being who becomes the god of our idolatrous cult.

This god is always revealed to be a false god and is overthrown, broken, only to be replaced by another, and yet another. When she recalls her first love, Lélia tells Pulchérie that the beloved became the focus of all her energies: "[I] carried over onto him the enthusiasm that I had had for the other creations of the Divinity." She goes on to describe a particularly female way of loving, one that is reminiscent of Indiana's tortured and misguided love for Raymon.

> C'était un état inexprimable de douleur et de joie, de désespoir et d'énergie. Mon âme orageuse se plaisait à ce ballottement funeste qui l'usait sans fruit et sans retour. . . . Il lui fallait des obstacles, des fatigues, des jalousies dévorantes à concentrer. . . . C'était une carrière, une gloire; homme, j'eusse aimé les combats . . . ; peut-être l'ambition de régner par l'intelligence, de dominer les autres hommes par des paroles puissantes, m'eût-elle souri aux jours de ma jeunesse. Femme, je n'avais qu'une destinée noble sur la terre, c'était d'aimer.

> I experienced an inexpressible state of sadness and joy, of despair and energy. My afflicted soul took pleasure in this ill-starred tossing that consumed me fruitlessly. . . . I demanded obstacles, fatigues, devouring jealousies to repress. . . . This was a glorious career. Had I been a man, I would have loved combat. . . . Perhaps in my youth I might have sought to reign by intelligence and to dominate others by powerful speeches. As a woman, I had only one noble destiny on earth, which was to love.

Love is woman's only vocation, whereas men can choose combat or power; men can produce but women merely waste their energies. When Lélia in the monastery imagines death near, she sees it as a "death worthy of heroes and saints," a glorious end, not a servile one. In particular, men can dominate by their words, a poignant admission that she does not see her own writing as having the same impact as a man's. Indeed, although Sand was enormously influential, even outside of France, her force would not be felt for several years, since she had only been writing for the public for a year and a half. Yet Sand might already have felt that her first two novels were too well received, that male critics were patting her on the head rather than helping put into effect her program of social reform.

Woman in love is masochistic and self-effacting; she cannot assert herself in the relationship. "I know that I have used up my strength in devotion, that I have abjured my pride, effaced my existence behind another's." Further on, she states: "The more he made me feel his domination, the more I cherished it, the greater pride I took in wearing my fetters," the word fetters (*chaîne*) being the one that appears in **Indiana** as the synonym for marriage both with Delmare and (potentially) with Raymon. As in **Indiana,** too, Lélia discovers that her masochism is scornfully received by men and not appreciated, so that she derives neither personal satisfaction nor outside regard for her self-abnegation. The flaw in this model of woman's submersion in her lover and suppression of her own self stems from the inevitable resurfacing of what Lélia calls egotism, but what more properly might be termed self-love, as opposed to selfishness. This self-love is not limited to women but applies to both sexes. ". . . [H]uman egotism is ferocious, it is indomitable. . . ." Lélia articulates the dialectic of love as defined by the culture, in which the needs of the self are at war with the demands of the other: "[I] felt that one could both love another, to the point of submitting to him, and love oneself, to the point of hating him who subjugates us." For women, no equilibrium between these conflicting urges is thought necessary or desirable by society.

Woman's needs extend beyond the spiritual to the physical, as anyone who has ever heard of **Lélia** knows, for the scandal surrounding the novel was due largely to its sexual frankness. While literature had portrayed women as sexual beings before (Corinne is a perfect example of a sympathetic character who is evidently sexually experienced), Lélia is the first woman to speak of her sex life and, what is more, to do so in a critical way. Lélia launches two accusations against men's bedroom technique. Men are brutal, interested only in their own pleasure, and do not hesitate to engage in what today is called "conjugal rape" to satisfy themselves. "But he would pursue me, and claimed that he did not want to have been awakened for no reason. He savored his fierce pleasure on the breast of a woman who had fainted and was half dead." This last image recalls that of the idiot Denise, attacked by Horace in **Rose et Blanche. Lélia** expresses the same fears of male sexual power and physical force as **Rose et Blanche.** Once, when Sténio abandons his passive stance and takes Lélia in his arms, forcing her to kiss him, Lélia pushes him away and says: "Leave me alone, I don't like you when you are like this!" Later, after Sténio's death, Lélia recalls the past and her feelings for him. "I would have liked to be your mother and be able to clasp you in my arms without awakening in you a man's desires."

The corollary of male crudeness is the lack of sexual pleasure and fulfillment felt by women. "When he was asleep, satisfied and gratified, I remained immobile and dismayed at his side." It is not that women do not feel desire, nor is it their fault that they cannot respond sexually; rather, men are indifferent to women's needs. This is the crucial distinction between Lélia and Balzac's Foedora, with whom Reboul compares Lélia. Balzac criticizes Foedora's coquetry and coldness; she makes a virtue out of her frigidity and uses it as a weapon against men. This image is that of the man-eater and man-hater, common in our culture. Sand shows a woman who wants to feel sexual pleasure but to whom it is denied and who therefore loses all hope of ever finding satisfaction. Surely Sand's negative depiction of men's lack of sensitivity and inability to please women must have insulted and infuriated the French male critical fraternity, who prided themselves on their prowess in love and contributed heavily to the excoriation of the novel and its author.

By the end of the novel, Sténio has come to much the same conclusions as Lélia regarding woman's condition. In the "Don Juan" section of Part V, he expresses his disillusionment with debauchery and with women; yet in accusing woman of being merely a figment of man's imagination and of having the potential to be as unfaithful as man, he nonetheless repeats Lélia's earlier arguments about the conflict between masochism and self-love in woman's soul. Sténio points out that don juanism is based on the man's eternal conquest of a willing victim and insists that woman's own desires and demands will not remain repressed but will eventually burst forth. He apostrophizes Don Juan:

> Avais-tu lu quelque part dans les Conseils de Dieu que la femme est une chose faite pour le plaisir de l'homme, incapable de résistance ou de changement? Pensais-tu que cette perfection idéale de renoncement existait sur la terre et devait assurer l'inépuisable renouvellement de tes joies?

> Did you read somewhere in the Counsels of God that woman is a thing made for man's pleasure, incapable of resistance or change? Did you think that this ideal womanly perfection of renunciation existed on earth and would assure the inexhaustible renewal of your joys?

Sténio has discovered the other side of Lélia's dilemma, namely that if masochism is untenable, so is sadism. Just as Lélia was not grandiose in her self-denial, as Pulchérie tells her, but merely foolish, Sténio and his ilk are not heroes and conquerors, but merely libertines who are rightly condemned. Although Sténio's words have a further structural function in the novel, they complete the portrait developed by Sand of love as total misunderstanding between the sexes.

Because of her lofty talents and unusual sensibility, Lélia cannot find refuge in the kind of love available in the culture. Nor is prostitution the answer, although Pulchérie finds her own justification as a courtesan. Like Lélia the artist, Pulchérie the courtesan is presented without elaborate explanation. We see her at the ball, surrounded by admirers, and later in her villa; although the ignominy and opprobrium attached to prostitutes are alluded to, they are never shown in the novel. Pulchérie simply *is* a courtesan and is neither castigated nor punished. Unlike Manon

Lescaut, who paid for her profligate ways with her death, or Hugo's repentant heroines such as Marion Delorme, Pulchérie neither dies nor repents but simply lives her life as she knows how, doing good where she can and taking her pleasure, physical and spiritual, when possible. This positive, unembarrassed, and nonjudgmental depiction of the courtesan departs sharply from those of prostitution before or after, at least until Colette, whose Léa of the *Chéri* novels is as unsentimentally and unapologetically drawn as Pulchérie. Sand's perspective differs from the male viewpoint, in which the courtesan is a danger to society and the family and must be neutralized, either through repentance, death, or social exclusion; her creation of Pulchérie contributed not a little to the controversy surrounding the novel.

The traditional distinction between "good" women and "bad" does not exist in *Lélia.* In a phrase that anticipates Proudhon's famous dictum "housewife or courtesan," but in an entirely opposite spirit, Pulchérie assimilates lovers, mothers, and courtesans, "three conditions of woman's destiny that no woman can escape, whether she sells herself to a man as a prostitute or as a wife, by a marriage contract." Pulchérie even goes so far as to suggest that the prostitute is superior to the mother, whom society reinforces in her choice of career while the prostitute is an outcast despite the fact that her profession is utilized, even made necessary, by that same society. It is as outsiders that Pulchérie and Lélia find their spiritual as well as real sisterhood, for neither is accepted by proper society. Pulchérie, though, has created a fulfilling life for herself within her own sphere, and like Trenmor, the other character of the novel who has found peace and equilibrium by circumscribing his life, serves as both conscience and reproach to Lélia, who will not bend and cannot compromise, and thus is consumed with regret and impotence. Yet it is clear that it is not Lélia's fault, but society's, that the exceptional woman cannot find an acceptance of her gifts and a match for her soul; the narrator states that the crowd at Spuela's ball was offended by Lélia's independence. The courtesan, the mother, and the lover, whatever the hardships of their lives, are happier than the woman artist.

I never asked myself why I wanted this or that. The inner me always proudly answered: Because I want it. That said everything.

—George Sand, as quoted in Ruth Jordan's George Sand: A Biography, *1976.*

Like love, religion offers little solace to women, for the church is a profoundly misogynist institution, as *Rose et Blanche* and *Indiana* had already shown. On her supposed deathbed, Lélia is refused absolution by Magnus, who denies her a place in heaven or hell. In any case, Lélia does not believe in the trappings of religion and thus cannot ac-

cept Pulchérie's suggestion that she enter a convent if she cannot make a life for herself in the world. It is a measure of the gulf between the two editions of *Lélia* that in the later one, Lélia becomes an abbess. Magnus, the priest maddened by his lust for Lélia, calls her the enemy and strangles her while repeating words of exorcism, convinced she is Satan. In Magnus's tortured mind, Lélia is a temptress and the test of his faith, a test he fails every time, to the point of doubting the existence of God. Magnus presents Lélia as a "hideous monster, a harpy," and imagines her as a succubus who entices him in his bed. This depiction of woman as the source of evil and sexual debasement is an old one in the church, going back to Saint Paul. While a clear criticism of the effects of priestly celibacy, which is openly reproved by Lélia in Part V, *Lélia* also demonstrates how women are blamed by religion for the effects they produce in men and condemned by these same men as unnatural.

Sténio, too, sees Lélia as a monster. When she describes the monster of the Apocalypse, the Whore of Babylon riding a hydra, Sténio exclaims, "Are you not this unfortunate and terrible apparition?" Lélia tells Trenmor that for Sténio, she is a "monstrous exception," who enables him to believe in his own dreams as normal and usual.

Viewed as an oddity by Magnus and Sténio, Lélia becomes a monster in her own as well as in society's eyes. She makes the connection explicit in Part III, where she describes her stay in an abandoned monastery, ornamented with "these monstrous sculptures with which Catholicism used to adorn its places of worship." Like her in her impotence, these grotesques are imprisoned in stone, images of desire and fury unable to move or act.

> Au-dessous de moi, ces bizarres allégories allongeaient leurs têtes noircies par le temps et semblaient comme moi se pencher vers la plaine pour regarder silencieusement couler les flots, les siècles et les générations. Ces guivres couvertes d'écailles, ces lézards au tronc hideux, ces chimères pleines d'angoisses, tous ces emblèmes du péché, de l'illusion et de la souffrance, vivaient avec moi d'une vie fatale, inerte, indestructible. . . . [J]e m'identifiais avec ces images d'une lutte éternelle entre la douleur et la nécessité, entre la rage et l'impuissance.

> Beneath me these bizarre allegories stretched out their heads, blackened by time. They seemed to stretch toward the plain and silently to watch the flow of waves, centuries, and generations. These fantastic scaly serpents, these lizards with their hideous bodies, these chimeras full of anguish, all these emblems of sin, illusion, and suffering lived a life that was inert and indestructible. . . . [I] identified myself with these images of eternal struggle between suffering and necessity, between rage and impotence.

Lélia, in her song in Part II called "A Dieu," asks God why he created her a woman, only to turn her to stone. The image is a tragic inversion of Galatea's transformation from Pygmalion's stone sculpture into a live woman. In *Lélia* a woman becomes frozen, useless to others and herself; in *André,* Sand will create a further variant of this legend, the awakening of a woman who becomes not her creator's equal but his superior. Sténio evokes Pygmalion directly in Part V, when he asks: "Why should I henceforth bend my knee before this marble idol? Even if I had Pygmalion's burning glance and the gods' assent to animate her, what would I do with her?" Reboul sees the word "stone" as an allusion to Lélia's "frigidity," but it is wrong to limit Lélia to a mere reference to sexual dysfunction in this passage, as she so obviously places her insufficiencies in a social and artistic context.

Lélia speaks specifically of her soul, not her body: "Is that what is called a poet's soul? . . . O life, o torment! to aspire to everything and to grasp nothing, to understand everything and possess nothing!" She longs to feel, but she also wishes to act, to be able to use her gifts. She does not know why she has been chosen to suffer. "If this is the fate of the chosen, let it be sweet and let me bear it without suffering; if it is a life of punishment, why have you inflicted it on me?" Her invocation to God is followed by a section entitled "Dans le Désert," in which Lélia, who has become a female Christ figure, a prophet of doom who is unheeded, paints a dismal picture of civilization. The world is old and exhausted, and its population does not become better with progress. "The arts, industry and science, the whole scaffolding of civilization, what are they if not the continued effort of human weakness to hide its evils and cover its misery?" Man and nature are in conflict, with man despoiling beauty and creating chaos out of God's order. ". . . [W]e couldn't spend three days here without spoiling the vegetation and polluting the air. . . . You would call it making a garden." Lélia foresees the results of the Industrial Revolution in the pollution and destruction of nature: ". . . [T]his wild valley . . . blossoms beautiful and proud without dreaming that in a single day the plow and the hundred-armed monster called industry could rip open its breast to steal its treasures. . . . " This is not the picture of lush nature, either on the île Bourbon or in the Berry, and of unconventional marriages breaking down class barriers and creating new wealth and prosperity; rather, it is an apocalyptic vision of a world beyond redemption. Again the word "monster" appears alongside the image of the rape of nature perpetrated by progress.

Decidedly, Sand's imagination was obsessed with the unnatural while she wrote *Lélia.* The world as she described it is filled with horrible creatures and suffering; even the warm, meridional regions commonly thought to be paradisiacal are ruled by ferocious, bloodthirsty animals. Humans are themselves compared to animals, and their anxieties described as grotesques. Not only do people pillage their environment, but they flay animals to use the skins and feathers for clothing and covering. In a passage that might have influenced Baudelaire and that anticipates Freud's work on neuroses and the unconscious, Lélia characterizes the poet's imagination as necrophilic, teratogenic:

> Ce que les peintres et les poètes ont inventé de plus hideux dans les fantaisies grotesques de leur imagination et, il faut bien le dire, ce qui nous apparaît le plus souvent dans le cauchemar, c'est un sabat de cadavres vivants, de squelettes d'animaux, décharnés, sanglants, avec des er-

> reurs monstrueuses, des superpositions bizarres, des têtes d'oiseau sur des troncs de cheval, des faces de crocodile sur des corps de chameau; c'est toujours un pêle-mêle d'ossements, une orgie de la peur qui sent le carnage et des cris de douleur, des paroles de menace proférées par des animaux mutilés.

The most hideous things poets and painters have invented in their grotesque fantasies also appear most often, it must be said, in our nightmares. We dream of witches' sabbaths of living corpses, animal skeletons, emaciated, bloody, with monstrous deformities and bizarre superpositions— bird heads on horse trunks, crocodile faces on camel bodies; there are heaps of bones, it is an orgy of fear that smells of carnage and the cries of suffering, the threats proffered by mutilated animals.

Lélia describes what can be termed the collective unconscious detailed by artists and dreams:

> Croyez-vous que les rêves soient une pure combinaison du hasard? Ne pensez-vous pas qu'en dehors des lois d'association et des habitudes consacrées chez l'homme par le droit et par le pouvoir, il peut exister en lui de secrets remords, vagues, instinctifs, que nul ordre d'idées reçues n'a voulu avouer ou énoncer et qui se révèlent par les terreurs de la superstition ou les hallucinations du sommeil? Alors que les moeurs, l'usage et la croyance ont détruit certaines réalités de notre vie morale, l'empreinte en est restée dans un coin du cerveau et s'y réveille quand les autres facultées intelligentes s'endorment.

Do you think that dreams are a pure combination of chance? Don't you think that outside of the laws of association and the habits that man endows with right and power, there can exist in him secret, vague, instinctive remorse which he has not wanted to admit rationally and which reveals itself through the terrors of superstition or the hallucinations of sleep? Although customs and belief have destroyed certain realities of our moral life, the imprint remains in a corner of the brain and awakens when the other intelligent faculties sleep.

In *Histoire de ma vie,* Sand pursues this syncretic thought when she asks: "Is the life of the individual not the summary of the life of the species?" Here, the collective life is the terrifying underside of the mind's capacity. The woman artist not only is a monster; she creates monsters in her language, in her imagination; her work, by extension, must also be seen as monstrous. Sand, like her British and American contemporaries, fits the pattern discerned by Sandra Gilbert and Susan Gubar of the social and self-image of the woman writer as monster giving birth to unhealthy progeny.

Lélia thus repeats in radically intensified form Aurore Dudevant's doubts about her career as an artist, expressed in her very first works. Despite the acclaim awarded to *Indiana* and *Valentine,* Sand obviously did not feel successful herself. She felt vulnerable and insecure, without a niche in society or a clear identity, social or sexual. The first line of the book, significantly a question, raises the issue explicitly: "Who are you?" As Pulchérie tells Lélia: "[I] only saw that you had a problematic life as a woman." *Lélia* posits again Sand's androgynous self-image as man-woman even as it explores her uncertainties concerning her vocation and explicitly links the two in a way the earlier works did not because Lélia speaks for herself. The artist as man and woman appears twice in *Lélia,* for both Lélia and Sténio are artists and androgynous figures. It should be noted also that Lélia's name is a pseudonym, and that Pulchérie is called La Zinzolina by her friends, so that the same connection between name and identity is made in *Lélia* as in *Rose et Blanche.*

Pulchérie and Lélia share a crucial scene in the novel that specifically asserts Lélia's male side. Pulchérie describes her sexual and social awakening as an adolescent thanks to Lélia, a confession that has no previous literary model, as Reboul rightly points out. Pulchérie reaches the stage where she is able to perceive herself as other, to differentiate herself from her sister and to break out of her own narcissism. The use of the mirror shows Pulchérie's evolution; at first, she only looks at herself and wants to kiss her own reflection, but after her dream, she finds her sister more beautiful because Lélia resembles a man. The adolescent Pulchérie moves from self-love (and love of the same—the mother) to love for a man, the usual path of female development, while Lélia does not. When Lélia looks into the water, which functions as a mirror, she does not recognize her own beauty or appreciate her androgyny; it is as though the mirror remains empty for her. The young Lélia has no self-image, or at least not the traditional one, and cannot develop like Pulchérie. Lélia specifically states that nothing happened for her that day, whereas Pulchérie's life was changed. Later, Lélia does assume her androgyny, appearing early in the novel in a man's costume at Spuela's ball, as Sand's first heroines had played male roles in the theater.

The scene between the two sisters, which has sometimes been interpreted as a lesbian confession, instead continues Sand's self-portrait not only as androgynous but as the alter ego of her father. It is significant that Pulchérie dreams first of a man, "a man with black hair," and then sees Lélia, on whom she projects the description of her dream lover, and not the other way around. Lélia is described as a man by Pulchérie: her skin is tanned, her arms hairy, her expression masculine. "I thought you resembled this beautiful black-haired child of whom I had just dreamed, and, trembling, I kissed your arm." There is again constituted a triangle consisting of the two women and a man, with an equivalence established between the man and Lélia as doubles.

This dream triangle prepares the next one, where Lélia and Pulchérie switch roles so that Sténio makes love to Pulchérie when he thinks he is with Lélia at last. Even though *Lélia* is as far from Sand's previous works in plot and narrative form as possible, the novel nonetheless presents the same kind of structure as its predecessors: two sisters are involved with the same man, one briefly and sexually, while the other is eventually united with him, in this case in death. The first triangle resembles this one in that sexuality is also present, if only in fantasy: Pulchérie and

her imaginary lover exchange a kiss. Pulchérie insists that she has become Lélia by possessing Sténio, while Sténio has nonetheless consummated his relationship with Lélia through Pulchérie. Pulchérie is therefore the link through whom Lélia and Sténio achieve oneness, just as earlier it was through her that the identity of the dream man and Lélia was created.

After this encounter, Sténio becomes explicitly Lélia's double and equal. Earlier, he had been a younger version of Lélia, a poet, too, but one who had not yet produced. He was optimistic, whereas she was disillusioned. In his farewell letter to Lélia after his discovery that he had spent the night with her sister, he uses language that repeats Lélia's earlier formulations. "But God set me higher or lower than the rest of them." The fifth part of the novel makes the equivalence between Sténio and Lélia even clearer. Sténio, too, is physically impotent; he rejects his model Don Juan, the way Lélia had repudiated romantic love, as we have already seen. He has also become an outsider; even as he shares the orgies with his supposed friends, they mock him. Like Lélia, Sténio has become "sceptical and cold." Unable to find any meaning in his life, Sténio commits suicide.

Lélia joins him in the grotto where his body has been laid out, another of the enclosed spaces dear to Sand's imagination. There, she is called "the corpse's worthy fiancée"; further on in the text, she imagines their reunion with God at some future point and says, "Perhaps then we will be equals, perhaps we will be lovers and siblings." Their imagined union is incestuous, as was overtly stated by Lélia after Sténio's night with Pulchérie: "Be just my brother and my son, and let the thought of any marriage appear incestuous and bizarre." Their union takes place sooner than Lélia dreams, for Magnus, now mad with remorse over Sténio's death and with desire for Lélia, strangles her. Although Magnus clearly represents many things in the novel, he most symbolizes physical desire and is in many ways a foil for Lélia, who also desires but in a more metaphysical way, without achieving satisfaction. Here, Magnus incarnates the forbidden, wild desire that allows Lélia and Sténio to come together. Their marriage in death is made concrete in the image of the two meteors that Trenmor sees on the surface of the lake: "He spent the entire night watching those inseparable lights, which sought and followed each other like two souls in love."

Lélia and Sténio's union is that of two androgynes, rather than the marriage of a woman and a man; if Lélia is shown as androgynous, so is Sténio depicted as a young girl as well as a young man, at the beginning, where Trenmor describes Sténio as a child, feminine in appearance, and at the end, where Magnus takes the cadaver, dressed in a white winding-sheet and wearing a crown of flowers, like a bride, for that of a woman. Lélia prefers this nonvirile Sténio to the sexually avid, demanding lover he became at times.

> Lélia se rappela les jours où elle l'avait aimé le plus. C'était lorsqu'il était plutôt poète qu'amant. Dans ces premiers temps de leur affection, la passion de Sténio avait quelque chose de romanesque et d'angélique. . . . Plus tard,

son oeil s'était animé d'un feu plus viril, sa lèvre plus avide avait cherché et demandé le baiser, sa poésie avait exprimé des transports plus sauvages; c'est alors que l'impuissante Lélia s'était sentie effrayée, fatiguée et presque dégoûtée de cet amour qu'elle ne partageait pas.

> Lélia remembered when she had loved him most. It was when he was poet rather than lover. In those first days of their affection, Sténio's passion had a romantic, angelic quality. . . . Later his eyes would grow animated with a more virile fire. His greedy lips would seek and demand kisses. His poetry would express more savage outbursts of feeling. Then the impotent Lélia had felt frightened, fatigued, and nearly disgusted with this love she did not share.

Lélia's fear of the kind of brutal virility described in Part III as well as here leads to a desire for a more maternal, less threatening relationship with Sténio and perhaps sheds some light on Sand's own penchant for younger men whose pattern of sexual behavior was not yet fixed, and thus open to modifications by her.

The final couple in *Lélia* is thus similar to those of *Indiana* and *Valentine.* Both partners are equals and, furthermore, they resemble each other. The man is not the patriarchal father figure, but a gentle, kind friend. In *Indiana,* Ralph and Indiana were an explicitly oedipal couple whose incestuous bonds were alluded to throughout the novel. The case in *Lélia* is much more subtle and, as in *Valentine,* relies on internal, structural evidence. Yet in addition to the triangular relationships I have defined as oedipal, *Lélia* seems obsessed with secrets and with the dead to such a degree that this theme must be taken into account when dealing with the novel's oedipal content.

We have already looked at Lélia's evocation of monsters and cadavers as forming the basis of the dreams of poets. With an admirable prescience, Sand distinguishes between two categories of dreams: those which are healthy and allow the soul to renew itself through sleep, and those nightmares which reveal troubles with which the dreamer cannot cope, the "secret remorse" of the unconscious that surfaces in sleep.

> Mes rêves ont un effroyable caractère de vérité; les spectres de toutes mes déceptions y repassent sans cesse, plus lamentables, plus hideux chaque nuit. Chaque fantôme, chaque monstre évoqué par le cauchemar est une allégorie claire et saisissante qui répond à quelque profonde et secrète souffrance de mon âme.

> Instead, my dreams have a frightful character of truth. The ghosts of all my disappointments pass continually back and forth. Each phantom evoked by nightmare is a clear, gripping allegory that responds to some deep, secret suffering in my soul.

She then recounts a dream of her own, in which she pursues her sister, whom she thinks dead (this is before her meeting with Pulchérie); as she follows what she thinks is her sister's form, another ghost appears, described as "some hideous object, an ironic demon, a bloody cadaver, a temptation or a remorse." There is again set up a trian-

gular situation with the two women and this horrible phantom, seen as both temptation and guilt.

Cadavers and the "living dead" reappear constantly in *Lélia.* Lélia's account of her year spent in the deserted abbey gives two very revealing examples of Lélia's contact with the dead. In the first, she talks about her desires and need for action. "Stretched out on the tombstones, I gave in to the fury of my imagination. I dreamed of the embraces of an unknown demon; I felt his hot breath burn my breast, and I dug my nails into my shoulders, thinking I felt the bite of his teeth." Her position on top of the tombstones, like a *gisante,* is a reminiscence of the more frenetic Gothic literature, but in the context of Sand's own psychology it implies much more, particularly when the second instance of Lélia's communication with the dead is examined.

In an underground chapel, whose entrance has been blocked by debris, Lélia finds a monk on his knees in an attitude of prayer. At first, she thinks he is alive, but then she realizes that he has been dead for thirty years and preserved in the airless cave. Or rather, his clothes have remained and become dust when Lélia touches them, revealing a skeleton underneath. "It was both frightening and sublime to see for the first time this monk's head whose tufts of grey hair were still stirred by the wind and whose beard was entwined in the emaciated fingers of his hands folded under his chin." This scene is not ghoulish, as was the earlier one, but rather touching, particularly as Lélia goes on to make the dead monk her friend.

> J'enveloppai d'un nouveau vêtement la dépouille sacrée du prêtre. Je m'agenouillai chaque jour auprès d'elle. Souvent je lui parlai à haute voix dans les agitations de ma souffrance, comme à un compagnon d'exil et de douleur. Je me pris d'une sainte et folle affection pour ce cadavre. Je me confessai à lui: je lui racontai les angoisses de mon âme; je lui demandai de se placer entre le ciel et moi pour nous réconcilier; et souvent, dans mes rêves, je le vis passer devant mon grabat comme l'esprit des visions de Job et je l'entendis murmurer d'une voix faible comme la brise des paroles de terreur ou d'espoir.

> I covered the priest's remains with new clothing. Each day I knelt down beside him. He became the companion of my exile and sadness, to whom I spoke out loud of my suffering. I developed a saintly and crazy affection for this cadaver. I confessed to him. I told him of my spiritual anguish. I asked that he place himself as intermediary between heaven and me. And often in my dreams I saw him pass before my pallet like a spirit out of Job's visions, and I heard him murmur words of terror or hope in a voice as feeble as the breeze.

What is particularly interesting about this monk's return from the dead, so to speak, is that the scene recalls one told by George Sand in *Histoire de ma vie* about her and Deschartres's visit to her father's grave when it was opened to receive her grandmother's body. " 'You are going to see him who was your father . . . I've seen the skeleton. The head has already detached itself. I lifted it, I kissed it.' . . . We entered the crypt and I performed piously this act of devotion, as had Deschartres." Lélia's friend from beyond the grave is identifiable with Sand's father, with whom she communicated in spirit, as she does here with the monk.

The special affinity between Lélia and Sand's private scenarios is made clear in *Histoire de ma vie,* where Sand ascribes the novel to what she calls the "school of Corambé."

> Il portait trop le caractère du rêve, il était trop de l'école de *Corambé* pour être goûté par de nombreux lecteurs. Je ne me pressais donc pas, et j'éloignais de moi, à dessein, la préoccupation du public, éprouvant une sorte de soulagement triste à céder à l'imprévu de ma rêverie, et m'isolant même de la réalité du monde actuel, pour tracer la synthèse du doute et de la souffrance, à mesure qu'elle se présentait à moi sous une forme quelconque.

> It bore too strongly the character of a dream, it was too much of the school of Corambé to be appreciated by many readers. I was therefore not in a hurry, and I deliberately did not take the public into account, feeling a sort of sad satisfaction in giving in to the unforeseen train of my reverie, and isolating myself from the reality of contemporary life to trace the synthesis of doubt and suffering, as it presented itself to me in whatever form it liked.

The same vocabulary of reverie that characterizes Aurore Dudevant's childish creations, the evocation of Corambé and the intimation that *Lélia* is the product of a kind of automatic writing inspired by her innermost feelings, links the novel's content with that of Sand's other oedipal fantasies. Unlike Corambé, the childhood stories, the convent romance, or the last two novels, however, *Lélia* is not a positive, nurturing, and life-affirming creation. Rather, it is the inverse of what came before, the surfacing of the underside of Sand's usually benign vision.

Lélia links narrative, society, and personal psychology, as did *Indiana* and *Valentine,* but in a negative way. Just as Sand describes two kinds of dreams, two kinds of collective unconscious, one dark, the other healthy, so does *Lélia* express what the previous works had not, at least not to the same extent: the guilt, the despair, the fear occasioned both by her secret dreams and by her condition as author, which was so dependent on these imaginings. Written in a period of depression, when nothing seemed to go right and when the suicidal urges present in her mind for the past ten years were strongest, *Lélia* decries the very impulses that made Sand's strength and defined her character, precisely because that force and identity were ill received by others, in the professional and personal spheres. Having been repudiated by society, she turns that criticism upon herself but makes it obvious that it was society that rejected her first.

Temptations, remorse, skeletons from the past, monsters within and without, *Lélia* is clearly not the kind of novel that is usually associated with Sand. Intensely personal and original, *Lélia* has no parallel in Sand's *oeuvre,* partly because, as Sainte-Beuve noted, *Lélia* "is a work one only writes once," which served as a kind of purgative, and partly because the book was so badly received, even by its

defenders. It is perhaps the final irony that the novel was condemned for its negativity and scandalous frankness, just as its heroine had been refused a place in the world. Ultimately, the criticism leveled against *Lélia* concerned its unremitting pessimism and its lack of constructive suggestions for change. "The general tone of the book is one of anger in the mouth of Lélia, and one only has Trenmor's cold stoicism to relieve it, to refresh oneself from this bitter and contrary wind," wrote Sainte-Beuve. In *La France Littéraire,* Alfred Désessarts concluded: "Must I admit my whole opinion: this book strikes me as dangerous, not because it destroys some modern prevailing ideas (what is the importance of today's system?), but because it prepares nothing." Past literary renderings of the *mal du siècle* had contained some glimmer of hope and consolation; at the end of René's story, Father Souël and Chactas reprove the young man's hypersensitivity. If, as D. G. Charlton points out, the *romans de l'individu* "are above all dialogues, not monologues from a single character or the author himself," preaching "moral affirmation," then *Lélia* clearly does not fit the paradigm on either score; although dialogic in form, the combat is largely conducted between Lélia and Sténio, similar characters who become identified at the end. Furthermore, the two characters who are satisfied with their lives, the reformed criminal and the courtesan, have no secret formula to share with others, no hints to communicate to those who would emulate them, and are by definition social outcasts. Chateaubriand's faith in religion is not shared by Sand, who has no other palliative to offer. On the contrary, she demonstrates that for a woman, the Catholic church, at least as constituted in her time, is an impossible refuge. While she does not present Lélia as a model, any more than René was a model, Sand does intend her and the novel as a condemnation of the society that rejects her, and thereby goes beyond the individual to the general.

Sand's open expression of the despair of the woman artist was censured, leading to her own self-censorship. Sand took these criticisms of *Lélia* to heart and returned in her next works to the forms, style, and themes previously elaborated. She did not let the reactions to *Lélia* in the press go without protest, however. In her 1834 preface to a new edition of *Romans et nouvelles,* she states: "For the last several months, the attacks aimed at the author of *Lélia* have taken on such a coarse and personal nature, that a public response has become necessary." What follows is less a justification of *Lélia* than a serious discussion of the inconsistencies of critics, who take back their praise of an author when a new work does not suit their tastes or ideas. Still chafing from the calumnies, in her 1842 preface to the Perrotin edition of the *Oeuvres complètes* she again mentions the fury of the critics and serenely asserts her right as an author to raise in her novel the questions she deems essential. After *Lélia,* though, Sand's female voice went underground again and just a few years later she undertook to revise, indeed denature, the novel, which (re)appeared in 1839; as Jules Janin had recommended, she became a man once more in her fiction. She continued to express her own ideals and explore her particular themes, but more covertly, as in *Indiana* and *Valentine.* Significantly, her next openly "feminist" project, the one-sided fictional correspondence related in form to *Lélia,* the

Lettres à Marcie (1837), aroused the antagonism of Lamennais, in whose journal *Le Monde* it appeared; because it advocated divorce, it was eventually censored by him.

Although *Lélia,* like *René, Obermann,* and similar novels that express the *mal du siècle,* is much less readable today than it was one hundred and fifty years ago, and the supposedly scandalous passages have lost most of their shock value, it is still a novel that was worth daring, to use Sainte-Beuve's phrase. It remains a searingly honest cry of a woman artist's soul, an indictment of, and a curse upon, a society in which she had no place. (pp. 95-114)

> *Kathryn J. Crecelius, in her* Family Romances: George Sand's Early Novels, *Indiana University Press, 1987, 183p.*

Donna Dickenson   (essay date 1988)

[*In the essay below, Dickenson explores the extent to which Sand could be described as a feminist, examining in particular the heroines of* Lélia *and* La petite Fadette.]

> They [women] are mistreated, reproached for the stupidity imposed on them, scorned as ignorant, their wisdom mocked. In love they are treated like courtesans, in conjugal friendship like servants. They are not loved, they are used, they are exploited.
> Sand, *Intimate Journal,* 25 June 1837

> Too proud of their recently acquired education, certain women have shown signs of personal ambition. . . . The smug daydreams of modern philosophies have encouraged them, and these women have given sad proof of the powerlessness of their reasoning. . . . In vain do they gather into clubs, in vain do they engage in polemics, if the expression of their discontent proves that they are incapable of properly managing their affairs and of governing their affections.
> Sand, "Third Letter to Marcie," March 1837

Sand wrote this apparently contradictory pair of quotations in the same year; the second mocking women's rationality and wisdom in exactly the manner the first detests. Although 1837 was difficult for Sand, with her mother's death, the public humiliation of her court case for separation and the dissolution of her affair with the radical lawyer Michel de Bourges, there is no reason to think that Sand's confusion over feminism was confined to one bad year. At many other times in her life she gave voice to the crusading fellow-feeling for women which characterises the first excerpt. In 1838, for example, she wrote to Chopin's friend Albert Grzymala that she always took the part of wronged or violated women, and that she was rightfully thought to be the advocate of her sex. In *La Comtesse de Rudolstadt* (1843-4) she battled against the double standard: 'Virtue, imposed on women, you will never be more than a name until men take up their half of the task'. Adultery in women was punishable by solitary confinement in prison, she noted bitterly, but congratulated in men. In the 1842 preface to *Indiana*—in which the publisher had requested that she restrain herself—she

stuck to her guns about 'the injustice and barbarity of the laws which govern women's existence in marriage, the family, and society'. Is it any wonder that in her lifetime Sand was reputed an opponent of marriage and of what modern feminists have called 'the anti-social family'?

But Sand always denied that she was a partisan of 'free love': she once answered a critic of her supposedly earth-shattering views with the untranslatable aphorism that she was indeed an enemy of *maris* but not of *marriage,* of husbands but not of marriage. Nor was she by any means a 'man-hater': *husbands* (as the law defined their duties and powers) were her enemy, but *men* she often venerated above women. The second quotation [at the beginning of this essay] is woman-hating, not man-hating. Without any apparent awareness that she was condemning herself out of her own mouth, she wrote: 'We must ask the ladies' pardon if, judging from current examples, we plump for the intellectual superiority of men. . . . The greatest women in science and literature—with no exceptions—have never been and are not at present anything more than second-rate men'. She could be very patronising towards her female acquaintances. To the spinster Marie de Rozières she sent this rather hypocritical explanation of why she had decided her daughter Solange should not come on a visit:

> In the old days you were not a coquette, but now, my love, your eyes have become terribly voluptuous. . . . All the men have noticed it, though of course if you do not mind, why should I? . . . All the same, I have decided that Solange had better not see quite so much of you—until this little nervous trouble of yours is over, and you have taken either a lover or a husband *ad libitum.*

Rejecting the chivalry of a minority of male Académie Française members who proposed her candidature to that female-excluding body in 1863, Sand wrote that women were not worthy of the honour: 'The majority of women in this generation fall into one of two camps: the religious and the worldly. The nonentities don't count and never have done. . . . Everything of spark and fire in women tends to be joined to something excessive, either religious intolerance or infatuation with luxury and flirtatiousness'. This lack of identification with her own sex is borne out by her admission that:

> With very few exceptions, I do not long endure the company of women. Not that I feel them inferior to me in intelligence: I consume so few of them in the habitual commerce of my life that everyone has more of them around than I. But women, generally speaking, are nervous, anxious beings who, my resistance notwithstanding, communicate their eternal disquiet to me apropos of everything. I begin by listening to them with regret, then I let myself be caught up in a natural interest for what they are saying, only to perceive that there was really nothing to get worked up about in their puerile agitations. . . . I thus like men better than women, and I say so without malice.

A 'lack of malice' like this would be interpreted as rabid malevolence in a man, and rightly so. At best, Sand emerges from this second set of quotations as a woman of the self-made sort who has little sympathy for females who have *not* succeeded against the odds of poor education for girls, rigid marriage laws for wives, and a male-centred literary world. At the strangest, she appears to have no inkling that she *is* a woman at all. . . . I suggest that Sand's pen name may indeed have created some confusion in her mind over her own gender identity. By this I do not mean to suggest that she had a 'masculinity complex', as has been argued. I doubt there is any such thing: it is not neurotic but perfectly rational to want to be a man in a world of male privilege. For the moment, however, I want to consider whether Sand was a feminist in her *works,* not whether she was liberated in her *life.* . . . To do this I shall need to separate her works of non-fiction—her twenty volumes of political pamphlets and literary essays, her twelve-volume autobiography—from her sixty or seventy novels. I argue that the latter are more obviously feminist than the former, but that both are rooted in Sand's unchanging and not necessarily feminist conviction that women and men possess separate identities and roles. In the essays, this dogma of 'separate but equal' often degenerates into 'certainly separate, and not so equal as all that'. In the novels, paradoxically, women are often presented as different and *superior.*

Sand never argued that biology was destiny in the simpleminded reductionist way, but she did offer a conventional basis for distinguishing between male and female 'natures'. Very roughly speaking, she equated man with head and woman with heart. This is a very loose categorisation, and Sand always denied that there was any real opposition between heart and head—as in *Laura.* She viewed the division between 'the masculine' and 'the feminine' as created by Providence and intractable to change, but she did *not* equate it with her society's standard gender roles. In this passage she sounds quite modern in her refusal to take her contemporaries' prejudices about male and female *roles* as timeless truths about male and female *natures:*

> *There is only one sex.* Men and women are exactly the same, so much so that I can make no sense of the welter of distinctions and subtle arguments raised on this score by society. I watched my son and daughter develop. My son was like me, and therefore a woman—more so than my daughter, who was a failed man.

But the modern feminism this resembles is an Eighties variant, not a Sixties version. Sand was sure that women were more sensitive than men, due largely to their mothering role. She doubted that better education would entirely dissolve women's tendency to set more store—perhaps too much—by the affairs of the heart. Therefore she would not have accepted Wollstonecraft's argument that male and female minds would reason identically if male and female education were identical. Nevertheless, she certainly proposed a far less limited schooling for women than was current in her own youth. Her novel *Gabriel* (1840) concerns a princess who is given a boy's education by mistake, and turns out a perfectly capable 'prince'. She complained that women were scorned if they remained in squalid ignorance and mocked as 'femmes savantes' if they tried to acquire any learning. And she castigated Rousseau for his unimaginativeness towards girls' education—just as

Wollstonecraft had done. Particularly degrading, she argued, was Rousseau's scornful granting of *carte blanche* for women to continue their irrational faith in organised religion. The educated man, he asserted, would have no need of such shibboleths.

In these aspects Sand thought women just as rational as men—or to be more precise, she reckoned that women were as capable of arriving at truth and justice through sensibility as men were through reason. Since the division between heart and head was artificial to her, it would be surprising to find her making it airtight in her theory of gender. It was the union of the two she valued, and she urged society to honour both natures equally. When she browbeat feminists—as in the second quotation at the start of the [essay]—it was usually for neglecting their crucial feminine sensibilities. As a Christian humanist she hoped that pacifistic 'female' values would come to carry more weight, and she often speculated that women were the better devotees of St Paul, despite his aversion to them. Society's claim to value Christian love and to esteem women as guardians of a higher ethic was hypocritical, in her mind. Although women were placed on pedestals—recall this argument in *Laura*—and motherhood officially venerated, in fact most women were their husband's slaves, and most mothers glorified wet-nurses.

However, Sand made frequent tactical retreats from these reasonably advanced positions. Not all the male writers and critics of her day were as comparatively enlightened as Jules Sandeau, Alfred de Vigny, and Prosper Mérimée, the triumvirate plotting Sand's election to the Académie Française. Sand wrote three *Letters to Marcie*—advice to a putative young woman on female roles and male rights—for the Abbé Félicité Robert de Lamennais, an egalitarian priest, editor of *Le Monde.* Lamennais's anarchistic *Paroles d'un croyant* has been called 'a lyrical version of the *Communist Manifesto'.* Sand met him through Liszt, at a dinner party also attended by the poet Heinrich Heine. (The glamour of Sand's life lies in her treasure trove of famous and intellectually challenging acquaintances, I think, not in the roster of her often unsatisfactory lovers.) Although she was favourably struck by Lamennais's socialism and his defiance of the papal establishment, and though she came to view him as her spiritual advisor, she was to find that his progressivism stopped short of equal rights for women. This troubled Sand, particularly when Lamennais later brought out a misogynous pamphlet, *Discussions pratiques et pensées diverses sur la religion et la philosophie.* Sand confided her doubts to her journal:

> I would attribute this inferiority [of women, which Lamennais had laid down as a natural law], which is a real fact, in general, to the inferiority which society would like to consecrate in perpetuity as a principle, in order to prey on women's weakness, ignorance, and vanity, in a word, on all the failings produced by education. This is not to say that the evil is part of our nature, but rather . . . that it arises from the way in which your sex has governed us.

Although Sand was little bolder than this in the *Letters to Marcie*—condemning contemporary feminists and apostrophising an angelic ideal of motherhood—she was still not reactionary enough for Lamennais, who excised the most progressive bits of the *Letters,* on divorce.

It is only fair to Lamennais to point out that Sand's consciousness was only raised on issues which had affected her personally, such as divorce and separation. Elsewhere her delineation of male and female roles is quite conventional, as is the stereotype at the root of them: that women are creatures of emotion, whether noble or trivial, and that men are blessed with all the brainpower. Her elaborate division of the human psyche into these two components often sounds very platitudinous when applied to particulars. For example, in her autobiography she speculates that men's honour centres on business affairs and women's on marriage. It is unsurprising that most women, even the ostensibly pious, cheat at cards: there is no question of honour in it for them. Men can cheat on their wives with no risk to their reputation; indeed, they may gain honour as casanovas. Both men and women would be better advised, she thinks, to practice a little more honesty in their respective spheres; but she does not challenge the basis of the spheres themselves. In another excerpt she describes how she learned to ride by hanging onto her unschooled filly's mane. But rather than making a feminist point about women's equal courage, she shrugs off her achievement by putting it down to 'woman's nervous will'.

At worst, Sand allows female superiority in understanding, tact and commitment to become an apologia for female submission. In a letter written during the early days of her marriage, she enthuses about the joys of obeying her husband:

> What an unquenchable source, obeying the one you love. Each privation is a new pleasure. One sacrifices to God and to conjugal love at the same time, doing one's duty and ensuring one's happiness. The only question remaining is whether the man or the woman ought to re-mould themselves so, and since all power is on the side of the beard, and men aren't capable of such an attachment, we are perforce the ones who must bend in obedience.

Sand was only eighteen when she wrote this protesting-too-much letter, and she could have been expected to echo pietistic homilies—particularly if she was trying to convince herself as much as her friend. Later in life she was more hard-headed—and much more assertively feminist—about marriage. When her foster-daughter's suitor, the artist Théodore Rousseau, insisted that his intended had to have a clean bill of virginity and a promissory note for her dowry, Sand cut him down: 'We are *women,* and for this reason we are not weak, and we do not reply as we could do to men who believe themselves strong. You have doubts about the frankness of the mother and the purity of the daughter. . . . They will not humble themselves further'. Sand *could* see sisterhood as powerful, but most often in her own particular strong-minded case. In the abstract she continued to have mixed and often hackneyed views of women. While writing her first novel, she described its heroine Indiana as

> a typical woman, weak as well as strong, at once

weary of the air she breathes and capable of shouldering the heavens, timid in everyday life and yet bold in days of battle. . . . Such, I believe, is woman in general, an incredible mixture of weakness and energy, greatness and pettiness, a being forever composed of two opposed natures, now sublime, now wretched, skilled in deceiving, yet easily deceived.

Most to the point, Sand always regarded woman as the Other, to use de Beauvoir's formulation—as the negative end of a scale whose middle and positive pole are both occupied by 'man'. 'Woman' was an entity which could be compassed in such generalisations as that about Indiana, a paradox which needed explanation. No one would make such speculations about 'man' in general; that would be read as 'the human species'—which is certainly not what Sand meant.

But in her novels Sand does not distance herself from her women in this way; perhaps that explains why her female figures are rounded, compelling personnages—so much so that male critics complained. The women in Sand make Madame Bovary—usually regarded as a sympathetic and tragic figure—appear stupid and tiresome. One of the most robust women in Sand's novels is Lélia, and it was on her account that the novel was variously slammed as 'stinking of mud and prostitution' and admired as liberating for women. Lélia is such a powerful character that she has had to be contained by sexual boxing-in, then as now. The modern convention is that *Lélia* is a book about a frigid woman. Now of course this is a bit of post-Freudian anachronism, although Sand seems to have had a premonition that her heroine would be slurred like this—perhaps because her own professionalism was so often taken for granted and her sexual peccadilloes magnified. Men call women frigid when they are frightened of their rightful demands, she says. 'Now a self-respecting woman cannot experience pleasure without love; that is why she will never find either one in the arms of most men. As for the male sex, it is far more difficult for them to respond to our noble instincts and to nourish our generous desires than to accuse us of coldness.'

It is not too extreme to say that Lélia has been slandered as frigid for the same reason that Sand herself has been insulted: because she terrifies men—and perhaps more conventional women—with her capability. Lélia is a superior logician and supremely skilled orator who defeats her would-be seducer Sténio in a debate on nineteenth-century permissive society, as embodied in Don Juan—whom Sand abominates, interestingly enough. Lélia considers taking the sexual initiative—rather than settling for the more decorous occupation of being pursued—and defines the male sex in relation to the female, not the orthodox reverse. She refuses to pray, preferring to rely 'on a columnar Self', as Emily Dickinson put it. More broadly, she always remains symbolically standing, never bends the knee, never lowers the eye. She is allowed some scathing lines about masculine vanity, as when, describing her previous lover, she remarks to her sister: 'He reproached me with the sin of being less childish than he was, he who enjoyed treating me like a child. And then at last he turned his anger against my race, because he was furious at feel-

George Sand's painting of her estate Nohant.

ing smaller than me, and cursed my entire sex so as to have the right to curse me'. She and her sister, the courtesan Pulchérie, tell each other hen-party-raunchy stories about men, bemoaning premature ejaculation and satirising male hypocrisy towards prostitutes. Lélia accuses her demanding admirer, the poet Sténio, of wanting her only for her admittedly superb body—primarily so that he can boast about it afterwards to his mates. She pronounces men and women equal before God, and challenges the religious and social ethic which restricts women's lives: 'Is woman's role necessarily bounded by the transports of love?' She regrets the limited opportunities in her own life which have turned her into a female Werther, a useless dreamer, when she was cut out for crusades and cannon-fire.

> If I were a man, I should have gloried in combat, the smell of blood, the strictures of danger; perhaps my youth would have been blessed by the dream of ruling through my intelligence, of dominating other men through my powerful words. As a woman, I had only one noble destiny on earth, that is, loving. So I loved *valiantly. . . .*

Men, she scolds Sténio, have no excuse for Romantic *ennui:*

> You have a goal in life; if I were a man, I should have one too, and however perilous it was, I

should advance towards it calmly. But you fail to remember that I am a woman and that my career is limited by uncrossable bounds. I was supposed to content myself with that which is the pride and joy of other women [conventional romantic love]; I could have done so, were I not cursed with a serious mind and a yearing for affections which I have not found.

This last quotation raises another ground for doubting that Lélia is frigid: she wants more love, not less. In particular, she demands a more genuine and high-minded love than the shallow society of her time offers her in the person of the self-centred, pestering Sténio. Sand did exemplify the Romantic in so far as she longed for this ideal of love. By it she measured the mean-minded Napoleonic Code on women's property rights, the double standard, and the legalised prostitution which she identified as contemporary marriage. (The law appears to have reflected and ensured the truth of Napoleon's famous remark: 'Nature has made women our slaves'.) This search for the ideal was to occupy the female sensibility, in Sand's thought, and this is what Lélia teaches her novices when she becomes abbess of the convent of the Camaldules.

> Lélia knew how to escort them towards her ideas without shocking their prejudices or putting their piety on guard. She found some aid in Christian ethics for teaching her most heartfelt beliefs: purity of thought, elevation of sentiment,

SAND   *NINETEENTH-CENTURY LITERATURE CRITICISM, Vol. 42*

disdain for the little vanities that destroy women, aspiration towards an infinite love of a sort they knew and understood but poorly.

It is almost as inappropriate to charge Lélia with frigidity as it would be the Virgin Mary. Indeed, Sand makes the parallel herself: Lélia's raiment is always spotless, 'without stain or fold, with something fantastical about it, as if she were an immaterial existence, a serenity out of reach of the laws of the possible'. Sténio is afraid to look into the face of a marble Virgin he passes because he knows he will see Lélia's features there. He invokes her support for the ex-convict Trenmor in these Marian terms: 'You voluntarily became his friend, his consolation, his good angel; you went to him, you said, "Come unto me, you who are accursed, I shall return to you the heaven you have lost! Come to me, who am without spot or blame, I shall make clean your sins with my hands!" ' When Lélia becomes a nun, the Church gives her the name of Annunziata—either she unto whom the Annunciation is made, or even, perhaps, a female Messiah. In a pairing of two characters which is a frequent device in Sand, she is doubled with her long-lost sister Pulchérie, who represents Mary Magdalen. This is ironically limited if Sand really is a feminist, since, as Marina Warner points out in her excellent *Alone of All Her Sex,* the Virgin and the Magdalen have compassed and restricted the gamut of female roles for two millennia.

But Lélia is not translated heavenwards at the end of the novel. In both editions of the book, she ends badly—in the first, strangled by a monk with a rosary in the worst traditions of 1830s 'frenetic literature', in the second hounded by the Church establishment, vilified with sexual rumours from which her chastity cannot protect her, and left to die of pneumonia in a remote and cold convent to which she is exiled. Cold is a recurring theme in the book, and if Lélia cannot be accused of frigidity, Sand does portray her will as glacial. (Interestingly, Sand called Lélia *impotent,* not frigid, in her journal, but then rebutted that charge too.) Lélia is ultimately incomplete because she represents the masculine, reasoning side of human nature too narrowly. By presenting a chilly, over-cerebral nature in a *woman,* Sand highlights its inadequacy in a *man* when it is unmatched by 'feminine' sensibility. She keeps to her Platonic theme, drawn from the myth in *The Symposium* (*The Banquet*) which relates that all human creatures were originally hermaphroditic until the two sexes were split, and that the halves have been searching for each other since then. This necessary union of the rational and the spiritual may appear trite and platitudinous in Sand's essays and autobiography, but the device Sand uses in the novel *Lélia* gives it sudden force. Lélia's lack of fellow-feeling with humankind evokes the young Raskolnikov, but it is even more terrifying in her—because it knocks our expectations of women into a cocked hat—than in *Crime and Punishment,* where it terminates in a blood-soaked axe.

Sand denied that *Lélia* was any sort of manifesto for women. In 1834, the year after its publication, she wrote to a friend:

> *Lélia* is not a book: it is a scream of pain, or a bad dream, or a splenetic digression full of both

truth and paradox, injustice and warning. It has everything except calm. And without calm there can be no acceptable conclusion. One should no more ask Lélia to enunciate a moral code than require witty remarks of a dying man. If a few women of spirit thought they should try to be either exactly like or perfectly unlike her, they were mistaken. You understood her better . . . because you saw in her nothing but a woman to be pitied.

Sand refused to accept that Lélia *was* a superior character, despite her tragic stature. This appears to contradict my earlier point: that female nature is depicted as different from men's nature in the novels, but superior, whereas it is usually piddling and inferior in her non-fiction. But of course Lélia is not the embodiment of *ideal* female nature: this is exactly the tragedy of the novel. She does enjoy the higher masculine attributes and lacks male violence—which kills her in the first edition. If she could wed to the better male qualities a greater sense of feminine compassion, then she would be a whole creature.

Sand often made this common philosophical error in discussing women's questions: confusing the descriptive with the normative, mixing up how women are with how they ought to be. It is a failing to which modern feminists are not immune when they idealise female nature, it has been argued. Nevertheless, if Lélia as she *is* cannot be termed a morally enlightened being, she is certainly the book's fulcrum. She and Pulchérie have all the best lines, some very outrageous indeed. One critic of the time warned readers to lock the book away from their daughters, and another thought it so licentious and cynical that it had certainly put paid to the rumours that George Sand was really a woman. But of course *Lélia* could only have been written by a woman: it puts the 'female question' centre stage. As Pulchérie remarks to Lélia: 'You have had a problematic existence, being a woman'.

Tillie Olsen claims [in her *Silences,* 1979] that George Sand was the only nineteenth-century woman writer who viewed her sex's position as problematic. I am not sure this is true, particularly not of American writers: Harriet Beecher Stowe tends more and more to be read as a feminist as well as an abolitionist; Margaret Fuller wrote a bestseller on 'the woman question'. Elizabeth Barrett Browning also presented the creative woman's dilemma in *Aurora Leigh.* But whether or not what Sand *said* was feminist—and I doubt that it was—the fact of her *concern* for women is feminist. Lélia is the incarnation of this interest, the Daughter rather than the Son of Man, a female Job, Hamlet or Werther. It was the casting of a woman in these plum roles which was revolutionary—and which has had to be minimised by scaling Lélia down to the comfortably low level of a sexually maladjusted female. The same tactic has often been used against Sand herself. Indeed, Sand is often equated with Lélia even by her sympathetic biographers, such as André Maurois, who actually calls his account of Sand's life *Lélia.* But Sand denied that she was Lélia any more than she was one of the book's other characters. Some critics have reproached her for letting her own personality dominate Pulchérie's—and Pulchérie is presented as Lélia's opposite. Sand wrote in her autobiography that she had never appeared on her own stage in female guise—though her acknowledgement that if she was anyone, it was the monk Spiridion, did not exclude the possibility of a bit of literary transvestism. Why not, when Flaubert used to say that he was Madame Bovary? But in general the tendency to read Sand's novels as purely autobiographical leads to ridiculous contradictions and denigrates her professionalism.

La Petite Fadette, though written fifteen years after *Lélia* and demonstrating a master craftsman's unity of themes and delicacy of expression, is also stereotypically read as autobiographical. (Never mind that this makes Sand a tall Italian countess who was also a diminutive French provincial ragamuffin.) Fadette, the tomboy who mends her hoydenish ways and gets her man, is thought by proponents of the 'masculinity complex' view to represent Sand, the betrousered cigar-smoking virago. According to this thesis, Sand's myriad maladjustments—ranging in contradictory plenitude from frigidity to nymphomania—stemmed from her grandmother's harrowing revelations about her mother's scarlet past.

'Masculinity complex' adherents see in *Fadette* the tale of a girl awakened to proper feminine mental health by the love of a good man. If this were the course of the story, it would be hard to regard Sand's message as feminist, even though a female character stars in the title. But the novel is much more to do with the reform of a *man*— indeed, of two men—by a woman. This theme of woman as moral educator is very common in Sand. *Mauprat* (1837) concerns a Heathcliff-like wolf boy who is taught to control his temper and libido by his cousin, herself equally prone to the family fiery spirits but saved by feminine sensibility—as he is, too, in the end, by hers. *Laura* likewise uses a woman to symbolise the just middle way between extremes and to save the narrator from the excesses of his own fantasies. In *La Mare au diable* the chirpy peasant girl Marie inspires the virtuous but bovine Germain with her stoicism and cheer when they are lost together at night in an evil marsh. Unlike Dickens's women, Sandian heroines are not legless angels. They have faults, and it is these minor wrinkles which Fadette has to iron out of her character. But they are not sufficient vices to brand her as neurotic, or to threaten the superiority of female nature, as she typifies it.

La Petite Fadette actually begins with the heroine well off-stage: a year before her birth, when the twin boys Sylvinet and Landry are born to a wealthy peasant family, the Barbeaus. The identical twins develop a profound affinity which the family encourages despite the midwife's warning that treating two twins as one person can only bring grief. (The theme of the wise woman recurs in this novel: Fadette herself is a sort of good witch, having been tutored in taming will o' the wisps and discerning medicinal virtues in plants by her grandmother.) When the farm can no longer support both sons, one has to go 'away'—to work on the neighbouring farm, which Sand correctly portrays as an immense distance to the country mind. The twin left behind, Sylvinet, develops an insatiable jealousy of his brother, whose life no longer revolves solely around him. Described by his mother as having 'the heart of a girl,

tender and gentle', Sylvinet is also prey to unreasonable possessiveness, usually depicted as feminine. (Recall the cartoons in *Mad* magazine: a man stands with his arm tightly clasped around a woman, and in the background a spectator whispers admiringly: 'Isn't he protective?' In the next frame a woman assumes the same posture with a man, and the onlooker clucks: 'Isn't she possessive?') Here once again Sand reverses the stereotypes of masculine and feminine. Landry tries to reason with his brother but makes no headway, although he warns Sylvinet that '[love,] through being too great, can sometimes become a sickness'.

Though stoical and devoted, Landry has his own failings: he is superstitious, rather condescending, materialistic, and ungrateful to Fadette, who overturns the usual knightly myth by saving the boys twice—once when Sylvinet goes missing and she locates him for Landry, once when Landry has been deluded off the safe track through a ford at night by a will o' the wisp. (Fadette's name is a diminutive for fairy or will o' the wisp, and it is clear that she possesses considerable powers, though Sand leaves open the question of whether their 'otherworldliness' is only a figment of peasant imagination.) When Fadette encounters Landry at the dangerous ford, she pulls him through the dark night and the water that he cannot swim with a force she looks too slight to possess. Later, Sand remarks that 'she taught him reason'; she is learned in country lore and has a scientific enquiring mind.

Thus most of the story concerns the men's awakening: they are the sleeping beauties, and Fadette the prince. Her own transformation from an ugly duckling she effects without any help from Landry other than a bit of frank advice, and all in the space of a week. All she has to do is reform her appearance, which is ill-kempt because she has no mother to teach her basic cleanliness and no money to buy herself girlish gewgaws. She could obtain work as a servant if she were concerned to buy such fripperies. But this she refuses to do because she will not leave her lame younger brother, who has been likewise deprived of his mother. Although the villagers judge the daughter by the sins of the mother, who has run off to follow the soldiers, in fact she has the best of feminine virtues under her tomboy appearance. It is maternal concern for her brother which has kept her in tatters. She washes and irons a little more frequently, puts a stop to the swearing at which she was proficient, and learns to curb her over-hasty wit; this is the extent of her 'taming'. Another local girl, Madelon—contrasted with Fadette in a typical Sandian doubling, as indeed is the device of twins—conceals a selfish and perfidious nature under her belle's looks. Even in her gaucherie Fadette is the superior character: coquetterie is selfish, and unconcern over a proper feminine appearance at least has the merit of humility.

By the end of the novel, Fadette, initially better endowed with spirit than with charity, has expanded in kindliness without shrinking in wit—much the same progression that Elizabeth Bennett undergoes in *Pride and Prejudice*. She is still devilish, playing pranks on her mercenary prospective father-in-law. Old Barbeau forbids Landry to see Fadette because he does not know that her grandmother has left her wealthy—until she brings him the coffers to tally up, with the demure fib that she is not adept at counting over 100. Actually her head for business is better than anyone's, and her 'heart and blood' stronger than Landry's. Most tellingly, at the climax of the book she alone can cure Sylvinet of his jealousy, which has provoked a psychosomatic fever after Sylvinet learns that Fadette and Landry are to be married. Although she is skilled in herbal cures, she uses no drugs with him: only touching, in both a literal and a symbolic sense. This casting out of devils, this touching Sylvinet deep down in his heart, has been called a proto-Freudian analysis session. It is treated with the psychological acuity and sympathy for both characters which mark most of Sand's novels. The female nature is certainly superior here—an ideal female nature now, though a believable one. But Sylvinet is made credible and likeable in both his weakness and his willingness to be cured of it.

> He felt that she was right, deep down, and that she was not over-strict except on one point: she seemed to think that he had never fought his sickness and that he was perfectly aware of his own egotism; whereas he had been selfish without knowing or wishing it. That pained and shamed him a good deal, and he wished he could give her a better opinion of his good conscience. As for her, she knew perfectly well that she was exaggerating, and she did it deliberately, to plague his spirit and soften him up for kindness and consolation. She forced herself to talk harshly to him and to seem angry with him, whilst in her heart she felt so much pity and sympathy for him that she was quite sick with her own deception, and she was more exhausted than he when she left.

The two boys grow up through achieving separateness from each other; Fadette, through establishing her connection with ordinary femaleness by renouncing her superficial oddities of dress and manner. (Sand herself was a self-sacrificing, good-listening, 'womanly woman', despite her aberrant costume in her youth—though as I have said, the autobiographical parallels with Fadette should not be exaggerated.) In *La Petite Fadette* male and female sentimental educations are separate but only unequal in that the men have much more work to do. This distinction fits Sand's emphasis on different natures, which will remain even after education and maturation. (pp. 45-60)

> *Donna Dickenson, in her* George Sand: A Brave Man—The Most Womanly Woman, *Berg, 1988, 190 p.*

Anne Berger   (essay date 1988)

[*In the following essay, Berger explores Sand's conception of language, particularly noting the oral tradition of the French peasantry as depicted in Sand's works.*]

George Sand wrote her autobiography and a series of novels of country life during the same period. Having gone through a double apprenticeship in the art of living and writing, she decided, in the late 1840s, to tell the story of her life. She no longer needed, at that point, to learn in order to live. She had 'reached an age of tranquility when her personality had nothing to gain by displaying itself'. She no longer 'sought the key words'. It was when she ceased to believe that the subject could grasp itself through speculation that she undertook to 'communicate herself' to others in a pedagogical and maternal gesture. At this moment, she definitively assumed the position of the artist, identifying herself with a destiny which she neither foresaw nor wanted, tying the thread of her life to the thread of the text. It was as an artist that she proceeded to reveal a reality without which the teaching provided by fiction remained, according to her, incomplete. But, she said: 'It is costly for an artist to touch on this reality . . . it is not, without a great effort that *I will descend into the prose of my subject* (added emphasis).

Thus the novels of country life coincide with her accession to the peak of art. From this point, the artist then undertakes a difficult descent in order to once again touch the reality of 'his' subject, indeed of *the* subject.

George Sand's aesthetic concerns in the prefaces to her rustic novels seem to display the success of her ascent. Indeed she comes close to formulating an aesthetic theory when she examines the complex connections between art and nature on the one hand and art and history on the other. The degree to which she idealizes her rustic characters adds further evidence. Idealization is an essential part of artistic representation and activity, as she repeatedly stresses. Finally, the apparent lack of autobiographical concern in her rustic novels at the moment when *The Story of My Life* is written contrasts with the extensive use of personal material in her other novels. (The personal stance in the prefaces to her other novels, such as *Lelia, Indiana* or *Mauprat,* accounts for their ideological cast as well as their tone, which is either apologetic or polemic.)

If the novels of country life seem to assume a stance at odds with the prosaic reality of her subject, they are at the same time the most singular and most accomplished expression of her artistic language. Whereas George Sand often indulges in the novelistic conventions of her time by offering the reader a mixture of realistic description and 'Rocambolesque' adventures, she has an entirely different purpose in her 'études champêtres'. Condemning the novelistic production of her time as an unfortunate offspring of bourgeois ideology, she presents the rustic novel as a reversal of the contemporary novel which delights in the disfiguration of reality and uses the pen as a 'dagger' in the services of a 'brutal and fiery art'.

George Sand opposes the study of the quiet 'mystery of primitive simplicity' to the violence of bourgeois representation. Indeed, she writes most of her rustic novels in Nohant, her native village, far from the tumults of history and the seductions of society. She will return there more and more often in the second and non-written part of her life. In this sense, she departs from the implacable law, epitomized in Balzac's novels, which governs the course of all social and artistic education. This law commands a break with native land and attachments. It demands that artistic success be defined through social accomplishment, the symbol of which is the conquest of Paris. On the contrary, artistic maturation seems to coincide for George

Sand with a return to her original location. I would also like to read this return as an attempt to recover her own language. George Sand does not intend to revive the aristocratic tradition of the 'pastoral' whose idyllic representations are obviously part of an idealistic denial, if not a refusal, of history. She dismisses both the parricidal dagger of the bourgeoisie and the shepherd's crook of Marie-Antoinette. Indeed, her rustic novels, with the exception of *Jeanne,* have some features in common with fairy tales: all is well that ends well; obstacles (such as the money problems which threaten the story with the phantom of bourgeois society) are magically overcome; marriage sanctifies the abolition of the contradictions and rifts imposed by history. However, even if she explicitly resorts to the strategies of fairy tales, George Sand insists on the truth of her endeavour. François Rollinat, her friend and the interlocutor of her preface to *François le Champi,* recalls that the priest's housekeeper and the man who twines hemp told them a 'true story':

> 'Between the two of them they told us a true story, rather long, which looked like an intimate novel. Do you remember it?'

> 'Perfectly, and I could retell it word for word in their language.'

At the end of the novel, someone who has just heard the story echoes Rollinat's remark:

> 'Then the story is completely true?' Sylvine Courtioux asked.

> 'If it isn't, it could well be', answered the twiner of hemp. 'And if you don't believe me, go and see for yourself.'

Thus the 'truth' of its narrative conditions guarantees the truthfulness of the rustic tale. It is a true story because it is directly recounted by real peasants. All the difficulty and originality of George Sand's project lie in her desire to make the language of peasants heard. Ethnographic critics have tried to determine the extent to which she was faithful to this project. She has been declared faithful because her tale is studded with regional Berrichon expressions and unfaithful because she occasionally invented such expressions.

The contradictory necessity of faithfulness and unfaithfulness to the peasant language is precisely the central issue. The peasant mode of expression is fundamentally oral. The relation of 'our literature'—which 'only knows how to amplify or disguise'—to 'rustic songs, narratives and tales' emblematizes the relation of written to oral language. Since we learn to speak before we learn to read or write, the passage to writing can be experienced as a shift to a second language. In any case, it opens a division internal to linguistic practice: it requires translation, inevitably unfaithful. It provokes a defiant distancing, if not the total obliteration of all traces of an orality improper to the code of writing. Therefore, although George Sand is able to 'recount word for word in their language' François le Champi's story as it was told by the peasants, she must translate it from the moment she writes it down: 'Their language demands to be translated; one has to write in French and

not allow oneself any word that is not unless it is so intelligible that a footnote would be useless for the reader.'

What should then be found in the rustic novels is a way to articulate a language doubly primitive and thus doubly menaced by disappearance: primitive or primary because it is oral and primitive because it is spoken by the most primitive layer of society.

I want rapidly to list the linguistic devices which, by emphasizing the primacy of the oral, enable George Sand to be faithful to peasant language. She particularly likes to place the narration in the mouths of peasants, a device she uses in other novels as well. Even in the case of *Jeanne,* the first and least strictly rustic of her rustic novels, where the sad fate of the heroine could be linked to the failure to restore an original language, she invents the following dedication:

> To Françoise Meillant
> You cannot read, my quiet friend. But your daughter and mine have been to school. Some day, at a gathering on a winter evening, while you spin, they will tell you the story which will become much prettier by passing through their mouths.

Despite the denaturing quality of writing, the possibility of passing the tale through the mouths of the daughters to the mother might save, if not Jeanne, at least her story. The great importance granted to dialogue in George Sand's novels as well as in all her writings—for example, her insistence on considering written correspondence as 'chatter'—seems to me another indication of her desire to inscribe or represent orality.

Dialogue represents the simplest form of oral communication. It also functions as a main diegetic tool in her novels. Whether we think of the dialogue between the narrator and 'his' friend in the prefaces to *François le Champi* and *La petite Fadette* or of the dialogues between François and Madeleine, Landry and Fadette, Bernard and Edmée, or even She and Him in the novel of that name, in every case their maieutic virtue is essential to the development of the story. Every time women speak, with the exception of the prefaces where the male-friend plays the role of initiator and maieutician, it allows the other to give birth to his own speech. The dialogue guarantees his coming to the world; introspection is practically non-existent in the rustic novels. When it does occur, it means that received speech is interiorized. Above all, dialogue is the royal path of love; through it the essence of love manifests itself. Landry falls in love with the speech of 'la petite Fadette' at a moment when the two find themselves outside the social scene. It is just at the point in 'la petite Fadette' 's speech when she tells him that she takes care of her little brother as though she were his mother (thus revealing the maternal figure hidden under her rags and her boyishness), that Landry falls madly in love with her. In a similar way, one could read the story of François le Champi as another instance of love at first speech. It tells of the coming to speech, thanks to Madeleine, of a poor nameless child who 'did not know how to say a word'. By addressing herself to him and by loving him, Madeleine literally gives him speech.

In *The Story of My Life* George Sand associates the moment when she was forced by her paternal grandmother to stop speaking the Berrichon patois with her mother's departure. The grandmother forced the mother to leave after the death of their common love object, Maurice Dupin, George Sand's father. She provided her granddaughter with a second education, following the primary education under the mother's guidance, which George Sand describes as an attempt to break original ties. Thus began a period of suppression which she evokes in these terms:

> She (the grandmother) was eager to cast off my inveterate sloppiness which my mother had never bothered to correct. I wasn't to roll on the ground any more, or to laugh so loud, or to talk our broad Berrichon dialect.

The repression of the mother coincides with the prohibition of Berrichon.

The distance between the 'base' and the 'summit', between *The Story of My Life* and the Berrichon novels, between 'the reality of the subject' and the artistic ideal, is clearly marked. However, perhaps one could say that, reaching the summit of art, George Sand directs herself toward the mother's tongue as though it were the living source of her artistic language.

The statement which opens the actual narrative of *The Story of My Life* is often forgotten:

> One is not only one's father's child, *one is also a bit, I believe, one's mother's.* It seems to me one is even more so; we are held to the womb which bore us in the most immediate, powerful and sacred way (added emphasis).

This phrase is forgotten because it emerges with such pain, and comes with such reticence before it affirms itself. By contrast one does not forget, particularly if one is a critic by profession, this other sentence, which is so assertive: 'I will go on with my father's story since he is, without punning, the real author of the story of my life.' It resonates all the more in memory since *The Story of My Life* indeed begins with the story of George Sand's father. Moreover the word 'author' seems to clearly establish the symbolic affiliation between 'the author of life' ('l'auteur de ses jours') and the author of novels. It has always been easier, and this was even more true then, to have oneself recognized as the child of one's father.

But were we to look more closely, we could avoid a precipitous interpretation which would make George Sand, a writer with a masculine pseudonym, the worthy daughter, if not the son, of her father, Maurice. For the story of the father George Sand recounts so ardently is in fact the marvellous story of a mother and a son and their reciprocal passion. Maurice, the beloved and loving son, later displayed these treasures of love transmitted to him by his mother for Sophie-Victoire, mother of George Sand. A woman of the people, older than him, Sophie-Victoire could have matched the revolutionary ideals of his mother if the latter had not been jealous of her. He remained faithful to the mother, from then on torn between two loyalties which were one in their origin. I would like to recall two

important moments in George Sand's narrative. In the first, she evokes Maurice's voluntary enlistment in the service of the Revolution while his mother was in gaol during the Terror:

> Although suffering from the Revolution in his very entrails because he felt his adored mother under the knife, I never see him curse the Mother-ideas ('les Idées mères') of the Revolution.

Maurice Dupin is faithful to the maternal principle even when it entails contradiction.

The second moment seems to me most significant. It follows the recounting of a heartrending separation, again provoked by revolutionary events:

> This poor child had never left his mother, he had never known, never foreseen pain. *He was as beautiful as a flower and as chaste as a maid.* He was sixteen . . . *At that age, a boy raised by a tender mother is an exceptional being in creation. He belongs, so to speak, to no gender. He loves his mother in a way a daughter does not love her and will never be able to love her.* Drowned in the bliss of being exclusively loved and adoringly cherished, this mother is the object of a kind of cult for him. This is love without the storms and the faults he will be dragged into later by love for another woman. Yes, this is ideal love, and it lasts only a moment in a man's life (added emphasis).

Thus the ideal son is indeed a daughter; the loving son represents the ideal daughter of the mother, the one George Sand did not have but the one she was herself. It is in this way that George Sand identifies herself with her father; not with a paternal figure but with the son of the mother, even of two mothers. For, George Sand adds, if he is 'capable of ardently and nobly loving a new idol' (his wife), it is because 'he will have gone through the sacred apprenticeship of true love with his mother'. Was not George Sand the adored and adoring daughter of her own mother and the 'son' of her grandmother, who recognized in her the living image of her late son? After a few sentences the story that George Sand tells us ceases to be strictly biographical and turns into a subjectless reverie, a prelude to a novelistic creation. Can one not recognize in this narrative the very story of *François le Champi* that George Sand started to write in 1847, the year she started to put down her own story? Does not François le Champi, with his 'mother' Madeleine, experience the sacred apprenticeship of a true and ideal love? Nothing is more sublime, indeed more sublimated, than this novel of love, the most perfect and the least erotic of all romantic novels. It tells the story of a son 'as well behaved as a good girl', endowed with the extraordinary capacity to act as the mother in his turn. He takes care of Madeleine in all the ways she took care of him; he looks after the house, he cures her and feeds her. This story could well represent the originary scene of George Sand's fantasy since this term relates the realm of the poetic to the unconscious. In *François le Champi* one finds the primary system of the writer's ego-identifications as well as the source of her romantic imagination. 'In my opinion', she writes as a conclusion to her description of this sacred apprenticeship, 'poets and novelists have not sufficiently recognized this observable topic, this swift and unique moment in the life of a man, which is a source of poetry.' Then she interrupts the dream-story of a father eternally kept by death in the guise of a young man, a faithful lover and faithfully loved, with the exclamation: 'This existence would have made such a beautiful topic for a novel, had not the principal characters been my father, my mother and my grandmother!' I leave George Sand with her paraliptical statement. I will only note that it could lead us to rethink the connections between the biographical and the novelist in her work. Whether it concerns Maurice Dupin, George Sand herself, or Maurice Sand, the son who took his mother's name, what she tells is indeed the story of the mother's child. For the first two characters of this intimate novel, it is a story about the restoration of ties broken by history. Is not history itself the sad account of innumerable separations?

George Sand describes the catastrophic separation, inevitable in our cultural system, which initiates the historical process, precisely as a separation from original language. In the passage we are concerned with, she engages in a diatribe against the damage of the second education, the education the boy gets no longer from his mother but at school. The school-boy becomes ugly, he begins to fear women, 'his mother's caresses make him blush,' 'the most beautiful languages of the world', those of the poets, disgust him. And, George Sand concludes,

> It will take him years to lose the fruit of his detestable education, *to learn his own language,* forgetting the Latin he hardly knows and the Greek he does not know at all, so he can form his taste and have the right idea of history . . . *Only then will he love his mother.* But the passions instantly seize him and he will never have known this heavenly love I was talking about, which is like a pause for a man's soul in the bosom of an enchanting oasis (added emphasis).

Thus the writer advocates a third moment of apprenticeship aimed at unlearning the lessons of the social in order to recover the taste of one's own tongue. In my opinion, this educational project is the most subtle and the most revolutionary aspect of George Sand's thought. She does not conceive of the return to the mother as a regression to a state of nature, a recrossing of the threshold of language acquisition. Rather she thinks of it as a passage beyond divisions (nature/culture, body/language) created precisely by placing the mother outside the socio-cultural order.

Contrary to what a Lacanian or Kristevan analysis would have us believe, in George Sand's life and work it is the mother who guarantees access to the symbolic order and the maintenance of meaning through the gift of speech made to the child. As evidence, I want to refer the reader to the many anecdotes of language acquisition told by George Sand in *The Story of My Life.* They are all connected with the mother, whether they concern the first utterance of the verb 'to love' or the endless fairy tales little Aurore invents for her mother. The latter, 'a natural artist', helps her daughter keep hold of the thread of her speech. I would add to these examples the reading lessons in her novels. In *Mauprat,* for instance, Patience learns

how to read poetry under the direction of the maternal Edmée. Madeleine teaches François how to read in *François le Champi;* the fact that she can read is considered her most striking feature by the peasant narrators. The scene of the reading lesson always shows two people reading aloud, as when the mother reads her child a bedtime story, like the story of François le Champi that Proust's mother tells him in a voice which penetrates him forever. Thus the dimension of speech is maintained and founds the pleasure of consuming the book in the union of mouths and ears. Through speech, both the primitive maternal and the cultural, pleasure and the production of meaning, are linked. Thus the 'problem' Lacan evokes for us might be addressed. 'The problem is that of the relationship in the subject between speech and language': 'speech', by which the subject believes he expresses himself as the subject of his desire, and 'language', which, by separating the subject from his own body, abolishes desire as it sanctions it. 'Speech indeed is a gift of language', Lacan writes. But if 'in the gift of speech resides all the reality of its effects' still Lacan gives us no indication of how we are to consider the gift. He does not qualify the gift; he does not say 'who' gives. Rather he suggests that language gives itself, that the Word, in enunciating itself, makes a present of itself, just as the law, God, or the analyst according to Lacan, do. But if Lacan is right to say that the *gift* of speech, by generating transference, founds the 'efficacy of linguistic symbols', is not what gives or what provokes giving or what is given, under the name of transference, love? And if this gift of speech was the gift of the mother's love, it would give, as to George Sand or to François le Champi, the gift of love as well as the gift of speech.

It is from this perspective that I would read the thematic of the promise (*parole donnée*) in George Sand's work. The promise inaugurates many love stories. Even before being acknowledged as a gift or a bond of love, the gift of a word unites Landry and Fadette or Bernard and Edmée and guarantees their everlasting fidelity. I would say that George Sand conceives of language not as *Verbum* but as *Fides,* as oath (*foi jurée*), binding speech, responsible for repairing the rents of history, which inscribes the subject in the social at the expense of the body. This is why the nuptials, at the end of the rustic narratives, coincide with reunion; the wedding ceremony celebrates the return of the hero who, for a while, has lived in an unfamiliar social scene. It consecrates the victory of the original love bond, the end of separation and its threats, the retaking of the first paths. This last issue is underlined by the Sandian topology of lost paths, paths leading astray or straight to their goal: to the point of departure. In *François le Champi, La Petite Fadette* or *La Mare au Diable,* all these paths lead back to the mother.

One can always find one's way back to the mother. Such, too, is the lesson of *Mauprat.* That life offers more than one path, that education can always modify tendencies and allow 'a soul plunged in the depths of an unclean mire as it emerges from the cradle' none the less to develop, illustrates the orientation of this particular apprenticeship: Bernard Mauprat, removed early from the maternal cradle and left to the feudal and masculine barbarity of his uncles, will find in Edmée the educating mother who will help him to unlearn the lessons of his caste, in order to learn how to speak well and to love well.

The direct connection between the maternal tongue and the poetic tongue can be attributed to George Sand's own mother's predispositions. She was the daughter of a bird-seller and a singing bird herself. A 'bird song' that 'his mother Zabelle used to tell him to put him to sleep, in the parlance of the old days of our country' comes to François' mind on his way back to his 'second' 'mother'. Madeleine, whom he has decided to marry.

> Une pive
> cortive,
> Anc ses piviots,
> Cortiviots,
> Livardiots,
> S'en va pivant
> Livardiant
> Cortiviant

It is also in relation to the mother's desire—at least George Sand's mother—that I would interpret the writer's characterization of the road of creation: the path of idealization which she represents as an ascent toward the summit. Here is what she says about it, in a letter to her friend Flaubert, at the moment when she reaches the summit, some months before her death:

> As for me I want to gravitate up to my last breath, not with the certitude nor the need of finding elsewhere a good place, but because my sole joy is in keeping myself and mine on an upward road.

> In other words *I flee the sewer and I seek the dry and the clean,* certain that it is the law of my existence (added emphasis).

Is not the learning of the dry and the (neat and) clean (*propre*) the paradigm of all first education and the indication of the child's submission to the mother's desire which, in matters of cleanliness, has the force of law? We can confirm this by referring to the scene George Sand describes as a traumatic memory of her early childhood, when her mother snatched her from the pleasure of splashing about in an imaginary river which she called a sewer. We should no longer be surprised by the story George Sand addresses to 'those interested in the making of works of art' in the forward to *François le Champi.* Here she describes how she took a path 'no one is likely ever to take' which led to a muddy pond she again calls a sewer. Suddenly a wild child sprang over the sewer as if to illustrate Freud's remarks on children's theories of birth. The narrator helped him across the sewer and began to ask him questions, as Madeleine did in the first conversation she had with the Champi, when she found him on the bank of the river. The child, who had no name and no parents, did not know how to answer. George Sand concluded with the necessity for education, recalling that she herself had 'had several Champi of both sexes brought up'.

Does not the law of existence of George Sand's characters consist in having them march in the direction of the dry and the clean (*propre*)? Is not learning to speak well a way of pleasing the mother by sublimating the erotic impulses and displacing them from the anal-genital zone to the mouth? Under the benevolent protection of the first god of George Sand's first religion, Corambé, the mouth tells stories which are so clean the body is nearly absent from them. 'Let's make a novel which would be a religion, or a religion which would be a novel'. Thus was born Corambé, about whom George Sand tells us that she imagined him sometimes with the features of her mother, sometimes with those of a swineherd named Pleasure!

Education, according to George Sand, begins and ends near the river. 'Let's go to the fountain. Maybe I will find my tongue there', François says at the end of the novel. This is where he first met Madeleine, where he was born, so to speak. In the meantime he has learned not to throw himself into the river, not to plunge back into it in a gesture of deadly regression. François and François the Fadette, or even Bernard Mauprat, dirty children of the river, the sewer and the swamp, thus learn, through love, to live, to speak, to wash themselves and to become well behaved (*propres*)—as well behaved and pure as François Rollinat, George Sand's devoted friend, her favourite interlocutor in the rustic novels, the co-singer of a long amebean song, the ultimate addressee of *The Story of My Life,* the representative of an asexual love, the most faithful and perfect of George Sand's life. Indeed George Sand may have taken him for the mother's intermediary: was he not charged with watching over the realization of a desire which had become the law of her existence, the desire transmitted by the mother for a *proper* tongue? (pp. 54-64)

> *Anne Berger, "Let's Go to the Fountain: On George Sand and Writing," in* Writing Differences: Readings from the Seminar of Hélène Cixous, *edited by Susan Sellers, Open University Press, 1988, pp. 54-65.*

George A. Kennedy   (essay date 1989)

[*In the following excerpt, Kennedy examines the philosophy and characters of Sand's* Seven Strings of the Lyre, *comparing it to Goethe's* Faust *and placing it in the context of nineteenth-century Romantic literature.*]

The Seven Strings of the Lyre is a reaction by a major French writer to Goethe's *Faust* and one of the very few treatments of the Faust legend by a woman (another is Dorothy Sayers's 1939 play, *The Devil to Pay*). It was written in 1838 during the early stages of Sand's romantic liaison with Frédéric Chopin, and one of its themes is the nature of music: the ability of music to express ideas, and its relationship to other arts. One character in the work may be thought to represent Chopin and another, to a more limited extent, Franz Liszt. Sand's treatment of music seems to have been inspired by recent discussions with Liszt. The work thus has a small place in the history of romantic aesthetics and musicology. Philosophically, and this is a very philosophic work, it is a reaction against eighteenth-century rationalism—the tradition of Cartesianism and Voltaire—and an assertion of the existence of some higher truth to be found in music, poetry, and a sympathetic response to nature. As often in Sand's novels, this higher vision is most easily obtained by a woman innocent of the complexities and pedantry of learning, but the lot of women is suffering, and the threat of a brutalizing marriage hangs over them, as Sand knew from personal experience. Yet a woman may lead a man to fuller knowledge and a fuller life through love.

Politically, *The Lyre* presents an idealized socialism in the tradition of Rousseau and the Saint-Simoneans, founded on faith in the perfectibility of human society and hostile to both the aristocracy of the *ancien régime* and the bourgeois monarchy of Louis-Philippe. Though deeply romantic, it is also opposed to the art-for-art's-sake romanticism of Gautier and other writers of the time in that it demands social responsibility of an artist. In Sand's view, the arts should lead society to awareness of truth, freedom, and the meaning of life, and this is what she here attempts to do. The primary value of the work is as a document in literary, aesthetic, and intellectual history. As a purely literary achievement it falls below many of Sand's novels and plays, but her technical skills of composition were always great. With minor exceptions identified in the notes, the plot is well worked out, the characters are vividly realized, some of the scenes are dramatically effective, and at times Helen and the Spirit of the Lyre rise to a poetic eloquence that may move those readers who can enter into the romantic mind of the early nineteenth century. Sand has attempted a difficult task: to cast into words the effect of music and to give dramatic interest to philosophical abstractions. Readers of the work, both at the time of publication and since, have usually thought that she was only partially successful, but the attempt deserves respect, and *The Lyre* makes an interesting contrast to Sand's treatment of similar themes elsewhere. (pp. 1-2)

Sand's Lyre *and Goethe's* Faust

The Seven Strings of the Lyre (Les septs cordes de la lyre) is a philosophical play, not intended for production on stage, written in simple but poetic prose in the late summer of 1838, soon after the beginning of Sand's relationship with Chopin. It was published in *La Revue des deux mondes,* a journal to which Sand was then under contract, in the issues of 15 April and 1 May 1839, then as a separate book by F. Bonnaire in Paris in 1840 and in later collected editions of Sand's works. (p. 5)

The time and place of the action of *The Lyre* are not specified in the stage directions. The time, however, is clearly the present or recent past, thus about 1838: the reigning king in act 1, scene 7, much resembles Louis-Philippe; Helen's vision of the earth in act 4, scene 1, includes steam locomotives and railways, a development of the 1830s; in act 3, scene 3, the eighteenth century is referred to as the past. The place is less consistently maintained. Throughout most of the action it appears to be a small German university town where Albertus is a teacher of philosophy: the students and townspeople have German names; the countryside is nearby; people seem to know others in a way not characteristic of large cities. This is clearly adopted from the Faust legend. But the scenes mentioned above as fixing the time of the action are inconsistent with such a location, for act 1, scene 7, seems to suggest that the city is a royal residence, and the first of Helen's views from the cathedral tower in act 4, scene 1, seems clearly to overlook Paris. Yet the cathedral cannot be Notre-Dame de Paris,

for its high bell tower is surmounted by a tapering spire. Strasbourg Cathedral would better fit the description. Clearly, although the basic setting is a German-speaking university town, Sand freely departs from this locale to bring in contemporary French allusions.

The action of the play describes the efforts of the devil, Mephistopheles (Méphistophélès), to win the soul of Master Albertus (Maître Albertus); the latter, as Mephistopheles tells us in act 1, scene 3, is a descendant of Faust and perhaps also of Faust's mistress, Marguerite. To reach his goal, Mephistopheles discovers he must first destroy a remarkable lyre in Albertus's possession, "the symbol that here lights the flames of the heart," and secure the spirit that dwells within the lyre. His task is aided by the fact that the middle-aged Albertus has come to feel that, in his dedication to philosophy, life and love have passed him by; it is complicated, however, by differences between Albertus's character and that of Faust ("He has more conscience than the other; pride has taken greater hold of him, vanity none"), by the fact that the lyre is magical and cannot be broken by the agents the devil first tries to employ, and by the presence of Helen (Hélène).

Helen of Troy is a traditional character in the Faust legend (derived from stories of Helen and Faustus in early Christian accounts of Simon Magus), and is often a *femme fatale* conjured up from hell to awaken Faust's passions and secure his damnation. This is the role she plays in Christopher Marlowe's *Doctor Faustus,* in which she appears but never speaks. In the second part of Goethe's *Faust,* however, she plays a benign role as a symbol of the beauty and naturalness of classical antiquity, and her union with Faust represents the synthesis of the classic and antique with the Gothic and Germanic. In Sand's play, Helen is a beautiful young woman who has come to live with Albertus as his ward on the death of her father, Meinbaker the instrument maker. Her only inheritance is the magic lyre, made by her ancestor Adelsfreit. Albertus has sought to teach her philosophy, but she is bewildered by books. Her intelligence responds instead to nature, to virtue, and to music, and in the course of the play she achieves and expresses a knowledge of God and understanding of nature, a sympathy for human life and suffering, and finally love, which is impossible within the system of rational philosophy. She awakens the love of the Spirit of the Lyre and ultimately frees him from his prison and thus from the clutches of Mephistopheles. She also innocently awakens the love of Albertus. Mephistopheles has sought to encourage this as a way of leading Albertus into fleshly lust or disgusting him by a degradation of Helen, but he is ultimately unsuccessful. Albertus learns from Helen what he had never learned from books, and though she departs with the Spirit of the Lyre to the heavenly empyrean and the infinite, Albertus is left with a new motivation to study and to teach a more profound and more sensitive view of philosophy.

George Sand's judgment of Goethe, influenced by her mentor at the time, Pierre Leroux, is set out in an article entitled **"Essai sur le drame fantastique,"** which she published in *La Revue des deux mondes* at the end of 1839, a year after her composition of *The Lyre.* . . . Sand viewed Goethe as an able artist and *Faust* as a considerable achievement, but she felt Goethe was lacking in "enthusiasm, belief, and passion." To her, he was not an ideal poet, for she thought he himself lacked an ideal, and she regarded him as a skeptic and as a German descendant of Voltaire. She also identified him with the art-for-art's-sake movement as she knew it in France and criticized him for a lack of social conscience. Some of her views clearly influenced her recasting of the Faust story in *The Lyre.* She criticizes Goethe's Mephistopheles as not adequately wicked; her character showed what a devil should be. She finds Goethe's Faust, as a character, too cold; her Albertus is considerably more emotional. For Goethe's simple village girl, Marguerite, or for the dangerous Helen of the earlier Faust legend, she substituted the angelic Helen, who becomes the central figure in the action.

Sand seems to have based her judgments on a reading of the first part of *Faust* and of the separately published Helen Act in part two during the spring of 1838. The complete second part of *Faust,* first published in German in 1832, did not appear in French until the version by Henri Blaze in 1840. If Sand had known the complete part two of *Faust,* her judgments, especially of Goethe's social conscience, might well have been different, for it is in the later part of the work that Faust commits himself to service to society. On the positive side, Goethe's portrayal of Euphorion may possibly have influenced Sand's conception of the spirit of the Lyre. Although the two are rather different in character, Euphorion, the offspring of Faust and Helen, is the personification of poetry and is associated with music, and he is reminiscent of Lord Byron much as the Spirit can be regarded as reminiscent of Chopin. (pp. 5-8)

Music and Philosophy

Music was an important part of George Sand's life. In her autobiography, *My Life,* she tells of a small harp that she had in her student days, and she also played the piano. Her serious interest in music was enhanced by conversations and correspondence with Franz Liszt in 1836. Liszt may appear in *The Lyre* as the student Hanz, who has a special understanding of music. When Helen plays the lyre, the other characters hear only the music of the instrument, but Sand verbalizes the meaning for the benefit of the reader, implying that musical sounds convey ideas, both abstract and concrete. Moreover, music and words are analogous to visual images; being is both a harmony and a prism. Liszt, however, did not like the play. He wrote later that it left "a painful impression" and spoke of its "lassitude, enervation, and decadence." What Chopin thought, I do not know. Immediately after Sand completed *The Lyre* he went with her for the winter to Majorca, already showing signs of tuberculosis and under pressure to complete some compositions for his publishers. The unconventional couple was not well received on the island, the climate was less agreeable than they expected, and they both had a difficult winter.

Music and musicians appear in a number of Sand's works, for example *Consuelo* (1842-43), which centers around the life of an opera singer. In *Les Maîtres sonneurs* (1857) Sand tells the story of a young man who seems taciturn and dull but who is able, by playing the bagpipes, to convey thoughts, resemblances, and moods. Her heroines, like Helen, are often intelligent, sensitive people with a feeling for nature and the arts who, despite lack of formal education, have wisdom, insight, and understanding. A good example is found in one of her last novels, *Marianne.*

The songs of Helen and the Spirit of the Lyre adumbrate a system of philosophy, though many of the details remain vague. The seven strings of the Lyre together speak the harmony of all being. The two golden strings sing of the mystery of the infinite, one being identified with the ideal and with intelligence, the other with faith and the ardor of the soul, as explained in act 2, scene 4. When Albertus, urged on by Mephistopheles, has disconnected these strings, Helen plays the silver strings, which sing of terrestrial creation and nature. The first silver string is dedicated to the contemplation of nature, the second to Providence (see act 3, scene 3.) After Albertus disconnects the silver strings, Helen plays the steel strings, and the Spirit now sings of the grandeur and genius of man, while Helen sings of man's crimes and misfortunes (see act 4, scene 3.) With the removal of the steel strings there remains one brazen string (*corde d'airain*) that sings of love.

Antecedents for the metaphysics here expressed can be found in Platonism, in writings of Spinoza, and in the mysticism of the seventeenth and eighteenth centuries, especially in the writings of Emanuel Swedenborg, but more immediate sources for George Sand are the writings and conversations she had with Hughes Felicité de Lamennais (1782-1854) and especially with Pierre Leroux (1797-1848). Leroux's treatise *De l'humanité,* though not published until 1840, represents his teaching at this time. It sets out a view of life as aspiration and speaks of an indivisible trinity of sensation, sentiment, and reason, moving through history toward an eventual perfection. Death is a veil that separates us from a new phenomenal manifestation and a new knowledge of man, and we eventually return to God, who contains our latent being. In a letter to Ferdinand Guillon in 1844 (*Correspondance,* 4, no. 2835), Sand describes herself as "only a pale reflection of Leroux, a fantastic disciple of the same ideal, but a disciple mute and ravished before his word, always ready to throw in the fire all her works, to write, to think, to pray, and to act under his inspiration." She claims, with considerable exaggeration, that she only seeks to translate into novels the philosophy of her master. I say "exaggeration" because it seems to me that Sand's most important inspiration lay in her own experience and its imaginative development. What Leroux provided her was a conceptualization of what she already instinctively believed.

The lyre, as a symbol of the union of music and poetry, was already a commonplace in classical times, for example in the poetry of Pindar or Horace, and the figure of the broken or unstrung lyre is occasionally found as well. One example that George Sand would have known occurs in book 2, chapter 3, of Victor Hugo's *Notre-Dame de Paris* (1831), in which a woman's voice interrupts the song of the Bohemian and Grégoire exclaims, "Cursed notched saw that comes to break the lyre!" The specific source, however, for a lyre on which different strings have different meanings apparently came to Sand from Michel de Bourges, whom she called "Everard." Among his papers was found a sketch of a lyre with the inscription "The lyre of George Sand after the plan of her friend Everard. Nohant, 11 August 1835." This date is exactly three years before composition of *The Lyre.* On the strings are the following labels: (1) peace, sciences, agriculture; (2) war or liberty and tyranny; (3) sufferings or death, crime; (4) joys, or belief, the martyrs, virtue; (5) evocation, tombs; (6) love of the elements; the sea, the sky, the earth, water, fire; (7) God, or prayer, and adoration. Sand has apparently rearranged the ideas into a different sequence, but most of the motifs appear at some point in the songs of Helen and the Spirit. (pp. 9-12)

The Characters

It seems possible that the Spirit of the Lyre, imprisoned in the instrument, in some sense represents Frédéric Chopin. Whatever Sand's conscious intent, such an identification is reasonable on the part of a reader. The Spirit of the Lyre, like Chopin, speaks with music; Helen, with whom Sand herself may be identified, alone fully understands him. A harmony and unity emerge in their thought, they learn from each other and come to love one another, and together they escape from the constraints and suffering of the world into an ideal union of bliss and harmony. In contrast to them are the worldly poet, painter, composer, and critic of act 1, scene 7; these are caricatures of professional types and apparently do not satirize specific individuals.

The figure of Albertus evokes many connotations. He is called a descendant of Faust and is, first of all, Sand's version of that traditional character. He may in part be modeled on philosophers Sand knew, for example Lamennais, and he may even incorporate some memories of her tutor, François Deschartres, who had tried to teach her Latin and who dabbled in theology, medicine, and magic. The choice of Albertus in its Latin form, however, easily recalls Albertus Magnus (ca. 1206-1280), scholastic philosopher and theologian, an archetype of the man of learning of the past. He is cast in the latter role in Edgar Quinet's epic, *Ahasvérus* (1833). Another Albert in Sand's mind at this time was Count Albert Grzymala (1793-1855), a Polish émigré, a close friend of Chopin, and a confidant to Sand in her relationship with the composer, as her letters indicate. Albertus has nothing of Grzymala's character, but that he had made some contribution to the work is suggested by the strange quotation Sand set on the first page of *The Lyre.* It purports to be Grzymala's translation of a Slavic (Polish?) song in which there is reference to the Son of the Lyre, Spirits of Light, and Spirits of Harmony. Thus some of the figures of the play are attributed to Grzymala. The quotation is very unlike any Slavic folk poetry, and no such translation by Grzymala is otherwise known. Perhaps there is some private allusion here; something Grzymala had said may have met a response in Sand's thinking. The song is addressed to an unidentified "Eugene," but it is interesting that "Eugene" and "Albert," the one Greek in origin, the other Germanic, have the same basic meaning of "well-born."

There are still other Alberts who have some connection with *The Lyre* or with how it might be read in Sand's cir-

cle. If *The Lyre* is in part a reaction to Goethe's *Faust,* it is also in some sense a response to writings by Théophile Gautier, and especially to his role as a leading spokesman in the art-for-art's-sake movement. Although George Sand and Gautier (1811–1872) were not especially intimate, they knew each other and had many friends in common. In 1832 Gautier had published *Albertus, or the Soul and Sin,* a narrative poem in 122 stanzas. As a result, some of his friends gave him the nickname "Albertus." In Gautier's poem, a wicked woman named Véronique, by nature ugly in the extreme, disguises herself to appear young and beautiful, magically transforms her black cat into the figure of Don Juan, and goes to live in Leyden, where she becomes the mysterious center of a luxurious, hedonistic circle. Albertus is a young painter obsessed with memories of a beautiful woman he had known in Venice (where Sand had lived with Musset a few years earlier). He is summoned to Véronique's home, instantly falls in love with her, and declares that to possess her he would give his soul to the devil (stanza 94). In a highly erotic scene, she offers herself to him, but at the moment of sexual climax, naked in his arms, she suddenly turns back into the hideous old woman she really is. One might compare this scene with Mephistopheles' experience with the beautiful Lamiae in Goethe's *Faust* (pt. 2, l. 7770). Albertus then discovers himself in a filthy room with Don Juan, who has again become a cat, "like the dog of Faust," and who ties him in magic bonds with his black tail, from which radiates a strange blue light. There follows an assembly in hell before the devil, accompanied by a fiendish symphony of cacophonous music. The end of act 2, scene 7, of *The Lyre* could recall this scene. Albertus's soul is lost, and in the morning his dead body is found on the Appian Way near Rome. In the last stanza the narrator speaks of the poem as an "allegory" but coyly leaves its interpretation to the reader. The sensuality and irony of the poem really make it a parody of a moral allegory. In the last line the narrator calls for a volume of Rabelais' *Pantagruel,* thereby seeming to assert the spirit of Rabelaisian humor and its intoxication with life.

Again, in a story entitled "Celle-ci et celle-là," included in *Les jeunes France* (1833), Gautier introduced a central character named Albert, a sophisticated young man who, on the last page, is ironically described as "true reason, intimate friend of true poetry, himself fine and delicate prose who holds at his finger tips poetry that wishes to fly from the solid earth of reality into clouds of dreams and chimeras. He is Don Juan who gives a hand to Childe-Harold." Sand may have amused herself by taking the name of a character twice identified with Gautier and inverting the presentation for her own purposes. In 1836 Gautier published *Mademoiselle de Maupin,* the most brilliant and controversial novel of the period, immediately preceding Sand's composition of *The Lyre.* Its long preface is one of the most famous romantic declarations of art for art's sake, and the novel throughout is sensuous, physical, and amoral. Although there is no Albert in this story, there are some passages that provide background for Sand's *Lyre.* The narrator says, for example, "What use is a lyre without strings to a poet, or life without love to a man?" (chap. 2). And the description of moonlight, in chapter 4, bears some resemblance to the passage about the moon in act 3 of *The Lyre.*

Sand fundamentally disagreed with Gautier's view of art. Some of the issues of this disagreement are brought out in the debate between the poet, the painter, the composer, and the critic in act 1, scene 7 (perhaps the best single scene in *The Lyre*), and *The Lyre* as a whole is an example of the use of literature for philosophical and social purposes that Gautier rejected. The name "Albertus" thus draws attention to the difference. Sand again used the name "Albert" for the philosopher in *Consuelo* and its sequel, *The Countess of Rudolstadt.* Yet Gautier so wittily undercuts any serious meaning in his own treatments that the philosophizing on art and love in *The Lyre*— especially to an audience that had enjoyed his poem, story, and novel—could easily have seemed strained, prudish, and now even irrelevant. The reaction was indeed generally negative. It is a mark of Sand's basic seriousness, and of her naiveté, that she expected *The Lyre* to be an artistic success in the aftermath of *Mademoiselle de Maupin.*

Gautier may be said, however, to have paid her the compliment of imitation much later in his short 1865 novel, *Spirite,* a very uncharacteristic and not very successful work that takes up some of *The Lyre*'s themes. In *Spirite,* a young nobleman, Guy de Malivert, falls in love with a spirit (actually a deceased young woman who had secretly loved him in life). Her love of him is sometimes expressed through music, and he calls her playing of the piano a comment on her words, analogous in color and sentiment, that prolong the passage in sonorous or melancholy vibrations. Spirite's playing is said to surpass the music of Chopin or Liszt, and just as Helen plays without touching the strings of the lyre, Spirite plays without touching the keys. Eventually Malivert and Spirite are, like Helen and the Spirit of the Lyre, joined in the spirit world. Swedenborgianism is an explicit theme in this story, and since some of the ideas of *The Lyre* resemble those of Swedenborg, that too can be thought of as a link between the two works.

Publication and Reception of **The Lyre**

On 8 August 1838, Sand wrote to Christine Buloz, wife of her publisher, François Buloz, reporting that though she was having difficulty completing the last twenty pages of *Spiridion* she had instead written about half of "a little fantastic drama," which was to become *The Lyre.* "I have been passionately working on it for five or six nights, and I can promise you that in a week at the most you will have it" (*Correspondance,* 4, no. 1775). Sand often did much of her writing at night and seems to have required little sleep. The half she had written, she pointed out, would be enough for one issue of *La Revue des deux mondes,* to which she was under contract.

It was not until 7 September, however, that she announced completion of *The Lyre* in a letter to Félix Bonnaire, again describing the work as "a kind of fantastic drama" (*Correspondance,* 4, no. 1784). She wanted Buloz to announce it and to publish it before *Spiridion.* Problems arose, however. Buloz did not like the play; it was too mystical and philosophical, and he was especially uncomfortable with the passage in act 1, scene 7, describing "the king's" pref-

erence for picture-frames over the pictures themselves. This could be easily taken as ridicule of Louis-Philippe's collection at Versailles, and was probably so intended. Buloz at the time was seeking appointment from the king as commissioner of the Comédie Française. At the beginning of October, Sand wrote a curt note to Buloz demanding immediate publication before she left Paris on 20 October. She also asked for payment of "five to six thousand francs" (*Correspondance,* 4, no. 1790).

Although Buloz continued to postpone publication, by 15 February 1839 he had paid Sand five thousand francs for *The Lyre* (*Correspondance,* 4, no. 1827). On 17 March, Sand assured Charlotte Marliani that *The Lyre* was actually going to appear and was as suitable for the review as any other material, though "our Buloz hesitates and recoils because there are five or six passages too risky and because the dear man fears to embroil himself with our dear government" (*Correspondance,* 4, no. 1843), but later that month she again wrote to Buloz revealing the fear that he would renege and questioning his literary judgment (*Correspondance,* 4, no. 1846). At the beginning of April, now in Marseilles, she told Charlotte to assure Buloz that she was writing a novel "to his taste," but first he must pay her something on the account he owed her and must publish *The Lyre* (*Correspondance,* 4, no. 1850).

By about 19 April, Sand had seen the first installment of *The Lyre* and wrote to Emmanuel Arago asking him to proofread the second half. The first half, she said, somewhat tongue-in-cheek, "must have bored you to death, for you are too much a beast to understand anything of this sublime, monumental, pyramidal, amazing, luxuriant, and lavish work. What follows, though ravishing, is less remarkable, and as a result will displease you less." She was particularly nervous that Buloz would tamper with the scene where Helen appears on the cathedral tower and sees all humanity spread out before her. He would not believe that Helen could see so far, and Sand made fun of his weak eyes. "You must understand," she said, "that I attach some importance to these four or five lines [actually as many pages]. I have continued to work for this ignoble journal only on the condition that I have the most complete liberty" (*Correspondance,* 4, no. 1857).

Pierre Leroux had corrected the proofs of act 1, but apparently act 2 had not been carefully corrected by anybody. Sand complained to Buloz about it on 21 April, saying that she had marked out how the pages ought to be set so that the reader would understand that when Helen is in ecstasy the sound of the lyre, but not her words, are heard by the other characters (*Correspondance,* 4, no. 1859). Buloz was to ask Arago to proofread the remaining pages, if Leroux was still away. In a conciliatory tone, she told Buloz that he knew French better than she did, but he didn't have time for this task. In any event, *nobody* else was even to see the proofs except Buloz and his wife—the latter in case they were useful in curing her insomnia! Writing to Buloz on 23 June, however, she was in a bitter mood over his treatment of her. He pretended to understand what he edited! She was very doubtful that he could understand the second part of *Faust,* and she offered to pay him for all the money he had lost on *The Lyre.* "I'm not the jew Shylock, and I don't know what I would do with your skin," she says (**Correspondance**, 4, no. 1888). Buloz had written earlier that he did not like the second part of *Faust* any better than **The Lyre.** Writing again in December, she waived any payment for her new novel, **Pauline:** "I believe I owe it to you to make up for the bad success of **The Lyre,** which rests on my conscience" (**Correspondance,** 4, no. 1971).

Publication of **The Lyre** was greeted with silence by the critics, though Sand's productivity was so great it was easily overlooked in the flood of other works she was turning out, and its failure had no adverse effects on her reputation. Almost the only person who admired it was a young poet named Leconte de Lisle. In a short poem dedicated to George Sand (1839) he addressed her as "mystic Helen," and in the socialist journal *La Phalange* (2 [July 1845]: 179-82), he published his own "Hélène," inspired by **The Lyre.** In this work, he imagines a trip to Greece, where he is moved by the landscape and the art to a new vision of humanity. But subsequently Leconte de Lisle disowned the poem and, in authoritative editions of his works, replaced it with a new "Hélène," composed in 1852. In the new version, Helen of Troy has become the symbol of black destiny, the pessimism that the poet felt about politics and society when the Revolution of 1848 failed to advance his ideals. He turned to a view of art for art's sake and became a major figure in the Parnasse movement. (pp. 12-19)

There are occasional traces of **The Lyre** in nineteenth-century French literature, showing that it was not entirely forgotten, especially among Sand's own friends. . . . To me, the most striking allusion to Sand's work is found in part 3, chapter 6, of the most famous novel of the century, Flaubert's *Madame Bovary*—though the reference would easily escape a reader who did not know Sand's play. Emma Bovary is thinking aloud and asks, "But if there was somewhere a strong beautiful being, a valorous nature, full at one and the same time of exaltation and refinements, the heart of a poet under the form of an angel, *lyre with brazen strings,* sounding epithalamia toward the sky, why, by chance, could she not find it?" It is Flaubert's tribute to his friend George Sand and to her creation.

Sand's Feminism

The significance of Sand's **Lyre** for early nineteenth-century romanticism, and its relationship to some of her own works and those of others, are perhaps clear from what has been said above. Obviously the connection between its philosophical ideas and those of contemporary works, or its musical theory, could be worked out in greater detail than seemed appropriate here. I do not know what to say about the anti-Semitism of the play; on the one hand, Sand seems to go out of her way to stress the identification of Mephistopheles as a Jew; yet anti-Semitism is also a part of the late medieval atmosphere, inherited from the Faust legend, that hangs over the play, and in that sense the attitude is rather conventional.

The feminism of **The Lyre** is clear from the treatment of the character of Helen, on which some comments have already been made. Beginning in act 1, scene 8, Helen is re-peatedly referred to as "daughter of men," suggesting that she may be viewed as a sacrificial figure representing all women. There are doubtless other features of the play that could be discussed in the light of modern feminist criticism. For example, in act 1, scene 8, Helen is identified with the sibyl. The sibyl is a recurring symbol of feminine literary creativity, seen also in the introduction of Mary Shelley's *The Last Man* (1826), as discussed by Sandra M. Gilbert in *The Madwoman in the Attic* (1979). It might be argued that whereas the male characters of the play, including Albertus and the Spirit of the Lyre, take a positive view of historical progress and technology, Helen seems to live and think in space outside of history and with an acute sense of human suffering. Alice A. Jardine's theory of gynesis (*Diacritics* 12 [1982]) could perhaps be applied to **The Lyre,** in the sense that technology and time are here associated with the male, nature and space with the female. (On this see also Julia Kristeva, "Woman's Time," *Signs* 7 [1981].)

In conclusion, and without exaggerating the profundity of **The Lyre,** it seems appropriate to note that some of its themes, often passionately treated, are still significant one hundred and fifty years later. The experience of Helen as a woman is clearly one of these. Especially, perhaps, to an academic, the midlife crisis of Albertus, professor of philosophy, also cuts near the bone. The phenomenon of the scholar who loses confidence in his or her own knowledge and regrets choices of the past is not unknown today. Sand holds out hope that wisdom is attainable. The more general issue of the nature of knowledge still vexes us in the aftermath of the controversy between C. P. Snow and F. R. Leavis over "the two cultures," as it did the nineteenth century in the aftermath of Kant's aesthetic. Does there, in fact, exist a kind of poetic knowledge, complementary to but quite different from scientific knowledge? Sand, again passionately, believed there does, and that it is the more important of the two. Though especially available to a woman, a man may achieve it with effort. (pp. 20-22)

> *George A. Kennedy, in an introduction to* A Woman's Version of the Faust Legend: 'The Seven Strings of the Lyre' *by George Sand, translated by George A. Kennedy, The University of North Carolina Press, 1989, pp. 1-22.*

Brigitte Lane (essay date 1991)

[*Lane is an educator and critic who has extensively studied French expression and culture. In the essay below, she discusses Sand's unconventional treatment of the traditional folktale genre in her novel* La petite Fadette.]

In her 1848 preface to **La Petite Fadette,** George Sand establishes from the very start, and not without irony, a relationship between her novel and the folktale tradition, by declaring: "We dedicate this work to our friends in prison; since we are forbidden to discuss politics with them, we can only create *tales* to entertain them or put them to sleep."

Thus, the novelist, whose declared goal is to create "a series of village tales," returns to the familiar style of *François le champi* (1846) and, as in the earlier work, hides behind a male narrator: the traditional hemp-beater (*chanvreur* or *chanvreux*) of the Berry region, through whom she expresses herself throughout the narrative.

From this beginning, one could therefore expect a very ordinary story dominated by the conventions of the popular tale. This is not the case, however, for beyond the staged figure of her male narrator, the author (an invisible female presence) performs, throughout the work, a subtle manipulation of the usual traditional elements to establish as part of her discourse a subversive (almost feminist) dialectic of the conventions of the traditional folktale and of oral tradition in general.

This [essay] will therefore attempt to show how the novel *La Petite Fadette,* which came to be considered as children's literature, especially in the eyes of the French public, is in fact a deeply modern and original work that presented a somewhat revolutionary view of life and society for its time, for beyond the narration (and even beyond the action), George Sand repeatedly counters the accepted male conventions of the traditional folktale. She does so at three different levels.

At the conceptual level, the novelist deals first with the notion of "metamorphosis"—a notion that is usually associated, in the realm of traditional literature, with the concept of magic or the idea of "divine" (supernatural) intervention.

One of the best examples of the use of this concept is the well-known story of "Beauty and the Beast," as well as its seventeenth-century literary variants which (for the most part) are mere copies or offshoots of the traditional tale classified as Type 425 by Aarne-Thompson. All of these narratives are more or less derived from the very ancient story of "Amor and Psyche," related by Apuleïus in *The Golden Ass* as early as the middle of the second century.

La Petite Fadette, like the traditional tale, narrates the story of a "monstrous" being (or rather of a being perceived as "monstrous" by others, because of its dual nature: half-human, half-animal). However, the "monster's" inner, spiritual beauty and thoroughly human nature are ultimately revealed through the generous and redeeming love of a human being of the opposite sex. This redemption is usually accompanied by a physical transformation that finally allows physical appearances and spiritual reality to coincide. Meanwhile, the character involved has gone through a physical mutation which has brought him from the animal (and supernatural) realm to a purely human realm.

A similar ambiguity of nature is found in *La Petite Fadette,* for Fanchon Fadet and her little brother, *le sauteriot* (the little grasshopper) are viewed, all the way through the first part of the book, through animal (or even "sub-animal") metaphors, given the fact that they are usually associated with insect imagery or compared with other small animals. George Sand writes, when Fanchon Fadet first appears: "Whether 'Fadette' means a little fairy or the female of the elf . . . she was thin and tiny, dishevelled and bold. She was a highly talkative and mocking child,

as lively as a butterfly, as inquisitive as a red-robin and as black as a cricket." She further adds: "And when I compare Little Fadette to a cricket, it amounts to saying that she was no beauty, for that poor little cricket of the fields is even uglier than that of the chimney-corner."

Later, when the Saint-Andoche dance takes place, Sand stresses again the physical ugliness of Fadette, "the little cricket" (*grelet* or *grillon*). She writes: "Poor Cricket was so badly dressed that she seemed ten times uglier than usual. Landry . . . thought her far uglier than in her everyday rags. She had meant to make herself pretty but her efforts to tame her wild appearance only served to provoke laughter."

Here Fanchon Fadet's ugliness touches on the ridiculous and the author concludes her description by stating that the girl "looked like a little old woman in her Sunday best." Moreover, the term *dressage* (taming) stresses Fadette's almost savage, antisocial dimension, bring out again her animal attributes. However, in some respect, the so-called "ugliness" of Fanchon is associated in the villagers' eyes with her daring nonconformism and her boyish manners, which were obviously unacceptable in the nineteenth century. "She always behaved like a boy," writes Sand.

Landry himself, in one of his first surges of sympathy toward Fadette, evokes the contradiction between her physical appearance and her "soul" (if it is true that the eyes are the mirror of the soul), by telling her:

> If your nose were not so short, your mouth so large and your complexion so dark, you would not be bad looking at all. For people also say that, in the country hereabouts, there is not a pair of eyes equal to yours, and if you didn't have that bold and derisive look, many would like to be viewed kindly by those eyes.

Similar to the metamorphosis of the Beast, in the well-known folktale, Fanchon Fadet's metamorphosis corresponds both to a spectacular physical change and to a general change in attitude—to a "humanization" of the character.

It is the love Landry feels for Fadette, as well as her secret love for him, that bring Fadette to this utter transformation in "dress as well as manners." So great is the change that Landry himself, astonished, attributes this phenomenon to witchcraft: "She is a witch, he says. She has wanted to become beautiful instead of ugly as she used to be; and here she is, beautiful by a miracle."

Fadette's newly acquired beauty is also viewed as a form of socialization since she is described as having become "pleasant in her speech and dress, and her bearing towards people." This double metamorphosis, which causes the villagers great astonishment, nevertheless gains her their general favor.

Unlike the metamorphosis of the Beast in the popular tale (and although this latter is partly due to "the magic of love"), Fadette's metamorphosis is not instantaneous, but rather takes place in several phases. The first phase (as mentioned earlier) is provoked by Landry's generous love, which happens to be shared by Fadette; the second phase results from the willed and essentially initiatory journey (and one-year stay) that the girl makes to Château-Meillant. To that must be added the unexpected (and almost miraculous) discovery of the treasure left by old grandmother Fadet. All this contributes to the fact that, when Fanchon returns to the village, she is perceived by the community as a totally different person and even as "the best match in the region." George Sand writes: "Two days afterwards, Little Fadette dressed very neatly, for she was no longer poor and wretched and her mourning was made of fine cloth. She walked through La Cosse, and, as she had grown a good deal, those who saw her did not recognize her at first. She had become considerably lovelier during her stay in town." However, eager to make it clear that this incredible transformation had nothing to do with magic or witchcraft, the novelist explains right away: "Being better lodged and fed, she had gained color and flesh as much as was suitable for her age, and she could no longer be taken for a boy in disguise, so handsome and pleasant to look at was her figure. Love and happiness, too, had given her face and person something which is at once perceived but not so easily described."

The hypothesis of a magical intervention is therefore totally eliminated by Sand and, magic being excluded in favor of realism, the extraordinary changes witnessed in Fadette are attributed to highly practical causes: social acceptance, the love of another being (who is socially integrated), unexpected material wealth, better living conditions, and a better diet. The universe of the folktale, which implies magic and supernatural intervention, is therefore subsumed under the rules of the rustic novel which, for its part, relies on daily life and the reality of the peasant world.

One can wonder, moreover, whether the subtitle of the novel should not be "Beauty" (here, in the masculine) and "the Beast" (in the feminine), for the truth is that the basic dynamics of the book depend on female (rather than male) action, and on the central character of Fadette whose outer transformation, indirectly symbolic of her new social acceptance and, therefore, of her entry into collective life, forms the basis of the story. On the other hand are the twins (male characters); Landry plays a relatively passive role while Sylvinet assumes a totally paralyzing function in relation to the plot and the triangle of influence formed by the three main characters.

In *La Petite Fadette,* therefore, the nineteenth-century middle-class male/female stereotypes are not only questioned, but the male/female roles are also somewhat reversed in relation to tradition.

THE THEMATIC LEVEL

On the thematic level, George Sand simultaneously plays with the themes of magic, religion, and even magic as the opposite of religion.

At the beginning of the novel, if one takes into account the superstitions of the Berry region, Fadette is perceived by the village community as an ambivalent being having ties with both the animal and supernatural worlds. A number of metaphors (previously cited) define her "animal" di-

mension, but her name (*la Fadette*) links her even more to the supernatural world, on the one hand with the *fadets, farfadets,* or *follets,* defined by Sand as "sweet but rather malicious elves," and on the other hand, with the *fades* (or fairies) in whom "around here," writes Sand, "nobody much believes any more." The novelist herself insists on the double meaning of the name "Fadette" which (at the supernatural level) can equally mean "little elf " (in the feminine) and "little fairy" and, therefore, can designate a beneficial as well as a malefic being at the level of the conventional role. Mother Fadet (Little Fadette's grandmother) is also well known in the area for her skills as a healer and perhaps a sorceress. The tradition from the Berry region requires that secrets of witchcraft be transmitted orally, from generation to generation. Fadette can therefore be viewed as a potential witch.

Furthermore, her social marginality; her poverty; the fact that, as a child, she was abandoned by her mother (who was considered by the village as far from respectable); her premature role as a substitute mother to her little brother Jeanet; and finally her physical ugliness are so many elements that seem to justify the villagers' prejudices, along with the suspicion and scorn they display toward her.

Moreover, by means of the revelations she makes to Landry regarding her healing talents, Fadette (and with her, George Sand) demystifies all belief in magic (or sorcery), presenting her botanical knowledge as a form of science: "As for me, she says, without being a sorceress, I know the properties of the least herbs you crush beneath your feet." She later adds:

> It is true that God has made me curious, if that
> means wanting to know things that are hidden.
> But if people had been good and humane to me,
> I would never have dreamed of satisfying my cu-
> riosity at their expense. I would have confined
> my amusement to the knowledge of the secrets
> my grandmother teaches me for the healing of
> the human body.

It is also Fadette who tells about her inventiveness in the art of healing. She seems indeed to have an even greater knowledge of the subject than her grandmother, since she states: "I find virtues in herbs myself which she [Mother Fadet] does not know they have, and she is quite astonished when I make drugs and she subsequently sees their good effect."

George Sand insists several times on the fact that the knowledge and the use of plants for healing the human body (or even animals) is a kind of science and not magic. She had already stated earlier, wishing to denounce peasant superstitions: "In the countryside, one is never knowledgeable without being some kind of witch." By that, she means, without being *considered* a witch.

Little Fadette obviously is *not* a witch, as Sand reiterates at the end of the novel: "It [her knowledge] did not make her a witch, and she was right in denying the charge; but she had an observant mind, one that made comparisons, notes, trials, and that is undeniably a natural gift."

Fanchon's great curiosity of mind, her early maturity (acquired through suffering), her keen sense of observation, and even her desire to help others, constitute what would be called, in the twentieth century, an innate scientific mind.

To the knowledge acquired in the countryside due to her great freedom will be added another type of knowledge, acquired during her stay at Château-Meillant. Religion will then complement, or rather be superimposed, on magic, for Fanchon's mistress and friend, a former nun, will teach her "a number of fine [medical] secrets which [she] had learned in her convent, in the days before the Revolution."

Since this ex-nun also depicts Fanchon as a "perfect Christian," and therefore the best one can find in terms of religion, all uncertainty is removed regarding the source of the "talents" and "powers" of the young woman. The city (removed from peasant superstitions) has played, at the same time, an initiatory and liberating role for Fadette. It has made it possible for her to create a new social image of herself: an image reflecting her true nature and drawing both from science and religion, while excluding magic.

A healer of the body, Fadette will soon reveal herself as also being able to heal the mind. Sylvinet's first recovery (from "delirium and fever") is accomplished thanks to her medical knowledge but also through religious techniques (imposition of hands and prayers) practiced in a total spirit of self-sacrifice. Another technique she uses is a process close to hypnosis: "His body is not very ill; it is with his mind that I need to deal; I am going to try to make mine enter it," she says to Mother Barbeau.

Science and religion having replaced magic in Sand's dialectical system, the witch has become a saint and the elf both a fairy and a princess, since the reader is told at the very end of the novel that Fadette "had a pretty house built . . . in order to gather in all the distressed children of the commune for four hours every weekday."

As for traditional beliefs regarding twins, they are similarly demystified by George Sand (through Fadette herself, and in the name of religion) when Fanchon says to Sylvinet:

> Don't you fall back on the fact of your being a twin. There's been far too much said around you about this fondness of twins being a law of nature and how you would die, if it were thwarted. So you thought you were obeying your destiny by carrying this fondness to extremes; but God is not so unjust as to mark us for a bad fate when we still are in our mother's womb. He is not so evil as to give us ideas that we can never overcome, and you insult him, superstitious man that you are, by believing that the blood in your body contains more strength and evil destiny than there is power of resistance and reason in your mind.

Fanchon Fadet (and, with her, George Sand) is thus attacking the superstitions of the Berry region, as well as popular traditional philosophy in general and the belief in fate in particular. She indirectly asserts that every human being (man or woman) can (and must) take his life into his hands and shape it himself. Here, the novel (unlike the popular folktale) denies the mythology of evil usually em-

bodied, in oral tradition, by negative creatures such as Georgeon, the devil figure of the Berry region. Thus, if the rustic novel goes against the conventions of the folktale, it also goes against its ideology.

THE STRUCTURAL LEVEL

At the structural level, it is most revealing that the character of Fadette (which gives the novel its title) only appears in the eighth chapter of the book and disappears again (or rather fades into the background) at the end of the narrative. Drawing from a well-known narrative device, which is often used in traditional literature, George Sand uses the male storyteller figure as intermediary and inserts the story of Fadette within a broader story which provides, at the same time, a frame and a context. It is the story of the Barbeau twins and of their excessive attachment to each other—according to the superstitions of Berry—that functions as a framing story. In her article "Métamorphoses du conte, du conteur et du conté, dans 'La fleur sacrée' de George Sand" [in *George Sand: Collected Essays*, edited by Janis Glasgow, 1985], Edith Jonsson-Devillers refers to it as "metanarrative" (*méta-récit*). Actually, the narrative frame here reflects the contribution (as well as the ideological perspective) of the hemp-beater narrator, whereas the invisible female author surreptitiously enters the novel with the Fadette character. This framing process, which consists of inserting one narrative within another, is very old. It can be found in *The Thousand and One Nights* and also (in literary form) in numerous medieval narratives or even in more recent popular tales. What makes Sand's use of this process particularly original is the fact that she draws from it a subplot giving her novel what could be called a double focus.

The action of the inner narrative, which is essentially dynamic in nature (and can be tied up with the heroic narrative tradition, although expressed here in the feminine) demands reflection. According to the folktale type number 425 (to which the story of "Amor and Psyche" belongs), the journey of the female character should be a desperate quest in search of a lost husband. According to the heroic tradition, the journey should be a male initiatory journey in search of a wife (in order to provide descendants who will assume the continuity of the family name), or "wisdom" (which is supposed to be a privilege of adulthood), and of power. From a female point of view, following the model of "Beauty and the Beast," this journey should also be an irresponsible one. What is George Sand's perspective, however? She stages a female initiatory journey by means of which the heroine moves away from the man she loves, in order to protect him and give them both the eventual opportunity to build their future together. It is not a quest for a lost husband; it is not an escape, nor a family visit. It is rather a willed transfer of the heroine into "another world" (the world outside her village), in order to allow a victorious return (as in the case of Ulysses in *The Odyssey*). The goal is to make possible the future union of those who share a common love and have been faithful to one another in order to promote community peace and social harmony around the main protagonists of the story. The only traditional element left out by George Sand is revenge.

In conclusion, the novelist structures her narrative around the feats of a female character who is neither passive nor deceitful; neither a victim nor a fool, as some traditional patterns would require. On the contrary, she is fully aware, in complete control of her life, and able to take action. With this reversal of the male/female values usually present in traditional narratives (and, particularly, in folktales), Sand asserts and demonstrates the equality of men and women along with the possible superiority of the latter. Fadette is, to a point, Landry's teacher: She shares with him her knowledge of "herbal properties" as well as her "recipes for healing people and animals." She is endlessly full of good advice, and frees him from his superstitions, thanks to her positive approach to the world. Having "taught" Landry, she also "liberates" Sylvinet by forcing him to enter life. Fadette completely dominates the action of the novel, whether from a psychological or a dynamic point of view. She is omnipresent; she is an endless source of light. However, once again, her triumph over her life's circumstances is not due to any kind of supernatural intervention but exclusively to her own qualities: her intelligence, sensitivity, awareness, and willpower. Only the discovery of an unexpected fortune (her grandmother's hidden treasure) can be viewed as a providential event.

Subtle manipulator of the conventions of the folktale, Sand uses it as she does folklore in general: She puts it "through the filter of her own imagination and feelings" as writes Nicole Belmont in her article "L'Académie celtique et George Sand." However, the novelist is willing to draw on definite elements of the genre when they fulfill her ideology. For example, the story has a happy ending (as does any genuine folktale) since the heroine finds love, marriage, wealth, and experiences at the same time—social integration and promotion—as would any central character of a folktale who was originally the victim of his community. Moreover, in *La Petite Fadette,* the surrounding community benefits from the girl's social ascension (both in a material and a spiritual sense) since she helps the villagers get rid of some of their superstitions and dedicates part of her newly acquired fortune to the local children in distress.

In the rustic novel, contrary to the folktale, the negative characters (Madelon and Sylvinet) are neither punished nor destroyed, but rather they disappear in the end. As for the positive characters, in agreement with the folktale tradition, they find their reward: Cadet Caillaud (Landry's faithful companion in the days of hardship) marries Nanette (Landry's sister), and the two weddings are symbolically celebrated on the same day. Obviously, Sand has thwarted, twisted, and fragmented the conventions of the popular tale to integrate them in her novel. However, she has done so in order to promote an ideology of good and make possible a generous ending that illustrates her philosophy of life and her idea of an ideal society.

Invisible (but powerful and omnipresent) beyond the voice of her narrator, the hemp-beater, George Sand dismantles the conventions of popular tradition. In *La Petite Fadette,* she presents us with the poetic figure of a young country maiden "liberated" from the superstitions of her time: Fanchon Fadet.

The notion of metamorphosis which is constantly used by the novelist in her narrative can also be viewed as a metaphor describing Fadette's passage from adolescence to adulthood (a particularly original approach, since Marilyn Yalom tells us that there was no such thing as the concept of adolescence in the nineteenth century). However, such a partial interpretation only corresponds to a minor level of the story. The truth is that the main function of the whole dialectical system elaborated by Sand, in the architecture of her novel, is to show us a female character who, once she has overcome social antagonism and assumed a position of power, is able to act in a totally just, positive, and generous way. In the modern literary tale entitled *La Petite Fadette,* "Cinderella" assumes power and liberates herself: due to her intelligence, her wisdom, and her strength of will. She has no need for the protection of a fairy godmother (or any other supernatural creature) in order to establish her life. She is fully conscious that her life is in her hands.

Such a reading of *La Petite Fadette,* derived from the conventional popular folktale elements, first brings to light George Sand's extraordinary knowledge and deeply romantic understanding of the oral tradition of Berry, as well as of the larger popular tradition. If the folklorist Arnold Van Gennep (founder of French ethnography) wrote most surprisingly in 1926 that the one gift George Sand had was to drown the simplest ideas and the simplest facts in an unattractive prolixity, he was nonetheless right when he stated: "George Sand's goal was not to describe local customs for their own sake or for the sake of science; she only saw in these practices a canvas upon which she could weave 'human' as well as 'humanitarian' generalizations" [*Mercure de France,* June 1, 1926].

Foremost among these humanitarian preoccupations was probably, in George Sand's mind, what Hippolyte Taine has called, in a few beautiful lines paying homage to the novelist, her quest for "social truth."

The idealized peasant world depicted for us by George Sand in *La Petite Fadette* seems quite removed from the Berry country world of "misery and feasting" which came out of the hunger riots around the year 1845, as described by Marc Baroli in his work *La Vie quotidienne en Berry au temps de George Sand.* It is not a realistic depiction but rather a mythical context well suited to the folktale genre. However, Fadette is an extremely modern character given the fact that her passage from the state of a frustrated *fadet* (elf) to that of a stereotyped *fade* (good fairy) might easily symbolize the evolution of women in modern society and their craving for benevolent power. If the novel *La Petite Fadette* can be read as a folktale, it is therefore only as a modern, social and prefeminist narrative, since the term *feminism* had already appeared in France in 1837. It may be considered, in that respect, to serve a utopian ideal that has today become an accepted goal. As Victor Hugo stated at George Sand's funeral: "Beings like George Sand are public benefactors. They pass, but hardly have they passed, that in their empty space surges a new form of progress. . . . George Sand has died, but she is leaving behind for us the belief in women's rights which draws its evidence from the genius of women." (pp. 15-23)

Brigitte Lane, " 'La Petite Fadette': A Pre-Feminist Dialectic of Tradition," in The World of George Sand, *Natalie Datlof, Jeane Fuchs, David A. Powell, eds., Greenwood Press, 1991, pp. 15-26.*

Elizabeth Drew on Sand's varied and abundant output:

Her . . . creative faculty is staggering in its proportions. She produced eighty works of fiction and wrote an average of two books a year for fifty years. The output of Scott, Dickens, Balzac, of even the prolific Mrs. Oliphant, appear positively meagre beside her prodigious fecundity. She produced books with the ease and exuberance and variety with which a conjuror produces rabbits and watches and paper streamers out of a top hat. She had no individual manner, she created no world which is her own. Her subject matter is as wide as the interests of the reading public, and she presents that public with sensationalism as thorough-going as Mrs. Radcliffe's, with personal emotion as whole-hearted as Charlotte Bronte's, with propaganda as careful as Kingsley's, with pastoralism as simple as George Eliot's, with historical romance as coloured as Scott's.

Elizabeth Drew, in an introduction to Letters of George Sand, *selected and translated by Veronica Lucas, 1976.*

Isabelle Hoog Naginski   (essay date 1991)

[*In the excerpt below, Naginski examines the structure of* Indiana, *discussing the work as an "apprenticeship novel" in which Sand sought to establish her literary voice.*]

"Un Début dans la vie"

The embryonic ***Histoire du rêveur*** was abandoned and remained unfinished, never to be published in Sand's lifetime. It was the earliest manifestation of her exploration of the nocturnal landscape and her first articulation of a hero in search of artistic integration. Nevertheless, its fragmented form revealed that Aurore Dupin, the *rêveuse*, was still a long way away from George Sand, the *écrivaine*. And although after ***Histoire du rêveur*** she published a full-length novel and several short stories in collaboration with Jules Sandeau and under the truncated pseudonym J. Sand, it was not until the publication of ***Indiana,*** on 19 May 1832 that G. Sand burst upon the literary scene in her own "write." The event precipitated its anonymous and unknown author (whose enigmatic signature Gustave Planche deciphered as denoting a certain "Georgina Sand") into immediate celebrity. The book was proclaimed the literary event of the year by almost all the critics of the time. The writer and journalist H. de Latouche, who had been Sand's mentor when she first came to Paris, wrote to his young protégée that ***Indiana*** placed her "in one leap, at the head of contemporary writers." An anonymous article in the June issue of *La France littéraire* announced that the novel was "worthy of being included among the best novels of our time." In the July 9 feuilleton of the *Journal des débats*, Jules Janin declared that ***Indi-***

ana was "the most splendid *roman de moeurs* that has been published in France in the last twenty years." Certain intrinsic qualities of ***Indiana*** and the particular situation of the novel in France in the beginning of the 1830s combined to make the work's publication a sensation.

The French novel found itself in a period of rapid expansion around 1832. The years 1832 to 1834 represent the culminating point in an ascending curve of published novels. From 179 novels published in 1831, the number jumped to 282 for 1832 and reached 345 for 1834. This fertile period witnessed the emergence of three young novelists: Stendhal (*Le Rouge et le noir* came out only two months before ***Indiana*** which was favorably compared with it); Balzac (Sand was constantly compared to him); and Sand. This period also coincided with a "prise de conscience" on the part of the critics concerning the possibilities of the novel. Since there existed remarkably little theory of the novel before 1830 and almost no *ars poetica* for fiction, the Romantic generation saw itself increasingly associated with the valorization of fictional forms.

This is not to say that suddenly, in the critical discourse concerning the novel, opposition or antagonism or disparagement ceased to be heard. The novel continued to be defined by its adversaries as marginal literature, the pulp genre of the day. As late as 1821, for instance, the table of contents of the literary journal *L'Abeille* (formerly *La Minerve Littéraire*) did not include the category "novels" under the general rubric of "literature." By 1832, however, the opinions of such a critic as Louis-Simon Auger—for whom the novelistic genre was "a kind of monster, born of the adulterous coupling of Falsehood and Truth," and writing novels a feminine occupation barely superior to sewing ("We must let women have . . . the tasks best suited to their physical and moral constitutions. . . . I am therefore of the opinion that they should be allowed to scribble their novels as they do their needlework")—were on the way out. The novel, now worthy of men's attention, was being taken more and more seriously. Its lack of imposed formal conventions was now valued for its potential, seen as a sign of maximal flexibility, rather than as a defect. Eugène Pelletan, in a review of Sand's ***Le Meunier d'Angibault*** (1845) for example, praised the novel genre for being "the most complete, the most comprehensive": "What constitutes the superiority of the novel in our era is its triple universality. It deals with all subjects, addresses all readers, and encompasses all literary forms. The novel has no limits, no barriers, no fixed path." The novel was increasingly being considered as the great reservoir of endless possibilities, one that could accommodate all forms, all subjects, all styles. When in our day Mikhail Bakhtin claims that "it is only in the novel that discourse can reveal all its specific potential and achieve its true depth," he also is asserting the genre's unlimited range of possibilities.

But, whether the novel was considered a sign of literary decadence or of literary renewal (both opinions can be found in the press of the time), it was invading the entire literary domain. And with examples such as Sand making her literary début in 1832 with a novel, the genre's respectability seemed increasingly secure. Before the 1830s in

France, a young writer who sought to become established in the sacred realm of literature, was obliged to display his or her talents in a tragedy. After 1830, increasingly, a young writer's debut tended to be in the form of a novel.

The dazzling success of Sand's *Indiana* derived in part from the critics' perception of the work as the "prototype of the new novel." The press of 1832 judged it, with its blend of history, poetry, drama, and politics, to be profoundly modern. *Indiana* represented "the official chronicle of the passions of our time"; it contributed to the elaboration of "the charter (la charte) of what is going to become the modern novel"; it was a sign of the author's "original and independent mind." It also prefigured *Lélia,* which would be defined as "the most innovative and revolutionary novel that our civilization has produced".

Today this ascription of modernity may seem somewhat excessive. In fact, the word modernity in the critical usage of 1832 was used to convey two main concepts. First, it alluded to Romanticism. *Indiana* represented the story of a "modern passion," said the *Figaro* of May 31, the drama of an "enfant du siècle." It was a study, among other things, of the almost pathological hypersensitivity of the time, which the comparatist Paul Van Tieghem has called Romanticism's "hypertrophy of the imagination and sensibility." The novel probed Indiana's sickly sensibility as she succumbed to 'l'instinct du malheur," and "[le] magnétisme de la souffrance." As a chronicle of the splenetic ideal of the day, *Indiana* appeared modern. Sand's even more innovative transposition of the Romantic hero into a feminine incarnation only accentuates *our* impression of newness.

Second, and paradoxically, modernity was also used as a synonym for realism. And in this sense as well *Indiana* was modern. It could readily be seen as belonging to the fashionable category of the "études de moeurs," which characterized many novels of the 1830s. Stendhal's subtitle for *Le Rouge et le noir,* "Chronique de 1830," could apply just as easily to *Indiana.* In fact, a variant of the first edition referred to the text as "cette chronique." The subtitle of another Stendhal novel, *Armance,* "Quelques scènes d'un salon de Paris en 1827," could be slightly altered to read "Scenes from a Parisian and a provincial salon in 1830" and would fit *Indiana* equally well. Sand's novel could be read as another illustration of Balzac's "Scènes de la vie privée." *Indiana* also integrated contemporary historical events into the fiction, specifically the political crisis that led to the three frenetic days—"les Trois Glorieuses"—of the July revolution of 1830. But, although one should not neglect this "documentary" aspect of *Indiana,* critics traditionally have been overly concerned with the mimetic aspect of the text and with the role that historical events play in it. The historical dimension, it is true, documents a given moment in French society in precise fashion, but above all it serves to illustrate symbolically the central subject of the novel, which is not so much History as the Word. It is this symbolic subject that ensures the true and lasting modernity of the novel.

Indiana is remarkable in that it does not appear to be a first novel, but rather the product of an already mature talent. Numerous critics were surprised by this quasi-miraculous birth of George Sand the novelist. As far as the reading public was concerned, the young novelist, like Athena emerging in adult form from Zeus's thigh or head, had suddenly appeared out of nowhere, with a fully-formed voice and a fully-developed talent. Even Henry James, years later, was to comment upon this brilliant literary "début dans la vie," marveling at the unexpected plentitude of the author's talent and voice:

> About this sudden entrance into literature, into philosophy, into rebellion . . . there are various different things to be said. Very remarkable, indeed, was the immediate development of the literary faculty in this needy young woman who lived in cheap lodgings and looked for "employment." She wrote as a bird sings; but unlike most birds, she found it unnecessary to indulge, by way of prelude, in twitterings and vocal exercises; she broke out at once with her full volume of expression. [*Literary Criticism,* 1884]

Three points need to be made here in reference to the unusual virtuosity of this literary début. First, *Indiana,* at least in the early pages, contains clear indications of being written by a reader of Chateaubriand. The novel opens with a brilliantly constructed scene evoking Romantic spleen, a subject that inevitably conjures up the author of *René* as Sand's literary forefather. Second, Henry James expressed his regret that the author of *Indiana* had not shed more light on its gestation when he writes: "[there is] no account of how she learned to write, no record of effort or apprenticeship . . . the thing about which she had least to say was the writer's, the inventor's, the romancer's art. She possessed it by the gift of God, but she seems never to have felt the temptation to examine the pulse of the machine." Yet *Histoire de ma vie* does contain several passages that James seems to have skimmed over too quickly or not read at all which offer some insight into the "pulse of the machine." Third, while many readers and critics considered Sand's bursting onto the literary scene as a kind of artistic parthenogenesis, *Indiana,* in an unusual way, is very much a work of apprenticeship. The novel can be seen as a series of narrative experimentations which culminates in the writer's acquisition of a voice to match her point of view. Embedded within the novel, the story of Ralph recapitulates the writer's progress from initial uncertainty and hesitation to ultimate assurance and eloquence. The deep structure of *Indiana,* which contains a reflection on the genesis of Sand's literary voice, will be examined in this [essay].

A Feminized mal du siècle

Indiana opens with a tableau of the heroine, her cousin Ralph, and her husband Delmare sitting in silence, immediately conveying the characters' dominant mood of melancholic gloom:

> Par une soirée d'automne pluvieuse et fraîche, trois personnes rêveuses étaient gravement occupées, au fond d'un petit castel de la Brie, à regarder brûler les tisons du foyer et cheminer lentement l'aiguille de la pendule. Deux de ces hôtes silencieux semblaient s'abandonner en toute soumission au vague ennui qui pesait sur eux; mais le troisième donnait des marques de

rébellion ouverte: il s'agitait sur son siège, étouffait à demi haut quelques baîllements mélancoliques, et frappait la pincette sur les bûches pétillantes.

(On a rainy and cool autumn evening, three pensive people in a small chateau in Brie were solemnly watching the embers burning in the hearth and the slow rotation of the clock hand. Two of these silent inhabitants seemed submissively resigned to the vague boredom that weighed down on them; but the third gave signs of open rebellion: he fidgeted in his chair, he half-stifled several melancholic yawns, and hit the tongs against the smoldering logs.)

Sand frames her characters in an atmosphere of mal du siècle, placing **Indiana** in the tradition of *René,* with its reference to the gloomy "paternal castle" in "a remote province," home to the hero's sickly and hypersensitive soul. Chateaubriand's "château gothique" like Sand's, is described in its autumnal incarnation. Clearly *René* was important to Sand, as we see from several allusions in *Histoire de ma vie.* Sand's first reading of the novel in adolescence prompted her to identify with the hero ("it seemed to me that *René* was myself"). And of her decision to live the bohemian life in Paris, she wrote: "Cela valait mieux qu'une cellule et j'aurais pu dire avec *René* . . . que je me promenais dans le *désert des hommes*" ("It was preferable to a cell and I could have said, as in *René,* . . . that I was wandering in the *desert of men*"). But if at first René was a character to emulate in her own life, he was quickly transformed into an exemplar for her first authentic literary heroine.

Inclined to be more inspired by male rather than female literary models, Sand expressed this fascination for Chateaubriand's splenetic character in **Indiana.** Her heroine, therefore, was modeled on René rather than on his sister, Amélie, too peripheral a character with too simplistic a mental life. Indiana possessed "comme René, le coeur mort avant d'avoir vécu" ("like René, a dead heart even before having lived"). Like him she was prey to the "goût du siècle," attributing to herself an exceptional sensibility and wallowing in self-absorbed suffering:

> [Indiana] avait dix-neuf ans, et, si vous l'eussiez vue enfoncée sous le manteau de cette vaste cheminée de marbre blanc incrusté de cuivre doré; si vous l'eussiez vue, toute fluette, toute pâle, toute triste, le coude appuyé sur son genou, elle toute jeune . . . à côté de ce vieux mari, semblable à une fleur née d'hier qu'on fait éclore dans un vase gothique, vous eussiez plaint la femme du colonel Delmare.

> ([Indiana] was nineteen years old, and if you had seen her huddled beneath the mantelpiece of that vast, white marble fireplace encrusted with brass; if you had seen her, so thin, pale, sad, her elbow propped up on her knee, she who was so young . . . next to this old husband, she who resembled a fresh, budding flower made to bloom in a Gothic vase, you would have pitied Colonel Delmare's wife.)

This elaborate portrait highlights the character of Indiana and focuses the reader's attention on the author's main reason for using *René* as a model. Sand wished to elaborate on the theme of a feminized agony. Chateaubriand's text served not so much to guide the young writer stylistically as much as to offer a model to emulate and subvert simultaneously. Chateaubriand had articulated the mal du siècle in its heretofore unambiguously masculine form—as a metaphysical malady so poetic and sophisticated that it could only be suffered by men. Sand's hidden agenda was to cross the boundaries of gender-defined moral ailments. By identifying her heroine from the first as a kind of female René, Sand was attempting, in her first novel, to feminize the mal du siécle.

From *Rêveuse* to *Ecrivaine*

Sand's correspondence for 1832 is a good source of information about the period encompassing the writing and publication of **Indiana.** But, surprisingly, what is singularly missing in these letters is much information on Sand's apprenticeship as a writer and on the gestation of her first novel. Between 1832 and 1837 only a very few letters discuss the book's impact, its subject matter, or her intentions when composing it. Most references discuss it as an object, a consumer product. Her most pressing problems are the reedition, the sale price, the number of copies sent out and sold.

To make matters more difficult, even when Sand does touch on her writing and literary life in her correspondence from this early period, she most often does so in an offhand manner and with a lightness of tone which seem intended to discourage taking the subject entirely seriously. Talking about her pseudonym, for instance, in a letter of May 1832 to Charles Duvernet, she writes: "Les commerçants littéraires nous [disent] prenez un nom. Un nom vous le savez c'est une marchandise, une denrée, un fonds de commerce" ("Literary merchants tell us to take a name. A name, as you know, is a kind of merchandise, a commodity, a business"). Such passages clearly convey Sand's characteristic stance of not taking herself seriously as a writer, at least in her public statements. The tone of self-mockery which shows through in her correspondence is frequently reinforced by a profound ambivalence in *Histoire de ma vie* when the discussion turns to the birth of her literary career. She writes, for example: "quand je parlais d'écrire, c'était en riant et en me moquant de la chose et de moi-même. Une sorte de destinée me poussait cependant . . . une destinée de liberté morale et d'isolement poétique" ("when I spoke of writing, it was in jest and I joked about it and about myself. Something like destiny was pushing me in spite of it all . . . a destiny of moral freedom and poetic isolation"). Here the tone is less playful, but the self-ddeprecation remains, as Sand ennobles the writer's vocation on which she is embarking, while undermining her own literary ambitions through ironic juxtaposition.

In the last chapters of Part 4 [of *Histoire de ma vie*] Sand refers to what she called her "vie d'écolier littéraire" or "vie de gamin" to describe the period of her life when she had just come to Paris to become a writer. She uses a playful, lighthearted tone that belies the seriousness of her subject. For example, she chats amusingly about the Ecole Frénétique, the Romantic school that took as its model

English Gothic prose and was the height of fashion in the 1830s:

> On cherchait des titres impossibles, des sujets dégoûtants, et, dans cette course au clocher d'affiches ébouriffantes, des gens de talent eux-mêmes subissaient la mode, et, couverts d'oripeaux bizarres, se précipitaient dans la mêlée. J'étais bien tentée de faire comme les autres écoliers, puisque les maîtres donnaient le mauvais exemple, et je cherchais des bizarreries que je n'eusse jamais pu exécuter.

> ([Writers] went in pursuit of impossible titles, revolting subjects, and in this obstacle race in search of shocking placards; even talented people were enslaved by fashion, and dressed in bizarre and flashy costumes, they rushed into the fray. I was tempted to act like the other schoolboys, since the masters were setting a bad example, and I searched for oddities that I would never have been able to carry off.)

Thanks to the guidance of Latouche, she informs us, she did not let herself be carried along down the slippery path of frenetic literature, in imitation of Pétrus Borel or Charles Lassailly. At the same time, by his repeated insults and mockery of her as a "cerveau creux," Latouche discouraged her from further literary endeavors. Downhearted, she returned to Nohant, ready to abandon literature. Then, as she presents it, unexpectedly the subject of *Indiana* surged up ex nihilo, haunting her, invading her entire being. She started to write "sans projet, sans espoir, sans aucun plan . . . et ne fouillant ni dans la matière des autres ni dans ma propre individualité pour le sujet et les types" ("without a preliminary design, without hope, without a plan . . . and delving neither into the material of others nor into my own individuality for the subject and the characters"). The abrupt passage from discouragement to euphoria is noted, but not elucidated. Nothing in Sand's description clarifies for the reader the nature of the literary miracle. One moment she is still a hollow brain; the next she has been metamorphosed into a fertile one. This transformation is presented as instantaneous and mysterious. Furthermore, in her description of the way she composed *Indiana,* the negative aspects of writing are stressed: the need to start afresh, to make a clean slate. She empties her mind of any apprenticeship, any influence, any acquired technique: "mettant résolument à la porte de mon souvenir tout ce qui m'avait été posé en précepte ou en exemple" ("resolutely putting out of my mind the memory of everything that had been set before me as a precept or as an example"). Highlighting inspiration rather than methodology, she eludes any discussion of genesis, of gestation, of development. She presents herself as possessed by a "powerful emotion," which sustains her during a prolonged period of creative hallucination. As Sand explains it in *Histoire de ma vie,* the text of *Indiana* suddenly emerged, fully formed, as she found herself fully a writer overnight:

> J'écrivis tout d'un jet, sans plan . . . et littéralement sans savoir où j'allais. . . . J'avais en moi seulement, comme un sentiment bien net et bien ardent, l'horreur de l'esclavage brutal et bête. . . . J'écrivis donc ce livre sous l'empire d'une émotion et non d'un système.

> (I wrote in one stroke, without a plan . . . and literally without knowing where I was going. . . . I had only a very distinct and vehement feeling, and this was the horror of brutal and stupid enslavement. . . . I therefore wrote this book in the grip of an emotion and not according to a system.)

Any notion of effort, labor, correction, hesitation, or groping is absent from this lyrical description of the creation of *Indiana.* The reader is not given any view of the writing process—but only the finished product on the table. Sand's persona remains hidden.

Whether Sand's version about the composition of *Indiana* represents the "truth" or not matters little. What is important is how faithfully it coincides with the image she draws of herself as a writer who depended on improvisation and the inspiration of the moment. Her sense that she did not write *Indiana,* but that in some way it wrote itself may well be a self-protective device, but such an attitude served her public persona well. So we will not find sufficient information about this literary period of experimentation which so intrigued James, either in her autobiography or in her correspondence. We have to look for it elsewhere, inscribed metaphorically in another text. It is in *Indiana* itself, where the embedded theme of the search for a literary voice emerges as a crucial structural element, that we can read about it.

The Search for a Literary Voice

Indiana is a novel about writing a first novel. Sand inscribes this theme into her text through an examination of each character's language system. Some characters are already eloquent, such as Raymon. Others are resolutely dull in their speech, as in the case of Delmare. Finally, some such as Ralph, come to master a certain elegance of expression in the course of the novel. To listen to these three men discuss politics in the early pages of the novel is to get a sense of the importance the author accords each individual's phraseology. As critics have already noted, these male characters represent the three main political tendencies in the last years of the Restoration. On the right, the "Ultras," "plus royalistes que le roi," in Louis XVIII's own words. Against them, the liberal opposition, in two factions: the heirs of the eighteenth-century *philosophes,* those whom Napoleon called the "idéologues"; and the mass of Bonapartist ex-soldiers and ex-officers, unemployed and dissatisfied, who remained faithful to the emperor's memory. Colonel Delmare is the old Bonapartist whose dreams have been broken. He has retreated into moodiness and glumness as a way of life and as a way of talking politics. Ralph Brown, Indiana's phlegmatic cousin, is a democrat who argues for the return of a republic. Raymon de la Ramière, whom Gustave Planche defined as the representative of corruption in the nineteenth century, is politically to the right, attached to the "Charte," walking a fine line between "l'abus du pouvoir et celui de la licence." As for the women, they do not discuss politics.

The text, however, does more than simply present a spectrum of political positions. It allows the reader to glimpse

A photograph of Sand surrounded by Nadar's sketches illustrating her career.

the author's search for a language that is at once powerful and authentic. Each man is not so much defined as an emblematic representative of the political realities of the day as identified with a specific mode of speech, which in turn is linked inextricably with a particular political position.

Colonel Delmare's language is fossilized. He interminably rehashes the same stale formulas, the same ready-made ideas, the same refrains: "treason," "motherland betrayed." Unlike Balzac's positive portrayal of Colonel Chabert or Goguelat (in *Le Médecin de campagne*), both of whom, like Delmare, have their ideological roots in the good old days of the Empire, Sand's depiction of her character as a man who has become petrified in the old ideas is drawn with no sympathy: "Il n'avait pas fait un pas depuis 1815. C'était un vieux stationnaire encroûté" ("He hadn't moved forward since 1815. He was an old fossil set in his ways"). Since the narrator expresses his belief that "l'opinion politique d'un homme, c'est l'homme tout entier" ("a man's entire identity is to be found in his political opinions"). We are prompted to see Delmare's reactionary political stance [as] the index of his reactionism in all aspects of life. In this light, the reader can begin to understand the importance of each character's political world view. It stands as a metonymy for temperament. Politics provide a privileged insight into each protagonist's psychological makeup. Delmare's political vocabulary is the expression of his mummified character.

The opposing political views of the two protagonists, Raymon and Ralph, are exemplified in their antithetical rhetorical talents. The first is a "champion of the existing society"; the second attacks the "edifice on all points." Their confrontation on the political front in fact conceals the latent hostility they feel for each other in private life: "On n'eût pas osé se traiter de fourbe, d'imbécile, d'ambitieux et de poltron. On enferme les mêmes idées sous le nom de jésuite, de royaliste, de révolutionnaire . . ." ("They would not have dared to call each other rogue, imbecile, upstart, or coward. So the same ideas were couched in different terms: Jesuit, Royalist, Revolutionary . . ."). The confrontation of ideologies is at the same time a confrontation of antithetical rhetorics.

Ralph's power of speech, as the narrator reminds us more than once, is almost nonexistent: "[il] avait si peu le talent de la persuasion, il était si candide, si maladroit . . . sa franchise était si raboteuse, sa logique si aride, ses principes si absolus! Il ne ménageait personne, il n'adoucissait aucune vérité" ("He so completely lacked the ability to be persuasive, he was so naive, so awkward. . . . His candor was so unpolished, his logic so dry, his principles so absolute! He humoured no one, and never softened the truth"). The more he tries to convince his opponent, the more he gets tangled up in his arguments. This "maladresse d'élocution," a veritable existential handicap, prevents him from expressing fully his inner feelings. More serious still, it prevents him from recognizing the entire scope of his sentiments and thoughts. Ralph is a stranger unto himself. This drama of the spoken word embodied in Ralph, a kind of paralysis of the tongue which the text defines as "impotence," finds its opposition in Raymon's triumphant discourse. He speaks "skillfully," uses "vicious argu-

ments," "a flowered rhetoric" that always guarantees that he will be surrounded by a group of admiring listeners. He has at his disposal "all the subtleties of language, all the small-minded treacheries of civilization." As a partisan of the dominating ideology, Raymon is politically and linguistically identified with a rhetoric of falsehood which is proficient in manipulating the truth. The regime Raymon approves of is characterized, in the narrator's view, by a distortion of truth accompanied by a certain degradation of speech. The entire phraseology of this regime is, in the narrator's words,

> une reine prostituée qui descend et s'élève à tous les rôles, qui se déguise, se pare, se dissimule et s'efface . . . le plus honnête des hommes est celui qui pense et qui agit le mieux, mais *le plus puissant est celui qui sait le mieux écrire et parler.* (emphasis added)

> (a prostituted queen who is ready to assume all roles, be they noble or lowly, who disguises, adorns, conceals, and effaces herself . . . the most honest man is the one who thinks and acts in the best manner, but *the most powerful is the one who knows best how to write and speak.*)

To learn how to talk and how to write, that is the issue at the heart of Sand's first novel. The author's insistence on the supremacy of the word and of the signifier in the construction of her fictional universe makes for the modernity of *Indiana*. She strives to capture the various individualized languages of her milieu and to embody them in the different characters. Unlike Stendhal's mirror novel, whose fortune is to travel along a road in order to refract the outside world, *Indiana* can be considered as a recording machine. Stendhal articulates mimesis in terms of images, while Sand expresses the mimetic act through verbal reduplication. The precise manner by which Sand inscribes her initiation into writing metaphorically into her text deserves further elucidation.

The Coining of a Literary Vernacular

A lot of talking goes on in *Indiana*—long pronouncements, monologues, declarations of love, confessions, tirades, verbal seductions. To give one notable example, toward the end of the novel Ralph talks for some fifteen pages without a break. Much writing goes on as well, with many of these missives transcribed verbatim for the reader. I will return to one of them, from Indiana, later in the [essay]. Clearly verbal expression is a major element of the text. Furthermore, each of the principal characters speaks a language that embodies the role he or she plays.

Colonel Delmare wants to exercise fully the rights conferred upon him by his marital status. He believes in the absolute power of husbands. Their right is to govern: the wives' duty is to submit. He says to the heroine: "Qui donc est le maître ici, de vous ou de moi? Qui donc porte une jupe et doit filer une quenouille? Prétendez-vous m'ôter la barbe du menton? . . . femmelette" ("Who is the master here, you or I? Who wears a skirt and must spin the yarn? Do you dare take the beard from my chin? . . . weakling"). He formulates his contempt for women as a group in generalized declarations where all the clichés of misogyny are reiterated: "[les femmes sont] toutes menteuses et rusées pour le plaisir de l'être" ("[Women are] all liars and cunning simply for the pleasure of it"); or "Les femmes sont faites pour obéir" ("Women are meant to obey"). Finally, he often has recourse to violence, occasionaly in his actions—we see him beat Indiana and her pet dog (a female, the text carefully specifies)—and habitually in his speech: "Ses épigrammes favorites roulaient toujours sur des coups de bâton à donner et des affaires d'honneur à vider." ("His favorite epigrams always revolved around beatings to be administered and matters of honor to be settled"). Delmare, occupying the role of the overbearing husband, incarnates in his speech the brutalizing idiom of the master.

Noun, the maid, is almost without speech. As a woman, as a servant, and as a Creole, she is triply disempowered of her right to speak. Nearly mute, she is also barely literate. When, fearing that Raymon may have abandoned her, she commits the grave mistake of writing him a letter in which the "rules of grammar" are not respected, its style and orthography make the seducer blush. This letter, significantly not transcribed in the novel, but described by the narrator as a "chef-d'oeuvre de passion naïve et gracieuse" ("masterpiece of naive and graceful passion"), is the prologue to the definitive silence that Noun will seek in suicide, leaving behind no word of explanation to clarify the motive of her act. Noun speaks and writes in the language of female subjection. Her brief act of revolt against the system of masters and slaves reveals all the more starkly her fundamental powerlessness. Her suicide through drowning, an expression of her Ophelia complex, signifies passive acquiescence. Not surprisingly, her ultimate language is silence.

Laure de Nangy, the woman who finally marries Raymon, occupies only a small place in the novel, but she nevertheless fits into Sand's spectrum of speech types. She is first presented to the reader in the following symbolic situation:

> Dans le grand salon, à la place où madame Delmare se tenait d'ordinaire pour travailler, une jeune personne grande et svelte, au long regard à la fois doux et malicieux, caressant et moqueur, était assise devant un chevalet et s'amusait à copier à l'aquarelle les bizarres lambris de la muraille. C'était une chose charmante que cette copie, une fine moquerie tout empreinte du caractère railleur et poli de l'artiste. . . . A coté de cette oeuvre . . . elle avait écrit le mot *pastiche.*

> (In the main drawing room, at the place madame Delmare usually occupied when she was at work, sat a tall, svelte, young woman with a gaze that was both gentle and malicious, caressing and mocking. She was sitting before an easel, amusing herself by making a watercolor copy of the wall's bizarre ornamentation. It was a charming thing, this copy, a delicate mockery stamped with the artist's satirical and polite mark. . . . Next to this work . . . she had written the word *pastiche.*)

The obvious point here is that Laure has no authentic speech of her own. She imitates, makes a pastiche of, the

language of her class, with a self-aware touch of irony. Her language is uncreative, only a parody of preexisting forms. She is also, as critics have remarked before, a kind of Balzacian character. The author, then, presents a double pastiche. Laure drawing a pastiche of an original is analogous to Sand writing a pastiche of Balzac. In so doing she exorcizes the influence of her young fellow writer. As such, this little scene is not without mischief.

Meanwhile, within the novel itself, a different kind of parallelism is evident in the rhetorical fortunes of Raymon and Ralph. Raymon makes his debut in the novel as a skillful manipulator of a semantic system of lies. He ends up reduced to silence. Ralph, on the other hand, is depicted throughout as an awkward conversationalist, as a man who prefers silence to speech. But he dominates the conclusion with a fully articulated confession. *Indiana* ends with his voice, which at first glance may appear to be startling considering the novel's title and its underlying ideology of sympathy for woman's plight. But, as we shall see, Ralph's voice is androgynous, an echo of the author's own search for authorhood, a working model for the author's double-gendered voice. Ralph's and Raymon's destinies are antithetical and can be studied as mirror images of one another. This antithesis transcends the distinction of noble versus ignoble character, since Ralph represents a male projection of the author's own search for an authentically poetic voice, while Raymon stands for the artful but dangerously seductive voice of the literary establishment. The poet versus the political pamphleteer.

Undeniably, Raymon speaks the language of the seducer. His rhetoric manipulates people, notably women, and events. His letters are masterpieces of falsehood. As an aristocrat and a sometime political journalist, he has mastered the idiom of high society and power.

> Raymon avait une incroyable puissance sur tout ce qui l'entourait . . . c'était . . . un homme supérieur dans la société . . . vous avez été entraîné, en lisant les journaux du temps, par le charme irrésistible de son style, et les grâces de sa logique courtoise et mondaine.

> (Raymon had tremendous influence over everything that surrounded him . . . he was . . . a superior man in society . . . you have been carried away, while reading the newspapers of the day, by the irresistible charm of his style, and the grace of his courteous and worldly logic.)

In his first seduction scene with Indiana, this French Lovelace appropriates all the clichés of the fashionable rhetoric of the time which depicts woman as sylph, spirit, nymph, ethereal creature of men's desire:

> Tu es la femme que j'avais rêvée, la pureté que j'adorais; la chimère qui m'avait toujours fui, l'étoile brillante qui luisait devant moi. . . . De tout temps, tu m'étais destinée, ton âme était fiancée à la mienne, Indiana! . . . tu m'appartiens, tu es la moitié de mon âme, qui cherchait depuis longtemps à rejoindre l'autre. . . . Ne t'ai-je pas reconnu, ange, lorsque tu étanchais mon sang avec ton voile . . .

(You are the woman I have dreamed of, the pure soul I have adored, the chimera who has always escaped me, the brilliant star that shone before me. . . . You were always destined for me, your soul was betrothed to mine, Indiana! . . . You belong to me, you are the other half of my soul, which has been searching for its partner for so long. . . . Did I not recognize you, angel, as you stanched my blood with your veil . . .)

A master in the art of turning any situation to his advantage with words he excuses his brutality when a love scene turns violent by blaming it on the victim: "Pardon, Indiana, pardon! Si je t'effraye *c'est ta faute;* tu m'as fait tant souffrir que j'ai perdu la raison" (emphasis added; "Forgive me, Indiana, forgive me! If I frighten you, *it is your fault;* you have made me suffer so much that I have lost all reason"). Sometimes he acts out his passion with so much verisimilitude, he is so "puissant dans son langage" that he allows himself to be persuaded by his own rhetoric. He then comes to feel emotions that are not authentic.

Finally, he is an odious liar, without any concern for the relation between truth and the spoken word. In Raymon, Sand reveals the complicity between language and power. The stylized eloquence of his speech expresses his privileged status in the symbolic order. His powerful and haughty voice duplicates the discourse of the established newspapers in power at the time. The fascination Raymon exerts on both heroines of the novel also affected its young author. Raymon's rhetoric was fashioned by Sand so as to be exorcized, and transcended.

Ralph will exemplify this transcendence. Originally lacking both skill or elegance in his manner of speaking, laconic and lackluster in his correspondence, he undergoes a linguistic metamorphosis that constitutes the crucial episode of the book. Significantly, Ralph's transformation into a poet-philosopher is as brusque and unexplained in the novel as Sand's own transmutation into a novelist, a parallel that helps shed light on his key role in the novel as the figure around whom so much of the plot crystallizes.

Ralph's linguistic metamorphosis occurs during the initiatory voyage that brings him, accompanied by Indiana, back to the "désert" (read "wilderness") of the Ile Bourbon:

> Son âme, longtemps roidie contre la douleur, s'amollit à la chaleur vivifiante de l'espérance. Le ciel descendit aussi dans ce coeur amer et froissé. Ses paroles prirent l'empreinte de ses sentiments.

> (His soul, long hardened against pain, softened with the revitalizing warmth of hope. Heaven penetrated this injured and bitter heart. His words began to express his feelings.)

The scene in which Ralph finally begins to speak echoes the biblical episode in which the Apostles are touched by grace and start to communicate in many tongues. If, as she asserted in *Histoire de ma vie,* inspiration is "for artists what grace is for Christians," Ralph becomes in these pages the supreme Sandian artist. His newly found but already secure eloquence ensures that he can never again be reduced to silence.

The language he will use is the vernacular of poets. Here is an example of the lyricism of his prose:

> le baptême du malheur a bien assez purifié nos âmes: rendons-les à celui qui nous les a données. . . . Pour nous *l'univers est le temple* où nous adorons Dieu. C'est au sein d'une nature grande et vierge qu'on retrouve le sentiment de sa puissance, pure de toute profanation humaine. Retournons donc au désert, afin de pouvoir prier . . . (emphasis added)

> (The baptism of misfortune has purified our souls well enough: let us return them to the One who gave them to us. . . . For us, *the universe is the temple* in which we worship God. It is in the bosom of a great and pure nature that one rediscovers the feeling of His power, pure of any human profanation. Let us return to the desert, so that we can pray . . .)

Ralph's striking image in the phrase "l'univers est le temple" presages the well-known line in Baudelaire's sonnet "Correspondances," "la nature est un temple."

For Sand the spoken word, *la parole,* is the privileged path of thought. From a "crétin sans intelligence et sans voix," Ralph is transformed into a prophet (the one who announces a revelation). Because in Sand's cosmogony the creation of one's own authentic language is synonymous with self-knowledge, Ralph's tale, as he tells it to Indiana, with all its detailed information about his inner life, his affective and moral world view, is likened to "un moment d'ivresse intellectuelle, [un moment] d'exaltation et d'extase où [les] pensées s'épurent, se subtilisent, s'éthèrent" ("a moment of intellectual intoxication, of exaltation and ecstasy in which thoughts become purified, refined, ethereal"). The result of Ralph's confession is true self-discovery. His long speech constitutes a veritable talking cure. But this treatment goes beyond the purely psychological realm, since his passage from silence to the spoken word is also the decisive step in his life as an artist. The figure of Ralph has now come to symbolize the young author's metamorphosis from *cerveau creux* to *cerveau fertile.* In his confession scene, which takes place *in extremis,* on the verge of death, he translates his inner dreamworld into speech. In so doing, Ralph also articulates the writer's discovery of her own vernacular.

Ralph's confession dominates Part Four of ***Indiana,*** and leads directly to the culminating suicide pact between the two characters: "Alors Ralph prit sa fiancée dans ses bras, et l'emporta pour la précipiter avec lui dans le torrent" ("Ralph then took his fiancée in his arms, and carried her away in order to hurl her down into the torrent with him"). This scene, however, is not the end of the novel, although, according to Sand's biographer Wladimir Karénine, it was so in the author's original plan. All editions of the novel, including the first, contain a concluding chapter, an epilogue, which depicts Indiana and Ralph living the ideal life in a "chaumière indienne," an eighteenth-century dream reminiscent of both l'Abbé Laugier's "primitive hut" and Bernardin de Saint-Pierre's paradisiac Ile de France.

This double ending—suicides, an idyll—has always bothered the critics for its implausibility. But there is a legitimate reason for the false suicide to be transmuted into a happy ending. The heroes' flight to a paradise lost—far from society, far from history, into a circular mythological time—can be understood only in light of the metamorphosis that Indiana and Ralph undergo in this most poetic of scenes. Ralph's confession results in true self-discovery and thus the desire to live.

The paradox, of course, is that Sand's first novel is at the same time about suicide and survival. She plays with the powerful literary motif of suicide but recasts it in a symbolic system of her own coining. Ralph's cry "Mourons ensemble" ("Let us die together") is a leitmotif of Sand's imagination reappearing in *Valentine* and also in the fourth of the *Lettres d'un voyageur,* where the narrator imagines that her children are saying to her: "Oui, la vie est insupportable dans un monde ainsi fait; mourons ensemble! Montrez-nous le chemin de Bernica, ou le lac de Sténio, ou les glaciers de Jacques!" ("Yes, life is unbearable in the world such as it is; let us die together! Show us the path to Bernica or Stenio's lake, or the glaciers where Jacques chose to end his life"). Here this cry is transformed into "Vivons ensemble." Ralph articulates his life-affirming credo to the "voyageur" in the Epilogue: "nos jours . . . passent rapides et purs comme ceux de notre enfance. Chaque soir, nous bénissons le ciel; nous l'implorons chaque matin, nous lui demandons le soleil et les ombrages de la veille" ("our days . . . pass swiftly and innocently like those of our childhood. Each evening, we bless heaven; we turn to Him every morning, and we ask Him to provide again the sun and the shade of the day before"). *Indiana,* opening with a gloomy description evoking René's Gothic castle, begins under the sign of Chateaubriand, but it ends under the sign of Bernardin de Saint-Pierre. Between these two poles of inspiration the author's own double meditation on suicide—in its active and passive versions—constitutes a privileged insight into her imagination.

Sand in her autobiography clearly offers a parallel between the emotion she encountered in the remarkably short period of the novel's composition and the feelings Ralph experiences when discovering the miracle of speech:

> Cette émotion, lentement amassée dans le cours d'une vie de réflexions, déborda très impétueuse dès que le cadre d'une situation quelconque s'ouvrit pour la contenir; mais elle s'y trouva fort à l'étroit, et cette sorte de combat entre l'émotion et l'exécution me soutint pendant six semaines dans un état de volonté tout nouveau pour moi.

> (This emotion, built up slowly during the course of a life of meditation, overflowed quite impetuously as soon as some situation offered a framework to contain it; but this emotion was very confined, and the struggle between emotion and implementation kept me for six weeks in a sustained state of will power which was entirely new to me.)

During the composition of *Indiana,* two inner events took place. First, Sand discovered her true literary vocation, which marked *Indiana* off from all her preceding literary efforts: "Je sentis en commençant à écrire *Indiana* une émotion très vive et très particulière, ne ressemblant à rien de ce que j'avais éprouvé dans mes précédents essais . . ." ("When I began to write *Indiana,* I experienced a very powerful and distinctive emotion, totally different from what I had felt during my previous writing attempts . . ."). This event Sand incorporated in the novel in the form of Ralph's transformation. Second, she realized that the elaborate mythical world that she had created in her childhood and that had nourished her imagination up to that time had suddenly ceased to exist. Ever since she had been a child, the binary helix of Aurore's intellectual preoccupations had been religion and literature: "Religion and novel grew side by side in my soul," she wrote in *Histoire de ma vie.* Sand's instinctive rapprochement of literature and religion led her to express Ralph's poetic inspiration in theological terms, to equate the grace conferred on him by mystical ecstasy with a poetic state. At the center of her childhood mythical world, at once pagan and Christian, was Corambé, a private deity she had invented. The pacifist Corambé was androgynous, with a woman's face but referred to as "il" by the author. This creation now receded. The writing of *Indiana* had somehow brought about the disappearance of double-gendered Corambé and his or her world. Sand relates the episode in *Histoire de ma vie:*

> A peine eus-je fini mon livre, que je voulus retrouver le vague ordinaire de mes rêveries. Impossible! . . . j'espérai en vain voir reparaître . . . ces figures à moitié nettes, ces voix à moitié distinctes, qui flottaient autour de moi comme un tableau animé derrière un voile transparent. Ces chères visions n'étaient que les précurseurs de l'inspiration.

> (I had barely finished my book and I longed to return to the usual vagueness of my reveries. It was no longer possible! . . . I hoped in vain for the reemergence of . . . those half-discernible figures, half-distinct voices, which floated around me like an animated painting behind a transparent veil. Those precious visions had been nothing but the precursors of inspiration.)

This strange phenomenon can be understood as a very specific passage in Sand's mental life from an inexpressible but vividly present system of reveries (at the center of which stood Corambé) to an intellectualized and verbalized system of storytelling. From *rêveuse,* Sand had indeed become a full-fledged *écrivaine.* Sand's formulations—"le vague des rêveries," "figures à moitié nettes," "voix à moitié distinctes," "tableau derrière un voile"—are all metaphors for a preverbal language, for a prelinguistic state Julia Kristeva calls the semiotic. The composition of *Indiana* and the sudden dissipation of this "phénomène de demi-hallucination" which until that point Sand had experienced regularly in her life, marks an exceptional moment—Aurore's re-creation of herself as George Sand the writer.

If Ralph's coining of a personal phraseology coincides

with the birth of Sand's specifically literary voice, what are we to make of the character of Indiana and the symbolic function of her language? More complex than either Raymon or Ralph, Indiana at first speaks very little. In the course of the novel she employs three main forms of discourse. The most forceful of these she uses in a moment of heightened epiphany, when she becomes an impassioned letter writer. After her flawed suicide and in the novel's final pages, she falls silent. Of all the characters, she alone presents an enigma, since her linguistic evolution does not parallel her personal development. Whereas Ralph's loosened tongue signifies the author's own poetic unleashing of language, Indiana can be eloquent only in protest—against her tyrannical and exploitative husband, or the injustice of marriage. The moment she finds a solution to her mal du siècle she is overcome by contentment which results in silence.

First of all, she articulates a language of resistance, which she reserves for her husband. Her speeches condemning the patriarchal arbitrariness of power and its violence are perhaps the most famous passages of the novel. Contemporary critics drew great attention to them and went on to proclaim Sand as a champion of women's rights. This eloquent tirade of Indiana, often cited, is addressed to Delmare:

> Je sais que je suis l'esclave et vous le seigneur. La loi de ce pays vous a fait mon maître. Vous pouvez lier mon corps, garotter mes mains, gouverner mes actions. Vous avez le droit du plus fort, et la société vous le confirme; mais sur ma volonté, monsieur, vous ne pouvez rien, Dieu seul peut la courber et la réduire. Cherchez donc une loi, un cachot, un instrument de supplice qui vous donne prise sur moi! C'est comme si vous vouliez manier l'air et saisir le vide.

> (I know that I am the slave and you are the lord. The laws of this land have made you my master. You can tie up my body, bind my hands, govern my actions. You have the right of the strongest, and society confirms it; but over my will, monsieur, you have no hold, only God can curb and abate it. Search if you will a law, a prison, an instrument of torture that could give you a hold over me! It's as if you wanted to touch air and grasp nothingness.)

Many critics have used this passage to make of Indiana a double of the author and to accentuate Sand's feminism above all. Of course Sand was very much interested in denouncing the marital rights of men and in proclaiming women's rights both within and outside of marriage. Her hatred of physical brutality, whether the violence of husbands against their wives, of governments against political opposition, or of any majority's use of violence against any minority, was frequently a motivating force in her writing. Several years after *Indiana,* she was still fighting for the inclusion of women in what she called the social and moral order. In a letter written in the spring of 1837 to Frédéric Girerd [sic], for example, she wrote:

> le monde trouve fort naturel et fort excusable qu'on se joue avec les femmes de ce qu'il y a de plus sacré: les femmes ne comptent ni dans l'ordre social, ni dans l'ordre moral. Oh! J'en fais le serment, et voici la première lueur de courage et d'ambition de ma vie! Je relèverai le femme de son abjection, et dans ma personne et dans mes écrits.

> (society finds it quite natural and quite excusable to treat contemptuously what is most sacred about women: women have no status in the social order, or in the moral order. Oh! I make an oath of this, and here is the first glimmer of courage and ambition in my life! I will lift women out of their abjection, both in my person and in my writings.)

In spite of such statements and Indiana's demonstrated resistance to her husband's authority, it is somewhat shortsighted to equate heroine with author, or indeed to use Indiana's words as unequivocal proof of Sand's feminism. Sand's position was more complicated and more contradictory. Nor does Indiana herself always express a militant feminist view. In fact her language of resistance is counterbalanced by a second antithetical code, what we might call submissive discourse, the discourse she reserves for her lover Raymon:

> je viens pour te donner du bonheur, pour être tout ce que tu voudras, ta compagne, ta servante ou ta maitresse . . . je n'ai plus le droit de te refuser aucun sacrifice. Dispose de moi, de mon sang, de ma vie; je suis à toi corps et âme. J'ai fait trois mille lieues pour t'appartenir, pour te dire cela; prends-moi, je suis ton bien, tu es mon maître.

> (I come to offer you happiness, to be everything you wish, your companion, your servant or your mistress . . . I no longer have the right to refuse you any sacrifice. Dispose of me, of my blood, of my life; I am yours, body and soul. I have traveled three thousand leagues to belong to you, to say this to you; take me, I am your property, you are my master.)

This is a shocking text when viewed from a modern feminist perspective. It is also a passage not often quoted. But Indiana's words here translate the inherent subservient relationship of the woman-as-object to the male creator of a false rhetoric. It expresses a moment of weakness in which the heroine is attracted to the master code which the male embodies.

How can Indiana's two antithetical vocabularies be reconciled? The author illustrates in these two verbal systems the only two linguistic solutions available to a woman who finds herself in a position of inequality with a man. Her linguistic range can be only reactive—either in revolt or in resignation. The passages quoted are less examples of an authentic language than of an idiom made up of contradictions, an idiom common to all women living in a similar situation of dependence.

Indiana begins to fashion an authentic discourse for herself late in the novel (almost as late as does Ralph); in a letter addressed to Raymon she finally sees the seducer for what he really is. Here the heroine ceases to speak in reaction to another's word and takes the initiative to speak in her own right. This third language puts forward her claims; it articulates another law, another reality:

> je ne sers pas le même Dieu [que vous]. . . . Le vôtre, c'est *le dieu des hommes,* c'est le roi, le fondateur et l'appui de votre race; le mien, c'est le Dieu de l'univers, le créateur, le soutien et l'espoir de toutes les créatures. Le vôtre a tout fait pour vous seuls; le mien a fait toutes les espèces les unes pour les autres. Vous vous croyez *les maîtres du monde;* je crois que vous n'en êtes que les tyrans. Vous pensez que Dieu vous protège et vous autorise à usurper l'empire de la terre; moi je pense qu'il le souffre pour un peu de temps, et qu'un jour viendra où, comme des grains de sable, son souffle vous dispersera . . . la religion que vous avez inventée, je la repousse; toute votre morale, tous vos principes, ce sont les intérêts de votre société que vous avez érigés en lois et que vous prétendez faire émaner de Dieu . . . mais tout cela est mensonge et impiété. (emphasis added)

> (I do not serve the same God [as you]. . . . Yours is *the god of men,* he is the king, the founder and pillar of your race; mine is the God of the universe, the creator, support, and hope of all creatures. Yours has made everything for men alone; mine has made all creatures for each other. You believe yourselves to be *the masters of the world;* I believe you are nothing but its tyrants. You think that God protects you and authorizes you to usurp the earth; I think He endures it for a while, and the day will come when, like grains of sand, his breath will scatter you. . . . I reject the religion you have invented; your morals, your principles have been erected as law in the interest of your society, and you pretend that they emanate from God . . . but all this is nothing but lies and blasphemy.)

Through her heroine Sand denounces the absolute equation of language with masculine power. She replaces the passage through language into the symbolic phallocratic order with a feminine utopia—a structure that is both social and linguistic. The double *si* (if/yes) of Woman replaces the double *nom/non* (name/no) of the Father:

> Si [Dieu] daignait descendre jusqu'à intervenir dans nos chétifs intérêts, il briserait le fort et relèverait le faible; il passerait sa grande main sur nos têtes inégales et les nivellerait . . . il dirait à l'esclave: "Jette ta chaîne . . ." Il dirait aux rois: "Jetez la pourpre . . ." Il dirait aux puissants: "Courbez le genou . . ." Oui, *voilà mes rêves; ils sont tous d'une autre vie, d'un autre monde où la loi du brutal n'aura point passé sur la tête du pacifique* . . . (emphasis added)

> (Yes, if [God] deigned to take an interest in our paltry affairs, He would break the strong and uplift the weak; He would pass His great hand over our unequal heads and make them equal . . . He would say to the slave: "Cast your chain aside . . ." He would say to the kings: "Relinquish the scarlet robes . . ." He would say to the powerful: "Kneel down . . ." Yes, *these are my dreams: they are of another life, of another world*

> *in which the law of brutality will have no precedence over pacifism . . .*)

To denounce the "law of brutality", that is Indiana's definitive role. After having fallen prey to the passive reactive behavior that identifies her with regard to both husband and lover, Indiana finally comes into her own, articulating a utopian position of such force as to make this first of Sand's heroines authentically subversive and a fitting older sister of Lélia.

After the forceful tone of Indiana's letter, it is disappointing, if not incomprehensible, to witness her silence at the novel's conclusion. But it can be explained when examined in relation to the two male principal's patterns of speech. Dispelling once and for all the temptation to identify Indiana with Sand, the reader can clearly sense that the equilibrium of the book defines itself through the three main characters of the novel: Indiana, Ralph, and Raymon. Significantly Indiana is placed in a position where she must choose between the two discourses represented by Raymon and Ralph. First she chooses Raymon's code, seduced by skillful rhetoric; subsequently she will reduce him to silence. Then, when she decides to follow Ralph on his journey, she makes his awakening into language possible. The astonishing scene of Ralph's confession follows, taking place symbolically at Bernica Falls, "les gorges de Bernica." The word "gorge" can be read in two ways here, as a geological and a physiological term—gorges/falls and throat. In this desert, this other world from which "la loi du brutal" is banished, the poetic word appears. Sand certainly shares common traits with her heroine; she even perhaps shares certain faults with Raymon. But at the end it is with Ralph the poet, whose speech closes the book, that the writer finds the closest identification.

New ways of considering the characters of ***Indiana*** suggest themselves. The old theory, the search for the real-life models for any given character, needs to be transcended. In this naive perspective which has been so much abused, Indiana and Noun are the double transposition of George Sand; Colonel Delmare, a portrait of the hateful Casimir; Raymon, a combination of Aurélien de Sèze and Stéphane de Grandsagne; Ralph, Jules Néraud, nicknamed Le Malgache; and so on. A second approach, according to which a given character is the incarnation of a type, allows us to see in the novel the elaboration of a Romantic cast of characters fixed in a modern commedia dell'arte. In this interpretation Indiana is a romantic heroine; Ralph, a suffering Byronic hero; Raymon, a Lovelace; Laure, a woman of the world; Delmare, the brutal husband; Noun, the woman-slave. Yet a third approach is possible in ***Indiana,*** one where the character is the incarnation of a certain mode of being of the author. Each character symbolizes a possible solution to the central dilemma, the creation of a literary voice. From this perspective the six characters represent six possible solutions, ranging from the patriarchal code (in Delmare), on to false journalistic rhetoric (Raymon), through silence (Noun) and parody (Laure), to arrive at the language of protest (Indiana) and poetic discourse (Ralph).

The novel's double ending, which has always bothered the critics for its implausibility now finds its true significance.

I do not agree with Planche that the novel should have ended with Raymon's marriage and Indiana's abandonment. There is a legitimate reason for the false suicide to be transmuted into a happy ending, a logic behind the two heroes' flight to a paradise lost, as they engulf themselves in a circular mythological time. The solution reached in the novel regarding the creation of an authentic language system is represented metaphorically in the novel's ending. Indiana can finally realize her dream of a voyage initiatique: "Si j'écoutais la voix que Dieu a mise au fond de mon coeur, je fuirais au désert" ("If I listened to the voice that God has placed at the bottom of my heart, I would escape to the desert"). Ralph, taking her back to Ile Bourbon, can finally express the plentitude of his being.

Paradoxically, the exile motif at the close of the novel is also an expression of the underhanded way in which Sand enters as a full-fledged member into the masculine world of literature. In the desert of Ile Bourbon a new system of communication has been hammered out, through Ralph. The author can now return to Paris, with a finished novel under her arm. Sand leaves Indiana and Ralph in their "chaumiére indienne" (a direct allusion to Bernardin de Saint-Pierre's text of 1790), but she herself comes back from exile and into the world of letters.

In conclusion, Sand's fictional text is less the story of unrequited love than the triumph of the spoken (and written) word, the triumph of the text. The conclusion does not so much advocate recourse to solitude and the renunciation of society, or the stopgap measure of friendship at the expense of true love, as it proclaims the triumph of language, the discovery of the power of the word, and the transfiguration of silence into speech. As a novel of apprenticeship, then, *Indiana* is an instance of what Henry James called the breaking of a spell of silence. Through the character of Ralph—in whom the critic Eugène Morisseau (read Balzac) correctly saw "la grande figure du livre"—Sand expressed her own coming into language. When the narrator says of Ralph, "c'était la première fois, peut-être, depuis qu'il était né, que sa pensée tout entière venait se placer sur ses lèvres" ("it was maybe the first time since he had been born that all his thought managed to form itself whole on his lips"), this observation equally refers to Sand's discovery and articulation of a "parole bienfaisante." All evidence in the novel points to the equation of spoken and written discourse with healing.

Sand will mention this unleashing of verbal power again, with emotion, in her 1832 preface to *Indiana.* There, not surprisingly, she expresses the twin themes of freedom and verbal expression:

> Liberté de la pensée, liberté d'écrire et de parler, sainte conquête de l'esprit humain! Que sont les petites souffrances et les soucis éphémères engendrés par tes erreurs ou tes abus, au prix des bienfaits infinis que tu prépares au monde.

> (Freedom of thought, freedom to write and to speak, sacred conquest of the human spirit! The small sufferings and the ephemeral worries engendered by your mistakes or your excesses are meaningless, when compared to the infinite benefits that you bestow upon the world.)

Every woman who writes, Julia Kristeva has remarked, is "an eternal disident in relation to the social and political consensus, *exiled in relation to power,* and therefore always eccentric, fragmented." Fragmentation and exile: Sand experienced them both cruelly. *Indiana* is at the same time the locus of her psychic integration and the expression of her return from exile. Here she started in actuality writing for her life. (pp. 53-76)

> *Isabelle Hoog Naginski, in her* George Sand: Writing for Her Life, *Rutgers University Press, 1991, 281 p.*

FURTHER READING

Biography

Barry, Joseph. *Infamous Woman: The Life of George Sand.* Garden City, N. Y.: Doubleday & Co., 1977, 436 p.
    Addresses Sand's achievement in terms of her works and the events of her life, asserting that she was "quintessentially the modern woman."

West, Anthony. "George Sand." In his *Mortal Wounds,* pp. 225-306. New York: McGraw-Hill Book Co., 1973.
    Provides an analysis of Sand's life and an interpretation of her fiction based on behavioral psychology.

Winegarten, Renee. *The Double Life of George Sand, Woman and Writer.* New York: Basic Books, Inc., 1978, 339 p.
    Critical biography of Sand, examining in particular her struggle "to understand herself as a woman and as a human being."

Criticism

Crecelius, Kathryn J. "Writing A Self: From Aurore Dudevant to George Sand." *Tulsa Studies in Women's Literature* 4, No. 1 (Spring 1985): 47-59.
    Traces Sand's literary development through her early writings, most of which were not published in her lifetime.

——. "Female Fantastic: The Case of George Sand." *L'Esprit Createur* XXVIII, No. 3 (Fall 1988): 49-62.
    Considers Sand's fiction in the context of nineteenth-century fantastic literature.

——. " 'Fille majeure, établie, maitresse de ses actions': George Sand's Unusual Heroines." In *Women in French Literature,* edited by Michel Guggenheim. Saratoga, Calif.: Anma Libri and Co., 1988.
    Investigates the range of Sand's female protagonists, suggesting that her "lesser-known heroines, women from the peasant and working classes, are perhaps her most intriguing."

Danahy, Michael. "*La Petite Fadette:* The Dilemma of Being a Heroine." In his *The Feminization of the Novel,* pp. 159-91. Gainesville, Fla.: University of Florida Press, 1991.
    Analyzes Fadette as a heroine without role models or social support.

Davis, Mary Byrd. "George Sand and the Poetry of Matthew Arnold." *Texas Studies in Language and Literature* XIX, No. 2 (Summer 1977): 204-26.

Contends that Sand "was a central influence on Arnold's life and writing."

Deutelbaum, Wendy, and Huff, Cynthia. "Class, Gender, and Family System: The Case of George Sand." In *The (M)other Tongue: Essays in Feminist Psychoanalytic Interpretation,* edited by Shirley Nelson Garner, Claire Kahane, and Madelon Sprengnether, pp. 260-79. Ithaca, N. Y.: Cornell University Press, 1985.

Feminist psychoanalytic essay arguing that Sand's internalized "family drama" profoundly shaped her work.

Grant, Richard B. "George Sand's *La Petite Fadette* and the Problem of Masculine Individuation." In *L'Hénaurme Siècle: A Miscellany of Essays on Nineteenth-Century French Literature,* edited by Will L. McLendon, pp. 47-61. Heidelberg: Carl Winter Universitätsverlag, 1984.

Psychoanalytic reading of Sand's *La Petite Fadette.*

————. "George Sand's *Lélia* and the Tragedy of Dualism." *Nineteenth-Century French Studies* 19, No. 4 (Summer 1991): 499-516.

Studies the pattern of Romantic dualism in Sand's *Lélia* which separates "higher" spiritual values from "lower" material ones.

James, Henry. "George Sand." In his *Notes on Novelists, with Some Other Notes,* pp. 127-47. J. M. Dent & Sons, 1914.

Discusses Sand's character and verbal genius as demonstrated in her letters to poet Alfred de Musset.

Jurgrau, Thelma. "Autobiography in General and George Sand's in Particular." *Nineteenth-Century French Studies* 17, Nos. 1-2 (1988-89): 196-207.

Presents Sand's autobiography as a text which combines factual events and fiction.

Karp, Carole. "George Sand, Balzac, and the Russian Soul." *Michigan Academician* X, No. 3 (Winter 1978): 347-59.

Explores Sand's literary influence on Russian writers including Turgenev and Dostoevsky.

Manifold, Gay. *George Sand's Theatre Career.* Theater and Dramatic Studies, No. 28. Ann Arbor, Mich.: UMI Research Press, 1983, 188 p.

Overview of Sand's theater career, which involved writing, producing, and directing plays.

Miller, Nancy K. "Writing (from) the Feminine: George Sand and the Novel of Female Pastoral." In *The Representation of Women in Fiction,* edited by Carolyn G. Heilbrun and Margaret R. Higonnet. Baltimore, Md.: Johns Hopkins University Press, 1983.

Feminist analysis of Sand's novel *Valentine.*

Schor, Naomi. "Female Fetishism: The Case of George Sand." In *The Female Body in Western Culture,* edited by Susan Rubin Suleiman, pp. 363-72. Cambridge, Mass.: Harvard University Press, 1986.

Feminist psychoanalytic examination of the "striking representation of the female body" in several of Sand's works.

————. "Idealism in the Novel: Recanonizing Sand." *Yale French Studies,* No. 75 (1988): 56-73.

Discusses Sand's representation of idealism in *Indiana* and how it differs from that of her contemporaries.

————. "*Lélia* and the Failures of Allegory." *L'Esprit Createur* XXIX, No. 3 (Fall 1989): 76-83.

Interprets Sand's novel *Lélia* as a hybrid genre combining "metaphysical allegory" with "physical love story."

Sonnenfeld, Albert. "George Sand: Music and Sexuality." *Nineteenth-Century French Studies* XVI, No. 3 (Spring/Summer 1988): 310-21.

Contends that music plays a central role in Sand's novels *Consuelo* and *Les Maitres sonneurs.*

Wren, Keith. " 'The Education of the Heart': The Moral and Social Dimensions of George Sand's *Mauprat*." In *Studies in French Fiction in Honour of Vivienne Mylne,* edited by Robert Gibson, pp. 357-71. Valencia, Spain: Grant and Cutler, 1988.

Argues that *Mauprat* "stands at the crossroads of George Sand's . . . output" in its representation of her early and late social visions.

Nineteenth-Century
Literature Criticism

Cumulative Indexes
Volumes 1-42

How to Use This Index

The main references

Calvino, Italo
    1923-1985.....CLC 5, 8, 11, 22, 33, 39,
                                    73; SSC 3

---

list all author entries in the following Gale Literary Criticism series:

CLC = *Contemporary Literary Criticism*
CLR = *Children's Literature Review*
CMLC = *Classical and Medieval Literature Criticism*
DC = *Drama Criticism*
LC = *Literature Criticism from 1400 to 1800*
NCLC = *Nineteenth-Century Literature Criticism*
PC = *Poetry Criticism*
SSC = *Short Story Criticism*
TCLC = *Twentieth-Century Literary Criticism*

The cross-references

See also CANR 23; CA 85-88;
    obituary CA 116

---

list all author entries in the following Gale biographical and literary sources:

AAYA = *Authors & Artists for Young Adults*
AITN = *Authors in the News*
BLC = *Black Literature Criticism*
BW = *Black Writers*
CA = *Contemporary Authors*
CAAS = *Contemporary Authors Autobiography Series*
CABS = *Contemporary Authors Bibliographical Series*
CANR = *Contemporary Authors New Revision Series*
CAP = *Contemporary Authors Permanent Series*
CDALB = *Concise Dictionary of American Literary Biography*
CDBLB = *Concise Dictionary of British Literary Biography*
DA = *DISCovering Authors*
DLB = *Dictionary of Literary Biography*
DLBD = *Dictionary of Literary Biography Documentary Series*
DLBY = *Dictionary of Literary Biography Yearbook*
HW = *Hispanic Writers*
MAICYA = *Major Authors and Illustrators for Children and Young Adults*
MTCW = *Major 20th-Century Writers*
SAAS = *Something about the Author Autobiography Series*
SATA = *Something about the Author*
WLC = *World Literature Criticism, 1500 to the Present*
YABC = *Yesterday's Authors of Books for Children*

Literary Criticism Series
Cumulative Author Index

A.
See Arnold, Matthew

A. E. . . . . TCLC 3, 10
See also Russell, George William
See also DLB 19

A. M.
See Megged, Aharon

Abasiyanik, Sait Faik 1906-1954
See Sait Faik
See also CA 123

Abbey, Edward 1927-1989 . . . . . . CLC 36, 59
See also CA 45-48; 128; CANR 2, 41

Abbott, Lee K(ittredge) 1947- . . . . . . CLC 48
See also CA 124; DLB 130

Abe, Kobo 1924-1993 . . . . CLC 8, 22, 53
See also CA 65-68; 140; CANR 24; MTCW

Abelard, Peter c. 1079-c. 1142 . . . CMLC 11
See also DLB 115

Abell, Kjeld 1901-1961 . . . . CLC 15
See also CA 111

Abish, Walter 1931- . . . . CLC 22
See also CA 101; CANR 37; DLB 130

Abrahams, Peter (Henry) 1919- . . . . . CLC 4
See also BW; CA 57-60; CANR 26;
DLB 117; MTCW

Abrams, M(eyer) H(oward) 1912-. . . CLC 24
See also CA 57-60; CANR 13, 33; DLB 67

Abse, Dannie 1923-. . . . . CLC 7, 29
See also CA 53-56; CAAS 1; CANR 4;
DLB 27

Achebe, (Albert) Chinua(lumogu)
1930- . . . . . CLC 1, 3, 5, 7, 11, 26, 51, 75
See also BLC 1; BW; CA 1-4R; CANR 6,
26; CLR 20; DA; DLB 117; MAICYA;
MTCW; SATA 38, 40; WLC

Acker, Kathy 1948- . . . . CLC 45
See also CA 117; 122

Ackroyd, Peter 1949-. . . . . CLC 34, 52
See also CA 123; 127

Acorn, Milton 1923-. . . . . CLC 15
See also CA 103; DLB 53

Adamov, Arthur 1908-1970 . . . . . . CLC 4, 25
See also CA 17-18; 25-28R; CAP 2; MTCW

Adams, Alice (Boyd) 1926- . . . CLC 6, 13, 46
See also CA 81-84; CANR 26; DLBY 86;
MTCW

Adams, Douglas (Noel) 1952- . . . CLC 27, 60
See also AAYA 4; BEST 89:3; CA 106;
CANR 34; DLBY 83; JRDA

Adams, Francis 1862-1893 . . . . NCLC 33

Adams, Henry (Brooks)
1838-1918 . . . . TCLC 4, 52
See also CA 104; 133; DA; DLB 12, 47

Adams, Richard (George)
1920- . . . . CLC 4, 5, 18
See also AITN 1, 2; CA 49-52; CANR 3,
35; CLR 20; JRDA; MAICYA; MTCW;
SATA 7, 69

Adamson, Joy(-Friederike Victoria)
1910-1980 . . . . CLC 17
See also CA 69-72; 93-96; CANR 22;
MTCW; SATA 11, 22

Adcock, Fleur 1934-. . . . . CLC 41
See also CA 25-28R; CANR 11, 34;
DLB 40

Addams, Charles (Samuel)
1912-1988 . . . . CLC 30
See also CA 61-64; 126; CANR 12

Addison, Joseph 1672-1719 . . . . LC 18
See also CDBLB 1660-1789; DLB 101

Adler, C(arole) S(chwerdtfeger)
1932-. . . . . CLC 35
See also AAYA 4; CA 89-92; CANR 19,
40; JRDA; MAICYA; SAAS 15;
SATA 26, 63

Adler, Renata 1938-. . . . . CLC 8, 31
See also CA 49-52; CANR 5, 22; MTCW

Ady, Endre 1877-1919 . . . . TCLC 11
See also CA 107

Aeschylus 525B.C.-456B.C. . . . . . . CMLC 11
See also DA

Afton, Effie
See Harper, Frances Ellen Watkins

Agapida, Fray Antonio
See Irving, Washington

Agee, James (Rufus)
1909-1955 . . . . TCLC 1, 19
See also AITN 1; CA 108;
CDALB 1941-1968; DLB 2, 26

A Gentlewoman in New England
See Bradstreet, Anne

A Gentlewoman in Those Parts
See Bradstreet, Anne

Aghill, Gordon
See Silverberg, Robert

Agnon, S(hmuel) Y(osef Halevi)
1888-1970 . . . . CLC 4, 8, 14
See also CA 17-18; 25-28R; CAP 2; MTCW

Aherne, Owen
See Cassill, R(onald) V(erlin)

Ai 1947-. . . . . CLC 4, 14, 69
See also CA 85-88; CAAS 13; DLB 120

Aickman, Robert (Fordyce)
1914-1981 . . . . CLC 57
See also CA 5-8R; CANR 3

Aiken, Conrad (Potter)
1889-1973 . . . CLC 1, 3, 5, 10, 52; SSC 9
See also CA 5-8R; 45-48; CANR 4;
CDALB 1929-1941; DLB 9, 45, 102;
MTCW; SATA 3, 30

Aiken, Joan (Delano) 1924-. . . . . CLC 35
See also AAYA 1; CA 9-12R; CANR 4, 23,
34; CLR 1, 19; JRDA; MAICYA;
MTCW; SAAS 1; SATA 2, 30, 73

Ainsworth, William Harrison
1805-1882 . . . . NCLC 13
See also DLB 21; SATA 24

Aitmatov, Chingiz (Torekulovich)
1928-. . . . . CLC 71
See also CA 103; CANR 38; MTCW;
SATA 56

Akers, Floyd
See Baum, L(yman) Frank

Akhmadulina, Bella Akhatovna
1937-. . . . . CLC 53
See also CA 65-68

Akhmatova, Anna
1888-1966 . . . . CLC 11, 25, 64; PC 2
See also CA 19-20; 25-28R; CANR 35;
CAP 1; MTCW

Aksakov, Sergei Timofeyvich
1791-1859 . . . . NCLC 2

Aksenov, Vassily . . . . CLC 22
See also Aksyonov, Vassily (Pavlovich)

Aksyonov, Vassily (Pavlovich)
1932-. . . . . CLC 37
See also Aksenov, Vassily
See also CA 53-56; CANR 12

Akutagawa Ryunosuke
1892-1927 . . . . TCLC 16
See also CA 117

Alain 1868-1951 . . . . TCLC 41

Alain-Fournier . . . . TCLC 6
See also Fournier, Henri Alban
See also DLB 65

Alarcon, Pedro Antonio de
1833-1891 . . . . NCLC 1

Alas (y Urena), Leopoldo (Enrique Garcia)
1852-1901 . . . . TCLC 29
See also CA 113; 131; HW

Albee, Edward (Franklin III)
1928-. . . CLC 1, 2, 3, 5, 9, 11, 13, 25, 53
See also AITN 1; CA 5-8R; CABS 3;
CANR 8; CDALB 1941-1968; DA;
DLB 7; MTCW; WLC

Alberti, Rafael 1902-. . . . . CLC 7
See also CA 85-88; DLB 108

Alcala-Galiano, Juan Valera y
See Valera y Alcala-Galiano, Juan

Alcott, Amos Bronson 1799-1888 . . NCLC 1
See also DLB 1

Alcott, Louisa May 1832-1888 . . . . NCLC 6
See also CDALB 1865-1917; CLR 1; DA;
DLB 1, 42, 79; JRDA; MAICYA; WLC;
YABC 1

Aldanov, M. A.
See Aldanov, Mark (Alexandrovich)

Antoine, Marc
   See Proust, (Valentin-Louis-George-Eugene-) Marcel

Antoninus, Brother
   See Everson, William (Oliver)

Antonioni, Michelangelo 1912- ..... **CLC 20**
   See also CA 73-76

Antschel, Paul 1920-1970. ...... **CLC 10, 19**
   See also Celan, Paul
   See also CA 85-88; CANR 33; MTCW

Anwar, Chairil 1922-1949 .... **TCLC 22**
   See also CA 121

Apollinaire, Guillaume .. **TCLC 3, 8, 51; PC 7**
   See also Kostrowitzki, Wilhelm Apollinaris de

Appelfeld, Aharon 1932- .... **CLC 23, 47**
   See also CA 112; 133

Apple, Max (Isaac) 1941-. .... **CLC 9, 33**
   See also CA 81-84; CANR 19; DLB 130

Appleman, Philip (Dean) 1926- ..... **CLC 51**
   See also CA 13-16R; CAAS 18; CANR 6, 29

Appleton, Lawrence
   See Lovecraft, H(oward) P(hillips)

Apteryx
   See Eliot, T(homas) S(tearns)

Apuleius, (Lucius Madaurensis)
   125(?)-175(?) .... **CMLC 1**

Aquin, Hubert 1929-1977. .... **CLC 15**
   See also CA 105; DLB 53

Aragon, Louis 1897-1982. .... **CLC 3, 22**
   See also CA 69-72; 108; CANR 28; DLB 72; MTCW

Arany, Janos 1817-1882. .... **NCLC 34**

Arbuthnot, John 1667-1735. .... **LC 1**
   See also DLB 101

Archer, Herbert Winslow
   See Mencken, H(enry) L(ouis)

Archer, Jeffrey (Howard) 1940- .... **CLC 28**
   See also BEST 89:3; CA 77-80; CANR 22

Archer, Jules 1915- .... **CLC 12**
   See also CA 9-12R; CANR 6; SAAS 5; SATA 4

Archer, Lee
   See Ellison, Harlan

Arden, John 1930- .... **CLC 6, 13, 15**
   See also CA 13-16R; CAAS 4; CANR 31; DLB 13; MTCW

Arenas, Reinaldo 1943-1990 .... **CLC 41**
   See also CA 124; 128; 133; HW

Arendt, Hannah 1906-1975 .... **CLC 66**
   See also CA 17-20R; 61-64; CANR 26; MTCW

Aretino, Pietro 1492-1556 .... **LC 12**

Arguedas, Jose Maria
   1911-1969 .... **CLC 10, 18**
   See also CA 89-92; DLB 113; HW

Argueta, Manlio 1936-........... **CLC 31**
   See also CA 131; HW

Ariosto, Ludovico 1474-1533. .... **LC 6**

Aristides
   See Epstein, Joseph

Aristophanes
   450B.C.-385B.C. .... **CMLC 4; DC 2**
   See also DA

Arlt, Roberto (Godofredo Christophersen)
   1900-1942 .... **TCLC 29**
   See also CA 123; 131; HW

Armah, Ayi Kwei 1939-......... **CLC 5, 33**
   See also BLC 1; BW; CA 61-64; CANR 21; DLB 117; MTCW

Armatrading, Joan 1950-......... **CLC 17**
   See also CA 114

Arnette, Robert
   See Silverberg, Robert

Arnim, Achim von (Ludwig Joachim von Arnim) 1781-1831 .... **NCLC 5**
   See also DLB 90

Arnim, Bettina von 1785-1859. .... **NCLC 38**
   See also DLB 90

Arnold, Matthew
   1822-1888 .... **NCLC 6, 29; PC 5**
   See also CDBLB 1832-1890; DA; DLB 32, 57; WLC

Arnold, Thomas 1795-1842 ...... **NCLC 18**
   See also DLB 55

Arnow, Harriette (Louisa) Simpson
   1908-1986 .... **CLC 2, 7, 18**
   See also CA 9-12R; 118; CANR 14; DLB 6; MTCW; SATA 42, 47

Arp, Hans
   See Arp, Jean

Arp, Jean 1887-1966. .... **CLC 5**
   See also CA 81-84; 25-28R; CANR 42

Arrabal
   See Arrabal, Fernando

Arrabal, Fernando 1932- ...**CLC 2, 9, 18, 58**
   See also CA 9-12R; CANR 15

Arrick, Fran. .... **CLC 30**

Artaud, Antonin 1896-1948 ..... **TCLC 3, 36**
   See also CA 104

Arthur, Ruth M(abel) 1905-1979. .... **CLC 12**
   See also CA 9-12R; 85-88; CANR 4; SATA 7, 26

Artsybashev, Mikhail (Petrovich)
   1878-1927 .... **TCLC 31**

Arundel, Honor (Morfydd)
   1919-1973 .... **CLC 17**
   See also CA 21-22; 41-44R; CAP 2; SATA 4, 24

Asch, Sholem 1880-1957 .... **TCLC 3**
   See also CA 105

Ash, Shalom
   See Asch, Sholem

Ashbery, John (Lawrence)
   1927- ...... **CLC 2, 3, 4, 6, 9, 13, 15, 25, 41, 77**
   See also CA 5-8R; CANR 9, 37; DLB 5; DLBY 81; MTCW

Ashdown, Clifford
   See Freeman, R(ichard) Austin

Ashe, Gordon
   See Creasey, John

Ashton-Warner, Sylvia (Constance)
   1908-1984 .... **CLC 19**
   See also CA 69-72; 112; CANR 29; MTCW

Asimov, Isaac
   1920-1992 ...... **CLC 1, 3, 9, 19, 26, 76**
   See also BEST 90:2; CA 1-4R; 137; CANR 2, 19, 36; CLR 12; DLB 8; DLBY 92; JRDA; MAICYA; MTCW; SATA 1, 26, 74

Astley, Thea (Beatrice May)
   1925- .... **CLC 41**
   See also CA 65-68; CANR 11

Aston, James
   See White, T(erence) H(anbury)

Asturias, Miguel Angel
   1899-1974 .... **CLC 3, 8, 13**
   See also CA 25-28; 49-52; CANR 32; CAP 2; DLB 113; HW; MTCW

Atares, Carlos Saura
   See Saura (Atares), Carlos

Atheling, William
   See Pound, Ezra (Weston Loomis)

Atheling, William, Jr.
   See Blish, James (Benjamin)

Atherton, Gertrude (Franklin Horn)
   1857-1948 .... **TCLC 2**
   See also CA 104; DLB 9, 78

Atherton, Lucius
   See Masters, Edgar Lee

Atkins, Jack
   See Harris, Mark

Atticus
   See Fleming, Ian (Lancaster)

Atwood, Margaret (Eleanor)
   1939- ..... **CLC 2, 3, 4, 8, 13, 15, 25, 44; SSC 2**
   See also BEST 89:2; CA 49-52; CANR 3, 24, 33; DA; DLB 53; MTCW; SATA 50; WLC

Aubigny, Pierre d'
   See Mencken, H(enry) L(ouis)

Aubin, Penelope 1685-1731(?). .... **LC 9**
   See also DLB 39

Auchincloss, Louis (Stanton)
   1917- .... **CLC 4, 6, 9, 18, 45**
   See also CA 1-4R; CANR 6, 29; DLB 2; DLBY 80; MTCW

Auden, W(ystan) H(ugh)
   1907-1973 ...... **CLC 1, 2, 3, 4, 6, 9, 11, 14, 43; PC 1**
   See also CA 9-12R; 45-48; CANR 5; CDBLB 1914-1945; DA; DLB 10, 20; MTCW; WLC

Audiberti, Jacques 1900-1965 ...... **CLC 38**
   See also CA 25-28R

Auel, Jean M(arie) 1936-............ **CLC 31**
   See also AAYA 7; BEST 90:4; CA 103; CANR 21

Auerbach, Erich 1892-1957. ...... **TCLC 43**
   See also CA 118

Augier, Emile 1820-1889 .... **NCLC 31**

August, John
   See De Voto, Bernard (Augustine)

Augustine, St. 354-430. .... **CMLC 6**

Aurelius
   See Bourne, Randolph S(illiman)

Austen, Jane
    1775-1817 . . . . **NCLC 1, 13, 19, 33**
    See also CDBLB 1789-1832; DA; DLB 116;
    WLC

Auster, Paul 1947- . . . . **CLC 47**
    See also CA 69-72; CANR 23

Austin, Frank
    See Faust, Frederick (Schiller)

Austin, Mary (Hunter)
    1868-1934 . . . . **TCLC 25**
    See also CA 109; DLB 9, 78

Autran Dourado, Waldomiro
    See Dourado, (Waldomiro Freitas) Autran

Averroes 1126-1198 . . . . **CMLC 7**
    See also DLB 115

Avison, Margaret 1918- . . . . **CLC 2, 4**
    See also CA 17-20R; DLB 53; MTCW

Axton, David
    See Koontz, Dean R(ay)

Ayckbourn, Alan
    1939- . . . . **CLC 5, 8, 18, 33, 74**
    See also CA 21-24R; CANR 31; DLB 13;
    MTCW

Aydy, Catherine
    See Tennant, Emma (Christina)

Ayme, Marcel (Andre) 1902-1967 . . . **CLC 11**
    See also CA 89-92; CLR 25; DLB 72

Ayrton, Michael 1921-1975 . . . . **CLC 7**
    See also CA 5-8R; 61-64; CANR 9, 21

Azorin . . . . **CLC 11**
    See also Martinez Ruiz, Jose

Azuela, Mariano 1873-1952 . . . . **TCLC 3**
    See also CA 104; 131; HW; MTCW

Baastad, Babbis Friis
    See Friis-Baastad, Babbis Ellinor

Bab
    See Gilbert, W(illiam) S(chwenck)

Babbis, Eleanor
    See Friis-Baastad, Babbis Ellinor

Babel, Isaak (Emmanuilovich)
    1894-1941(?) . . . . **CLC 73**
    See also CA 104; TCLC 2, 13

Babits, Mihaly 1883-1941 . . . . **TCLC 14**
    See also CA 114

Babur 1483-1530 . . . . **LC 18**

Bacchelli, Riccardo 1891-1985 . . . . . **CLC 19**
    See also CA 29-32R; 117

Bach, Richard (David) 1936- . . . . **CLC 14**
    See also AITN 1; BEST 89:2; CA 9-12R;
    CANR 18; MTCW; SATA 13

Bachman, Richard
    See King, Stephen (Edwin)

Bachmann, Ingeborg 1926-1973 . . . . . **CLC 69**
    See also CA 93-96; 45-48; DLB 85

Bacon, Francis 1561-1626 . . . . **LC 18**
    See also CDBLB Before 1660

Bacovia, George . . . . **TCLC 24**
    See also Vasiliu, Gheorghe

Badanes, Jerome 1937- . . . . **CLC 59**

Bagehot, Walter 1826-1877 . . . . . . **NCLC 10**
    See also DLB 55

Bagnold, Enid 1889-1981 . . . . **CLC 25**
    See also CA 5-8R; 103; CANR 5, 40;
    DLB 13; MAICYA; SATA 1, 25

Bagrjana, Elisaveta
    See Belcheva, Elisaveta

Bagryana, Elisaveta
    See Belcheva, Elisaveta

Bailey, Paul 1937- . . . . **CLC 45**
    See also CA 21-24R; CANR 16; DLB 14

Baillie, Joanna 1762-1851 . . . . **NCLC 2**
    See also DLB 93

Bainbridge, Beryl (Margaret)
    1933- . . . . **CLC 4, 5, 8, 10, 14, 18, 22, 62**
    See also CA 21-24R; CANR 24; DLB 14;
    MTCW

Baker, Elliott 1922- . . . . **CLC 8**
    See also CA 45-48; CANR 2

Baker, Nicholson 1957- . . . . **CLC 61**
    See also CA 135

Baker, Ray Stannard 1870-1946 . . . **TCLC 47**
    See also CA 118

Baker, Russell (Wayne) 1925- . . . . . . **CLC 31**
    See also BEST 89:4; CA 57-60; CANR 11,
    41; MTCW

Bakshi, Ralph 1938(?)- . . . . **CLC 26**
    See also CA 112; 138

Bakunin, Mikhail (Alexandrovich)
    1814-1876 . . . . **NCLC 25**

Baldwin, James (Arthur)
    1924-1987 . . . . . . **CLC 1, 2, 3, 4, 5, 8, 13,
            15, 17, 42, 50, 67; DC 1; SSC 10**
    See also AAYA 4; BLC 1; BW; CA 1-4R;
    124; CABS 1; CANR 3, 24;
    CDALB 1941-1968; DA; DLB 2, 7, 33;
    DLBY 87; MTCW; SATA 9, 54; WLC

Ballard, J(ames) G(raham)
    1930- . . . . **CLC 3, 6, 14, 36; SSC 1**
    See also AAYA 3; CA 5-8R; CANR 15, 39;
    DLB 14; MTCW

Balmont, Konstantin (Dmitriyevich)
    1867-1943 . . . . **TCLC 11**
    See also CA 109

Balzac, Honore de
    1799-1850 . . . . **NCLC 5, 35; SSC 5**
    See also DA; DLB 119; WLC

Bambara, Toni Cade 1939- . . . . **CLC 19**
    See also AAYA 5; BLC 1; BW; CA 29-32R;
    CANR 24; DA; DLB 38; MTCW

Bamdad, A.
    See Shamlu, Ahmad

Banat, D. R.
    See Bradbury, Ray (Douglas)

Bancroft, Laura
    See Baum, L(yman) Frank

Banim, John 1798-1842 . . . . **NCLC 13**
    See also DLB 116

Banim, Michael 1796-1874 . . . . . . **NCLC 13**

Banks, Iain
    See Banks, Iain M(enzies)

Banks, Iain M(enzies) 1954- . . . . . . **CLC 34**
    See also CA 123; 128

Banks, Lynne Reid . . . . **CLC 23**
    See also Reid Banks, Lynne
    See also AAYA 6

Banks, Russell 1940- . . . . **CLC 37, 72**
    See also CA 65-68; CAAS 15; CANR 19;
    DLB 130

Banville, John 1945- . . . . **CLC 46**
    See also CA 117; 128; DLB 14

Banville, Theodore (Faullain) de
    1832-1891 . . . . **NCLC 9**

Baraka, Amiri
    1934- . . . **CLC 1, 2, 3, 5, 10, 14, 33; PC 4**
    See also Jones, LeRoi
    See also BLC 1; BW; CA 21-24R; CABS 3;
    CANR 27, 38; CDALB 1941-1968; DA;
    DLB 5, 7, 16, 38; DLBD 8; MTCW

Barbellion, W. N. P. . . . . **TCLC 24**
    See also Cummings, Bruce F(rederick)

Barbera, Jack 1945- . . . . **CLC 44**
    See also CA 110

Barbey d'Aurevilly, Jules Amedee
    1808-1889 . . . . **NCLC 1**
    See also DLB 119

Barbusse, Henri 1873-1935 . . . . **TCLC 5**
    See also CA 105; DLB 65

Barclay, Bill
    See Moorcock, Michael (John)

Barclay, William Ewert
    See Moorcock, Michael (John)

Barea, Arturo 1897-1957 . . . . **TCLC 14**
    See also CA 111

Barfoot, Joan 1946- . . . . **CLC 18**
    See also CA 105

Baring, Maurice 1874-1945 . . . . **TCLC 8**
    See also CA 105; DLB 34

Barker, Clive 1952- . . . . **CLC 52**
    See also AAYA 10; BEST 90:3; CA 121;
    129; MTCW

Barker, George Granville
    1913-1991 . . . . **CLC 8, 48**
    See also CA 9-12R; 135; CANR 7, 38;
    DLB 20; MTCW

Barker, Harley Granville
    See Granville-Barker, Harley
    See also DLB 10

Barker, Howard 1946- . . . . **CLC 37**
    See also CA 102; DLB 13

Barker, Pat 1943- . . . . **CLC 32**
    See also CA 117; 122

Barlow, Joel 1754-1812 . . . . **NCLC 23**
    See also DLB 37

Barnard, Mary (Ethel) 1909- . . . . **CLC 48**
    See also CA 21-22; CAP 2

Barnes, Djuna
    1892-1982 . . . **CLC 3, 4, 8, 11, 29; SSC 3**
    See also CA 9-12R; 107; CANR 16; DLB 4,
    9, 45; MTCW

Barnes, Julian 1946- . . . . **CLC 42**
    See also CA 102; CANR 19

Barnes, Peter 1931- . . . . **CLC 5, 56**
    See also CA 65-68; CAAS 12; CANR 33,
    34; DLB 13; MTCW

Baroja (y Nessi), Pio 1872-1956 . . . . **TCLC 8**
    See also CA 104

Baron, David
    See Pinter, Harold

Bellamy, Edward   1850-1898 . . . . . .   **NCLC 4**
See also DLB 12

Bellin, Edward J.
See Kuttner, Henry

Belloc, (Joseph) Hilaire (Pierre)
1870-1953 . . . .   **TCLC 7, 18**
See also CA 106; DLB 19, 100; YABC 1

Belloc, Joseph Peter Rene Hilaire
See Belloc, (Joseph) Hilaire (Pierre)

Belloc, Joseph Pierre Hilaire
See Belloc, (Joseph) Hilaire (Pierre)

Belloc, M. A.
See Lowndes, Marie Adelaide (Belloc)

Bellow, Saul
1915- . . . . . .   **CLC 1, 2, 3, 6, 8, 10, 13, 15,
25, 33, 34, 63, 79**
See also AITN 2; BEST 89:3; CA 5-8R;
CABS 1; CANR 29; CDALB 1941-1968;
DA; DLB 2, 28; DLBD 3; DLBY 82;
MTCW; WLC

Belser, Reimond Karel Maria de
1929- . . . .   **CLC 14**

Bely, Andrey . . . .   **TCLC 7**
See also Bugayev, Boris Nikolayevich

Benary, Margot
See Benary-Isbert, Margot

Benary-Isbert, Margot   1889-1979 . . .   **CLC 12**
See also CA 5-8R; 89-92; CANR 4;
CLR 12; MAICYA; SATA 2, 21

Benavente (y Martinez), Jacinto
1866-1954 . . . .   **TCLC 3**
See also CA 106; 131; HW; MTCW

Benchley, Peter (Bradford)
1940- . . . .   **CLC 4, 8**
See also AITN 2; CA 17-20R; CANR 12,
35; MTCW; SATA 3

Benchley, Robert (Charles)
1889-1945 . . . .   **TCLC 1**
See also CA 105; DLB 11

Benedikt, Michael   1935- . . . .   **CLC 4, 14**
See also CA 13-16R; CANR 7; DLB 5

Benet, Juan   1927- . . . .   **CLC 28**

Benet, Stephen Vincent
1898-1943 . . . .   **TCLC 7; SSC 10**
See also CA 104; DLB 4, 48, 102; YABC 1

Benet, William Rose   1886-1950 . . .   **TCLC 28**
See also CA 118; DLB 45

Benford, Gregory (Albert)   1941- . . . .   **CLC 52**
See also CA 69-72; CANR 12, 24;
DLBY 82

Bengtsson, Frans (Gunnar)
1894-1954 . . . .   **TCLC 48**

Benjamin, David
See Slavitt, David R(ytman)

Benjamin, Lois
See Gould, Lois

Benjamin, Walter   1892-1940 . . . . .   **TCLC 39**

Benn, Gottfried   1886-1956 . . . .   **TCLC 3**
See also CA 106; DLB 56

Bennett, Alan   1934- . . . .   **CLC 45, 77**
See also CA 103; CANR 35; MTCW

Bennett, (Enoch) Arnold
1867-1931 . . . .   **TCLC 5, 20**
See also CA 106; CDBLB 1890-1914;
DLB 10, 34, 98

Bennett, Elizabeth
See Mitchell, Margaret (Munnerlyn)

Bennett, George Harold   1930-
See Bennett, Hal
See also BW; CA 97-100

Bennett, Hal . . . .   **CLC 5**
See also Bennett, George Harold
See also DLB 33

Bennett, Jay   1912- . . . .   **CLC 35**
See also AAYA 10; CA 69-72; CANR 11,
42; JRDA; SAAS 4; SATA 27, 41

Bennett, Louise (Simone)   1919- . . . . .   **CLC 28**
See also BLC 1; DLB 117

Benson, E(dward) F(rederic)
1867-1940 . . . .   **TCLC 27**
See also CA 114

Benson, Jackson J.   1930- . . . .   **CLC 34**
See also CA 25-28R; DLB 111

Benson, Sally   1900-1972 . . . .   **CLC 17**
See also CA 19-20; 37-40R; CAP 1;
SATA 1, 27, 35

Benson, Stella   1892-1933 . . . .   **TCLC 17**
See also CA 117; DLB 36

Bentham, Jeremy   1748-1832 . . . . .   **NCLC 38**
See also DLB 107

Bentley, E(dmund) C(lerihew)
1875-1956 . . . .   **TCLC 12**
See also CA 108; DLB 70

Bentley, Eric (Russell)   1916- . . . .   **CLC 24**
See also CA 5-8R; CANR 6

Beranger, Pierre Jean de
1780-1857 . . . .   **NCLC 34**

Berger, Colonel
See Malraux, (Georges-)Andre

Berger, John (Peter)   1926- . . . . . .   **CLC 2, 19**
See also CA 81-84; DLB 14

Berger, Melvin H.   1927- . . . .   **CLC 12**
See also CA 5-8R; CANR 4; CLR 32;
SAAS 2; SATA 5

Berger, Thomas (Louis)
1924- . . . .   **CLC 3, 5, 8, 11, 18, 38**
See also CA 1-4R; CANR 5, 28; DLB 2;
DLBY 80; MTCW

Bergman, (Ernst) Ingmar
1918- . . . .   **CLC 16, 72**
See also CA 81-84; CANR 33

Bergson, Henri   1859-1941 . . . .   **TCLC 32**

Bergstein, Eleanor   1938- . . . .   **CLC 4**
See also CA 53-56; CANR 5

Berkoff, Steven   1937- . . . .   **CLC 56**
See also CA 104

Bermant, Chaim (Icyk)   1929- . . . . . .   **CLC 40**
See also CA 57-60; CANR 6, 31

Bern, Victoria
See Fisher, M(ary) F(rances) K(ennedy)

Bernanos, (Paul Louis) Georges
1888-1948 . . . .   **TCLC 3**
See also CA 104; 130; DLB 72

Bernard, April   1956- . . . .   **CLC 59**
See also CA 131

Bernhard, Thomas
1931-1989 . . . .   **CLC 3, 32, 61**
See also CA 85-88; 127; CANR 32;
DLB 85, 124; MTCW

Berrigan, Daniel   1921- . . . .   **CLC 4**
See also CA 33-36R; CAAS 1; CANR 11;
DLB 5

Berrigan, Edmund Joseph Michael, Jr.
1934-1983
See Berrigan, Ted
See also CA 61-64; 110; CANR 14

Berrigan, Ted . . . .   **CLC 37**
See also Berrigan, Edmund Joseph Michael,
Jr.
See also DLB 5

Berry, Charles Edward Anderson   1931-
See Berry, Chuck
See also CA 115

Berry, Chuck . . . .   **CLC 17**
See also Berry, Charles Edward Anderson

Berry, Jonas
See Ashbery, John (Lawrence)

Berry, Wendell (Erdman)
1934- . . . .   **CLC 4, 6, 8, 27, 46**
See also AITN 1; CA 73-76; DLB 5, 6

Berryman, John
1914-1972 . . . . . .   **CLC 1, 2, 3, 4, 6, 8, 10,
13, 25, 62**
See also CA 13-16; 33-36R; CABS 2;
CANR 35; CAP 1; CDALB 1941-1968;
DLB 48; MTCW

Bertolucci, Bernardo   1940- . . . .   **CLC 16**
See also CA 106

Bertrand, Aloysius   1807-1841 . . . .   **NCLC 31**

Bertran de Born   c. 1140-1215 . . . . .   **CMLC 5**

Besant, Annie (Wood)   1847-1933 . . .   **TCLC 9**
See also CA 105

Bessie, Alvah   1904-1985 . . . .   **CLC 23**
See also CA 5-8R; 116; CANR 2; DLB 26

Bethlen, T. D.
See Silverberg, Robert

Beti, Mongo . . . .   **CLC 27**
See also Biyidi, Alexandre
See also BLC 1

Betjeman, John
1906-1984 . . . .   **CLC 2, 6, 10, 34, 43**
See also CA 9-12R; 112; CANR 33;
CDBLB 1945-1960; DLB 20; DLBY 84;
MTCW

Bettelheim, Bruno   1903-1990 . . . . . .   **CLC 79**
See also CA 81-84; 131; CANR 23; MTCW

Betti, Ugo   1892-1953 . . . .   **TCLC 5**
See also CA 104

Betts, Doris (Waugh)   1932- . . . .   **CLC 3, 6, 28**
See also CA 13-16R; CANR 9; DLBY 82

Bevan, Alistair
See Roberts, Keith (John Kingston)

Beynon, John
See Harris, John (Wyndham Parkes Lucas)
Beynon

Bialik, Chaim Nachman
1873-1934 . . . .   **TCLC 25**

Bickerstaff, Isaac
See Swift, Jonathan

Bidart, Frank 1939- . . . . CLC 33
See also CA 140

Bienek, Horst 1930- . . . . CLC 7, 11
See also CA 73-76; DLB 75

Bierce, Ambrose (Gwinett)
1842-1914(?) . . . . . TCLC 1, 7, 44; SSC 9
See also CA 104; 139; CDALB 1865-1917;
DA; DLB 11, 12, 23, 71, 74; WLC

Billings, Josh
See Shaw, Henry Wheeler

Billington, Rachel 1942- . . . . CLC 43
See also AITN 2; CA 33-36R

Binyon, T(imothy) J(ohn) 1936- . . . . CLC 34
See also CA 111; CANR 28

Bioy Casares, Adolfo 1914- . . . . CLC 4, 8, 13
See also CA 29-32R; CANR 19; DLB 113;
HW; MTCW

Bird, C.
See Ellison, Harlan

Bird, Cordwainer
See Ellison, Harlan

Bird, Robert Montgomery
1806-1854 . . . . NCLC 1

Birney, (Alfred) Earle
1904- . . . . CLC 1, 4, 6, 11
See also CA 1-4R; CANR 5, 20; DLB 88;
MTCW

Bishop, Elizabeth
1911-1979 . . . . . . CLC 1, 4, 9, 13, 15, 32;
PC 3
See also CA 5-8R; 89-92; CABS 2;
CANR 26; CDALB 1968-1988; DA;
DLB 5; MTCW; SATA 24

Bishop, John 1935- . . . . CLC 10
See also CA 105

Bissett, Bill 1939- . . . . CLC 18
See also CA 69-72; CANR 15; DLB 53;
MTCW

Bitov, Andrei (Georgievich) 1937- . . . CLC 57

Biyidi, Alexandre 1932-
See Beti, Mongo
See also BW; CA 114; 124; MTCW

Bjarme, Brynjolf
See Ibsen, Henrik (Johan)

Bjornson, Bjornstjerne (Martinius)
1832-1910 . . . . TCLC 7, 37
See also CA 104

Black, Robert
See Holdstock, Robert P.

Blackburn, Paul 1926-1971 . . . . . . CLC 9, 43
See also CA 81-84; 33-36R; CANR 34;
DLB 16; DLBY 81

Black Elk 1863-1950 . . . . TCLC 33

Black Hobart
See Sanders, (James) Ed(ward)

Blacklin, Malcolm
See Chambers, Aidan

Blackmore, R(ichard) D(oddridge)
1825-1900 . . . . TCLC 27
See also CA 120; DLB 18

Blackmur, R(ichard) P(almer)
1904-1965 . . . . CLC 2, 24
See also CA 11-12; 25-28R; CAP 1; DLB 63

Black Tarantula, The
See Acker, Kathy

Blackwood, Algernon (Henry)
1869-1951 . . . . TCLC 5
See also CA 105

Blackwood, Caroline 1931- . . . . CLC 6, 9
See also CA 85-88; CANR 32; DLB 14;
MTCW

Blade, Alexander
See Hamilton, Edmond; Silverberg, Robert

Blaga, Lucian 1895-1961 . . . . CLC 75

Blair, Eric (Arthur) 1903-1950
See Orwell, George
See also CA 104; 132; DA; MTCW;
SATA 29

Blais, Marie-Claire
1939- . . . . CLC 2, 4, 6, 13, 22
See also CA 21-24R; CAAS 4; CANR 38;
DLB 53; MTCW

Blaise, Clark 1940- . . . . CLC 29
See also AITN 2; CA 53-56; CAAS 3;
CANR 5; DLB 53

Blake, Nicholas
See Day Lewis, C(ecil)
See also DLB 77

Blake, William 1757-1827 . . . . NCLC 13
See also CDBLB 1789-1832; DA; DLB 93;
MAICYA; SATA 30; WLC

Blasco Ibanez, Vicente
1867-1928 . . . . TCLC 12
See also CA 110; 131; HW; MTCW

Blatty, William Peter 1928- . . . . CLC 2
See also CA 5-8R; CANR 9

Bleeck, Oliver
See Thomas, Ross (Elmore)

Blessing, Lee 1949- . . . . CLC 54

Blish, James (Benjamin)
1921-1975 . . . . CLC 14
See also CA 1-4R; 57-60; CANR 3; DLB 8;
MTCW; SATA 66

Bliss, Reginald
See Wells, H(erbert) G(eorge)

Blixen, Karen (Christentze Dinesen)
1885-1962
See Dinesen, Isak
See also CA 25-28; CANR 22; CAP 2;
MTCW; SATA 44

Bloch, Robert (Albert) 1917- . . . . CLC 33
See also CA 5-8R; CANR 5; DLB 44;
SATA 12

Blok, Alexander (Alexandrovich)
1880-1921 . . . . TCLC 5
See also CA 104

Blom, Jan
See Breytenbach, Breyten

Bloom, Harold 1930- . . . . CLC 24
See also CA 13-16R; CANR 39; DLB 67

Bloomfield, Aurelius
See Bourne, Randolph S(illiman)

Blount, Roy (Alton), Jr. 1941- . . . . . CLC 38
See also CA 53-56; CANR 10, 28; MTCW

Bloy, Leon 1846-1917 . . . . TCLC 22
See also CA 121; DLB 123

Blume, Judy (Sussman) 1938- . . . CLC 12, 30
See also AAYA 3; CA 29-32R; CANR 13,
37; CLR 2, 15; DLB 52; JRDA;
MAICYA; MTCW; SATA 2, 31

Blunden, Edmund (Charles)
1896-1974 . . . . CLC 2, 56
See also CA 17-18; 45-48; CAP 2; DLB 20,
100; MTCW

Bly, Robert (Elwood)
1926- . . . . CLC 1, 2, 5, 10, 15, 38
See also CA 5-8R; CANR 41; DLB 5;
MTCW

Bobette
See Simenon, Georges (Jacques Christian)

Boccaccio, Giovanni 1313-1375
See also SSC 10

Bochco, Steven 1943- . . . . CLC 35
See also CA 124; 138

Bodenheim, Maxwell 1892-1954 . . . TCLC 44
See also CA 110; DLB 9, 45

Bodker, Cecil 1927- . . . . CLC 21
See also CA 73-76; CANR 13; CLR 23;
MAICYA; SATA 14

Boell, Heinrich (Theodor) 1917-1985
See Boll, Heinrich (Theodor)
See also CA 21-24R; 116; CANR 24; DA;
DLB 69; DLBY 85; MTCW

Boerne, Alfred
See Doeblin, Alfred

Bogan, Louise 1897-1970 . . . . . CLC 4, 39, 46
See also CA 73-76; 25-28R; CANR 33;
DLB 45; MTCW

Bogarde, Dirk . . . . CLC 19
See also Van Den Bogarde, Derek Jules
Gaspard Ulric Niven
See also DLB 14

Bogosian, Eric 1953- . . . . CLC 45
See also CA 138

Bograd, Larry 1953- . . . . CLC 35
See also CA 93-96; SATA 33

Boiardo, Matteo Maria 1441-1494 . . . . LC 6

Boileau-Despreaux, Nicolas
1636-1711 . . . . LC 3

Boland, Eavan 1944- . . . . CLC 40, 67
See also DLB 40

Boll, Heinrich (Theodor)
1917-1985 . . . . CLC 2, 3, 6, 9, 11, 15, 27,
39, 72
See also Boell, Heinrich (Theodor)
See also DLB 69; DLBY 85; WLC

Bolt, Lee
See Faust, Frederick (Schiller)

Bolt, Robert (Oxton) 1924- . . . . CLC 14
See also CA 17-20R; CANR 35; DLB 13;
MTCW

Bomkauf
See Kaufman, Bob (Garnell)

Bonaventura . . . . NCLC 35
See also DLB 90

Bond, Edward 1934- . . . . CLC 4, 6, 13, 23
See also CA 25-28R; CANR 38; DLB 13;
MTCW

Bonham, Frank 1914-1989 . . . . **CLC 12**
See also AAYA 1; CA 9-12R; CANR 4, 36;
JRDA; MAICYA; SAAS 3; SATA 1, 49,
62

Bonnefoy, Yves 1923- . . . . **CLC 9, 15, 58**
See also CA 85-88; CANR 33; MTCW

Bontemps, Arna(ud Wendell)
1902-1973 . . . . **CLC 1, 18**
See also BLC 1; BW; CA 1-4R; 41-44R;
CANR 4, 35; CLR 6; DLB 48, 51; JRDA;
MAICYA; MTCW; SATA 2, 24, 44

Booth, Martin 1944- . . . . **CLC 13**
See also CA 93-96; CAAS 2

Booth, Philip 1925- . . . . **CLC 23**
See also CA 5-8R; CANR 5; DLBY 82

Booth, Wayne C(layson) 1921- . . . . . **CLC 24**
See also CA 1-4R; CAAS 5; CANR 3;
DLB 67

Borchert, Wolfgang 1921-1947 . . . . . **TCLC 5**
See also CA 104; DLB 69, 124

Borel, Petrus 1809-1859 . . . . **NCLC 41**

Borges, Jorge Luis
1899-1986 . . . **CLC 1, 2, 3, 4, 6, 8, 9, 10,
13, 19, 44, 48; SSC 4**
See also CA 21-24R; CANR 19, 33; DA;
DLB 113; DLBY 86; HW; MTCW; WLC

Borowski, Tadeusz 1922-1951 . . . . . . **TCLC 9**
See also CA 106

Borrow, George (Henry)
1803-1881 . . . . **NCLC 9**
See also DLB 21, 55

Bosman, Herman Charles
1905-1951 . . . . **TCLC 49**

Bosschere, Jean de 1878(?)-1953 . . . **TCLC 19**
See also CA 115

Boswell, James 1740-1795 . . . . **LC 4**
See also CDBLB 1660-1789; DA; DLB 104;
WLC

Bottoms, David 1949- . . . . **CLC 53**
See also CA 105; CANR 22; DLB 120;
DLBY 83

Boucicault, Dion 1820-1890 . . . . . . **NCLC 41**

Boucolon, Maryse 1937-
See Conde, Maryse
See also CA 110; CANR 30

Bourget, Paul (Charles Joseph)
1852-1935 . . . . **TCLC 12**
See also CA 107; DLB 123

Bourjaily, Vance (Nye) 1922- . . . . **CLC 8, 62**
See also CA 1-4R; CAAS 1; CANR 2;
DLB 2

Bourne, Randolph S(illiman)
1886-1918 . . . . **TCLC 16**
See also CA 117; DLB 63

Bova, Ben(jamin William) 1932- . . . . **CLC 45**
See also CA 5-8R; CAAS 18; CANR 11;
CLR 3; DLBY 81; MAICYA; MTCW;
SATA 6, 68

Bowen, Elizabeth (Dorothea Cole)
1899-1973 . . . . . . **CLC 1, 3, 6, 11, 15, 22;
SSC 3**
See also CA 17-18; 41-44R; CANR 35;
CAP 2; CDBLB 1945-1960; DLB 15;
MTCW

Bowering, George 1935- . . . . **CLC 15, 47**
See also CA 21-24R; CAAS 16; CANR 10;
DLB 53

Bowering, Marilyn R(uthe) 1949- . . . **CLC 32**
See also CA 101

Bowers, Edgar 1924- . . . . **CLC 9**
See also CA 5-8R; CANR 24; DLB 5

Bowie, David . . . . **CLC 17**
See also Jones, David Robert

Bowles, Jane (Sydney)
1917-1973 . . . . **CLC 3, 68**
See also CA 19-20; 41-44R; CAP 2

Bowles, Paul (Frederick)
1910- . . . . **CLC 1, 2, 19, 53; SSC 3**
See also CA 1-4R; CAAS 1; CANR 1, 19;
DLB 5, 6; MTCW

Box, Edgar
See Vidal, Gore

Boyd, Nancy
See Millay, Edna St. Vincent

Boyd, William 1952- . . . . **CLC 28, 53, 70**
See also CA 114; 120

Boyle, Kay
1902-1992 . . . . . **CLC 1, 5, 19, 58; SSC 5**
See also CA 13-16R; 140; CAAS 1;
CANR 29; DLB 4, 9, 48, 86; MTCW

Boyle, Mark
See Kienzle, William X(avier)

Boyle, Patrick 1905-1982 . . . . **CLC 19**
See also CA 127

Boyle, T. Coraghessan 1948- . . . . **CLC 36, 55**
See also BEST 90:4; CA 120; DLBY 86

Boz
See Dickens, Charles (John Huffam)

Brackenridge, Hugh Henry
1748-1816 . . . . **NCLC 7**
See also DLB 11, 37

Bradbury, Edward P.
See Moorcock, Michael (John)

Bradbury, Malcolm (Stanley)
1932- . . . . **CLC 32, 61**
See also CA 1-4R; CANR 1, 33; DLB 14;
MTCW

Bradbury, Ray (Douglas)
1920- . . . . **CLC 1, 3, 10, 15, 42**
See also AITN 1, 2; CA 1-4R; CANR 2, 30;
CDALB 1968-1988; DA; DLB 2, 8;
MTCW; SATA 11, 64; WLC

Bradford, Gamaliel 1863-1932 . . . . . **TCLC 36**
See also DLB 17

Bradley, David (Henry, Jr.) 1950- . . **CLC 23**
See also BLC 1; BW; CA 104; CANR 26;
DLB 33

Bradley, John Ed 1959- . . . . **CLC 55**

Bradley, Marion Zimmer 1930- . . . . . **CLC 30**
See also AAYA 9; CA 57-60; CAAS 10;
CANR 7, 31; DLB 8; MTCW

Bradstreet, Anne 1612(?)-1672 . . . . **LC 4**
See also CDALB 1640-1865; DA; DLB 24

Bragg, Melvyn 1939- . . . . **CLC 10**
See also BEST 89:3; CA 57-60; CANR 10;
DLB 14

Braine, John (Gerard)
1922-1986 . . . . **CLC 1, 3, 41**
See also CA 1-4R; 120; CANR 1, 33;
CDBLB 1945-1960; DLB 15; DLBY 86;
MTCW

Brammer, William 1930(?)-1978 . . . . **CLC 31**
See also CA 77-80

Brancati, Vitaliano 1907-1954 . . . . . **TCLC 12**
See also CA 109

Brancato, Robin F(idler) 1936- . . . . . **CLC 35**
See also AAYA 9; CA 69-72; CANR 11;
CLR 32; JRDA; SAAS 9; SATA 23

Brand, Max
See Faust, Frederick (Schiller)

Brand, Millen 1906-1980 . . . . **CLC 7**
See also CA 21-24R; 97-100

Branden, Barbara . . . . **CLC 44**

Brandes, Georg (Morris Cohen)
1842-1927 . . . . **TCLC 10**
See also CA 105

Brandys, Kazimierz 1916- . . . . **CLC 62**

Branley, Franklyn M(ansfield)
1915- . . . . **CLC 21**
See also CA 33-36R; CANR 14, 39;
CLR 13; MAICYA; SAAS 16; SATA 4,
68

Brathwaite, Edward (Kamau)
1930- . . . . **CLC 11**
See also BW; CA 25-28R; CANR 11, 26;
DLB 125

Brautigan, Richard (Gary)
1935-1984 . . . . **CLC 1, 3, 5, 9, 12, 34, 42**
See also CA 53-56; 113; CANR 34; DLB 2,
5; DLBY 80, 84; MTCW; SATA 56

Braverman, Kate 1950- . . . . **CLC 67**
See also CA 89-92

Brecht, Bertolt
1898-1956 . . . . . **TCLC 1, 6, 13, 35; DC 3**
See also CA 104; 133; DA; DLB 56, 124;
MTCW; WLC

Brecht, Eugen Berthold Friedrich
See Brecht, Bertolt

Bremer, Fredrika 1801-1865 . . . . . **NCLC 11**

Brennan, Christopher John
1870-1932 . . . . **TCLC 17**
See also CA 117

Brennan, Maeve 1917- . . . . **CLC 5**
See also CA 81-84

Brentano, Clemens (Maria)
1778-1842 . . . . **NCLC 1**

Brent of Bin Bin
See Franklin, (Stella Maraia Sarah) Miles

Brenton, Howard 1942- . . . . **CLC 31**
See also CA 69-72; CANR 33; DLB 13;
MTCW

Breslin, James 1930-
See Breslin, Jimmy
See also CA 73-76; CANR 31; MTCW

Breslin, Jimmy . . . . **CLC 4, 43**
See also Breslin, James
See also AITN 1

Bresson, Robert 1907- . . . . **CLC 16**
See also CA 110

Cameron, Peter 1959-............ **CLC 44**
See also CA 125

Campana, Dino 1885-1932........ **TCLC 20**
See also CA 117; DLB 114

Campbell, John W(ood, Jr.)
1910-1971 .... **CLC 32**
See also CA 21-22; 29-32R; CANR 34;
CAP 2; DLB 8; MTCW

Campbell, Joseph 1904-1987 ...... **CLC 69**
See also AAYA 3; BEST 89:2; CA 1-4R;
124; CANR 3, 28; MTCW

Campbell, (John) Ramsey 1946- .... **CLC 42**
See also CA 57-60; CANR 7

Campbell, (Ignatius) Roy (Dunnachie)
1901-1957 .... **TCLC 5**
See also CA 104; DLB 20

Campbell, Thomas 1777-1844 .... **NCLC 19**
See also DLB 93

Campbell, Wilfred................. **TCLC 9**
See also Campbell, William

Campbell, William 1858(?)-1918
See Campbell, Wilfred
See also CA 106; DLB 92

Campos, Alvaro de
See Pessoa, Fernando (Antonio Nogueira)

Camus, Albert
1913-1960 .... **CLC 1, 2, 4, 9, 11, 14, 32,
63, 69; DC 2; SSC 9**
See also CA 89-92; DA; DLB 72; MTCW;
WLC

Canby, Vincent 1924-............. **CLC 13**
See also CA 81-84

Cancale
See Desnos, Robert

Canetti, Elias 1905- ...... **CLC 3, 14, 25, 75**
See also CA 21-24R; CANR 23; DLB 85,
124; MTCW

Canin, Ethan 1960-............... **CLC 55**
See also CA 131; 135

Cannon, Curt
See Hunter, Evan

Cape, Judith
See Page, P(atricia) K(athleen)

Capek, Karel
1890-1938 .... **TCLC 6, 37; DC 1**
See also CA 104; 140; DA; WLC

Capote, Truman
1924-1984 ...... **CLC 1, 3, 8, 13, 19, 34,
38, 58; SSC 2**
See also CA 5-8R; 113; CANR 18;
CDALB 1941-1968; DA; DLB 2;
DLBY 80, 84; MTCW; WLC

Capra, Frank 1897-1991.......... **CLC 16**
See also CA 61-64; 135

Caputo, Philip 1941-.............. **CLC 32**
See also CA 73-76; CANR 40

Card, Orson Scott 1951- .... **CLC 44, 47, 50**
See also CA 102; CANR 27; MTCW

Cardenal (Martinez), Ernesto
1925- .... **CLC 31**
See also CA 49-52; CANR 2, 32; HW;
MTCW

Carducci, Giosue 1835-1907...... **TCLC 32**

Carew, Thomas 1595(?)-1640....... **LC 13**
See also DLB 126

Carey, Ernestine Gilbreth 1908- .... **CLC 17**
See also CA 5-8R; SATA 2

Carey, Peter 1943-............ **CLC 40, 55**
See also CA 123; 127; MTCW

Carleton, William 1794-1869...... **NCLC 3**

Carlisle, Henry (Coffin) 1926-...... **CLC 33**
See also CA 13-16R; CANR 15

Carlsen, Chris
See Holdstock, Robert P.

Carlson, Ron(ald F.) 1947-........ **CLC 54**
See also CA 105; CANR 27

Carlyle, Thomas 1795-1881 ..... **NCLC 22**
See also CDBLB 1789-1832; DA; DLB 55

Carman, (William) Bliss
1861-1929 .... **TCLC 7**
See also CA 104; DLB 92

Carossa, Hans 1878-1956........ **TCLC 48**
See also DLB 66

Carpenter, Don(ald Richard)
1931- .... **CLC 41**
See also CA 45-48; CANR 1

Carpentier (y Valmont), Alejo
1904-1980 .... **CLC 8, 11, 38**
See also CA 65-68; 97-100; CANR 11;
DLB 113; HW

Carr, Emily 1871-1945.......... **TCLC 32**
See also DLB 68

Carr, John Dickson 1906-1977 ...... **CLC 3**
See also CA 49-52; 69-72; CANR 3, 33;
MTCW

Carr, Philippa
See Hibbert, Eleanor Alice Burford

Carr, Virginia Spencer 1929-...... **CLC 34**
See also CA 61-64; DLB 111

Carrier, Roch 1937- .... **CLC 13, 78**
See also CA 130; DLB 53

Carroll, James P. 1943(?)-......... **CLC 38**
See also CA 81-84

Carroll, Jim 1951- .... **CLC 35**
See also CA 45-48; CANR 42

Carroll, Lewis .... **NCLC 2**
See also Dodgson, Charles Lutwidge
See also CDBLB 1832-1890; CLR 2, 18;
DLB 18; JRDA; WLC

Carroll, Paul Vincent 1900-1968.... **CLC 10**
See also CA 9-12R; 25-28R; DLB 10

Carruth, Hayden 1921- .... **CLC 4, 7, 10, 18**
See also CA 9-12R; CANR 4, 38; DLB 5;
MTCW; SATA 47

Carson, Rachel Louise 1907-1964... **CLC 71**
See also CA 77-80; CANR 35; MTCW;
SATA 23

Carter, Angela (Olive)
1940-1992 ...... **CLC 5, 41, 76; SSC 13**
See also CA 53-56; 136; CANR 12, 36;
DLB 14; MTCW; SATA 66;
SATA-Obit 70

Carter, Nick
See Smith, Martin Cruz

Carver, Raymond
1938-1988 ... **CLC 22, 36, 53, 55; SSC 8**
See also CA 33-36R; 126; CANR 17, 34;
DLB 130; DLBY 84, 88; MTCW

Cary, (Arthur) Joyce (Lunel)
1888-1957 .... **TCLC 1, 29**
See also CA 104; CDBLB 1914-1945;
DLB 15, 100

Casanova de Seingalt, Giovanni Jacopo
1725-1798 .... **LC 13**

Casares, Adolfo Bioy
See Bioy Casares, Adolfo

Casely-Hayford, J(oseph) E(phraim)
1866-1930 .... **TCLC 24**
See also BLC 1; CA 123

Casey, John (Dudley) 1939-........ **CLC 59**
See also BEST 90:2; CA 69-72; CANR 23

Casey, Michael 1947-.............. **CLC 2**
See also CA 65-68; DLB 5

Casey, Patrick
See Thurman, Wallace (Henry)

Casey, Warren (Peter) 1935-1988 ... **CLC 12**
See also CA 101; 127

Casona, Alejandro................. **CLC 49**
See also Alvarez, Alejandro Rodriguez

Cassavetes, John 1929-1989........ **CLC 20**
See also CA 85-88; 127

Cassill, R(onald) V(erlin) 1919-... **CLC 4, 23**
See also CA 9-12R; CAAS 1; CANR 7;
DLB 6

Cassity, (Allen) Turner 1929- .... **CLC 6, 42**
See also CA 17-20R; CAAS 8; CANR 11;
DLB 105

Castaneda, Carlos 1931(?)-......... **CLC 12**
See also CA 25-28R; CANR 32; HW;
MTCW

Castedo, Elena 1937- .... **CLC 65**
See also CA 132

Castedo-Ellerman, Elena
See Castedo, Elena

Castellanos, Rosario 1925-1974..... **CLC 66**
See also CA 131; 53-56; DLB 113; HW

Castelvetro, Lodovico 1505-1571..... **LC 12**

Castiglione, Baldassare 1478-1529 ... **LC 12**

Castle, Robert
See Hamilton, Edmond

Castro, Guillen de 1569-1631....... **LC 19**

Castro, Rosalia de 1837-1885 ..... **NCLC 3**

Cather, Willa
See Cather, Willa Sibert

Cather, Willa Sibert
1873-1947 ...... **TCLC 1, 11, 31; SSC 2**
See also CA 104; 128; CDALB 1865-1917;
DA; DLB 9, 54, 78; DLBD 1; MTCW;
SATA 30; WLC

Catton, (Charles) Bruce
1899-1978 .... **CLC 35**
See also AITN 1; CA 5-8R; 81-84;
CANR 7; DLB 17; SATA 2, 24

Cauldwell, Frank
See King, Francis (Henry)

Caunitz, William J. 1933- .... **CLC 34**
See also BEST 89:3; CA 125; 130

Collier, Christopher 1930- .... **CLC 30**
See also CA 33-36R; CANR 13, 33; JRDA;
MAICYA; SATA 16, 70

Collier, James L(incoln) 1928- ..... **CLC 30**
See also CA 9-12R; CANR 4, 33; JRDA;
MAICYA; SATA 8, 70

Collier, Jeremy 1650-1726 .... **LC 6**

Collins, Hunt
See Hunter, Evan

Collins, Linda 1931- .... **CLC 44**
See also CA 125

Collins, (William) Wilkie
1824-1889 .... **NCLC 1, 18**
See also CDBLB 1832-1890; DLB 18, 70

Collins, William 1721-1759 .... **LC 4**
See also DLB 109

Colman, George
See Glassco, John

Colt, Winchester Remington
See Hubbard, L(afayette) Ron(ald)

Colter, Cyrus 1910- .... **CLC 58**
See also BW; CA 65-68; CANR 10; DLB 33

Colton, James
See Hansen, Joseph

Colum, Padraic 1881-1972 .... **CLC 28**
See also CA 73-76; 33-36R; CANR 35;
MAICYA; MTCW; SATA 15

Colvin, James
See Moorcock, Michael (John)

Colwin, Laurie (E.)
1944-1992 .... **CLC 5, 13, 23**
See also CA 89-92; 139; CANR 20;
DLBY 80; MTCW

Comfort, Alex(ander) 1920- .... **CLC 7**
See also CA 1-4R; CANR 1

Comfort, Montgomery
See Campbell, (John) Ramsey

Compton-Burnett, I(vy)
1884(?)-1969 ...... **CLC 1, 3, 10, 15, 34**
See also CA 1-4R; 25-28R; CANR 4;
DLB 36; MTCW

Comstock, Anthony 1844-1915 .... **TCLC 13**
See also CA 110

Conan Doyle, Arthur
See Doyle, Arthur Conan

Conde, Maryse .... **CLC 52**
See also Boucolon, Maryse

Condon, Richard (Thomas)
1915- .... **CLC 4, 6, 8, 10, 45**
See also BEST 90:3; CA 1-4R; CAAS 1;
CANR 2, 23; MTCW

Congreve, William
1670-1729 .... **LC 5, 21; DC 2**
See also CDBLB 1660-1789; DA; DLB 39,
84; WLC

Connell, Evan S(helby), Jr.
1924- .... **CLC 4, 6, 45**
See also AAYA 7; CA 1-4R; CAAS 2;
CANR 2, 39; DLB 2; DLBY 81; MTCW

Connelly, Marc(us Cook)
1890-1980 .... **CLC 7**
See also CA 85-88; 102; CANR 30; DLB 7;
DLBY 80; SATA 25

Connor, Ralph .... **TCLC 31**
See also Gordon, Charles William
See also DLB 92

Conrad, Joseph
1857-1924 ...... **TCLC 1, 6, 13, 25, 43;
SSC 9**
See also CA 104; 131; CDBLB 1890-1914;
DA; DLB 10, 34, 98; MTCW; SATA 27;
WLC

Conrad, Robert Arnold
See Hart, Moss

Conroy, Pat 1945- .... **CLC 30, 74**
See also AAYA 8; AITN 1; CA 85-88;
CANR 24; DLB 6; MTCW

Constant (de Rebecque), (Henri) Benjamin
1767-1830 .... **NCLC 6**
See also DLB 119

Conybeare, Charles Augustus
See Eliot, T(homas) S(tearns)

Cook, Michael 1933- .... **CLC 58**
See also CA 93-96; DLB 53

Cook, Robin 1940- .... **CLC 14**
See also BEST 90:2; CA 108; 111;
CANR 41

Cook, Roy
See Silverberg, Robert

Cooke, Elizabeth 1948- .... **CLC 55**
See also CA 129

Cooke, John Esten 1830-1886 ..... **NCLC 5**
See also DLB 3

Cooke, John Estes
See Baum, L(yman) Frank

Cooke, M. E.
See Creasey, John

Cooke, Margaret
See Creasey, John

Cooney, Ray .... **CLC 62**

Cooper, Henry St. John
See Creasey, John

Cooper, J. California .... **CLC 56**
See also BW; CA 125

Cooper, James Fenimore
1789-1851 .... **NCLC 1, 27**
See also CDALB 1640-1865; DLB 3;
SATA 19

Coover, Robert (Lowell)
1932- .... **CLC 3, 7, 15, 32, 46**
See also CA 45-48; CANR 3, 37; DLB 2;
DLBY 81; MTCW

Copeland, Stewart (Armstrong)
1952- .... **CLC 26**
See also Police, The

Coppard, A(lfred) E(dgar)
1878-1957 .... **TCLC 5**
See also CA 114; YABC 1

Coppee, Francois 1842-1908 ...... **TCLC 25**

Coppola, Francis Ford 1939- .... **CLC 16**
See also CA 77-80; CANR 40; DLB 44

Corcoran, Barbara 1911- .... **CLC 17**
See also CA 21-24R; CAAS 2; CANR 11,
28; DLB 52; JRDA; SATA 3

Cordelier, Maurice
See Giraudoux, (Hippolyte) Jean

Corelli, Marie 1855-1924 .... **TCLC 51**
See also Mackay, Mary
See also DLB 34

Corman, Cid .... **CLC 9**
See also Corman, Sidney
See also CAAS 2; DLB 5

Corman, Sidney 1924-
See Corman, Cid
See also CA 85-88

Cormier, Robert (Edmund)
1925- .... **CLC 12, 30**
See also AAYA 3; CA 1-4R; CANR 5, 23;
CDALB 1968-1988; CLR 12; DA;
DLB 52; JRDA; MAICYA; MTCW;
SATA 10, 45

Corn, Alfred 1943- .... **CLC 33**
See also CA 104; DLB 120; DLBY 80

Cornwell, David (John Moore)
1931- .... **CLC 9, 15**
See also le Carre, John
See also CA 5-8R; CANR 13, 33; MTCW

Corrigan, Kevin .... **CLC 55**

Corso, (Nunzio) Gregory 1930- ... **CLC 1, 11**
See also CA 5-8R; CANR 41; DLB 5, 16;
MTCW

Cortazar, Julio
1914-1984 ...... **CLC 2, 3, 5, 10, 13, 15,
33, 34; SSC 7**
See also CA 21-24R; CANR 12, 32;
DLB 113; HW; MTCW

Corwin, Cecil
See Kornbluth, C(yril) M.

Cosic, Dobrica 1921- .... **CLC 14**
See also CA 122; 138

Costain, Thomas B(ertram)
1885-1965 .... **CLC 30**
See also CA 5-8R; 25-28R; DLB 9

Costantini, Humberto
1924(?)-1987 .... **CLC 49**
See also CA 131; 122; HW

Costello, Elvis 1955- .... **CLC 21**

Cotter, Joseph S. Sr.
See Cotter, Joseph Seamon Sr.

Cotter, Joseph Seamon Sr.
1861-1949 .... **TCLC 28**
See also BLC 1; BW; CA 124; DLB 50

Coulton, James
See Hansen, Joseph

Couperus, Louis (Marie Anne)
1863-1923 .... **TCLC 15**
See also CA 115

Court, Wesli
See Turco, Lewis (Putnam)

Courtenay, Bryce 1933- .... **CLC 59**
See also CA 138

Courtney, Robert
See Ellison, Harlan

Cousteau, Jacques-Yves 1910- ...... **CLC 30**
See also CA 65-68; CANR 15; MTCW;
SATA 38

Coward, Noel (Peirce)
1899-1973 .... **CLC 1, 9, 29, 51**
See also AITN 1; CA 17-18; 41-44R;
CANR 35; CAP 2; CDBLB 1914-1945;
DLB 10; MTCW

Cowley, Malcolm 1898-1989 .... **CLC 39**
See also CA 5-8R; 128; CANR 3; DLB 4,
48; DLBY 81, 89; MTCW

Cowper, William 1731-1800 .... **NCLC 8**
See also DLB 104, 109

Cox, William Trevor 1928- ... **CLC 9, 14, 71**
See also Trevor, William
See also CA 9-12R; CANR 4, 37; DLB 14;
MTCW

Cozzens, James Gould
1903-1978 .... **CLC 1, 4, 11**
See also CA 9-12R; 81-84; CANR 19;
CDALB 1941-1968; DLB 9; DLBD 2;
DLBY 84; MTCW

Crabbe, George 1754-1832 .... **NCLC 26**
See also DLB 93

Craig, A. A.
See Anderson, Poul (William)

Craik, Dinah Maria (Mulock)
1826-1887 .... **NCLC 38**
See also DLB 35; MAICYA; SATA 34

Cram, Ralph Adams 1863-1942 .... **TCLC 45**

Crane, (Harold) Hart
1899-1932 .... **TCLC 2, 5; PC 3**
See also CA 104; 127; CDALB 1917-1929;
DA; DLB 4, 48; MTCW; WLC

Crane, R(onald) S(almon)
1886-1967 .... **CLC 27**
See also CA 85-88; DLB 63

Crane, Stephen (Townley)
1871-1900 ..... **TCLC 11, 17, 32; SSC 7**
See also CA 109; 140; CDALB 1865-1917;
DA; DLB 12, 54, 78; WLC; YABC 2

Crase, Douglas 1944- .... **CLC 58**
See also CA 106

Craven, Margaret 1901-1980 ...... **CLC 17**
See also CA 103

Crawford, F(rancis) Marion
1854-1909 .... **TCLC 10**
See also CA 107; DLB 71

Crawford, Isabella Valancy
1850-1887 .... **NCLC 12**
See also DLB 92

Crayon, Geoffrey
See Irving, Washington

Creasey, John 1908-1973 .... **CLC 11**
See also CA 5-8R; 41-44R; CANR 8;
DLB 77; MTCW

Crebillon, Claude Prosper Jolyot de (fils)
1707-1777 .... **LC 1**

Credo
See Creasey, John

Creeley, Robert (White)
1926- ..... **CLC 1, 2, 4, 8, 11, 15, 36, 78**
See also CA 1-4R; CAAS 10; CANR 23;
DLB 5, 16; MTCW

Crews, Harry (Eugene)
1935- .... **CLC 6, 23, 49**
See also AITN 1; CA 25-28R; CANR 20;
DLB 6; MTCW

Crichton, (John) Michael
1942- .... **CLC 2, 6, 54**
See also AAYA 10; AITN 2; CA 25-28R;
CANR 13, 40; DLBY 81; JRDA;
MTCW; SATA 9

Crispin, Edmund .... **CLC 22**
See also Montgomery, (Robert) Bruce
See also DLB 87

Cristofer, Michael 1945(?)- .... **CLC 28**
See also CA 110; DLB 7

Croce, Benedetto 1866-1952 ...... **TCLC 37**
See also CA 120

Crockett, David 1786-1836 .... **NCLC 8**
See also DLB 3, 11

Crockett, Davy
See Crockett, David

Croker, John Wilson 1780-1857 .. **NCLC 10**
See also DLB 110

Crommelynck, Fernand 1885-1970 .. **CLC 75**
See also CA 89-92

Cronin, A(rchibald) J(oseph)
1896-1981 .... **CLC 32**
See also CA 1-4R; 102; CANR 5; SATA 25,
47

Cross, Amanda
See Heilbrun, Carolyn G(old)

Crothers, Rachel 1878(?)-1958 ..... **TCLC 19**
See also CA 113; DLB 7

Croves, Hal
See Traven, B.

Crowfield, Christopher
See Stowe, Harriet (Elizabeth) Beecher

Crowley, Aleister .... **TCLC 7**
See also Crowley, Edward Alexander

Crowley, Edward Alexander 1875-1947
See Crowley, Aleister
See also CA 104

Crowley, John 1942- .... **CLC 57**
See also CA 61-64; DLBY 82; SATA 65

Crud
See Crumb, R(obert)

Crumarums
See Crumb, R(obert)

Crumb, R(obert) 1943- .... **CLC 17**
See also CA 106

Crumbum
See Crumb, R(obert)

Crumski
See Crumb, R(obert)

Crum the Bum
See Crumb, R(obert)

Crunk
See Crumb, R(obert)

Crustt
See Crumb, R(obert)

Cryer, Gretchen (Kiger) 1935- ..... **CLC 21**
See also CA 114; 123

Csath, Geza 1887-1919 .... **TCLC 13**
See also CA 111

Cudlip, David 1933- .... **CLC 34**

Cullen, Countee 1903-1946 ..... **TCLC 4, 37**
See also BLC 1; BW; CA 108; 124;
CDALB 1917-1929; DA; DLB 4, 48, 51;
MTCW; SATA 18

Cum, R.
See Crumb, R(obert)

Cummings, Bruce F(rederick) 1889-1919
See Barbellion, W. N. P.
See also CA 123

Cummings, E(dward) E(stlin)
1894-1962 ...... **CLC 1, 3, 8, 12, 15, 68;**
PC 5
See also CA 73-76; CANR 31;
CDALB 1929-1941; DA; DLB 4, 48;
MTCW; WLC 2

Cunha, Euclides (Rodrigues Pimenta) da
1866-1909 .... **TCLC 24**
See also CA 123

Cunningham, E. V.
See Fast, Howard (Melvin)

Cunningham, J(ames) V(incent)
1911-1985 .... **CLC 3, 31**
See also CA 1-4R; 115; CANR 1; DLB 5

Cunningham, Julia (Woolfolk)
1916- .... **CLC 12**
See also CA 9-12R; CANR 4, 19, 36;
JRDA; MAICYA; SAAS 2; SATA 1, 26

Cunningham, Michael 1952- .... **CLC 34**
See also CA 136

Cunninghame Graham, R(obert) B(ontine)
1852-1936 .... **TCLC 19**
See also Graham, R(obert) B(ontine)
Cunninghame
See also CA 119; DLB 98

Currie, Ellen 19(?)- .... **CLC 44**

Curtin, Philip
See Lowndes, Marie Adelaide (Belloc)

Curtis, Price
See Ellison, Harlan

Cutrate, Joe
See Spiegelman, Art

Czaczkes, Shmuel Yosef
See Agnon, S(hmuel) Y(osef Halevi)

D. P.
See Wells, H(erbert) G(eorge)

Dabrowska, Maria (Szumska)
1889-1965 .... **CLC 15**
See also CA 106

Dabydeen, David 1955- .... **CLC 34**
See also BW; CA 125

Dacey, Philip 1939- .... **CLC 51**
See also CA 37-40R; CAAS 17; CANR 14,
32; DLB 105

Dagerman, Stig (Halvard)
1923-1954 .... **TCLC 17**
See also CA 117

Dahl, Roald 1916-1990 ..... **CLC 1, 6, 18, 79**
See also CA 1-4R; 133; CANR 6, 32, 37;
CLR 1, 7; JRDA; MAICYA; MTCW;
SATA 1, 26, 73; SATA-Obit 65

Dahlberg, Edward 1900-1977 ... **CLC 1, 7, 14**
See also CA 9-12R; 69-72; CANR 31;
DLB 48; MTCW

Dale, Colin .... **TCLC 18**
See also Lawrence, T(homas) E(dward)

Dale, George E.
See Asimov, Isaac

Daly, Elizabeth 1878-1967 .... **CLC 52**
See also CA 23-24; 25-28R; CAP 2

Daly, Maureen 1921-. . . . . **CLC 17**
See also AAYA 5; CANR 37; JRDA;
MAICYA; SAAS 1; SATA 2

Daniels, Brett
See Adler, Renata

Dannay, Frederic 1905-1982 . . . . **CLC 11**
See also Queen, Ellery
See also CA 1-4R; 107; CANR 1, 39;
MTCW

D'Annunzio, Gabriele
1863-1938 . . . . **TCLC 6, 40**
See also CA 104

d'Antibes, Germain
See Simenon, Georges (Jacques Christian)

Danvers, Dennis 1947-. . . . . **CLC 70**

Danziger, Paula 1944-. . . . . **CLC 21**
See also AAYA 4; CA 112; 115; CANR 37;
CLR 20; JRDA; MAICYA; SATA 30,
36, 63

Dario, Ruben . . . . **TCLC 4**
See also Sarmiento, Felix Ruben Garcia

Darley, George 1795-1846 . . . . **NCLC 2**
See also DLB 96

Daryush, Elizabeth 1887-1977. . . . **CLC 6, 19**
See also CA 49-52; CANR 3; DLB 20

Daudet, (Louis Marie) Alphonse
1840-1897 . . . . **NCLC 1**
See also DLB 123

Daumal, Rene 1908-1944 . . . . **TCLC 14**
See also CA 114

Davenport, Guy (Mattison, Jr.)
1927- . . . . **CLC 6, 14, 38**
See also CA 33-36R; CANR 23; DLB 130

Davidson, Avram 1923-
See Queen, Ellery
See also CA 101; CANR 26; DLB 8

Davidson, Donald (Grady)
1893-1968 . . . . **CLC 2, 13, 19**
See also CA 5-8R; 25-28R; CANR 4;
DLB 45

Davidson, Hugh
See Hamilton, Edmond

Davidson, John 1857-1909 . . . . **TCLC 24**
See also CA 118; DLB 19

Davidson, Sara 1943-. . . . . **CLC 9**
See also CA 81-84

Davie, Donald (Alfred)
1922- . . . . **CLC 5, 8, 10, 31**
See also CA 1-4R; CAAS 3; CANR 1;
DLB 27; MTCW

Davies, Ray(mond Douglas) 1944- . . **CLC 21**
See also CA 116

Davies, Rhys 1903-1978. . . . . **CLC 23**
See also CA 9-12R; 81-84; CANR 4

Davies, (William) Robertson
1913- . . . . **CLC 2, 7, 13, 25, 42, 75**
See also BEST 89:2; CA 33-36R; CANR 17,
42; DA; DLB 68; MTCW; WLC

Davies, W(illiam) H(enry)
1871-1940 . . . . **TCLC 5**
See also CA 104; DLB 19

Davies, Walter C.
See Kornbluth, C(yril) M.

Davis, Angela (Yvonne) 1944-. . . . . . **CLC 77**
See also BW; CA 57-60; CANR 10

Davis, B. Lynch
See Bioy Casares, Adolfo; Borges, Jorge
Luis

Davis, Gordon
See Hunt, E(verette) Howard, Jr.

Davis, Harold Lenoir 1896-1960. . . . **CLC 49**
See also CA 89-92; DLB 9

Davis, Rebecca (Blaine) Harding
1831-1910 . . . . **TCLC 6**
See also CA 104; DLB 74

Davis, Richard Harding
1864-1916 . . . . **TCLC 24**
See also CA 114; DLB 12, 23, 78, 79

Davison, Frank Dalby 1893-1970 . . . **CLC 15**
See also CA 116

Davison, Lawrence H.
See Lawrence, D(avid) H(erbert Richards)

Davison, Peter 1928-. . . . . **CLC 28**
See also CA 9-12R; CAAS 4; CANR 3;
DLB 5

Davys, Mary 1674-1732. . . . . **LC 1**
See also DLB 39

Dawson, Fielding 1930-. . . . . **CLC 6**
See also CA 85-88; DLB 130

Dawson, Peter
See Faust, Frederick (Schiller)

Day, Clarence (Shepard, Jr.)
1874-1935 . . . . **TCLC 25**
See also CA 108; DLB 11

Day, Thomas 1748-1789. . . . . **LC 1**
See also DLB 39; YABC 1

Day Lewis, C(ecil)
1904-1972 . . . . **CLC 1, 6, 10**
See also Blake, Nicholas
See also CA 13-16; 33-36R; CANR 34;
CAP 1; DLB 15, 20; MTCW

Dazai, Osamu . . . . **TCLC 11**
See also Tsushima, Shuji

de Andrade, Carlos Drummond
See Drummond de Andrade, Carlos

Deane, Norman
See Creasey, John

de Beauvoir, Simone (Lucie Ernestine Marie
Bertrand)
See Beauvoir, Simone (Lucie Ernestine
Marie Bertrand) de

de Brissac, Malcolm
See Dickinson, Peter (Malcolm)

de Chardin, Pierre Teilhard
See Teilhard de Chardin, (Marie Joseph)
Pierre

Dee, John 1527-1608 . . . . **LC 20**

Deer, Sandra 1940-. . . . . **CLC 45**

De Ferrari, Gabriella . . . . **CLC 65**

Defoe, Daniel 1660(?)-1731 . . . . **LC 1**
See also CDBLB 1660-1789; DA; DLB 39,
95, 101; JRDA; MAICYA; SATA 22;
WLC

de Gourmont, Remy
See Gourmont, Remy de

de Hartog, Jan 1914-. . . . . **CLC 19**
See also CA 1-4R; CANR 1

de Hostos, E. M.
See Hostos (y Bonilla), Eugenio Maria de

de Hostos, Eugenio M.
See Hostos (y Bonilla), Eugenio Maria de

Deighton, Len . . . . **CLC 4, 7, 22, 46**
See also Deighton, Leonard Cyril
See also AAYA 6; BEST 89:2;
CDBLB 1960 to Present; DLB 87

Deighton, Leonard Cyril 1929-
See Deighton, Len
See also CA 9-12R; CANR 19, 33; MTCW

Dekker, Thomas 1572(?)-1632. . . . . . **LC 22**
See also CDBLB Before 1660; DLB 62

de la Mare, Walter (John)
1873-1956 . . . . **TCLC 4, 52**
See also CDBLB 1914-1945; CLR 23;
DLB 19; SATA 16; WLC

Delaney, Franey
See O'Hara, John (Henry)

Delaney, Shelagh 1939-. . . . . **CLC 29**
See also CA 17-20R; CANR 30;
CDBLB 1960 to Present; DLB 13;
MTCW

Delany, Mary (Granville Pendarves)
1700-1788 . . . . **LC 12**

Delany, Samuel R(ay, Jr.)
1942- . . . . **CLC 8, 14, 38**
See also BLC 1; BW; CA 81-84; CANR 27;
DLB 8, 33; MTCW

Delaporte, Theophile
See Green, Julian (Hartridge)

De La Ramee, (Marie) Louise 1839-1908
See Ouida
See also SATA 20

de la Roche, Mazo 1879-1961 . . . . . . **CLC 14**
See also CA 85-88; CANR 30; DLB 68;
SATA 64

Delbanco, Nicholas (Franklin)
1942- . . . . **CLC 6, 13**
See also CA 17-20R; CAAS 2; CANR 29;
DLB 6

del Castillo, Michel 1933-. . . . . **CLC 38**
See also CA 109

Deledda, Grazia (Cosima)
1875(?)-1936 . . . . **TCLC 23**
See also CA 123

Delibes, Miguel . . . . **CLC 8, 18**
See also Delibes Setien, Miguel

Delibes Setien, Miguel 1920-
See Delibes, Miguel
See also CA 45-48; CANR 1, 32; HW;
MTCW

DeLillo, Don
1936- . . . . . **CLC 8, 10, 13, 27, 39, 54, 76**
See also BEST 89:1; CA 81-84; CANR 21;
DLB 6; MTCW

de Lisser, H. G.
See De Lisser, Herbert George
See also DLB 117

De Lisser, Herbert George
1878-1944 . . . . **TCLC 12**
See also de Lisser, H. G.
See also CA 109

Deloria, Vine (Victor), Jr.　1933-....**CLC 21**
See also CA 53-56; CANR 5, 20; MTCW;
SATA 21

Del Vecchio, John M(ichael)
1947- ....**CLC 29**
See also CA 110; DLBD 9

de Man, Paul (Adolph Michel)
1919-1983 ....**CLC 55**
See also CA 128; 111; DLB 67; MTCW

De Marinis, Rick　1934-..........**CLC 54**
See also CA 57-60; CANR 9, 25

Demby, William　1922-............**CLC 53**
See also BLC 1; BW; CA 81-84; DLB 33

Demijohn, Thom
See Disch, Thomas M(ichael)

de Montherlant, Henry (Milon)
See Montherlant, Henry (Milon) de

de Natale, Francine
See Malzberg, Barry N(athaniel)

Denby, Edwin (Orr)　1903-1983.....**CLC 48**
See also CA 138; 110

Denis, Julio
See Cortazar, Julio

Denmark, Harrison
See Zelazny, Roger (Joseph)

Dennis, John　1658-1734...........**LC 11**
See also DLB 101

Dennis, Nigel (Forbes)　1912-1989....**CLC 8**
See also CA 25-28R; 129; DLB 13, 15;
MTCW

De Palma, Brian (Russell)　1940-....**CLC 20**
See also CA 109

De Quincey, Thomas　1785-1859 ...**NCLC 4**
See also CDBLB 1789-1832; DLB 110

Deren, Eleanora　1908(?)-1961
See Deren, Maya
See also CA 111

Deren, Maya ....**CLC 16**
See also Deren, Eleanora

Derleth, August (William)
1909-1971 ....**CLC 31**
See also CA 1-4R; 29-32R; CANR 4;
DLB 9; SATA 5

de Routisie, Albert
See Aragon, Louis

Derrida, Jacques　1930-............**CLC 24**
See also CA 124; 127

Derry Down Derry
See Lear, Edward

Dersonnes, Jacques
See Simenon, Georges (Jacques Christian)

Desai, Anita　1937- ....**CLC 19, 37**
See also CA 81-84; CANR 33; MTCW;
SATA 63

de Saint-Luc, Jean
See Glassco, John

de Saint Roman, Arnaud
See Aragon, Louis

Descartes, Rene　1596-1650 ....**LC 20**

De Sica, Vittorio　1901(?)-1974 .....**CLC 20**
See also CA 117

Desnos, Robert　1900-1945........**TCLC 22**
See also CA 121

Destouches, Louis-Ferdinand
1894-1961 ....**CLC 9, 15**
See also Celine, Louis-Ferdinand
See also CA 85-88; CANR 28; MTCW

Deutsch, Babette　1895-1982 ....**CLC 18**
See also CA 1-4R; 108; CANR 4; DLB 45;
SATA 1, 33

Devenant, William　1606-1649 ....**LC 13**

Devkota, Laxmiprasad
1909-1959 ....**TCLC 23**
See also CA 123

De Voto, Bernard (Augustine)
1897-1955 ....**TCLC 29**
See also CA 113; DLB 9

De Vries, Peter
1910- ....**CLC 1, 2, 3, 7, 10, 28, 46**
See also CA 17-20R; CANR 41; DLB 6;
DLBY 82; MTCW

Dexter, Martin
See Faust, Frederick (Schiller)

Dexter, Pete　1943-............**CLC 34, 55**
See also BEST 89:2; CA 127; 131; MTCW

Diamano, Silmang
See Senghor, Leopold Sedar

Diamond, Neil　1941- ....**CLC 30**
See also CA 108

di Bassetto, Corno
See Shaw, George Bernard

Dick, Philip K(indred)
1928-1982 ....**CLC 10, 30, 72**
See also CA 49-52; 106; CANR 2, 16;
DLB 8; MTCW

Dickens, Charles (John Huffam)
1812-1870 ....**NCLC 3, 8, 18, 26**
See also CDBLB 1832-1890; DA; DLB 21,
55, 70; JRDA; MAICYA; SATA 15

Dickey, James (Lafayette)
1923- ....**CLC 1, 2, 4, 7, 10, 15, 47**
See also AITN 1, 2; CA 9-12R; CABS 2;
CANR 10; CDALB 1968-1988; DLB 5;
DLBD 7; DLBY 82; MTCW

Dickey, William　1928-..........**CLC 3, 28**
See also CA 9-12R; CANR 24; DLB 5

Dickinson, Charles　1951-..........**CLC 49**
See also CA 128

Dickinson, Emily (Elizabeth)
1830-1886 ....**NCLC 21; PC 1**
See also CDALB 1865-1917; DA; DLB 1;
SATA 29; WLC

Dickinson, Peter (Malcolm)
1927- ....**CLC 12, 35**
See also AAYA 9; CA 41-44R; CANR 31;
CLR 29; DLB 87; JRDA; MAICYA;
SATA 5, 62

Dickson, Carr
See Carr, John Dickson

Dickson, Carter
See Carr, John Dickson

Didion, Joan　1934-.....**CLC 1, 3, 8, 14, 32**
See also AITN 1; CA 5-8R; CANR 14;
CDALB 1968-1988; DLB 2; DLBY 81,
86; MTCW

Dietrich, Robert
See Hunt, E(verette) Howard, Jr.

Dillard, Annie　1945-............**CLC 9, 60**
See also AAYA 6; CA 49-52; CANR 3;
DLBY 80; MTCW; SATA 10

Dillard, R(ichard) H(enry) W(ilde)
1937- ....**CLC 5**
See also CA 21-24R; CAAS 7; CANR 10;
DLB 5

Dillon, Eilis　1920-...............**CLC 17**
See also CA 9-12R; CAAS 3; CANR 4, 38;
CLR 26; MAICYA; SATA 2, 74

Dimont, Penelope
See Mortimer, Penelope (Ruth)

Dinesen, Isak..........**CLC 10, 29; SSC 7**
See also Blixen, Karen (Christentze
Dinesen)

Ding Ling.......................**CLC 68**
See also Chiang Pin-chin

Disch, Thomas M(ichael)　1940-...**CLC 7, 36**
See also CA 21-24R; CAAS 4; CANR 17,
36; CLR 18; DLB 8; MAICYA; MTCW;
SAAS 15; SATA 54

Disch, Tom
See Disch, Thomas M(ichael)

d'Isly, Georges
See Simenon, Georges (Jacques Christian)

Disraeli, Benjamin　1804-1881 ..**NCLC 2, 39**
See also DLB 21, 55

Ditcum, Steve
See Crumb, R(obert)

Dixon, Paige
See Corcoran, Barbara

Dixon, Stephen　1936-............**CLC 52**
See also CA 89-92; CANR 17, 40; DLB 130

Doblin, Alfred ....**TCLC 13**
See also Doeblin, Alfred

Dobrolyubov, Nikolai Alexandrovich
1836-1861 ....**NCLC 5**

Dobyns, Stephen　1941-............**CLC 37**
See also CA 45-48; CANR 2, 18

Doctorow, E(dgar) L(aurence)
1931-.....**CLC 6, 11, 15, 18, 37, 44, 65**
See also AITN 2; BEST 89:3; CA 45-48;
CANR 2, 33; CDALB 1968-1988; DLB 2,
28; DLBY 80; MTCW

Dodgson, Charles Lutwidge　1832-1898
See Carroll, Lewis
See also CLR 2; DA; MAICYA; YABC 2

Dodson, Owen (Vincent)
1914-1983 ....**CLC 79**
See also BLC 1; BW; CA 65-68; 110;
CANR 24; DLB 76

Doeblin, Alfred　1878-1957........**TCLC 13**
See also Doblin, Alfred
See also CA 110; 141; DLB 66

Doerr, Harriet　1910- ....**CLC 34**
See also CA 117; 122

Domecq, H(onorio) Bustos
See Bioy Casares, Adolfo; Borges, Jorge
Luis

Domini, Rey
See Lorde, Audre (Geraldine)

Dominique
See Proust, (Valentin-Louis-George-Eugene-)
Marcel

Don, A
See Stephen, Leslie

Donaldson, Stephen R. 1947-...... **CLC 46**
See also CA 89-92; CANR 13

Donleavy, J(ames) P(atrick)
1926-............. **CLC 1, 4, 6, 10, 45**
See also AITN 2; CA 9-12R; CANR 24;
DLB 6; MTCW

Donne, John 1572-1631...... **LC 10; PC 1**
See also CDBLB Before 1660; DA;
DLB 121; WLC

Donnell, David 1939(?)-........... **CLC 34**

Donoso (Yanez), Jose
1924-............... **CLC 4, 8, 11, 32**
See also CA 81-84; CANR 32; DLB 113;
HW; MTCW

Donovan, John 1928-1992........ **CLC 35**
See also CA 97-100; 137; CLR 3;
MAICYA; SATA 29

Don Roberto
See Cunninghame Graham, R(obert)
B(ontine)

Doolittle, Hilda
1886-1961..... **CLC 3, 8, 14, 31, 34, 73;**
PC 5
See also H. D.
See also CA 97-100; CANR 35; DA;
DLB 4, 45; MTCW; WLC

Dorfman, Ariel 1942-......... **CLC 48, 77**
See also CA 124; 130; HW

Dorn, Edward (Merton) 1929-... **CLC 10, 18**
See also CA 93-96; CANR 42; DLB 5

Dorsan, Luc
See Simenon, Georges (Jacques Christian)

Dorsange, Jean
See Simenon, Georges (Jacques Christian)

Dos Passos, John (Roderigo)
1896-1970... **CLC 1, 4, 8, 11, 15, 25, 34**
See also CA 1-4R; 29-32R; CANR 3;
CDALB 1929-1941; DA; DLB 4, 9;
DLBD 1; MTCW; WLC

Dossage, Jean
See Simenon, Georges (Jacques Christian)

Dostoevsky, Fedor Mikhailovich
1821-1881.... **NCLC 2, 7, 21, 33; SSC 2**
See also DA; WLC

Doughty, Charles M(ontagu)
1843-1926.................. **TCLC 27**
See also CA 115; DLB 19, 57

Douglas, Ellen
See Haxton, Josephine Ayres

Douglas, Gavin 1475(?)-1522....... **LC 20**

Douglas, Keith 1920-1944....... **TCLC 40**
See also DLB 27

Douglas, Leonard
See Bradbury, Ray (Douglas)

Douglas, Michael
See Crichton, (John) Michael

Douglass, Frederick 1817(?)-1895.. **NCLC 7**
See also BLC 1; CDALB 1640-1865; DA;
DLB 1, 43, 50, 79; SATA 29; WLC

Dourado, (Waldomiro Freitas) Autran
1926-................... **CLC 23, 60**
See also CA 25-28R; CANR 34

Dourado, Waldomiro Autran
See Dourado, (Waldomiro Freitas) Autran

Dove, Rita (Frances) 1952-... **CLC 50; PC 6**
See also BW; CA 109; CANR 27, 42;
DLB 120

Dowell, Coleman 1925-1985....... **CLC 60**
See also CA 25-28R; 117; CANR 10;
DLB 130

Dowson, Ernest Christopher
1867-1900.................. **TCLC 4**
See also CA 105; DLB 19

Doyle, A. Conan
See Doyle, Arthur Conan

Doyle, Arthur Conan
1859-1930......... **TCLC 7; SSC 12**
See also CA 104; 122; CDBLB 1890-1914;
DA; DLB 18, 70; MTCW; SATA 24;
WLC

Doyle, Conan 1859-1930
See Doyle, Arthur Conan

Doyle, John
See Graves, Robert (von Ranke)

Doyle, Sir A. Conan
See Doyle, Arthur Conan

Doyle, Sir Arthur Conan
See Doyle, Arthur Conan

Dr. A
See Asimov, Isaac; Silverstein, Alvin

Drabble, Margaret
1939-........ **CLC 2, 3, 5, 8, 10, 22, 53**
See also CA 13-16R; CANR 18, 35;
CDBLB 1960 to Present; DLB 14;
MTCW; SATA 48

Drapier, M. B.
See Swift, Jonathan

Drayham, James
See Mencken, H(enry) L(ouis)

Drayton, Michael 1563-1631........ **LC 8**

Dreadstone, Carl
See Campbell, (John) Ramsey

Dreiser, Theodore (Herman Albert)
1871-1945.......... **TCLC 10, 18, 35**
See also CA 106; 132; CDALB 1865-1917;
DA; DLB 9, 12, 102; DLBD 1; MTCW;
WLC

Drexler, Rosalyn 1926-......... **CLC 2, 6**
See also CA 81-84

Dreyer, Carl Theodor 1889-1968.... **CLC 16**
See also CA 116

Drieu la Rochelle, Pierre(-Eugene)
1893-1945.................. **TCLC 21**
See also CA 117; DLB 72

Drop Shot
See Cable, George Washington

Droste-Hulshoff, Annette Freiin von
1797-1848.................. **NCLC 3**
See also DLB 133

Drummond, Walter
See Silverberg, Robert

Drummond, William Henry
1854-1907.................. **TCLC 25**
See also DLB 92

Drummond de Andrade, Carlos
1902-1987................... **CLC 18**
See also Andrade, Carlos Drummond de
See also CA 132; 123

Drury, Allen (Stuart) 1918-........ **CLC 37**
See also CA 57-60; CANR 18

Dryden, John 1631-1700.... **LC 3, 21; DC 3**
See also CDBLB 1660-1789; DA; DLB 80,
101, 131; WLC

Duberman, Martin 1930-........... **CLC 8**
See also CA 1-4R; CANR 2

Dubie, Norman (Evans) 1945-...... **CLC 36**
See also CA 69-72; CANR 12; DLB 120

Du Bois, W(illiam) E(dward) B(urghardt)
1868-1963............ **CLC 1, 2, 13, 64**
See also BLC 1; BW; CA 85-88; CANR 34;
CDALB 1865-1917; DA; DLB 47, 50, 91;
MTCW; SATA 42; WLC

Dubus, Andre 1936-........... **CLC 13, 36**
See also CA 21-24R; CANR 17; DLB 130

Duca Minimo
See D'Annunzio, Gabriele

Ducharme, Rejean 1941-.......... **CLC 74**
See also DLB 60

Duclos, Charles Pinot 1704-1772..... **LC 1**

Dudek, Louis 1918-........... **CLC 11, 19**
See also CA 45-48; CAAS 14; CANR 1;
DLB 88

Duerrenmatt, Friedrich
1921-1990..... **CLC 1, 4, 8, 11, 15, 43**
See also Durrenmatt, Friedrich
See also CA 17-20R; CANR 33; DLB 69,
124; MTCW

Duffy, Bruce (?)-................. **CLC 50**

Duffy, Maureen 1933-............ **CLC 37**
See also CA 25-28R; CANR 33; DLB 14;
MTCW

Dugan, Alan 1923-.............. **CLC 2, 6**
See also CA 81-84; DLB 5

du Gard, Roger Martin
See Martin du Gard, Roger

Duhamel, Georges 1884-1966....... **CLC 8**
See also CA 81-84; 25-28R; CANR 35;
DLB 65; MTCW

Dujardin, Edouard (Emile Louis)
1861-1949.................. **TCLC 13**
See also CA 109; DLB 123

Dumas, Alexandre (Davy de la Pailleterie)
1802-1870.................. **NCLC 11**
See also DA; DLB 119; SATA 18; WLC

Dumas, Alexandre
1824-1895............. **NCLC 9; DC 1**

Dumas, Claudine
See Malzberg, Barry N(athaniel)

Dumas, Henry L. 1934-1968..... **CLC 6, 62**
See also BW; CA 85-88; DLB 41

du Maurier, Daphne
1907-1989.............. **CLC 6, 11, 59**
See also CA 5-8R; 128; CANR 6; MTCW;
SATA 27, 60

Dunbar, Paul Laurence
1872-1906.... **TCLC 2, 12; PC 5; SSC 8**
See also BLC 1; BW; CA 104; 124;
CDALB 1865-1917; DA; DLB 50, 54, 78;
SATA 34; WLC

Dunbar, William   1460(?)-1530(?) .... **LC 20**

Duncan, Lois   1934-............... **CLC 26**
  See also AAYA 4; CA 1-4R; CANR 2, 23,
  36; CLR 29; JRDA; MAICYA; SAAS 2;
  SATA 1, 36, 75

Duncan, Robert (Edward)
  1919-1988 .... **CLC 1, 2, 4, 7, 15, 41, 55;**
                                              PC 2
  See also CA 9-12R; 124; CANR 28; DLB 5,
  16; MTCW

Dunlap, William   1766-1839....... **NCLC 2**
  See also DLB 30, 37, 59

Dunn, Douglas (Eaglesham)
  1942-..................... **CLC 6, 40**
  See also CA 45-48; CANR 2, 33; DLB 40;
  MTCW

Dunn, Katherine (Karen)   1945-..... **CLC 71**
  See also CA 33-36R

Dunn, Stephen   1939-............. **CLC 36**
  See also CA 33-36R; CANR 12; DLB 105

Dunne, Finley Peter   1867-1936.... **TCLC 28**
  See also CA 108; DLB 11, 23

Dunne, John Gregory   1932-....... **CLC 28**
  See also CA 25-28R; CANR 14; DLBY 80

Dunsany, Edward John Moreton Drax
    Plunkett   1878-1957
  See Dunsany, Lord; Lord Dunsany
  See also CA 104; DLB 10

Dunsany, Lord................. **TCLC 2**
  See also Dunsany, Edward John Moreton
    Drax Plunkett
  See also DLB 77

du Perry, Jean
  See Simenon, Georges (Jacques Christian)

Durang, Christopher (Ferdinand)
  1949-.................... **CLC 27, 38**
  See also CA 105

Duras, Marguerite
  1914- ...... **CLC 3, 6, 11, 20, 34, 40, 68**
  See also CA 25-28R; DLB 83; MTCW

Durban, (Rosa) Pam   1947-........ **CLC 39**
  See also CA 123

Durcan, Paul   1944-............ **CLC 43, 70**
  See also CA 134

Durrell, Lawrence (George)
  1912-1990 .... **CLC 1, 4, 6, 8, 13, 27, 41**
  See also CA 9-12R; 132; CANR 40;
  CDBLB 1945-1960; DLB 15, 27;
  DLBY 90; MTCW

Durrenmatt, Friedrich
  .... **CLC 1, 4, 8, 11, 15, 43**
  See also Duerrenmatt, Friedrich
  See also DLB 69, 124

Dutt, Toru   1856-1877.......... **NCLC 29**

Dwight, Timothy   1752-1817...... **NCLC 13**
  See also DLB 37

Dworkin, Andrea   1946- .... **CLC 43**
  See also CA 77-80; CANR 16, 39; MTCW

Dwyer, Deanna
  See Koontz, Dean R(ay)

Dwyer, K. R.
  See Koontz, Dean R(ay)

Dylan, Bob   1941- ...... **CLC 3, 4, 6, 12, 77**
  See also CA 41-44R; DLB 16

Eagleton, Terence (Francis)   1943-
  See Eagleton, Terry
  See also CA 57-60; CANR 7, 23; MTCW

Eagleton, Terry .... **CLC 63**
  See also Eagleton, Terence (Francis)

Early, Jack
  See Scoppettone, Sandra

East, Michael
  See West, Morris L(anglo)

Eastaway, Edward
  See Thomas, (Philip) Edward

Eastlake, William (Derry)   1917-..... **CLC 8**
  See also CA 5-8R; CAAS 1; CANR 5;
  DLB 6

Eberhart, Richard (Ghormley)
  1904-.............. **CLC 3, 11, 19, 56**
  See also CA 1-4R; CANR 2;
  CDALB 1941-1968; DLB 48; MTCW

Eberstadt, Fernanda   1960-........ **CLC 39**
  See also CA 136

Echegaray (y Eizaguirre), Jose (Maria Waldo)
  1832-1916 .... **TCLC 4**
  See also CA 104; CANR 32; HW; MTCW

Echeverria, (Jose) Esteban (Antonino)
  1805-1851 .... **NCLC 18**

Echo
  See Proust, (Valentin-Louis-George-Eugene-)
    Marcel

Eckert, Allan W.   1931-........... **CLC 17**
  See also CA 13-16R; CANR 14; SATA 27,
  29

Eckhart, Meister   1260(?)-1328(?) .. **CMLC 9**
  See also DLB 115

Eckmar, F. R.
  See de Hartog, Jan

Eco, Umberto   1932-........... **CLC 28, 60**
  See also BEST 90:1; CA 77-80; CANR 12,
  33; MTCW

Eddison, E(ric) R(ucker)
  1882-1945 .... **TCLC 15**
  See also CA 109

Edel, (Joseph) Leon   1907-...... **CLC 29, 34**
  See also CA 1-4R; CANR 1, 22; DLB 103

Eden, Emily   1797-1869 .... **NCLC 10**

Edgar, David   1948-.............. **CLC 42**
  See also CA 57-60; CANR 12; DLB 13;
  MTCW

Edgerton, Clyde (Carlyle)   1944-.... **CLC 39**
  See also CA 118; 134

Edgeworth, Maria   1767-1849...... **NCLC 1**
  See also DLB 116; SATA 21

Edmonds, Paul
  See Kuttner, Henry

Edmonds, Walter D(umaux)   1903-.. **CLC 35**
  See also CA 5-8R; CANR 2; DLB 9;
  MAICYA; SAAS 4; SATA 1, 27

Edmondson, Wallace
  See Ellison, Harlan

Edson, Russell .... **CLC 13**
  See also CA 33-36R

Edwards, G(erald) B(asil)
  1899-1976 .... **CLC 25**
  See also CA 110

Edwards, Gus   1939-.............. **CLC 43**
  See also CA 108

Edwards, Jonathan   1703-1758....... **LC 7**
  See also DA; DLB 24

Efron, Marina Ivanovna Tsvetaeva
  See Tsvetaeva (Efron), Marina (Ivanovna)

Ehle, John (Marsden, Jr.)   1925-.... **CLC 27**
  See also CA 9-12R

Ehrenbourg, Ilya (Grigoryevich)
  See Ehrenburg, Ilya (Grigoryevich)

Ehrenburg, Ilya (Grigoryevich)
  1891-1967 .... **CLC 18, 34, 62**
  See also CA 102; 25-28R

Ehrenburg, Ilyo (Grigoryevich)
  See Ehrenburg, Ilya (Grigoryevich)

Eich, Guenter   1907-1972 .... **CLC 15**
  See also CA 111; 93-96; DLB 69, 124

Eichendorff, Joseph Freiherr von
  1788-1857 .... **NCLC 8**
  See also DLB 90

Eigner, Larry..................... **CLC 9**
  See also Eigner, Laurence (Joel)
  See also DLB 5

Eigner, Laurence (Joel)   1927-
  See Eigner, Larry
  See also CA 9-12R; CANR 6

Eiseley, Loren Corey   1907-1977..... **CLC 7**
  See also AAYA 5; CA 1-4R; 73-76;
  CANR 6

Eisenstadt, Jill   1963-............. **CLC 50**
  See also CA 140

Eisner, Simon
  See Kornbluth, C(yril) M.

Ekeloef, (Bengt) Gunnar
  1907-1968 .... **CLC 27**
  See also Ekelof, (Bengt) Gunnar
  See also CA 123; 25-28R

Ekelof, (Bengt) Gunnar............. **CLC 27**
  See also Ekeloef, (Bengt) Gunnar

Ekwensi, C. O. D.
  See Ekwensi, Cyprian (Odiatu Duaka)

Ekwensi, Cyprian (Odiatu Duaka)
  1921-...................... **CLC 4**
  See also BLC 1; BW; CA 29-32R;
  CANR 18, 42; DLB 117; MTCW;
  SATA 66

Elaine........................ **TCLC 18**
  See also Leverson, Ada

El Crummo
  See Crumb, R(obert)

Elia
  See Lamb, Charles

Eliade, Mircea   1907-1986 .... **CLC 19**
  See also CA 65-68; 119; CANR 30; MTCW

Eliot, A. D.
  See Jewett, (Theodora) Sarah Orne

Eliot, Alice
  See Jewett, (Theodora) Sarah Orne

Eliot, Dan
  See Silverberg, Robert

Eliot, George
  1819-1880 .... **NCLC 4, 13, 23, 41**
  See also CDBLB 1832-1890; DA; DLB 21,
  35, 55; WLC

Fairbairns, Zoe (Ann) 1948- .... **CLC 32**
See also CA 103; CANR 21

Falco, Gian
See Papini, Giovanni

Falconer, James
See Kirkup, James

Falconer, Kenneth
See Kornbluth, C(yril) M.

Falkland, Samuel
See Heijermans, Herman

Fallaci, Oriana 1930- .... **CLC 11**
See also CA 77-80; CANR 15; MTCW

Faludy, George 1913- .... **CLC 42**
See also CA 21-24R

Faludy, Gyoergy
See Faludy, George

Fanon, Frantz 1925-1961 .... **CLC 74**
See also BLC 2; BW; CA 116; 89-92

Fanshawe, Ann .... **LC 11**

Fante, John (Thomas) 1911-1983 ... **CLC 60**
See also CA 69-72; 109; CANR 23;
DLB 130; DLBY 83

Farah, Nuruddin 1945- .... **CLC 53**
See also BLC 2; CA 106; DLB 125

Fargue, Leon-Paul 1876(?)-1947 ... **TCLC 11**
See also CA 109

Farigoule, Louis
See Romains, Jules

Farina, Richard 1936(?)-1966 .... **CLC 9**
See also CA 81-84; 25-28R

Farley, Walter (Lorimer)
1915-1989 .... **CLC 17**
See also CA 17-20R; CANR 8, 29; DLB 22;
JRDA; MAICYA; SATA 2, 43

Farmer, Philip Jose 1918- .... **CLC 1, 19**
See also CA 1-4R; CANR 4, 35; DLB 8;
MTCW

Farquhar, George 1677-1707 .... **LC 21**
See also DLB 84

Farrell, J(ames) G(ordon)
1935-1979 .... **CLC 6**
See also CA 73-76; 89-92; CANR 36;
DLB 14; MTCW

Farrell, James T(homas)
1904-1979 .... **CLC 1, 4, 8, 11, 66**
See also CA 5-8R; 89-92; CANR 9; DLB 4,
9, 86; DLBD 2; MTCW

Farren, Richard J.
See Betjeman, John

Farren, Richard M.
See Betjeman, John

Fassbinder, Rainer Werner
1946-1982 .... **CLC 20**
See also CA 93-96; 106; CANR 31

Fast, Howard (Melvin) 1914- ...... **CLC 23**
See also CA 1-4R; CAAS 18; CANR 1, 33;
DLB 9; SATA 7

Faulcon, Robert
See Holdstock, Robert P.

Faulkner, William (Cuthbert)
1897-1962 ..... **CLC 1, 3, 6, 8, 9, 11, 14,
18, 28, 52, 68; SSC 1**
See also AAYA 7; CA 81-84; CANR 33;
CDALB 1929-1941; DA; DLB 9, 11, 44,
102; DLBD 2; DLBY 86; MTCW; WLC

Fauset, Jessie Redmon
1884(?)-1961 .... **CLC 19, 54**
See also BLC 2; BW; CA 109; DLB 51

Faust, Frederick (Schiller)
1892-1944(?) .... **TCLC 49**
See also CA 108

Faust, Irvin 1924- .... **CLC 8**
See also CA 33-36R; CANR 28; DLB 2, 28;
DLBY 80

Fawkes, Guy
See Benchley, Robert (Charles)

Fearing, Kenneth (Flexner)
1902-1961 .... **CLC 51**
See also CA 93-96; DLB 9

Fecamps, Elise
See Creasey, John

Federman, Raymond 1928- ...... **CLC 6, 47**
See also CA 17-20R; CAAS 8; CANR 10;
DLBY 80

Federspiel, J(uerg) F. 1931- .... **CLC 42**

Feiffer, Jules (Ralph) 1929-.... **CLC 2, 8, 64**
See also AAYA 3; CA 17-20R; CANR 30;
DLB 7, 44; MTCW; SATA 8, 61

Feige, Hermann Albert Otto Maximilian
See Traven, B.

Fei-Kan, Li
See Li Fei-kan

Feinberg, David B. 1956-.......... **CLC 59**
See also CA 135

Feinstein, Elaine 1930-............ **CLC 36**
See also CA 69-72; CAAS 1; CANR 31;
DLB 14, 40; MTCW

Feldman, Irving (Mordecai) 1928-.... **CLC 7**
See also CA 1-4R; CANR 1

Fellini, Federico 1920-............ **CLC 16**
See also CA 65-68; CANR 33

Felsen, Henry Gregor 1916- .... **CLC 17**
See also CA 1-4R; CANR 1; SAAS 2;
SATA 1

Fenton, James Martin 1949-....... **CLC 32**
See also CA 102; DLB 40

Ferber, Edna 1887-1968.......... **CLC 18**
See also AITN 1; CA 5-8R; 25-28R; DLB 9,
28, 86; MTCW; SATA 7

Ferguson, Helen
See Kavan, Anna

Ferguson, Samuel 1810-1886..... **NCLC 33**
See also DLB 32

Ferling, Lawrence
See Ferlinghetti, Lawrence (Monsanto)

Ferlinghetti, Lawrence (Monsanto)
1919(?)- .... **CLC 2, 6, 10, 27; PC 1**
See also CA 5-8R; CANR 3, 41;
CDALB 1941-1968; DLB 5, 16; MTCW

Fernandez, Vicente Garcia Huidobro
See Huidobro Fernandez, Vicente Garcia

Ferrer, Gabriel (Francisco Victor) Miro
See Miro (Ferrer), Gabriel (Francisco
Victor)

Ferrier, Susan (Edmonstone)
1782-1854 .... **NCLC 8**
See also DLB 116

Ferrigno, Robert 1948(?)-......... **CLC 65**
See also CA 140

Feuchtwanger, Lion 1884-1958 ..... **TCLC 3**
See also CA 104; DLB 66

Feydeau, Georges (Leon Jules Marie)
1862-1921 .... **TCLC 22**
See also CA 113

Ficino, Marsilio 1433-1499 .... **LC 12**

Fiedler, Leslie A(aron)
1917- .... **CLC 4, 13, 24**
See also CA 9-12R; CANR 7; DLB 28, 67;
MTCW

Field, Andrew 1938-.............. **CLC 44**
See also CA 97-100; CANR 25

Field, Eugene 1850-1895 .... **NCLC 3**
See also DLB 23, 42; MAICYA; SATA 16

Field, Gans T.
See Wellman, Manly Wade

Field, Michael .... **TCLC 43**

Field, Peter
See Hobson, Laura Z(ametkin)

Fielding, Henry 1707-1754 .... **LC 1**
See also CDBLB 1660-1789; DA; DLB 39,
84, 101; WLC

Fielding, Sarah 1710-1768 .... **LC 1**
See also DLB 39

Fierstein, Harvey (Forbes) 1954- ... **CLC 33**
See also CA 123; 129

Figes, Eva 1932-................. **CLC 31**
See also CA 53-56; CANR 4; DLB 14

Finch, Robert (Duer Claydon)
1900- .... **CLC 18**
See also CA 57-60; CANR 9, 24; DLB 88

Findley, Timothy 1930- .... **CLC 27**
See also CA 25-28R; CANR 12, 42;
DLB 53

Fink, William
See Mencken, H(enry) L(ouis)

Firbank, Louis 1942-
See Reed, Lou
See also CA 117

Firbank, (Arthur Annesley) Ronald
1886-1926 .... **TCLC 1**
See also CA 104; DLB 36

Fisher, M(ary) F(rances) K(ennedy)
1908-1992 .... **CLC 76**
See also CA 77-80; 138

Fisher, Roy 1930-................ **CLC 25**
See also CA 81-84; CAAS 10; CANR 16;
DLB 40

Fisher, Rudolph 1897-1934 .... **TCLC 11**
See also BLC 2; BW; CA 107; 124; DLB 51,
102

Fisher, Vardis (Alvero) 1895-1968.... **CLC 7**
See also CA 5-8R; 25-28R; DLB 9

Fiske, Tarleton
See Bloch, Robert (Albert)

ﾉ

Glassman, Joyce
See Johnson, Joyce

Glendinning, Victoria 1937- .... **CLC 50**
See also CA 120; 127

Glissant, Edouard 1928- .... **CLC 10, 68**

Gloag, Julian 1930- .... **CLC 40**
See also AITN 1; CA 65-68; CANR 10

Gluck, Louise (Elisabeth)
1943- .... **CLC 7, 22, 44**
See also Glueck, Louise
See also CA 33-36R; CANR 40; DLB 5

Glueck, Louise .... **CLC 7, 22**
See also Gluck, Louise (Elisabeth)
See also DLB 5

Gobineau, Joseph Arthur (Comte) de
1816-1882 .... **NCLC 17**
See also DLB 123

Godard, Jean-Luc 1930- .... **CLC 20**
See also CA 93-96

Godden, (Margaret) Rumer 1907- ... **CLC 53**
See also AAYA 6; CA 5-8R; CANR 4, 27,
36; CLR 20; MAICYA; SAAS 12;
SATA 3, 36

Godoy Alcayaga, Lucila 1889-1957
See Mistral, Gabriela
See also CA 104; 131; HW; MTCW

Godwin, Gail (Kathleen)
1937- .... **CLC 5, 8, 22, 31, 69**
See also CA 29-32R; CANR 15; DLB 6;
MTCW

Godwin, William 1756-1836 ...... **NCLC 14**
See also CDBLB 1789-1832; DLB 39, 104

Goethe, Johann Wolfgang von
1749-1832 .... **NCLC 4, 22, 34; PC 5**
See also DA; DLB 94; WLC 3

Gogarty, Oliver St. John
1878-1957 .... **TCLC 15**
See also CA 109; DLB 15, 19

Gogol, Nikolai (Vasilyevich)
1809-1852 ...... **NCLC 5, 15, 31; DC 1;**
                                      SSC 4
See also DA; WLC

Gold, Herbert 1924- .... **CLC 4, 7, 14, 42**
See also CA 9-12R; CANR 17; DLB 2;
DLBY 81

Goldbarth, Albert 1948- .... **CLC 5, 38**
See also CA 53-56; CANR 6, 40; DLB 120

Goldberg, Anatol 1910-1982 .... **CLC 34**
See also CA 131; 117

Goldemberg, Isaac 1945- .... **CLC 52**
See also CA 69-72; CAAS 12; CANR 11,
32; HW

Golden Silver
See Storm, Hyemeyohsts

Golding, William (Gerald)
1911- ..... **CLC 1, 2, 3, 8, 10, 17, 27, 58**
See also AAYA 5; CA 5-8R; CANR 13, 33;
CDBLB 1945-1960; DA; DLB 15, 100;
MTCW; WLC

Goldman, Emma 1869-1940 ...... **TCLC 13**
See also CA 110

Goldman, Francisco 1955- .... **CLC 76**

Goldman, William (W.) 1931- .... **CLC 1, 48**
See also CA 9-12R; CANR 29; DLB 44

Goldmann, Lucien 1913-1970 ...... **CLC 24**
See also CA 25-28; CAP 2

Goldoni, Carlo 1707-1793 .... **LC 4**

Goldsberry, Steven 1949- .... **CLC 34**
See also CA 131

Goldsmith, Oliver 1728-1774 .... **LC 2**
See also CDBLB 1660-1789; DA; DLB 39,
89, 104, 109; SATA 26; WLC

Goldsmith, Peter
See Priestley, J(ohn) B(oynton)

Gombrowicz, Witold
1904-1969 .... **CLC 4, 7, 11, 49**
See also CA 19-20; 25-28R; CAP 2

Gomez de la Serna, Ramon
1888-1963 .... **CLC 9**
See also CA 116; HW

Goncharov, Ivan Alexandrovich
1812-1891 .... **NCLC 1**

Goncourt, Edmond (Louis Antoine Huot) de
1822-1896 .... **NCLC 7**
See also DLB 123

Goncourt, Jules (Alfred Huot) de
1830-1870 .... **NCLC 7**
See also DLB 123

Gontier, Fernande 19(?)- .... **CLC 50**

Goodman, Paul 1911-1972 .... **CLC 1, 2, 4, 7**
See also CA 19-20; 37-40R; CANR 34;
CAP 2; DLB 130; MTCW

Gordimer, Nadine
1923- .... **CLC 3, 5, 7, 10, 18, 33, 51, 70**
See also CA 5-8R; CANR 3, 28; DA;
MTCW

Gordon, Adam Lindsay
1833-1870 .... **NCLC 21**

Gordon, Caroline
1895-1981 .... **CLC 6, 13, 29**
See also CA 11-12; 103; CANR 36; CAP 1;
DLB 4, 9, 102; DLBY 81; MTCW

Gordon, Charles William 1860-1937
See Connor, Ralph
See also CA 109

Gordon, Mary (Catherine)
1949- .... **CLC 13, 22**
See also CA 102; DLB 6; DLBY 81;
MTCW

Gordon, Sol 1923- .... **CLC 26**
See also CA 53-56; CANR 4; SATA 11

Gordone, Charles 1925- .... **CLC 1, 4**
See also BW; CA 93-96; DLB 7; MTCW

Gorenko, Anna Andreevna
See Akhmatova, Anna

Gorky, Maxim .... **TCLC 8**
See also Peshkov, Alexei Maximovich
See also WLC

Goryan, Sirak
See Saroyan, William

Gosse, Edmund (William)
1849-1928 .... **TCLC 28**
See also CA 117; DLB 57

Gotlieb, Phyllis Fay (Bloom)
1926- .... **CLC 18**
See also CA 13-16R; CANR 7; DLB 88

Gottesman, S. D.
See Kornbluth, C(yril) M.; Pohl, Frederik

Gottfried von Strassburg
fl. c. 1210- .... **CMLC 10**

Gottschalk, Laura Riding
See Jackson, Laura (Riding)

Gould, Lois .... **CLC 4, 10**
See also CA 77-80; CANR 29; MTCW

Gourmont, Remy de 1858-1915 .... **TCLC 17**
See also CA 109

Govier, Katherine 1948- .... **CLC 51**
See also CA 101; CANR 18, 40

Goyen, (Charles) William
1915-1983 .... **CLC 5, 8, 14, 40**
See also AITN 2; CA 5-8R; 110; CANR 6;
DLB 2; DLBY 83

Goytisolo, Juan 1931- ...... **CLC 5, 10, 23**
See also CA 85-88; CANR 32; HW; MTCW

Gozzi, (Conte) Carlo 1720-1806 .. **NCLC 23**

Grabbe, Christian Dietrich
1801-1836 .... **NCLC 2**
See also DLB 133

Grace, Patricia 1937- .... **CLC 56**

Gracian y Morales, Baltasar
1601-1658 .... **LC 15**

Gracq, Julien .... **CLC 11, 48**
See also Poirier, Louis
See also DLB 83

Grade, Chaim 1910-1982 .... **CLC 10**
See also CA 93-96; 107

Graduate of Oxford, A
See Ruskin, John

Graham, John
See Phillips, David Graham

Graham, Jorie 1951- .... **CLC 48**
See also CA 111; DLB 120

Graham, R(obert) B(ontine) Cunninghame
See Cunninghame Graham, R(obert)
B(ontine)
See also DLB 98

Graham, Robert
See Haldeman, Joe (William)

Graham, Tom
See Lewis, (Harry) Sinclair

Graham, W(illiam) S(ydney)
1918-1986 .... **CLC 29**
See also CA 73-76; 118; DLB 20

Graham, Winston (Mawdsley)
1910- .... **CLC 23**
See also CA 49-52; CANR 2, 22; DLB 77

Grant, Skeeter
See Spiegelman, Art

Granville-Barker, Harley
1877-1946 .... **TCLC 2**
See also Barker, Harley Granville
See also CA 104

Grass, Guenter (Wilhelm)
1927- .. **CLC 1, 2, 4, 6, 11, 15, 22, 32, 49**
See also CA 13-16R; CANR 20; DA;
DLB 75, 124; MTCW; WLC

Gratton, Thomas
See Hulme, T(homas) E(rnest)

Grau, Shirley Ann 1929- .... **CLC 4, 9**
See also CA 89-92; CANR 22; DLB 2;
MTCW

Gunn, Bill .... **CLC 5**
See also Gunn, William Harrison
See also DLB 38

Gunn, Thom(son William)
1929- .... **CLC 3, 6, 18, 32**
See also CA 17-20R; CANR 9, 33;
CDBLB 1960 to Present; DLB 27;
MTCW

Gunn, William Harrison 1934(?)-1989
See Gunn, Bill
See also AITN 1; BW; CA 13-16R; 128;
CANR 12, 25

Gunnars, Kristjana 1948- .... **CLC 69**
See also CA 113; DLB 60

Gurganus, Allan 1947- .... **CLC 70**
See also BEST 90:1; CA 135

Gurney, A(lbert) R(amsdell), Jr.
1930- .... **CLC 32, 50, 54**
See also CA 77-80; CANR 32

Gurney, Ivor (Bertie) 1890-1937 ... **TCLC 33**

Gurney, Peter
See Gurney, A(lbert) R(amsdell), Jr.

Gustafson, Ralph (Barker) 1909- .... **CLC 36**
See also CA 21-24R; CANR 8; DLB 88

Gut, Gom
See Simenon, Georges (Jacques Christian)

Guthrie, A(lfred) B(ertram), Jr.
1901-1991 .... **CLC 23**
See also CA 57-60; 134; CANR 24; DLB 6;
SATA 62; SATA-Obit 67

Guthrie, Isobel
See Grieve, C(hristopher) M(urray)

Guthrie, Woodrow Wilson 1912-1967
See Guthrie, Woody
See also CA 113; 93-96

Guthrie, Woody .... **CLC 35**
See also Guthrie, Woodrow Wilson

Guy, Rosa (Cuthbert) 1928- .... **CLC 26**
See also AAYA 4; BW; CA 17-20R;
CANR 14, 34; CLR 13; DLB 33; JRDA;
MAICYA; SATA 14, 62

Gwendolyn
See Bennett, (Enoch) Arnold

H. D. .... **CLC 3, 8, 14, 31, 34, 73; PC 5**
See also Doolittle, Hilda

Haavikko, Paavo Juhani
1931- .... **CLC 18, 34**
See also CA 106

Habbema, Koos
See Heijermans, Herman

Hacker, Marilyn 1942- .... **CLC 5, 9, 23, 72**
See also CA 77-80; DLB 120

Haggard, H(enry) Rider
1856-1925 .... **TCLC 11**
See also CA 108; DLB 70; SATA 16

Haig, Fenil
See Ford, Ford Madox

Haig-Brown, Roderick (Langmere)
1908-1976 .... **CLC 21**
See also CA 5-8R; 69-72; CANR 4, 38;
CLR 31; DLB 88; MAICYA; SATA 12

Hailey, Arthur 1920- .... **CLC 5**
See also AITN 2; BEST 90:3; CA 1-4R;
CANR 2, 36; DLB 88; DLBY 82; MTCW

Hailey, Elizabeth Forsythe 1938-... **CLC 40**
See also CA 93-96; CAAS 1; CANR 15

Haines, John (Meade) 1924- .... **CLC 58**
See also CA 17-20R; CANR 13, 34; DLB 5

Haldeman, Joe (William) 1943-..... **CLC 61**
See also CA 53-56; CANR 6; DLB 8

Haley, Alex(ander Murray Palmer)
1921-1992 .... **CLC 8, 12, 76**
See also BLC 2; BW; CA 77-80; 136; DA;
DLB 38; MTCW

Haliburton, Thomas Chandler
1796-1865 .... **NCLC 15**
See also DLB 11, 99

Hall, Donald (Andrew, Jr.)
1928- .... **CLC 1, 13, 37, 59**
See also CA 5-8R; CAAS 7; CANR 2;
DLB 5; SATA 23

Hall, Frederic Sauser
See Sauser-Hall, Frederic

Hall, James
See Kuttner, Henry

Hall, James Norman 1887-1951 ... **TCLC 23**
See also CA 123; SATA 21

Hall, (Marguerite) Radclyffe
1886(?)-1943 .... **TCLC 12**
See also CA 110

Hall, Rodney 1935- .... **CLC 51**
See also CA 109

Halliday, Michael
See Creasey, John

Halpern, Daniel 1945- .... **CLC 14**
See also CA 33-36R

Hamburger, Michael (Peter Leopold)
1924- .... **CLC 5, 14**
See also CA 5-8R; CAAS 4; CANR 2;
DLB 27

Hamill, Pete 1935- .... **CLC 10**
See also CA 25-28R; CANR 18

Hamilton, Clive
See Lewis, C(live) S(taples)

Hamilton, Edmond 1904-1977 .... **CLC 1**
See also CA 1-4R; CANR 3; DLB 8

Hamilton, Eugene (Jacob) Lee
See Lee-Hamilton, Eugene (Jacob)

Hamilton, Franklin
See Silverberg, Robert

Hamilton, Gail
See Corcoran, Barbara

Hamilton, Mollie
See Kaye, M(ary) M(argaret)

Hamilton, (Anthony Walter) Patrick
1904-1962 .... **CLC 51**
See also CA 113; DLB 10

Hamilton, Virginia 1936- .... **CLC 26**
See also AAYA 2; BW; CA 25-28R;
CANR 20, 37; CLR 1, 11; DLB 33, 52;
JRDA; MAICYA; MTCW; SATA 4, 56

Hammett, (Samuel) Dashiell
1894-1961 .... **CLC 3, 5, 10, 19, 47**
See also AITN 1; CA 81-84; CANR 42;
CDALB 1929-1941; DLBD 6; MTCW

Hammon, Jupiter 1711(?)-1800(?).. **NCLC 5**
See also BLC 2; DLB 31, 50

Hammond, Keith
See Kuttner, Henry

Hamner, Earl (Henry), Jr. 1923- ... **CLC 12**
See also AITN 2; CA 73-76; DLB 6

Hampton, Christopher (James)
1946- .... **CLC 4**
See also CA 25-28R; DLB 13; MTCW

Hamsun, Knut .... **TCLC 2, 14, 49**
See also Pedersen, Knut

Handke, Peter 1942- .. **CLC 5, 8, 10, 15, 38**
See also CA 77-80; CANR 33; DLB 85,
124; MTCW

Hanley, James 1901-1985 ... **CLC 3, 5, 8, 13**
See also CA 73-76; 117; CANR 36; MTCW

Hannah, Barry 1942- .... **CLC 23, 38**
See also CA 108; 110; DLB 6; MTCW

Hannon, Ezra
See Hunter, Evan

Hansberry, Lorraine (Vivian)
1930-1965 .... **CLC 17, 62; DC 2**
See also BLC 2; BW; CA 109; 25-28R;
CABS 3; CDALB 1941-1968; DA;
DLB 7, 38; MTCW

Hansen, Joseph 1923-............. **CLC 38**
See also CA 29-32R; CAAS 17; CANR 16

Hansen, Martin A. 1909-1955..... **TCLC 32**

Hanson, Kenneth O(stlin) 1922- .... **CLC 13**
See also CA 53-56; CANR 7

Hardwick, Elizabeth 1916- .... **CLC 13**
See also CA 5-8R; CANR 3, 32; DLB 6;
MTCW

Hardy, Thomas
1840-1928 ...... **TCLC 4, 10, 18, 32, 48;**
SSC 2
See also CA 104; 123; CDBLB 1890-1914;
DA; DLB 18, 19; MTCW; WLC

Hare, David 1947- .... **CLC 29, 58**
See also CA 97-100; CANR 39; DLB 13;
MTCW

Harford, Henry
See Hudson, W(illiam) H(enry)

Hargrave, Leonie
See Disch, Thomas M(ichael)

Harlan, Louis R(udolph) 1922- ..... **CLC 34**
See also CA 21-24R; CANR 25

Harling, Robert 1951(?)- .... **CLC 53**

Harmon, William (Ruth) 1938- ..... **CLC 38**
See also CA 33-36R; CANR 14, 32, 35;
SATA 65

Harper, F. E. W.
See Harper, Frances Ellen Watkins

Harper, Frances E. W.
See Harper, Frances Ellen Watkins

Harper, Frances E. Watkins
See Harper, Frances Ellen Watkins

Harper, Frances Ellen
See Harper, Frances Ellen Watkins

Harper, Frances Ellen Watkins
1825-1911 .... **TCLC 14**
See also BLC 2; BW; CA 111; 125; DLB 50

Harper, Michael S(teven) 1938- .. **CLC 7, 22**
See also BW; CA 33-36R; CANR 24;
DLB 41

Harper, Mrs. F. E. W.
See Harper, Frances Ellen Watkins

Harris, Christie (Lucy) Irwin
1907- .... **CLC 12**
See also CA 5-8R; CANR 6; DLB 88;
JRDA; MAICYA; SAAS 10; SATA 6, 74

Harris, Frank 1856(?)-1931 .... **TCLC 24**
See also CA 109

Harris, George Washington
1814-1869 .... **NCLC 23**
See also DLB 3, 11

Harris, Joel Chandler 1848-1908 ... **TCLC 2**
See also CA 104; 137; DLB 11, 23, 42, 78,
91; MAICYA; YABC 1

Harris, John (Wyndham Parkes Lucas)
Beynon 1903-1969 .... **CLC 19**
See also CA 102; 89-92

Harris, MacDonald
See Heiney, Donald (William)

Harris, Mark 1922- .... **CLC 19**
See also CA 5-8R; CAAS 3; CANR 2;
DLB 2; DLBY 80

Harris, (Theodore) Wilson 1921-.... **CLC 25**
See also BW; CA 65-68; CAAS 16;
CANR 11, 27; DLB 117; MTCW

Harrison, Elizabeth Cavanna 1909-
See Cavanna, Betty
See also CA 9-12R; CANR 6, 27

Harrison, Harry (Max) 1925- ...... **CLC 42**
See also CA 1-4R; CANR 5, 21; DLB 8;
SATA 4

Harrison, James (Thomas) 1937-
See Harrison, Jim
See also CA 13-16R; CANR 8

Harrison, Jim .... **CLC 6, 14, 33, 66**
See also Harrison, James (Thomas)
See also DLBY 82

Harrison, Kathryn 1961- .... **CLC 70**

Harrison, Tony 1937-............. **CLC 43**
See also CA 65-68; DLB 40; MTCW

Harriss, Will(ard Irvin) 1922-...... **CLC 34**
See also CA 111

Harson, Sley
See Ellison, Harlan

Hart, Ellis
See Ellison, Harlan

Hart, Josephine 1942(?)- .... **CLC 70**
See also CA 138

Hart, Moss 1904-1961 .... **CLC 66**
See also CA 109; 89-92; DLB 7

Harte, (Francis) Bret(t)
1836(?)-1902 .... **TCLC 1, 25; SSC 8**
See also CA 104; 140; CDALB 1865-1917;
DA; DLB 12, 64, 74, 79; SATA 26; WLC

Hartley, L(eslie) P(oles)
1895-1972 .... **CLC 2, 22**
See also CA 45-48; 37-40R; CANR 33;
DLB 15; MTCW

Hartman, Geoffrey H. 1929-....... **CLC 27**
See also CA 117; 125; DLB 67

Haruf, Kent 19(?)- .... **CLC 34**

Harwood, Ronald 1934-........... **CLC 32**
See also CA 1-4R; CANR 4; DLB 13

Hasek, Jaroslav (Matej Frantisek)
1883-1923 .... **TCLC 4**
See also CA 104; 129; MTCW

Hass, Robert 1941-............ **CLC 18, 39**
See also CA 111; CANR 30; DLB 105

Hastings, Hudson
See Kuttner, Henry

Hastings, Selina. .... **CLC 44**

Hatteras, Amelia
See Mencken, H(enry) L(ouis)

Hatteras, Owen .... **TCLC 18**
See also Mencken, H(enry) L(ouis); Nathan,
George Jean

Hauptmann, Gerhart (Johann Robert)
1862-1946 .... **TCLC 4**
See also CA 104; DLB 66, 118

Havel, Vaclav 1936-........ **CLC 25, 58, 65**
See also CA 104; CANR 36; MTCW

Haviaras, Stratis .... **CLC 33**
See also Chaviaras, Strates

Hawes, Stephen 1475(?)-1523(?) ..... **LC 17**

Hawkes, John (Clendennin Burne, Jr.)
1925- ...... **CLC 1, 2, 3, 4, 7, 9, 14, 15,**
27, 49
See also CA 1-4R; CANR 2; DLB 2, 7;
DLBY 80; MTCW

Hawking, S. W.
See Hawking, Stephen W(illiam)

Hawking, Stephen W(illiam)
1942- .... **CLC 63**
See also BEST 89:1; CA 126; 129

Hawthorne, Julian 1846-1934 ..... **TCLC 25**

Hawthorne, Nathaniel
1804-1864 .... **NCLC 39; SSC 3**
See also CDALB 1640-1865; DA; DLB 1,
74; WLC; YABC 2

Haxton, Josephine Ayres 1921- .... **CLC 73**
See also CA 115; CANR 41

Hayaseca y Eizaguirre, Jorge
See Echegaray (y Eizaguirre), Jose (Maria
Waldo)

Hayashi Fumiko 1904-1951 ...... **TCLC 27**

Haycraft, Anna
See Ellis, Alice Thomas
See also CA 122

Hayden, Robert E(arl)
1913-1980 ...... **CLC 5, 9, 14, 37; PC 6**
See also BLC 2; BW; CA 69-72; 97-100;
CABS 2; CANR 24; CDALB 1941-1968;
DA; DLB 5, 76; MTCW; SATA 19, 26

Hayford, J(oseph) E(phraim) Casely
See Casely-Hayford, J(oseph) E(phraim)

Hayman, Ronald 1932-............ **CLC 44**
See also CA 25-28R; CANR 18

Haywood, Eliza (Fowler)
1693(?)-1756 .... **LC 1**

Hazlitt, William 1778-1830 ...... **NCLC 29**
See also DLB 110

Hazzard, Shirley 1931- .... **CLC 18**
See also CA 9-12R; CANR 4; DLBY 82;
MTCW

Head, Bessie 1937-1986........ **CLC 25, 67**
See also BLC 2; BW; CA 29-32R; 119;
CANR 25; DLB 117; MTCW

Headon, (Nicky) Topper 1956(?)- ... **CLC 30**
See also Clash, The

Heaney, Seamus (Justin)
1939- .... **CLC 5, 7, 14, 25, 37, 74**
See also CA 85-88; CANR 25;
CDBLB 1960 to Present; DLB 40;
MTCW

Hearn, (Patricio) Lafcadio (Tessima Carlos)
1850-1904 .... **TCLC 9**
See also CA 105; DLB 12, 78

Hearne, Vicki 1946-.............. **CLC 56**
See also CA 139

Hearon, Shelby 1931-............. **CLC 63**
See also AITN 2; CA 25-28R; CANR 18

Heat-Moon, William Least.......... **CLC 29**
See also Trogdon, William (Lewis)
See also AAYA 9

Hebert, Anne 1916- .... **CLC 4, 13, 29**
See also CA 85-88; DLB 68; MTCW

Hecht, Anthony (Evan)
1923- .... **CLC 8, 13, 19**
See also CA 9-12R; CANR 6; DLB 5

Hecht, Ben 1894-1964 .... **CLC 8**
See also CA 85-88; DLB 7, 9, 25, 26, 28, 86

Hedayat, Sadeq 1903-1951........ **TCLC 21**
See also CA 120

Heidegger, Martin 1889-1976 ...... **CLC 24**
See also CA 81-84; 65-68; CANR 34;
MTCW

Heidenstam, (Carl Gustaf) Verner von
1859-1940 .... **TCLC 5**
See also CA 104

Heifner, Jack 1946-.............. **CLC 11**
See also CA 105

Heijermans, Herman 1864-1924 ... **TCLC 24**
See also CA 123

Heilbrun, Carolyn G(old) 1926-..... **CLC 25**
See also CA 45-48; CANR 1, 28

Heine, Heinrich 1797-1856 .... **NCLC 4**
See also DLB 90

Heinemann, Larry (Curtiss) 1944- .. **CLC 50**
See also CA 110; CANR 31; DLBD 9

Heiney, Donald (William) 1921-..... **CLC 9**
See also CA 1-4R; CANR 3

Heinlein, Robert A(nson)
1907-1988 ...... **CLC 1, 3, 8, 14, 26, 55**
See also CA 1-4R; 125; CANR 1, 20;
DLB 8; JRDA; MAICYA; MTCW;
SATA 9, 56, 69

Helforth, John
See Doolittle, Hilda

Hellenhofferu, Vojtech Kapristian z
See Hasek, Jaroslav (Matej Frantisek)

Heller, Joseph
1923- .... **CLC 1, 3, 5, 8, 11, 36, 63**
See also AITN 1; CA 5-8R; CABS 1;
CANR 8, 42; DA; DLB 2, 28; DLBY 80;
MTCW; WLC

Hellman, Lillian (Florence)
1906-1984 ...... **CLC 2, 4, 8, 14, 18, 34,**
44, 52; DC 1
See also AITN 1, 2; CA 13-16R; 112;
CANR 33; DLB 7; DLBY 84; MTCW

Helprin, Mark 1947- ..... **CLC 7, 10, 22, 32**
See also CA 81-84; DLBY 85; MTCW

Helyar, Jane Penelope Josephine 1933-
See Poole, Josephine
See also CA 21-24R; CANR 10, 26

Hemans, Felicia 1793-1835 ...... NCLC 29
See also DLB 96

Hemingway, Ernest (Miller)
     1899-1961 .... CLC 1, 3, 6, 8, 10, 13, 19,
              30, 34, 39, 41, 44, 50, 61; SSC 1
See also CA 77-80; CANR 34;
     CDALB 1917-1929; DA; DLB 4, 9, 102;
     DLBD 1; DLBY 81, 87; MTCW; WLC

Hempel, Amy 1951- .... CLC 39
See also CA 118; 137

Henderson, F. C.
See Mencken, H(enry) L(ouis)

Henderson, Sylvia
See Ashton-Warner, Sylvia (Constance)

Henley, Beth .... CLC 23
See also Henley, Elizabeth Becker
See also CABS 3; DLBY 86

Henley, Elizabeth Becker 1952-
See Henley, Beth
See also CA 107; CANR 32; MTCW

Henley, William Ernest
     1849-1903 .... TCLC 8
See also CA 105; DLB 19

Hennissart, Martha
See Lathen, Emma
See also CA 85-88

Henry, O. .... TCLC 1, 19; SSC 5
See also Porter, William Sydney
See also WLC

Henryson, Robert 1430(?)-1506(?).... LC 20

Henry VIII 1491-1547 .... LC 10

Henschke, Alfred
See Klabund

Hentoff, Nat(han Irving) 1925- ..... CLC 26
See also AAYA 4; CA 1-4R; CAAS 6;
     CANR 5, 25; CLR 1; JRDA; MAICYA;
     SATA 27, 42, 69

Heppenstall, (John) Rayner
     1911-1981 .... CLC 10
See also CA 1-4R; 103; CANR 29

Herbert, Frank (Patrick)
     1920-1986 .... CLC 12, 23, 35, 44
See also CA 53-56; 118; CANR 5; DLB 8;
     MTCW; SATA 9, 37, 47

Herbert, George 1593-1633 .... PC 4
See also CDBLB Before 1660; DLB 126

Herbert, Zbigniew 1924- .... CLC 9, 43
See also CA 89-92; CANR 36; MTCW

Herbst, Josephine (Frey)
     1897-1969 .... CLC 34
See also CA 5-8R; 25-28R; DLB 9

Hergesheimer, Joseph
     1880-1954 .... TCLC 11
See also CA 109; DLB 102, 9

Herlihy, James Leo 1927- .... CLC 6
See also CA 1-4R; CANR 2

Hermogenes fl. c. 175- .... CMLC 6

Hernandez, Jose 1834-1886 ...... NCLC 17

Herrick, Robert 1591-1674 .... LC 13
See also DA; DLB 126

Herring, Guilles
See Somerville, Edith

Herriot, James 1916- .... CLC 12
See also Wight, James Alfred
See also AAYA 1; CANR 40

Herrmann, Dorothy 1941- .... CLC 44
See also CA 107

Herrmann, Taffy
See Herrmann, Dorothy

Hersey, John (Richard)
     1914-1993 .... CLC 1, 2, 7, 9, 40
See also CA 17-20R; 140; CANR 33;
     DLB 6; MTCW; SATA 25

Herzen, Aleksandr Ivanovich
     1812-1870 .... NCLC 10

Herzl, Theodor 1860-1904 .... TCLC 36

Herzog, Werner 1942- .... CLC 16
See also CA 89-92

Hesiod c. 8th cent. B.C.- .... CMLC 5

Hesse, Hermann
     1877-1962 .... CLC 1, 2, 3, 6, 11, 17, 25,
              69; SSC 9
See also CA 17-18; CAP 2; DA; DLB 66;
     MTCW; SATA 50; WLC

Hewes, Cady
See De Voto, Bernard (Augustine)

Heyen, William 1940- .... CLC 13, 18
See also CA 33-36R; CAAS 9; DLB 5

Heyerdahl, Thor 1914- .... CLC 26
See also CA 5-8R; CANR 5, 22; MTCW;
     SATA 2, 52

Heym, Georg (Theodor Franz Arthur)
     1887-1912 .... TCLC 9
See also CA 106

Heym, Stefan 1913- .... CLC 41
See also CA 9-12R; CANR 4; DLB 69

Heyse, Paul (Johann Ludwig von)
     1830-1914 .... TCLC 8
See also CA 104; DLB 129

Hibbert, Eleanor Alice Burford
     1906-1993 .... CLC 7
See also BEST 90:4; CA 17-20R; 140;
     CANR 9, 28; SATA 2; SATA-Obit 74

Higgins, George V(incent)
     1939- .... CLC 4, 7, 10, 18
See also CA 77-80; CAAS 5; CANR 17;
     DLB 2; DLBY 81; MTCW

Higginson, Thomas Wentworth
     1823-1911 .... TCLC 36
See also DLB 1, 64

Highet, Helen
See MacInnes, Helen (Clark)

Highsmith, (Mary) Patricia
     1921- .... CLC 2, 4, 14, 42
See also CA 1-4R; CANR 1, 20; MTCW

Highwater, Jamake (Mamake)
     1942(?)- .... CLC 12
See also AAYA 7; CA 65-68; CAAS 7;
     CANR 10, 34; CLR 17; DLB 52;
     DLBY 85; JRDA; MAICYA; SATA 30,
     32, 69

Hijuelos, Oscar 1951- .... CLC 65
See also BEST 90:1; CA 123; HW

Hikmet, Nazim 1902-1963 .... CLC 40
See also CA 141; 93-96

Hildesheimer, Wolfgang
     1916-1991 .... CLC 49
See also CA 101; 135; DLB 69, 124

Hill, Geoffrey (William)
     1932- .... CLC 5, 8, 18, 45
See also CA 81-84; CANR 21;
     CDBLB 1960 to Present; DLB 40;
     MTCW

Hill, George Roy 1921- .... CLC 26
See also CA 110; 122

Hill, John
See Koontz, Dean R(ay)

Hill, Susan (Elizabeth) 1942- .... CLC 4
See also CA 33-36R; CANR 29; DLB 14;
     MTCW

Hillerman, Tony 1925- .... CLC 62
See also AAYA 6; BEST 89:1; CA 29-32R;
     CANR 21, 42; SATA 6

Hillesum, Etty 1914-1943 .... TCLC 49
See also CA 137

Hilliard, Noel (Harvey) 1929- ...... CLC 15
See also CA 9-12R; CANR 7

Hillis, Rick 1956- .... CLC 66
See also CA 134

Hilton, James 1900-1954 .... TCLC 21
See also CA 108; DLB 34, 77; SATA 34

Himes, Chester (Bomar)
     1909-1984 .... CLC 2, 4, 7, 18, 58
See also BLC 2; BW; CA 25-28R; 114;
     CANR 22; DLB 2, 76; MTCW

Hinde, Thomas .... CLC 6, 11
See also Chitty, Thomas Willes

Hindin, Nathan
See Bloch, Robert (Albert)

Hine, (William) Daryl 1936- .... CLC 15
See also CA 1-4R; CAAS 15; CANR 1, 20;
     DLB 60

Hinkson, Katharine Tynan
See Tynan, Katharine

Hinton, S(usan) E(loise) 1950- ..... CLC 30
See also AAYA 2; CA 81-84; CANR 32;
     CLR 3, 23; DA; JRDA; MAICYA;
     MTCW; SATA 19, 58

Hippius, Zinaida .... TCLC 9
See also Gippius, Zinaida (Nikolayevna)

Hiraoka, Kimitake 1925-1970
See Mishima, Yukio
See also CA 97-100; 29-32R; MTCW

Hirsch, E(ric) D(onald), Jr. 1928-... CLC 79
See also CA 25-28R; CANR 27; DLB 67;
     MTCW

Hirsch, Edward 1950- .... CLC 31, 50
See also CA 104; CANR 20, 42; DLB 120

Hitchcock, Alfred (Joseph)
     1899-1980 .... CLC 16
See also CA 97-100; SATA 24, 27

Hoagland, Edward 1932- .... CLC 28
See also CA 1-4R; CANR 2, 31; DLB 6;
     SATA 51

Hoban, Russell (Conwell) 1925- .. CLC 7, 25
See also CA 5-8R; CANR 23, 37; CLR 3;
     DLB 52; MAICYA; MTCW; SATA 1, 40

Hobbs, Perry
See Blackmur, R(ichard) P(almer)

Howells, William Dean
1837-1920 . . . . **TCLC 41, 7, 17**
See also CA 104; 134; CDALB 1865-1917;
DLB 12, 64, 74, 79

Howes, Barbara 1914- . . . . **CLC 15**
See also CA 9-12R; CAAS 3; SATA 5

Hrabal, Bohumil 1914- . . . . **CLC 13, 67**
See also CA 106; CAAS 12

Hsun, Lu . . . . **TCLC 3**
See also Shu-Jen, Chou

Hubbard, L(afayette) Ron(ald)
1911-1986 . . . . **CLC 43**
See also CA 77-80; 118; CANR 22

Huch, Ricarda (Octavia)
1864-1947 . . . . **TCLC 13**
See also CA 111; DLB 66

Huddle, David 1942- . . . . **CLC 49**
See also CA 57-60; DLB 130

Hudson, Jeffrey
See Crichton, (John) Michael

Hudson, W(illiam) H(enry)
1841-1922 . . . . **TCLC 29**
See also CA 115; DLB 98; SATA 35

Hueffer, Ford Madox
See Ford, Ford Madox

Hughart, Barry 1934- . . . . **CLC 39**
See also CA 137

Hughes, Colin
See Creasey, John

Hughes, David (John) 1930- . . . . **CLC 48**
See also CA 116; 129; DLB 14

Hughes, (James) Langston
1902-1967 . . . . . **CLC 1, 5, 10, 15, 35, 44;**
DC 3; PC 1; SSC 6
See also BLC 2; BW; CA 1-4R; 25-28R;
CANR 1, 34; CDALB 1929-1941;
CLR 17; DA; DLB 4, 7, 48, 51, 86;
JRDA; MAICYA; MTCW; SATA 4, 33;
WLC

Hughes, Richard (Arthur Warren)
1900-1976 . . . . **CLC 1, 11**
See also CA 5-8R; 65-68; CANR 4;
DLB 15; MTCW; SATA 8, 25

Hughes, Ted
1930- . . . . **CLC 2, 4, 9, 14, 37; PC 7**
See also CA 1-4R; CANR 1, 33; CLR 3;
DLB 40; MAICYA; MTCW; SATA 27,
49

Hugo, Richard F(ranklin)
1923-1982 . . . . **CLC 6, 18, 32**
See also CA 49-52; 108; CANR 3; DLB 5

Hugo, Victor (Marie)
1802-1885 . . . . **NCLC 3, 10, 21**
See also DA; DLB 119; SATA 47; WLC

Huidobro, Vicente
See Huidobro Fernandez, Vicente Garcia

Huidobro Fernandez, Vicente Garcia
1893-1948 . . . . **TCLC 31**
See also CA 131; HW

Hulme, Keri 1947- . . . . **CLC 39**
See also CA 125

Hulme, T(homas) E(rnest)
1883-1917 . . . . **TCLC 21**
See also CA 117; DLB 19

Hume, David 1711-1776 . . . . **LC 7**
See also DLB 104

Humphrey, William 1924- . . . . **CLC 45**
See also CA 77-80; DLB 6

Humphreys, Emyr Owen 1919- . . . . . **CLC 47**
See also CA 5-8R; CANR 3, 24; DLB 15

Humphreys, Josephine 1945- . . . . **CLC 34, 57**
See also CA 121; 127

Hungerford, Pixie
See Brinsmead, H(esba) F(ay)

Hunt, E(verette) Howard, Jr.
1918- . . . . **CLC 3**
See also AITN 1; CA 45-48; CANR 2

Hunt, Kyle
See Creasey, John

Hunt, (James Henry) Leigh
1784-1859 . . . . **NCLC 1**

Hunt, Marsha 1946- . . . . **CLC 70**

Hunter, E. Waldo
See Sturgeon, Theodore (Hamilton)

Hunter, Evan 1926- . . . . **CLC 11, 31**
See also CA 5-8R; CANR 5, 38; DLBY 82;
MTCW; SATA 25

Hunter, Kristin (Eggleston) 1931- . . . **CLC 35**
See also AITN 1; BW; CA 13-16R;
CANR 13; CLR 3; DLB 33; MAICYA;
SAAS 10; SATA 12

Hunter, Mollie 1922- . . . . **CLC 21**
See also McIlwraith, Maureen Mollie
Hunter
See also CANR 37; CLR 25; JRDA;
MAICYA; SAAS 7; SATA 54

Hunter, Robert (?)-1734 . . . . **LC 7**

Hurston, Zora Neale
1903-1960 . . . . . . **CLC 7, 30, 61; SSC 4**
See also BLC 2; BW; CA 85-88; DA;
DLB 51, 86; MTCW

Huston, John (Marcellus)
1906-1987 . . . . **CLC 20**
See also CA 73-76; 123; CANR 34; DLB 26

Hustvedt, Siri 1955- . . . . **CLC 76**
See also CA 137

Hutten, Ulrich von 1488-1523 . . . . . . **LC 16**

Huxley, Aldous (Leonard)
1894-1963 . . . . . **CLC 1, 3, 4, 5, 8, 11, 18,**
35, 79
See also CA 85-88; CDBLB 1914-1945; DA;
DLB 36, 100; MTCW; SATA 63; WLC

Huysmans, Charles Marie Georges
1848-1907
See Huysmans, Joris-Karl
See also CA 104

Huysmans, Joris-Karl . . . . **TCLC 7**
See also Huysmans, Charles Marie Georges
See also DLB 123

Hwang, David Henry 1957- . . . . **CLC 55**
See also CA 127; 132

Hyde, Anthony 1946- . . . . **CLC 42**
See also CA 136

Hyde, Margaret O(ldroyd) 1917- . . . **CLC 21**
See also CA 1-4R; CANR 1, 36; CLR 23;
JRDA; MAICYA; SAAS 8; SATA 1, 42

Hynes, James 1956(?)- . . . . **CLC 65**

Ian, Janis 1951- . . . . **CLC 21**
See also CA 105

Ibanez, Vicente Blasco
See Blasco Ibanez, Vicente

Ibarguengoitia, Jorge 1928-1983 . . . . **CLC 37**
See also CA 124; 113; HW

Ibsen, Henrik (Johan)
1828-1906 . . . . **TCLC 2, 8, 16, 37, 52;**
DC 2
See also CA 104; 141; DA; WLC

Ibuse Masuji 1898-1993 . . . . **CLC 22**
See also CA 127; 141

Ichikawa, Kon 1915- . . . . **CLC 20**
See also CA 121

Idle, Eric 1943- . . . . **CLC 21**
See also Monty Python
See also CA 116; CANR 35

Ignatow, David 1914- . . . . . . **CLC 4, 7, 14, 40**
See also CA 9-12R; CAAS 3; CANR 31;
DLB 5

Ihimaera, Witi 1944- . . . . **CLC 46**
See also CA 77-80

Ilf, Ilya . . . . **TCLC 21**
See also Fainzilberg, Ilya Arnoldovich

Immermann, Karl (Lebrecht)
1796-1840 . . . . **NCLC 4**
See also DLB 133

Inclan, Ramon (Maria) del Valle
See Valle-Inclan, Ramon (Maria) del

Infante, G(uillermo) Cabrera
See Cabrera Infante, G(uillermo)

Ingalls, Rachel (Holmes) 1940- . . . . . **CLC 42**
See also CA 123; 127

Ingamells, Rex 1913-1955 . . . . **TCLC 35**

Inge, William Motter
1913-1973 . . . . **CLC 1, 8, 19**
See also CA 9-12R; CDALB 1941-1968;
DLB 7; MTCW

Ingelow, Jean 1820-1897 . . . . **NCLC 39**
See also DLB 35; SATA 33

Ingram, Willis J.
See Harris, Mark

Innaurato, Albert (F.) 1948(?)- . . **CLC 21, 60**
See also CA 115; 122

Innes, Michael
See Stewart, J(ohn) I(nnes) M(ackintosh)

Ionesco, Eugene
1912- . . . . **CLC 1, 4, 6, 9, 11, 15, 41**
See also CA 9-12R; DA; MTCW; SATA 7;
WLC

Iqbal, Muhammad 1873-1938 . . . . . **TCLC 28**

Ireland, Patrick
See O'Doherty, Brian

Irland, David
See Green, Julian (Hartridge)

Iron, Ralph
See Schreiner, Olive (Emilie Albertina)

Irving, John (Winslow)
1942- . . . . **CLC 13, 23, 38**
See also AAYA 8; BEST 89:3; CA 25-28R;
CANR 28; DLB 6; DLBY 82; MTCW

Johnson, James Weldon
1871-1938 . . . . TCLC 3, 19
See also BLC 2; BW; CA 104; 125;
CDALB 1917-1929; CLR 32; DLB 51;
MTCW; SATA 31

Johnson, Joyce 1935- . . . . CLC 58
See also CA 125; 129

Johnson, Lionel (Pigot)
1867-1902 . . . . TCLC 19
See also CA 117; DLB 19

Johnson, Mel
See Malzberg, Barry N(athaniel)

Johnson, Pamela Hansford
1912-1981 . . . . CLC 1, 7, 27
See also CA 1-4R; 104; CANR 2, 28;
DLB 15; MTCW

Johnson, Samuel 1709-1784 . . . . LC 15
See also CDBLB 1660-1789; DA; DLB 39,
95, 104; WLC

Johnson, Uwe
1934-1984 . . . . CLC 5, 10, 15, 40
See also CA 1-4R; 112; CANR 1, 39;
DLB 75; MTCW

Johnston, George (Benson) 1913- . . . CLC 51
See also CA 1-4R; CANR 5, 20; DLB 88

Johnston, Jennifer 1930- . . . . CLC 7
See also CA 85-88; DLB 14

Jolley, (Monica) Elizabeth 1923- . . . CLC 46
See also CA 127; CAAS 13

Jones, Arthur Llewellyn 1863-1947
See Machen, Arthur
See also CA 104

Jones, D(ouglas) G(ordon) 1929- . . . . CLC 10
See also CA 29-32R; CANR 13; DLB 53

Jones, David (Michael)
1895-1974 . . . . CLC 2, 4, 7, 13, 42
See also CA 9-12R; 53-56; CANR 28;
CDBLB 1945-1960; DLB 20, 100; MTCW

Jones, David Robert 1947-
See Bowie, David
See also CA 103

Jones, Diana Wynne 1934- . . . . CLC 26
See also CA 49-52; CANR 4, 26; CLR 23;
JRDA; MAICYA; SAAS 7; SATA 9, 70

Jones, Edward P. 1951- . . . . CLC 76

Jones, Gayl 1949- . . . . CLC 6, 9
See also BLC 2; BW; CA 77-80; CANR 27;
DLB 33; MTCW

Jones, James 1921-1977 . . . . CLC 1, 3, 10, 39
See also AITN 1, 2; CA 1-4R; 69-72;
CANR 6; DLB 2; MTCW

Jones, John J.
See Lovecraft, H(oward) P(hillips)

Jones, LeRoi . . . . CLC 1, 2, 3, 5, 10, 14
See also Baraka, Amiri

Jones, Louis B. . . . . CLC 65
See also CA 141

Jones, Madison (Percy, Jr.) 1925- . . . CLC 4
See also CA 13-16R; CAAS 11; CANR 7

Jones, Mervyn 1922- . . . . CLC 10, 52
See also CA 45-48; CAAS 5; CANR 1;
MTCW

Jones, Mick 1956(?)- . . . . CLC 30
See also Clash, The

Jones, Nettie (Pearl) 1941- . . . . CLC 34
See also CA 137

Jones, Preston 1936-1979 . . . . CLC 10
See also CA 73-76; 89-92; DLB 7

Jones, Robert F(rancis) 1934- . . . . CLC 7
See also CA 49-52; CANR 2

Jones, Rod 1953- . . . . CLC 50
See also CA 128

Jones, Terence Graham Parry
1942- . . . . CLC 21
See also Jones, Terry; Monty Python
See also CA 112; 116; CANR 35; SATA 51

Jones, Terry
See Jones, Terence Graham Parry
See also SATA 67

Jong, Erica 1942- . . . . CLC 4, 6, 8, 18
See also AITN 1; BEST 90:2; CA 73-76;
CANR 26; DLB 2, 5, 28; MTCW

Jonson, Ben(jamin) 1572(?)-1637 . . . . . . LC 6
See also CDBLB Before 1660; DA; DLB 62,
121; WLC

Jordan, June 1936- . . . . CLC 5, 11, 23
See also AAYA 2; BW; CA 33-36R;
CANR 25; CLR 10; DLB 38; MAICYA;
MTCW; SATA 4

Jordan, Pat(rick M.) 1941- . . . . CLC 37
See also CA 33-36R

Jorgensen, Ivar
See Ellison, Harlan

Jorgenson, Ivar
See Silverberg, Robert

Josipovici, Gabriel 1940- . . . . CLC 6, 43
See also CA 37-40R; CAAS 8; DLB 14

Joubert, Joseph 1754-1824 . . . . NCLC 9

Jouve, Pierre Jean 1887-1976 . . . . . . CLC 47
See also CA 65-68

Joyce, James (Augustine Aloysius)
1882-1941 . . . . TCLC 3, 8, 16, 35; SSC 3
See also CA 104; 126; CDBLB 1914-1945;
DA; DLB 10, 19, 36; MTCW; WLC

Jozsef, Attila 1905-1937 . . . . TCLC 22
See also CA 116

Juana Ines de la Cruz 1651(?)-1695 . . . LC 5

Judd, Cyril
See Kornbluth, C(yril) M.; Pohl, Frederik

Julian of Norwich 1342(?)-1416(?) . . . . LC 6

Just, Ward (Swift) 1935- . . . . CLC 4, 27
See also CA 25-28R; CANR 32

Justice, Donald (Rodney) 1925- . . CLC 6, 19
See also CA 5-8R; CANR 26; DLBY 83

Juvenal c. 55-c. 127 . . . . CMLC 8

Juvenis
See Bourne, Randolph S(illiman)

Kacew, Romain 1914-1980
See Gary, Romain
See also CA 108; 102

Kadare, Ismail 1936- . . . . CLC 52

Kadohata, Cynthia . . . . CLC 59
See also CA 140

Kafka, Franz
1883-1924 . . . . TCLC 2, 6, 13, 29, 47;
SSC 5
See also CA 105; 126; DA; DLB 81;
MTCW; WLC

Kahn, Roger 1927- . . . . CLC 30
See also CA 25-28R; SATA 37

Kain, Saul
See Sassoon, Siegfried (Lorraine)

Kaiser, Georg 1878-1945 . . . . TCLC 9
See also CA 106; DLB 124

Kaletski, Alexander 1946- . . . . CLC 39
See also CA 118

Kalidasa fl. c. 400- . . . . CMLC 9

Kallman, Chester (Simon)
1921-1975 . . . . CLC 2
See also CA 45-48; 53-56; CANR 3

Kaminsky, Melvin 1926-
See Brooks, Mel
See also CA 65-68; CANR 16

Kaminsky, Stuart M(elvin) 1934- . . . CLC 59
See also CA 73-76; CANR 29

Kane, Paul
See Simon, Paul

Kane, Wilson
See Bloch, Robert (Albert)

Kanin, Garson 1912- . . . . CLC 22
See also AITN 1; CA 5-8R; CANR 7;
DLB 7

Kaniuk, Yoram 1930- . . . . CLC 19
See also CA 134

Kant, Immanuel 1724-1804 . . . . . . NCLC 27
See also DLB 94

Kantor, MacKinlay 1904-1977 . . . . . . CLC 7
See also CA 61-64; 73-76; DLB 9, 102

Kaplan, David Michael 1946- . . . . . . CLC 50

Kaplan, James 1951- . . . . CLC 59
See also CA 135

Karageorge, Michael
See Anderson, Poul (William)

Karamzin, Nikolai Mikhailovich
1766-1826 . . . . NCLC 3

Karapanou, Margarita 1946- . . . . CLC 13
See also CA 101

Karinthy, Frigyes 1887-1938 . . . . . . TCLC 47

Karl, Frederick R(obert) 1927- . . . . . CLC 34
See also CA 5-8R; CANR 3

Kastel, Warren
See Silverberg, Robert

Kataev, Evgeny Petrovich 1903-1942
See Petrov, Evgeny
See also CA 120

Kataphusin
See Ruskin, John

Katz, Steve 1935- . . . . CLC 47
See also CA 25-28R; CAAS 14; CANR 12;
DLBY 83

Kauffman, Janet 1945- . . . . CLC 42
See also CA 117; DLBY 86

Kaufman, Bob (Garnell)
1925-1986 . . . . CLC 49
See also BW; CA 41-44R; 118; CANR 22;
DLB 16, 41

Kingston, Maxine (Ting Ting) Hong
  1940- .... **CLC 12, 19, 58**
  See also AAYA 8; CA 69-72; CANR 13,
    38; DLBY 80; MTCW; SATA 53

Kinnell, Galway
  1927- .... **CLC 1, 2, 3, 5, 13, 29**
  See also CA 9-12R; CANR 10, 34; DLB 5;
    DLBY 87; MTCW

Kinsella, Thomas 1928- .... **CLC 4, 19**
  See also CA 17-20R; CANR 15; DLB 27;
    MTCW

Kinsella, W(illiam) P(atrick)
  1935- .... **CLC 27, 43**
  See also AAYA 7; CA 97-100; CAAS 7;
    CANR 21, 35; MTCW

Kipling, (Joseph) Rudyard
  1865-1936 .... **TCLC 8, 17; PC 3; SSC 5**
  See also CA 105; 120; CANR 33;
    CDBLB 1890-1914; DA; DLB 19, 34;
    MAICYA; MTCW; WLC; YABC 2

Kirkup, James 1918- .... **CLC 1**
  See also CA 1-4R; CAAS 4; CANR 2;
    DLB 27; SATA 12

Kirkwood, James 1930(?)-1989 ...... **CLC 9**
  See also AITN 2; CA 1-4R; 128; CANR 6,
    40

Kis, Danilo 1935-1989 .... **CLC 57**
  See also CA 109; 118; 129; MTCW

Kivi, Aleksis 1834-1872 .... **NCLC 30**

Kizer, Carolyn (Ashley) 1925-... **CLC 15, 39**
  See also CA 65-68; CAAS 5; CANR 24;
    DLB 5

Klabund 1890-1928.............. **TCLC 44**
  See also DLB 66

Klappert, Peter 1942-............. **CLC 57**
  See also CA 33-36R; DLB 5

Klein, A(braham) M(oses)
  1909-1972 .... **CLC 19**
  See also CA 101; 37-40R; DLB 68

Klein, Norma 1938-1989 .... **CLC 30**
  See also AAYA 2; CA 41-44R; 128;
    CANR 15, 37; CLR 2, 19; JRDA;
    MAICYA; SAAS 1; SATA 7, 57

Klein, T(heodore) E(ibon) D(onald)
  1947- .... **CLC 34**
  See also CA 119

Kleist, Heinrich von 1777-1811.... **NCLC 2**
  See also DLB 90

Klima, Ivan 1931-............... **CLC 56**
  See also CA 25-28R; CANR 17

Klimentov, Andrei Platonovich 1899-1951
  See Platonov, Andrei
  See also CA 108

Klinger, Friedrich Maximilian von
  1752-1831 .... **NCLC 1**
  See also DLB 94

Klopstock, Friedrich Gottlieb
  1724-1803 .... **NCLC 11**
  See also DLB 97

Knebel, Fletcher 1911-1993 .... **CLC 14**
  See also AITN 1; CA 1-4R; 140; CAAS 3;
    CANR 1, 36; SATA 36; SATA-Obit 75

Knickerbocker, Diedrich
  See Irving, Washington

Knight, Etheridge 1931-1991 .... **CLC 40**
  See also BLC 2; BW; CA 21-24R; 133;
    CANR 23; DLB 41

Knight, Sarah Kemble 1666-1727 ..... **LC 7**
  See also DLB 24

Knowles, John 1926- ...... **CLC 1, 4, 10, 26**
  See also AAYA 10; CA 17-20R; CANR 40;
    CDALB 1968-1988; DA; DLB 6; MTCW;
    SATA 8

Knox, Calvin M.
  See Silverberg, Robert

Knye, Cassandra
  See Disch, Thomas M(ichael)

Koch, C(hristopher) J(ohn) 1932- ... **CLC 42**
  See also CA 127

Koch, Christopher
  See Koch, C(hristopher) J(ohn)

Koch, Kenneth 1925- .... **CLC 5, 8, 44**
  See also CA 1-4R; CANR 6, 36; DLB 5;
    SATA 65

Kochanowski, Jan 1530-1584 .... **LC 10**

Kock, Charles Paul de
  1794-1871 .... **NCLC 16**

Koda Shigeyuki 1867-1947
  See Rohan, Koda
  See also CA 121

Koestler, Arthur
  1905-1983 .... **CLC 1, 3, 6, 8, 15, 33**
  See also CA 1-4R; 109; CANR 1, 33;
    CDBLB 1945-1960; DLBY 83; MTCW

Kogawa, Joy Nozomi 1935-........ **CLC 78**
  See also CA 101; CANR 19

Kohout, Pavel 1928-............. **CLC 13**
  See also CA 45-48; CANR 3

Koizumi, Yakumo
  See Hearn, (Patricio) Lafcadio (Tessima
    Carlos)

Kolmar, Gertrud 1894-1943....... **TCLC 40**

Konrad, George
  See Konrad, Gyoergy

Konrad, Gyoergy 1933- ...... **CLC 4, 10, 73**
  See also CA 85-88

Konwicki, Tadeusz 1926-..... **CLC 8, 28, 54**
  See also CA 101; CAAS 9; CANR 39;
    MTCW

Koontz, Dean R(ay) 1945-........ **CLC 78**
  See also AAYA 9; BEST 89:3, 90:2;
    CA 108; CANR 19, 36; MTCW

Kopit, Arthur (Lee) 1937- .... **CLC 1, 18, 33**
  See also AITN 1; CA 81-84; CABS 3;
    DLB 7; MTCW

Kops, Bernard 1926-.............. **CLC 4**
  See also CA 5-8R; DLB 13

Kornbluth, C(yril) M. 1923-1958.... **TCLC 8**
  See also CA 105; DLB 8

Korolenko, V. G.
  See Korolenko, Vladimir Galaktionovich

Korolenko, Vladimir
  See Korolenko, Vladimir Galaktionovich

Korolenko, Vladimir G.
  See Korolenko, Vladimir Galaktionovich

Korolenko, Vladimir Galaktionovich
  1853-1921 .... **TCLC 22**
  See also CA 121

Kosinski, Jerzy (Nikodem)
  1933-1991 .... **CLC 1, 2, 3, 6, 10, 15, 53,
                                          70**
  See also CA 17-20R; 134; CANR 9; DLB 2;
    DLBY 82; MTCW

Kostelanetz, Richard (Cory) 1940-.. **CLC 28**
  See also CA 13-16R; CAAS 8; CANR 38

Kostrowitzki, Wilhelm Apollinaris de
  1880-1918
  See Apollinaire, Guillaume
  See also CA 104

Kotlowitz, Robert 1924-............ **CLC 4**
  See also CA 33-36R; CANR 36

Kotzebue, August (Friedrich Ferdinand) von
  1761-1819 .... **NCLC 25**
  See also DLB 94

Kotzwinkle, William 1938- ... **CLC 5, 14, 35**
  See also CA 45-48; CANR 3; CLR 6;
    MAICYA; SATA 24, 70

Kozol, Jonathan 1936-............ **CLC 17**
  See also CA 61-64; CANR 16

Kozoll, Michael 1940(?)- .... **CLC 35**

Kramer, Kathryn 19(?)- .... **CLC 34**

Kramer, Larry 1935- .... **CLC 42**
  See also CA 124; 126

Krasicki, Ignacy 1735-1801 .... **NCLC 8**

Krasinski, Zygmunt 1812-1859 .... **NCLC 4**

Kraus, Karl 1874-1936........... **TCLC 5**
  See also CA 104; DLB 118

Kreve (Mickevicius), Vincas
  1882-1954 .... **TCLC 27**

Kristeva, Julia 1941- .... **CLC 77**

Kristofferson, Kris 1936-.......... **CLC 26**
  See also CA 104

Krizanc, John 1956-............... **CLC 57**

Krleza, Miroslav 1893-1981........ **CLC 8**
  See also CA 97-100; 105

Kroetsch, Robert 1927- ...... **CLC 5, 23, 57**
  See also CA 17-20R; CANR 8, 38; DLB 53;
    MTCW

Kroetz, Franz
  See Kroetz, Franz Xaver

Kroetz, Franz Xaver 1946- .... **CLC 41**
  See also CA 130

Kroker, Arthur 1945-............. **CLC 77**

Kropotkin, Peter (Aleksieevich)
  1842-1921 .... **TCLC 36**
  See also CA 119

Krotkov, Yuri 1917-.............. **CLC 19**
  See also CA 102

Krumb
  See Crumb, R(obert)

Krumgold, Joseph (Quincy)
  1908-1980 .... **CLC 12**
  See also CA 9-12R; 101; CANR 7;
    MAICYA; SATA 1, 23, 48

Krumwitz
  See Crumb, R(obert)

Krutch, Joseph Wood 1893-1970.... **CLC 24**
  See also CA 1-4R; 25-28R; CANR 4;
    DLB 63

Krutzch, Gus
  See Eliot, T(homas) S(tearns)

Krylov, Ivan Andreevich
1768(?)-1844 . . . . NCLC 1

Kubin, Alfred 1877-1959 . . . . TCLC 23
See also CA 112; DLB 81

Kubrick, Stanley 1928- . . . . CLC 16
See also CA 81-84; CANR 33; DLB 26

Kumin, Maxine (Winokur)
1925- . . . . CLC 5, 13, 28
See also AITN 2; CA 1-4R; CAAS 8;
CANR 1, 21; DLB 5; MTCW; SATA 12

Kundera, Milan
1929- . . . . CLC 4, 9, 19, 32, 68
See also AAYA 2; CA 85-88; CANR 19;
MTCW

Kunitz, Stanley (Jasspon)
1905- . . . . CLC 6, 11, 14
See also CA 41-44R; CANR 26; DLB 48;
MTCW

Kunze, Reiner 1933- . . . . CLC 10
See also CA 93-96; DLB 75

Kuprin, Aleksandr Ivanovich
1870-1938 . . . . TCLC 5
See also CA 104

Kureishi, Hanif 1954(?)- . . . . CLC 64
See also CA 139

Kurosawa, Akira 1910- . . . . CLC 16
See also CA 101

Kuttner, Henry 1915-1958 . . . . TCLC 10
See also CA 107; DLB 8

Kuzma, Greg 1944- . . . . CLC 7
See also CA 33-36R

Kuzmin, Mikhail 1872(?)-1936 . . . . TCLC 40

Kyd, Thomas 1558-1594 . . . . LC 22; DC 3
See also DLB 62

Kyprianos, Iossif
See Samarakis, Antonis

La Bruyere, Jean de 1645-1696 . . . . . . LC 17

Lacan, Jacques (Marie Emile)
1901-1981 . . . . CLC 75
See also CA 121; 104

Laclos, Pierre Ambroise Francois Choderlos
de 1741-1803 . . . . NCLC 4

La Colere, Francois
See Aragon, Louis

Lacolere, Francois
See Aragon, Louis

La Deshabilleuse
See Simenon, Georges (Jacques Christian)

Lady Gregory
See Gregory, Isabella Augusta (Persse)

Lady of Quality, A
See Bagnold, Enid

La Fayette, Marie (Madelaine Pioche de la Vergne Comtes 1634-1693 . . . . . . LC 2

Lafayette, Rene
See Hubbard, L(afayette) Ron(ald)

Laforgue, Jules 1860-1887 . . . . NCLC 5

Lagerkvist, Paer (Fabian)
1891-1974 . . . . CLC 7, 10, 13, 54
See also Lagerkvist, Par
See also CA 85-88; 49-52; MTCW

Lagerkvist, Par
See Lagerkvist, Paer (Fabian)
See also SSC 12

Lagerloef, Selma (Ottiliana Lovisa)
1858-1940 . . . . TCLC 4, 36
See also Lagerlof, Selma (Ottiliana Lovisa)
See also CA 108; CLR 7; SATA 15

Lagerlof, Selma (Ottiliana Lovisa)
See Lagerloef, Selma (Ottiliana Lovisa)
See also CLR 7; SATA 15

La Guma, (Justin) Alex(ander)
1925-1985 . . . . CLC 19
See also BW; CA 49-52; 118; CANR 25;
DLB 117; MTCW

Laidlaw, A. K.
See Grieve, C(hristopher) M(urray)

Lainez, Manuel Mujica
See Mujica Lainez, Manuel
See also HW

Lamartine, Alphonse (Marie Louis Prat) de
1790-1869 . . . . NCLC 11

Lamb, Charles 1775-1834 . . . . NCLC 10
See also CDBLB 1789-1832; DA; DLB 93,
107; SATA 17; WLC

Lamb, Lady Caroline 1785-1828 . . NCLC 38
See also DLB 116

Lamming, George (William)
1927- . . . . CLC 2, 4, 66
See also BLC 2; BW; CA 85-88; CANR 26;
DLB 125; MTCW

L'Amour, Louis (Dearborn)
1908-1988 . . . . CLC 25, 55
See also AITN 2; BEST 89:2; CA 1-4R;
125; CANR 3, 25, 40; DLBY 80; MTCW

Lampedusa, Giuseppe (Tomasi) di . . . TCLC 13
See also Tomasi di Lampedusa, Giuseppe

Lampman, Archibald 1861-1899 . . NCLC 25
See also DLB 92

Lancaster, Bruce 1896-1963 . . . . CLC 36
See also CA 9-10; CAP 1; SATA 9

Landau, Mark Alexandrovich
See Aldanov, Mark (Alexandrovich)

Landau-Aldanov, Mark Alexandrovich
See Aldanov, Mark (Alexandrovich)

Landis, John 1950- . . . . CLC 26
See also CA 112; 122

Landolfi, Tommaso 1908-1979 . . . CLC 11, 49
See also CA 127; 117

Landon, Letitia Elizabeth
1802-1838 . . . . NCLC 15
See also DLB 96

Landor, Walter Savage
1775-1864 . . . . NCLC 14
See also DLB 93, 107

Landwirth, Heinz 1927-
See Lind, Jakov
See also CA 9-12R; CANR 7

Lane, Patrick 1939- . . . . CLC 25
See also CA 97-100; DLB 53

Lang, Andrew 1844-1912 . . . . TCLC 16
See also CA 114; 137; DLB 98; MAICYA;
SATA 16

Lang, Fritz 1890-1976 . . . . CLC 20
See also CA 77-80; 69-72; CANR 30

Lange, John
See Crichton, (John) Michael

Langer, Elinor 1939- . . . . CLC 34
See also CA 121

Langland, William 1330(?)-1400(?) . . . LC 19
See also DA

Langstaff, Launcelot
See Irving, Washington

Lanier, Sidney 1842-1881 . . . . NCLC 6
See also DLB 64; MAICYA; SATA 18

Lanyer, Aemilia 1569-1645 . . . . LC 10

Lao Tzu . . . . CMLC 7

Lapine, James (Elliot) 1949- . . . . CLC 39
See also CA 123; 130

Larbaud, Valery (Nicolas)
1881-1957 . . . . TCLC 9
See also CA 106

Lardner, Ring
See Lardner, Ring(gold) W(ilmer)

Lardner, Ring W., Jr.
See Lardner, Ring(gold) W(ilmer)

Lardner, Ring(gold) W(ilmer)
1885-1933 . . . . TCLC 2, 14
See also CA 104; 131; CDALB 1917-1929;
DLB 11, 25, 86; MTCW

Laredo, Betty
See Codrescu, Andrei

Larkin, Maia
See Wojciechowska, Maia (Teresa)

Larkin, Philip (Arthur)
1922-1985 . . . . CLC 3, 5, 8, 9, 13, 18, 33,
39, 64
See also CA 5-8R; 117; CANR 24;
CDBLB 1960 to Present; DLB 27;
MTCW

Larra (y Sanchez de Castro), Mariano Jose de
1809-1837 . . . . NCLC 17

Larsen, Eric 1941- . . . . CLC 55
See also CA 132

Larsen, Nella 1891-1964 . . . . CLC 37
See also BLC 2; BW; CA 125; DLB 51

Larson, Charles R(aymond) 1938- . . . CLC 31
See also CA 53-56; CANR 4

Latham, Jean Lee 1902- . . . . CLC 12
See also AITN 1; CA 5-8R; CANR 7;
MAICYA; SATA 2, 68

Latham, Mavis
See Clark, Mavis Thorpe

Lathen, Emma . . . . CLC 2
See also Hennissart, Martha; Latsis, Mary
J(ane)

Lathrop, Francis
See Leiber, Fritz (Reuter, Jr.)

Latsis, Mary J(ane)
See Lathen, Emma
See also CA 85-88

Lattimore, Richmond (Alexander)
1906-1984 . . . . CLC 3
See also CA 1-4R; 112; CANR 1

Laughlin, James 1914- . . . . CLC 49
See also CA 21-24R; CANR 9; DLB 48

Laurence, (Jean) Margaret (Wemyss)
1926-1987 .. **CLC 3, 6, 13, 50, 62; SSC 7**
See also CA 5-8R; 121; CANR 33; DLB 53;
MTCW; SATA 50

Laurent, Antoine 1952- .... **CLC 50**

Lauscher, Hermann
See Hesse, Hermann

Lautreamont, Comte de
1846-1870 .... **NCLC 12**

Laverty, Donald
See Blish, James (Benjamin)

Lavin, Mary 1912- ...... **CLC 4, 18; SSC 4**
See also CA 9-12R; CANR 33; DLB 15;
MTCW

Lavond, Paul Dennis
See Kornbluth, C(yril) M.; Pohl, Frederik

Lawler, Raymond Evenor 1922- .... **CLC 58**
See also CA 103

Lawrence, D(avid) H(erbert Richards)
1885-1930 ...... **TCLC 2, 9, 16, 33, 48;**
SSC 4
See also CA 104; 121; CDBLB 1914-1945;
DA; DLB 10, 19, 36, 98; MTCW; WLC

Lawrence, T(homas) E(dward)
1888-1935 .... **TCLC 18**
See also Dale, Colin
See also CA 115

Lawrence Of Arabia
See Lawrence, T(homas) E(dward)

Lawson, Henry (Archibald Hertzberg)
1867-1922 .... **TCLC 27**
See also CA 120

Lawton, Dennis
See Faust, Frederick (Schiller)

Laxness, Halldor .... **CLC 25**
See also Gudjonsson, Halldor Kiljan

Layamon fl. c. 1200- .... **CMLC 10**

Laye, Camara 1928-1980 .... **CLC 4, 38**
See also BLC 2; BW; CA 85-88; 97-100;
CANR 25; MTCW

Layton, Irving (Peter) 1912- ..... **CLC 2, 15**
See also CA 1-4R; CANR 2, 33; DLB 88;
MTCW

Lazarus, Emma 1849-1887 .... **NCLC 8**

Lazarus, Felix
See Cable, George Washington

Lazarus, Henry
See Slavitt, David R(ytman)

Lea, Joan
See Neufeld, John (Arthur)

Leacock, Stephen (Butler)
1869-1944 .... **TCLC 2**
See also CA 104; 141; DLB 92

Lear, Edward 1812-1888 .... **NCLC 3**
See also CLR 1; DLB 32; MAICYA;
SATA 18

Lear, Norman (Milton) 1922- ...... **CLC 12**
See also CA 73-76

Leavis, F(rank) R(aymond)
1895-1978 .... **CLC 24**
See also CA 21-24R; 77-80; MTCW

Leavitt, David 1961- .... **CLC 34**
See also CA 116; 122; DLB 130

Leblanc, Maurice (Marie Emile)
1864-1941 .... **TCLC 49**
See also CA 110

Lebowitz, Fran(ces Ann)
1951(?)- .... **CLC 11, 36**
See also CA 81-84; CANR 14; MTCW

le Carre, John .... **CLC 3, 5, 9, 15, 28**
See also Cornwell, David (John Moore)
See also BEST 89:4; CDBLB 1960 to
Present; DLB 87

Le Clezio, J(ean) M(arie) G(ustave)
1940- .... **CLC 31**
See also CA 116; 128; DLB 83

Leconte de Lisle, Charles-Marie-Rene
1818-1894 .... **NCLC 29**

Le Coq, Monsieur
See Simenon, Georges (Jacques Christian)

Leduc, Violette 1907-1972 .... **CLC 22**
See also CA 13-14; 33-36R; CAP 1

Ledwidge, Francis 1887(?)-1917 ... **TCLC 23**
See also CA 123; DLB 20

Lee, Andrea 1953- .... **CLC 36**
See also BLC 2; BW; CA 125

Lee, Andrew
See Auchincloss, Louis (Stanton)

Lee, Don L. .... **CLC 2**
See also Madhubuti, Haki R.

Lee, George W(ashington)
1894-1976 .... **CLC 52**
See also BLC 2; BW; CA 125; DLB 51

Lee, (Nelle) Harper 1926- ...... **CLC 12, 60**
See also CA 13-16R; CDALB 1941-1968;
DA; DLB 6; MTCW; SATA 11; WLC

Lee, Julian
See Latham, Jean Lee

Lee, Larry
See Lee, Lawrence

Lee, Lawrence 1941-1990 .... **CLC 34**
See also CA 131

Lee, Manfred B(ennington)
1905-1971 .... **CLC 11**
See also Queen, Ellery
See also CA 1-4R; 29-32R; CANR 2

Lee, Stan 1922- .... **CLC 17**
See also AAYA 5; CA 108; 111

Lee, Tanith 1947- .... **CLC 46**
See also CA 37-40R; SATA 8

Lee, Vernon .... **TCLC 5**
See also Paget, Violet
See also DLB 57

Lee, William
See Burroughs, William S(eward)

Lee, Willy
See Burroughs, William S(eward)

Lee-Hamilton, Eugene (Jacob)
1845-1907 .... **TCLC 22**
See also CA 117

Leet, Judith 1935- .... **CLC 11**

Le Fanu, Joseph Sheridan
1814-1873 .... **NCLC 9**
See also DLB 21, 70

Leffland, Ella 1931- .... **CLC 19**
See also CA 29-32R; CANR 35; DLBY 84;
SATA 65

Leger, (Marie-Rene) Alexis Saint-Leger
1887-1975 .... **CLC 11**
See also Perse, St.-John
See also CA 13-16R; 61-64; MTCW

Leger, Saintleger
See Leger, (Marie-Rene) Alexis Saint-Leger

Le Guin, Ursula K(roeber)
1929- .... **CLC 8, 13, 22, 45, 71; SSC 12**
See also AAYA 9; AITN 1; CA 21-24R;
CANR 9, 32; CDALB 1968-1988; CLR 3,
28; DLB 8, 52; JRDA; MAICYA;
MTCW; SATA 4, 52

Lehmann, Rosamond (Nina)
1901-1990 .... **CLC 5**
See also CA 77-80; 131; CANR 8; DLB 15

Leiber, Fritz (Reuter, Jr.)
1910-1992 .... **CLC 25**
See also CA 45-48; 139; CANR 2, 40;
DLB 8; MTCW; SATA 45;
SATA-Obit 73

Leimbach, Martha 1963-
See Leimbach, Marti
See also CA 130

Leimbach, Marti .... **CLC 65**
See also Leimbach, Martha

Leino, Eino .... **TCLC 24**
See also Loennbohm, Armas Eino Leopold

Leiris, Michel (Julien) 1901-1990 ... **CLC 61**
See also CA 119; 128; 132

Leithauser, Brad 1953- .... **CLC 27**
See also CA 107; CANR 27; DLB 120

Lelchuk, Alan 1938- .... **CLC 5**
See also CA 45-48; CANR 1

Lem, Stanislaw 1921- .... **CLC 8, 15, 40**
See also CA 105; CAAS 1; CANR 32;
MTCW

Lemann, Nancy 1956- .... **CLC 39**
See also CA 118; 136

Lemonnier, (Antoine Louis) Camille
1844-1913 .... **TCLC 22**
See also CA 121

Lenau, Nikolaus 1802-1850 ...... **NCLC 16**

L'Engle, Madeleine (Camp Franklin)
1918- .... **CLC 12**
See also AAYA 1; AITN 2; CA 1-4R;
CANR 3, 21, 39; CLR 1, 14; DLB 52;
JRDA; MAICYA; MTCW; SAAS 15;
SATA 1, 27, 75

Lengyel, Jozsef 1896-1975 .... **CLC 7**
See also CA 85-88; 57-60

Lennon, John (Ono)
1940-1980 .... **CLC 12, 35**
See also CA 102

Lennox, Charlotte Ramsay
1729(?)-1804 .... **NCLC 23**
See also DLB 39

Lentricchia, Frank (Jr.) 1940- ...... **CLC 34**
See also CA 25-28R; CANR 19

Lenz, Siegfried 1926- .... **CLC 27**
See also CA 89-92; DLB 75

Leonard, Elmore (John, Jr.)
1925- .... **CLC 28, 34, 71**
See also AITN 1; BEST 89:1, 90:4;
CA 81-84; CANR 12, 28; MTCW

Malraux, (Georges-)Andre
1901-1976 ..... **CLC 1, 4, 9, 13, 15, 57**
See also CA 21-22; 69-72; CANR 34;
CAP 2; DLB 72; MTCW

Malzberg, Barry N(athaniel) 1939-... **CLC 7**
See also CA 61-64; CAAS 4; CANR 16;
DLB 8

Mamet, David (Alan)
1947- .... **CLC 9, 15, 34, 46**
See also AAYA 3; CA 81-84; CABS 3;
CANR 15, 41; DLB 7; MTCW

Mamoulian, Rouben (Zachary)
1897-1987 .... **CLC 16**
See also CA 25-28R; 124

Mandelstam, Osip (Emilievich)
1891(?)-1938(?) .... **TCLC 2, 6**
See also CA 104

Mander, (Mary) Jane 1877-1949... **TCLC 31**

Mandiargues, Andre Pieyre de...... CLC 41
See also Pieyre de Mandiargues, Andre
See also DLB 83

Mandrake, Ethel Belle
See Thurman, Wallace (Henry)

Mangan, James Clarence
1803-1849 .... **NCLC 27**

Maniere, J.-E.
See Giraudoux, (Hippolyte) Jean

Manley, (Mary) Delariviere
1672(?)-1724 .... **LC 1**
See also DLB 39, 80

Mann, Abel
See Creasey, John

Mann, (Luiz) Heinrich 1871-1950... **TCLC 9**
See also CA 106; DLB 66

Mann, (Paul) Thomas
1875-1955 .... **TCLC 2, 8, 14, 21, 35, 44;**
                        SSC 5
See also CA 104; 128; DA; DLB 66;
MTCW; WLC

Manning, David
See Faust, Frederick (Schiller)

Manning, Frederic 1887(?)-1935... **TCLC 25**
See also CA 124

Manning, Olivia 1915-1980 ...... **CLC 5, 19**
See also CA 5-8R; 101; CANR 29; MTCW

Mano, D. Keith 1942- .... **CLC 2, 10**
See also CA 25-28R; CAAS 6; CANR 26;
DLB 6

Mansfield, Katherine... TCLC 2, 8, 39; SSC 9
See also Beauchamp, Kathleen Mansfield
See also WLC

Manso, Peter 1940- .... **CLC 39**
See also CA 29-32R

Mantecon, Juan Jimenez
See Jimenez (Mantecon), Juan Ramon

Manton, Peter
See Creasey, John

Man Without a Spleen, A
See Chekhov, Anton (Pavlovich)

Manzoni, Alessandro 1785-1873.. **NCLC 29**

Mapu, Abraham (ben Jekutiel)
1808-1867 .... **NCLC 18**

Mara, Sally
See Queneau, Raymond

Marat, Jean Paul 1743-1793....... **LC 10**

Marcel, Gabriel Honore
1889-1973 .... **CLC 15**
See also CA 102; 45-48; MTCW

Marchbanks, Samuel
See Davies, (William) Robertson

Marchi, Giacomo
See Bassani, Giorgio

Margulies, Donald................. CLC 76

Marie de France c. 12th cent. -.... **CMLC 8**

Marie de l'Incarnation 1599-1672.... **LC 10**

Mariner, Scott
See Pohl, Frederik

Marinetti, Filippo Tommaso
1876-1944 .... **TCLC 10**
See also CA 107; DLB 114

Marivaux, Pierre Carlet de Chamblain de
1688-1763 .... **LC 4**

Markandaya, Kamala .... CLC 8, 38
See also Taylor, Kamala (Purnaiya)

Markfield, Wallace 1926-.......... **CLC 8**
See also CA 69-72; CAAS 3; DLB 2, 28

Markham, Edwin 1852-1940 ..... **TCLC 47**
See also DLB 54

Markham, Robert
See Amis, Kingsley (William)

Marks, J
See Highwater, Jamake (Mamake)

Marks-Highwater, J
See Highwater, Jamake (Mamake)

Markson, David M(errill) 1927-.... **CLC 67**
See also CA 49-52; CANR 1

Marley, Bob...................... CLC 17
See also Marley, Robert Nesta

Marley, Robert Nesta 1945-1981
See Marley, Bob
See also CA 107; 103

Marlowe, Christopher
1564-1593 .... **LC 22; DC 1**
See also CDBLB Before 1660; DA; DLB 62;
WLC

Marmontel, Jean-Francois
1723-1799 .... **LC 2**

Marquand, John P(hillips)
1893-1960 .... **CLC 2, 10**
See also CA 85-88; DLB 9, 102

Marquez, Gabriel (Jose) Garcia...... CLC 68
See also Garcia Marquez, Gabriel (Jose)

Marquis, Don(ald Robert Perry)
1878-1937 .... **TCLC 7**
See also CA 104; DLB 11, 25

Marric, J. J.
See Creasey, John

Marrow, Bernard
See Moore, Brian

Marryat, Frederick 1792-1848 .... **NCLC 3**
See also DLB 21

Marsden, James
See Creasey, John

Marsh, (Edith) Ngaio
1899-1982 .... **CLC 7, 53**
See also CA 9-12R; CANR 6; DLB 77;
MTCW

Marshall, Garry 1934-........... **CLC 17**
See also AAYA 3; CA 111; SATA 60

Marshall, Paule 1929-.. **CLC 27, 72; SSC 3**
See also BLC 3; BW; CA 77-80; CANR 25;
DLB 33; MTCW

Marsten, Richard
See Hunter, Evan

Martha, Henry
See Harris, Mark

Martin, Ken
See Hubbard, L(afayette) Ron(ald)

Martin, Richard
See Creasey, John

Martin, Steve 1945- .... **CLC 30**
See also CA 97-100; CANR 30; MTCW

Martin, Violet Florence
1862-1915 .... **TCLC 51**

Martin, Webber
See Silverberg, Robert

Martin du Gard, Roger
1881-1958 .... **TCLC 24**
See also CA 118; DLB 65

Martineau, Harriet 1802-1876.... **NCLC 26**
See also DLB 21, 55; YABC 2

Martines, Julia
See O'Faolain, Julia

Martinez, Jacinto Benavente y
See Benavente (y Martinez), Jacinto

Martinez Ruiz, Jose 1873-1967
See Azorin; Ruiz, Jose Martinez
See also CA 93-96; HW

Martinez Sierra, Gregorio
1881-1947 .... **TCLC 6**
See also CA 115

Martinez Sierra, Maria (de la O'LeJarraga)
1874-1974 .... **TCLC 6**
See also CA 115

Martinsen, Martin
See Follett, Ken(neth Martin)

Martinson, Harry (Edmund)
1904-1978 .... **CLC 14**
See also CA 77-80; CANR 34

Marut, Ret
See Traven, B.

Marut, Robert
See Traven, B.

Marvell, Andrew 1621-1678......... **LC 4**
See also CDBLB 1660-1789; DA; DLB 131;
WLC

Marx, Karl (Heinrich)
1818-1883 .... **NCLC 17**
See also DLB 129

Masaoka Shiki.................... TCLC 18
See also Masaoka Tsunenori

Masaoka Tsunenori 1867-1902
See Masaoka Shiki
See also CA 117

Masefield, John (Edward)
1878-1967 .... **CLC 11, 47**
See also CA 19-20; 25-28R; CANR 33;
CAP 2; CDBLB 1890-1914; DLB 10;
MTCW; SATA 19

Maso, Carole 19(?)- .... **CLC 44**

Mason, Bobbie Ann
1940- .... **CLC 28, 43; SSC 4**
See also AAYA 5; CA 53-56; CANR 11,
31; DLBY 87; MTCW

Mason, Ernst
See Pohl, Frederik

Mason, Lee W.
See Malzberg, Barry N(athaniel)

Mason, Nick 1945- .... **CLC 35**
See also Pink Floyd

Mason, Tally
See Derleth, August (William)

Mass, William
See Gibson, William

Masters, Edgar Lee
1868-1950 .... **TCLC 2, 25; PC 1**
See also CA 104; 133; CDALB 1865-1917;
DA; DLB 54; MTCW

Masters, Hilary 1928- .... **CLC 48**
See also CA 25-28R; CANR 13

Mastrosimone, William 19(?)- ...... **CLC 36**

Mathe, Albert
See Camus, Albert

Matheson, Richard Burton 1926- ... **CLC 37**
See also CA 97-100; DLB 8, 44

Mathews, Harry 1930- .... **CLC 6, 52**
See also CA 21-24R; CAAS 6; CANR 18,
40

Mathias, Roland (Glyn) 1915- ...... **CLC 45**
See also CA 97-100; CANR 19, 41; DLB 27

Matsuo Basho 1644-1694 .... **PC 3**

Mattheson, Rodney
See Creasey, John

Matthews, Greg 1949- .... **CLC 45**
See also CA 135

Matthews, William 1942- .... **CLC 40**
See also CA 29-32R; CAAS 18; CANR 12;
DLB 5

Matthias, John (Edward) 1941- ...... **CLC 9**
See also CA 33-36R

Matthiessen, Peter
1927- .... **CLC 5, 7, 11, 32, 64**
See also AAYA 6; BEST 90:4; CA 9-12R;
CANR 21; DLB 6; MTCW; SATA 27

Maturin, Charles Robert
1780(?)-1824 .... **NCLC 6**

Matute (Ausejo), Ana Maria
1925- .... **CLC 11**
See also CA 89-92; MTCW

Maugham, W. S.
See Maugham, W(illiam) Somerset

Maugham, W(illiam) Somerset
1874-1965 .... **CLC 1, 11, 15, 67; SSC 8**
See also CA 5-8R; 25-28R; CANR 40;
CDBLB 1914-1945; DA; DLB 10, 36, 77,
100; MTCW; SATA 54; WLC

Maugham, William Somerset
See Maugham, W(illiam) Somerset

Maupassant, (Henri Rene Albert) Guy de
1850-1893 .... **NCLC 1, 42; SSC 1**
See also DA; DLB 123; WLC

Maurhut, Richard
See Traven, B.

Mauriac, Claude 1914- .... **CLC 9**
See also CA 89-92; DLB 83

Mauriac, Francois (Charles)
1885-1970 .... **CLC 4, 9, 56**
See also CA 25-28; CAP 2; DLB 65;
MTCW

Mavor, Osborne Henry 1888-1951
See Bridie, James
See also CA 104

Maxwell, William (Keepers, Jr.)
1908- .... **CLC 19**
See also CA 93-96; DLBY 80

May, Elaine 1932- .... **CLC 16**
See also CA 124; DLB 44

Mayakovski, Vladimir (Vladimirovich)
1893-1930 .... **TCLC 4, 18**
See also CA 104

Mayhew, Henry 1812-1887 ...... **NCLC 31**
See also DLB 18, 55

Maynard, Joyce 1953- .... **CLC 23**
See also CA 111; 129

Mayne, William (James Carter)
1928- .... **CLC 12**
See also CA 9-12R; CANR 37; CLR 25;
JRDA; MAICYA; SAAS 11; SATA 6, 68

Mayo, Jim
See L'Amour, Louis (Dearborn)

Maysles, Albert 1926- .... **CLC 16**
See also CA 29-32R

Maysles, David 1932- .... **CLC 16**

Mazer, Norma Fox 1931- ...... **CLC 26**
See also AAYA 5; CA 69-72; CANR 12,
32; CLR 23; JRDA; MAICYA; SAAS 1;
SATA 24, 67

Mazzini, Guiseppe 1805-1872 .... **NCLC 34**

McAuley, James Phillip
1917-1976 .... **CLC 45**
See also CA 97-100

McBain, Ed
See Hunter, Evan

McBrien, William Augustine
1930- .... **CLC 44**
See also CA 107

McCaffrey, Anne (Inez) 1926- ...... **CLC 17**
See also AAYA 6; AITN 2; BEST 89:2;
CA 25-28R; CANR 15, 35; DLB 8;
JRDA; MAICYA; MTCW; SAAS 11;
SATA 8, 70

McCann, Arthur
See Campbell, John W(ood, Jr.)

McCann, Edson
See Pohl, Frederik

McCarthy, Cormac, Jr. .... **CLC 4, 57**
See also McCarthy, Charles, Jr.
See also DLB 6

McCarthy, Mary (Therese)
1912-1989 ... **CLC 1, 3, 5, 14, 24, 39, 59**
See also CA 5-8R; 129; CANR 16; DLB 2;
DLBY 81; MTCW

McCartney, (James) Paul
1942- .... **CLC 12, 35**

McCauley, Stephen (D.) 1955- ..... **CLC 50**
See also CA 141

McClure, Michael (Thomas)
1932- .... **CLC 6, 10**
See also CA 21-24R; CANR 17; DLB 16

McCorkle, Jill (Collins) 1958- ...... **CLC 51**
See also CA 121; DLBY 87

McCourt, James 1941- .... **CLC 5**
See also CA 57-60

McCoy, Horace (Stanley)
1897-1955 .... **TCLC 28**
See also CA 108; DLB 9

McCrae, John 1872-1918 .... **TCLC 12**
See also CA 109; DLB 92

McCreigh, James
See Pohl, Frederik

McCullers, (Lula) Carson (Smith)
1917-1967 .. **CLC 1, 4, 10, 12, 48; SSC 9**
See also CA 5-8R; 25-28R; CABS 1, 3;
CANR 18; CDALB 1941-1968; DA;
DLB 2, 7; MTCW; SATA 27; WLC

McCulloch, John Tyler
See Burroughs, Edgar Rice

McCullough, Colleen 1938(?)- ...... **CLC 27**
See also CA 81-84; CANR 17; MTCW

McElroy, Joseph 1930- .... **CLC 5, 47**
See also CA 17-20R

McEwan, Ian (Russell) 1948- ... **CLC 13, 66**
See also BEST 90:4; CA 61-64; CANR 14,
41; DLB 14; MTCW

McFadden, David 1940- .... **CLC 48**
See also CA 104; DLB 60

McFarland, Dennis 1950- .... **CLC 65**

McGahern, John 1934- .... **CLC 5, 9, 48**
See also CA 17-20R; CANR 29; DLB 14;
MTCW

McGinley, Patrick (Anthony)
1937- .... **CLC 41**
See also CA 120; 127

McGinley, Phyllis 1905-1978 ...... **CLC 14**
See also CA 9-12R; 77-80; CANR 19;
DLB 11, 48; SATA 2, 24, 44

McGinniss, Joe 1942- .... **CLC 32**
See also AITN 2; BEST 89:2; CA 25-28R;
CANR 26

McGivern, Maureen Daly
See Daly, Maureen

McGrath, Patrick 1950- .... **CLC 55**
See also CA 136

McGrath, Thomas (Matthew)
1916-1990 .... **CLC 28, 59**
See also CA 9-12R; 132; CANR 6, 33;
MTCW; SATA 41; SATA-Obit 66

McGuane, Thomas (Francis III)
1939- .... **CLC 3, 7, 18, 45**
See also AITN 2; CA 49-52; CANR 5, 24;
DLB 2; DLBY 80; MTCW

McGuckian, Medbh 1950- .... **CLC 48**
See also DLB 40

McHale, Tom 1942(?)-1982 .... **CLC 3, 5**
See also AITN 1; CA 77-80; 106

McIlvanney, William 1936- .... **CLC 42**
See also CA 25-28R; DLB 14

McIlwraith, Maureen Mollie Hunter
See Hunter, Mollie
See also SATA 2

Morgan, Edwin (George) 1920-..... **CLC 31**
See also CA 5-8R; CANR 3; DLB 27

Morgan, (George) Frederick
1922-...................... **CLC 23**
See also CA 17-20R; CANR 21

Morgan, Harriet
See Mencken, H(enry) L(ouis)

Morgan, Jane
See Cooper, James Fenimore

Morgan, Janet 1945- .... **CLC 39**
See also CA 65-68

Morgan, Lady 1776(?)-1859...... **NCLC 29**
See also DLB 116

Morgan, Robin 1941-............. **CLC 2**
See also CA 69-72; CANR 29; MTCW

Morgan, Scott
See Kuttner, Henry

Morgan, Seth 1949(?)-1990 .... **CLC 65**
See also CA 132

Morgenstern, Christian
1871-1914 .... **TCLC 8**
See also CA 105

Morgenstern, S.
See Goldman, William (W.)

Moricz, Zsigmond 1879-1942 ..... **TCLC 33**

Morike, Eduard (Friedrich)
1804-1875 .... **NCLC 10**
See also DLB 133

Mori Ogai .... **TCLC 14**
See also Mori Rintaro

Mori Rintaro 1862-1922
See Mori Ogai
See also CA 110

Moritz, Karl Philipp 1756-1793 ...... **LC 2**
See also DLB 94

Morland, Peter Henry
See Faust, Frederick (Schiller)

Morren, Theophil
See Hofmannsthal, Hugo von

Morris, Bill 1952-............... **CLC 76**

Morris, Julian
See West, Morris L(anglo)

Morris, Steveland Judkins 1950(?)-
See Wonder, Stevie
See also CA 111

Morris, William 1834-1896 .... **NCLC 4**
See also CDBLB 1832-1890; DLB 18, 35, 57

Morris, Wright 1910-... **CLC 1, 3, 7, 18, 37**
See also CA 9-12R; CANR 21; DLB 2;
DLBY 81; MTCW

Morrison, Chloe Anthony Wofford
See Morrison, Toni

Morrison, James Douglas 1943-1971
See Morrison, Jim
See also CA 73-76; CANR 40

Morrison, Jim .... **CLC 17**
See also Morrison, James Douglas

Morrison, Toni 1931-..... **CLC 4, 10, 22, 55**
See also AAYA 1; BLC 3; BW; CA 29-32R;
CANR 27, 42; CDALB 1968-1988; DA;
DLB 6, 33; DLBY 81; MTCW; SATA 57

Morrison, Van 1945- .... **CLC 21**
See also CA 116

Mortimer, John (Clifford)
1923-................... **CLC 28, 43**
See also CA 13-16R; CANR 21;
CDBLB 1960 to Present; DLB 13;
MTCW

Mortimer, Penelope (Ruth) 1918-.... **CLC 5**
See also CA 57-60

Morton, Anthony
See Creasey, John

Mosher, Howard Frank 1943-...... **CLC 62**
See also CA 139

Mosley, Nicholas 1923-........ **CLC 43, 70**
See also CA 69-72; CANR 41; DLB 14

Moss, Howard
1922-1987 .... **CLC 7, 14, 45, 50**
See also CA 1-4R; 123; CANR 1; DLB 5

Mossgiel, Rab
See Burns, Robert

Motion, Andrew 1952-............ **CLC 47**
See also DLB 40

Motley, Willard (Francis)
1912-1965 .... **CLC 18**
See also BW; CA 117; 106; DLB 76

Mott, Michael (Charles Alston)
1930-..................... **CLC 15, 34**
See also CA 5-8R; CAAS 7; CANR 7, 29

Mowat, Farley (McGill) 1921- ..... **CLC 26**
See also AAYA 1; CA 1-4R; CANR 4, 24,
42; CLR 20; DLB 68; JRDA; MAICYA;
MTCW; SATA 3, 55

Moyers, Bill 1934-............... **CLC 74**
See also AITN 2; CA 61-64; CANR 31

Mphahlele, Es'kia
See Mphahlele, Ezekiel
See also DLB 125

Mphahlele, Ezekiel 1919-......... **CLC 25**
See also Mphahlele, Es'kia
See also BLC 3; BW; CA 81-84; CANR 26

Mqhayi, S(amuel) E(dward) K(rune Loliwe)
1875-1945 .... **TCLC 25**
See also BLC 3

Mr. Martin
See Burroughs, William S(eward)

Mrozek, Slawomir 1930-........ **CLC 3, 13**
See also CA 13-16R; CAAS 10; CANR 29;
MTCW

Mrs. Belloc-Lowndes
See Lowndes, Marie Adelaide (Belloc)

Mtwa, Percy (?)-................. **CLC 47**

Mueller, Lisel 1924-........... **CLC 13, 51**
See also CA 93-96; DLB 105

Muir, Edwin 1887-1959 .... **TCLC 2**
See also CA 104; DLB 20, 100

Muir, John 1838-1914 .... **TCLC 28**

Mujica Lainez, Manuel
1910-1984 .... **CLC 31**
See also Lainez, Manuel Mujica
See also CA 81-84; 112; CANR 32; HW

Mukherjee, Bharati 1940-........ **CLC 53**
See also BEST 89:2; CA 107; DLB 60;
MTCW

Muldoon, Paul 1951-.......... **CLC 32, 72**
See also CA 113; 129; DLB 40

Mulisch, Harry 1927-............. **CLC 42**
See also CA 9-12R; CANR 6, 26

Mull, Martin 1943-............... **CLC 17**
See also CA 105

Mulock, Dinah Maria
See Craik, Dinah Maria (Mulock)

Munford, Robert 1737(?)-1783 .... **LC 5**
See also DLB 31

Mungo, Raymond 1946-........... **CLC 72**
See also CA 49-52; CANR 2

Munro, Alice
1931-........ **CLC 6, 10, 19, 50; SSC 3**
See also AITN 2; CA 33-36R; CANR 33;
DLB 53; MTCW; SATA 29

Munro, H(ector) H(ugh) 1870-1916
See Saki
See also CA 104; 130; CDBLB 1890-1914;
DA; DLB 34; MTCW; WLC

Murasaki, Lady .... **CMLC 1**

Murdoch, (Jean) Iris
1919-...... **CLC 1, 2, 3, 4, 6, 8, 11, 15,**
22, 31, 51
See also CA 13-16R; CANR 8;
CDBLB 1960 to Present; DLB 14;
MTCW

Murphy, Richard 1927-........... **CLC 41**
See also CA 29-32R; DLB 40

Murphy, Sylvia 1937-............. **CLC 34**
See also CA 121

Murphy, Thomas (Bernard) 1935-... **CLC 51**
See also CA 101

Murray, Albert L. 1916- .... **CLC 73**
See also BW; CA 49-52; CANR 26; DLB 38

Murray, Les(lie) A(llan) 1938- ..... **CLC 40**
See also CA 21-24R; CANR 11, 27

Murry, J. Middleton
See Murry, John Middleton

Murry, John Middleton
1889-1957 .... **TCLC 16**
See also CA 118

Musgrave, Susan 1951- .... **CLC 13, 54**
See also CA 69-72

Musil, Robert (Edler von)
1880-1942 .... **TCLC 12**
See also CA 109; DLB 81, 124

Musset, (Louis Charles) Alfred de
1810-1857 .... **NCLC 7**

My Brother's Brother
See Chekhov, Anton (Pavlovich)

Myers, Walter Dean 1937- .... **CLC 35**
See also AAYA 4; BLC 3; BW; CA 33-36R;
CANR 20, 42; CLR 4, 16; DLB 33;
JRDA; MAICYA; SAAS 2; SATA 27, 41,
70, 71

Myers, Walter M.
See Myers, Walter Dean

Myles, Symon
See Follett, Ken(neth Martin)

Nabokov, Vladimir (Vladimirovich)
1899-1977 ..... **CLC 1, 2, 3, 6, 8, 11, 15,**
23, 44, 46, 64; SSC 11
See also CA 5-8R; 69-72; CANR 20;
CDALB 1941-1968; DA; DLB 2;
DLBD 3; DLBY 80, 91; MTCW; WLC

Norton, Andre 1912- .... **CLC 12**
See also Norton, Alice Mary
See also CA 1-4R; CANR 2, 31; DLB 8, 52;
JRDA; MTCW

Norway, Nevil Shute 1899-1960
See Shute, Nevil
See also CA 102; 93-96

Norwid, Cyprian Kamil
1821-1883 .... **NCLC 17**

Nosille, Nabrah
See Ellison, Harlan

Nossack, Hans Erich 1901-1978 ..... **CLC 6**
See also CA 93-96; 85-88; DLB 69

Nosu, Chuji
See Ozu, Yasujiro

Nova, Craig 1945-............. **CLC 7, 31**
See also CA 45-48; CANR 2

Novak, Joseph
See Kosinski, Jerzy (Nikodem)

Novalis 1772-1801 .... **NCLC 13**
See also DLB 90

Nowlan, Alden (Albert) 1933-1983 .. **CLC 15**
See also CA 9-12R; CANR 5; DLB 53

Noyes, Alfred 1880-1958 .... **TCLC 7**
See also CA 104; DLB 20

Nunn, Kem 19(?)- .... **CLC 34**

Nye, Robert 1939- .... **CLC 13, 42**
See also CA 33-36R; CANR 29; DLB 14;
MTCW; SATA 6

Nyro, Laura 1947- .... **CLC 17**

Oates, Joyce Carol
1938- ...... **CLC 1, 2, 3, 6, 9, 11, 15, 19,
33, 52; SSC 6**
See also AITN 1; BEST 89:2; CA 5-8R;
CANR 25; CDALB 1968-1988; DA;
DLB 2, 5, 130; DLBY 81; MTCW; WLC

O'Brien, E. G.
See Clarke, Arthur C(harles)

O'Brien, Edna
1936- ... **CLC 3, 5, 8, 13, 36, 65; SSC 10**
See also CA 1-4R; CANR 6, 41;
CDBLB 1960 to Present; DLB 14;
MTCW

O'Brien, Fitz-James 1828-1862... **NCLC 21**
See also DLB 74

O'Brien, Flann....... **CLC 1, 4, 5, 7, 10, 47**
See also O Nuallain, Brian

O'Brien, Richard 1942- .... **CLC 17**
See also CA 124

O'Brien, Tim 1946-......... **CLC 7, 19, 40**
See also CA 85-88; CANR 40; DLBD 9;
DLBY 80

Obstfelder, Sigbjoern 1866-1900... **TCLC 23**
See also CA 123

O'Casey, Sean
1880-1964 .... **CLC 1, 5, 9, 11, 15**
See also CA 89-92; CDBLB 1914-1945;
DLB 10; MTCW

O'Cathasaigh, Sean
See O'Casey, Sean

Ochs, Phil 1940-1976............. **CLC 17**
See also CA 65-68

O'Connor, Edwin (Greene)
1918-1968 .... **CLC 14**
See also CA 93-96; 25-28R

O'Connor, (Mary) Flannery
1925-1964 .... **CLC 1, 2, 3, 6, 10, 13, 15,
21, 66; SSC 1**
See also AAYA 7; CA 1-4R; CANR 3, 41;
CDALB 1941-1968; DA; DLB 2;
DLBY 80; MTCW; WLC

O'Connor, Frank.......... **CLC 23; SSC 5**
See also O'Donovan, Michael John

O'Dell, Scott 1898-1989........... **CLC 30**
See also AAYA 3; CA 61-64; 129;
CANR 12, 30; CLR 1, 16; DLB 52;
JRDA; MAICYA; SATA 12, 60

Odets, Clifford 1906-1963 .... **CLC 2, 28**
See also CA 85-88; DLB 7, 26; MTCW

O'Doherty, Brian 1934-........... **CLC 76**
See also CA 105

O'Donnell, K. M.
See Malzberg, Barry N(athaniel)

O'Donnell, Lawrence
See Kuttner, Henry

O'Donovan, Michael John
1903-1966 .... **CLC 14**
See also O'Connor, Frank
See also CA 93-96

Oe, Kenzaburo 1935-.......... **CLC 10, 36**
See also CA 97-100; CANR 36; MTCW

O'Faolain, Julia 1932-....... **CLC 6, 19, 47**
See also CA 81-84; CAAS 2; CANR 12;
DLB 14; MTCW

O'Faolain, Sean
1900-1991 .... **CLC 1, 7, 14, 32, 70;
SSC 13**
See also CA 61-64; 134; CANR 12;
DLB 15; MTCW

O'Flaherty, Liam
1896-1984 .... **CLC 5, 34; SSC 6**
See also CA 101; 113; CANR 35; DLB 36;
DLBY 84; MTCW

Ogilvy, Gavin
See Barrie, J(ames) M(atthew)

O'Grady, Standish James
1846-1928 .... **TCLC 5**
See also CA 104

O'Grady, Timothy 1951-.......... **CLC 59**
See also CA 138

O'Hara, Frank
1926-1966 ....**CLC 2, 5, 13, 78**
See also CA 9-12R; 25-28R; CANR 33;
DLB 5, 16; MTCW

O'Hara, John (Henry)
1905-1970 ...... **CLC 1, 2, 3, 6, 11, 42**
See also CA 5-8R; 25-28R; CANR 31;
CDALB 1929-1941; DLB 9, 86; DLBD 2;
MTCW

O Hehir, Diana 1922- .... **CLC 41**
See also CA 93-96

Okigbo, Christopher (Ifenayichukwu)
1932-1967 ....**CLC 25; PC 7**
See also BLC 3; BW; CA 77-80; DLB 125;
MTCW

Olds, Sharon 1942-............. **CLC 32, 39**
See also CA 101; CANR 18, 41; DLB 120

Oldstyle, Jonathan
See Irving, Washington

Olesha, Yuri (Karlovich)
1899-1960 .... **CLC 8**
See also CA 85-88

Oliphant, Margaret (Oliphant Wilson)
1828-1897 .... **NCLC 11**
See also DLB 18

Oliver, Mary 1935-............ **CLC 19, 34**
See also CA 21-24R; CANR 9; DLB 5

Olivier, Laurence (Kerr)
1907-1989 .... **CLC 20**
See also CA 111; 129

Olsen, Tillie 1913- ..... **CLC 4, 13; SSC 11**
See also CA 1-4R; CANR 1; DA; DLB 28;
DLBY 80; MTCW

Olson, Charles (John)
1910-1970 ..... **CLC 1, 2, 5, 6, 9, 11, 29**
See also CA 13-16; 25-28R; CABS 2;
CANR 35; CAP 1; DLB 5, 16; MTCW

Olson, Toby 1937- .... **CLC 28**
See also CA 65-68; CANR 9, 31

Olyesha, Yuri
See Olesha, Yuri (Karlovich)

Ondaatje, (Philip) Michael
1943-.............. **CLC 14, 29, 51, 76**
See also CA 77-80; CANR 42; DLB 60

Oneal, Elizabeth 1934-
See Oneal, Zibby
See also CA 106; CANR 28; MAICYA;
SATA 30

Oneal, Zibby .... **CLC 30**
See also Oneal, Elizabeth
See also AAYA 5; CLR 13; JRDA

O'Neill, Eugene (Gladstone)
1888-1953 .... **TCLC 1, 6, 27, 49**
See also AITN 1; CA 110; 132;
CDALB 1929-1941; DA; DLB 7; MTCW;
WLC

Onetti, Juan Carlos 1909-....... **CLC 7, 10**
See also CA 85-88; CANR 32; DLB 113;
HW; MTCW

O Nuallain, Brian 1911-1966
See O'Brien, Flann
See also CA 21-22; 25-28R; CAP 2

Oppen, George 1908-1984 .... **CLC 7, 13, 34**
See also CA 13-16R; 113; CANR 8; DLB 5

Oppenheim, E(dward) Phillips
1866-1946 .... **TCLC 45**
See also CA 111; DLB 70

Orlovitz, Gil 1918-1973........... **CLC 22**
See also CA 77-80; 45-48; DLB 2, 5

Orris
See Ingelow, Jean

Ortega y Gasset, Jose 1883-1955 ... **TCLC 9**
See also CA 106; 130; HW; MTCW

Ortiz, Simon J(oseph) 1941- .... **CLC 45**
See also CA 134; DLB 120

Orton, Joe .... **CLC 4, 13, 43; DC 3**
See also Orton, John Kingsley
See also CDBLB 1960 to Present; DLB 13

Orton, John Kingsley 1933-1967
See Orton, Joe
See also CA 85-88; CANR 35; MTCW

Paustovsky, Konstantin (Georgievich)
1892-1968 .... CLC **40**
See also CA 93-96; 25-28R

Pavese, Cesare 1908-1950 .... TCLC **3**
See also CA 104; DLB 128

Pavic, Milorad 1929- .... CLC **60**
See also CA 136

Payne, Alan
See Jakes, John (William)

Paz, Gil
See Lugones, Leopoldo

Paz, Octavio
1914- .... CLC **3, 4, 6, 10, 19, 51, 65;**
PC **1**
See also CA 73-76; CANR 32; DA;
DLBY 90; HW; MTCW; WLC

Peacock, Molly 1947- .... CLC **60**
See also CA 103; DLB 120

Peacock, Thomas Love
1785-1866 .... NCLC **22**
See also DLB 96, 116

Peake, Mervyn 1911-1968 .... CLC **7, 54**
See also CA 5-8R; 25-28R; CANR 3;
DLB 15; MTCW; SATA 23

Pearce, Philippa .... CLC **21**
See also Christie, (Ann) Philippa
See also CLR 9; MAICYA; SATA 1, 67

Pearl, Eric
See Elman, Richard

Pearson, T(homas) R(eid) 1956- .... CLC **39**
See also CA 120; 130

Peck, John 1941- .... CLC **3**
See also CA 49-52; CANR 3

Peck, Richard (Wayne) 1934- ...... CLC **21**
See also AAYA 1; CA 85-88; CANR 19,
38; JRDA; MAICYA; SAAS 2; SATA 18,
55

Peck, Robert Newton 1928- .... CLC **17**
See also AAYA 3; CA 81-84; CANR 31;
DA; JRDA; MAICYA; SAAS 1;
SATA 21, 62

Peckinpah, (David) Sam(uel)
1925-1984 .... CLC **20**
See also CA 109; 114

Pedersen, Knut 1859-1952
See Hamsun, Knut
See also CA 104; 119; MTCW

Peeslake, Gaffer
See Durrell, Lawrence (George)

Peguy, Charles Pierre
1873-1914 .... TCLC **10**
See also CA 107

Pena, Ramon del Valle y
See Valle-Inclan, Ramon (Maria) del

Pendennis, Arthur Esquir
See Thackeray, William Makepeace

Pepys, Samuel 1633-1703.......... LC **11**
See also CDBLB 1660-1789; DA; DLB 101;
WLC

Percy, Walker
1916-1990 .... CLC **2, 3, 6, 8, 14, 18, 47,**
65
See also CA 1-4R; 131; CANR 1, 23;
DLB 2; DLBY 80, 90; MTCW

Perec, Georges 1936-1982 .... CLC **56**
See also CA 141; DLB 83

Pereda (y Sanchez de Porrua), Jose Maria de
1833-1906 .... TCLC **16**
See also CA 117

Pereda y Porrua, Jose Maria de
See Pereda (y Sanchez de Porrua), Jose
Maria de

Peregoy, George Weems
See Mencken, H(enry) L(ouis)

Perelman, S(idney) J(oseph)
1904-1979 ... CLC **3, 5, 9, 15, 23, 44, 49**
See also AITN 1, 2; CA 73-76; 89-92;
CANR 18; DLB 11, 44; MTCW

Peret, Benjamin 1899-1959 .... TCLC **20**
See also CA 117

Peretz, Isaac Loeb 1851(?)-1915... TCLC **16**
See also CA 109

Peretz, Yitzkhok Leibush
See Peretz, Isaac Loeb

Perez Galdos, Benito 1843-1920 ... TCLC **27**
See also CA 125; HW

Perrault, Charles 1628-1703 .... LC **2**
See also MAICYA; SATA 25

Perry, Brighton
See Sherwood, Robert E(mmet)

Perse, Saint-John
See Leger, (Marie-Rene) Alexis Saint-Leger

Perse, St.-John .... CLC **4, 11, 46**
See also Leger, (Marie-Rene) Alexis
Saint-Leger

Peseenz, Tulio F.
See Lopez y Fuentes, Gregorio

Pesetsky, Bette 1932- .... CLC **28**
See also CA 133; DLB 130

Peshkov, Alexei Maximovich 1868-1936
See Gorky, Maxim
See also CA 105; 141; DA

Pessoa, Fernando (Antonio Nogueira)
1888-1935 .... TCLC **27**
See also CA 125

Peterkin, Julia Mood 1880-1961.... CLC **31**
See also CA 102; DLB 9

Peters, Joan K. 1945-............. CLC **39**

Peters, Robert L(ouis) 1924-....... CLC **7**
See also CA 13-16R; CAAS 8; DLB 105

Petofi, Sandor 1823-1849........ NCLC **21**

Petrakis, Harry Mark 1923-........ CLC **3**
See also CA 9-12R; CANR 4, 30

Petrov, Evgeny .... TCLC **21**
See also Kataev, Evgeny Petrovich

Petry, Ann (Lane) 1908- ...... CLC **1, 7, 18**
See also BW; CA 5-8R; CAAS 6; CANR 4;
CLR 12; DLB 76; JRDA; MAICYA;
MTCW; SATA 5

Petursson, Halligrimur 1614-1674 .... LC **8**

Philipson, Morris H. 1926- .... CLC **53**
See also CA 1-4R; CANR 4

Phillips, David Graham
1867-1911 .... TCLC **44**
See also CA 108; DLB 9, 12

Phillips, Jack
See Sandburg, Carl (August)

Phillips, Jayne Anne 1952- ..... CLC **15, 33**
See also CA 101; CANR 24; DLBY 80;
MTCW

Phillips, Richard
See Dick, Philip K(indred)

Phillips, Robert (Schaeffer) 1938-... CLC **28**
See also CA 17-20R; CAAS 13; CANR 8;
DLB 105

Phillips, Ward
See Lovecraft, H(oward) P(hillips)

Piccolo, Lucio 1901-1969.......... CLC **13**
See also CA 97-100; DLB 114

Pickthall, Marjorie L(owry) C(hristie)
1883-1922 .... TCLC **21**
See also CA 107; DLB 92

Pico della Mirandola, Giovanni
1463-1494 .... LC **15**

Piercy, Marge
1936- .... CLC **3, 6, 14, 18, 27, 62**
See also CA 21-24R; CAAS 1; CANR 13;
DLB 120; MTCW

Piers, Robert
See Anthony, Piers

Pieyre de Mandiargues, Andre 1909-1991
See Mandiargues, Andre Pieyre de
See also CA 103; 136; CANR 22

Pilnyak, Boris .... TCLC **23**
See also Vogau, Boris Andreyevich

Pincherle, Alberto 1907-1990 ... CLC **11, 18**
See also Moravia, Alberto
See also CA 25-28R; 132; CANR 33;
MTCW

Pinckney, Darryl 1953- .... CLC **76**

Pineda, Cecile 1942- .... CLC **39**
See also CA 118

Pinero, Arthur Wing 1855-1934 ... TCLC **32**
See also CA 110; DLB 10

Pinero, Miguel (Antonio Gomez)
1946-1988 .... CLC **4, 55**
See also CA 61-64; 125; CANR 29; HW

Pinget, Robert 1919- .... CLC **7, 13, 37**
See also CA 85-88; DLB 83

Pink Floyd...................... CLC **35**
See also Barrett, (Roger) Syd; Gilmour,
David; Mason, Nick; Waters, Roger;
Wright, Rick

Pinkney, Edward 1802-1828 ..... NCLC **31**

Pinkwater, Daniel Manus 1941- .... CLC **35**
See also Pinkwater, Manus
See also AAYA 1; CA 29-32R; CANR 12,
38; CLR 4; JRDA; MAICYA; SAAS 3;
SATA 46

Pinkwater, Manus
See Pinkwater, Daniel Manus
See also SATA 8

Pinsky, Robert 1940- .... CLC **9, 19, 38**
See also CA 29-32R; CAAS 4; DLBY 82

Pinta, Harold
See Pinter, Harold

Pinter, Harold
1930- .. CLC **1, 3, 6, 9, 11, 15, 27, 58, 73**
See also CA 5-8R; CANR 33; CDBLB 1960
to Present; DA; DLB 13; MTCW; WLC

Pritchett, V(ictor) S(awdon)
1900- . . . . **CLC 5, 13, 15, 41**
See also CA 61-64; CANR 31; DLB 15;
MTCW

Private 19022
See Manning, Frederic

Probst, Mark 1925- . . . . **CLC 59**
See also CA 130

Prokosch, Frederic 1908-1989 . . . . **CLC 4, 48**
See also CA 73-76; 128; DLB 48

Prophet, The
See Dreiser, Theodore (Herman Albert)

Prose, Francine 1947- . . . . **CLC 45**
See also CA 109; 112

Proudhon
See Cunha, Euclides (Rodrigues Pimenta) da

Proust, (Valentin-Louis-George-Eugene-)
Marcel 1871-1922 . . . . **TCLC 7, 13, 33**
See also CA 104; 120; DA; DLB 65;
MTCW; WLC

Prowler, Harley
See Masters, Edgar Lee

Prus, Boleslaw . . . . **TCLC 48**
See also Glowacki, Aleksander

Pryor, Richard (Franklin Lenox Thomas)
1940- . . . . **CLC 26**
See also CA 122

Przybyszewski, Stanislaw
1868-1927 . . . . **TCLC 36**
See also DLB 66

Pteleon
See Grieve, C(hristopher) M(urray)

Puckett, Lute
See Masters, Edgar Lee

Puig, Manuel
1932-1990 . . . . **CLC 3, 5, 10, 28, 65**
See also CA 45-48; CANR 2, 32; DLB 113;
HW; MTCW

Purdy, Al
See Purdy, Al(fred Wellington)
See also CAAS 17; DLB 88

Purdy, Al(fred Wellington)
1918- . . . . **CLC 3, 6, 14, 50**
See also CA 81-84; CANR 42

Purdy, James (Amos)
1923- . . . . **CLC 2, 4, 10, 28, 52**
See also CA 33-36R; CAAS 1; CANR 19;
DLB 2; MTCW

Pure, Simon
See Swinnerton, Frank Arthur

Pushkin, Alexander (Sergeyevich)
1799-1837 . . . . **NCLC 3, 27**
See also DA; SATA 61; WLC

P'u Sung-ling 1640-1715 . . . . **LC 3**

Putnam, Arthur Lee
See Alger, Horatio, Jr.

Puzo, Mario 1920- . . . . **CLC 1, 2, 6, 36**
See also CA 65-68; CANR 4, 42; DLB 6;
MTCW

Pym, Barbara (Mary Crampton)
1913-1980 . . . . **CLC 13, 19, 37**
See also CA 13-14; 97-100; CANR 13, 34;
CAP 1; DLB 14; DLBY 87; MTCW

Pynchon, Thomas (Ruggles, Jr.)
1937- . . **CLC 2, 3, 6, 9, 11, 18, 33, 62, 72**
See also BEST 90:2; CA 17-20R; CANR 22;
DA; DLB 2; MTCW; WLC

Qian Zhongshu
See Ch'ien Chung-shu

Qroll
See Dagerman, Stig (Halvard)

Quarrington, Paul (Lewis) 1953- . . . . **CLC 65**
See also CA 129

Quasimodo, Salvatore 1901-1968 . . . **CLC 10**
See also CA 13-16; 25-28R; CAP 1;
DLB 114; MTCW

Queen, Ellery . . . . **CLC 3, 11**
See also Dannay, Frederic; Davidson,
Avram; Lee, Manfred B(ennington);
Sturgeon, Theodore (Hamilton); Vance,
John Holbrook

Queen, Ellery, Jr.
See Dannay, Frederic; Lee, Manfred
B(ennington)

Queneau, Raymond
1903-1976 . . . . **CLC 2, 5, 10, 42**
See also CA 77-80; 69-72; CANR 32;
DLB 72; MTCW

Quevedo, Francisco de 1580-1645 . . . . **LC 23**

Quin, Ann (Marie) 1936-1973 . . . . **CLC 6**
See also CA 9-12R; 45-48; DLB 14

Quinn, Martin
See Smith, Martin Cruz

Quinn, Simon
See Smith, Martin Cruz

Quiroga, Horacio (Sylvestre)
1878-1937 . . . . **TCLC 20**
See also CA 117; 131; HW; MTCW

Quoirez, Francoise 1935- . . . . **CLC 9**
See also Sagan, Francoise
See also CA 49-52; CANR 6, 39; MTCW

Raabe, Wilhelm 1831-1910 . . . . **TCLC 45**
See also DLB 129

Rabe, David (William) 1940- . . . **CLC 4, 8, 33**
See also CA 85-88; CABS 3; DLB 7

Rabelais, Francois 1483-1553 . . . . **LC 5**
See also DA; WLC

Rabinovitch, Sholem 1859-1916
See Aleichem, Sholom
See also CA 104

Radcliffe, Ann (Ward) 1764-1823 . . **NCLC 6**
See also DLB 39

Radiguet, Raymond 1903-1923 . . . . **TCLC 29**
See also DLB 65

Radnoti, Miklos 1909-1944 . . . . **TCLC 16**
See also CA 118

Rado, James 1939- . . . . **CLC 17**
See also CA 105

Radvanyi, Netty 1900-1983
See Seghers, Anna
See also CA 85-88; 110

Raeburn, John (Hay) 1941- . . . . **CLC 34**
See also CA 57-60

Ragni, Gerome 1942-1991 . . . . **CLC 17**
See also CA 105; 134

Rahv, Philip . . . . **CLC 24**
See also Greenberg, Ivan

Raine, Craig 1944- . . . . **CLC 32**
See also CA 108; CANR 29; DLB 40

Raine, Kathleen (Jessie) 1908- . . . **CLC 7, 45**
See also CA 85-88; DLB 20; MTCW

Rainis, Janis 1865-1929 . . . . **TCLC 29**

Rakosi, Carl . . . . **CLC 47**
See also Rawley, Callman
See also CAAS 5

Raleigh, Richard
See Lovecraft, H(oward) P(hillips)

Rallentando, H. P.
See Sayers, Dorothy L(eigh)

Ramal, Walter
See de la Mare, Walter (John)

Ramon, Juan
See Jimenez (Mantecon), Juan Ramon

Ramos, Graciliano 1892-1953 . . . . . **TCLC 32**

Rampersad, Arnold 1941- . . . . **CLC 44**
See also CA 127; 133; DLB 111

Rampling, Anne
See Rice, Anne

Ramuz, Charles-Ferdinand
1878-1947 . . . . **TCLC 33**

Rand, Ayn 1905-1982 . . . . . **CLC 3, 30, 44, 79**
See also AAYA 10; CA 13-16R; 105;
CANR 27; DA; MTCW; WLC

Randall, Dudley (Felker) 1914- . . . . . . **CLC 1**
See also BLC 3; BW; CA 25-28R;
CANR 23; DLB 41

Randall, Robert
See Silverberg, Robert

Ranger, Ken
See Creasey, John

Ransom, John Crowe
1888-1974 . . . . **CLC 2, 4, 5, 11, 24**
See also CA 5-8R; 49-52; CANR 6, 34;
DLB 45, 63; MTCW

Rao, Raja 1909- . . . . **CLC 25, 56**
See also CA 73-76; MTCW

Raphael, Frederic (Michael)
1931- . . . . **CLC 2, 14**
See also CA 1-4R; CANR 1; DLB 14

Ratcliffe, James P.
See Mencken, H(enry) L(ouis)

Rathbone, Julian 1935- . . . . **CLC 41**
See also CA 101; CANR 34

Rattigan, Terence (Mervyn)
1911-1977 . . . . **CLC 7**
See also CA 85-88; 73-76;
CDBLB 1945-1960; DLB 13; MTCW

Ratushinskaya, Irina 1954- . . . . **CLC 54**
See also CA 129

Raven, Simon (Arthur Noel)
1927- . . . . **CLC 14**
See also CA 81-84

Rawley, Callman 1903-
See Rakosi, Carl
See also CA 21-24R; CANR 12, 32

Rawlings, Marjorie Kinnan
1896-1953 . . . . **TCLC 4**
See also CA 104; 137; DLB 9, 22, 102;
JRDA; MAICYA; YABC 1

Ray, Satyajit 1921-1992 . . . . **CLC 16, 76**
See also CA 114; 137

Read, Herbert Edward 1893-1968.... **CLC 4**
See also CA 85-88; 25-28R; DLB 20

Read, Piers Paul 1941- ...... **CLC 4, 10, 25**
See also CA 21-24R; CANR 38; DLB 14;
SATA 21

Reade, Charles 1814-1884 .... **NCLC 2**
See also DLB 21

Reade, Hamish
See Gray, Simon (James Holliday)

Reading, Peter 1946- .... **CLC 47**
See also CA 103; DLB 40

Reaney, James 1926- .... **CLC 13**
See also CA 41-44R; CAAS 15; CANR 42;
DLB 68; SATA 43

Rebreanu, Liviu 1885-1944 .... **TCLC 28**

Rechy, John (Francisco)
1934- .... **CLC 1, 7, 14, 18**
See also CA 5-8R; CAAS 4; CANR 6, 32;
DLB 122; DLBY 82; HW

Redcam, Tom 1870-1933 .... **TCLC 25**

Reddin, Keith .... **CLC 67**

Redgrove, Peter (William)
1932- .... **CLC 6, 41**
See also CA 1-4R; CANR 3, 39; DLB 40

Redmon, Anne .... **CLC 22**
See also Nightingale, Anne Redmon
See also DLBY 86

Reed, Eliot
See Ambler, Eric

Reed, Ishmael
1938- .... **CLC 2, 3, 5, 6, 13, 32, 60**
See also BLC 3; BW; CA 21-24R;
CANR 25; DLB 2, 5, 33; DLBD 8;
MTCW

Reed, John (Silas) 1887-1920 ...... **TCLC 9**
See also CA 106

Reed, Lou .... **CLC 21**
See also Firbank, Louis

Reeve, Clara 1729-1807 .... **NCLC 19**
See also DLB 39

Reid, Christopher (John) 1949- ..... **CLC 33**
See also CA 140; DLB 40

Reid, Desmond
See Moorcock, Michael (John)

Reid Banks, Lynne 1929-
See Banks, Lynne Reid
See also CA 1-4R; CANR 6, 22, 38;
CLR 24; JRDA; MAICYA; SATA 22, 75

Reilly, William K.
See Creasey, John

Reiner, Max
See Caldwell, (Janet Miriam) Taylor
(Holland)

Reis, Ricardo
See Pessoa, Fernando (Antonio Nogueira)

Remarque, Erich Maria
1898-1970 .... **CLC 21**
See also CA 77-80; 29-32R; DA; DLB 56;
MTCW

Remizov, A.
See Remizov, Aleksei (Mikhailovich)

Remizov, A. M.
See Remizov, Aleksei (Mikhailovich)

Remizov, Aleksei (Mikhailovich)
1877-1957 .... **TCLC 27**
See also CA 125; 133

Renan, Joseph Ernest
1823-1892 .... **NCLC 26**

Renard, Jules 1864-1910 .... **TCLC 17**
See also CA 117

Renault, Mary .... **CLC 3, 11, 17**
See also Challans, Mary
See also DLBY 83

Rendell, Ruth (Barbara) 1930- .. **CLC 28, 48**
See also Vine, Barbara
See also CA 109; CANR 32; DLB 87;
MTCW

Renoir, Jean 1894-1979 .... **CLC 20**
See also CA 129; 85-88

Resnais, Alain 1922- .... **CLC 16**

Reverdy, Pierre 1889-1960 .... **CLC 53**
See also CA 97-100; 89-92

Rexroth, Kenneth
1905-1982 ...... **CLC 1, 2, 6, 11, 22, 49**
See also CA 5-8R; 107; CANR 14, 34;
CDALB 1941-1968; DLB 16, 48;
DLBY 82; MTCW

Reyes, Alfonso 1889-1959 .... **TCLC 33**
See also CA 131; HW

Reyes y Basoalto, Ricardo Eliecer Neftali
See Neruda, Pablo

Reymont, Wladyslaw (Stanislaw)
1868(?)-1925 .... **TCLC 5**
See also CA 104

Reynolds, Jonathan 1942- ...... **CLC 6, 38**
See also CA 65-68; CANR 28

Reynolds, Joshua 1723-1792 .... **LC 15**
See also DLB 104

Reynolds, Michael Shane 1937- .... **CLC 44**
See also CA 65-68; CANR 9

Reznikoff, Charles 1894-1976 .... **CLC 9**
See also CA 33-36; 61-64; CAP 2; DLB 28,
45

Rezzori (d'Arezzo), Gregor von
1914- .... **CLC 25**
See also CA 122; 136

Rhine, Richard
See Silverstein, Alvin

R'hoone
See Balzac, Honore de

Rhys, Jean
1890(?)-1979 .... **CLC 2, 4, 6, 14, 19, 51**
See also CA 25-28R; 85-88; CANR 35;
CDBLB 1945-1960; DLB 36, 117; MTCW

Ribeiro, Darcy 1922- .... **CLC 34**
See also CA 33-36R

Ribeiro, Joao Ubaldo (Osorio Pimentel)
1941- .... **CLC 10, 67**
See also CA 81-84

Ribman, Ronald (Burt) 1932- .... **CLC 7**
See also CA 21-24R

Ricci, Nino 1959- .... **CLC 70**
See also CA 137

Rice, Anne 1941- .... **CLC 41**
See also AAYA 9; BEST 89:2; CA 65-68;
CANR 12, 36

Rice, Elmer (Leopold)
1892-1967 .... **CLC 7, 49**
See also CA 21-22; 25-28R; CAP 2; DLB 4,
7; MTCW

Rice, Tim 1944- .... **CLC 21**
See also CA 103

Rich, Adrienne (Cecile)
1929- .... **CLC 3, 6, 7, 11, 18, 36, 73, 76;
PC 5**
See also CA 9-12R; CANR 20; DLB 5, 67;
MTCW

Rich, Barbara
See Graves, Robert (von Ranke)

Rich, Robert
See Trumbo, Dalton

Richards, David Adams 1950- ...... **CLC 59**
See also CA 93-96; DLB 53

Richards, I(vor) A(rmstrong)
1893-1979 .... **CLC 14, 24**
See also CA 41-44R; 89-92; CANR 34;
DLB 27

Richardson, Anne
See Roiphe, Anne Richardson

Richardson, Dorothy Miller
1873-1957 .... **TCLC 3**
See also CA 104; DLB 36

Richardson, Ethel Florence (Lindesay)
1870-1946
See Richardson, Henry Handel
See also CA 105

Richardson, Henry Handel .... **TCLC 4**
See also Richardson, Ethel Florence
(Lindesay)

Richardson, Samuel 1689-1761 .... **LC 1**
See also CDBLB 1660-1789; DA; DLB 39;
WLC

Richler, Mordecai
1931- .... **CLC 3, 5, 9, 13, 18, 46, 70**
See also AITN 1; CA 65-68; CANR 31;
CLR 17; DLB 53; MAICYA; MTCW;
SATA 27, 44

Richter, Conrad (Michael)
1890-1968 .... **CLC 30**
See also CA 5-8R; 25-28R; CANR 23;
DLB 9; MTCW; SATA 3

Riddell, J. H. 1832-1906 .... **TCLC 40**

Riding, Laura .... **CLC 3, 7**
See also Jackson, Laura (Riding)

Riefenstahl, Berta Helene Amalia 1902-
See Riefenstahl, Leni
See also CA 108

Riefenstahl, Leni .... **CLC 16**
See also Riefenstahl, Berta Helene Amalia

Riffe, Ernest
See Bergman, (Ernst) Ingmar

Riley, James Whitcomb
1849-1916 .... **TCLC 51**
See also CA 118; 137; MAICYA; SATA 17

Riley, Tex
See Creasey, John

Rilke, Rainer Maria
1875-1926 .... **TCLC 1, 6, 19; PC 2**
See also CA 104; 132; DLB 81; MTCW

Rimbaud, (Jean Nicolas) Arthur
1854-1891 . . . . **NCLC 4, 35; PC 3**
See also DA; WLC

Rinehart, Mary Roberts
1876-1958 . . . . **TCLC 52**
See also CA 108

Ringmaster, The
See Mencken, H(enry) L(ouis)

Ringwood, Gwen(dolyn Margaret) Pharis
1910-1984 . . . . **CLC 48**
See also CA 112; DLB 88

Rio, Michel 19(?)- . . . . **CLC 43**

Ritsos, Giannes
See Ritsos, Yannis

Ritsos, Yannis 1909-1990 . . . . . **CLC 6, 13, 31**
See also CA 77-80; 133; CANR 39; MTCW

Ritter, Erika 1948(?)- . . . . **CLC 52**

Rivera, Jose Eustasio 1889-1928 . . . **TCLC 35**
See also HW

Rivers, Conrad Kent 1933-1968 . . . . . . **CLC 1**
See also BW; CA 85-88; DLB 41

Rivers, Elfrida
See Bradley, Marion Zimmer

Riverside, John
See Heinlein, Robert A(nson)

Rizal, Jose 1861-1896 . . . . **NCLC 27**

Roa Bastos, Augusto (Antonio)
1917- . . . . **CLC 45**
See also CA 131; DLB 113; HW

Robbe-Grillet, Alain
1922- . . . . . . **CLC 1, 2, 4, 6, 8, 10, 14, 43**
See also CA 9-12R; CANR 33; DLB 83;
MTCW

Robbins, Harold 1916- . . . . **CLC 5**
See also CA 73-76; CANR 26; MTCW

Robbins, Thomas Eugene 1936-
See Robbins, Tom
See also CA 81-84; CANR 29; MTCW

Robbins, Tom . . . . **CLC 9, 32, 64**
See also Robbins, Thomas Eugene
See also BEST 90:3; DLBY 80

Robbins, Trina 1938- . . . . **CLC 21**
See also CA 128

Roberts, Charles G(eorge) D(ouglas)
1860-1943 . . . . **TCLC 8**
See also CA 105; DLB 92; SATA 29

Roberts, Kate 1891-1985 . . . . **CLC 15**
See also CA 107; 116

Roberts, Keith (John Kingston)
1935- . . . . **CLC 14**
See also CA 25-28R

Roberts, Kenneth (Lewis)
1885-1957 . . . . **TCLC 23**
See also CA 109; DLB 9

Roberts, Michele (B.) 1949- . . . . **CLC 48**
See also CA 115

Robertson, Ellis
See Ellison, Harlan; Silverberg, Robert

Robertson, Thomas William
1829-1871 . . . . **NCLC 35**

Robinson, Edwin Arlington
1869-1935 . . . . **TCLC 5; PC 1**
See also CA 104; 133; CDALB 1865-1917;
DA; DLB 54; MTCW

Robinson, Henry Crabb
1775-1867 . . . . **NCLC 15**
See also DLB 107

Robinson, Jill 1936- . . . . **CLC 10**
See also CA 102

Robinson, Kim Stanley 1952- . . . . . . **CLC 34**
See also CA 126

Robinson, Lloyd
See Silverberg, Robert

Robinson, Marilynne 1944- . . . . **CLC 25**
See also CA 116

Robinson, Smokey . . . . **CLC 21**
See also Robinson, William, Jr.

Robinson, William, Jr. 1940-
See Robinson, Smokey
See also CA 116

Robison, Mary 1949- . . . . **CLC 42**
See also CA 113; 116; DLB 130

Rod, Edouard 1857-1910 . . . . **TCLC 52**

Roddenberry, Eugene Wesley 1921-1991
See Roddenberry, Gene
See also CA 110; 135; CANR 37; SATA 45

Roddenberry, Gene . . . . **CLC 17**
See also Roddenberry, Eugene Wesley
See also AAYA 5; SATA-Obit 69

Rodgers, Mary 1931- . . . . **CLC 12**
See also CA 49-52; CANR 8; CLR 20;
JRDA; MAICYA; SATA 8

Rodgers, W(illiam) R(obert)
1909-1969 . . . . **CLC 7**
See also CA 85-88; DLB 20

Rodman, Eric
See Silverberg, Robert

Rodman, Howard 1920(?)-1985 . . . . . **CLC 65**
See also CA 118

Rodman, Maia
See Wojciechowska, Maia (Teresa)

Rodriguez, Claudio 1934- . . . . **CLC 10**

Roelvaag, O(le) E(dvart)
1876-1931 . . . . **TCLC 17**
See also CA 117; DLB 9

Roethke, Theodore (Huebner)
1908-1963 . . . . . . **CLC 1, 3, 8, 11, 19, 46**
See also CA 81-84; CABS 2;
CDALB 1941-1968; DLB 5; MTCW

Rogers, Thomas Hunton 1927- . . . . . **CLC 57**
See also CA 89-92

Rogers, Will(iam Penn Adair)
1879-1935 . . . . **TCLC 8**
See also CA 105; DLB 11

Rogin, Gilbert 1929- . . . . **CLC 18**
See also CA 65-68; CANR 15

Rohan, Koda . . . . **TCLC 22**
See also Koda Shigeyuki

Rohmer, Eric . . . . **CLC 16**
See also Scherer, Jean-Marie Maurice

Rohmer, Sax . . . . **TCLC 28**
See also Ward, Arthur Henry Sarsfield
See also DLB 70

Roiphe, Anne Richardson 1935- . . . **CLC 3, 9**
See also CA 89-92; DLBY 80

Rojas, Fernando de 1465-1541 . . . . . . **LC 23**

Rolfe, Frederick (William Serafino Austin
Lewis Mary) 1860-1913 . . . . . **TCLC 12**
See also CA 107; DLB 34

Rolland, Romain 1866-1944 . . . . . . **TCLC 23**
See also CA 118; DLB 65

Rolvaag, O(le) E(dvart)
See Roelvaag, O(le) E(dvart)

Romain Arnaud, Saint
See Aragon, Louis

Romains, Jules 1885-1972 . . . . **CLC 7**
See also CA 85-88; CANR 34; DLB 65;
MTCW

Romero, Jose Ruben 1890-1952 . . . **TCLC 14**
See also CA 114; 131; HW

Ronsard, Pierre de 1524-1585 . . . . **LC 6**

Rooke, Leon 1934- . . . . **CLC 25, 34**
See also CA 25-28R; CANR 23

Roper, William 1498-1578 . . . . **LC 10**

Roquelaure, A. N.
See Rice, Anne

Rosa, Joao Guimaraes 1908-1967 . . . **CLC 23**
See also CA 89-92; DLB 113

Rosen, Richard (Dean) 1949- . . . . **CLC 39**
See also CA 77-80

Rosenberg, Isaac 1890-1918 . . . . . . **TCLC 12**
See also CA 107; DLB 20

Rosenblatt, Joe . . . . **CLC 15**
See also Rosenblatt, Joseph

Rosenblatt, Joseph 1933-
See Rosenblatt, Joe
See also CA 89-92

Rosenfeld, Samuel 1896-1963
See Tzara, Tristan
See also CA 89-92

Rosenthal, M(acha) L(ouis) 1917- . . . **CLC 28**
See also CA 1-4R; CAAS 6; CANR 4;
DLB 5; SATA 59

Ross, Barnaby
See Dannay, Frederic

Ross, Bernard L.
See Follett, Ken(neth Martin)

Ross, J. H.
See Lawrence, T(homas) E(dward)

Ross, Martin
See Martin, Violet Florence

Ross, (James) Sinclair 1908- . . . . **CLC 13**
See also CA 73-76; DLB 88

Rossetti, Christina (Georgina)
1830-1894 . . . . **NCLC 2; PC 7**
See also DA; DLB 35; MAICYA;
SATA 20; WLC

Rossetti, Dante Gabriel
1828-1882 . . . . **NCLC 4**
See also CDBLB 1832-1890; DA; DLB 35;
WLC

Rossner, Judith (Perelman)
1935- . . . . **CLC 6, 9, 29**
See also AITN 2; BEST 90:3; CA 17-20R;
CANR 18; DLB 6; MTCW

Rostand, Edmond (Eugene Alexis)
1868-1918 . . . . **TCLC 6, 37**
See also CA 104; 126; DA; MTCW

Roth, Henry   1906- . . . . **CLC 2, 6, 11**
See also CA 11-12; CANR 38; CAP 1;
DLB 28; MTCW

Roth, Joseph   1894-1939 . . . . **TCLC 33**
See also DLB 85

Roth, Philip (Milton)
1933- . . . . . . **CLC 1, 2, 3, 4, 6, 9, 15, 22,
31, 47, 66**
See also BEST 90:3; CA 1-4R; CANR 1, 22,
36; CDALB 1968-1988; DA; DLB 2, 28;
DLBY 82; MTCW; WLC

Rothenberg, Jerome   1931- . . . . **CLC 6, 57**
See also CA 45-48; CANR 1; DLB 5

Roumain, Jacques (Jean Baptiste)
1907-1944 . . . . **TCLC 19**
See also BLC 3; BW; CA 117; 125

Rourke, Constance (Mayfield)
1885-1941 . . . . **TCLC 12**
See also CA 107; YABC 1

Rousseau, Jean-Baptiste   1671-1741 . . . **LC 9**

Rousseau, Jean-Jacques   1712-1778 . . . **LC 14**
See also DA; WLC

Roussel, Raymond   1877-1933 . . . . . **TCLC 20**
See also CA 117

Rovit, Earl (Herbert)   1927- . . . . **CLC 7**
See also CA 5-8R; CANR 12

Rowe, Nicholas   1674-1718 . . . . **LC 8**
See also DLB 84

Rowley, Ames Dorrance
See Lovecraft, H(oward) P(hillips)

Rowson, Susanna Haswell
1762(?)-1824 . . . . **NCLC 5**
See also DLB 37

Roy, Gabrielle   1909-1983 . . . . . . **CLC 10, 14**
See also CA 53-56; 110; CANR 5; DLB 68;
MTCW

Rozewicz, Tadeusz   1921- . . . . **CLC 9, 23**
See also CA 108; CANR 36; MTCW

Ruark, Gibbons   1941- . . . . **CLC 3**
See also CA 33-36R; CANR 14, 31;
DLB 120

Rubens, Bernice (Ruth)   1923- . . . **CLC 19, 31**
See also CA 25-28R; CANR 33; DLB 14;
MTCW

Rudkin, (James) David   1936- . . . . . . **CLC 14**
See also CA 89-92; DLB 13

Rudnik, Raphael   1933- . . . . **CLC 7**
See also CA 29-32R

Ruffian, M.
See Hasek, Jaroslav (Matej Frantisek)

Ruiz, Jose Martinez . . . . **CLC 11**
See also Martinez Ruiz, Jose

Rukeyser, Muriel
1913-1980 . . . . **CLC 6, 10, 15, 27**
See also CA 5-8R; 93-96; CANR 26;
DLB 48; MTCW; SATA 22

Rule, Jane (Vance)   1931- . . . . **CLC 27**
See also CA 25-28R; CAAS 18; CANR 12;
DLB 60

Rulfo, Juan   1918-1986 . . . . **CLC 8**
See also CA 85-88; 118; CANR 26;
DLB 113; HW; MTCW

Runeberg, Johan   1804-1877 . . . . . . **NCLC 41**

Runyon, (Alfred) Damon
1884(?)-1946 . . . . **TCLC 10**
See also CA 107; DLB 11, 86

Rush, Norman   1933- . . . . **CLC 44**
See also CA 121; 126

Rushdie, (Ahmed) Salman
1947- . . . . **CLC 23, 31, 55**
See also BEST 89:3; CA 108; 111;
CANR 33; MTCW

Rushforth, Peter (Scott)   1945- . . . . . **CLC 19**
See also CA 101

Ruskin, John   1819-1900 . . . . **TCLC 20**
See also CA 114; 129; CDBLB 1832-1890;
DLB 55; SATA 24

Russ, Joanna   1937- . . . . **CLC 15**
See also CA 25-28R; CANR 11, 31; DLB 8;
MTCW

Russell, George William   1867-1935
See A. E.
See also CA 104; CDBLB 1890-1914

Russell, (Henry) Ken(neth Alfred)
1927- . . . . **CLC 16**
See also CA 105

Russell, Willy   1947- . . . . **CLC 60**

Rutherford, Mark . . . . **TCLC 25**
See also White, William Hale
See also DLB 18

Ruyslinck, Ward
See Belser, Reimond Karel Maria de

Ryan, Cornelius (John)   1920-1974 . . . **CLC 7**
See also CA 69-72; 53-56; CANR 38

Ryan, Michael   1946- . . . . **CLC 65**
See also CA 49-52; DLBY 82

Rybakov, Anatoli (Naumovich)
1911- . . . . **CLC 23, 53**
See also CA 126; 135

Ryder, Jonathan
See Ludlum, Robert

Ryga, George   1932-1987 . . . . **CLC 14**
See also CA 101; 124; DLB 60

S. S.
See Sassoon, Siegfried (Lorraine)

Saba, Umberto   1883-1957 . . . . **TCLC 33**
See also DLB 114

Sabatini, Rafael   1875-1950 . . . . **TCLC 47**

Sabato, Ernesto (R.)   1911- . . . . . . **CLC 10, 23**
See also CA 97-100; CANR 32; HW;
MTCW

Sacastru, Martin
See Bioy Casares, Adolfo

Sacher-Masoch, Leopold von
1836(?)-1895 . . . . **NCLC 31**

Sachs, Marilyn (Stickle)   1927- . . . . . **CLC 35**
See also AAYA 2; CA 17-20R; CANR 13;
CLR 2; JRDA; MAICYA; SAAS 2;
SATA 3, 68

Sachs, Nelly   1891-1970 . . . . **CLC 14**
See also CA 17-18; 25-28R; CAP 2

Sackler, Howard (Oliver)
1929-1982 . . . . **CLC 14**
See also CA 61-64; 108; CANR 30; DLB 7

Sacks, Oliver (Wolf)   1933- . . . . **CLC 67**
See also CA 53-56; CANR 28; MTCW

Sade, Donatien Alphonse Francois Comte
1740-1814 . . . . **NCLC 3**

Sadoff, Ira   1945- . . . . **CLC 9**
See also CA 53-56; CANR 5, 21; DLB 120

Saetone
See Camus, Albert

Safire, William   1929- . . . . **CLC 10**
See also CA 17-20R; CANR 31

Sagan, Carl (Edward)   1934- . . . . **CLC 30**
See also AAYA 2; CA 25-28R; CANR 11,
36; MTCW; SATA 58

Sagan, Francoise . . . . **CLC 3, 6, 9, 17, 36**
See also Quoirez, Francoise
See also DLB 83

Sahgal, Nayantara (Pandit)   1927- . . . **CLC 41**
See also CA 9-12R; CANR 11

Saint, H(arry) F.   1941- . . . . **CLC 50**
See also CA 127

St. Aubin de Teran, Lisa   1953-
See Teran, Lisa St. Aubin de
See also CA 118; 126

Sainte-Beuve, Charles Augustin
1804-1869 . . . . **NCLC 5**

Saint-Exupery, Antoine (Jean Baptiste Marie
Roger) de   1900-1944 . . . . **TCLC 2**
See also CA 108; 132; CLR 10; DLB 72;
MAICYA; MTCW; SATA 20; WLC

St. John, David
See Hunt, E(verette) Howard, Jr.

Saint-John Perse
See Leger, (Marie-Rene) Alexis Saint-Leger

Saintsbury, George (Edward Bateman)
1845-1933 . . . . **TCLC 31**
See also DLB 57

Sait Faik . . . . **TCLC 23**
See also Abasiyanik, Sait Faik

Saki . . . . **TCLC 3; SSC 12**
See also Munro, H(ector) H(ugh)

Salama, Hannu   1936- . . . . **CLC 18**

Salamanca, J(ack) R(ichard)
1922- . . . . **CLC 4, 15**
See also CA 25-28R

Sale, J. Kirkpatrick
See Sale, Kirkpatrick

Sale, Kirkpatrick   1937- . . . . **CLC 68**
See also CA 13-16R; CANR 10

Salinas (y Serrano), Pedro
1891(?)-1951 . . . . **TCLC 17**
See also CA 117

Salinger, J(erome) D(avid)
1919- . . . . **CLC 1, 3, 8, 12, 55, 56; SSC 2**
See also AAYA 2; CA 5-8R; CANR 39;
CDALB 1941-1968; CLR 18; DA;
DLB 2, 102; MAICYA; MTCW;
SATA 67; WLC

Salisbury, John
See Caute, David

Salter, James   1925- . . . . **CLC 7, 52, 59**
See also CA 73-76; DLB 130

Saltus, Edgar (Everton)
1855-1921 . . . . **TCLC 8**
See also CA 105

Saltykov, Mikhail Evgrafovich
1826-1889 . . . . **NCLC 16**

Schwartz, Muriel A.
See Eliot, T(homas) S(tearns)

Schwarz-Bart, Andre 1928- . . . . **CLC 2, 4**
See also CA 89-92

Schwarz-Bart, Simone 1938- . . . . **CLC 7**
See also CA 97-100

Schwob, (Mayer Andre) Marcel
      1867-1905 . . . . **TCLC 20**
See also CA 117; DLB 123

Sciascia, Leonardo
      1921-1989 . . . . **CLC 8, 9, 41**
See also CA 85-88; 130; CANR 35; MTCW

Scoppettone, Sandra 1936- . . . . **CLC 26**
See also CA 5-8R; CANR 41; SATA 9

Scorsese, Martin 1942- . . . . **CLC 20**
See also CA 110; 114

Scotland, Jay
See Jakes, John (William)

Scott, Duncan Campbell
      1862-1947 . . . . **TCLC 6**
See also CA 104; DLB 92

Scott, Evelyn 1893-1963 . . . . **CLC 43**
See also CA 104; 112; DLB 9, 48

Scott, F(rancis) R(eginald)
      1899-1985 . . . . **CLC 22**
See also Scott, Frank
See also CA 101; 114; DLB 88

Scott, Frank
See Scott, F(rancis) R(eginald)
See also CA 141

Scott, Joanna 1960- . . . . **CLC 50**
See also CA 126

Scott, Paul (Mark) 1920-1978 . . . . **CLC 9, 60**
See also CA 81-84; 77-80; CANR 33;
      DLB 14; MTCW

Scott, Walter 1771-1832 . . . . **NCLC 15**
See also CDBLB 1789-1832; DA; DLB 93,
      107, 116; WLC; YABC 2

Scribe, (Augustin) Eugene
      1791-1861 . . . . **NCLC 16**

Scrum, R.
See Crumb, R(obert)

Scudery, Madeleine de 1607-1701 . . . . . **LC 2**

Scum
See Crumb, R(obert)

Scumbag, Little Bobby
See Crumb, R(obert)

Seabrook, John
See Hubbard, L(afayette) Ron(ald)

Sealy, I. Allan 1951- . . . . **CLC 55**

Search, Alexander
See Pessoa, Fernando (Antonio Nogueira)

Sebastian, Lee
See Silverberg, Robert

Sebastian Owl
See Thompson, Hunter S(tockton)

Sebestyen, Ouida 1924- . . . . **CLC 30**
See also AAYA 8; CA 107; CANR 40;
      CLR 17; JRDA; MAICYA; SAAS 10;
      SATA 39

Secundus, H. Scriblerus
See Fielding, Henry

Sedges, John
See Buck, Pearl S(ydenstricker)

Sedgwick, Catharine Maria
      1789-1867 . . . . **NCLC 19**
See also DLB 1, 74

Seelye, John 1931- . . . . **CLC 7**

Seferiades, Giorgos Stylianou 1900-1971
See Seferis, George
See also CA 5-8R; 33-36R; CANR 5, 36;
      MTCW

Seferis, George . . . . **CLC 5, 11**
See also Seferiades, Giorgos Stylianou

Segal, Erich (Wolf) 1937- . . . . **CLC 3, 10**
See also BEST 89:1; CA 25-28R; CANR 20,
      36; DLBY 86; MTCW

Seger, Bob 1945- . . . . **CLC 35**

Seghers, Anna . . . . **CLC 7**
See also Radvanyi, Netty
See also DLB 69

Seidel, Frederick (Lewis) 1936- . . . . . **CLC 18**
See also CA 13-16R; CANR 8; DLBY 84

Seifert, Jaroslav 1901-1986 . . . . . **CLC 34, 44**
See also CA 127; MTCW

Sei Shonagon c. 966-1017(?) . . . . . . **CMLC 6**

Selby, Hubert, Jr. 1928- . . . . . **CLC 1, 2, 4, 8**
See also CA 13-16R; CANR 33; DLB 2

Selzer, Richard 1928- . . . . **CLC 74**
See also CA 65-68; CANR 14

Sembene, Ousmane
See Ousmane, Sembene

Senancour, Etienne Pivert de
      1770-1846 . . . . **NCLC 16**
See also DLB 119

Sender, Ramon (Jose) 1902-1982 . . . . **CLC 8**
See also CA 5-8R; 105; CANR 8; HW;
      MTCW

Seneca, Lucius Annaeus
      4B.C.-65 . . . . **CMLC 6**

Senghor, Leopold Sedar 1906- . . . . . . **CLC 54**
See also BLC 3; BW; CA 116; 125; MTCW

Serling, (Edward) Rod(man)
      1924-1975 . . . . **CLC 30**
See also AITN 1; CA 65-68; 57-60; DLB 26

Serna, Ramon Gomez de la
See Gomez de la Serna, Ramon

Serpieres
See Guillevic, (Eugene)

Service, Robert
See Service, Robert W(illiam)
See also DLB 92

Service, Robert W(illiam)
      1874(?)-1958 . . . . **TCLC 15**
See also Service, Robert
See also CA 115; 140; DA; SATA 20; WLC

Seth, Vikram 1952- . . . . **CLC 43**
See also CA 121; 127; DLB 120

Seton, Cynthia Propper
      1926-1982 . . . . **CLC 27**
See also CA 5-8R; 108; CANR 7

Seton, Ernest (Evan) Thompson
      1860-1946 . . . . **TCLC 31**
See also CA 109; DLB 92; JRDA; SATA 18

Seton-Thompson, Ernest
See Seton, Ernest (Evan) Thompson

Settle, Mary Lee 1918- . . . . **CLC 19, 61**
See also CA 89-92; CAAS 1; DLB 6

Seuphor, Michel
See Arp, Jean

Sevigne, Marie (de Rabutin-Chantal) Marquise
      de 1626-1696 . . . . **LC 11**

Sexton, Anne (Harvey)
      1928-1974 . . . . **CLC 2, 4, 6, 8, 10, 15, 53;
                                                         PC 2**
See also CA 1-4R; 53-56; CABS 2;
      CANR 3, 36; CDALB 1941-1968; DA;
      DLB 5; MTCW; SATA 10; WLC

Shaara, Michael (Joseph Jr.)
      1929-1988 . . . . **CLC 15**
See also AITN 1; CA 102; DLBY 83

Shackleton, C. C.
See Aldiss, Brian W(ilson)

Shacochis, Bob . . . . **CLC 39**
See also Shacochis, Robert G.

Shacochis, Robert G. 1951-
See Shacochis, Bob
See also CA 119; 124

Shaffer, Anthony (Joshua) 1926- . . . . **CLC 19**
See also CA 110; 116; DLB 13

Shaffer, Peter (Levin)
      1926- . . . . **CLC 5, 14, 18, 37, 60**
See also CA 25-28R; CANR 25;
      CDBLB 1960 to Present; DLB 13;
      MTCW

Shakey, Bernard
See Young, Neil

Shalamov, Varlam (Tikhonovich)
      1907(?)-1982 . . . . **CLC 18**
See also CA 129; 105

Shamlu, Ahmad 1925- . . . . **CLC 10**

Shammas, Anton 1951- . . . . **CLC 55**

Shange, Ntozake
      1948- . . . . **CLC 8, 25, 38, 74; DC 3**
See also AAYA 9; BLC 3; BW; CA 85-88;
      CABS 3; CANR 27; DLB 38; MTCW

Shanley, John Patrick 1950- . . . . **CLC 75**
See also CA 128; 133

Shapcott, Thomas William 1935- . . . **CLC 38**
See also CA 69-72

Shapiro, Jane . . . . **CLC 76**

Shapiro, Karl (Jay) 1913- . . **CLC 4, 8, 15, 53**
See also CA 1-4R; CAAS 6; CANR 1, 36;
      DLB 48; MTCW

Sharp, William 1855-1905 . . . . **TCLC 39**

Sharpe, Thomas Ridley 1928-
See Sharpe, Tom
See also CA 114; 122

Sharpe, Tom . . . . **CLC 36**
See also Sharpe, Thomas Ridley
See also DLB 14

Shaw, Bernard . . . . **TCLC 45**
See also Shaw, George Bernard

Shaw, G. Bernard
See Shaw, George Bernard

Shaw, George Bernard
      1856-1950 . . . . **TCLC 3, 9, 21**
See also Shaw, Bernard
See also CA 104; 128; CDBLB 1914-1945;
      DA; DLB 10, 57; MTCW; WLC

Shaw, Henry Wheeler
1818-1885 .... **NCLC 15**
See also DLB 11

Shaw, Irwin 1913-1984 ...... **CLC 7, 23, 34**
See also AITN 1; CA 13-16R; 112;
CANR 21; CDALB 1941-1968; DLB 6,
102; DLBY 84; MTCW

Shaw, Robert 1927-1978 .... **CLC 5**
See also AITN 1; CA 1-4R; 81-84;
CANR 4; DLB 13, 14

Shaw, T. E.
See Lawrence, T(homas) E(dward)

Shawn, Wallace 1943- .... **CLC 41**
See also CA 112

Sheed, Wilfrid (John Joseph)
1930- .... **CLC 2, 4, 10, 53**
See also CA 65-68; CANR 30; DLB 6;
MTCW

Sheldon, Alice Hastings Bradley
1915(?)-1987
See Tiptree, James, Jr.
See also CA 108; 122; CANR 34; MTCW

Sheldon, John
See Bloch, Robert (Albert)

Shelley, Mary Wollstonecraft (Godwin)
1797-1851 .... **NCLC 14**
See also CDBLB 1789-1832; DA; DLB 110,
116; SATA 29; WLC

Shelley, Percy Bysshe
1792-1822 .... **NCLC 18**
See also CDBLB 1789-1832; DA; DLB 96,
110; WLC

Shepard, Jim 1956- .... **CLC 36**
See also CA 137

Shepard, Lucius 1947- .... **CLC 34**
See also CA 128; 141

Shepard, Sam
1943- ...... **CLC 4, 6, 17, 34, 41, 44**
See also AAYA 1; CA 69-72; CABS 3;
CANR 22; DLB 7; MTCW

Shepherd, Michael
See Ludlum, Robert

Sherburne, Zoa (Morin) 1912- ...... **CLC 30**
See also CA 1-4R; CANR 3, 37; MAICYA;
SATA 3

Sheridan, Frances 1724-1766 .... **LC 7**
See also DLB 39, 84

Sheridan, Richard Brinsley
1751-1816 .... **NCLC 5; DC 1**
See also CDBLB 1660-1789; DA; DLB 89;
WLC

Sherman, Jonathan Marc .... **CLC 55**

Sherman, Martin 1941(?)- .... **CLC 19**
See also CA 116; 123

Sherwin, Judith Johnson 1936- ... **CLC 7, 15**
See also CA 25-28R; CANR 34

Sherwood, Robert E(mmet)
1896-1955 .... **TCLC 3**
See also CA 104; DLB 7, 26

Shiel, M(atthew) P(hipps)
1865-1947 .... **TCLC 8**
See also CA 106

Shiga, Naoya 1883-1971 .... **CLC 33**
See also CA 101; 33-36R

Shimazaki Haruki 1872-1943
See Shimazaki Toson
See also CA 105; 134

Shimazaki Toson .... **TCLC 5**
See also Shimazaki Haruki

Sholokhov, Mikhail (Aleksandrovich)
1905-1984 .... **CLC 7, 15**
See also CA 101; 112; MTCW; SATA 36

Shone, Patric
See Hanley, James

Shreve, Susan Richards 1939- ...... **CLC 23**
See also CA 49-52; CAAS 5; CANR 5, 38;
MAICYA; SATA 41, 46

Shue, Larry 1946-1985 .... **CLC 52**
See also CA 117

Shu-Jen, Chou 1881-1936
See Hsun, Lu
See also CA 104

Shulman, Alix Kates 1932- ...... **CLC 2, 10**
See also CA 29-32R; SATA 7

Shuster, Joe 1914- .... **CLC 21**

Shute, Nevil .... **CLC 30**
See also Norway, Nevil Shute

Shuttle, Penelope (Diane) 1947- ..... **CLC 7**
See also CA 93-96; CANR 39; DLB 14, 40

Sidney, Mary 1561-1621 .... **LC 19**

Sidney, Sir Philip 1554-1586 .... **LC 19**
See also CDBLB Before 1660; DA

Siegel, Jerome 1914- .... **CLC 21**
See also CA 116

Siegel, Jerry
See Siegel, Jerome

Sienkiewicz, Henryk (Adam Alexander Pius)
1846-1916 .... **TCLC 3**
See also CA 104; 134

Sierra, Gregorio Martinez
See Martinez Sierra, Gregorio

Sierra, Maria (de la O'LeJarraga) Martinez
See Martinez Sierra, Maria (de la
O'LeJarraga)

Sigal, Clancy 1926- .... **CLC 7**
See also CA 1-4R

Sigourney, Lydia Howard (Huntley)
1791-1865 .... **NCLC 21**
See also DLB 1, 42, 73

Siguenza y Gongora, Carlos de
1645-1700 .... **LC 8**

Sigurjonsson, Johann 1880-1919 ... **TCLC 27**

Sikelianos, Angelos 1884-1951 .... **TCLC 39**

Silkin, Jon 1930- .... **CLC 2, 6, 43**
See also CA 5-8R; CAAS 5; DLB 27

Silko, Leslie Marmon 1948- .... **CLC 23, 74**
See also CA 115; 122; DA

Sillanpaa, Frans Eemil 1888-1964 ... **CLC 19**
See also CA 129; 93-96; MTCW

Sillitoe, Alan
1928- .... **CLC 1, 3, 6, 10, 19, 57**
See also AITN 1; CA 9-12R; CAAS 2;
CANR 8, 26; CDBLB 1960 to Present;
DLB 14; MTCW; SATA 61

Silone, Ignazio 1900-1978 .... **CLC 4**
See also CA 25-28; 81-84; CANR 34;
CAP 2; MTCW

Silver, Joan Micklin 1935- .... **CLC 20**
See also CA 114; 121

Silver, Nicholas
See Faust, Frederick (Schiller)

Silverberg, Robert 1935- .... **CLC 7**
See also CA 1-4R; CAAS 3; CANR 1, 20,
36; DLB 8; MAICYA; MTCW; SATA 13

Silverstein, Alvin 1933- .... **CLC 17**
See also CA 49-52; CANR 2; CLR 25;
JRDA; MAICYA; SATA 8, 69

Silverstein, Virginia B(arbara Opshelor)
1937- .... **CLC 17**
See also CA 49-52; CANR 2; CLR 25;
JRDA; MAICYA; SATA 8, 69

Sim, Georges
See Simenon, Georges (Jacques Christian)

Simak, Clifford D(onald)
1904-1988 .... **CLC 1, 55**
See also CA 1-4R; 125; CANR 1, 35;
DLB 8; MTCW; SATA 56

Simenon, Georges (Jacques Christian)
1903-1989 .... **CLC 1, 2, 3, 8, 18, 47**
See also CA 85-88; 129; CANR 35;
DLB 72; DLBY 89; MTCW

Simic, Charles 1938-... **CLC 6, 9, 22, 49, 68**
See also CA 29-32R; CAAS 4; CANR 12,
33; DLB 105

Simmons, Charles (Paul) 1924- ..... **CLC 57**
See also CA 89-92

Simmons, Dan 1948- .... **CLC 44**
See also CA 138

Simmons, James (Stewart Alexander)
1933- .... **CLC 43**
See also CA 105; DLB 40

Simms, William Gilmore
1806-1870 .... **NCLC 3**
See also DLB 3, 30, 59, 73

Simon, Carly 1945-................ **CLC 26**
See also CA 105

Simon, Claude 1913-....... **CLC 4, 9, 15, 39**
See also CA 89-92; CANR 33; DLB 83;
MTCW

Simon, (Marvin) Neil
1927-........... **CLC 6, 11, 31, 39, 70**
See also AITN 1; CA 21-24R; CANR 26;
DLB 7; MTCW

Simon, Paul 1942(?)- .... **CLC 17**
See also CA 116

Simonon, Paul 1956(?)- .... **CLC 30**
See also Clash, The

Simpson, Harriette
See Arnow, Harriette (Louisa) Simpson

Simpson, Louis (Aston Marantz)
1923- .... **CLC 4, 7, 9, 32**
See also CA 1-4R; CAAS 4; CANR 1;
DLB 5; MTCW

Simpson, Mona (Elizabeth) 1957-... **CLC 44**
See also CA 122; 135

Simpson, N(orman) F(rederick)
1919- .... **CLC 29**
See also CA 13-16R; DLB 13

Sinclair, Andrew (Annandale)
1935- .... **CLC 2, 14**
See also CA 9-12R; CAAS 5; CANR 14, 38;
DLB 14; MTCW

Sinclair, Emil
See Hesse, Hermann

Sinclair, Iain 1943-.............. **CLC 76**
See also CA 132

Sinclair, Iain MacGregor
See Sinclair, Iain

Sinclair, Mary Amelia St. Clair 1865(?)-1946
See Sinclair, May
See also CA 104

Sinclair, May................. **TCLC 3, 11**
See also Sinclair, Mary Amelia St. Clair
See also DLB 36

Sinclair, Upton (Beall)
1878-1968 .... **CLC 1, 11, 15, 63**
See also CA 5-8R; 25-28R; CANR 7;
CDALB 1929-1941; DA; DLB 9; MTCW;
SATA 9; WLC

Singer, Isaac
See Singer, Isaac Bashevis

Singer, Isaac Bashevis
1904-1991 .... **CLC 1, 3, 6, 9, 11, 15, 23,**
38, 69; SSC 3
See also AITN 1, 2; CA 1-4R; 134;
CANR 1, 39; CDALB 1941-1968; CLR 1;
DA; DLB 6, 28, 52; DLBY 91; JRDA;
MAICYA; MTCW; SATA 3, 27;
SATA-Obit 68; WLC

Singer, Israel Joshua 1893-1944 ... **TCLC 33**

Singh, Khushwant 1915-........... **CLC 11**
See also CA 9-12R; CAAS 9; CANR 6

Sinjohn, John
See Galsworthy, John

Sinyavsky, Andrei (Donatevich)
1925-...................... **CLC 8**
See also CA 85-88

Sirin, V.
See Nabokov, Vladimir (Vladimirovich)

Sissman, L(ouis) E(dward)
1928-1976 .... **CLC 9, 18**
See also CA 21-24R; 65-68; CANR 13;
DLB 5

Sisson, C(harles) H(ubert) 1914-..... **CLC 8**
See also CA 1-4R; CAAS 3; CANR 3;
DLB 27

Sitwell, Dame Edith
1887-1964 .... **CLC 2, 9, 67; PC 3**
See also CA 9-12R; CANR 35;
CDBLB 1945-1960; DLB 20; MTCW

Sjoewall, Maj 1935-.............. **CLC 7**
See also CA 65-68

Sjowall, Maj
See Sjoewall, Maj

Skelton, Robin 1925-............. **CLC 13**
See also AITN 2; CA 5-8R; CAAS 5;
CANR 28; DLB 27, 53

Skolimowski, Jerzy 1938-........ **CLC 20**
See also CA 128

Skram, Amalie (Bertha)
1847-1905 .... **TCLC 25**

Skvorecky, Josef (Vaclav)
1924- .... **CLC 15, 39, 69**
See also CA 61-64; CAAS 1; CANR 10, 34;
MTCW

Slade, Bernard................. **CLC 11, 46**
See also Newbound, Bernard Slade
See also CAAS 9; DLB 53

Slaughter, Carolyn 1946-......... **CLC 56**
See also CA 85-88

Slaughter, Frank G(ill) 1908- ...... **CLC 29**
See also AITN 2; CA 5-8R; CANR 5

Slavitt, David R(ytman) 1935-.... **CLC 5, 14**
See also CA 21-24R; CAAS 3; CANR 41;
DLB 5, 6

Slesinger, Tess 1905-1945 .... **TCLC 10**
See also CA 107; DLB 102

Slessor, Kenneth 1901-1971....... **CLC 14**
See also CA 102; 89-92

Slowacki, Juliusz 1809-1849 ..... **NCLC 15**

Smart, Christopher 1722-1771....... **LC 3**
See also DLB 109

Smart, Elizabeth 1913-1986....... **CLC 54**
See also CA 81-84; 118; DLB 88

Smiley, Jane (Graves) 1949- .... **CLC 53, 76**
See also CA 104; CANR 30

Smith, A(rthur) J(ames) M(arshall)
1902-1980 .... **CLC 15**
See also CA 1-4R; 102; CANR 4; DLB 88

Smith, Betty (Wehner) 1896-1972... **CLC 19**
See also CA 5-8R; 33-36R; DLBY 82;
SATA 6

Smith, Charlotte (Turner)
1749-1806 .... **NCLC 23**
See also DLB 39, 109

Smith, Clark Ashton 1893-1961 .... **CLC 43**

Smith, Dave................... **CLC 22, 42**
See also Smith, David (Jeddie)
See also CAAS 7; DLB 5

Smith, David (Jeddie) 1942-
See Smith, Dave
See also CA 49-52; CANR 1

Smith, Florence Margaret
1902-1971 .... **CLC 8**
See also Smith, Stevie
See also CA 17-18; 29-32R; CANR 35;
CAP 2; MTCW

Smith, Iain Crichton 1928- .... **CLC 64**
See also CA 21-24R; DLB 40

Smith, John 1580(?)-1631 .... **LC 9**

Smith, Johnston
See Crane, Stephen (Townley)

Smith, Lee 1944-.............. **CLC 25, 73**
See also CA 114; 119; DLBY 83

Smith, Martin
See Smith, Martin Cruz

Smith, Martin Cruz 1942-........ **CLC 25**
See also BEST 89:4; CA 85-88; CANR 6, 23

Smith, Mary-Ann Tirone 1944-..... **CLC 39**
See also CA 118; 136

Smith, Patti 1946-.............. **CLC 12**
See also CA 93-96

Smith, Pauline (Urmson)
1882-1959 .... **TCLC 25**

Smith, Rosamond
See Oates, Joyce Carol

Smith, Sheila Kaye
See Kaye-Smith, Sheila

Smith, Stevie .... **CLC 3, 8, 25, 44**
See also Smith, Florence Margaret
See also DLB 20

Smith, Wilbur A(ddison) 1933- ..... **CLC 33**
See also CA 13-16R; CANR 7; MTCW

Smith, William Jay 1918- .... **CLC 6**
See also CA 5-8R; DLB 5; MAICYA;
SATA 2, 68

Smith, Woodrow Wilson
See Kuttner, Henry

Smolenskin, Peretz 1842-1885.... **NCLC 30**

Smollett, Tobias (George) 1721-1771 .. **LC 2**
See also CDBLB 1660-1789; DLB 39, 104

Snodgrass, W(illiam) D(e Witt)
1926- .... **CLC 2, 6, 10, 18, 68**
See also CA 1-4R; CANR 6, 36; DLB 5;
MTCW

Snow, C(harles) P(ercy)
1905-1980 .... **CLC 1, 4, 6, 9, 13, 19**
See also CA 5-8R; 101; CANR 28;
CDBLB 1945-1960; DLB 15, 77; MTCW

Snow, Frances Compton
See Adams, Henry (Brooks)

Snyder, Gary (Sherman)
1930- .... **CLC 1, 2, 5, 9, 32**
See also CA 17-20R; CANR 30; DLB 5, 16

Snyder, Zilpha Keatley 1927- ...... **CLC 17**
See also CA 9-12R; CANR 38; CLR 31;
JRDA; MAICYA; SAAS 2; SATA 1, 28,
75

Soares, Bernardo
See Pessoa, Fernando (Antonio Nogueira)

Sobh, A.
See Shamlu, Ahmad

Sobol, Joshua.................... **CLC 60**

Soderberg, Hjalmar 1869-1941 .... **TCLC 39**

Sodergran, Edith (Irene)
See Soedergran, Edith (Irene)

Soedergran, Edith (Irene)
1892-1923 .... **TCLC 31**

Softly, Edgar
See Lovecraft, H(oward) P(hillips)

Softly, Edward
See Lovecraft, H(oward) P(hillips)

Sokolov, Raymond 1941-........... **CLC 7**
See also CA 85-88

Solo, Jay
See Ellison, Harlan

Sologub, Fyodor .... **TCLC 9**
See also Teternikov, Fyodor Kuzmich

Solomons, Ikey Esquir
See Thackeray, William Makepeace

Solomos, Dionysios 1798-1857 ... **NCLC 15**

Solwoska, Mara
See French, Marilyn

Solzhenitsyn, Aleksandr I(sayevich)
1918- ...... **CLC 1, 2, 4, 7, 9, 10, 18, 26,**
34, 78
See also AITN 1; CA 69-72; CANR 40;
DA; MTCW; WLC

Somers, Jane
See Lessing, Doris (May)

Somerville, Edith 1858-1949 ...... **TCLC 51**

Somerville & Ross
See Martin, Violet Florence; Somerville, Edith

Sommer, Scott 1951- . . . . **CLC 25**
See also CA 106

Sondheim, Stephen (Joshua)
1930- . . . . **CLC 30, 39**
See also CA 103

Sontag, Susan 1933-. . . **CLC 1, 2, 10, 13, 31**
See also CA 17-20R; CANR 25; DLB 2, 67; MTCW

Sophocles
496(?)B.C.-406(?)B.C.. . . . **CMLC 2; DC 1**
See also DA

Sorel, Julia
See Drexler, Rosalyn

Sorrentino, Gilbert
1929- . . . . **CLC 3, 7, 14, 22, 40**
See also CA 77-80; CANR 14, 33; DLB 5; DLBY 80

Soto, Gary 1952-. . . . . **CLC 32**
See also AAYA 10; CA 119; 125; DLB 82; HW; JRDA

Soupault, Philippe 1897-1990 . . . . . . **CLC 68**
See also CA 116; 131

Souster, (Holmes) Raymond
1921- . . . . **CLC 5, 14**
See also CA 13-16R; CAAS 14; CANR 13, 29; DLB 88; SATA 63

Southern, Terry 1926- . . . . **CLC 7**
See also CA 1-4R; CANR 1; DLB 2

Southey, Robert 1774-1843 . . . . **NCLC 8**
See also DLB 93, 107; SATA 54

Southworth, Emma Dorothy Eliza Nevitte
1819-1899 . . . . **NCLC 26**

Souza, Ernest
See Scott, Evelyn

Soyinka, Wole
1934- . . . . **CLC 3, 5, 14, 36, 44; DC 2**
See also BLC 3; BW; CA 13-16R; CANR 27, 39; DA; DLB 125; MTCW; WLC

Spackman, W(illiam) M(ode)
1905-1990 . . . . **CLC 46**
See also CA 81-84; 132

Spacks, Barry 1931-. . . . . **CLC 14**
See also CA 29-32R; CANR 33; DLB 105

Spanidou, Irini 1946-. . . . . **CLC 44**

Spark, Muriel (Sarah)
1918- . . . . **CLC 2, 3, 5, 8, 13, 18, 40; SSC 10**
See also CA 5-8R; CANR 12, 36; CDBLB 1945-1960; DLB 15; MTCW

Spaulding, Douglas
See Bradbury, Ray (Douglas)

Spaulding, Leonard
See Bradbury, Ray (Douglas)

Spence, J. A. D.
See Eliot, T(homas) S(tearns)

Spencer, Elizabeth 1921-. . . . . **CLC 22**
See also CA 13-16R; CANR 32; DLB 6; MTCW; SATA 14

Spencer, Leonard G.
See Silverberg, Robert

Spencer, Scott 1945-. . . . . **CLC 30**
See also CA 113; DLBY 86

Spender, Stephen (Harold)
1909- . . . . **CLC 1, 2, 5, 10, 41**
See also CA 9-12R; CANR 31; CDBLB 1945-1960; DLB 20; MTCW

Spengler, Oswald (Arnold Gottfried)
1880-1936 . . . . **TCLC 25**
See also CA 118

Spenser, Edmund 1552(?)-1599 . . . . **LC 5**
See also CDBLB Before 1660; DA; WLC

Spicer, Jack 1925-1965 . . . . . . **CLC 8, 18, 72**
See also CA 85-88; DLB 5, 16

Spiegelman, Art 1948-. . . . . **CLC 76**
See also AAYA 10; CA 125; CANR 41

Spielberg, Peter 1929-. . . . . **CLC 6**
See also CA 5-8R; CANR 4; DLBY 81

Spielberg, Steven 1947-. . . . . **CLC 20**
See also AAYA 8; CA 77-80; CANR 32; SATA 32

Spillane, Frank Morrison 1918-
See Spillane, Mickey
See also CA 25-28R; CANR 28; MTCW; SATA 66

Spillane, Mickey . . . . **CLC 3, 13**
See also Spillane, Frank Morrison

Spinoza, Benedictus de 1632-1677 . . . . **LC 9**

Spinrad, Norman (Richard) 1940-. . . **CLC 46**
See also CA 37-40R; CANR 20; DLB 8

Spitteler, Carl (Friedrich Georg)
1845-1924 . . . . **TCLC 12**
See also CA 109; DLB 129

Spivack, Kathleen (Romola Drucker)
1938- . . . . **CLC 6**
See also CA 49-52

Spoto, Donald 1941-. . . . . **CLC 39**
See also CA 65-68; CANR 11

Springsteen, Bruce (F.) 1949- . . . . . . **CLC 17**
See also CA 111

Spurling, Hilary 1940-. . . . . **CLC 34**
See also CA 104; CANR 25

Squires, (James) Radcliffe
1917-1993 . . . . **CLC 51**
See also CA 1-4R; 140; CANR 6, 21

Srivastava, Dhanpat Rai 1880(?)-1936
See Premchand
See also CA 118

Stacy, Donald
See Pohl, Frederik

Stael, Germaine de
See Stael-Holstein, Anne Louise Germaine Necker Baronn
See also DLB 119

Stael-Holstein, Anne Louise Germaine Necker Baronn 1766-1817 . . . . **NCLC 3**
See also Stael, Germaine de

Stafford, Jean 1915-1979 . . . **CLC 4, 7, 19, 68**
See also CA 1-4R; 85-88; CANR 3; DLB 2; MTCW; SATA 22

Stafford, William (Edgar)
1914- . . . . **CLC 4, 7, 29**
See also CA 5-8R; CAAS 3; CANR 5, 22; DLB 5

Staines, Trevor
See Brunner, John (Kilian Houston)

Stairs, Gordon
See Austin, Mary (Hunter)

Stannard, Martin. . . . . **CLC 44**

Stanton, Maura 1946- . . . . **CLC 9**
See also CA 89-92; CANR 15; DLB 120

Stanton, Schuyler
See Baum, L(yman) Frank

Stapledon, (William) Olaf
1886-1950 . . . . **TCLC 22**
See also CA 111; DLB 15

Starbuck, George (Edwin) 1931-. . . . **CLC 53**
See also CA 21-24R; CANR 23

Stark, Richard
See Westlake, Donald E(dwin)

Staunton, Schuyler
See Baum, L(yman) Frank

Stead, Christina (Ellen)
1902-1983 . . . . **CLC 2, 5, 8, 32**
See also CA 13-16R; 109; CANR 33, 40; MTCW

Stead, William Thomas
1849-1912 . . . . **TCLC 48**

Steele, Richard 1672-1729. . . . . **LC 18**
See also CDBLB 1660-1789; DLB 84, 101

Steele, Timothy (Reid) 1948-. . . . . . . **CLC 45**
See also CA 93-96; CANR 16; DLB 120

Steffens, (Joseph) Lincoln
1866-1936 . . . . **TCLC 20**
See also CA 117

Stegner, Wallace (Earle)
1909-1993 . . . . **CLC 9, 49**
See also AITN 1; BEST 90:3; CA 1-4R; 141; CAAS 9; CANR 1, 21; DLB 9; MTCW

Stein, Gertrude
1874-1946 . . . . **TCLC 1, 6, 28, 48**
See also CA 104; 132; CDALB 1917-1929; DA; DLB 4, 54, 86; MTCW; WLC

Steinbeck, John (Ernst)
1902-1968 . . . . . . **CLC 1, 5, 9, 13, 21, 34, 45, 75; SSC 11**
See also CA 1-4R; 25-28R; CANR 1, 35; CDALB 1929-1941; DA; DLB 7, 9; DLBD 2; MTCW; SATA 9; WLC

Steinem, Gloria 1934-. . . . . **CLC 63**
See also CA 53-56; CANR 28; MTCW

Steiner, George 1929-. . . . . **CLC 24**
See also CA 73-76; CANR 31; DLB 67; MTCW; SATA 62

Steiner, Rudolf 1861-1925. . . . . **TCLC 13**
See also CA 107

Stendhal 1783-1842. . . . . **NCLC 23**
See also DA; DLB 119; WLC

Stephen, Leslie 1832-1904. . . . . **TCLC 23**
See also CA 123; DLB 57

Stephen, Sir Leslie
See Stephen, Leslie

Stephen, Virginia
See Woolf, (Adeline) Virginia

Stephens, James 1882(?)-1950. . . . . . **TCLC 4**
See also CA 104; DLB 19

Summers, Andrew James 1942-..... **CLC 26**
See also Police, The

Summers, Andy
See Summers, Andrew James

Summers, Hollis (Spurgeon, Jr.)
1916-...................... **CLC 10**
See also CA 5-8R; CANR 3; DLB 6

Summers, (Alphonsus Joseph-Mary Augustus)
Montague 1880-1948....... **TCLC 16**
See also CA 118

Sumner, Gordon Matthew 1951-.... **CLC 26**
See also Police, The

Surtees, Robert Smith
1803-1864 .... **NCLC 14**
See also DLB 21

Susann, Jacqueline 1921-1974...... **CLC 3**
See also AITN 1; CA 65-68; 53-56; MTCW

Suskind, Patrick
See Sueskind, Patrick

Sutcliff, Rosemary 1920-1992...... **CLC 26**
See also AAYA 10; CA 5-8R; 139;
CANR 37; CLR 1; JRDA; MAICYA;
SATA 6, 44; SATA-Obit 73

Sutro, Alfred 1863-1933.......... **TCLC 6**
See also CA 105; DLB 10

Sutton, Henry
See Slavitt, David R(ytman)

Svevo, Italo .... **TCLC 2, 35**
See also Schmitz, Aron Hector

Swados, Elizabeth 1951- .... **CLC 12**
See also CA 97-100

Swados, Harvey 1920-1972 .... **CLC 5**
See also CA 5-8R; 37-40R; CANR 6;
DLB 2

Swan, Gladys 1934- .... **CLC 69**
See also CA 101; CANR 17, 39

Swarthout, Glendon (Fred)
1918-1992 .... **CLC 35**
See also CA 1-4R; 139; CANR 1; SATA 26

Sweet, Sarah C.
See Jewett, (Theodora) Sarah Orne

Swenson, May 1919-1989..... **CLC 4, 14, 61**
See also CA 5-8R; 130; CANR 36; DA;
DLB 5; MTCW; SATA 15

Swift, Augustus
See Lovecraft, H(oward) P(hillips)

Swift, Graham 1949- .... **CLC 41**
See also CA 117; 122

Swift, Jonathan 1667-1745.......... **LC 1**
See also CDBLB 1660-1789; DA; DLB 39,
95, 101; SATA 19; WLC

Swinburne, Algernon Charles
1837-1909 .... **TCLC 8, 36**
See also CA 105; 140; CDBLB 1832-1890;
DA; DLB 35, 57; WLC

Swinfen, Ann .... **CLC 34**

Swinnerton, Frank Arthur
1884-1982 .... **CLC 31**
See also CA 108; DLB 34

Swithen, John
See King, Stephen (Edwin)

Sylvia
See Ashton-Warner, Sylvia (Constance)

Symmes, Robert Edward
See Duncan, Robert (Edward)

Symonds, John Addington
1840-1893 .... **NCLC 34**
See also DLB 57

Symons, Arthur 1865-1945 .... **TCLC 11**
See also CA 107; DLB 19, 57

Symons, Julian (Gustave)
1912-.................. **CLC 2, 14, 32**
See also CA 49-52; CAAS 3; CANR 3, 33;
DLB 87; DLBY 92; MTCW

Synge, (Edmund) J(ohn) M(illington)
1871-1909 .... **TCLC 6, 37; DC 2**
See also CA 104; 141; CDBLB 1890-1914;
DLB 10, 19

Syruc, J.
See Milosz, Czeslaw

Szirtes, George 1948-............. **CLC 46**
See also CA 109; CANR 27

Tabori, George 1914-............. **CLC 19**
See also CA 49-52; CANR 4

Tagore, Rabindranath 1861-1941.... **TCLC 3**
See also CA 104; 120; MTCW

Taine, Hippolyte Adolphe
1828-1893 .... **NCLC 15**

Talese, Gay 1932-................. **CLC 37**
See also AITN 1; CA 1-4R; CANR 9;
MTCW

Tallent, Elizabeth (Ann) 1954- ..... **CLC 45**
See also CA 117; DLB 130

Tally, Ted 1952-................. **CLC 42**
See also CA 120; 124

Tamayo y Baus, Manuel
1829-1898 .... **NCLC 1**

Tammsaare, A(nton) H(ansen)
1878-1940 .... **TCLC 27**

Tan, Amy 1952- .... **CLC 59**
See also AAYA 9; BEST 89:3; CA 136;
SATA 75

Tandem, Felix
See Spitteler, Carl (Friedrich Georg)

Tanizaki, Jun'ichiro
1886-1965 .... **CLC 8, 14, 28**
See also CA 93-96; 25-28R

Tanner, William
See Amis, Kingsley (William)

Tao Lao
See Storni, Alfonsina

Tarassoff, Lev
See Troyat, Henri

Tarbell, Ida M(inerva)
1857-1944 .... **TCLC 40**
See also CA 122; DLB 47

Tarkington, (Newton) Booth
1869-1946 .... **TCLC 9**
See also CA 110; DLB 9, 102; SATA 17

Tarkovsky, Andrei (Arsenyevich)
1932-1986 .... **CLC 75**
See also CA 127

Tartt, Donna 1964(?)-............. **CLC 76**

Tasso, Torquato 1544-1595 .... **LC 5**

Tate, (John Orley) Allen
1899-1979 .... **CLC 2, 4, 6, 9, 11, 14, 24**
See also CA 5-8R; 85-88; CANR 32;
DLB 4, 45, 63; MTCW

Tate, Ellalice
See Hibbert, Eleanor Alice Burford

Tate, James (Vincent) 1943- ... **CLC 2, 6, 25**
See also CA 21-24R; CANR 29; DLB 5

Tavel, Ronald 1940-.............. **CLC 6**
See also CA 21-24R; CANR 33

Taylor, Cecil Philip 1929-1981 ..... **CLC 27**
See also CA 25-28R; 105

Taylor, Edward 1642(?)-1729....... **LC 11**
See also DA; DLB 24

Taylor, Eleanor Ross 1920-......... **CLC 5**
See also CA 81-84

Taylor, Elizabeth 1912-1975 ... **CLC 2, 4, 29**
See also CA 13-16R; CANR 9; MTCW;
SATA 13

Taylor, Henry (Splawn) 1942-...... **CLC 44**
See also CA 33-36R; CAAS 7; CANR 31;
DLB 5

Taylor, Kamala (Purnaiya) 1924-
See Markandaya, Kamala
See also CA 77-80

Taylor, Mildred D. .... **CLC 21**
See also AAYA 10; BW; CA 85-88;
CANR 25; CLR 9; DLB 52; JRDA;
MAICYA; SAAS 5; SATA 15, 70

Taylor, Peter (Hillsman)
1917- ...... **CLC 1, 4, 18, 37, 44, 50, 71;
SSC 10**
See also CA 13-16R; CANR 9; DLBY 81;
MTCW

Taylor, Robert Lewis 1912-........ **CLC 14**
See also CA 1-4R; CANR 3; SATA 10

Tchekhov, Anton
See Chekhov, Anton (Pavlovich)

Teasdale, Sara 1884-1933.......... **TCLC 4**
See also CA 104; DLB 45; SATA 32

Tegner, Esaias 1782-1846......... **NCLC 2**

Teilhard de Chardin, (Marie Joseph) Pierre
1881-1955 .... **TCLC 9**
See also CA 105

Temple, Ann
See Mortimer, Penelope (Ruth)

Tennant, Emma (Christina)
1937-.................... **CLC 13, 52**
See also CA 65-68; CAAS 9; CANR 10, 38;
DLB 14

Tenneshaw, S. M.
See Silverberg, Robert

Tennyson, Alfred
1809-1892 .... **NCLC 30; PC 6**
See also CDBLB 1832-1890; DA; DLB 32;
WLC

Teran, Lisa St. Aubin de .... **CLC 36**
See also St. Aubin de Teran, Lisa

Teresa de Jesus, St. 1515-1582 ...... **LC 18**

Terkel, Louis 1912-
See Terkel, Studs
See also CA 57-60; CANR 18; MTCW

Terkel, Studs . . . . CLC 38
See also Terkel, Louis
See also AITN 1

Terry, C. V.
See Slaughter, Frank G(ill)

Terry, Megan 1932- . . . . CLC 19
See also CA 77-80; CABS 3; DLB 7

Tertz, Abram
See Sinyavsky, Andrei (Donatevich)

Tesich, Steve 1943(?)- . . . . CLC 40, 69
See also CA 105; DLBY 83

Teternikov, Fyodor Kuzmich 1863-1927
See Sologub, Fyodor
See also CA 104

Tevis, Walter 1928-1984 . . . . CLC 42
See also CA 113

Tey, Josephine . . . . TCLC 14
See also Mackintosh, Elizabeth
See also DLB 77

Thackeray, William Makepeace
1811-1863 . . . . NCLC 5, 14, 22
See also CDBLB 1832-1890; DA; DLB 21,
55; SATA 23; WLC

Thakura, Ravindranatha
See Tagore, Rabindranath

Tharoor, Shashi 1956- . . . . CLC 70
See also CA 141

Thelwell, Michael Miles 1939- . . . . . CLC 22
See also CA 101

Theobald, Lewis, Jr.
See Lovecraft, H(oward) P(hillips)

The Prophet
See Dreiser, Theodore (Herman Albert)

Theriault, Yves 1915-1983 . . . . CLC 79
See also CA 102; DLB 88

Theroux, Alexander (Louis)
1939- . . . . CLC 2, 25
See also CA 85-88; CANR 20

Theroux, Paul (Edward)
1941- . . . . CLC 5, 8, 11, 15, 28, 46
See also BEST 89:4; CA 33-36R; CANR 20;
DLB 2; MTCW; SATA 44

Thesen, Sharon 1946- . . . . CLC 56

Thevenin, Denis
See Duhamel, Georges

Thibault, Jacques Anatole Francois
1844-1924
See France, Anatole
See also CA 106; 127; MTCW

Thiele, Colin (Milton) 1920- . . . . CLC 17
See also CA 29-32R; CANR 12, 28;
CLR 27; MAICYA; SAAS 2; SATA 14,
72

Thomas, Audrey (Callahan)
1935- . . . . CLC 7, 13, 37
See also AITN 2; CA 21-24R; CANR 36;
DLB 60; MTCW

Thomas, D(onald) M(ichael)
1935- . . . . CLC 13, 22, 31
See also CA 61-64; CAAS 11; CANR 17;
CDBLB 1960 to Present; DLB 40;
MTCW

Thomas, Dylan (Marlais)
1914-1953 . . . . . . TCLC 1, 8, 45; PC 2;
SSC 3
See also CA 104; 120; CDBLB 1945-1960;
DA; DLB 13, 20; MTCW; SATA 60;
WLC

Thomas, (Philip) Edward
1878-1917 . . . . TCLC 10
See also CA 106; DLB 19

Thomas, Joyce Carol 1938- . . . . CLC 35
See also BW; CA 113; 116; CLR 19;
DLB 33; JRDA; MAICYA; MTCW;
SAAS 7; SATA 40

Thomas, Lewis 1913- . . . . CLC 35
See also CA 85-88; CANR 38; MTCW

Thomas, Paul
See Mann, (Paul) Thomas

Thomas, Piri 1928- . . . . CLC 17
See also CA 73-76; HW

Thomas, R(onald) S(tuart)
1913- . . . . CLC 6, 13, 48
See also CA 89-92; CAAS 4; CANR 30;
CDBLB 1960 to Present; DLB 27;
MTCW

Thomas, Ross (Elmore) 1926- . . . . . . CLC 39
See also CA 33-36R; CANR 22

Thompson, Francis Clegg
See Mencken, H(enry) L(ouis)

Thompson, Francis Joseph
1859-1907 . . . . TCLC 4
See also CA 104; CDBLB 1890-1914;
DLB 19

Thompson, Hunter S(tockton)
1939- . . . . CLC 9, 17, 40
See also BEST 89:1; CA 17-20R; CANR 23;
MTCW

Thompson, Jim 1906-1977(?) . . . . CLC 69

Thompson, Judith . . . . CLC 39

Thomson, James 1700-1748 . . . . LC 16

Thomson, James 1834-1882 . . . . . . NCLC 18

Thoreau, Henry David
1817-1862 . . . . NCLC 7, 21
See also CDALB 1640-1865; DA; DLB 1;
WLC

Thornton, Hall
See Silverberg, Robert

Thurber, James (Grover)
1894-1961 . . . . CLC 5, 11, 25; SSC 1
See also CA 73-76; CANR 17, 39;
CDALB 1929-1941; DA; DLB 4, 11, 22,
102; MAICYA; MTCW; SATA 13

Thurman, Wallace (Henry)
1902-1934 . . . . TCLC 6
See also BLC 3; BW; CA 104; 124; DLB 51

Ticheburn, Cheviot
See Ainsworth, William Harrison

Tieck, (Johann) Ludwig
1773-1853 . . . . NCLC 5
See also DLB 90

Tiger, Derry
See Ellison, Harlan

Tilghman, Christopher 1948(?)- . . . . . CLC 65

Tillinghast, Richard (Williford)
1940- . . . . CLC 29
See also CA 29-32R; CANR 26

Timrod, Henry 1828-1867 . . . . . . NCLC 25
See also DLB 3

Tindall, Gillian 1938- . . . . CLC 7
See also CA 21-24R; CANR 11

Tiptree, James, Jr. . . . . CLC 48, 50
See also Sheldon, Alice Hastings Bradley
See also DLB 8

Titmarsh, Michael Angelo
See Thackeray, William Makepeace

Tocqueville, Alexis (Charles Henri Maurice
Clerel Comte) 1805-1859 . . . . . NCLC 7

Tolkien, J(ohn) R(onald) R(euel)
1892-1973 . . . . CLC 1, 2, 3, 8, 12, 38
See also AAYA 10; AITN 1; CA 17-18;
45-48; CANR 36; CAP 2;
CDBLB 1914-1945; DA; DLB 15; JRDA;
MAICYA; MTCW; SATA 2, 24, 32;
WLC

Toller, Ernst 1893-1939 . . . . TCLC 10
See also CA 107; DLB 124

Tolson, M. B.
See Tolson, Melvin B(eaunorus)

Tolson, Melvin B(eaunorus)
1898(?)-1966 . . . . CLC 36
See also BLC 3; BW; CA 124; 89-92;
DLB 48, 76

Tolstoi, Aleksei Nikolaevich
See Tolstoy, Alexey Nikolaevich

Tolstoy, Alexey Nikolaevich
1882-1945 . . . . TCLC 18
See also CA 107

Tolstoy, Count Leo
See Tolstoy, Leo (Nikolaevich)

Tolstoy, Leo (Nikolaevich)
1828-1910 . . . . . . TCLC 4, 11, 17, 28, 44;
SSC 9
See also CA 104; 123; DA; SATA 26; WLC

Tomasi di Lampedusa, Giuseppe 1896-1957
See Lampedusa, Giuseppe (Tomasi) di
See also CA 111

Tomlin, Lily . . . . CLC 17
See also Tomlin, Mary Jean

Tomlin, Mary Jean 1939(?)-
See Tomlin, Lily
See also CA 117

Tomlinson, (Alfred) Charles
1927- . . . . CLC 2, 4, 6, 13, 45
See also CA 5-8R; CANR 33; DLB 40

Tonson, Jacob
See Bennett, (Enoch) Arnold

Toole, John Kennedy
1937-1969 . . . . CLC 19, 64
See also CA 104; DLBY 81

Toomer, Jean
1894-1967 . . . . . . CLC 1, 4, 13, 22; PC 7;
SSC 1
See also BLC 3; BW; CA 85-88;
CDALB 1917-1929; DLB 45, 51; MTCW

Torley, Luke
See Blish, James (Benjamin)

Tornimparte, Alessandra
See Ginzburg, Natalia

Torre, Raoul della
See Mencken, H(enry) L(ouis)

Torrey, E(dwin) Fuller 1937-....... **CLC 34**
See also CA 119

Torsvan, Ben Traven
See Traven, B.

Torsvan, Benno Traven
See Traven, B.

Torsvan, Berick Traven
See Traven, B.

Torsvan, Berwick Traven
See Traven, B.

Torsvan, Bruno Traven
See Traven, B.

Torsvan, Traven
See Traven, B.

Tournier, Michel (Edouard)
1924-................. **CLC 6, 23, 36**
See also CA 49-52; CANR 3, 36; DLB 83;
MTCW; SATA 23

Tournimparte, Alessandra
See Ginzburg, Natalia

Towers, Ivar
See Kornbluth, C(yril) M.

Townsend, Sue 1946-............. **CLC 61**
See also CA 119; 127; MTCW; SATA 48,
55

Townshend, Peter (Dennis Blandford)
1945-.................... **CLC 17, 42**
See also CA 107

Tozzi, Federigo 1883-1920....... **TCLC 31**

Traill, Catharine Parr
1802-1899 .... **NCLC 31**
See also DLB 99

Trakl, Georg 1887-1914.......... **TCLC 5**
See also CA 104

Transtroemer, Tomas (Goesta)
1931- .... **CLC 52, 65**
See also CA 117; 129; CAAS 17

Transtromer, Tomas Gosta
See Transtroemer, Tomas (Goesta)

Traven, B. (?)-1969............. **CLC 8, 11**
See also CA 19-20; 25-28R; CAP 2; DLB 9,
56; MTCW

Treitel, Jonathan 1959- .... **CLC 70**

Tremain, Rose 1943-............. **CLC 42**
See also CA 97-100; DLB 14

Tremblay, Michel 1942-........... **CLC 29**
See also CA 116; 128; DLB 60; MTCW

Trevanian (a pseudonym) 1930(?)-... **CLC 29**
See also CA 108

Trevor, Glen
See Hilton, James

Trevor, William
1928-............ **CLC 7, 9, 14, 25, 71**
See also Cox, William Trevor
See also DLB 14

Trifonov, Yuri (Valentinovich)
1925-1981 .... **CLC 45**
See also CA 126; 103; MTCW

Trilling, Lionel 1905-1975.... **CLC 9, 11, 24**
See also CA 9-12R; 61-64; CANR 10;
DLB 28, 63; MTCW

Trimball, W. H.
See Mencken, H(enry) L(ouis)

Tristan
See Gomez de la Serna, Ramon

Tristram
See Housman, A(lfred) E(dward)

Trogdon, William (Lewis) 1939-
See Heat-Moon, William Least
See also CA 115; 119

Trollope, Anthony 1815-1882 .. **NCLC 6, 33**
See also CDBLB 1832-1890; DA; DLB 21,
57; SATA 22; WLC

Trollope, Frances 1779-1863 ..... **NCLC 30**
See also DLB 21

Trotsky, Leon 1879-1940........ **TCLC 22**
See also CA 118

Trotter (Cockburn), Catharine
1679-1749 .... **LC 8**
See also DLB 84

Trout, Kilgore
See Farmer, Philip Jose

Trow, George W. S. 1943-........ **CLC 52**
See also CA 126

Troyat, Henri 1911-.............. **CLC 23**
See also CA 45-48; CANR 2, 33; MTCW

Trudeau, G(arretson) B(eekman) 1948-
See Trudeau, Garry B.
See also CA 81-84; CANR 31; SATA 35

Trudeau, Garry B................... **CLC 12**
See also Trudeau, G(arretson) B(eekman)
See also AAYA 10; AITN 2

Truffaut, Francois 1932-1984....... **CLC 20**
See also CA 81-84; 113; CANR 34

Trumbo, Dalton 1905-1976 .... **CLC 19**
See also CA 21-24R; 69-72; CANR 10;
DLB 26

Trumbull, John 1750-1831...... **NCLC 30**
See also DLB 31

Trundlett, Helen B.
See Eliot, T(homas) S(tearns)

Tryon, Thomas 1926-1991 .... **CLC 3, 11**
See also AITN 1; CA 29-32R; 135;
CANR 32; MTCW

Tryon, Tom
See Tryon, Thomas

Ts'ao Hsueh-ch'in 1715(?)-1763....... **LC 1**

Tsushima, Shuji 1909-1948
See Dazai, Osamu
See also CA 107

Tsvetaeva (Efron), Marina (Ivanovna)
1892-1941 .... **TCLC 7, 35**
See also CA 104; 128; MTCW

Tuck, Lily 1938-................. **CLC 70**
See also CA 139

Tunis, John R(oberts) 1889-1975 ... **CLC 12**
See also CA 61-64; DLB 22; JRDA;
MAICYA; SATA 30, 37

Tuohy, Frank.................... **CLC 37**
See also Tuohy, John Francis
See also DLB 14

Tuohy, John Francis 1925-
See Tuohy, Frank
See also CA 5-8R; CANR 3

Turco, Lewis (Putnam) 1934- ... **CLC 11, 63**
See also CA 13-16R; CANR 24; DLBY 84

Turgenev, Ivan
1818-1883 .... **NCLC 21; SSC 7**
See also DA; WLC

Turner, Frederick 1943-........... **CLC 48**
See also CA 73-76; CAAS 10; CANR 12,
30; DLB 40

Tusan, Stan 1936-................ **CLC 22**
See also CA 105

Tutuola, Amos 1920- .... **CLC 5, 14, 29**
See also BLC 3; BW; CA 9-12R; CANR 27;
DLB 125; MTCW

Twain, Mark
.... **TCLC 6, 12, 19, 36, 48; SSC 6**
See also Clemens, Samuel Langhorne
See also DLB 11, 12, 23, 64, 74; WLC

Tyler, Anne
1941-........ **CLC 7, 11, 18, 28, 44, 59**
See also BEST 89:1; CA 9-12R; CANR 11,
33; DLB 6; DLBY 82; MTCW; SATA 7

Tyler, Royall 1757-1826.......... **NCLC 3**
See also DLB 37

Tynan, Katharine 1861-1931 .... **TCLC 3**
See also CA 104

Tytell, John 1939- .... **CLC 50**
See also CA 29-32R

Tyutchev, Fyodor 1803-1873..... **NCLC 34**

Tzara, Tristan .... **CLC 47**
See also Rosenfeld, Samuel

Uhry, Alfred 1936-............... **CLC 55**
See also CA 127; 133

Ulf, Haerved
See Strindberg, (Johan) August

Ulf, Harved
See Strindberg, (Johan) August

Unamuno (y Jugo), Miguel de
1864-1936 .... **TCLC 2, 9; SSC 11**
See also CA 104; 131; DLB 108; HW;
MTCW

Undercliffe, Errol
See Campbell, (John) Ramsey

Underwood, Miles
See Glassco, John

Undset, Sigrid 1882-1949......... **TCLC 3**
See also CA 104; 129; DA; MTCW; WLC

Ungaretti, Giuseppe
1888-1970 .... **CLC 7, 11, 15**
See also CA 19-20; 25-28R; CAP 2;
DLB 114

Unger, Douglas 1952-............. **CLC 34**
See also CA 130

Unsworth, Barry (Forster) 1930-.... **CLC 76**
See also CA 25-28R; CANR 30

Updike, John (Hoyer)
1932- ...... **CLC 1, 2, 3, 5, 7, 9, 13, 15,
23, 34, 43, 70; SSC 13**
See also CA 1-4R; CABS 1; CANR 4, 33;
CDALB 1968-1988; DA; DLB 2, 5;
DLBD 3; DLBY 80, 82; MTCW; WLC

Upshaw, Margaret Mitchell
See Mitchell, Margaret (Munnerlyn)

Upton, Mark
See Sanders, Lawrence

Voigt, Cynthia 1942- .... **CLC 30**
See also AAYA 3; CA 106; CANR 18, 37,
40; CLR 13; JRDA; MAICYA;
SATA 33, 48

Voinovich, Vladimir (Nikolaevich)
1932- .... **CLC 10, 49**
See also CA 81-84; CAAS 12; CANR 33;
MTCW

Voltaire 1694-1778 .... **LC 14; SSC 12**
See also DA; WLC

von Daeniken, Erich 1935- .... **CLC 30**
See also von Daniken, Erich
See also AITN 1; CA 37-40R; CANR 17

von Daniken, Erich .... **CLC 30**
See also von Daeniken, Erich

von Heidenstam, (Carl Gustaf) Verner
See Heidenstam, (Carl Gustaf) Verner von

von Heyse, Paul (Johann Ludwig)
See Heyse, Paul (Johann Ludwig von)

von Hofmannsthal, Hugo
See Hofmannsthal, Hugo von

von Horvath, Odon
See Horvath, Oedoen von

von Horvath, Oedoen
See Horvath, Oedoen von

von Liliencron, (Friedrich Adolf Axel) Detlev
See Liliencron, (Friedrich Adolf Axel)
Detlev von

Vonnegut, Kurt, Jr.
1922- ...... **CLC 1, 2, 3, 4, 5, 8, 12, 22,
40, 60; SSC 8**
See also AAYA 6; AITN 1; BEST 90:4;
CA 1-4R; CANR 1, 25;
CDALB 1968-1988; DA; DLB 2, 8;
DLBD 3; DLBY 80; MTCW; WLC

Von Rachen, Kurt
See Hubbard, L(afayette) Ron(ald)

von Rezzori (d'Arezzo), Gregor
See Rezzori (d'Arezzo), Gregor von

von Sternberg, Josef
See Sternberg, Josef von

Vorster, Gordon 1924- .... **CLC 34**
See also CA 133

Vosce, Trudie
See Ozick, Cynthia

Voznesensky, Andrei (Andreievich)
1933- .... **CLC 1, 15, 57**
See also CA 89-92; CANR 37; MTCW

Waddington, Miriam 1917- .... **CLC 28**
See also CA 21-24R; CANR 12, 30;
DLB 68

Wagman, Fredrica 1937- .... **CLC 7**
See also CA 97-100

Wagner, Richard 1813-1883 .... **NCLC 9**
See also DLB 129

Wagner-Martin, Linda 1936- ...... **CLC 50**

Wagoner, David (Russell)
1926- .... **CLC 3, 5, 15**
See also CA 1-4R; CAAS 3; CANR 2;
DLB 5; SATA 14

Wah, Fred(erick James) 1939-...... **CLC 44**
See also CA 107; 141; DLB 60

Wahloo, Per 1926-1975 .... **CLC 7**
See also CA 61-64

Wahloo, Peter
See Wahloo, Per

Wain, John (Barrington)
1925- .... **CLC 2, 11, 15, 46**
See also CA 5-8R; CAAS 4; CANR 23;
CDBLB 1960 to Present; DLB 15, 27;
MTCW

Wajda, Andrzej 1926-............. **CLC 16**
See also CA 102

Wakefield, Dan 1932-.............. **CLC 7**
See also CA 21-24R; CAAS 7

Wakoski, Diane
1937- .... **CLC 2, 4, 7, 9, 11, 40**
See also CA 13-16R; CAAS 1; CANR 9;
DLB 5

Wakoski-Sherbell, Diane
See Wakoski, Diane

Walcott, Derek (Alton)
1930- .... **CLC 2, 4, 9, 14, 25, 42, 67, 76**
See also BLC 3; BW; CA 89-92; CANR 26;
DLB 117; DLBY 81; MTCW

Waldman, Anne 1945- .... **CLC 7**
See also CA 37-40R; CAAS 17; CANR 34;
DLB 16

Waldo, E. Hunter
See Sturgeon, Theodore (Hamilton)

Waldo, Edward Hamilton
See Sturgeon, Theodore (Hamilton)

Walker, Alice (Malsenior)
1944- .... **CLC 5, 6, 9, 19, 27, 46, 58;
SSC 5**
See also AAYA 3; BEST 89:4; BLC 3; BW;
CA 37-40R; CANR 9, 27;
CDALB 1968-1988; DA; DLB 6, 33;
MTCW; SATA 31

Walker, David Harry 1911-1992.... **CLC 14**
See also CA 1-4R; 137; CANR 1; SATA 8;
SATA-Obit 71

Walker, Edward Joseph 1934-
See Walker, Ted
See also CA 21-24R; CANR 12, 28

Walker, George F. 1947- .... **CLC 44, 61**
See also CA 103; CANR 21; DLB 60

Walker, Joseph A. 1935- .... **CLC 19**
See also BW; CA 89-92; CANR 26; DLB 38

Walker, Margaret (Abigail)
1915- .... **CLC 1, 6**
See also BLC 3; BW; CA 73-76; CANR 26;
DLB 76; MTCW

Walker, Ted .... **CLC 13**
See also Walker, Edward Joseph
See also DLB 40

Wallace, David Foster 1962- .... **CLC 50**
See also CA 132

Wallace, Dexter
See Masters, Edgar Lee

Wallace, Irving 1916-1990 ...... **CLC 7, 13**
See also AITN 1; CA 1-4R; 132; CAAS 1;
CANR 1, 27; MTCW

Wallant, Edward Lewis
1926-1962 .... **CLC 5, 10**
See also CA 1-4R; CANR 22; DLB 2, 28;
MTCW

Walpole, Horace 1717-1797......... **LC 2**
See also DLB 39, 104

Walpole, Hugh (Seymour)
1884-1941 .... **TCLC 5**
See also CA 104; DLB 34

Walser, Martin 1927-............. **CLC 27**
See also CA 57-60; CANR 8; DLB 75, 124

Walser, Robert 1878-1956 .... **TCLC 18**
See also CA 118; DLB 66

Walsh, Jill Paton.................. **CLC 35**
See also Paton Walsh, Gillian
See also CLR 2; SAAS 3

Walter, William Christian
See Andersen, Hans Christian

Wambaugh, Joseph (Aloysius, Jr.)
1937- .... **CLC 3, 18**
See also AITN 1; BEST 89:3; CA 33-36R;
CANR 42; DLB 6; DLBY 83; MTCW

Ward, Arthur Henry Sarsfield 1883-1959
See Rohmer, Sax
See also CA 108

Ward, Douglas Turner 1930-....... **CLC 19**
See also BW; CA 81-84; CANR 27; DLB 7,
38

Ward, Peter
See Faust, Frederick (Schiller)

Warhol, Andy 1928(?)-1987........ **CLC 20**
See also BEST 89:4; CA 89-92; 121;
CANR 34

Warner, Francis (Robert le Plastrier)
1937- .... **CLC 14**
See also CA 53-56; CANR 11

Warner, Marina 1946-............ **CLC 59**
See also CA 65-68; CANR 21

Warner, Rex (Ernest) 1905-1986.... **CLC 45**
See also CA 89-92; 119; DLB 15

Warner, Susan (Bogert)
1819-1885 .... **NCLC 31**
See also DLB 3, 42

Warner, Sylvia (Constance) Ashton
See Ashton-Warner, Sylvia (Constance)

Warner, Sylvia Townsend
1893-1978 .... **CLC 7, 19**
See also CA 61-64; 77-80; CANR 16;
DLB 34; MTCW

Warren, Mercy Otis 1728-1814... **NCLC 13**
See also DLB 31

Warren, Robert Penn
1905-1989 .... **CLC 1, 4, 6, 8, 10, 13, 18,
39, 53, 59; SSC 4**
See also AITN 1; CA 13-16R; 129;
CANR 10; CDALB 1968-1988; DA;
DLB 2, 48; DLBY 80, 89; MTCW;
SATA 46, 63; WLC

Warshofsky, Isaac
See Singer, Isaac Bashevis

Warton, Thomas 1728-1790 .... **LC 15**
See also DLB 104, 109

Waruk, Kona
See Harris, (Theodore) Wilson

Warung, Price 1855-1911........ **TCLC 45**

Warwick, Jarvis
See Garner, Hugh

Washington, Alex
See Harris, Mark

Washington, Booker T(aliaferro)
1856-1915 . . . . TCLC 10
See also BLC 3; BW; CA 114; 125;
SATA 28

Wassermann, (Karl) Jakob
1873-1934 . . . . TCLC 6
See also CA 104; DLB 66

Wasserstein, Wendy 1950- . . . . . . CLC 32, 59
See also CA 121; 129; CABS 3

Waterhouse, Keith (Spencer)
1929- . . . . CLC 47
See also CA 5-8R; CANR 38; DLB 13, 15;
MTCW

Waters, Roger 1944- . . . . CLC 35
See also Pink Floyd

Watkins, Frances Ellen
See Harper, Frances Ellen Watkins

Watkins, Gerrold
See Malzberg, Barry N(athaniel)

Watkins, Paul 1964- . . . . CLC 55
See also CA 132

Watkins, Vernon Phillips
1906-1967 . . . . CLC 43
See also CA 9-10; 25-28R; CAP 1; DLB 20

Watson, Irving S.
See Mencken, H(enry) L(ouis)

Watson, John H.
See Farmer, Philip Jose

Watson, Richard F.
See Silverberg, Robert

Waugh, Auberon (Alexander) 1939- . . CLC 7
See also CA 45-48; CANR 6, 22; DLB 14

Waugh, Evelyn (Arthur St. John)
1903-1966 . . . CLC 1, 3, 8, 13, 19, 27, 44
See also CA 85-88; 25-28R; CANR 22;
CDBLB 1914-1945; DA; DLB 15;
MTCW; WLC

Waugh, Harriet 1944- . . . . CLC 6
See also CA 85-88; CANR 22

Ways, C. R.
See Blount, Roy (Alton), Jr.

Waystaff, Simon
See Swift, Jonathan

Webb, (Martha) Beatrice (Potter)
1858-1943 . . . . TCLC 22
See also Potter, Beatrice
See also CA 117

Webb, Charles (Richard) 1939- . . . . . . CLC 7
See also CA 25-28R

Webb, James H(enry), Jr. 1946- . . . . CLC 22
See also CA 81-84

Webb, Mary (Gladys Meredith)
1881-1927 . . . . TCLC 24
See also CA 123; DLB 34

Webb, Mrs. Sidney
See Webb, (Martha) Beatrice (Potter)

Webb, Phyllis 1927- . . . . CLC 18
See also CA 104; CANR 23; DLB 53

Webb, Sidney (James)
1859-1947 . . . . TCLC 22
See also CA 117

Webber, Andrew Lloyd . . . . CLC 21
See also Lloyd Webber, Andrew

Weber, Lenora Mattingly
1895-1971 . . . . CLC 12
See also CA 19-20; 29-32R; CAP 1;
SATA 2, 26

Webster, John 1579(?)-1634(?) . . . . DC 2
See also CDBLB Before 1660; DA; DLB 58;
WLC

Webster, Noah 1758-1843 . . . . NCLC 30

Wedekind, (Benjamin) Frank(lin)
1864-1918 . . . . TCLC 7
See also CA 104; DLB 118

Weidman, Jerome 1913- . . . . CLC 7
See also AITN 2; CA 1-4R; CANR 1;
DLB 28

Weil, Simone (Adolphine)
1909-1943 . . . . TCLC 23
See also CA 117

Weinstein, Nathan
See West, Nathanael

Weinstein, Nathan von Wallenstein
See West, Nathanael

Weir, Peter (Lindsay) 1944- . . . . CLC 20
See also CA 113; 123

Weiss, Peter (Ulrich)
1916-1982 . . . . CLC 3, 15, 51
See also CA 45-48; 106; CANR 3; DLB 69,
124

Weiss, Theodore (Russell)
1916- . . . . CLC 3, 8, 14
See also CA 9-12R; CAAS 2; DLB 5

Welch, (Maurice) Denton
1915-1948 . . . . TCLC 22
See also CA 121

Welch, James 1940- . . . . CLC 6, 14, 52
See also CA 85-88; CANR 42

Weldon, Fay
1933(?)- . . . . CLC 6, 9, 11, 19, 36, 59
See also CA 21-24R; CANR 16;
CDBLB 1960 to Present; DLB 14;
MTCW

Wellek, Rene 1903- . . . . CLC 28
See also CA 5-8R; CAAS 7; CANR 8;
DLB 63

Weller, Michael 1942- . . . . CLC 10, 53
See also CA 85-88

Weller, Paul 1958- . . . . CLC 26

Wellershoff, Dieter 1925- . . . . CLC 46
See also CA 89-92; CANR 16, 37

Welles, (George) Orson
1915-1985 . . . . CLC 20
See also CA 93-96; 117

Wellman, Mac 1945- . . . . CLC 65

Wellman, Manly Wade 1903-1986 . . CLC 49
See also CA 1-4R; 118; CANR 6, 16;
SATA 6, 47

Wells, Carolyn 1869(?)-1942 . . . . . . TCLC 35
See also CA 113; DLB 11

Wells, H(erbert) G(eorge)
1866-1946 . . . . . . TCLC 6, 12, 19; SSC 6
See also CA 110; 121; CDBLB 1914-1945;
DA; DLB 34, 70; MTCW; SATA 20;
WLC

Wells, Rosemary 1943- . . . . CLC 12
See also CA 85-88; CLR 16; MAICYA;
SAAS 1; SATA 18, 69

Welty, Eudora
1909- . . . . CLC 1, 2, 5, 14, 22, 33; SSC 1
See also CA 9-12R; CABS 1; CANR 32;
CDALB 1941-1968; DA; DLB 2, 102;
DLBY 87; MTCW; WLC

Wen I-to 1899-1946 . . . . TCLC 28

Wentworth, Robert
See Hamilton, Edmond

Werfel, Franz (V.) 1890-1945 . . . . . . TCLC 8
See also CA 104; DLB 81, 124

Wergeland, Henrik Arnold
1808-1845 . . . . NCLC 5

Wersba, Barbara 1932- . . . . CLC 30
See also AAYA 2; CA 29-32R; CANR 16,
38; CLR 3; DLB 52; JRDA; MAICYA;
SAAS 2; SATA 1, 58

Wertmueller, Lina 1928- . . . . CLC 16
See also CA 97-100; CANR 39

Wescott, Glenway 1901-1987 . . . . CLC 13
See also CA 13-16R; 121; CANR 23;
DLB 4, 9, 102

Wesker, Arnold 1932- . . . . CLC 3, 5, 42
See also CA 1-4R; CAAS 7; CANR 1, 33;
CDBLB 1960 to Present; DLB 13;
MTCW

Wesley, Richard (Errol) 1945- . . . . . . CLC 7
See also BW; CA 57-60; CANR 27; DLB 38

Wessel, Johan Herman 1742-1785 . . . . LC 7

West, Anthony (Panther)
1914-1987 . . . . CLC 50
See also CA 45-48; 124; CANR 3, 19;
DLB 15

West, C. P.
See Wodehouse, P(elham) G(renville)

West, (Mary) Jessamyn
1902-1984 . . . . CLC 7, 17
See also CA 9-12R; 112; CANR 27; DLB 6;
DLBY 84; MTCW; SATA 37

West, Morris L(anglo) 1916- . . . . . . CLC 6, 33
See also CA 5-8R; CANR 24; MTCW

West, Nathanael
1903-1940 . . . . TCLC 1, 14, 44
See also CA 104; 125; CDALB 1929-1941;
DLB 4, 9, 28; MTCW

West, Owen
See Koontz, Dean R(ay)

West, Paul 1930- . . . . CLC 7, 14
See also CA 13-16R; CAAS 7; CANR 22;
DLB 14

West, Rebecca 1892-1983 . . CLC 7, 9, 31, 50
See also CA 5-8R; 109; CANR 19; DLB 36;
DLBY 83; MTCW

Westall, Robert (Atkinson)
1929-1993 . . . . CLC 17
See also CA 69-72; 141; CANR 18;
CLR 13; JRDA; MAICYA; SAAS 2;
SATA 23, 69; SATA-Obit 75

Westlake, Donald E(dwin)
1933- . . . . CLC 7, 33
See also CA 17-20R; CAAS 13; CANR 16

Westmacott, Mary
See Christie, Agatha (Mary Clarissa)

Weston, Allen
See Norton, Andre

Wetcheek, J. L.
See Feuchtwanger, Lion

Wetering, Janwillem van de
See van de Wetering, Janwillem

Wetherell, Elizabeth
See Warner, Susan (Bogert)

Whalen, Philip 1923- . . . . **CLC 6, 29**
See also CA 9-12R; CANR 5, 39; DLB 16

Wharton, Edith (Newbold Jones)
1862-1937 . . . . **TCLC 3, 9, 27; SSC 6**
See also CA 104; 132; CDALB 1865-1917;
DA; DLB 4, 9, 12, 78; MTCW; WLC

Wharton, James
See Mencken, H(enry) L(ouis)

Wharton, William (a pseudonym)
. . . . **CLC 18, 37**
See also CA 93-96; DLBY 80

Wheatley (Peters), Phillis
1754(?)-1784 . . . . **LC 3; PC 3**
See also BLC 3; CDALB 1640-1865; DA;
DLB 31, 50; WLC

Wheelock, John Hall 1886-1978 . . . . **CLC 14**
See also CA 13-16R; 77-80; CANR 14;
DLB 45

White, E(lwyn) B(rooks)
1899-1985 . . . . **CLC 10, 34, 39**
See also AITN 2; CA 13-16R; 116;
CANR 16, 37; CLR 1, 21; DLB 11, 22;
MAICYA; MTCW; SATA 2, 29, 44

White, Edmund (Valentine III)
1940- . . . . **CLC 27**
See also AAYA 7; CA 45-48; CANR 3, 19,
36; MTCW

White, Patrick (Victor Martindale)
1912-1990 . . **CLC 3, 4, 5, 7, 9, 18, 65, 69**
See also CA 81-84; 132; MTCW

White, Phyllis Dorothy James 1920-
See James, P. D.
See also CA 21-24R; CANR 17; MTCW

White, T(erence) H(anbury)
1906-1964 . . . . **CLC 30**
See also CA 73-76; CANR 37; JRDA;
MAICYA; SATA 12

White, Terence de Vere 1912- . . . . . . **CLC 49**
See also CA 49-52; CANR 3

White, Walter F(rancis)
1893-1955 . . . . **TCLC 15**
See also White, Walter
See also CA 115; 124; DLB 51

White, William Hale 1831-1913
See Rutherford, Mark
See also CA 121

Whitehead, E(dward) A(nthony)
1933- . . . . **CLC 5**
See also CA 65-68

Whitemore, Hugh (John) 1936- . . . . . **CLC 37**
See also CA 132

Whitman, Sarah Helen (Power)
1803-1878 . . . . **NCLC 19**
See also DLB 1

Whitman, Walt(er)
1819-1892 . . . . **NCLC 4, 31; PC 3**
See also CDALB 1640-1865; DA; DLB 3,
64; SATA 20; WLC

Whitney, Phyllis A(yame) 1903- . . . . **CLC 42**
See also AITN 2; BEST 90:3; CA 1-4R;
CANR 3, 25, 38; JRDA; MAICYA;
SATA 1, 30

Whittemore, (Edward) Reed (Jr.)
1919- . . . . **CLC 4**
See also CA 9-12R; CAAS 8; CANR 4;
DLB 5

Whittier, John Greenleaf
1807-1892 . . . . **NCLC 8**
See also CDALB 1640-1865; DLB 1

Whittlebot, Hernia
See Coward, Noel (Peirce)

Wicker, Thomas Grey 1926-
See Wicker, Tom
See also CA 65-68; CANR 21

Wicker, Tom . . . . **CLC 7**
See also Wicker, Thomas Grey

Wideman, John Edgar
1941- . . . . **CLC 5, 34, 36, 67**
See also BLC 3; BW; CA 85-88; CANR 14,
42; DLB 33

Wiebe, Rudy (Henry) 1934- . . . **CLC 6, 11, 14**
See also CA 37-40R; CANR 42; DLB 60

Wieland, Christoph Martin
1733-1813 . . . . **NCLC 17**
See also DLB 97

Wieners, John 1934- . . . . **CLC 7**
See also CA 13-16R; DLB 16

Wiesel, Elie(zer) 1928- . . . . . **CLC 3, 5, 11, 37**
See also AAYA 7; AITN 1; CA 5-8R;
CAAS 4; CANR 8, 40; DA; DLB 83;
DLBY 87; MTCW; SATA 56

Wiggins, Marianne 1947- . . . . **CLC 57**
See also BEST 89:3; CA 130

Wight, James Alfred 1916-
See Herriot, James
See also CA 77-80; SATA 44, 55

Wilbur, Richard (Purdy)
1921- . . . . **CLC 3, 6, 9, 14, 53**
See also CA 1-4R; CABS 2; CANR 2, 29;
DA; DLB 5; MTCW; SATA 9

Wild, Peter 1940- . . . . **CLC 14**
See also CA 37-40R; DLB 5

Wilde, Oscar (Fingal O'Flahertie Wills)
1854(?)-1900 . . . . **TCLC 1, 8, 23, 41;**
SSC 11
See also CA 104; 119; CDBLB 1890-1914;
DA; DLB 10, 19, 34, 57; SATA 24; WLC

Wilder, Billy . . . . **CLC 20**
See also Wilder, Samuel
See also DLB 26

Wilder, Samuel 1906-
See Wilder, Billy
See also CA 89-92

Wilder, Thornton (Niven)
1897-1975 . . . . . . **CLC 1, 5, 6, 10, 15, 35;**
DC 1
See also AITN 2; CA 13-16R; 61-64;
CANR 40; DA; DLB 4, 7, 9; MTCW;
WLC

Wilding, Michael 1942- . . . . **CLC 73**
See also CA 104; CANR 24

Wiley, Richard 1944- . . . . **CLC 44**
See also CA 121; 129

Wilhelm, Kate . . . . **CLC 7**
See also Wilhelm, Katie Gertrude
See also CAAS 5; DLB 8

Wilhelm, Katie Gertrude 1928-
See Wilhelm, Kate
See also CA 37-40R; CANR 17, 36; MTCW

Wilkins, Mary
See Freeman, Mary Eleanor Wilkins

Willard, Nancy 1936- . . . . **CLC 7, 37**
See also CA 89-92; CANR 10, 39; CLR 5;
DLB 5, 52; MAICYA; MTCW;
SATA 30, 37, 71

Williams, C(harles) K(enneth)
1936- . . . . **CLC 33, 56**
See also CA 37-40R; DLB 5

Williams, Charles
See Collier, James L(incoln)

Williams, Charles (Walter Stansby)
1886-1945 . . . . **TCLC 1, 11**
See also CA 104; DLB 100

Williams, (George) Emlyn
1905-1987 . . . . **CLC 15**
See also CA 104; 123; CANR 36; DLB 10,
77; MTCW

Williams, Hugo 1942- . . . . **CLC 42**
See also CA 17-20R; DLB 40

Williams, J. Walker
See Wodehouse, P(elham) G(renville)

Williams, John A(lfred) 1925- . . . . **CLC 5, 13**
See also BLC 3; BW; CA 53-56; CAAS 3;
CANR 6, 26; DLB 2, 33

Williams, Jonathan (Chamberlain)
1929- . . . . **CLC 13**
See also CA 9-12R; CAAS 12; CANR 8;
DLB 5

Williams, Joy 1944- . . . . **CLC 31**
See also CA 41-44R; CANR 22

Williams, Norman 1952- . . . . **CLC 39**
See also CA 118

Williams, Tennessee
1911-1983 . . . . . **CLC 1, 2, 5, 7, 8, 11, 15,**
19, 30, 39, 45, 71
See also AITN 1, 2; CA 5-8R; 108;
CABS 3; CANR 31; CDALB 1941-1968;
DA; DLB 7; DLBD 4; DLBY 83;
MTCW; WLC

Williams, Thomas (Alonzo)
1926-1990 . . . . **CLC 14**
See also CA 1-4R; 132; CANR 2

Williams, William C.
See Williams, William Carlos

Williams, William Carlos
1883-1963 . . . . **CLC 1, 2, 5, 9, 13, 22, 42,**
67; PC 7
See also CA 89-92; CANR 34;
CDALB 1917-1929; DA; DLB 4, 16, 54,
86; MTCW

Williamson, David (Keith) 1942- . . . . **CLC 56**
See also CA 103; CANR 41

Williamson, Jack . . . . **CLC 29**
See also Williamson, John Stewart
See also CAAS 8; DLB 8

Williamson, John Stewart 1908-
See Williamson, Jack
See also CA 17-20R; CANR 23

Wurlitzer, Rudolph 1938(?)- ... **CLC 2, 4, 15**
See also CA 85-88

Wycherley, William 1641-1715 .... **LC 8, 21**
See also CDBLB 1660-1789; DLB 80

Wylie, Elinor (Morton Hoyt)
1885-1928 .... **TCLC 8**
See also CA 105; DLB 9, 45

Wylie, Philip (Gordon) 1902-1971 ... **CLC 43**
See also CA 21-22; 33-36R; CAP 2; DLB 9

Wyndham, John
See Harris, John (Wyndham Parkes Lucas)
Beynon

Wyss, Johann David Von
1743-1818 .... **NCLC 10**
See also JRDA; MAICYA; SATA 27, 29

Yakumo Koizumi
See Hearn, (Patricio) Lafcadio (Tessima
Carlos)

Yanez, Jose Donoso
See Donoso (Yanez), Jose

Yanovsky, Basile S.
See Yanovsky, V(assily) S(emenovich)

Yanovsky, V(assily) S(emenovich)
1906-1989 .... **CLC 2, 18**
See also CA 97-100; 129

Yates, Richard 1926-1992 ..... **CLC 7, 8, 23**
See also CA 5-8R; 139; CANR 10; DLB 2;
DLBY 81, 92

Yeats, W. B.
See Yeats, William Butler

Yeats, William Butler
1865-1939 .... **TCLC 1, 11, 18, 31**
See also CA 104; 127; CDBLB 1890-1914;
DA; DLB 10, 19, 98; MTCW; WLC

Yehoshua, Abraham B. 1936- ... **CLC 13, 31**
See also CA 33-36R

Yep, Laurence Michael 1948- ...... **CLC 35**
See also AAYA 5; CA 49-52; CANR 1;
CLR 3, 17; DLB 52; JRDA; MAICYA;
SATA 7, 69

Yerby, Frank G(arvin)
1916-1991 .... **CLC 1, 7, 22**
See also BLC 3; BW; CA 9-12R; 136;
CANR 16; DLB 76; MTCW

Yesenin, Sergei Alexandrovich
See Esenin, Sergei (Alexandrovich)

Yevtushenko, Yevgeny (Alexandrovich)
1933- .... **CLC 1, 3, 13, 26, 51**
See also CA 81-84; CANR 33; MTCW

Yezierska, Anzia 1885(?)-1970 ..... **CLC 46**
See also CA 126; 89-92; DLB 28; MTCW

Yglesias, Helen 1915- .... **CLC 7, 22**
See also CA 37-40R; CANR 15; MTCW

Yokomitsu Riichi 1898-1947 ...... **TCLC 47**

Yonge, Charlotte (Mary)
1823-1901 .... **TCLC 48**
See also CA 109; DLB 18; SATA 17

York, Jeremy
See Creasey, John

York, Simon
See Heinlein, Robert A(nson)

Yorke, Henry Vincent 1905-1974 ... **CLC 13**
See also Green, Henry
See also CA 85-88; 49-52

Young, Al(bert James) 1939- .... **CLC 19**
See also BLC 3; BW; CA 29-32R;
CANR 26; DLB 33

Young, Andrew (John) 1885-1971 .... **CLC 5**
See also CA 5-8R; CANR 7, 29

Young, Collier
See Bloch, Robert (Albert)

Young, Edward 1683-1765 .... **LC 3**
See also DLB 95

Young, Neil 1945- .... **CLC 17**
See also CA 110

Yourcenar, Marguerite
1903-1987 .... **CLC 19, 38, 50**
See also CA 69-72; CANR 23; DLB 72;
DLBY 88; MTCW

Yurick, Sol 1925- .... **CLC 6**
See also CA 13-16R; CANR 25

Zabolotskii, Nikolai Alekseevich
1903-1958 .... **TCLC 52**
See also CA 116

Zamiatin, Yevgenii
See Zamyatin, Evgeny Ivanovich

Zamyatin, Evgeny Ivanovich
1884-1937 .... **TCLC 8, 37**
See also CA 105

Zangwill, Israel 1864-1926 .... **TCLC 16**
See also CA 109; DLB 10

Zappa, Francis Vincent, Jr. 1940-
See Zappa, Frank
See also CA 108

Zappa, Frank .... **CLC 17**
See also Zappa, Francis Vincent, Jr.

Zaturenska, Marya 1902-1982 .... **CLC 6, 11**
See also CA 13-16R; 105; CANR 22

Zelazny, Roger (Joseph) 1937- ..... **CLC 21**
See also AAYA 7; CA 21-24R; CANR 26;
DLB 8; MTCW; SATA 39, 57

Zhdanov, Andrei A(lexandrovich)
1896-1948 .... **TCLC 18**
See also CA 117

Zhukovsky, Vasily 1783-1852 .... **NCLC 35**

Ziegenhagen, Eric .... **CLC 55**

Zimmer, Jill Schary
See Robinson, Jill

Zimmerman, Robert
See Dylan, Bob

Zindel, Paul 1936- .... **CLC 6, 26**
See also AAYA 2; CA 73-76; CANR 31;
CLR 3; DA; DLB 7, 52; JRDA;
MAICYA; MTCW; SATA 16, 58

Zinov'Ev, A. A.
See Zinoviev, Alexander (Aleksandrovich)

Zinoviev, Alexander (Aleksandrovich)
1922- .... **CLC 19**
See also CA 116; 133; CAAS 10

Zoilus
See Lovecraft, H(oward) P(hillips)

Zola, Emile (Edouard Charles Antoine)
1840-1902 .... **TCLC 1, 6, 21, 41**
See also CA 104; 138; DA; DLB 123; WLC

Zoline, Pamela 1941- .... **CLC 62**

Zorrilla y Moral, Jose 1817-1893 .. **NCLC 6**

Zoshchenko, Mikhail (Mikhailovich)
1895-1958 .... **TCLC 15**
See also CA 115

Zuckmayer, Carl 1896-1977 .... **CLC 18**
See also CA 69-72; DLB 56, 124

Zuk, Georges
See Skelton, Robin

Zukofsky, Louis
1904-1978 .... **CLC 1, 2, 4, 7, 11, 18**
See also CA 9-12R; 77-80; CANR 39;
DLB 5; MTCW

Zweig, Paul 1935-1984 .... **CLC 34, 42**
See also CA 85-88; 113

Zweig, Stefan 1881-1942 .... **TCLC 17**
See also CA 112; DLB 81, 118

Literary Criticism Series
Cumulative Topic Index

This index lists all topic entries in the Gale Literary Criticism Series *Contemporary Literary Criticism, Literature Criticism from 1400 to 1800, Nineteenth-Century Literature Criticism,* and *Twentieth-Century Literary Criticism.*

Topic Index

Spasmodic School of Poetry NCLC 24: 307-52
  history and major figures, 307-21
  the Spasmodics on poetry, 321-27
  Firmilian and critical disfavor, 327-39
  theme and technique, 339-47
  influence, 347-51

Steinbeck, John, Fiftieth Anniversary of *The Grapes of Wrath* CLC 59: 311-54

Sturm und Drang NCLC 40: 196-276
  definitions, 197-238
  poetry and poetics, 238-58
  drama, 258-75

Supernatural Fiction in the Nineteenth Century NCLC 32: 207-87
  major figures and influences, 208-35
  the Victorian ghost story, 236-54
  the influence of science and occultism, 254-66
  supernatural fiction and society, 266-86

Supernatural Fiction, Modern TCLC 30: 59-116
  evolution and varieties, 60-74
  "decline" of the ghost story, 74-86
  as a literary genre, 86-92
  technique, 92-101
  nature and appeal, 101-15

Surrealism TCLC 30: 334-406
  history and formative influences, 335-43
  manifestos, 343-54
  philosophic, aesthetic, and political principles, 354-75
  poetry, 375-81
  novel, 381-86
  drama, 386-92
  film, 392-98
  painting and sculpture, 398-403
  achievement, 403-05

Symbolism, Russian TCLC 30: 266-333
  doctrines and major figures, 267-92
  theories, 293-98
  and French Symbolism, 298-310
  themes in poetry, 310-14
  theater, 314-20
  and the fine arts, 320-32

Symbolist Movement, French NCLC 20: 169-249
  background and characteristics, 170-86
  principles, 186-91
  attacked and defended, 191-97

  influences and predecessors, 197-211
  and Decadence, 211-16
  theater, 216-26
  prose, 226-33
  decline and influence, 233-47

Theater of the Absurd TCLC 38: 339-415
  "The Theater of the Absurd," 340-47
  major plays and playwrights, 347-58
  and the concept of the absurd, 358-86
  theatrical techniques, 386-94
  predecessors of, 394-402
  influence of, 402-13

Tin Pan Alley
  See **American Popular Song, Golden Age of**

Transcendentalism, American NCLC 24: 1-99
  overviews, 3-23
  contemporary documents, 23-41
  theological aspects of, 42-52
  and social issues, 52-74
  literature of, 74-96

Travel Writing in the Twentieth Century TCLC 30: 407-56
  conventions and traditions, 407-27
  and fiction writing, 427-43
  comparative essays on travel writers, 443-54

Ulysses **and the Process of Textual Reconstruction** TCLC 26: 386-416
  evaluations of the new *Ulysses,* 386-94
  editorial principles and procedures, 394-401
  theoretical issues, 401-16

Utopian Literature, Nineteenth-Century NCLC 24: 353-473
  definitions, 354-74
  overviews, 374-88
  theory, 388-408
  communities, 409-26
  fiction, 426-53
  women and fiction, 454-71

Vampire in Literature TCLC 46: 391-454
  origins and evolution, 392-412
  social and psychological perspectives, 413-44
  vampire fiction and science fiction, 445-53

Victorian Autobiography NCLC 40: 277-363
  development and major characteristics 278-88
  themes and techniques 289-313
  the autobiographical tendency in Victorian prose and poetry 313-47
  Victorian women's autobiographies 347-62

Victorian Novel NCLC 32: 288-454
  development and major characteristics, 290-310
  themes and techniques, 310-58
  social criticism in the Victorian novel, 359-97
  urban and rural life in the Victorian novel, 397-406
  women in the Victorian novel, 406-25
  Mudie's Circulating Library, 425-34
  the late-Victorian novel, 434-51

World War I Literature TCLC 34: 392-486
  overview, 393-403
  English, 403-27
  German, 427-50
  American, 450-66
  French, 466-74
  and modern history, 474-82

Yellow Journalism NCLC 36: 383-456
  overviews, 384-96
  major figures, 396-413
  the role of reporters, 413-28
  the Spanish-American War, 428-48
  Yellow Journalism and society, 448-54

Young Playwrights Festival
  1988—CLC 55: 376-81
  1989—CLC 59: 398-403
  1990—CLC 65: 444-48

NCLC Cumulative Nationality Index

Nationality Index

ISBN 0-8103-8475-2

90000